n	i = 11%	12%	13%	14%	15%	16%	17%	18%	19%	20%
1	0.901	0.893	0.885	0.877	0.870	0.862	0.855	0.847	0.840	0.833
2	0.812	0.797	0.783	0.769	0.756	0.743	0.731	0.718	0.706	0.694
3	0.731	0.712	0.693	0.675	0.658	0.641	0.624	0.609	0.593	0.579
4	0.659	0.636	0.613	0.592	0.572	0.552	0.534	0.516	0.499	0.482
5	0.593	0.567	0.543	0.519	0.497	0.476	0.456	0.437	0.419	0.402
6	0.535	0.507	0.480	0.456	0.432	0.410	0.390	0.370	0.352	0.333
7	0.482	0.452	0.425	0.400	0.376	0.354	0.333	0.314	0.296	0.279
8	0.434	0.404	0.376	0.351	0.327	0.305	0.285	0.266	0.249	0.233
9	0.391	0.361	0.333	0.308	0.284	0.263	0.243	0.225	0.209	0.194
10	0.352	0.322	0.295	0.270	0.247	0.227	0.208	0.191	0.176	0.162
11	0.317	0.287	0.261	0.237	0.215	0.195	0.178	0.162	0.148	0.135
12	0.286	0.257	0.231	0.208	0.187	0.168	0.152	0.137	0.124	0.112
13	0.258	0.229	0.204	0.182	0.163	0.145	0.130	0.116	0.104	0.093
14	0.232	0.205	0.181	0.160	0.141	0.125	0.111	0.099	0.088	0.078
15	0.209	0.183	0.160	0.140	0.123	0.108	0.095	0.084	0.074	0.065
16	0.188	0.163	0.142	0.123	0.107	0.093	0.081	0.071	0.062	0.054
17	0.170	0.146	0.125	0.108	0.093	0.080	0.069	0.060	0.052	0.045
18	0.153	0.130	0.111	0.095	0.081	0.069	0.059	0.051	0.044	0.038
19	0.138	0.116	0.098	0.083	0.070	0.060	0.051	0.043	0.037	0.031
20	0.124	0.104	0.087	0.073	0.061	0.051	0.043	0.037	0.031	0.026
21	0.112	0.093	0.077	0.064	0.053	0.044	0.037	0.031	0.026	0.022
22	0.101	0.083	0.068	0.056	0.046	0.038	0.032	0.026	0.022	0.018
23	0.091	0.074	0.060	0.049	0.040	0.033	0.027	0.022	0.018	0.015
24	0.082	0.066	0.053	0.043	0.035	0.028	0.023	0.019	0.015	0.013
25	0.074	0.059	0.047	0.038	0.030	0.024	0.020	0.016	0.013	0.010
30	0.044	0.033	0.026	0.020	0.015	0.012	0.009	0.007	0.005	0.004
35	0.026	0.019	0.014	0.010	0.008	0.006	0.004	0.003	0.002	0.002
40	0.015	0.011	0.008	0.005	0.004	0.003	0.002	0.001	0.001	0.001
45	0.009	0.006	0.004	0.003	0.002	0.001	0.001	0.001	*	*
50	0.005	0.003	0.002	0.001	0.001	0.001	*	*	*	*

*Value less than 0.001.

Jim'

Especially Parts II, IV, V.

Enjoy!

Jim Gardner

Second Edition

Essentials of Managerial Finance

Second Edition

Essentials of Managerial Finance

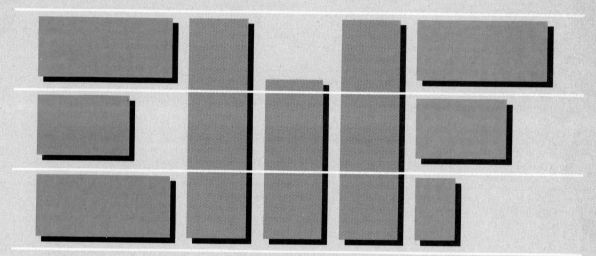

John J. Pringle
The University of North Carolina, Chapel Hill

Robert S. Harris
The University of North Carolina, Chapel Hill

Scott, Foresman and Company
Glenview, Illinois
London, England

To Our Families

Library of Congress Cataloging-in-Publication Data

Pringle, John J.
  Essentials of managerial finance.
  Includes bibliographies and indexes.
  1. Business enterprises—Finance.   2. Corporations—
Finance.   I. Harris, Robert S.,
II. Title.
HG4026.P73   1987   658.1'5   86-31333
ISBN 0-673-18331-9

1 2 3 4 5 6 RRC 91 90 89 88 87 86

Credits

Figure 1–2 on page 10: "Certificate of Deposit" by Bank of Virginia. Courtesy of Bank of Virginia, Richmond, Virginia.

Tables on pages 14–15 from *The Fortune 500* Listing. Copyright © 1986 Time, Inc. All rights reserved.

Table 2-3 on page 38 reprinted by permission from *Introduction to Taxation* by James E. Parker; copyright © 1986 by West Publishing Company. All rights reserved.

Figure 4–2 on page 101: "Money Multiplier Notes" from General Mills, Inc. Copyright © 1982 by General Mills, Inc. Reprinted by permission.

Figure 4–3 on page 103 from "Treasury Bonds, Notes & Bills," *The Wall Street Journal,* 8/16/85. Reprinted by permission of *The Wall Street Journal.* Copyright © Dow Jones & Company, Inc. 1985. All Rights Reserved.

Figure 4–6 on page 122 from "Bond Yields: September 1985," *The Wall Street Journal,* 9/9/85. Reprinted by permission of *The Wall Street Journal.* Copyright © Dow Jones & Company, Inc. 1985. All Rights Reserved.

Tables 5–7 on pages 152 and 163 reprinted by permission of the *Harvard Business Review* from "Does the Capital Asset Pricing Model Work?" by David D. Mullins, Jr. (January/February 1982). Copyright © 1982 by the President and Fellows of Harvard College; all rights reserved.

Figure 4–7 on page 123, Table 5–9 on page 166, and Table 10–9 on page 386 from "Common Stocks: Year-by-Year Returns 1926–1980" and "Past Returns in U.S. Financial Markets" from *Stocks, Bonds, Bills and Inflation: The Past and the Future* by Roger G. Ibbotson and Rex A. Sinquefield, 1982. Copyright © 1982 by R. G. Ibbotson and R. A. Sinquefield. Reprinted by permission of the authors.

Table in example on page 216 based upon a *Fortune* Magazine chart, 1981; figures updated by the authors. Copyright © 1981 by *Fortune* Magazine. Reprinted by permission.

Figure 7–2 on page 234 from "What To Look For On the Balance Sheet," *Business Week.* Reprinted from the June 7, 1976 issue of *Business Week* by special permission. Copyright © 1976 by McGraw-Hill, Inc.

Figure on page 237, "Int'l Bus. Mach.," from *Value Line Investment Survey,* May 9, 1986, p. 1107. Copyright © 1986 Value Line, Inc. Reprinted by permission.

Table in example on page 335 from "Survey and Analysis of Capital Budgeting Methods" by L. D. Schall, G. L. Sundem, and W. R. Geijsbeck, Jr., *Journal of Finance* 33 (March 1978): 281–87. Copyright © 1978. Reprinted by permission of the American Financial Association.

Table on page 398 from "Spending Plans Shrink In Major Economic Sectors," *Business Week.* Reprinted from March 22, 1982 issue of *Business Week* by special permission. Copyright © 1982 by McGraw-Hill, Inc.

Table 12–4 on page 453, "Interest Rates and Spreads of Long-Term Utility Bonds, 1965–1984," from *Moody's Public Utility Manual,* Vol. 1, 1985. Copyright © 1985 Moody's Investors Service, Inc. All rights reserved. Reprinted by permission.

Tables on page 532 from "Financing Policies and Practices in Large Corporations" by D. F. Scott and D. J. Johnson, *Financial Management,* Summer 1982, pp. 51–58. Copyright © 1982 Financial Management Association. Reprinted by permission of the publishers and the authors.

Tables on pages 554-55, "Twelve Firms that Paid No Dividends, 1971-80" "Nineteen Firms that Increased Their Dividends, 1971-80" from "Fresh Evidence that Dividends Don't Matter" by Linda Snyder Hayes, *Fortune,* May 4, 1981. Copyright © 1981 by Fortune Magazine. Reprinted by Permission.

Table on page 810 from "How Tax Reform Changes the Rules," *Business Week.* Reprinted from the September 1, 1986 issue of *Business Week* by special permission. Copyright © 1986 by McGraw-Hill, Inc.

Table 21-2 on pages 756–57 from "Foreign Exchange Rates," *The Wall Street Journal,* 7/15/85. Reprinted by permission of *The Wall Street Journal.* Copyright © Dow Jones & Company, Inc. 1985. All Rights Reserved.

Preface

Essentials of Managerial Finance, second edition, is intended for beginning students in financial management, whether in undergraduate or MBA programs. The book can also be useful to practicing managers who wish to review financial concepts and their applications. Throughout the book, financial management is viewed as part of a broader management process linking the firm with the external markets in which it must raise its funds, purchase its inputs, and sell its products. We place great emphasis on developing a sound conceptual framework along with learning specific skills and techniques so that students leave the first course with an ability to deal with problems that do not match exactly those addressed in the course itself. Our motive in presenting conceptual material always is pragmatic: to help managers make better decisions. We take care also to avoid overstating the benefits of quantitative applications of theoretical models and in the process undermining their credibility for qualitative and conceptual purposes.

Essentials of Managerial Finance has a number of distinctive features, in terms of pedagogy and subject coverage and emphasis. We provide a clear presentation of future and present values and discounted-cash-flow techniques. Early in the text, we introduce the capital-asset-pricing model (CAPM), not only to provide a basis for quantitative measures of return and risk, but also for the qualitative insights it provides regarding the risk/return relationship. We take care to discuss both strengths and weaknesses of CAPM and of other finance theories as aids to decision making as part of our emphasis on financial *management*. The financial analysis and planning chapters of the text are presented in the context of a financial manager's need to develop information. In our comprehensive coverage of capital-budgeting criteria and the capital-budgeting process, we place special emphasis on the idea that the required return depends on the risk of the individual project undertaken. The problem of applying risk-adjustment techniques is approached realistically. In the treatment of financing, there is extensive coverage of financing mix, both as theory and as a practical policy. There is full treatment of dividends and financial policy, working-capital management, international finance, and the recent wave of mergers (with a public-policy perspective).

NEW TO THE SECOND EDITION

The second edition of *Essentials of Managerial Finance* covers the latest issues and developments in the field of managerial finance, including

- the tax-reform legislation passed in 1986 (in a special appendix at the end of the book);
- the latest approaches to cash management and accounts-receivable analysis (in Chapters 19 and 20);
- stock repurchases and hostile takeovers (in Chapters 17 and 22);
- the issues of market efficiency (in Chapters 4, 5, 10, and 12);
- the use of financial forecasting (in Chapters 8 and 10);
- the management of interest rates through futures and options (in Appendix 16A and Chapter 21);
- the role of asymmetric information, agency relationships, and signaling in financing decisions (Chapter 13).

In addition, Chapter 11, "Dealing With Risk in Capital Budgeting," has been streamlined to focus on the key implications of risk for capital budgeting, with the more detailed description of how to use the capital-asset-pricing model to adjust return targets for risk moved to an appendix following Chapter 14. Many new "Finance in Practice" examples have been added, and each chapter contains new problems.

ORGANIZATION OF THE TEXT

There are many ways to teach financial management and a number of alternative ways to organize the material in a finance textbook. We have organized the material in *Essentials of Managerial Finance* into seven parts in a way that we hope will make alternative sequencing easy. The Introduction in Part One comprises two chapters that deal with the scope and objectives of financial management and the environment in which financial-management decisions must be made. The introduction is followed by chapters on "Time and Risk" in Part Two because dealing with these two factors is what finance is all about. Only in the context of time and risk does finance make its distinctive contribution to the management process. Part Two is more general than the rest of the book in that it deals with concepts of *finance* as distinct from *business financial management*. Chapter 3 develops the notion of the time value of money and discounted-cash-flow techniques. Chapter 4 shows how the concepts of discounted cash flow can be applied to values determined in financial markets. Chapter 5 focuses on risk and introduces portfolio theory and the capital-asset-pricing model.

In Part Three, "Financial Analysis and Planning," we develop basic accounting information and the techniques of financial analysis and planning that will be used throughout the remainder of the book. Along with an understanding of time and risk, we regard the ability to develop information (Chapter 6), analyze performance (Chapter 7), and make pro-forma projections (Chapter 8) as prerequisites for capital-budgeting and financing decisions.

Given the background provided by Parts Two and Three, the student should be prepared for "Analyzing Investment Decisions," the topic of Part Four. This sequencing is consistent with a view that, in spite of the theoretical interdependence between investment and financing, successful firms typically put commercial strategy first and then tailor the financial structure to fit the commercial strategy. Hence, our treatment of capital budgeting precedes discussion of financing decisions. The three chapters of Part Four provide a comprehensive introduction to the topic, with coverage of decision criteria and cash-flow estimation in Chapter 9, return targets in Chapter 10, and techniques for dealing with risk in Chapter 11.

Having discussed ways to analyze *uses* of funds in Part Four, we then turn to the analysis of *sources* of funds in Part Five. Decisions related to "Financing the Firm's Assets" are covered in six chapters: sources of funds in Chapter 12, the effects of financial leverage in Chapter 13, debt policy in Chapter 14, dividend policy in Chapter 15, and leases, convertible securities, and warrants in Chapter 16. Chapter 17 covers more applied problems of issuing new securities and managing outstanding issues.

Part Six focuses on "Managing Working Capital." Chapter 18 covers sources of short-term financing and alternative strategies for financing a variable asset structure. Chapter 19 covers cash management, and Chapter 20 discusses both accounts receivable and inventories. Part Seven, "Special Topics in Financial Management," provides coverage of two important special areas—international finance and mergers—both of which have become an important part of financial management.

While the organization of the book reflects our own views as to the best sequencing of material, we recognize that others may prefer different sequences. We discuss some alternative sequences in the introduction to the *Instructor's Manual.*

A good grounding in basic financial accounting is an essential prerequisite to the use of *Essentials of Managerial Finance.* A course in basic microeconomics is helpful but not essential. Certain parts of the book require some background in statistics and probability concepts, but these can be omitted without loss of continuity. In Chapter 5 (and its appendix), we develop probability concepts for those wishing to take up this material.

PEDAGOGICAL FEATURES OF THE TEXT

Essentials of Managerial Finance has the following features:

- Each chapter starts with learning objectives.
- Key terms appear in boldface in text, are defined in color in the margins, and are listed in the glossary.
- Key equations appear in shaded boxes and are numbered for easy reference.
- Key points are highlighted in bold color type inside shaded boxes.
- Sample Problems with solutions are integrated throughout the text.
- "Finance in Practice" sections provide real-world applications of concepts and techniques.
- End-of-chapter material includes a listing of key concepts, a summary, questions, problems, and references.
- Extensive problem sections contain two types of problems: those that *reinforce* the concepts and techniques presented and those that *enrich* the discussion. Answers to odd-numbered questions and solutions to odd-numbered problems are given at the end of the text.
- The end-of-text glossary contains chapter references for each item.

THE INSTRUCTIONAL PACKAGE

Essentials of Managerial Finance is supplemented by a complete instructional package. The *Instructor's Manual/Test Bank* is composed of two parts. The first part, the *Instructor's Manual,* prepared by the authors, is composed of alternative course outlines, chapter commentaries, capsule statements of important topics covered in each chapter, teaching tips (often including supplemental class handouts), and answers or solutions to all of the questions and problems in the text. The second part, the *Test Bank,* was prepared by James Gentry, University of Illinois, Champaign-Urbana, and contains many analytical, challenging questions. The class-tested *Study Guide,* prepared by David Durst of the University of Akron, contains (for each chapter) learning objectives, key terms and concepts, fill-in questions for these key terms, a complete and extensive chapter outline, true/false questions, a multiple-choice review, and review problems, with full solutions to every question and problem; also included are calculator solutions for those students who use business calculators. The *Transparency Masters* supplement contains more than 75 figures from the text.

DIPLOMA is a set of four computer programs—EXAM, GRADEBOOK, STUDY GUIDE, and CALENDAR—that assist instructors in testing, grading, and other classroom functions. The programs operate on IBM, Apple IIc and IIe, and compatible microcomputers. A *"Financial Toolkit for the IBM PC"* disk provides most of the tools students need to work problems in financial management. Built-in spread sheets and strong graphing capabilities allow the student to work problems by changing the problem assumptions. The *"Microcomputer Problem-Solving Disk"* is a computer-assisted instruction program that presents problem sets for those chapters that lend themselves to analytical solution.

ACKNOWLEDGMENTS

Anyone who has worked on a textbook knows what a huge undertaking it is. We are fortunate to have benefited from the comments and criticisms of many excellent reviewers in preparing this second edition:

Gregory A. Brauer, *University of Iowa*
Larry Y. Dann, *University of Oregon*
Mona J. Gardner, *Illinois State University*
John Hammermeister, *Augustana College*
Del Hawley, *Michigan State University*
Daniel L. Knox, *Iowa State University*
Donald G. Margotta, *Northeastern University*
Dixie Mills, *Illinois State University*
William G. Modrow, *University of South Florida*
David L. Schalow, *St. Cloud State University*
Les Strickler, *Oregon State University*
Joseph M. Sulock, *University of North Carolina at Asheville*
Rolf Tedefalk, *University of North Dakato*
Gary R. Wells, *Idaho State University*
J. Kenton Zumwalt, *University of Illinois, Champaign*

As do all writers of finance textbooks, we owe an intellectual debt to those who have contributed to the development of the field of finance over the past decades. We have included specific references to literature throughout the text where doing so seemed useful to instructors or to students, and extensive references are provided at the ends of chapters. We are grateful to our colleagues at the University of North Carolina at Chapel Hill and elsewhere who have influenced our thinking on the subject of finance and who have contributed specific suggestions for the book. Special thanks go to Jennifer Conrad, Bob Conroy, Mustafa Gultekin, Dick Rendleman, and Michael Selby. We are grateful also to our students who have stimulated our interest in teaching over the years.

We wish to thank especially those who contributed directly to the preparation of the manuscript. Kathy Hevert provided invaluable assistance in updating text material, end-of-chapter problems, and the *Instructor's Manual*. Her care and good cheer were an inspiration. We also thank Bill Nance for help in preparation of *Test Bank* materials.

George Lobell of Scott, Foresman provided great enthusiasm as well as sound advice and guidance for the project, and (in retrospect) provided just the right pressure at crucial points. Mary LaMont provided expert editorial assistance and kept track of the seemingly endless flow of materials associated with the project.

To assist us in future revisions, we invite users of the book, students as well as instructors, to send us their comments and suggestions for improvement.

John J. Pringle
Robert S. Harris

Second Edition

Essentials of Managerial Finance

Contents

xi

Second Edition

Essentials of
Managerial Finance

Part **One**

Introduction

Financial managers must make important decisions about how to raise and use funds. In a corporation, for example, financial managers may obtain funds by borrowing money from a bank or by selling shares of stock to the public. Among other things, money may be used to build a new plant or to refurbish an old facility. In Part One, we discuss the basic problems facing financial managers in making such decisions, the objectives that managers pursue, and the financial environment in which managers operate.

Chapter 1 discusses the basic goals and problems of financial managers. There we see that, as shareholders' representatives, financial managers should make decisions that increase the *value* of the firm to those shareholders. Such value, established in financial markets, reflects both the timing and riskiness of benefits that the corporation can provide to shareholders. As a result, we see that dealing with time and risk is important for financial managers. In addition, Chapter 1 outlines the rest of the book.

Chapter 2 details the environment in which financial managers operate. It describes forms of business organization, types of financial markets, participants in financial markets, government regulation, taxes, and inflation. This chapter examines the institutional and financial surroundings in which financial managers find themselves.

The two chapters of Part One provide background on the goals and environment of financial managers so that we can better appreciate the decisions they face. These decisions are analyzed in subsequent parts of this book.

1

Financial Management: Goals and Problems

This chapter examines the goals of financial managers and some of the problems these managers face. As representatives of shareholders, managers should attempt to maximize the value of the firm to these shareholders. This value is determined in financial markets and depends upon both risk and the time value of money.

- In 1984, Chevron, a large oil company, paid more than $13 billion to acquire Gulf Oil.
- If you have taken a trip by plane recently, a bank or insurance company—not the airline—probably owned the plane in which you flew.
- In recent years, General Mills and many other large U.S. corporations borrowed money and promised to pay back double (or more) the amount borrowed.

What do these three statements have in common? They each describe the result of a basic management decision about how either to *use* money (the case of Chevron) or to *raise* money (the case of General Mills). This book will talk about how to explain and analyze such financial decisions. Why were the decisions made? Do the decisions make sense (and cents, too)? Do the decisions make more sense than other attractive decisions? We will get to Chevron's acquisition in Chapter 22, leasing of airplanes in Chapter 16, and General Mills's borrowing promise in Chapter 4, but in the meantime there is a wealth of descriptive and analytical material to explore.

For now we will set the stage for what follows by discussing the role of financial managers, their environment, and their decisions.

THE FINANCE FUNCTION

In most business organizations, there is no single individual who is designated as the "financial manager" and who has all the responsibilities of financial management.

Firms have controllers and corporate treasurers, vice-presidents of finance, and heads of finance committees, and sometimes all four titles are found within a single enterprise. On the other hand, we may find only one and sometimes none of these titles in the organizational structure of a firm. Yet, the financial-management function is always performed in some fashion, regardless of whether anyone has a job with the title of financial manager. Each firm must decide how to raise and invest money. A simplified, but useful, characterization of the financial manager's job is to think of a financial manager as making decisons that tie a firm to financial markets. Figure 1–1 displays the situation.

Figure 1–1
The Role of Financial Management

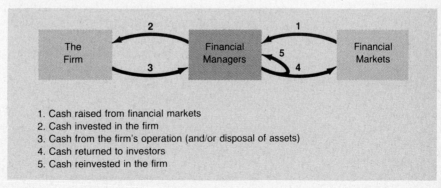

1. Cash raised from financial markets
2. Cash invested in the firm
3. Cash from the firm's operation (and/or disposal of assets)
4. Cash returned to investors
5. Cash reinvested in the firm

Financial markets—are markets where firms can raise funds and where their securities are valued, if they are publicly owned.

Stock—is a legal claim to ownership in a corporation and is usually divided into shares and represented by transferable certificates.

On the one hand, a financial manager must understand the operations and problems of the firm—the products produced, the technological capabilities, and the personalities of individuals. On the other hand, a financial manager must know a great deal about **financial markets**, the markets in which the firm can raise funds (for example, by borrowing money) and in which the firm itself may be valued. For example, **stocks**—shareholder ownership claims—of many large U.S. corporations are traded each day on the New York Stock Exchange, and the prices of these stocks fluctuate daily. Such prices represent the financial-market assessments of the value of the firm.

Being in such a position, financial managers operate in financial markets when they must decide on the best way to raise money. For example, should the firm raise money by borrowing from a bank in New York for a year, by borrowing from a bank in London for 6 months, or by selling new shares of stock? The possibilities are almost endless in a complex economy. Of course, the money being raised is to be used (invested); thus, the financial manager must make decisions about how to allocate the funds to be spent inside the corporation. Should a new plant be built, or should an old one be refurbished? Is an oil heating system better than a coal-burning system? At what rate should the firm expand (if at all)? If all goes well, the financial manager will also have to decide what to do with funds earned from profitable investments. Should they be paid to the corporation's owners or reinvested in hopes of even greater profits? To complicate the manager's life, all the decisions about using and raising money are interdependent and must be coordinated over time.

Although most of our discussion will concern financial management in business firms, business firms are not the only organizations that face financial decisions about how to invest and raise money. Other important organizations include federal, state, and local governments and government-owned enterprises; nonprofit organizations, such as churches, educational institutions, and hospitals; mutual associations owned by their customers, such as farm cooperatives and mutual insurance companies, savings banks, and savings-and-loan associations. Businesses owned by single individuals (for example, independent lawyers, doctors, and accountants) face financial decisions. All of these entities must make economic choices about how to raise and spend money.

This book is designed to help financial managers learn how to make better decisions. Some of the material in the book is descriptive—explaining the nature of financial markets—and can (and should!) be usefully supplemented by a regular reading of financial news, such as the *Wall Street Journal*. Other sections in the book explain the analytical tools that a manager can use.

Before we jump ahead of the story, we first need to establish what objectives a manager does or should have in making decisions. After all, a "good" decision is one that in some sense furthers the manager's and firm's objectives. In finance, we typically assume that a manager's objective is to maximize the value of the firm to existing *shareholders,* or owners. This important concept requires a bit of background explanation about the economic role of corporations.

A financial manager's objective is to maximize the value of the firm to existing shareholders.

PROFITS AND VALUE

Profit—is the excess of revenues over costs for a given project or time period.

Profit maximization—is the goal of making a firm's profits as large as possible.

A **market economy**—is an economic system in which resources are allocated and prices are determined through the interaction of buyers and sellers in markets.

The **equilibrium price**—is the price that equates quantity supplied and quantity demanded for a particular good or service.

The **price system**—is the coordination of economic activity through free trading of goods and services at prices set in markets by producers and consumers.

In practically any business endeavor, one common goal is to bring in more money than is paid out; that is, to make a **profit. Profit maximization**—making such profits as large as possible—seems to be a fairly reasonable goal for an entrepreneur who owns a firm because increases in such profits generally increase the entrepreneur's well-being.

In most economic studies of the way a **market economy** (economy in which goods are bought and sold at prices determined in markets) operates, profit maximization is viewed as the goal of corporate activity. Managers of firms have been found to direct their efforts toward areas of attractive profit potential, using prices as their signals.

Goods and services valued highly by consumers command higher prices, which in turn result in higher profits for producers. Other producers are attracted by profit opportunities, and supplies of the valued goods and services increase. In principle, a point of equilibrium is reached at which price and profit opportunities are just sufficient to bring forth the quantity demanded by consumers at that price. In the jargon of the economist, the **equilibrium price** is the price that *clears the market*, or equates quantity supplied and quantity demanded.

In the case of goods and services not highly valued or for other reasons in abundant supply, the process works in reverse. Prices and profits fall, producers drop out to search for better opportunities, and supply decreases. As a case in point, have you seen many new manual typewriters recently?

Thus, in a market economy, decisions to produce and consume are guided by prices set in markets by the actions of producers and consumers themselves. That is, the **price system** guides economic activity.

This important role for prices—signaling what consumers want and bringing forth quantity supplied—has not gone unnoticed even in centrally planned economies. In recent years, some parts of the economy in mainland China have been freed to allow prices to act as signals for production and investment. The planners recognize the useful role of prices in at least some areas of economic activity.

A central feature of a market economy is the decentralization of decision making. Decisions with respect to production and consumption are made by millions of economic units acting independently.

As a member of one of these independent economic units, a financial manager would desire to maximize profits. Unfortunately, profit maximization, in its simplest form, cannot be used as the basic criterion for decisions made by the financial managers of privately owned and controlled firms because of two main problems: *time* and *risk*.

Time

A major shortcoming of the simple profit-maximization criterion is that it does not take into account the fact that the timing of benefits expected from investments varies widely. For example, suppose your company is introducing a new product, and you anticipate a total of $100 profit (add as many zeros as you require) over the next two years. If you speed up production now (using production policy ''Fast''), you expect

Table 1–1
Timing of Anticipated Profit

	Anticipated Profit (dollars)	
Production Policy	Year 1	Year 2
"Fast"	100	0
"Slow"	0	100

to realize the entire $100 in the first year and none in the second. If you continue with your present schedule (production policy "Slow"), however, you expect to realize no profits in the first year and $100 in the second. Table 1–1 summarizes the situation. Which strategy should you, as a financial manager, select?

Simply adding the profits over time and picking the alternative with the highest total profit does not answer the question because both alternatives provide $100. However, one of the strategies is clearly better because it supplies the money earlier— namely, the "Fast" policy of speeding up production. To see why this policy is clearly better, consider that if you increased the speed of production and received $100 in year one, this $100 could be invested elsewhere between years one and two. For example, an available (if unexciting) possibility would be to put the $100 in a bank account and earn interest. Even at an interest rate of 6 percent a year, investing this $100 for one year would produce $100 + 0.06($100) = $106 in year two, an amount $6 larger than the $100 available in year two from the "Slow" policy.

Money has a time value.

Money can be put to work to earn a return, so savers and investors are not indifferent to the timing of cash receipts. As a result, cash flows in early years are valued more highly than equivalent cash flows in later years. For this reason, the "Fast" policy in Table 1–1 is superior to the "Slow" policy even though both provide a total of $100 profit. The profit-maximization criterion, thus, must be modified to take into account differences in timing of cash flows and the time value of money.

In practice, most investment and financing decisions involve much more complex patterns of cash flows over many periods, but the same message applies: a dollar today is worth more than a dollar tomorrow.

Risk

The second problem with assuming that financial managers are motivated simply by profit maximization is the problem of *uncertainty,* or *risk*. In this book, when discussing future events, we will use these two terms interchangeably. *Uncertainty* is present when we are not certain about what will happen in the future, and in most decisions (both personal and business) uncertainty is the rule, not the exception.

Table 1–2
Uncertainty About Outcomes

	Outcome of Investment (dollars)	
State of Economy	Investment A	Investment B
Recession	$ 90	$ 0
Normal	$100	$100
Boom	$110	$200

Consider two investment opportunities, A and B, whose profits depend on the state of the economy, as indicated in Table 1–2. If a normal economy is the most likely prospect, then the most likely profit from alternatives A and B is the same, $100. However, profit from A will lie between $90 and $110, whereas that from B can vary from 0 to $200, a much wider range. The most likely outcome is the same, but B is far more risky.

A decision criterion that considers only the most likely outcomes (the $100 in Table 1–2) provides no basis for choosing between alternatives A and B, whereas few investors would be indifferent between the two. As we will see later, nearly all investors who provide capital funds to firms are *risk-averse*, meaning that, other things being equal, they prefer less uncertainty to more. A risk-averse investor would prefer A to B in Table 1–2.[1] Risk preferences of investors are reflected in the financial markets and must be taken into account by firms when they make decisions.

As a decision criterion for practical use, profit maximization, thus, has two main shortcomings. It does not take into account either the time value of money or risk. For these reasons, **value maximization** has advantages over profit maximization as the operational criterion for financial-management decisions.

> **Value maximization has advantages over profit maximization as a decision criterion because it considers risk and the time value of money.**

Measuring Value

The **value** of certain assets is relatively easy to see and define. For example, the value of a $100 bill is that it can be exchanged for other assets given the prices of those assets (admittedly prices that are higher now than they once were). In a sense, the value of a dollar derives from its command over purchasing power. The value of a

Value maximization—is the goal of making a firm's value as large as possible and can be used as a criterion for making financial-management decisions.

The **value**—of an asset is the dollar amount a person would have to receive today to be just as well off as he or she would be owning the asset.

---

1. Daniel Bernoulli demonstrated the critical role of uncertainty in decision making in 1738 in a classic paper entitled ''Exposition of a New Theory on the Measurement of Risk.'' Bernoulli's paper, originally published in Latin, is as applicable to financial management today as it was 250 years ago. An English translation can be found in S. H. Archer and C. D'Ambrosio, eds., *The Theory of Business Finance,* 2nd ed. (New York: MacMillan, 1976).

college education is a bit harder to explain; surely, it brings both monetary and psychic rewards. In discussing financial assets or decisions in this book, we will talk of value in terms of cash benefits. Specifically, we will define the value of an asset as the dollar amount that persons would have to have today to be just as well off as they would be owning the asset. For example, suppose your favorite banker gave you a piece of paper that allowed you to receive $120 from her at any time. As long as the banker's credit is good, that piece of paper has a value of $120, since you can exchange it for $120 today if you desire. If, however, you were not sure that the banker could pay up upon demand, you might decide that you would be just as well off having $115 in your hand (for certain) as the piece of paper. If this were the case, the value of the paper would be $115. In the language of finance, because you are *risk-averse*, you have imposed a $120 − $115 = $5 penalty because of your uncertainty about the banker's ability to pay.

Figure 1–2
An Advertisement for a Certificate of Deposit

This announcement is not an offer to sell or a solicitation of an offer to buy any of these securities. The offering is made only by the Offering Circular.

NEW ISSUE   May 21, 1982

$60,000,000
Bank of Virginia

CERTIFICATES OF DEPOSIT*
(Zero Coupon)

	Price to the Public	Principal Amount at Maturity
Certificate of Deposit Maturing September 18, 1987 Totaling $20,000,000	$500	$1,000
Certificate of Deposit Maturing February 1, 1993 Totaling $40,000,000	$250	$1,000

*The Certificates of Deposit are insured by the Federal Deposit Insurance Corporation to a maximum amount of $100,000 for each depositor.

Copies of the Offering Circular may be obtained in any State in which this announcement is circulated only from such of the Underwriters as are qualified to act as dealers in securities in such State.

Wheat, First Securities, Inc.

Alex. Brown & Sons   A.G. Edwards & Sons, Inc.

J.C. Bradford & Co.   Butcher & Singer, Inc.   Craigie Incorporated

Davenport & Co. of Virginia, Inc.   Interstate Securities Corporation

Investment Corporation of Virginia   Johnston, Lemon & Co.   Legg Mason Wood Walker
                                             Incorporated   Incorporated

Scott & Stringfellow, Inc. Cecil, Waller & Sterling, Inc. Ferris & Company Strader & Company
                                                                          Incorporated   Incorporated

Source: Bank of Virginia.

Fortunately, in the United States, the Federal government guarantees many promises made by banks; however, most bank promises involve time delays. Returning to our example, suppose the banker promised to pay you $120 one year from today. Even if you were certain that the banker would pay up, it would take less than $120 today to make you just as happy as you would be if you received $120 in one year—because of the time value of money, which we discussed earlier. Suppose, for example, you knew that you could earn 20 percent interest per year; having just $100 today would allow you to accumulate $120 at the end of one year. That is, your $100 plus the $20 of interest would give you $120. In this instance, the $100 today is the value of the banker's promise because it will make you just as well off as the banker's promise (assuming you can earn interest of 20 percent per year). In the language of finance, time has a value, and you have imposed a $120 − $100 = $20 penalty for having to wait a year. Chapter 3 will discuss the time value of money in more detail.

Present value—is the value today of a future payment or stream of payments, discounted at the appropriate interest rate.

In general, values will reflect both time and risk, and the value of an asset is best viewed not in terms of its costs but in terms of the *future benefits* it can produce. The longer one has to wait for a benefit and the more uncertain is the benefit, the lower will be the **present value** of that benefit.

> **Value depends on the future benefits an asset can produce.**

The value-maximization decision criterion involves a comparison of value to cost. An action that has a present value, reflecting both time and risk, that exceeds its cost can be said to create value. Such actions increase the value of the firm and should be undertaken. Conversely, actions with value less than cost reduce the value of the firm and should be rejected. In the case of mutually exclusive alternatives, when only one is to be chosen, the alternative with the greatest net present value (excess of value over cost) should be selected. The objective of financial management is to maximize the value of the firm to existing shareholders.

Note that value maximization is simply the extension of profit maximization to a world where time and uncertainty are important. Where the time period is short and the degree of uncertainty is not great, value maximization and profit maximization amount to essentially the same thing.

VALUE AND MARKETS

Making an estimate of the value of an asset is often a difficult task. One useful guide, however, is the fact that many assets are traded in financial markets. For example, on May 21, 1982, the Bank of Virginia (see Figure 1–2) advertised a promise (similar to our earlier example of a banker's promise) in the *Wall Street Journal*. The bank promised to pay the owner of a piece of paper lump sum (**principal** payment) of $1,000 on February 1, 1993. The price of obtaining such a piece of paper was $250. That is, if you bought the paper in May 1982 you could get back $4 for every dollar invested ($1,000/$250 = 4). Why was there a $4-to-$1 ratio and a $750 difference between the promise to pay $1,000 and the price of obtaining the promise? The answer again is the importance of time and risk. Suppose that the Bank of Virginia has priced its promises well and that $250 is the maximum price that people will pay for the promise. In financial markets, the $750 penalty reflects the fact that $250 today (May 1982) is as good as this particular promise of $1,000 to be received more than 10 years later.

The **principal**—is a dollar amount borrowed, loaned, or deposited upon which interest is owed or earned.

In other words, as of May 1982, $250 is one estimate of the present value of the $1,000 to be received in 1993.

Although we'll spend more time in Chapters 3 through 5 developing specific techniques to derive present values of future cash amounts, the important point now is that financial markets place values on assets, values that often we can observe. The interaction of buyers and sellers determines a market price for an asset—in this case, the asset is a promise of $1,000 in the future, and the market price is $250 today. This price is one measure of value because it tells us what present dollar amount we would have to have in order to obtain the $1,000 in the future. Because of their role in establishing or reflecting value, financial markets will be extremely important to financial managers attempting to maximize value.

The value of assets is determined in financial markets.

> A **certificate of deposit(CD)**—is a bank's promise to make certain future cash payments to the person who buys the CD for a stated price.

The Bank of Virginia's promise is called a zero-coupon **certificate of deposit (CD).** A CD is a promise by the bank to make certain future cash payments to the owner of the CD. Typically, the payments consist of a series of interest payments and a larger final lump-sum payment. The interest payments (sometimes called *coupon payments*) on this particular CD are zero (because it is a *zero-coupon* CD), so only the lump-sum payment of $1,000 has been promised.

Is the value of a firm to its shareholders equal to the market price of its stock quoted in the financial pages of the daily newspaper? For example, on April 8, 1986, one share of IBM stock sold for $152. During the preceding 12 months, however, a share of IBM had sold for as much as $161 and as little as $118. The extent to which market prices fairly reflect true value is a complex and difficult issue about which we will have much to say later.

In the short run, stock-market prices are influenced by many factors beyond the control of management, such as general economic conditions, government actions, and the emotions of investors. Over the long run, market prices are a function of underlying economic variables: earning power and cash flows. Using valuation as a conceptual framework does not require that we consider every change in stock price as an indicator of the wisdom of our policies. Even though external factors may cause short-run fluctuations, our valuation criterion assumes that eventually wise managerial decisions will be recognized and reflected in market prices. In other words, in the long run, "true value will out."

VALUE AND MANAGERS: THEORY VERSUS PRACTICE

So far we have established that financial managers should have the objective of increasing their firm's value to shareholders. In a small firm with a single shareholder, this view of a manager's job is clear-cut. The owner of a corner drug store would have every right to expect the store manager to work on the owner's behalf—especially if the owner and manager happen to be the same person. The modern corporation (which we will discuss further in the next chapter) is, however, much more complex than the corner store. As an example, as of the early 1980s, IBM had more than 20 divisions and subsidiaries, operations in more than 100 countries, more than 350,000 employees, and more than 700,000 stockholders.

In such a complex organization, there is typically no single shareholder who can control corporate decisions. Instead share ownership is spread over thousands of individuals. Shareholders take on the role of suppliers of funding, while managers specialize in evaluating and making the firm's decisions. Managers are directly responsible to the board of directors elected by shareholders. This compact in forming a corporation gives managers the role of agents. But instead of representing a handful of professional athletes, corporate managers may be agents working on behalf of thousands of shareholders. Such a set of agreements has real benefits. It allows knowledgeable managers to use their specialized information and talents to make good business decisions. It allows shareholders to invest their money without having to learn about and keep track of the day-to-day operations of the firm. On the other hand, as with any set of agreements, the legal details can fast become complex. Managers are empowered to exercise their authority subject to the approval of the board of directors. If shareholders do not agree with managers' or directors' decisions, they have the right to vote for new members of the board of directors, which is empowered to change management.

If a manager's compensation were directly tied to whether or not he or she furthered shareholder interests, we probably would not have to worry about managers deviating from the pursuit of shareholder best interests—maximizing the value of the firm to existing shareholders. However, in a world where measurement of performance is difficult and information is costly, managers' interests do not always coincide with those of shareholders. For example, managers might be tempted to support the decision to acquire another company if they viewed their income and prestige as being based on the size of their corporation, even if the purchase provided no benefits (or perhaps losses) to existing shareholders. As another example, a manager may focus on achieving a short-term profit (even at the expense of overall shareholder value) if management compensation were based on that profit figure. In practice, situations arise in which the interests of owners and managers may diverge, and it is undoubtedly true that managers do not always act in the interests of owners.

When managers fail to act in behalf of those whose interests they represent (normally the shareholders of the firm), we would expect those managers ultimately to be replaced. Just how well the system of managerial selection works in practice is an important question, but it is beyond the scope of this book. We will assume in our discussion that a manager's job is to act in the interests of those for whom he or she is trustee, recognizing the interests of other parties as well. We will discuss analytical techniques, concepts, and policies that are useful to managers in discharging this responsibility.

Even if managers adopt value maximization as their goal, their job is difficult. In most corporate decisions, obtaining and interpreting information is a large problem. How does one measure the future benefits of the decision to enter the business of making personal computers? For that matter, how can we measure benefits even after they have occurred? As a result, some of our discussion in this book will focus on accounting tools as a means of gathering useful information. Even the best of accounting techniques, however, will not solve all the problems of dealing with time and risk.

In a world of costly and imperfect information it is not possible to analyze quantitatively the effects of every corporate decision. In fact, given the costs involved in gathering information on possible decisions, firms frequently state their goals (what they intend to accomplish) in qualitative, mission-oriented terms.

A firm might see itself as a builder of commercial aircraft, a provider of financial services, or a provider of equipment and technology for processing information. Around such a basic statement of purpose is built the firm's commercial strategy, which defines its markets, products, and production technology. From these follow supporting policies in operations, marketing, accounting, personnel, financial management, and so on.

That firms operate in such a mission-oriented fashion is not inconsistent with our notion of value maximization. Firms decide that they do a certain set of activities best and that the way to create value is to concentrate on these activities.

Another real-world factor complicating financial management is that there typically is no single financial manager. The functions of financial management may be diffused throughout the organization. Operating managers frequently have a considerable say in proposing and analyzing investment opportunities that lead to the commitment of corporate funds in plant, equipment, inventory, or acquisition of other firms. Central staff

---

Finance in Practice 1—1

The Performance of the Fortune 500

Each year in the spring, *Fortune* magazine publishes an extensive analysis of the 500 largest corporations in the United States, a listing that has come to be known as the "*Fortune* 500." In 1985, General Motors unseated Exxon for the top spot, having lost the title to Exxon in 1979. In fact, GM and Exxon are the only two companies to have held the top ranking since the listing was established in 1954. GM held it undisputed until 1974, when Exxon first took the lead. GM regained the title in 1977, then lost it again in 1979. In 1985, GM's sales were $96.4 billion, well above Exxon's $86.7 billion but still below Exxon's 1981 record of $108 billion. The accompanying Table A gives the top 10 companies in the 1985 *Fortune* 500 rankings.

Fortune designates its largest company winner based on total sales. If total profits had been the criterion, a different company would have won: IBM Corporation. For the second year in a row, IBM led all firms in profits. In 1985, IBM produced profits of $6.6 billion on sales of $50 billion versus GM's $4 billion profit on sales of $96.4 billion. In terms of profitability, or profits per dollar of sales, IBM was the clear winner. In fact, IBM has been a consistent leader in profitability (profits in relation to sales) over a period of many years.

But dollar profits are not the whole story, either. Another important measure of performance is *return on investment*, which measures profits per dollar of assets, or (alternatively) profits per dollar of shareholder investment. Using return on stockholder investment, IBM and Ford shared top honors in 1985 among the larger firms, although there were some smaller firms that did better on this measure.

Another important measure of performance is *return to shareholders*, which measures not company profits but the return actually received by shareholders. Shareholders receive part of their

Table A

	Sales (millions of dollars)	Assets (millions of dollars)	Profits (millions of dollars)
General Motors	96,372	63,833	3,999
Exxon	86,673	69,160	4,870
Mobil Corporation	55,960	41,752	1,040
Ford Motor Co.	52,774	31,604	2,515
IBM	50,056	52,634	6,555
Texaco	46,297	37,703	1,233
Chevron	41,741	38,899	1,547
AT&T	34,910	40,463	1,557
DuPont	29,483	25,140	1,118
General Electric	28,285	26,432	2,336

groups—sometimes under the treasurer, but just as frequently under the controller or an executive in charge of planning—play a large role in analyzing investment and financing ideas. Investment and financing decisions often involve committees of senior officers of the firm and, in the case of most major decisions, the board of directors as well.

Not only are financial-management functions frequently diffused among many individuals, but the functions are also diverse in character. Some of these functions— such as the receipt, disbursement, and custody of funds and **securities** (claims to ownership, such as stocks and bonds); the preparation of confidential payrolls; the supervision of how securities are registered or transferred; the payment of various taxes; the negotiation and placement of insurance policies—are better classified as administrative functions incidental to finance, rather than as financial management proper. Other functions are more central to financial management: the preparation and review of cash budgets; the investment of temporarily idle funds; the hedging of foreign-exchange

Securities—are claims to ownership, such as stocks and bonds.

---

return through dividends paid by the corporation and part through an increase in the value of their shares of stock. Looking now at industries rather than individual companies, the 1985 winner in total return to shareholders was a surprise—not electronics, not computers, not aerospace, but furniture! The furniture industry chalked up a total return to shareholders of 57.1 percent for the year, the best among 25 industry groups measured by *Fortune* and well above the all-industry average of 24.1 percent. It was not just a one-year phenomenon, either; furniture came in first among the 25 industries over the 10-year period 1976–85, delivering an average return to shareholders of 28.1 percent per year versus an all-industry average of 15.3 percent. The accompanying Table B gives the average annual return to shareholders for the 10-year period for the 25 industry groups.

There are many ways to measure performance. Looking at sales, profits, return on investment, and return to shareholders are just some of the possibilities. This book will examine these and other measures of performance but will also explore how to achieve excellence over the long run.

Table B

Industry	Average Annual Return (percent)
Furniture	28.1%
Publishing, Printing	25.0
Apparel	22.7
Aerospace	22.1
Beverages	21.2
Rubber Products	19.3
Food	17.5
Electronics	17.0
Transportation Equipment	16.9
Tobacco	16.7
Metal Products	15.4
All-Industry Average	**15.3**
Motor Vehicles and Parts	15.0
Mining, Oil Production	14.7
Forest Products	14.3
Textiles	13.4
Computers and Office Equipment	13.1
Chemicals	13.0
Petroleum Refining	12.7
Building Materials	11.6
Pharmaceuticals	11.5
Scientific & Photographic Equipment	11.4
Metals	8.3
Industrial and Farm Equipment	7.7
Soaps, Cosmetics	6.9

Source: Adapted from "Thin Profits in a Lean, Mean Year," and "The 500 Largest U.S. Industrial Corporations," *Fortune*, April 28, 1986, pp. 174–232.

risks; the arrangement of bank credit; the supervision of the company's pension funds; the decision to change the company's dividend rate or to issue new securities; the task of explaining the company's performance and prospects to groups of financial analysts.

The criterion for financial-management decisions in nonprofit organizations requires careful consideration. Benefits often are difficult or even impossible to measure. Dollar values cannot be attached to the output of churches or schools, for example. Where both benefits and costs of a course of action can be quantified, value maximization can still be used to guide decisions. Where only costs can be quantified, a cost/benefit approach still is useful, with cost estimates compared to benefits in qualitative terms. Where mutually exclusive alternatives are under consideration—that is, where two or more alternatives exist but only one can be chosen—**cost minimization** is the appropriate criterion. Where cash flows occur over long periods, techniques for dealing with the time value of money are as useful to a university or a church as to a business firm.

Cost minimization—is the goal of making a firm's costs as low as possible and can be used as a criterion for making financial-management decisions.

PLAN OF THE BOOK

To discuss the essentials of financial management, we have divided this book into seven parts.

Part One: Introduction

The present chapter and Chapter 2 are designed to give both an overview of financial management and to examine the legal, tax, and financial environments of a financial manager.

Part Two: Time and Risk

As already discussed, time and risk are two fundamental problems for a manager attempting to make decisions that will maximize the value of the firm. Chapter 3 develops the *discounted-cash-flow* method of valuing cash that comes in or goes out at different points in time. Chapter 4 shows how the concepts of discounted cash flow can be applied to values placed on securities in financial markets. One of the major difficulties in applying valuation techniques, such as discounted cash flow, is accounting for risk. Chapter 5 examines methods that can be used in dealing with risk. By the end of Part Two, we have thus developed some key tools and ways of thinking in finance.

Part Three: Financial Analysis and Planning

To apply any technique, one needs to have some sort of information or data. Part Three examines some of the standard ways in which information about a firm's performance (both past and prospective) is developed, reported, and analyzed. Chapters 6, 7, and 8 discuss basic accounting statements and tools of financial analysis and planning using these statements.

Part Four: Analyzing Investment Decisions

Having developed tools for dealing with time and risk (Part Two) and for analyzing information (Part Three), we turn in Part Four to an examination of how to make the basic decision of financial management—how to use funds. Chapters 9, 10, and 11 look at ways to decide which (if any) of the investment opportunities facing a firm should be undertaken. Making such investments involves allocating scarce funds among competing uses and requires an understanding that investment opportunities are typically risky and involve benefits and costs that are spread over time.

Part Five: Financing the Firm's Assets

Having discussed ways to analyze the *uses* of funds in Part Four, we turn in Part Five to an analysis of *sources* of funds. Chapters 12 through 17 examine what forms of financing are available to the firm. What are the differences between the various sources? Which sources are best for the corporation to use?

Chapter 12 descibes the types of long-term financing available in financial markets and discusses the efficiency of those markets in valuing securities (such as common stock) issued by corporations. Chapter 13 focuses on basic differences between debt (borrowing) and equity (stock) financing, leading to our discussion in Chapter 14 of the appropriate amount of borrowing for a firm. Chapter 15 examines the basic decision of whether to pay out money to shareholders or reinvest in the firm—the dividend decision. Chapters 16 and 17 are devoted to the large number of specialized financing methods and the practical side of actually issuing and managing the long-term securities, such as bonds, that the corporation may issue.

Part Six: Managing Working Capital

Since our discussion in Parts Four and Five focuses on the long-term investment and financing decisions of the firm, Part Six is devoted to a discussion of making decisions about certain shorter-term investments, such as inventory. Chapter 18 examines the different types of short-term financing; Chapter 19 looks at the management of cash; Chapter 20 analyzes the management of accounts receivable and inventory.

Part Seven: Special Topics

Having concluded our discussion of the major types of corporate decisions about investing and obtaining funds, we turn to a discussion of two specialized topics in Part Seven: international financial management (Chapter 21) and mergers and acquisitions (Chapter 22).

Guide to the Reader

In moving from chapter to chapter in a textbook, it is often easy to lose track of how the individual parts contribute to the whole process. As you read through this text, a useful reference point is Figure 1–1. Everything is this book is directed at developing an understanding of how financial managers can best make decisions about the *uses* and *sources* of money. To that end, we provide some background on the environment of the manager (Part One), basic tools of dealing with time, risk, and information (Parts Two and Three), and application of these tools to specific corporate decisions (Parts Four through Seven).

KEY CONCEPTS

1. Financial managers make decisions about the *sources* (financing decisions) and *uses* (investment decisions) of funds. In both situations, financial management ties the firm to financial markets.

2. Financial managers use value maximization as the basic decision rule to help them make "good" decisions. Value maximization is an extension of profit maximization.

3. Value is based on future benefits and reflects both time and risk.

4. Money has a time value: a dollar today is worth more than a dollar in the future. Generally, participants in financial markets are risk-averse.

5. The discipline of financial management encourages a long-range view in dealing with the fundamental issue of efficient use of capital funds.

SUMMARY

Financial management is the use of capital funds by firms and other organizations. Financial-management decisions link the firm to financial markets and establish both *sources* and *uses* of funds. Financial decisions are interdependent and must be coordinated over time as part of the process of financial planning.

Value maximization has replaced profit maximization as the operational criterion for financial-management decisions. Values reflect the facts that (1) money has a time value: dollars received today are more valuable than dollars received in the future; and (2) financial-market participants typically are risk-averse.

Although the theory and practice of financial management have developed around business firms, many of the concepts are applicable to the decisions of nonprofit organizations and individuals as well.

QUESTIONS

1. What is the role of business firms in a market economy? Contrast profit maximization and value maximization as criteria for financial-management decisions in practice.

2. Explain why money has *time value*.

3. How does risk affect value?

4. What problems do you see in using concepts such as profit maximization and value maximization in practice?

The Environment of Financial Decision Making

In this chapter we will discuss the environment in which financial managers have to operate. We will examine various types of financial markets, government regulations, and taxes. Additionally, we will see how inflation affects this environment.

In Chapter 1 we discussed the scope and objectives of financial management and the conceptual framework within which financial-management decisions are made. We found that modern financial management focuses on making decisions in a world that is uncertain and changing over time.

The environment in which financial managers actually must operate is far more complex than the world of microeconomic theory. It is a world of laws, regulations, taxes, institutions, and highly competitive financial markets. This chapter discusses some of the important factors that shape the environment in which financial-management decisions are made in practice.

As a guide to that discussion, Figure 2–1 is an expansion of Figure 1–1 from the last chapter that showed the role of a financial manager. Figure 2–1 diagrams a specific corporate decision: borrowing money from a bank (a source of funds) and investing the funds in a new piece of equipment (a use of funds).

In exchange for signing a loan agreement, the financial manager obtains funds. The colored arrows in Figure 2–1 show the deal struck between the financial manager as the corporation's representative and the bank. The funds (usually along with funds from other sources) are then invested in the firm in hopes of future cash benefits. The financial manager realizes, however, that part of the future benefits will go to the government in the form of taxes. Looking at the right side of Figure 2–1, we see that the bank actually obtained its money from individual savers as a result of savings-account deposits (dashed arrows). Both the bank and the savers also know they will owe taxes to the government.

Actually, Figure 2–1 is much too simplified. Financial managers can work for all sorts of business organizations, not just corporations. Financial managers have numerous ways to obtain money from other **financial institutions** (besides banks) and in **financial markets** (for example, by selling shares of stock). Banks can also obtain

A **financial institution**—is an institution, such as an insurance company, a leasing company, a mutual fund, a savings-and-loan association, or a commercial bank, that channels funds from savers to borrowers.

A **financial market**—is a market where firms can raise funds and where firms may be valued; it is a vast network linking institutions, instruments, and submarkets; it brings together millions of buyers and sellers of financial instruments.

Figure 2–1
The Environment of the Financial Manager

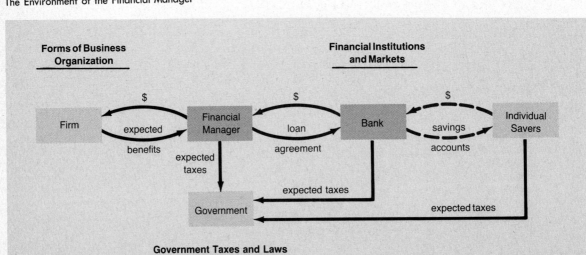

Government Taxes and Laws

funds in a variety of ways in these markets. For example, recall the Bank of Virginia zero-coupon certificate of deposit (CD) discussed in Chapter 1. A CD is one way banks can obtain funds. Finally, the government's regulation of business activity and its tax laws are quite complicated. In fact, some have claimed that the U.S. tax code is the most complex document in the history of civilization.

Before we can discuss whether a financial manager's decisions about sources and uses of funds are good ones, we need to get some idea of the environment in which the manager operates. In this chapter we will discuss various forms of business organizations, financial institutions, financial markets, government regulations, and taxes.

FORMS OF BUSINESS ORGANIZATION

A sole proprietorship—is a business owned and operated by a single individual that is not incorporated.

A corporation—is an entity created by law that owns assets, incurs liabilities, enters into contracts, and engages in on-going activities.

A partnership—is an unincorporated business owned by two or more persons.

There are three major forms of business organization: the sole proprietorship, the partnership, and the corporation.

More than 16 million firms operate in the United States. In terms of the number of firms, the **sole proprietorship** is the most prevalent organizational form, representing about 74 percent of all firms. A sole proprietorship is a business owned and operated by a single individual. On the other hand, the **corporation** is by far the dominant form in terms of income, output, and assets. For example, corporations account for about 90 percent of all business (as measured by dollar value of business receipts) in the United States.

The form of business organization varies widely by the line of business. In agriculture, for example, proprietorships account for the majority in terms of both number and sales. In manufacturing and transportation, however, corporations account for more than 90 percent of sales. In retail trade and services, proprietorships account for more in number of firms, and corporations account for more in sales. In many of these fields, the **partnership** is found less often than is either the proprietorship or the corporation, but partnerships do find wide use in professions such as law and architecture.

Even among corporations, small firms outnumber large ones, but the large firms dominate in sales and output. *Fortune's* list of the 500 largest industrial corporations in the United States in 1985 represented only a small fraction of the active manufacturing corporations in the United States but generated sales in 1984 that accounted for 47 percent of the gross national product.[1]

Sole Proprietorship

In a sole proprietorship, one individual owns all the assets of the firm and is responsible for all its liabilities. The proprietor is entitled to all profits and must stand all losses. He or she is responsible for all actions of the firm and is personally liable in the event of civil damage suits against the firm. With respect to such suits and debts of the firm, the proprietor's liability is *unlimited*; that is, it is not limited to his or her investment in the firm. Creditors or plaintiffs can proceed in legal actions against the personal assets of the proprietor.

---

[1]"Fortune's Directory of the 500 Largest U.S. Industrial Corporations," *Fortune Magazine* (April 29, 1985): 265–316.

The principal virtue of the proprietorship is its simplicity; in most cases, it is necessary only to set up shop and begin operations. The principal disadvantages of the proprietorship are unlimited liability and limitations on size. Generally, a proprietorship can raise funds only to the extent that the individual proprietor can do so. Often, this keeps the firm from raising large amounts of money.

A proprietorship itself is not subject to taxation of income. Rather, the income or loss derived from the proprietorship is included and taxed in the personal tax return of the proprietor.

Partnership

A **general partnership**—is a partnership in which all partners have unlimited liability for the debts and actions of the firm.

Partnerships are similar to proprietorships in all essential aspects except one: partnerships involve two or more owners. In a **general partnership**, all partners have unlimited liability for the debts and acts of the firm. Normally, a partnership agreement is made that specifies the capital contribution of the partners, the share of each partner both in the assets and in the profits of the firm, and provisions for the withdrawal or death of a partner. Aside from the need for an agreement, partnerships are about as easy to form as are proprietorships. As in the case of a proprietorship, the income of a partnership is included in the personal tax returns of the partners.

A **limited partnership**—is a partnership in which there is at least one general partner and one or more limited partners. Limited partners contribute capital, share in the profits, have limited liability for debts, and have no voice in directing the firm.

Some states permit the formation of a **limited partnership**, which consists of at least one general partner and one or more limited partners. The general partner (or partners) manages the firm and has the responsibilities of a partner described above, including unlimited liability. The limited partners' main function is to contribute capital; they share in the profits but have no voice in directing the operations of the firm; their liability is limited to their investment.

Relative to proprietorships, a partnership has the advantages of allowing a number of individuals to share expenses and work but to remain as owners. In addition, often a combination of partners will be able to raise more money than can a single individual. On the other hand, partners, like proprietors, often have unlimited liability and may face limitations in obtaining funds.

Corporations

By far the dominant form of business organization in the United States is the corporation. Although only about one in six firms is a corporation, corporations account for more than 80 percent of business sales. Large U.S. companies, such as IBM, General Motors, and Exxon are corporations. As defined more than a century and a half ago by John Marshall, Chief Justice of the U.S. Supreme Court, "A corporation is an artificial being, invisible, intangible, and existing only in contemplation of the law." A corporation is, thus, an entity created by law that is empowered to own assets, to incur liabilities, and to engage in certain specified activities.

The corporate form differs from the proprietorship and partnership forms in several important respects. First, and probably most important, the liability of owners for debts and actions of the firm is limited to their investment in the firm. Creditors and plaintiffs in damage suits can proceed against the assets of the corporation but not against the personal assets of the owners. Second, ownership in a corporation is easily

Stock—is the legal claim to ownership of a business corporation and is divided into shares and represented by certificates that can be transferred from one owner to another.

transferable, which is not true for a partnership. The corporation is a perpetual entity. Shares of **stock** give the shareowner certain claims of ownership in the corporation, such as receiving dividend payments and voting on the election of directors who monitor the activity of corporate managers. Generally, owners may sell their shares without affecting the operation of the firm. Third, because the corporation itself may incur liabilities, the corporate form provides better access to external sources of capital. As noted earlier, the corporation is the dominant form of business organization in the United States in terms of total output of goods and services. This dominance is due to the advantages of limited liability, transferability of ownership, continuous long-term existence, and access to capital.

A disadvantage of the corporate form is that, because it is a legal entity, the corporation itself pays taxes on its income—and, as we will discuss later, corporate tax rates are different from personal tax rates. In addition, choosing the corporate form of organization may subject owners' income to a form of double taxation. Income is taxed once at the corporate level and once more as part of personal income when income is distributed to shareholders as dividends.

Corporations are formed under the laws of the various states. A charter is issued by the state, establishing the corporation as a legal entity and setting forth its purpose and its relationship to the state. Corporate bylaws, governing the internal management of the firm, then are established. A board of directors is elected by the owners to set policy and oversee the firm in the owners' behalf. The directors appoint the executive officers of the firm, often referred to as the management, who normally are full-time employees of the firm. Managers are charged with executing the policies established by the directors and administering the operations of the firm. Selecting the firm's top management personnel and evaluating their performance are major functions of the board of directors.

Subchapter S Corporations

A **subchapter S corporation**—is a small corporation that may legally be treated as if it were a partnership for income-tax purposes.

Under a provision of the tax law known as "Subchapter S," certain small business corporations may elect to be treated in a manner similar to partnerships for income-tax purposes. Although such a corporation enjoys limited liability, the corporation's income is taxed directly at the shareholder level and not at the corporate and personal levels. This form of organization is widely used in the professional-service sector of the economy. In 1982, the Subchapter Revision Act redefined rules for **subchapter S corporations** and expanded the maximum number of shareholders allowed under the subchapter S rule to 35.

THE FINANCIAL ENVIRONMENT: FINANCIAL MARKETS

No matter what form of business organization is chosen, a firm's managers will be making decisions that affect the firm's relationship to the financial market—decisions about raising and using money. Recall our diagram of a simplified decision of a financial manager in Figure 2–1. In a fundamental sense, financial management is a continuing two-way interaction between the firm and its financial environment.

In the financial market, the firm raises the funds required for its current operations and for its capital expenditures. Here also the firm temporarily invests its surplus funds, pending their more long-term disposition. Finally, and most important, it is the financial market that ultimately determines whether the firm's policies are a success or failure.

> **The ultimate determination of the success or failure of a firm's policies is made in the financial market.**

The financial market is not a single, physical place. It comprises millions of participants spread across the world along with offices linked by an extensive telecommunication network that brings buyers and sellers together and sets prices in the process of doing so. In order to understand the complex institutions, instruments, and submarkets that collectively make up the financial market, it is useful to break down the financial market into smaller components. There are many ways of doing this; one way is to address the following questions:

1. What functions does the financial market perform?
2. What major types of financial claims or instruments are traded in the financial market?
3. Who are the principal participants?
4. What are the major submarkets with which the financial manager deals?

The Functions of the Financial Market

Financial claims—are promises to pay money in the future and are exchanged in financial markets for money. Examples are stocks, bonds and loans.

Surplus spending units—are individuals, companies, or government bodies who have excess funds.

Deficit spending units—are individuals, companies, or government bodies who need funds.

Like most markets, the financial market is where buyers and sellers meet in order to exchange things for money and vice versa. The things exchanged in financial markets are **financial claims**, or promises to pay money in the future. Individuals, companies, or government bodies who have excess funds exchange these funds in return for claims to future sums of money. Traders with excess funds are also known as **surplus spending units**. On the other side of the equation, individuals, companies, or government bodies who need funds sell claims that promise to pay money in the future in exchange for present funds. Traders who need funds are also known as **deficit spending units**. For example, as we saw in Chapter 1, an individual could pay $250 to the Bank of Virginia in exchange for the bank's promise to pay back $1,000 in the future. This specific type of financial claim is a certificate of deposit. Many other types of financial claims exist.

Figure 2–1 depicts a corporation's decision to borrow money from a bank, which in turn has received deposits from individual savers. The individual savers had excess funds that were ultimately channeled to a corporation that needed money. Organized financial markets make this process seem rather routine, but it does involve two sets of trades in which claims to *future* sums of money are exchanged for money today. In the first trade (dashed arrows), the bank promises to pay savers their money back (plus interest) in the future in exchange for the savers' making a deposit. The financial claim here might be a savings-account passbook showing the right of the saver to withdraw money from the bank. Alternatively, the bank could have used a certificate of deposit, as did the Bank of Virginia. In the second trade(colored arrows), the company promises to pay back the loan from the bank at some future date (also paying interest on the loan) in exchange for receiving the money today. The bank serves an important

A **financial intermediary**—is a financial go-between, such as a bank, that makes possible the easy transfer of funds from savers to spenders. Financial intermediaries gather funds, analyze credit possibilities, evaluate risk, and handle administrative and legal details for borrowers and lenders.

Capital formation—is investment in real assets, such as new buildings, machinery or technology, and is facilitated by financial markets.

Current saving—is any income not spent on consumption in the current period.

The **secondary market**—is the market where existing financial claims (such as stocks or bonds), as compared to new claims, can be bought and sold.

The **new-issues market**, or **primary market**,—is the market in which issues of new securities are offered for sale by companies to investors.

role as the financial go-between, or **financial intermediary**, that enables funds from surplus spending units (individual savers in Figure 2–1) to be easily channeled to deficit spending units (the corporation).

Of course, financial-market transactions can become much more complicated than those outlined in Figure 2–1, and there are all sorts of other financial claims traded and other financial intermediaries. Basically, however, the financial market performs several functions essential to a society.

1. The financial market allows those who wish to defer consumption (that is, to save) a convenient way of doing so.

2. The financial market allows those who wish to accelerate consumption (that is, to dissave) to do so conveniently. Consumer credit, credit cards, and mortgage loans enable millions of individuals to enjoy cars, appliances, and homes now, rather than later.

3. The financial market provides a channel through which new savings can flow into productive investment. If a firm needs money to build a new plant or develop a new technology, it may raise those funds by borrowing money from a bank, by selling new stock, or in numerous other ways. The financial market provides a ready source of funds and, thus, makes it possible for some organizations, mainly firms, to specialize in investing in real assets. Such investment is called **capital formation**. In order for living standards to rise, an economy has to add to its stock of tangible capital; that is, it must create additional residences, roads, plants, equipment, and inventory. The resources required for these purposes must come from **current saving**—that part of current output (gross national product) not immediately consumed. A major purpose of the financial market is to gather the current saving of millions of surplus spending units and put this saving to productive use.

4. Another important function of the financial market is to provide a **secondary market** where existing financial claims can be bought and sold so that decisions to save and dissave are not irrevocable. For example, if a person saves money and buys a share of IBM stock, that person would want to be able to sell that stock at some future date in case the money became needed for consumption. On the other hand, IBM would not want to sell off its plant and equipment to satisfy the desires of shareholders who want to cash in on their stock. The secondary market solves this problem by allowing shareholders to sell their IBM stock to other individuals without requiring IBM to take any action at all. The better the secondary market, the more likely it is that people will be willing to save and transfer their current saving to those who can use it.

The financial market can be divided functionally into two connected parts. One is the **new-issues market**, or **primary market**, through which society's annual saving eventually flows from the surplus spending units in society to the deficit spending units in exchange for newly issued claims. The other is the secondary market in which units that hold previously issued claims can exchange them for money. For example, IBM's sale of new stock in exchange for money would be an exchange in the new-issues market. The purchase of old IBM stock from another individual would be a secondary-market transaction. As might be expected, the size of the new-issues market is small relative to the size of the secondary market because the latter includes all past issues still outstanding.

5. In the process of facilitating saving and investment, financial markets also set prices, or values. For example, when people buy and sell shares of stock in IBM, the natural forces of supply and demand determine a market price, or *market value*, for a

share of stock. On July 31, 1985, for example, the value of a share of IBM stock was about $131.40 per share. Similarly, the financial market also determines how much money a person can receive one year hence if he or she is willing to give up a dollar today. In this case, the market value is an interest rate. At an interest rate of 15 percent per year, a person can obtain $1.15 in one year for each dollar saved today. As mentioned in Chapter 1, value plays a critical role in financial-management decisions when the objective is to maximize the value of the firm to existing shareholders. We will return to valuation in detail in Chapters 3 through 5.

Major Types of Financial Claims

A **corporate bond**—is a long-term debt claim representing a corporation's promise to repay with interest money borrowed from a bond holder.

A **mortgage**—is a loan in which designated property is pledged as security.

A **commercial loan**—is the transfer of funds from a bank to a business firm in exchange for the firm's promise to repay the funds with interest according to a specified schedule.

Table 2–1 shows the major types of financial claims outstanding as of the end of 1984. The last column shows the net new issues of each type of claim during 1984.

Corporate stocks represent shareholder claims to the ownership of a corporation. A **corporate bond** is a debt claim representing a corporation's promise to pay interest plus principal to the bondowner. At the time of the original issue of a bond, the corporation receives money (borrows) in return for its promise to make future cash payments. Bondholders have a legal right to receive their interest and principal payments but are not legal owners of the corporation. The U.S. government also borrows money by issuing bonds. In addition, it issues shorter-term debt claims in the form of notes and bills. U.S. government agencies and state and local governments raise funds by issuing debt claims such as bonds. Both individual homeowners (residents) and business firms take out **mortgages**, which supply them with the money they need now to buy property or buildings in return for promised interest payments and repayment of the borrowed amount. Finally, commercial banks make large numbers of **commercial loans** to business concerns. While Table 2–1 shows the major types of financial claims—stocks and forms of borrowing (bonds, notes, bills, mortgages, and loans)—there are many other sorts of specialized claims that are traded in the financial market. Chapters 12 and 18 will discuss the details of the ways corporations can raise money and will describe some of these additional claims.

Table 2–1
Major Financial Claims (billions of dollars)

	Outstanding 12/31/84	New Issues During 1984
Corporate stocks	2,030.0	−89.1
Corporate bonds	594.1	48.7
U.S. government securities (bonds, notes, bills)	1231.8	180.9
U.S. government-agency securities	531.3	71.3
State and local government securities	542.8	66.5
Residential mortgages	1518.4	155.1
Business and farm mortgages	512.2	53.2
Commercial bank loans	931.7	119.8

Source: Salomon Brothers, *1985 Prospects for Financial Markets* (New York: Salomon Brothers, 1985). Copyright © 1985 Salomon Brothers, Inc. Reprinted by permission.

Principal Participants in the Financial Market

Who are the participants in the financial market? The answer is almost everybody. But it is convenient to distinguish among three categories of participants: operating sectors, financial intermediaries, and specialized institutions.

Operating Sectors.   The first group consists of the ultimate providers and users of society's flow of savings—namely, households (or individuals), businesses (including corporations), and government. To complete the picture, we add a fourth operating sector classified in the accounts as the "rest of the world," which lumps together our net transactions with entities outside the United States. In general, the household sector, which collects the largest part of income generated by economic activity, is a net saver and, hence, a net provider of funds to the other three sectors. However, while these other sectors are net users of funds on balance, they also participate on an individual basis as providers of funds to the market. For example, a corporation with a temporary excess of funds will typically lend those funds in the market rather than use them to reduce its indebtedness to the rest of society. Likewise, although households as a group are net providers of funds to the market, many individual households borrow from the market in order to purchase homes and cars.

Financial Intermediaries.   The transfer of funds from surplus units (mainly households) to deficit units (mainly business, government, and some households) can take place directly, but **direct finance** is inconvenient for both the ultimate provider and the ultimate user of funds. Although the aggregate flow of annual saving in the United States is very large, individual households save in relatively small amounts—usually a few hundred or a few thousand dollars a year. Imagine a firm or a government attempting to borrow millions of dollars under conditions of direct finance. Financial officers would be busy indeed, for they would have to knock on hundreds or thousands of doors in order to obtain the total amount. Each lender would be issued an IOU. The cost to the firm for search and acquisition obviously would be quite high, significantly increasing the cost of borrowing. The higher is the cost of obtaining funds, the smaller is the number of investment opportunities that can be undertaken, and the lower is the level of investment that can be undertaken by the firm.

Direct finance is also a problem from the saver's standpoint. Suppose a household has saved $1,000 that it wishes to lend. Lending the entire amount to one borrower exposes the lender to considerable risk. To get reasonable diversification, the saver must lend to a number of firms rather than only one, analyzing the credit and evaluating the risk of each and making a separate contract with each. The costs to the saver in terms of time and effort would be quite large in relation to the amount of interest that could be earned. Also, the claims held by the saver would be highly *illiquid*, meaning that they could not be turned back into cash quickly at low cost.

Direct finance between savers and investors, thus, involves very significant transaction costs of search, acquisition, analysis, and diversification. The net return to savers would be so small (perhaps negative) that lending simply would not be worth the effort. Borrowing costs to firms would be so high that investment would be very low. In short, the losses due to **financial friction** would be so great that very little saving and investment would take place. As always, saving would equal real investment after the fact, but at a very low level of each. Economic growth would be very slow indeed,

Direct finance—is the direct transfer of funds from savers to investors without going through a financial intermediary.

Financial friction—refers to the costs for search, acquisition, analysis, and sale involved with financial transactions.

Figure 2–2
Direct Finance Versus Intermediation

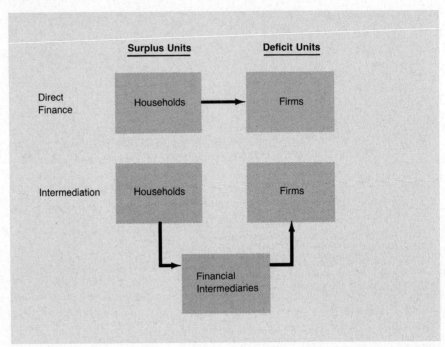

for few capital assets would be accumulated. Thus, financial intermediaries came into being to collect funds from savers and to transfer them to ultimate users. Today the largest part of saving goes into investment through financial intermediaries, such as commercial banks, mutual-savings banks, savings-and-loan associations, and life-insurance companies. Figure 2–2 shows the role of a financial intermediary.

With intermediation, savers lend to intermediaries, who in turn lend to firms and other fund-using units. The saver holds a claim against the intermediary in the form of a deposit, rather than against the firm. The financial officer of a firm who wishes to borrow a large sum of money now makes a single trip to the bank or insurance company and negotiates with only one lender, or at most a few. The cost of borrowing funds is much lower. Many investment opportunities that before were uneconomical now can be undertaken.

The saver also needs to make only one trip. The saver with $100 to save deposits it in a bank or savings-and-loan association and indirectly holds a claim against all the units to which the intermediary lends. The hundreds or even thousands of loans made by the intermediary comprise its loan **portfolio**, and the investor has a claim on that portfolio. The claim, therefore, is far more diversified than under direct finance, and at the same time the claim is far more liquid because it can be turned into cash on short notice at negligible cost. For a given degree of risk and liquidity, that saver's costs are far lower, and the net return far higher, than under direct finance.

The financial intermediary, thus, performs many of the tasks formerly performed by lender and borrower—tasks of gathering funds, analyzing credit, evaluating risk,

A **portfolio**—is the collection of securities (stocks, bonds, loans, etc.) held by an investor.

and handling administrative and legal details. These tasks involve costs, and the intermediary can perform them much more efficiently and at much lower total cost than can individual lenders and borrowers.

By their actions, financial intermediaries provide higher returns to lenders for a given degree of risk and liquidity and a lower cost to borrowers than would be possible with direct finance. Higher saving rates encourage saving, and lower borrowing costs permit greater investment. Saving and investment are equated at a much higher level; capital assets are accumulated more rapidly; economic growth is faster. Thus, financial intermediaries in conjunction with well-developed financial markets have a great influence on economic growth and development.

> **In comparison to direct finance, financial intermediation usually provides higher returns to lenders and lower costs to borrowers.**

Table 2–2 shows the relative importance of various types of intermediaries classified by broad types. It also indicates the relative change over time in the position of each type. While Table 2–2 shows little change in relative position in the past, the roles of financial intermediaries are now undergoing large changes.

Specialized Institutions.   The financial intermediaries just discussed channel the flow of saving from surplus to deficit units. Another tier of specialized institution in the

Table 2–2
Total Assets of Selected Financial Intermediaries, Year-End = 1965, 1982 and 1984

	Total Assets, 1965		Total Assets, 1982		Total Assets, 1984	
	Billions of Dollars	*Percent*	*Billions of Dollars*	*Percent*	*Billions of Dollars*	*Percent*
Depository types						
Commercial banks	336	38.6	1435	40.0		
Savings-and-loan					1664	37.9
associations	130	14.9	601	16.9	827	18.8
Mutual savings banks	58	6.6	151	4.2	178	4.1
Credit unions	9	1.0	64	1.8	102	2.3
Contractual types						
Life insurance companies	154	17.6	456	12.8	572	13.0
Pension and retirement						
funds[a][b]	106	12.1	455	12.8	543	12.4
Other						
Mutual funds[b][c]	35	4.0	164	4.6	220	5.0
Finance companies	45	5.2	225	6.3	278	6.3
Real estate trusts	0	0.0	2	0.1	4	0.1
Total	**873**	**100.0**	**3553**	**100.0**[d]	**4388**	**100.0**[d]

[a]Excludes Social Security and other federal retirement funds.
[b]Influenced by the level of stock prices.
[c]Includes money-market funds.
[d]Subtotals do not add to 100 due to rounding.
Source: Board of Governors, Federal Reserve System, *Flow of Funds, Assets and Liabilities Outstanding.*

financial market facilitates the flow of funds among the intermediaries themselves as well as to and from the ultimate operating sectors. These include institutions such as investment bankers, securities dealers and brokers, the organized securities exchanges, and mortgage bankers, to name just a few of the many types of highly specialized financial institutions within the market.

An **investment banker**—is a financial intermediary that underwrites and distributes new securities offerings and helps a business obtain financing.

When a corporation or a municipality issues a new security, it generally sells that issue through a syndicate of **investment bankers**. In effect, the bankers buy the issue and then wholesale and retail it to financial intermediaries and individuals. Investment bankers often provide advice to their customers on a wide range of financial issues, ranging from how to set a price on a newly issued share of stock to how to go about acquiring another company. Most of the largest investment-banking firms are based in New York, although there are many regional firms as well.

Securities brokers and dealers—are financial intermediaries that buy and sell stocks, bonds, and other financial claims in return for a commission fee.

The major investment-banking houses (referred to in England as merchant banks) resell new issues through their own branches or through the branch network of hundreds of **securities brokers and dealers**. This same group of brokers and dealers provides the marketplace in which individuals and institutions can sell or buy stocks and bonds.

Government-bond dealers—are financial intermediaries that buy and sell government bonds.

The federal government does not use investment bankers, but rather sells directly to **government-bond dealers** through the Federal Reserve System. The government bond dealers buy the bulk of each new government issue and eventually retail it to institutions and individuals.

Exchanges—are actual organizations with physical locations where financial claims are bought and sold.

Organized **exchanges** are actual organizations that have physical locations where financial claims are bought and sold. Exchanges such as the New York Stock Exchange (NYSE) and the American Stock Exchange (AMEX), both located in New York City, provide the means through which the public can buy and sell existing stocks and bonds listed on those exchanges. In addition to the NYSE and AMEX, there are other regional exchanges, each having its own rules and building.

To be listed on an exchange, a firm must satisfy certain financial requirements. For example, for listing purposes the NYSE requires firms to have at least 2,000 stockholders (owning 100 shares or more each), a minimum of 1 million shares of stock outstanding that is publicly held, a total market value of its publicly traded shares of at least $16 million, and certain standards of demonstrated earning power. In addition, certain governmental requirements imposed by the Securities and Exchange Commission (SEC) must be met. Other exchanges, including the AMEX and other regional exchanges, have less stringent requirements. Most larger corporations are listed by the NYSE or AMEX.

The **over-the-counter (OTC) market**—is the network of buyers, sellers and brokers who interact by means of telecommunication and deal in securities not listed on an organized exchange.

Bonds (corporate and government) and all stocks not listed on the major exchanges are bought and resold on the **over-the-counter (OTC) market**. The OTC market is not an actual organization with a physical location. It is a way of trading securities. The participants here are many of the same brokers, dealers, and investment-banking houses mentioned earlier. Rather than trading at a physical location, as is done on an organized exchange, the participants are linked by a telecommunications network. The National Association of Securities Dealers Automated Quotation System (NASDAQ) is an automated system that provides up-to-date prices on thousands of securities and is an important link between participants in the OTC markets.

A **mortgage banker**—is a financial intermediary who transfers funds from institutions who want to invest in mortgages to institutions or individuals who wish to borrow mortgage funds.

The mortgage market is large and complex, with its own set of specialized institutions. Among them is the **mortgage banker** who serves as an intermediary between institutions that want to place some of their funds in mortgages rather than in securities and individuals and institutions who wish to borrow mortgage funds.

Finally, there are several groups of specialized dealers in the financial market—such as dealers in commercial paper, in federal funds, or in foreign exchange. Virtually every function and subfunction that can be specialized has been specialized.

Major Submarkets: The Money Market and the Capital Market

The **money market**—is the market for transactions in short-term loans.

The **capital market**—is the market for transactions in longer-term debt issues and stock.

One widely used classification divides the financial market as a whole into the **money market** and the **capital market**. The money market makes possible open-market transactions in highly marketable short-term debt instruments, while the capital market is reserved for transactions in longer-term debt issues and stocks. The dividing line between short-term and long-term is necessarily arbitrary. By convention, short-term claims are those financial claims with maturities of less than one year. By this definition, a 60-day certificate of deposit (CD), with payment promised in 60 days, issued by a commercial bank would be a short-term security traded in the money market, while a 20-year government bond would be traded in the capital market. There is, however, no physical distinction between money and capital markets. In addition, a bond maturing in 1.5 years, which is by standard convention part of the capital market, is in many ways more like a 60-day CD than it is like a 20-year bond. Recognizing these difficulties, this book will adopt the standard convention of a maturity of one year as the dividing line between the money and capital markets.

The Money Market.   The principal participants in the money market are commercial banks (especially the large money-center banks located in New York, Chicago, and San Francisco), the U.S. government, and nonfinancial corporations.

A **commercial bank**—is a depository financial institution that offers checking-account services, accepts savings and other types of deposits, and makes loans.

In recent years, **commercial banks** have also become major borrowers in the money market through the sale of short-term negotiable certificates of deposit (CDs). The CDs issued by the larger banks are now actively traded and have emerged as a major money-market instrument. By the end of 1984, the volume of CDs outstanding reached $416.2 billion.[2] It should be noted that in recent years banks have also started issuing long-term CDs, such as the Bank of Virginia zero-coupon CD (mentioned in Chapter 1), which matures in 1993.

The **federal-funds market**—is the market in which excess bank reserves are borrowed and lent by federal banks.

Banks are also the principal participants in a highly specialized submarket known as the **federal-funds market**. Member banks of the Federal Reserve system are required by law to hold legal reserves—that is, deposits at the Federal Reserve Bank. Given the large ebb and flow of payments into and out of each bank, an active market has developed through which banks with excess reserves on a given day lend these funds to banks with deficient reserves. Such day-to-day transactions among banks are known as federal-funds transactions.

The U.S. government is a major demander of funds in the money market. A large part of the federal debt has been financed by the issuance of short-term marketable securities. For example, at the end of 1984, there were more than $374 billion worth

---

[2]This figure represents the amount outstanding of large time deposits (those in denominations of $100,000 or more) issued by commercial banks and thrift institutions as reported by the Federal Reserve.

of short-term (maturities of less than one year) U.S. Treasury bills outstanding. A large volume of this government short-term debt matures every week and has to be refinanced, which the Treasury does through its weekly auction of new short-term bills or certificates. The interest rates set in these auctions, especially the 3-month Treasury bill rate, are key rates in the money market and are followed closely both by government economists and participants in financial markets.

Commercial paper—is short-term borrowing, typically notes of less than 6 months' maturity.

Business corporations have become important participants in the money market, both as borrowers and lenders. Two types of commercial borrowers use the open market as a continuing source of short-term funds. Well-known nonfinancial firms issue short-term notes, typically of less than 6 months' maturity, known as **commercial paper** to finance short-term fund needs. Large finance companies, such as General Motors Acceptance Corporation, issue commercial paper (known as *finance paper* when issued by a financial firm) either directly or through dealers. We will discuss commercial paper in more depth in Chapter 18.

In addition to the major money-market participants discussed above, there are several other sectors that use the market regularly. Securities brokers and dealers, who have to hold inventories of securities in the course of their businesses, finance themselves through money-market borrowing. Brokers also need funds to lend to customers who desire to purchase securities on margin (that is, with a cash down payment less than the market value of the purchase). Exporters and importers require short-term funds to finance goods in transit or in warehouses. State and local governments borrow in the money market when they need current funds for brief periods pending the expected arrival of large, periodic tax receipts.

The Capital Market.   The capital market makes possible the flow of the long-term financing required for such purposes as long-term investment in business plant and equipment, residential construction, municipal building projects, and financing portions of the debt of the U.S. government. It also provides a place where investors who hold long-term instruments can sell them expeditiously to other groups; thus, the capital market gives long-term instruments a degree of liquidity.

The major borrowers in the capital market are: business corporations, who issue various forms of debt and stock; federal, state, and local governments (or their agencies), who issue bonds and notes; and apartment and home buyers, who borrow money by taking out mortgages. Most of the supply of long-term funds is channeled to the capital market through financial intermediaries such as insurance companies, pension funds, savings institutions and commercial banks. The instruments themselves will be discussed more fully in Chapter 12, which deals with long-term financing instruments.

International Financial Markets.   Our discussion to this point has focused on U.S. financial markets. Today, however, an increasing amount of financial activity is taking place in international financial markets. These markets bring together different economies and have flourished with the explosive growth in international trade and investment. For example, many large U.S. corporations now borrow some of their funds not from U.S. banks but from banks in other countries. Sometimes these borrowings may be denominated in dollars, other times in other currencies such as the French franc or the German mark. Chapter 21 will discuss in more detail international capital markets and their impact on financial managers.

GOVERNMENT REGULATION

We have examined the role of financial markets and intermediaries as part of the environment facing managers. Another important feature of this environment is the set of government rules and regulations.

Business firms are affected by the actions of a wide range of federal and state regulatory agencies. For many top managers, especially of larger companies, dealing with governmental regulation has become the single most attention-consuming function.

In fact, perhaps the largest financial-management challenge in U.S. history was a direct result of the interaction of corporate activity and government regulation. On January 1, 1984, the U.S. telecommunications industry was transformed by the breakup of the Bell System. For generations, most local telephone service had been provided by one giant corporation, American Telephone and Telegraph (AT&T), which was the parent company of local telephone companies throughout the country as well as of manufacturing and research subsidiaries. AT&T also dominated the market for long-distance phone service and telephone equipment. Due to its monopoly position in many markets and the importance of telephone service, this Bell System of companies was subject to government regulation. In 1984, however, AT&T was divided into eight new companies: seven operating companies that provide phone service on a regional basis and a new AT&T, which retains the long-distance services as well as manufacturing and research facilities. This corporate divestiture resulted when AT&T agreed to participate in a corporate restructuring rather than continue to fight legal action taken against AT&T by the U.S. government on the grounds that AT&T was in violation of antitrust laws (discussed below). The corporate reorganization involved more than $100 billion worth of assets and fundamentally changed the telecommunications market in the United States. Critics of the breakup argued "if it ain't broke, don't fix it" and pointed to the high standards of phone service provided in the United States up to that time. On the other hand, proponents of divestiture pointed to the likely benefits of increased competition in telecommunications markets. Needless to say, financial managers in the telephone business have new challenges in the new telecommunications environment.

We cannot begin to cover in this textbook all the numerous and complex effects of government regulation on the business environment. We will, therefore, confine what follows to a brief review of those aspects of current regulation that have direct implications for financial decisions.

Antitrust Regulation

In the United States, one of the oldest forms of economic regulation, antitrust policy, is designed to prevent the development of monopoly power and to promote competitive behavior. This responsibility is shared between the Department of Justice and the Federal Trade Commission. Many of the issues involved are structural factors, concerning the concentration of market power within one or more firms in an industry, or financial factors, such as rates of return on investment.

For example, the antitrust statutes dictate that "no corporation engaged in commerce shall acquire . . . another corporation . . . where the effect of such acquisition may be to lessen competition, or to tend to create a monopoly."[3] The enforcement of this law effectively limits business decisions by corporations. In some instances, they are unable to acquire other firms in the industry in which they presently operate.

Franchised Monopolies

The financial performance of public utilities, which are granted franchises to operate in specific service areas, are closely controlled by state and federal commissions and agencies. These controls cover the rates (prices) utilities may charge, their accounting practices, and their dividend and financing policies. Many of the regulatory issues are financial issues. For example, a key concern in regulation deliberations is what "fair" rate of return should be allowed to shareholders of the regulated companies. Most rate cases (in which a company or an industry appeals for a change in rates) draw heavily on financial theory and on the skills of the financial experts involved.

Some of the regulated monopolies that are subject to detailed regulation by state utility commissions include: electric and gas utilities, which provide power or gas for cities; telephone and telegraph companies, which provide communications services; and pipelines, which transport natural gas. Where interstate commerce is involved, these monopolies are also regulated by the Federal Power Commission (now part of the Federal Energy Regulatory Commission) and the Federal Communications Commission.

A major change in some traditionally regulated industries has been government's decision to deregulate. Since the late 1970s both the trucking and airline industries in the United States have undergone major deregulation. In addition, the AT&T divestiture in 1984 has been accompanied by loosening of many regulatory restrictions on companies providing telecommunications services. Such shifts have dramatically affected the business decisions of managers who must now respond to market forces rather than to decisions made by regulators.

Financial Institutions

All major types of financial institutions are subject to close controls by a large number of regulatory agencies. Commercial banks are regulated by state banking commissions, the Federal Reserve Board, the Comptroller of the Currency in the case of national banks, and the Federal Deposit Insurance Corporation. Federal savings-and-loan associations are regulated by the Federal Home Loan Bank Board, and mutual savings banks and insurance companies are regulated by state authorities. In the case of most of these institutions, regulation extends to capital positions that must be maintained, activities in which the institutions may engage, and credit standards. As a result, these regulations affect the financial environment in which financial managers must raise funds. Regulatory agencies in many cases act also as the lender of last resort in the event of serious difficulties.

The financial environment is in the process of major change. The U.S. Congress passed the Depository Institutions Deregulation and Monetary Control Act of 1980 (DIDMCA) which, in effect, changed many of the traditional boundaries between fi-

---

[3]Excerpted from the Celler-Kefauver Act of 1950 that amended Section 7 of the Clayton Act originally passed by Congress in 1914.

A **thrift institution**—is a financial intermediary that accepts savings deposits and makes certain types of loans.

A **negotiable-order-of-withdrawal (NOW) account**—is a type of checking account at a depository institution that pays interest.

A **money-market deposit account (MMDA)**—is a deposit account offered by a bank or depository institution that offers money-market interest rates but restricts check writing.

nancial institutions. For many years commercial banks were prohibited by law from paying interest on checking accounts, and there were major restrictions on the types of services specific financial institutions could provide. Prior to the enactment of DIDMCA, commercial banks were effectively isolated from competition; they were the only type of federally chartered depository institution able to accept demand deposits from consumers or businesses. They also had the unique authority to issue commercial loans.

DIDMCA represented an important step in relaxing many of these restrictions. It permitted **thrift institutions** the same range of consumer services as commercial banks, including consumer demand deposits, and granted them limited commercial loan power. It also allowed interest-bearing checking accounts, called **negotiable-order-of-withdrawal (NOW) accounts**, to be established nationwide. Finally, it provided for the phasing out of interest-rate ceilings and imposed uniform reserve requirements on all depository institutions.

The Garn/St.Germain Depository Institutions Act of 1982 (DIA) altered further the traditional boundaries between financial institutions. It granted commercial demand-deposit authority to savings-and-loan associations and augmented their commercial- and consumer-loan power. It also allowed commercial banks and savings-and-loan institutions to issue **money-market deposit accounts (MMDA)**. These accounts, designed to compete with money-market mutual funds, offer money-market rates but restrict check writing. Super NOW accounts, authorized in January 1983, allow unrestricted check writing but offer returns somewhat below those offered on MMDAs.

Social Regulatory Agencies

Starting in the late 1960s and continuing with accelerated speed in the 1970s, the scope of regulation was widened significantly to embrace previously uncovered areas. Unlike most of the older agencies that had jurisdiction over specific industries, the more recent legislation cuts across all businesses and industries. To mention just three major agencies: the passage of the Equal Employment Opportunity Act led to the Equal Employment Opportunity Commission (EEOC); the Clean Air and Clean Water Acts created the Environmental Protection Agency (EPA); the Occupational Safety and Health Act gave birth to the Occupational Safety and Health Administration (OSHA). Each of these agencies has major powers of control over many areas of a corporation's activity. All of these agencies have such profound effects on the future course of corporate investment and financing needs that any modern manager must take them into account in developing financial plans for the future. For example, some corporations must make investments to modify plant and equipment or production techniques to meet standards set by the EPA and or by OSHA. The magnitude of such investments affects both the profitability of the corporation as well as its need for financing.

Another major piece of social legislation passed in the 1970s that intimately affects future financial planning for most corporations is the Employee Retirement-Income Security Act (ERISA). Among other things, this act, which became law in 1974, strengthened the legal obligation of employers to make annual contributions to pension funds that are designed to pay pension benefits to employees. Contributions to pension funds have become a major addition to annual labor costs, and the continuing responsibility for seeing that the funds themselves are invested prudently and profitably has emerged as a major responsibility for the chief financial officer of many large corporations.

The Securities and Exchange Commission

The **Securities and Exchange Commission (SEC)**—regulates (1) the markets where stocks and bonds are traded, (2) the issuance of new securities, and (3) the merger of firms.

The business-regulating agency that most frequently affects the financial manager of publicly owned firms is the **Securities and Exchange Commission (SEC)**. The commission directly regulates (1) all the securities markets in which corporate stocks and bonds are traded, (2) all major new issues of securities, and (3) mergers between existing firms (or acquisitions of one firm by another). In addition, it indirectly regulates communications between a firm and its bondholders and shareholders, including financial and other statements released to the public. In recent years, the SEC has been active in influencing accounting practices underlying financial statements as well as practices related to the internal control of a company's financial flows, including the composition and function of the audit committees of a firm's board of directors.

Although the SEC has the power to set accounting standards, it has thus far delegated this task to self-regulation by the private sector. Private bodies such as the American Institute of Certified Public Accountants (AICPA), the Financial Accounting Standards Board (FASB), and the New York Stock Exchange (NYSE) now share responsibility for seeing that disclosure of a firm's financial affairs is as full and complete as the SEC deems sufficient. Nonetheless, almost nothing a financial officer says or does that might be related to the value placed on a company's securities is outside the potential purview of the commission.

Regulation and the Changing Financial Environment

It is almost certain that the relationship between government regulation and the financial environment will change over time. In recent years we have seen significant changes in the roles of some specific financial institutions, at least in part due to changes in regulations. For example, for most of U.S. history commercial banks were the only institutions providing checking accounts, and most Americans who saved relatively small amounts of money placed their deposits in savings accounts at either banks or savings-and-loan associations. In the 1980s, things have changed. Sears, a retail chain, provides checking services and bill paying by telephone, will sell you insurance, and has one of the largest credit-card operations in the country. American Express, of credit-card renown, has acquired a stock-brokerage house and owns a Boston bank. As a result, American Express can do just about everything a commercial bank can, plus more. Banking firms, once confined to specific geographic locations for some of their operations, have diversified by acquiring banks in other states.

In such a dynamic changing financial environment, financial managers face the continuing challenge of keeping abreast of new developments.

TAXES

As one cynical observer of life in the United States has observed, "There are only two things an individual can be sure about—death and taxes."

In fact, tax considerations affect nearly every decision a firm makes and are especially important in financial-management decisions. Tax considerations also affect many decisions of individuals. Most nonprofit organizations, on the other hand, are exempt from many of the taxes to which firms and individuals are subject.

Different chapters in this book will be dealing with many different aspects of taxation; here we will mention only some general considerations. The tax laws are so complex and their impact is so important that nearly all firms and many individuals require expert tax advice that goes far beyond the discussion in this book.

Personal Taxes

In the United States, as in most other countries, the income of individuals is subject to taxes. Both the federal government and many states levy personal taxes. Usually the tax bill is based on both (1) a (sometimes complicated) calculation of taxable income and (2) some (almost always complicated) schedule of tax rates. For example, based on 1985 tax rates, a single individual with a taxable income of $50,000 would owe the U.S. government about $13,600 in personal income taxes—or an **average tax rate** of $13,600/$50,000 = 27.2 percent. Needless to say, if the U.S. government had claim to more than one out of every four dollars a person earns, taxes would be a major concern to that person.

The **average tax rate**—is a taxpayer's tax payment divided by taxable income.

Actually, a look at the Internal Revenue Service (IRS) Form 1040 (the personal income-tax form individuals must file with the U.S. government) will quickly reveal that tax calculations can be very complicated. Returning to our example, the $50,000 figure for taxable income is the result of subtracting **tax-deductible expenses** from one's taxable sources of income. Such expenses range from medical bills to interest costs on a loan taken to buy a home. Taxable sources of income include salaries and wages as well as "unearned" income, such as dividends received from owning stock or interest received from owning a corporate bond or a bank certificate of deposit.

Tax-deductible expenses—are expenses that can legally be subtracted from total income to determine taxable income.

The U.S. personal-income-tax code taxes income at **progressive tax rates**—that is, the higher is the amount of one's taxable income, the higher is the percentage payable as taxes. Table 2–3 displays the rates in effect for income received in 1985. As the table shows, a person earning an income of $50,000 pays taxes at a 42 percent rate for all income over $43,190. The tax rate on the last dollar of one's income is one's **marginal tax rate**. Despite this 42 percent marginal tax rate, this $50,000 earner pays total taxes of only $13,600, for an average tax rate of 27.2 percent. This figure is calculated as $10,740 + 0.42 ($50,000 − $42,190) = $13,600. The difference between the 27.2 percent and 42 percent figures is a result of the lower marginal tax rates on the first dollars of this earner's income.

Progressive tax rates—are tax rates where the higher is the amount of taxable income, the higher is the percentage payable as taxes.

The **marginal tax rate**—is the tax rate on the last dollar of income, or the change in a taxpayer's tax payment divided by the change in taxable income.

Tax laws are subject to considerable revision from year to year. During 1986–87, a major overhaul of the U.S. tax code was being implemented, as discussed in the Appendix, "Tax Reform in 1986," at the end of this book. Under any set of tax regulations, there are numerous legal complications in defining what are taxable sources of income and what are tax-deductible expenses. This set of complex issues goes far beyond the scope of this text, but fortunately there are a number of useful sources of information on the tax code.[4] In fact, quite a few lawyers and accountants make a comfortable living (at least financially comfortable) specializing in the details of tax laws.

---

[4]For detailed discussions, see either *Federal Tax Course* (New York: Commerce Clearing House) or *Federal Tax Course* (Englewood Cliffs, N.J.: Prentice Hall), which are both published annually.

Table 2–3

1985 Tax Rates for Single Taxpayers

Income Range (dollars)		Tax =	
Over	But not Over	Base Amount (dollars)	+ Percentage of the Difference Between Income and Amount in first column
0	2,390	0	0
2,390	3,540	0	11
3,540	4,580	127	12
4,580	6,760	251	14
6,760	8,850	557	15
8,850	11,240	870	16
11,240	13,430	1,252	18
13,430	15,610	1,647	20
15,610	18,940	2,083	23
18,940	24,460	2,849	26
24,460	29,970	4,284	30
29,970	35,490	5,937	34
35,490	43,190	7,814	38
43,190	57,550	10,740	42
57,550	85,130	16,771 +	48
85,130 and up		30,009 +	50

Source: James E. Parker, *Introduction to Taxation* (St. Paul: West Publishing Company, 1985).

Business Taxes

The income of all firms is also taxed by the federal government and by most state governments. The income of proprietorships and partnerships is taxed as part of the owners' personal income. Corporations, on the other hand, pay specific corporate taxes on their income. The rate at which the income of proprietorships and partnerships is taxed depends on the personal-tax status of the owners. Corporate income is taxed by the federal government at specified rates.

The laws affecting corporate taxes change over time. In order to spur business growth, the Revenue Act of 1978 lowered corporate tax rates and installed a graduated rate structure that favors smaller corporations. The Economic Recovery Tax Act of 1981 made further substantial changes in tax rates and other provisions of the tax code. The 1984 Tax Reform Act imposed an additional tax of 5 percent on taxable income in excess of $1 million but not more than $1,405,000. This additional tax hit larger businesses without eroding certain tax benefits to smaller corporations. At taxable-income levels of $1,405,000 and above, the tax schedule with this additional tax is identical to a flat-rate system that imposes a rate of 46 percent on all levels of a large corporation's income, thereby eliminating for large firms the benefits of a graduated scheme intended for small corporations.[5] The top panel of Table 2–4 compares the corporate tax rates currently in effect with rates for earlier periods.

Based on tax rates in effect for 1985 income (shown in the top panel of Table 2–4), the tax payable for small corporations on the first $100,000 of income would be $25,750. That is, the first $25,000 of income would be taxed at a 15 percent rate, the next $25,000 at an 18 percent rate, and so on. Thus, 0.15($25,000) + 0.18($25,000) + 0.30($25,000) + 0.40($25,000) = $25,750. This $25,750 (an average of 25.75 percent) represents a substantial reduction from $41,500 (an average rate of 41.5 percent), which reflects the rate that prevailed prior to 1975. For large corporations, the major changes are the reduction in the marginal tax rate from 48 percent to 46 percent beginning in the 1979 tax year, and the additional 5 percent tax on large corporations beginning in the 1985 tax year.

As the preceding calculations show, there can be quite a difference between marginal and average tax rates for small corporations. The lower panel of Table 2–4 reports both marginal and average tax rates for different levels of taxable income using the 1985 marginal tax rates. Note that the left-most column in this lower panel shows taxable-income levels that fall inside different income categories used for determining marginal tax rates. The marginal and average tax rates can be quite different for corporations with smaller amounts of taxable income. On extra income the government collects tax dollars at the marginal rate; the average tax rate simply reflects the total tax bill as a fraction of taxable income. As taxable income becomes large, however, the average and marginal rates begin to converge because the first $100,000 of income is all that is subject to less than the 46 percent marginal-tax rates. For taxable incomes in excess of $1,000,000, the marginal and average tax rates approach equality, due to the provisions of the 1984 Tax Reform Act discussed above. Finally, at taxable-income levels of $1,405,000 and above, marginal and average tax rates are identical.

Net income—is a firm's revenues minus its expenses.

Income tax is a key issue in the determination of **net income**—that is, revenues less expenses. Where the applicable marginal tax rate is T, of each $1 of revenue, the government gets T and the firm keeps $1(1 - T)$. Likewise, $1 of expense costs the firm only $1(1 - T)$. To illustrate, if $T = 0.46$ (46 percent), then out of $100 of revenue, the government gets $46 and the owners keep $54. A $100 expense item reduces taxes by $46, so the net outlay by the owners is only $54. If IBM hires a new financial manager at a salary of $50,000 a year, the salary costs IBM only $50,000 $(1 - 0.46) = $27,000$ on an after-tax basis since salaries are tax-deductible (assuming that IBM is paying taxes at a 46 percent marginal rate). On the other hand, 46 percent of any new taxable income earned as a result of the new manager's efforts will go to the government as tax payments. Ultimately, cash flow after taxes is of greater concern to owners than before-tax cash flow. As the tax rates in Tables 2–3 and 2–4 suggest, tax considerations loom large in investment and financing decisions.

Interest and dividends deserve special mention. Interest paid on the debt obligations of a firm is deductible as an expense item to the firm for income-tax purposes, whereas

---

[5]Note that at a taxable income of $1,405,000, the additional tax amounts to 5 percent (0.05 in decimal notation) of $405,000 (the difference between $1,405,000 and $1,000,000), which is $20,250. This amount is the difference in total tax liability between the graduated tax schedule shown in Table 2–3 and a fixed rate schedule of 46 percent on all income levels, as shown below:

$(0.46 - 0.15)($25,000) + (0.46 - 0.18)($25,000) +$

$$(0.46 - 0.30)($25,000) + (0.46 - 0.40)($25,000) = $20,250.$$

Table 2–4
Corporate Tax Rates

Panel A Marginal Tax Rate (percent per year)

Taxable Income	Before 1975	1975–79	1979–81	1982	1983	1984–85
$ 0–25,000	22	20	17	16	15	15
$ 25,001–50,000	48	22	20	19	18	18
$ 50,001–75,000	48	48	30	30	30	30
$ 75,001–100,000	48	48	40	40	40	40
$ 100,001–1,000,000	48	48	46	46	46	46
$1,000,001–1,405,000	48	48	46	46	46	51
$1,405,001 and over	48	48	46	46	46	46

Panel B 1985 Marginal and Average Tax Rates

Taxable Income	Marginal Tax Rate (percent)	Average Tax Rate (percent)
$20,000	15	15
$40,000	18	16.13
$60,000	30	18.75
$80,000	40	22.19
$120,000	46	29.13
$200,000	46	35.88
$1,250,000	51	45.38
$10,000,000	46	46

For example, on $60,000 of income, taxes would be $0.15(\$25,000) + 0.18(\$25,000) + .30(\$10,000) = \$11,250$, for an *average* tax rate of $\$11,250 \div \$60,000 = 0.1875 = 18.75\%$.

Source: U.S. Department of the Treasury, Internal Revenue Service, *Tax Guides* (various issues).

Capital-gains tax—is the tax applied to the gain on a sale of assets not used or bought and sold in the ordinary course of the firm's business.

dividends paid on common and preferred stock are not. Because this differential tax treatment has very important implications for the financing decisions of firms, we will discuss these matters in more depth later in this book. With respect to dividend income, present federal tax law exempts from taxation 85 percent of dividends received by a corporation on its holdings of preferred or common stock of other firms. This 85 percent exclusion is intended to reduce the effect of multiple taxation of the same income, since it already has been taxed once when earned by the corporation before the dividend was determined.

Business firms are subject to a variety of taxes other than income tax. One of the most important of these is the **capital-gains tax**, which is lower than the tax on income and is applied to gain or loss on the sale of assets that are not used or bought and sold in the ordinary course of the firm's business.[6] For example, consider a manufacturing

---

[6]Capital-gains taxes are extremely complex. Roughly speaking, the Economic Recovery Tax Act of 1981 reduced the maximum rate of tax on capital gains for corporations to 28 percent.

firm that acquires some land for a proposed plant site and later sells it because it decides not to construct the plant. Any proceeds of the sale in excess of the original cost would be subject to capital-gains tax. The firm's primary business is presumed to be manufacturing, not buying and selling land, so the gain on the sale is taxed as a capital gain and not as ordinary income. In the case of a firm dealing in land, on the other hand, the difference between selling price and cost of goods purchased for resale is taxed as income. In this latter case, purchase or sale of the good in question (land) represents the firm's principal business. The capital-gains tax is important in many decisions involving investment in capital assets where an existing asset is to be disposed of. Besides capital gains, certain business assets, such as real estate, usually are subject to state and local property taxes.

An **investment tax credit (ITC)**—is a specified percentage of capital expenditures that a firm is permitted to subtract from its tax liability.

The **investment tax credit (ITC)** is a special provision in the tax laws that permits a firm to subtract from its **tax liability** (the amount it owes in taxes, not its taxable income) a specified percentage of the purchase price of new capital assets of certain types. Limited investment tax credits are also available on purchases of used property. The investment tax credit was first instituted in 1962, eliminated in 1966, reinstituted in 1971, significantly liberalized in 1978, and modified again in 1981. At least one of the several tax-reform bills under consideration by the Congress in the Spring of 1986 calls for the repeal of the investment tax credit, and its ultimate fate is still uncertain. The allowable percentage of credit presently is 6 percent on equipment with a three-year life and 10 percent on five-year equipment.

Tax liability—is the amount of tax a taxpayer must pay in a given period.

To illustrate the impact of the ITC, suppose a machine were purchased for $50,000 and were classified as five-year equipment by the tax authorities. Under the current rules, the company could take a one-time tax credit of 0.10($50,000) = $5,000. In other words, the amount of tax dollars owed the government in the year the asset was purchased would be reduced directly by $5,000. Certain kinds of real property (specifically land) do not qualify for the investment tax credit under present law. The tax credit has the effect of lowering the purchase price of the asset and, thus, all other things equal, increasing the profitability of the investment. In the above example, the after-tax cost of the equipment would be $50,000 − $5,000 = $45,000; $50,000 is paid for the machine but is partially offset by a $5,000 reduction in taxes paid. From a public-policy viewpoint, the tax credit lowers the effective cost of certain investments and has been used to stimulate such investment and, hence, to stimulate economic growth.

As the preceding discussion shows, the tax laws can affect dramatically the cash that a corporation or individual will receive as a result of any business decision. As a result, financial managers must be careful to incorporate the effects of taxes in analyzing corporate investment and financing decisions.

INTEREST RATES

The **interest rate**—is the price of borrowing funds over time, usually a percentage of the amount borrowed.

One item of major interest to individual investors and corporate financial managers is the rate at which they can lend or borrow money—that is, the **interest rate**. Actually, there is no single interest rate; rather, there are a multitude of interest rates in financial markets. For example, the *Wall Street Journal* reported the August 1, 1985 prime bank-loan rate (the rate charged by commercial banks to their prime customers) to be 9.5 percent (by tradition in financial circles, an interest rate will always refer to a one-year period unless explicitly stated otherwise). At the same time, commercial paper maturing in 30 to 59 days placed directly by General Motors Acceptance Corporation (a financial arm of General Motors) carried an interest rate of 7.75 percent, and high-quality long-term bonds issued by public utilities, such as power companies, had interest rates of around 9.5 percent. Figure 2–3 displays the interest rates on a number of different financial instruments.

There is no single interest rate, but rather a multitude of interest rates in financial markets.

Natural questions are: Why do the rates differ over time? Why is the rate on one sort of security different from that on another? Why, for example, on August 1, 1985 could state and local governments issue municipal bonds and as a result borrow money at 9.3 percent while credit-worthy corporations had to pay 11.70 percent interest on their bonds?

Figure 2–3
Interest Rates on Selected Securities

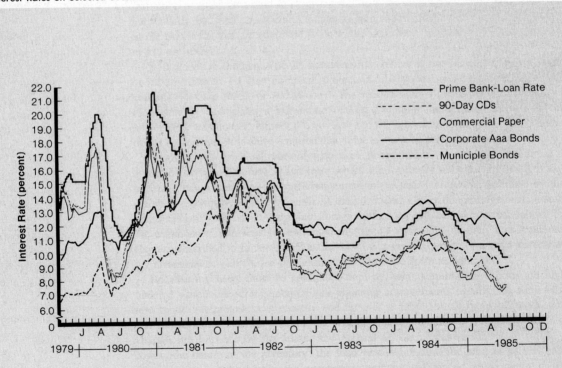

In an idealized world, all securities should have about the same interest rate because of the natural pressures of buying and selling. If one security had a higher interest rate than all other securities, it would be in high demand by investors. Facing such high demand, the issuer of the security would be able to sell it at a lower interest rate, eventually driving down the interest rate on this security until it was equal to interest rates on other securities. In one sense, an interest rate is nothing more than the price of borrowing; in an ideal financial market, we would expect there to be only one price—that is, one interest rate. This idealized world, however, assumes away most of what makes a financial manager's job interesting and difficult. Major differences in interest rates on securities can be understood by examining such factors as the tax status, risk, and maturity of a security.

For example, the income received from owning a municipal bond is generally tax-free, while income from corporate bonds is taxable. As a result, a lower before-tax interest return on a municipal bond may be just as good to a taxed investor as a higher before-tax interest rate on a corporate bond. Given this differential tax treatment, municipal bonds typically carry lower interest rates than do U.S. government bonds.

Maturity—is the time period over which interest and principal payments are to be made on a loan or bond.

A more subtle difference between interest rates depends on the **maturity** of the security. A 90-day certificate of deposit promises a given interest rate for only a 90-day period (even though it might be stated in annual terms, a rate of 12 percent per year is equivalent to 12 percent/4 = 3 percent for the next 90 days, or 1/4 of a year). A long-term corporate bond, on the other hand, promises a given annual interest rate over a 20-year period. If a buyer were comparing investment in a 90-day CD to investment in a 20-year corporate bond, he or she would have to compare two very different time horizons, and in the resultant comparison there is no assurance that the same stated interest rate on the two securities would make the buyer equally happy. For example, if I thought interest rates would go up 90 days from now, I might take a lower current interest rate on a 90-day CD (relative to a 20-year bond) in order to take best advantage of the ability to have money to invest at the higher rate 3 months hence. In practice, interest rates on different securities differ for a variety of reasons, including taxes, risk, and maturity.

At numerous points in our discussion of a financial manager's job, we will again have reason to discuss interest rates. After all, one of a financial manager's primary decisions is how best to raise money; interest rates reflect the cost of raising funds by borrowing.

In addition, rates of return required by individuals on their investments in shares of stock will be affected by interest rates, since individuals have the ability to shift funds between stocks and bonds depending on the opportunities for return available in each.

The financial market plays a critical role in determining the interest rates that affect managers' decisions.

THE ENVIRONMENT OF THE 1980s: UNCERTAIN INFLATION

Inflation—is the general rate of increase in the level of prices of goods and services in the economy.

One factor that has had a tremendous impact on financial managers in recent years is **inflation**—the general rate of increase in the level of prices of goods and services in the economy. During most of the 1950s and 1960s, inflation was not a problem for financial managers, or for nearly anyone else for that matter. For the period 1926–

Table 2–5

Inflation Rates

Year	Inflation Rate (percent per year)
1955	0.4
1960	1.5
1965	1.9
1970	5.5
1971	3.4
1972	3.4
1973	8.8
1974	12.2
1975	7.0
1976	4.8
1977	6.8
1978	9.4
1979	13.4
1980	12.4
1981	8.9
1982	3.9
1983	3.8
1984	4.0
1985	3.7

Source: Federal Reserve Bank of St. Louis.

1980, inflation averaged only about 3 percent per year, but in recent U.S. financial history, things have changed. Consider the data in Table 2–5 and compare inflation rates in the 1970s and early 1980s with those of earlier years. Not only was the rate of general price increase much higher in the later period, but it was much more variable. As a result, financial managers have faced a much more uncertain environment in which to operate. Predicting the course of future inflation has become a much more difficult task in recent years, adding to the complexity of a financial manager's job.

Inflation has become pervasive in its impact on individuals, firms, and other organizations. It affects everything from the revenues, costs, and profits of large corporations to the price of hotdogs at a ball game. Let us consider the problem of inflation from the viewpoint of the financial manager. Inflation has a number of important effects on financial markets, on interest rates, on returns to investors, on capital investment by firms, on corporate projects, and on debt and dividend policies.

Impact of Inflation on the Financial Market

For the financial manager, inflation has a very important effect on interest rates.

Figure 2–4 displays the rate of change in consumer prices (inflation) and the level of short-term interest rates, as represented by the rates paid on commercial paper (a type of short-term borrowing) issued by large creditworthy corporations. Note how interest rates rose during the late 1970s as inflation increased, and then fell during the

Figure 2–4
Inflation and Short-Term Interest Rates

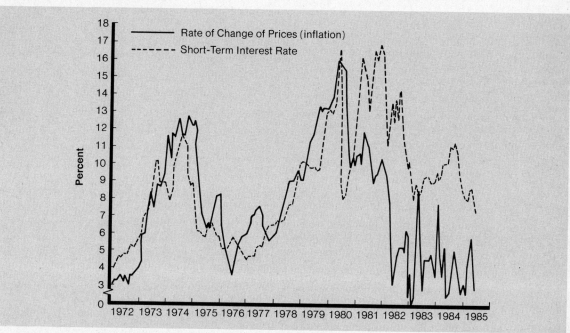

Source: National Economic Trends, U.S. Financial Data, Federal Reserve Bank of St. Louis, various dates. Inflation is measured as the rate of change in the Consumer Price Index. The short-term interest rate is measured as the rate for 4- to 6-month prime commercial paper prior to Nov. 1, 1979; beginning Nov. 1, 1979, the rate is for 4-month commercial paper; beginning Jan. 1, 1983, the rate is for 1-month commercial paper.

early 1980s as inflation declined. Let us explore the relationship between inflation and interest rates.

Consider a lender and a borrower about to make a deal for a $1,000 loan. The lender asks the borrower to pay 3 percent interest in addition to the $1,000 principal when the borrower repays the loan in one year, and the borrower agrees. Both expect zero inflation. But suppose that inflation unexpectedly occurs, and prices rise by 2 percent over the ensuing year. The borrower repays the lender a total of $1,030, as agreed. The lender discovers that this $1,030 is worth in real terms, after inflation, only $1,030/1.02 = $1,009.80. The lender's real return, adjusted for inflation, is only about 1 percent.[7]

An **inflation premium**—is an additional charge for anticipated or expected inflation that investors add to the real rate of return they are requiring.

The lender expected 3 percent but received only 1 percent. What does he or she do next time? The answer is, he or she includes an **inflation premium** in the contract rate. If he or she expects 2 percent inflation over the next year, he or she asks 5 percent. If inflation does turn out to be 2 percent, he or she will receive a real return of 5 − 2 = 3 percent, which is the required rate.

---

[7]We can determine the real return approximately, and fairly accurately, by subtracting the inflation rate from the nominal return: 3 percent minus 2 percent = 1 percent. The exact method is to divide one by the other: 1.03/1.02 = 1.00980, or 0.980 percent.

Table 2–6

Interest Rates and Inflation (percent per year)

	1955	1981	1982	1983	1984	1985
Interest rate on 90-day Treasury bill	2.4	11.4	8.0	8.9	7.7	7.0
Interest rate on long-term Treasury bond	3.0	13.7	10.5	11.78	11.4	9.5
Interest rate on Aaa corporate bond	3.2	14.5	11.8	12.5	12.2	10.0
Inflation rate	0.4	8.9	3.9	3.8	4.0	3.7

Note: Interest rates are year-end. Inflation rate is for prior 12 months.

Source: Federal Reserve Bank of St. Louis.

The **nominal interest rate**—is the interest rate observed in financial markets.

The **real interest rate**—is the rate of increase in the ability to purchase goods and services, or the nominal interest rate minus the expected rate of inflation.

Is the borrower willing to pay the extra 2 percent? If he or she can invest the funds in something that itself generates a return that includes the inflation premium, or in assets (such as inventories) whose price is rising with inflation, the answer is yes. The borrower's real cost, adjusted for inflation, is 5 − 2 = 3 percent.

Imagine this sort of reasoning and negotiating process being repeated in thousands of individual transactions throughout the economy. The result is that expectations regarding inflation gradually work themselves into the entire structure of market interest rates, affecting the relationship between **nominal interest rates** and **real interest rates**. The *nominal* interest rate is the rate we observe in the financial markets, the actual contract rate on the loan, bond, or savings account. The *real* interest rate is the nominal rate minus the inflation rate.

When inflation is widely anticipated in the future, all nominal rates move up to include an inflation premium. In the absence of inflation, the rate on long-term U.S. government bonds would undoubtedly be rather low, as would the rate on corporate bonds with the best credit ratings, such as IBM bonds. Where were these rates in the early 1980s? Table 2–6 provides some interest-rate figures.

Expectations about inflation are incorporated in market interest rates.

Rates are higher in the 1980s than they were in the 1950s for one main reason: inflation. At certain times in the early 1980s, lenders expected inflation on the order of 10 percent per year. To protect themselves, they included an inflation premium (of about 10 percent) in the rate they demanded. Borrowers, anticipating the receipt of an inflation premium themselves, were willing to pay it.

The result is that all market rates include an inflation premium reflecting the market's consensus judgment regarding future inflation rates. This premium is best seen in long-term rates because short-term rates are more subject to supply and demand pressures induced by the monetary policy of the Federal Reserve. The course of future inflation is unknown, and we hope that in the future, we will discuss high levels of inflation totally in the past tense. The rapid decline in oil prices during early 1986 was a hopeful sign for future inflation, and interest rates responded by falling further. Inflation remains an ever-present prospect, however, and a critical consideration for financial managers.

Table 2–7
Real Returns After Taxes (percent per year)

Inflation Rate (1)	Market Interest Rate (2)	Tax at 40 Percent (3)	Return after tax (4) = (2) − (3)	Real Return after Tax (5) = (4) − (1)
0.0	5.0	2.0	3.0	3.0
4.0	9.0	3.6	5.4	1.4
8.0	13.0	5.2	7.8	−0.2
12.0	17.0	6.8	10.2	−1.8

Table 2–8
Effective Tax Rate (percent per year)

Inflation Rate (1)	Market Interest Rate (2)	Real Pretax Return (3) = (2) − (1)	Tax [from Table 2–7] (4)	Effective Tax Rate (5) = (4) ÷ (3)
0.0	5.0	5.0	2.0	40
4.0	9.0	5.0	3.6	72
8.0	13.0	5.0	5.2	104
12.0	17.0	5.0	6.8	136

Impact of Inflation on Returns to Investors

In practice, the relationship between inflation and interest rates is very complex and not yet well understood. In order to explore an important issue—namely, the effect of inflation on returns to investors—let us for the moment suppose that for each 1 percent of expected inflation, market interest rates rise roughly 1 percent.[8] Consider an investor in, say, a 40 percent personal-tax bracket. Table 2–7 shows the returns he or she will receive.

As inflation rises, the real return falls. Why? Because the government is *taxing the inflation premium*. The inflation premium is not really income; it is a payment received to maintain the real value of the lender's claim. So the inflation premium in every true sense is a principal payment, yet the tax system treats it as income.

As prices go up, the real return to investors falls because the inflation premium is taxed.

Let us look at the data in Table 2–7 another way by considering Table 2–8.

---

[8]Some studies indicate that rates rise by less than 1 percent for each 1 percent of inflation, but the issue is not settled. See B. Friedman, ''Who Puts the Inflation Premium into Nominal Interest Rates,'' *Journal of Finance* 33, June 1978. For our purposes here, the one-to-one relationship is close enough to display the nature of the effect. In fact, if interest rates go up by less than 1 percent for each 1 percent of inflation, the impact of inflation on returns to investors is even more devastating.

The figures in Table 2–8 are sobering. At an inflation rate of 4 percent, the investor pays tax of 3.6 percent, which is 72 percent of the real return of 5 percent. The tax rate has risen from 40 percent, the rate intended by the tax code, to 72 percent. At an inflation rate of 8 percent, the effective tax rate is more than 100 percent! Small wonder that heavy doses of inflation can reduce the rate of saving.

The interaction of high inflation and a tax structure designed for zero inflation can be devastating to savers and investors, small and large alike. Many small savers have seen all of their real earnings taxed away, and then some. Inflation also has proved to be the deadly enemy of investors in the stock market, although to fully understand the reasons we must wait until we have developed the theory of valuation in chapters 3 and 4.

Impact of Inflation on Investment by Firms

Depreciation—is the allocation of the cost of a long-lived asset to different time periods over the life of the asset.

Inflation also affects return on investment inside the firm. Current accounting and tax procedures require that **depreciation** on capital assets—plant and equipment—be calculated on the basis of historical cost. A machine purchased for, say, $50,000 generates $50,000 in depreciation charges over its lifetime. For example, one way to depre-

---

Finance in Practice 2–1

The Real Rate of Interest

The real rate of return actually earned on financial assets depends on two things: (1) payments received by investors (interest and principal on bonds, dividends and price appreciation on stocks), and (2) the rate of inflation. If the rate of inflation turns out to be high, realized real returns will be low, assuming no change in payments received.

Looking ahead, no one knows what the real return on financial assets is going to be, in part because no one knows what the inflation rate will turn out to be. In the case of risky assets, such as common stocks and real estate, the payments themselves are uncertain. Some uncertainty is also attached to corporate bonds because companies sometimes do default. There is no uncertainty, we all fervently hope, in the payments to be made on U.S. government securities. Nevertheless, the real return to be earned in the future on government securities is

uncertain because future inflation is uncertain.

Since future inflation is so important to the real returns to be earned looking ahead, investors are constantly attempting to estimate what the inflation rate will turn out to be. Investors' estimates of future inflation are reflected in market (stated) interest rates. If investors expect inflation to be low, they will add a small inflation premium to the required real rate, and stated rates will be only slightly above real rates. This situation prevailed in the mid-1950s, as shown in Table 2–6. When inflation increased rapidly during the 1970s, investors consistently underestimated it, and nominal rates rose less rapidly than inflation. During some periods in the late 1970s, the realized real rate was actually negative! By 1981, investors had learned a lot, estimates of inflation had caught up, and market rates reflected a substantial infla-

ciate the cost of a $50,000 machine would be to spread the $50,000 evenly over 5 years, charging off $50,000/5 = $10,000 a year as a tax-deductible expense representing a cost of using the machine. By deducting the depreciation before computing taxes, the intent is to tax only income generated by the machine over and above its cost. But in an inflationary world, $10,000 five years in the future has less purchasing power than $10,000 today. As a result, the real value of the future depreciation charges is less in an inflationary environment. As a result, inflation reduces the real expense that the corporation can legitimately claim as an offset against revenues in calculating taxable income. The result is an increase in the effective tax rate charged to the corporation. The impact of inflation on investment by firms will be investigated more fully in Part Four.

Impact of Inflation on Financial Statements

In an inflationary world, measuring things accurately, like corporate earnings, becomes a difficult problem. In addition to the problems of measuring depreciation described in the preceding section, inflation also causes problems in the measuring the value of inventories. Profits made through price increases on inventories are not real profits at

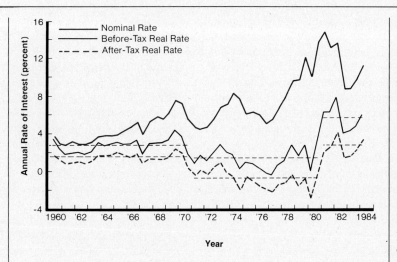

Year

tion premium, as indicated in Table 2–6.

Thus, realized real interest rates are affected by actual inflation rates, while nominal market interest rates are affected by anticipated inflation, looking ahead. Many years ago, a well-known economist, Irving Fisher, suggested that the nominal rate of interest would always equal the real rate plus the expected rate of inflation.

Nominal rates can be determined by looking them up in the newspaper. The real rate, however, like the inflation rate, we can only estimate looking ahead. If we can estimate one of the two, we can use Fisher's relationship to estimate the third. If we knew the real rate, we could infer the inflation rate the markets appear to expect. If we knew what inflation the market expected, we could calculate the real rate of interest. Fisher's relationship is used in both of these ways.

In one recent study, opinions of a large group of economists regarding expected inflation were collected, averaged, and used as the estimate of future inflation in Fisher's equation. The study yielded the estimates of real interest rates in the accompanying figure. (The dashed lines represent average levels of before- and after-tax real interest rates over selected time periods.)

Source: Irving Fisher, *The Theory of Interest* (New York: Macmillan, 1930); A.S. Holland, "Real Interest Rates— What Accounts for Their Recent Rise?" *Review*, Federal Reserve Bank of St. Louis, December 1984, 18–29. The data for the figure comes from the Federal Reserve Bank of St. Louis.

all but rather are simply the increased revenues necessary to offset inflation. Another problem arises from the fact that the inflation premium embedded in interest payments is treated as an expense by traditional accounting methods; yet, in reality, it is a principal payment. The accounting profession is struggling to develop better ways to deal with these and other problems of performance measurement under inflationary conditions. We will examine these problems of measurement in more detail in Chapter 7.

Inflation also greatly complicates financial planning within firms: estimating requirements for funds and obtaining those funds when needed. High inflation can cause balance-sheet relationships between financing done by shareholders and financing done by borrowing to become distorted. As a result, firms find it necessary to alter their policies regarding use of debt and payment of dividends. We will return to these issues in Part Five.

Coping With Inflation

Firms respond to high inflation in a number of ways. Many choose an inventory accounting method that is advantageous under high inflation rates. Some firms publish inflation-adjusted financial statements.[9] In fact, certain large, publicly held enterprises currently are required to disclose supplementary accounting information on an inflation-adjusted basis. Accelerated depreciation, by which companies charge off more of the cost of a machine early in its lifetime, can serve to offset some of the effects of basing depreciation on historical costs in an inflationary world. The Economic Recovery Tax Act of 1981 liberalized the depreciation rules and made the use of accelerated depreciation even more attractive. Further changes in depreciation rules are being considered by the Congress as part of the major tax-reform effort during 1985 and 1986.

Other steps can be taken. Pricing policies can be revised to anticipate future inflation. Return targets can and should be revised to include an inflation premium. Debt and dividend policies should reflect the effects of future inflation. We will return to these and other issues at various points throughout the book. Although inflation declined markedly during the early 1980s, the ability to cope with inflation remains an important skill for financial managers—a skill we hope the modern financial manager will have less opportunity to practice in the future.

---

[9]For a discussion of general-price-level-adjusted accounting and current-value accounting, see S. Davidson, C.P. Stickney, and R.L. Weil, *Inflation Accounting* (New York: McGraw-Hill Book Company, 1976). The Financial Accounting Standards Board issued FASB Statement No. 33 in 1979, which outlined requirements for inflation-adjusted reporting.

KEY CONCEPTS

1. Financial managers must operate in a complex world of laws, regulations, taxes, institutions, and highly competitive financial markets.
2. The main forms of business organization are the sole proprietorship, the partnership, and the corporation. Corporations are by far the dominant form in terms of income, output, and assets.
3. A major function of financial markets is to allow surplus spending units to provide funds to deficit spending units.
4. Financial intermediaries facilitate the flow of funds from surplus to deficit units. There are many types of financial intermediaries, including banks, insurance companies, mutual funds, and investment bankers.
5. The financial market is divided into the money market (the forum for trades of securities of less than one year's maturity) and the capital market (the forum for trades of longer-term securities).
6. An increasing amount of financial activity is taking place in international financial markets.
7. Government regulation and taxes play an important role in many business decisions.
8. Interest rates in financial markets differ for a variety of reasons, including taxes, risk, and maturity.
9. Uncertain inflation has a major impact on financial decisions.

SUMMARY

Business firms may be organized as sole proprietorships, partnerships, or corporations. Proprietorships are the simplest and most prevalent in terms of the number of firms. Corporations, though fewer in number, are much larger, on the average, and produce by far the largest part of the nation's output of goods and services. The major distinctions among the three forms of organization concern taxes and the liability of owners for debts of the firm. Proprietorships and partnerships pay no taxes themselves; taxes on income earned by such firms are paid by the owners personally. Corporations pay taxes on income earned, and, under present law, any profits distributed as dividends are taxed again as income to owners. Proprietors and general partners have unlimited liability for the debts and acts of the firm. The liability of shareholders of corporations, on the other hand, is limited to their investment in the firm. The corporate form provides other advantages in terms of transferability of ownership and access to capital markets.

An appreciation of the financial environment in which the firm operates is important to the financial manager. The financial system transmits the savings of surplus spending units (mainly households) to investing units (mainly firms and government). Financial markets provide the meeting place for suppliers and users of funds to make their transactions. Suppliers of funds receive claims against the assets and future income of borrowers. The participants in the financial markets include the operating sectors, the financial intermediaries, and the specialized institutions. The operating sectors comprise the ultimate suppliers and users of funds. Financial intermediaries act as conduits to channel funds from suppliers to users. Financial intermediaries play a key role in the economy by reducing the costs to lenders and borrowers of search, acquisition, analysis, and diversification. By their actions, financial intermediaries provide higher interest returns to lenders and lower interest costs to borrowers. The third category of participants, the specialized institutions, acts to facilitate the flow of funds. Some, though not all, financial claims are publicly traded in markets that can be classified under two general headings, the money market and the capital market. The money market makes possible transactions involving short-term, highly marketable debt instruments. The capital market makes possible longer-term debt issues and stocks.

Government regulation is another important factor in the financial-management decisions of certain specialized types of firms, such as public utilities and financial institutions. All firms whose securities are publicly owned are subject to regulation by the Securities and Exchange Commission.

Taxes on income and capital gains are an important factor in business decisions. Ultimately, owners are concerned about after-tax cash flow. Tax laws are so complex that tax implications constitute an important aspect of financial analysis.

One important responsibility of the financial manager is to be familiar with the levels and movement of interest rates, because interest rates reflect the cost of borrowing funds.

Inflation has profound effects on financial markets, on the level of interest rates, on returns to investors, on returns to capital investment by firms, and on financial planning. The ability to cope with inflation is an important skill for financial managers.

QUESTIONS

1. What are the three basic forms of business organization in the United States? In what essential respects do they differ?

2. How does a limited partnership differ from a general partnership?

3. Why is it said that income earned by corporations is subject to double taxation?

4. In terms of the number of firms, sole proprietorships represent the dominant form of business organization in the United States. Can you explain why this is so?

5. Economists sometimes argue that a reduction in the marginal tax rate on income leads to more efficient decisions by individuals and firms (leaving aside the effect on government revenues). Why might this be so?

6. What are the principal functions of the financial market?

7. What economic units are, in the aggregate, the net providers of funds in the U.S. economy? Which are the net users?

8. What is the function of financial intermediaries in the financial system?

9. What are the major types of financial intermediaries in the financial system?

10. What are the major types of financial intermediaries in the United States?

11. How does inflation affect interest rates?

12. How does inflation affect returns to investors? What implications do you see in this relationship for aggregate capital formation in the economy?

REFERENCES

Baumol, W. J., *The Stock Market and Economic Efficiency*. New York: Fordham University Press, 1965.

Board of Governors. Federal Reserve System. *Flow of Funds Accounts* (quarterly bulletins).

Bodie, Z., A., Kane, and R. McDonald. "Why Haven't Nominal Rates Declined?" *Financial Analysts Journal* (March-April 1984): 16–27.

Bowsher, N. M., "The Rise and Fall of Interest Rates." Federal Reserve Bank of St. Louis *Review,* 62, (August-September 1980), 16–23.

Dougall, H. E., and J. E. Gaumnitz. *Capital Markets and Institutions*. 4th ed. Englewood Cliffs, N.J.: Prentice-Hall, 1980.

Henning, C. N., W. Pigott, and R. H. Scott. *Financial Markets and the Economy*. 2nd ed. Englewood Cliffs, N.J.: Prentice-Hall, 1980.

Light, J. O., and W. White. *The Financial System*. Homewood, Il: Richard D. Irwin, 1979.

Parker, James E. *Introduction to Taxation*. St. Paul: West Publishing Company, 1985.

Ritter, L. S., *The Flow of Funds Accounts: A Framework for Financial Analysis*. New York: Graduate School of Business, New York University, 1968.

Salomon Brothers. *1985 Prospects for Financial Markets*. New York: Salomon Brothers, 1985.

Part Two

Time and Risk

The next three chapters will lay some important groundwork for much of this book. Part Two focuses on two main topics: *time* and *risk*.

As we saw in Chapter 1, the value of any asset is affected by both the time you have to wait to receive the benefits of owning that asset and the risk that those benefits will not be received at all. For example, suppose I promise to pay you $100. How much is that promise worth? Among other things, that depends on how long you have to wait to get the money and how likely you think it is that I will honor my promise in full. That is, the value of the promise depends on time and risk.

Since time and risk affect value, they are especially important to financial managers because, as we discussed earlier in Chapter 1, the objective of financial managers is to maximize the value of the firm to existing shareholders. Financial-management decisions about how to invest money or raise money will affect the value of the firm. Since these decisions involve both time and risk, we must understand the effects of time and risk on value.

Consider an automobile company that is analyzing a proposal to redesign its cars to increase gas mileage. Such a project will require huge dollar outlays now. The benefits will come in future years *if* the redesigning effort works and *if* the company's automobile sales improve as a result of the redesign effort. Should the company adopt the proposal? The answer is yes if the proposal will increase the value of the firm. The financial manager's job is to estimate the likelihood of an increase in value. This estimate requires trading off dollar costs today against risky dollar benefits in future time periods.

Chapter 3 will develop the concepts of discounted cash flow, our basic technology for dealing with time. Chapter 4 then can use this tool to develop *valuation* as the basic conceptual framework of financial management. Chapter 4 also discusses how *risk* and *risk aversion* affect values. Chapter 5 provides a more thorough discussion of risk.

The tools and concepts developed in these three chapters will give us an ability to deal with time and risk. Developing this ability will set the stage for analyzing corporate decisions and their effects on the value of the firm.

Chapter

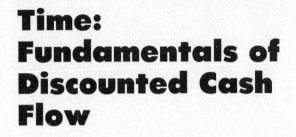

Time: Fundamentals of Discounted Cash Flow

This chapter will examine the time value of money. The chapter begins with the basic concepts of compound interest and uses these concepts to develop the notions of future value and present value. The chapter outlines the steps for calculating the future and present values of both single sums of money and streams of payments over time and explains how to value level streams of equal payments (annuities) and level streams that continue forever (perpetuities). Finally, this chapter shows how these basic techniques of discounted cash flow can be applied to practical problems in finance.

Most financial decisions involve risky benefits and costs that are spread out over time. When people buy stocks, they pay money today (the price of the stock) and expect benefits in the future (dividends plus a rising stock price). When financial managers consider purchasing a new piece of equipment, money is spent today and benefits (for example, cost savings) are expected in the future. Facing such decisions, we need to have some way of gauging whether the decisions are good ones. In terms of financial management, does the decision create value? Restated, does the positive value of the benefits exceed the negative value of the costs?

Discounted cash flow (DCF)—is a method of estimating the value of an asset by taking the cash flows associated with the asset and discounting them for time and risk.

Getting estimates of value is a difficult task. In finance, one of the essential methods of obtaining such estimates is **discounted cash flow (DCF)**. DCF assumes that the value of an asset depends not on its cost or its past usefulness, but on its *future* usefulness. For example, suppose you own a share of stock in IBM. Its value today depends on what dividend payments IBM may make in the future and on the price for which you can sell the stock—not on what you paid for the stock when you bought it. This value is obtained by taking the *cash* flows associated with the assets and penalizing them, or *discounting* them, if you have to wait for the cash or if you are uncertain about whether the cash will actually be there even if you wait. Thus, discounted cash flow is a way of evaluating future benefits in terms of time and risk.

TIME VALUE OF MONEY

Opportunity cost—is the return on the best alternative investment forgone by making the chosen investment.

The **interest rate**—is the rate at which individuals or firms will be compensated for exchanging money now for money to be received later.

This chapter will focus on the way discounted cash flow handles time. The key point to understanding the time value of money is that a dollar today is worth more than a dollar in the future because waiting for future dollars involves forgoing the opportunity to earn a rate of return on money while you are waiting. If, for example, I gave you $1 today and you could put it in the bank and earn 6 percent interest per year, at the end of a year you would have $1.06. As a result, a dollar today is able to become more than a dollar in one year because of the interest rate. In this case, the interest rate of 6 percent per year is the **opportunity cost** of waiting for future dollars—it is a return that you would have to forgo if you choose to receive money in the future rather than receive money today.

Principal—is the initial amount of money loaned or borrowed.

> **Money has time value: a dollar today is worth more than a dollar in the future.**

Compound Interest

Compound interest—means that interest is figured on both the initial principal and interest earned in prior periods. Interest on interest is the key feature of compound interest.

The **interest rate** is simply the rate at which an individual or firm will be compensated for exchanging money it has now for money it will receive later. The original amount is known as the **principal**. At the end of the first time period, a dollar amount of interest is calculated and added to the principal amount. This dollar amount of interest is calculated as the interest rate times the principal. **Compound interest** is interest that is earned in the next period on the prior period's interest as well as on the principal.

To illustrate, suppose you deposited $100.00 (the principal amount) in a bank account that promised to pay 6 percent per year compounded annually; that is, the account promises to pay 6 percent interest on the principal balance and on any accumulated interest at the end of each year. At the end of the first year, you would have $100.00 principal plus $6.00 interest(6 percent of $100.00), or $106.00 total.

The bank has simply paid you interest of 6 percent (or 0.06 in decimal notation) of the principal amount ($0.06 \times \$100 = \$6.00$). In total, the bank owes you $106.00—your original balance plus interest. This $106.00 balance can also be calculated as $100(1 + 0.06) = $106.00 where the 1 in the parentheses represents the repayment of principal and the 0.06 figure represents the addition of interest at 6 percent per year.

The distinguishing feature of compound interest can be seen by looking at how much money you would have in the bank at the end of two years. At the end of the second year, the bank would calculate your balance as $106.00 (the balance at the beginning of the second year) plus $6.36 interest (6 percent of $106.00), or $112.36 total.

Note that the bank compounds your account at the end of the first year, calculating a balance of $106.00. You then earn interest during the second year on this entire $106.00, not just on the original deposit of $100.00. As a result, at the end of two years you have a balance of $112.36. This amount is $0.36 more than the $112 you would get if you earned only the same interest in year two as you did in year one ($100 + $6 + $6 = $112). The $0.36 difference is precisely the interest earned during the second year on the interest paid in the first year ($0.36 = 0.06 \times $6). Of course, you have to leave this $6 in the bank account to earn the $0.36. While this $0.36 doesn't seem like much, we'll soon see that the power of compounding, or earning interest on interest, can be quite amazing. Table 3–1, for example, shows our bank account extended over a 10-year period. As can be seen in column (3) of Table 3–1, interest in year 10 is $10.14, or $4.14 greater than the $6.00 interest in year one. The $4.14 difference is interest on the interest paid in the first 9 years.

Table 3–1
Illustration of Compound Interest Calculations

Year (1)	Beginning Value (dollars) (2)	Interest Earned at 6 Percent (dollars) (3) = (2) × 0.06	Ending Value (dollars) (4) = (2) + (3)
1	100.00	6.00	106.00
2	106.00	6.36	112.36
3	112.36	6.74	119.10
4	119.10	7.15	126.25
5	126.25	7.57	133.82
6	133.82	8.03	141.85
7	141.85	8.51	150.36
8	150.36	9.02	159.38
9	159.38	9.56	168.94
10	168.94	10.14	179.08

Figure 3—1

Time Line of Compound-Interest Calculations: Hypothetical Figures

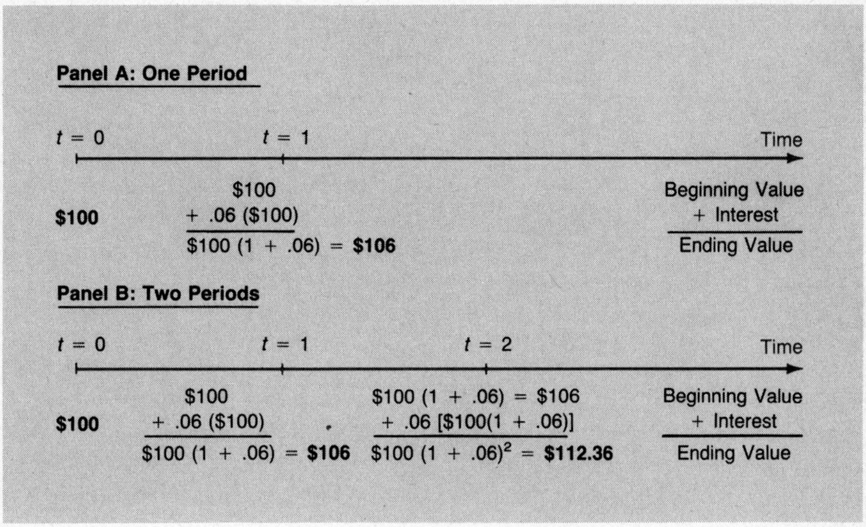

Panel A: One Period

$t = 0$	$t = 1$	Time
	$100	Beginning Value
$100	+ .06 ($100)	+ Interest
	$100 (1 + .06) = **$106**	Ending Value

Panel B: Two Periods

$t = 0$	$t = 1$	$t = 2$	Time
	$100	$100 (1 + .06) = $106	Beginning Value
$100	+ .06 ($100)	+ .06 [$100(1 + .06)]	+ Interest
	$100 (1 + .06) = **$106**	$100 (1 + .06)^2 = **$112.36**	Ending Value

A useful way to look at the process of compound interest is to use a time line that shows cash amounts at different points in time. Figure 3–1 shows the bank-account example on a time line. Moving to the right on the time line means moving forward in time. For convenience, we have chosen to divide time into one-year periods (time 0 = now, time 1 = 1 year from now, and so on), although we could have chosen any other time interval (day, month, quarter) that suited our purposes. A year is convenient because in this case, compounding occurs at the end of each year. Panel A in Figure 3–1 shows the status of the bank account after one year, while Panel B carries the account through two years.

Figure 3–1 simply restates our earlier calculations and shows that at the end of one year the bank balance will be $106.00 (Panel A) and that at the end of two years the bank-account balance will be $112.36 (Panel B). The notation in Figure 3–1 shows some specific relationships between the initial deposit ($100) and the bank-account balance at any future time. Specifically, the balance at the end of the second year could be calculated as $112.36 = $100(1 + 0.06)^2. Figure 3–2 shows the relationship between the amount of interest and the amount of time in more general terms. In Figure 3–2, P_t stands for the principal balance at time t. For example, P_0 is the original principal balance at time 0 and equals $100 in our example, P_1 is the balance at time 1 and equals $106 in our example, and so on. The interest rate in decimal form is represented by i. In this example, $i = 0.06$.

In general terms, we can write the relationships shown in Figure 3–1 and Figure 3–2 as $P_1 = P_0(1 + i)$ at the end of the first year, and $P_2 = P(1 + i)^2$ at the end of

Figure 3–2

Time Line of Compound-Interest Calculations: General Notation

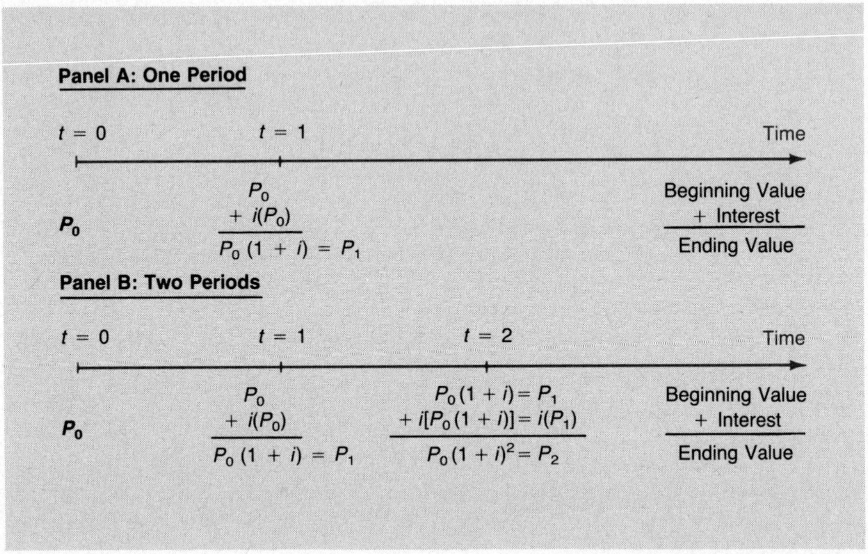

Panel A: One Period

$t = 0$	$t = 1$	Time

	P_0	Beginning Value
P_0	$+ \ i(P_0)$	$+$ Interest
	$P_0 \ (1 + i) = P_1$	Ending Value

Panel B: Two Periods

$t = 0$	$t = 1$	$t = 2$	Time

	P_0	$P_0 (1 + i) = P_1$	Beginning Value
P_0	$+ \ i(P_0)$	$+ \ i[P_0 (1 + i)] = i(P_1)$	$+$ Interest
	$P_0 (1 + i) = P_1$	$P_0 (1 + i)^2 = P_2$	Ending Value

the second year.[1] Once we get beyond, say, 3 periods, the period-by-period hand calculations, such as those in Figure 3–1, become cumbersome, and a general formula—Equation (1)—makes the calculations easier.

The future value (P_n) of a certain present dollar amount (P_0) that earns interest at rate i compounded periodically for n periods can be calculated as

$$P_n = P_0 \ (1 + i)^n \tag{1}$$

where $P_0 =$ the initial principal amount, $P_n =$ the amount accumulated n periods later, $n =$ the number of interest periods, and $i =$ the interest rate per period.

---

[1]To see this pattern, note that, as shown in Figure 3–2, we can keep rearranging terms as follows:

$$P_2 + P_1 + i \ (P_1).$$

Since $P_1 = P_0 + i(P_0)$, we can substitute for P_1:

$$P_2 = P_0 \ (1 + i) + i[P_0(1 + i)].$$

Regrouping, we see that
$$P_2 = P_0[1 + i + i(1 + i)]$$
$$= P_0(1 + 2i + i^2).$$

From basic algebra theory, we know that
$$(1 + 2i + i^2) = (1 + i)^2.$$

Therefore,
$$P_2 = P_0(1 + i)^2.$$

Table 3–2

Excerpt from Appendix Table III: Future Value (at interest rate of i per period) at the End of n Periods of One Dollar Received Today

n	$i = 1\%$	2%	3%	4%	5%	6%	7%	8%	9%	10%
01	1.010	1.020	1.030	1.040	1.050	1.060	1.070	1.080	1.090	1.100
02	1.020	1.040	1.061	1.082	1.103	1.124	1.145	1.166	1.188	1.210
03	1.030	1.061	1.093	1.125	1.158	1.191	1.225	1.260	1.295	1.331
04	1.041	1.082	1.126	1.170	1.216	1.263	1.311	1.361	1.417	1.464
05	1.051	1.104	1.159	1.217	1.276	1.338	1.403	1.469	1.539	1.611
06	1.062	1.126	1.194	1.265	1.340	1.419	1.501	1.587	1.677	1.772
07	1.072	1.149	1.230	1.316	1.407	1.504	1.606	1.714	1.828	1.949
08	1.083	1.172	1.267	1.369	1.478	1.594	1.718	1.851	1.993	2.144
09	1.094	1.195	1.305	1.423	1.551	1.690	1.839	1.999	2.172	2.358
10	1.105	1.219	1.344	1.480	1.629	**1.791**	1.967	2.159	2.367	2.594
11	1.116	1.243	1.384	1.540	1.710	1.898	2.105	2.332	2.580	2.853
12	1.127	1.268	1.426	1.602	1.796	2.012	2.252	2.518	2.813	3.138
13	1.138	1.294	1.469	1.665	1.886	2.133	2.410	2.720	3.066	3.452
14	1.150	1.320	1.513	1.732	1.980	2.261	2.579	2.937	3.342	3.798
15	1.161	1.346	1.558	1.801	2.079	2.397	2.759	3.172	3.643	4.177
16	1.173	1.373	1.605	1.873	2.183	2.540	2.952	3.426	3.970	4.595
17	1.184	1.400	1.653	1.948	2.292	2.693	3.159	3.700	4.328	5.054
18	1.196	1.428	1.702	2.026	2.407	2.854	3.380	3.996	4.717	5.560
19	1.208	1.457	1.754	2.107	2.527	3.026	3.617	4.316	5.142	6.116
20	1.220	1.486	1.806	2.191	2.653	3.207	3.870	4.661	5.604	6.728
21	1.232	1.516	1.860	2.279	2.786	3.400	4.141	5.034	6.109	7.400
22	1.245	1.546	1.916	2.370	2.925	3.604	4.430	5.437	6.659	8.140
23	1.257	1.577	1.974	2.465	3.072	3.820	4.741	5.871	7.258	8.954
24	1.270	1.608	2.033	2.563	3.225	4.049	5.072	6.341	7.911	9.850
25	1.282	1.641	2.094	2.666	3.386	4.292	5.427	6.849	8.623	10.835

Note: Future value is calculated as $(1 + i)^n$.

Future Value

Future value (*FV*)—is the value of a certain dollar amount compounded forward through time at an appropriate interest rate. It is the amount to which a payment or series of payments will grow by a given future date.

Equation (1) allows us to calculate directly the **future value (*FV*)** that we can accumulate if we have a certain present dollar amount and can earn interest at rate i for n periods. For example, if you deposited $100 in a bank account in 1986 at 6 percent annual interest and it was compounded annually for 10 years, the money will grow by 1996 to $100(1 + 0.06)^{10}$. Fortunately, computers and many hand calculators can perform such a calculation almost instantly. Additionally, Appendix Table III at the end of this book provides **future-value factors**—the calculated values of $(1 + i)^n$ for different interest rates and periods. Table 3–2 reproduces part of Appendix Table III and shows that $(1 + 0.06)^{10} = 1.791$. In 10 years, we would have accumulated 1.791

A **future-value factor**— for a single cash flow is the number by which a given present value is multiplied to determine the amount into which that present value will grow in the future (future value). A future-value factor is calculated as $(1 + i)^n$.

dollars for each dollar deposited in year 0. In our example, we deposited $100 in year 0, so we would have $100(1.791) = $179.10 in year 10.

Except for rounding, this $179.10 is precisely the same figure shown in year 10 of Table 3–1.[2] Using the numbers in Table 3–2, we can also see the results of increases in either the interest rate or the length of time money is invested. For example, after 20 years $100 invested at 6 percent per year would have grown to $100(1 + 0.06)^{20} = $100(3.207) = $320.70, or to more than three times the original principal. At 10 percent per year, the same deposit of $100 would grow to more than $600 in 20 years—specifically, to $100(1 + 0.10)^{20} = $100(6.728) = $672.80. As these calculations show, the higher is the interest rate and the longer is the length of the investment, the more money an investor can obtain for each dollar invested.

The future value(*FV*) of a certain present dollar amount can be determined from a future-value table, such as Appendix Table III at the end of this book, as

$$FV = \text{present dollar value} \times \text{future-value factor},$$

where the future-value factor is that figure found at the intersection of the appropriate interest-rate column and time-period row.

The Power of Compound Interest

Over long periods, compound interest is very powerful. Adding 6 percent each year does not sound like much, but after 25 years, $1 will have grown by a factor of 4; after 50 years, it will have grown by a factor of 18. If a generous friend had set aside $1,000 at the time of your birth and invested it at 6 percent per year, that money would have grown to $59,000 by the time you reached age 70. Over longer periods, the results are even more interesting, as Figure 3–3 shows.

Where time periods are very long, the results can be spectacular, as an example will show. As the story goes, in 1626 William Verhlhurst bought the land that is now Manhattan, New York, from the Canarsee Indians in exchange for trinkets worth $24.00—a real steal. How much would that $24.00 be worth today? Of course, the answer depends on the rate of interest that could be earned. Suppose 6 percent per year could have been earned for the 360 years between 1626 and 1986. Using Equation (1), it is possible to calculate[3]

$$P_{360} = \$24(1 + 0.06)^{360}$$

$$= \$30,925,927,728.$$

That is, the $24 would have grown into $30.93 billion, or to much more than $100 for every man, woman, and child in the United States!

---

[2]The figures in Table 3–2 are rounded to three decimals and are, thus, less accurate than the calculations done by most calculators. The reader should be aware that such rounding differences are not important when small amounts of money are involved but may represent huge sums of money when millions of dollars are involved.

[3]Unfortunately, the tables in this book don't go up to 360 years, but many hand calculators have no problem with the computation.

Figure 3–3
Compound Growth of $1 at 6 Percent Annual Interest

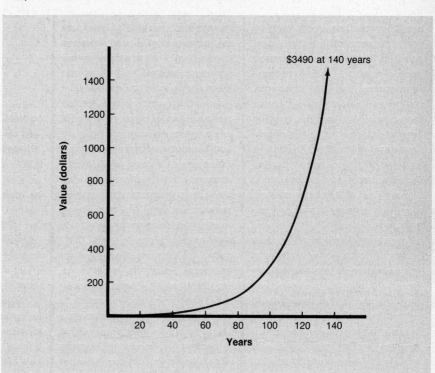

Over long time periods, the rate of increase in value is extremely sensitive to the interest rate. For example, at 3 percent per year, the $24 would become only $24(1 + 0.03)^{360} = $1,003,719 by 1986—just over $1 million. Needless to say, over long time periods, there is quite a difference between 3 percent and 6 percent a year, compounded annually. Unfortunately for the Carnarsees, interest rates have typically been closer to 3 percent per year than to 6 percent (over long time periods), meaning that the purchase of Manhattan really was a steal.

In an inflationary world, however, we must be careful in interpreting such results. Table 3–3 displays some useful numbers. Suppose that you could earn 6 percent interest for each of the next 50 years but that you expected the rate of inflation to be 3 percent per year. Over a 50-year period, $1 would grow to $18.42 at 6 percent per year, but the cost of living would go up by a factor of 4.384. The figures in Table 3–3 are determined by looking at future values 50 years hence at 6 percent (18.420) and 3 percent (4.384), respectively. As a result, your $18.42 in 50 years could buy as much (in terms of goods and services) as $18.42/4.384 = $4.202 could today, a much more modest number. In other words, with 6 percent interest and 3 percent inflation, the *real rate of interest* (rate of increase in your ability to purchase goods and services) is much less than 6 percent.

Table 3—3
Future Values

Years Hence	Future Value of $1 (dollars)	
	At 6 Percent Interest	At 3 Percent Interest
1	1.060	1.030
5	1.338	1.159
10	1.791	1.344
25	4.292	2.094
50	18.420	4.384
75	79.057	9.179
100	339.302	19.219
200	115,125.904	369.356

Length of Time to Double

Suppose I offer you a contract that promises to pay you double your money back in 20 years. Am I being generous? The answer can be found by knowing what interest rate I am offering. In this and other situations it is sometimes useful to know how long it will take something to double in value. Table 3—4 shows selected interest rates and how long it takes money to double at those rates. A rough rule of thumb for calculating the time to double is to divide the interest rate into 70. We get 70 years at 1 percent, 35 years at 2 percent, 17.5 years at 4 percent, and so on. We can see from Table 3—4 that the approximation is fairly close at low interest rates but not so good at rates above 10 percent.

Now let us return to the question of whether a promise to double your money in 20 years is generous. Using our rule of thumb, if money doubles in 20 years, the interest rate being offered is approximately 3.5 percent per year—70 divided by 20 = 3.5. If you can earn higher interest rates than 3.5 percent by investing elsewhere, the promise of doubling your money in 20 years is not so generous. For example, if you can earn 5 percent per year, Table 3—2 (or Appendix Table III at the end of the book) shows that you could accumulate $2.653 in year 20 for every dollar invested today—clearly better than just doubling your funds.

Frequency of Compounding

In Equation (1) above, we carefully defined n as the number of periods and i as the rate per period. In many financial contracts, the period is a year. However, the period can be defined any way we wish: as a year, a quarter, a month, or even a day. Sometimes we will find situations in which interest is compounded over a period shorter than one year.

In practice, interest rates are expressed in terms of percent per year. For example, a savings-and-loan association might offer interest at the rate of 8 percent per year but might offer to compound interest *semiannually*. If we deposit $100 in such an account,

Table 3–4
Time for Money to Double

Interest Rate (percent)	Time Required to Double (years)
1	69.7
2	35.0
4	17.7
6	11.9
8	9.0
10	7.3
15	5.0
20	3.8

how much will we have at the end of a year (2 six-month periods)? To use Equation (1), we need to make sure that n corresponds to the number of time periods in the future and that i corresponds to the interest rate relevant for each of those time periods. Since we are looking 2 six-month periods into the future ($n = 2$) and the interest rate is 4 percent per six-month period ($i = 0.08/2 = 0.04$), we can apply Equation (1) to determine that the future value of $100 invested today will be $100 $(1 + 0.04)^2 =$ $108.16 in one year.

Note that the interest rate per period is 8 percent divided by 2, or 4 percent, and that the number of periods is 2. Also note that we get $108.16 and not the $108.00 we would get if we used 8 percent per year and did not worry about semiannual compounding. Let's explore the issue of compounding in more detail.

In general, in developing Equation (1) we assumed that the interest rate was named over the same time period as it was compounded—for example, 8 percent per *year* compounded *annually*. When we encounter a situation like 8 percent interest per year compounded semiannually, we need to distinguish between the **interest period**, or the calendar period over which the interest rate is named, and the **compounding period**, or the calendar period over which compounding occurs.

The **interest period**— is the calendar period over which an interest rate is named.

The **compounding period**—is the calendar period over which compounding occurs.

> To calculate future value when the compounding period is not the same as the interest period, as a rule we (1) convert the named interest rate to the rate per compounding period and then (2) use Equation (1), letting n be the number of compounding periods that have elapsed and letting i be the interest rate per compounding period.

For example, suppose we deposited $100 in a bank account paying 8 percent per year compounded quarterly. Since a quarter (3 months) is a compounding period, the bank would give us one fourth of the annual interest rate ($0.08/4 = 0.02 = 2$ percent) for the first quarter and then compound our account; the bank would pay us (2 percent) for the second quarter and then compound our account; and so on. As Figure 3–4 displays, at the end of a year (four quarters), the bank would owe us an amount we could calculate from Equation (1) as 100(1 + 0.02)^4 =$ $108.24. In our example, $n = 4$ quarters in a year and $i = 0.08/4 = 0.02 =$ the interest rate per quarter. In fact,

Finance in Practice 3–1

DCF Techniques for Buying Insurance

A well-known insurance company offers a policy known as the "estate creator, 6 pay." Typically, the policy is bought by an individual, usually a parent or grandparent, for the benefit of a young child. The motive is to "create an estate" for the child when he or she reaches an age when such things become important.

According to the provisions of the policy, the purchaser (say, a parent) makes six payments to the insurance company, as follows: $730 each year in years 1, 2, and 3 followed by $855 each year in years 4, 5, and 6.

After year 6, no more payments are made. When the child reaches age 65, he or she receives from the insurance company a single lump-sum payment of $143,723, which becomes his or her "estate." If the beneficiary were to die before age 65, the insurance company would pay a greater amount to another beneficiary named in the policy (for example, the child's brother or sister).

Does it make sense for the parent to buy the contract, agree to make the six payments, and thereby guarantee the child at least $143,723 for future delivery 65 years later? The six payments total $4,755, a sum far surpassed by the future benefit. Common sense tells us that the answer does not lie in simply comparing the two sums.

How can the parent decide whether the insurance contract is a good investment, a wise use of funds? DCF techniques are pre-

cisely the tools necessary to make this decision.

The critical issue in deciding whether the insurance contract is a wise investment is to consider what else might be done with the money. Suppose, as an alternative to buying the insurance contract, the parent considered putting the same six payments in a savings account at 5 percent interest. By applying Equation (1), we can calculate the total future value of the savings account at the end of year 65.

$730 for 64 years at 5 percent = $730 $(1.05)^{64}$ = $16,574

$730 for 63 years at 5 percent = $730 $(1.05)^{63}$ = $15,785

$730 for 62 years at 5 percent = $730 $(1.05)^{62}$ = $15,033

$855 for 61 years at 5 percent = $855 $(1.05)^{61}$ = $16,769

$855 for 60 years at 5 percent = $855 $(1.05)^{60}$ = $15,971

$855 for 59 years at 5 percent = $855 $(1.05)^{59}$ = $15,210

The value of the 6 payments at year 65 if they had been placed in a savings account would be the sum of the future values of the 6 payments, or

$$FV = \$16,574 + \$15,785$$
$$+ \$15,033 + \$16,769$$
$$+ \$15,971 + \$15,210$$
$$= \$95,342$$

Thus, the insurance contract is superior to an alternative of putting the same six payments in a savings account at 5 percent interest, since $143,723 exceeds $95,343. What about at 6 per-

| Discount Rate | Present Value (dollars) | |
(percent)	Of Six Payments	Of Final Payoff
5	4,199	6,036
6	4,102	3,451
5.7	4,131	4,137

cent? Following the same procedure, we would find the value of the same 6 payments if placed in a savings account at 6 percent interest to be $170,849 at age 65. Quite a difference, again showing that small differences in the interest rate are important over long time periods. At a rate of 5.7 percent, the value at year 65 is $143,501, essentially equal to the insurance payment. So we conclude that the insurance contract is equivalent to investing at 5.7 percent. We can say that 5.7 percent is the *rate of return* on the investment in the insurance contract.

Rather than looking at future (terminal) values, an alternative approach to evaluating this insurance policy would be to calculate the present value of the six payments, using Equation (2). The present value of the 6 cash payments, or outflows, would be calculated as

$$PV = \$730/(1 + i) +$$
$$\$730/(1 + i)^2 +$$
$$\$730/(1 + i)^3 +$$
$$\$855/(1 + i)^4 +$$
$$\$855/(1 + i)^5 +$$
$$\$855/(1 + i)^6$$

The present value of the payoff, or cash inflow, from the insurance policy at year 65 would be calculated as

$$PV = \$143,732/(1 + i)^{65}$$

(While Appendix Table I only goes up to 50 years, we can determine the value of $1/(1 + i)^{65}$ by using a calculator or by noting from algebra theory that $1/(1 + i)^{65} = 1/(1 + i)^{50}$ multiplied by $1/(1 + i)^{15}$.)

Substituting different discount rates for i, we find the results shown in the accompanying table. As the table shows, the present value of the final payoff, at 5 percent, is $6,036. That is, if a person put $6,036 in the bank at 5 percent per year it would take 65 years for the bank-account balance to reach $143,732. As before, we find that the insurance policy is equivalent to earning 5.7 percent. At a 5.7 percent discount rate, the present value of the six payments is approximately equal to the present value of the final payoff. The present-value approach tells us exactly the same thing as looking at the future values.

What is our conclusion regarding the insurance policy? We conclude that if the funds can be invested at a rate greater than 5.7 percent for the 65 years, the insurance policy is inferior as an investment. There is an important qualification to this conclusion: we have ignored personal taxes in our calculation. Implicitly, we have assumed that the cash flows from the insurance policy will be treated for personal tax purposes in the same fashion as the cash flows from other investment opportunities. If this is the case, we can compare directly the 5.7 percent return on the insurance policy to the rate of return on an alternative investment.

In practice, personal tax calculations can be quite different depending on the type of investment. If, for example, the cash flows on the insurance policy were cash flows after the payment of personal taxes, then the 5.7 percent must be interpreted as an after-tax figure; that is, an alternative investment opportunity must return 5.7 percent per year after payment of personal taxes to be superior to the insurance policy. Suppose, for example, that a bank account paid 8 percent annual interest, but the interest was taxable income and the marginal tax rate was 40 percent. The after-tax return on this bank account would be only 8 percent − 0.40(8 percent) = 4.8 percent. In complicated, real-world personal-finance decisions, it would be appropriate to use DCF techniques on the after-tax cash flows associated with any investment. The investor could then compare after-tax rates of return on alternative investments.

Figure 3–4
Quarterly Compounding

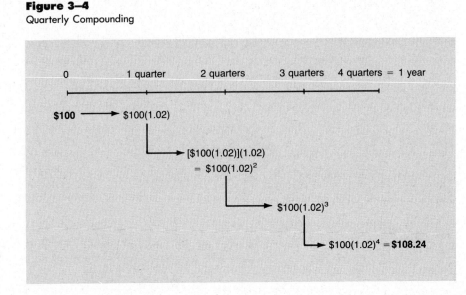

Figure 3–4 is like Figure 3–1 or 3–2, except we divide time into three-month periods rather than into years.

Thus, Equation (1) can handle all sorts of compounding situations as long as we are careful to think of dividing time into compounding periods. How much money would you have at the end of two years if the bank offered you 4 percent per six months compounded quarterly on a deposit of $100? First, since the compounding period is a quarter and there are two quarters every six months, the interest rate per quarter is $i = 0.04/2 = 0.02$. Second, since two years is eight quarters, $n = 8$. As a result, the amount at the end of two years can be found using Equation (1) as $100(1 + 0.02)^8 = \$117.17$.

While, fortunately, most institutions don't quote interest rates for six-month periods, the above example shows that Equation (1) can handle such definitions as long as we use the compounding period as the way to divide time on our time line.

Effective Interest Rates

One thing that is clear from the example above is that 8 percent per year can mean different things depending on the compounding period assumed.

Consider the results for annual, semiannual, quarterly, and monthly compounding shown in Table 3–5. When interest is compounded semiannually on a $100 deposit at a rate of 8 percent, the depositor has accumulated $108.16 by the end of one year. The annual **effective interest rate** is 8.16 percent per year: $100(1 + 0.0816) = \$108.16$. In other words, 8 percent per year compounded semiannually is the equivalent of 8.16 percent per year compounded annually. For any form of financial contract (such as a bank account), the effective interest rate of the contract is the rate compounded *once* per interest period that provides the same dollar payoff as the financial

The **effective interest rate**—is the rate compounded *once* per interest period that provides the same dollar payoff as a financial contract (such as a bank account).

Table 3–5
Comparison of Results for Different Compounding Periods

Initial Investment (dollars)	Interest Rate per Year (percent)	Frequency of Compounding	Money at the End of One Year (dollars)	Effective Annual Interest Rate (percent)
100	8	Annually	$100(1 + 0.08) = 108$	8
100	8	Semiannually	$100\left(1 + \dfrac{0.08}{2}\right)^2 = 108.16$	8.16
100	8	Quarterly	$100\left(1 + \dfrac{0.08}{4}\right)^4 = 108.24$	8.24
100	8	Monthly	$100\left(1 + \dfrac{0.08}{12}\right)^{12} = 108.30$	8.30

contract. In our example, the interest period is one year, and 8.16 percent is the effective annual rate (compounded once per year).

Similarly, 8 percent per year compounded quarterly has an annual effective interest rate of 8.24 percent. Obviously, the more frequent the compounding, the more interest is earned on interest, and the higher is the effective interest rate.

Frequency of compounding is discussed in more depth in Appendix 3B at the end of this chapter. In the case of savings accounts in banks or savings-and-loan associations, the frequency of compounding is an important consideration. In many other cases, it is not so important. Unless otherwise noted, this book will express interest rates in terms of percent per year and assume annual compounding.

This convention of assuming annual compounding will simplify matters. In many decisions facing financial managers—for example, a decision to purchase a new machine—the difficulties in picking an appropriate interest rate are so large that concern for frequency of compounding is a misplaced emphasis.

Sample Problem 3–1

The Future Value of Savings for a Rainy Day

A. Suppose you invested $1,000 savings for a rainy day, and it earned interest of 10 percent per year compounded annually for the next 5 years. How much money, P_5, would you have at the end of the 5-year period?

Solution
Using Equation (1) and Appendix Table III,

$$P_5 = \$1,000(1 + 0.10)^5$$

$$= \$1,000(1.611)$$

$$= \$1,611.00 \text{ at the end of 5 years.}$$

B. How much money would you have at the end of the 5 years if interest were compounded semiannually rather than annually?

Solution

The interest rate is $(0.10/2) = 0.05$ per six-month period, and there are 10 six-month periods in 5 years. Again using Equation (1) and Appendix Table III,

$$P_{10} = \$1,000(1 + 0.05)^{10}$$

$$= \$1,000(1.629)$$

$$= \$1,629.00 \text{ at the end of 5 years.}$$

Note that in part (B) the answer is \$18.00 higher than in part (A). This \$18.00 is the extra interest earned on interest when compounding occurs semiannually instead of annually. ᴲꞁⵑꟽ

Sample Problem 3–2

Effective Interest Rates on Two Bank Accounts

Suppose you are trying to decide between two bank accounts. Bank A offers 12 percent per year compounded quarterly on all your deposits, while Bank B offers 12.1 percent per year compounded annually. You plan to deposit \$100 in one of the two accounts and to leave it there for the next year. Which account should you choose?

Solution

To solve this problem, we need to determine which account accumulates more money by the end of the year. Alternatively, we can find out which account has the higher effective annual interest rate and choose that account. Because compounding occurs quarterly at Bank A, we must divide time into 3-month(quarterly) periods; hence, $i = (0.12/4) = 0.03$, and $n = 4$ (quarters). Using Equation (1) and Appendix Table III, the future value at the end of one year of the \$100 deposited at Bank A can be calculated as

$$P_4 = \$100(1 + 0.03)^4 = \$100(1.126) = \$112.60.$$

Because the compounding period at Bank B is the same as the interest period (one year), we can use Equation (1) and assume that $i = 0.121$ and that $n = 1$. The future value at the end of one year of the \$100 deposited at Bank B can then be calculated as

$$P_1 = \$100(1.121)^1 = \$112.10.$$

Thus, Bank A offers the better deal because \$112.60 is larger than \$112.10. Note also that Bank A provides an effective annual interest rate of 12.6 percent(that is, a \$100 deposit accumulates interest of \$12.60 in a year's time), which is higher than Bank B's effective annual interest rate of 12.1 percent. ᴲꞁⵑꟽ

PRESENT VALUE

The time value of money—is the opportunity to earn interest on money one receives now rather than later. Because of the time value of money, a dollar today is worth more than a dollar in the future.

Our discussion to this point has shown how a dollar today will grow into more than a dollar in the future because of the **time value of money**—that is, there is an opportunity to earn interest if money is received now rather than later. Equation (1) provided the necessary mechanics to determine the future value of today's dollars.

If we reverse our thought process, we can pose the question: How much money is needed today in order to get a certain dollar amount in the future? For example, earlier in Table 3–1 we showed that if you had \$100.00 today and could earn 6 percent annual interest compounded annually for 10 years you would have $179.10 at the end of 10 years. (If you did not round off your calculations you would get $179.08, but the difference is not important for present purposes.) In other words, at a 6 percent annual interest rate, $100.00 today is just as good as $179.10 to be received 10 years from now. Having $100.00 today would allow us to have $179.10 in 10 years if we can earn 6 percent annual interest. As a result, $100 is the **present value (PV)** of $179.10 to be received in 10 years if the interest rate is 6 percent per year. The present value of a future sum of money is the amount of money today (at present) that has the same value as the future sum.

The mechanics of calculating present value are simply the inverse of the mechanics of calculating future value. In general, Equation (1) stated that future value equals present value times $(1 + i)^n$.

Dividing both sides of the relationship by $(1 + i)^n$, Equation (2) shows how a present value can be calculated if we know a future value.[4]

Present value (PV)—is the value today of a future payment or stream of payments, discounted at the appropriate discount rate.

The present value (P_0) of a certain future dollar amount (P_n) to be received n periods in the future when the discount rate is i can be calculated as

$$P_0 = \frac{P_n}{(1 + i)^n} = P_n (1 + i)^{-n} \qquad \textbf{(2)}$$

where P_0 = the present value of a future sum, P_n = an amount to be received in the future, n = the number of periods, and i = the discount rate per period.

Let us consider an example. Suppose we have an opportunity to receive $100 a year from now. What is its value today if the interest rate is 6 percent? Applying Equation (2), the present value of $100 to be received a year from now is $100/$(1.06)^1$, or $94.34.

What is the present value of the same amount if it is to be received two years from today? Applying Equation (2), the present value of $100 to be received two years from now is $100/(1.06)^2$, or $89.00.

Whereas we spoke of **compounding** cash flows forward in time earlier in the chapter, this section speaks of **discounting** cash flows backward in time. In calculating a present value, the interest rate usually is referred to as the **discount rate**.

Compounding—is the evaluation of how a certain interest rate will cause a certain present dollar amount to grow in the future.

Discounting—is the evaluation of how a certain discount rate will decrease the value of a certain future dollar amount to convert it to its present value.

To calculate the *future* value of a present cash flow, we *compound* the cash flow forward in time. To calculate the *present* value of a future cash flow, we *discount* the cash flow back in time.

The **discount rate**—is the rate of exchange between the future and the present time period, or the interest rate used in the discounting process.

The above examples demonstrated how to calculate the present value of a future sum. If 6 percent represents the rate that we can earn on savings, then we would pay no more than $94.34 for an opportunity to receive $100 a year from now, and we would pay no more than $89.00 to receive the $100 in 2 years. In other words, $100 a year from now is equivalent to $94.34 today; we would be indifferent between the two sums. The same can be said of $89.00 now versus $100.00 in 2 years; we would

---

[4]From algebra theory, recall that negative exponents denote division. As a result, $(1 + i)^{-2}$ is just another way to write $1/(1 + i)^2$.

be as happy with one sum as the other. Note that we are assuming that 6 percent correctly expresses our time preference—that is, the rate at which we are willing to exchange present for future sums and vice versa. Note also that as the interest rate increases, the present value will decrease. In Equation (2), increases in the interest rate, i, increase the denominator. For example, the present value at 6 percent of $100 to be received in 1 year is $94.34, as we calculated above. At 10 percent, however, the present value is only $100/1.10 = $90.91—more than $3 less than the figure calculated at 6 percent. Common sense tells us that an inverse relationship should exist between interest rates and present value. The higher is the interest rate you can earn, the less money you need today to accumulate a given amount of money in the future.

Finance in Practice 3–2

Using DCF Techniques to Evaluate a Corporate Investment

A firm is planning to purchase and install some new equipment at a cost of $500,000. It is expected that the equipment will have an economic life of 5 years, after which it will be sold in the secondhand market, bringing in an expected $60,000 in year 5. During the next 5 years, the firm has a fixed-price 5-year contract to manufacture a definite number of artillery shells for the U.S. Army. The new equipment is expected to save the firm material, energy, and labor costs each year. The engineering and accounting departments estimate that the total after-tax cash savings will be $80,000 in year 1, $100,000 in year 2, $125,000 in year 3, $150,000 in year 4, and $200,000 in year 5. The annual benefits rise over time because material costs, energy costs, and labor costs are all expected to rise rapidly.

The firm has set a 15 percent per annum after-tax rate as a required rate of return on cost-saving investment. What is the present value of the benefits expected from the equipment?

To answer this question, we need to find the present value, at 15 percent per year, of the stream of cost savings as estimated. In addition, we must remember that the used equipment is to be sold for an estimated $60,000 at the end of year 5.

The calculation is shown in the accompanying table. Column (1) shows the stream of expected benefits (including the sale value of the used equipment in year 5). Column (2), drawn from Appendix Table I at the end of this book, shows the present-value factor at a 15 percent discount rate. Assuming for computational simplicity that the benefits accrue at the end of each year, column (3) shows the present value of each year's total benefit. The sum of those benefits is shown at the foot of column (3). The present value of all the benefits is $442,470. This is lower than the cost of the equipment ($500,000), so the proposed investment should be rejected. The value of the dollars going out more than offsets the cost savings anticipated. Chapter 9 will discuss such corporate-investment decisions and related tax issues in more detail.

Year	Expected Benefit (dollars) (1)	Present-Value Factor at Interest Rate of 15 Percent a Year (percent) (2)	Present Value of Benefits (dollars) (3) = (1) × (2)
1	80,000	0.870	69,600
2	100,000	0.756	75,600
3	125,000	0.658	82,250
4	150,000	0.572	85,800
5	260,000	0.497	129,220
Total (1–5)			442,470

Present-Value Tables

For use in calculating present values, tables have been constructed for various commonly encountered discount rates and time periods. For convenience, these tables are reproduced at the end of this book. Appendix Table I gives the present value of $1 to be received n years in the future at an interest rate of i per year. Values for Appendix Table I are calculated using Equation (2). As such, the values in Appendix Table I are simply the reciprocals of the values in Appendix Table III.[5]

That is, $1/(1 + i)^n$ (Appendix Table I) is the reciprocal of $(1 + i)^n$ (Appendix Table III). To illustrate, the present value (PV) of $1 to be received 4 years from now, at a discount rate of 6 percent, is $1/(1.06)^4 = \$0.792$.

From Appendix Table I, we can see that 0.792 is the present value factor in the 6 percent column opposite 4 years. Other values in Appendix Table I are calculated similarly using Equation (2).

To illustrate the use of the present-value tables, let us calculate the present value of $100 in 4 years at a discount rate of 6 percent. This present value is simply $100 multiplied by the **present-value factor** from Appendix Table I that corresponds to a discount rate of 6 percent and a time period of 4 years:

$$PV = \$100 \times 0.792 = \$79.20.$$

The present value (PV) of a certain dollar amount to be received n periods in the future when the discount rate is i can be determined from a present-value table, such as Appendix Table I at the end of this book, as

$$PV = \text{future dollar value} \times \text{present-value factor}$$

where the present-value factor is that figure found at the intersection of the appropriate n row and i column. Using this equation is, of course, equivalent to using Equation (2), where the present-value factor of 0.792 is equal to $1/(1 + 0.06)^4 = (1.06)^{-4}$.

A **present-value factor**— is the number by which a given future value is multiplied to determine that future value's present value and is calculated as $(1 + i)^{-n}$.

Sample Problem 3–3

Present Value and the Frequency of Compounding

Calculate the present value of $2,000 to be received 2 years from now, assuming

A. a 5 percent discount rate, compounded annually and
B. an 8 percent discount rate, compounded semiannually.

Solution
A. The present value of $2,000 to be received in 2 years when the discount rate is 5 percent and interest is compounded annually can be calculated, using Equation (2) and Appendix Table I, as

$$P_0 = \$2,000/(1.05)^{-2}$$

$$= \$2,000(0.907)$$

$$= \$1,814.00.$$

---

[5]In calculating present values, one can either multiply by the figures in Appendix Table I or divide by those in Appendix Table III. Except for rounding, the answers will be identical.

Thus, if today we deposited $1,814.00 in a bank account and earned 5 percent annual interest(compounded annually) our bank balance would be $2,000 in 2 years. Note that dividing by $(1.05)^2$ is equivalent to multiplying by 0.907.

B. When interest is compounded semiannually, the interest rate per period becomes $0.08/2 = 0.04$, and there are 4 six-month periods in 2 years. Using Equation (2) and Appendix Table I, where $i = 0.04$ and $n = 4$, the present value of $2,000 to be received in 2 years when the discount rate is 8 percent and interest is compounded semiannually can be calculated as

$$P_0 = \$2,000/(1.04)^4$$

$$= \$2,000(0.855)$$

$$= \$1,710.00.$$

Thus, if we have $1,710.00 today and could earn 8 percent per year(compounded semiannually), we could accumulate $2,000.00 at the end of 2 years. ∃⦀⫤

Present Value of a Stream of Payments

A **stream of payments**—is a series of cash payments at specified (although not necessarily regular) intervals of specified (although not always necessarily the same) amounts.

In the examples above, we calculated the present value of a single sum to be received in the future. How do we calculate the present value of a **stream of payments** to be received at different dates in the future? The answer is that we simply calculate the present value of each payment separately and add the results. Thus, the present value of $100 to be received at the end of 1 year and $200 to be received at the end of 2 years, at a discount rate of 6 percent, is

$$PV = \$100/(1.06)^1 + \$200/(1.06)^2$$

$$= 94.34 + 178.00 = \$272.34.$$

Using the symbol Σ (the Greek capital letter *sigma*) to indicate summation, we can generalize the above to get Equation (3).

The present value (PV) of a stream of future payments can be calculated as

$$PV = \sum_{t=0}^{n} \frac{C_t}{(1 + i)^t} \tag{3}$$

where t = the period in which a payment is received, C_t = the amount to be received in period t, n = the number of periods, and i = the discount rate.

The expression in the denominator of Equation (3) is the reciprocal of the present-value factor described above. Figure 3–5 displays the process defined by Equation (3).

The Σ notation simply indicates that t = time should take on different values from 0 (note that $t = 0$ at the bottom of the Σ) to n (note the n at the top of the Σ) and that these values should then be added up. For example, suppose that you were promised payments of $100 a year for each of the next two years and $200 in year 3 and that the interest rate was $i = 8$ percent per year. The present value of this stream of payments could be calculated, with the help of Appendix Table I, as

$$PV = \$0/(1 + 0.08)^0 + \$100/(1 + 0.08)^1 + \$100/(1 + 0.08)^2 + \$200/(1 + 0.08)^3$$

$$= \$0 + \$92.60 + \$85.70 + \$158.80 = \$337.10.$$

The sigma notation of Equation (3) is simply a shorthand way of expressing this kind of calculation. In period 0, the amount to be received is 0. In period 1, the amount to be received is \$100, and it is to be discounted at 8 percent for one period. In period 2, the amount to be received is \$100, and it is to be discounted at 8 percent for 2 periods. In period 3, the amount to be received is \$200, and it is to be discounted at 8 percent for 3 periods. The sigma notation of Equation (3) says we should add up the ratio of the future value to the reciprocal of the present-value factor for each time period. In other words, we should add

$$\$0/(1 + 0.08)^0 + \$100/(1 + 0.08)^1 + \$100/(1 + 0.08)^2 + \$200/(1 + 0.08)^3,$$

which is exactly what we did to get the \$337.10 amount as the present value of the three cash flows. Note that $(1 + i)^0$ is exactly equal to one: there is no discounting of cash flows in period 0 since they are already present dollars.

Figure 3–5
Present Values of a Stream of Cash Payments

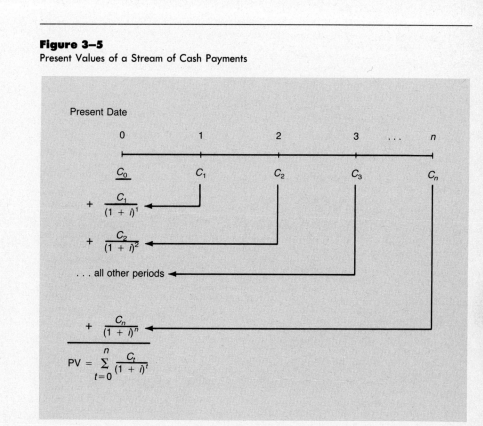

FUTURE VALUE OF A STREAM OF PAYMENTS

Just as we can calculate the present value of a stream of payments, we can also calculate the *future value* of a series of cash flows occurring at different times. The process is simply to add up the cash amounts plus any interest that is earned on the amounts—as of the future date. For example, suppose you put $5,000 in the bank today and $3,000 in the bank one year from today. How much money would you have in the bank at the end of four years if you made no further deposits or withdrawals and if the bank paid interest of 10 percent per year compounded annually?

In this case we can calculate two future values, using Equation (1) above, and then add them up. The $5,000 will earn interest for four years(from now to the end of year 4), and the $3,000 will earn interest for three years (from the end of year 1 to the end of year 4). The total amount in the bank, or future value (*FV*), can be calculated with the help of Appendix Table III as

$$FV = \$5,000(1 + 0.10)^4 + \$3,000(1 + 0.10)^3$$

$$= \$5,000(1.464) + \$3,000(1.331)$$

$$= \$7,320 + \$3,993 = \$11,313.00.$$

Figure 3–6
Future Value of a Stream of Cash Payments

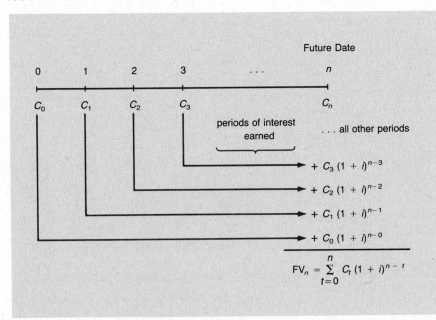

Using the sigma notation, we can generalize the calculation of the future value of a stream of cash flows as shown in Equation (4).

The future value (FV_n) of a stream of cash payments can be calculated as

$$FV_n = \sum_{t=0}^{n} C_t(1 + i)^{n-t} \qquad (4)$$

where $n - t$ = the number of periods in which interest is earned on a given payment amount, C_t = the amount to be paid in period t, and i = the interest rate.

Equation (4) is diagrammed in Figure 3–6, which shows that the future value as of time n is simply found by adding up each individual cash flow and adjusting for the number of periods of interest that is earned. The exponent, $n - t$, shows the number of periods of interest earned. Note that cash deposited at time 0 will earn n years of interest ($n - t = n - 0 = n$); cash deposited at time 1 will earn $n - 1$ years of interest; and so forth.

Sample Problem 3–4

Present and Future Values of a Stream of Education Payments

Suppose you needed to spend $2,000 next year, $3,000 two years from now, and $3,500 three years from now in order to finish your current education. Also suppose that you could invest your money in a bank account earning 6 percent annual interest compounded annually.

A. How much money would you have to put in the bank account today in order to be able to make all three payments out of that account?

B. If, instead of spending these three dollar amounts on education, you place them in the bank account, what would your balance be at the end of three years(right after depositing the $3,500)?

Solution

A. The present value of this stream of cash flows is the amount needed in the bank today. For this problem, $i = 0.06$, $C_0 = 0$, $C_1 = \$2,000$, $C_2 = \$3,000$, and $C_3 = \$3,500$. Using Equation (3) and Appendix Table I, we can calculate the present value as

$$PV = \$0/(1.06)^0 + \$2,000/(1.06)^1 + \$3,000/(1.06)^2 + \$3,500/(1.06)^3$$

$$= \$2,000(0.943) + \$3,000(0.890) + \$3,500(0.840)$$

$$= \$1,886 + \$2,670 + \$2,940 = \$7,496.$$

Thus, depositing $7,496 in the bank today will make it possible to accumulate the money for the three future payments.

B. The future value of the stream of payments would be the bank balance in three years if the three payments were deposited in a bank account at the three specified times. Using Equation (4) and Appendix Table III, this future value can be calculated as

$$FV_3 = \$0(1.06)^3 + \$2,000(1.06)^2 + \$3,000(1.06)^1 + \$3,500(1.06)^0$$

$$= \$2,000(1.124) + \$3,000(1.06) + \$3,500$$

$$= \$2,248 + \$3,180 + \$3,500 = \$8,928.$$

This future value of $8,928 is the amount that would have accumulated in the bank account in three years. Note that this future value is also equal to the present value, calculated in part (A), plus interest for three years at 6 percent. That is,

$$FV_3 = PV(1 + i)^3$$

$$\$8,928 = \$7,496(1.06)^3$$

Annuities: Streams of Level Payments

Equations (3) and (4) will always allow us to calculate present or future values of any stream of payments given an interest rate. Unfortunately, when there are many payments, the adding up process can be quite tedious. For some special cases of cash flows we can develop shortcuts. The most common of such patterns is an annuity. An **annuity** is a stream of equal payments at regular time intervals. For example, many commonly encountered payments, such as apartment rent, mortgage payments, and life-insurance premiums, take the form of an annuity when equal payments are evenly spaced out over time.

An **annuity**—is a stream of equal payments at regular time intervals.

Building on Equation (3), we can calculate the present value of an annuity as shown in Equation (5).

The present value (PV_A) of an annuity, where the amount to be received at each period in the future is a constant value (A), can be calculated as

$$PV_A = \sum_{t=1}^{n} \frac{A}{(1 + i)^t} \qquad (5a)$$

where A = the annuity payment per period, i = the discount rate, t = the time period, and n = the number of periods. Factoring out the constant A, we can write

$$PV_A = A \sum_{t=1}^{n} \frac{1}{(1 + i)^t}. \qquad (5b)$$

Note that in Equation (5), we start our adding up process at $t = 1$ (not at the present, $t = 0$) because the standard definition of an annuity is a payment stream that begins one period from today and goes on for n periods; that is, $C_0 = 0$, $C_1 = A$, $C_2 = A, \ldots, C_n = A$.

In Equation (5), we see that we can get the present value of an annuity by multiplying the annuity payment, A, by the sum of the present-value factors for each payment period. To illustrate, the present value of $1 per year for 3 years at a discount rate of 6 percent can be calculated with the help of Appendix Table I as

$$PV_A = \$1[1/(1 + 0.06)^1 + 1/(1 + 0.06)^2 + 1/(1 + 0.06)^3]$$

$$= \$1(0.943 + 0.890 + 0.840)$$

$$= \$1(2.673) = \$2.673.$$

The benefit of working the problem this way is that special tables can be constructed that allow us to skip the adding up we did above. Thus, Appendix Table II at the end of this book gives present-value factors for annuities. In Appendix Table II, we see 2.673 in the 6 percent column in the row for 3 periods—precisely the totaled term we needed for the above calculation. The remaining factors in Appendix Table II were calculated in exactly the same way, by adding up the present-value factors (from Appendix Table I) for various interest rates (i) and periods (n). The values assume compounding once per period, with the $1 payment received at the end of each period.

To illustrate the use of Appendix Table II, suppose we want to find the present value of $15,000 received each year for the next 4 years at a discount rate of 10 percent. In the 10 percent column in the row for 4 years, we find a present-value factor of 3.170. Therefore, the present value equals the payment amount times the present-value factor, or

$$PV = \$15,000 \times 3.170 = \$47,550.$$

Note that this present-value result is equivalent to

$$PV = \$15,000/(1.10)^1 + \$15,000/(1.10)^2 + \$15,000/(1.10)^3 + \$15,000/(1.10)^4$$

$$= \$47,550.$$

In Appendix Table II, as in Appendix Table I, we assume that payments are made or received at the end of the period in question.

Sample Problem 3–5

The Present Value of a Lifetime Annuity

Suppose David Brown, aged 70, wanted to buy an insurance contract that would assure him of an annual income of $10,000 for the rest of his life. Life-insurance companies sell annuity contracts, a special form of which is called a *lifetime annuity*. Insurance companies estimate average life expectancy for persons of all ages. Persons 70 years old might have a life expectancy of, say, 15 more years. Some will live longer, and some will live not as long, but the average 70-year-old person will live 15 more years.

Solution

An insurance company would base the annuity contract's purchase price on a 15-year life expectancy and a particular rate of interest based on what it would expect to earn over the following 15 years. Let us assume that this rate is 6 percent. Ignoring commissions and other expenses, the purchase price of the annuity contract would be the present value of $10,000 per year for 15 years at a discount rate of 6 percent. Using Equation (5) and Appendix Table II, the purchase price of the annuity would be calculated as

$$PV_A = \$10,000(9.712) = \$97,120.$$

Suppose David Brown does not have $97,000 but has saved $50,000. How large an annual annuity could he purchase? Rearranging Equation (5), the amount of the annuity payment Brown would receive each year could be calculated as

$$\text{Annuity payment} = \text{present value} \div \text{present-value factor for an annuity}$$

$$= \$50,000/9.712 = \$5,148.27.$$

Brown's $50,000 would buy him a lifetime annuity of $5,148.27 per year. ▦▥▦

Future Value of an Annuity

Suppose you plan to work hard over the next 4 years and anticipate saving $1,000 each year. You plan to put your savings in the bank at 6 percent interest. If your plan is to deposit $1,000 at the end of each of the next 4 years, how much would you have accumulated by the end of the fourth year? We can calculate the final sum by applying Equation (4), keeping in mind that there is no payment at time zero, as

$$FV = \$1,000(1.06)^3 + \$1,000(1.06)^2 + \$1,000(1.06)^1 + \$1,000$$

$$= \$4,374.62.$$

Alternatively, we could factor out the $1,000 payment amount ($A = \$1,000$) when we add up the future value that corresponds to each payment, as shown in Equation (6).

The future value (FV_A) of an annuity, where the amount being paid at each period is a constant value (A), can be calculated as

$$FV_A = A \sum_{t=1}^{n} (1 + i)^{n-t} \tag{6}$$

where A = the payment amount per period, i = the interest rate, t = the time period, n = the number of time periods, $n - t$ = the numbers of periods on which interest is earned on a given payment amount.

Applying Equation (6) to our current example, the future value of the four $1,000 payments could be calculated with the help of Appendix Table III as

$$FV_A = \$1,000[(1 + 0.06)^3 + (1 + 0.06)^2 + (1 + 0.06)^1 + 1]$$

$$= \$1,000(1.191 + 1.124 + 1.06 + 1)$$

$$= \$1,000(4.375) = \$4,375.00$$

Appendix Table IV shows the 4.375 figure at the intersection of the interest-rate column for 6 percent and the time-period row for 4 periods. The 4.375 is simply the addition of the appropriate figures in Appendix Table III. The future value (FV) of an annuity can be calculated from a future-value table for annuities, such as Appendix Table IV at the end of this book, as

$$FV = \text{annuity payment} \times \text{future-value factor for an annuity},$$

where the future-value factor is that figure found at the intersection of the appropriate interest-rate row and time-period column.

Sample Problem 3–6

The Future Value of a Savings Annuity

What would be the future value of $500 deposited at the end of each year for 5 years in a savings account offering 5 percent interest, compounded annually?

Solution

The first deposit of $500(the deposit made at the end of year 1) will be earning interest for 4 periods; the second deposit will be earning interest for 3 periods; the third deposit will earn interest for 2 periods; the fourth deposit will earn interest for 1 period; the final deposit(made at the end of year 5) will not earn any interest by the end of year 5. Using Equation (4) and Appendix Table III, the future value can be calculated as

$$FV_A = \$500(1.05)^4 + \$500(1.05)^3 + \$500(1.05)^2 + \$500(1.05)^1 + \$500$$

$$= \$2,762.82.$$

We can also use Appendix Table IV, which gives the future-value factor for annuities, assuming an interest rate of 5 percent and 5 time periods, to calculate the future value as

$$FV_A = \$500(5.526) = \$2,763.00.$$

The two answers are the same except for rounding.   ∃⊪⸩

Perpetuities

A **perpetuity**—is an annuity that continues forever.

An annuity that goes on forever is called a **perpetuity**. The present value of a perpetuity of A dollars per year can be calculated as shown in Equation (7).

The present value (PV_p) of a perpetuity, or a stream of equal $A payments that is to continue for an infinite number of time periods, can be calculated as

$$PV_p = \frac{A}{(1 + i)} + \frac{A}{(1 + i)^2} + \cdots + \frac{A}{(1 + i)^\infty}$$

$$= \sum_{t=1}^{\infty} \frac{A}{(1 + i)^t}$$

$$= A\sum_{t=1}^{\infty} \frac{1}{(1 + i)^t} \tag{9a}$$

where ∞ denotes infinity and i denotes the discount rate. It can be shown, with the help of mathematics, that the infinite series above adds up to a finite sum. Thus,

$$\sum_{t=1}^{\infty} \frac{1}{(1 + i)^t} = \frac{1}{i}.$$

Hence

$$PV_p = \frac{A}{i}. \tag{7}$$

To illustrate, the present value of $5 per year to be received each year forever at a 6 percent discount rate can be calculated, using Equation (7), as

$$PV_P = \$5/0.06 = \$83.33.$$

We will find later that the valuation equation for a perpetuity—Equation (7)—is very useful in valuing certain kinds of income streams. It also has a common-sense interpretation. Consider a bank account that promised to pay 10 percent interest per year compounded annually. How much money would you have to put in the bank if you would like to withdraw $8.00 per year without ever cutting into your original deposit? A bit of thinking suggests that you would have to deposit enough money so that the interest was $8.00—that way you could withdraw all the interest leaving the original deposit intact. Clearly, an $80 deposit is necessary to get $8 interest a year at 10 percent interest. Note that Equation (7) produces exactly this $80 figure as the present value of $8 a year to be received forever at an annual 10 percent discount rate:

$$PV_P = \$8/0.10 - \$80.$$

This initial $80 could generate $8 of annual interest forever (as long as the interest rate is 10 percent and you withdraw only $8 per year). It is, thus, equivalent to a perpetuity of $8 per year.

Since a perpetuity, by definition, continues indefinitely, there is no well-defined future value of a perpetuity. Since it doesn't stop, there is no date at which we can calculate a future value that includes all of the perpetuity payments.

THE DISCOUNT RATE: MOVING MONEY THROUGH TIME

In our discussion of the time value of money, the *discount rate* plays a central role. The discount rate is the rate of exchange between time periods. If we know the rate of exchange over time, we can use it to discount a stream of payments to a single present value that is exactly equivalent in value, or to compound the stream forward to a single terminal value that also is equivalent in value. The discount rate, thus, is the rate at which we can shift cash flows between time periods without changing their present value.

Assume a hypothetical depositor will deposit in a bank account $200 in period 1, $350 in period 2, and $250 in period 3. Assuming, for example, that 6 percent represents the rate of exchange over time, we can apply Equation (3) to shift the three flows back to period 0 and thereby determine the present value of the stream, which we find to be $710. Receipt of $710 at period 0 is equivalent to receiving the three amounts at the dates indicated. Likewise, we can shift the three flows forward in time, finding them equivalent to $846 received at the end of period 3. The three alternative but equivalent cash-flow patterns are shown in Table 3–6.

Provided that we have correctly chosen the discount rate, the three cash-flow patterns—A, B, and C in Table 3–6—are exactly equivalent; we would as soon receive one as another. This example demonstrates the real utility of discounted cash flow. With proper choice of the discount rate, we can shift cash flows through time while maintaining value equivalence. Complex patterns of cash flows can be reduced to an equivalent single figure, and decisions with respect to those cash flows are made far easier. If, for example, we can obtain pattern B in Table 3–6 for an outlay less than

Table 3–6
Equivalent Cash Flows

	Cash Flows (dollars)			
Investment	Period 0	Period 1	Period 2	Period 3
A	710	0	0	0
B	0	200	350	250
C	0	0	0	846

$710, we know that we have a good investment. In addition, by calculating present values (and future values) for a number of different possible investments, we can compare alternative investments.

SOLVING FOR AN UNKNOWN INTEREST RATE

The **rate of return**—on an investment project is the percentage benefit earned per dollar invested.

So far we have solved problems in which the interest rate is known, and we calculated either the present value or the future value of payments. In many cases, however, you may be interested in what **rate of return**, or interest rate, you either have earned or expect to earn. Suppose you are buying a share of stock today for $100 and expect its price to be $115 at the end of 2 years (assume, for simplicity, that the stock pays no dividends). What annual rate of return are you expecting on the investment? Equation (1) can be used to determine what interest rate would give a present amount of $100 a future value of $115:

$$\$115 = \$100 \,(1 + i)^2.$$

To solve for i, we must do some rearranging:

$$(1 + i)^2 = \$115/\$100 = 1.15$$

$$1 + i = \sqrt{1.15}$$

$$i = \sqrt{1.15} - 1$$

$$i = 1.072 - 1 = 0.072$$

A return of 7.2 percent per year (compounded annually) would produce $115 by the end of 2 years. This calculation is the basis for determining the rate of return on an investment.

We can also make the rate-of-return calculation using either Appendix Table I or Appendix Table III at the end of this book. For example, from the above we know that $(1 + i)^2 = 1.15$. Remember that $(1 + i)^2$ is simply the future-value factor at i percent per year for 2 years. Looking in Appendix Table III in the row for 2 years, we see that at 7 percent the FV factor is 1.145 and that at 8 percent it is 1.166. Therefore, the interest rate corresponding to a future-value factor of 1.15 must be slightly above 7 percent.

To estimate the rate, we can interpolate the figures in Appendix Table III. The figure 1.15 is a bit less than one quarter of the way between 1.145 (the *FV* factor at 7 percent) and 1.166 (the *FV* factor at 8 percent), as can be seen by noting that

$$(1.15 - 1.145)/(1.166 - 1.145) = 0.238.$$

Rounding to the nearest tenth, we can say 1.15 is 0.2 of the way between the two future-value factors. As a result we can approximate that the rate of return is 7.2 percent—0.2 of the way between 7 percent and 8 percent in Appendix Table III. This is the same 7.2 percent we obtained earlier by rearranging Equation (1).

We can perform the same sort of calculation with an annuity. Suppose an annuity of $1,000 per year for 3 years costs $2,500 today. What is the implied rate of return? From Equation (5), we know that the present value of an annuity can be calculated, with the help of Appendix Table II, as

$$PV = \text{annuity payment} \times \text{present-value factor for annuity}$$

Therefore,

$$\$2,500 = \$1,000 \times PV \text{ factor}$$

$$\text{Factor} = \$2,500/\$1,000$$

$$= 2.500$$

In Appendix Table II in the row for 3 years, we find a *PV* factor of 2.531 when the discount rate is 9 percent and a *PV* factor of 2.487 when the discount rate is 10 percent. Therefore, the discount rate corresponding to a *PV* factor of 2.500 must lie

---

Finance In Practice 3–3

Using DCF Techniques to Evaluate a U.S. Government Bond

When the U.S. Treasury borrows money, it may sell a bond, which is a promise to repay a certain *face value* to the owner at the end of a certain number of years— when the bond reaches its *maturity*. In addition, the bond's owner receives annual interest payments (sometimes called *coupon payments*). (In practice, half of the annual interest payment is made every six months, as the next chapter will discuss.) Consider a U.S. government bond

with a face value of $1,000 and a maturity of 20 years issued in 1977 and maturing in 1997 that carries a coupon rate of 8 percent (that is, there are annual interest payments of 8 percent of the face value, or 0.08($1,000) = $80). Suppose that at the end of year 1986, the bond is selling for $840, and you are considering purchasing it. You feel you can earn 10 percent per year on investments that are similar in risk to the bond. Is the bond a good buy?

We can use the present-value formulas to see what the present value of the bond is at 10 percent per year. In essence, this figure is the amount of money we would

need today to duplicate the cash flows on the bond (if we can earn 10 percent per year).

As of 1986, the bond promises an annuity of $80 a year for 11 years (1987–1997) and a repayment of $1,000 at 11 years in the future. Using Equation (5) and Appendix Table II, we can calculate the present-value of the annuity of $80 coupon payments as

$$PV = \$80 \,(6.495) = \$519.60.$$

Using Equation (2) and Appendix Table I, we can calculate the present value of the $1,000 repayment of face value as

$$PV = \$1,000(.350) = \$350.00.$$

Adding the two present-value

somewhere between 9 percent and 10 percent. By interpolation we find the unknown rate as

$$\text{Rate} = 9 + (2.531 - 2.500)/(2.531 - 2.487)$$

$$= 9 + 0.705$$

$$= 9.705 \text{ percent}$$

If we had an opportunity to invest $2,500 and earn $1,000 per year for 3 years, we would say the investment promises a rate of return of 9.705 percent per year.

USING DISCOUNTED CASH FLOW IN PRACTICE

We have developed the mechanics of discounted cash flow (DCF), and we have discussed the details of calculating both future values and present values. "Finance in Practice" examples 3–1, 3–2, and 3–3 show the power of these techniques when they are applied to personal-finance, corporate-investment, and bond-market decisions.

In each of these three "Finance in Practice" examples, discounted-cash-flow techniques were used to make a decision. Such techniques will be important throughout this book because they provide a specific way to place a value on cash flows. DCF techniques assume that the value of an asset is the sum of all the payments that the asset will generate in the future, discounted back to their present value. The DCF valuation model is quite general in its applicability and can be used in any situation in which value is a function of future cash payments. For example, the value of a bond

amounts together, the total present value of the bond is

$$PV = \$519.60 + \$350.00$$
$$= \$869.60.$$

This means that if we had $869.60 in 1986 and put it in a bank account paying 10 percent interest, we could withdraw $80 a year for each of the next 11 years, and in year 11 (1997) we would still have $1,000 left in our account to withdraw from the bank. That is, at an interest rate of 10 percent, $869.60 can duplicate the cash flows from the bond.

Since you can purchase the bond for $840, the bond is a good buy. Buying the bond, in effect, puts you ahead of the game by $29.60—the difference between $869.60 and $840.00. In the absence of the bond, we would have had to put up $869.60 in our alternative investments earning 10 percent to get the same cash flows as those the bond promises. In a real sense, the bond has a positive *net present value* (value in excess of cost) of $29.60 and is, thus, a wise purchase, given our assumptions.

Note that one of these assumptions was that our required rate of return on the bond was 10 percent. At a 10 percent required return the bond has a positive net present value. Suppose other people also required 10 percent on the bond. They would also see the bond as a good buy. If many such buyers saw the bond as a good buy at its current price, we would expect them to try to buy the bond. This increased demand for the bond would drive up the bond's price until, at the new higher price, the bond is likely to have a net present value of zero—value equal to costs. This process is precisely what happens in well-developed financial markets. Chapter 4 will elaborate more on using DCF techniques to evaluate bonds.

is simply the present value of all interest and principal payments that the holder of the bond expects to receive. The value of a share of stock is the present value of all payments that its holder expects to receive—namely, dividends and the proceeds from sale at some future date. The value of an entire company may be thought of as the present value of all future cash flows that the company will generate. Again and again throughout this book, we will find applications for the DCF valuation model. Chapter 1 noted that the general criterion for financial-management decisions is value maximization; that is, financial managers do things that increase value and avoid things that decrease it. The DCF valuation model provides the basic conceptual framework for the valuation criterion.

"Finance in Practice" examples 3–1, 3–2, and 3–3 make discounted cash flow look like pretty powerful medicine. Indeed, it is useful, but it is not the answer to every manager's prayer. It has its limitations, especially in situations involving uncertainty. Two of the three examples involved cash flows that were fixed in amount by contract: the insurance policy and the bond. The corporate-investment example treated the cash savings as if they were known with certainty. In practice, DCF techniques often must be applied in cases where the cash flows are subject to a great deal of uncertainty.

Suppose you are the top managers of Apple Computer, contemplating introducing a new computer designed for executives in medium and large companies. It is a market quite different from the markets for computers for small business, home, and education use—Apple's main markets to that time. The market for computers for executives is potentially huge, but it will put Apple into competition with Xerox, Digital Equipment Corporation, and, alas, with mighty IBM. Development costs will be very high and subject to great uncertainty. The commercial success of the venture and, hence, the sales and profits it will generate, are subject to even more uncertainty.

Will the use of DCF techniques to evaluate the decision guarantee that Apple will do the right thing? It most certainly will not. If Apple's management makes mistakes in estimating the cash flows of the project, they can easily make the wrong decision. Even if they make good cash-flow estimates, there remains a second problem—what discount rate to apply. A mistake here could also lead to the wrong decision. Discounted cash flow is more difficult to use as a valuation model if discount rates are uncertain. If the discount rate is far off, a project that was initially considered worthwhile may, in fact, decrease value rather than increase it.

A critical issue in deciding whether an investment is wise is to consider what else might be done with the money.

DCF is a useful tool, but it is no substitute for careful analysis and sound judgment. The numbers that go into a DCF analysis must be based on reasonable assumptions and a full assessment of the facts; otherwise, the numbers that come out will be unreliable.

KEY CONCEPTS

1. Current value depends on future benefits.
2. Money has time value. A dollar now is more valuable than a dollar in the future.
3. The interest rate represents the rate of exchange over time—that is, the rate of exchange between money now and money later.
4. Present value is future value discounted back to the present.
5. The present value of a stream of payments equals the sum of the present values of the individual elements.
6. The interest rate that equates a present sum with a future sum can be viewed as the rate of return on the present sum if invested.
7. The notion of present value provides the basic valuation framework on which the theory of financial management rests. The general DCF valuation model is fundamental in its importance.
8. The discount rate in a present-value calculation represents the rate of exchange between time periods. Using discounted-cash-flow techniques, cash flows can be moved forward or backward in time.

SUMMARY

The notion that money has time value is a basic concept of finance. The sooner funds are received, the sooner they can be put to work in other new investments. If funds are received later rather than sooner, the recipient forgoes the interest that could have been earned in the meantime. Therefore, to analyze the economic worth of investment opportunities, managers must take into account the *timing* of cash flows as well as their amounts.

The rate of interest represents the rate at which present funds can be exchanged for future funds, and vice versa. The interest rate is the rate of exchange over time and is the tool for adjusting cash flows to account for differences in timing. Time affects cash flows through the mechanism of compound interest.

The future value of a sum of money equals its present value compounded forward through time at the appropriate interest rate. Similarly, the present value of a future sum is its future value discounted back to the present. The present value of a stream of payments is the sum of the present values of its separate elements. In the case of level streams (annuities), the computation of present value can be simplified using present-value tables especially designed for annuities.

The general discounted-cash-flow (DCF) valuation model expresses the value of an asset as the sum of all payments that the asset will generate, discounted to their present value. Using DCF techniques, a complex pattern of cash flows extending over many time periods can be reduced to a single figure that is equivalent in value. The present value of a stream of cash inflows can be compared to the outlay required to generate it. Similarly, two or more alternative investments (each of which generates a complex cash-flow stream) can be reduced to present values and compared directly. DCF techniques greatly simplify the evaluation of complex cash-flow patterns.

QUESTIONS

1. Why does money have time value?
2. What does the rate of interest represent? Who establishes the rate of interest and by what mechanism?
3. What happens to the effective rate of interest as the frequency of compounding is increased?
4. What is an annuity? A perpetuity?
5. If you have a choice between a savings account that pays 5 percent compounded quarterly and one that pays 5 percent compounded daily, which would you prefer? Why?

PROBLEMS

Unless otherwise stated, assume annual interest rates compounded once per year. Problems preceded by one asterisk (*) assume knowledge of Appendix 3A.

1. $100 today is equivalent in value to how much at the end of 3 years,
   a. assuming an interest rate of 10 percent?
   b. assuming an interest rate of 30 percent?
   c. assuming an interest rate of 0 percent?

2. $100 at the end of 3 years is equivalent in value to how much today,
   a. assuming an interest rate of 10 percent?
   b. assuming an interest rate of 30 percent?
   c. assuming an interest rate of 0 percent?

3. $500 received at the end of each of the next 3 years is equivalent in value to how much today,
   a. assuming an interest rate of 4 percent?
   b. assuming an interest rate of 25 percent?

4. $500 received at the end of the next 3 years is equivalent in value to how much at the end of the third year,
   a. assuming an interest rate of 4 percent?
   b. assuming an interest rate of 25 percent?

5. $100 is to be received at the end of 1 year, $400 at the end of 2 years, and $800 at the end of 3 years. These receipts are equivalent in value to how much today,
   a. assuming an interest rate of 6 percent?
   b. assuming an interest rate of 20 percent?

6. $800 is to be received at the end of 1 year, $400 at the end of 2 years, and $100 at the end of 3 years. These receipts are equivalent in value to how much today,
   a. assuming an interest rate of 6 percent?
   b. assuming an interest rate of 20 percent?
   c. Contrast the results with those of Problem (5). Why are the results different?

7. Find the effective annual rate of interest for:
   a. 8 percent compounded semiannually.
   b. 8 percent compounded quarterly.
   c. 8 percent compounded monthly.

8. Calculate (without using tables) the future value of:
   a. $1,000 invested for 2 years at 4 percent per year, compounded annually.
   b. $1,000 invested for 1 year at 4 percent per year, compounded semiannually.
   c. $4,000 invested for 6 months at 8 percent per year, compounded quarterly.
   d. $2,000 invested for 10 months at 6 percent per year, compounded monthly.

9. Calculate (without using tables) the present value of:
   a. $1,000 to be received at the end of 2 years at 6 percent compounded annually.
   b. $4,000 to be received at the end of 1 year at 4 percent compounded quarterly.
   c. $1,000 to be received at the end of 6 months at 12 percent compounded monthly.
   d. $3,000 to be received at the end of 2 years at 8 percent compounded semiannually.

10. Rework Problem (9) using the present-value tables (Appendix Tables I and II at the end of the book).

11. Calculate the present value of the stream of payments given in Table A, assuming discount rates of 4 percent, 8 percent, and 12 percent.

12. Calculate the present value of the following annuities if the annual discount rate is 8 percent.
   a. $1,000 per year for 5 years.
   b. $3,000 per year for 7 years.
   *c. $1,000 every 6 months for 2 years. (Assume semiannual compounding.)
   *d. $500 per quarter for 3 years. (Assume quarterly compounding.)

13. Find the present value of the cash flows given in Table B using a discount rate of 8 percent.

*14. Calculate the price of a 10-year bond paying a 6 percent annual coupon (half of the 6 percent semiannually) on a face value of $1,000 if investors

Table A

Period	Cash Flow (dollars)
1	300
2	400
3	600
4	100

Table B

Year	Cash Flow (dollars per year)
1–4	100
5	200
6	300
7–15	100
16	400

can earn 8 percent per year on alternative investments. That is, suppose investors require an 8 percent return on the bond in setting the market price. Assume semiannual compounding.

15. Consider cash flows of $100 at the end of year 1, $300 at the end of year 2, and $200 at the end of year 3. Assuming an interest rate of 10 percent, calculate the single amount that is equivalent in value

    a. if received today.
    b. if received at the end of year 1.
    c. if received at the end of year 2.
    d. if received at the end of year 3.

16. Consider cash flows of $200 at the end of year 1, −$100 at the end of year 2, $100 at the end of year 3, and $300 at the end of year 4. Calculate the present value of these cash flows.

    a. an interest rate of 5 percent.
    b. at an interest rate of 20 percent.

17. South Philadelphian Sylvester Ballone has agreed to make four $600 payments, the first now and the rest at annual intervals, to Pennsylvania Fried Chicken, Inc. in repatriation for damages he inflicted upon chicken carcasses while practicing his left hook. Pennsylvania Fried Chicken, Inc. assumed an effective annual interest rate of 10 percent in specifying the $600 figure. How much do the damages total in present terms?

18. What is the present value of cash flows of $80 per year forever (in perpetuity),

    a. assuming an interest rate of 8 percent?
    b. assuming an interest rate of 10 percent?

19. Jan Francis deposited her most recent paycheck in Hometown National Bank's Big H account that pays interest at a rate of 6 percent compounded quarterly. What is the effective annual rate of interest on the Big H account?

20. According to a local department store, the store charges customers 1 percent per month on the outstanding balance. Is this equivalent to 12 percent per year? What is the effective annual rate on such consumer credit? Assume the store recalculates your account balance at the end of each month.

21. Suppose you are 16 years old and plan to start college exactly 2 years hence. You now have $2,000 in the bank earning 10 percent per year. Your first college tuition payment (due in 2 years) will be $2,500. Do you presently have enough saved to finance that payment?

22. Cameron, Inc. has just obtained a $10 million loan from a local insurance company. The terms of the loan require repayment in 5 annual payments of $2,773,925 each. The first payment is to be paid one year after receipt of the $10 million.

    a. What is the effective annual interest cost of the loan?
    b. Suppose that Cameron, Inc. has just made the second of the five payments. What is the smallest amount of money that Cameron would have to put into a bank account on the date of this payment in order for this bank account to contain a large enough balance to be the only source of funds to make the last three payments? Assume that the bank pays 10 percent per year compounded annually.

23. You have purchased a new $8,000 sailboat and have the option of paying the entire $8,000 now or making equal, annual payments for the next 4 years, with the first payment due one year from now. If your time value of money is 7 percent, what would be the largest amount for the annual payments that you would be willing to undertake?

24. You have just borrowed some money from Sam the friendly loan maker. To pay off the debt, you will make three annual payments of $3,000 (the first payment made one year from today) *and* you will make a "balloon" payment of $20,000 four years from now. If Sam charged you 8 percent per year compounded annually, how much money must you have borrowed?

25. Your bank has offered you a $15,000 loan. The terms of the loan require you to pay back the

loan in five equal annual installments of $4,161.00. The first payment will be made a year from today. What is the effective rate of interest on this loan?

26. Suppose you plan to purchase a new stereo system. Burk and Chirp, a local sound shop, has offered the following terms. The *cash* price (including all taxes plus free home delivery) is $600. Alternatively, you can make 12 monthly payments (the first coming one month from the date of purchase) of $56.76 each. What is the effective annual interest rate on this financing?

27. The Canadian Pacific Railroad has outstanding an issue of 4 percent perpetual bonds—that is, bonds that have no maturity and promise to pay $20 semiannually forever. If the market rate of interest is 9 percent per year (compounded semiannually) for bonds of this risk class, at what price should the Canadian Pacific "Perpetual 4s" sell?

28. As a graduation present, a wealthy relative has given you $5,000 to be put into one of three investment opportunities. The cash flows generated by each investment are given in Table C. If you must invest the entire $5,000 in only one of these alternatives and if all three have the same risk, which alternative offers the highest rate of return? (Assume you cannot sell your rights to these opportunities and that you will hold any investment to its maturity in year 5.)

29. Lefty Smith paid $1,000 for 10 shares of stock 12 years ago ($100 per share). He received dividends of $6 a share at the end of each of the first 7 years and $3 a share at the end of each of the next 5 years. He just sold the stock for $860 (immediately after he received the last dividend). What rate of return did he make on his investment? Set up a formula to solve.

Table C

Investment	Cash Flows Received, Year-End (dollars)				
	Year 1	Year 2	Year 3	Year 4	Year 5
A	1500	1500	1500	1500	1500
B	650	650	650	650	5650
C	0	0	0	0	9000

30. The Friendly Finance Company offers you a $5,000 loan. After a bit of fast talking, Friendly's chief loan officer tells you that the repayment schedule will be four annual payments of $1,416.00. The first payment will be deducted from the loan amount, the second payment is due one year from now, etc. What is the approximate effective annual rate of interest on this loan?

31. You have a checking account at WizFizz National Bank that you established two years ago when you entered college. You have found it necessary to keep an average balance of $450 in the account to cover your checks. Now you learn that if you are willing to leave an additional $500 in a savings account at WizFizz you can establish a NOW account; that is, you will receive interest on both checking *and* savings balances at the rate of 5.5 percent per year compounded on a daily basis. Presently you have the additional $500 in a six-month certificate, which pays 10 percent per year (5 percent per six months) and is about to mature. You can buy another identical certificate. Will you make the switch to the NOW account? (Assume the bank uses a 365-day year in all its daily compounding calculations.)

32. Slow Learners Publishing Company is trying to decide whether to revise its popular textbook *Financial Psychoanalysis Made Simple*. They have estimated that the revisions will cost $40,000 initially but after-tax cash flow from increased sales will be $10,000 the first year and will increase by 8 percent per year for two years and then remain stable for two more years, at which time the book will go out of print. If the company requires a 10 percent return for such an investment, should it undertake the revision?

33. You are 35 years old and wish to provide for your old age. Suppose you invest $1,000 per year at an effective rate of 5 percent per year for the next 25 years, with the first deposit beginning one year hence. Beginning at age 60 you start withdrawing $X per year for the next 20 years. How large will X be in order to use up all of your funds?

34. You have agreed to pay a creditor $5,000 one year hence, $4,000 two years hence, $3,000 three years hence, $2,000 four years hence, and a final payment of $1,000 five years from now.

Because of budget considerations, you would like to make five equal annual payments (X) to satisfy your contract. If the agreed-upon interest is 5 percent effective per year, what will X be?

35. Suppose you have decided to start saving money to take a long-awaited world cruise, which you estimate will cost you $6,000. You want to take your cruise 5 years from today. The savings account you established for your trip offers 6 percent interest, compounded annually.

   a. How much will you have to deposit each year (at year-end) to have your $6,000 if your first deposit is made one year from today and the final deposit is made on the day the cruise departs?

   b. How much will you have to deposit each year if the final deposit is made one year before the cruise departs?

   c. Suppose the cost of living increases 4 percent per year over the next 5 years. What would be the effective purchasing power in year 5 of your deposits calculated in part (a)?

36. A U.S. government bond, maturing exactly 5 years from now, pays annual interest of 7 percent payable once a year. The first interest payment is due exactly one year hence. The face value of the bond is $1,000. Suppose you can earn an effective annual rate of 8 percent for 5 years in what you considered to be an investment of the same risk class as the government bond. How much would you be willing to pay for the 7 percent bond? What if you could earn only 5 percent on your money in alternative investments?

37. Hoe Downs, a 60-year-old penniless freelance gardener, quite unexpectedly found himself named the beneficiary in the estate proceedings of a woman whose roses he used to prune. After all pertinent fees had been extracted from Hoe's largesse, he found he had netted $87,500. Hoe immediately retired and placed $80,500 of his inheritance in a savings account on which he would earn 6 percent per year compounded annually. He planned to extract $7,000 from the account at yearly intervals commencing one year from the date of his deposit, to satisfy the modest needs of his retirement years. Given that Hoe lives long enough, about how old will he be when his money runs out?

38. Susan Potter put $5,000 into a savings account that paid 8 percent annual interest. She then let the money grow (no deposits or withdrawals) for 10 years. At that point, she decided to reap some of the rewards of her thrift and planned to begin systematic annual withdrawals from the account. Each withdrawal would be the same dollar amount. The first withdrawal would be in one year (on the 11th anniversary of her initial deposit) and Sue planned to make 12 of these withdrawals, the last of which would clean out her account. How large a withdrawal (Y) could Sue make in each of the 12 years?

*39. Suppose you decide to purchase a $3,500 car, pay $1,500 in cash, and assume a 13.5 percent add-on installment contract for the remaining $2,000. Your installment contract runs for one year and requires you to pay [$2,000 + 0.135($2,000)]/12 = $189.17 per month for one year. What is the effective monthly rate you pay on the outstanding balance? The effective yearly rate?

40. At a New Year's party, a friend approaches you for some financial advice. Your friend is celebrating his 30th birthday and wants to start saving for his anticipated retirement at age 65. He wants to be able to withdraw $10,000 from his savings account at the end of each year for 10 years following his retirement (the first withdrawal will be at the end of his 65th year). Your friend is very risk averse and will invest his money only in the local savings bank, which offers 8 percent interest compounded annually. He wants to make equal, annual deposits at the end of each year in a new savings account he will establish for his retirement fund.

   a. If he starts making these deposits at the end of this year and continues to make deposits until he is 65 (the last deposit will be at the end of his 64th year), what amount must he deposit annually to be able to make the desired withdrawals upon retirement?

   b. Suppose your friend has just inherited a large sum of money and has decided to make one lump-sum payment at the end of this year to cover his retirement needs rather than make equal annual payments. What amount would he have to deposit?

Appendix 3A

Annuities

As Chapter 3 explained, an annuity is simply a level stream of payments. This appendix will describe annuities in more detail.

PRESENT VALUE OF AN ANNUITY

Equation (5) in Chapter 3 gave the basic formula for the present value of an annuity. Equation (5) is reproduced here as this appendix's Equation (A–1).

> The present value (PV_A) of an annuity, where the amount to be received at each period in the future is a constant value (A), can be calculated as
>
> $$PV_A = \sum_{t=1}^{n} \frac{A}{(1 + i)^t} \qquad \text{(A–1a)}$$
>
> where A = the annuity payment per period, i = the discount rate, t = the time period, and n = the number of periods. Factoring out the constant A, we can write
>
> $$PV_A = A \sum_{t=1}^{n} \frac{1}{(1 + i)^t} \qquad \text{(A–1b)}$$

When the payments are received or paid at the end of each period, the annuity is called an *ordinary annuity*. An annuity the payments of which are received or paid at the beginning of each period is called an *annuity due*. This appendix will discuss only ordinary annuities.

Equation (A–1) shows the present-value-of-an-annuity formula in two forms, (a) and (b). As Chapter 3 noted, Appendix Table II at the end of this book is constructed using Equation (A–1b) with A equal to $1.

Technically, the summation in Equation (A–1b) is a geometric progression that adds up to a finite sum. Therefore, Equation (A–1b) can be rewritten as shown in Equation (A–2).

> An alternative way to calculate the present value (PV_A) of an annuity is to calculate it as
>
> $$PV_A = A \left[\frac{1 - (1 + i)^{-n}}{i} \right] \qquad \text{(A–2)}$$
>
> where A = the annuity payment per period, i = the discount rate, and n = the number of periods.

When annuity tables, such as those in Appendix Table II at the end of this book, are not available, Equation (A–2) can be used to solve any type of ordinary-annuity problem.

For example, suppose someone wishes to borrow $40,000 by means of a mortgage loan in order to buy a house. A savings-and-loan association offers terms of 10.5 percent annual interest and monthly payments over 25 years. The monthly payment could be determined by applying Equation (A–2) and solving for A. In this case, i will be 10.5 divided by 12 = 0.875 percent per (monthly) period, and n will be 12 × 25 = 300 periods. Thus,

$$\$40,000 = A \left[\frac{1 - (1.00875)^{-300}}{0.00875} \right]$$

$$A = \$40,000 \div \left[\frac{1 - (1.00875)^{-300}}{0.00875} \right]$$

$$= \$377.67 \text{ per month.}$$

In doing this calculation, note that we have used an interest rate of 0.00875 (or 0.875 percent) per month. Equation (A–2), along with Appendix Tables II and IV at the end of the book, assume compounding once per period. In this case, the period is one month, so we have calculated a mortgage loan at 0.875 percent per month compounded monthly—an effective *annual* interest rate of more than 10.5 percent. Annuity formulas assume that compounding occurs once per period, where the period is the length of time between annuity payments. Therefore, the interest rate, i, to be used in annuity problems should be the effective interest rate for the time period between payments.

As another example, suppose you borrowed $6,000 to buy a car at an interest rate of 12 percent per year (1 percent per month). If you were making 48 monthly payments to repay the loan, what would be the amount (A) of each monthly payment? In this case i = 12 percent divided by 12 months = 1 percent per period, and n = 48 periods. The payments must be such that their present value is equal to $6,000. Using Equation (A–2), we can calculate the amount of the payment as

$$\$6,000 = A \left[\frac{1 - (1.01)^{-48}}{0.01} \right]$$

$$\$6,000 = A \, (37.974)$$

$$A = \$6,000/37.974 = \$158.00 \text{ per month.}$$

FUTURE VALUE OF AN ANNUITY

Chapter 3 also discussed the future value of an annuity. If you planned on depositing a certain amount each month or each year in a savings account, you might want to know what the balance will be as of a certain future date. Or at some point in your life, you might wish to contract with an insurance company for a qualified tax-deferred annuity for retirement purposes. Under such a plan, the payments are deductible for tax purposes, and taxes that would have been due on income that you used to make the payments are deferred until some future date.

Equation (6) in Chapter 3 showed how to calculate the future value of any ordinary annuity (in which payments are made at the end of the period). Chapter 3's Equation (6) is reproduced here as this appendix's Equation (A–3).

The future value (FV_A) of an annuity, where the amount being paid at each period is a constant value (A), can be calculated as

$$FV_A = A \sum_{t=1}^{n} (1 + i)^{n-t} \qquad \text{(A–3)}$$

where A = the payment amount per period, i = the interest rate, t = the time period, n = the number of time periods, $n - t$ = the numbers of periods on which interest is earned on a given payment amount.

Here again, because the summation is a geometric progression that adds up to a finite sum, it can be rewritten as shown in Equation (A–4).

An alternative way to calculate the future value (FV_A) of an annuity is to calculate it as

$$FV_A = A \left[\frac{(1 + i)^n - 1}{i} \right] \qquad \text{(A–4)}$$

where A = the annuity amount per period, i = the interest rate, and n = the number of time periods.

Suppose you decide to save $1,500 per year for 15 years. Under a qualified individual-retirement-account (IRA) plan, you can deposit the money with an insurance company at 8.5 percent interest. At the end of 15 years, you would have

$$FV_A = \$1,500 \left[\frac{(1.085)^{15} - 1}{0.085} \right]$$

$$= \$42,348.40.$$

Suppose you wish to begin immediately saving for your child's college education as soon as your child is born. You figure that, on the child's 18th birthday, you will need $20,000. You locate an insurance company offering annuity contracts at 8 percent interest. How much would you have to deposit each year (at year-end) to accumulate $20,000 by your child's 18th birthday? Using Equation (A–4), you could calculate your yearly payment (A) as follows:

$$\$20,000 = A \left[\frac{(1.08)^{18} - 1}{0.08} \right]$$

$$A = \$534.04 \text{ per year.}$$

Sometimes the payment necessary to produce a given future sum is called a *sinking-fund payment*. This term is often used in connection with amounts set aside by corporations to retire a bond at some future date.

Appendix 3B

Compounding

Equation (1) from Chapter 3 gave the general formula for calculating future value and is reproduced here as this appendix's Equation (B–1).

> The future value (P_n) of a certain present dollar amount (P_0) that earns interest at rate i compounded periodically for n periods can be calculated as
>
> $$P_n = P_0 (1 + i)^n \qquad \text{(B–1)}$$
>
> where P_0 = the initial principal amount, P_n = the amount accumulated n periods later, n = the number of interest periods, and i = the interest rate per period.

Chapter 3 considered the cases of semiannual and quarterly compounding. In principle, we can compound as often as we wish: monthly, weekly, daily, hourly, or by the minute! At the limit, we can compound continuously. To explore the effects of increasing the frequency of compounding, we can assume P_0 equals $1 and modify Equation (B–1) as shown in Equation (B–2).

> The future value (P_n) of $1 that earns interest at rate i compounded periodically for n periods can be calculated as
>
> $$P_n = \$1 \left(1 + \frac{i}{x}\right)^{xn} \qquad \text{(B–2)}$$
>
> where P_n = the amount accumulated n interest periods later, n = the number of *interest* periods, i = the interest rate, x the number of compoundings per interest period, i/x = the interest rate per compounding period, and xn = the number of *compounding periods*.

For example, with an interest period of a year and semiannual compounding, x will be 2 in Equation (B–2). How much money would you have after 3 years if you invested $1 today at 10 percent per year compounded semiannually? In Equation (B–2), n would be 3, x would be 2, xn would be 2 times 3, or 6, and i would be 0.10. Therefore, the future value can be calculated, with the help of Appendix Table III, as

$$FV = \$1(1 + 0.05)^6$$

$$= \$1(1.34)$$

$$= \$1.34.$$

Now we can examine the effects of increasing the frequency of compounding. As x increases, we compound more often over shorter intervals. If we let x increase without limit, we find that the future value of $1 if interest is compounded continuously for n years can be calculated as shown in Equation (B–3).

The future value of $1 at the end of n years if interest is compounded continuously (that is, the limit to x is infinity) can be calculated as

$$\lim_{x \to \infty} \left(1 + \frac{i}{x}\right)^{xn} = e^{in} \tag{B–3}$$

where e is a constant approximately equal to 2.718.

To illustrate, we can calculate the future value (FV) in one year, $n = 1$, of $100 at 6 percent interest per year compounded continuously as

$$FV = \$100(e^{0.06}) = \$106.18.$$

The *effective rate*, if interest is compounded continuously, is 6.18 percent. Compare this figure to effective rates of 6.09 percent if compounded semiannually and 6.14 percent if compounded quarterly.

In practice, we seldom encounter situations in which interest is compounded continuously, although there have been cases in which savings-and-loan associations have offered to calculate interest as if it were compounded continuously. There are, however, situations in which an assumption of continuous compounding is useful for analytical purposes. For example, where economic variables grow over time, an assumption of continuous growth is a better model of reality than an assumption of growth in discrete steps. Equation (B–4) shows how to calculate the continuous growth of a quantity at a rate of g per period.

Where a quantity, P_0, grows continuously at a rate of g percent per period, its future value, P_n, can be calculated n periods in the future as

$$P_n = P_0 \, e^{gn} \tag{B–4}$$

where e is a constant value 2.718.

For example, $100 growing continuously at 6 percent per year would become, after 4 years,

$$P_4 = \$100(e^{0.24}) = \$127.12.$$

Note that in the above calculation the figure 0.24 is calculated as 0.06 multiplied by 4. For comparison, $100 at 6 percent for 4 years with annual compounding would total $126.25.

It is worth noting that the quantity e is the base for the system of natural logarithms, which finds wide use in mathematics and engineering as well as in economics. By modifying Equation (B–3) to reflect an assumption of $n = 1$, e can be calculated as

$$\lim_{x \to \infty} \left(1 + \frac{i}{x}\right)^{x} = e = 2.718281828.$$

Chapter

4

Value in Markets

This chapter applies the discounted-cash-flow model to assets traded in financial markets. The DCF model is applied to both single and multiple cash flows and to the valuation of bonds. The chapter also develops one version of the general DCF model, the dividend-valuation model, that can be applied to stocks. Later in the chapter, we discuss the risk of investments and its relation to risk aversion by investors, and we explore the central role of financial markets in pricing securities and determining the required rate of return.

Chapter 3 developed discounted-cash-flow (DCF) techniques as a way to estimate the value of a stream of cash flows. DCF techniques are one of the most important tools financial managers can use since they allow us to collapse a whole series of cash flows into one present value—the value in today's dollars.

To apply the DCF model we need estimates of cash flows and some interest rate, or discount rate. In practice, estimating cash flows and choosing discount rates are complex and difficult tasks. Nevertheless, the effort often leads to handsome rewards in terms of improved decisions.

This chapter shows how values observed in financial markets can be explained in terms of DCF techniques. In Chapter 1, we settled on value maximization as the objective of financial management. Values are determined in financial markets by thousands of investors making decisions about whether to buy or sell assets. DCF techniques allow us to explain and estimate values and, thus, make operable our objective of value maximization. Extending the DCF model to market values provides us with a number of very useful insights. First, it gives financial managers a better understanding of the financial environment in which they operate. Second, it forces us to confront a second important dimension of financial problems—risk. Looking at market values in a DCF context helps us find ways to deal with risk, as we will see later in this chapter. Specifically, we will discuss how rates of return available on financial securities vary with the risk of the securities.

THE DISCOUNTED-CASH-FLOW MODEL

The last chapter developed the basic DCF model to determine the present value (*PV*) of a stream of payments. Here we repeat the basic DCF model as Equation (1), but here we assume that the first cash flow is at time 1.

The present value (*PV*) of a stream of future payments can be calculated as

$$PV = \sum_{t=1}^{n} \frac{C_t}{(1 + i)^t} \qquad (1)$$

where t = the period in which a payment is received, C_t = the amount to be received in period t, n = the number of periods, and i = the discount rate.

The basis for the discounted-cash-flow model is: present value equals the sum of all of the cash flows at various times, each discounted back to the present.

In all the problems considered so far we have glossed over the fact that cash flows are typically only estimates—we often (in fact, usually) don't know what the cash flow will be. For now, let us call C_t the expected cash flow. For example, suppose I offered you the following bet. I'll toss a coin. If it comes up heads I'll pay you $10; if it comes up tails I'll pay you $0. What is your expected cash flow? If you believe that the coin is fair and that there is an equal chance for either heads or tails, you could say the expected (average) cash flow is the average outcome of $5; that is, 0.5($10) + 0.5($0) = $5. Later we'll have more to say about expected values. If there is no uncertainty about payment at all, the expected cash flow is just the cash flow promised.

The value for the discount rate, i, has also been assumed in the discussions thus far, but the discount rate can vary from situation to situation.

DETERMINING VALUE IN MARKETS

A Single Cash Flow

Before going into more detail about cash flows and discount rates, let us turn back to the Bank of Virginia's zero-coupon certificate of deposit(CD) discussed in Chapter 1. On May 21, 1982, the Bank of Virginia asked a price of $250 for a certificate of deposit that promised to make a single payment—$1,000—on February 1, 1993. The Bank of Virginia was selling this CD, and, in a real sense, the market said that $250 was the value today of the $1,000 in the future. That is, $250 today will allow the CD holder to receive $1,000 in the future and is, thus, the *present value* of the $1,000.

Our DCF model allows us to interpret what the market is saying about the CD.

Since there is only one future cash flow associated with owning this CD, we can rewrite Equation (1) as follows.

$$PV = \sum_{t=1}^{n} \frac{C_t}{(1 + i)^t} = \frac{C_n}{(1 + i)^n}$$

Thus, $250 = $1,000/(1 + i)^{10\text{-}2/3}$. In this case, we know that $PV = 250 and that the initial amount $= $1,000$ receivable about 10-2/3 years later (10 years and 8 months between the end of May 1982 and the beginning of February 1993). Figure 4–1 displays the situation.

Unfortunately for us, the time period involved is 10-2/3 years—a slightly awkward figure with which to work. On the other hand, that's the way the world is—the numbers don't always come in neat packages. Rearranging our equation, and substituting the appropriate numbers for the variables we know, we can see that

$$(1 + i)^{10\text{-}2/3} = $1,000/$250 = 4.$$

Rearranging in this manner is very useful because it allows us to solve for the rate, i, that the market used to equate $1,000 to its present value of $250. Here, i is the market's discount rate on this CD. The only awkwardness is that we have $n = 10\text{-}2/3$. In Appendix Table III at the end of this book, we have values of $(1 + i)^n$—the future-value factor—but only for integer values of n. Looking at Appendix Table III, we see that at a time period of 11 years, the future-value factor is 3.836 for an interest rate of 13 percent, and the FV factor is 4.226 for an interest rate of 14 percent. Thus, we know that, roughly speaking, the interest rate is between 13 and 14 percent

Figure 4–1
Present Value of Zero-Coupon Certificate of Deposit

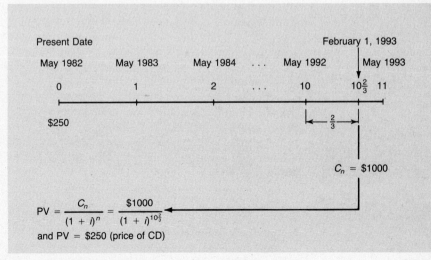

per year. Of course, with many calculators we can solve for i directly because we can write

$$(1 + i) = \sqrt[10^{2/3}]{4}$$
$$i = \sqrt[10^{2/3}]{4} - 1 = 1.1388 - 1 = 0.1388 = 13.88 \text{ percent}$$

The above mathematical manipulation should not cloud the main point of the illustration—that the market puts a value of $250 today on the $1,000 to be received in the future. This present value is equivalent to discounting the $1,000 at 13.88 percent per year for 10-2/3 years. Stated another way, an investor paying $250 at the end of May 1982 expects to earn 13.88 percent per year if he or she holds the CD and receives $1,000 on February 1, 1993. Computers and specialized calculators easily can handle messy calculations. The key point is that investment in this CD promises about a 13.88 percent annual return. This rate of return can be compared to other investments available in financial markets.

The discount rate, such as the 13.88 percent we calculated above, also goes by other names. Frequently this rate is called the **capitalization rate** because it allows us to transform a stream of expected cash flows into a single number called *present value*, **capital value**, or simply *value*. In the DCF valuation framework, the capitalization rate is simply another term for the discount rate.

The 13.88 percent rate of return on this CD can also be thought of as the market's **required rate of return** on this type of investment. The interaction of buyers and sellers in financial markets established a price of $250. In trading at this price, investors in the CD are revealing what rate of return they require on such an investment—the minimum return the investor will accept on the investment. As a result, this book will use the term *required rate of return*, or *required return*, to refer to the discount rate applied to future cash flows. When market prices are used to estimate this rate, the rate is the *market's required return*.

Figure 4–2 shows how General Mills could in July 1982 advertise to pay back $100 million in November 1987 in order to borrow $50 million in 1982.[1] General Mills was borrowing money just as was the Bank of Virginia. In General Mills's case, it promised to pay back double the money it received. As noted in Figure 4–2, this doubling of money in a little more than 5 years represents about a 13.50 percent annual return (compounded semiannually) to someone lending money to General Mills. The relevant calculations are just like those we did for the Bank of Virginia.

General Mills's borrowing scheme is called a *zero-coupon money-multiplier note*, which makes no payment except for the lump-sum payment at maturity. Such an investment may be especially desirable for people trying to accumulate money at a future date through retirement plans, such as an *individual retirement account (IRA)*. IRAs are retirement-savings plans with special tax-savings provisions. IRAs allow individuals to avoid paying taxes on portions of income that are placed in these special accounts.

The **capitalization rate**—or discount rate, is the rate of exchange between various time periods.

Capital value—is the present value of a stream of expected cash flows.

The **required rate of return**—is the *minimum* return prospective investors should accept evaluating an investment.

---

[1]Later, in the summer of 1982, when General Mills actually issued the notes, the maturity was set at January 4, 1988. Since the payment was later than November, General Mills was able to pay a lower interest rate than the 13.5 percent figure indicated in Figure 4–2. General Mills paid 13.30 percent because interest rates had dropped from the higher levels of earlier months.

Figure 4–2
Request for Funds to Borrow, Issued by General Mills

A registration statement relating to debt securities of which these securities are a part has been filed with the Securities and Exchange Commission and has become effective, but a final prospectus supplement with respect to the offering of these securities has not yet been filed. These securities may not be sold nor may offers to buy be accepted prior to the time a final prospectus supplement is delivered. This advertisement shall not constitute an offer to sell or the solicitation of an offer to buy nor shall there be any sale of these securities in any State in which such offer, solicitation or sale would be unlawful prior to registration or qualification under the securities laws of such State.

$100,000,000
General Mills, Inc.
Money Multiplier Notes*
(Zero Coupon)

Price to the Public per Note	Amount Payable at Maturity per Note	Approximate Maturity
$500	$1,000	November 1987

In lieu of interest payments, a purchaser of Money Multiplier Notes will receive double the original investment if the Notes are held to maturity. Money Multiplier Notes will be offered at $500 per Note and will be payable at maturity at $1,000 per Note. The actual maturity of the Notes will be established on the offering date expected to be in late July 1982. Based on current market conditions, the anticipated yield to maturity for the Notes, computed on a semiannual basis, would be approximately 13.50% per annum. The final selection of the maturity will reflect the then current market conditions and demand for the Notes, and the actual resultant yield for the Notes may vary significantly from that given above.

This proposed new issue of securities is designed primarily for purchase by IRA's, Keogh plans, IRA rollovers, pension plans and other investors not subject to federal income taxes.

General Mills, Inc. is a diversified consumer products company with operations in consumer foods, restaurants, toys, fashion and specialty retailing.

A Preliminary Prospectus Supplement, which gives details of the offering and includes a prospectus dated July 16, 1982, is available. To obtain a copy, please contact your broker, dealer or investment advisor.

Copies of the Preliminary Prospectus Supplement may be obtained in any State from securities dealers who may legally offer these securities in compliance with the securities laws of such State.

Salomon Brothers, Inc.
Dillon, Read & Co. Inc.
Merrill Lynch White Weld Capital Markets Group
Merrill Lynch, Pierce, Fenner & Smith Incorporated

*Trademark of Salomon Brothers Inc.

Source: General Mills money-multiplier notes. Reproduced by courtesy of General Mills, Inc.

Multiple Cash Flows

"Finance in Practice" 3–3 in the last chapter used a simplified example to illustrate the valuation of U.S. government bonds. We can learn a bit more by examining a few additional details of U.S.-government-bond valuation in terms of DCF analysis.

Figure 4–3, taken from the *Wall Street Journal*, shows the prices of a number of U.S. government bonds and notes. Like bonds, notes pay interest and principal but when issued are of shorter maturity than bonds. Since a note is essentially the same thing as a bond, notes are often referred to as bonds. These prices are for transactions of at least $1 million (a bit expensive for most private individuals!), reflecting trades made by large institutions, such as insurance companies, pension funds and brokerage houses. An individual could also participate in the market by purchasing shares (for much less than $1 million) in mutual funds specializing in bonds. Such funds pool money from individual investors.

A few details of the way figures are reported need to be discussed in order to understand the pricing of bonds. For example, look at the entry marked with colored arrows in Figure 4–3.

The **coupon rate**—is the stated percentage of the face value of a bond or note paid in interest each period.

The rate of "10-3/4S," called the **coupon rate**, means that this Treasury obligation pays 10-3/4 percent of its face value in interest each year. Treasury obligations pay half of these coupon payments every six months. For example, if the face value of the bond is $1,000, the bond will pay annual interest of $0.1075 \times \$1,000 = \$107.50$. Half of this amount, $\$107.50/2 = \$53.75$, would be paid every six months. Most bonds, both corporate and government, make semiannual payments of interest.

The maturity date of "2005 Aug" means that the last interest payment will be made in August 2005 along with repayment of the face value. The "k," a special footnote code in the newspaper, signals that those who are not U.S. citizens are exempt from withholding taxes on this bond.

Figure 4–4 displays the cash flows the purchaser of the bond would receive on a bond with a face value of $1,000 if it were bought in August 1985 and held until maturity in 2005 (assuming, of course, that the U.S. government makes all the promised payments). Note that Figure 4–4 divides time into six-month periods because for this Treasury security interest is paid every six months (in February and August of each year).

The next figures in the highlighted row of Figure 4–3, "99.22 (Bid)" and "99.26 (Asked)," require some explanation. They are quotes by government-bond dealers in the over-the-counter market (see Chapter 2) and indicate the price at which the dealers would buy this bond (the *bid price*) or sell this bond (the *asked price*). Both prices are quoted in terms of the percentage of face value of the bond and use a special convention for decimals. As stated at the top of Figure 4–3, decimals represent 32nds—not tenths; thus, 99.22 for a bid price means that dealers have bid, or offered to pay, 99-22/32 percent of the face value of the bond to buy the bond.[2] In the case of a $1,000-

---

[2]This convention can lead to what are, at first, confusing results. For example, as this convention is used, 99.22 is greater than 99.9 because 99.22 = 99-22/32 and 99.9 = 99-9/32. Also, 99.20 is not equal to 99.2.

Figure 4–3

Treasury Issues as of August 15, 1985: Bonds, Notes, and Bills

Source: Wall Street Journal, August 16, 1985, p. 29.

Figure 4–4

Cash Flows from a U.S. Government Note

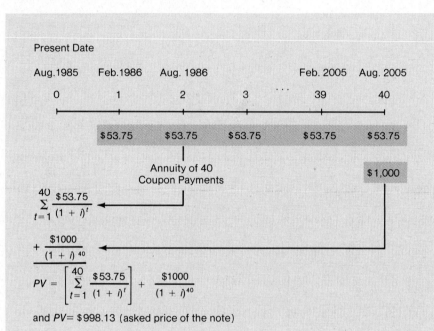

and $PV = \$998.13$ (asked price of the note)

face-value bond, this amount is 99.6875 percent of $1,000, or $996.88. The bid change, "−.3," is the change (in 32nds) in the bid price since the previous day.

Note that the bid price of 99.22 is less than the asked price of 99.26. This means that dealers are asking 99-26/32 percent of face value to sell you the note, but they are willing to pay only 99-22/32 percent of face value to buy the same note from you. The difference between the bid and asked price of 4/32 percent = 0.125 percent (or $1.25 per $1,000 face value) is called the *spread* and represents one of the ways a government-bond dealer would make money by buying securities at a slightly lower price (bid price) and selling them at a higher (asked) price.[3]

At what price could you buy this bond? While a large, powerful buyer, such as a major investment bank, might be able to negotiate and buy the bond at less than the asked price, a good assumption is that most buyers would have to pay the full amount of the asked price—that is, 99-26/32 percent of face value, or $998.13 for a note with a $1,000 face value. In the market, the value in today's dollars of this note maturing in August 2005 is $998.13.

---

[3]Bid prices will never be greater than asked prices unless the dealer wants to lose money continuously. If the bid price were greater than the asked price, a buyer could buy at the asked price and turn right around and sell at the bid price, making an instant and riskless profit.

We can now put the cash flows from this note into the DCF model as shown in Figure 4–4 by using Equation (1).

$$\$998.13 = \left[\sum_{t=1}^{40} \frac{\$53.75}{(1 + i)^t} \right] + \frac{\$1,000}{(1 + i)^{40}}$$

Note that in applying the DCF model, we have broken the cash flow in period 40 into two parts—the coupon payment of $53.75 and the principal repayment of $1,000. Note also that there are a total of 40 periods from August 1985 to August 2005. The one unknown in the equation above is the discount rate, i. What discount rate is the market using to value the cash flows from this bond? Note that because our time line in Figure 4–4 is divided into six-month periods, the rate i for this problem is defined for only a six-month period compounded once per six months.

Finding the value of i to satisfy the above equation is mechanical but not very interesting. Some calculators will solve the problem, and there are even bond tables that give interest rates that will equate price to the present value of interest and principal payments.

In general, the problem is to find the value of i in Appendix Tables I and II at the end of the book that will work. For example, at an discount rate of 5 percent, Appendix Table II gives a PV factor of 17.159 and Appendix Table I gives a PV factor of 0.142. Thus, at 5 percent,

$$PV = \$53.75(17.159) + \$1,000(0.142) = \$1,064.29.$$

At a discount rate of 6 percent, the appropriate PV factor from Appendix Table II is 15.046 and from Appendix Table I is 0.097. Thus, at 6 percent,

$$PV = \$53.75(15.046) + \$1,000(0.097) = \$905.72.$$

We can see from the above that the correct value of i must lie somewhere between 5 percent and 6 percent because $998.13, the actual present value of the note in the market, lies between $1,064.29 (the PV at 5 percent) and $905.72 (the PV at 6 percent). In fact, with precise tables, i could be calculated as 5.386 percent. Remember, however, that this value for i is per six months. On an annual basis the rate is double that, or $2 \times 5.386 = 10.77$ percent.[4] Note also that the compounding period would

---

[4]Note that $998.13 is about 0.4 of the way between a present value at 5 percent and a present value at 6 percent; that is,

$$(1064.29 - 998.13)/(1064.29 - 905.72) = 0.4172.$$

As a result, we can guess that the correct value for i is about 40 percent of the way between 5 percent and 6 percent; hence, i is approximately 5.4 percent. Of course, more precise calculations are necessary to get the exact answer of 5.386 percent. This text follows the convention used in the market for U.S. government securities that yields to maturity are quoted assuming semiannual compounding. As a result, we refer to an annual rate of 10.77 percent, which is double 5.386 percent. A rate of 10.77 percent per year compounded semiannually has an *effective* annual rate of $(1.05386)^2 - 1$, or about 11.1 percent. The difference between 11.1 and 10.77 reflects the semiannual compounding.

be 6 months because Figure 4–4 is divided into six-month periods. Thus, we can finally state that the market's discount rate on this note is 10.77 percent per year compounded semiannually. In the government-bond market, this rate is called the **yield to maturity**. The yield to maturity is the rate a bondholder could earn on the bond (or note) if he or she bought it at the current price, held the bond to maturity, and received all the cash flows promised by the bond. This yield to maturity, sometimes shortened to *yield*, is understood to be compounded semiannually, so the August 2005 bond would be said to have a yield of 10.77 percent. Note that this yield figure of 10.77 percent is precisely the last number in the *Wall Street Journal* entry for the August 2005 bond.

> The **yield to maturity**—is the rate that could be earned on a bond or note if the investor bought it at the current price, held it to maturity, and received all the cash flows promised.

An initial reaction might be, why go to all the trouble of calculating the yield when it is right there in the newspaper? In fact, the benefit of seeing a yield calculation (at least once) is in understanding exactly what that number does and does not mean. The yield is a rate of return that you can earn on this Treasury note *if you hold it to maturity*.

VALUATION OF STOCKS

In the case of the U.S. government note analyzed above, the cash flows (at least if you held the note to maturity) are fairly easy to predict—the payment of interest and face value. The same is the case for most bonds issued by corporations that have stated coupon rates, maturities, and face amounts.

We now move one step further to see how the same DCF model provides a basis for valuing the stream of benefits associated with owning a firm or a share in that firm. Shareholders purchase a share of a firm when they acquire common stock. Shareholders are also referred to as *equity owners* of the corporation because stock is sometimes called *equity*. The stream of cash flows associated with stock is much more uncertain than that associated with bonds (unlike a bond, common stock offers no contractual payment), and common stock offers no specified date for repayment of principal.

> **Common stocks offer an uncertain stream of cash flows (dividends) with no repayment of principal, while bonds offer a contractually fixed stream of cash flows (interest) with a specified repayment date for principal.**

Does the same general DCF valuation formula apply? It does. The formula allows us to convert a *stream* of expected benefits (or cash flows), whether finite or infinite, whether riskless or risky, whether equal or unequal, into a *single* present value. The big difference in using the valuation formula for equity securities (common stock) is that the future stream of benefits expected on equities is much harder to predict than have been the cash flows we analyzed so far. Although it may be a difficult task, predicting future benefits is important for managers in making decisions that will increase the value of their firm's stock and, hence, the well-being of the firm's shareholders.

Dividend-Valuation Model

The general DCF model tells us that value is a function of the future cash flows to be received. The cash flows that the owner of shares in a firm actually stands to receive are dividends plus the proceeds from the sale of the shares at some future date. The dividend is the only cash payment made by the firm to the shareholder. In most cases, firms pay out part of their earnings in the form of dividends and retain a part for reinvestment. The value of a share of stock at time-period 0(the present) can be calculated as shown in Equation (2).

The Dividend-Valuation Model

The present value (P_0) of a share of stock can be calculated as

$$P_0 = \frac{D_1}{(1 + K_e)} + \frac{D_2}{(1 + K_e)^2} + \cdots + \frac{D_n + P_n}{(1 + K_e)^n}$$ (2)

$$= \left[\sum_{t=1}^{n} \frac{D_t}{(1 + K_e)^t} \right] + \frac{P_n}{(1 + K_e)^n}$$

where D_t = the dividend expected in period t, P_n = the price at which the share is expected to be sold at the end of the final period, and K_e = the rate of return required by the market on the firm's stock.

The **dividend-valuation model**—is the discounted-cash-flow model applied to the valuation of stock, or equity.

The required rate of return is simply the discount rate that shareholders in the market are applying to the stock. The subscript e refers to the fact that stocks are also called equities. Note that the value of the shares depends only on *cash payments that the holder expects to receive*. Equation (2) is a straightforward application of the DCF model to the valuation of equity securities and has come to be known as the **dividend-valuation model**.

Sample Problem 4–1

Applying the Dividend-Valuation Model to TMI Stock

Triangle Microsystems Inc. (TMI), producer of both business and home computers, is expected to pay a dividend of $1 per share in 1987. In addition, shareholders expect this dividend to grow steadily at 7 percent per year for the next 3 years. At the end of the 3-year period, financial experts expect TMI stock to be selling for between $12 and $16 per share; let's assume an average expectation of $14 per share. If the market's required rate of return(discount rate) on TMI stock is 15 percent, what would be the market price of TMI stock at the end of 1986?

Solution
First, let's summarize the relevant cash flows to the nearest penny. In year 1—1987—the expected dividend is $1.00; in year 2—1988—the expected dividend is $1(1 + 0.07) = $1.07; in year 3—1989—the expected dividend is $1(1 + 0.07)^2 = $1.14 and the return from the sale of stock is expected to be $14.00.

Applying Equation (2), the current(1986) price (P_0) for a share of TMI stock can be calculated as

$$P_0 = \$1.00/(1.15) + \$1.07/(1.15)^2 + \$1.14/(1.15)^3 + \$14.00/(1.15)^3$$

$$= \$1.00(0.870) + \$1.07(0.756) + \$1.14(0.658) + \$14.00(0.658)$$

$$= \$0.87 + \$0.81 + \$0.75 + \$9.21$$

$$= \$11.64.$$

From the above calculations, we see that TMI's market price must be $11.64 if shareholders require a 15 percent annual return on the expected cash flows. This $11.64 is the sum of the present value of dividends for the next three years (a present value of $2.43) plus the present value of the proceeds of selling the stock for $14.00 in 1989(a present value of $9.21).

Companies often pay dividends on a quarterly basis, so we have simplified the problem by using annual figures. Further, the cash flows are only guesses about what might occur. In practice, obtaining such cash-flow estimates is a major difficulty. Anyone who buys TMI at $11.64 will likely get either more or less than the cash flows(dividends and stock price) projected. The cash flows are, however, the best guesses presently available. ≡III≡

Looking at Equation (2), a natural question is: On what does the share price, P_n, in period n depend? This price depends on dividends to be received from that point further into the future and on the proceeds from a sale at an even further point. Value at that further point in turn depends on dividends from that point on. So we can say that the value of a share of stock is simply the present value of *all* future dividends expected on the share. In other words, the present value of a share of stock can also be calculated as shown in Equation (3).

The present value, P_0, of a share of stock can also be calculated as simply the present value of all future dividends expected, or as

$$P_0 = \sum_{t=1}^{\infty} \frac{D_t}{(1 + K_e)^t} \qquad (3)$$

where D_t = the dividend expected in period t and K_e = the rate of return required by the market.

Equation (3) assumes that the stock is held forever. Since it is never sold, P_n disappears from the equation. In practice, no individual can hold a stock forever (at least given the current state of medical practice); nonetheless, when one individual sells the stock the next owner will receive dividends. In the final analysis, a company will pay out dividends only to shareholders, so Equation (3) expresses the value of a company's stock. While Equation (3) is an abstraction of the way any individual views stock ownership, it provides a useful way to look at market values.

Constant-Growth Dividend-Valuation Model

Estimating future dividends for a two- or three-year period is difficult enough; Equation (3) requires an estimate of dividends forever. A pragmatic way of providing such estimates is to assume that the dividend is going to grow steadily at the constant rate, g. Making this assumption, we can rewrite Equation (3), as shown in Equation (4).[5]

> **The Constant-Growth Dividend-Valuation Model**
>
> The present value, P_0, of a share of stock, when calculated as simply the present value of all future dividends expected and assuming that the dividend will grow steadily at the constant rate, g, is
>
> $$P_0 = \sum_{t=1}^{\infty} \frac{D_0(1 + g)^t}{(1 + K_e)^t}$$
>
> which can be simplified mathematically to
>
> $$P_0 = \frac{D_1}{K_e - g} \qquad (4)$$
>
> where D_1 = the dividend expected in the first year, K_e = the rate of return required by the market, and g = the expected rate of growth in dividends.

The **constant-growth dividend-valuation model**—is a method for valuing stock that assumes that the dividend will grow at a constant rate.

Equation (4) is known as the **constant-growth dividend-valuation model.**

Sample Problem 4-2

Applying the Constant-Growth Dividend-Valuation Model to TMI Stock

Let's return to Triangle Microsystems Inc. and make some different assumptions about its future. Suppose that TMI is expected to pay a dividend of $1 per share in 1987 and that future dividends are expected to grow steadily at 7 percent per year. The market's required rate of return(the discount rate) on TMI stock is 15 percent. Assume that this growth in dividends is expected to continue indefinitely. Apply the constant-growth dividend-valuation model from Equation (4) to determine the market price of TMI stock at the end of 1986.

---

[5]Except for the growth rate, g, Equation (4) is just like the perpetuity formula in Equation (7) of Chapter 3. Stated another way, a perpetuity has a growth rate of zero—it is a payment that is the same each period. Chapter 3's Equation (7) indicated that for a perpetuity, present value was just the payment amount divided by the discount rate, which is equivalent to this chapter's Equation (4) because $g = 0$ for a perpetuity. With growth, the denominator in Equation (4) becomes smaller than without growth. The lower denominator with growth implies a higher present value. This makes common sense—all other things equal, a stock with growth in dividends is worth more than one without growth. Equation (4) reflects this fact. Technically speaking, Equation (4) holds only when K_e exceeds g. If g exceeds K_e forever, the present value, P_0, becomes infinitely large. In financial markets, we don't find stocks with infinite prices, which means that in practice g does not exceed K_e.

Solution

The market price of the stock can be calculated as

$$P_0 = \$1.00/(0.15 - 0.07) = \$1.00/0.08 = \$12.50 \text{ per share.}$$

This price differs from the answer to Sample Problem 4–1 of $11.64 because we made different assumptions about cash flows. ▛▙▜

Equation (4) allows us to estimate the value of a share of stock assuming we can make assumptions about future dividend growth and shareholders' required return. We can use the same relationships to look at shareholders' required return by rearranging Equation (4) as shown in Equation (5).

The capitalization rate, or discount rate, that equates the present value of a share of stock and the stream of all future dividends expected, assuming that the dividend will grow at a steady rate, can be calculated as

$$K_e - g = \frac{D_1}{P_0}$$

$$K_e = \frac{D_1}{P_0} + g \tag{5}$$

where D_1 = expected dividend per share at time 1, P_0 = current market price per share, g = expected growth rate in dividends, and K_e = the discount rate, or capitalization rate.

That is, the capitalization rate implied by a given dividend rate, D_1/P_0, and a given growth rate, g, is simply the sum of the two. Equation (5) shows that the shareholder's required return will be equated to the sum of next period's dividend yield (D_1/P_0 = dividends as a percentage of share price) and the expected growth (g) in dividends.

In interpreting Equation (5) we must realize that it is the stock price, P_0, that adjusts in financial markets so that the relationship shown in Equation (5) will hold. If little growth is expected in dividends (if g is low), share price (P_0) will be low, and hence dividend yield (D_1/P_0) will be high. The result will be that the shareholder's required return will be satisfied largely by dividend yield. In contrast, if dividend growth is expected to be high, the share price will (all other things constant) be higher, and, as a result, the dividend yield will be lower. In the higher-growth case, the shareholder's required return may be satisfied largely by expected growth even if current dividend yield is low.

Sample Problem 4–3

The Capitalization Rate Applicable to TMI Stock

Given the information supplied about TMI stock in Sample Problem 4–2, what capitalization rate is applicable to the relationship between stock price and expected future benefits?

Solution

Equation (5) can be used to interpret the data in Sample Problem 4–2. Note that TMI's current dividend yield is the $1 dividend divided by the stock price of $12.50, or 8 percent. Adding this figure to the expected growth rate of 7 percent gives us 15 percent, which is the market's required rate of return (K_e) on TMI stock. In other words, investors expect to receive a total return on TMI stock of 15 percent—8 percent in current yield plus an additional 7 percent through capital gain achieved through a growing stock price as dividends grow. ∎

Variable-Growth Dividend-Valuation Models

The constant-growth dividend-valuation model is an oversimplified depiction of a complex world. The insights that these models provide are useful, and, in fact, they are widely used to estimate the rate of return required by the marketplace on equity securities. Nonetheless, no simple model can give us the ultimate truth. There will always be situations in which the assumptions of the model do not hold.

The weakness of the constant-growth dividend-valuation model is its assumption that a single growth rate will persist into the future indefinitely. This assumption can be especially misleading when it is applied to companies that have grown very rapidly.

As an extreme example, consider Teledyne, a company in the business of industrial electronics, specialty metals, and consumer products. According to the 1985 *Fortune 500* directory, the company's earnings per share grew at a rate of more than 52 percent per year between 1974 and 1984.

Common sense tells us that we cannot project an observed 52 percent growth rate very far into the future and certainly not to infinity. At 52 percent growth a year, the company's sales (which were $3.494 billion in 1984) will grow past the $15 trillion mark in 20 years, a figure more than four times the 1984 gross national product of the United States!

One way to resolve the issue is to use a **variable-growth dividend-valuation model** based on Equation (3). Such a model would assume that rapid growth can continue for only a short period into the future, beyond which growth declines to a more normal level close to the growth of the economy as a whole. One problem with this approach is that there are few objective methods for estimating how long above-normal growth will continue.

The **variable-growth dividend-valuation model**—is a method for valuing stock that assumes that a rapid growth in the dividend can continue for only a short period and will then decline to a more normal growth level.

Estimating Returns on Stocks

We can also use the DCF model to estimate what returns we have earned on past investments in securities. If we have data on past dividends and prices, we can modify Equation (2) slightly as shown in Equation (6).

The realized (actual) rate of return, R_e, received in the past on a share of stock can be calculated using known data on past dividends and prices as

$$P_0 = \frac{D_1}{(1 + R_e)} + \frac{D_2}{(1 + R_e)^2} + \cdots + \frac{D_n + P_n}{(1 + R_e)^n}$$

$$= \left[\sum_{t=1}^{n} \frac{D_t}{(1 + R_e)^t} \right] + \frac{P_n}{(1 + R_e)^n}$$

(6)

where D_t = the dividend actually received in period t, P_n = the price at which the share could be sold at the end of the final period, and P_0 = the price of the share at the beginning of the historical period.

Table 4—1
TMI Stock Prices and Dividends Paid-1981 through 1986, Year End (dollars)

	Stock Price	Dividend Paid
1981	6.50	0.50
1982	9.00	0.50
1983	9.75	0.75
1984	11.25	0.75
1985	10.00	0.75
1986	11.50	0.90

The **actual rate of return**—on an investment project is the return investors in fact receive, as distinct from the return they decide to require before undertaking the investment.

The only difference between Equations (6) and (2) is that R_e signifies *actual* return (looking back in time), while K_e signifies *required* return (looking ahead). If we know beginning price (P_0), dividends actually paid (D_1, D_2, D_n), and price at the end of the period (P_n), we can solve for R_e, the **actual rate of return**.

Sample Problem 4—4

Actual Return on TMI Stock

Suppose we have the data on TMI stock that are listed in Table 4–1. If someone bought a share of TMI stock for $6.50 per share at the end of 1981 and sold it for $11.50 at the end of 1986, what actual rate of return did he or she receive?

Solution
Applying Equation (6), P_0 is $6.50, five dividends were received in years 1981-1986, and P_n is $11.50. To solve for R_e, we set the problem up and solve by trial and error for the discount rate that makes the present value of the five dividends plus the final price exactly equal to the purchase price:

$$\$6.50 = \frac{\$0.50}{1 + R_e} + \frac{\$0.75}{(1 + R_e)^2} + \frac{\$0.75}{(1 + R_e)^3} + \frac{\$0.75}{(1 + R_e)^4} + \frac{\$0.90 + \$11.50}{(1 + R_e)^5}$$

The only way to use the Appendix Tables (Appendix Table I in this case) to find R_e is by trial and error. In this case, an actual return of 20 percent results in a present value of dividends plus sale price greater than $6.50 and is, therefore, too low. An actual return of 21 percent results in a present value that is less than $6.50 and is, therefore, too high. Many calculators can be used to calculate the actual return more precisely as 20.9 percent. ∃III∃

USING THE DCF MODEL TO VALUE SECURITIES

In previous examples, we have applied the basic DCF model to place a value on a number of different types of securities—CDs, bonds, and stocks. In the process we saw that the DCF formula relates three critical sets of variables—the projected *cash flows*, the *discount rate*, and the *value* of the security. Given an estimate of cash flows and given a discount rate, we can determine the value of an asset. Alternatively, given a value and a set of projected cash flows, we can infer what the market's discount rate must have been.

> **The DCF model relates three critical variables: cash flows, the discount rate, and the value of the security.**

These relationships are especially important to financial managers. Most investment decisions facing a manager involve paying out cash in hopes of receiving future cash. These cash trade-offs will directly affect the value of the firm, as our DCF formula suggests. If a financial manager wants to increase the value of the firm, he or she must understand how values are determined.

Risk Characteristics

Risk—is the degree of uncertainty about an outcome.

Default risk—is the risk that the issuer of a bond will not meet promised payments.

Interest-rate risk—is uncertainty about future interest rates as they affect future value.

So far so good. The main problem with valuation arises when we remember that the assets we were valuing (and will value in the future) are characterized by very different sorts of **risk**—or the degree of uncertainty about an outcome. A U.S. government bond is almost certain to pay off the promised interest and face value if we hold it to maturity. A bond issued by a corporation is typically very safe, but occasionally some corporations are not able to meet their promised payments and, thus, *default* on their promise.

Even ownership of a bond that has for practical purposes no **default risk** (such as a U.S. government bond) is not without its uncertainties. Suppose you buy a 20-year bond and must sell it one year later. Your actual return will depend on the price of the bond in one year—and that price will depend on next year's market required rate of return on government bonds, a rate that you can now only guess. Such uncertainty about future interest rates is called **interest-rate risk**.

Sample Problem 4–5

Interest-Rate Risk on a U.S. Government Bond

Suppose that in August 1985 you bought the August 2005 10-3/4 U.S. government bond highlighted in Figure 4–3 for the asked price of $998.13 (the dollar equivalent of 99-26/32 percent of the $1,000 face value of the bond). We already know that the bond has a yield of 10.77 percent, so 10.77 percent will be your annual return if you hold it until it matures in August 2005. Suppose, however, that you have to sell the bond in August 1990, at which time yields on such notes have risen to 16 percent per year. What would be the price, *P*, of the bond in August 1990? What would be your annual rate of return, *R*, over the five years that you owned the bond?

Solution

As of August 1990 (right after the August coupon payment), the note will have 30 more semiannual coupon payments of $53.75 each to make as well as repayment of the $1,000 face value in August 2005. Using the DCF model as shown in Equation (1), the present value of the stream of payments associated with the bond can be calculated, with the help of Appendix Tables II and I at the end of this book, as

$$P = \left[\sum_{t=1}^{30} \frac{\$53.75}{(1 + 0.08)^t}\right] + \frac{\$1,000}{(1 + 0.08)^{30}}$$

$$= \$53.75 (11.258) + \$1,000 (0.099)$$

$$= \$605.12 + \$99.00 = \$704.12$$

Note that $i = 0.16/2 = 0.08$ because we are dealing with six-month periods rather than years. We use the 16 percent rate(8 percent every 6 months) because the market now requires 16 percent interest on notes such as this: 16 percent is the opportunity cost of money for this security.

Since we paid $998.13 for the note, received 10 coupon payments of $53.75 each, and then sold the note for $P_1 = \$704.12$, our return, R, must satisfy the equation

$$\$998.13 = \left[\sum_{t=1}^{9} \frac{\$53.75}{(1 + R)^t} \right] + \frac{\$53.75 + \$704.12}{(1 + R)^{10}}$$

By trial and error, we find that R is approximately equal to 0.028 per six months, or 0.056 per year. The price of the note dropped as interest rates went up from 10.77 percent to 16 percent. As a result, the actual return, R, earned on the note from August 1985 to August 1990 was low—only 5.6 percent per year. Considering only principal and not interest, we actually lost $294.01 on the transaction because we bought the bond at $998.13 and sold it for $704.12. But we collected $537.50 in interest, so our total return was positive—in this case 5.6 percent. Even though the note had no default risk, its return from August 1985 to August 1990 was substantially lower than the yield to maturity because of *interest-rate risk*. ▪▪▪

Purchasing-power risk— is the risk that money received in the future will not purchase the same goods and services as it can today, or the risk that inflation will decrease the value of future cash flows.

Even if you know what dollar amounts you will receive, you can't be sure of what goods and services those dollars will be able to purchase because purchasing power depends on future prices—that is, on the rate of inflation. Thus, there is some **purchasing-power risk** associated with the uncertainties of inflation.

The true returns to stocks can be even more difficult to predict than those to bonds. Future dividends depend on many variables: corporate earnings, economic conditions, and management decisions. Stock prices can fluctuate dramatically. The investment risk borne by shareholders is the sum of a company's **financial risk** and its **operating risk**. Operating risk, sometimes referred to as *business risk*, is the uncertainty associated with a firm's product markets and operations. For example, a firm planning to enter the fast-food business faces unknowns about trends in the fast-food market. Will health-conscious consumers start to avoid hamburgers? A new firm might also face uncertainty about how its products will fare against competition from market giants like McDonalds, Burger King, or Wendy's. Financial risk is the additional risk, over and above operating risk, to which shareholders are exposed when a company uses debt(or debt-like) financing. As the portion of future earnings committed to such fixed-cost obligations increases, so do risks to shareholders.

Financial risk—is the additional risk to shareholders, over and above operating risk, that results from the use of debt (or debt-like) financing.

Operating risk—or *business risk*, is the risk to shareholders that arises from uncertainty about a firm's product markets or operations.

For example, suppose a project required an outlay of $100 now, and the financial manager expects that at the end of one year the project will end and earn either 20 percent($120 for $100 invested) in a good outcome or 5 percent($105 for $100 invested) in a bad outcome. Each of the outcomes is equally likely. While real-world operating risk is more complex, the uncertainty about the good or bad outcomes for the project is the underlying operating risk in this example. Given this operating risk, a firm has a number of options about how to finance the project. Table 4–2 describes two of these options. One option is to raise all money from shareholders (all-equity financing). The All-Equity Plan in Table 4–2 shows the returns to shareholders if the firm follows this strategy and uses no debt. The shareholders' returns exactly mirror those of the project. Another alternative is to use **financial leverage**—to finance part of the project with borrowing. Plan B in Table 4–2 traces through the shareholder

Financial leverage—is the use of debt, or borrowing, to finance investment.

returns if shareholders put up $10 for the project, with the remaining $90 being borrowed at a market interest rate of 10 percent per year. At time 1, the shareholders' return comes after repayment of the loan ($90 principal plus $9 interest). Table 4–2 shows that if the project turns out well (the good outcome is achieved) using Plan B, shareholders earn a whopping 110 percent, more than doubling their $10 investment. Financial leverage has magnified a 20 percent return on the project into more than a 100 percent return to shareholders—quite a profitable prospect that often provides a powerful incentive for borrowing when you expect the underlying investment will earn a rate of return higher than the interest rate charged on borrowing.

A further look at the results of using Plan B shows, however, that financial leverage is a two-edged sword. If the project turns sour (the bad outcome results), shareholders will experience a 40 percent loss because they end up borrowing money at 10 percent to invest it in a project that earned 5 percent—clearly a raw deal for shareholders. What should the firm do? If it knows the project outcome is going to be good, it should borrow. Because of operating risk, however, the project's future is uncertain. We'll return to the firm's choice of financing in Part Four of this book. What is clear is that a firm's use of debt increases risks to shareholders. This extra risk over and above operating risk is the financial risk to shareholders. As a result, even if two companies have basically the same operating risk, the stock of one may be more risky if that firm uses more debt financing than its counterpart. Also, individuals do not have to rely on firms to supply financial leverage. They can borrow for themselves (for example, from the bank) to increase the potential rewards and risks of investments. As Table 4–2 shows, the use of financial leverage adds financial risk to the operating risk already inherent in a firm's activities.

How can our valuation model take into account these different types of uncertainties?

Table 4–2

Financial Leverage and Financial Risk

Financing Plan (1)	Shareholder Investment (dollars) at $t = 0$ (2)	Outcome	Dollars to Shareholder at $t = 1$ (3)	Percent Return to Shareholder at $t = 1$ (4) = [(3) − (2)]/(2)
A. All-Equity Plan (entire $100 investment financed by shareholders)	$100	Good	$120	20
		Bad	$105	5
B. Financial-Leverage Plan ($10 financed by shareholders; $90 borrowed at 10 percent annual interest)	$ 10	Good	$120 − $99 (loan) = $21	110
		Bad	$105 − $99 (loan) = $6	−40

Some help in answering this question can be found by returning to some basic elements of value outlined in Chapter 1—time and risk. There we defined the *value* of an asset as "the dollar amount that people would have to have today to make them just as well off as they would be owning the asset."

As we developed our DCF model in Chapter 3, the discount rate reduced the value of future cash dollars relative to present dollars. That is, future dollars were discounted back to their present value to reflect the forgone opportunity to earn a rate of return on money while we wait. We must remember that to fit our definition of *value* there must also be a penalty imposed for any uncertainty that we have to bear as a result of holding the asset. Fortunately, the DCF model can also incorporate this penalty for risk by applying a higher discount rate. In effect, investors require higher returns (a higher discount rate) to compensate them for additional risks—and as the discount rate goes up, value goes down in the DCF model.

Required Return and Value

Suppose you expect the price of a certain share of stock in one year to be $50 and *require* a 19 percent annual return; that is, 19 percent is the minimum return you will accept. The stock is not expected to pay a dividend in the next year. What is the maximum price you would pay today for the stock? This price can be calculated using Equation (2) as

$$P_0 = \$50/(1 + 0.19) = \$42.$$

Suppose, however, that you become more uncertain about the company's prospects. (For example, foreign competition increases.) While you still expect a price of $50 in one year, you now require a 25 percent return (an additional 6 percent over the previous 19 percent to compensate you for the new uncertainty). The maximum price you would now pay today for the stock can also be calculated using Equation (2) as

$$P_0 = \$50/(1 + 0.25) = \$40.$$

The higher required return (25 percent versus 19 percent) lowered the value of the stock from $42 to $40 per share—that is, there was a penalty for the new uncertainty associated with the company.

The DCF model can, thus, be used to capture the effects of both time and risk on value. The discount rate, or the *required rate of return* on an investment, becomes larger to compensate investors for greater risk.

> **The required rate of return on an investment opportunity depends on the riskiness of the investment. The required rate of return is the minimum expected return the investor will accept on the investment. The required return compensates investors for the passage of time and for risk.**

The **risk/expected-return trade-off**—is that the greater is the risk of an investment opportunity, the greater is the return required by an investor.

Figure 4–5 illustrates the **risk/expected-return trade-off** explained by the DCF model. The greater the risk of the investment opportunity, the greater is the return required by the investor. The line in Figure 4–5 symbolizes the terms of the risk/

Figure 4–5
The Risk/Expected Return Trade-Off

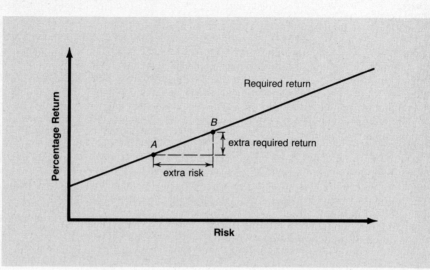

expected-return trade-off.[6] At point B, a higher return is required than at point A because there is extra return required for bearing extra risk. To economize on words, we will sometimes refer to this trade-off as simply the *risk/return trade-off*.

Note that the risk/return trade-off depicted in Figure 4–5 assumes that people do not like risk. Because they are risk-averse, they require compensation for bearing risk. The fact that an investment has zero risk, however, does not mean it will have a required return of zero.[7] As shown in Figure 4–5, even at zero risk there is a positive required return; investors still require compensation for the passage of time. Thus, the required return compensates the investor for both the passage of time and risk. In symbolic terms, the required return can be represented as shown in Equation (7), where the **risk premium** (*rp*) is the extra return required as compensation for risk.

A **risk premium** (*rp*)—is the extra return required as compensation for risk.

The required rate of return can be represented symbolically as

$$K = R_f + rp \qquad (7)$$

where K = the required rate of return, R_f = the risk-free rate of return, and *rp* = the risk premium.

---

[6]In Figure 4–5, the risk/return trade-off is drawn as a positively sloped straight line. While the trade-off need not be a straight line, there must be a positive relationship between risk and required return—the higher is the risk, the higher is the required return.

[7]In reality, there is no such thing as a riskless investment. U.S. government bonds are widely used as the risk-free benchmark. While such bonds are relatively free of default risk, they are not free of the risk of price fluctuations as the level of interest rates rises and falls. The term *risk-free* is used in this chapter to be consistent with common usage in the finance literature. When referring to investment alternatives that actually exist in practice, ''risk-free'' should be interpreted to mean ''least-risk.''

RISK AND RISK AVERSION

To explain adequately how risky benefits are valued in the financial markets, we must draw a clear distinction between the *risk* of investments and the *attitude toward risk* of investors. Since investors will buy and sell the firm's stock and thereby determine the stock's value in financial markets, it is important for financial managers to consider investors' attitudes toward risk.

Risk

As mentioned earlier in the chapter, *risk* is the degree of uncertainty about an outcome. Consider two investments, A and B, that have the possible payoffs listed in Table 4–3, depending on the state of the economy. Assuming that the three states of the economy are equally likely, the average expected return from both investments is $100. But the return from investment A will range between $90 and $110, whereas that from B may vary between $0 and $200. Thus, there is considerably more uncertainty about the return from B. As a result, we say that B is riskier than A.

Risk Aversion

Now let us consider the effect of investor attitudes toward risk. Suppose you were offered an opportunity to choose one of the two investments, A or B, in Table 4–3 above. Both investments are expected to have a $100 payoff. If your choice is A, you are *risk-averse* with respect to this decision—you dislike risk. If your choice is B, you are *risk-preferent*—you like risk. If you are indifferent between A and B, you are *risk-neutral* with respect to this decision. Consider another illustration. Suppose you are offered an opportunity to undertake investment B in return for a cash payment. The **expected value** of investment B is $100, as calculated in Table 4–4. This $100 figure comes from adding up each possible payoff multiplied by the probability that the payoff will occur, as shown in the last column of Table 4–4.

What is the maximum you would be willing to pay for an opportunity to invest in B? If your maximum were less than $100, you would be exhibiting risk-averse behavior with respect to this investment opportunity. If your maximum were more than

> The **expected value**—of an investment project is the weighted average of possible outcomes where each weight is the probability associated with the outcome.

Table 4–3
Estimating Outcomes for Investments Based on States of the Economy

State of Economy	Outcome (dollars) Investment A	Investment B
Recession	90	0
Normal	100	100
Boom	110	200

Table 4–4
Calculating the Expected Value of an Investment

Payoff (dollars) (1)	Probability (percent) (2)	Weighted Outcome (dollars) (3) = (1) × (2)
0	0.333	0
100	0.333	33.33
200	0.333	66.67
Expected Value of Payoff		100.00

$100, you would be exhibiting risk preference. If your maximum were exactly $100, you would be exhibiting risk neutrality. In general, an unwillingness to pay an amount as great as the expected value of an uncertain investment opportunity indicates risk-averse behavior; a willingness to pay exactly the expected value indicates risk neutrality; a willingness to pay more indicates risk-preference.

Any given individual may exhibit risk-averse behavior toward some decisions and risk-preferent behavior toward others. An individual who plays roulette at Las Vegas, an example of risk-preferent behavior, also may own fire insurance on a house, an example of risk-averse behavior. The size of the gamble also may be a factor. The same individual may be risk-preferent toward small gambles, such as flipping coins for nickels, and risk-averse toward large gambles, such as flipping coins for $1,000 a flip.

There is nothing inconsistent or irrational about the behavior of an individual who exhibits risk aversion toward some gambles and risk preference toward others. In the case of an individual who is risk-averse toward most financial decisions but who also occasionally exhibits risk-preferent behavior, it is likely that the risk-preferent behavior contains elements of entertainment—for example, gambling at Las Vegas.

Where matters of income and wealth are concerned, as distinct from entertainment, we can safely assume risk aversion to be characteristic of nearly all individuals. An individual making an investment decision affecting only himself or herself can determine his or her own attitude toward risk. With respect to investors in general, studies of the securities markets provide convincing evidence that the majority of investors in stocks and bonds are risk-averse. This suggests that they are unwilling to pay an amount equal to the expected value of an investment opportunity; that is, they demand a premium for bearing risk.[8] The greater is the perceived risk, the lower is the value placed on uncertain benefits.

Risk aversion, risk neutrality, and risk preference are three types of investor attitude toward risk. A risk-averse investor requires compensation for bearing risk. A risk-preferent investor will pay for the opportunity to gamble. A risk-neutral investor is indifferent toward risk; that is, he or she requires no compensation for bearing risk.

---

[8]For evidence of risk aversion, see I. Friend and M. Blume, "The Demand for Risky Assets," *American Economic Review* 55 (December 1975): 900-22.

Risk aversion does not imply complete avoidance of risk; it merely implies that compensation is required. The greater the risk, the greater the compensation must be. A risk-averse person will undertake a risky investment, even an investment of very high risk, provided the compensation is sufficiently high.

The concept of risk aversion has very important implications for investment decisions. A higher expected return is required to motivate individual investors to take on greater risk. Similarly, if shareholders of a professionally managed firm are risk-averse (and, in general, they are), and if management is to act as agent of those shareholders, then investments of differing risk must be evaluated using different required rates of return. In applying the DCF method, the discount rate used must vary with the riskiness of the investment opportunity, which is determined by the degree of uncertainty surrounding the stream of cash flows that the investment generates.

Finance in Practice 4—1

How Portfolio Managers Use the Dividend-Valuation Model

"This is a very hysterical business," remarked an executive with a major investment-counseling firm in describing his industry. "Emotion rides high, and things tend to get exaggerated, and that creates opportunities."

To help identify the opportunities that emotion creates, a number of major investment-management firms since the late 1970s have been making heavy use of the dividend-valuation model, or *dividend-discount model(DDM)*, as many practitioners call it. The success of those using the dividend-valuation model has spawned a boom in what one observer called "born-again value players," who have brought the model into wider popularity. "The user universe for our dividend-discount model has gone straight up," commented a vice-president of one of several Wall Street firms offering the models to outside users. An analyst at one firm making heavy use of the div-idend-valuation model stated that the top 20 percent of stocks ranked by the model from 1970 through 1983 would have outperformed the Standard & Poors (S&P) 500 stock index by 7 to 8 percentage points. The S&P 500 index is a widely followed average of 500 stocks.

Advocates of the dividend-valuation model differ in the ways they use it and in the extent to which they rely on it. For some firms, it is the core of their approach. One uses the model to rank a universe of about 500 stocks from highest expected returns to lowest. The top 100 stocks become buy candidates. Stocks become candidates for sale once they drop out of the top 20 percent and are automatic sells when they drop below the top 40 percent. Performance in 1984 for this firm was an average return of 11 percent versus 6.3 percent for the Standard & Poor's 500 index; for the five years ending in 1983,

THE DISCOUNT RATE, RISK, AND FINANCIAL MARKETS

Increasing discount rates to provide compensation for risk is not just a mechanical device to use in DCF calculations: rates of return in markets reflect these risk differentials. Consider the data in Figure 4–6, which show that in mid-1985 the yield (required return) on long-term U.S. government obligations averaged about one percentage point less than yields on long-term bonds issued by public utilities (for example, power companies). At least part of the reason is that U.S. government bonds are safer than those issued by individual corporations. U.S. Treasury bonds are backed by the full taxing authority and financial power of the U.S. government. While public utilities are typically not small companies, they certainly don't have the financial resources of the federal government. The yield on municipal bonds was fully one percentage point

performance for this firm was 26 percent per year versus 17.3 for the S&P index.

A larger group of firms, estimated by some to be between 50 and 100 in number, use the dividend-valuation model as one tool among several upon which they rely heavily. One firm uses the model as one of five equally weighted screens, along with measures of momentum, current and historical price/earnings ratios, and normalized measures of earnings (that is, measures adjusted for the effects of the business cycle). Finally, there is an even larger group of firms that use the model as a cross-check, or an indicator to be heeded or ignored at will. One analyst commented that "two out of three institutional money managers are casual DDM practitioners."

Users of the dividend-valuation model are quick to point out that the model has its limitations. The model tends to underperform in comparison to some other techniques at times when emotion rules the stock market. That means that users of the model will not always lead the pack. Also, the model is only as good as the data that go into it. One early user of the dividend-valuation model pointed to a case in which his firm was badly burned in energy stocks in spite of use of the model because of one analyst's euphoric predictions for the industry. "It is impossible to stress too strongly the importance of consistent inputs and the political integration of the process," commented an executive of one firm.

In summing up use of the dividend-valuation model in investment management over the past six to eight years, an analyst stated that the model has gone from "a hard (thing to) sell in 1979 to part of the landscape today." Some users expect it ultimately to become the standard way of doing investment analysis.

Source: Material for this section was adapted from the article by B. Donnelly, "The Dividend Discount Model Comes Into Its Own," *Institutional Investor*, March 1985, pp. 77–82.

Figure 4–6
Bond Yields: September 1985

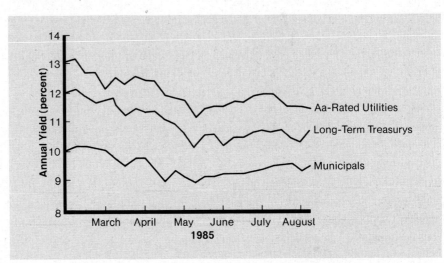

Source: Merrill Lynch Securities Research, as reported in *Wall Street Journal*, September 9, 1985, p. 34.

below that on long-term U.S. government obligations, largely due to the tax advantages on these securities. As discussed in Chapter 2, such advantages motivate investors to require a lower before-tax rate of return on municipal bonds.

Such risk-related return differences are also reflected in past returns that investors have earned. Table 4–5 shows some average rates of return earned by investors in different sorts of securities over a long period of U.S. financial history—1926–1981. As one would expect, common stocks have, on average, provided higher returns (11.4 percent) than have corporate bonds (3.7 percent), which in turn have provided higher

Table 4–5
Average Annual Returns for Various Types of Investments, 1926–1981

Type of Investment	Percentage Annual Return (arithmetic average)
Long-Term U.S. Government Bonds	3.1
Long-Term Corporate Bonds	3.7
Common Stocks	11.4

Source: R. Ibbotson and R. Sinquefield, *Stocks, Bonds, Bills and Inflation: The Past and the Future* (The Financial Analysts Research Foundation, 1982).

returns than have long-term government bonds (3.1 percent). These results are consistent with the notion of higher returns for higher risks.

There is, however, a critical difference between *required return* and *actual return*. Our reasoning suggests that required returns ought to be higher the higher are the risks perceived by investors. That does not mean, however, that investors will always receive their required return. For example, Table 4–5 shows that shareholders averaged 11.4 percent per year over the period 1926–1981. Figure 4–7 shows the numbers that went into that average. As Figure 4–7 shows, anyone owning stocks takes risks. The average of 11.4 percent does not capture the nature of what happened to someone who happened to invest in stocks during a year like 1974, when the return was −26.5 percent, or in 1980, when the return was 32.4 percent. After all, risk implies that the outcome may not be as good as you expect it to be.

> **The required return of an investment may differ from the actual return investors receive after they make an investment; for example, stocks may perform better or worse than expected.**

Figure 4–7
Year-by-Year Returns on Common Stocks, 1926–1981

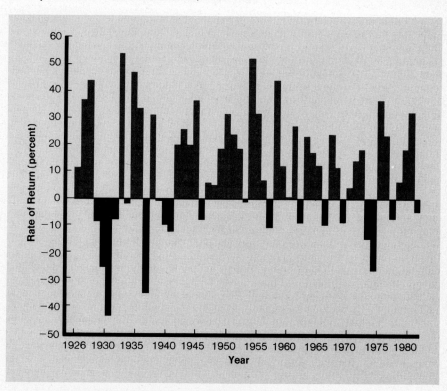

Source: R. Ibbotson and R. Sinquefield, *Stocks, Bonds, Bills, and Inflation: The Past and the Future* (The Financial Analysts Research Foundation, 1982).

The Role of Markets

The **equilibrium price,** or **market-clearing price**—of a good or service is the price at which the quantity demanded equals the quantity supplied.

The **demand curve**—for a good or service shows the amounts of the good or service buyers are prepared to purchase at different prices during a specified time period.

The **supply curve**—for a good or service shows the amounts of the good or service suppliers are willing to offer for sale at different prices during a specified time period.

It is no accident that returns in financial markets reflect differences in risk. A major function of financial markets is to establish prices for financial assets; as a result, markets determine returns on those assets.

In a market for goods and services, trading takes place until an **equilibrium price**, or **market-clearing price**, is established; that is, the price equates quantity demanded by buyers with quantity supplied by sellers. Figure 4–8 illustrates the typical supply and demand curves of microeconomic theory. The **demand curve** shows the amounts of a given item buyers are prepared to purchase at different prices during a specified time period. The **supply curve** shows the amounts of the item offered for sale at different prices during a specified time period.

> **In a market for goods or services, trading occurs until a price is established that clears the market (equates quantity supplied with quantity demanded).**

As a result of buying and selling decisions by market participants, an equilibrium price of P^* is established. At a price of P^*, exactly Q^* units are both demanded and supplied. If the price falls below the equilibrium level, some demand is left unsatisfied, so the price is bid back up. If the price rises above the equilibrium level, excess supply results, causing the price to fall. Thus, the equilibrium price of P^* equates quantity supplied and quantity demanded.

For financial assets such as stocks and bonds, demand and supply curves like those in Figure 4–8 depend on the expectations of market participants about future rewards

Figure 4–8
The Equilibrium Price

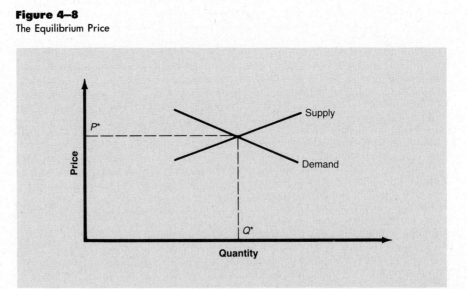

from owning those assets. All investors will be hoping to earn superior returns—after all, that is most of the potential fun in picking stocks. One strategy to earn such returns would be to buy stocks currently "underpriced" by the market. If an investor believes a certain stock is underpriced, he or she believes that the current price is below the equilibrium level—perhaps because of unwarranted market pessimism about the company's prospects. Buying at the low price, the smart investor could reap a capital gain when the market realizes the error of its ways and the stock price goes up. Sounds like a great strategy, but is it possible consistently to pick underpriced stocks? The answer to that question is the subject of considerable controversy. Clearly, many brokers feel that they can pick winners—doing so is part of their business, and many fortunes have been made in the stock market. On the other hand, there is substantial evidence that many financial markets (such as the well-organized stock and bond markets in the United States) are highly efficient. An **efficient market** is one in which current market prices impound all available information and are, as a result, a fair reflection of the true value of a financial asset. Facing such prices, an investor is unlikely consistently to pick assets that turn out to be underpriced. After the fact, some prices will turn out to have been too high, and some too low; the difficulty lies in determining in advance which ones are which. Similarly, in an efficient market, a financial manager of a firm need not worry that his or her company's stock is underpriced when considering raising funds through the sale of new shares unless, of course, that manager has some unannounced information not yet available to the market. In short, the manager relies on an efficient market to price the firm's shares fairly.

We'll return to a more detailed discussion of market efficiency (and possible inefficiencies) in Part Four. For present purposes, it is important to remember that in well-organized financial markets information is readily available, and literally thousands of investors compete in the buying and selling of assets to establish prices. As a result of that competition, prices reflect a wealth of information. This does not mean that financial markets have perfect forecasting ability. In the future, some stocks will provide high financial returns and others will produce losses—the question is which one to buy now. No one wants to buy a stock to lose money. The basic uncertainty associated with securities is that the future is unknown. The key is that if markets are efficient, current prices will appropriately reflect this uncertainty.

An **efficient market**—is a market in which current market prices impound all available information and are a fair reflection of the true value of a financial asset.

The Market Required Rate of Return

Earlier this chapter discussed the relationship between prices and returns on financial assets. A higher current price, other factors equal, implies a lower return, and vice versa. In establishing prices of financial assets, the market simultaneously is establishing expected returns. Given that investors are risk-averse, different rates of return are established for different degrees of risk. In effect, investments of differing risk are different commodities, each having a different price—that is, a different required rate of return. In principle, a different rate is established by the market for each degree of risk, thus resulting in a **market risk/return schedule**, as illustrated in Figure 4–9. Figure 4–9 shows that as the risk of an asset increases, the risk premium (*rp*) on that asset will increase. This increased risk premium is necessary to compensate risk-averse

A **market risk/return schedule**—for a given investment project shows the return required by investors at different levels of risk.

Figure 4–9
The Market Risk/Return Schedule

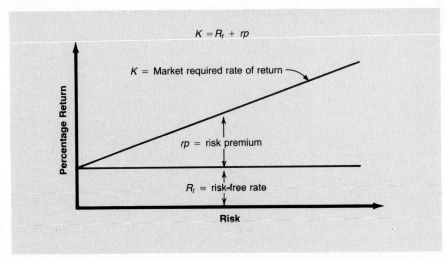

individuals for investing in risky securities. As the risk and risk premium increase, the required return (K) also increases. Chapter 5 will examine the measurement of risk and the nature of the risk/return trade-off more carefully.

A major function of financial markets is to establish prices. In principle, the market establishes a different required rate of return for each degree of risk.

Opportunities to invest exist for all assets for which there are organized and public markets. Such markets exist for a wide variety of financial and real (physical) assets. Financial assets at the low end of the risk spectrum (left portion of Figure 4–9) include savings accounts and, for those with sufficient funds, U.S. government securities. Of slightly greater, but still low, risk are bonds issued by corporations. Then come common stocks, varying widely as to risk. Next there are investments, such as *commodity futures* (agreements about purchasing and selling commodities such as wheat at future dates), *financial futures* (agreements to purchase or sell financial assets at future dates), and *options* to purchase or sell financial assets at future dates. These latter investments usually are considered to be of high risk. (We will return in a later chapter to a discussion of financial futures and options.) The point we need to focus on here is that markets for all these assets are public and highly organized; information is readily available to participants, and costs of entering and transacting are relatively low. Other markets for investment assets, such as real estate, present additional opportunities for some investors but are less highly organized.

> Returns in organized and public markets, which are available at low cost and little effort, represent the minimum that an investor should accept on any investment opportunity. Hence, organized markets establish, for every degree of risk, the required rate of return. Since everyone faces essentially the same set of opportunities in the markets, the opportunity cost for any given degree of risk is the same for every investor.

Applying the DCF Model

The DCF model provides a conceptual framework for handling both time and risk. The difficulty in practice is getting more specific. How do we estimate cash flows? How do we measure risk? How do we translate risk into appropriate required rates of return?

There are no easy answers to these questions. Useful tools for the analysis, however, can be borrowed from the field of statistics, as Chapter 5 will show. Using such tools, we can be more precise about dealing with risk.

KEY CONCEPTS

1. To make decisions that will increase the value of the firm, financial managers need to understand how values are determined in financial markets.

2. Discounted-cash-flow techniques provide a method for analyzing the value of assets.

3. The value of any asset depends on the future benefits of owning or using the asset. Present value, discussed in Chapter 3, provides the basic analytical framework for valuation of financial assets, the benefits of which are future cash flows.

4. The value of a future cash-flow stream depends on its size, its timing, and its risk. The greater is the risk, the higher is the discount rate used to calculate its present value.

5. Risk is uncertainty about an outcome and is a characteristic of investment opportunities.

6. Shareholder returns are subject to operating risk, which is uncertainty related strictly to the firm's operations. This risk is magnified by financial risk, which is the additional uncertainty caused by the use of financial leverage.

7. Risk aversion, risk neutrality, and risk preference are three types of investor attitudes toward risk.

8. In general, suppliers of capital are risk-averse and demand a risk premium for bearing risk. The greater is the risk, the higher is the rate of return required by the investor.

9. Required rates of return are established in the financial markets.

SUMMARY

Chapter 1 established value maximization as the objective of financial managers. To make decisions that will increase value, financial managers need to understand how values are determined in financial markets.

The DCF model can be used to value assets, such as stocks and bonds. To estimate value, we need a set of estimated cash flows and a discount rate that reflects the risks associated with those cash-flow estimates. The higher is the risk, the higher is the discount rate, which is also called the required rate of return.

Financial markets can give financial managers guidance on appropriate discount rates because a wide array of alternative investment opportunities are available in such markets.

QUESTIONS

1. What determines the value of an asset?
2. Explain how operating risk and financial risk affect shareholder returns. How are these risks related to financial leverage?
3. Explain the differences between risk aversion, risk neutrality, and risk preference.
4. How does risk-averse behavior by investors affect returns in the financial markets?
5. What is the dividend-valuation model? How can it be used?
6. Who determines the value of firms? Explain.
7. Which characteristic of financial markets assures that financial-asset prices are a fair reflection of their true value?

PROBLEMS

Note: To work problems preceded by an asterisk requires knowledge of material in Appendix 4A.

1. Please refer to Table 4-2 in this chapter to respond to the following questions.

   a. What is the expected return to shareholders if Plan A (all-equity financing) is used?
   b. What is the expected return to shareholders if Plan B (financial-leverage strategy) is used?
   c. Which is a better strategy? Why?

   (*Hint:* The expected return is calculated as an *expected value*, which will be discussed in detail in the following chapter. The expected value is defined by multiplying the payoff of each outcome by the probability of that outcome and then summing these products over all possible outcomes.)

2. You own rights to a lottery with the probabilities and payoffs shown in Table A. Someone has offered to buy your rights to the lottery for cash. What is the minimum amount you would accept? (Note: your answer depends upon your individual attitude about risk.)

3. Repeat Problem (2) for each of the lotteries given in Table B. Based on your results, what can you say about your own attitude toward risk?

4. Suppose that 5 individuals are offered a lottery ticket that pays either $0 or $1,000 and that each of these outcomes is equally likely. The 5 individuals are willing to pay the amounts for this lottery ticket that are indicated in Table C. What may we conclude about the attitude toward risk held by each of these individuals?

5. In 1738, Daniel Bernoulli presented to the Imperial Academy of Sciences in Petersburg a clas-

Table A

Lottery 1 Payoff (dollars)	Probability (percent)	Weighted Outcome (dollars)
400	0.5	
600	0.5	
	Expected value	

Table B

Lottery	Payoff (dollars)	Probabilities (percent)	Expected Value (dollars)	Sale Price (dollars)
2	0/1000	0.5/0.5		
3	−1000/2000	0.5/0.5		
4	−25,000/26,000	0.5/0.5		

Table C

Individual	Amount Individual Is Willing to Pay for Lottery Ticket (dollars)
1	376
2	515
3	500
4	478
5	189

Table D

Opportunity	Anticipated Cash Inflow (dollars)	Probability (percent)
A	0	0.333
	500	0.333
	1000	0.333
B	0	0.05
	500	0.90
	1000	0.05
C	0	0.15
	500	0.70
	1000	0.15
D	0	0.0
	500	1.0
	1000	0.0

sic paper on probability[9] in which he discussed the following problem (known as the *Petersburg Paradox*): "Peter tosses a coin and continues to do so until it should land 'heads.' He agrees to give Paul one ducat if he gets heads on the first toss, two ducats if he gets heads on the second, four if on the third, eight if on the fourth, and so on, so that with each additional toss the number of ducats that Peter must pay is doubled." Therefore, if Peter gets heads on the first toss, he receives one ducat and the game is over. If he gets heads on the second toss, he gets two ducats and the game is over. The game terminates when Peter lands a head. Answers to (b) and (c) depend on your individual attitude about risk.

a. What is the expected value of the above gamble (to Paul)?
b. What is the maximum amount you would pay to Peter for a chance to play?
c. If you were Peter (offering the gamble), what is the minimum entrance fee you would charge?

6. Consider the investment opportunities in Table D, each of which requires the same outlay.

a. Rank the four investments in order of riskiness.
b. Rank the four investments in descending order of value, assuming that a risk-averse investor is valuing them.

c. Repeat part (b) assuming that a risk-neutral investor is valuing the investments.

7. Rework Sample Problem 4–5 on interest-rate risk assuming that the interest rate on government bonds has dropped to 12 percent.

8. Rework Sample Problem 4–2 on the constant-growth dividend-valuation-model assuming a required rate of return of 17 percent.

*9. The Dow Jones Industrial Average (DJIA) provides information on stock prices, earnings, and dividends for the 30 companies included in the average. On June 18, 1979, the "price" for the DJIA was $839.40; earnings for 1979 were estimated at $124.10. Use the simple earnings model from Appendix 4A to calculate what rate of return the market was requiring on the stocks of the DJIA companies.

10. DJIA dividends for 1979 were estimated at $49.48. Thirteen years earlier in 1966 dividends were $30.42. Use the constant-growth dividend-valuation model (assuming past and future growth will be at the same rate) to calculate what rate of return the market was requiring on the stocks of the DJIA companies. You will need some information from Problem (9).

11. Explain why the two valuation models in Problems (9) and (10) give different answers to the same question.

[9]Daniel Bernoulli, "Exposition of a New Theory on the Measurement of Risk," reprinted in S. H. Archer and C. D'Ambrosio, eds., *The Theory of Business Finance*, 2nd ed.(New York: Macmillan, 1976).

12. Suppose that the dividends per share of common stock of Ron's Marine Supply, Inc. are expected to grow indefinitely at a rate of 4 percent per year. The company's current *price/earnings ratio*—defined here as this year's ($t = 0$) price per share divided by next year's ($t = 1$) earnings per share (EPS)—has been and will continue to be 10. Furthermore, Ron's dividend payout ratio (dividend/share) is expected to remain at 0.75 EPS. What rate of return is required by rational investors on an investment in this stock?

*13. According to the judgment of an investment banker, the common stock of Eastman Kodak should sell at 12 times current earnings. Translate this statement into what rate of return the investment banker thinks the market should expect from an investment in Eastman Kodak stock.

14. Suppose you read in the *Wall Street Journal* that a U.S. government bond is selling at *par* (price = face value), matures in 5 years, and carries a coupon rate of 14 percent.

   a. What is the present yield to maturity on that bond?

   b. What would the bond sell for if its yield to maturity were 8 percent? (Assume a face value of $1,000). Suppose the lower yield to maturity was due to lower required returns as people expected the inflation rate to decrease.

   c. What would the bond sell for if its yield to maturity increased to 20 percent?

   d. What would be your rate of return (one year) if you bought the bond today at face value and sold the bond next year? Assume that next year the yield to maturity on the bond (then maturing in four years) has dropped to 8 percent.

   e. Repeat part (d) assuming the yield to maturity next year is 20 percent.

15. Suppose Apple Computer Core Incorporated (ACC, Inc.) sold its new 10-year bonds at face value ($1,000) to provide a yield to maturity of 12 percent. Suppose, at the same time, 10-year U.S. government bonds were yielding 9 percent. In terms of dollars per bond, for how much less is an ACC bond trading because it is more risky than government debt? (To simplify matters, assume annual interest payments and yields compounded only once per year. In addition, assume that ACC bonds are in all respects except risk similar to U.S. government bonds.)

16. Last year Wolfpack Whistles Corporation had earnings per share of $4. WWC pays out half of its earnings in dividends. The firm's earnings and dividends are expected to grow at 7 percent per year for the foreseeable future.

   a. Suppose you bought the stock at the end of last year for $35 and expect to hold it for 4 years and then sell it. You believe that the stock will then sell at a *P/E* ratio (price per share divided by earnings per share) of 10 times. What is your expected rate of return?

   b. Suppose you do not know what the *P/E* ratio will be. Use the constant-growth dividend-valuation model to calculate the expected rate of return on the stock. Why does this differ from your answer in part (a)?

   c. Suppose the earnings and dividends are expected to grow at 7 percent for 3 years, 10 percent for the following 2 years, and 8 percent indefinitely after that. If your required return is 14 percent, how much will you pay for the stock?

REFERENCES

Bernoulli, D. "Exposition of a New Theory on the Measurement of Risk." Reprinted in S. H. Archer and C. D'Ambrosio (eds.), *The Theory of Business Finance*. 2d ed. New York: Macmillan, 1976.

Boldt, B. L. and H. L. Arbit, "Efficient Markets and the Professional Investor." *Financial Analysts Journal* (July–August 1984):22–34.

Friend, I. and M. Blume, "The Demand for Risky Assets." *American Economic Review* 55 (Dec. 1975): 900–922.

Ibbotson, R. and R. A. Sinquefield *Stocks, Bonds, Bills and Inflation: The Past and the Future*. The Financial Analysts Research Foundation, 1982.

Kelly, W. A. and J. A. Miles, "Darby and Fisher: Resolution of a Paradox." *Financial Review*, forthcoming.

Seligman, D. "Can You Beat the Stock Market?" *Fortune* (December 26, 1983): 82–96.

Appendix 4A

The Earnings Model

Under certain circumstances, a variant of the dividend-valuation model, called the *earnings model,* can be useful. Consider a firm that pays out 100 percent of its earnings, so that earnings (*E*) and dividends (*D*) are one and the same. Assume that the firm plans no new issues of common stock and, to keep things as simple as possible, that there is no inflation.

In theory, with level prices, the firm's depreciation charges each year should be just sufficient to maintain its plant and equipment in a constant condition, so reinvestment of depreciation should maintain constant net investment. Assuming that the productivity of the firm's plant remains constant over time and that profit margins remain constant, the firm's sales and earnings should be level indefinitely.

The stream of dividends, or earnings, is, therefore, a *perpetuity*, and we can use Equation (7) from Chapter 3 as a model for valuing this stream. Equations (A–1a) and (A–1b) show how to use this model to calculate the present value of this earnings stream.

The present value(*PV*) of a share of stock can be calculated by discounting the perpetual stream of dividends as

$$PV = D/K \qquad \text{(A–1a)}$$

where *D* = the expected dividend and *K* = the market's required rate of return. In the case where 100 percent of earnings are paid out as dividends, this present value can also be calculated as

$$PV = E/K \qquad \text{(A–1b)}$$

where *E* represents earnings per dividend period.

It is not often that we encounter a firm that pays out 100 percent of its earnings, and certainly we do not live in a world of no inflation. But the simple earnings model in Equation (A–1) can be useful as a rough valuation technique in certain circumstances. Suppose we want to estimate the value of XYZ Corporation, which currently is earning $3.00 per share and paying a dividend of $0.75. The company is reinvesting $2.25 per share over and above depreciation charges, and this net investment should result in growth.

We could use Equation (2) from Chapter 4 to apply the dividend-valuation model to estimate the value of the company's stock. To do so we would project dividends (which should grow), estimate a terminal value for the stock some years in the future (which should be higher than the value today), and then apply Equation (2). Alternatively, we could apply Equation (A–1) from this appendix. Let us assume that the market required rate of return on the firm's stock is 9 percent. If we value the stock *as if* the company were paying out 100 percent of its earnings and as if, therefore, its earnings were going to be level, we would calculate the value of the stock as

$$PV = \$3.00/0.09 = \$33.33 \text{ per share.}$$

This calculation would give a rough idea of the value of the earnings stream the company currently is generating if it could be maintained indefinitely into the future. Reinvesting a portion of those earnings, if done wisely, should increase the firm's value. So the simple earnings model often can be useful to give a rough idea of the lower end of a range of reasonable values.

Chapter

5

Risk

This chapter investigates the measurement of risk and how risk affects required returns and the value of assets. After developing some statistical tools to deal with risk, we then examine the effects of diversification when a number of assets are combined in a portfolio. The chapter also examines the capital asset pricing model, which attempts to explain how risk affects expected returns.

Chapters 3 and 4 developed one way to estimate value, taking time and risk into account. In this discounted-cash-flow method, the discount rate is used to reflect both time and risk. We saw how such a method is useful in explaining the way in which various assets, such as stocks and bonds, are valued in financial markets. Thus, we have come a long way in providing one of the tools necessary for financial management—a way to place values *on sets of cash flows.*

This chapter analyzes risk more carefully, using some of the basic tools of statistics. In the process, we can obtain a better appreciation of exactly how we might define and measure risk.

An appreciation of risk is especially important to financial managers making decisions about investing and raising corporate funds. These decisions should increase the value of the firm. From our earlier discussion, we know that this value will depend upon risk. Suppose a company planned to spend billions of dollars to build a 500-mile gas pipeline from Alaska through Canada to deliver gas to both the midwestern and west-coast regions of the United States. As we will discuss later in Chapter 11, that pipeline is a real, not hypothetical, financial-management problem. Is the plan a good investment? The answer depends on weighing the costs and benefits of the pipeline. Both these costs and benefits are, however, unknown. Managers can at best make educated guesses about the magnitude of cash flows associated with the pipeline. One thing is certain: risk (and its analysis) plays a large role in the decision.

THE RISK/RETURN TRADE-OFF

Figure 5–1 reproduces the risk/return trade-off line from Figure 4–5 in the last chapter. We have already explained the reasoning behind the trade-off. People generally dislike risk; because they are risk-averse, they require higher returns to compensate them for bearing risk. If a set of cash flows is characterized by A units of risk, as measured along the horizontal axis in Figure 5–1, the appropriate required return is K_A, as measured along the vertical axis.

The problems with using the concepts depicted in Figure 5–1 are (1) providing some way to measure risk (how do we measure the risk associated with a point like A?) and (2) establishing how such risk translates into a required return (what does the risk/return trade-off look like?)

Figure 5–1
The Risk/Return Trade-Off

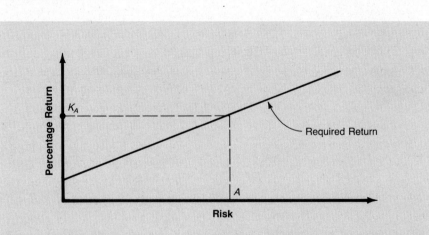

CASH FLOWS, RISK, AND STATISTICS

The field of statistics assumes that we can describe the nature of our uncertainty about a future event—say, a set of cash flows—in measurable terms.

Let us return to our basic DCF model developed in the last two chapters. Equation (1) reproduces Equation (1) from Chapter 4, which shows how to calculate the present value of a stream of future cash payments.

The present value (*PV*) of a stream of future payments can be calculated as

$$PV = \sum_{t=1}^{n} \frac{C_t}{(1 + i)^t} \qquad (1)$$

where t = the period in which a payment is received, C_t = the amount to be received in period t, n = the number of periods, and i = the discount rate.

As already mentioned, in most cases we are not sure of the value of a cash flow but can only make educated guesses.

Suppose you were considering investment in a new solar technology that would reduce your company's expenditures on fuel in the upcoming year. The actual dollar savings would depend both on the success of the technology (how much fuel could actually be saved) and on the price of fuel during the next year. After some analysis, your staff has estimated that there are only four possible outcomes, which are detailed in Panel A of Table 5–1, where C is the cash flow (cost savings).

Table 5–1
Possible Cost Savings of Solar Technology

Panel A

Possible Outcome	Value of Cost Savings (C) (dollars)	Probability of Outcome (proportion of total)
1	1,000	1/10 = 0.1
2	2,000	2/10 = 0.2
3	3,000	4/10 = 0.4
4	4,000	3/10 = 0.3

Panel B

Possible Outcome, j	Value of C (dollars), C_j	Probability (proportion of total), p_j
1	$C_1 = 1,000$	$p_1 = 0.1$
2	$C_2 = 2,000$	$p_2 = 0.2$
3	$C_3 = 3,000$	$p_3 = 0.4$
4	$C_4 = 4,000$	$p_4 = 0.3$
		$\sum_{j=1}^{M} p_j = 1.0$

Figure 5–2
Possible Cost Savings of Solar Technology

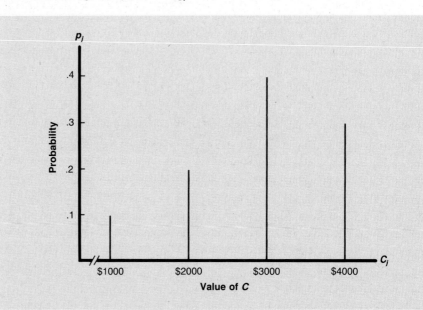

A **discrete random variable**—is a variable that can take on a finite number of possible values.

A **probability distribution**—is a function that assigns probabilities to the possible values of a random variable.

In the terminology of statistics, the cash flow, C, is a **discrete random variable**— a variable that can take on a finite number of possible values. In this case, C can be $1,000, $2,000, $3,000, or $4,000. Panel A of Table 5–1 is a discrete **probability distribution**—a function that assigns probabilities to possible values of a random variable. Note that in this example, C can take on only four values while in other cases a random variable could take on 5, 1,000, or any number of values. Panel B of Table 5–1 develops a bit of general notation to describe what a probability distribution looks like. Specifically, j is the number assigned to each outcome ($j = 1, 2, 3, 4$); M is the number of possible outcomes ($M = 4$); C_j is the amount of the cash flow in outcome j; p_j is the probability of outcome j.

The probability distribution is nothing more than a way to characterize the uncertainty associated with this cash flow. There is only a 30 percent chance of a cost savings of $4,000, but there is also a 10 percent chance that only $1,000 may be saved. Figure 5–2 is a line chart that gives a graphical display of the same probability distribution.

The probabilities for the four possible outcomes must add up to one; that is,

$$0.1 + 0.2 + 0.4 + 0.3 = 1.0.$$

In general, the sum of the probabilities of all possible outcomes must equal one:

$$\sum_{j=1}^{M} p_j = 1$$

where j = the number of the outcome, M = the number of possible outcomes, and p_j = the probability of outcome j.

In other words, it is certain that one of the outcomes will occur. Note that if there were no uncertainty, there would be only one possible outcome, and it would have a probability of 1.0.

Developing a probability distribution is sometimes easy. For example, given a fair coin, on any given flip, there is a 50 percent chance of heads and a 50 percent chance of tails. In most financial problems, however, our estimates are necessarily subjective and involve predictions about a whole array of future events. The difficulty of making these estimates should not be underestimated; nevertheless, a probability distribution gives us a useful way to organize our thoughts about uncertain events.

> A probability distribution is a useful way to organize estimates about uncertain events.

Using Probability Distributions

Looking at Table 5–1 and Figure 5–2, we get some rough idea of the range of likely cost savings and the uncertainty in those flows. One of the primary benefits of statistics is that it allows us to develop measures that summarize the information contained in a probability distribution. We can obtain summary measures of the cash flows we expect and of the uncertainty associated with those flows.

Measuring Probable Outcomes: Expected Values

The expected value, or mean,—is the weighted average of the possible outcomes, where the weights are the probabilities of the outcomes, and provides a measure of the expected outcome of a random variable.

The **expected value,** or **mean,** of a random variable is a measure of an expected cash flow. As Equation (2) indicates, the expected value is nothing more than a weighted average of the possible outcomes where the weights are the probabilities of the outcome.

> The expected value, $E(C)$, of a cash flow, can be expressed as
>
> $$E(C) = \sum_{j=1}^{M} p_j C_j \tag{2}$$
>
> where j = the outcome number, p_j = the probability of outcome j, C_j = the cash flow that results from outcome j, M = the number of possible outcomes, and $E(C)$ = the expected value of the random variable, C.

From the data in Table 5–1, we can calculate the expected value of the cost savings, using Equation (2), as

$$E(C) = 0.1(\$1,000) + 0.2(\$2,000) + 0.4(\$3,000) + 0.3(\$4,000)$$
$$= \$2,900.$$

The expected-value operator—the letter E in the expected-value equation—is a signal to take the probability-weighted average of the outcomes.

As used above, the capital letter E is frequently called an **expected-value operator** and simply says to take the probability-weighted average. Note that the expected value allows different outcomes to have different probabilities—the p_j terms need not all be equal. If each of M possible outcomes were equally probable, each probability would be $1/M$. The expected value of a cash flow, when each of the possible outcomes is equally probable, can be expressed as

$$E(C) = \sum_{j=1}^{M} \frac{1}{M} C_j = \frac{1}{M} \sum_{j=1}^{M} C_j$$

where $1/M$ = the probability of each equally probable outcome.

An examination of this equation shows that this calculation produces the normal **arithmetic average.**

The expected value, or mean, is a measure of the expected outcome of a random variable. In our specific case of cost savings, the mean of $2,900 weighs all the possible outcomes given their probabilities and can be used as the single number that characterizes the likely outcome. This $2,900 figure is precisely the type of number we should use in the numerator of DCF applications.

Such a measure of estimated cash flows is by no means perfect, however. First of all, note that the single *most likely* outcome in our example is not the mean of $2,900 but is $3,000, which will occur 40 percent of the time. In fact, while $2,900 is in some sense our best statistical guess of cash flow, in this example $2,900 will never be the cash flow that actually occurs. As Table 5–1 shows, the cash flow will be either $1,000, $2,000, $3,000, or $4,000—never $2,900! Nonetheless, the mean does incorporate all our information about possible outcomes; in making financial decisions in practice, normally there will be little, if any, difference between the expected value of the distribution and the most likely value.

A second feature of the expected value is that it only summarizes one bit of information about a distribution—the *average* outcome. As a summary measure, the mean does not give us any indication of how dispersed the outcomes are likely to be. For example, suppose someone offers you the following bet. A fair coin will be flipped. If it comes up heads (a 50 percent chance), you win $1.00. If it comes up tails (a 50 percent chance), you lose $1.00. The expected value of the bet is $0. Now suppose the bet is changed, and you either win $1,000.00 or lose $1,000.00. The expected value of the bet is still $0, but you probably would have different attitudes about the two bets because the outcomes of the second gamble are much more dispersed. Without some measure of this dispersion, we have no idea of how confident we can be that the cash flow that actually occurs will be close to the expected value. We need some measure of the variability of possible outcomes.

> **One problem with the expected value as a summary measure is that it gives no indication of the dispersion of outcomes.**

Measuring Variability of Outcomes

Suppose that in addition to the estimates in Table 5–1, your staff has provided cost-savings estimates for another technology (hydroelectric), as shown in Table 5–2. Table 5–2 indicates that the mean cost savings, $E(C)$, is equal to $2,900—the same expected value as that for solar technology in Table 5–1. It is obvious, however, that there is much less chance of being very far from our expected value with the hydroelectric technology (data in Table 5–2) than there is with the solar technology (data in Table 5–1). In Table 5–2, we can at worst be above or below our mean by $200. In Table

The **arithmetic average**—is a summary measure obtained by adding the values observed and dividing their sum by the number of values.

Table 5–2
Possible Cost Savings of Hydroelectric Technology

Possible Outcome, j	Value of C (dollars), C_j	Probability (percentage of total), p_j
1	2700	0.25
2	2900	0.5
3	3100	0.25

$$E(C) = \sum_{j=1}^{3} p_j C_j$$
$$= 0.25(\$2700) + 0.5(\$2900) + 0.25(\$3100)$$
$$E(C) = \$2900$$

5–1, we have a 1 in 10 chance of being below the mean by a full $1,900, because $2,900 − $1,000 = $1,900. In a real sense, there is more variability for one of the probability distributions even if the two distributions have the same expected value— $2,900.

The **standard deviation—** is the probability-weighted measure of the dispersion of possible outcomes around an expected value and is a statistical measure of variability, or risk.

One statistical measure of variability is the **standard deviation.** The standard deviation is simply a probability-weighted measure of the dispersion of possible outcomes around the expected value and can be expressed as shown in Equation (3).

The standard deviation, σ, of possible outcomes around an expected value can be expressed as

$$\sigma = \sqrt{\sum_{j=1}^{M} p_j [C_j - E(C)]^2} \qquad (3)$$

where M = the number of possible outcomes, j = the outcome number, p_j = the probability of outcome j, C_j = the cash flow that results from outcome j, $E(C)$ = the expected value of the random variable, C.

In words, the standard deviation says subtract the expected value of C from the value that C takes on with outcome j; square this difference; add up these squared terms, weighting by the probability of the outcome; finally, take the square root of the sum you have just created. Taking the square root is useful because it gives the standard deviation the same units of measurement as the random variable. In our example, the squared difference between C_j and $E(C)$ would be expressed in terms of dollars squared whereas taking the square root of the entire sum converts units back to dollars.

We can use Equation (3) to calculate the standard deviations for the data in Tables 5–1 and 5–2. The standard deviation of possible outcomes around the expected value in the case of hydroelectric power (Table 5–2) can be calculated as

$$\sigma = \sqrt{0.25\,(\$2,700 - \$2,900)^2 + 0.50\,(\$2,900 - \$2,900)^2 + 0.25\,(\$3,100 - \$2,900)^2}$$
$$= \sqrt{0.25\,(-\$200)^2 + 0.50\,(\$0)^2 + 0.25\,(\$200)^2}$$
$$= \sqrt{\$20,000}$$
$$= \$141.42.$$

Following a similar procedure, we can calculate the standard deviation for the solar technology from the data in Table 5–1 to be σ = \$943.40.

As the line charts in Figure 5–3 show, the hydroelectric technology has much less variability than does the solar technology. The outcomes for hydroelectric technology are clustered between \$2,700 and \$3,100, while the cost savings for solar technology may be as low as \$1,000 or as high as \$4,000. Clearly, the outcome for solar technology is subject to much more variation. And as the calculations show, the standard deviation is much higher for the solar technology than for its hydroelectric counterpart. The larger standard deviation of \$943.40 for solar technology (versus a standard deviation of \$141.42 for hydroelectric) is simply a numerical measure of the dispersion that Figure 5–3 displays graphically. The higher is the standard deviation, the more dispersed are the possible outcomes and, as a result, the larger is the chance that the actual outcome will be substantially different from the expected value. In this sense, standard deviation can serve as a measure of the risks, or uncertainty, associated with an outcome. Standard deviation is simply a summary measure of variability.

The mean and standard deviation are two extremely useful bits of summary information about a probability distribution. In our example, the mean, or expected value, tells us the likely *magnitude* of the dollar flows, while the standard deviation reflects the potential *variability* associated with those flows. Of course these two measures don't always tell us everything we would like to know, and other statistical measures can be developed.[1] For many purposes in finance, however, these two measures can be useful.

> **The mean indicates the likely *magnitude* of an expected outcome; the standard deviation indicates the potential *variability*, or risk, associated with an outcome.**

For example, the expected cash flow to put in a DCF calculation can be measured by the expected value of the probability distribution of that cash flow. As we calculated earlier, the possible cost savings of solar technology displayed in Table 5–1 can be summarized as an expected cost savings of \$2,900.

In our example of solar and hydroelectric technologies in Figure 5–3, the standard deviation of the cost savings for the hydroelectric technology is less than the standard deviation for the solar technology. We can, thus, speak of the solar technology as being the riskier of the two choices. The higher is the standard deviation, the more dispersed are the possible outcomes and, as a result, the larger is the chance that the actual outcome will be substantially different from the expected value.

The **coefficient of variation**—is the standard deviation divided by the expected value and is a measure of risk relative to return.

When it is necessary to compare situations with very different levels of expected outcome, it is sometimes useful to look at the **coefficient of variation,** which is the standard deviation divided by the expected value. For example, the solar technology has a coefficient of variation equal to \$943.40/\$2,900 = 0.3253. The higher is the coefficient of variation, the higher is the risk relative to the expected outcome.

---

[1]Technically speaking, the expected value and standard deviation are measures of the first two *moments* of a probability distribution. One can develop even higher *moments,* but that is beyond the scope of this text. Later this chapter will consider standard deviation as a measure of risk when investors hold a number of assets.

Figure 5–3
Possible Cost Savings

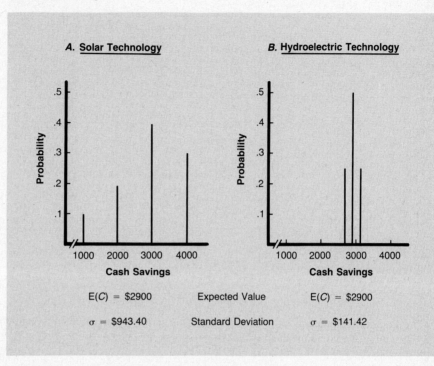

A. Solar Technology   B. Hydroelectric Technology

E(C) = \$2900	Expected Value	E(C) = \$2900
σ = \$943.40	Standard Deviation	σ = \$141.42

To this point, we have used the expected value and standard deviation to measure attributes of projected cash flows. These statistical measures can be applied to all kinds of random variables, including those events we already observed.

Suppose we thought annual returns on IBM stock would be the same in the future as they have been in the past. If so, we might assume that the past distribution of returns on IBM's stock is a good guess about what the future probability distribution for that stock looks like. Table 5–3 shows IBM's record for the 10-year period from 1975 to 1984. Annual returns have ranged from −13 percent in 1979 and 1981 to a whopping 75 percent in 1982. If we assume that each year's return is equally likely (that is, the probability of each year is the same) we can compute the expected return and standard deviation as illustrated in the caption to Table 5–3. Thus, we find an expected return of 18.1 percent with a standard deviation of 25.04 percent.

An important cautionary word is in order. Note that we computed this expected return and standard deviation from past data. As a result, they are useful predictions about future return and risk *only* if we think the future will be like the past. In many cases, past data may help with future projections, but always remember that there is no rule that says that history must repeat itself. For purposes of making most financial decisions, we must think in terms of the future course of events.

Table 5–3

Annual Rate of Return from Owning Stock in IBM, 1975–1984

Year, j	Rate of Return (percent), R_j	Year, j	Rate of Return (percent), R_j
1975	38	1980	16
1976	26	1981	−13
1977	1	1982	75
1978	17	1983	30
1979	−13	1984	4

$$E(R) = \sum_{j=1}^{M} p_j R_j$$

$$= \frac{1}{M} \sum_{j=1}^{M} R_j = 18.1\% \text{ assuming each year's return is equally likely } (M = 10)$$

$$\sigma = \sqrt{\sum_{j=1}^{M} p_j(R_j - E(R))^2} = 25.04\%$$

Diversification

There is an old piece of advice that says, "Don't put all your eggs in one basket." That advice is especially applicable to financial management because it tells us that risk can be reduced by **diversification,** or investing in more than one type of asset. A simple sort of diversification would be to put half of your money in one stock—say, Sunglasses, Inc.—and half in another—say, Umbrellas, Inc. If the weather were especially rainy during a particular year, the earnings of Sunglasses, Inc. would decline. With a decline in earnings, the stock price and return to stockholders would decline. On the other hand, in a rainy year, the return to stockholders of Umbrellas, Inc. would be up. In a sunny year, the situation would be reversed.

While the return on each individual stock might vary quite a bit, depending on the weather, the return on your **portfolio** of the two stocks could be quite stable. Bad returns on one stock are offset by good returns on the other.

In fact, at least in theory, the offsetting process could eliminate risk entirely. Consider, for example, the situation depicted in Table 5–4. With half your money in each stock, 50 percent of your money would earn R_s (the return on Sunglasses, Inc.) and 50 percent of your money would earn R_u (the return on Umbrellas, Inc.). Your portfolio rate of return (R_p) could, thus, be calculated for each possible outcome(sunny weather, normal weather, or rainy weather). The portfolio rate of return for sunny weather would be

$$R_p = 0.5R_s + 0.5R_u = 0.5(0.2) + 0.5(0) = 10 \text{ percent;}$$

the portfolio rate of return for normal weather would be

$$R_p = 0.5R_s + 0.5R_u = 0.5(0.1) + 0.5(0.1) = 10 \text{ percent;}$$

the portfolio return for rainy weather would be

$$R_p = 0.5R_s + 0.5R_u = 0.5(0) + 0.5(0.2) = 10 \text{ percent.}$$

Diversification—is investing in more than one type of asset in order to reduce risk. When risky assets are combined in a portfolio, risk reduction is achieved through diversification.

A **portfolio**—is the combination of securities held by any one investor.

Table 5—4
Effects of Diversification on Rates of Return

Weather Conditions	Return on Sunglasses, Inc. (percent), R_s	Return on Umbrellas, Inc. (percent), R_u	Return on Portfolio (percent) $R_p = 0.5R_s + 0.5R_u$
Rainy Weather	0	20	10
Normal Weather	10	10	10
Sunny Weather	20	0	10

Note that the portfolio earns 10 percent no matter what the weather is. Through diversification, two risky stocks (note R_s and R_u both depend on the weather) can be combined to make a riskless portfolio.

Our previous discussion alerts us to an important fact. Even if variability, as measured by standard deviation, is a good measure of risk, it can be quite misleading to look at the standard deviation of returns on any single asset as a measure of the asset's risk *if* that asset can be placed in a portfolio. Let us return to our example in Table 5–4. Assuming rainy, normal, and sunny weather are equally likely events (that each will happen 1/3 of the time) we can calculate the expected return and standard deviation of returns on (1) the return, R_s, on Sunglasses, Inc., (2) the return, R_u, on Umbrellas, Inc. and (3) the return, R_p, on the portfolio of the two stocks. Table 5–5 uses Equations (3) and (5) to make these calculations. Because the portfolio is risk-free, its standard deviation—our measure of risk—is equal to zero, even though each stock in the portfolio has a standard deviation of 8.16 percent. As the calculations in Table 5–5 show, by combining two stocks in a portfolio we can reduce risk, as measured by standard deviation.

Table 5—5
Expected Returns and Standard Deviations

Sunglasses, Inc. (R_s)

$$E(R_s) = \tfrac{1}{3}(0\%) + \tfrac{1}{3}(10\%) + \tfrac{1}{3}(20\%) = 10\%$$

$$\sigma_s = \sqrt{\tfrac{1}{3}(0\% - 10\%)^2 + \tfrac{1}{3}(10\% - 10\%)^2 + \tfrac{1}{3}(20\% - 10\%)^2}$$
$$= \sqrt{66.67} = 8.16\%$$

Umbrellas, Inc. (R_u)

$$E(R_u) = \tfrac{1}{3}(20\%) + \tfrac{1}{3}(10\%) + \tfrac{1}{3}(0\%) = 10\%$$

$$\sigma_u = \sqrt{\tfrac{1}{3}(20\% - 10\%)^2 + \tfrac{1}{3}(10\% - 10\%)^2 + \tfrac{1}{3}(0\% - 10\%)^2}$$
$$= \sqrt{66.67} = 8.16\%$$

Portfolio (R_p)

$$R_p = \tfrac{1}{3}(10\%) + \tfrac{1}{3}(10\%) + \tfrac{1}{3}(10\%) = 10\%$$

$$\sigma_p = \sqrt{\tfrac{1}{3}(10\% - 10\%)^2 + \tfrac{1}{3}(10\% - 10\%)^2 + \tfrac{1}{3}(10\% - 10\%)^2}$$
$$= \sqrt{0} = 0\%$$

Correlation—is the relationship between variables indicating how they move relative to each other.

In practice, one can seldom find assets that perfectly offset one another and are, thus, perfectly negatively correlated. All stocks, practically speaking, have some degree of positive **correlation** and tend to, on average, rise and fall together because all are influenced to some extent by general economic conditions. Fluctuations in economic activity tend to affect nearly everyone.

> **All stocks tend to have some degree of positive correlation (they rise and fall together) because all are influenced to some extent by general economic conditions.**

But the good news is that we do not have to have perfect negative correlation in order to reduce risk through diversification. All we need is for stocks not to move up and down *exactly* together—in other words, all we need is the absence of perfect positive correlation.

As long as the returns of different stocks do not move in perfect lockstep, we can combine those stocks into a portfolio and achieve some risk reduction. We find in practice that returns on different stocks normally do show some association (because of the influence of the business cycle), but because it is not perfect correlation, we can achieve significant risk reduction by diversifying.

The risk-reduction effects of diversification are important both for financial managers and for investors in stocks or bonds. After all, the market value of a firm to shareholders is determined by investors buying and selling a company's stock. It is this market value that financial managers are attempting to maximize.

THE STATISTICS OF THE MATTER: PORTFOLIO THEORY

The basic insight that assets can be combined into portfolios has long been recognized in finance.[2] Beginning in the 1950s, significant contributions were made in finance by applying statistical and quantitative techniques to formalize what happens in such portfolio combinations. Perhaps the most influential contribution was made by Harry Markowitz, one of the founders of modern portfolio theory.[3] While Markowitz's work and that which has followed it has been developed through rather complicated mathematics, the basic concepts are straightforward.

Statistical tools again allow us to show exactly what the effects of combining two random variables (such as two stocks in a portfolio) will be. The expected return on

---

[2]This first half of this section may be skipped, and the reader can jump ahead to the subsection headed "Diversifiable and Nondiversifiable Risk" if a formal treatment of portfolio theory is beyond the scope of the reader's desires.

[3]Markowitz's work appeared in a famous 1952 article, H. M. Markowitz, "Portfolio Selection," *Journal of Finance* (March 1952): 77–91. Many of his early contributions are in his book, *Portfolio Selection: Efficient Diversification of Investments* (New York: John Wiley & Sons, 1959). Many financial texts, such as *Investment: Concepts, Analysis, and Strategy* by Robert Radcliffe (Glenview, Ill.: Scott, Foresman and Company, 1986), provide extensive treatment of portfolio theory.

our portfolio of Sunglasses, Inc. stock and Umbrellas, Inc. stock can be thought of as the weighted sum of two random variables, where in this case the weights are each 0.5—half of our money in each stock. For purposes of statistics, we can, thus, think of the portfolio return as a random variable, R_p, which itself is simply a weighted sum of other random variables, R_s and R_u:

$$R_p = W_s R_s + W_u R_u$$

$$= 0.5R_s + 0.5R_u$$

where in this case both of the weights, W_s and W_u, are 0.5.

Now we can use statistical techniques to determine the expected value and standard deviation of the return on a stock portfolio, R_p, that contains two stocks. Equation (4) shows the expected return on the portfolio.

The expected value of the return (R_p) on a portfolio containing two stocks, a and b, can be expressed as

$$E(R_p) = W_a E(R_a) + W_b E(R_b) \qquad (4)$$

where W = the weight (the proportion of the portfolio invested in the stock), and $E(R)$ = the expected rate of return on the stock.

In words, the expected value of a weighted sum of two random variables is simply the weighted sum of the expected values of each individual random variable.

In the case of our portfolio of Sunglasses, Inc. and Umbrellas, Inc. stock, the expected value of the return on the portfolio, from Equation (4), would be

$$E(R_p) = W_s E(R_s) + W_u E(R_u)$$

In Table 5–5, we calculated $E(R_p)$ to be 10 percent. Equation (4) gives the same answer:

$$E(R_p) = 0.5E(R_s) + 0.5E(R_u)$$

$$= 0.5(0.10) + 0.5(0.10) = 0.10 = 10 \text{ percent.}$$

The expected value of a portfolio return is a weighted sum of random variables, which is calculated as the weighted sum of the expected values of each individual random variable.

The more interesting point concerns the standard deviation of the return on our portfolio, which is expressed in Equation (5). In Equation (5), ρ_{ab} represents the **correlation coefficient,** or the measure of the degree of correlation, between two stocks. Appendix 5A at the end of this chapter provides details on the calculation of correlation coefficients. A correlation coefficient can range from -1 to $+1$. The correlation coefficient measures the extent to which two random variables move together (perfect positive correlation $= +1$) or move in opposite directions (perfect negative correlation $= -1$). Note in Equation (5) that the standard deviation of the portfolio depends not

The **correlation coefficient, ρ,**—is a measure of the degree of correlation that exists between two variables.

only on the standard deviations of the individual stocks, but also on the correlation between the stocks as measured by the correlation coefficient.

> The standard deviation, σ, of the return on a 2-stock portfolio can be expressed as
>
> $$\sigma_p = \sqrt{W_a^2\sigma_a^2 + W_b^2\sigma_b^2 + 2W_aW_b\rho_{ab}\sigma_a\sigma_b} \qquad (5)$$
>
> where ρ_{ab} is the correlation coefficient between the return on stock a and the return on stock b.

In our example, we have two stocks that perfectly offset one another. Because they are perfectly negatively correlated, $\rho_{su} = -1$. Using Equation (5), we can now calculate the standard deviation of the portfolio to be

$$\sigma_p = \sqrt{[(0.5)^2(8.16)^2] + [(0.5)^2(8.16)^2] + [2(0.5)(0.5)(-1)(8.16)(8.16)]}$$

$$= 0 \text{ percent.}$$

The standard deviation on the return to the portfolio is 0, as we calculated earlier in Table 5–5. The calculation using Equation (5) highlights the reason that $\sigma_p = 0$. Because $\rho_{su} = -1$, the last term of Equation (5) cancels out the first two terms.

On the other hand, suppose the two stocks had been perfectly positively correlated; that is, suppose $\rho_{su} = +1$ and the stock returns always moved together. From Equation (5), we can calculate σ_p as

$$\sigma_p = \sqrt{[(0.5)^2(8.16)^2] + [(0.5)^2(8.16)^2] + [2(0.5)(0.5)(1)(8.16)(8.16)]}$$

$$= \sqrt{66.67} \qquad = 8.16 \text{ percent.}$$

Note that this standard-deviation figure is exactly the same as the calculated figure for the standard deviation of each of the individual stocks. With perfect positive correlation, there is absolutely no risk reduction from diversification. Stocks that are perfectly correlated always move together, so they never offset one another. With perfect positive correlation ($\rho = +1$), the standard deviation of the portfolio is simply a weighted average of the standard deviations of the component securities.

> **The standard deviation, or risk, of the portfolio depends both on the standard deviations of the individual stocks and on the correlation between the stocks.**

By studying Equation (5) carefully, we can see that as long as ρ_{ab} is less than $+1.0$, the standard deviation of the portfolio is always less than a simple weighted average of the standard deviations of the securities making up the portfolio. The key to risk reduction through diversification is that the *mean* portfolio return is a simple weighted average, while the *standard deviation* is less than a simple weighted average, provided the component securities are not perfectly positively correlated.

Figure 5–4
Portfolio Combinations of Stocks

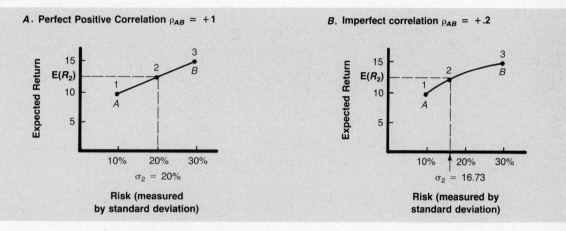

A. **Perfect Positive Correlation** $\rho_{AB} = +1$

B. **Imperfect correlation** $\rho_{AB} = +.2$

Risk (measured by standard deviation)

$\sigma_2 = 20\%$

$\sigma_2 = 16.73$

Portfolios of Two Securities

Figure 5–4 provides a graphical display of the effects of combining two stocks (A and B) in a portfolio and plots the data displayed in Table 5–6. Stock B is the riskier of the two stocks.

Let us consider possible portfolios that could be formed using only these two stocks by varying the percentage of our money invested in each. In Table 5–6 and Figure 5–4, three possible ways of investing our money are referred to as portfolios 1, 2, and 3. If all our money is invested in stock B ($W_A = 0$; $W_B = 1$), obviously our portfolio has the same return and risk as does stock B. Of course we could divide our money up in any other fashion as long as the weights added up to one—that is, as long as we invested all our money. As we discussed previously, however, when we divide our money between two stocks, the risk of our portfolio depends upon the correlation of the stocks going into our portfolio.

Let us consider an example. In Panel A of Table 5–6 and Figure 5–4, we assume that the returns on stocks A and B are perfectly positively correlated: $\rho_{AB} = +1$. In Panel B of Table 5–6 and Figure 5—4, we assume there is some positive correlation but that it is much lower: $\rho_{AB} = 0.2$.

In practice, the correlation would be only one figure—here we focus on what difference the correlation coefficient makes. In portfolio 2, we are splitting our money evenly between the two stocks ($W_A = 0.5$; $W_B = 0.5$). With perfect positive correlation, we find the expected value of the return on portfolio 2 to be 12.5 percent and

---

[4]The calculations of the many-variable case are more complicated and beyond the scope of this text. Many finance texts in investments discuss portfolio formation in more detail. For example, see William F. Sharpe, *Investments,* 2nd ed. (Englewood Cliffs, N.J.: Prentice-Hall, 1981), and Robert Radcliffe, *Investment: Concepts, Analysis, and Strategy* (Glenview, Ill.: Scott, Foresman and Company, 1986).

Table 5—6
Effects of Combining Two Stocks in a Portfolio

Panel A: Perfect Positive Correlation $\rho_{AB} = +1$.

Portfolio	Investment Weight, W		$E(R_p)$ (percent)	σ_p (percent)
	Stock A	Stock B		
1	1	0	10	10
2	0.5	0.5	12.5	20
3	0	1	15	30

Panel B: Imperfect Correlation ($\rho_{AB} = +0.2$)

Portfolio	Investment Weight, W		$E(R_p)$ (percent)	σ_p (percent)
	Stock A	Stock B		
1	1	0	10	10
2	0.5	0.5	12.5	16.73
3	0	0	15	30

Assumptions are that for Stock A the expected return, or $E(R_A)$, is 10 percent and the standard deviation, or σ_A, is 10 percent; for stock B the $E(R_B)$ is 15 percent and the σ_B is 30 percent. Calculations use Equations (4) and (5) from this chapter.

the risk, or standard deviation, of the return on portfolio 2 to be 20 percent. These figures are listed in the third and fourth columns of Panel A of Table 5–6 and are plotted (as point 2) in Panel A of Figure 5–4. If we looked at other portfolios of these 2 stocks with perfect positive correlation—for example, a portfolio in which 20 percent of our money is invested in stock A and 80 percent is invested in stock B—we would get other points on the straight line between points 1 and 3.

In Panel B of Table 5–6 and Figure 5–4, however, we are assuming that stocks A and B have a smaller positive correlation: $\rho_{AB} = +0.2$. Under these circumstances, the expected value of the return on portfolio 2 would be 12.5 percent, and the risk, or standard deviation, of the return on portfolio 2 would be 16.73 percent. This expected value/standard deviation combination is plotted as point 2 in Panel B of Figure 5–4. The curved line traces out the points that would result from other portfolios with different allocations of our investment funds.

The key difference in the two situations—perfect positive correlation versus smaller positive correlation—is now apparent. In both situations, portfolio 2 provides the same expected return of = 12.5 percent, but there is less portfolio risk when we do not have perfect positive correlation. Specifically, when $\rho = 0.2$, $\sigma_2 = 16.73$ percent, which is 3.27 percent lower than the $\sigma_2 = 20$ percent calculated when $\rho = +1.0$. This difference of 3.27 percent is precisely the risk reduction of diversification by combining stocks in a portfolio.

Figure 5–5 shows the two cases—$\rho = 1.0$ and $\rho = 0.2$—on the same graph. When there is less than perfect positive correlation between two stocks, portfolios are represented by a curved line (colored line in Figure 5–5), while perfect positive correlation produces portfolios that lie along a straight line. Note that the curved line lies to the left of the straight line and, thus, shows less risk for given levels of expected return. The reduction in risk is the benefit of diversification—the partial offsetting of variability because stocks don't move exactly together.

Portfolios of Three or More Securities

While we have presented our calculations using only two securities (stocks A and B), the same sort of process can be done for any number of securities.[4] The results are similar to those in the two-asset cases. For example, Figure 5–6 adds a third stock, C, to stocks A and B that we have already analyzed. Note that we now need to keep track of 3 correlation coefficients: ρ_{AB}, ρ_{BC}, and ρ_{AC}. While the actual calculations become tedious, Figure 5–6 shows the basic results in three separate panels.

In Panel A, we see that, taking two stocks at a time, we can get the lines AB, AC, and BC, which all correspond to portfolios of two stocks, just like our results in Figure 5–5 when we had only two stocks at a time.

In Panel B, we allow 3 stocks to be in a portfolio. For example, point D (along line AB), which represents a portfolio half of which is invested in stock A and half in B, can be treated as if it were representing a new stock, D. We can put some of our money in portfolio D and some in stock C and trace out the points on line DC. Points on line DC are portfolios formed with some of all three stocks (A, B, and C). Thus, we can obtain points like A that represent only one stock, points like D (on line AB) that represent 2 stocks (A and B), and points like F (on line DC) where we own three stocks (A, B, and C).

Figure 5–5
The Risk Reduction from Portfolio Formation with Two Imperfectly Correlated Stocks

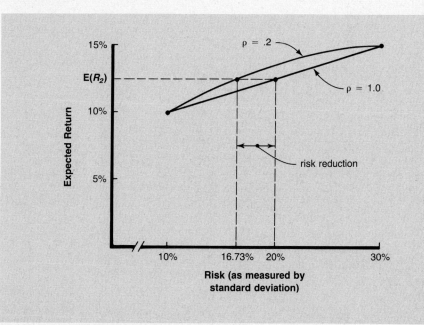

If we traced out all possible portfolio combinations of the three stocks we would have the situation depicted in Panel C of Figure 5–6. The shaded area is the set of all possible portfolio combinations. A similar graph would result if we add more stocks.

Fortunately, only a small subset of these portfolios really needs our attention—namely, the heavy line that forms the upper boundary of the shaded area. This line represents those portfolios that for a given level of risk provide the most return. Given that investors like higher expected returns, they would always prefer points on this line to points below it. This line is sometimes called an **efficient frontier** because it represents the set of portfolios that provide the most return for a given level of risk.

The **efficient frontier**—is the line that represents the set of portfolios that provides the most expected return for a given level of risk.

The Investor's Risk/Return Trade-Off

Figure 5–7 shows possible portfolios from which an investor might choose. Facing the situation depicted in Figure 5–7, what should an investor do? Which of the points (representing portfolios of stocks) would best suit his or her needs? A point to the left, like G, represents a portfolio with low expected return but low risk, while a point farther to the right, like H, represents a portfolio with higher expected returns and higher risks.

Figure 5–6
Portfolio Combinations of Many Stocks

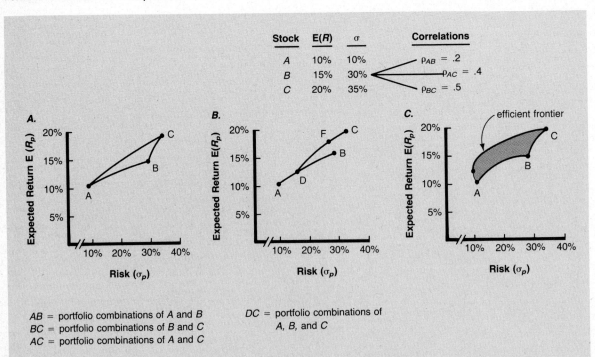

Stock	E(R)	σ
A	10%	10%
B	15%	30%
C	20%	35%

Correlations

$\rho_{AB} = .2$
$\rho_{AC} = .4$
$\rho_{BC} = .5$

AB = portfolio combinations of A and B
BC = portfolio combinations of B and C
AC = portfolio combinations of A and C
DC = portfolio combinations of A, B, and C

Figure 5—7
Portfolio Choice

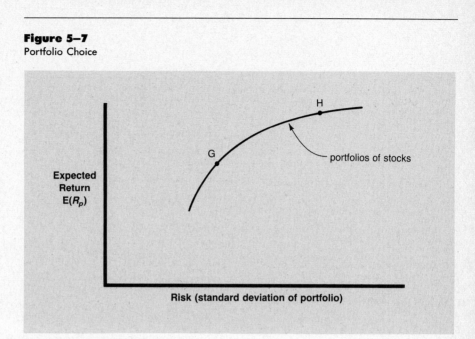

There is no clear-cut answer. Each individual's choice would depend upon his or her attitude toward risk. That is, the choice would depend on the individual's risk/return trade-off. A very risk-averse person might choose the portfolio represented by point *G*, while a less risk-averse person might pick the one represented by *H*. Remember that the measure of risk is the standard deviation (variability) of the portfolio return, which measures uncertainty about whether that return will be close to its expected value.

From our previous discussion we know that the standard deviation of the return on a portfolio depends upon both the variability of the returns on the stocks in the portfolio (the stocks' standard deviations) and on the correlation among the returns on the stocks (the stocks' correlation with each other). The less correlated are the stocks, the more risk reduction is achieved through diversification.

Diversifiable and Nondiversifiable Risk

The fact that returns on stocks do not move in lockstep means that risk can be reduced by diversification. But the fact that there is *some* association among the returns means that risk cannot be reduced to zero. Even a very well-diversified portfolio will show some variability of return as economic conditions change and as stock prices in general fluctuate. For example, stock prices declined by 12 percent from December 1983 through June 1984 and then rose by 19 percent over the next 15 months.[5] Few portfolios, no matter how well diversified, escaped the decline in early 1984, and most benefitted from the subsequent rise.

---

[5]These percentage changes were measured by the Dow Jones Industrial Average.

Table 5–7
Examples of Risk Factors

Nondiversifiable (Market) Risk Factors

A major change in tax rates
A war
An increase or decrease in inflation rates
An increase in international oil prices
A significant change in monetary policy by the Federal Reserve

Diversifiable (Specific) Risk Factors

A labor contract that grants above-average wage increases
A strike
Bankruptcy of a major supplier
Death of a key company officer
Unexpected entry of a new competitor into the market

Source: Based on D. W. Mullins, Jr., "Does the Capital Asset Pricing Model Work?" *Harvard Business Review* 60 (Jan./Feb. 1982): 105–114.

So there is a limit to the amount by which risk can be reduced by diversifying, and that limit depends on how closely the returns on the stocks are associated with one another. In technical terms, the amount of risk reduction depends on the degree of positive correlation between stocks. The lower is the correlation, the greater is the amount of risk reduction that is possible.

> **The lower is the degree of positive correlation between stocks in a portfolio, the greater is the amount of risk reduction possible.**

Nondiversifiable risk,—or *market risk,* is the part of total risk that is related to the general economy or to the stock market as a whole and is, therefore, the risk that *cannot* be eliminated by diversification.

The common element linking returns on stocks is their degree of association with general economic activity and the stock market overall. The extent to which a stock or a group of stocks moves with the market in general sets the lower limit on the amount of risk reduction possible through diversification. Risk that is unique to an individual firm or industry can be eliminated by diversifying, while risk arising from the link to the general market cannot. This notion of a common link suggests that the risk of any individual stock can be separated into two components: **nondiversifiable risk** and **diversifiable risk.**

Nondiversifiable risk is that part of the total risk that is related to the general economy or the stock market as a whole and, hence, *cannot* be eliminated by diversification. Nondiversifiable risk is also known as *market risk,* or *systematic risk.*

Diversifiable risk,—or *specific risk,* is the part of total risk that is unique to the company or asset and is, therefore, the risk that *can* be eliminated by diversification.

Diversifiable risk is that part of total risk that is unique to the company or industry and that, therefore, *can* be eliminated by diversification. Diversifiable risk is sometimes also referred to as *unsystematic risk,* or *specific risk.*

Table 5–7 gives some examples of factors that give rise to diversifiable and nondiversifiable risk.

The Number of Stocks in the Portfolio

The amount of risk reduction achieved by diversification depends not only on the degree of correlation with the general market, but also on the number of stocks in the portfolio. As the number of stocks increases, the diversifying effect of each additional stock diminishes, as shown in Figure 5–8.

As Figure 5–8 indicates, the major benefits of diversification are obtained with the first couple of dozen stocks, provided they are drawn from industries that are not closely related. Increases beyond this point continue to reduce risk, but the benefits are diminishing. Since the remaining risk is nearly all market-related, diversified portfolios tend to move together and in step with the stock market as a whole. The widely followed stock-market averages, such as the Dow Jones Industrial Average and the Standard & Poors 500 Stock Index, are themselves diversified portfolios and tend to move together. These indices often are used as surrogates for the market as a whole. Thus, any reasonably well diversified portfolio tends to move with market indices.

> **As the number of stocks increases, the diversifying effect of each additional stock diminishes.**

Figure 5–8
Risk Reduction through Diversification

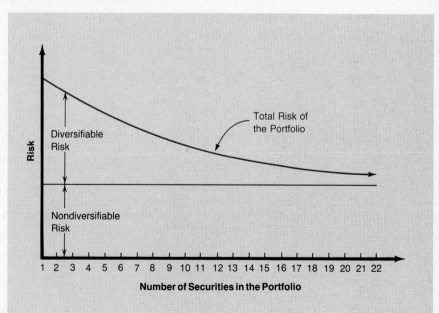

Sources: Based on D. W. Mullins, Jr., "Does the Capital Asset Pricing Model Work?" *Harvard Business Review* 60 (Jan./Feb. 1982): 105–14; J. L. Evans and S. H. Archer, "Diversification of the Reduction of Dispersion," *Journal of Finance* 23 (December 1968): 29–40.

Portfolios and Risk

Discussion of portfolio combinations, thus, provides us with a further insight into measurement of risk. We can think of standard deviation (a measure of variability) as a good indicator of the risk of a portfolio; to the extent that adding a stock to that portfolio increases the portfolio's standard deviation, the stock adds risk. Such addition of risk must be considered in analyzing the value of the stock to the purchaser.

If an investor were to hold only one stock, his or her risk would be the standard deviation of that stock. An important insight of portfolio theory is that if an investor holds a number of stocks, not all of an individual stock's standard deviation will ultimately be added to portfolio risk—some of it will be diversified away. In practice, holding a number of stocks is made quite easy because investors can buy shares of mutual funds, which are themselves portfolios containing many stocks.

> **A measure of a stock's risk is the risk it adds to a portfolio.**

The risk a stock adds to a portfolio will depend not only on the stock's *total risk*— its standard deviation—but also on how that risk breaks down into diversifiable risk and nondiversifiable risk. Ultimately, it is the nondiversifiable risk that an investor must bear.

As a result, when we speak of a risk/return trade-off, such as the one displayed in Figure 5–1, risk (as measured along the horizontal axis) is appropriately defined as the risk actually borne by the investor. If an investor owns only one stock, he or she has no diversification, and risk is, therefore, the standard deviation of the stock. For a diversified investor, the risk of a stock is only that portion of the stock's standard deviation that cannot be diversified away.

These comments about stocks also apply to corporate projections about future cash flows, such as the ones we used in the discounted-cash-flow model. Only when the risk associated with corporate cash flows is evaluated on the basis of how much risk the cash flows add to the holdings of the corporation's owners will managers have an appropriate measure of risk.

In evaluating a prospective investment project, financial managers should not be satisfied with looking only at the variability of the project's cash flow as a measure of risk. It is also important to determine how the project affects the risks facing the corporation's owners. The answer to this question depends not only on the variability of the project's cash flows but also on how these cash flows are correlated with returns to other assets of the corporation's owners. These assets may include existing projects in the corporation as well as stocks and bonds in other corporations because many shareholders hold a wide variety of assets in their personal investment portfolio.

THE CAPITAL-ASSET-PRICING MODEL

Our earlier discussion of portfolios shows that risk can be measured by the standard deviation of portfolio returns and that the relevant risk for each individual asset (be it a stock or an investment project) is the amount of risk it contributes to an investor's portfolio. These points add to our conceptual understanding of the risk/return trade-off

The **capital-asset-pricing model (CAPM)**—provides useful insights about how market values and discount rates are determined in financial markets, describes the valuation process in a portfolio context, and analyzes how risk/return trade-offs work in financial markets.

that we discussed in Chapter 4. What we need are explicit ways to incorporate these insights into our analysis of decisions. How much extra return does the market require as compensation for extra risk? How can financial managers estimate required returns that are appropriate for projects of different risk?

Some headway in answering these questions can be made by exploring the implications of the **capital-asset-pricing model (CAPM).**[6] The CAPM is one of the major developments in modern financial theory, and despite its shortcomings provides extremely useful insights into how market values and discount rates are determined in financial markets. Rather than viewing the return and value of each security in isolation, the capital-asset-pricing model sets the valuation process in a *portfolio* context on the assumption that an investor usually holds securities in a portfolio.

Assumptions

The capital-asset-pricing model is one theory about the way return and risk are related and about how market values of risky assets are determined. As are most theories, the CAPM is based on a list of critical assumptions, including those that follow.

1. Investors are risk-averse and are willing to use the expected value of return and standard deviation of return as the appropriate measures of return and risk for their portfolio. In other words, the greater is the perceived risk of a portfolio (as measured by σ_p), the higher must be the expected return on the portfolio for a risk-averse individual.
2. Investors make their investment decisions based on a single-period horizon. The risk and return they foresee for the next time period facing them drives their decisions.
3. Financial markets are essentially *frictionless;* that is, transactions costs (for example, commissions on stock sales and purchases) are low enough to ignore, and assets can be bought and sold in any unit desired. Any investor has the ability to buy any asset at the going market price and is limited only by his or her wealth and the price of the asset.
4. All returns are taxed in exactly the same fashion in a way such that taxes do not affect the choice of buying one asset versus another.
5. All individuals can borrow and lend unlimited amounts of money at a single-period riskless rate of interest.
6. All individuals assume that they can buy assets at the going market price, and they all agree on the nature of the return and risk associated with each investment.

Some of these assumptions don't fit reality and require a bit of discussion. Looking at the first three assumptions, we can agree that most people *are* risk-averse and that well

---

[6]The capital-asset-pricing model was developed by three principal researchers: William F. Sharpe, "Capital Asset Prices: A Theory of Market Equilibrium Under Conditions of Risk," *Journal of Finance 19(1964): 425–42;* John Lintner, "The Evaluation of Risky Assets and the Selection of Risky Investments in Stock Portfolios and Capital Budgets," *Review of Economics Statistics* 47(February 1965): 13-77; and Jan Mossin, "Equilibrium in a Capital Asset Market," *Econometrics* 34(October 1966): 768–55. For an excellent discussion of the model and its practical applications, see D. W. Mullins, Jr., "Does the Capital Asset Pricing Model Work?" *Harvard Business Review* 60(Jan./Feb. 1982): 105–114.

The **riskless rate of return**—is the rate of return that would be received on a riskless asset and is estimated using a current interest rate on a U.S. Treasury bond or note—the closest available approximation of a riskless asset.

A **frictionless market**—is a market in which there are no costs, such as commissions or information costs, involved in financial transactions.

A **market portfolio**—is the portfolio that includes all risky assets.

A **risk premium**—is the difference between the required rate of return on a particular risky asset and the rate of return on a riskless asset with the same expected life, or the additional return that compensates an investor for bearing additional risk.

developed financial markets don't involve large transactions costs. In addition, looking only one period into the future may not be too bad an approximation as long as we remember that the return we expect for the next period (say, the next year) depends on the price we expect one period (year) from today, which should reflect our opinion about events in the more distant future (two, three, and more periods hence).

The last three major assumptions are, admittedly, harder to square with the real world. Assumption 4 downplays the role of what is a rather complicated tax system. For example, as we discussed in Chapter 2, dividends are typically taxed at higher rates than are capital gains (increases in an asset's price) even though both constitute a form of return to investment. Assumption 5 says there is some **riskless rate of interest** at which persons can borrow and lend money. As a first approximation, lending money to the U.S. government (say, by buying a U.S. Treasury obligation) may be close to risk-free. But even on Treasury bills we can't be sure what *real return* (adjusted for inflation) we'll get because of purchasing-power risk if we don't know what future prices will be. Borrowing money at a riskless rate is impossible; at best, individuals and corporations pay interest at a rate commensurate with the perceived risk of the loan. Finally, assumption 6 says that everyone agrees—a result that is almost never an accurate description of what a group of people manage to do. For example, Assumption 6 means that if the president of IBM (an investor himself) thinks that IBM stock will have an 18 percent return in the next year with a standard deviation of 25 percent, all other investors agree with him. While no one is certain of what the return will be (the standard deviation is not zero), assumption 6 implies that everyone would at least agree on the nature of the uncertainty.

Goals

The assumptions listed above are limiting, but they do allow us to develop a very useful set of results. Namely, the CAPM lets us be much more precise about how risk/return trade-offs are determined in financial markets.[7]

The general idea of the CAPM is that in **frictionless markets,** people will buy and sell securities until an equilibrium is reached where current market prices of assets reflect people's assessments about the cash flow they might receive from owning those assets. In theory, this equilibrium requires that trade-offs be established between *all* possible assets—stocks, bonds, real estate, gold, etc. In such an equilibrium, we would expect risk-averse investors to require higher expected returns to compensate them for owning assets that are riskier. A 20 percent return on a very risky asset might be just as good to an investor as a 10 percent return on a fairly safe asset. The strength of the CAPM is that it specifies how this risk/expected return trade-off will work. Here we concentrate on the main results of the theory.

Results

The **market portfolio** is the portfolio of *all* risky assets. Because investors are risk averse, they will require a **risk premium** to invest in the market portfolio rather than

---

[7]A number of scholars have relaxed some of the assumptions of the CAPM, producing different variations of asset-pricing models. The CAPM is by far the most widely used of these models. For a discussion of some of the variants of the CAPM, see T. Copeland and F. Weston, *Financial Theory and Corporate Policy* (Reading, Mass.: Addison-Wesley, 1983).

in a riskless asset. In terms of our notation, we can express this risk premium expected to be earned on the market portfolio as

$$\text{Risk premium} = E(R_m) - R_f.$$

Hence, the risk premium *per unit of risk* is given in Equation (6).

The risk premium (*rp*) per unit of risk (or *reward/risk ratio*) for the market portfolio can be expressed as

$$\frac{E(R_m) - R_f}{\sigma_m} \qquad (6)$$

where R_f = the risk-free rate of return, $E(R_m)$ = the expected rate of return on the market portfolio, and σ_m = the risk, or standard deviation, on the market portfolio.

Equation (6) simply gives the risk premium that the market expects to earn on the portfolio of all risky assets relative to the risk of that portfolio.

Now let's look at the implications of the CAPM. In the CAPM, an expected return—for example, $E(R_m)$—can also be thought of as a *required return,* the minimum acceptable return defined in Chapter 4, because of the nature of market equilibrium. The CAPM assumes that investors buy and sell securities and that market prices adjust until they are in equilibrium. In equilibrium, demand and supply pressures will ensure that expected returns and required returns will be one and the same. If the expected return on the market portfolio of risky assets exceeded the required return, there would be extra demand to buy the securities. As prices were driven up, the expected return would fall. Given the same future cash flows from owning an asset, one's expected rate of return is lower the higher is the price one has to pay for that asset. If expected returns were lower than required returns, prices would fall and expected rates of return would rise. Thus, in equilibrium, the expected return is equal to the required return, as Equation (7) indicates.

In equilibrium, the expected return on the market portfolio, $E(R_m)$, will be such that

$$E(R_m) = K_m \qquad (7)$$

where K_m = the required rate of return on the market portfolio.

Based on Equation (7), Equation (6) can be rewritten in terms of required returns, as shown in Equation (8).

The risk premium *(rp)* per unit of risk for the market portfolio can be expressed in terms of required returns as

$$rp \text{ per unit of risk} = \frac{K_m - R_f}{\sigma_m} \qquad (8)$$

where K_m = the required rate of return on the market portfolio, R_f = the risk-free rate of return, and σ_m = the risk, or standard deviation, on the market portfolio.

For any asset or portfolio of assets (denoted by the subscript j), the risk premium per unit of risk is given by Equation (9).

> The risk premium (rp) per unit of risk for any asset or portfolio of assets, j, can be expressed as
>
> $$rp \text{ per unit of risk } = \frac{K_j - R_f}{Risk_j} \qquad (9)$$
>
> where K_j = required return on asset j (or portfolio j), R_f = the risk-free rate of return, and $Risk_j$ = the risk associated with asset j (or portfolio j).

Since investors are risk-averse, the risk premium varies with the risk; the higher the risk associated with an asset or portfolio, the higher is its risk premium.

There is one very important difference between Equation (8) for the market portfolio and Equation (9) for any asset j—that difference is in how we measure risk. In the case of the market portfolio, we have done all the diversification possible (since the market portfolio includes all risky assets); thus, the standard deviation, σ_m, is an appropriate measure of risk. Because all the benefits of risk reduction through diversification have already occurred, σ_m is all *nondiversifiable risk*—risk that an investor cannot avoid.

We know, however, that some of the variability of returns on individual assets can be diversified away so that the standard deviation of an asset is *not* an appropriate measure of the risk it adds to a portfolio. As long as the asset's returns are not perfectly positively correlated with other assets, there will be some way to diversify away some of the individual asset's risk. The question is, how should we measure $Risk_j$ in Equation (9)? The capital-asset-pricing model provides an answer. Specifically, the results of CAPM show that the appropriate measure of risk for any individual asset or portfolio can be written as shown in Equation (10).

> The risk associated with any individual asset or portfolio, j, can be expressed as
>
> $$Risk_j = \rho_{jm}\sigma_j \qquad (10)$$
>
> where ρ_{jm} = the correlation coefficient between the return on asset j and the return on the market portfolio and σ_j = the standard deviation of the return on the asset.

The risk of an asset (or portfolio) is the correlation coefficient between that asset and the market portfolio multiplied by the standard deviation of the return on the asset.

Equation (10) shows the capital-asset-pricing model's measure of nondiversifiable risk. Note that as portfolio considerations suggest, the appropriate risk measure depends both on the asset's standard deviation and on how that asset correlates with other assets. If the asset returns correlated perfectly with the market (if $\rho_{jm} = 1$), there would be no risk-reducing benefits of diversification, and the asset's entire standard deviation would be nondiversifiable risk:

$$\rho_{jm}\sigma_j = 1(\sigma_j) = \sigma_j.$$

Note that this is the case for the market portfolio because it would be perfectly correlated with itself. As the correlation drops, however, the appropriate measure of risk becomes less than the asset's standard deviation.

The **beta coefficient**—is a measure of the risk of an asset relative to the market portfolio.

Frequently, $Risk_j$ is converted to a relative-risk measure by expressing it relative to the risk of the market portfolio. This relative-risk measure has come to be known as the asset's **beta coefficient,** which can be expressed as shown in Equation (11).

> The relative risk associated with any individual asset or portfolio, j, as measured in relation to the risk of the market portfolio, can be expressed as
>
> $$\beta_j = \frac{Risk_j}{\sigma_m}$$
>
> $$= \frac{\rho_{jm}\sigma_j}{\sigma_m}$$
>
> (11)
>
> where ρ_{jm} = the correlation coefficient between the return on asset j and the return on the market portfolio, σ_j = the standard deviation of the return on asset j, σ_m = the risk, or standard deviation, on the market portfolio.

The beta coefficient is a measure of the nondiversifiable risk of an asset relative to that of the market portfolio. A beta of 1.0 indicates an asset of average risk. A beta coefficient greater than 1.0 indicates above-average risk—stocks whose returns tend to be more risky than the market. Stocks with beta coefficients less than 1.0 are below-average risk. Later we will return to the use of the beta coefficient.

Sample Problem 5—1 Calculating Nondiversifiable Risk for TMI Stock

Suppose we have data on annual returns on the stock for Triangle Microsystems, Inc. for the period 1965–1985, along with returns on the market portfolio for each of those years. From these data, we can calculate the standard deviation, σ_j, of return on TMI stock as 0.20 and the coefficient of correlation, ρ_{jm}, between the TMI returns and those of the market as 0.55. (Appendix 5A at the end of this chapter explains the calculation techniques.)

Solution
The nondiversifiable risk associated with TMI stock can be calculated, using Equation (10), as

$$Risk_{TMI} = 0.55 \times 0.20 = 0.11.$$

Thus, TMI's *total risk is 0.20, while the nondiversifiable* component—that part that cannot be eliminated by diversification—is 0.11. Where ρ_{jm} is less than 1.0 (which, in practice, is almost always), nondiversifiable risk will be less than total risk. ∃⃘⃘⃘

Market Equilibrium

The capital-asset-pricing model assumes that the movement of the market for all capital assets toward **market equilibrium** will establish the return/risk relationship for individual financial assets. In theory, investors will buy and sell individual securities

Market equilibrium—in the market for risky capital assets is achieved when investors buy and sell assets until each asset offers the same reward/risk ratio. In market equilibrium, the market risk premium per unit of nondiversifiable risk is the same for all risky assets.

until each offers the same **reward/risk ratio**—that is, the same expected risk premium per unit of risk. Once equilibrium is reached in the market, the reward/risk ratio for every financial asset will be the same and will equal that for the market as a whole. The equilibrium relationship is represented symbolically in Equation (12).

> According to the capital-asset-pricing model, the market for capital assets is in equilibrium when
>
> $$\frac{K_j - R_f}{Risk_j} = \frac{K_j - R_f}{\rho_{jm}\sigma_j} = \frac{K_m - R_f}{\sigma_m} \qquad (12)$$

Equation (12) represents an equilibrium condition that must hold in a rational financial market. In equilibrium, the market risk premium per unit of nondiversifiable risk is the same for all risky assets. In theory, investors will buy or sell securities (thus, changing the price and the expected return on each) until each security or mix of securities offers the same reward/risk ratio. In equilibrium, investors' expected rates of return will be equal to their required rates of return.

The **reward/risk ratio**—is the expected risk premium per unit of risk and equals the market risk premium (expected rate of return on the market portfolio minus the risk-free rate of return) divided by the risk of the market portfolio.

Let us now apply this reasoning to the common stock of an individual firm. If we assume that the market treats all firms rationally (and there is no reason to think otherwise), then the risk premium per unit of risk should be the same for all common stocks. As Equation (12) already told us, in equilibrium, for every stock:

$$\frac{K_j - R_f}{\rho_{jm}\sigma_j} = \frac{K_m - R_f}{\sigma_m},$$

where K_j now represents the expected return on the asset, which in this case is the common stock of the particular firm under discussion. The quantity

$$\frac{K_m - R_f}{\sigma_m}$$

The **market standard**—is the rate of return per unit of risk against which all risky investments are judged and is expressed as $(K_m - R_f)/\sigma_m$.

has special significance: it is the **market standard** against which all prospective risky investments are judged. If any risky asset provides a return per unit of risk greater than the market standard, investors will seek it out and, in so doing, drive its price up until its reward/risk ratio is equal to the market standard.

THE REQUIRED RATE OF RETURN

Equation (12) can be arranged to give us an expression for the required rate of return on an asset in market equilibrium, as Equation (13) demonstrates.

> According to the capital-asset-pricing model, the expected rate of return, K_j, on asset j in market equilibrium can be expressed as
>
> $$K_j = R_f + (K_m - R_f)\left(\frac{\rho_{jm}\sigma_j}{\sigma_m}\right)$$
>
> $$= R_f + [(K_m - R_f)(\beta_j)] \qquad (13)$$

In Equation (13), K_j is the required rate of return on asset j in equilibrium. It is made up of two components: the risk-free rate of return, R_f, plus a risk premium. The risk premium is the product of the risk premium required on the market portfolio ($K_m - R_f$) and the relative risk, or beta coefficient, of asset j (β_j).

This beta coefficient, which we expressed earlier in Equation (11), is the nondiversifiable risk of the asset relative to the risk of the market. If the asset is greater in risk than the market, the beta coefficient exceeds 1, and Equation (13) tells us to assign a higher risk premium to asset j than to the market. For example, suppose that a chemical company had a beta coefficient of 1.20, that the required rate of return on the market (K_m) was 15 percent per year, and that the risk-free interest rate(R_f) was 6 percent per year. We can use Equation (13) to estimate the required return on the stock as

$$K_j = 0.06 + [(0.15 - 0.06)(1.20)]$$

$$= 0.06 + 0.108$$

$$= 0.168 = 16.8 \text{ percent.}$$

As calculated above, we see that the required return on this stock would be 16.8 percent—the sum of the 6 percent risk-free rate and a 10.8 percent risk premium. This 16.8 percent is larger than the 15 percent required return on the market because the chemical stock is riskier than the market. As a result, investors require a larger risk premium on the stock than on the market in general. The capital-asset-pricing model provides a specific estimate of how much larger this risk premium is.

The Market Line

The **market line**—shows the relationship between required return and risk.

We can plot the relationship between required return and nondiversifiable risk, as expressed in Equation (13), to produce a graph of the **market line,** as shown in Figure 5–9.

The vertical axis of the figure measures required return, and the horizontal axis measures nondiversifiable risk. Figure 5–9 tells us in graphic form the same thing that Equation (13) tells us—namely, that in equilibrium the required return on any security, K_j, depends on its nondiversifiable risk. The market line in Figure 5–9 is simply the risk/return trade-off implied by the capital-asset-pricing model. It measures risk and return more precisely than does the general model of the risk/return trade-off depicted in Chapter 4 and earlier in this chapter. In equilibrium, all securities would lie along the upward-sloping line. High-risk securities would lie on the upper part of the line, and low-risk securities would lie along the lower part.[8] Figure 5–9 shows that only nondiversifiable risk is important in determining required return. Because the capital-asset-pricing model assumes that all diversifiable risk can be diversified away by holding portfolios and need not be borne by investors, there is no need for the market to "pay" for bearing diversifiable risk by granting a higher expected return. Only nondiversifiable risk is important.

---

[8]Technically, the line in Figure 5–9 is called the *security market line*. For a discussion, see W. F. Sharpe, *Portfolio Theory and Capital Markets* (New York: McGraw-Hill, 1970).

> **According to the capital-asset-pricing model, in equilibrium, the required return of any security depends on its nondiversifiable risk.**

Risk and Beta Coefficients

In Equation (13), the beta coefficient, β_j, is a measure of an asset's nondiversifiable risk relative to the market. If an asset has a beta coefficent of 2.0, it is twice as risky as the market, and according to Equation (13), investors will require twice as large a risk premium on this asset as on the market. It is important to remember that the beta coefficient reflects nondiversifiable risk—that part of total risk that cannot be eliminated by diversification. Because beta coefficients already reflect the benefits of diversification, the beta coefficient of any portfolio can be calculated as the average of the beta coefficients of the individual assets in that portfolio. As an example, if you invested 30 percent of your money in Risky Business Inc. (with a beta coefficient of 2.0) and the remaining 70 percent in No Frills Limited (with a beta coefficient of 0.5), the beta coefficient of your portfolio would be calculated as

$$\beta_p = 0.30(2.0) + 0.70(0.5) = 0.60 + 0.35 = 0.95.$$

By combining a risky and a safe asset, you have created a portfolio with nondiversifiable risk only slightly smaller than the market's beta coefficient of 1.0.

Beta coefficients can be estimated using the statistical technique of *regression analysis*. Returns for a particular stock would be obtained for specific time periods—normally months or weeks—and related using regression analysis to returns for identical periods on a widely diversified portfolio, such as the Standard & Poors 500 stock

Figure 5–9
The Market Line

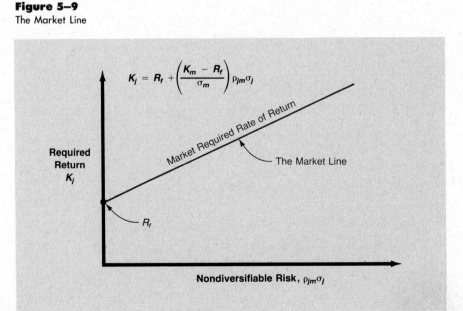

Nondiversifiable Risk, $\rho_{jm}\sigma_j$

Table 5–8
Examples of Beta Coefficients

	Industry	Beta Coefficient
High Risk	Airlines	1.80
	Electronics	1.60
	Consumer durables	1.45
	Producer goods	1.30
	Chemicals	1.25
	Shipping	1.20
Medium Risk	Steel	1.05
	Containers	1.05
	Nonferrous metals	1.00
	Agriculture	1.00
	Food	1.00
	Liquor	0.90
Low Risk	Banks	0.85
	International oil	0.85
	Tobacco	0.80
	Telephone utilities	0.75
	Energy utilities	0.60
	Gold	0.35

Source: D. W. Mullins, Jr., ''Does the Capital Asset Pricing Model Work?'' *Harvard Business Review* 60 (Jan./Feb. 1982): 105–114.

index, which is a proxy for the market portfolio.[9] Beta coefficients also are available from many investment-brokerage firms and advisory services, such as the Value Line Investment Survey. Often it is safe to assume that a beta coefficient estimated using a company's past stock returns is a good indicator of future risks. If, however, a major change in the operation or risks of a company takes place, there would be a need for further care in estimating beta. For example, if an oil company purchases an electronics firm, the postmerger firm will likely have a level of beta risk that reflects an average of risks in both the oil and electronics industries. The risk relevant to investors is *future risk*.

Table 5–8 gives examples of beta coefficients for selected industries. Airlines head the list of high-risk stocks, with an average beta coefficient for the industry of 1.80. Airlines have revenues that fluctuate considerably with economic activity. This basic variability is amplified by high fixed costs, including interest payments, that result from corporate borrowing. At the other end of the spectrum are telephone and electric utilities. Electric utilities are regulated, and the demand for electricity tends to grow in a steady manner. Because the revenues and earnings of electric-utility companies are very stable, they have low beta coefficients. Gold-mining stocks have the lowest beta coefficients of all at 0.35. The nonferrous metals, agriculture, and food industries fall in the middle of the risk spectrum, with beta coefficients of 1.00.

[9]We noted earlier that the market portfolio theoretically consists of *all* risky assets, but because of the difficulty of obtaining data, a proxy for the market portfolio must be used in practice. All-equity portfolios, such as the Standard & Poors 500 stock index, or the New York Stock Exchange Index, are widely used as surrogates in practice.

Sample Problem 5–2   Calculating the Required Return on WPNA Stock

Word Processors of North America(WPNA) has a beta coefficient (relative-risk ratio) of 1.2. If the required return on the market (K_m) is 0.17 and the risk-free interest rate (R_f) is 0.09, apply Equation (13) to calculate the market's required rate of return on WPNA stock.

Solution

According to Equation (13), the required return on a capital asset equals the risk-free rate plus a risk premium:

$$K_j = 0.09 + [(0.17 - 0.09)(1.2)]$$

$$= 0.09 + 0.096$$

$$= 0.186 = 18.6 \text{ percent.}$$

The market requires a 0.096 risk premium on WPNA stock. When this risk premium is added to the risk-free rate of return, the result is a required rate of return on WPNA stock of 18.6 percent. ∃⫙⊏

Implementing the Capital-Asset-Pricing Model

In Sample Problem 5–2, we made a number of important assumptions to implement Equation (13). *First,* we assumed a value for the beta coefficient. In practice, this value is often estimated using past data on returns to a particular stock relative to returns on some market index. Estimated betas were given in Table 5–8. There is no

---

Finance in Practice 5–1

Where Do Betas Come From?

Beta coefficients have come into use in a number of applications where future returns on financial assets must be estimated. Analysts and executives are using beta coefficients:

- as an input to the CAPM to estimate expected returns on stocks.
- in public-utility rate cases as a basis for setting the rates that electric, telephone, and other utilities can charge the public.

- to aid in setting return targets— that is, minimum acceptable returns—for capital-investment projects.
- to identify overvalued and undervalued stocks.
- in portfolio management(by institutions such as insurance companies, pension funds, and mutual funds) to construct portfolios with particular risk characteristics.

The standard way to estimate a beta coefficient on a particular stock is to use historical data on the stock and some index of general market performance. Commonly used indexes are the Standard & Poors 500 stock index and the New York Stock Exchange

Composite index. The S&P 500 measures the total return—dividends plus capital gains (or losses!)—on a portfolio of 500 common stocks broadly diversified across many industries. The NYSE Composite index measures returns on all stocks listed on the NYSE, approximately 1600 companies.

Whichever index is chosen plays the role of the "market portfolio" in the capital-asset-pricing model. To estimate a company's beta coefficent, actual returns are gathered for a large historical period—most commonly, by monthly intervals. Data are also gathered on returns on the index. For each month, the analyst has a pair of returns: a reassurance, however, that past relationships are good indicators of future risks. Frequently, the basic nature of a company does not change, so measurement of past risk in such cases is a good indication of future risk. On the other hand, we have to be especially careful to see if there is any reason to believe that the future pattern of risk will differ from the past since only future risk is important to investors.

Second, to calculate required returns using the capital-asset-pricing model's Equation (13), we need estimates of both a risk-free rate of return, R_f, and a market risk premium, $K_m - R_f$. Typically, the risk-free rate of return is estimated using a current interest rate on U.S. government Treasury obligations because these are probably the closest things to riskless assets that one can find. Even then, however, the choice of the appropriate interest rate is not an easy one. For example, what happens if short-term U.S. government notes yield 11 percent interest but long-term U.S. government bonds yield 14 percent interest? Which is the best estimate of the risk-free rate—11 percent or 14 percent? The capital-asset-pricing model doesn't help us out here because it considers only one time horizon, while the 11 percent and 14 percent rates are for two very different periods of time. In practice, probably the best advice is to use a time period for choosing the risk-free rate of return that approximates the time period for which you are considering investment in an asset. Thus, if you as an investor are considering a stock as a long-term investment, you might use a long-term government bond rate as your risk-free interest rate.

The estimate of the market risk premium is even more problematic. One starting point is to look at past market risk premiums, such as those that are displayed in Table 5–9. Panel A shows average returns for a long period of time, while Panel B converts these returns into risk-premium form by subtracting an estimate of the risk-free rate of

---

turn for the stock in question and a return for the index.

The next step is to use statistical *regression analysis* to determine the relationship between the returns on the stock and the returns on the index. The slope coefficient out of that regression is an estimate of the stock's beta coefficient. As noted earlier, a beta coefficient is a measure of the volatility of a particular stock *relative to* the market. Some analysts go further to adjust the regression results to get an "improved" value for beta.

Every time a security analyst or a portfolio manager needs a beta coefficient, does he or she go off and do some regression analysis? The answer is no. A number of firms provide beta coefficients commercially as a service. As of this writing, beta coefficients are available on a large number of stocks from The Value Line Investment Survey, Merrill Lynch, Drexel Burnham Lambert, and Barr Rosenberg Associates.

The good news is that there are a number of sources for beta coefficients. The bad news is that the beta coefficients for a given company often vary, depending on which source one picks. In calculating the beta coefficient, a number of options exist with respect to the statistical technique used, the time period covered by the analysis, the interval chosen (such as monthly or quarterly), and the index used as a market proxy. Different choices for these parameters can give rise to different results. The different firms offering beta coefficients don't all do things the same way, so beta coefficients from different sources often vary. In using commercially available beta coefficients, a financial manager must pay attention to the details and be sure that the particular beta chosen fits the job at hand.

Source: Adapted from D. R. Harrington, "Whose Beta Is Best?" *Financial Analysts Journal,* July-August 1983, pp. 67-73.

Table 5—9
Past Returns in U.S. Financial Markets

Panel A: Investment Total Annual Returns, 1926–1981

Series	Arithmetic Mean (percent)	Standard Deviation (percent)
Common stocks	11.4	21.9
Long-term corporate bonds	3.7	5.6
Long-term government bonds	3.1	5.7
U.S. Treasury bills	3.1	3.1
Inflation	3.1	.5.1

Panel B: Annual Market Risk Premia (for Common Stocks)

	Arithmetic Mean (percent)
Common stocks minus long-term U.S. government bonds	8.3
Common stocks minus U.S. Treasury bills	8.3

Source: Data in Panel A from R. Ibbotson and R. A. Sinquefield, *Stocks, Bonds, Bills, and Inflation: The Past and the Future* (The Financial Analysts Research Foundation, 1982).

return from each type of market return. Note that the market risk premium on common stocks has stayed between 8 percent and 9 percent as measured by the arithmetic average of annual returns. If the future is like the past, shareholders might require similar risk premiums, but there is no assurance. We will return to problems of estimating required returns in Chapters 10 and 11.

Validity of the Capital-Asset-Pricing Model

Obviously, there are many difficulties in attempting to use the capital-asset-pricing model. In addition, the model has been extensively tested with mixed results. Some researchers have found evidence that returns do seem to be related to nondiversifiable risks, as the theory suggests. Others studying the problem have cast doubts on the model's validity.[10] Whether the model perfectly explains relationships between return

---

[10]For a review of much of the testing of the CAPM, see T. Copeland and F. Weston, *Financial Theory and Corporate Policy* (Reading, Mass.: Addison-Wesley, 1983). For a critique of empirical tests of the CAPM, see R. Roll, "A Critique of the Capital Asset Pricing Theory's Tests," *Journal of Financial Economics* 4 (March 1977): 129–76. For a pragmatic discussion of the shortcomings of the CAPM, see Mullins, "Does the CAPM Work?" As an outgrowth of criticism of the CAPM, a new theory of asset pricing, called the *arbitrage-pricing theory (APT)*, has been developed. Like the CAPM, the APT relies on competition among investors to produce a market equilibrium. Its appeal lies in the fact that its assumptions are less restrictive than those of the CAPM, and it allows for more than one source of risk. Unfortunately, APT offers no economic insight into what the sources of risk ought to be. Research is under way to put APT to the test, and it is too early to tell what its ultimate impact will be. The seminal work on APT was done by S. A. Ross in "The Arbitrage Theory of Capital Asset Pricing," *Journal of Economic Theory* 13 (December 1976): 341–60. Copeland and Weston review some of the work on APT, but much of it is still coming to press in academic circles.

and risk (which it does not), however, is not a fair test of the theory's usefulness. The capital-asset-pricing model is important for the qualitative insights it brings to light.

> **The capital-asset-pricing model brings to light a number of important insights:**
>
> 1. **The values (prices) placed on financial assets are determined in the financial market by the actions of investors, lenders, and borrowers competing against one another.**
> 2. **Expected returns and perceived risk are related. The market is dominated by the risk-averse investors who demand higher expected returns on riskier investments.**
> 3. **The market as a whole functions so that all financial assets are, roughly speaking, "equally good buys"; that is, prices are set so the reward/risk ratio is the same for all financial assets.**
> 4. **The market standard developed in the model is useful for evaluating investments in physical assets just as it is for evaluating financial assets. Investors require extra return for bearing nondiversifiable risk.**

The capital-asset-pricing model is a theory about the way risk and required return should be related. Given its assumptions, the CAPM leads to a very useful risk/return equation—Equation (13)—that allows one to estimate required rates of return.

In practice we'll find that the CAPM is only one way to "skin the cat" in dealing with risk. Practitioners also deal with risk in other ways, as Chapter 11 will discuss.

The capital-asset-pricing model provides many useful insights for the financial manager attempting to maximize the value of the firm. The model shows the type of risk (nondiversifiable) for which shareholders require compensation in the form of a higher risk premium and, hence, a higher required return. Because financial managers are investing funds on behalf of shareholders (for example, by building a new plant), managers must keep sight of the returns shareholders will require as a result of the project's risks.

KEY CONCEPTS

1. Financial management provides tools for dealing with two difficult problems involved in most management decisions: time and risk.
2. In placing a value on an asset, the basic discounted-cash-flow model must reflect the fact that the value of a future cash flow stream depends on its size, its timing, and its risk. The greater is the risk, the higher is the discount rate used to calculate its present value.
3. Statistical techniques allow us to provide summary measures of return and risk. *Expected value* can be used as a measure of the size of a cash flow or return. The *standard deviation,* the statistical measure of variability, can be used as a measure of the amount of risk associated with an outcome.
4. When risky assets are combined in a portfolio, some risk can be diversified away. An appropriate measure of an individual asset's risk is the risk it adds to a portfolio.
5. The total risk of any asset can be thought of as the sum of diversifiable risk and nondiversifiable risk.
6. The capital-asset-pricing model (CAPM) is a theory about how risky assets are valued in financial markets. It shows us the specific relationship between required return and risk that can exist in financial markets. Thus, it provides insight about the risk/return trade-off.

SUMMARY

A major problem in finance is dealing with risk. The standard deviation is a statistical tool that can be used to measure variability, or the amount of risk associated with an outcome.

When we extend our analysis of risk to portfolios of assets, we find that some risk can be diversified away if investors hold a number of assets in a portfolio. As a result, it is important to focus on that nondiversifiable component of risk that an investor must ultimately bear.

The capital-asset-pricing model (CAPM) provides a specific way to relate risk to required return. It shows that required returns should depend only upon nondiversifiable risk. There are, however, many questions about the validity of the CAPM. We should, thus, view its insights with a grain of salt as we attempt to apply them to real-world problems. The model does, however, provide useful insights for financial managers about risk/return trade-offs.

QUESTIONS

1. What are some shortcomings of the standard deviation as a measure of risk?

2. How does the correlation between two stocks affect the risk of a portfolio formed by investing money in the two stocks?

3. What is the capital-asset-pricing model (CAPM)? Why is it important to financial management?

4. Explain the difference between diversifiable and nondiversifiable risk.

5. The capital-asset-pricing model implies that investors are compensated by means of a risk premium only for bearing nondiversifiable risk and that diversifiable risk is not reflected in market required rates of return. Why should this be so?

6. Give some examples of factors that could increase (or decrease) diversifiable risk for a firm. Do the same for nondiversifiable risk.

7. What is a *beta coefficient?* How can beta coefficients be used?

8. You are the treasurer of a large corporation. As treasurer, you sit on the Pension Fund Committee. The committee is concerned with investing the pension-fund money. At a recent meeting concerning the investments to be made for the current fiscal year, various members of the committee put forward the following proposals:

Primus: I think we should invest the pension-fund money available this year in the stocks of companies making video games. This is a high-growth area, and the returns will be enormous.

Secundus: I don't agree with this. The video-game market is becoming saturated with companies making games. It is very risky. While the ex-pected return may be great, the chances are high that we will pick the wrong companies. I suggest we invest in the home-computer market, which is likely to have considerable growth in the future, but won't be risky.

Tertius: I don't agree with either of you. We should aim for a well-diversified portfolio. What if video games or home computers don't do as well as expected? We have to balance the stocks with stocks in U.S. steel companies. The steel companies are not doing well, so these stocks should offset growth stocks, such as home computers, and give us a well-diversified portfolio.

Quartus: I suggest a different approach. These are troubled times. The inflation rate has fluctuated. Who knows what will happen in the future? As trustees for all of the people who will eventually receive pensions from this company, we must be extremely risk-averse. We must invest the pension-fund money in U.S. Treasury bills, which are as risk-free as you can get.

Quintus: Why do we have to pick our stocks carefully? Look at the data for the returns on stocks over the past 60 years. The arithmetic average is at least 8.5 percent more than the risk-free rate. The stocks we pick are irrelevant, as long as they are not perfectly correlated. If they don't do well this year, they will rebound the next, because the 60 years' data show that we don't have to worry.

Sixtus: We should seek a well-diversified portfolio, but being well diversified means choosing stocks with low dispersion of results (low standard deviations). I suggest we load the portfolio with these blue-chip stocks.

As a member of the Pension Fund Committee, how would you respond to each of your colleagues? What policy would you recommend?

9. The Simpson and Menzies Company is a large Scottish publisher. Most of their revenue comes from publishing health books, such as exercise and running books. They also own a London publishing company, Conquest and Champion, which publishes books on popular psychology. As one of the key financial officers of this company, you are called in to discuss the possible sale of the London company. The president of Simpson and Menzies, Farquhar Fraser, wants to know what you and Lachlan MacTavish, the chief of corporate planning, think of his proposal:

"I want to sell this London company. We are publishers of health books. It is nice to publish popular psych books and make a lot of money, but this is not our specialty. We should publish books in fields where we have extensive expertise. If we sell the psych company, we can use the proceeds to beef up our health books, the backbone of our company."

"Farquhar," replies Lachlan MacTavish, "I don't agree that this is the best way to go. By selling the company and concentrating in health-book publishing, we are not diversifying. By diversifying into other companies, we cut our risks for the future. What if health-book publishing declines or we cannot keep our market leadership? By keeping the psych company, we diversify our risk."

How would you evaluate these proposals? Evaluate in the context of the goals and strategies of a corporation discussed in Chapter 1 and the portfolio theory discussed in this chapter.

10. As a financial manager of Lobell and Howard, you sit on the committee that invests funds used for the employee profit-sharing plan. Fiona Campbell, of the planning department, also sits on this committee, and has made the following recommendation:

"Okay, Financial Whiz, I have the perfect investment for us. You talk about diversifiable and non-diversifiable risk. You tell me that *all* stocks have some nondiversifiable risk because they all move to some degree with the market. Well, you are wrong. I have the perfect stock: the Chicago Cubs baseball team. The Cubs haven't won a pennant in 37 years, yet those suckers known as Cubs fans keep flocking to Cubs Park as if they were a bunch of lemmings. And this gullibility is passed on from generation to generation. Oh, they can raise prices and the fans might moan a bit, but they will still come out and see their beloved Cubs fold in August and September, if they haven't already folded by that time each year. The stock has absolutely no risk. It is better than Treasury bonds. We can't lose with this one. It's market-proof." How would you reply to this?

PROBLEMS

Note: To solve problems preceded by an asterisk requires a knowledge of material in Appendix 5A.

1. Two investments, A and B, have the probability distributions of returns given in Table A. Calculate the expected return and standard deviation for each investment. Which is the riskier investment? What can you say about the expected return relative to the riskiness of each investment?

2. Calculate the expected return and standard deviation of a portfolio which is composed of 50 percent stock A and 50 percent stock B when the correlation coefficient is

   a. $\rho_{AB} = 1$. b. $\rho_{AB} = .5$. c. $\rho_{AB} = 0$.

How does the correlation coefficient affect the standard deviation of the portfolio?

Table A

A		B	
Probability	Return	Probability	Return
0.10	0.10	0.15	0.08
0.20	0.12	0.15	0.10
0.30	0.15	0.15	0.18
0.40	0.20	0.55	0.24

Table B

State	Return on X (percent)	Return on Y (percent)	Probability
A	40	28	0.2
B	−10	20	0.2
C	35	41	0.2
D	−5	−17	0.2
E	15	3	0.2

3. Suppose you are given the data in Table B for securities X and Y.

   a. Calculate the expected return and standard deviation (σ) for securities X and Y.

   *b. If a portfolio is composed of equal amounts of X and Y, calculate the correlation coefficient and the covariance of the securities in this portfolio.

   c. If a portfolio contains equal amounts of X and Y, calculate the expected return and risk of the portfolio.

   d. If a risk-averse investor who presently owns no securities were able to choose to invest in (1) security X alone, (2) security Y alone, or (3) portfolio XY, which would he or she choose? Graph the three choices in risk/expected return space to explain your answer.

4. An analyst calculates the beta coefficient for XYZ corporation to be 1.3. Suppose $K_m = 0.17$ and $R_f = .09$. Suppose further that the analyst calculates the expected return on XYZ's shares to be 22 percent. Is XYZ a good buy?

5. Suppose that a shareholder had just paid $50 per share for XYZ company stock. The stock will pay a $2.00 per share dividend in the upcoming year, and this dividend is expected to grow at an annual rate of 10 percent for the indefinite future. The shareholder felt that the price paid was an appropriate price given an assessment of XYZ's risks.

   a. What is the annual required rate of return of this shareholder?

   b. Assume that the capital-asset-pricing model holds and that the expected return on the market portfolio was 12 percent and the risk-free rate was 8 percent. What is the beta coefficient (β) of XYZ's stock?

6. Suppose you are considering investing in two different stocks. One has had a standard deviation of returns $\sigma_A = 0.03$ and a correlation with market returns of $\rho_{Am} = .6$. The other has $\sigma_B = 0.05$ and $\rho_{Bm} = 0.35$. Suppose $\sigma_m = 0.04$. Which is the riskier stock if you hold a well-diversified portfolio?

7. Calculate K_j for the companies listed in Table C. Assume the government bond rate (R_f) is 11 percent and the expected return on the market portfolio (K_m) is 19 percent.

Table C

Industry	Beta Coefficient
Airline	1.75
Electronics manufacturer	1.62
Shipping company	1.18
Packaged-foods producer	1.00
Liquor distiller	0.93
Tobacco company	0.82
Telephone utility	0.77
Electric utility	0.64

8. Suppose K_m, the expected return on the market portfolio, is 17 percent; the U.S. government bond rate, R_f, is 11 percent; σ_m, the standard deviation of return on the market portfolio, is 0.22. Calculate and interpret the implied market standard.

9. Draw the market risk/return schedule implied by the data in problem (8).

10. The data in problem (8) assume an inflation rate of 8.5 percent per year. Redo problem (9) assuming an inflation rate of zero and no change in real rates of return.

REFERENCES

Evans, J. L. and S. H. Archer, "Diversification and the Reduction of Dispersion." *Journal of Finance* 23 (Dec. 1968): 29–40.

Fama, E. F. "Efficient Capital Markets—A Review of Theory and Empirical Work." *Journal of Finance* 25 (May 1970): 383–417.

Fama, E. F. and J. D. Macbeth, "Risk, Return and Equilibrium: Empirical Tests." *Journal of Political Economy* 81 (May 1973): 607–631.

Gordan, M. J. and L. I. Gould. "Comparison of the DCF and HPR Measures of the Yield on Common Shares." *Financial Management* 13 (Winter 1984): 40–47.

Ibbotson, R. and R. A. Sinquefield. *Stocks, Bonds, Bills and Inflation: The Past and the Future.* The Financial Analysts Research Foundation, 1982.

Jensen, M. C. (ed.), *Studies in the Theory of Capital Markets.* New York: Frederick A. Praeger, Inc., 1972.

Kripke, H. "Inside Information and Efficient Markets." *Financial Analysts Journal* (March–April 1980): 20–24.

Lintner, J. "The Evaluation of Risk Assets and the Selection of Risky Investments in Stock Portfolios and Capital Budgets." *Review of Economics and Statistics 47* (Feb. 1965) 13–77.

Markowitz, H. M. "Portfolio Selection." *Journal of Finance* (Mar. 1952): 77–91.

Markowitz, H. M. *Portfolio Selection: Efficient Diversification of Investments.* New York: John Wiley & Sons, Inc., 1959.

Mossin, J. "Equilibrium in a Capital Asset Market." *Econometrica* 34, 4 (Oct. 1966): 768–775.

Mullins, D. W. Jr., "Does the Capital Asset Pricing Model Work?" *Harvard Business Review* (January–February 1982): 105–114.

Radcliffe, R. *Investment.* Glenview, Illinois: Scott, Foresman and Company, 1986.

Ramakrishnan, R. T. and A. V. Thakor. "The Valuation of Assets Under Moral Hazard." *Journal of Finance* 39 (March 1984): 229–238.

Reiganum, M. R. "A Direct Test of Roll's Conjecture on the Firm Size Effect." *Journal of Finance* 36 (Mar. 1982): 27–36.

Roll, R. W. and S. A. Ross. "The Arbitrage Pricing Theory Approach to Strategic Portfolio Planning." *Financial Analysts Journal* (May–June 1984): 14–26.

Roll, R. W. "A Critique of the Capital Asset Pricing Theory's Tests." *Journal of Financial Economics* (March 1977): 129–176.

Roll, R. W. and S. A. Ross. "An Empirical Investigation of Arbitrage Pricing Theory." *Journal of Finance* 35 (December 1980): 1073–1104.

Ross, S. A. "The Arbitrage Theory of Capital Asset Pricing." *Journal of Economic Theory* 13 (Dec. 1976): 341–360.

Rubinstein, M. "A Mean-Variance Synthesis of Corporate Financial Theory." *Journal of Finance* 28 (Mar. 1973): 167–182.

Shanken, J. "The Arbitrage Pricing Theory: Is It Testable?" *Journal of Finance* 37 (December 1982): 1129–1140.

Sharpe, W. F. "Capital Asset Prices: A Theory of Market Equilibrium Under Conditions of Risk." *Journal of Finance,* 19, 3 (1964): 425–442.

Sharpe, W. F. *Investments.* 3rd ed. Englewood Cliffs, New Jersey: Prentice-Hall, Inc., 1985.

Sharpe, W. F. *Portfolio Theory and Capital Markets.* New York: McGraw-Hill, 1970.

Wallace, A. "Is Beta Dead?" *Institutional Investor* (July 1980): 23–30.

Appendix 5A

CORRELATION AND COVARIANCE

In discussing the risk of a portfolio, Chapter 5 used the correlation coefficient, ρ—see Equations (7) and (13). This appendix will investigate correlation and the calculation of a correlation coefficient in more detail.

The term *correlation* implies that a relationship exists between two variables. For example, sales of television sets may be correlated with personal disposable income. Sales of a particular product are likely to be correlated with the level of advertising expenditures for the product.

The notion of correlation is especially important in economics and finance because many economic and financial variables are related to one another. At the level of the economy as a whole, gross national product (GNP), personal consumption, business sales, personal income, and corporate profits, to name just a few macroeconomic variables, all tend to move together. At the level of the individual firm, sales, expenses, and profits are correlated both among themselves and very likely also with measures of aggregate economic activity, such as GNP. The many complex interdependencies in our economy contribute to this moving together and give rise to business and monetary cycles. Projections of sales, cash flow, and costs require an understanding of the relationship between the individual firm's activity and that of the general economy.

COEFFICIENT OF CORRELATION

Intuitively, correlation between two variables implies that they move together. The *coefficient of correlation*, ρ, gives us a more precise statistical measure. The correlation coefficient can range from $+1.0$ to -1.0. Perfect positive correlation, a coefficient of $+1.0$, indicates that the two variables move together in perfect lockstep. Consider the data in Table 5A–1 that describe variables A and B, which have, by

Table 5A–1
Hypothetical Values of Variables A and B

	Value of Variable	
	A	B
	4	7
	3	6
	5	8
	7	10
	6	9
Arithmetic mean	5	8

Table 5A–2
Hypothetical Values of Variables C and D

	Value of Variable	
	C	D
	4	11
	7	8
	6	9
	8	7
	5	10
Arithmetic mean	6	9

design, a correlation coefficient of $+1.0$. In each pair of observations, A and B deviate from their respective means by the same amount. Thus, when A is 7 (2 above its mean), B is 10 (2 above its mean). So A and B move by equal amounts about their respective means.

Now consider the data in Table 5A–2, which describe variables C and D. These two variables are perfectly *negatively* correlated ($\rho = -1.0$). In each pair of observations, C and D deviate from their respective means by the same absolute amount, but in opposite directions. Thus, when C is above its mean by 2, D is below its mean by 2. So C and D move in perfect opposition about their respective means.

Two variables that are completely unrelated to one another would have a correlation coefficient of zero. To illustrate, suppose that we roll two dice a very large number of times; each time we record the outcome of each die roll separately. Because the outcome of one die is independent of the outcome of the other, we would expect the numbers representing the pairs of outcomes to be uncorrelated.

Table 5A–3
Correlation and Causation

Year	Egg Production (millions)	Sales of Television Sets (thousands)
1975	15,750	4,720
1976	15,895	4,910
1977	16,210	4,920
1978	16,350	4,850
1979	16,590	5,040
1980	16,880	5,110
1981	17,050	5,095
1982	17,125	5,020

CORRELATION, DEPENDENCE, AND CAUSATION

Events that are independent are always uncorrelated; that is, they have a correlation coefficient of zero. However, the reverse is not necessarily true. It is possible to conceive of events that are dependent but related in such a way as to have a zero correlation coefficient. Thus, independence implies zero correlation, but zero correlation does not necessarily imply independence. In finance and economics, we do not often encounter variables that are uncorrelated yet dependent.

In interpreting correlation, we must be especially careful in drawing inferences about *causation*. Two variables may be highly correlated even when no causal relationship exists between them. Such statistical relationships often occur when two variables are both related to a third variable. Consider the hypothetical data given in Table 5A–3.

The coefficient of correlation between egg production and sales of television sets in the table is 0.86. We will see how to calculate this coefficient shortly. Does a causal relationship exist? Probably not. Both variables, however, probably are related to population growth. Many economic variables that have no causal relationship may grow over time and, therefore, may exhibit positive correlation. In contrast, suppose we examine data on sales of stereo equipment and personal disposable income and find them to be correlated. Here we probably would conclude that a causal relationship does exist.

Correlation does not imply causation.

CALCULATING THE CORRELATION COEFFICIENT

The coefficient of correlation between two random variables, X and Y is defined as shown in Equation (A–1).

The coefficient of correlation, ρ, between two random variables X and Y can be defined as

$$\rho_{XY} = \frac{COV\ (X,Y)}{\sigma_X \sigma_Y} \qquad \textbf{(A–1)}$$

where $COV(X, Y)$ is the covariance of X and Y, σ_X is the standard deviation of X, and σ_Y is the standard deviation of Y.

The *covariance* to which Equation (A–1) refers is defined as shown in Equation (A–2).

The covariance of X and Y, $COV(X,Y)$, can be defined as
$$COV(X,Y) = E[(X - \overline{X})(Y - \overline{Y})] \qquad \textbf{(A–2)}$$
where E is the expected-value operator, $\overline{X}$ is the mean of X, and $\overline{Y}$ is the mean of Y. (Note that $\overline{X}$ is just another way to write $E(X)$, or the expected value of X.)

We can rewrite (A–2), in terms of the probability of an individual observation, as

$$COV(X,Y) = \sum_{i=1}^{n} p_i[(X_i - \overline{X})]\ (Y_i - \overline{Y})]$$

where the subscript i denotes an individual observation of the variables X and Y, p_i is the probability of each observation i, and n is the number of pairs of observations.

If all observations are equally likely (that is, if $p_i = 1/n$ for each observation), the above equation simplifies to

$$COV(X,Y) = \frac{1}{n} \sum_{i=1}^{n} [(X_i - \overline{X})(Y_i - \overline{Y})]$$

which further simplifies to

$$COV(X,Y) = \frac{1}{n} \sum_{i=1}^{n} (X_i Y_i - \overline{X}\overline{Y})$$

We can rewrite the definition of ρ from Equation (A–1) using the simplified definition of covariance above, as shown in Equation (A–3).

The coefficient of correlation, ρ, between two random variables, X and Y, when all observations are equally likely (that is, $p_i = 1/n$ for each observation) can be defined using the simplified definition of $COV(X,Y)$ as

$$\rho_{XY} = \frac{\dfrac{1}{n} \displaystyle\sum_{i=1}^{n} (X_i Y_i) - \overline{X}\,\overline{Y}}{\sigma_X \sigma_Y} \qquad \text{(A–3)}$$

where X_i = an individual X observation, Y_i = an individual Y observation, $\overline{X}$ = the expected value of the random variable X, $\overline{Y}$ = the expected value of the random variable Y, σ_X = the standard deviation of X, and σ_Y = the standard deviation of Y.

Let us now calculate the correlation coefficient for the data in Table 5A–4, assuming each outcome is equally likely. We can first calculate the mean of X as 5 and the mean of Y as 11. After setting up Table 5A–5, we see that

$$\frac{1}{n}\sum_{i=1}^{n}(X_i Y_i) = \frac{1}{5}(305) = 61.0.$$

Table 5A–4
Hypothetical Values X and Y

Value of Variable	
X	Y
4	8
2	7
5	11
6	14
8	15

Table 5A–5
Calculating the Correlation Coefficient ($\overline{X} = 5$; $\overline{Y} = 11$)

i	X_i	Y_i	$X_i Y_i$	$X_i - \overline{X}$	$(X_i - \overline{X})^2$	$Y_i - \overline{Y}$	$(Y_i - \overline{Y})^2$
1	4	8	32	−1	1	−3	9
2	2	7	14	−3	9	−4	16
3	5	11	55	0	0	0	0
4	6	14	84	1	1	3	9
5	8	15	120	3	9	4	16
			305		20		50

Applying Equation (A–3), the coefficient of correlation is

$$\sigma_X = \sqrt{\frac{1}{n}(X_i - \overline{X})^2} = \sqrt{\frac{1}{5}(20)} = 2.0.$$

$$\sigma_Y = \sqrt{\frac{1}{n}(Y_i - \overline{Y})^2} = \sqrt{\frac{1}{5}(50)} = 3.16.$$

$$\rho_{XY} = \frac{61.0 - [(5)(11)]}{(2.0)(3.16)} = 0.95.$$

We see that variables X and Y are almost perfectly positively correlated because X and Y move together.

As Chapter 5 illustrates, correlation coefficients are very important in determining the risks of a portfolio that combines different assets.

Part Three

Financial Analysis and Planning

Part One examined the role of financial management and the environment in which firms operate. Part Two explored time and risk and their relation to value in financial markets. The basic discounted-cash-flow model provides a way to measure the value of an asset (such as a bond) in a way that takes both time and risk into account. To use such a model, however, we need information. In the case of a U.S. government bond, we may only need to read the *Wall Street Journal* to get the relevant information about the cash flows we should expect if we buy the bond and hold it to maturity.

For corporate financial managers, however, the problems of obtaining usable information are much more difficult. What will be the effects of an investment in a new computer? For that matter, how efficient are the company's current methods of operation? We need to be able to predict the future effects of possible courses of action among which we must choose in order to make good decisions.

In practice, we often build our predictions about future events on what we know about the present and the past. The chapters in Part Three examine some of the basic ways in which corporate managers measure and evaluate the past, present, and future results of a corporation's activity. Such techniques are also widely used by people outside the corporation, such as bank loan officers and investors, who may be trying to evaluate a company.

We begin our analysis in Chapter 6 by discussing the basic financial statements of a corporation—balance sheets, income statements, and source-and-use-of-funds statements. These provide the basic framework for measuring the profit or cash flow of a corporation.

Chapter 7 outlines the basic techniques of *financial analysis* for evaluating the health of a firm or other organization. Is the firm profitable? What have been the trends in profitability? How does profitability compare with that of the industry or other similar companies?

Following our discussion of financial analysis in Chapter 7, Chapter 8 turns to the future and a discussion of *financial planning*. The primary focus in Chapter 8 is on near-term financial planning (a time horizon of one to two years), but it also examines long-run financial planning. Financial planning is important for all firms, and especially critical for small firms with small amounts of cash and with heavy borrowing. In Chapter 8, we will learn how to estimate financial requirements and to prepare a comprehensive financial plan, including pro-forma income statements, balance sheets, and cash budgets. These plans provide the type of information we need to begin analyzing corporate decisions in more detail.

Chapter

6

Measuring Profit and Cash Flow

This chapter describes the basic financial statements of a corporation—balance sheets, income statements, and source-and-use-of-funds statements. These statements provide a basic framework for developing information about a company, including data on profit and cash flow.

Part Two focused on how financial markets place *values* on assets, such as a firm's common stock. We saw that investors in these markets valued assets based on the future cash flows that those assets might provide. To make projections about the future, however, we need to develop and interpret information. What is the future financial performance of a company likely to be? We can start answering this question only if we can evaluate what the company has done in the past and is doing currently. From this base, we are in a much better position to make projections about the future.

Accounting—is the system of recording and summarizing business and financial transactions and analyzing, verifying, and reporting the results.

One of the main sources of information on business entities is accounting data. A basic concern of **accounting** is measurement. For example, one of the most difficult problems facing the accountant is measurement of income. In economic terms, **economic income** equals the change in wealth. The income to an economic unit, an individual, or a firm during any period of time is the change in that unit's wealth during the period. For example, suppose you bought a share of stock for $100 at the end of 1986. Suppose also that during 1987 the stock paid you a dividend of $5 and that its price increased to $120 by year-end 1987. As a result of owning that stock, your wealth went up from $100 to $125 ($120 stock price plus $5 dividend). This increase of $25 is the *economic income* earned from owning the stock in 1987.

Economic income—of an economic unit during a period of time is the change in the net worth of that economic unit during the period.

The income to an economic unit, an individual, or a firm during any period of time is the change in that unit's wealth during the period.

Accounting income—is the income figure that results from the application of generally accepted accounting principles to the problem of allocating receipts and expenditures to particular time periods.

In the case of the stock price, the economic income is fairly easy to calculate. When we turn to the actual operations of the firm, however, the problem becomes more complicated. We can think of income as the difference between revenues and expenses during a time period, but making specific judgments can be difficult. As a result we must draw a distinction between *accounting income* and economic income.[1] **Accounting income** refers to the income figure resulting from the application of generally accepted accounting principles. This figure, however, is the product of a number of essentially arbitrary judgments. The amount of an economic unit's accounting income depends on how receipts and expenditures are allocated to particular time periods as revenue or expense. As goods are sold, when is the revenue earned? Is it earned when the order is placed by the customer, when the goods are shipped, when the invoice is mailed, or when the customer's check is received? Most firms keep their books using an **accrual accounting system:** that is, they recognize the sale as a transaction and record the revenue as earned in the accounting period during which the goods are shipped. Some smaller firms keep books using a **cash accounting system;** that is, they recognize the sale only when the customer's payment is received.

An accrual accounting system—is an accounting system that assigns revenues and expenses to particular time periods according to a predetermined set of rules.

A cash accounting system—is an accounting system that assigns revenues and expenses to particular time periods according to the timing of receipts and expenditures.

Over long time periods, economic income and accounting income converge, because problems of allocation to particular time periods disappear. Over short time periods, the differences between the two can be substantial. An objective of accounting should be to measure the true economic income of the firm; however, the state of the art is not adequate to deal with all the problems involved. Later in this chapter we will discuss some of the problems of measurement with which accountants must deal in practice. For now, let us realize that the accounting records kept by a firm provide

---

[1]For further discussion of this distinction, see R. K. Jaedicke and R. T. Sprouse, *Accounting Flows: Income, Funds, Cash* (Englewood Cliffs, N.J.: Prentice-Hall, 1965).

important information about the firm's past and current operations. As such, these records (reported in financial statements) provide useful information for developing assumptions about what might happen in the future.

> **Economic income and accounting income converge over long time periods. Over short time periods, the difference between the two can be substantial.**

FINANCIAL STATEMENTS

An **income statement,**—or *profit-and-loss statement,* is a record of financial events between two points in time. The income statement is an attempt to measure the change in net worth over time.

The **balance sheet**—is a "snapshot" summary of the firm's financial position at a single point in time.

A **flow variable**—is a variable whose value is measured during a period of time.

Large firms typically have quite thorough accounting systems that provide a wide array of information to corporate managers. With the increasing sophistication of computers, such accounting services are also becoming available to smaller firms. This chapter will focus on the three basic financial statements used by a firm: the income statement, the balance sheet, and the source-and-use-of-funds statement. These statements provide a type of financial model for the firm that provides the starting point for both the analysis of the past and the prediction of the future.

Consider the income statement in Table 6–1 and balance sheet in Table 6–2 for Sparta Manufacturing Company, a manufacturer of paints and varnishes. We will work here with these two statements and turn to the source-and-use-of-funds statement later in this chapter.

The **income statement** (which is also known as a *profit-and-loss statement*) represents a record of events between two points in time, in this case December 31, 1985, to December 31, 1986. The **balance sheet** represents a "snapshot" of the firm's position at a single point in time: December 31, 1986. The income statement measures *flows* of dollars per unit of time, because income is a **flow variable.** In contrast, the items in the balance sheet are **stock variables;** that is, they represent dollar values at a given point in time.

Accounting ground rules govern the construction of financial statements. One way

---

Table 6–1
Sparta Manufacturing Company Income Statement, Calendar Year 1986

Sales	$1,140,000
Cost of goods sold	(730,000)
Gross profit	$ 410,000
Depreciation	(15,000)
Selling, general, and administrative expense	(340,100)
Operating profit	$ 54,900
Interest	(12,900)
Profit before taxes	42,000
Income taxes	(8,400)
Profit after taxes	$ 33,600

Note: Figures in parentheses represent expenses which are to be subtracted.

A **stock variable**—is a variable whose value is measured at a given moment in time.

Net worth—of a firm is the value of total assets minus total liabilities, or the value of the owners' claim on assets.

to think of the distinction between the income statement and the balance sheet is to focus on the effect of a particular transaction on the firm's owners, the shareholders. In accounting, a measure of a firm's worth to shareholders is represented by the **net worth** of the corporation. The net worth is simply the total assets of the company minus the total liabilities of the company—that is, net worth is the shareholders' claim on the company after all other claims have been settled. Transactions that would increase or decrease net worth appear in the income statement. The income statement is, thus, an attempt to measure the change in the wealth of owners over a period of time—that is, it measures income.

> **The income statement records events during a *period* of time. The balance sheet represents a "snapshot" at a *point* in time.**

For example, looking at Table 6–1, in 1986 Sparta Manufacturing sold goods in exchange for $1,140,000, but those goods cost Sparta $730,000. The sales revenue increased net worth while the cost of the goods sold decreased net worth. The transaction of the sale increased net worth on balance by $410,000—the difference between the revenue ($1,140,000) and the cost ($730,000). Both types of transactions are recorded in the income statement. If the firm is doing well, the increases in net worth (for example, sales revenues) exceed the decreases in net worth (for example, salaries paid), so the shareholders experience an increase in wealth, at least as measured by accounting standards. This increase in wealth represents an accounting profit earned on income. In 1986, Sparta had a profit after taxes—that is, an increase in net worth—of $33,600 as shown in Table 6–1.

The balance sheet catalogs all the assets and liabilities of the company at a single point in time. At year-end 1986, Table 6-2 shows that Sparta had $722,500 worth of

Table 6–2
Sparta Manufacturing Company Balance Sheet, December 31, 1986

Cash	$ 2,500
Accounts receivable	152,500
Inventory	420,000
Total current assets	$575,000
Fixed assets, net of depreciation	112,500
Other assets	35,000
Total assets	$722,500
Note payable (bank)	$144,100
Accounts payable	122,500
Taxes payable	7,500
Miscellaneous accruals	50,000
Total current liabilities	$324,100
Mortgage payable	26,000
Total liabilities	$350,100
Common stock	155,000
Retained earnings	217,400
Total liabilities and net worth	$722,500

assets and $350,100 worth of total liabilities. The difference between the two figures of $372,400 is the claim of shareholders, which is precisely the net worth of Sparta. Thus, the balance sheet shows the net worth of shareholders at a point in time, while the income statement measures *changes* in net worth.

> **The balance sheet shows the net worth (total assets minus total liabilities) of shareholders at a point in time, while the income statement measures *changes* in net worth.**

Note that in Table 6–2 this net worth is broken into two categories—common stock and retained earnings. These two accounts add up to net worth for Sparta ($155,000 + $217,400 = $372,400). The *common-stock account* represents amounts of money received from shareholders who have put money directly into the business by buying shares of the firm's stock; the *retained-earnings account* represents profits that have been earned in the past and retained in the business rather than being paid out to owners. For example, to raise money, Sparta may have originally sold 10,000 shares of stock for $15.50 a share to generate a common-stock figure of 10,000 × $15.50 = $155,000, as reported in Table 6–2.

The retained-earnings account in the balance sheet plays a critical role in linking the balance sheet and the income statement. If Sparta kept all of its profits in the business and paid out no dividends, balance-sheet retained earnings as of year-end 1986 would be retained earnings as of year-end 1985 plus profits after taxes earned during 1986. Assuming no dividends, in this case, we can infer that Sparta's 1985 balance sheet retained earnings were $183,800 because Sparta's profits in 1986 were $33,600 (from the Table 6–1 income statement), Sparta's 1986 retained earnings were $217,400 (from the Table 6–2 balance sheet), and $217,400 − $33,600 = $183,800. Assuming the shareholders make no further actual contributions to Sparta in 1986 (assuming, in other words, that the common-stock account would be unchanged), Sparta's net worth on the balance sheet would, thus, increase by $33,600 in 1986— precisely the figure of profits after taxes found in the income statement.

> **The retained earnings account in the balance sheet plays the critical role of linking the balance sheet with the income statement.**

If dividends are paid, retained earnings would increase in a year by only the amount of profits actually retained—that is, by profit after taxes minus dividends. Thus, the net worth on the balance sheet would go up by less than profit after taxes from the income statement. The shareholders would, however, have received the dividend payment so their wealth (at least as measured by accounting data) would be increased by the full amount of profits after taxes. For example, if profits after taxes were $100,000 and dividends were $40,000, shareholders would see balance-sheet net worth increase by $60,000 (which is $100,000 - $40,000), but they would also get dividends of $40,000 for a total dollar figure of $100,000. As a result, the $100,000 profit-after-tax figure is still a measure of the effect of the year's operation on shareholder wealth. The important point for our purposes is that the income statement feeds into the balance sheet.

Expenses—are only those expenditures that appear in the income statement (only those that affect net worth).

Expenditures—are all cash outflows.

Receipts—are all cash inflows.

Revenues—are only those receipts that appear in the income statement (only those that affect net worth).

Current assets—are assets with a maturity of less than one year, such as cash holdings, inventories of raw materials, accounts receivable, goods in process, and finished goods.

Fixed assets—are normally defined as assets with a maturity of more than one year.

Working capital—is composed of the firm's current assets, normally with maturities of less than one year.

To understand the distinction between income-statement and balance-sheet transactions, it is important to understand the accounting meaning of the names of various categories in the statements.

All cash outflows are **expenditures,** but only those expenditures that affect net worth and, therefore, appear in the income statement are **expenses.** All cash inflows are **receipts,** but only those receipts that appear in the income statement are **revenues.**

For example, suppose a company borrows $1 million from a bank, receiving a check for the full amount. While the $1 million is certainly a *receipt* of cash, it is not *revenue*. The cash receipt is offset by the firm's owing the bank $1 million. Shareholder net worth is not changed.

Working Capital

Within the balance-sheet total it is useful to distinguish between **current,** or circulating, **assets** and **fixed assets.** Current assets include the firm's holdings of cash, accounts receivable, and the inventory of raw materials, goods in process, and finished goods. The term **working capital** often is used to refer to the firm's current assets, and the term **net working capital** is used to refer to current assets less current liabilities. Short-term assets, such as accounts receivable and inventories, are considered working capital because they are part of the basic workings of the company's day-to-day business. Using these definitions, we can see from Table 6–2 that Sparta Manufacturing Company had $575,000 worth of working capital as of December 31, 1986. Table 6–2 also tells us that the company's **current liabilities** on that date amounted to $324,100. Subtracting this figure from total current assets of $575,000 gives us net working capital of $250,900. If we wish, we can restate Sparta's balance sheet as shown in Table 6–3.

Net working capital—is the firm's current assets minus its current liabilities.

Current liabilities—are the short-term debt obligations of a firm, with maturities of less than one year.

Accounts receivable—are amounts of money owed to the firm by its customers and shown as current assets on the balance sheet.

The balance-sheet format in Table 6–3 makes clear the fact that *net* working capital—that portion of current assets not financed by current liabilities—must of necessity be financed by long-term funds—such as common stock or long-term borrowing. If the firm is a growing one, both the net working capital and its attendant financing requirement also increase.

Net Operating Capital

It is also useful to separate the current liabilities that arise directly out of the firm's operations from those that do not. To support sales, the firm needs inventories and working cash balances. But sales also generate cash and **accounts receivable.** These

Table 6–3
Sparta Manufacturing Company Balance Sheet, December 31, 1986

Assets		*Liabilities and Net Worth*	
Net working capital	$250,900	Mortgage payable	$ 26,000
Net fixed assets	112,500	Common stock	155,000
Other assets	35,000	Retained earnings	217,400
Total assets	$398,400	**Total liabilities and net worth**	$398,400

Accounts payable—are amounts of money owed by the firm to its creditors and shown as current liabilities on the balance sheet.

Net operating capital—is current assets minus operating liabilities (those liabilities that arise directly out of the firm's operations, such as taxes payable).

working assets normally are partially financed by **accounts payable** and various other accrual accounts, such as taxes payable, wages payable, and certain other expenses that at any point in time are owed but not yet paid. We will refer to current assets less these operating liabilities as **net operating capital.** For Sparta Manufacturing Company, we can rearrange the balance sheet shown in Table 6–2 to indicate the required level of financing from nonoperating sources. For Sparta, the operating liabilities are $180,000, consisting of the sum of accounts payable ($122,500), taxes payable ($7,500), and miscellaneous accrual accounts ($50,000). In short, $180,000 worth of total current assets ($575,000) were financed spontaneously by operations, leaving $395,000 of net operating capital to be financed from other sources.

Such spontaneous sources of financing operations can be temporarily increased or decreased by slowing down or speeding up the punctuality with which bills due are paid. But generally, the remaining $395,000 must be financed by other means. In effect, as Table 6–4 shows, Sparta has a total capital requirement (including net operating capital and fixed capital) of $542,500. Of this, $400,820 is financed by long-term sources and $144,100 by bank loans.[2]

The concept of net operating capital is useful in planning or making projections. If a firm's operations are managed consistently and it remains in more or less the same line of business, the relationship between its net operating capital and its sales should remain fairly stable, perhaps declining somewhat with growth. To generate $1,140,000 in sales during 1986, Sparta Manufacturing Company required $395,000 in net operating capital as of year-end 1986, or approximately $0.35 per $1 of sales. Given a projection of future sales, we can quickly generate an estimate of the requirement for net operating capital. We will discuss financial projections in Chapter 8.

INCOME MEASUREMENT

As we discussed at the beginning of this chapter, a basic concern of accounting is measurement. Measuring income is extremely difficult. Already we have distinguished between economic and accounting income. The figures in Table 6–1 show us that Sparta Manufacturing earned profits of $33,600 after taxes in 1986.

As do practically all firms, Sparta uses an accrual accounting system, rather than a cash accounting system, so it recognizes sales as transactions and records the revenue as earned in the accounting period during which the goods are shipped.

Determining the Appropriate Accounting Period

There are a number of difficult problems in calculating a measured income, as Table 6–1 does for Sparta. When a firm purchases materials, it must determine in which particular time period the expenditure should be recorded as an expense. Is the expense incurred when the materials are ordered, received, consumed, or paid for? Again, the answer depends on whether the firm is using a cash or an accrual system of accounting. The firm also needs to determine whether the outlay is to be treated as a *product*

---

[2]Some firms hold liquid assets (assets, such as certificates of deposit, that are easily turned into cash) far above their actual requirements. Such assets (Sparta has none) should be excluded from net operating capital and shown as a separate item on the balance sheet because they are not essential to the basic operations of the company.

Table 6—4
Sparta Manufacturing Company Balance Sheet, December 31, 1986

Assets		Liabilities and Net Worth	
Net operating capital	$395,000	Notes payable (bank)	$144,100
Net fixed assets	112,500	Mortgage payable	26,000
Other assets	35,000	Common stock	155,000
		Retained earnings	217,400
Total assets	**$542,500**	**Total liabilities and net worth**	**$542,500**

cost and recognized when the product is sold or as a *period cost* that is assigned to a time period.

One of the major problems in recording accounting information is deciding how the costs of long-lived assets, such as equipment, are to be treated. Suppose a company purchased a machine for $100,000 that was expected to last five years and then be worthless. While there is a cash expenditure of $100,000 now, the company also has an asset worth $100,000 so it has not incurred a cost. It simply traded one asset (cash) for another (the machine). As the machine wears out (or becomes technologically obsolete) in the next five years, however, the company does incur a depreciation cost—the erosion of the value of a valuable asset. But at what rate does this value decrease? Is it spread evenly over five years? Does it occur mostly in the first few years? Accountants deal with this problem by calculating **depreciation** allowances that allocate the cost of the asset to different time periods. While, ideally, accountants would use economic depreciation (the reduction in the machine's value), practical difficulties in applying the concept of economic depreciation have led to the adoption of mechanical calculations of depreciation. For example, the *straight-line* method of depreciation calculation allocates the historical cost of a machine evenly over its useful life. In the example above, the annual depreciation allowance by the straightline method would be ($100,000 − $0)/5 = $20,000. This $20,000 figure implicitly assumes that the machine loses $20,000 of its value each year until it has zero value in five years.

To produce financial statements, many other judgments are required that affect the allocation of revenue and expense to particular time periods. A number of options usually are open with respect to the treatment of depreciation. For example, straight-line depreciation spreads the original cost of an asset evenly over a number of years while accelerated methods of depreciation allocate a larger percentage of the asset's cost to early time periods. Research-and-development (R&D) expenditures generally are expensed as they occur, but in some cases they are treated as an asset and *amortized* (depreciated) over several accounting periods. For example, suppose a company had made total cash outlays of $200,000 on research and development to produce new products. Since the benefits of these outlays will be spread out over future time periods, the company may treat the outlays as creating an asset (that is, they may *capitalize* the outlay as an asset) and subsequently spread the $200,000 out as costs over a number of time periods in the same way depreciation allowances spread the cost of a machine over its useful life. Likewise, the acquisition of patents and goodwill (value that cannot be attributed to any specific tangible asset or assets) may be capitalized and subsequently amortized over several accounting periods. Taxes may be treated one

Depreciation—is the allocation of the cost of an asset to different time periods.

way for reporting to the Internal Revenue Service (IRS) and another for financial reporting to investors. In all these cases, the question is not the total amount involved over the life of a transaction, but the time period to which the receipt or expenditure is to be allocated as revenue or expense.

> **In producing financial statements, numerous judgments are made that affect the allocation of revenue and expense to particular time periods.**

Reflecting Changes in Market Value and Inflation

Other difficulties in measurement arise from changes in market value. If the securities owned by a firm rise in value during a particular period, should the increase be treated as income? In an economic sense, assuming no inflation, the increase does constitute income, and a decline in value would constitute a real economic loss. For accounting purposes, however, such gains and losses usually are not recognized until the securities are sold.

A problem of major proportion in income measurement is the treatment of inflation. Inflation affects the market value of all the firm's assets. During inflationary periods, "profits" are earned on inventories while held by the firm. Fixed assets rise in value. Replacement costs of new fixed assets to maintain the firm's earning power can exceed depreciation allowances, because the depreciation allowances are based on historical cost. When price levels are rising, the use of historical-cost depreciation and the emergence of inventory profits (the gain due to inflation on inventories while held by the firm) overstate earnings. On the other hand, if a firm had debt outstanding, the real value of this debt declines during inflationary periods because the firm will eventually repay the debt in cheaper dollars. Because historical-cost accounting conventions do not recognize this debt effect, the firm's reported earnings will tend to understate its economic income when price levels rise. The net effect of these several forces of overstatement and understatement will depend, of course, on the particular mix of assets and liabilities in the individual balance sheet under consideration. To determine the true change in the firm's net worth during any period under such circumstances is a difficult problem indeed.

> **The treatment of inflation is a major problem in financial accounting.**

While on the subject of income, let us note that income to a corporate firm is not the same as income to the firm's shareholders. Income to shareholders consists of dividends paid on the shares plus capital gains (or losses) that result from changes in the market value of the shares. In theory, in the case of a firm with shares that are publicly traded, the market value of the firm's shares should reflect all elements of value—those not measured directly by traditional financial statements as well as those that are. *Market value of a firm* often deviates substantially from the figure for *book net worth of a firm* (assets minus liabilities) given in a financial statement.

> **Income to a corporate firm is not the same as income to the firm's shareholders.**

To compute market value, all the firm's outstanding shares are valued at the market quotation of the shares on the stock exchange where they are traded. If market value at any point in time is a good estimate of the firm's true value (in other words, if the market value of the stock is an *unbiased estimate*), then the change in market value between two points in time along with changes in dividends paid should represent a good, or unbiased, estimate of the firm's economic income for the period.

OPERATING CASH FLOW

Profit—is the excess of revenues over expenses during a given time period.

Cash flow—is the total change in the firm's cash account, the actual cash flowing into and out of a firm over a particular time period, and is measured as operating cash flow plus all balance sheet changes.

Operating cash flows— are the flows of cash arising from the operation of the firm, normally defined as profit after taxes plus non-cash charges.

A firm must also distinguish between **profit** as reported and **cash flow** in recording information about the firm. Let us first consider **operating cash flow**—cash flow generated by the firm's operations. In most cases, cash flow from operations during any period will exceed profit after tax by the amount of noncash expenses charged during the period—mainly depreciation—but part of the difference between profit and cash flow may also include the amortization of goodwill, patents, or research-and-development expenditures previously capitalized. In the case of Sparta Manufacturing Company, we have only depreciation to consider. As noted above, depreciation is the process of allocating the cost of a long-lived asset to the time periods during which it is used up. Cash changes hands at the time the machine is purchased, but subsequent depreciation charges represent *noncash* expenses. To determine the cash flow generated by a firm's operations during any period, we must adjust the profit figure by *adding back* depreciation. Consider Sparta Manufacturing's profit-and-loss statement for 1986, given in Table 6–5.

Column (1) in Table 6–5 shows the results of profit and loss calculations using accrual accounting. Profit after taxes for Sparta is $33,600. Column (2) enters only cash items. Note that because depreciation is a noncash expense, no depreciation figure is entered in column (2). Doing the arithmetic in column (2), we see that cash flow from operations is $48,600. This cash-flow figure is precisely the amount of the de-

Table 6–5

Profit-and-Loss Statement for Sparta Manufacturing Company, 1986

	Profit and Loss (Accrual) (1)	Cash Flow (Cash Only) (2)
Sales	$1,140,000	$1,140,000
minus Cost of goods sold	− 730,000	− 730,000
minus Depreciation	− 15,000	—
minus Selling, general, and administrative expense	− 340,100	− 340,100
minus Interest	− 12,900	− 12,900
minus Taxes	− 8,400	− 8,400
equals Profit after taxes	$ 33,600	
plus Depreciation	+ 15,000	
equals After tax cash flow from operations	$ 48,600	$ 48,600

preciation expense plus the profit after taxes ($15,000 + $33,600 = $48,600) because depreciation is a noncash item and, hence, is not subtracted in column (2). The last entries in column (1) show that we can also get this cash-flow number ($48,600) by adding the depreciation expense back to profits after taxes.

Adding back depreciation to profit after tax, as is done in column (1), is a handy way to arrive at an approximate measure of cash flow from operations. In some cases—for example, when a capital asset is sold—correctly identifying all the noncash charges can be confusing. We can always arrive at the right answer simply by starting with cash revenues and subtracting all cash expenses (including taxes) required to generate those revenues, as is done in column (2). Because taxes are figured as a percentage of profits, however, the accrual-accounting figures in column (1) are needed to know what taxes will be entered in column (2).

> **To obtain a quick approximate measure of cash flow from operations, one can add back depreciation to profit after tax.**

Profit Versus Cash Flow

Let us examine more closely the distinction between operating cash flow and profit. In principle, the profit figure is intended to measure change in value, albeit imperfectly. The operating-cash-flow figure measures funds generated by the firm's operations and available for expenditure. The funds might be used to expand the investment in fixed assets, to pay dividends, to expand working capital, to retire debt, or for a variety of other purposes.

Taking a long view, however, there are claims against operating cash flow that must be met. To sustain its earning power, the firm must reinvest to replace assets that wear out. Let us suppose that a particular firm reinvests exactly enough to sustain its real earning power—that is, its earning power adjusted for inflation. If we subtract the reinvestment requirement from operating cash flow, the remainder over the long run should approximately equal the firm's earnings. To generate a growing earnings stream (again, in real terms, adjusted for inflation), the firm must reinvest an amount over and above replacement requirements.

Our interpretation of operating cash flow and its uses, thus, depends on our time frame, whether we take a short or long view. In the short run, operating cash flow can be used for any purpose. In the long run, a large part must be earmarked for reinvestment if the cash flow itself is to be sustained.

Sample Problem 6–1   Operating Cash Flow and Profit for Montana Lumber

Montana Lumber Company raises timber and manufactures lumber products and furniture components. Projected 1987 sales are $530 million, with cost of goods sold 76 percent of sales. Selling, administrative, and research expenses should reach $50 million. Montana Lumber pays 8.5 percent interest on $5 million worth of long-term debt. Annual depreciation on fixed assets is $8 million. The 1986 balance sheet reflected a $530 million balance in the lumber and timber account. It is expected that 4 percent of this balance will be depleted in 1987. The company pays 46 percent corporate income taxes. What amount of funds generated by Montana Lumber's operations should management consider to be available for expenditure? (*Note: Depletion* of timber is a noncash charge analogous to depreciation of machinery or other fixed assets.)

Solution

This problem illustrates the difference between operating cash flow and accounting profit. After arranging the given revenue and expense information into profit-and-loss-statement format, those figures that represent cash items are combined to find the operating cash flow. Depreciation and depletion are noncash expenses. We can arrive at the cash-flow figure in two ways: by adding noncash expenses to the profit-after-tax figure, as in column (1) of Table 6–6, or by starting with cash revenues and subtracting all cash expenses required to generate those revenues, as in column (2). As Table 6–6 shows, the cash flow from operations is $54,890 as calculated in either column (1) or column (2). ∃ꟾꟾᖴ

Total Cash Flow Versus Operating Cash Flow

The source-and-use-of-funds statement—is a summary of the flow of the financial activity of the firm, as recorded in the income statement and the balance sheet, that shows where a firm obtains cash and how it uses it.

The firm's total cash flow—the total change in the firm's cash account—during a period, as distinct from operating cash flow, is affected by balance-sheet changes. Let us examine the balance-sheet data for Sparta Manufacturing Company for two successive years, as given in Table 6–7. In Table 6–5, we calculated Sparta's cash flow from *operations* during 1986 as $48,600. Yet Table 6–7 shows that the cash balance *declined* by $7,500, from $10,000 in 1985 to $2,500 in 1986. The difference arises from the fact that cash flow from operations is only part of the picture. The firm's cash balance is affected by other changes taking place in the balance sheet. To see all of these changes we need to examine the **source-and-use-of-funds statement**, the third major type of financial statement.

Table 6–6
Profit-and-Loss Statement for Montana Lumber Company

	Profit and Loss (thousands of dollars) (1)	Cash Flow (thousands of dollars) (2)
Sales	530,000	530,000
minus Cost of goods sold	− 402,800	− 402,800
equals Gross profit	127,200	127,200
minus Expenses		
Selling, administrative, research	− 50,000	− 50,000
Interest	− 425	− 425
Depreciation	− 8,000	—
Depletion	− 21,200	—
equals Pretax profit	47,575	
minus Taxes (46 percent)	− 21,885	− 21,885
equals Profit after tax	25,690	
plus Noncash expense	+ 29,200	
equals After-tax cash flow from operations	54,890	54,890

Table 6—7

Sparta Manufacturing Company Year-End Balance Sheets, 1985 and 1986

	December 31, 1985	*December 31, 1986*
Cash	$ 10,000	$ 2,500
Accounts receivable	147,500	152,500
Inventories	410,000	420,000
Total current assets	$567,500	$575,000
Fixed assets, net of depreciation	55,000	112,500
Other assets	15,000	35,000
Total assets	$637,500	$722,500
Notes payable (bank)	$ 88,100	$144,100
Accounts payable	117,500	122,500
Taxes payable	7,600	7,500
Miscellaneous accruals	57,500	50,000
Total current liabilities	$270,700	$324,100
Mortgage payable	28,000	26,000
Total liabilities	$298,700	$350,100
Common stock	155,000	155,000
Retained earnings	183,800	217,400
Total liabilities and net worth	$637,500	$722,500

SOURCES AND USES OF FUNDS

To produce goods and services, firms acquire assets and put these assets to work productively. Assets are paid for initially by using capital funds provided by owners or by issuing liabilities (such as bonds) in exchange for cash and then using the cash to acquire assets. As the goods and services produced by the firm are sold, more assets are acquired, and a cycle is established. We can view the cyclical flow of cash in the simplified terms illustrated in Figure 6–1. A useful first step in analyzing a firm's performance often is to use the the income statement and balance sheet to prepare a source-and-use-of-funds statement. Here, we are defining *funds* to mean cash, although the term is not always so defined.[3] Through source-and-use-of-funds analysis, we can determine over any period of time where a firm obtained its funds and what it did with them—in other words, what has been going on financially in a firm.

Balance-Sheet Changes

Source-and-use analysis begins with an analysis of balance-sheet changes over the period of time in which we are interested. Tables 6–8 and 6–9 present six years of Sparta's financial history as captured by its income statements and balance sheets. Using balance-sheet data from Table 6–9, we can prepare a statement of balance-sheet

---

[3]An alternative is to define *funds* as working capital. Our purposes here are better served by defining funds as cash.

Figure 6—1
The Flow of Cash from a Firm

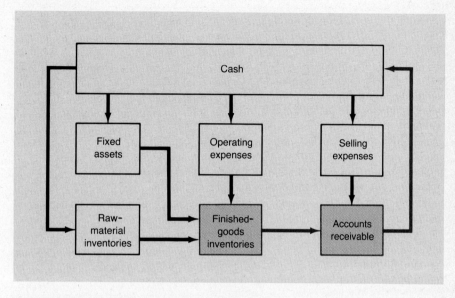

changes for the Sparta Manufacturing Company over the period of December 31, 1981, to December 31, 1986, as in Table 6–10.

Table 6—8
Sparta Manufacturing Company Income Statements, 1981–1986

	1981	1982	1983	1984	1985	1986
Sales	$515,000	$557,500	$647,500	$930,000	$990,000	$1,140,000
Cost of goods sold	335,000	355,000	387,500	592,500	622,500	730,000
Material	167,500	177,500	192,500	300,000	317,500	375,000
Labor	77,500	80,000	90,000	147,500	157,500	205,000
Overhead	90,000	97,500	105,000	145,000	147,500	150,000
Gross profit	$180,000	$202,500	$260,000	$337,500	$367,500	$410,000
Depreciation	7,500	5,000	5,000	5,000	10,000	15,000
Selling, general, and administrative expense	149,400	181,100	190,600	282,400	307,900	340,100
Operating profit before taxes	$ 23,100	$ 16,400	$ 64,400	$ 50,100	$ 49,600	$ 54,900
Interest	8,100	3,900	4,400	5,100	9,600	12,900
Net profit before taxes	$ 15,000	$ 12,500	$ 60,000	$ 45,000	$ 40,000	$ 42,000
Taxes	3,000	2,500	12,000	9,000	8,000	8,400
Profit after taxes	$ 12,000	$ 10,000	$ 48,000	$ 36,000	$ 32,000	$ 33,600

Note: Taxes are computed at a tax rate of 20 percent.

Table 6—9

Sparta Manufacturing Company Year-End Balance Sheets, 1981–1986

	1981	1982	1983	1984	1985	1986
Assets						
Cash	$ 1,000	$ 1,000	$ 2,500	$ 12,500	$ 10,000	$ 2,500
Accounts receivable	125,000	90,000	95,000	107,500	147,500	152,500
Inventory	187,500	180,000	250,000	325,000	410,000	420,000
Total current assets	$313,500	$271,000	$347,500	$445,000	$567,500	$575,000
Fixed assets, net of depreciation	55,000	50,000	45,000	52,500	55,000	112,500
Other assets	17,500	15,000	15,000	17,500	15,000	35,000
Total assets	$386,000	$336,000	$407,500	$515,000	$637,500	$722,500
Liabilities and net worth						
Notes payable (bank)	$ 66,200	$ 16,400	$ 28,200	$ 34,700	$ 88,100	$144,100
Accounts payable (trade)	52,500	42,500	42,500	110,000	117,500	122,500
Taxes payable	3,500	2,800	14,000	8,500	7,600	7,500
Miscellaneous accruals	15,000	17,500	20,000	25,000	57,500	50,000
Total current liabilities	$137,200	$ 79,200	$104,700	$178,200	$270,700	$324,100
Mortgage payable	36,000	34,000	32,000	30,000	28,000	26,000
Total liabilities	$173,200	$113,200	$136,700	$208,200	$298,700	$350,100
Common stock	155,000	155,000	155,000	155,000	155,000	155,000
Retained earnings	57,800	67,800	115,800	151,800	183,800	217,400
Total liabilities and net worth	$386,000	$336,000	$407,500	$515,000	$637,500	$722,500

The Source-and-Use-of-Funds Statement

Table 6–10 can be reorganized into a statement of the sources and uses of Sparta's funds. In addition to acquisition of assets, funds may be used to reduce liabilities. Sources of funds include reductions in assets as well as increases in liabilities. **Sources of funds** can be defined as

1. increases in liabilities (for example, through additional bank borrowing or an increase in accounts payable);
2. increases in net worth achieved through retained earnings or additional capital contributions by owners;
3. reductions in assets (for example, through the liquidation of inventory or the sale of plant).

Uses of funds can be defined as

1. reductions in liabilities (for example, the payment of debt);
2. reductions in net worth achieved through the payment of dividends, the retirement of stock, or operating losses (the latter can also be viewed as a negative source);
3. increases in assets (for example, the purchase of fixed assets, the extension of more credit to customers, or expansion of inventories).

Reorganizing the changes in the balance sheet into this format gives us the source-

Table 6–10

Sparta Manufacturing Company Balance Sheet Changes, December 31, 1981–December 31, 1986

	1981	1986	Change
Assets			
Cash	$ 1,000	$ 2,500	+ $ 1,500
Accounts receivable	125,000	152,500	+ 27,500
Inventory	187,500	420,000	+ 232,500
Total current assets	$313,500	$575,000	+ $261,500
Fixed assets, net of depreciation	55,000	112,500	+ 57,500
Other assets	17,500	35,000	+ 17,500
Total assets	$386,000	$722,500	+ $336,500
Liabilities and net worth			
Notes payable (bank)	$ 66,200	$144,100	+ $ 77,900
Accounts payable (trade)	52,500	122,500	+ 70,000
Tax payable	3,500	7,500	+ 4,000
Miscellaneous accruals	15,000	50,000	+ 35,000
Total current liabilities	$137,200	$324,100	+ $186,900
Mortgage payable	36,000	26,000	− 10,000
Total liabilities	$173,200	$350,100	+ $176,900
Common stock	155,000	155,000	—
Retained earnings	57,800	217,400	+ 159,600
Total liabilities and net worth	$386,000	$722,500	+ $336,500

Sources of funds—are (1) increases in liabilities, (2) increases in net worth through retained earnings or additional capital contributions by owners, and (3) reductions in assets.

Uses of funds—are (1) reductions in liabilities, (2) reductions in net worth through the payment of dividends, retirement of stock, or operating losses, and (3) increases in assets.

and-use-of-funds statement of Table 6–11. In Table 6–11, cash is treated as the residual item. Since Sparta's sources exceed its uses, the statement shows an increase in cash. As an alternative to this format, we could interpret the change in cash as a use or a source, depending on whether it increases or decreases—in which case, total uses would equal total sources. In Sparta's case, the increase in cash would then be classified as a $1,500 use (increase in assets) of funds.

In Table 6–11, all of Sparta's asset accounts increased over the period 1981-1986, so all of these changes represented *uses* of funds. This was not the case for the year 1982, viewed individually, as we can see by constructing a source-and-use statement for the period December 31, 1981, to December 31, 1982.

Table 6–12 shows that changes in accounts receivable, inventories, and fixed assets during 1982 represented *sources* of funds rather than uses as in Table 6–11. When an asset account increases, it uses funds; when it decreases, it releases, or *provides,* funds and, hence, becomes a source.

Similarly, when a liability account increases, it provides funds (acts as a source), as does the accounts-payable category in Table 6–11. But in Table 6–12, accounts payable is a *use* of funds because $10,000 in funds had to be used to reduce the amount owed to trade creditors. Likewise, bank debt was reduced by $49,800 (a use), and the mortgage was reduced by $2,000 (another use). When a liability account increases, it provides funds (it is a source); when it decreases, funds are required to make the reduction (the account is a use).

Table 6—11

Sparta Manufacturing Company Source-and-Use-of-Funds
Statement, December 31, 1981–December 31, 1986

Sources	
Bank borrowing	$ 77,900
Increase in accounts payable	70,000
Increase in taxes payable	4,000
Increase in miscellaneous accruals	35,000
Retained earnings	159,600
Total sources	**$346,500**

Uses	
Increase in accounts receivable	$ 27,500
Increase in inventories	232,500
Net increase in fixed assets	57,500
Increase in other assets	17,500
Reduction in mortgage	10,000
Total uses	**$345,000**

Increase in cash	$ 1,500

Table 6—12

Sparta Manufacturing Company Source-and-Use-of-Funds
Statement, December 31, 1981–December 31, 1982

Sources	
Reduction in accounts receivable	$35,000
Reduction in inventory	7,500
Reduction in fixed assets	5,000
Reduction in other assets	2,500
Increase in miscellaneous accruals	2,500
Retained earnings	10,000
Total sources	**$62,500**

Uses	
Reduction in bank borrowing	$49,800
Reduction in accounts payable	10,000
Reduction in mortgage	2,000
Reduction in taxes payable	700
Total uses	**$62,500**

Change in cash balance	$ 0

Table 6—13

Alamance Corporation's Balance Sheet, Year-End 1985 and Year-End 1986 (thousands of dollars)

	December 31, 1985	December 31, 1986
Assets		
Cash	435	239
Marketable securities	648	378
Accounts receivable	1,079	1,459
Inventory	3,593	4,253
Other current assets	435	525
Total current assets	6,190	6,854
Net fixed assets	6,765	7,336
Total assets	**12,955**	**14,190**
Liabilities		
Accounts payable (trade)	3,537	3,932
Taxes payable	340	189
Other current liabilities	1,200	1,220
Total current liabilities	5,077	5,341
Long-term debt	3,012	3,000
Preferred stock	900	800
Common stock	1,500	1,700
Retained earnings	2,466	3,349
Total liabilities and owners' equity	**12,955**	**14,190**

Sample Problem 6–2   Alamance Corporation's Sources and Uses of Funds

Alamance Corporation's balance sheet for the period from December 31, 1985, to December 31, 1986, is given in Table 6–13.

A. Compute the balance-sheet changes for Alamance Corporation from year-end 1985 to year-end 1986.
B. List the various sources and uses of funds for 1986.
C. Construct a source-and-use-of-funds statement similar to the one in Table 6–11.

Solution

A. The balance-sheet changes are given in Table 6–14.
B. The various sources and uses of funds are listed in Table 6–15.
C. The source-and-use-of-funds statement is given as Table 6–16.

Table 6–14
Balance-Sheet Changes for Alamance Corporation (thousands of dollars)

Assets	Change	Liabilities	Change
Cash	− 196	Accounts payable	+ 395
Marketable securities	− 270	Taxes payable	− 151
Accounts receivable	+ 380	Other current liabilities	+ 20
Inventory	+ 660	Long-term debt	− 12
Other current assets	+ 90	Preferred stock	− 100
Fixed assets	+ 571	Common stock	+ 200
		Retained earnings	+ 883
Total assets	+1,235	**Total liabilities and net worth**	+1,235

Table 6–15
Alamance Corporation's Sources and Uses of Funds

Sources	Uses
Changes in liabilities	Changes in liabilities
Increase in accounts payable	Decrease in taxes payable
Increase in other current liabilities	Decrease in long-term debt
Changes in assets	Changes in assets
Decrease in cash	Increase in accounts receivable
Decrease in marketable securities	Increase in inventory
	Increase in other current assets
	Increase in fixed assets
Changes in net worth	Changes in net worth
Increase in common stock	Decrease in preferred stock
Increase in retained earnings	

Table 6–16
Source-and-Use-of-Funds Statement for Alamance Corporation (thousands of dollars)

Sources	
Increase in accounts payable	395
Increase in other current liabilities	20
Decrease in marketable securities	270
Increase in common stock	200
Increase in retained earnings	883
Total sources	1,768
Uses	
Decrease in taxes payable	151
Decrease in long-term debt	12
Increase in accounts receivable	380
Increase in inventory	660
Increase in other current assets	90
Increase in fixed assets	571
Decrease in preferred stock	100
Total uses	1,964
Decrease in cash	196

As Tables 6–14 to 6–16 show, in 1986 Alamance Corporation had total sources of funds of $1,768,000 and total uses of funds of $1,964,000. Because uses exceeded sources, Alamance experienced a decrease in cash of $196,000. ▪▥▦

Interpreting the Source-and-Use-of-Funds Statement

What do we learn from the source-and-use analysis? Let us again examine the data in Table 6–11 for Sparta Manufacturing for the entire period 1981–1986. First, we see that the largest use of funds by far was to expand inventories. Was the increase due to growth of the firm, or are inventories being managed ineffectively? We cannot tell from the data in Table 6–11, but we can put inventory management on our list for further investigation. We see also that that increase in cash was quite small relative to other asset categories. Has the firm's ability to come up with cash (liquidity) declined? If so, that decline could be dangerous if the firm faces unexpected costs—another question for our list. With respect to sources, we see retained earnings providing the largest single source, with bank borrowing and accounts payable also providing large amounts. Has Sparta Manufacturing Company borrowed too heavily? Is trade credit being used to the point that relations with suppliers might be damaged? More questions for our list. Techniques for answering some of these questions will be developed in the next chapter.

We can see that the source-and-use statement provides valuable insights into the firm's operations. In addition to the questions raised above, we can examine the expansion of accounts receivable and fixed assets, the mix of internal versus external financing, and the mix of short-term versus long-term financing relative to the kinds of assets being financed. If, for example, we were to find a large expansion in fixed assets financed primarily by short-term sources of funds, we would want to investigate further. Perhaps the company will have trouble paying off short-term debt before the expansion becomes profitable. The source-and-use statement, thus, provides valuable information. Information about how a company has raised and used its funds in the past is extremely useful in trying to make "good" decisions in the present. Should a bank loan officer lend money to a company? Should a company be interested in buying another company in a merger? The source-and-use statement presents information in concise, accessible form that can be useful in answering such questions.

The source-and-use analysis should be performed over that particular time period in which we are interested. It may be any length, from a month or even a shorter period up to several years. The relevant period may be defined by events in the life of the firm, such as a period of growth or a period of decline. Sometimes it is useful to break the time period into two or more smaller periods to determine whether there were significant differences in fund flows. In addition to being useful for analyzing historical performance, source-and-use analysis may be useful in connection with planning for the future. (Chapter 8 will discuss financial planning.)

Some Refinements

Some refinements of the source-and-use statement are often desirable under certain conditions. The payment of dividends, for example, is sometimes an important use of funds that we would not detect by examining only the changes in the retained-earnings account on the balance sheet. If we cannot obtain data on dividend payments directly, we may be able to draw some inferences from the income-statement and balance-sheet data we have available. We know that the transfer to retained earnings each year, in the absence of other complicating transactions, will equal profit after taxes for the year minus dividends paid. If we examine the change in the retained-earnings account for Sparta Manufacturing Company from December 31, 1981, to December 31, 1982, we find it to be $10,000—exactly the amount of profit after taxes in 1982. Thus, we infer that Sparta paid no dividends in 1982. Repeating this analysis over the remaining years indicates that no dividends were paid over the period 1981-1986.

We also may wish to look further into the fixed-asset account. In our balance sheet for Sparta, fixed assets are measured after depreciation. Our source-and-use statement, thus, gives the expenditures on fixed assets, *net* of depreciation over the period. We know from the income statements in Table 6–8 that depreciation charges during 1982–1986 totaled $40,000. Thus, we can infer that Sparta's total expenditures for fixed assets from December 31, 1981, to December 31, 1986, were $97,500, rather than $57,500, as indicated by the net figure in Table 6–11.

Let us now revise our source-and-use statement to take into account the refinement just discussed. Under the heading of *Sources,* we will list *Funds from operations* rather than *Increase in retained earnings*. Funds from operations is equal to profit after taxes plus depreciation for the period. Under the heading of *Uses,* we will list *Gross* (rather

Finance in Practice 6—1

Credit Ratings

A number of organizations rate the credit worthiness of firms or governments that want to borrow money. For example, Standard and Poors Corporation rates corporate and municipal bonds in various categories ranging from Aaa (the rating given bond-issuing organizations whose capacity to pay interest and repay principal is extremely strong) to D (the rating given to bond-issuing organizations whose debt is in default and whose payment of interest

and/or repayment of principal is in arrears). Such ratings, according to Standard and Poors, "help investors by providing an easily recognizable, simple tool that couples a possibly unknown issuer with an informative and meaningful symbol of credit quality." These ratings are of particular importance to financial managers because the better the ratings (Aaa being the best), the lower the interest rate charged on borrowing.

How do credit-rating agencies determine their ratings? According to Standard & Poors, "a funds statement provides information which is of central importance in credit analysis . . . examination of sources and uses of

cash is basic to an evaluation. Such examination aids in identifying the financial nature of an enterprise (fixed versus working capital intensive), in evaluating historical financial performance, and in projecting future financial direction."

While Standard & Poors uses many other ways to develop information, a source-and-use-of-funds statement is clearly one important tool. Chapter 12 will mention credit ratings again in discussing characteristics of debt used by corporations.

Source: Standard and Poors Corporation, *Credit Overview: Corporate and International Ratings.*

---

than *Net*) *increase in fixed assets,* expenditures and dividends (even though Sparta paid no dividends). The result is shown in Table 6–17.

In addition to taking into account dividends and expenditures for fixed assets, other refinements sometimes may be appropriate, such as the sale of stock, sales of fixed assets, and payment of stock dividends.[4]

Where longer-term changes in the balance-sheet account, rather than changes in current assets and liabilities, are of primary importance, we can prepare a statement of sources and uses of *working capital,* defined earlier. Net working capital is equal to current assets *less* current liabilities. By the same token, *changes* in net working capital (or sources and uses of net working capital) are obtained by adding *changes* in the current-asset accounts and subtracting *changes* in the current-liability accounts. In Table 6–17, we can see that current assets increased by $261,500, which is the sum of the $1,500 cash increase, the $27,500 change in accounts receivable, and the $232,500 change in inventories. Over the same period, current liabilities increased by $184,480, which is the sum of the $77,900 change in bank borrowing, the $70,000 change in accounts payable, the $4,000 change in taxes payable, and the $35,000 change in miscellaneous accruals. Thus, net working capital increased by $261,500 *less* $186,900, or by $74,600.

We can, therefore, recast the data in Table 6–17 according to the format shown in Table 6–18. Table 6–18 simply records in net form the working-capital elements

---

[4]For a discussion of these and other refinements of the source-and-use statement, see Erich A. Helfert, *Techniques of Financial Analysis,* 4th ed. (Homewood, Ill.: Richard D. Irwin, 1977). Dividends are typically cash payments to shareholders. Stock dividends, in contrast, are distributions of additional shares of stock (not cash) to the existing shareholders. Cash and stock dividends are discussed in Chapter 15.

Table 6–17

Sparta Manufacturing Company Revised Source-and-Use Statement, December 31, 1981–
December 31, 1986

Sources		
Bank borrowing		$ 77,900
Increase accounts payable		70,000
Increase taxes payable		4,000
Increase miscellaneous accruals		35,000
Funds from operations		
Profit after taxes	$159,600	
Depreciation	40,000	199,600
Total sources		$386,500
Uses		
Increase in accounts receivable		$ 27,500
Increase in inventories		232,500
Gross increase in fixed assets		97,500
Increase in other assets		17,500
Reduction in mortgage		10,000
Dividends		0
Total uses		$385,000
Increase in cash		$ 1,500

Table 6–18

Sparta Manufacturing Company's Sources and Uses of Working Capital, December 31, 1981–
December 31, 1986

Sources of working capital	
Funds from operations	$199,600
Uses of working capital	
Gross increase in fixed assets	97,500
Increase in other assets	17,500
Reduction in mortgage	10,000
Dividends	0
Total uses	$125,000
Increase in net working capital	$ 74,600

shown in detail in Table 6–17. All current-asset and current-liability items are combined into the single net figure of $74,600 shown at the bottom of Table 6–18.

In addition to giving a financial picture of a firm's activities, source-and-use analysis identifies potential trouble spots that may need further investigation. Source-and-use analysis, thus, is an important tool in developing information to be used in financial decisions. The next chapter now turns to an exploration of techniques for analyzing financial performance.

KEY CONCEPTS

1. Financial statements are the basic raw material of financial analysis.
2. *Net working capital* is the difference between current assets and current liabilities.
3. Operating cash flow is the total cash generated by the firm's operations, or the sum of profit after tax and depreciation.
4. The total cash flow of a firm during any period can be determined as operating cash flow plus the effects of balance-sheet changes.
5. A source-and-use-of-funds statement shows where a firm's money came from and where it went. It provides a useful framework for learning about a company's activity and is a good beginning point for financial analysis.

SUMMARY

The firm's financial statements provide a starting point for developing information about a company. The income statement presents a record of events between two points in time, while the balance sheet presents a "snapshot" of the firm's position at a particular point in time. The source-and-use-of-funds statement shows where the firm obtained and used its money.

A basic concern of accounting is measurement. Measurement of income requires allocation of receipts and expenditures to particular time periods. Recognition of income and expense often involves arbitrary judgments. Inflation greatly complicates the measurement problem. For these and other reasons, accounting income often is an imperfect measure of economic income.

An important distinction in financial analysis is that between profit and cash flow. Operating cash flow is cash revenues less cash expenses. A shorthand way of calculating operating cash flow is by adding depreciation back to after-tax profits. Total cash flow during any period includes balance-sheet changes in addition to operating cash flow.

The source-and-use statement shows patterns in total cash flow and gives a good picture of what has been going on financially in a firm. It is therefore a good beginning point for financial analysis.

QUESTIONS

1. What is the general rule for determining whether an accounting transaction appears in the income statement as opposed to the balance sheet?
2. What is the difference between an *expenditure* and an *expense?* What is the difference between a *receipt* and *revenue?*
3. Define *working capital, net working capital,* and *net operating capital.*
4. Contrast *profit* and *operating cash flow.*
5. In terms of balance-sheet changes, what are the principal sources of funds to a firm? What are the principal uses of funds?

PROBLEMS

1. Calculate the amount of working capital, the amount of net working capital, and the amount of net operating capital for the Acme Manufacturing Corporation for each of the four years given the data in the income statement and balance sheet shown in Tables A and B.
2. Acme's sales are expected to increase by 15 percent in year 5 over year 4. Assuming that the relationship between net operating capital and sales remains the same in year 5 as in year 4, how much additional net operating capital will Acme require in year 5?

Table A

	Year 1 (thousands of dollars)	Year 2 (thousands of dollars)	Year 3 (thousands of dollars)	Year 4 (thousands of dollars)
Sales	48,200	60,600	72,500	81,400
Cost of goods sold	35,600	46,000	56,200	63,100
Gross profit	12,600	14,600	16,300	18,300
Depreciation	2,200	2,400	2,400	2,900
Amortization of goodwill*	200	200	200	200
Selling, general, and administrative expense	4,100	5,500	7,100	7,700
Income from operations	6,100	6,500	6,600	7,500
Interest	1,525	1,650	1,530	1,686
Profit before taxes	4,575	4,850	5,070	5,814
Taxes	2,100	2,200	2,400	2,700
Profit after taxes	2,475	2,650	2,670	3,114

*Amortization of goodwill is not deducted in computing taxes.

Table B

	Year End as of December 31 (thousands of dollars)			
	1	2	3	4
Cash	1,900	2,800	4,600	2,700
Accounts receivable	7,900	9,600	11,400	13,600
Inventory	5,000	6,600	7,200	8,900
Other	1,000	1,100	1,100	1,200
Current assets	15,800	20,100	24,300	26,400
Plant and equipment	42,000	45,500	45,500	54,500
Less: Accumulated depreciation	12,900	15,300	17,700	20,000
Net fixed assets	29,100	30,200	27,800	34,500
Goodwill	6,600	6,400	6,200	6,000
Total assets	51,500	56,700	58,300	66,900
Notes payable	5,550	5,700	4,500	5,600
Accounts payable	6,500	6,300	7,400	8,900
Accruals	2,600	2,900	3,000	3,200
Tax payable	900	1,200	1,000	1,800
Current liabilities	15,550	16,100	15,900	19,500
Senior debentures*	7,000	9,000	9,000	9,000
Subordinated debentures	7,000	7,000	7,000	8,000
Common stock ($5 par)	7,000	7,000	7,000	8,000
Capital surplus	3,500	3,500	3,500	4,500
Retained earnings	11,450	14,100	15,900	17,900
Total liabilities and net worth	51,500	56,700	58,300	66,900

*Debentures are a type of bond issued by many corporations and are discussed in Chapter 12.

3. Calculate the after-tax cash flow from operations for Acme for each of the four years. Use both the long method of subtracting all cash expenses from revenues and the shortcut method of adding back noncash expenses to profit after tax.

4. Consider the balance sheet data for the Grainger Company for year-end 1985 and 1986 shown in Table C.

    a. Compute working capital, net working capital and net operating capital for 1985 and 1986.

    b. Suppose you are told that profit after taxes for the Grainger Company was $38,000 in 1986. How much was paid out as dividends in that year?

    c. Suppose you are told that profit after taxes in 1985 was $27,000 and that $8,000 in dividends were paid in that year. What were the company's retained earnings in 1984?

d. Prepare a sources-and-uses-of-funds statement for the Grainger Company for 1986.

e. Prepare a statement of sources and uses of working capital for the Grainger Company for 1986.

f. Summarize in a few sentences what you have learned about Grainger's operations.

5. In Table D are year-end balance sheet data for Fuelish Motors, Inc. Arrange the data in a sources-and-uses format like that used in Table 6–11.

6. A balance sheet for the Downtown Hardware Company is given in Table E.

    a. Prepare a statement of balance sheet changes.

    b. Organize the results of Part (a) into a sources-and-uses format like that used in Table 6–11.

    c. What further analysis does the sources-and-uses statement suggest?

Table C

	1985	1986
Cash	$ 15,000	$ 7,000
Marketable securities	11,000	0
Accounts receivable	22,000	30,000
Inventories	53,000	75,000
Total current assets	$101,000	$112,000
Gross fixed assets	$ 75,000	$150,000
Less depreciation	26,000	41,000
Net fixed assets	$ 49,000	$109,000
Total assets	$150,000	$221,000
Accounts payable	$ 15,000	$ 18,000
Notes payable	15,000	3,000
Taxes payable	7,000	15,000
Total current liabilities	$ 37,000	$ 36,000
Long-term debt	8,000	26,000
Common stock	38,000	64,000
Retained earnings	67,000	95,000
Total liabilities and net worth	$150,000	$221,000

Table D

	1985	1986	Change
Assets			
Cash	$ 434,400	$ 234,200	− $ 200,200
Marketable securities	647,800	371,700	− 276,100
Accounts receivable	1,078,800	1,457,100	+ 378,300
Inventory	3,592,700	4,253,000	+ 660,300
Other current assets	435,800	525,200	+ 89,400
Total current assets	$ 6,189,500	$ 6,841,200	+ $ 651,700
Net buildings and equipment	5,192,700	5,684,000	+ 491,300
Other assets	1,571,800	1,648,400	+ 76,600
Total assets	$12,954,000	$14,173,600	+ $1,219,600
Liabilities			
Accounts payable	$ 3,537,100	$ 3,932,300	+ $ 395,200
Taxes payable	340,100	189,300	− 150,800
Other current liabilities	651,800	1,219,300	+ 567,500
Total current liabilities	$ 4,529,000	$ 5,340,900	+ $ 811,900
Accrued liabilities	921,300	1,087,500	+ 166,200
Deferred income tax	121,600	27,200	− 94,400
Long-term debt	977,000	1,476,700	+ 499,700
Total liabilities	$ 6,548,900	$ 7,932,300	+ $1,383,400
Owners' equity			
Common stock	$ 628,500	$ 595,900	− $ 32,600
Retained earnings	5,776,600	5,645,400	− 131,200
Liabilities and owners' equity	$12,954,000	$14,173,600	+ $1,219,600

Table E

	December 31, 1985	December 31, 1986
Cash	$ 60	$ 1,420
Accounts receivable	60,290	118,826
Inventory	92,305	233,568
Total current assets	$152,655	$353,814
Net fixed assets	6,500	10,560
Total assets	$159,155	$364,374
Notes payable	$ 30,000	$ 51,000
Accounts payable	52,640	215,685
Accrued expense	1,500	2,110
Total current liabilities	$ 84,140	$268,795
Net worth	75,015	95,579
Total liabilities and net worth	$159,155	$364,374

Table F

	December 31, 1985		December 31, 1986	
Cash		$ 10,850		$ 431
Accounts receivable		41,614		68,313
Inventory		82,892		80,710
Miscellaneous current assets		7,681		6,413
Total current assets		$143,037		$155,867
Land		42,000		42,000
Plant and equipment	$217,575		$231,820	
Less depreciation	−36,816	180,759	−42,015	189,805
Total assets		$365,796		$387,672
Accounts payable		$ 52,218		$ 50,946
Taxes payable		18,416		22,840
Accrued expenses		15,823		13,908
Total current liabilities		$ 86,457		$ 87,694
Mortgage payable		110,000		103,500
Paid-in capital		95,000		105,000
Retained earnings		74,339		91,478
Total liabilities and net worth		$365,796		$387,672

7. A balance sheet for the Madison Company is shown in Table F. Prepare a sources-and-uses statement for the Madison Company for the year 1986. Interpret the result.

8. Prepare a sources-and-uses statement for Sparta Manufacturing Company for the year 1986 using data in Table 6–9.

9. Assume that Acme Manufacturing Corporation, referred to in problem (1), retired assets during year 4 that originally cost the company $600,000 and were carried at a zero book value. No new goodwill has been entered on the books since year 0.

a. Prepare sources-and-uses-of-funds statements for Acme for each of the three years 2–4.

b. Prepare a single sources-and-uses-of-funds statement for the entire 3-year period.

c. What areas of additional investigation are suggested by these sources-and-uses-of-funds statements?

10. Using the information given in Problem 9, prepare sources-and-uses-of-working-capital statements for Acme for each of the years 2–4. Prepare a single sources-and-uses-of-working-capital statement for the entire 3-year period.

REFERENCES

Helfert, E. A. *Techniques of Financial Analysis*. 4th ed. Homewood, Ill.: Richard D. Irwin, 1977.

Jaedicke, R. K. and R. T. Sprouse. *Accounting Flows: Income, Funds, and Cash*. Englewood Cliffs, N.J.: Prentice-Hall, 1965.

Chapter

7

Analyzing Financial Performance

This chapter develops the basic tools for evaluating the financial condition of a company and for measuring its performance, past and future. The chapter explains how to measure profitability, return on investment, activity rates and turnover, liquidity, and indebtedness. We will look at some of the key measures used by investors in the stock market. We also will explore relationships between costs, volume, and profits, and learn how to calculate break-even points. The tools developed in this chapter will be used throughout the remainder of the book and have many applications in practice.

Financial analysis is never a simple task. In order to understand fully a company, either from the outside or the inside, it is necessary to go through the investigations of a financial detective. The clues include various financial ratios for a company—at least 20 of them and in some cases more. The ratios are compared with the company's own past and also against those of other companies in the same or similar industries.

THE REQUIREMENTS OF FINANCIAL ANALYSIS

Like any dissection of data, the purpose of financial analysis is to develop an underlying understanding of what is going on. Students frequently wonder if this effort is really necessary. Later, when they serve as security analysts, commercial-bank loan officers, hospital administrators, investment-banking executives, or assistants to corporate management, they invariably find that the effort is not only worthwhile but is essential.

Although the analysis of past events cannot, in itself, provide an accurate forecast of the future, it can provide a warning about difficulties that might lie ahead. The bankruptcy of the Penn Central Railroad and of W. T. Grant and Company, as well as Chrysler Corporation's financial problems, were all foreshadowed by trends in their balance sheets and income statements.

For decision makers—whether managers, investors, or creditors—the future usually is of more interest than the past. However, analysis of the future often begins with analysis of the past to uncover trends. The question then becomes: Will the trends continue? This chapter focuses on history. The next chapter will look ahead and develop a financial plan. The performance-measurement techniques developed here can be applied to a forward-looking financial plan as well as to historical data.

Table 7–1

Sparta Manufacturing Company Income Statements, 1981–1986

	1981	1982	1983	1984	1985	1986
Sales	$515,000	$557,500	$647,500	$930,000	$990,000	$1,140,000
Cost of goods sold	$335,000	$355,000	$387,500	$592,500	$622,500	$ 730,000
Material	167,500	177,500	192,500	300,000	317,500	375,000
Labor	77,500	80,000	90,000	147,500	157,500	205,000
Overhead	90,000	97,500	105,000	145,000	147,500	150,000
Gross profit	$180,000	$202,500	$260,000	$337,500	$367,500	$ 410,000
Depreciation	7,500	5,000	5,000	5,000	10,000	15,000
Selling, general, and administrative expense	149,400	181,100	190,600	282,400	307,900	340,100
Operating profit before taxes	$ 23,100	$ 16,400	$ 64,400	$ 50,100	$ 49,600	$ 54,900
Interest	8,100	3,900	4,400	5,100	9,600	12,900
Net profit before taxes	$ 15,000	$ 12,500	$ 60,000	$ 45,000	$ 40,000	$ 42,000
Taxes	3,000	2,500	12,000	9,000	8,000	8,400
Profit after taxes	$ 12,000	$ 10,000	$ 48,000	$ 36,000	$ 32,000	$ 33,600

Note: Taxes are computed at a tax rate of 20 percent.

FINANCIAL STATEMENTS AND RATIO ANALYSIS

The starting points for analyzing financial performance are the basic financial statements of the firm: the income statement, the balance sheet, and the source-and-use-of-funds statement.

Chapter 6 showed how the source-and-use-of-funds statement revealed important information about Sparta Manufacturing's activities in past years. This statement is one of the tools needed by a financial manager.

We need not stop with the basic forms of the financial statements because we can often repackage the information to reveal new and important features about a company's past—features that may improve our ability to evaluate its future. One of the primary ways of repacking the information is to use **ratio analysis.** *Ratios* simply measure one variable relative to another. For example, to know whether a company is highly profitable, a financial manager needs to look not just at the dollar amount of its profits but at its dollar profits relative to the assets used in the business. This ratio (profits divided by assets) shows how profitable the company is per dollar of assets invested in the business. As we'll see in this chapter, many such ratios can aid in doing the detective work required in financial analysis.

Ratio analysis—is the analysis of financial performance based on the comparison of one financial variable to another.

Tables 7–1 and 7–2 duplicate the income statements and balance sheets for Sparta Manufacturing that we used in the last chapter. The information contained in these statements can be manipulated to reveal different dimensions of corporate activity, such as profitability to shareholders, return on investment, liquidity, and indebtedness.

While all of these dimensions are related and important, different financial investigators may focus on different characteristics. For example, a prospective shareholder

Table 7–2

Sparta Manufacturing Company Year-End Balance Sheets, 1981–1986

	1981	*1982*	*1983*	*1984*	*1985*	*1986*
Assets						
Cash	$ 1,000	$ 1,000	$ 2,500	$ 12,500	$ 10,000	$ 2,500
Accounts receivable	125,000	90,000	95,000	107,500	147,500	152,500
Inventory	187,500	180,000	250,000	325,000	410,000	420,000
Total current assets	$313,500	$271,000	$347,500	$445,000	$567,500	$575,000
Fixed assets, net of depreciation	55,000	50,000	45,000	52,500	55,000	112,500
Other assets	17,500	15,000	15,000	17,500	15,000	35,000
Total assets	$386,000	$336,000	$407,500	$515,000	$637,500	$722,500
Liabilities and net worth						
Notes payable (bank)	$ 66,200	$ 16,400	$ 28,200	$ 34,700	$ 88,100	$144,100
Accounts payable (trade)	52,500	42,500	42,500	110,000	117,500	122,500
Taxes payable	3,500	2,800	14,000	8,500	7,600	7,500
Miscellaneous accruals	15,000	17,500	20,000	25,000	57,500	50,000
Total current liabilities	$137,200	$ 79,200	$104,700	$178,200	$270,700	$324,100
Mortgage payable	36,000	34,000	32,000	30,000	28,000	26,000
Total liabilities	$173,200	$113,200	$136,700	$208,200	$298,700	$350,100
Common stock	155,000	155,000	155,000	155,000	155,000	155,000
Retained earnings	57,800	67,800	115,800	151,800	183,800	217,400
Total liabilities and net worth	$386,000	$336,000	$407,500	515,000	$637,500	$722,500

might focus primarily on whether the company will be *profitable* and, hence, able to benefit shareholders. In analyzing whether to make a short-term loan, a bank loan officer might focus on the company's *liquidity* because liquid assets might be turned into cash to repay loans. The loan officer would also look at existing borrowing, or indebtedness, to see whether the company has to repay other existing loans before the bank could get its money back. An analyst evaluating another company as a potential merger candidate might place equal emphasis on all dimensions.

As we will see, there are a number of ways to measure each facet of a corporation. While we will restrict our focus here to private-sector firms, the same techniques can be used for other types of organizations as well, including not-for-profit organizations.

MEASURING PROFITS AND PROFITABILITY

Chapter 6 noted the importance of profits as a measure of performance and described some of the difficulties of measuring profits and the possible divergence between true economic profit and measured accounting profit. Here we will be using the terms *profit, income,* and *earnings* as synonyms.

Dollar Profits

Let us return now to the Sparta Manufacturing Company analyzed in Chapter 6. From Table 7–1, we see that Sparta earned $33,600 after taxes in 1986. From this figure alone, we can draw few conclusions about whether Sparta's performance was good or bad. Dollar profit figures for another similar company or for the relevant industry grouping would be of little additional help. One way of evaluating the flow of profits is to compare the 1986 profit to corresponding figures from prior years. From such comparisons we can determine *trends*.

Several different measures of profit are available in Table 7–1. On the bottom line, we have *profit after taxes (PAT)*, which takes into account all factors influencing earnings. We see that Sparta's profit after taxes increased rapidly from 1981 to 1983, then declined somewhat and remained essentially flat from 1984 to 1986. In the next section, when we measure *profitability*—profits in relation to sales—we will see a different picture.

Operating profit, or earnings before interest and taxes (EBIT),— measures the firm's performance before the effects of financing or taxes.

Tax rates are beyond the control of management. To factor out the effects of taxes, we can look at *profit before taxes (PBT)*. **Operating profit** measures the performance of the firm's commercial activities without regard to financing. Operating profit gives us an indication of the success of the basic operations of the company before we analyze how the company chose to finance these operations. (We'll examine the financing issues later in this chapter.) In 1982, operating profit declined by 29 percent relative to 1981, while profit after taxes declined by only about 17 percent. In 1986, operating profit rose, while profit after taxes remained essentially flat. Operating profit often is referred to as **earnings before interest and taxes (EBIT).**

Earnings per share (EPS)—is profit after taxes (PAT) divided by the number of shares of stock outstanding and is a widely used performance measure.

Another widely used earnings measure is **earnings per share (EPS),** which is profit after taxes divided by the number of shares of stock outstanding. EPS figures allow a shareholder to keep track of his or her claim on the company's total earnings. When the number of shares remains constant, earnings per share and profit after taxes tell the same story.

Table 7–3

Sparta Manufacturing Company Normalized Income Statement, 1981–1986

	1981 (percent)	1982 (percent)	1983 (percent)	1984 (percent)	1985 (percent)	1986 (percent)
Sales	100.0	100.0	100.0	100.0	100.0	100.0
Cost of goods sold	65.0	63.7	59.8	63.7	62.9	64.0
Materials	32.5	31.8	29.7	32.3	32.1	32.9
Labor	15.0	14.3	13.9	15.9	15.9	18.0
Overhead	17.5	17.5	16.2	15.6	14.9	13.2
Gross profit	35.0	36.3	40.2	36.3	37.1	36.0
Depreciation	1.5	0.9	0.8	0.5	1.0	1.3
Selling, general, and administrative expense	29.0	32.5	29.4	30.4	31.1	29.8
Operating profit	4.5	2.9	9.9	5.4	5.0	4.8
Interest	1.6	0.7	0.7	0.5	1.0	1.1
Profit before taxes	2.9	2.2	9.3	4.8	4.0	3.7
Taxes	0.6	0.4	1.9	1.0	0.8	0.7
Profit after taxes	2.3	1.8	7.4	3.9	3.2	2.9

Note: Details may not add to totals because of rounding.

The Normalized Income Statement

Profits per dollar of sales—is a useful measure of a firm's performance that measures profits in relation to the sales necessary to generate those profits.

A **normalized income statement**—is an income statement in which all items are expressed as percentages of sales.

We can learn still more about a firm's performance by measuring profits in relation to the sales necessary to generate those profits. **Profits per dollar of sales** is a measure of *profitability*. A convenient way to analyze profitability is to prepare a **normalized income statement** in which all items are expressed as percentages of sales. We then can examine the behavior of various elements of cost as well as the behavior of profits. Table 7–3 shows normalized income statements for Sparta Manufacturing Company, prepared from the data in Table 7–1. What conclusions can we draw from the data in Table 7–3? As before, single figures mean little; we need a standard of comparison.

We can look at the figures over time to identify trends. Sparta's profit after tax per dollar of sales declined from 3.2 percent in 1985 to 2.9 percent in 1986; dollar profits rose in absolute terms. Materials costs remained more or less a constant percentage of sales, labor costs rose, and overhead costs fell. Gross profit and operating profit both rose during 1981–1983, then fell during 1983–1986. By looking at trends, we cannot tell whether a particular element is too high or too low, but we can tell whether it is getting better or worse. Trouble spots can be identified, and management can determine causes. Normalized income statements can be prepared in any format and at any level of detail for which data are available.

To make a judgment as to whether an element of cost or profit in a given year is too high or too low, we can compare Sparta to another firm with similar characteristics or to an industry average. Sparta manufactures a wide variety of paints and varnishes, some of which are produced to specifications set forth by customers. We may have some difficulty finding comparable firms or groupings of firms. In the case of a department store or a lumber wholesaler or an electric utility, interfirm comparisons may be more meaningful.

Industry averages are available from at least two sources: Dun & Bradstreet and Robert Morris Associates (RMA), a national association of bank lending and credit officers. The RMA industry grouping that best fits Sparta is the paint, varnish, and lacquer industry. RMA data for this industry indicate a profit-before-taxes-per-dollar-of-sales figure of 2.9 percent, somewhat lower than Sparta's recent experience.[1] We must make such comparisons cautiously, however, because the firms in the RMA sample may not be exactly comparable to Sparta.

MEASURING RETURN ON INVESTMENT

It is also useful to relate profits and sales to the investment required to generate these flows. Capital is one of society's scarce resources. A measure of the efficiency with which these resources are being utilized is return per dollar of investment, known as **return on investment (ROI).** Return on investment is widely used as a measure of financial performance.

Return on Investment (ROI)

Return on investment (ROI)—is the return per dollar of investment per unit of time, a measure of the efficiency with which the firm utilizes capital.

Return on investment can be calculated in many ways. Some are based on standard accounting data and others on discounted-cash-flow techniques, which we discussed in Chapters 3 and 4. Accounting-based measures of ROI involve some measure of profit or return divided by some measure of outlay or investment. The resulting ratio is usually expressed in percentage terms. The general expression for calculating return on investment using accounting data is given in Equation (1).

> The general expression for return on investment (ROI) calculated using accounting data is
>
> $$ROI = \frac{Return}{Investment}. \tag{1}$$

For example, suppose a bank advertises savings accounts that pay interest of 6 percent per year. A deposit, or investment, of $100 today would yield $106 in 1 year, of which $6 is interest and $100 is the original principal. In this case, ROI would be calculated, using Equation (1), as

$$ROI = \$6/\$100 = 0.06 = 6 \text{ percent per year.}$$

In Equation (1), the numerator, *Return,* has a time dimension—dollars per unit of time—in this case, dollars per year. The denominator is in dollars. The quotient, ROI, is, therefore, a rate or percentage per unit of time—in this case, percent per year.

Return on investment based on accounting data sometimes is referred to as the *accounting rate of return.* Both the numerator and the denominator can be calculated in a number of ways. These alternatives provide flexibility but can result in ambiguity. Let us consider another example. Suppose an investment of $1,000 made at time 0 generates the earnings listed in Table 7–4 over its 4-year life.

---

[1]For an example of Robert Morris Associates data, see "Finance in Practice" 7–3 in this chapter.

Table 7-4

Return on an Investment Project over Its 4-Year Life

	Return			
	Year 1	Year 2	Year 3	Year 4
Revenue	$670	$700	$730	$750
Cash expenses	200	200	200	200
Depreciation	250	250	250	250
Profit before taxes	$220	$250	$280	$300
Taxes at 46 percent	101	115	129	138
Profit after taxes	$119	$135	$151	$162

To calculate accounting ROI, we first must determine the return. We can choose profits either before tax or after tax. We also see that profit is different each year. Which profit figure do we pick? We can calculate an average over the 4 years, or we can calculate ROI for each year if we wish.

Now for the investment. Should we define it as the initial outlay of $1,000? Alternatively, we might argue that the funds actually devoted to the project decline over time as the outlay is recovered through depreciation. In each year, we subtract depreciation allowances in calculating profit after tax and also reduce the **book value** (as opposed to the **market value**) of the asset on the balance sheet by the amount of the annual depreciation charge. The book value of the investment is $1,000 just after the investment is made, but falls to $750 at the end of year 1, and $500, $250, and $0 at the ends of years 2, 3, and 4, respectively. We might define the investment as the average of these book values over the life of the investment for an *average* investment of $500.

Thus, we see that there are many ways to calculate accounting ROI. We can calculate it pretax or after tax. We can calculate ROI for each year or an average over the 4 years. If we calculate an average, we still have alternative ways to define the investment. Which method of calculating ROI is correct? All are correct—that is, each answers a different question. There is no standard, generally agreed-upon calculation. Therefore, when we use accounting ROI, in order to avoid confusion, we must specify exactly how it is calculated.

Calculating Return on Investment for a Firm

The **book value**—of a firm is a measure of net asset value (after all liabilities), valued at historical cost.

The **market value**—of a firm is the value placed by investors on the future cash flows a company is expected to generate.

The **return on assets (ROA)**—is one measure of return on investment in which investment is defined as the total assets of the firm. ROA is calculated as profit after taxes divided by total assets.

How do we measure a firm's overall return on investment? One alternative is to define investment as the total assets of the firm and then calculate the firm's **return on assets (ROA),** as shown in Equation (2).

A firm's overall return on investment (ROI) can be calculated as return on assets (ROA) by defining investment as total assets:

$$ROA = \frac{\text{Profit after taxes}}{\text{Total assets}}. \qquad (2)$$

Table 7–5
Operating Assets

Assets	Liabilities and Net Worth
Net operating assets	Short-term borrowing
Fixed assets	Long-term debt
	Equity

The **operating return on assets (OROA)**—is a measure of return on investment that reflects the total dollars of profit from operations relative to the assets devoted to those operations. OROA is calculated as *operating profit,* or earnings before interest and taxes (EBIT), divided by total assets.

Usually it is desirable to purge the total-assets figure of intangible assets, such as goodwill or patents. A variation on the calculation above would be to substitute *operating profit before interest and taxes* in the numerator to get **operating return on assets (OROA)** before taxes. The use of this operating-profit figure in the numerator is often desirable because it represents dollars available to pay both debtholders and stockholders. Both sets of these owners have claims on the total assets (denominator) of the company. As a result, calculating return on assets as the ratio of operating profit to total assets reflects the total dollars of profit from operations relative to the total assets devoted to those operations. Use of profit after taxes, on the other hand, only shows profitability to the shareholders.

We might also subtract from assets all current liabilities that arise directly from operations, such as accounts payable, taxes payable, and various other accrual accounts. We then have a type of balance sheet, as shown in Table 7–5. From this balance sheet, we then can calculate **net operating return on assets (NOROA),** using either net profit or operating profit. Each of these variations allows us to focus on a slightly different aspect of the company's returns.

Another alternative for calculating a firm's overall return on investment is to calculate **return on equity (ROE),** as shown in Equation (3).

Another measure of a firm's overall return on investment can be determined by calculating return on equity (ROE) as

$$\text{ROE} = \frac{\text{Profit after taxes}}{\text{Net worth}}, \tag{3}$$

where net worth is the book value of the shareholder's equity claim on the balance sheet.

The **net operating return on assets (NOROA)**—is a measure of return on investment that subtracts from operating assets all current liabilities. NOROA is calculated as operating profit divided by net operating assets.

Return on equity explicitly takes into account the effects of the firm's use of debt, or financial leverage, while the various return-on-assets measures described above do so only indirectly (when profit is measured after interest). By incurring debt, a firm can affect its return on equity.

For example, suppose a company earned operating profit before taxes and interest of $12 on assets of $100, which were financed by borrowing $60 at 6 percent and by $40 of equity (net worth). By subtracting interest charges of $0.06($60) = $3.60, we could calculate profits before taxes to be $12 − $3.60 = $8.40. Assuming no taxes for simplicity, profit after taxes would also be $8.40. Now we can see the effects of

Table 7–6
Sparta Manufacturing Company Return on Investment, 1981–1986

	1981	1982	1983	1984	1985	1986
1. Return on assets (ROA)						
$ROA = \dfrac{\text{Profit after taxes}}{\text{Total assets}}$	3.1%	3.0%	11.8%	7.0%	5.0%	4.7%
2. Operating ROA, before taxes (OROA)						
$OROA = \dfrac{\text{Operating profit}}{\text{Total assets}}$	6.0%	4.9%	15.8%	9.7%	7.8%	7.6%
3. Net operating ROA, before taxes (NOROA)						
Net operating assets (thousands)[a]	$315	$273	$331	$372	$455	$543
$NOROA = \dfrac{\text{Operating profit}}{\text{Net operating assets}}$	7.3%	6.0%	19.5%	13.5%	10.9%	10.1%
4. Return on equity (ROE)						
Net worth (thousands)[b]	$213	$223	$271	$307	$340	$375
$ROE = \dfrac{\text{Profit after taxes}}{\text{Net worth}}$	5.6%	4.5%	17.7%	11.7%	9.4%	9.0%

[a]Net operating assets equal total assets less accounts payable, taxes payable, and miscellaneous accruals.
[b]Net worth equals common stock plus retained earnings.

The **return on equity (ROE)**—is a measure of return on investment in which investment is defined as the net worth of the firm. ROE is calculated as profit after taxes divided by net worth.

using debt. While operating return on assets would be $12/$100 = 12 percent, return on equity would be $8.40/$40 = 21 percent. Clearly, the use of debt made a difference.

We will discuss in depth the effects of using debt (financial leverage) in Part Five, where we will find that, although an increase in financial leverage (use of more debt) typically increases return on equity, it also increases *risk*. For now, let us note that the return-on-equity measure must be used with great caution as a performance measure. Return on equity gives us a measure of return but ignores the riskiness, or variability, of that return.

> **An increase in financial leverage (use of debt) typically increases return on equity (ROE), but it also increases risk.**

The various measures of return on investment are calculated for the Sparta Manufacturing Company in Table 7–6, using data from Tables 7–1 and 7–2.

Each of the four return-on-investment measures answers a different question, but all tell much the same story. Sparta's return on investment rose from 1981 to 1983 and then declined from 1983 to 1986. This downward trend after 1984 suggests that the company may be having difficulties. In practice, financial analysts would look further to see why profitability has declined. Has the company lost control of its costs? Are Sparta's markets becoming more competitive, putting downward pressure on prices and profits? Have other firms in the industry experienced the same decrease in profits? Answers to these and other questions are necessary before financial managers can make forecasts about how Sparta is likely to do in the future.

Finance in Practice 7–1

The Return on Equity of the
Fortune 500

	Return on Stockholders' Equity (percent)					
	1971–75	1976–80	1981	1982	1983	1984
Aerospace	10.4	16.0	15.0	11.7	13.4	13.9
Apparel	8.3	13.1	16.2	12.3	13.0	13.9
Office equipment	9.5	14.2	13.3	12.1	11.1	12.6
Textiles	6.4	10.1	7.8	6.3	8.7	8.2
Petroleum refining	12.1	15.6	16.4	12.5	9.5	9.5
Chemicals	11.3	13.9	13.5	8.9	9.8	12.2
Food	12.0	13.7	14.4	15.3	14.5	16.2
Pharmaceuticals	16.4	17.2	18.0	16.9	17.5	18.1
Beverages	14.1	13.9	19.2	16.7	16.9	15.7
Mining & crude-oil production	15.6	15.3	17.6	9.0	9.8	13.8
Rubber & plastic products	10.0	8.5	10.4	1.9	10.0	12.1
Average, all industries	**11.4**	**14.3**	**13.8**	**10.9**	**10.7**	**13.6**

During the five-year period from 1976 to 1980, the return on equity (ROE) for the 500 largest industrial companies in the United States averaged 14.3 percent per year. For the first time since the average was first calculated in 1958, ROE exceeded 12 percent over a five-year period. The 14.3 percent figure compared to 9.7 percent on A-rated industrial bonds. (*Aaa* is the top bond rating using the Standard and Poors rating scale. An *A* rating would be more typical for the majority of companies in the *Fortune 500* list.)

During the early 1960s, return on equity had substantially exceeded the return on bonds. As inflation increased during the late 1960s and early 1970s, corporate ROE did not rise commensu-rately. Rather, ROE seemed to get stuck at about 12 percent, while bond yields rose to that level and above. In the 1976-1980 period, the companies in the *Fortune 500* list collectively improved their returns and sustained that improvement over a five-year period. Returns then declined somewhat in 1982 and 1983 but were up to 13.6 percent in 1984.

Data for return on equity (in percent) for selected industries are given in the accompanying table. As indicated, the 1984 return varied from a low of 8.2 percent for textile products to 18.1 percent for the pharmaceuticals industry.

Source: Data for table adapted from C. J. Loomis, ''Profitability Goes Through a Ceiling,'' *Fortune,* May 4, 1981, figures updated by the authors. Copyright © 1981 by *Fortune* Magazine. Reprinted by permission.

Margin Versus Turnover

The return generated by a firm's assets represents the difference between revenues and total expenses, including taxes. This difference, when divided by the firm's level of sales, often is referred to as the firm's **profit margin.** Over a period of time—say, a

Table 7–7
Sparta Manufacturing Company Profit Margin and Sales Turnover, 1981–1986

	Profit Margin $\left(\dfrac{\text{Profit after Taxes}}{\text{Sales}}\right)$ (percent) (1)	Sales Turnover $\left(\dfrac{\text{Sales}}{\text{Assets}}\right)$ (2)	Return on Assets (percent) (3) = (1) × (2)
1981	2.33	1.33	3.11
1982	1.79	1.66	2.98
1983	7.41	1.59	11.78
1984	3.87	1.81	7.00
1985	3.23	1.55	5.01
1986	2.95	1.58	4.66

Profit margin—is the difference between revenues and total expenses (including taxes) divided by sales.

year—the total return depends not only on the profit margin per dollar of sales but also on the rate at which sales are generated. The rate of sales in relation to assets often is called the **sales turnover** rate. Thus, Equation (4) can represent return on assets (ROA) as the product of two components, margin and turnover.

A firm's return on assets (ROA) can be represented as

$$\text{ROA} = \text{profit margin} \times \text{Sales turnover.}$$

In other words,

$$\frac{\text{Profit}}{\text{Assets}} = \frac{\text{Profit}}{\text{Sales}} \times \frac{\text{Sales}}{\text{Assets}}. \tag{4}$$

Sales turnover—is the rate of sales in relation to assets.

For example, we can apply Equation (4) to Sparta Manufacturing's 1986 data found in Sparta's income statement and balance sheet (Tables 7–1 and 7–2) to determine Sparta's return on assets:

$$\text{ROA} = \frac{\$33,600}{\$1,140,000} \times \frac{\$1,140,000}{\$722,500}$$

$$= 0.0295 \times 1.58 = 0.0466 = 4.66 \text{ percent.}$$

As the calculations show, Sparta had a profit margin of 2.95 percent. Since it had $1.58 worth of sales for each dollar of assets (a turnover rate of 1.58), this profit margin translated into a 4.66 percent return on assets.

By decomposing ROA into margin and turnover components, we can better analyze changes over time. If ROA is decreasing, for example, we can determine whether the decrease is a result of a declining profit margin or a declining turnover rate. Such information is useful for planning corrective action. We also can compare data on margin and turnover with industry averages. Table 7–7 breaks down ROA into profit margin and sales turnover for each year from 1981 to 1986 for Sparta Manufacturing Company. Note that column (3) is the product of columns (1) and (2), with differences due to rounding. Now some new conclusions emerge. The big increase in ROA in 1983 resulted primarily from improved profit margins. The big drop in ROA in 1984 resulted from a sharp decline in margins, offset somewhat by an increase in sales turnover. With the exception of 1984, sales turnover remained more or less constant from 1982 to 1986. Differences in ROA, thus, were attributable to variations in margin. Of particular significance is the conclusion that the deterioration of ROA from 1982 to 1986 is a result of a decline in profit margin, not sales turnover. Knowing this, Sparta's management can focus its efforts to improve ROA.

The principal factors that determine the profit margin and the sales turnover rate can themselves be traced to more detailed changes in subfactors. A system of financial analysis and control designed to pinpoint the salient elements underlying the ROA achieved during any given period was developed by the DuPont Company many decades ago. It is a summary presentation that captures in one page (or one photographic slide) a concise picture of how and why ROA changes from one period to another. This system, adapted to suit the particular needs of individual companies, is widely used today to present results, both by major divisions and for the company as a whole, at periodic board meetings.

Figure 7-1 presents one adaptation of the DuPont system to report the results for Sparta Manufacturing for 1986. Each figure used in calculating ROA is broken down in detail. Compared with a similar presentation for the preceding year or several preceding years, it helps us determine why ROA for Sparta fell between 1983 and 1986.

In Figure 7-1, we can trace through the determinants of ROA. For example, by looking at the right portion of Figure 7-1 we see that Sparta's 1986 cost of goods sold was $730,000, or about $730,000/$1,140,000 = 64 percent of sales. To determine if this percentage is high relative to sales, financial managers could look at data from past years to see if the decline in ROA was the result of a higher cost of goods sold. By looking at other figures compared to past years, we could continue our detective work in analyzing what has been going on at Sparta and what is likely to happen in the future.

MEASURING ACTIVITY AND TURNOVER

This section explores some measures of turnover other than the sales turnover rate discussed above. Such turnover ratios give some indication of how efficiently managers use assets. The measures discussed below pertain to three specific areas of managerial performance: accounts receivable, inventory, and accounts payable.

Accounts-Receivable Turnover

The majority of firms sell on credit. Credit terms often are viewed as a marketing tool to be used to increase the firm's profits. Sales transacted but not collected appear on the balance sheet as accounts receivable. Accounts receivable must be financed. A

Figure 7–1
DuPont System of Financial Control Applied to Sparta Manufacturing Company, 1986

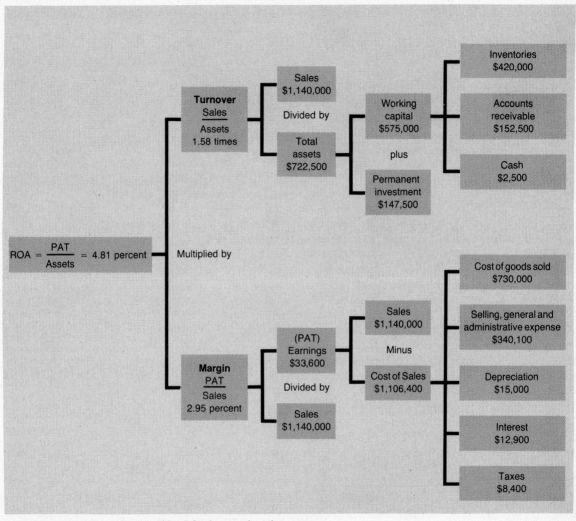

Note: Permanent assets are here considered fixed assets plus other assets.

loose credit policy may increase sales and operating profits, but it also increases accounts receivable and, therefore, the firm's financing costs. For example, if a company has to borrow money from a bank to finance its accounts receivable, there will be interest costs on this borrowing. The objective of credit policy should be to trade off costs and benefits and, thus, to maximize the value of the firm.

The discussion in this section will be limited to techniques for measuring the effectiveness with which receivables are being collected. We will measure collection experience against credit terms, but we will not discuss how credit terms should be set; credit policy will be discussed later in Part Six.

One useful measure of collection experience is the number of **days sales outstanding (DSO)** at any point in time, which is determined as shown in Equation (5).

> The average number of days it takes to receive payment from sales made on credit, or days sales outstanding (DSO), is calculated as
>
> $$DSO = \frac{\text{Accounts Receivable}}{\text{Credit sales per day}}. \qquad (5)$$

Days sales outstanding (DSO)—is the ratio of accounts receivable to credit sales per day and is also called the *average collection period.*

The DSO figure is also referred to as the *average collection period*. To calculate DSO, we consider only sales made on credit, excluding sales for cash. Sometimes accounts receivable will be reported on a net basis, after subtracting a reserve for bad debts; other times both the gross receivables outstanding and the reserve will be given. When available, the gross receivables figure should be used to calculate DSO.

Selecting the period over which to calculate sales per day also is important. Usually it is best to use the shortest and most recent period for which data are available—say, a quarter or even a month. Managers must be especially careful in selecting the averaging period when sales are seasonal or growing rapidly. Where a seasonal sales pattern exists, variations in the sales rate over the year will cause the DSO figure to vary even when there is no change in the underlying collection rate; the DSO figures computed at different points during the year, therefore, must be interpreted with caution. Where the firm is growing rapidly, managers should select a short averaging period to reflect the most recent sales rate. Part Six will present more refined techniques for monitoring accounts receivable.

For Sparta Manufacturing Company, we have only annual sales data, so we must use a year as our averaging period. Using Equation (5), we can calculate DSO figures for Sparta Manufacturing Company for December 31, 1986, as

$$DSO = \frac{\$152,500}{\$1,140,000/365 \text{ days}} = \frac{\$152,500}{\$3,123/\text{day}} = 49 \text{ days}.$$

Assuming all sales were on credit, Sparta's average daily sales rate during 1986 was $3,123 per day. Thus, the receivables balance of $152,500 on December 31, 1986, represented about 49 days of sales.

As financial analysts, our principal objective in calculating DSO is to determine whether Sparta is managing its receivables effectively. To answer this question, we must compare Sparta's DSO with its terms of sale. Sparta sells on two different terms, depending on competition and the bargaining power of customers. Some sales are on a *net 30* basis; that is, payment is due within 30 days. Other sales are on a *net 60* basis.[2] If all sales were net 30, a DSO figure of 49 would indicate laxity in Sparta's collection procedures. In this case, Sparta's sales are approximately half net 30 and half net 60. We would, therefore, expect a DSO figure of about 45 if all customers were paying exactly on time. If data are available, we might compare Sparta's DSO figure against an industry average.

It is useful also to examine the DSO data over time, as given in Table 7–8, to

---

[2]Chapter 20 provides a more detailed discussion of credit terms.

Table 7–8
Sparta Manufacturing Company Year-End Days Sales Outstanding, 1981–1986

Year	Days Sales Outstanding (DSO)
1981	89
1982	59
1983	54
1984	42
1985	54
1986	49

The **receivables/sales ratio**—is a tool for analyzing collection trends and is calculated as accounts receivable divided by sales.

identify any trends in collection experience. We find some variability but, excluding 1981, no clear trend. The variability might result either from variations in the sales mix, from changes in economic conditions, or from some inconsistency on Sparta's part in managing its receivables.

> **Comparing days sales outstanding (DSO) to credit terms indicates whether or not a firm is effectively managing its accounts receivable.**

The DSO figure is useful in part because it can be compared to credit terms. We converted sales to a daily basis in calculating DSO. If we had not converted sales to a daily basis, we would obtain an alternative measure relevant for analyzing the firm. This measure, the **receivables/sales ratio** can be calculated and expressed as a percentage. While this ratio bears no intuitive relationship to credit terms, for analyzing trends it serves about as well as DSO. The reciprocal figure—the ratio of sales to receivables—is referred to as the **receivables turnover rate.** Note that the average collection period divided into 365 also gives us the turnover rate in annual terms. All of these calculations convey basically the same information. Since the DSO figure can be compared to credit terms, it is the most useful figure.

The **receivables turnover rate**—is sales divided by accounts receivable.

The **aging schedule**—is a technique for analyzing accounts receivable by categorizing receivables outstanding by the length of time outstanding.

Another technique for analyzing accounts receivable is to prepare an **aging schedule.** To do this, the financial manager must categorize the receivables outstanding at any point in time according to the length of time outstanding. Table 7–9 breaks down

Table 7–9
Sparta Manufacturing Company Accounts-Receivable Aging Schedule, December 31, 1986

Month of Sale	Age of Account (days)	Proportion of Total Receivables (percent)
December	0–30	40
November	31–60	30
October	61–90	17
September	91–120	10
Before September	Over 120	3
		100

Sparta's receivables on December 31, 1986. The aging schedule, thus, gives us considerably more information than does the DSO figure. The DSO figure of 49 days masks the fact that 30 percent of Sparta's receivables on December 31, 1986, were more than 60 days old. The aging schedule tells Sparta's management to look further at collection procedures.

Inventory Turnover

An important aspect of managerial performance is the efficiency with which inventories are utilized. The basic function of inventories is to decouple the production process from purchases on the one hand and from sales on the other. To reduce purchasing costs, firms buy raw materials in quantity and hold them until needed. Since sales and production seldom are exactly synchronized on a daily basis, inventories of finished goods are held to avoid lost sales due to lack of stocks. Inventory policy requires a trade-off between the costs of purchasing and the cost of lost sales on the one hand and inventory-carrying costs (primarily storage and financing) on the other. Chapter 20 will address the issue of how much to invest in inventory. Here, we are concerned only with measuring inventory utilization.

> The **inventory-turnover ratio**—is a measure of the efficiency with which inventories are utilized and is calculated as the cost of goods sold divided by average inventory.

Inventory management must be judged relative to some overall measure of firm output. A widely used measure is the **inventory-turnover ratio,** defined in Equation (6).

The efficiency of inventory utilization, as measured by the inventory-turnover ratio is

$$\text{Inventory turnover} = \frac{\text{Cost of goods sold}}{\text{Average inventory}}. \tag{6}$$

Cost of goods sold, rather than sales, is the appropriate activity measure because it contains elements of cost comparable to those included in the inventory figure. We can pick any period over which to measure turnover—a month, a quarter, or a year. Here again, we must be careful to take into account seasonal patterns. The average-inventory figure often must be calculated as simply the average of beginning and ending figures for the period in question. Sometimes it is necessary to settle for only a beginning or an ending inventory figure.

We can compare turnover to industry averages or examine it over time. The inventory-turnover figure for Sparta Manufacturing for December 31, 1986, would be calculated, using Equation (6), as

$$
\begin{aligned}
\text{inventory turnover} &= \frac{\$730,000}{(\$410,000 + \$420,000)/2} \\
&= \frac{\$730,000}{\$415,000} \\
&= 1.76 \text{ times.}
\end{aligned}
$$

Table 7–10

Sparta Manufacturing Company Inventory Turnover, 1982–1986

Year	Inventory Turnover
1982	1.93
1983	1.80
1984	2.06
1985	1.69
1986	1.76

Sparta's inventory-turnover figures for the period 1982–1986 are given in Table 7–10. In our discussion of source-and-use analysis in the previous chapter, we found inventories to be the largest single user of funds. Now we can see why. Sparta is turning over its inventory less than twice a year, far below the industry average, which we find from Robert Morris Associates data to be 5.4 times per year in 1985 and much more than 5 times per year during previous years. Another interpretation is that on average, materials are remaining in inventory for more than 6 months. In addition, the data in Table 7–10 indicate a worsening trend. Inventory management seems to be a major problem area for Sparta.

Payment Period

Days purchases outstanding (DPO)—is a measure of how promptly a firm pays its bills. DPO is calculated as accounts payable divided by purchases per day (also known as the *average payment period).*

Creditors, especially trade creditors, are interested in how promptly a firm pays its bills. If a firm is known for paying its bills promptly, it is more likely to obtain credit and to obtain it on more favorable terms. We can calculate the number of **days purchases outstanding (DPO),** also known as the *payment period,* as shown in Equation (7).

> The average number of days it takes for a firm to make payments for purchases it makes on credit, or days purchases outstanding (DPO), is calculated as
>
> $$DPO = \frac{\text{Accounts payable}}{\text{Purchases per day}}. \qquad (7)$$

If we do not have data on purchases, we may have to improvise. In the case of Sparta Manufacturing Company, we have (in Table 7–1) data on the materials component of cost of goods sold. If usage and purchasing rates were about the same, and if selling, general, and administrative expense does not include significant purchases (for office supplies, etc.), we can then use the cost of material as a proxy for purchases. The payment period for Sparta for December 31, 1986, can then be calculated, using Equation (7), as

Table 7–11

Sparta Manufacturing Company Year-End Days Purchases Outstanding, 1981–1986

	Days Purchases Outstanding (DPO)
1981	114
1982	87
1983	81
1984	134
1985	135
1986	119

$$\text{DPO} = \frac{\$122,500}{\$375,000/365 \text{ days}}$$

$$= \frac{\$122,500}{\$1,027/\text{day}}$$

$$= 119 \text{ days.}$$

Table 7–11 gives the results of calculating the payment period for each of the other years.

Days purchases outstanding also can be interpreted as the average payment period. Since Sparta's terms of purchase are net 30 in most cases, we find Sparta far overdue on its trade credit. Our earlier source-and-use analysis raised the question of whether Sparta was relying too heavily on trade credit to finance its operations. Analysis of Sparta's payment period confirms that this indeed is the case.

Sparta's management should immediately look further into the accounts-payable situation to determine the reason for the slow payment and to plan corrective action. A potential lender or supplier should look much more deeply into Sparta's treatment of its trade creditors before advancing credit. One technique for looking further is the aging schedule, constructed in the same manner as that for accounts receivable in Table 7–9. As before, seasonal patterns and growth can seriously distort the calculation of the payment period. To avoid such distortion, it is best to use purchase data for the shortest and most recent period available.

MEASURING LIQUIDITY

Liquidity—measures a firm's ability to come up with cash quickly to meet expected and unexpected cash requirements.

The **liquidity** of a firm measures its ability to meet expected and unexpected cash requirements, expand its assets, reduce its liabilities, or cover any operating losses. Liquidity measures the company's ability to come up with cash quickly. The most obvious way to achieve liquidity is to have cash on hand, but liquidity is also increased by holding assets that can be easily turned into cash.

Ratio Measures of Liquidity

The **current ratio**—is a measure of liquidity that is calculated as current assets divided by current liabilities.

One of the most widely used liquidity measures is the **current ratio,** defined in Equation (8).

> The current ratio, a measure of a firm's liquidity, is defined as
> $$\text{Current ratio} = \frac{\text{Current assets}}{\text{Current liabilities}}. \tag{8}$$

Current assets and current liabilities, according to standard accounting convention, have maturities shorter than one year. The ratio of the one to the other, thus, gives a measure of the firm's ability to make ends meet in the short run. The current ratio for Sparta for December 31, 1986, can be calculated, using Equation (8), as

$$\text{current ratio} = \frac{\$575{,}000}{\$324{,}100} = 1.77.$$

The **acid-test ratio,**—or *quick ratio,* is a more stringent measure of liquidity than the current ratio because it includes only the most liquid of current assets and is calculated as cash plus marketable securities plus receivables, divided by current liabilities.

The current ratio is a crude measure of liquidity, however, because it does not take into account differences among categories of assets. Inventories, for example, may not be as quickly and readily turned into cash as accounts receivable. The **acid-test ratio,** or *quick ratio,*—defined in Equation (9)—is a more stringent measure because it includes only the most liquid of current assets.

> The acid-test ratio, a measure of a firm's liquidity that includes only the most liquid of current assets, is defined as
> $$\text{Acid-test ratio} = \frac{\text{Cash} + \text{Marketable securities} + \text{Receivables}}{\text{Current liabilities}}. \tag{9}$$

For Sparta, which has no marketable securities, the acid-test ratio for December 31, 1986, can be calculated from Equation (9) as

$$\text{acid-test ratio} = \frac{\$155{,}000}{\$324{,}100} = 0.48.$$

The same calculation for the year 1985 shows that in that year Sparta's acid-test ratio was 0.58.

The industry's average value for the acid-test ratio has been 1.0 or 1.1 for each year from 1981 to 1985. The fact that Sparta's acid-test ratio is substantially less than average may indicate that Sparta is not as liquid as other firms and would have difficulty coming up with cash in an emergency. Before we could know whether Sparta does have a liquidity problem, more detective work would be needed.

Table 7–12

Sparta Manufacturing Company Liquidity Measures, 1981–1986

	Current Ratio	Acid-Test Ratio	Net Working Capital (thousands of dollars)	Net Working Capital / Sales
1981	2.28	0.92	176	0.34
1982	3.42	1.15	192	0.34
1983	3.32	0.93	243	0.38
1984	2.50	0.67	267	0.29
1985	2.10	0.58	297	0.30
1986	1.77	0.48	251	0.22

Dollar Measures of Liquidity

Net working capital (NWC)—is a dollar measure of liquidity and is calculated as current assets minus current liabilities.

Net liquid assets—is a more stringent dollar measure of liquidity than net working capital and is calculated as short-term marketable securities minus discretionary debt maturing in less than one year.

In some cases, it is useful to measure liquidity in dollar terms. One widely used dollar measure is simply **net working capital (NWC),** defined as current assets minus current liabilities. Dividing by sales yields *net working capital per dollar of sales.*

A much more stringent dollar measure of liquidity is **net liquid assets,** defined as short-term marketable securities minus discretionary debt maturing in less than one year. The term *discretionary debt* refers to debt that excludes operating liabilities, such as accounts payable and other accruals. An example of discretionary debt would be a short-term bank loan. The net-liquid-assets figure gives a measure of the firm's ability to respond to unexpected cash demands without reducing operating assets, such as cash, receivables, and inventories. By subtracting discretionary short-term debt, we obtain the net liquid assets available after repayment of current debt.

The principal liquidity measures for the Sparta Manufacturing Company have been calculated and listed in Table 7–12. The net-liquid-assets measure has been omitted because Sparta holds no marketable securities. According to our ratio measures, Sparta's liquidity has declined steadily since 1982. Net working capital increased moderately in dollar terms through 1985 but has declined steadily in relation to sales except in 1983. Overall, we see a picture of declining liquidity. Our analysis of liquidity, thus, confirms the suspicion raised earlier in our source-and-use analysis.

Liquidity may be declining, but is it too low? Perhaps Sparta had excess liquidity during the early 1980s. Small growing firms have excess liquidity so infrequently that we can dismiss this as a possibility. We may be able to get a better feel for Sparta's liquidity by comparing its current and acid-test ratios with industry standards, but we must take care that the industry data are from similar firms.

In measuring liquidity as well as other aspects of financial performance, it is important to avoid being too mechanical. Financial managers should be less concerned with standard labels and methods of calculation and more concerned with what they are trying to measure. Sometimes financial managers may find that they can devise their own tailor-made measures in situations that standard measures do not fit.

MEASURING INDEBTEDNESS

Indebtedness, or financial leverage,—is the mix of debt and equity used to finance a firm's activities.

It is often of interest to creditors, investors, or management to measure a firm's indebtedness. **Indebtedness,** sometimes called **financial leverage,** represents the amount of money a corporation owes to various parties and can be measured in two ways. **Debt ratios** are based on the balance-sheet relationships between debt and asset value and are of particular concern in the event of liquidation. The higher the level of debt relative to the liquidating or sale value of assets, the less likely it is that all creditors will receive all payments due them in the event of liquidation. **Coverage ratios** are based on income-statement relationships between debt and income. They measure the ability of a firm to meet periodic payments due on its debt obligations. The larger the annual debt burden (the sum of interest and partial return of capital due each year) relative to the size and stability of the annual income flow, the higher is the probability that a fall in income might push the firm into default.

Debt ratios—are measures of indebtedness calculated using balance-sheet data and reflect the degree to which creditors are protected in the event of the liquidation of the firm.

Debt Ratios

Coverage ratios—are measures of indebtedness calculated using income-statement data and reflect a firm's ability to meet periodic payments due on its debt obligations.

The **ratio of debt to total assets**—measures percentage of total assets financed by creditors and is calculated as total liabilities (current liabilities plus long-term debt) divided by total assets.

The **ratio of debt to total assets** measures the percentage of total assets financed by creditors. Debt includes all current liabilities plus long-term debt. A variation on the debt/assets ratio is the **debt/net worth ratio,** also known as the *debt/equity ratio*. The debt/assets ratio is defined in Equation (10), and the debt/net worth ratio is defined in Equation (11).

A firm's use of borrowing can be measured by the debt/assets ratio as

$$\frac{\text{Debt}}{\text{Total assets}} = \frac{\text{Total liabilities}}{\text{Total assets}}. \tag{10}$$

The **debt/net worth ratio,**—or *debt/equity ratio,* is a variation of the ratio of debt to total assets and is calculated as total liabilities divided by net worth.

A firm's use of borrowing can be measured by the debt/net worth ratio, or debt/equity ratio, as

$$\frac{\text{Debt}}{\text{Net worth}} = \frac{\text{Total liabilities}}{\text{Common stock} + \text{Retained earnings}}. \tag{11}$$

For Sparta, these two debt ratios for December 31, 1986, can be calculated using the balance-sheet data in Table 7–2 as

$$\frac{\text{debt}}{\text{total assets}} = \frac{\$350,100}{\$722,500} = 0.48.$$

$$\frac{\text{debt}}{\text{net worth}} = \frac{\$350,100}{\$155,000 + \$217,400} = \frac{\$350,100}{\$372,400} = 0.94.$$

The debt/assets and debt/net worth ratios tell essentially the same story, because net worth is total assets less debt. Both ratios measure the protection afforded to creditors in the event of liquidation. A debt/assets ratio of 0.50 (debt/net worth of 1.0) indicates that assets need bring only $0.50 on the dollar in liquidation to fully protect creditors. The market value of assets in liquidation, however, may be substantially less than

Table 7–13
Sparta Manufacturing Company Year-End Debt Ratios, 1981–1986

	Debt / Total Assets	Debt / Net Worth	Long-Term-Debt / Capital
1981	0.45	0.81	0.14
1982	0.34	0.51	0.13
1983	0.34	0.50	0.11
1984	0.40	0.68	0.09
1985	0.47	0.88	0.08
1986	0.48	0.94	0.07

The **ratio of long-term debt to total capital**—measures the proportion of total long-term funds supplied by creditors as opposed to owners and is calculated as long-term debt divided by the sum of long-term debt and net worth.

book value. When using debt ratios to measure protection in liquidation, it is usually wise to eliminate from the balance sheet any intangible assets, such as goodwill.

A third debt ratio that is sometimes useful is the **ratio of long-term debt to total capital. Total capital** is the sum of long-term debt and net worth, where net worth includes common stock, retained earnings, and preferred stock, if any. **Long-term debt (LTD)** includes both **secured debt** (such as a mortgage) and **unsecured debt** (such as debentures). The LTD/capital ratio is defined in Equation (12) and tells us the proportion of total long-term funds supplied by creditors as opposed to owners.

A firm's use of borrowing can be measured by the long-term debt/capital ratio as

$$\frac{\text{Long-term debt}}{\text{Capital}} = \frac{\text{Long-term debt}}{\text{Long-term debt} + \text{Net worth}}. \tag{12}$$

For Sparta, this LTD/capital ratio for December 31, 1986 is

$$\frac{\text{LTD}}{\text{Capital}} = \frac{\$26,000}{\$26,000 + \$372,400} = \frac{\$26,000}{\$398,400} = 0.07.$$

Total capital—is the sum of long-term debt and net worth, where net worth includes common stock, paid-in surplus, retained earnings, and preferred stock, if any.

In many situations, adjustments of the data are necessary to get an accurate picture of a firm's debt ratios. For example, firms using last-in, first-out (LIFO) inventory accounting will find their inventories, and therefore total assets and net worth, understated during periods of inflation because the remaining inventory will be carried on the balance sheet at a value that does not reflect recent price increases of the inventory items. The value of plant and equipment may exceed its balance-sheet cost. Leases and unfunded pension benefits are contractual liabilities that are not carried on the balance sheet. Adjustments such as these are too complex for us to take up here, but they can be quite important in some situations.[3]

Table 7–13 lists the calculated values of the three debt ratios just discussed for each

---

[3]For an excellent discussion of these issues, see D. A. Lasman and R. L. Weil, "Adjusting the Debt/Equity Ratio," *Financial Analysts Journal*, Sept./Oct. 1978, pp. 49–58.

Long-term debt (LTD)—includes both secured and unsecured debt maturing beyond one year.

of the six years from 1981–1986 for Sparta Manufacturing Company. Beginning in 1983, Sparta's total debt has been increasing relative to assets and net worth. The increase has been in short-term debt, with the long-term debt ratio declining as the mortgage was paid down. From the standpoint of creditors, the trends are in the wrong direction. Some additional conclusions might be drawn from a comparison of Sparta's debt ratios against industry standards.

Coverage Ratios

Secured debt—is debt against which certain property is pledged to satisfy the debt in the event of borrower default.

Unsecured debt—is debt that is not backed with a pledge of property in the event of borrower default.

Coverage ratios examine indebtedness in terms of *flows*—that is, using income-statement relationships. In contrast to balance-sheet debt ratios, which measure protection of creditors in the event of liquidation, coverage ratios examine the ability of the firm to meet its debt obligations as a going concern.

The **times-interest-earned ratio** measures the margin by which current earnings cover interest charges and the extent to which operating earnings can decline before interest is threatened. The higher is the ratio, the greater is the margin of safety for creditors. One version of this ratio, shown as Equation (13), is calculated by dividing earnings before interest and taxes (EBIT) by interest charges on all debt, both short-term and long-term.

Interest coverage can be determined by calculating the times-interest-earned ratio which measures the margin by which earnings cover interest charges, as

$$\text{Times interest earned} = \frac{\text{EBIT}}{\text{Interest}} \qquad (13)$$

where EBIT is earnings before interest and taxes.

For Sparta in 1986, we find that the times-interest-earned ratio can be calculated from income-statement data as

$$\text{times interest earned} = \frac{\$54,900}{\$12,900} = 4.3 \text{ times.}$$

The **times-interest-earned ratio**—measures the margin by which current earnings cover interest charges on debt and is calculated as current earnings divided by interest charges.

When a firm has several debt issues outstanding and some are senior to others, we may wish to calculate coverage of each issue separately because senior debt must be paid before junior debt can receive its interest payments. Here we must proceed with care. Suppose a firm has outstanding two bond issues, A and B; A is senior to B, meaning that A's interest is paid in full before any of B's. We calculate the interest coverage for issue A using Equation (13) with only the interest on A in the denominator. To determine coverage on B, we include total interest (on both A and B) in the denominator because senior debt must be paid before junior. If we (mistakenly) calculated the coverage of B as earnings available after payment of interest on A, divided by interest on B, B would appear to have a higher coverage than A. The correct calculation gives B's coverage as the same as overall coverage of both issues.

To illustrate, assume (hypothetically) that Sparta's total interest payments of $12,900 in 1986 consist of a *senior* obligation of $8,000 that must be satisfied in full before any other interest payments may be made and a *junior* obligation of $4,900.

The times-interest-earned ratio for the first obligation would be $54,900/$8,000, or 6.9 times. For the junior obligation it is *not* ($54,900 − $8,000)/$4,900, which would give 9.6 times and would wrongly suggest that the junior obligation is safer than the senior; rather, the times-interest-earned ratio for the junior obligation is $54,900/$12,900, or 4.3 times—exactly the same as the overall coverage of both issues together.

A variation on the times-interest-earned ratio is the ratio of interest to profit after taxes (PAT) plus interest. Profit after taxes plus interest constitutes the total payments going to creditors and owners together. The proportion of this figure going to interest gives a measure of financial leverage—the counterpart, in flow terms, of the debt/net worth ratio. For 1986, we can calculate this ratio for Sparta as:

$$\frac{\text{interest}}{\text{PAT} + \text{interest}} = \frac{\$12,900}{\$33,600 + \$12,900} = 0.28.$$

The reciprocal of this ratio is also used by some analysts as a type of times-interest-earned ratio.

The **fixed-charge-coverage (FCC) ratio**—is a more comprehensive coverage measure than the times-interest-earned ratio because it measures the margin by which a firm's current earnings can cover debt and all other contractual obligations, including lease payments.

A more comprehensive coverage measure is **fixed-charge coverage (FCC),** which includes all contractual obligations rather than interest alone. Other contractual obligations include rent, lease payments, and principal repayments on long-term debt. The latter often are referred to as *sinking-fund payments,* about which we will have more to say in Part Five. There are two complications involved in calculating fixed-charge coverage, which is given in Equation (14). Because lease payments and rent are *subtracted* before we arrive at EBIT, we have to add them back both to the numerator and to the denominator of the ratio. Also, because principal repayments on fixed debt are not deductible for tax purposes, we have to convert this number to a before-tax basis when we include it in the calculation by dividing by the factor $(1 - T)$, where T is the marginal income tax rate (which is 20 percent for Sparta).

Coverage of debt and other contractual obligations can be measured by the fixed-charge-coverage (FCC) ratio, which is calculated as

$$FCC = \frac{\text{EBIT} + \text{Lease} + \text{Rent}}{\text{Lease} + \text{Rent} + \text{Interest} + [\text{Principal}/(1 - T)]} \qquad \textbf{(14)}$$

where T = the firm's marginal tax rate.

With these two factors included, the fixed-charge coverage for Sparta for 1986 can be calculated as

$$FCC = \frac{\$54,900 + \$0 + \$0}{\$0 + \$0 + \$12,900 + (\$2,000/0.80)}$$

$$= \frac{\$54,900}{\$15,400}$$

$$= 3.6 \text{ times.}$$

Note that Sparta has neither lease payments nor rental payments.

Table 7-14
Sparta Manufacturing Company Coverage Ratios, 1981-1986

	Times-Interest-Earned Ratio	*Fixed-Charge-Coverage Ratio*
1981	2.9	2.2
1982	4.2	2.6
1983	14.6	9.3
1984	9.8	6.6
1985	5.2	4.1
1986	4.3	3.6

A variation on Equation (14) is to add depreciation and other noncash charges to the numerator, thus providing a coverage measure in terms of operating cash flow rather than earnings. Over the long run, however, fixed charges must be covered by earnings.

The concept of coverage can be extended to dividends on preferred and common stock. Although dividends are not contractual, as are interest and principal payments, dividends are an important obligation that should be covered except in times of serious financial difficulty. Coverage of dividends by earnings gives a measure of the likelihood of their being discontinued or reduced during hard times. The usual procedure in calculating dividend coverage is to add the before-tax equivalent of the dividend— dividend divided by $(1 - T)$—to the denominator of Equation (14).

Table 7-14 lists the coverage ratios for each year from 1981 to 1986 for Sparta Manufacturing Company.[4] Sparta's principal payments on the outstanding mortgage amounted to $2,000 per year. We see from Table 7-14 that Sparta still is covering interest and fixed charges with some margin to spare, but a bad earnings year could put fixed charges in jeopardy. Also, the trend since 1983 is worrisome. Industry comparisons again might be helpful.

Before leaving coverage ratios, let us note some limitations. First, coverage ratios consider only operating earnings and cash flows. During a financial emergency, fixed charges can be met from other sources of cash, such as a cut in planned capital expenditures or a reduction in working capital. Second, coverage ratios tell us nothing about the likelihood of a decline in earnings sufficient to put fixed charges in jeopardy. Part Five will consider the firm's cash flows in analyzing debt capacity. The various performance measures we have discussed thus far are summarized in Table 7-15. Figure 7-2 shows the relationship of certain ratios to a firm's financial statements.

Sparta Manufacturing Company is a privately owned company, which means that its stock does not trade in public stock markets. Many companies are publicly owned, and for these companies there are some additional performance measures that are of interest. Some of these measures use a company's stock price as well as its financial-statement data to provide further insights. Finance in Practice 7-2 shows how indicators such as the **price/earnings (P/E) ratio** or the **market/book ratio** can provide valuable information about the performance of a company.

The **price/earnings (P/E) ratio**—is the ratio of current market price per share to the most recently reported annual earnings per share and gives an indication of the market's assessment of a company's growth prospects and riskiness.

The **market/book ratio**—is the ratio of share price to book value per share and relates the value to shareholders of the firm's future cash flows (market value) to the historical costs to shareholders of acquiring the firm's assets.

[4]For a critique of alternative coverage ratios, see M. C. Findlay III and E. E. Williams, "Toward More Adequate Debt Service Coverage Ratios" *Financial Analysts Journal* 31 (Nov./Dec. 1975): 58–61.

Table 7–15
Summary of Performance Measures

Measure	Calculation
Profits	
1. Dollar profits	Profit after taxes (PAT); profit before taxes (PBT); operating profit
2. Earnings per share	$\dfrac{\text{PAT} - \text{Preferred dividends}}{\text{Average common shares outstanding}}$
3. Earnings per share (fully diluted)	$\dfrac{\text{PAT} - \text{Preferred dividends}}{\text{Potential shares outstanding*}}$
Profitability	
4. Gross margin	$\dfrac{\text{Sales} - \text{Cost of goods sold}}{\text{Sales}}$
5. Operating expenses	$\dfrac{\text{Operating expenses}}{\text{Sales}}$
6. Net margin	$\dfrac{\text{PAT}}{\text{Sales}}$
7. Normalized income statement	$100 \times \dfrac{\text{Each item in income statement}}{\text{Sales}}$
Return on Investment (ROI)	
8. Accounting rate of return	$\dfrac{\text{PAT}}{\text{Average investment}}$ (typically)
9. Return on assets (ROA)	$\dfrac{\text{PAT}}{\text{Total assets}} = \dfrac{\text{PAT}}{\text{Sales}} \times \dfrac{\text{Sales}}{\text{Total assets}}$
10. Return on equity (ROE)	$\dfrac{\text{PAT}}{\text{Net worth}} = \dfrac{\text{PAT}}{\text{Sales}} \times \dfrac{\text{Sales}}{\text{Net worth}}$
Activity and Turnover	
11. Days sales outstanding (DSO) (also *average collection period*)	$\dfrac{\text{Accounts receivable}}{\text{Average credit sales per day}}$

*Assuming all convertible securities are converted.

INFLATION AND PERFORMANCE MEASURES

Inflation causes serious distortions in financial reporting. Before the mid-1960s, when the rate of inflation was below 2 percent, the problem could be ignored without serious error. During the 1970s and early 1980s, inflation rates got very high (13 percent in 1979), and distortions in financial data were a major problem. Inflation has declined significantly in the mid-1980s, but even moderate inflation rates of 3 to 5 percent, probably the minimum we can expect for the rest of this decade, can cause difficulty.

Measure	Calculation
12. Inventory turnover rate	$\dfrac{\text{Cost of goods sold}}{\text{Average inventory}}$
13. Days purchases outstanding (also *average payment period*)	$\dfrac{\text{Accounts payable}}{\text{Average purchases per day}}$
Liquidity	
14. Current ratio	$\dfrac{\text{Current assets}}{\text{Current liabilities}}$
15. Acid test ratio	$\dfrac{\text{Cash} + \text{Marketable securities} + \text{Receivables}}{\text{Current liabilities}}$
16. Net working capital to sales	$\dfrac{\text{Current assets} - \text{Current liabilities}}{\text{Sales}}$
17. Net liquid assets	Short-term marketable securities − Discretionary short-term debt
Indebtedness	
18. Debt to total assets	$\dfrac{\text{Total liabilities}}{\text{Total assets}}$
19. Debt to net worth	$\dfrac{\text{Total liabilities}}{\text{Net worth}}$
20. Long-term debt to capital	$\dfrac{\text{Long-term debt}}{\text{Long-term debt} + \text{Net worth}}$
21. Times interest earned	$\dfrac{\text{Earnings before interest and taxes (EBIT)}}{\text{Interest}}$
22. Fixed-charge coverage	$\dfrac{\text{EBIT} + \text{Lease} + \text{Rent}}{\text{Lease} + \text{Rent} + \text{Interest} + \text{Principal}/(1 - T)}$

Distortions in Income-Statement Data

How are financial reports affected by inflation? First, measurement of income is distorted in several ways. Increases in the prices of items held in inventory tend to overstate true earnings. Calculating depreciation based on historical rather than replacement costs also overstates earnings. As a result of these distortions, firms pay taxes on "phantom" profits.

Offsetting these distortions is the impact of inflation on borrowed funds. During inflationary times, interest rates incorporate an *inflation premium*. This premium ac-

Figure 7–2

What to Look for on the Balance Sheet

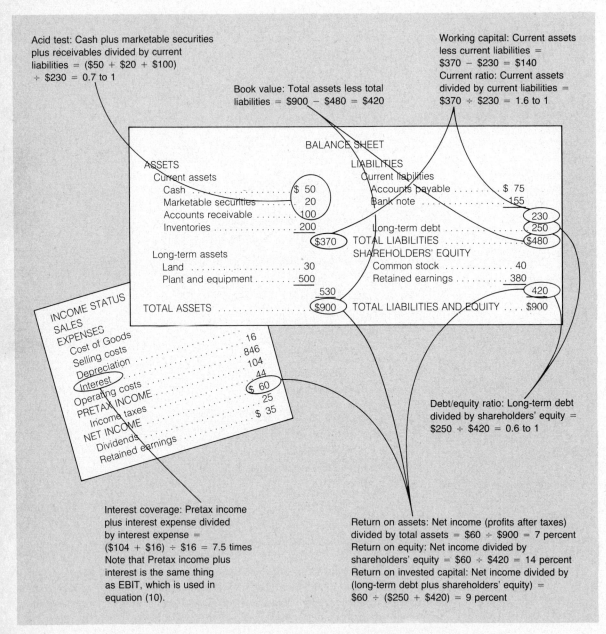

Note: All dollar figures are in thousands.

Source: "What To Look for on the Balance Sheet," *Business Week* 58 (June 7, 1976).

tually is not interest at all; rather, it is a repayment of principal to maintain the purchasing power of the lender's claim. Principal payments on debt should not be deducted from income, but the inflation premium included in the interest rate is so deducted under current accounting rules. Unless some adjustment is made, taking the interest inflation premium through the income statement understates earnings.

Distortions such as these affect many of the measures discussed in this chapter. Measurement of profits and profitability clearly are affected. So too are measures of ROI and debt coverage. Methods of dealing with these distortions are too complex for us to consider here, but financial analysts need to be aware of them.[5]

Distortions of Balance-Sheet Data

Inflation also causes distortion of balance-sheet data. Firms using LIFO (last-in, first-out) inventory accounting find their inventories understated on their balance sheet relative to firms using the first-in, first-out (FIFO) method.[6] Plant and equipment may have market values far above their balance-sheet costs.

Changes in interest rates that result from inflation affect the real value of previously incurred long-term indebtedness. All of these distortions add up to more headaches for the financial analyst. Both the accounting profession (through the Financial Accounting Standards Board) and the Securities and Exchange Commission (SEC) have been developing reporting procedures that provide financial data adjusted for changes in the price level. However, a final acceptable system has not yet been devised to replace the existing system of historical-cost accounting for tax and reporting purposes.

> **A single performance figure means little without comparison to data over time or to data for other similar firms.**

COST/VOLUME/PROFIT RELATIONSHIPS

Thus far the chapter has demonstrated techniques for evaluating various dimensions of a company, ranging from profitability to indebtedness. The system initiated by Du-Pont, depicted in Figure 7–1, pointed out some of the key relationships between measures of profitability, such as return on assets (ROA), and the sales that a firm could generate per dollar of assets. Specifically, in Equation (4), ROA was broken down as the product of margin and turnover.

---

[5]For an excellent discussion of the problem of accounting for the cost of borrowed funds, see G. M. Von Furstenberg and B. G. Malkiel, "Financial Analysis in an Inflationary Environment," *Journal of Finance* 32 (May 1977): 575–88.

[6]Under a FIFO inventory system, raw materials are charged into cost-of-goods-sold (CGS) at the "oldest" prices; hence, CGS is understated relative to replacement costs when prices are rising. Firms using LIFO charge raw materials at the most recent prices paid, leaving "older" items in inventory and, hence, understating the value of inventory on the balance sheet in times of inflation. Thus, under a FIFO system, when prices and inventories are rising, CGS tends to be understated and inventories correct; under a LIFO system, inventories are understated and CGS is correct.

Finance in Practice 7–2

Performance Measures for IBM Corporation

The accompanying page is reproduced from the *Value Line Investment Survey.* Value Line, Inc. publishes on a regular basis similar data on about 1,700 companies and is used by many investors, both professional and amateur alike.

The first six rows under the diagram on the sample page give annual data for key indicators on a per-share basis: revenues per share, earnings per share, book value per share, and so on. The figures are computed by taking the total figure for, say, earnings and dividing it by the number of shares of common stock outstanding. Most shareholders in IBM, with the exception of a few large institutional investors, such as pension funds, own only a small percentage of the company. Each shareholder, thus, has an interest in knowing his or her share of the total earnings. The *earnings per share (EPS)* number, multiplied by the number of shares owned, gives the shareholder's share of earnings. In 1986, IBM had 616.0 million shares of stock outstanding and earnings per share of $11.85.

A firm's EPS is widely watched as a performance measure. Also widely watched is the stock price, which is quoted on a per share basis. After all, the value of the holding of stock is really what matters to most investors. As we found in our discussions of valuation in Chapters 4 and 5, the market value of a stock is the present value of all the cash flows that investors expect to receive on the stock in the future. The trend in EPS is one important factor investors take into account in forecasting future cash flows. Note that Value Line forecasts cash flow along with sales revenue, earnings, dividends, and book value.

Value Line also forecasts future stock price. Later in the book we will talk about just how difficult it is to forecast stock prices. In the aggregate, all investors can receive returns equal to only what firms actually earn. Although some investors may forecast better than others, the number of investors who can "outforecast" all others consistently over extended periods is very small.

Another widely used indicator is the *price/earnings (P/E) ratio,* the ratio of current market price per share to the most recently reported annual earnings per share. If a company is growing rapidly in sales and, more important, in earnings, it is likely to have a higher stock price (present value of future cash flows to shareholders) than a similar company growing less rapidly. Thus, other factors equal, higher growth normally results in a higher P/E ratio. So, a high P/E may indicate that the market expects the company to grow rapidly.

A second important factor in interpreting P/E ratios is *risk.* Other factors equal, lower risk will result in a lower market required rate of return, or discount rate (the denominator in our valuation models in Chapters 4 and 5), and hence in a higher stock price. So a high P/E ratio could

---

> **To understand the effects of various actions on profit, one must use techniques for analyzing the response of revenues, costs, and profits to changes in sales volume.**

For planning and decision making, a further understanding of the effects of various actions on profit is clearly important. Such an understanding requires techniques for analyzing the response of revenues, costs, and profits to changes in sales volume. We will begin with costs.

indicate an assessment of relatively low risk or high expected growth or both.

Book value per share and the *market/book ratio*—the ratio of share price to book value per share—also are useful indicators. Market value, in principle, is the present value of the future cash flows the company is expected to generate for shareholders. Book value, on the other hand, represents the cost of the assets financed by shareholders to produce those cash flows. Book value has many shortcomings as a measure of cost, especially in an inflationary world, but in a rough sense, book value represents the cost of inputs used by the firm, and market price represents the value of the outputs it produces. Using the market/book ratio as a guide, the market seems to be telling IBM that they have done a good job. In February 1986, the time of the Value Line data in the accompanying entry, IBM's stock price was $156 and its book value $59.65, a market/book ratio of 2.73. It would be nice for investors if all firms did so well.

Source: Value Line Investment Survey, Value Line, Inc., New York, May, 1986.

INT'L BUS. MACH. NYSE-IBM RECENT PRICE **156** P/E RATIO **13.9** (Trailing: 14.6, Median: 13.0) RELATIVE P/E RATIO **0.94** DIV'D YLD **2.8%** VALUE LINE **1107**

[Value Line data sheet for International Business Machines Corp. — financial chart and statistical tables, May 9, 1986.]

BUSINESS: International Business Machines Corp. is the largest supplier of data processing equipment. Also makes typewriters, dictating machines, copiers. In 1984, purchased Rolm Corp., now a wholly-owned subsidiary. Foreign business accounted for 43% of 1985 revenues; 48% of pretax earnings. Research & Development costs equaled 6.9% of revenues; estimated payroll costs. 35%. '85 depreciation rate: 8.9%. Estimated plant age: 4 years. Has 405,535 employees. 798,100 shareholders. Insiders control .6% of stock. Chairman: J.R. Opel. President and Chief Executive Officer: J.F. Akers. Incorporated: New York. Address: Armonk, New York 10504. Telephone: 914 765 1900.

The Armonk brass is urging caution. While economic seers generally predict accelerating growth ahead, IBM—along with its competitors—has yet to witness a measurable order upturn. March-quarter product shipments actually declined .3% year to year, and the interim's weak share-net tally would have been more anemic but for a 23¢ benefit arising from the lower value of the dollar. Company efforts to light the demand fire through broad-based price cuts and accelerated delivery schedules haven't appreciably fattened the backlog; accordingly, we've cut our 1986 earnings estimate to $11.85 a share.

With revenue growth stalled, the focus is now on the cost side. At its mid-April debut of new PC-family products, IBM hinted at what we believe will become a cornerstone of its future strategy by showing a film of its automated manufacturing facility in Austin, where the new PC Convertible is fully assembled in about six minutes by computer-controlled robots. We expect that this technology will be incorporated throughout IBM plants over the years ahead (implying that capital investment is likely to remain high), enabling Big Blue to compete effectively against lower-cost producers such as those found in the Far East and Japan. **IBM copycats are likely to find rough sailing ahead.** In recent years, IBM products utilized a large number of off-the-shelf components, making the reverse-engineering job of competitors relatively easy. In an attempt to capture market share, however, we expect to see IBM integrate more hardware functions at the chip level, thus squeezing the clone crowd out of the fray. Too, we believe the recent trend toward more in-house component manufacturing will continue, which, over the long haul, should result in plumper margins.

Though IBM—and its stock—is currently languishing, a solid foundation is being laid for future gains. We applaud IBM for maintaining its investment pace throughout the recent industry slump, and believe that substantial benefits will accrue to the company for maintaining this prudent course. Likewise, we believe that this top-quality equity—though currently mired in a narrow trading range—will reach much higher ground by decade's end, and our advice to shareholders is to hold on for the ride.

Jerry P. Melin

Factual material is obtained from sources believed to be reliable but cannot be guaranteed.   © 1986 VALUE LINE, INC.   711 Third Avenue, New York, N.Y. 10017

Fixed Versus Variable Costs

Variable costs are costs that vary directly with changes in production volume.

How do costs respond to changes in sales volume? Some costs, known as **variable costs,** vary directly with production volume, and their variations are roughly proportionate to changes in production volume. For example, every passenger car that General Motors builds needs five tires; thus, the *cost* of this component of the final product rises either in proportion or almost in proportion to the total number of cars built in a period. In contrast, the total cost of tools and dies used for stamping the body parts

Figure 7–3
Behavior of Costs

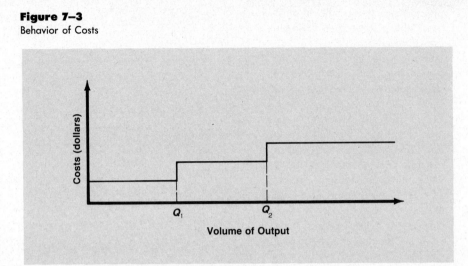

Fixed costs are costs that remain the same over a given wide range of production.

for a new model would be a **fixed cost** because it does *not* change with the volume of bodies produced but remains *fixed* over a very wide range of production levels. In a wholesale or retail business, variable costs would include the cost of goods purchased for resale and commissions paid to salespersons. In a manufacturing firm, variable costs include materials used in the manufacturing process, direct labor, supplies, energy costs, packaging, freight, and sales commissions.

What costs are fixed with respect to sales volume? Here we must be cautious. We might begin by identifying such costs as executive salaries, depreciation, rent, property taxes, insurance, and interest. The next section will have more to say about how fixed a fixed cost really is.

The **break-even point**—is that quantity of firm output at which sales revenues just cover total fixed costs, or the quantity of output at which revenue equals operating costs and operating profit is zero.

Accepting for the moment that some costs vary with sales volume and that some do not, we can define the concept of *contribution*. Suppose a manufacturing firm makes a product that is priced at $10 per unit. If variable cost per unit is $6, then each unit sold contributes $4 toward payment of fixed costs. If enough units are sold, total fixed costs will be covered. Sales above that **break-even point** contribute to profits.

How Fixed Are Fixed Costs?

Returning to our discussion of fixed costs, suppose a pencil-manufacturing firm operates a plant that has the capacity to produce 50,000 pencils per year. Suppose further that adequate managerial and supervisory personnel are available to produce at full plant capacity and that the accounting department, sales department, and company cafeteria also are staffed to support that level of operation. At any production level below 50,000 pencils per year, all these support or overhead costs remain fixed in total dollars per unit in time.

Suppose production is to be expanded above 50,000 units. New plant capacity is needed and possibly an additional supervisor for additional production personnel. Additional personnel may be needed in the accounting department, and the cafeteria may have to be expanded.

Figure 7–4
A Typical Break-Even Chart

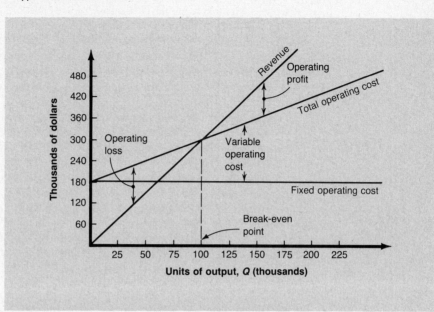

When we say that a particular element of cost is fixed, we mean that it is fixed over some *range* of sales volume. In the long run, all costs are variable. In the long run, the firm can go out of business and eventually eliminate all costs. It is necessary, therefore, when speaking of fixed costs to specify the relevant range of output. When output goes beyond the relevant range, types of costs that previously did not change with output increase, often as a step function, as shown in Figure 7–3. The costs depicted in Figure 7–3 are *fixed* (constant) for volumes less than Q_1, but they increase when output exceeds Q_1 and increase again when output exceeds Q_2.

Even over the relevant range of output, any classification of costs as either fixed or variable often is an oversimplification of reality. Some costs contain both fixed and variable components. A part of the electric power bill, for example, may be fixed, but part may vary with the level of output.

BREAK-EVEN ANALYSIS

Break-even analysis—is a technique for analyzing the relationship between revenue and profit that examines the proportion of fixed costs to total costs.

The ratio of fixed costs to total costs is an important factor in the relationship between revenue and profit. **Break-even analysis** is a technique for analyzing this relationship by examining the ratio of fixed costs to total costs. At this point, we will restrict our attention to the relationship between revenue and *operating profit,* often referred to as earnings before interest and taxes, or EBIT. In this way, we can separate the effects of operating and financial leverage, both of which we will discuss shortly.

Figure 7–4 shows a break-even diagram constructed for a product with a selling price of $3.00 and variable costs of $1.20 per unit. Fixed operating costs are $180,000 per year and plot as a horizontal line that intersects the vertical axis at $180,000.

Because the selling price for the product in question is $3.00 per unit, the total revenue produced at each level of output, Q, can be calculated as $3Q$. The total-revenue line is constructed by plotting each output level against each total-revenue amount ($3Q$) associated with that output level. Because variable cost is $1.20 per unit, total variable cost is calculated as $1.2Q$ for each level of output, Q. Total cost for each level of output is calculated by adding the variable cost, $1.20Q$, for each level of output to the fixed cost of $180,000, and then plotting the result to get the total-cost line in the diagram. In cases where it would be useful, we can construct a break-even chart with sales dollars or percent of production capacity, rather than units of output, on the horizontal axis.

The *break-even point* is the level of production at which sales just cover fixed costs. The break-even point in this case is 100,000 units of production. At that output level, sales revenue is $300,000, variable costs are $120,000, fixed costs are $180,000, and operating profit is zero.

We can also calculate the break-even point algebraically. At the break-even point, we know that total fixed costs are covered. Each unit sold can contribute to covering these costs to the extent that the unit sells for a price (P) more than its unit variable cost (VC). In this example, the contribution of each unit sold is $P - VC = \$3.00 - \$1.20 = \$1.80$. If Q_b is break-even volume, $\$1.80(Q_b)$ must equal fixed costs (FC) of $180,000. Algebraically, break-even volume of output can be calculated as shown in Equation (15).

> The break-even volume (Q_b) of a firm's output can be calculated as
>
> $$(P - VC)\, Q_b = FC \qquad\qquad (15)$$
>
> $$Q_b = \frac{FC}{P - VC}$$
>
> where P = price per unit sold, VC = variable cost per unit, and FC = fixed cost.

In our example, the break-even volume of output (Q_b) would be

$$Q_b = \frac{\$180,000}{\$3.00 - \$1.20} = \frac{\$180,000}{\$1.80} = 100,000 \text{ units per year.}$$

Some Limitations of Break-Even Analysis

Break-even analysis is a very useful tool, but it is important to keep its limitations firmly in mind. First, let us recall our earlier conclusion that fixed costs usually are fixed only over some relevant range of output. Our analysis, therefore, is valid only over that range. Also, we assumed in the discussion above that selling price is constant over the range of output analyzed. In practice, output and price are often related. Variable costs may not be absolutely constant per unit over the entire range. When such assumptions do not hold, the cost and revenue lines in Figure 7–4 are not linear. Where refinement of the analysis is necessary and justified, nonlinear relationships can be approximated by a series of straight-line segments.

Another limitation concerns multiple products. The analysis in Figure 7–4 is carried out for a single product. The fixed costs are those to be incurred because of a decision

Figure 7–5
Break-Even Analysis on a Cash Basis

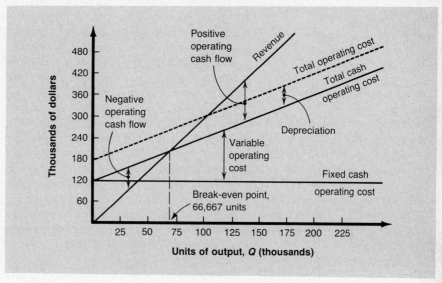

to market that product. In a multiproduct firm, break-even analysis can be applied to each product; allocating expenses that are jointly attributable to all products—for example, a supervisor's salary—presents problems. To perform break-even analysis for the firm as a whole, we must define output as the total for all products, assuming a stable product mix over the entire range of output. In some cases, such an assumption may not be realistic.

An additional shortcoming of simple break-even analysis is that it ignores the time value of money. Costs and revenues are treated as if they all occur at the same time. For analysis of relatively short time periods, ignoring the time value of money may not cause large problems. For long-range analysis, however, the time value of money can be an important factor. Taking the time value of money into account would require an adjustment of costs and revenues to their present value.

Finally, problems may be encountered in obtaining the data necessary for a break-even analysis. Some elements of cost may be uncertain. Cost relationships may change over time, and historical data may not always provide good estimates of future costs. Problems in using historical data are especially troublesome when rates of inflation are high.

Break-Even Analysis on a Cash Basis

Since companies are concerned with cash flow, it is often useful to know the point at which a product will break-even on a cash basis. To perform the analysis on a cash basis, we subtract all noncash expenses—in most cases, only depreciation—from operating costs. In the case of the product analyzed in Figure 7–4 let us assume that the fixed-cost figure of $180,000 included $60,000 in depreciation. Figure 7–5 shows the new fixed-*cash*-cost line at $120,000 and the new break-even diagram that results.

Finance in Practice 7–3

Sources of Data on Firms and Industries

This chapter has emphasized the necessity for benchmarks, or standards of comparison, in analyzing performance. A single figure for a single period or point in time is of little use unless it can be compared either to data for the same firm over time or to data for other similar firms.

Firm Data. Publicly owned firms are required by the Securities and Exchange Commission (SEC) to report financial data to investors on a regular basis. A firm's *annual report* to stockholders is the primary reporting vehicle and is often supplemented by quarterly reports. Even more detail is provided in the annual 10-K and quarterly 10-Q reports that must be filed with the SEC. Such reports contain the basic financial information that is the starting point for financial analysis. Annual reports sometimes are collected by libraries and usually can be obtained directly from the firm.

Publications issued by Moody's Investors Service and Standard & Poors Corp. can also be found in many libraries. Moody's

Investor's Service publishes financial data on thousands of publicly owned firms organized by type of business. Moody's data go back many years and provide a valuable historical source. Standard & Poors also publishes data on individual firms. In addition, the Standard & Poors Compustat Tapes provide a machine-readable source of standard financial data on a large number of public companies.

Another widely used source is the *Value Line Investment Survey*. Recall the data for IBM presented earlier in Finance in Practice 7–2, which shows a page from a recent edition of the *Survey*. Note that the extensive tabular data is accompanied by additional comments. The *Value Line Investment Survey* is aimed primarily at investors, and one can see this orientation both in the choice of data presented and in the nature of the comments, which present Value Line's opinion regarding the likely future returns from investing in IBM stock. Value Line provides data on approximately 1,700 companies along with summary data on a number of major industries. The *Survey* represents a compact and useful source for certain data. Like the publications of Moody's Investors Service and Standard & Poors, the *Value Line Investment Survey* is relatively expensive but normally can be found in libraries with a good business section.

Industry Data. As noted earlier, Robert Morris Associates (RMA) compiles data for a large number of different industries. Included in RMA data are basic balance-sheet and income-statement information and standard ratios of the type discussed in this chapter, broken down by size of firm. A sample of data available from RMA covering the paints, varnish, and lacquer segment of industry (in which Sparta Manufacturing would belong) is reproduced in the accompanying sample entry. In the entry, the firms are broken into size categories based on dollar value of assets for purposes of reporting current data. Sparta would fall in the smallest category since its assets are less than $1 million. (*MM* in the table denotes millions of dollars.)

The entry reports normalized income statements and balance sheets for the firms in the industry. In addition, Robert Morris Associates provides a number of calculated ratios. Three values are given for each ratio. For example, the current ratio in Sparta's size class ($0 to $1 million in assets) is given as 2.9, 1.8, and 1.3. The middle number, 1.8, represents the *median* current ratio of the reporting firms; that is, there are as many firms with current ratios above 1.8 as there are firms with current ratios below 1.8. Looking back at Table 7–12 in the chapter, we see that Sparta's current ratio for 1984 is 2.50. This puts Sparta above the industry median figure for the current ratio. The other two numbers give further information on how different current ratios are among firms. For example, 25 percent have current ratios below 1.3.

Dun & Bradstreet compiles data on both individual firms and industries. They compile and publish 14 key financial ratios on 125 different lines of business, including manufacturing, wholesaling, and retailing.

The Federal Trade Commission (FTC) and the SEC jointly publish the *Quarterly Financial Report for Manufacturing Corporations*. The report contains balance-sheet and income-statement data broken down by industry group and by asset size.

Trade associations represent another source of industry data. Many industries maintain trade associations with a staff that collects data and makes the data available on request.

Fortune magazine, *Forbes* magazine, and *Business Week* also provide summary data on the largest corporations.

A word of warning is in order regarding the use of industry data. Industry averages and data on other individual companies reflect what other companies *have done* and *are doing,* but not necessarily what they *should be doing.* In no sense should industry averages be viewed as targets toward which a company should aspire.

MANUFACTURERS - PAINT, VARNISH & LACQUER SIC# 2851

Current Data: 0-1MM / 31	1-10MM / 73	10-50MM / 19	50-100MM / 7	ALL / 130	ASSET SIZE / NUMBER OF STATEMENTS	6/30/79 ALL 148	6/30/80 ALL 155	6/30/81 ALL 142	6/30/82 ALL 136	6/30/83 ALL 130
%	%	%	%	%	**ASSETS**	%	%	%	%	%
6.4	8.8	8.2		8.6	Cash & Equivalents	6.5	7.6	6.7	8.3	8.6
29.5	30.4	30.4		29.8	Accts & Notes Rec - Trade(net)	29.4	29.8	28.6	29.1	29.8
29.9	29.8	28.9		29.2	Inventory	33.1	31.4	30.9	29.3	29.2
3.7	.9	1.2		1.6	All Other Current	1.2	1.4	2.1	1.9	1.6
69.6	69.9	68.7		69.2	Total Current	70.2	70.0	68.3	68.5	69.2
22.9	22.9	23.8		23.6	Fixed Assets (net)	21.9	22.1	23.3	22.0	23.6
.5	.2	.7		.4	Intangibles (net)	.9	.6	.6	.8	.4
7.0	7.0	6.8		6.9	All Other Non-Current	7.1	7.2	7.8	8.7	6.9
100.0	100.0	100.0		100.0	Total	100.0	100.0	100.0	100.0	100.0
					LIABILITIES					
8.2	8.2	3.7		7.1	Notes Payable-Short Term	6.6	6.3	6.7	6.8	7.1
4.6	2.7	2.1		3.0	Cur. Mat.-L/T/D	2.2	2.0	2.6	2.5	3.0
18.4	17.5	17.5		17.4	Accts & Notes Payable - Trade	19.3	17.3	17.3	16.9	17.4
4.0	6.4	8.3		6.3	Accrued Expenses	6.5	7.2	6.4	5.6	6.3
3.5	2.1	2.9		2.5	All Other Current	3.6	2.7	3.2	2.9	2.5
38.8	36.9	34.4		36.3	Total Current	38.3	35.5	36.2	34.7	36.3
13.9	14.2	9.9		13.1	Long Term Debt	12.8	12.5	15.0	12.7	13.1
2.9	1.9	2.7		2.4	All Other Non-Current	2.3	2.5	1.7	1.8	2.4
44.5	47.0	53.0		48.2	Net Worth	46.6	49.5	47.1	50.8	48.2
100.0	100.0	100.0		100.0	Total Liabilities & Net Worth	100.0	100.0	100.0	100.0	100.0
					INCOME DATA					
100.0	100.0	100.0		100.0	Net Sales	100.0	100.0	100.0	100.0	100.0
69.2	69.9	66.9		68.7	Cost Of Sales	71.1	70.4	70.1	69.3	68.7
30.8	30.1	33.1		31.3	Gross Profit	28.9	29.6	29.9	30.7	31.3
27.9	26.6	28.2		27.5	Operating Expenses	24.3	25.0	25.3	27.2	27.5
2.9	3.5	4.9		3.8	Operating Profit	4.6	4.6	4.6	3.4	3.8
1.6	.8	.4		.9	All Other Expenses (net)	.8	.7	1.3	1.0	.9
1.2	2.7	4.5		2.9	Profit Before Taxes	3.8	4.0	3.3	2.5	2.9
					RATIOS					
2.9	2.9	2.5		2.8	Current	2.5	2.7	2.9	3.1	2.8
1.8	2.0	2.2		2.1		2.0	2.1	2.0	2.2	2.1
1.3	1.4	2.0		1.5		1.4	1.6	1.5	1.6	1.5
1.5	1.8	1.4		1.7	Quick	1.3	1.6	1.5	1.7	1.7
(30) 1.0	1.1	1.3	(129) 1.1			1.0	1.1	1.0	1.1	(129) 1.1
.7	.7	1.0		.8		.7	.8	.7	.8	.8
35 10.5	38 9.7	44 8.3		39 9.4	Sales/Receivables	35 10.5	35 10.3	32 11.5	34 10.7	39 9.4
49 7.4	49 7.5	51 7.2		49 7.4		42 8.6	43 8.4	41 8.8	45 8.1	49 7.4
68 6.3	59 6.2	68 6.3		59 6.2		56 6.6	54 6.7	54 6.7	54 6.8	59 6.2
36 10.2	45 8.1	48 7.7		45 8.2	Cost of Sales/Inventory	51 7.2	48 7.6	50 7.3	49 7.5	45 8.2
80 6.1	69 5.3	83 4.4		68 5.4		69 5.3	66 5.5	66 5.5	66 5.5	68 5.4
91 4.0	101 3.6	91 4.0		94 3.9		96 3.8	96 3.8	89 4.1	91 4.0	94 3.9
20 18.4	25 14.6	31 11.8		26 14.3	Cost of Sales/Payables	26 14.3	21 17.2	19 18.9	22 16.7	26 14.3
46 8.0	37 9.9	41 8.8		40 9.1		36 10.2	32 11.3	30 12.0	33 11.1	40 9.1
63 5.8	51 7.2	54 6.8		54 6.8		51 7.1	51 7.5	48 7.6	49 7.4	54 6.8
4.8	4.6	4.7		4.8	Sales/Working Capital	4.7	4.8	5.2	4.9	4.8
6.4	7.2	5.5		6.4		7.6	7.0	7.4	6.9	6.4
16.0	11.8	7.3		10.6		12.1	10.6	11.6	9.2	10.6
6.8	6.7	9.9		8.7	EBIT/Interest	8.6	9.4	7.8	6.3	8.7
(23) 2.2	(58) 3.0	(14) 7.2	(99) 3.2			(112) 4.5	(131) 4.1	(113) 3.4	(110) 2.6	(99) 3.2
-1.0	2.0	2.8		1.9		1.5	1.8	1.3	.8	1.9
9.5	8.4	16.4		10.3	Cash Flow/Cur. Mat. L/T/D	9.1	9.8	10.8	9.3	10.3
(25) 2.2	(47) 3.6	(17) 7.5	(96) 5.0			(90) 3.7	(100) 3.9	(96) 4.3	(91) 3.3	(96) 5.0
-.3	2.2	2.9		2.0		1.7	1.9	1.6	1.2	2.0
.3	.3	.4		.3	Fixed/Worth	.3	.3	.3	.3	.3
.4	.5	.4		.5		.5	.4	.5	.4	.5
.9	.7	1.0		.9		.7	.7	.8	.7	.7
.6	.5	.6		.5	Debt/Worth	.6	.6	.6	.5	.5
1.2	1.1	.8		1.0		1.1	1.0	1.2	.9	1.0
3.0	1.9	1.0		1.8		2.0	1.9	1.9	2.1	1.8
21.5	27.9	30.8		28.4	% Profit Before Taxes/Tangible Net Worth	31.3	30.2	31.8	23.6	28.4
(28) 11.3	(72) 14.8	18.4	(127) 14.7			(145) 19.2	(154) 16.2	(140) 19.9	(133) 11.0	(127) 14.7
-4.9	7.9	10.4		7.1		6.8	6.8	5.8	3.2	7.1
11.4	10.6	16.6		13.0	% Profit Before Taxes/Total Assets	15.4	15.8	15.1	11.0	13.0
3.8	6.7	9.6		6.8		8.7	8.6	7.9	5.6	6.8
-2.1	3.2	3.8		2.8		2.7	2.5	2.0	.7	2.8
23.2	19.6	11.1		19.4	Sales/Net Fixed Assets	19.6	20.3	17.3	17.3	19.4
14.6	11.9	8.6		11.3		11.2	10.3	11.1	11.8	11.3
7.5	6.8	6.5		6.4		7.8	7.1	7.4	7.4	6.4
2.8	2.7	2.5		2.7	Sales/Total Assets	2.8	2.7	3.0	2.7	2.7
2.5	2.2	2.2		2.3		2.4	2.3	2.4	2.3	2.3
2.0	1.8	1.7		1.8		1.9	1.9	1.9	1.9	1.8
1.1	1.1	1.1		1.2	% Depr., Dep., Amort./Sales	.9	.9	.9	1.1	1.2
(28) 1.5	(65) 1.7	(18) 1.7	(118) 1.6			(131) 1.3	(141) 1.3	(130) 1.4	(126) 1.5	(118) 1.6
2.1	2.3	2.4		2.3		1.9	1.9	1.9	2.0	2.3
.5	.5			.7	% Lease & Rental Exp/Sales	.6	.6	.6	.7	.7
(12) 1.8	(24) 1.0		(47) 1.4			(55) 1.1	(70) 1.2	(69) 1.1	(63) 1.5	(47) 1.4
2.1	2.0			1.9		1.9	2.4	1.9	2.4	1.9
2.6	1.5			2.0	% Officers' Comp/Sales	1.5	1.2	1.3	2.3	2.0
(13) 4.2	(18) 3.3		(31) 3.4			(44) 3.2	2.7	(47) 3.1	(38) 3.6	(31) 3.4
10.2	4.7			5.5		4.5	4.7	4.8	5.5	
40010M	576520M	895043M	811623M	2123198M	Net Sales ($)	1793129M	3189046M	2836601M	2275490M	2123198M
16883M	271627M	339272M	448662M	1074444M	Total Assets ($)	807121M	1411596M	1314517M	1084171M	1074444M

M = $thousand   MM = $million

Source: Excerpted page Copyright © 1984 by Robert Morris Associates. Reprinted by permission. *Disclaimer Statement:* RMA cautions that the studies be regarded only as a general guideline and not as an absolute industry norm. This is due to limited samples within categories, the categorization of companies by their primary Standard Industrial Classification (SIC) number only, and different methods of operations by companies within the same industry. For these reasons, RMA recommends that the figures be used only as general guidelines in addition to other methods of financial analysis.

Break-even volume on a cash basis (Q_c) is calculated algebraically as shown in Equation (16).

The break-even volume, Q_c, of firm output determined on a cash basis, can be calculated as

$$Q_c = \frac{FC_c}{P - VC} \qquad \text{(16)}$$

where FC_c = fixed cash operating cost, P = price per unit, and VC = variable cost per unit.

In our example, break-even volume, determined on a cash basis, would be

$$Q_c = \frac{\$120,000}{\$3.00 - \$1.20} = \frac{\$120,000}{\$1.80} = 66,667 \text{ units per year.}$$

To cover total cash expenses, the firm must sell only 66,667 units versus 100,000 to cover all costs.

Sample Problem 7–1 Break-Even Analysis for Benchmark Corporation

Benchmark Corporation sells a single product for $30.00 with variable costs per unit of $18.00. If fixed costs are $3 million, calculate the break-even point in units. If fixed costs include $900,000 of noncash expenses (depreciation and amortization), what is the break-even point on a cash basis?

Solution
Using Equation (15), the break-even volume of output would be

$$Q_b = \frac{\$3,000,000}{\$30 - \$18} = 250,000 \text{ units.}$$

On a cash basis, the break-even volume of output would be determined using Equation (16) as

$$Q_c = \frac{\$2,100,000}{\$30 - \$18} = 175,000 \text{ units.} \;\; \blacksquare$$

OPERATING LEVERAGE AND FINANCIAL LEVERAGE

In Figure 7–4, we can see that above the break-even point, operating profits rise rapidly. At output levels above the break-even point, a given change in volume of output produces a larger percentage change in operating profit. For example, a 10 percent change in volume, from 125,000 units to 137,500 units, produces a 10 percent change in sales revenue. Operating profit, however, increases by 50 percent, from $45,000 at 125,000 units to $67,500 at 137,500 units. Below break-even volume, we have the same relationship, but in the opposite direction.

Operating Leverage

Operating leverage—
measures the sensitivity of
operating profit to changes
in sales and can be
calculated as the
percentage change in
operating profits divided
by the percentage change
in sales.

Operating leverage is the sensitivity of operating profit to changes in sales. Earlier in the book, Chapter 4 discussed a firm's operating risk as the risk to shareholders that results from the nature of a firm's product markets and production facilities. Shortly, we will define operating risk more carefully and show how overall operating risk depends in part on operating leverage. The framework of break-even analysis provides a useful way to see the relationship. The degree of operating leverage at any level of output is given in Equation (17).

The degree of operating leverage (DOL) at any level of output is calculated as

$$\text{DOL} = \frac{\text{Percentage change in operating profits}}{\text{Percentage change in sales}}. \qquad (17)$$

Operating leverage is a function of the firm's cost structure, specifically the ratio of fixed operating costs to total operating costs. If a firm had no fixed costs, it would have operating leverage equal to 1.0, and a given change in sales would produce the same percentage change in operating profit. Where fixed costs do exist, the firm has operating leverage greater than 1.0, and a given change in sales produces a larger percentage change in operating profit. The higher the ratio of fixed to total operating costs, the greater is the degree of operating leverage.

For example, as we stated earlier, for the example depicted in Figure 7–4, a 10 percent change in sales (from 125,000 to 137,500 units) produced a 50 percent change in operating profit (from $45,000 to $67,500). Using Equation (17), we calculate the degree of operating leverage in this case as

$$\text{DOL} = \frac{50 \text{ percent}}{10 \text{ percent}} = 5.0.$$

This degree of operating leverage exceeds 1.0 because the firm has fixed costs.

The concept of operating leverage is illustrated in Figure 7–6, which plots the data from Table 7–16. Panel B of the figure repeats the break-even diagram presented earlier in Figure 7–4. The diagram in Panel B was constructed for a product with a selling price of $3.00, variable costs of $1.20 per unit, and fixed operating costs of $180,000 per year. Panel A of Figure 7–6 is constructed for a product with a selling price of $3.00, variable costs of $2.20 per unit, and fixed operating costs of $40,000 per year. Panel A illustrates low operating leverage, and Panel B illustrates high operating leverage. Any given change in sales produces a much larger percentage change in B's operating profit than in A's. When sales are rising, high operating leverage is desirable; when sales are falling, high operating leverage is not desirable. The sword has two edges.

The degree of operating leverage (DOL) at any level of sales can be expressed directly in terms of the cost structure as shown in Equation (18).

Figure 7–6

Operating Leverage

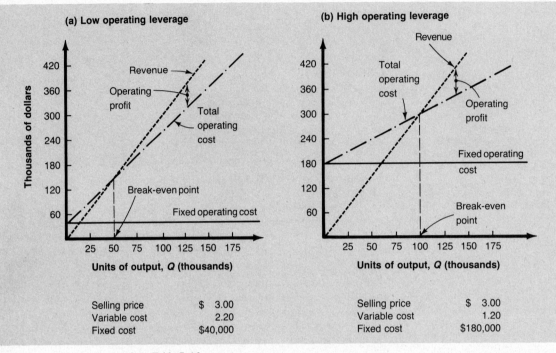

Note: This figure plots the data from Table 7–16.

The degree of operating leverage (DOL) at any level of sales can be expressed in terms of the cost structure as

$$DOL = \frac{S - VC}{S - VC - FC} \tag{18}$$

where S = sales in dollars, VC = total variable cost in dollars, and FC = total fixed cost in dollars.

Using data from Figure 7–6 as an example, at a sales level of $450,000, the DOL for the firms in Panel A and B would be calculated as

$$DOL_A = \frac{\$450,000 - \$330,000}{\$450,000 - \$330,000 - \$40,000} = 1.5.$$

$$DOL_B = \frac{\$450,000 - \$180,000}{\$450,000 - \$180,000 - \$180,000} = 3.0.$$

Equation (18) makes it clear that the DOL for a given firm is different at different levels of operations.

A good example of a firm with high operating leverage is an airline. Fixed operat-

Table 7–16

Comparison of Low Operating Leverage with High Operating Leverage

Panel A: Low Operating Leverage

Units (thousands)	Sales (thousands of dollars)	Variable Cost (thousands of dollars)	Total Cost (thousands of dollars)	Operating Profit (thousands of dollars)
25	75	55	95	−20
50	150	110	150	0
75	225	165	205	20
100	300	220	260	40
125	375	275	315	60
150	450	330	370	80
175	525	385	425	100

Panel B: High Operating Leverage

Units (thousands)	Sales (thousands of dollars)	Variable Cost (thousands of dollars)	Total Cost (thousands of dollars)	Operating Profit (thousands of dollars)
25	75	30	210	−135
50	150	60	240	−90
75	225	90	270	−45
100	300	120	300	0
125	375	150	330	45
150	450	180	360	90
175	525	210	390	135

Note: Panel A assumptions include a selling price of $3.00, a variable cost of $2.20, and a fixed cost of $40,000. Panel B assumptions include a selling price of $3.00, a variable cost of $1.20, and a fixed cost of $180,000.

ing costs are very high and include, primarily, salaries, fuel, maintenance, and depreciation. All these costs are incurred no matter how many passengers are carried. Variable costs are minimal, perhaps involving not much more than the cost of inflight meals and ticket blanks. Once above the break-even passenger load, each additional dollar of revenue is practically all operating profit. Operating profit is very sensitive to the number of passengers carried.

A typical retail business, on the other hand, has much lower operating leverage. Variable costs are high and are, primarily, the cost of goods purchased for resale. A wholesaler might have even lower operating leverage, with fixed salaries a smaller proportion of total costs.

In an uncertain world, sales revenue is likely to vary over time and will be uncertain for any period in the future. Variable sales result in variable operating profits. Variability of operating profits over time, and uncertainty as to what future operating profits will be, is referred to as **operating risk,** or as *business risk.* Chapter 4 discussed operating risk and its relation to financial risk. We can see from Figure 7–6

Operating risk,—or *business risk,* is the risk inherent in the firm's commercial activities. Operating risk affects the variability of operating profits over time.

that operating leverage is an important determinant of operating risk. For any given level of variability of sales, the higher the operating leverage, the more variable is operating profit and, thus, the higher is the operating risk. We will find in later chapters that the degree of operating risk is an important consideration in formulating many financial policies.

Financial Leverage

Thus far, this chapter has focused on operating costs and operating profits, with interest excluded from consideration, in order to draw a distinction between *operating leverage* and *financial leverage*.

Operating leverage is determined by the firm's cost structure and, therefore, by the nature of the business. The firm's commercial strategy dictates the markets in which it operates and, therefore, the technology of its production and marketing operations and their resulting cost structures.

Financial leverage, on the other hand, is determined by the mix of debt and equity funds used to finance the firm's assets. We discussed financial leverage briefly in Chapter 4 and will return to this important concept later in this book. Here we make only a few brief observations. The income statement for Sparta Manufacturing Company in Table 7–1 shows that interest is subtracted from operating profit to obtain net profit before taxes. The more debt a firm employs, the more interest it pays. Interest cost is fixed with respect to output and, therefore, is directly analogous to fixed operating costs. In the presence of financial leverage, a given change in operating profit produces a larger percentage change in net profit before taxes. The analogy with operating leverage is direct. The sensitivity of net profit before (and after) taxes to changes in sales, thus, depends on the combined effects of both operating and financial leverage. Operating leverage affects the sensitivity of operating profit to changes in sales. In turn, financial leverage affects the sensitivity of net profit before (and after) taxes to changes in operating profit.

> **Operating leverage is determined by the firm's cost structure and, therefore, by the nature of the firm's business. Financial leverage is determined by the mix of debt and equity funds used to finance the firm's assets.**

Applications of Cost/Volume/Profit Analysis

Cost/volume/profit analysis has many applications. It is useful in making projections of cash flow and profits for the period ahead. It is also useful in analyzing decisions regarding new products or decisions to expand or contract or drop existing products. It sometimes is useful in make-or-buy decisions. Break-even analysis also may be useful in decisions involving equipment selection and replacement, especially where fixed costs are being substituted for variable costs through automation. It may find use also in marketing decisions involving pricing, promotion and advertising, and distribution channels.

KEY CONCEPTS

1. Profitability can be analyzed effectively using the normalized income statement, which measures elements relative to sales.

2. Return on investment, or profit per dollar of capital invested, is an efficiency measure.

3. The turnover rates for inventory, accounts receivable, and accounts payable are measures of activity and efficiency.

4. Liquidity measures are useful in assessing a firm's ability to meet its cash obligations in the short run.

5. Measures of indebtedness give an indication of a firm's ability to meet obligations over the longer term.

6. Separating costs into fixed and variable components is necessary in order to calculate break-even volumes.

7. Operating leverage depends on the relationship between a firm's fixed and variable costs.

8. Financial leverage depends on the mix of debt and equity funds used to finance the firm's assets. The greater is the use of debt, the higher is the financial leverage.

9. The sensitivity of profits after taxes to changes in sales depends on the combined effects of both operating and financial leverage.

SUMMARY

Financial analysis begins with the examination of information to determine past trends. Fundamentally, financial analysis seeks to use the knowledge of the past to improve decisions for the future. The income statement, balance sheet, and source-and-use statement provide basic data for analyzing financial performance.

Profits are measured in dollar terms by the income statement. Profitability (profit per dollar of sales) is measured by the normalized income statement. Such a statement also is useful for examining the behavior of costs over time in relation to sales. Return on investment (ROI) measures profit per dollar of investment. There are many different ways to calculate ROI, so care must be taken to avoid ambiguity. Often it is useful to decompose ROI into two components, profit margin and sales turnover. Margin and turnover themselves can be decomposed using the DuPont system of financial control. The effectiveness of accounts-receivable management can be measured by calculating *days sales outstanding,* also known as the *average collection period,* or by constructing an accounts-receivable aging schedule. Inventory management can be analyzed by calculating an inventory turnover ratio. Accounts payable can be analyzed by calculating *days purchases outstanding.* Activity and turnover measures must be interpreted very carefully where seasonal patterns and growth trends are present.

The ability of a firm to meet its obligations as they come due can be judged through the use of liquidity ratios. The *current ratio* (current assets divided by current liabilities) and the *acid-test ratio* are the most widely used liquidity ratios. Dollar measures of liquidity are net working capital per dollar of sales and net liquid assets. Indebtedness can be measured both in stock terms, using various ratios of debt to other balance-sheet data, and in flow terms, using coverage ratios calculated from income-statement data. Two widely used coverage ratios are *times interest earned* and *fixed-charge coverage.* For publicly owned companies, market performance measures are also useful tools in financial analysis.

Benchmarks, or standards of comparison, are necessary for analyzing financial performance. Single figures for a single point in time are of little use by themselves and must be compared either to data for the same firm over time (to identify trends) or to data for other similar firms (to make industry comparisons).

Analysis of a company also requires an understanding of the response of revenues, costs, profits, and cash flows to changes in sales volume. In the short run, some costs vary with sales volume, and some do not. Some costs are fixed within a given range of sales volume and are variable outside that range. In the long run, over wide ranges of sales volume, all costs are variable.

Break-even analysis is a technique for examining the relationship between operating profit and sales volume. Its usefulness, however, sometimes is limited where costs cannot be separated into fixed and variable components or where joint costs are attributable to more than one product.

Operating leverage is the sensitivity of a firm's operating profit to changes in sales. The degree of operating leverage of a firm is a function of its cost structure (the ratio of fixed to total operating costs) and, hence, is determined by the nature of its business. *Financial leverage*, the subject of Part Five of this book, depends on the mix of debt and equity used to finance the firm's assets.

QUESTIONS

1. Why is return on investment (ROI) sometimes ambiguous as a measure of performance?
2. Return on assets can be viewed as a product of which two components?
3. What are the problems of measuring the performance of accounts receivable and inventory management in a firm with a seasonal sales pattern?
4. What sources of information are available that provide data on firms? On industries?
5. Is it possible for a firm to earn a profit consistently and yet always be short of cash?
6. Can you imagine a firm having difficulty paying its bills when its current ratio is between 2.0 and 3.0? Can you think of a firm that could operate successfully with an acid-test ratio considerably lower than 1.0?
7. Define the terms *fixed costs* and *variable costs*. Is a *fixed cost* constant over all ranges of output?
8. What are some of the limitations of break-even analysis?
9. Why would a firm's break-even point for operating profit differ from its break-even point on a cash basis?
10. What is *operating leverage*? Give some examples both of businesses with high operating leverage and those with low operating leverage.
11. How does financial leverage differ from operating leverage?

PROBLEMS

1. Prepare normalized income statements for Acme using the data from problem (1) in Chapter 6 for each of the four years 1–4. What questions are answered? What additional questions are raised?
2. Assume that all sales for Acme are on credit and that the company averaged $58,000 per day in credit purchases from suppliers in year 1, $80,000 per day in year 2, $95,000 per day in year 3, and $108,000 per day in year 4.
   a. Calculate the return on assets, the operating return on assets before tax, the net operating return on assets before tax, and the return on equity for each of the four years. (Exclude goodwill in this calculation.)

Table A

	Return on Assets (percent)	Sales (thousands of dollars)	Profit after Taxes (thousands of dollars)
1982	8.4	3,500	175
1983	8.0	4,600	225
1984	7.2	6,000	280
1985	4.8	9,200	415
1986	3.1	11,000	465

Table B

Balance Sheet (thousands of dollars), 12/31/86

Cash	230	Notes payable	1,015
Accounts receivable	9,380	Accounts payable	3,545
Inventories	7,515	Accrued taxes	225
Current assets	17,125	Current liabilities	4,784
Net fixed assets	34,125	Long-term debt	18,036
Total assets	51,250	Deferred income taxes	2,840
		Total liabilities	20,876
		Common stock (par)	575
		Capital in excess of par	7,945
		Retained earnings	17,070
		Common equity	25,590
		Total liabilities	
		and net worth	51,250

b. Calculate the following ratios for the December 31 balance sheet dates in each of the four years: DSO, receivables turnover rate, inventory turnover, days purchases outstanding, current ratio, acid test ratio, net working capital per dollar of sales, debt to total assets, debt to net worth, and the times interest earned on both long-term debt issues. Assume year 0 ending inventory of $3,900,000.

c. Do these ratios point out any potential problems or weak spots?

3. The Beech Company has been suffering a severe decline in return on assets over the last 5 years, and management has asked you to recommend corrective action. Based on the preliminary infor-

mation in Table A, where would you begin your initial investigative efforts?

4. The balance sheet and income statement for Harrington Incorporated for the year 1986 in addition to various financial ratios for the industry in which Harrington operates are given in Tables B, C, and D.

a. Compute the ratios given above for the Harrington Company. The inventories were $6,800,000 and the receivables were $8,400,000 for Harrington on December 31, 1985.

b. Discuss briefly the liquidity and leverage position of Harrington in relation to the industry norms. Compare its profitability to that of the industry.

Table C

Income Statement (thousands of dollars), Year-End 1986

Net sales (credit)	46,235
Cost of goods sold	33,167
Gross profit	13,068
General and administrative expense	9,590
Operating income	3,478
Interest expense	1,120
Net income before taxes	2,358
Income taxes	1,130
Net income	1,228

Table D

	Industry Ratio
Current ratio	4.02
Acid-test ratio	3.00
Inventory turnover	7.50 times
Average collection period	63.10 days
Profit margin (pretax)	5.0 percent
Return on assets (ROA)	2.5 percent
Debt-to-total-assets ratio	30.0 percent
Times-interest-earned ratio	3.90

Table E

		Ratios		
	1984	*1985*	*1986*	*Industry Norm*
Days sales outstanding (DSO)	31	34	32	33
Inventory-turnover	4.1 times	3.6 times	3.2 times	4.0 times
Days purchases outstanding (DPO)	25	32	41	26
Current ratio	2.04	1.88	1.64	2.11
Acid-test ratio	1.18	1.14	1.06	1.24
Debt/total assests ratio	0.46	0.49	0.54	0.44
Debt/net worth ratio	1.15	1.17	1.18	1.13
Times-interest-earned ratio	11 times	9 times	7 times	9 times

5. The ABC Company has enjoyed rapid growth in assets over the last 5 years although profits have been declining since 1984. Eight key ratios are shown in Table E for the years 1984, 1985 and 1986. The median ratios for the industry are shown in a separate column.

   a. Evaluate the company's situation and suggest the problem areas most promising for further investigation.

   b. What problems do you see in relying on a strict comparison with median ratios for the industry?

6. Selected information from the Warm-Glow Light Company's financial records is summarized in Table F. Using ratios discussed in this chapter, analyze the company's financial conditions and performance. Does the analysis reveal any problems?

7. The data in Table G were taken from the financial statements of two companies.

   a. Which company has the better current position? Why?

   b. Which company has the greater working-capital turnover? (This ratio was not defined in the chapter and must be provided by the student.)

Table F

	1984	*1985*	*1986*
Sales	$10,385,000	$10,750,000	$9,495,000
Cost of goods sold	$ 8,100,000	$ 9,000,000	$8,450,000
Net profit	$ 750,000	$ 500,000	$ 250,000
Cash	$ 83,000	$ 50,000	$ 35,500
Accounts receivable	500,000	650,000	725,000
Inventory	1,000,000	1,200,000	1,500,000
Net fixed assets	2,000,000	2,000,000	2,000,000
Total assets	$ 3,583,000	$ 3,900,000	$4,260,500
Accounts payable	$ 583,000	$ 750,000	$ 973,000
Miscellaneous accruals	500,000	525,000	562,500
Short-term bank loan	250,000	250,000	350,000
Long-term debt	750,000	750,000	750,000
Common stock	250,000	250,000	250,000
Retained earnings	1,250,000	1,375,000	1,375,000
Total liabilities and owners' equity	$ 3,583,000	$ 3,900,000	$4,260,500

Table G

	(thousands of dollars)	
	Company A	Company B
Sales	3,000	9,000
Cost of goods sold	1,900	6,900
Operating expenses	400	1,600
Interest expense	10	110
Income taxes	240	300
Cash	1,000	4,000
Inventory	4,000	2,000
Net fixed assets	5,000	19,000
Long-term investments	400	100
Current liabilities	1,000	2,000
Long-term liabilities	100	1,800
Capital stock ($100 par value)	3,000	18,000
Retained earnings	6,300	3,300

c. Which company has the better profit margin?
d. Which company has the highest book value (net worth) per share?
e. Which company is earning the better rate of return on resources available to the management?

Table H

Balance Sheet (thousands of dollars), 12/31/86	
Cash	220
Accounts receivable	275
Inventory	825
Total current assets	1,320
Net fixed assets	605
Total assets	1,925
Accounts payable	165
Notes payable	220
Other current liabilities	110
Total current liabilities	495
Long-term debt	220
Common equity	1,210
Total claims on assets	1,925

8. The balance sheet and income statement for the Apple Core Computer (ACC) Company and its industry averages for the year 1986 are given in Tables H, I, and J.

a. Calculate the ratios for which ACC's industry averages are given in Table J.
b. Outline ACC's strengths and weaknesses as revealed by your analysis.

Table I

Income Statement, Year-End 1986		
Sales		$2,750,000
Cost of goods sold		
Materials	$1,045,000	
Labor	660,000	
Heat, light and power	99,000	
Indirect labor	165,000	
Depreciation	60,500	2,029,500
Gross profit		$ 720,000
Selling expenses		275,000
General and administrative expenses		316,800
Earnings before interest and taxes		$ 128,700
Less interest expense		− 13,200
Net profit before taxes		$ 115,500
Less federal income taxes (at 50 percent)		57,750
Profit after taxes		$ 57,750

Table J

Performance Measure	Industry Average
Current ratio	2.4
Average collection period	43 days
Sales/inventories	9.8
Sales/total assets	2
Profit margin	3.3 percent
Return on assets	6.6 percent
Return on equity	18.1 percent
Debt to total assets	63.5 percent

c. Suppose ACC had doubled its sales and also its inventories, accounts receivable, and common equity during 1986. How would that information affect the validity of your ratio analysis?

9. During 1986 the Theta Company purchased a warehouse for $2 million cash. The company also acquired an office building for $3 million, giving a long-term note for that amount. In addition, the company issued common stock to retire a $4 million long-term note and retired other long-term notes totaling $3 million by paying cash. Net income during 1986 was $10 million. No assets were retired or sold during 1986. Balance sheets are given in Table K.

a. Determine the change in working capital during the year 1986.

b. Construct a detailed source-and-use statement for 1986 similar to that in Table 6–12.

10. Selected data from three companies are provided in Table L. Calculate the return on assets. Using the Dupont system, compare and contrast the three companies.

11. Benchmark Corporation sells a single product for $30.00 with variable costs per unit of $18.00. If fixed costs are $3,000,000, calculate the break-even point in units. If fixed costs include $900,000 of noncash expenses (depreciation and amortization), what is the break-even point on a cash basis?

Table K

	December 31, 1985	December 31, 1986
Cash	$ 4,000	$ 5,000
Accounts receivable	5,000	4,000
Inventory	10,000	14,000
Net fixed assets	25,000	28,000
Total assets	$44,000	$51,000
Accounts payable	$ 3,000	$ 5,000
Short-term notes payable	4,000	3,000
Long-term notes payable	10,000	6,000
Common stock	15,000	19,000
Retained earnings	12,000	18,000
Total liabilities and owners' equity	$44,000	$51,000

Table L

	Company A	Company B	Company C
Sales	$100,000	$375,000	$500,000
Profit after taxes	$ 1,500	$ 3,000	$ 4,500
Total assets	$ 50,000	$100,000	$400,000

12. Using the data in problem (11), prepare a break-even chart following the format of Figure 7–5 in the text.

13. If we assume that the information given in problem (11) remains valid over all levels of output, would you expect the degree of operating leverage to remain constant over all levels of output? Calculate the degree of operating leverage at sales levels of 300,000 units and 400,000 units in order to answer the question.

14. Assume the Benchmark Corporation, referred to in problem (11), decides to automate its production process by replacing some of the manual production tasks with a robot. If fixed costs increase to $3,300,000 because of the added depreciation while variable costs decrease to $17 per unit because of the lower labor expense, what is the effect on the break-even point? What would be the effect on operating profit at an output of 400,000 units?

15. The Lakeland Manufacturing Company is determining its budget for 1987. There is some concern about expected profits. Three alternatives that may improve profits are being considered. The proposed budget, in thousands of dollars, is given in Table M.

a. Compute the break-even point using a break-even chart.

b. Alternative 1 for improving profits requires a 5 percent increase in sales prices. Evaluate its effect on profits and the break-even point when the number of units sold is unchanged.

c. Alternative 2 would reduce fixed costs by 5 percent. Evaluate the effect on profits and the

Table M

Sales (14,000,000 units at $1)		$14,000
Cost of goods sold		
Fixed	$5,325	
Variable	3,150	8,475
Gross margin		$ 5,525
Selling and general expenses		
Fixed	$2,800	
Variable	2,500	5,300
Net income		$ 225

break-even point, assuming alternative 1 is not put into effect.

d. Alternative 3 would reduce variable costs by 5 percent. Evaluate the effect on profits and the break-even point when neither alternative 1 nor 2 is put into effect.

e. Evaluate the effect on profits and the break-even point when all three alternatives are implemented simultaneously.

16. Competition in the small kitchen appliance industry has forced Home Products Company to consider two different product-line strategies. Plan 1 involves the elimination of two of the four existing food-processor models. This would result in decreased start-up and packaging costs. Plan 2 would retain all four models but would replace the current hand assembly of the three-piece body with a one-piece, injection-molded body. A large initial investment for the molds would pay off in the form of lower labor and material costs. The costs for the current sales volume and the projected costs of each plan are given in Table N.

Table N

	Estimated Costs (dollars)		
	Current	Plan 1	Plan 2
Raw materials	440,000	390,000	265,000
Factory labor	615,000	500,000	215,000
Depreciation on fixed assets	800,000	980,000	1,257,500
Salary expense	640,000	700,000	775,000
Variable selling expense	70,600	72,012	70,600
Property taxes	36,000	45,000	63,000
Other fixed expenses	52,000	75,000	103,000

Table O

Sales (12,200,000	
units at $1)	$12,200,000
Cost of sales	
Fixed	$3,910,000
Variable	4,240,000
Gross margin	4,050,000
Selling and	
general expenses	
Fixed	1,500,000
Variable	1,950,000
Income	$ 600,000

The current annual sales level is about 60,000 units. Half of these are sold at $40 each and half at $60 each. Plan 1 would eliminate one $40 and one $60 model. It is expected that unit sales would remain at 60,000 with the $40 model comprising 45 percent of unit sales. Management is primarily concerned with the relative riskiness of profits under each plan.

a. Compute the degree of operating leverage at current volume (60,000 units) for each of the three possibilities.

b. What is the effect on profit of a 5 percent decrease in dollar sales?

Table P

	(thousands of dollars)
Advertising expense	275
Depreciation and insurance on plant	450
Interest expense	120
Fixed factory overhead	150
Salaries expense	500

c. Rank the possibilities according to their degree of riskiness, as measured by operating leverage.

17. The income statement of Tarrytown Corporation for 1986 is given in Table O. Tarrytown plans an expansion of its production facilities to allow for projected sales of $20,000,000 (at $1 per unit) for 1987. The expansion is expected to increase expenses by the amounts shown in Table P.

a. Prepare a projected income statement for the expected (1987) sales and expenses.

b. Compare break-even points at present (1986) and projected (1987) operating levels.

c. Compare profits before and after expansion if sales remain at the 1986 level.

REFERENCES

Altman, E. I., R. G. Haldeman, and P. Narayanan. "Zeta Analysis: A New Model to Identify Bankruptcy Risk of Corporations." *Journal of Banking and Finance* 1 (June 1977): 29–54.

Beaver, W. H. "Financial Ratios as Predictors of Failure." *Empirical Research in Accounting, Selected Studies, 1966* (January 1967): 71–111.

Edmister, R. O. "An Empirical Test of Financial Ratio Analysis for Small Business Failure Prediction." *Journal of Financial and Quantitative Analysis* 7 (March 1973) 1477–1493.

Findlay, M. C., III and E. E. Williams. "Toward More Adequate Debt Service Coverage Ratios." *Financial Analysts Journal* 31 (November–December 1975) 58–61.

Gordon, M. J. "Towards a Theory of Financial Distress." *Journal of Finance* 26 (May 1971) 347–356.

Helfert, E. A. *Techniques of Financial Analysis*. 4th ed. Homewood, Ill.: Richard D. Irwin, 1977.

Ketz, J. E. "Are Constant-Dollar Disclosures Informative?" *Financial Analysts Journal* (March–April 1983) 52–55.

Lasman, D. A., and R. L. Weil. "Adjusting the Debt/Equity Ratio." *Financial Analysts Journal* (September–October 1978) 49–58.

Lev, B. *Financial Statement Analysis: A New Approach*. Englewood Cliffs, N.J.: Prentice-Hall, 1974.

Levin, R. I., and C. A. Kirkpatrick. *Quantitative Approaches to Management*. 3d ed. New York: McGraw-Hill, 1975, chap. 2.

Loomis, C. J. "Profitability Goes Through a Ceiling." *Fortune* (May 4, 1981).

Murray, R. F. "The Penn-Central Debacle: Lessons for Financial Analysis." *Journal of Finance* 26 (May 1971) 327–332.

Smith, K. V., and J. F. Weston. "Further Evaluation of Conglomerate Performance." *Journal of Business Research* 5 (March 1977) 5–14.

Von Furstenberg, G. M., and B. G. Malkiel. "Financial Analysis in an Inflationary Environment." *Journal of Finance* 32 (May 1977) 575–588.

Chapter

8

Financial Planning

This chapter discusses techniques for developing and using financial plans and explains how to estimate requirements for funds using pro-forma analysis. The chapter examines different financing patterns, including seasonal and long-term growth patterns, and shows how to develop a cash budget. As we will see, financial plans can be used for communications and control in addition to decision making. Finally, the chapter explores the impact of inflation on financial plans.

Figure 8–1
A Planning System

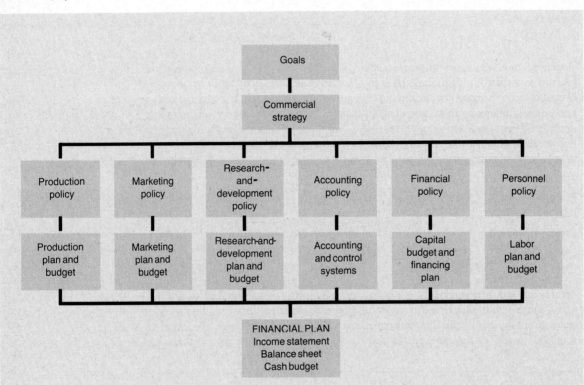

Chapters 6 and 7 were concerned primarily with analyzing past and current performance. The tools developed there, such as source-and-use analysis and ratio analysis, were diagnostic in purpose, and the orientation was mainly historical, although we noted that the same analytical tools could be applied to plans for the future as well.

Another task of financial management is to look ahead—*to plan*. In simplest terms, a **financial plan** is a statement of what is to be done in some future period and of effective ways of doing it. Why should a firm plan? Planning requires effort and, therefore, is not without cost. In an uncertain world, events are likely to deviate from even the most carefully formulated plan. Are the benefits of planning worth the cost? For most firms, planning of the type discussed in this chapter very definitely is worth the cost. A planning system improves coordination in an organization and encourages the kind of thinking that identifies difficulties before they occur. Many potential problems can be avoided and significant operating and financing economies achieved. A rather modest planning system usually will pay for itself many times over in terms of efficiency and lower costs.

A **financial plan**—describes in dollar terms the activities that the firm intends to engage in over some future period. An income statement and balance sheet are key components of the financial plan.

Financial planning is one part of a larger planning process within an organization.

A **commercial strategy**—is the firm's definition of the products and services it will produce and the markets it will serve.

A complete planning system begins at the highest level of policy with a statement of the firm's basic goal or purpose, usually expressed in qualitative, mission-oriented, terms. From this statement of purpose is derived the firm's **commercial strategy,** defining the products or services it will produce and the markets it will serve. Supporting policies then are developed in production, marketing, research and development, accounting, finance, and personnel. The extent to which the system is formalized with detailed planning and budgeting systems in each area depends in part on the firm's size and on the complexity of its operations. A planning system might be represented schematically as in Figure 8–1.

Financial planning—is part of a larger planning process within an organization; the complete planning system begins at the highest policy level with the statement of the firm's key goal or purpose.

Broadly conceived, **financial planning** can be viewed as the representation of an overall plan for the firm in financial terms. Narrowly conceived, financial planning may refer only to the process of determining the financing requirements necessary to support a given set of plans in other areas. This chapter will discuss technqiues for accomplishing both types of financial planning.

The basic elements of the financial plan are the *projected income statement* and the *projected balance sheet*. Supporting elements may include a cash budget, personnel budget, production budget, purchasing budget, income and expense budget, and so on. These may be prepared by various organizational units within the firm and may be stated in terms of dollars, physical units, or people. These detailed budgets represent time-phased schedules of the expenditures, people, materials, and activities required to accomplish the objectives set forth in the overall financial plan.

The **operating plan**—describes in detail the activities in which the firm plans to engage and consists of the sales, production, marketing, research-and-development, and personnel plans required to carry out the firm's commercial strategy.

The starting point for the financial-planning process is the firm's commercial strategy and the associated production, marketing, and research-and-development plans. We will refer to these plans collectively as the firm's **operating plan** because they describe the activities in which the firm plans to engage. Initially, we will take the operating plan as given, although later we will see that operating plans sometimes must be modified in light of financing implications. In addition to the operating plan, we will also take as given the firm's long-term financial structure, its fixed assets, and its long-term liabilities. Decisions with respect to these areas are taken up later in this book.

Given the firm's long-term asset/liability structure and its operating plan, our objective is to represent its plans in financial terms and at the same time to determine financing requirements. We will first focus our attention on financial planning over the near term, specifically the coming 12-month period, and will discuss financial planning over longer periods later in the chapter.

As our vehicle for discussion and illustration, we will leave our old friend, Sparta Manufacturing Company, and use a new firm, Aquatic Systems, Inc., a manufacturer of swimming-pool equipment and accessories, including pumps, filters, and ancillary cleaning and maintenance equipment. Aquatic was established in the 1960s and pursued innovative design and marketing policies coupled with conservative production and financing policies. It found this combination to be quite profitable. Financial statements for the year ending December 31, 1986, are given in Tables 8–1 and 8–2.

Aquatic's sales pattern was highly seasonal, with nearly 50 percent of sales concentrated in the four months from May to August. More than 90 percent of sales were in standard products, and Aquatic followed a policy of level production throughout the year. The seasonal sales pattern coupled with level production resulted in a highly variable financing requirement over the year. A firm with these particular characteristics will give us a good workout in financial planning. We also will see the flow of

Table 8–1

Aquatic Systems, Inc. Income Statement, Year Ending December 31, 1986 (thousands of dollars)

Sales		5080
Cost of goods sold		
Materials and labor	3150	
Manufacturing overhead	290	
Total cost of goods sold		3440
Gross profit		1640
Depreciation		260
Selling and administrative expense		600
Profit before taxes		780
Income taxes at 30 percent*		234
Profit after taxes		546
Dividends		240
To retained earnings		306

*The tax rate of 30 percent is chosen for illustrative purposes only. Given the many changes in tax laws in recent years, this rate is not intended to match current statutes.

funds through the current section of the balance sheet as current assets expand and contract, and we will have a good illustration of the effect of operating policies on financial requirements.

Aquatic normally begins its annual planning cycle each October and develops a financial plan for the 12-month period from January to December. To simplify matters for purposes of illustration, we will assume that the time is now early January 1987: the financial statements we need for 1986 appear in Tables 8–1 and 8–2. We will (1) estimate financing requirements for each month during 1987, (2) discuss patterns of funds requirements, (3) develop a cash budget, and (4) discuss the uses of the financial plan before turning to a discussion of long-run financial planning and the impact of inflation at the end of the chapter.

ESTIMATING REQUIREMENTS FOR FUNDS

Pro-forma analysis—is the projection into the future or past of a firm's financial statements to depict a firm's financial condition *as if* certain prospective events (such as a given sales and production plan) had taken place.

Given Aquatic's long-term asset/liability structure, what are the requirements for financing its operating plan over the next 12 months? Will outside bank financing be required? If so, how much? And when? When will it be repaid? The best way to answer such questions is to project the balance sheet to each date in question. The loan required to make the balance sheet balance is the answer to our question. The process requires painstaking work, but it is essential to good financial management.

The technique we will use often is referred to as **pro-forma analysis.** As used in finance, the term *pro forma* can be translated to mean "as if." Pro-forma analysis is projecting an income statement or balance sheet or cash budget into the future to depict the firm's financial condition *as if* certain prospective events—namely, a given sales and production plan—had taken place. The term *pro forma* usually pertains to projections, but the concept is equally applicable to current or prior periods. A pro-forma balance sheet could be constructed for some prior date depicting the state of affairs as

Table 8–2
Aquatic Systems, Inc. Balance Sheet, December 31, 1986 (thousands of dollars)

Assets	
Cash	50
Marketable securities	94
Accounts receivable	353
Inventories	1,080
Total current assets	1,577
Plant and equipment, gross	4,960
Less accumulated depreciation	− 1,850
Net	3,110
Total assets	4,687
Liabilities and Net Worth	
Note payable (bank)	0
Accounts payable	148
Income taxes payable[a]	40
Other accruals	50
Total current liabilities	238
Mortgage[b]	960
Common stock	1,500
Retained earnings	1,989
Total liabilities and net worth	4,687

[a]Taxes payable of $40,000 represent the amount remaining to be paid on 1986 income taxes, payable on April 15, 1987.
[b]Principal payments of $100,000 per year are due in equal installments in June and December.

if a prospective merger had taken place, or as if a particular division or subsidiary had been sold. Pro-forma analysis is a very useful concept, with applications beyond those discussed in this chapter.

In constructing pro-forma financial statements by month for 1987, our starting point is the operating plan. In Aquatic's case, the operating plan consists of sales and production plans and the expenditures for plant and equipment, materials, labor, overhead, marketing, and administration necessary to carry out those plans. The operating plan completely determines all items in Aquatic's projected income statement, except interest and taxes, and all items in the current section of the balance sheet, except cash and the bank loan. In other words, the operating plan determines the short-term financing requirements. Our objective is to ascertain the amounts and timing of those financing requirements. To do so we will project, on the basis of the operating plan, the income statement and balance sheet, with cash and the bank loan as the balancing figures.

Operating Plan

Based on several economic forecasts, knowledge of its markets and its historical seasonal sales pattern, and predictions about summer weather, Aquatic's marketing department estimated 1987 sales as listed in Table 8–3.

In order to minimize costs, production was scheduled at a level rate throughout the

Table 8–3

Aquatic Systems, Inc. 1987 Sales Plan (thousands of dollars)

December 1986	$250		
January 1987	$220	July	715
February	275	August	605
March	385	September	495
April	495	October	385
May	605	November	275
June	770	December	275
		1987 total	$5,500

year. Aquatic historically had followed a policy of maintaining a high inventory level, and in the past, inventory turnover averaged only about 3.0 times per year. In an effort to improve turnover, management decided to reduce finished-goods inventories gradually in 1987 by holding production at the 1986 rate, even though a sales increase of about 8 percent was forecast for 1987. Accordingly, 1987 purchases were scheduled at $125,000 per month, and production was scheduled at a level rate of $285,000 per month ($125,000 in materials, $135,000 in labor, and $25,000 in manufacturing overhead).

Materials and labor historically had averaged 62 percent of sales. For 1987 as a whole, cost of goods sold should, therefore, total $3,411,000 for materials and labor (0.62 × $5,500,000) plus $300,000 for manufacturing overhead, or $3,711,000 in total. With production scheduled at $285,000 × 12 = $3,420,000 for the year, inventories should decline over the year.

Selling and administrative expenses, including interest, were expected to average approximately $55,000 per month in 1987. Work was expected to be completed in February on a $500,000 expansion and modernization program, with payments to be made in equal installments in January and February. No further capital expenditures were planned in 1987. Depreciation, with that for the new facilities and equipment included, was expected to average $25,000 per month.

All of Aquatic's sales were made on credit, with approximately half on terms of *net 30* (payment due in 30 days) and half on terms of *net 60*—the latter terms being made necessary by competitive pressures. Aquatic's credit manager had determined that, historically, essentially 100 percent of a month's sales remained outstanding at month end, about 50 percent were collected in the first month following, and about 50 percent were collected in the second month following. With respect to disbursements, accounts payable at the end of any month were settled in the following month. Payments for direct labor, manufacturing overhead, and selling and administrative expenses were generally made with a time lag of about one week, giving rise to accrual accounts that remained constant at about $50,000 at the current rate of operations.

Internal Revenue Service regulations required that estimated taxes for any year be paid in four equal installments during the year in the months of April, June, September, and December. Mortgage principal payments of $50,000 were due in June and December. Dividend policy was to remain unchanged, with payments of $60,000 in March, June, September, and December.

Aquatic followed a policy of maintaining a minimum cash balance of $50,000, borrowing where necessary to maintain that figure and investing all amounts over that figure in U.S. Treasury bills. Holdings of bills amounted to $94,000 on December 31, 1986. Aquatic historically had used bank credit to finance its seasonal buildup of receivables and inventories. Relations with a local bank were excellent, and Aquatic currently had access to a seasonal line of credit of $1 million secured by a *blanket lien* on inventories and receivables; that is, Aquatic used all of its inventories and receivables as collateral for the loan. Under the agreement, Aquatic could borrow up to $1 million at any time, provided only that inventories plus receivables exceeded the loan by 75 percent and that the loan was ''off the books''—that is, reduced to zero—for at least 2 months per year.

Pro-Forma Income Statement

A **pro-forma income statement**—is an income statement constructed by projecting as if a certain sales and production plan had taken place.

We now have the information necessary to construct pro-forma financial statements for Aquatic Systems. It is necessary to begin with the **pro-forma income statement,** because in order to do the balance sheet we need the transfer to retained earnings, and to get this figure we must know the profit after tax (PAT). We will use the same format as in Table 8–1. Our sales projection, as we noted, is given in Table 8–3. Assuming no change in prices relative to costs, we can project cost of goods sold at the historical figure of 62 percent of sales for materials and labor plus $25,000 per month for manufacturing overhead. Subtracting depreciation and selling and administrative expenses gives profit before taxes (PBT). Taxes are computed at 30 percent. The complete pro-forma income statement for each month in 1987 is given in Table 8–4.

To get the transfer to retained earnings each month, we subtract dividends from PAT. Dividends normally are not included in the pro-forma income statement because they are not expenses, but we have shown them in Table 8–4 for convenience. This transfer to retained earnings will become an input to our pro-forma balance sheet.

The **sales plan**—is the projection of sales into the future for a specified period and forms the basis for planning production levels, marketing programs, and other firm activities.

The **sales plan** plays the critical role of providing the basis for the production levels, marketing programs, and a variety of activities within the firm. In a firm with good management controls, particularly on expenses, most of the uncertainty about future profits results from uncertainty about future sales. As we will see shortly, the sales and production plans together determine a good part of the balance sheet. If actual sales deviate significantly from planned levels, the effects on the firm's financial condition are likely to be substantial.

> **The sales plan plays a critical role in financial planning in many firms, forming the basis for other supporting plans.**

Sample Problem 8–1   Developing a Pro-Forma Income Statement for Madison International

Prepare a pro-forma income statement for 1987 for Madison International assuming that (1) projected sales are $19.5 million, (2) the cost of goods sold is 58 percent of sales, (3) selling and administrative expenses are $2.5 million a year, (4) depreciation is $80,000 a month, (5) interest expense is $200,000 a year, and (6) the tax rate is 46 percent.

Table 8–4
Aquatic Systems, Inc. Pro-Forma Income Statements, 1987 (thousands of dollars)

	Actual 1986	Jan.	Feb.	Mar.	Apr.	May	June	July	Aug.	Sept.	Oct.	Nov.	Dec.	Total[b] 1987
Sales	5,080	220	275	385	495	605	770	715	605	495	385	275	275	5,500
Cost of goods sold (CGS)														
Materials and labor at 62 percent	3,150	136	171	239	307	375	477	443	375	307	239	171	171	3,411
Manufacturing overhead	290	25	25	25	25	25	25	25	25	25	25	25	25	300
Total CGS	3,440	161	196	264	332	400	502	468	400	332	264	196	196	3,711
Gross profit	1,640	59	79	121	163	205	268	247	205	163	121	79	79	1,789
Depreciation	260	25	25	25	25	25	25	25	25	25	25	25	25	300
Selling and administrative expense[a]	600	55	55	55	55	55	55	55	55	55	55	55	55	660
Profit before taxes	780	(21)	(1)	41	83	125	188	167	125	83	41	(1)	(1)	829
Taxes at 30 percent	234	(6)	0	12	25	38	56	50	38	25	12	0	0	250
Profit after taxes	546	(15)	(1)	29	58	87	132	117	87	58	29	(1)	(1)	579
Dividends	240			60			60		60		60		60	240
To retained earnings	306	(15)	(1)	(31)	58	87	72	117	87	(2)	29	(1)	(61)	339

[a]Includes interest.
[b]Totals for 1987 are found by adding together figures for each month. Due to rounding of monthly figures, this procedure may produce minor differences from totals obtained if monthly figures were left unrounded.

Table 8–5
Madison International Pro-Forma Income Statement, 1987

Sales		$19,500,000
Cost of goods sold		11,310,000
Gross margin		$ 8,190,000
Selling and administrative expense	$2,500,000	
Depreciation ($80,000 × 12)	960,000	3,460,000
Earnings before interest and taxes (EBIT)		$ 4,730,000
Interest		200,000
Profit before taxes (PBT)		$ 4,530,000
Taxes		2,083,800
Net profit		$ 2,446,200

Solution
Madison International's completed pro-forma income statement for 1987 is given in Table 8–5. ▤▥▰

Pro-Forma Balance Sheet

If our objective is to determine the amounts and timing of financing required to carry out the operating plan over the next 12 months, our procedure will be to project all items other than cash and the bank loan, leaving the latter two as our balancing figures. The items to be projected are determined either directly or indirectly by the operating plan or by external commitment (taxes and mortgage payments). We will proceed item by item to create a **pro-forma balance sheet,** using the format in Table 8–2. We will give particular attention to accounts receivable and to inventories, because we can expect these items to be highly variable where sales are seasonal and production is level.

In situations in which sales are not seasonal and the collection pattern is stable, we can project accounts receivable using historical relationships to sales. Perhaps the simplest method is to determine the historical receivables/sales ratio and multiply this figure by sales in each period of the projection. We get the same result by assuming that the number of days sales outstanding (DSO) remains constant over time.

Where sales are highly seasonal, as in the case of Aquatic Systems, neither of these methods is sufficiently accurate for projecting receivables balances during the year. In such cases, we must look more deeply into the relationship between sales and collections. In the case of Aquatic Systems, we know that about 50 percent of any month's sales are collected in the first month following and the remainder in the second month following. Therefore, at the end of any month there will be outstanding that month's sales plus half of the prior month's sales. At the end of January, the receivables balance will include January's sales of $220,000 plus half of December's sales of $250,000, for a total of $345,000. At the end of February, we have outstanding February sales of $275,000 plus half of January's, and so on. The complete projection of receivables is given later in Table 8-7. When we discuss the cash budget, we will develop a schedule of collections that can be used as an alternative method of projecting receivables.

A **pro-forma balance sheet**—is a balance sheet constructed by projecting the firm's financial condition as if a certain sales and production plan had taken place.

Table 8—6

Aquatic Systems, Inc. Projection of Inventories (thousands of dollars)

Inventory, December 31, 1986	1080
plus January production	+ 285
minus January cost of goods sold	− 161
equals Inventory, January, 31, 1987	1204
plus February production	+ 285
minus February cost of goods sold	− 196
equals Inventory, February 28, 1987	1293
plus March production	+ 285
minus March cost of goods sold	− 264
equals Inventory, March 31, 1987	1314

Inventories also require special attention. When production and sales follow approximately the same pattern—for example, when both are level or when both are seasonal—inventories can be projected using a simple inventory/sales ratio. In the case of Aquatic Systems, production and sales are not in step, and we must take into account the relationship between the two in each month in order to project inventories. At the end of any month, inventory will equal inventory at the beginning of the month, plus production for the month, less cost of goods sold during the month. We know that production each month is $285,000 at cost: $125,000 for materials, $135,000 for direct labor, and $25,000 for manufacturing overhead. Table 8–4 lists the cost of goods sold in each month. Using the months of January through March to illustrate, we can calculate inventory levels as shown in Table 8–6. The complete inventory projection is given in Table 8–7.

In the case of Aquatic Systems, the problem is simplified somewhat by the fact that purchases are scheduled at $125,000 per month, exactly the rate at which raw materials are to be consumed. Were this not the case, it might be necessary to project raw-materials, work-in-process, and finished-goods inventories separately.

To project plant and equipment, we add the planned outlays of $250,000 in January and February to the gross-plant-and-equipment figure for December. Depreciation accumulates at $25,000 per month.

Since payments for purchases are made in the month following, accounts payable at the end of each month will equal purchases made during the month. Other accruals should remain constant at $50,000.

Income taxes payable require a complete schedule. We know that 1987 estimated taxes of $250,000 must be paid in advance in equal installments in April, June, September, and December. Taxes payable at the end of any month equal the balance at the beginning of the month, plus taxes due on income for the month (Table 8-4), minus tax payments made during the month. In April, in addition to $62,500 on 1987 income (one-fourth of $250,000), Aquatic Systems also must pay the $40,000 still due as of December 31, 1986, on 1986 income.

The mortgage-payable balance can be projected by subtracting the $50,000 payments due in June and December. Retained earnings are projected by adding to each month's beginning balance the amount retained during the month (from Table 8–4).

Common stock remains constant at $1.5 million because no new issues are planned during 1987.

Table 8-7

Aquatic Systems, Inc. Pro-Forma Balance Sheets, 1987 (thousands of dollars)

	Actual 12/31/86	Jan.	Feb.	Mar.	Apr.	May	June	July	Aug.	Sept.	Oct.	Nov.	Dec.
Cash	50	50	50	50	50	50	50	50	50	50	50	50	50
Marketable securities	94	0	0	0	0	0	0	0	0	172	382	482	301
Accounts receivable	353	345	385	523	688	853	1,073	1,100	963	798	633	468	413
Inventories	1,080	1,204	1,293	1,314	1,267	1,152	935	752	637	590	611	700	789
Total current assets	1,577	1,599	1,728	1,887	2,005	2,055	2,058	1,902	1,650	1,610	1,676	1,700	1,553
Gross plant and equipment	4,960	5,210	5,460	5,460	5,460	5,460	5,460	5,460	5,460	5,460	5,460	5,460	5,460
Less accumulated depreciation	−1,850	−1,875	−1,900	−1,925	−1,950	−1,975	−2,000	−2,025	−2,050	−2,075	−2,100	−2,125	−2,150
Net plant	3,110	3,335	3,560	3,535	3,510	3,485	3,460	3,435	3,410	3,385	3,360	3,335	3,310
Total assets	4,687	4,934	5,288	5,422	5,515	5,540	5,518	5,337	5,060	4,995	5,036	5,035	4,863
Notes payable (bank)	0	291	646	799	912	812	775	427	25	0	0	0	0
Accounts payable	148	125	125	125	125	125	125	125	125	125	125	125	125
Taxes payable[a]	40	34	34	46	(32)	6	(1)	49	87	49	61	61	0
Other accruals	50	50	50	50	50	50	50	50	50	50	50	50	50
Total current liabilities	238	500	855	1,020	1,055	993	949	651	287	224	236	236	175
Mortgage[b]	960	960	960	960	960	960	910	910	910	910	910	910	860
Common stock	1,500	1,500	1,500	1,500	1,500	1,500	1,500	1,500	1,500	1,500	1,500	1,500	1,500
Retained earnings	1,989	1,974	1,973	1,942	2,000	2,087	2,159	2,276	2,363	2,361	2,390	2,389	2,328
Total liabilities and net worth	4,687	4,934	5,288	5,422	5,515	5,540	5,518	5,337	5,060	4,995	5,036	5,035	4,863

[a]The December 31, 1986, figure of $40,000 is the amount remaining on 1986 taxes and is payable on April 15, 1987. The 1987 estimated tax is payable in equal installments in April, June, September, and December. The negative figures in April and June represent prepaid taxes.

[b]The mortgage principal payment of $100,000 per year is payable in June and December.

We now have projected all items except cash, marketable securities, and the bank loan, with the final results given in Table 8–7. To complete the balance sheet for each month, we must determine whether Aquatic Systems must borrow that month. We know that Aquatic maintains a minimum cash balance of $50,000 and borrows from the bank to prevent cash from falling below that figure. When cash rises above $50,000, the loan is paid down and any excess is invested in U.S. Treasury bills, so the cash figure on the balance sheet remains at $50,000 each month. When cash plus marketable securities are more than $50,000, the loan balance will be zero.

To determine the marketable securities and loan balances in any month, we first assume a figure of zero for each. We then add all the asset accounts to get a trial figure for total assets, and add all the liability accounts and net worth to get a trial figure for total liabilities plus net worth. If the resulting trial total-asset figure exceeds the trial total of liabilities plus net worth, then the loan makes up the difference. If the trial total-asset figure is less than trial total liabilities plus net worth, marketable securities make up the difference. Hence, in any given month, the firm may have marketable securities or a loan, but never both simultaneously.

In January, for example, total assets including $50,000 cash are $4,934,000 (from Table 8–7). Total liabilities plus net worth excluding the loan are $4,643,000, so a loan of $291,000 is needed to balance. Proceeding this way, we can calculate the marketable-securities and loan balances for February through August. In September, total liabilities plus net worth exceed trial total assets (excluding marketable securities), so the loan will be zero; marketable securities of $172,000 are needed to balance. Figures for October through December are found in like manner. The complete balance sheet is shown in Table 8–7.

We see from Table 8–7 that Aquatic Systems must begin borrowing in January and borrow additional amounts each month through April, after which the loan declines to zero by the end of September. Aquatic Systems is borrowing for 8 months out of the year, and the loan reaches a maximum of $912,000 in April. By increasing its long-term financing by means of common stock or mortgages or other long-term debt, Aquatic Systems could reduce both its level of short-term borrowing and the length of time each year during which it must borrow. Should Aquatic Systems rely more on long-term and less on short-term financing? Here we raise the important question of the appropriate *maturity structure* of a firm's liabilities and the closely related question of *liquidity*. Chapter 18 will deal with these questions in more detail.

Let us note again the critical importance of the sales plan in constructing the pro-forma balance sheet. To meet a given sales plan, managers must develop a production plan and programs of other kinds throughout the firm. The sales and production plans together determine much of the pro-forma balance sheet.

Note also that in Table 8–4 interest is lumped in with general selling and administrative expense, and the total is projected at $55,000 per month. In reality, of course, interest expense depends on the size of the loan, which varies from month to month (see Table 8–7). The size of the loan in turn depends on retained earnings, which depends on profits, which depends on interest. So interest depends on the size of the loan, which depends (indirectly, through profits) on interest. The problem is circular; in other words, the income statement and the balance sheet are *simultaneously determined*. Dealing with this problem can get tricky, so we defer a discussion of the problem to Appendix 8A, which discusses the use of computer-based planning models to solve this and other problems.

Sample Problem 8–2

Developing a Pro-Forma Balance Sheet for Madison International

Madison International's balance sheet for December 31, 1986 is shown in Table 8–8. Use the information from Sample Problem 8–1 plus the data in Table 8–8 to construct a December 31, 1987 pro-forma balance sheet (round off all numbers to the nearest thousand). Assume that:

1. The collection period for accounts receivable is 61 days, and all sales are on credit.
2. Inventory turnover is projected to be 6.5 times.
3. Dividends of $1.5 million will be paid on December 31,1987.
4. Accrued labor expense is expected to be $950,000, and taxes payable will be $800,000.
5. Purchases equal 75 percent of the cost of goods sold, and the company's payment period is expected to be 36.5 days.
6. No changes are expected in the common-stock account, in the plant-and-equipment account, or in bonds.

Solution

The accounts on the balance sheet can be calculated one item at a time.

1. The collection period for accounts receivable is 61 days, which is 1/6 of a year, and sales are $19.5 million. Therefore, the ending balance for accounts receivable is $19.5 million/6 = $3.25 million.
2. With turnover of 6.5 times, and cost of goods sold equaling $11,310,000, the average inventory during 1987 will be $11,310,000/6.5 = $1,740,000. With be-

Table 8–8
Madison International Balance Sheet, December 31, 1986

Assets			
Cash		$2,290,000	
Accounts receivable		2,850,000	
Inventory		1,900,000	
Total current assets			$7,040,000
Gross plant and equipment	$6,400,000		
Less accumulated depreciation	−3,860,000		
Net plant and equipment			2,540,000
Total assets			$9,580,000
Liabilities and net worth			
Accounts payable	$1,100,000		
Accrued labor	870,000		
Taxes payable	760,000		
Total current liabilities			$2,730,000
Bonds at 10 percent			2,000,000
Common stock			1,500,000
Retained earnings			3,350,000
Total liabilities and net worth			$9,580,000

Table 8–9
Madison International Pro-Forma Balance Sheet, December 31, 1987

Assets		
Cash	$3,984,200	
Accounts receivable	3,250,000	
Inventory	1,580,000	
Total current assets		$ 8,814,200
Gross plant and equipment	6,400,000	
Less accumulated depreciation	−4,820,000	
Net plant and equipment		1,580,000
Total assets		$10,394,200
Liabilities and net worth		
Accounts payable	$ 848,000	
Accrued labor	950,000	
Taxes payable	800,000	
Total current liabilities		$ 2,598,000
Bonds at 10 percent		2,000,000
Common stock		1,500,000
Retained earnings		4,296,200
Total liabilities and net worth		$10,394,200

ginning inventory equal to $1,900,000, ending inventory will be ($1,740,000 × 2) − $1,900,000 = $1,580,000.

3. The gross amount for plant and equipment will not change, but the net amount will be $960,000 less than in 1986 due to 1986 depreciation; that is, $2,540,000 − $960,000 = $1,580,000.

4. Because purchases equal 75 percent of the cost of goods sold, or $8,482,500, ending accounts payable equals purchases per day times 36.5 days purchases outstanding, or ($8,482,500/365) × 36.5 = $848,000 (rounded).

5. Accrued labor and taxes payable are given as $950,000 and $800,000.

6. Bonds will remain at $2 million.

7. Common stock will remain at $1.5 million.

8. Retained earnings will be $3,350,000 (beginning balance) + $2,446,200 (earnings) − $1,500,000 (dividends) = $4,296,200.

9. Cash can be calculated by finding the value that will balance the balance sheet. The completed pro-forma balance sheet is given in Table 8–9. ▣

Pro-Forma Source-and-Use-of-Funds Statement

Because of seasonality, a source-and-use statement for a single month is not likely to be useful in the case of Aquatic Systems. Over a full year, the effect of seasonality is eliminated. Following procedures discussed in Chapter 6, we can construct a source-and-use statement for the year 1987, as shown in Table 8–10. In Table 8–10, we vary our procedure from Chapter 6 and lump together cash plus marketable securities because they represent the firm's most liquid assets.

Table 8–10

Aquatic Systems, Inc. Source-and-Use-of-Funds Statement, December 31, 1986–December 31, 1987 (thousands of dollars)

Sources		
Funds from operations		
Profit after taxes	579	
Depreciation	300	879
Reduce inventories		291
Total sources		1,170
Uses		
Increase in accounts receivable		60
Expansion of plant and equipment		500
Reduction in accounts payable		23
Reduction in taxes payable		40
Reduction in mortgage		100
Payment of dividends		240
Total uses		963
Increase in cash plus marketable securities		207

A source-and-use statement quickly reveals any changes in balance-sheet relationships resulting from the financial plan. We see, for example, that Aquatic is reducing inventories while receivables and other categories of assets are expanding. Although it is not always necessary in connection with a financial plan, a source-and-use analysis sometimes reveals aspects of the plan that are not otherwise apparent.

Shortcuts

Preparing financial plans is time-consuming and, therefore, costly. We must keep in mind costs as well as benefits and look for ways to streamline the procedure without sacrificing too much accuracy. In general, we should spend our time on items that are large and difficult to estimate—receivables and inventories, in Aquatic's case. We should not spend excessive time on items that either are small or easily estimated with reasonable accuracy. It is important, however, to be *consistent*—to base all projected financial statements on a single consistent set of assumptions.

> **It is important to base all projected financial statements on a single *consistent* set of assumptions.**

Monthly balance sheets were necessary in the case of Aquatic Systems because of its highly seasonal sales pattern. Often quarterly statements will do the job, and sometimes annual estimates are all that is required. Where we need only annual statements, seasonality is of no concern, because we are looking at the same point in each year.

Where seasonality is not a problem, we often can use simpler techniques than those used in the case of Aquatic Systems. One such technique is the *percentage-of-sales approach*. Since the sales plan is nearly always the critical element in a financial plan, when relationships remain fairly stable over time, many items can be projected using historical percentage relationships to sales. Several of the major operating items in the income statement and balance sheet can be projected in this manner. For example, as a first approximation, we can assume that the cost of materials and labor in 1987 will be in the same proportion to 1987 sales as they were in 1986. Thus, using the 1986 ratio of 62 percent of sales, we apply the 62 percent factor to projected sales of $5.5 million expected in 1987 and get a figure of $3,410,000 as our estimate for cost of materials and labor in 1987 (see Table 8-4—the slight difference is due to rounding).

Other items for which the percentage-of-sales method generally works well are (1) administrative and selling expenses, (2) accounts receivable, and (3) accounts payable. Of course, if there are specific reasons to believe that the ratio of these items to sales will change, the percentage factor can be adjusted up or down to get a better approximation.

Some items are not closely sales-related. For example, items such as interest on debt, principal payments on debt, and depreciation can be projected more accurately on the basis of independent facts. In summary, the extent to which the simple percent-of-sales approach to projection is used depends on the characteristics of the firm itself and on the degree of accuracy required. As always, the approach should be suited to the task and the available information.

PATTERNS OF FUND REQUIREMENTS

A firm's requirement for external financing depends on the nature of its business and the operating plan it adopts. This section will examine some of the more common patterns of financing.

Seasonal Requirements

Seasonality—is the annually recurring pattern of changes within a year.

The financing requirement for Aquatic Systems is strongly seasonal, rising rapidly in the spring and falling to zero by September. **Seasonality** is the regular, annually recurring pattern of changes that occur within a year. By definition, seasonal movements are predictable.

Table 8–7 showed the flow of funds into and out of accounts receivable and inventory for Aquatic Systems. The sales peak comes in June; the receivables peak in July. Because production is level, inventories rise when the sales rate (figured at cost) is below the production rate, as is the case during the period from October to March. When the cost of goods sold rises above production in April, inventories begin to decline from the March peak of $1,314,000. Thus, the inventory peak comes before the sales peak, and the receivables peak comes after the sales peak. The financing requirement is related to the sum of the receivables and inventory figures, and the peak financing requirement occurs in April.

Any firm with a seasonal sales pattern is likely to exhibit a similar seasonal pattern in receivables, probably with a slight lag. If production and sales are not synchronized, inventories also will exhibit a seasonal pattern. The resulting financing requirement may be handled entirely by outside sources, such as bank credit. Alternatively, as in the case of Aquatic Systems, part may be handled by bank credit and part by expanding and contracting holdings of liquid assets. Where external financing is used, the requirement is short-term in nature, existing over only part of a year.

The Growing Firm

The 1987 sales for Aquatic Systems were projected to increase about 8.3 percent over 1986. To generate sustained sales growth over long periods, additional assets normally are required—fixed assets as well as working capital. Where working capital is managed effectively, it should grow at approximately the same rate as sales, assuming the product mix and operating plan remain stable.

These increasing asset requirements must be financed. A portion of these requirements normally will be financed spontaneously by current liabilities that expand along with sales.

For example, as a firm expands its output, it will generally require larger inventories and it will make larger purchases of materials. As a result, its accounts payable will also increase, and this increase represents a source of funds. Also, if employment and profits rise along with increased output, then wages payable and taxes payable will rise automatically, representing another source of funds. The remaining requirement must be financed by earnings retention or through outside sources.

To examine the financing requirement induced by growth, consider a firm with sales that are growing at a steady rate. Let us assume that a *steady-state growth* is attained, and earnings retention is such that every item on the balance sheet grows at exactly the same percentage rate each year. The firm may require additional outside financing, but creditors are willing to supply the funds because balance-sheet relationships and relative risk remain stable through time.

Since retained earnings represent a source of long-term equity funds generated internally, over the long run, with no outside equity financing, the rate of growth in equity (retained earnings plus common stock) can be expressed as given in Equation (1).

With no outside equity financing, a firm's long-run rate of growth of equity (retained earnings plus common stock), g, will approximately equal the product of after-tax return on equity and the percentage of earnings retained; that is,

$$g = \frac{\text{PAT}}{\text{Equity}} \times \frac{\text{Dollars retained}}{\text{PAT}} \qquad (1)$$

where PAT = profit after taxes.

An example will illustrate this effect. Suppose a company's 1987 return on equity (ROE = PAT/Equity) was 20 percent. For equity (retained earnings plus common stock) of \$500,000 in 1986, this ROE figure resulted in 1987 profits after taxes of 0.20(\$500,000) = \$100,000. As is the company's policy, 40 percent of the profits (\$40,000) were retained, and the rest (\$60,000) were paid in dividends. We can calculate the equity figure at year-end 1987 as

$$\text{Equity (1987)} = \text{Equity (1986)} + \text{Earnings retained (1987)}$$

$$= \$500,000 + \$40,000$$

$$= \$540,000.$$

This represents a $40,000 increase over 1986, or a growth rate, g, of $40,000/$500,000 = 8$ percent. Note that this g value could also have been calculated by applying Equation (1) as

$$g = \frac{\$100,000}{\$500,000} \times \frac{\$40,000}{\$100,000}$$

$$= 0.20 \times 0.40 = 0.08 = 8 \text{ percent.}$$

If, in the future, the company continues earning 20 percent on equity, issues no new shares of stock, and retains 40 percent of earnings, then the growth in equity, g, will remain at 8 percent per year.

One measure of **profitability**—is profits per dollar of sales.

The rate of growth in equity, thus, depends on both **profitability** and **retention.** The higher is the profitability, the higher is the payout that still permits equity to grow at the same rate as sales. Where sales growth is especially high, or where profitability is particularly low, even a zero-dividend payout may not permit equity to grow as rapidly as sales. Such a situation often is encountered in small, rapidly growing firms.

The **retention rate**—is dollars retained divided by profits after taxes.

> **The rate of growth in equity depends on both profitability and retention.**

When net worth grows less rapidly than sales and assets, balance-sheet relationships change over time. Something other than net worth must grow at a faster rate. Often the deficit is made up for a time by bank credit or by trade credit or by some combination of the two. If bank credit is used and growth continues, the loan is a permanent one, growing larger each year. If trade credit is used, the lengthening of the firm's payment period is likely to have two undesirable consequences. First, relations with suppliers are likely to become strained; second, the firm will be unable to take advantage of any prompt-payment discounts offered.

Current liabilities can expand more rapidly than other parts of the balance sheet for short periods—but not for long. At some point, suppliers and bankers will call a halt because of risk considerations. If the firm reaches the point where it has reduced its dividend payout and has increased its profitability as much as possible, it has two alternatives: obtain external long-term funds or change commercial strategy and slow the rate of sales growth.

Thus, we see that growth must be financed, and that the financing requirement is *long-term* in nature. The faster the growth in sales and assets, the more severe the financing problem is likely to become. Growth normally is desirable, but the financing requirements induced by growth must not be overlooked.

Unpredictable Financing Requirements

Financing requirements induced by seasonality or growth usually can be anticipated. Some financing requirements, however, cannot. Most firms are subject to the swings of the business and monetary cycle that occur in the U.S. economy over periods of three to five years. In spite of advances in the state of the economic art, booms and recessions still cannot be anticipated with accuracy. Cyclical variations resulting from economic swings are common to all firms and may induce financing requirements in addition to those normally encountered.

Most firms are subject to other unpredictable events as well, some affecting an entire industry and some affecting only individual firms. Strikes, product failure, changes in supply prices, sudden opportunities, or problems arising from changes in technology or consumer preferences—all are events that may affect a firm's financing requirements. Where assets must be expanded suddenly, or where profitability suddenly is reduced, outside financing at above-normal levels may be required.

Unexpected financing requirements may be short or intermediate in term. Requirements induced by the business cycle may persist for longer than a year, after which relationships return to normal. Unpredictable events arising from temporary phenomena, such as strikes, may be short-term in nature.

> **A firm's requirement for external financing depends on the nature of its business and on the operating plan that it adopts.**

Operating Decisions and Financing Requirements

It is apparent that a firm's financing requirements are determined primarily by its commercial strategy and operating plan. Because firms exist to produce goods and services, commercial strategy normally comes first, and financing is tailored to fit.

Though financing requirements are normally subordinate to the operating plan, they nevertheless must be considered when the operating plan is formulated. Changes in the operating plan must take into account the effects they may have on financing requirements. Sometimes financing requirements themselves may become a constraint and may necessitate the modification of the operating plan. Some operating plans may be too risky to finance. For example, consider a plan calling for level production of a product with a seasonal sales pattern that is subject to fashion or fad risk, such as toys or women's fashion garments. The risk involved in accumulating large inventories of such products may be unacceptable to suppliers of funds.

The case of Aquatic Systems provides a good example of the impact of production decisions on financing requirements. The decision to produce at a level rate lowers production costs and provides a better balance between people and equipment. But offsetting these benefits are the costs of storing and financing the large inventories and the added risk of obsolescence, which in the case of Aquatic Systems was not excessive.

Marketing decisions also affect financing requirements. Advertising and selling efforts affect sales and accounts receivable and indirectly affect inventories and production schedules. Changes in credit terms, likewise, may affect sales and, therefore, receivables and inventories. Where receivables and inventories are affected, financing requirements will also be affected.

In theory, operating plans and financing requirements should be determined jointly. The optimal combination maximizes the value of the firm. In practice, it is often necessary first to formulate an operating plan, then to calculate its financing requirements, and finally to determine whether the financing is feasible. If the financing is not considered feasible, the operating plan is modified, and the process is repeated. Such an iterative process can be greatly facilitated by the use of a computer to generate financial statements. By using a computer-based planning model, the financial implications of different operating plans can be analyzed quickly and inexpensively. With the advent in the early 1980s of planning models available for small, inexpensive computers, computer-based planning models have become available to a wide range of financial managers, as explained in Appendix 8A, which follows this chapter.

From the financial plan, we can determine the nature of the financing requirement. It is important to both the firm and its suppliers of funds that this determination be made so that the right kind of financing arrangement can be negotiated. If the situation is one of growth, requiring long-term financing, it is best to recognize it as such at the outset. If the need is for short-term financing, it can be tailored accordingly, and unnecessary borrowing will be avoided.

THE CASH BUDGET OF RECEIPTS AND DISBURSEMENTS

A **budget**—is a time-phased schedule of activities, events, or transactions, usually in dollar terms.

A **cash budget**—is a time-phased schedule of cash receipts and disbursements.

The cash budget is one of several specialized supporting components of the overall financial plan. Others include the advertising budget, the materials budget, the capital-expenditures budget, the income-and-expense budget by organizational unit, and so on. A **budget** is simply a time-phased schedule of activities or events or transactions, usually in dollar terms. A budget can be prepared for any activity of the firm to describe exactly what is to be done and when.

The **cash budget** is a time-phased schedule of cash receipts and disbursements. Its primary purpose is to provide control of cash at a level of detail not possible with the balance sheet alone. With a complete schedule of all planned receipts and disbursements, deviations from the plan can be detected promptly and the reasons for the deviations can be ascertained. The balance sheet will tell us when cash is higher or lower than planned; the cash budget will pinpoint the reason for the variance.

The cash budget is similar to the income statement in that it is constructed in flow terms and describes activities that are to take place during some specified period of time. It differs from the income statement in that it includes cash items only and is prepared on a cash basis, whereas the income statement is prepared on an accrual basis. The criterion for deciding whether a particular item belongs in the cash budget is whether it affects the cash balance. If it goes in the cash drawer or is deposited to the checking account, or if a check is written for it, then it goes in. Depreciation has no place in a cash budget, nor do other noncash charges or accruals of any sort, revenue or expense. Only *cash received* or *cash disbursed* goes in.

Preparing the Cash Budget

We will now prepare a cash budget for Aquatic Systems, Inc., for each month in 1987. Looking first at cash *receipts,* we see that the only receipts in this case will come from collection of accounts receivable and increases in the bank loan. We will handle the bank loan as a balancing figure to maintain the cash balance at the appropriate figure. Using our knowledge of the patterns of payment by Aquatic Systems customers, we can prepare the collection schedule given in Table 8–11. In this table, December sales of $250,000 are collected half in January and half in February; January sales of $220,000 are collected half in February and half in March, and so on.

The collections figures derived in Table 8–11 for the cash budget must be consistent with the sales and accounts receivable figures on the income statement and balance

Table 8–11

Aquatic Systems, Inc. Collection of Accounts Receivable, 1987 (thousands of dollars)

Sales		Time of Collection						
		Jan.	Feb.	Mar.	Apr.	May	June	July
Nov.	206	103						
Dec.	250	125	125					
Jan.	220	0	110	110				
Feb.	275		0	137	138			
Mar.	385			0	192	193		
Apr.	495				0	247	248	
May	605					0	302	303
June	770						0	385
Total collections		228	235	247	330	440	550	688

Sales		Aug.	Sept.	Oct.	Nov.	Dec.	Jan.
June	770	385					
July	715	357	358				
Aug.	605	0	302	303			
Sept.	495		0	247	248		
Oct.	385			0	192	193	
Nov.	275				0	137	138
Dec.	275					0	137
Total collections		742	660	550	440	330	275

sheet. The relationship can be expressed as: accounts receivable as of December 31, 1986 *plus* January 1987 sales *minus* January 1987 collections will equal accounts receivable as of January 31, 1987. In other words,

$$\$353,000 + \$220,000 - \$228,000 = \$345,000.$$

If we know sales and receivables for each month, we can calculate collections. If we know sales and collections and the initial receivables balance, we can project receivables for each month.

Now let us focus on *cash disbursements*. Each month, checks will be written to settle accounts payable at the end of the prior month. In January, for example, payments to suppliers will be made totaling $148,000. Payments for direct labor, manufacturing overhead, and selling and administrative expense are made approximately one week after the expenses are incurred. Payment schedules for plant-and-equipment expenditures, taxes, mortgage principal, and dividends were given earlier.

Given the schedule of receipts and disbursements, we can construct the cash budget as shown in Table 8–12. The row labeled "Receipts less disbursement" indicates the gross change in the cash balance each month before increases or decreases in the bank loan. To this figure we add the beginning cash balance and marketable securities and then determine the loan increase or decrease required to maintain the ending cash balance at $50,000 or higher. The loan must be increased each month from January

Table 8–12
Aquatic Systems, Inc. Pro-Forma Cash Budget, 1987 (thousands of dollars)

	Jan.	Feb.	March	April	May	June	July	Aug.	Sept.	Oct.	Nov.	Dec.
Receipts												
Collection of accounts receivable	228	235	247	330	440	550	688	742	660	550	440	330
Disbursements												
Payment of accounts payable	148	125	125	125	125	125	125	125	125	125	125	125
Direct labor	135	135	135	135	135	135	135	135	135	135	135	135
Manufacturing overhead	25	25	25	25	25	25	25	25	25	25	25	25
Selling and administrative expenses	55	55	55	55	55	55	55	55	55	55	55	55
Plant and equipment	250	250		103								
Taxes						63			63			61
Mortgage principal						50						50
Dividends			60			60			60			60
Total disbursements	613	590	400	443	340	513	340	340	463	340	340	511
Receipts less disbursements	−385	−355	−153	−113	100	37	348	402	197	210	100	−181
plus Beginning cash and marketable securities	+144	+50	+50	+50	+50	+50	+50	+50	+50	+222	+432	+532
equals Subtotal	−241	−305	−103	−63	150	87	398	452	247	432	532	351
plus Loan increase	+291	+355	+153	+113	−100	−37	−348	−402	−25	0	0	0
Ending cash and marketable securities	50	50	50	50	50	50	50	50	222	432	532	351
Ending loan balance	291	646	799	912	812	775	427	25	0	0	0	0

through April, and then reduced each month until it reaches zero by the end of September. Note especially that the ending balances for cash plus marketable securities and the loan match those in the pro-forma balance sheet. If they did not, we would know that an error existed somewhere, either in the cash budget or in the pro-forma statements.

In the case of Aquatic Systems, the only receipts were collections of accounts receivable and borrowings from the bank; the latter appear toward the end of Table 8–12 rather than under "Receipts." In other situations, other types of receipts may be encountered. Some part of a firm's sales may be for cash, although sales by Aquatic Systems were all for credit. Fixed assets sometimes are sold, in which case the proceeds are treated as a receipt and any change in tax payments is treated as an increase or decrease in disbursements for taxes. Cash discounts received on purchases sometimes are treated as a receipt. Finally, proceeds of any issues of long-term securities by the firm—stock or long-term debt—should be included as receipts.

Relationships of Cash Budget to Other Pro-Forma Statements

We noted above that the ending cash and loan figures in the cash budget must match those in the balance sheet and that the collections figure must be consistent with the sales and receivables figures. Upon close inspection, we will see also that the payment of accounts payable in the cash budget should be consistent with the accounts-payable and inventory figures in the balance sheet and with the planned level of purchases and the cost-of-goods-sold figure in the income statement. Disbursements for labor and overhead should be consistent with the cost of goods sold and inventory; disbursements for plant and equipment should be consistent with fixed assets and depreciation; disbursements for taxes should be consistent with taxes on the income statement and taxes payable on the balance sheet; and so on.

It is apparent that the cash budget, the pro-forma income statement, and the pro-forma balance sheet all are mutually interdependent. With consistent assumptions and accurate preparation, all the figures will mesh. If they do not, an error exists somewhere. Errors often become apparent when the ending cash and loan figures are calculated in the cash budget and the figures do not match those in the balance sheet. The cash and loan figures constitute our controls in preparing the statements.

> **The cash budget, the pro-forma income statement, and the pro-forma balance sheet are all mutually interdependent. With consistent assumptions and accurate preparation, all the figures will mesh.**

A cash budget can be prepared to cover any time period. In the case of Aquatic Systems, we prepared a monthly cash budget covering the entire year in order to demonstrate the interlocking character of the financial statements. In practice, Aquatic Systems might prepare a cash budget for only those months in which the loan is high and control of cash is most critical. At other times during the year, the pro-forma balance sheet, coupled with an income-and-expense budget, might provide adequate control. Firms with especially acute cash shortages may find it useful to prepare a cash budget by week or even by day. Firms that employ detailed income-and-expense budgets by organizational units may find a cash budget unnecessary.

USING THE FINANCIAL PLAN

The pro-forma income statement, the pro-forma balance sheet, and the cash budget constitute the basic elements of the firm's financial plan. Some of the uses of the financial plan are apparent from the discussion thus far. Here we will elaborate a bit.

Planning

Planning, essentially, is making decisions in advance about what is to be done in the future. As a plan is developed, decisions are made. Hence, the very process of developing the plan yields a major part of the overall benefits, regardless of what is done with the final product.

> **Because developing a plan necessitates the making of decisions, the very process of developing a plan yields a major part of the overall benefits of financial planning.**

Development of a financial plan requires good coordination and communication throughout the firm. To support the sales plan, programs and budgets are developed in production, marketing, personnel, and finance. During the process, the feasibility of alternative operating plans can be examined. Performance measures, such as those discussed in Chapter 7, can be applied, and judgments can be made as to the plan's acceptability with respect to profitability, return on investment, inventory and receivables management, liquidity, and debt coverage. The feasibility of obtaining financing can be ascertained. Where necessary, the operating plan can be modified, and performance and feasibility tests can be applied again. Sometimes a firm may find it desirable to develop one or more alternative plans to allow for certain outcomes. To deal with uncertainty, a firm might develop one set of plans representing the most favorable set of circumstances and another representing the least favorable.

The amounts, timing, and nature of the financing requirement can be determined from the financial plan. Appropriate sources of funds can be selected, and borrowing and repayment schedules can be prepared. Chapter 18 will discuss sources of short-term and intermediate financing in more detail.

> **The final product of the financial-planning process is a description in financial terms of what the firm intends to accomplish over the period of time in question.**

Besides providing a record of decisions made, the financial plan has other important uses.

Communications

One such use is in communications with outside parties, including investors and other suppliers of funds. After the management of Aquatic Systems completes the financial plan, we can imagine the financial vice-president going to the bank to negotiate the loan arrangement for 1987. The plan contained in Tables 8–4, 8–7, and 8–12 would be discussed in detail with the loan officer. The vice-president would be able to tell the loan officer exactly how much money Aquatic Systems needs, when it is needed, how it will be used, and when and how the bank will be repaid.

Contrast the above bargaining session with one in which a potential borrower approaches a bank for a loan without a detailed financial plan. The borrower is unable to be specific with respect to how much, when it is needed, how it will be used, and when and how it will be repaid.

By coming to the bargaining table equipped with a comprehensive financial plan, a firm's management sends an important message to the supplier of funds: "This management is in control of its business and knows what it is doing." Lenders and investors like to do business with such firms. The specific numbers can be less important to the supplier of funds than the fact that a comprehensive plan has been developed.

By coming in with a plan, a firm's management is likely to gain a psychological advantage in the bargaining process. A feeling of confidence in the firm may lead the lender to assign a lower risk and, therefore, a lower interest rate to the loan. Thus, an important use of the financial plan is as a communications device.

Control

The financial plan also is useful for purposes of control—that is, for seeing that the plans in fact are carried out. We should not allow the precise appearance of the numbers in Table 8–4, 8–7, and 8–12 to lead us to forget about uncertainty. The elements of the plan that depend directly or indirectly on revenue and expense estimates are subject to uncertainty. Usually, the plan represents our best guess as to the most likely set of outcomes, or the outcomes that management hopes to achieve. Deviations above or below the plan are bound to occur and should be expected. When they do occur, we want to find out immediately and determine the reasons.

Most management-control systems are based on comparisons of actual data versus plans. Such comparisons can be made at any level of detail and with any frequency. Expense-control systems often compare actual versus plan data on a monthly basis. In decentralized firms, reporting systems using computers often are designed to provide information by organizational unit in a timely manner. Subordinate managers are able to identify problems quickly in their own areas of responsibility.

For the firm as a whole, progress against the operating plan can be monitored using the consolidated pro-forma income statement and pro-forma balance sheet. Each month, or each quarter, actual income statements and balance sheets are compared to the plan, item by item, and deviations are calculated. The effects of a deviation from the sales plan will be seen in accounts receivable, inventories, cash, the bank loan (if any), profits, tax accruals, and perhaps other areas. Sometimes it is useful to examine deviations in a source-and-use format, categorizing balance-sheet changes as providing or using more or less funds than planned.

By comparing actual versus plan data at frequent intervals, deviations can be detected as events unfold, and corrective action can be taken in a timely manner. The control system tells management that things are off-track and identifies the problem areas. Production schedules can be modified, advertising budgets increased or decreased, collection efforts intensified, or expenses cut. As a control device, pro-forma financial statements are very useful. Indeed, there is no way of achieving good control without them.

Applicability of Financial-Planning Techniques

The financial-planning techniques discussed in this chapter are applicable to any type of business firm, regardless of its line of business. Pro-forma financial statements are always useful and usually necessary to the successful operation of any business, whether it is a manufacturer, a retailer, a wholesaler, a service establishment, or a financial institution. Any firm is likely to benefit from the process of developing a plan—from the improvement in internal communications, the requirement to think ahead and anticipate problems, the discipline of having to be specific, and the commitment to carry out the plan once formulated. The appropriate level of detail and sophistication will vary widely from one situation to another, as will procedures and the format for organizing and presenting information. The planning system appropriate for an appliance retailer will differ markedly from that appropriate for a manufacturer or a commercial bank. All, however, are likely to benefit from a financial-planning system of some sort.

Is the usefulness of financial planning confined to profit-making enterprises? Non-profit organizations also must plan and make decisions. Such organizations sometimes have no revenues, but nearly always have expenses and expenditures. A pro-forma income statement may not be applicable, but a pro-forma balance sheet and expense budget usually are. A cash budget often is very useful. Hospitals, schools, churches, and charitable organizations do not earn profits, but they do expend resources, handle large amounts of money, and invariably require financing. Although the procedures and details may differ, the basic techniques of financial planning and control are just as applicable to such organizations as to business firms.

LONG-RUN FINANCIAL PLANNING

Thus far we have discussed financial planning over the relatively near term—12 to perhaps 18 months. We took the commercial strategy and long-term asset/liability structure of Aquatic Systems as given. Our emphasis was on the operating and financing necessary to support the longer-term strategy.

Commercial Strategy

Over the long run, the firm's *commercial strategy* is not fixed. A major purpose of long-range planning is to examine alternative commercial strategies and to select the one most appropriate to the firm's overall goals. Should Aquatic Systems begin manufacturing saunas and hot tubs? Such products are related to swimming pools in that people fill them with water and get in, but marketing hot tubs to consumers is quite different from marketing pumps to pool contractors. What about diversifying into pumps for applications other than pools, such as pumping industrial chemicals? Such questions have long-range strategic implications, and the answers determine the nature of the business. The firm's prosperity and survival depend on wise choices by management in these areas, and mistakes can be very costly.

The purposes of long-range planning, thus, differ from those of short-range planning. More emphasis is placed on analysis of alternatives and decision making and less on communications and control. To draw an analogy, the focus is on deciding the ship's course rather than on tuning the engine for optimal fuel economy.

> **Long-range planning differs from short-range planning because more emphasis is placed on analysis of alternatives and on decision making, and less on communications and control.**

Long-range financial planning plays the same role in formulating commercial strategy as does short-range financial planning in formulating the operating plan. The financing requirements of alternative commercial strategies are examined, performance measures are applied, financing feasibility is examined, sources of financing are investigated, and the strategy is modified if necessary. The final product, as before, is a description in financial terms of what the firm intends to accomplish over the period in question.

An **investment plan**—is the set of decisions a firm makes about what products to produce, what manufacturing process to use, and what plant and equipment will be required as these questions relate to the acquisition of assets.

Over the long run, the firm's long-term asset/liability structure is not given. An important part of the long-range planning process is to develop the long-term **investment plan** necessary to execute the firm's commercial strategy. What products is the firm to offer? What kind of manufacturing process is to be used? What facilities are needed? What equipment is appropriate? Decisions of this sort involve acquisition of assets with long lives. Alternatives often involve complex patterns of cash flows spread over many time periods. Techniques for analyzing such investment decisions will be our principal concern in Part Four.

Preparing the Long-Range Financial Plan

Given a commercial strategy and its associated long-term investment plan, the approach to financial planning is essentially the same as that used for Aquatic Systems in the short run. The basic technique is pro-forma analysis, with the income statement and balance sheet again used as the basic planning vehicles. As before, the sales plan is the critical element, and financing requirements are determined by the commercial strategy and operating plan.

Uncertainty usually is greater over long time periods than over short periods. Some random elements may average out, but new elements of uncertainty enter. Consumer preferences change, new technologies develop, costs change, competition emerges, and entire industries rise and fall.

Given these greater uncertainties, different techniques are necessary for projecting sales and other uncertain elements of a long-range plan. Long-term trends and historical relationships between firm variables and general economic variables become more important. An economist may be better equipped to forecast sales over long periods than a sales manager. Sales of color television sets, for example, are likely to depend more on population and per-capita income in the long run than on advertising and sales effort. Statistical techniques, such as correlation and regression analysis, may be useful in developing sales-forecasting models. The economic technique of *input/output analysis* may be useful. Techniques of demand analysis, marketing research, and in-depth studies of markets may be appropriate in evaluating new products. Finally, computer-assisted planning models can be very useful in applying all of the approaches.[1]

---

[1]For an example of an operational planning model, see D. F. Rychel, "Capital Budgeting with Mixed Integer Linear Programming: An Application," *Financial Management* 6 (Winter 1977): 11–19.

Table 8–13

Example of a Pro-Forma Balance Sheet with No Inflation

	1987	1988	1989
Cash	$ 100	$ 106	$ 112
Accounts receivable	300	318	337
Inventories	400	424	449
Fixed assets	300	318	337
Total assets	$1,100	$1,166	$1,235
Debt	600	636	674
Net worth	500	530	561
Total liabilites and net worth	$1,100	$1,166	$1,235
Debt/assets	0.55	0.55	0.55
Δdebt/Δassets*	—	0.55	0.55

*This ratio represents the *change* in debt divided by the *change* in assets, or the marginal debt/assets ratio.

Once the long-range sales and production plans and other elements of the operating plan are determined, financing requirements can be evaluated. Over the long run, financing choices are much wider than before, and the decisions are more difficult. The appropriate mix of debt and equity must be determined, depending on the nature of the firm's business. The firm must choose between internal and external sources and, thereby, set its dividend policy. Once the appropriate debt policy is determined, a choice must be made with respect to maturity or the appropriate mix of short-term versus long-term debt. Where outside financing is necessary, a plan must be developed that indicates the types and amounts of securities to be sold and the timing of the issues. These difficult questions of long-term financing policy will occupy us in later chapters.

> **Over the long run, financing choices are much wider than in the short run, and decisions are more difficult.**

INFLATION AND FINANCIAL PLANNING

Inflation has a pronounced impact on firms' financial planning. If revenues and expenses are affected equally, then each increases faster than it otherwise would have. Profits also increase more rapidly. If the effect on revenues and expenses is uneven, profit growth may be affected in either direction.

Balance sheets are also affected by inflation. To see the effects, let us consider an example. Suppose every item in a firm's balance sheet and income statement is growing at 6 percent per year. There is no inflation. The balance sheet projected ahead 3 years would look like Table 8–13. Note that everything grows at the same rate of 6 percent. Note especially that the ratio of debt to assets remains the same and that debt

Table 8–14

Example of a Pro-Forma Balance Sheet with 5 Percent Inflation

	1987	1988	1989
Cash	$ 100	$ 111	$ 123
Accounts receivable	300	333	370
Inventories	400	444	493
Fixed assets	300	319	340
Total assets	$1,100	$1,207	$1,326
Debt	600	675	759
Net worth	500	532	567
Total liabilities and net worth	$1,100	$1,207	$1,326
Debt/assets	0.55	0.56	0.57
Δdebt/Δassets	—	0.70	0.71

provides 55 percent of the total new financing required to expand assets from $1,100 to $1,235 (see the last row in Table 8–13).

Now suppose we have inflation of 5 percent per year in 1988 and 1989. The cash balance will have to grow by 11 percent in 1988—6 percent to accommodate real growth in transactions and another 5 percent to accommodate inflation. So the cash balance will have to be $111 at the end of 1988, rather than $106 as it was originally planned. In 1989, cash must grow another 11 percent to $123.

Similarly, receivables and inventory now must grow at 11 percent per year rather than 6 percent. Fixed assets, however, are different. Only the *increment* to fixed assets is affected by inflation; with historical-cost accounting, fixed assets already in place are not affected. For example, with 5 percent inflation in 1988, fixed assets will increase by $18(1 + 0.05) = $19 (rounded), rather than by the $18 increase that would occur with no inflation. Table 8–14 reconstructs the complete pro-forma balance sheet from Table 8–13 under conditions of inflation.

Note that the net-worth figure in 1988 is $532 under conditions of inflation compared with $530 with no inflation. Inflation hardly affected net worth at all, whereas assets were affected very significantly. Why? Because inflation acts only on the *increment* to net worth each year—that is, profits retained. Existing net worth, like existing fixed assets, is not affected at all.

Thus, inflation has a much bigger impact on assets, specifically on current assets, than it does on net worth. With no inflation, net worth and assets grow at the same rate of 6 percent. Under conditions of inflation, net worth grows much more slowly than do assets. The growth rate of total assets from 1987 to 1989 with inflation is 9.8 percent per year, while the growth of net worth is only 6.5 percent.

Impact on Borrowing

When assets grow more rapidly than net worth during inflationary periods, debt must make up the difference. By 1989, debt is at $759, compared to $674 in the no-inflation case. Of the new financing required to expand assets, equity provides only 30 percent, so debt must provide 70 percent. The debt/asset ratio begins to rise.

Let us be clear about what is happening. Inflation affects fixed assets and net worth differently than it affects current assets because fixed assets and net worth are *long-maturity* items. Unlike fixed assets and net worth, cash, receivables, and inventory are quickly replaced by new items that reflect inflation. Existing fixed assets and net worth (in book-value terms) are unaffected by inflation; only the *increments* are affected.

> **Long-maturity items, such as fixed assets and net worth, are affected differently by inflation than are current assets. The balance-sheet values of current assets reflect inflation quickly, while those of fixed assets and net worth are affected much more slowly.**

Policy Implications

In practice, the effects of inflation are more complex than those portrayed above. However, our simple example points up the major implications. In general, inflation increases the need for outside financing. To maintain a desired balance between debt and the book value of equity, equity growth must be accelerated. To accomplish this acceleration of equity growth requires either greater retention of profits or additional outside equity financing. Greater retention requires a cut in the dividend paid, in the case of corporations, or a cut in owner withdrawals, in the case of proprietorships and partnerships.

All of these choices represent important policy changes. The problem can be especially acute for small firms that cannot sell stock publicly and must rely mainly on banks for their outside financing. A cut in withdrawals can be painful if owners need the money for living expenses. If withdrawals are not cut, debt rises to the point at which banks begin to become unhappy. The only alternative is to slow the firm's rate of growth.

> **The higher is the rate of inflation, the greater is the external financing requirement.**

This chapter has taken a top-down approach to planning; that is, it started with sales and developed a plan to achieve the sales projections. Chapter 9 begins a new part of the book that addresses a different set of planning issues. The emphasis in Chapter 9 differs from that here in two important ways: first, it focuses on a longer time horizon, and second, it takes a bottom-up rather than a top-down approach by focusing on individual capital-investment projects rather than on the firm as a whole.

KEY CONCEPTS

1. Financial planning is part of a larger planning process that begins with corporate strategy and includes planning all phases of the business.

2. Pro-forma analysis is a useful technique for evaluating the effects of actions before the actions are taken.

3. The operating plan is a description of what the company intends to do, with emphasis on sales and production.

4. Pro-forma financial statements (income statement, balance sheet, and cash budget) are determined essentially by the operating plan. The financial state-

ments are a financial representation of the activities the firm intends to carry out.

5. Growth requires financing. The faster the growth, the greater is the financing requirement.

6. The financial plan is very useful as a communications device both inside and outside the company

and as a control device against which actual performance can be measured.

7. Inflation complicates financial planning and distorts balance-sheet relationships. Often inflation increases a firm's need for outside financing.

SUMMARY

Planning is a major function of management. Financial planning is a part of the larger planning process within an organization. The basic elements of the financial plan are the income statement and the balance sheet. The starting point is the operating plan, which describes the activities in which the firm intends to engage. In developing short-term financial plans that cover a 12- to 18-month horizon, the operating plan and the long-term asset/liability structure are taken as given. The objective of the planning process is to represent the operating plan in financial terms and to determine short-term financing requirements.

The pro-forma (projected) balance sheet is the basic tool for estimating funds requirements. A standard approach is to project all items of the balance sheet except cash and the bank loan, which are left as balancing figures. The figure that brings the balance sheet into balance is the required loan or, alternatively, the excess cash balance. To project the balance sheet, the income statement must be projected first in order to provide the transfer to retained earnings. The operating plan (sales plan, production plan, and expenditures for plant, equipment, materials, labor, overhead, marketing, research and development, and administration) provides the basis for the income projection. The operating plan also determines the levels of current operating assets and liabilities (working cash balance, accounts receivable, inventories, accounts payable, and various accrual accounts). Projection of these items along with the addition to retained earnings and long-term assets and liabilities (taken as given) completes the balance sheet. Once the balance sheet has been projected, a pro-forma source-and-use statement can be prepared if necessary. In general, the sales plan is of central importance in financial planning because of the effect of sales on many income-statement and balance-sheet items.

A firm's financing requirements depend on the nature of its business and the operating plan that it adopts. A seasonal sales or expense pattern usually will give rise to a seasonal financing requirement. Growth in sales gives rise to a growing financing requirement that is long-term in nature. The faster the growth, the larger the financing requirement in each period. Financing requirements also can be affected by general economic conditions and by changes in technology, consumer preferences, and competitive factors. Normally, commercial strategy and the operating plan are determined first, and the financing plan is tailored to fit them. Nevertheless, financing requirements must be considered when the operating plan is formulated, and the operating plan sometimes must be modified to take into account financing constraints.

The cash budget is one of several specialized supporting components of the financial plan and consists of a time-phased schedule of cash receipts and expenditures. Its purpose is to control cash at a level of detail not possible with the pro-forma balance sheet alone. With consistent assumptions, all figures in the cash budget, in the pro-forma income statement, and in the pro-forma balance sheet will mesh.

A major benefit of financial planning is the process of preparing the plan itself because, once prepared, the plan is very useful for communicating with outside parties, especially suppliers of funds. It is also useful as a control device for monitoring the firm's progress in executing the plan. Financial planning is essential not only for business firms but also for nonprofit organizations.

Inflation has a very pronounced impact on financial plans. More external financing is often required in times of inflation. If equity growth is not increased through stock sales or higher retention of profits, firms can be forced to rely too heavily on debt.

QUESTIONS

1. How does financial planning fit into a larger planning process within a firm?

2. Why are the sales and production plans so important to financial planning?

3. What additional planning requirements does seasonality impose?

4. In a rapidly growing firm, sales and assets often grow more rapidly than does net worth. What is the likely result?

5. What is the relationship between operating plans and financing requirements?

6. What is a *cash budget?* What is the criterion for determining what goes into a cash budget?

7. What is the relationship of the cash budget to the pro-forma income statement and to the pro-forma balance sheet?

8. What are the major uses of the financial plan?

9. How does inflation affect financing requirements?

PROBLEMS

1. Prepare a pro forma income statement for 1987 for Hi-Tech Manufacturing Company using the following information:
   a. Projected sales: $2,025,000
   b. Cost of goods sold: 65.92 percent of sales
   c. Selling and administrative expense: $20,000 per month
   d. Depreciation: $10,000 per month January–April; $12,000 per month May–December
   e. Interest expense: $40,000
   f. Tax rate: 46 percent

   Balance sheet data for Hi-Tech are shown in Table A.

2. Whittenberg Medical Company has recently merged with Bailey and Lowe, Incorporated, producer of a specialized line of sports equipment, to form a new industrial concern—Wolf Group Enterprises (WG). Under president Jim Valvoline's guidance, WG has recently introduced its products into the Western portions of the U.S. under a new name—"Destiny Products." Satisfied with this new marketing concept, Valvoline plans an additional marketing push into the Southwest. WG is attempting to project funding needs for this new expansion. Income and balance sheets for last year, 1986, are reproduced in Tables B and C. WG feels that asset and current liability accounts, as well as costs, will remain constant percentages of sales as they have in the past. The company also plans to maintain its policy of paying out 70 percent of its earnings in the form of dividends. Valvoline projects 1987 sales of $150. Prepare an analysis of WG's needs for external financing in 1987.

3. Utilize all the information from problem (1) plus the balance sheet for December 31, 1986 given in Table A and the following information to construct a pro forma balance sheet for Hi-Tech Manufacturing Company for December 31, 1987.
   a. An addition to plant and equipment of $175,000 is due on April 15. The depreciation figure in problem (1) above already includes the depreciation charges for this addition.
   b. The company maintains an open line of credit with a local bank and was carrying an outstanding loan balance of $50,000 on December 31, 1986.
   c. The minimum cash balance desired by the company is $20,000.
   d. The accounts receivable collection period (days sales outstanding) is projected to be 55 days, the year having 365 days.
   e. Inventory turnover is projected to be 10.75 times.
   f. Purchases amount to 45.5 percent of cost of goods sold, and the company's payment period (days purchases outstanding) at year-end is expected to be 36 days.
   g. At December 31, 1987, accrued labor expense is expected to be $60,000, taxes payable zero, and accrued overhead expense $10,000.
   h. No change is expected in debentures or common stock.

4. Prepare a quarterly cash budget for the Chapel-on-

Table A

Assets	
Cash	$ 20,000
Accounts receivable	292,500
Inventory	118,000
Total current assets	$ 430,500
Gross plant and equipment	$1,800,000
Less accumulated depreciation	− 963,000
Net plant and equipment	837,000
Total assets	$1,267,500
Liabilities and net worth	
Bank loan	$ 50,000
Accounts payable	54,000
Accrued labor	54,000
Taxes payable	5,000
Accrued overhead	10,000
Total current liabilities	$ 173,000
Debentures	500,000
Common stock	300,000
Retained earnings	294,500
Total liabilities and net worth	$1,267,500

Table B

Assets	
Current assets	$20
Net fixed assets	30
Total assets	$50
Liabilities and owners' equity	
Accounts payable	$10
Long-term debt	20
Common stock	5
Retained earnings	15
Total liabilities and owner's equity	$50

the-Hill Church utilizing the following information and including any required borrowing. All annual receipts and disbursements are received or made in equal quarterly amounts unless otherwise noted.

a. Annual expenditures are projected as follows:

Salary, allowances, and expenses (Rector)	$24,480
Salary, allowances, and expenses (Assistant Rector)	$16,500
Clerical and janitorial expense	$32,160
Building maintenance and taxes	$12,800
Supplies and programs	$11,600
Work outside the parish	$25,000

b. In addition to the above expenditures, the church must make principal payments on the church mortgage of $2,000 in the second and fourth quarters, and interest payments of $700 per quarter.

c. Receipts are projected as $7,800 for plate collections and $121,000 for pledge payments, with plate collections evenly distributed throughout the year, and 40 percent of pledge payments to be received in quarter four and 20 percent in each of the other three quarters.

d. The cash balance at the beginning of the year is $4,200.

5. Consider the Harrington Incorporated data presented in problem (4) in Chapter 7. Suppose Harrington planned to increase net sales to $60,000,000 in 1987. Further, assume that all its asset, current liability and deferred income tax accounts would have the same relationship to sales as they had in 1986. Further assume that none of the long-term debt is due in 1987.

a. Assuming that Harrington has the same profit margin as it had in 1986, what amount of new external financing will Harrington need in 1987? Construct a pro forma balance sheet as part of your answer.

b. What after-tax profit margin would Harrington need in 1987 to support the $60,000,000 sales figure without new external financing?

c. If Harrington paid dividends, how would this affect your answers above?

d. What dangers do you see in using a year-end pro forma balance sheet to project financing needs?

6. Monthly sales of Orange Furniture, Inc. for 1987 are projected as shown in Table D. Accounts receivable are collected as follows: 25 percent within 10 days; 15 percent in days 11 through 30; 40 percent in the month after the sale (days 31–60); 15 percent in the second month after the sale; 5 percent will never be collected. How much cash will Orange receive from sales during each month

Table C

Income Statement, Year-End 1986	
Sales	$100
Cost of goods sold	80
Profit before tax	$ 20
Taxes at 40 percent	8
Profit after tax	$ 12

in 1987? The firm's first year in business is 1987, so there will be no cash receipts from prior years' sales. Orange offers credit terms of a discount of 2 percent if the invoice is paid within 10 days, otherwise the net (full amount) is due within 30 days. Assume all sales take place on the first day of each month. (Round to the nearest $1.)

7. Compute the projected accounts receivable balance on December 31, 1987 for Transylvania Corporation from the following information (round to the nearest $10):

   a. The December 31, 1986 accounts-receivable balance is $83,210.
   b. All sales are on credit, and are projected for 1987 in Table E.
   c. Accounts receivable are collected as follows: 35 percent in the month following the sale; 50 percent in the second month after the sale; and 15 percent in the third month after the sale.

8. Playtime Toy Company has projected sales as shown in Table F. The company's gross profit percentage is 40 percent. Seventy-five percent of cost

Table E

January	$36,300
February	$39,850
March	$45,700
April	$51,540
May	$48,390
June	$54,400
July	$52,230
August	$57,230
September	$53,710
October	$47,930
November	$44,260
December	$41,000

Table D

January	$26,500
February	$24,300
March	$28,600
April	$23,500
May	$28,700
June	$26,900
July	$30,200
August	$29,400
September	$31,200
October	$27,800
November	$29,900
December	$32,300

of goods sold are materials that are purchased, and 25 percent are labor. Parts must be ordered two months before they are assembled and sold. They are received one month after being ordered. Playtime pays all of its bills 30 days after they are received, and bills arrive when the parts are delivered.

   a. Compute the accounts payable balance for each month in 1987.
   b. Compute the parts inventory for each month in 1987. The inventory balance on December 31, 1986 was $6,200.

9. Prepare pro forma income statements for Hi-Tech Manufacturing Company for each month of 1987 using the information given in problem (1) above plus the following information:

Table F

January 1987	$5,400
February	$4,800
March	$4,100
April	$4,300
May	$3,600
June	$3,700
July	$2,200
August	$2,300
September	$3,900
October	$4,500
November	$6,600
December	$8,200
January 1988	$6,000

a. The monthly sales forecast for 1987 is as shown in Table G.

b. A total of 90 percent of sales are on credit terms of net 45 and the remaining 10 percent are for cash. Credit sales have historically been collected on the basis of 50 percent in the month following sale and the remaining 50 percent in the second month after sale. Bad debt losses are negligible.

c. Monthly production is scheduled at the level of forecasted sales for the following month. Materials expense and labor expense each average 30 percent of sales. Both expenses are payable in the month following production.

d. Overhead expense of $10,000 per month is paid in the following month.

e. Interest on bonds of $20,000 is due on June 5 and December 5.

f. Selling and administrative expenses average $20,000 per month and are paid in the month incurred.

g. Tax payments are due on April 15, June 15, September 15, and December 15, and are equal to the tax liability through the month of payment.

h. No dividends will be paid.

10. Prepare monthly pro forma balance sheets for 1987 for Hi-Tech using all the information given in problems (1), (3), and (9).

Table G (thousands)

1986 actual	
November	$190
December	$230
1987, forecasted	
January	$180
February	$150
March	$130
April	$120
May	$130
June	$160
July	$175
August	$200
September	$180
October	$160
November	$200
December	$240
1988 forecasted	
January	$200

11. Prepare a monthly cash budget for Hi-Tech for 1987 using all the information given in problems (1), (3), and (9).

12. Prepare an annual pro forma sources-and-uses-of-funds statement for Hi Tech for 1987 using all the information given in problems (1), (3), and (9).

REFERENCES

Carleton, W. T. "An Analytical Model for Long-Range Financial Planning." *Journal of Finance* 25, (May 1970) 291–315.

Carleton, W. T., C. L. Dick, and D. H. Downes. "Financial Policy Models: Theory and Practice." *Journal of Financial and Quantitative Analysis* 8, (Dec. 1973) 691–710.

Chambers, J. C., S. K. Mullick, and D. D. Smith. "How to Choose the Right Forecasting Techniques." *Harvard Business Review* 49, (July–Aug. 1971) 45–74.

Donaldson, G. *Strategy for Financial Mobility*. Homewood, Ill.: Richard D. Irwin, 1969.

Francis, J. C., and D. R. Rowel. "A Simultaneous Equation Model of the Firm for Financial Analysis and Planning." *Financial Management* 7 (Spring 1978) 29–44.

Helfert, E. A. *Techniques of Financial Analysis*. 4th ed. Homewood, Ill.: Richard D. Irwin, 1977.

Horngren, C. T. *Accounting for Management Control*. 3d ed. Englewood Cliffs, N.J.: Prentice-Hall, 1974.

Jaedicke, R. D., and R. T. Sprouse. *Accounting Flows: Income, Funds, and Cash*. Englewood Cliffs, N.J.: Prentice-Hall, 1965, chaps. 5 and 6.

McInnes, J. M., and W. T. Carleton. "Theory, Models and Implementation in Financial Management." *Management Science* 28, no. 9 (September 1982) 957–978.

Pappas, J. L., and G. P. Huber. "Probabilistic Short-Term Financial Planning." *Financial Management* 2 (Autumn 1973).

Parker, G. G. C., and E. L. Segura. "How to Get a Better Forecast." *Harvard Business Review* 49 (Mar.–Apr. 1971): 99–109.

Rychel, D. F. "Capital Budgeting with Mixed Integer Linear Programming: An Application." *Financial Management* 6 (Winter 1977) 11–19.

Appendix 8A

Financial Modeling

In preparing the pro-forma income statement for Aquatic Systems discussed in Chapter 8 (see Table 8–4), we took a shortcut. We lumped interest in with selling and administrative expense rather than treating it explicitly. Using this approach, we obtained a set of pro-forma statements that was accurate enough for the purpose at hand—namely, to estimate financing requirements for Aquatic Systems over the year 1987.

By projecting a selling-and-administrative-expense level of $55,000 each month, we were treating interest as if it were constant each month. In reality, of course, interest expense each month depends on the size of the loan—which, as we found, varied from a high of more than $900,000 in April to a low of $0 in September through December (see Table 8–7). At 14 percent interest—the rate Aquatic Systems estimated it would pay in 1987—interest expense would vary from more than $10,000 in April to $0 in September. For some planning purposes, we may need more accuracy than we obtained using our earlier shortcut, so we need a way to estimate interest each month.

To estimate interest in any given month—say, January—we need first to know the size of the loan in January. To estimate the loan we need to complete the entire balance sheet, which means that we need an estimate of retained earnings for January. The retained-earnings figure for January, in turn, depends on profit for the month, which depends on interest. Alas, interest depends on the size of the loan, which depends on interest. We have a *simultaneous* system, which is always the case where interest is being paid periodically on the unpaid balance of the loan—a common practice.

How do we deal with this problem? The usual approach is to do it the way we did in Tables 8–4 and 8–7: ignore interest initially, do a complete pro-forma income statement, figure retained earnings, and then do a pro-forma balance sheet and figure the loan. To achieve more accuracy, we then adopt an *iterative* technique. With the loan determined, we figure interest each month and revise the pro-forma income statement to include interest. This revision process changes the retained-earnings figure on the balance sheet, which means that the loan now must be recalculated. We then revise the interest estimate based on the new loan figure, revise the profit and retained-earnings figures, and recalculate the loan again. The process theoretically would go on forever, with each revision requiring another and each iteration moving closer to an exact solution. The changes get smaller with each iteration, and after two or three cycles, typically, we get close enough for practical use and we stop.

Table 8A–1

Aquatic Systems, Inc. Pro-Forma Income Statements, 1987, with Actual Interest (thousands of dollars)

	Actual 1986	Jan.	Feb.	March	April	May	June	July	Aug.	Sept.	Oct.	Nov.	Dec.	Total 1987
Sales	5,080	220	275	385	495	605	770	715	605	495	385	275	275	5,500
Cost of goods sold														
Materials and labor at 62 percent	3,150	136	171	239	307	375	477	443	375	307	239	171	171	3,411
Manufacturing overhead	290	25	25	25	25	25	25	25	25	25	25	25	25	300
Total cost of goods sold	3,440	161	196	264	332	400	502	468	400	332	264	196	196	3,711
Gross profit	1,640	59	79	121	163	205	268	247	205	163	121	79	79	1,789
Depreciation	260	25	25	25	25	25	25	25	25	25	25	25	25	300
Selling and administrative expense	560	52	52	52	52	52	52	52	52	52	52	52	52	624
Interest income	5	0	0	0	0	0	0	0	0	1	2	3	3	9
Interest expense	45	2	5	8	10	10	10	7	3	0	0	0	0	55
Profit before tax	780	(20)	(3)	36	76	118	181	163	125	87	46	5	5	819
Taxes at 30 percent	234	(6)	(1)	11	23	35	54	49	38	26	14	2	2	247
Profit after taxes	546	(14)	(2)	25	53	83	127	114	87	61	32	3	3	572
Dividends	240	0	0	60	0	0	60	0	0	60	0	0	60	240
To retained earnings	306	(14)	(2)	(35)	53	83	67	114	87	1	32	3	(57)	332

Table 8A-2

Aquatic Systems, Inc. Pro-Forma Balance Sheets, 1987, with Actual Interest (thousands of dollars)

	Actual 12/31/86	Jan.	Feb.	March	April	May	June	July	Aug.	Sept.	Oct.	Nov.	Dec.
Cash	50	50	50	50	50	50	50	50	50	50	50	50	50
Marketable securities	94	0	0	0	0	0	0	0	0	148	363	469	294
Accounts receivable	353	345	385	523	688	853	1,073	1,100	963	798	633	468	413
Inventories	1,080	1,204	1,293	1,314	1,267	1,152	935	752	637	590	611	700	789
Total current assets	1,577	1,599	1,728	1,887	2,005	2,055	2,058	1,902	1,650	1,586	1,657	1,687	1,546
Gross plant and equipment	4,960	5,210	5,460	5,460	5,460	5,460	5,460	5,460	5,460	5,460	5,460	5,460	5,460
Less accumulated depreciation	1,850	1,875	1,900	1,925	1,950	1,975	2,000	2,025	2,050	2,075	2,100	2,125	2,150
Net plant	3,110	3,335	3,560	3,535	3,510	3,485	3,460	3,435	3,410	3,385	3,360	3,335	3,310
Total assets	4,687	4,934	5,288	5,422	5,515	5,540	5,518	5,337	5,060	4,971	5,017	5,022	4,856
Notes payable (bank)	0	290	647	805	924	831	800	456	54	0	0	0	0
Accounts payable	148	125	125	125	125	125	125	125	125	125	125	125	125
Taxes payable[a]	40	34	33	44	(35)	0	(8)	41	79	43	57	59	0
Other accruals	50	50	50	50	50	50	50	50	50	50	50	50	50
Total current liabilities	238	499	855	1,024	1,064	1,006	967	672	308	218	232	234	175
Mortgage[b]	960	960	960	960	960	960	910	910	910	910	910	910	860
Common stock	1,500	1,500	1,500	1,500	1,500	1,500	1,500	1,500	1,500	1,500	1,500	1,500	1,500
Retained earnings	1,989	1,975	1,973	1,938	1,991	2,074	2,141	2,255	2,342	2,343	2,375	2,378	2,321
Total liabilities and net worth	4,687	4,934	5,288	5,422	5,515	5,540	5,518	5,337	5,060	4,971	5,017	5,022	4,856

[a]The December 31, 1986, figure of $40,000 is the amount remaining on 1986 taxes and is payable on April 15, 1987. The 1987 estimated tax is payable in equal installments in April, June, September and December. The negative figures in April and June represent prepaid taxes.
[b]The mortgage principal payment of $100,000 per year is payable in June and December.

COMPUTER-BASED MODELING PROGRAMS

A better way is to use a computer to do all the figuring. There now exist a number of very good *financial-modeling* programs that will solve problems of this sort quite nicely. Most use an iterative technique like that described above (but computers do it fast and do not complain about getting tired). Many programs are available that will run on desk-top computers costing less than $2,500.

Tables 8A–1 and 8A–2 show an exact solution for the Aquatic Systems pro-forma income statement and pro-forma balance sheet for 1987. Interest expense is figured at 14 percent and totals $55,000 for the year. During September through December, Aquatic Systems is investing excess cash in marketable securities at 9 percent interest, so we see interest income during those months. In constructing Tables 8–4 and 8–7, we assumed, in effect, that interest income and expense were level each month, whereas Table 8A–1 shows that interest expense is concentrated in the spring and interest income is concentrated in the late fall. Compare Table 8A–2 to Table 8–7 and note the differences in the projected loan level each month. Using the exact method, we find that the loan peaks at $924,000 in April, whereas Table 8–7 had estimated the peak at $912,000, a difference of $12,000.

CHANGING ASSUMPTIONS: WHAT IF?

The approximation method is entirely adequate for many purposes, but the use of computers to do this sort of thing has great advantages. Once a model of the firm's financial statements is constructed, the financial manager can ask "what if" questions very easily. What if the cost of goods sold runs to 65 percent of sales rather than 62 percent? With a computer model, this question can be answered with a couple of keyboard entries, and a *complete set* of financial statements will be generated in a few seconds showing the full impact of the higher cost-of-goods-sold figure. What would happen if accounts-receivable collections slowed down? Would the plan be affected significantly? Would Aquatic Systems have to borrow significantly more money in 1987? What if the sales pattern changed?

When pro-forma statements must be done by hand, even with the help of a calculator, there is a tendency to avoid asking such questions because it is too much work to answer them. With a computer model, answering them is easy, so the questions get asked more often.

Computer-based planning models have been around for a decade or more, but only in the early 1980s did they become available on small, relatively inexpensive computers. Tables 8A–1 and 8A–2 were generated using a *spreadsheet* program on a desk-top computer. Wide accessibility to computer-based financial-planning programs is one of the most important developments in financial management in many years. All financial managers should investigate their use. Chapter 11 will return to the topic of financial modeling in its discussion of sensitivity analysis.

Part Four

Analyzing Investment Decisions

Each year business firms commit huge sums of money for capital expenditures. In 1984, aggregate expenditures by U.S. firms for plant and equipment totaled about $425 billion. Exxon alone invested almost $8 billion. While Exxon's total was the largest for any single firm, many other individual firms also invested large sums. Table IV–1 gives estimates of capital expenditures for 1986 from the *Value Line Investment Survey*.

Business firms compete among themselves for the funds necessary to finance their investments. The business sector also competes for funds against other sectors: individuals who wish to build houses and buy automobiles and refrigerators; governments that wish to build schools, roads, and military aircraft; nonprofit organizations that wish to build universities or hospitals; foreigners who wish to invest in the United States.

Just as firms must compete among themselves and against other sectors of the economy for capital funds, so too do individual projects or proposals compete for funds within a single firm. The decision to select one investment over another is an important one—not just for the firm making the decision, but for society as a whole. Because investment decisions consume scarce capital, a steadily increasing standard of living depends very much on wise investment decisions by firms, governments, and other organizations.

Table IV–1
Capital Investment by U.S. Firms (millions of dollars)

Firm	1986 (estimated)
Exxon	6,497
IBM	5,996
GM	6,150
AT&T	3,870
Texaco	1,080
Mobil	2,652
GE	2,102
Ford	2,996

Source: Value Line Investment Survey.

As we will see, a key characteristic of capital-investment projects typically is that they have an impact over long periods of time—years or even decades. How should long-term investment opportunities be analyzed? Which opportunities represent wise and efficient uses of capital funds and which do not? As we develop our approach, the factors that we considered earlier in Parts Two and Three—time, risk, and information—will occupy center stage. We will devote three chapters in Part Four to the question of analyzing investment opportunities. Chapter 9 develops our basic approach. Chapters 10 and 11 then deal with the problem of setting performance standards—that is, minimum acceptable rates of return.

9

Fundamentals of Capital Budgeting

In this chapter, we will learn to analyze long-term investment opportunities using the basic techniques of capital budgeting. First we will discuss alternative decision criteria and their strengths and weaknesses. Then we will develop in detail the discounted-cash-flow approach. Next we will develop techniques for estimating the cash flows that an investment generates. Finally, we will discuss some practical problems in applying capital-budgeting techniques.

WHAT IS CAPITAL BUDGETING?

Suppose XYZ Corporation has three investment opportunities under consideration: (1) expanding a warehouse for $60,000, (2) purchasing a new truck for $35,000, or (3) purchasing a computer for $45,000.

Should XYZ undertake any of the three projects? All of them? Some subset of them? The firm must *budget* its funds (capital) among them. The term **capital budgeting** describes this process of *analyzing* capital investment opportunities and *deciding* which (if any) to undertake.

Capital budgeting—is the process of analyzing capital investment opportunities and deciding which (if any) to undertake; it includes the creative search for investment opportunities, the gathering of data and making of forecasts, the economic analysis, the decision, and the implementation.

In making such capital-budgeting decisions, we will assume that managers attempt to maximize the value of the firm to existing shareholders. With such an objective, managers need some way to estimate the value that a project might provide. If a project creates value, it will further the manager's pursuit of shareholder-wealth maximization and should be undertaken.

In this chapter, we focus on capital budgeting at the project level and show how to evaluate specific investment opportunities. Through this process, we can relate decisions directly to the value they may create for shareholders. The cumulative effect of undertaking specific projects ultimately defines a firm's assets and capabilities. This "bottom-up" project appraisal should be complemented with the type of financial planning discussed in the previous chapter, which analyzes the firm as a whole typically through the use of pro-forma financial statements. By viewing the firm in its entirety, managers can make sure that the collection of projects undertaken fits into a unified whole. Before we begin analysis of capital budgeting in detail, however, it is best to take one step back and look at the capital-budgeting *process* as it faces a firm. Table 9–1 outlines the three basic steps in the process.

Determination of Alternatives and Strategic Analysis

Strategic analysis—is the process of making fundamental decisions about a firm's basic goal or purpose and about the products or services it will produce and the markets it will serve.

First, investment alternatives don't arrive in neat bundles for managers to evaluate—the alternatives must be defined. The founders of Apple Computer had the insight to see that the opportunity to produce home computers was worth their consideration. In fact, many fortunes are made (or lost) at the initial stages of realizing what alternatives are even worth considering. In practice, a lot of the determination of alternatives takes place in the context of **strategic analysis** where a firm makes fundamental choices about its commercial strategy. Such strategic analysis may not consider the detailed attributes of each alternative.

Well-managed companies often impose a strategic test before they ever get to the economic analysis. A firm that builds aircraft is unlikely to be interested in opening a

Table 9–1
Steps in the Capital Budgeting Process

A. Determination of alternatives and strategic analysis
B. Economic analysis of remaining alternatives
C. Implementation of chosen alternatives (including performance assessment)

Finance in Practice 9–1

Taking a Long View

During the 1970s many companies achieved improvements in earnings per share (EPS) yet failed to provide shareholders with an adequate return. Return to shareholders (RTS), as we found in Chapter 4, is the sum of dividends plus capital gains. A firm's earnings may rise, but if the market does not value those earnings accordingly, the firm's stock price may not keep pace, and return to shareholders will lag behind.

Of the 400 companies in the Standard & Poors industrial stock index for the period 1974–1979, 232 had earnings growth of 10 percent per year or more over the period. Of those 232 companies, 39 had negative returns to shareholders *even though their earnings grew* during the period. A total of 89 of the 232 companies generated returns to shareholders lower than the rate of inflation.

Why did this happen, and what does it imply? The experience of these companies demonstrates that earnings growth does not necessarily lead to an increase in the market value of a company's shares.

Some observers of American business think that part of the problem arises from a preoccupation of American managers with short-term performance. Many companies continue to use FIFO (first-in, first-out) instead of LIFO (last-in, first-out) inventory accounting. LIFO can have large advantages in reducing taxes, but the disadvantage of causing *reported* profits to be lower even though cash flow is higher. Many companies measure the performance of managers using accounting return on investment even though accounting ROI is known to bias decision makers toward short-term results. If a manager has an opportunity to invest in a project that generates very large cash flows in the future but shows accounting losses in the early years, accounting ROI suffers in the near term. Knowing this, a manager may be tempted to forgo an attractive project— one that has an attractive rate of return (based on discounted cash flow) and clearly creates value for both shareholders and society— because it makes near-term accounting ROI look bad.

While U.S. companies have invested large dollar amounts, many economists have been concerned in the last decade over the low rate of capital investment in the United States. Relative to the size of the U.S. economy, capital investment fell during the 1970s and early 1980s. In recent years, capital investment in the United States has averaged only about 7 percent of gross national product versus 9 percent in earlier years. Many economists and managers are concerned that this drop in the rate of investment has hurt U.S. productivity and has reduced the ability of U.S. business to compete in international markets. Some of the tax initiatives of the Reagan Administration have been aimed in part at stimulating savings and capital investment. Preliminary results do not indicate that this attempt was successful, but more time must pass before we can fully judge the outcome.

The solution to America's problems with low capital investment may lie partly in reforms of tax laws and the regulatory environment. Officials in Washington, initially spurred by the Reagan administration, have placed such changes on the national agenda. But changes also are necessary in the attitudes of managers. To invest wisely, a long-range orientation is essential. Investment, by its very nature, involves committing scarce resources in the present in return for benefits in the future. A long view is necessary to give future benefits proper weight.

Source: A. Rappaport, ''Selecting Strategies that Create Shareholder Value,'' *Harvard Business Review* 59 (May/June 1981): 139–49; *Business Week,* June 1, 1981, pp. 60–71.

string of ice-cream parlors, no matter what the numbers look like. "We build air-planes," the chief executive would say, and a proposal to build ice-cream parlors would never make it to the economic-analysis stage.

In a world in which all information and analysis were costless, managers could quantitatively analyze every conceivable alternative. Given the costs in both dollars and time of gathering and analyzing information, managers are forced to eliminate many alternatives based on strategic grounds without a full economic evaluation of the investment.

Economic Analysis of Remaining Alternatives

Economic analysis—is the process of gathering and evaluating quantitative information about the costs and benefits of an investment project.

After alternatives are determined and some are eliminated on strategic grounds, the remaining investments should be subjected to a detailed scrutiny, or **economic analysis,** which is the step of the capital-budgeting process on which we will focus in detail.

Since managers are attempting to maximize the value of the firm to shareholders, they need some guidance as to what value a potential investment might have. The economic analysis is a gathering of specific quantitative information about a project. Suppose a textile firm is considering the purchase of a new loom versus the repair of an old one: should the new loom be purchased?

Answering this question involves measuring and weighing costs and benefits of each alternative to determine which (if either) alternative will best serve the sharehold-ers of the company. We'll have much more to say about the steps in the economic analysis of projects later in the chapter.

Implementation of Chosen Alternatives

Once an investment decision is made, it still must be implemented. The investment decision to build a new plant is only the beginning. Next the plant must be built and efficiently operated. Implementation involves communicating what is to be done in often complex organizations and being sure that the best efforts are made to carry out plans. Unexpected events occur, and original plans may have to be modified. Ob-viously, implementation is no trivial matter and absorbs the time and talents of cor-porate employees ranging from the executive level to manual labor.

In addition, it is important to evaluate the project after it is adopted. Did the project live up to expectations? If not, why? Answers to such questions provide critical infor-mation the firm needs to evaluate its existing employees and gain knowledge useful for future decisions. Information about why one project failed may spark an idea for a new alternative, and the whole capital-budgeting process then begins again. The three phases of capital budgeting depicted in Table 9–1 are interdependent.

Though we will focus here on economic analysis, it is important to remember that economic analysis is only part of the process. No amount of economic analysis can salvage a company that never comes up with decent alternatives to analyze. And poor implementation can foil the best-laid plans. On the other hand, economic analysis can improve decisions for all companies.

Finance in Practice 9–2

Innovation in the Mail Business

Need a package delivered halfway across the United States overnight? If you call Federal Express, the Memphis-based air courier, they will pick it up, deliver it to their company-owned planes, and bring it to the destination the next morning. If for some reason it doesn't get there the next day, you get a reduced rate, but that doesn't happen often. Federal Express claims that more than 99 percent of the shipments arrive overnight.

This type of service is the result of a major innovation in the mail business. Until the last few years, alternatives for mailing packages were limited to the U.S. Postal Service and a few other private package carriers. All of these private carriers picked up your package and promised delivery, but they used only scheduled airplane service. This method of operation kept capital requirements down—no hangars or airplanes had to be purchased.

Enter Federal Express, founded by chairman Fred Smith. Smith decided to concentrate on delivery of small packages, but instead of relying on scheduled airline service he decided to invest in company-owned planes to ensure control over shipments and, thus, to improve the speed and reliability of service. Packages are flown to a central location in Memphis, sorted during the night, and sent to their destinations aboard company planes.

The capital outlay for the planes and other facilities was large, but it has paid off. For example, earnings grew at an almost incredible 76 percent annual rate for the five-year period beginning in 1976, the company's stock price went from $6 to $65 a share (between 1978 and 1981), and Fred Smith's holdings of that stock grew in value to about $150 million by mid-1981—not a bad investment for Mr. Smith.

The key to this success was finding a new potentially profitable investment, analyzing its potential, and then carrying the project through—all basic steps in the capital-budgeting process. Clearly, a key was Smith's innovative idea of how to change the mail business by making a capital investment in planes and creating a dependable overnight service.

Source: Adapted from G. Colvin, "Federal Express Dives into Air Mail," *Fortune,* June 15, 1981, pp. 106–108.

ECONOMIC ANALYSIS OF INVESTMENT PROPOSALS

Given the framework depicted in Table 9–1, let's focus on economic analysis for specific proposals. If a manager's objective is to maximize the value of the firm to existing shareholders, we need a way to determine whether or not a project adds value to the firm. In short, we need a method to determine whether a project is or is not a good investment proposal. Let us examine a number of methods that are widely used by firms in practice.

Measuring the Payback Period

One simple and widely used method of analyzing investment opportunities is known as the **payback approach**. This approach addresses the question of how long a time it will take the cash inflows expected from an investment to repay the initial outlay.

Table 9–2

Payback Period for a Hypothetical Investment

	Year 0	Year 1	Year 2	Year 3
Cash out	1000	0	0	0
Cash in	0	500	400	300
Net cash to date	(1000)	(500)	(100)	200

The **payback approach**—is a method of analyzing investment opportunities that determines how long it will take the cash inflows expected from an investment to repay (pay back) the initial outlay.

Suppose an investment of $1,000 is expected to generate after-tax cash inflows of $500, $400, and $300 over a three-year period. As we can see in Table 9–2, the investment would be recovered part way through the third year.

As Table 9–2 shows, the investment has "paid back" all but $100 by the end of year 2. Since year 3 produces a cash inflow of $300, the final $100 will be paid back about one third of the way through year 3. So the payback period for this hypothetical investment is 2.33 years.

A company might use the payback period in investment analysis by establishing the criterion for investments of accepting projects that had payback periods of less than some critical value. For example, if a company's maximum acceptable payback period were 3 years, the project in Table 9–2 with a payback period of 2.33 years would be acceptable, whereas another project with a payback of 4 years would be rejected.

In making investments, it is often useful to know just how long it is going to take to recover the outlay. In general, the shorter the better. However, as a criterion for judging the economic worth of an investment, or its worth relative to other investments, payback has some serious shortcomings.

First, the payback period does not take into account differences in the *time pattern* of cash flows. Consider the two hypothetical investments in Table 9–3. Both investments have the same payback period—namely, 2 years. But most people would prefer investment A for two reasons. First, while the total flows in the first two years are equal, A has a larger flow in year 1. Anyone for whom money has time value (and that includes almost everyone) would prefer a pattern of $600 sooner and $400 later to a pattern of $400 sooner and $600 later. Second, although both investments have the same total payback for the first two years, A promises $300 in year 3 and B

Table 9–3

Time Pattern of Cash Flows for Two Investment Alternatives

Investment	Cash Out	Cash In		
		Year 1	Year 2	Year 3
A	1000	600	400	800
B	1000	400	600	100

promises only $100 in year 3. Thus, as a criterion for judging economic worth, the payback approach has two serious shortcomings: it ignores the time value of money, and it ignores cash flows occuring beyond the end of the payback period.

In addition, setting a maximum acceptable payback period is essentially an arbitrary decision: there is no easy way to relate payback period to more general criteria, such as profit maximization or value maximization.

> **Payback has two serious shortcomings as a criterion for judging economic worth: it ignores the time value of money, and it ignores the cash flows that occur after the end of the payback period.**

In spite of some shortcomings, the payback approach is still widely used because it answers an important question: how long is it expected to take to get the investment back? While useful for these purposes, most firms find it necessary to go beyond the simple payback measure before arriving at final decisions on important investments.[1] The payback approach is, thus, generally used in conjunction with other methods of analyzing projects.

Measuring Accounting Return on Investment (AROI)

The **AROI approach**—is a method of analyzing capital investments that relies on an accounting-based measure of return on investment, calculated as some measure of accounting profit divided by some measure of accounting investment.

The **straight-line method of depreciation**—allocates the cost of an asset equally over a period of years by dividing the historical cost of the asset by the number of years and allocating that equal fraction of the cost to each year in the recovery period.

The **AROI approach** to economic analysis of cash flows uses accounting-based return-on-investment calculations. Measures of *accounting-based return on investment (AROI),* as we discovered in Chapter 7, are calculated as some measure of accounting profit divided by some measure of accounting investment. Herein lies one of the problems with accounting-based ROI measures: ambiguity. There are many ways return can be measured—accounting profit, cash flow, before tax, after tax, and perhaps others we could devise. Likewise, investment can be measured in many ways—initial outlay, book value, average book value, and so on. ROI calculated with each of these different quantities would yield a different result. Even if we settled on particular choices for return and investment, these quantities themselves would be affected by accounting conventions, such as choice of depreciation method. (Depreciation can be calculated using the **straight-line method of depreciation** or an **accelerated method of depreciation.**) So, there are many ways to calculate accounting ROI, none of which are any more or less "correct" than the others.

Let us put aside these ambiguities for a moment and calculate AROI for the proposed project detailed in Table 9–4. The project requires investment in early 1987 and is expected to last through year-end 1989. (The assumed tax rate is 46 percent.)

Note the differences in the before-tax and after-tax calculations. Note also that the calculations were performed using *ending book value* in each year. They just as easily could have been performed using *beginning book value* or *average book value* in each year. And, of course, each of these methods would yield a different answer.

---

[1]For an analysis of the payback criterion and some arguments in favor of its use, see J. M. Blatt, "Investment Evaluation Under Uncertainty," *Financial Management* 8 (Summer 1979): 66–81.

Table 9—4
Accounting Return on Investment (AROI) for a Proposed Project, 1987–1989

	Return (thousands of dollars)		Investment (thousands of dollars)				Return on Investment (percent)	
Year (1)	Net Profit Before Tax (2)	Net Profit After Tax (3)	Beginning Book Value (4)	Gross Investment (5)	Deprecia- tion (6)	Ending Book Value (7) = (4) + (5) − (6)	AROI Before Tax (8) = (2) ÷ (7)	AROI After Tax (9) = (3) ÷ (7)
1987	−50	−27	0	320	100	220	−23	−12
1988	100	54	220	0	100	120	83	45
1989	100	54	120	0	100	20	500	270

An **accelerated method of depreciation**—allocates the cost of an asset over a period of years according to a schedule that allows a greater fraction of the historical cost to be allocated to earlier years and a smaller fraction of the historical cost to be allocated to later years.

Another interesting observation can be made about the AROI numbers in Table 9–4: they are different in each year. After-tax AROI starts out at −12 percent in 1987, rises first to 45 percent the following year and then to 270 percent in 1989. Is the project a good investment? It is difficult to tell looking only at the AROI numbers. Suppose our required return for the project—that is, the minimum return we would accept—was 15 percent after taxes. The return in Table 9–4 falls short of the target in 1987 but exceeds it in 1988 and 1989 by substantial margins. Should we undertake an investment whose projected return is inadequate in some years and very attractive in others? The answer is that we need a better measure.

One fairly obvious possibility is to compute the *average* AROI over the three-year period. One method of averaging is to divide average profit for the period by average investment. Averaging the figures in column (2) of Table 9–4, we see that average profit after tax (PAT) is $27,000, and using ending book values in column (6), average investment is $120,000. Average AROI would then be $27,000/$120,000 = 22.5 percent.

By *averaging* AROI over the three years, we have solved part of the ambiguity problem, but alas we have created another problem—we are not taking into account the time value of money. As Table 9–4 shows, the large cash outflow takes place in the early years, as reflected in column (4) of Table 9–4, whereas the cash inflows (the rewards) do not become large until the later years. Averaging the AROI figures over the three years does not take into account this timing difference, which can be very important, as it is in this case.

Thus, it turns out that the AROI method forces us to choose between the problem of ambiguity (if we calculate AROI in each year) and the problem of not considering the time value of money (if we average it). In view of these shortcomings, why use the AROI method? What questions does it answer? The AROI method gives a measure of accounting profit per dollar of investment, often a useful piece of information in measuring performance, especially over a relatively short time period (say, a year). The AROI method is especially useful in measuring the performance of firms and industries. But our goal in the case of this project is to *make a decision*, not to measure performance.

DISCOUNTED CASH FLOW AND INVESTMENT DECISIONS

As we've seen, the payback method and the AROI method have shortcomings as means for deciding on investment projects. While useful in some respects, neither measure directly addresses the issue of what value a project adds to the firm. If managers are to maximize the value of the firm, they need such value estimates to make good decisions about investment projects.

Fortunately, some of the tools we developed earlier will help in providing such estimates of value. Our basic discounted-cash-flow (DCF) model from Part Two showed how we might value a set of cash flows. The value is determined as the present value of future cash flows—discounted back to the present. We can, thus, think of investment projects as packages of cash flows and use DCF techniques to determine their value. Specifically, we can think of the value (V) of the project as shown in Equation (1).

> The value (V) of an investment project can be determined, using discounted-cash-flow techniques, as
>
> $$V = \sum_{t=0}^{n} \frac{C_t}{(1 + K)^t} \tag{1}$$
>
> where C_t = the expected cash the project contributes in time t and K = the required rate of return on the cash flows.

Equation (1) states that the value of the project can be found by adding up the present values of each of the expected cash flows. The Σ (sigma) notation is a directive to add all cash flows from time 0 through time n, where n would be the date of the last expected cash flow associated with the project. In finding these present values, we should use a required return (K) that will penalize cash flows for both *time* delay and greater *risk*. Remember that we have to wait to receive some of the cash flows and that the cash flows might not materialize at all if our projections about the future are wrong.

> **If we think of investment projects as bundles of cash flows, we can use discounted-cash-flow techniques to determine their value.**

To implement Equation (1) we have to estimate cash flows, for which the material from Part Three on financial analysis will be useful. We will also have to address the problem of what required return is to be used in our DCF calculations. What rate of return should be required on a project if managers are to serve shareholder interests? In choosing this rate we have to remember the risk/return trade-off. Thus, in talking about various approaches to analyzing investment opportunities we will build on basic tools of finance that have been developed in the first three parts of the book.

In actually implementing the DCF valuation concepts expressed in Equation (1), firms typically use one or both of two techniques: the net-present-value (*NPV*) technique and the internal-rate-of-return (*IRR*) technique.

Net Present Value (*NPV*)

The net-present-value (*NPV*) technique is a direct application of Equation (1), which can be rewritten as shown in Equation (2).

> The net present value (*NPV*) of an investment project can be determined, using discounted-cash-flow techniques, as
>
> $$NPV = \sum_{t=0}^{n} \frac{C_t}{(1 + K)^t} \qquad (2)$$
>
> where C_t = the expected cash flow in period t and K = the required rate of return.

Cash inflows in Equation (2) will be positive values of C_t, and cash outflows will be negative values. Note that we sum from $t = 0$ and thereby include any initial outlays on the project as negative values for C_0. Later in this chapter we will examine the methods of determining the cash flows, and in Chapters 10 and 11 we will examine methods of determining required return (K), but for the moment let us take these as given.

The **net present value** (*NPV*)—of an investment is the present value of the cash inflows less (net of) the required outlay.

The **net present value** (*NPV*) of an investment is simply the present value of the inflows less (net of) the required outlay. If *NPV* is positive, the project has a positive value (the benefits outweigh the costs) and should be accepted. Such a positive value will increase the value of the firm to shareholders and, thus, further the objective of maximizing shareholder wealth.

> The *NPV* investment rule is: in general, accept any investment that has a positive net present value when evaluated at the appropriate required rate of return.

Sample Problem 9–1

Calculation of Net Present Value for a Hypothetical Investment

Consider a hypothetical investment of $100 that is expected to yield cash inflows of $30, $50, and $40 over the next three years. Suppose the required rate of return (K) is 15 percent. Should the firm undertake the project?

Solution

Table 9–5 lays out the calculation of net present value. Because *NPV* is negative, the project should not be accepted.

The calculations in Table 9–5 are simply the application of DCF analysis in the context of an investment proposal. It is useful here to think for a moment of the project as a financial asset. It offers cash flows of $30, $50, and $40 in the next three years respectively. At a required rate of return of 15 percent per year, these flows have a present value of $90.22, which can be calculated as

Table 9–5
Calculating Net Present Value (NPV)—General Form

Period, t	Cash Flow, C_t (dollars)	Present-Value Factor at 15 Percent, $\left[\dfrac{1}{(1+K)^t}\right]$ (percent)	Present Value, $\left[\dfrac{C_t}{(1+K)^t}\right]$ (dollars)
0	−100	1.000	−100.00
1	30	0.870	26.10
2	50	0.756	37.80
3	40	0.658	26.32
			$NPV = -\underline{\underline{9.78}}$

$$PV = \frac{\$30}{(1+0.15)^1} + \frac{\$50}{(1+0.15)^2} + \frac{\$40}{(1+0.15)^3}$$

$$= \$30(0.870) + \$50(0.756) + \$40(0.658)$$

$$= \$90.22.$$

In other words, it would take $90.22 today in a bank account earning interest at 15 percent per year to enable us to make bank-account withdrawals of $30, $50, and $40 in the next three years. The catch is that the project requires an outlay of $100 to get the cash flows. Why pay $100 for the project if $90.22 will get you the same future cash flows when you can invest at 15 percent (your required return)? The answer is that you should *not* invest in the project; it has a negative value. Specifically, it has a net present value of $90.22 − $100 = −$9.78, as calculated in Table 9–5. ∃ⅢϜ

Internal Rate of Return (*IRR*)

The **internal rate of return** (*IRR*)—of an investment is the rate that discounts all of the cash flows of an investment, including all outlays, to exactly zero; it is the discount rate that makes the net present value of the project equal to zero; it is the discounted-cash-flow measure of the expected rate of return to be earned on an investment.

Net present value is a dollar measure of the net value of any project and is thus a direct application of DCF techniques developed earlier. For some purposes, however, rather than a dollar value, managers would prefer to estimate the *percentage* rate of return they expect to earn on an investment. For example, Chapter 4 showed how to calculate the yield to maturity on a bond. That yield was simply the DCF measure of the percentage rate of return you would earn on the bond if you purchased it and held it to maturity (assuming, of course, that the issuer of the bond did not default). This yield could be compared to your required rate of return to see if the bond was a desirable purchase.

In the analysis of investment projects within the firm, the rate of return analogous to a bond's yield to maturity is called an **internal rate of return** (*IRR*) and is simply the DCF measure of the rate of return expected to be earned on the investment in the project if the estimated cash flows actually materialize. In simplest terms, the *IRR* is the interest rate that discounts the future expected cash inflows to be exactly equal to the cash outlay. That is, an *IRR* is that discount rate which would make the net present value of the project equal to zero, as shown in Equation (3).

> The internal rate of return (*IRR*) that discounts all the cash flows of an investment, including all outlays, to exactly zero can be calculated by solving for *R* in the following equation:
>
> $$0 = \sum_{t=0}^{n} \frac{C_t}{(1 + R)^t} \tag{3}$$
>
> where $R = IRR$, and where C_0, the outlay in time period 0, is included in the summation.

The *IRR* is a *time-adjusted* rate of return. Its great virtue is that it takes into account the time value of money. In addition, its definition is standard, with no ambiguity as to the method of calculation as was true of the AROI method.

How do we use the internal rate of return to evaluate investment opportunities? We simply compare the *IRR* to the required rate of return.

> **The *IRR* investment rule is: in general, undertake any project that has an internal rate of return greater than the required rate of return.**

Like the *NPV* investment rule, the *IRR* investment rule is a general guide that should not be followed blindly. Some investments with an internal rate of return greater than the target rate may be unwise for other reasons, and some with an *IRR* below target may be necessary or desirable. For example, an investment in pollution-control equipment may have a low indicated *IRR* but may be essential to comply with the law or simply with good citizenship.

Sample Problem 9–2

Calculating the Internal Rate of Return for an Investment Proposal

Let us consider an investment proposal that is expected to yield cash inflows of $40, $50, and $30 in the next three years, respectively. The project requires an investment today of $100. Should the project be undertaken if the required rate of return is 15 percent?

Solution

Using the definition of *IRR* in Equation (3), we can set up the problem as follows, remembering that $(1 + R)^0 = 1$:

$$0 = -\$100 + \frac{\$40}{(1 + R)} + \frac{\$50}{(1 + R)^2} + \frac{\$30}{(1 + R)^3}$$

$$\$100 = \frac{\$40}{(1 + R)} + \frac{\$50}{(1 + R)^2} + \frac{\$30}{(1 + R)^3}$$

Table 9–6
Finding the Internal Rate of Return (IRR) of a Hypothetical Investment Proposal

		First Try		Second Try	
Year	Cash Flow (dollars)	Present Value Factor at 12 Percent (percent)	Present Value (dollars)	Present Value Factor at 8 Percent (percent)	Present Value (dollars)
1	40	0.893	35.72	0.926	37.04
2	50	0.797	39.85	0.857	42.85
3	30	0.712	21.26	0.794	23.82
			96.93		103.71

The rate, R, that solves the above equation—the rate that discounts the cash inflows to exactly equal the outlay of $100—is the internal rate of return of the investment.

When we calculated net present value, we started with a given discount rate and solved for the present value of the flows. To calculate the internal rate of return, we do the opposite—we start with the present value of the flows (the outlay) and solve for the discount rate. But how do we actually find R? The answer is by trial and error, unless we have a calculator with a solution method for *IRR* programmed into it.

Let us illustrate the method using the above problem. First we simply guess at the correct rate. Let us try 12 percent. Using the present-value tables, Appendix Table I at the back of the book, we get the result in the *First Try* columns of Table 9–6.

On our first try, at 12 percent, we get a present value of $96.93. At 12 percent, we have penalized the future cash flows too much because $96.93 is less than the outlay of $100. So we know we set the discount rate too high and need to use a figure less than 12 percent. For our second try, let us use 8 percent. Now we get $103.71, so we know 8 percent is too low. If we try 10 percent, we get $100.19; if we try 11 percent, we get $98.57. Hence, the internal rate of return lies between 10 percent and 11 percent. In many cases, it is sufficient to state that the internal rate of return is "about 10 percent," or "between 10 percent and 11 percent." Clearly, the internal rate of return is less than the required rate of return of 15 percent, so the project should be rejected.

If we need greater accuracy, we can either buy a calculator with DCF capability or interpolate using present-value tables.

We already saw that as we go from a discount rate of 10 percent to 11 percent, the resulting present value changes from $100.19 to $98.57 for a net change of $100.19 − $98.57 = $1.62. To solve our problem, however, we need a present value of $100, not $100.19 or $98.57. A way to proceed is to notice that $100 is just $0.19 less than the present value at 10 percent ($100.19 − $100.00 = $0.19). This $0.19 is equivalent to $0.19/$1.62 = 0.12 of the total change in present value resulting in a change in *IRR* from 10 percent to 11 percent. As a result, we could approximate the precise value of the internal rate of return as being 0.12 of the way between 10 percent and 11 percent, or as $10 + 0.12 (11 - 10) = 10.12$ percent. In doing this interpolation, we are assuming that changes in the *IRR* (as it moves from 10 percent to 11 percent) move in the same way as do changes in the present value. While not exactly correct, the assumption provides an answer that is close enough for our purposes. We can formalize this interpolation by stating that the precise value of the internal rate of return, *R*, can be interpolated given knowledge of a rate that is too high and one that is too low as

$$\left(\frac{R - \text{lower rate}}{\text{the actual difference in rates}}\right) = \left(\frac{\text{the desired difference in present value}}{\text{the actual difference in present value}}\right)$$

$$\frac{R - 10}{11 - 10} = \frac{\$100.19 - \$100}{\$100.19 - \$98.57}$$

$$R - 10 = \frac{\$0.19}{\$1.62} (11 - 10)$$

$$R = \frac{\$0.19}{\$1.62} + 10 = 0.12 + 10 = 10.12 \text{ percent}$$

At an internal rate of return of 10.12 percent, present value is $100.00; thus, at $R = 10.12$ percent, the net present value of the project is zero. ∃⊪╒

If the cash inflows are equal and the outlay occurs only in the initial year, there is a shortcut in calculating *IRR* that uses annuity tables.

Sample Problem 9–3

Calculating the Internal Rate of Return with Equal Cash Inflows

An investment of $1,000 yields $176.99 for 10 years. What is its internal rate of return?

Solution
$1,000 = $176.99 × the present-value annuity factor. Dividing $1,000 by $176.99 gives 5.650. Looking in Appendix Table II at the back of the book, we search in the row for year 10 until we find 5.650 in the column for 12 percent, which tells us that the investment has an *IRR* of 12 percent. Usually we will not be so lucky as to find an exact match, and we will have to interpolate between columns in the table. To do so, we use the procedure outlined in Sample Problem 9–2. ∃⊪╒

Profitability Index

In addition to net present value and internal rate of return, the **profitability index** is a third discounted-cash-flow technique used to evaluate investment projects. The profitability index is actually only a rearrangement of our net-present-value equation to put things in ratio form, as shown in Equation (4).

> The profitability index (*PI*) of an investment project can be calculated, using discounted-cash-flow techniques, as
>
> $$PI = \frac{PV \text{ of future cash benefits}}{\text{Dollar investment}} \qquad (4)$$
>
> $$= \frac{\sum_{t=1}^{n} C_t(1 + K)^{-t}}{-C_0}$$

The **profitability index** (*PI*)—is a ratio measure of an investment's benefits in relation to its costs that is calculated using discounted-cash-flow techniques.

As Equation (4) shows, the profitability index is a look at the present value of future cash flows from $t = 1$ onward relative to the cash costs of undertaking the project. Just as in the *NPV* calculation, K is the required return on the project. The minus sign before C_0 in the denominator converts a cash outflow to a positive dollar cost (a minus in front of a negative number makes it a positive number). For example, for the project in Table 9–5, the profitability index (at $K = 15$ percent) can be calculated as

$$PI = \frac{\left[\dfrac{\$30}{(1 + 0.15)} + \dfrac{\$50}{(1 + 0.15)^2} + \dfrac{\$40}{(1 + 0.15)^3}\right]}{-(-\$100)}$$

$$= \frac{\$30(0.870) + \$50(0.756) + \$40(0.658)}{\$100}$$

$$= \frac{\$90.22}{\$100} = 0.9022.$$

This profitability index gives us the ratio of benefits to costs. If $PI < 1$, the benefits (in present-value terms) are less than the costs, and the project should be rejected. If $PI > 1$, the project's benefits exceed its costs, and the project should be accepted.

The *PI* investment rule is: in general, undertake those investment projects with a profitability index greater than 1.

Note that whenever $NPV > 0$, the profitability index exceeds 1 and whenever $NPV < 0$, the profitability index is less than 1. As a result, the NPV and PI investment rules always give us the same accept/reject decision on projects. The only difference is that the profitability index gives the benefits per dollar of costs, while net present value gives the dollar value of benefits minus costs. As our above calculations show, the project in Table 9–5 has a net present value of $-\$9.78$ and a profitability index of 0.9022. Both calculations tell us to reject the project. The profitability index tells us that we get only about 90 cents of benefits per dollar invested, which makes the decision a bad one. Because of the similarities between net present value and the profitability index, we will not carry *PI* through further discussions in this chapter. In addition, the *PI* rule is not used in practice nearly as much as is the *NPV* rule or the *IRR* rule. We will use the internal rate of return and net present value as our basic discounted-cash-flow techniques for analyzing projects.

COMPARING NET PRESENT VALUE AND INTERNAL RATE OF RETURN

We now have two measures of investment worth based on discounted cash flow. Net present value is a dollar measure, internal rate of return is a percentage-return measure. Which is best? Both have their uses, and in many cases either will serve to measure investment worth. *IRR* is easy to interpret even by those unfamiliar with discounted cash flow, whereas *NPV* is reliable in some situations that *IRR* is not. Let us examine the two measures a bit more closely.

Investment decisions can be classified into two general categories:

1. *accept/reject decisions,* where the issue is whether to undertake a given investment opportunity, and
2. *ranking decisions,* where two or more investment opportunities exist but not all can be undertaken.

Accept/Reject Decisions

For accept/reject decisions, we can use either the *NPV* rule or the *IRR* rule and get the same signal. The result is the same because if the internal rate of return exceeds the required rate of return (*K*), net present value will be greater than zero, so both rules signal a decision to accept the investment. If the internal rate of return is less than the required rate of return, then net present value is greater than zero, so both rules call for a decision to reject the investment.

To see the equivalence of these two rules, let us consider an investment of $100 that yields inflows of $50, $60, and $40 over a three-year period, with net present value plotted against the required rate of return (*K*), as shown in Figure 9–1. For

Figure 9–1
Net Present Value (*NPV*) Versus Discount Rate (*K*)

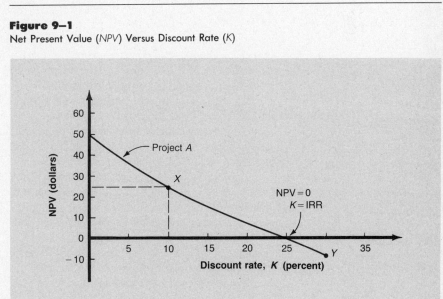

example, at a required return of 10 percent, we can calculate the net present value as

$$NPV = \$100 + \frac{\$50}{(1 + 0.10)} + \frac{\$60}{(1 + 0.10)^2} + \frac{\$40}{(1 + 0.10)^3}$$

$$= -\$100 + \$50(0.909) + \$60(0.826) + \$40(0.751)$$

$$= \$25.05$$

In Figure 9–1, point X represents a net present value of $25.05 at a required return of 10 percent. The other points on the line represent the *NPV* of project A calculated at other discount rates. Point Y shows a net present value of $-$8 at a required return of 30 percent. By looking at the figure, we can see that *NPV* is greater than 0 for any discount rate less than 25 percent, which is project A's internal rate of return (the point in Figure 9–1 where the graph crosses the horizontal axis making *NPV* equal to 0 at 25 percent). For example, at point X, the discount rate is 10 percent, which is less than the *IRR* of 25 percent. As a result, the *NPV* at point X is greater than zero. At point Y, however, the discount rate is 30 percent, which is above the *IRR* of 25 percent, and the *NPV* at Y is less than zero.

> For normal cash-flow patterns having a single internal rate of return, the *NPV* and *IRR* investment rules give identical signals in the case of accept/reject decisions.
>
> If *IRR* = K, then *NPV* = 0.
>
> If *IRR* > K, then *NPV* > 0.
>
> If *IRR* < K, then *NPV* < 0.

There is a technical difficulty with the *IRR* investment rule that deserves brief mention. Certain types of cash-flow patterns may have more than one positive discount rate that produces a zero *NPV*; that is, certain cash-flow patterns have more than one *IRR*. It turns out that the number of solutions may be as great as the number of sign reversals in the cash-flow stream. A stream with a pattern of $-, +, +, +, +$ has only one sign reversal and, therefore, no more than one positive *IRR*. A pattern of $-, +, -, +, +, +$ may have as many as three positive solutions.

Where multiple solutions occur, which solution is correct? The answer is that none is correct. Each solution discounts the cash flows to zero, but none is a meaningful measure of project return. In practice, cash-flow patterns that yield multiple *IRR*s are rare. Even patterns with more than one sign reversal usually have only one *IRR*, because it takes extreme cases to produce multiple solutions. Thus, usually the possibility of multiple solutions can be ignored, except for one important group of investments known as *acceleration projects*.

An example of an acceleration project is one in which a petroleum or mining company invests funds in order to accelerate the recovery of a given body of oil or minerals. In these situations, the typical cash flow associated with the investment always involves a major reversal of cash flows with the pattern $-, +, -$; that is, outlays now produce incremental positive flows in the near future (as recovery is accelerated relative to the status quo) followed by negative incremental flows (as the reserves are exhausted earlier than they would have been if the acceleration investment had not been made). The attempt to measure the *IRR* for such projects frequently yields multiple and, hence, meaningless solutions. In such cases, use of the *NPV* investment rule is recommended.

Ranking Decisions

In practice, investment opportunities often unfold over time in a way that presents each one as a decision to accept or not. Ranking becomes necessary in two situations: (1) where capital is *rationed*—that is, where capital funds are limited in amount and there are more investment opportunities than funds and (2), where two or more opportunities are *mutually exclusive*. Examples of mutually exclusive investments would be two machines to do the same job, two alternative plants to produce the same product, or two or more alternatives for accomplishing any given objective.

> **Ranking decisions are necessary where capital is rationed (where capital funds are limited and there are more good investment opportunities than funds) and where two or more opportunities are mutually exclusive.**

Mutually Exclusive Projects.   If forced to rank mutually exclusive projects, should we take the project with the higher net present value (as long as its *NPV* is greater than 0) or should we take the project with the higher internal rate of return? Fortunately, in most cases the project with the higher *NPV* also has the higher *IRR*, so there is no great difficulty involved. However, when projects differ greatly in their scale or useful life, complications may arise.

Let us look at an example where mutually exclusive projects differ in scale. To simplify matters, we look at two projects that each last only one time period. Project X requires an initial cash outlay of $100 and promises an expected cash flow of $120 in one year. Project Y requires a larger initial outlay of $200 but has an expected cash flow of $236 in one year. The company feels that the projects are equally risky and requires a return of 10 percent on both projects. Using Equations (2) and (3) we can calculate the net present value (at $K = 10$ percent) and internal rate of return for each project, as summarized in Table 9–7.

Table 9–7
Comparison of Two Investment Projects Based on Net Present Value and Internal Rate of Return

Project	Net Present Value at 10 Percent (dollars)	Internal Rate of Return (percent)
X	9.09	20
Y	14.55	18

As Table 9–7 reveals, project Y has the higher net present value, but project X has the higher internal rate of return. Which project should we choose? The answer is project Y. Because project Y has the higher net present value, it should contribute more to the value of the company and be the better choice in furthering the objective of value maximization. The *NPV* investment rule provides the right signal to select Y.

But how can project Y be better than X if Y has a lower internal rate of return (18 percent versus 20 percent)? The reason project Y is a better choice can be seen if we remember that the company feels that 10 percent is the appropriate discount rate. We must earn at least 10 percent to justify the investment. Now let us compare the results of selecting X or Y. If we adopt project X, we invest $100 today. Just to break even (earn only 10 percent), we will need to have a cash flow of $100(1 + 0.10) = $110 in one year. Fortunately, we expect to get $120 from project X so we expect to come out $10 ahead ($120 − $110 = $10) in year 1 with project X. Project Y, on the other hand, is of larger scale and allows us to invest $200. To earn 10 percent we will need a cash flow of $200 (1 + 0.10) = $220 in one year. Since we expect $236, we come out $16 ahead ($236 − $220 = $16) in year 1 with project Y. As the calculations show, project Y is expected to give us more money beyond our 10 percent requirement than is project X. That is, $16 is larger than $10. As a result, project Y is the better choice. Project Y allowed us to earn an internal rate of return of 18 percent on a *larger* investment than the investment on which we could earn the 20 percent *IRR* in project X. As a result, project Y gave us more extra value. The *NPV* calculations we did earlier already took this process into account. Note that the *NPV*s of projects X and Y are simply the present values (at 10 percent) of the $10 and $16 figures we calculated above.

Even if two projects are similar in scale, however, the *NPV* and *IRR* investment rules may rank them differently because of differences in the timing of the cash flows associated with the projects. To see this difference, let us compare two projects, one of which lasts longer than the other.

Earlier (in Figure 9–1) we considered an investment project (A) involving an outlay of $100 followed by inflows of $50, $60, and $40 over a three-year period. Let us now consider an alternative, project B, involving an outlay of $100 that generates inflows of $20, $30, $45, and $70 over a four-year period. Let us calculate the net present value of project B at different discount rates and plot its profile in Figure 9–2 as we did with project A in Figure 9–1. Now, the *IRR* rule tells us that project A is superior to project B because A's internal rate of return is 25 percent and B's *IRR* is about 19 percent. At a required return of, say, 15 percent, the *NPV* rule tells us the same thing: A is superior because A's *NPV* at 15 percent is greater than B's at 15 percent.

Suppose, however, that the required rate is not 15 percent but is 8 percent. The *IRR* rule still tells us that A is superior, but now the *NPV* rule tells us that B is superior because it has a net present value of $31.41 at 8 percent versus A's *NPV* of $29.49 at 8 percent. At any required rate of return less than approximately 10 percent—the point at which the net present value of A and B are approximately equal—the *IRR* and *NPV* rules give conflicting signals.

Why is this so? Because the time patterns of the cash-flow streams are different. Project B's cash inflows are greater in total than project A's, but they occur later in

Figure 9–2
Comparison of *NPV* Profiles

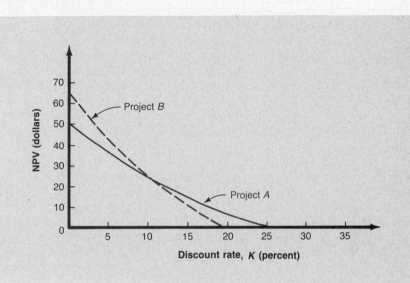

time. At low discount rates, the greater total outweighs later receipts, and project B is the more desirable project. If, on the other hand, the investor has opportunities to reinvest cash flows at high rates and, hence, has a higher required rate of return, project A is better because it delivers the cash flows sooner. So, the relative desirability of project A versus project B depends in part on the rate at which cash inflows can be reinvested. In Figure 9–2, we see that project B is better at low discount rates, while project A is better at high rates.

> The *NPV* rule and the *IRR* rule may give different signals for mutually exclusive projects when the scales of the projects are different or when time patterns of the cash-flow streams are different. In ranking mutually exclusive projects, if the signals given by the *NPV* and *IRR* rules conflict, the project chosen should be the one with the highest net present value.

The problem of conflicting signals is related to the *reinvestment of intermediate cash flows*. By definition, the required rate of return is the rate at which we assume that we have opportunities to reinvest. We use this rate as the discount rate in applying the *NPV* rule, as Equation (2) shows. So when we rank projects using the *NPV* rule, we automatically take the reinvestment rate into account (provided we use the reinvestment rate as the discount rate, as we should). If we rank using the *IRR* rule, on the other hand, we do not even need to know the reinvestment rate; we simply com-

Finance in Practice 9–3

Replacement Decisions

At the outset of the 1980s, many businesses were on the brink of what has been called the next industrial revolution—the use of new computer-age production techniques to replace older manufacturing processes. These new systems of production are called *flexible manufacturing systems (FMS)* because of the flexibility companies have in changing the amount and nature of the output produced at a given location.

These new systems consist of robots, remotely guided carts, and computer-controlled machines all linked and controlled by computer systems that dictate what will happen at each stage of the manufacturing process. For example, General Electric decided to transform a locomotive-frame factory into a modern automated manufacturing plant. With the old techniques, building a batch of locomotive frames took 16 days and 70 skilled machine operators. The new facility is designed to produce these frames in one day, untouched by human hands. The catch is that GE planned to invest $300 million to convert to the new technology.

Was GE's decision a good one? Clearly, the decision involves trading off large current expenditures for benefits in the future. This trade-off can be analyzed using the techniques we have discussed in this chapter. More important, the decision also involves tough, sometimes non-quantifiable, issues. For example, what about the 70 displaced machinists in the GE plant? In GE's case, these workers were retrained for other jobs. Sometimes, however, a company may be unable to provide employment for all displaced workers. U.S. machine-tool companies face tough competition from Japanese firms who have adopted automated systems and, as a result, have lower costs. In the next few years these companies will find it essential to analyze these investments in new production techniques.

Source: Adapted from G. Bylinsky, "The Race to the Automatic Factory," *Fortune,* February 21, 1983, pp. 52–64.

---

pare internal rates of return as calculated by Equation (3). Since it does not consider opportunities to reinvest, the *IRR* rule can (sometimes) give misleading signals in ranking projects with different time patterns of flows. We must simply remember that, when there is a conflict, the *NPV* rule gives the correct ranking.

Unequal Lives. How do we rank two or more mutually exclusive investments that have unequal lives? Project A described above had a life of 3 years, while B had a life of 4 years. Can the projects be directly compared? It depends.

If the useful life of the projects equals the time horizon over which they are being evaluated, we can compare them directly using the *NPV* rule. We evaluate both projects over a 4-year horizon and simply assume that project A generates an inflow of $0 in the fourth year.

Problems with unequal lives arise when we analyze activities that are expected to continue beyond the time horizon of the analysis. Cash flows may be expected to continue indefinitely, but for reasons of practicality we have to cut off our analysis at some point. If we are comparing two machines to do the same job and the machines have unequal useful lives, then one of the alternatives will require an additional out-flow for replacement before the other.

One way to handle such problems is to analyze both alternatives over a period equal to the shorter of the useful lives. The longer-lived project will still have some value remaining at that point. That remaining value should be estimated and treated as a cash inflow in the final period of the analysis.

Capital Rationing

In addition to having to compare two (or more) mutually exclusive projects because the projects use the same physical resource or serve the same function, a firm may sometimes have to choose between projects because there is a limitation on the amount of funds available for investment—in other words, capital is *rationed*. Appendix 9C discusses capital rationing in more detail. What is important for our purposes here is that the logic of the *NPV* rule can still be used. The manager should pick that set of projects that in combination have the highest total net present value. The *NPV* rule has the virtue of being consistent with the general criterion of value maximization. In the long run, value created by firms by means of wise investment decisions at some point will be reflected in the value of their shares.

Take the case of Apple Computer, Inc., a manufacturer of microcomputers for personal and professional use. The company did not exist prior to 1975. Two young men, Steven Jobs, then age 20, and Stephen Wozniak, 24, began to build small computers. Over the next five years, the decisions they made and the activities they initiated gave birth to an enterprise worth hundreds of millions of dollars. In fact, when stock was first sold to the public in December 1980, the market placed an aggregate value on the company of $1.2 billion! The value that Jobs, Wozniak, and others working with them created through their decisions and efforts ultimately was reflected in market value—a nice example for all budding entrepreneurs.[2]

ESTIMATING CASH FLOWS

Basic Concepts

As we've discussed above, the method we will apply to the economic analysis of projects is discounted cash flow. By calculating a project's net present value as expressed in Equation (2), we will be able to estimate whether the project will add to the value of the firm—that is, have a positive net present value.

To apply the *NPV* criterion, however, we must be able to estimate appropriate cash flows. The cash flows that we will use in our DCF analysis are **incremental after-tax cash flows**.

---

[2]For an interesting account of the Apple stock offering, see ''The Folks Who Brought You Apple,'' *Fortune*, January 12, 1981, pp. 66–79.

> The *incremental-cash-flow rule* is that the cash flows relevant in analyzing an investment opportunity are those after-tax cash flows and only those after-tax cash flows *directly attributable to the investment*.

An investment's **incremental after-tax cash flows**—are the after-tax cash flows directly attributable to the investment and are necessary information for performing a discounted-cash-flow analysis of an investment decision.

The words *incremental, after-tax,* and *cash* are critical. The term *cash* calls attention to the fact that we are interested in *cash flow* and not accounting profits. This important distinction was discussed in some detail back in Part Three. Ultimately, financial transactions must be carried out with cash, not profits, so we look to cash as the source of value.

The term *after-tax* emphasizes that we get to keep the cash only after payment of taxes. As we will see, we are interested in *all* cash flows affected by a decision under evaluation, no matter how those cash flows are classified for accounting purposes—whether as expenditures or expenses, receipts or income. If it is a cash item and it is affected by the decision we are analyzing, we are interested in it. Noncash items, such as depreciation, are important only if they affect cash flow—for example, by means of tax payments.

The word *incremental* is important because in deciding whether or not to do something, or whether to pick alternative A or alternative B, *differences* in outcomes are of interest. What changes as a result of the decision? If A is picked rather than B, what will be different? If a firm replaces a piece of machinery, will the firm's insurance costs change? If not, we can ignore the insurance premiums in our schedule of cash flows to analyze the decision about replacing the machinery.

Incremental analysis—is the evaluation of an investment decision that focuses only on differences in after-tax cash flows that result from the decision in question.

The concept of **incremental analysis** has wide applicability in decision making. Incremental analysis applies not just to investment decisions or to financial-management decisions, but to all decisions faced by individuals and firms. Only differences *resulting from the decision* need be considered. Other factors may be important, but not to the decision at hand.

Sample Problem 9–4

Incremental Cash Cost of Going to Summer School

Suppose you were living near a college campus and were considering the choice between going to a summer-school session for a month or continuing in your current summer job at a local bank. The bank pays you a salary of $1,000 a month. Your present apartment rent is $300 per month and you budget $400 for food and other miscellaneous expenses. You calculate that tuition, fees, and books for the summer session will be $500, and you contemplate no other changes in your living expenses as a result of going to school. Finally, assume you will not earn enough during the year to owe any income taxes. What is the incremental cash cost of going to summer school?

Solution

The relevant cost is $1,500. You lose $1000 because you will not be working at the bank and, in addition, must pay $500 in school fees. Your rent and other expenses will not change whether you go to the summer session or not and are, thus, not incremental cash costs. Your decision to go to school must be based on weighing the $1,500 cash costs versus your perceived net benefits of going to school. ∃⊪⫶

Table 9–8

Capital Outlay Requirements for Product 99 at Year-End 1986–1995 (thousands of dollars)

	1986	1987	1988	1989	1990	1991	1992	1993	1994	1995	Total
1. Land	0	0	0	0	0	0	0	0	0	0	0
2. New building construction	275	130	0	0	0	0	0	0	0	0	405
3. Modification of existing buildings	0	90	25	0	0	0	0	0	0	0	115
4. New equipment	50	160	0	0	0	0	0	0	0	0	210
5. Installation	5	25	0	0	0	0	0	0	0	0	30
6. Total	330	405	25	0	0	0	0	0	0	0	760
7. Less investment tax credit*	− 5	− 16	− 0	−0	−0	−0	−0	−0	−0	−0	− 21
8. Net capital outlay	325	389	25	0	0	0	0	0	0	0	739

*Credit consists of 10 percent of the outlay for new equipment.

Table 9–9

Estimated Annual Operating Flows for Product 99 (thousands of dollars)

	1987	1988	1989	1990	1991	1992	1993	1994	1995	1996
Sales	250	1,250	1,900	2,550	2,750	3,000	3,000	2,800	2,600	2,200
minus										
Cost of goods sold	− 137	− 687	−1,045	−1,402	−1,512	−1,650	−1,650	−1,540	−1,430	−1,210
equals										
Gross profit	113	563	855	1,148	1,238	1,350	1,350	1,260	1,170	990
minus										
Advertising and selling expense	− 138 −	438 −	665 −	765 −	825 −	900 −	900 −	840 −	780 −	660
minus										
Depreciation*	− 76 −	76 −	76 −	76 −	76 −	76 −	76 −	76 −	76 −	76
equals										
Profit before tax	− 101	49	114	307	337	374	374	344	314	254
minus										
Tax (at 46 percent)	−(−46) −	23 −	52 −	141 −	155 −	172 −	172 −	158 −	144 −	117
equals										
Profit after tax	−55	26	62	166	182	202	202	186	170	137

*In order to simplify the presentation, depreciation is calculated by the straight-line method over 10 years, using as the total to be depreciated the sum of lines 2–5 in Table 9–8. The straight-line method spreads the $760,000 evenly over the 10-year period for an annual depreciation expense of $760,000 ÷ 10 = $76,000. The actual rules covering depreciation are complex and provide for different depreciation lives for buildings and equipment. These distinctions are not important to the purpose at hand here; hence, the simpler approach of treating all depreciable items the same is taken. See Appendix 9E for further discussion of depreciation.

Working with the Data

While the incremental after-tax cash-flow rule is quite straightforward conceptually, a number of details require careful attention. To provide an illustration of cash flows, let us develop an extended example: a proposal to introduce a new dessert product—code-named Product 99—by American Foods, Inc. Tables 9–8 and 9–9 give some of the details of the project. In the case of Product 99, the question at issue is whether or not to implement the project. The time is fall 1986. The decision involves committing the company to large expenditures during the early years (1986–88) in return for benefits during the late 1980s and early to mid-1990s.

Our task is to relate these details to incremental after-tax cash flows and, ultimately, to determine (using the *NPV* rule) whether or not the proposal is acceptable. Table 9–8 shows the capital outlays necessary for Product 99. These outlays occur in 1986–1988. Table 9–9 shows the operating flows over the life of the project (through 1996).

INCREMENTAL CASH FLOWS

To estimate incremental cash flows for a project, such as American Food's Product 99 project, it is often useful to break the cash flows into three categories: initial-investment cash flows, operating cash flows, and terminal values.

Initial-Investment Cash Flows

Initial-investment cash flows—are the one-time outlays necessary to acquire the land, buildings, and equipment necessary to implement an investment project.

Initial-investment cash flows are the one-time outlays necessary to acquire land, buildings, and equipment. As rows (1) through (6) of Table 9–8 indicate, to introduce Product 99, American Foods will have initial-investment cash flows spread out over three years. The last column of Table 9–8 shows that American Foods will spend a total of $405,000 on new building construction ($275,000 in 1986 and $130,000 in 1987). In fact, a total of $760,000 will be spent on buildings, equipment, and installation. For illustrative purposes, we have assumed that American Foods will be able to take a major tax benefit as a result of its investment in new equipment. Specifically, we assume that a 10 percent investment tax credit is available that allows American Foods to reduce (take a credit against) its taxes by 10 percent of the amount of money spent on new equipment.[3] In this case, American Foods will spend $210,000 on equipment ($50,000 in 1986 and $160,000 in 1987) as shown in row (4) of Table 9–8, resulting in tax savings of 0.10($210,000) = $21,000 spread out over 1986 and 1987 and shown in row (7). This $21,000 is cash American Foods will not have to pay the government. As a result, the *after-tax* initial cash outflow is $760,000 less the $21,000 tax credit, or $739,000 spread over a three-year period. This figure is shown in the bottom row of the last column of Table 9–8.

During the period 1984–1985, American Foods conducted extensive market tests of Product 99 in six cities throughout the United States. The purpose of these tests was to gauge consumer reaction to the new product before making a final commitment

---

[3]Investment tax credits are special incentives passed by Congress to spur investment by providing tax relief. The laws on investment tax credits are subject to change both as to the allowable percentage of credit and the investments to which the credit applies. As of this writing, there is even serious discussion about eliminating such credits altogether. In our example, we assume a 10 percent investment tax credit to illustate how to deal with such credits in calculating cash flows. In practice, one would have to check current tax codes to see if an investment tax credit were available.

A **sunk cost**—is an expenditure that was made before a decision has been made and is unaffected by the decision under evaluation; it is not part of an investment's capital outlay and, in general, should be ignored in analyzing the investment.

to go ahead. Such *test marketing* is a widely used device for reducing the risk of new product introductions.

The market tests during 1984 and 1985 cost a total of $110,000. Should this expenditure be included in our analysis? The answer is no, because the time is now fall 1986 and the money for the test market has already been spent. This expenditure is a **sunk cost**.

Because the test-market outlay has already been made, it cannot be affected by our decision now, so the incremental cash-flow rule tells us that it is not relevant to the analysis of the decision at hand.

Operating Cash Flows

Operating cash flows— are the cash flows, such as sales, cost of goods sold, advertising, and taxes, generated by the operations associated with an investment project.

Operating cash flows—the cash flows generated by the operations associated with the project—are the next category of cash flows to consider. Table 9–9 lists the operating cash flows Product 99 is expected to generate. Note carefully the word *estimated* in the table's title. The items in the table represent management's best estimate of the flows that will be generated *if* Product 99 is introduced. If Product 99 is not introduced, none of the flows in Table 9–9 will take place. These flows are directly attributable to Product 99, so they are relevant to the decision. Note that sales are expected to rise to a maximum of $3 million in 1992–93 and then decline as competing products are introduced to replace Product 99.

Note that Table 9–9 reports the estimated operating results of Product 99 using accrual-accounting methods, not cash-accounting methods. Companies often base their analysis of cash flows on projections of accrual-accounting figures, such as those found in pro-forma income statements like the one that appears in Table 9–9. We must be careful to remember, however, that for purposes of our present evaluation of Product 99, we are interested in estimating cash flows, not profits—and many of the revenues and expenses recognized in accrual accounting do not present cash going in or out of the company. Cash flows, not profits, are required to apply discounted-cash-flow analysis to an investment decision such as the Product 99 project.

> **Discounted-cash-flow analysis of an investment decision must be applied to cash flows, not profits.**

Because depreciation is the major noncash item for most companies, let us assume for the moment that all the items in Table 9–9 are cash expenses and cash revenues except for the noncash expenses of depreciation. Table 9–10 shows the calculation of both profit after taxes (PAT) using accrual-accounting methods and operating cash flow for Product 99 in 1988. The cash flow is calculated in column (2) considering only cash items. Cash expenses (cost of goods sold plus advertising and selling expense) total $1,125,000 ($687,000 + $438,000 = $1,125,000). Note in Table 9–10 that the operating-cash-flow total in 1988 is $102,000, whereas the total profit after tax is only $26,000. This difference results from the subtraction of the depreciation figure of $76,000 in calculating 1988 PAT (using accrual accounting) even though depreciation is not a cash item. The cash flow associated with depreciation occurred when the assets

Table 9—10

Comparison of Accrual Accounting Adjustments and Cash Flows Estimated for 1988 for Product 99 (thousands of dollars)

	Calculation of Profit after Taxes by Accrual Accounting Method	Calculation of Operating Cash Flows by Cash Accounting Method
Cash revenues	1250	1250
Cash expenses	−1125	−1125
Depreciation (Noncash)	− 76	NA*
Profit before taxes	49	NA*
Taxes (at 46 percent)	− 23	− 23
	Profit after taxes = 26	Cash flow = 102

Note: This example assumes all accounting revenues and expenses except depreciation are cash items.

*This item is not applicable since it is not cash.

were purchased, not each year when the depreciation expense is subtracted in calculating profits.

As Table 9–10 shows, the operating cash flow in 1988 of $102,000 is exactly $76,000 (the amount of depreciation subtracted) higher than profit after tax. In fact, when depreciation is the only noncash item, we can estimate cash flow by simply adding depreciation back to PAT—that is, we add back the noncash item that was subtracted in calculating PAT. Table 9–11 shows this procedure for the first three years for Product 99. Note that the 1988 result in Table 9–11 is precisely the $102,000 figure we earlier obtained in Table 9–10.

Even though depreciation is a noncash charge, it does affect cash flow through its effect on taxes. Taxes are a cash flow, and taxes are calculated based on a profit figure—after the subtraction of depreciation. If 46 percent is the marginal tax rate, then every dollar of depreciation reduces taxes by $0.46. When companies that pay taxes include depreciation in their income calculation, they reduce their tax bills. For example, in 1988, Table 9–11 shows that American Foods expects taxes of $23,000— which is equal to 46 percent of profit before taxes (PBT) of $49,000. (Figures in the table have been rounded to the nearest thousand, as are all remaining figures in this paragraph.) If depreciation of $16,000 had not been tax deductible, American Foods would have had PBT of $125,000 and taxes of ($125,000)(0.46) = $58,000 (rounded). The depreciation charge, thus, saved American Foods $35,000 in taxes ($58,000 − $23,000 = $35,000). This tax savings is often referred to as the **depreciation tax shield** and is equal to the tax rate times the amount of the depreciation charge. In this case, the depreciation tax shield is equal to (0.46)($76,000) = $34,960 ($35,000 when rounded to the nearest thousand, as done above).

The depreciation and profit figures that are relevant to the determination of operating cash flows are those actually reported to the Internal Revenue Service. While the cost of the machine can be allocated equally over the years by means of straight-line depreciation, there are various accelerated methods of depreciation that allocate relatively more of the asset's cost to the early years and less to later years. The Internal

The **depreciation tax shield**—is the tax savings resulting from the subtraction of depreciation in calculating taxable income; it can be calculated as the tax rate multiplied by the amount of the depreciation charge.

Table 9–11
Calculating Operating Cash Flow for Product 99: Cash Flow = Profit after Tax +
Depreciation (thousands of dollars)

	1987	1988	1989
Sales	250	1,250	1,900
Cost of goods sold	137	687	1,045
Gross profit	113	563	855
Advertising and selling expense	138	438	665
Depreciation	76	76	76
Profit before tax	−101	49	114
Tax (at 46 percent)	−(−46)	− 23	− 52
Profit after tax	− 55	26	62
Add back depreciation	76	76	76
Cash flow from operations	21	102	138

Revenue Service sets the rules as to permissible depreciation methods for use in computing taxes in accordance with applicable laws passed by the Congress. Note that the choice of depreciation methods does not affect the total depreciation charged, only its time pattern. Because of the time value of money, however, corporations find it advantageous to use accelerated methods of depreciation and take their depreciation-related tax savings earlier rather than later. Appendix 9E discusses this issue in more detail.

Taxes are a central consideration in any discounted-cash-flow analysis, at least for organizations that pay taxes. One way to take taxes into account is shown in Table 9–11: simply arrange financial information in income-statement format and calculate the tax liability. Another way to skin the same cat is to convert all pre-tax cash flows to *after-tax equivalents*. Appendix 9A will discuss this method in more detail.

While depreciation is often the major noncash item relevant for a project's cash flows, other noncash revenues and expenses enter the calculations of accrual accounting. And some expenditures of cash do not find their way into the income statement for a given year.

For example, when Product 99 is marketed, some of the sales will be on credit terms. As a result, at the end of a year, sales revenues based on accrual accounting in the income statement might overstate the actual cash revenues. This overstatement would be particularly likely if accounts receivable based on the credit sales had increased during the year and were still not collected at the end of the year. Such an event would show up as an increase in accounts receivable for the year. Conceptually, adjusting for such noncash items is no more complicated than handling depreciation. First, we calculate PAT using the accrual-accounting numbers for revenues and expenses that the tax authorities allow. To estimate cash flow, noncash expenses (such as depreciation) should be added back to PAT, while noncash revenues (as reflected in an increase in accounts receivable) should be subtracted. Any cash expenditures that do not enter the income statement must be subtracted from PAT. Cash receipts not entering the income statement must be added to PAT. Appendix 9B provides a more detailed discussion of this issue.

Table 9–12
Operating Cash Flows for Product 99, 1987–1996 (thousands of dollars)

	1987	1988	1989	1990	1991	1992	1993	1994	1995	1996
Profit after tax	−55	26	62	166	182	202	202	186	170	137
Add back depreciation	76	76	76	76	76	76	76	76	76	76
Cash flow from operations	21	102	138	242	258	278	278	262	246	213

Sample Problem 9–5

Calculating Operating Cash Flow for Product 99

Calculate the cash flow from operations for Product 99 for each year 1987–1996 using the data in Table 9–9.

Solution

The solution is given in Table 9–12. Note that, while accounting profit is expected to be negative in 1987, total operating cash flow is positive. ▰▰▰

Terminal Values

In connection with many capital-budgeting projects, special steps must be taken to analyze cash flows in the final year. We noted earlier that American Foods management expected Product 99 sales and profits to decline during the mid 1990s as the product entered the late stages of its life cycle. Some profits might well be generated beyond 1996, but management decided that, in analyzing Product 99 as an investment opportunity, they would err on the side of conservatism and assume none. In effect, management assumed that 10 years was the useful life of Product 99.

Even if a product is expected to continue indefinitely, it still is necessary to pick a finite period over which to analyze it. The appropriate period depends on the nature of the decision, its size and complexity, and the amount of time management wishes to devote to its analysis. If a project is expected to continue to generate cash flows beyond the terminal point of the analysis, some estimate of the value of those subsequent cash flows should be made. This **terminal value** should be treated as a cash inflow in the final year of the product.

In the case of Product 99, management assumed not only zero cash flows beyond 1996, but also that buildings and equipment would have no value in that year. That is, Product 99 was assumed to have a terminal value of zero. Suppose, alternatively, management had assumed that the buildings and equipment would have a salvage value of $50,000 in 1996 and could be sold for that amount. Terminal cash flows then would appear as the salvage value of buildings and equipment less tax at 46 percent, or as $50,000 − $23,000 = $27,000.

The terminal value of $27,000 would be included as another inflow in year 1996. Note that tax is paid on the full $50,000 proceeds because buildings and equipment have been depreciated to zero book value by 1996. In general, taxes are paid on the

The **terminal value**—of an investment project is an estimate of the cash flows generated beyond the terminal point of the analysis and is treated as a cash inflow in the final year of the analysis.

Table 9–13

Cash Flows of Product 99 (thousands of dollars)

Year End	Initial Investment (Table 9–9) (1)	Operating Cash Flows (Table 9–13) (2)	Terminal Value (3)	Net Cash Flow (4) = (1) + (2) + (3)
1986	− 325	0		− 325
1987	− 389	21		− 368
1988	− 25	102		77
1989		138		138
1990		242		242
1991		258		258
1992		278		278
1993		278		278
1994		262		262
1995		246		246
1996		213	0	213

gain represented by the difference between the expected salvage value and the book value. For example, suppose the buildings and equipment had been depreciated to a book value of $20,000 by 1996. The tax levied would then be $13,800—46 percent of the $30,000 gain on the asset ($50,000 − $20,000 = $30,000). In this case, the after-tax cash proceeds would be $50,000 − $13,800 = $36,200.

The actual tax treatment of money received when assets are sold can become quite complicated, and in practice tax laws must be analyzed carefully. For example, under certain conditions the difference between the sale price and the purchase price of certain assets is taxed as a **capital gain** at a rate often lower than the ordinary income-tax rate. If the asset has been depreciated for tax purposes, the difference between the purchase price and the book value is taxed at ordinary income-tax rates as a recapture of depreciation.

A **capital gain**—is the difference between the sale price and the purchase price of certain assets.

Suppose the buildings and equipment associated with the Product 99 project could be sold for $800,000 in 1996. Because the original cost was only $760,000, there would be a capital gain of $40,000. For illustrative purposes, suppose that the capital-gains tax rate was 28 percent. The gain would lead to taxes of 0.28 ($40,000) = $11,200. The difference between the original cost and book value—in this case, $760,000 − 0 = $760,000 (book value equals zero)—would be taxed as ordinary income at a 46 percent rate, for taxes of 0.46 ($760,000) = $349,600. The total tax bill would, thus, be $11,200 + $349,600 = $360,800. As a result, the terminal value after payment of taxes would be $800,000 − $360,800 = $439,200. Because tax laws are subject to change, the estimation of cash flows dictates the need to keep aware of any major changes in these laws.

Summary of Incremental Cash Flows

Table 9–13 summarizes our results of estimating cash flows for Product 99. It brings together the initial investment (determined in Table 9–8), the operating cash flows

Table 9–14

Net Present Value (NPV) of Product 99

Period, t	Year End	Cash Flow (C_t) (thousands of dollars) (1)	Present-Value Factor at 15 Percent (percent) (2)	Present Value (thousands of dollars) (3) = (1) × (2)
0	1986	−325	1.000	−325
1	1987	−368	0.870	−320
2	1988	77	0.756	58
3	1989	138	0.658	91
4	1990	242	0.572	138
5	1991	258	0.497	128
6	1992	278	0.432	120
7	1993	278	0.376	105
8	1994	262	0.327	86
9	1995	246	0.284	70
10	1996	213	0.247	53
			$NPV =$	204

(determined in Table 9–12), and the terminal value. Note that management has assumed a terminal value of zero for Product 99.

The last column of Table 9–13 is a representation of Product 99 as a package of incremental after-tax cash flows. These cash flows are precisely the type of information necessary to use our DCF methods of evaluating the merits of the proposed investment.

Sample Problem 9–6

Determining the Net Present Value of Product 99

Is Product 99 a desirable investment if American Foods establishes a required rate of return for this investment of 15 percent?

Solution

To answer this question, we must recall the basic definition of net present value given in Equation (2). Table 9–13 provided the estimated cash flows (C_t), and in this case the required return, K, is 15 percent. Table 9–14 shows the results of using discounted-cash-flow techniques to calculate the net present value.

The *NPV* analysis tells us that the cash flows associated with Product 99, net of the required outlays, are worth $204,000 today. The *NPV* rule tells us to accept any investment project with a positive net present value. Using *NPV* analysis, we have reduced a very complex pattern of cash flows to a single time-adjusted figure that tells us whether Product 99 passes the economic test and, therefore, represents a wise use of capital funds. ∃▮▮⊧

Sample Problem 9–7

Determining the Internal Rate of Return for Product 99

From our earlier discussion we know that if the net present value of Product 99 at a 15 percent required return is positive, then the internal rate of return exceeds 15 percent. What is the internal rate of return for Product 99?

Table 9-15

Internal Rate of Return (IRR) for Product 99 (thousands of dollars)

Period, t	Cash Flow, C_t	Present Value at 15 Percent	Present Value at 25 Percent	
0	-325	-325	-325	
1	-368	-320	-294	
2	77	58	49	
3	138	91	71	
4	242	138	99	
5	258	128	85	
6	278	120	73	
7	278	105	58	
8	262	86	44	
9	246	70	33	
10	213	53	23	
Net present value* =		204	-85	$IRR = 21.3$ percent

*Due to rounding, individual figures may not add up exactly to totals.

Solution

We can calculate the internal rate of return of Product 99 using the cash flows in Table 9-13. The solution is given in Table 9-15. Suppose we pick 15 percent for our first try. We get a net present value of $204,000. Because this value is greater than zero, we know that 15 percent is too low a percentage for the internal rate of return. If we pick 25 percent for our second try, we get a negative net present value equal to −$85,000 so we know that the internal rate of return lies between 15 percent and 25 percent. With repeated trials, we can close in on the answer, which we find to be approximately 21.3 percent. Doing this by hand is a lot of work, so a calculator with DCF capability can come in handy!

Since the internal rate of return of 21.3 percent exceeds the American Foods required return of 15 percent, the *IRR* rule gives the same signal as the *NPV* rule: the project passes the economic test for acceptance. ∃⊔⊏

SEPARATING OPERATING FLOWS AND FINANCING FLOWS

Based on our calculations of net present value and internal rate of return, Product 99 looks like a good investment. Before we end our discussion of Product 99, however, we must underscore an important principle we adopted in calculating cash flows for Product 99: *operating flows and financing flows should be separated*. Recall that in our calculations we did not subtract any interest payments on debt or repayments on loans.

Suppose Product 99 is to be financed in part by a bank loan; a loan is to be arranged to pay for construction and equipment (see Table 9-8). Should the interest and principal payments on the loan be included among the cash flows to be analyzed? The

Financing cash flows—are the cash flows, such as interest, principal payments, and dividends to stockholders, arising from the financing arrangements associated with an investment project.

answer is no. In most cases, the best procedure is to analyze the *operating* cash flows of the project and to exclude **financing cash flows,** such as interest, principal payments, and dividends, from that analysis. Operating flows are those arising from the project itself, without regard to the way the project is financed.

> In most cases, operating cash flows should be considered in the analysis of an investment project, and the financing flows should be excluded from consideration. These financing flows will be reflected in the required rate of return.

The **target return**—is the rate of return required by the suppliers of funds to the investment project and is the rate with which the investment project's internal rate of return is compared to determine whether the project will return enough to satisfy those providing the funds.

The best approach is to view all the firm's sources of funds together and to charge projects with an average of the various interest and dividend costs. We will bring these financing costs into our analysis by means of the required rate of return *(K)*, sometimes called the **target return,** that we set for the project, as outlined below.

Suppose we have an investment opportunity, such as Product 99, and we need money to finance the construction and equipment. The money will come from some combination of lenders and stockholders, all of whom expect a return on their investment. Will Product 99 return enough to satisfy those providing the funds? To find out, we compare the *project return*—the *IRR*—to the *target* return demanded by the suppliers of funds. We calculate the project return looking only at the operating flows generated by the project itself and compare this return to the target rate of return. All the financing flows enter through the vehicle of the target return, *K*.

For example, in the case of Product 99 we calculated the *IRR*, which is the project return, to be 21.3 percent using operating flows. We compared this 21.3 percent to a required *target* return of 15 percent, which reflected the required returns of the suppliers of funds. Because the project return exceeded the target return, we concluded that Product 99 was a good investment.

Mixing operating and financing flows complicates the analysis. For one thing, most firms obtain their funds from many sources, and it is often hard to tell exactly from where the dollars for a particular outlay—say, equipment—came: whether from a bank loan negotiated last month, from profits earned this month, or from a mortgage arranged six months ago. In the case of Product 99, we would not know whether to charge interest at the rate on the bank loan or on the mortgage or what the appropriate mix of interest and dividends should be.

Sometimes projects arise in which financing arrangements are an integral part of the investment opportunity itself. A good example is a real-estate project, such as a shopping-center development, where a specially tailored mortgage loan will provide a major part of the financing. In such special cases, it sometimes proves necessary to analyze operating and financing flows together.[4] For our purposes here, however, the general rule is to analyze the project's operating flows distinct from its financing flows and to bring in financing considerations by means of the required rate of return.

---

[4]For an analysis of alternative methods of dealing with financing mix in investment analysis, see D. R. Chambers, R. S. Harris, and J. J. Pringle, "Treatment of Financing Mix in Analyzing Investment Opportunities," *Financial Management,* Summer 1982, pp. 24–41.

CAPITAL BUDGETING IN PRACTICE

In an uncertain world, estimating cash flows expected in the future often is an exceedingly difficult task. Frequently, investments must be analyzed where no historical model or example exists. Even where the opportunity is similar to others undertaken in the past, the world changes rapidly and events take place that often are completely unanticipated. Few anticipated the large increases in the prices of petroleum products that took place in 1973–74 and again in 1978–80, the severity of the 1981–82 recession, or the changes in weather that lead to localized crop failures in the 1980s.

Arranging figures neatly in tables can mislead the unwary in two ways—first, by obscuring the difficulty of making the estimates in the first place and, second, by giving a false impression of accuracy. All the sales and expense figures in Table 9–9 are subject to uncertainty; all are likely to turn out different from the projections, either higher or lower. If we only knew in which direction, we could improve our estimates now.

Not only is estimating cash flows difficult; it is also important. A good job of analyzing bad information still produces bad results. A careful job of estimating cash flows justifies the expenditure of considerable time and effort. Estimating cash flows is not a routine clerical task, but one that requires the attention of experts in accounting, economics, engineering, cost analysis, and perhaps other fields.

Finance in Practice 9–4 looks at the question of how capital-budgeting decisions are made in practice.

In our discussion thus far, we have been concerned primarily with the *economic analysis* of investment opportunities, but as we discussed at the outset of this chapter, there is more to capital budgeting than economic analysis.

The capital-budgeting process involves several major activities, including the creative search for investment opportunities, the gathering of data and the making of forecasts, economic analysis, decision making, and implementation.

In a small firm, all of these activities may be carried out by one or a few individuals. In large firms, many individuals and organizational units likely will be involved.

In a large organization, project proposals often are initiated by the *line units,* or operating units. Estimates of cash flows may be prepared by the initiating unit, calling on experts in marketing, production, accounting, finance, and other areas. A central unit, such as the corporate controller, may assist in preparing projections. Policies regarding decision criteria (the *NPV* rule, the *IRR* rule, the payback approach, etc.) and policies regarding return targets usually are set centrally by top management.

The review process in large organizations is likely to be complex. A proposal may be reviewed by executives in marketing, production, engineering, personnel, and legal departments as well as by staff officers in control and finance departments. Often the process is very formal, with committees, forms, and lengthy procedures. In addition to reviewing individual projects, management will typically be involved in financial planning at the firm and division level using year-by-year pro-forma projections of both financial statements and cash flows. Final decisions on funding projects will be made in the context of these larger-scale financial plans.

The responsibility for the final decision may lie with a division executive, with the

Table 9–16
Accounting Return on Investment (AROI) for Product 99, 1987–1990

Year (1)	Return: Net Profit After Tax (thousands of dollars) (2)	Investment (thousands of dollars)				Return on Investment (percent) (7) = (2) ÷ (6)
		Beginning Book Value (3)	Gross Investment (4)	Depreciation (5)	Ending Book Value (6) = (3) + (4) − (5)	
1987	− 55	0	330	76	254	− 22.0
1988	26	254	405	76	583	4.5
1989	62	583	25	76	532	12.0
1990	166	532	0	76	456	36.0

Note: Data are from Tables 9–8 and 9–9.

president or chairman of the board, or with the board of directors itself. Just where the decision is made depends on the size and nature of the project and on the firm's policies regarding decentralization. Although we have assumed that managers act to maximize the value of the firm to shareholders, it is important to remember that managers often face conflicting forces. Suppose for a moment that a division manager's compensation is based (at least in part) on some accounting figure, like AROI. Such compensation schemes are quite common. Consider such a manager's reaction to Product 99 as an addition to the division's line of products. We have already calculated that Product 99's net present value is $204,000 and represents a sound investment in terms of estimated future cash flows, but look at the calculation of Product 99's AROI shown in Table 9–16 and based on the first few years of data in Tables 9–8 and 9–9. In 1987, Product 99's AROI is − 22 percent; it will actually reduce the division profits. This reduction in profits may mean a lower compensation for our manager in 1987. The profit picture improves over time, and when we looked at the full life of the project, we saw it is a sound investment. The question is whether an individual manager who may have only a few more years on the job will also look past the next few years. It is a challenge to the corporation to make sure that managers' motivations channel their actions toward shareholder wealth maximization.[5]

Strategic analysis also enters into the process of capital budgeting. As we noted earlier, the kind of economic analysis described in this chapter should take place only *after* a prospective investment has been judged consistent with the firm's commercial strategy. If a firm is in business to manufacture and market industrial chemicals, it is not likely to spend much time analyzing proposals to go into the restaurant business.

---

[5]Many scholars have investigated the relationships between managers and shareholders. Recently, a large body of literature has developed that views managers as *agents* of shareholders. For a survey of some of that literature, see A. Barnea, R. Haugen, and L. Senbet, "Market Imperfections, Agency Problems, and Capital Structure: A Review," *Financial Management,* Summer 1981, pp. 7–22.

After all, if a firm has no competitive advantage in an area it is unlikely to be able to generate positive net present values on investments in that area.

Aside from factors relating directly to the interests of the firm and its owners, modern managers must consider other constituencies as well, including employees, customers, suppliers, creditors, the government, and the public at large. At the same time, qualitative considerations of ethics, social responsibility, relationships with local communities, and many other factors enter into investment decisions, and these factors often cannot be quantified in the economic analysis.

A **post audit**—is a review of the performance of an investment project in the years following its implementation, or a comparison of actual returns to projected returns.

Following up on a decision also is important in capital budgeting. Suppose American Foods decides to go ahead with Product 99. The project will have been justified in part on the basis of its prospective return. At some future date—say, two or three years after implementation—the performance of Product 99 ought to be reviewed to compare actual results with those projected initially when the decision to undertake the project was made. Such **post audits** are an important part of the capital-budgeting process.

Sample Problem 9–8

Decision Criteria for an Investment in Project Q

An investment in project Q requires an initial $15,000 cash outlay and will return $8,000 in year 1, $7,000 in year 2, and $5,000 in year 3. Calculate

A. the internal rate of return *(IRR)*,
B. the payback period, and
C. the net present value *(NPV)*, using a 10 percent discount rate.

Solution
A. Solving for the *IRR* involves a trial-and-error process. We want to find the rate, *R*, that will solve the equation

$$\$15,000 = \frac{\$8,000}{(1 + R)} + \frac{\$7,000}{(1 + R)^2} + \frac{\$5,000}{(1 + R^3}$$

Using the present-value factors from Appendix Table I at the back of the book, we can try a rate of 15 percent. Substituting 15 percent for *R* in the equation above results in a present value of $15,542:

$$\$8,000(0.870) + \$7,000(0.756) + \$5,000(0.658) = \$15,542.$$

With a 15 percent rate, the present value of the future cash streams exceeds the initial outlay of $15,000 by the net present value of $542 (the *IRR* is the rate that equates present value and the amount of the investment outlay), so we know that the 15 percent rate is too low. When we try higher discount rates, we find that the net present value is $77 at a discount rate of 17 percent but is −$153 at a discount rate of 18 percent. Thus, we know that the *IRR* is between 17 and 18 percent. If we interpolate, we can solve for a closer approximation of *IRR*:

$$IRR = 17 + \frac{77 - 0}{77 - (-153)} = 17.33 \text{ percent}$$

B. The payback period can be found by constructing Table 9–17. The payback period is 2 years. At that point, total payments received equal the outlay.

C. The net present value, using a 10 percent discount rate, can be found by using the present-value factors given in Appendix Table I at the back of this book as

$$NPV = -\$15,000 + \$8,000(0.909) + \$7,000(0.826) + \$5,000(0.751)$$

$$= -15,000 + \$16,809$$

$$= \$1,809$$

Table 9–17
Payback Period for an Investment

	Payback (dollars)			
	Year 0	Year 1	Year 2	Year 3
Cash flow	(15,000)	8,000	7,000	5,000
Cumulative cash flow	(15,000)	(7,000)	0	5,000

Techniques	Percentage of Firms
NPV rule	56
IRR rule	65
Payback approach	74
AROI approach	58

DCF analysis. For example, if a piece of machinery critical to a production process wears out, it is replaced. The managers don't go through a formal DCF analysis because they know without doing any analysis that they will get a large positive net present value if the alternative is to shut down operations. In the long run, however, assessment of such replacement investment is necessary. Other investments may be mandated by law (for example, environmental quality control) and are required for the firm to remain in operation. Another important factor to consider is the difficulty of applying the NPV and IRR rules, especially when very uncertain cash flows need to be projected. Some firms that are reluctant to project cash flows beyond a few years in the future use the payback method of evaluation.

What is clear is that the NPV and IRR rules are becoming more widely used. A similar survey in an earlier period (1970) found that only 57 percent of firms used the NPV or IRR rule—considerably less than the 86 percent observed in the more recent survey. In addition, it appears that larger companies tend to use DCF techniques more frequently than their smaller counterparts. With the increased level of management education and ease of using computers, DCF techniques, like the NPV rule or the IRR rule, have become a standard tool of financial management.

Source: Adapted from L. D. Schall, G. L. Sundem, and W. R. Geijsbeck, Jr., "Survey and Analysis of Capital-Budgeting Methods," *Journal of Finance,* March 1978, pp. 281–87.

Sample Problem 9–9

Preparing an Economic Analysis for an Investment in a New Machine

Your firm is considering replacing an existing machine with a newer piece of equipment. The existing machine has a book value of $4,000, annual depreciation charges of $800, and a remaining useful life of 5 years with an expected $0 salvage value. The machine could be sold today for $1,000. The new machine would cost $8,000, and it has an expected life of 5 years with a $0 salvage value. This new machine is expected to save $1,500 annually in operating expenses. The machine will be depreciated on a straight-line basis. That is, the annual depreciation on the new machine will be ($8,000 − 0)/5 = $1,600.

A. Assuming a tax rate of 46 percent and no investment tax credit, construct a table of the relevant incremental cash flows for the replacement decision.

B. If the firm's required rate of return on such investments is 10 percent, would you recommend replacement of the existing machine by the newer one?

Solution

A. There are several approaches to finding the incremental cash flows. One method is to convert the cash flows to their after-tax equivalents, as shown in Tables 9A–1 and 9A–3 of Appendix 9A, which follows this chapter. Using this method, we can construct Tables 9–18 and 9–19.

Table 9–18
Incremental Cash Flows Relevant to a Hypothetical Equipment-Replacement Decision

Annual Cash Flow	Existing Machine	New Machine	Incremental
Depreciation × Tax rate	$368	$736	$ 368
Operating savings × (1 − tax rate)			810
Total annual after-tax cash flow			$1,178

In Table 9–18, we calculate the depreciation tax shield as $800 × 0.46 = $368. Likewise the depreciation tax shield on the new machine is $1,600 × 0.46 = $736. The after-tax equivalent of the operating savings is $1,500(1 − 0.46) = $810.

If we sell the old machine, we show a book loss of $3,000 on the machine. This loss provides a tax shield of $3,000 × 0.46 = $1,380. Our taxes are reduced by this amount, so it represents a cash inflow. In year 0, we will have a net outflow of cash: $8,000 outflow for the new machine less the inflow of cash from the sale of the old machine and subsequent tax shield. The net cash outflow in year 0 is $5,620.

B. Using the *NPV* rule as our decision criterion, we would purchase the new machine if the net present value of the investment is greater than zero. Table 9–19 gives us the relevant cash flows. Because the cash flows in years 1–5 are equal, we can use the present-value factors (for 5 years and 10 percent) given in Appendix Table II at the back of this book to discount the cash flows:

$$NPV = -\$5,620 + \$1,178(3.791)$$

$$= -\$5,620 + \$4,465.80$$

$$= -\$1,154.20.$$

Because the incremental net present value is less than zero, we would not recommend the purchase of the machine. ∃∥⊧

Table 9–19
After-tax Cash Flows Generated by a Decision to Purchase New Equipment

	Cash Flows					
	Year 0	Year 1	Year 2	Year 3	Year 4	Year 5
Purchase of new machine	($8,000)					
Salvage value of old machine	1,000					
Salavage tax shield due to loss	1,380					
Annual cash flow	—	1,178	1,178	1,178	1,178	1,178
Net cash flow	(5,620)	1,178	1,178	1,178	1,178	1,178

KEY CONCEPTS

1. Capital budgeting is a process for analyzing investment opportunities.

2. Determining the payback period and determining accounting return on investment (AROI) are two methods often used in capital budgeting, but each method has some important shortcomings.

3. Using discounted-cash-flow techniques, complex cash-flow patterns can be reduced to single dollar *(NPV)*, ratio *(PI)*, or percentage *(IRR)* figures that can be more easily evaluated than can the payback period or AROI.

4. The *NPV* rule is the general criterion that is consistent with the objective of value maximization.

5. Projects with positive net present values pass the economic test of acceptance as sound investment proposals that will add to the value of the firm. Equivalently, projects with internal rates of return exceeding the required rate of return pass this test.

6. The *NPV* rule should be used to rank mutually exclusive projects, with the acceptable project being the one with the highest net present value.

7. The incremental-cash-flow rule is a general guide for estimating cash flows. The cash flows relevant in analyzing an investment opportunity are those after-tax cash flows and only those after-tax cash flows directly attributable to the investment.

8. Depreciation is a noncash charge that is relevant to the calculation of cash flows to the extent that it must be added back to accrual-accounting figures.

9. Operating flows and financing flows should be kept separate in the analysis of an investment project.

10. Capital budgeting is part of a larger system of planning that includes strategic as well as economic analysis.

SUMMARY

This chapter examined *capital budgeting,* or the process of making investment decisions in firms and other organizations, including nonprofit organizations. The process of investing is very important, because when firms and other organizations invest wisely, new value is created, meaning that the outputs of the investment are worth more than the cost of the inputs.

Capital budgeting is part of a larger planning process that includes strategic and other qualitative considerations as well as economic analysis. Economic analysis of investment opportunities, the major focus of this chapter, requires that we select a method of evaluating projects.

Criteria for investment decisions can be separated into two broad classes: those that are based on discounted-cash-flow (DCF) methods and those that are not. The two most widely used DCF criteria are the *NPV* rule and the *IRR* rule, both of which take into account the time value of money. The *NPV* rule has the additional advantage of always being consistent with the general objective of maximizing the value of the firm. Applied to investments, the *NPV* and *IRR*

rules constitute economic tests of investment worth. Both require that a return target—a minimum acceptable return on the investment—be established (a topic taken up in the next chapter). Investments pass the economic test if net present value is positive or, equivalently, if the internal rate of return exceeds the target return. Both rules give the same signals in accept/reject decisions but can sometimes give conflicting signals in ranking decisions. Where they do conflict, the *NPV* rule gives the correct ranking.

In using DCF decision criteria, it is cash flow that matters, rather than accounting profits. Careful cash-flow estimates are essential for good decisions. The incremental-cash-flow rule states that the cash flows that should be considered in analyzing an investment are those flows directly attributable to the investment. Cash flows that must be considered typically include the initial outlay, revenues and cash expenses, and taxes. The effect of depreciation on taxes must also be considered.

Sunk costs—that is, costs already incurred and unaffected by the decision under evaluation—are irrelevant in the economic analysis of an investment decision. The end objective of the cash-flow estimating process is the determination of *operating cash flows after taxes*. Financial flows (interest, principal, and dividends) in most cases should be kept out of the cash-flow analysis and taken into account in the return target (to be discussed in the next chapter).

DCF criteria encourage managers to take a long view and to make decisions that are best over the long run. A potential for conflict exists when DCF criteria, such as the *NPV* rule or the *IRR* rule, are used for

decisions while performance is measured using accounting measures, such as current profits or accounting return on investment.

Capital budgeting is part of a larger planning system. The *NPV* and *IRR* rules are decision criteria to be applied after a prospective investment has been judged consistent with the firm's commercial strategy. The firm's commercial strategy tells it where to look for attractive investment opportunities, and the *NPV* and *IRR* rules tell the firm which of those opportunities to select.

QUESTIONS

1. State and explain the incremental-cash-flow rule.
2. In some cases, investment opportunities involve outlays over several time periods. In such cases, what procedures should be followed to identify the "initial investment"?
3. A nonprofit organization not subject to income tax is considering an investment opportunity involving a labor-saving machine. How should depreciation be treated in the analysis?
4. How should sunk costs be treated in analyzing investment opportunities?
5. Many investment opportunities give rise to activities and to cash-flow streams that have no well-defined termination points. Over what time period should such investment opportunities be analyzed?
6. Why is it best to separate financing flows from an evaluation of the after-tax operating cash flows of an investment?

7. Define the internal rate of return of an investment opportunity.
8. Why is it sometimes necessary to rank investment opportunities?
9. How should allocated expenses, such as managers' salaries, be treated in analyzing investment opportunities?
10. When an investment opportunity makes use of existing facilities, how should costs associated with those existing facilities be treated in the analysis?
11. What are the shortcomings of the payback period as an investment criterion?
12. Why do the *NPV* and *IRR* rules sometimes give conflicting ranking signals?
13. What important shortcoming do you see in discounted-cash-flow techniques as applied to investment decisions?

PROBLEMS

To work problems preceded by an asterisk (*) requires knowledge of material in one of the five appendixes to Chapter 9.

1. A firm is considering the two competing proposals for the purchase of new equipment described in Table A. Assume straight-line depreciation and a tax rate of 40 percent.

a. Calculate the net present value of each alternative at a discount rate of 10 percent.
b. If 10 percent is the required rate of return, which alternative should be selected? Why?
2. Suppose that machine B in problem (1) is expected to have a salvage value of $1,000 at the end of year 5.

Table A

Proposal	Net Cash Outlay at Year 0 (dollars)	Salvage Value (dollars)	Estimated Life (years)	Net Cash Savings Before Depreciation and Taxes (dollars)	
				Years 1–3	Years 4–5
A	10,000	0	5	3,000	2,500
B	7,500	0	5	2,000	2,000

    a. Determine the effect of alternative B on the net present value (*NPV*) at 10 percent.

    b. Does this change the decision reached in problem (1), part (b)? Why or why not?

3. Suppose you are asked to rank a number of investment alternatives for which you have calculated the data shown in Table B. Each project is of approximately the same risk and, thus, you think 10 percent is an appropriate required rate of return for each project.

    a. Suppose that only one of the four projects (W, X, Y, Z) could be undertaken because all involve the use of the same land. Which of the projects would you choose?

    b. Suppose that you could spend no more than $300 on the projects but that this were the only constraint (that is, the projects are not mutually exclusive for physical reasons). What would be your decision?

4. International Company is considering replacing an old stamping machine with a newer and more efficient model. The old machine had an accounting book value of $12,000 and a projected life of 20 years when it was purchased 10 years ago. The projected salvage value was $2,000 at the time of purchase. The machine has recently begun causing problems with breakdowns and is costing the company $1,000 per year in maintenance expenses. The company has been offered $5,000 for the old machine as a trade-in on a newer model which has a delivered price (before allowance for trade-in) of $11,000. It has a projected life of 10 years and a projected salvage value of $1,000. The new machine will require installation modifications of $2,000 to existing facilities, but it is projected to have a cost savings in production materials of $4,000 per year. Maintenance costs are included in the purchase contract and are borne by the machine manufacturer. Assuming a marginal tax rate

Table B

Project	Net Present Value (dollars)	Internal Rate of Return (percent)	Initial Outlay (dollars)
W	15	11	150
X	70	30	200
Y	40	33	150
Z	−10	8	100

Table C

	Cash Flows (dollars)	
Year	Project X	Project Y
1	1,000	4,000
2	1,500	6,000
3	4,000	6,000
4	4,000	5,000
5	6,000	5,000

of 40 percent and all depreciation via the straight-line method, construct a summary table of relevant cash flows. For simplicity, assume that there is no investment tax credit and that installation costs will be depreciated over the life of the asset.

5. Chatham Manufacturing Corporation purchased an old building in Washington, D.C., 2 days ago and immediately contracted for $50,000 in exterior renovation. The building has a projected life of 30 years with zero salvage value, and Chatham paid $3,610,000 for it. Annual upkeep on the building is estimated at $25,000 and annual property taxes are $50,000. Chatham is considering using the building as a warehousing outlet to reduce current annual storage expenses by $400,000 per year. Alternatively, another firm has offered to lease the building for 30 years at $300,000 per year and assume all required maintenance expense. Assuming a marginal tax rate of 40 percent and all depreciation via the straight-line method, construct a summary table of relevant cash flows. Do you have enough information to be able to recommend what Chatham should do? If not, what additional information do you need?

6. Calculate the NPV for investment projects X and Y based on the cash flows shown in Table C. Project X requires an initial outlay of $12,000, and project Y requires an outlay of $16,500. Assume a required rate of return of 10 percent. Which of the two would you accept?

7. Calculate the internal rate of return (IRR) for the following investments:

a. An investment of $27,000 promising a return of $4,000 per year for 13 years.

b. An investment of $27,000 promising a return of $3,000 per year for 16 years.

c. An investment of $7,070 promising a return of $1,400 per year for 16 years.

8. Calculate the IRR for each of the two investments in problem (6).

9. Calculate the NPV for each of the three investments in problem (7) if the required rate of return is 12 percent. Which of the three investments would you accept?

10. Two mutually exclusive projects each involve an initial outlay of $800. Project A has cash inflows of $200 a year for 8 years, while project B has cash inflows of $325 per year for 4 years.

a. Calculate the NPV of each project at required rates of return of 0 percent, 7 percent, 14 percent, and 21 percent.

b. Calculate the IRR of each project.

c. Construct a plot of each project's NPV similar to the one shown in Figure 9–2.

d. Which project would you select? Why?

11. An investment requires an initial outlay of $1,000 and an additional outlay of $500 at the end of year 1. The investment generates cash inflows of $600, $800, and $800 at the ends of years 2, 3, and 4, respectively.

a. Calculate the NPV of the investment at a discount rate of 10 percent.

b. Calculate the IRR of the investment.

12. A bank lends $10,000 to a company to purchase a piece of equipment and requires the borrower to repay $2,637.97 per year (at year end) for 5 years.

a. Viewing the transaction as an investment decision from the standpoint of the bank, what is the internal rate of return to the bank?

b. Viewing the transaction from the standpoint of the borrower, calculate the effective interest cost of the loan.

13. You have arranged to borrow $1,000 from a bank. The bank offers two repayment plans: $402.09 per year for 3 years (payable at year end) or a single lump-sum repayment of $1,259.45 at the end of the third year.

Table D

Project	Initial Cash Outlay (dollars)	Annual Cash Revenues Before Taxes (dollars)	Annual Expenses* (dollars)	Tax Rate (percent)
A	1,500	2,000	1,500	40
B	2,100	2,300	1,600	40

*These expenses include both cash expenses *and* depreciation charges. Delta depreciates on a straight-line basis. All of the initial cash outlays are to purchase items that will be depreciated.

a. Calculate the effective interest cost (the rate that discounts cash flows to zero) of each alternative.

b. Which alternative would you prefer? Why?

14. You have an opportunity to purchase for $912 a bond promising to pay $40 semiannually for 6 years and $1,000 at maturity. What is the bond's yield to maturity?

15. A building contractor has estimated that using a higher grade of insulating material in your new home could save you $650 a year in heating costs over the next 10 years. If your required rate of return on such investments is 15 percent, what is the maximum amount you would be willing to pay for the higher grade material? (Ignore any possible tax credits, assume that after 10 years the savings differential between grades disappears, and assume that the contractor's estimates are accurate.)

16. Delta Inc., a highly profitable enterprise, is looking at two mutually exclusive investment projects—project A and project B. Each of the projects has an expected useful life of 3 years after which there will be zero salvage value. Information has been estimated for these projects and appears in Table D. Assume that Delta faces a cost of capital of 10 percent based on its operations in the food industry, and that projects A and B are in the food industry. Which (if either) would you recommend for acceptance by Delta?

17. Consider an investment of $5,000 that generates after-tax cash flows of $2,000 per year and net income of $1,000 per year over a 5-year life. Calculate the payback period and the accounting return on investment (AROI).

18. A company is trying to decide which of two machines to purchase for a new plant. Each machine requires an investment of $15,000. The after-tax cash flows and the net income figures are listed in Table E.

a. Calculate the payback period for each investment.

Table E

Year	Machine A Cash Flow (dollars)	Machine A Net Income (dollars)	Machine B Cash Flow (dollars)	Machine B Net Income (dollars)
1	3,000	1,000	6,000	2,000
2	4,000	2,000	7,000	3,000
3	5,000	3,000	8,000	4,000
4	6,000	4,000		
5	7,000	5,000		
6	8,000	6,000		

Table F

| | Cash Flow (dollars) | | | |
Investment	Period 0	Period 1	Period 2	Period 3
A	(10,000)	6,000	4,000	3,000
B	(5,000)	(2,000)	5,000	6,000
C	(15,000)	7,120	7,120	7,120

b. Calculate the AROI for each investment.

c. If machine B also had an after-tax cash flow of $5,000 in each of the last 3 years, would the payback period change? Why?

Guide for Table 9-E

19. An investment of $1,000 generates cash inflows of $301.93 per year for 4 years.

a. Calculate the payback period of the investment.

b. Calculate the net present value of the investment at a discount rate of 8 percent.

c. Note that the payback period and the present-value factor (from Appendix Table II at the end of the book) used in part (b) are equal. Suggest a way to interpret the present-value factors in Table II as payback periods.

20. An equipment manufacturer has marketed a new machine that promises to provide your company cash savings of $2,000 after taxes for each year the machine is operated. The useful life of this machine is not known with certainty. The machine will cost your firm $15,000.

a. If your firm's required rate of return on such investments is 14 percent, what is the minimum number of full years of life the machine must operate to make this investment acceptable? Ignore any tax effects that may result from the purchase or sale.

b. What would be the payback period for the machine?

c. Suppose your firm requires a payback period of 10 years for new equipment, and your production manager estimates this machine's useful life to be 12 years. Would you recommend purchasing the machine?

21. The Walters Company is considering the three mutually exclusive investments referred to in Table F.

a. Calculate the payback period and *IRR* for each investment.

b. If the firm's required rate of return is 15 percent, which investment would you recommend, using *NPV* analysis? If the firm selected the investment with the highest *IRR,* would it choose the investment you recommended using *NPV* as your decision criterion?

Guide for Table 9-F

22. Consider the following proposed investments with the cash flows indicated in Table G.

a. Can you say (by inspection rather than computation) that any of these investments are superior to any other?

b. Rank these investments using the following criteria: payback period; AROI (treat cash flows as income); *IRR* rule; the *NPV* rule, assuming a required rate of return of 4 percent; the *NPV* rule, assuming a required rate of return of 50 percent.

c. What conclusion can you draw from this problem? Why do the rankings differ?

23. Calculate the terminal value of the cash flows (by compounding the cash flows forward to the end of year 3) for each of the six investments in problem (22).

a. Assume an interest rate of 4 percent.

b. Assume an interest rate of 50 percent.

c. Rank the investments on the basis of terminal values and compare the rankings with those obtained in problem (22). What conclusions do you draw?

Table G

Investment	Initial Outlay (dollars)	Year-End Cash Inflows (dollars)		
		Year 1	Year 2	Year 3
A	200	200	0	0
B	200	100	100	100
C	200	20	100	300
D	200	200	20	20
E	200	140	60	100
F	200	160	160	80

24. Brown Bag Brewery is contemplating replacing one of its bottling machines with a newer and more efficient machine. The old machine has a book value of $500,000 and a remaining useful life of five years. The firm does not expect to realize any return from scrapping the old machine in five years, but if it is sold now to another firm in the industry, Brown Bag would receive $300,000 for it. The new machine has a purchase price of $1.1 million, an estimated useful life of five years, and an estimated salvage value of $100,000. The new machine is expected to economize on electric-power usage, labor, and repair costs, and also to reduce defective bottles; in total, an annual pre-tax cash savings of $200,000 will be realized if the new machine is installed. (Note: To calculate depreciation, assume that the salvage value is deducted from cost to get the depreciable cost.) The company is in the 40 percent tax bracket and uses straight-line depreciation. Brown Bag considers this a fairly safe project and feels it should earn at least 10 percent to justify its investment.

a. What is the incremental cash outlay (at time 0) necessary for the replacement?
b. What is the incremental annual cash flow (year 2) as a result of the replacement?
c. Should Brown Bag purchase the new machine?
d. How would your analysis be affected if the expected life of the existing machine was shorter than the expected life of the new machine?

*25. Your firm is considering an expansion project that will increase annual sales by $1 million. Aside from the usual project cash flows, you also recognize that working capital will have to be increased in order to support the new sales volume. Given the balance-sheet breakdown shown in Table H, expressed as a percentage of sales, and assuming that these percentages are expected to remain constant at the new sales level, what cash flow would you budget for the net increase in working capital? In what period would this outflow occur? (See Appendix 9B.)

Table H

Assets (percent of sales)		Liabilities (percent of sales)	
Cash	3	Accounts payable	12
Receivables	15	Accrued taxes	2
Inventories	22	Bonds	21
Net fixed assets	45	Common stock	20
		Retained earnings	20

26. The Cleveland Company is using an automated bench lathe that cost $120,000 five years ago. Its current market (salvage) value is only $10,000 due to the present marketing of a computerized bench lathe that is more economical and efficient. The old lathe had been straight-line depreciated over a ten-year life toward a zero salvage value. Management can purchase the new machine at a cost of $100,000. This new machine would be depreciated over a five-year life to a zero salvage value. Expected cash savings from the new machine are $7,000 a year (before tax) and the company's required rate of return is 10 percent per year (for projects of this risk). Assume a 40 percent tax rate and an estimated income of over $62,000 in either case.

   a. What will be the net cash *outflow* if the old lathe is sold and the new one is purchased?

   b. What is the present value of the net cash *inflows?*

   c. What do you think management should do?

27. Orange Manufacturing Company has an opportunity to replace an existing piece of equipment with a new machine that performs a particular manufacturing operation more efficiently. The purchase price of the new machine is $16,500. Shipping charges will be $900 and installation $600. Because of a high rate of technological obsolescence, the machine is expected to have a life of only 3 years and to have no salvage value. Direct savings from use of the new machine are expected to be $9,600 in the first year and $8,400 in each of the next 2 years. The old machine has a remaining book value of $2,100 and is being depreciated at a rate of $700 per year. Its remaining useful life is 3 years, at the end of which time it will have no salvage value. If sold now, it will bring $3,000. The applicable tax rate is 40 percent on both income and on gains on sales of equipment. The company uses straight-line depreciation and depreciates shipping and installation costs over the life of an asset.

   a. Calculate the net present value of the investment opportunity at a discount rate of 10 per-

cent. Calculate the internal rate of return. If 10 percent is the minimum acceptable rate of return on the investment opportunity, should the old machine be replaced?

   b. Suppose that the new machine has an estimated salvage value of $3,000 at the end of the third year, and that straight-line depreciation is calculated on this assumption. If all other assumptions are as in part (a) what are the *NPV* at 10 percent and the internal rate of return?

   c. Suppose that use of the new machine required an immediate investment in additional inventory of $2,500, and that this extra inventory can be liquidated at the end of year 3. If all other assumptions are those of part (a), what is the internal rate of return?

28. The Downtown Development Corporation plans to sell a vacant lot and receives two offers: the first, an offer of $800,000 cash; the second, an offer of $900,000 with $225,000 to be paid immediately and the balance in equal installments over 5 years (at year-end). Which offer should be accepted? Assume that opportunities exist to invest in riskless United States government bonds returning 12 percent.

29. The Allen Company, a manufacturer of inexpensive perfumes and toiletries, is considering an investment in a new perfume, Jasper. The company has spent $75,000 in developing and testing the new fragrance, and the final chemical formula and marketing plans have been decided upon. If Jasper is introduced, it will replace the Rosalyn product line, which has experienced declining sales over the past few years. Jasper can be manufactured and bottled using the same equipment and labor force currently used for Rosalyn without any adjustments or modifications. The equipment being used has a remaining book value of $160,000 and is being depreciated at a rate of $20,000 per year. An additional packaging machine will be required for the Jasper line to accommodate the product's more sophisticated package design. The machine required will cost $50,000 (delivered and in-

Table I

	Jasper Market Forecasts			Rosalyn Market Forecasts		
Year	Sales (number of bottles)	Price per Bottle (dollars)	Marketing Expenses* (dollars)	Sales (number of bottles)	Price per Bottle (dollars)	Marketing Expenses* (dollars)
1	100,000	5.00	200,000	75,000	4.00	50,000
2	100,000	5.00	200,000	75,000	4.00	40,000
3	75,000	5.00	120,000	50,000	3.50	40,000
4	60,000	4.00	50,000	30,000	3.50	0
5	30,000	4.00	20,000	20,000	3.00	0

*Assume marketing expenses are all cash outlays.

stalled) and has a projected life of 5 years with no salvage value. The machine is fully automated and will not require any additional personnel for operation. It is expected that this machine will increase overhead maintenance and power expenses by $1,000 per year. The raw material costs of Jasper are expected to be 15¢ per bottle compared to Rosalyn's cost of 10¢ per bottle. Labeling and packaging costs for Jasper are expected to be 20¢ per bottle compared to Rosalyn's 10¢ per bottle. The marketing department has provided projected sales levels and marketing expenses for the Jasper and Rosalyn lines for the next 5 years, which are shown in Table I. These forecasts assume that if Jasper is not introduced, Rosalyn will stay on the market, and if Jasper is introduced, Rosalyn will be taken off the market. At the end of 5 years, it is expected that either product will have exhausted its sales potential and will be taken off the market. No increases in working capital are expected to be needed to support the Jasper line.

a. Assuming a 50 percent tax rate and straight-line depreciation, construct a summary table of the relevant cash flows for making the decision of introducing Jasper or keeping Rosalyn.

b. If Allen's required rate of return is 20 percent, what is the incremental NPV of introducing Jasper? (For simplicity, assume all cash flows occur at the end of the year.)

*30. Smith and Company is considering a major new investment project. As Smith's new recruit on the finance staff, your challenge is to analyze the project. You are given the forecasts shown in Table J (figures are in thousands of dollars). The project requires an investment of $10 million in plant and machinery—column (2). This machinery can be dismantled and sold for net proceeds estimated at $1 million in year 7. This amount is the plant's salvage value. Suppose that the tax authorities allow Smith to depreciate the investment on a straight-line basis to an arbitrary book value of $500,000 at the end of the project. Assume that Smith requires a 20 percent rate of return on the project. (See Appendix 9B.)

a. Should the project be adopted?

b. Now assume that the figures in the table are based on an assumption of zero inflation. The 20 percent required return, on the other hand, assumes an inflation rate of 10 percent per year for the next six years on all sales, operating costs, working capital, and machinery values. In light of these inflation considerations, should Smith adopt the project?

31. Benson Enterprises, Inc., is evaluating alternative uses for a three-story manufacturing and warehousing building that had been purchased for $225,000. The company could continue to rent the

Table J

Period (1)	Capital Investment (2)	Accumulated Depreciation (3)	Year-End Book Value (4)	Working Capital (5)	Total Book Value (6) = (4) + (5)	Sales (7)	Operating Costs (8)	Other Costs (9)	Depreciation (10)	Profit Before Tax (11) = (7) − (8) − (9) − (10)	Tax at 46 Percent (12)	Profit After Tax (13) = (11) − (12)
0	10,000		10,000		10,000			4,000		−4,000	−1,840	−2,160
1		1,583	8,417	500	8,917	475	761	2,000	1,583	−3,869	−1,780	−2,089
2		3,167	6,833	1,065	7,898	10,650	6,388		1,583	2,679	1,232	1,447
3		4,750	5,250	2,450	7,700	24,500	14,690		1,583	8,227	3,784	4,443
4		6,333	3,667	3,340	7,007	33,400	20,043		1,583	11,774	5,416	6,358
5		7,917	2,083	2,225	4,308	22,250	13,345		1,583	7,322	3,368	3,954
6		9,500	500	1,130	1,630	11,130	6,678		1,583	2,869	1,320	1,549

building to the present occupants for $12,000 per year. The present occupants have indicated an interest in staying in the building for at least another 15 years. Alternatively, the company could modify the existing structure to use for its own manufacturing and warehousing needs. Benson's production engineer feels the building could be adapted to handle one of two new product lines. Cost and revenue data for the two product alternatives are given in Table K. The building will be used for only 15 years with either product A or B. After 15 years, the building will be too small for efficient production of either product line, and Benson plans to rent the building to firms similar to the current occupants. To rent the building again, Benson will have to restore the building to its present layout. The estimated cash cost of restoring the building if product A has been undertaken is $3,750; if product B has been produced, the cash cost will be $28,125. Benson will depreciate the original building shell (purchased for $225,000) over a 30-year life to zero salvage value regardless of which alternative is chosen. The building modifications and equipment purchases for either product are estimated to have a 15-year life and zero salvage value. All depreciation is done on a straight-line basis. The firm's tax rate is 50 percent, and its required rate of return on such investments is 12 percent, after taxes. Which use of the building for the next 15 years would you recommend to management? For simplicity, assume all cash flows for a given year occur at the end of the year, that the initial outlays for modifications and equipment will occur at $t = 0$, and the restoration outlays will occur at the end of year 15.

32. The Cartwright Company is considering replacing one of its existing machines with a new, more automated, and more efficient machine. The existing machine was purchased for $93,800 (installed) 4 years ago and is being depreciated on a straight-line basis over a 14-year life to a zero salvage value. The machine could be sold today for $20,000. The new machine could be purchased for $95,000. Installation costs would be an additional $3,000. It is estimated that the new machine could increase output by 10 percent, increasing sales

Table K

	Product A (thousands of dollars)	Product B (thousands of dollars)
Initial cash outlay for building modifications	36	54
Initial cash outlay for equipment	144	162
Annual pretax cash revenues (generated for 15 years)	105	127
Annual pretax cash expenditures (generated for 15 years)	60	75

revenue by $15,000 per year. In addition, the machine is expected to reduce operating costs by $18,000 annually. The machine has an expected 10-year life with a $13,000 salvage value and will be depreciated on a straight-line basis. Cartwright's required rate of return on such investments is 14 percent, and the firm's tax rate is 50 percent.

a. Should Cartwright purchase the new machine?

b. If the new machine did not reduce any costs but only increased output, what would be your recommendation?

c. If you do not advocate purchasing the new machine, what would the purchase price have to be to change your recommendation?

*33. National Foods is considering producing a new gelatin dessert, Tasty, of which management believes consumers will buy 5 million packages each year for 10 years at $0.40 per package. Equipment to produce Tasty will cost National $400,000, and $200,000 of additional net working capital will be required to support Tasty sales. National expects production costs to average 60 percent of Tasty's net revenues, with overhead and sales expenses totaling $500,000 per year. The equipment has a life of 10 years, at which time it will have no salvage value. Working capital is assumed to be fully recovered in year 10. Depreciation is straight-line, and National's tax rate is 50 percent. (See Appendix 9B.)

a. Determine the after-tax operating cash flows the Tasty project is expected to generate over its 10-year life.

b. Find the NPV of the operating cash flows at a required rate of return of 16 percent.

c. Calculate the IRR of the Tasty project.

d. Consider the effect on cash flows, NPV, and IRR if unit demand for Tasty were to fall 10 percent below management's expectations.

e. Consider the effect on cash flows, NPV, and IRR if unit demand were to be at the expected level but production costs were to average 70 percent of net revenues.

f. What conclusions do you draw from the changes in assumptions given in parts (d) and (e)?

34. Your firm is considering the purchase of a tractor. It has been established that this tractor will cost $32,000, will produce annual cash revenues in the neighborhood of $10,000 (before tax), and will be depreciated using the straight-line approach to zero in eight years. The board of directors, however, is having a heated debate as to whether the tractor can be expected to last eight years. Specifically, Wayne Seus insists that he knows of some that have lasted only five years. Tom Smith agrees with Wayne but argues that it is more likely that the tractor will give eight years of service. Wayne agrees. Finally, Ralph Evans says he has seen some last as long as ten years. Given this discussion, the board asks you to prepare a sensitivity analysis to ascertain how important the uncertainty about the life of the tractor is. Assume a 40 percent tax rate on both income and capital gains, zero salvage value, and a required rate of return of 10 percent.

a. Calculate the NPV if the tractor lasts 8 years.

b. Calculate the NPV if the tractor lasts only 5 years and then must be scrapped for zero salvage value.

Table L

Project	Net Present Value (NPV) (thousands of dollars)	Internal Rate of Return (IRR) (percent)	Required Initial Outlay (thousands of dollars)
A	30	28	100
B	10	20	75
C	8	14	75
D	40	15	300
E	8	13	100
F	5	17	50

c. Calculate the *NPV* if the tractor lasts 10 years and then is scrapped for zero salvage value.

d. Comment on the sensitivity of the purchase proposal to the life of the tractor.

35. After careful analysis, you have calculated *NPV* and *IRR* figures on a number of investment projects as shown in Table L. As division manager, you have authority to choose any of the projects you desire. But there is a catch. While the projects are not mutually exclusive, the chief financial officer of the company has decided that your division can spend no more than $350,000 on capital projects during the coming year. What set of projects would you choose? Why?

Guide for Table 9-L

*36. Suppose that the data given in problem (1) assume no inflation. Now assume that the firm expects inflation of 6 percent per year for the next five years. For example, cash savings before depreciation and taxes in year 1 with machine A are expected to be $3,000 (1 + 0.06) = $3,180 adjusted for inflation. Along with this inflation, assume the firm's required return is now 15 percent for each alternative. (See Appendix 9D.)

a. Calculate the NPV of each alternative.

b. Which alternative should be selected? Why?

*37. Look back at the Cartwright Company's replacement decision in problem (27). Suppose that the cash flow estimates stated in the problem had ignored the effects of inflation. In fact, Cartwright expected sales prices and salvage values to go up by 5 percent per year after year 1 due to inflation. For example, the $15,000 increase in sales revenue was based on next year's prices. In year 2, the same output increase would lead to $15,000(1 + 0.05) = $15,750 of revenues. Assume that Cartwright sticks to its original depreciation schedules for tax purposes even though it recalculates what it expects the new machine to be worth in 10 years. Assume a 14 percent required return. (See Appendix 9D.)

a. Should Cartwright purchase the new machine?

b. If the new machine did not reduce any costs but only increased output, what would be your recommendation?

REFERENCES

Ang, J. S., J. H. Chua, and R. Sellers. "Generating Cash Flow Estimates: An Actual Study Using the Delphi Technique." *Financial Management* 8 (Spring 1979): 64–67.

Bailey, A. D., and D. L. Jensen. "General Price Level Adjustments in the Capital Budgeting Decision." *Financial Management* 6 (Spring 1977): 26–32.

Barnea, A., R. Haugen, and L. Senbet. "Market Imperfections, Agency Problems, and Capital Structure: A Review." *Financial Management* (Summer 1981): 7–22.

Bernhard, R., "Mathematical Programming Models for Capital Budgeting—A Survey Generalization and Critique." *Journal of Financial and Quantitative Analysis* (June 1969).

Blatt, J. M., "Investment Evaluation Under Uncertainty." *Financial Management* 8 (Summer 1979): 66–81.

Brick, I. E., and D. G. Weaver. "A Comparison of Capital Budgeting Techniques in Identifying Profitable Investment." *Financial Management* 13 (Winter 1984): 29–39.

Business Week (June 1, 1981): 60–71.

Bylinsky, G., "The Race to the Automatic Factory." *Fortune* (Feb. 21, 1983): 52–64.

Callard, C. G., and D. C. Kleinman. "Inflation-Adjusted Accounting: Does It Matter?" *Financial Analysts Journal* (May-June 1985): 51–59.

Chambers, D. R., R. S. Harris, and J. J. Pringle. "Treatment of Financing Mix in Analyzing Investment Opportunities." *Financial Management* (Summer 1982): 24–41.

Colvin, G., "Federal Express Dives Into Air Mail." *Fortune* (June 15, 1981): 106–108.

Cooley, P. L., R. L. Roenfeldt, and I. Chew. "Capital Budgeting Procedures Under Inflation." *Financial Management* 4 (Winter 1975): 18–27.

Ezzell, J. R., and W. A. Kelly, Jr. "An APV Analysis of Capital Budgeting Under Inflation." *Financial Management* 13 (Autumn 1984): 49–53.

Feldstein, M. S., and J. Slemrod. "How Inflation Distorts the Taxation of Capital Gains." *Harvard Business Review* 56 (Sept.–Oct. 1978): 20–21.

Folger, H. R., "Ranking Techniques and Capital Rationing." *Accounting Review* 47 (Jan. 1972): 134–143.

"The Folks Who Brought You Apple." *Fortune* (Jan. 12, 1981): 66–79.

Gale, B. T., "Can More Capital Buy Higher Productivity?" *Harvard Business Review* 58 (July–Aug. 1980): 78–86.

Gitman, L. J., and J. R. Forrester, Jr. "A Survey of Capital Budgeting Techniques Used by Major U.S. Firms." *Financial Management* 6 (Fall 1977): 66–71.

Hertz, D. B., "Investment Policies that Pay Off." *Harvard Business Review* 46 (Jan.–Feb. 1968): 96–108.

Kim, M. H., "Inflationary Effects in the Capital Budgeting Process: An Empirical Examination." *Journal of Finance* 34 (September 1979): 941–950.

Lorie, J. H., and L. J. Savage. "Three Problems in Rationing Capital." *Journal of Business* 28 (Oct. 1955): 229–239.

McInness, M., and W. T. Carleton. "Theory, Models, and Implementation in Financial Management." *Management Science* (September 1982): 957–978.

Nelson, C. R., "Inflation and Capital Budgeting." *Journal of Finance* 31 (June 1976): 923–931.

Pratt, J. W., and J. S. Hammond, III. "Evaluating and Comparing Projects: Simple Detection of False Alarms." *Journal of Finance* 34 (December 1979): 1231–1242.

Rappaport, A., "Selecting Strategies that Create Shareholder Value." *Harvard Business Review* 59 (May-June 1981): 139–149.

Rappaport, A., and R. A. Taggart. "Evaluation of Capital Expenditure Proposals under Inflation." *Financial Management* 11 (Spring 1982): 5–13.

Reinhardt, U. E., "Breakeven Analysis for a Lockheed's TriStar—An Application of Financial Theory." *Journal of Finance* 28 (Sept. 1973): 821–838.

Sarnat, M., and H. Levy. "The Relationship of Rules of Thumb to the Internal Rate of Return: A Restatement and Generalization." *Journal of Finance* 24 (June 1969): 479–490.

Schall, L. D., and G. L. Sundem. "Capital Budgeting Methods and Risk: A Further Analysis." *Financial Management* 9 (Spring 1980): 7–11.

Schall, L. D, G. L. Sundem, and W. R. Geijsbeek. "Survey and Analysis of Capital Budgeting Methods." *Journal of Finance* 33 (Mar. 1978): 281–287.

Schwab, B., and P. Lusztig. "A Comparative Analysis of the Net Present Value and Benefit—Cost Ratios as Measures of Economic Desirability of Investment." *Journal of Finance* 24 (June 1969): 507–516.

Searby, F. W., "Return to Return on Investment." *Harvard Business Review* 53 (Mar.–Apr. 1975): 113–119.

Shapiro, A. C., "Capital Budgeting for the Multinational Corporation." *Financial Management* 7 (Spring 1978): 7–16.

Solomon, E., "Alternative Rate of Return Concepts and Their Implications for Utility Regulation." *Bell Journal of Economics and Management Science* 1 (Spring 1970): 65–81.

Solomon, E., "The Arithmetic of Capital Budgeting Decisions." *Journal of Business* 29 (Apr. 1956): 124–129.

Tatom, J. A., and J. E. Turley. "Inflation and Taxes: Disincentives for Capital Formation." *Monthly Review*, Federal Reserve Bank of St. Louis (Jan. 1978).

Appendix 9A

Tax Effects

Taxes are relevant to almost every financial decision that a firm or individual makes, unless the firm or individual is not subject to taxation. The incremental-cash-flow rule tells us that, if the decision at hand affects tax payments, those tax effects should be considered. In the final analysis, we are interested in the *net cash flow after taxes*.

While the details of tax laws change over time, tax effects remain very important in business decisions. For example, if the marginal tax rate is 46 percent, a dollar's worth of revenue becomes $0.54 after taxes, and a dollar's worth of depreciation saves $0.46 in taxes. Tax effects are important also to individuals because they often face high tax rates. Capital gains—the profits on the sale of capital assets—have traditionally been taxed by the federal government and by most state governments at rates below those on income, though such special treatment could change in the future.

There are two general approaches to dealing with tax effects in investment decisions. One way is to put financial information in income-statement format and determine taxes on net profit. This method was used earlier in Chapter 9, as we can recall by looking back at Table 9–11, which calculated operating cash flow for Product 99.

In a simple case, where depreciation is the only noncash item, we can represent the method used in Table 9–11 symbolically as shown in Equation (A–1).

Net operating cash flow (C) after taxes can be calculated from income-statement data as

$$C = \text{PAT} + DEP \tag{A-1}$$
$$= (CR - CE - DEP)(1 - T) + DEP$$

where CR = cash revenues, CE = cash expenses, PAT = profit after taxes, DEP = depreciation, and T = the corporate tax rate.

In Equation (A–1), we have simply stated that profit after taxes can be written as $(CR - CE - DEP)(1 - T)$ and that cash flow is profit after taxes plus depreciation. For example, using the 1987 data for Product 99 (from Table 9–10), we see that CR = $250,000; CE = $137,000 + $138,000 = $275,000; and DEP = $76,000. Using Equation (A–1), we can calculate operating cash flow after taxes as

$$C = (\$250,000 - \$275,000 - \$76,000)(1 - 0.46) + \$76,000$$

$$= \$21,000$$

This same result was given in the first column of Table 9–11.

A second method for calculating operating cash flow after taxes that many find useful can be expressed by rearranging Equation (A–1) as shown in Equation (A–2).

Table 9A–1

Calculating After-Tax Equivalent Cash Flows

	1987 Pre-Tax Cash Flow Item (thousands of dollars) (1)	Tax Effect (2)	After-Tax Equivalent (thousands of dollars) (3) = (1) × (2)
Sales (CR)	250	(1 − 0.46)	135
Cost of goods sold (CE)			
Advertising (CE)	− 137	(1 − 0.46)	− 74
Selling expense (CE)	− 138	(1 − 0.46)	− 75
Depreciation tax shield, (DEP) × T	76	0.46	35
Cash flow from operations after taxes			21

Net operating cash flow after taxes (C) can also be calculated, by converting each component cash flow to its after-tax equivalent flow, as

$$C = CR(1 - T) - CE(1 - T) - DEP(1 - T) + DEP \qquad \text{(A–2)}$$
$$= CR(1 - T) - CE(1 - T) + DEP(T)$$

where variables are defined as in Equation (A–1).

Note that Equation (A–2) is mathematically equivalent to Equation (A–1)—our first method of calculating after-tax operating cash flows—so we'll always get the same answer whether we use Equation (A–1) or Equation (A–2). The approach suggested in Equation (A–2) is to convert each cash flow to its *after-tax equivalent* flow. A cash revenue (for example, a sales figure) of $1,000 becomes $540, for that is the amount left over after the tax collector leaves. At a tax rate of 46 percent, $540 is the *after-tax equivalent* of the $1,000 revenue figure. In Equation (A–2), the after-tax equivalent of cash revenues is expressed as $CR(1 - T)$. Similarly, the after-tax equivalent of $600 in expenses is $CE(1 - T) = \$600(1 - 0.46) = \$324$.

As noted earlier, each dollar of depreciation saves taxes. This tax saving is called the *depreciation tax shield* and is the last term in Equation (A–2). To illustrate, $400 in depreciation generates a depreciation tax shield, or tax savings, of $(DEP \times T) = \$400 \times 0.46 = \$184$. Let us illustrate this method by applying it to Product 99. We will use 1987 data from Table 9–11, as reproduced in the first column of Table 9A–1. Using Equation (A–2), net operating cash flow can be calculated as

$$C = \$250,000(1 - 0.46) - \$275,000(1 - 0.46) + \$76,000(0.46)$$

$$= \$21,000.$$

Table 9A–1 demonstrates this result in more detail. Note that the result using the second method is the same as the one we obtained using the first method (in Table 9–11): $21,000. Note also that Table 9A–1 deals only with the pretax cash-flow items, plus depreciation. Note also that, while depreciation is an expense, the depreciation

Table 9A–2
Rules to Apply in Calculating After-Tax Equivalent Cash Flows

Type of Item	*Calculation Rule*
For cash items (sales, cash expenses, etc.)	Pretax amount $\times$ (1 $-$ T) = After-tax equivalent
For noncash items (depreciation, etc.)	Pretax amount $\times$ T = Tax shield

tax shield is a cash *inflow* because it reduces taxes. Table 9A–2 outlines the general rules we followed in constructing Table 9A–1.

It is important to keep in mind that tax effects could be quite different if the firm were losing money at the time and, therefore, were paying no taxes. Negative taxes are not paid to the firm by the government! Tax losses may be carried forward and applied against future income or may be carried back against prior years. Thus, even when a firm is losing money, tax effects can still be important, but the actual cash flows resulting from tax effects might take place in years other than the current one.

In addition, for a nonprofit organization such as a university or a church that pays no taxes, the tax rate, T, is 0 percent. Thus, while we could still use either approach—Equation (A–1) or Equation (A–2)—for calculating the nonprofit organization's operating cash flows, we would have to set T equal to zero.

One final note on depreciation. Depreciation can be calculated on a straight-line basis, or using one of several accelerated methods, such as the declining-balance method or the sum-of-the-year's-digits method. (See Appendix 9E for further discussion of depreciation expenses.) The more rapid is the depreciation, the lower are the taxes in early years and the greater are the taxes in later years. Deferring taxes by means of accelerated depreciation is advantageous because of the time value of money.

Sample Problem 9A–1

Determining the Net Operating Cash Flow and the Net Present Value of an Investment in a New Machine

Camino Industries is considering replacing an old machine with a newer model having lower maintenance expense. The old machine has a current book value of $200, depreciation charges of $500 per year, and a remaining life of 4 years, at which time it will have no salvage value. If the machine were sold today, proceeds would be $1,500. Annual maintenance is $1,500.

Table 9A–3
Comparison of Incremental Cash Flows For New and Old Machines, Camino Industries

Rule (from Table 9A–2)	*Existing* *(1)*	*Replacement* *(2)*	*Incremental* *(3) = (2) − (1)*
Maintenance			
Cash item:	$-\$1,500(1 - 0.46) = -\$810$	$-\$200(1 - 0.46) = -\$108$	$702
Pretax amount x (1 $-$ T)			
Depreciation			
Noncash item:	$500(0.46) = $230	$1,000(0.46) = $460	$230
Pretax amount $\times$ T		**Total**	$932

Table 9A–4

Total Cash Flows Generated by a New Machine Purchase

	Cash Flows				
	Year 0	Year 1	Year 2	Year 3	Year 4
Purchase of new machine	$(6,000)				
Salvage value of old machine	1,500				$2,000
Salvage tax shield*	230				
Annual new cash flow	0	$932	$932	$932	932
Total	**$(4,270)**	**$932**	**$932**	**$932**	**$2,932**

*Current book value of old machine is $2,000. Selling it today for $1,500 yields a book loss of $500 and thus a tax shield of $500 × 0.46 = $230. Salvage value of new machine equals book value at the end of year 4 ($2,000), so no tax shield is generated in year 4.

The new machine has a purchase price of $6,000, a life of 4 years, a salvage value at the end of 4 years of $2,000, and annual maintenance expense of $200. Assuming a tax rate of 46 percent, straight-line depreciation, and no investment tax credit, prepare a table of the relevant after-tax cash flows associated with the replacement. Calculate the net present value of the replacement assuming a required return of 10 percent.

Solution

As a first step, let us calculate the depreciation charge on the new machine. Assuming straight-line depreciation, we can calculate the annual depreciation expense as

$$\text{Depreciation} = \frac{\text{Amount to be depreciated}}{\text{Useful life}}$$

$$= \frac{\$6,000 - \$2,000}{4} = \$1,000 \text{ per year.}$$

Table 9A–3 shows the results of calculating the annual change in operating cash flow using the rules in Table 9A–2. Note that Table 9A–3 gives the *incremental* maintenance and depreciation flows determined by comparing the new machine with the old. As Table 9A–3 shows, there will be an annual after-tax cash savings of $932. Table 9A–4 shows the results of adding to the new operating cash flows the initial and terminal cash flows associated with the replacement.

The net present value at 10 percent can be calculated using the figures in Table

$$NPV = -\$4,270 + \frac{\$932}{(1.1)} + \frac{\$932}{(1.1)^2} + \frac{\$932}{(1.1)^3} + \frac{\$2932}{(1.1)^4}$$

$$= -\$4,270 + \$932(0.909) + \$932(0.826) + \$932(0.751) + \$2932(0.683)$$

$$= \$49.51$$

Because net present value is greater than 0, the replacement is a good decision, although it does not give an extremely large *NPV*. ∃▎╠

Appendix 9B

Working Capital and Incremental After-Tax Cash Flows

In calculating incremental after-tax cash flows, the guiding principle is to isolate the net amount of cash going in or out of the firm as a result of undertaking a project. Often we go about estimating such cash flows starting with accrual-accounting information. When we use information gathered on an accrual-accounting basis as our starting point, we must adjust our figures for differences between accrual-accounting figures and cash figures. For example, in Chapter 9 we noted that depreciation (a noncash charge) must be added back to profit after taxes (PAT) to get an estimate of cash flow. This estimate of cash flow assumes, however, that depreciation represents the only major difference between accrual revenues or expenses and cash revenues or expenses. In practice, there are often other differences between accrual and cash figures that must be handled in our cash-flow estimates.

Consider the following simplified situation. In January 1986, an investor plans to start XYZ Company by putting up $100 cash. XYZ will have no long-term assets; rather, it will retail goods that it buys directly from a wholesaler. During 1986, XYZ sales are expected to be $1,000, most of which will be made on credit terms to its customers, leading to significant accounts receivable. As of year-end 1986, XYZ anticipated $90 of accounts receivable. For that same year, XYZ plans to recognize $980 worth of expenses, although it will still owe $20 (accounts payable) to the wholesaler as of year-end 1986. Table 9B–1 summarizes XYZ's accounting for its planned operations.

While simplified, the situation depicted in Table 9B–1 is quite typical in that it shows a buildup of cash, accounts receivable, and accounts payable during the year. This buildup is common, especially in the early years of a project as sales build rapidly. The question is: what is the incremental after-tax cash flow during the year for our investor?

A quick look at the planned balance sheet in Table 9B–1 gives the answer. Our investor started with $100 in cash in January 1986, and by year-end 1986, the balance sheet shows a cash balance of $40—a net decrease of $60. In fact, however, if the $40 in cash is necessary to support normal business operations, the investor must leave it in the firm. As a result, the full $100 is tied up and net cash flow for the year is −$100.

Our task is to see how we can derive this −$100 figure using accrual-accounting methods. As always, we can start by adding depreciation to PAT. In this example, there is no depreciation, so we calculate a first-estimate cash flow of PAT + depreciation = $10 + $0 = $10.

Table 9B–1
Estimated Working Capital and Cash Flows for XYZ Company, 1985–1986 (thousands of dollars)

XYZ Balance Sheet (year end)	1985	1986	
Cash	$0	$ 40	
Accounts receivable	0	90	
Long-term assets	0	0	
Total Assets	$0	$130	
Accounts payable	$0	$ 20	
Long-term debt	0	0	
Owners equity			
Paid-in capital	0	100	
Retained earnings	0	10	
Total Liabilities and Net Worth	$0	$130	

XYZ Income Statement	Accrual Accounting	Cash	Reason for Difference
Sales	$1000	$910	Accounts receivable increased by $90
minus			
Expenses	−980	−960	Accounts payable increased by $20
equals			
Profit before taxes	$ 20	—	
minus			
Taxes (at 50 percent)	−10	−10	
equals			
Profit after taxes	$10	−$60	
		−40	Necessary cash balance of $40
	Cash flow	−$100	

This first estimate is not the −$100 figure we desire, however, because there are other noncash items besides depreciation. Specifically, the accrual sales revenues of $1,000 include $90 of noncash revenues—the $90 of accounts receivable as yet uncollected. In addition, the accrual expense figures include $20 of noncash expenses—the $20 of accounts payable as yet unpaid. Finally, the $40 in the cash account must be maintained at all times just to support XYZ's business. We can, thus, consider this $40 kept in a cash account to be a *cash use,* that does not enter the accrual-accounting system. Such a cash use must be subtracted from PAT to refine our estimate of cash flow.

Conceptually, the treatment of the example above is straightforward. We are ultimately interested only in cash flows. To use accrual accounting to estimate such flows we must make four basic types of adjustments to PAT. We must:

1. add back all noncash items that are "expensed" in the accrual-accounting process (including depreciation),
2. subtract all noncash items that are treated as revenues in the accrual-accounting process (in this case, increases in accounts receivable),

Table 9B–2

Estimated Cash Flow for XYZ Company

Item (type of adjustment)	Cash Flow (dollars)
Profit after taxes	+ 10
Depreciation (1)	+ 0
Noncash revenue (2)	− 90
Noncash expense (1)	+ 20
Required cash balance (4)	− 40
	− 100

3. add back cash receipts that are not recognized as revenues in the accrual-accounting process, and

4. subtract cash outflows that are not recognized as expenses in the accrual-accounting process (such cash outflows may include necessary investment in a cash account).

Note that item (4) above is exactly what we do in calculating initial outlays on long-term plant and equipment.

Applying these guidelines to the data for XYZ in Table 9B–1, we can estimate net operating cash flow as shown in Table 9B–2.

We, thus, see that we can use accrual accounting as a basis for estimating cash flow as long as we make the appropriate adjustments. In this case, we see that our investor had a cash outflow of $100 to start the XYZ Company.

Often the term *net working capital* is used in conjunction with some of the adjustments mentioned above. Net working capital is simply the difference between current assets and current liabilities. Increases or decreases in net working capital during a year reflect important noncash adjustments we must make in calculating cash flows. Net-working-capital figures are calculated for XYZ Company in Table 9B–3. Net working capital increased by $110 during 1986. Note that this $110 increase in net working capital is another representation of the total net adjustment we made in calculating cash flows for XYZ—arising from outflows in cash (− $40) and accounts receivable (− $90) and an inflow in accounts payable (+ $20)—that is, − $40 − $90 + $20 = $110. As a result we can alternatively estimate cash flow as

An alternative method for estimating net operating cash flow is

$$\text{Cash flow} = PAT + DEP - \text{Increase in Net working capital} \quad \textbf{(B–1)}$$

where PAT = profit after taxes and DEP = depreciation.

In the case of XYZ Company, this cash flow could be estimated using Equation (B–1) as $10 + $0 − $110 = − $100.

The adjustment for working capital is nothing more than an adjustment for differences between accrual-accounting and cash flows. In calculating cash flows starting with accrual-accounting figures, increases in net working capital must be subtracted out and decreases in net working capital must be added back.

Table 9B–3

Net Working Capital (NWC) for XYZ Company, 1985–1986: NWC = Current Assets (CA) − Current Liabilities (CL)

	1985	1986
Cash	$0	$ 40
Accounts receivable	0	90
Current assets (CA)	$0	$130
Accounts payable	0	20
Current liabilities (CL)	$0	$ 20
Net working capital (CA − CL)	$0	$110
Increase in net working capital		$110

In Chapter 9, we mentioned that we would include only operating cash flows for purposes of discounted-cash-flow analysis, allowing financing flows to enter the analysis only by means of the required rate of return, K. To keep this distinction, we will exclude from our working-capital adjustments any cash items that involve an explicit form of financial cost. For example, bank borrowing could create a short-term liability with cash coming to the bank as proceeds of a loan on which the company has to pay interest.

There are basically two ways to treat this loan. First, we could enter the loan proceeds, interest, and principal payments in the cash flows—a type of working-capital adjustment. If we adopt this procedure, the bank borrowing will already be explicitly entered into cash flows and we would not consider it in calculating our discount rate, K. The second alternative, and the one we adopt here, is not to make adjustments in the cash flow for the loan but rather to consider it as part of the financing flows.

Thus, our net-working-capital adjustments do not include interest-bearing loans or other types of financing involving financial charges.[1]

Adjustments associated with net working capital can be very important in analyzing investment opportunities. Earlier in our discussion of Product 99 we ignored working capital in order to keep things simple. Now we will return to the example of Product 99 and consider working capital in the analysis.

In analyzing an investment, only *incremental* net working capital is relevant. If an investment is expected to increase sales, it is likely that an increase will be required in accounts receivable, inventory, and perhaps cash. Part of the increase may be offset by increases in accounts payable and other current liabilities. The part that is not offset, the *net increase* in net working capital, should be treated as a cash outflow attributable to the project. Working-capital flows can be quite large and, therefore, important in analyzing investments.

---

[1]For a discussion of the general problem of alternative ways to define cash flows and discount rates, see D. Chambers, R. Harris, and J. Pringle, "Treatment of Financing Mix in Analyzing Investment Opportunities," *Financial Management,* Summer 1982, pp. 24–41.

Table 9B–4
Working Capital Flows for Product 99 (thousands of dollars)

	1987	1988	1989	1990	1991	1992	1993	1994	1995	1996
Cash	5	25	38	51	55	60	60	56	52	44
plus										
Accounts receivable	+21	+104	+158	+212	+229	+250	+250	+233	+217	+183
plus										
Inventory	+25	+125	+190	+255	+275	+300	+300	+280	+260	+220
minus										
Accounts payable	−14	−69	−104	−140	−151	−165	−165	−154	−143	−121
equals										
Net working capital (NWC)	37	185	282	378	408	445	445	415	386	326
Increase in cash	5	20	13	13	4	5	0	−4	−4	−8
plus										
Increase in accounts receivable	+21	+83	+54	+54	+17	+21	+0	+(−17)	+(−16)	+(−34)
plus										
Increase in inventory	+25	+100	+65	+65	+20	+25	+0	+(−20)	+(−20)	+(−40)
minus										
Increase in accounts payable	−14	−55	−35	−36	−11	−14	−0	+11*	+11*	+22*
equals										
Increase in NWC	37	148	97	96	30	37	0	−30	−29	−60

Note: In 1994, 1995, and 1996 accounts payable decrease. To show this decrease, we *add back* the decrease in accounts payable.

For a new product, such as Product 99, increases in net working capital usually are large in early years as sales build rapidly, tapering off some in later years. If a project has a definite life span and is terminated at some point, the net working capital at that terminal point is decreased as inventories are sold off, receivables collected, and payables paid. This *recapture* of working capital is treated as a cash inflow in the final year of the analysis. For a project with no anticipated terminal date, the amount of the net working capital can be treated as a cash inflow in the final year of the analysis (part of the project's terminal value) because it represents net claims on cash.

Table 9B–4 gives the net-working-capital figures for Product 99. The upper part of the table shows the anticipated levels of cash, accounts receivable, inventory, and payables required to support the project. The lower part shows the *changes* in these items each year.

In Table 9B–4, increases in *assets* (cash, accounts receivable, and inventory) represent cash outflows, or uses of funds, while increases in liabilities (accounts payable) represent inflows, or sources of funds.

Now let us redo the *NPV* analysis of Product 99 adjusting for changes in net working capital. The cash flows are given in Table 9B–5. Note that in 1996 net working capital of $326,000 (from Table 9B–4) is recaptured and treated as an inflow in that year.

Table 9B–5

Net Present Value with Net Working Capital (NWC) Adjustments for Product 99 (thousands of dollars)

	1986	1987	1988	1989	1990	1991	1992	1993	1994	1995	1996
Net profit after tax	0	− 55	26	62	166	182	202	202	186	170	137
plus											
Depreciation	+ 0	+ 76	+ 76	+ 76	+ 76	+ 76	+ 76	+ 76	+ 76	+ 76	+ 76
equals											
Cash flow from operations	0	21	102	138	242	258	278	278	262	246	213
minus											
Increase in NWC	− 0	− 37	−148	− 97	− 96	− 30	− 37	0	−(−30)	−(−29)	−(−60)
plus											
NWC recapture	+ 0	+ 0	+ 0	+ 0	+ 0	+ 0	+ 0	+ 0	+ 0	+ 0	+326
equals											
Net operating flow	0	− 16	− 46	41	146	228	241	278	292	275	599
minus											
Investment	−325	−389	− 25	− 0	− 0	− 0	− 0	− 0	− 0	− 0	− 0
equals											
Net cash flow	−325	−405	− 71	41	146	228	241	278	292	275	599

If we calculate the net present value of the net after-tax cash flows in Table 9B–5 (last line) at the target return for Product 99 of 15 percent, we get a net present value of $23,000. The internal rate of return is 15.6 percent, barely above the minimum acceptable figure of 15 percent. In Chapter 9, without net-working-capital adjustments, we got a net present value of $204,000 and an internal rate of return of 21.3 percent (see Tables 9–14 and 9–15). With working-capital flows included, Product 99 still passes the economic test, but only by an eyelash. Clearly, net-working-capital adjustments can make an important difference and in some cases could change the decision.

In the interest of simplicity, we have not complicated many of our example problems throughout Chapter 9 with working-capital considerations. In general, however, one should always make adjustments for changes in working capital when using accrual-accounting data to calculate cash flows.

Appendix 9C

Capital Rationing

In principle, the *NPV* rule tells us that a firm should undertake all investments that are attractive—that is, all investments that meet the test of increasing the firm's net present value. *Disinvestments,* such as selling existing assets, can also be judged by the *NPV* rule. In practice, top management, for other policy reasons, might want to restrain the growth (or decline) of the firm's assets to a different rate than the rate that would occur if the *NPV* rule is followed. One device that is frequently used to achieve growth (or orderly withdrawal from uneconomic activities) is to ration capital. Under a capital-rationing system, the top management of the firm decides on the size of the annual capital-expenditure budget. This size projection might be based on the volume of funds available to it for investment (without recourse to further long-term stock issues or borrowing), or it might be based on other considerations. In either case, the approach deviates from that suggested by the *NPV* rule—namely, that we should begin with the opportunities available, add up the total-funds requirements of all those that will increase the firm's net present value, and arrange for all these requirements to be financed in whatever way seems best.

Table 9C–1 illustrates a capital-rationing situation when the company has decided to spend only $250,000 on projects in the current year. A quick look at Table 9C–1 shows that all four projects have a positive net present value; the problem is that adopting all four projects would cost $500,000 and only $250,000 is available.

Under a capital-rationing system, it is no longer feasible to make simple accept or reject decisions for each project individually. The firm must rank the available projects and select the most attractive set of projects that can be financed within the predetermined budget. To do this, it should still use a variant of the broader *NPV* rule; in other words, it should select that subset of projects that contribute the highest combined net present value to the firm.

In Table 9C–1, we see that application of this rule would result in selecting projects B and C. In combination, they provide a net present value of $70,000, which is the highest possible *NPV* given the available budget and projects. Note that project A will not be chosen, even though it has the highest net present value ($60,000) of any individual project, because A would cost $200,000 of the $250,000 available. With the remaining $50,000, project D could be financed but the combined *NPV* of projects A and D would be only $65,000—which is $5,000 lower than the combined *NPV* of projects B and C.

Table 9C–1 has provided a very simple illustration. Capital-rationing problems can become much more complicated.[1] The basic rule, however, remains the same: select

---

[1]See R. Bernhard, "Mathematical Programming Models for Capital Budgeting—A Survey Generalization and Critique," *Journal of Financial and Quantitative Analysis,* June 1969, for some mathematical models developed to handle various capital-budgeting problems. For a perspective on the implementation of models, see M. McInness and W. T. Carleton, "Theory, Models, and Implementation in Financial Management," *Management Science,* September 1982.

Table 9C—1

Investment Projects Under Consideration by a Firm with a Capital Rationing System (thousands of dollars)

Project	Required Investment in Current Year	Net Present Value
A	200	60
B	125	35
C	125	35
D	50	5

Note: Capital spending is rationed to $250,000 in the current year.

the set of projects that in combination add the most to the value of the firm. We might pause for a moment to ask why capital rationing occurs in the first place. Why does management put a limit on capital spending even if discounted-cash-flow analysis indicates that such spending will increase value? In a world of perfect information, we should not reject a project with a positive net present value as long as it is not mutually exclusive to a project with an even higher net present value. We should raise the funds necessary for the investment. A problem is that in practice we may not know what other projects will be available to the firm in the upcoming years. In practice, investment opportunities often unfold more or less continuously through time. If a particular project is undertaken when it arises, it may preclude an even better project next quarter or next year. There is no good solution to this problem. Sometimes it may be feasible to postpone decisions and save up a list of projects for consideration all at once. This approach is often used in practice, but it can delay projects where time might be an important factor for competitive or other reasons. In such a case, managers may preserve flexibility by limiting capital spending in the current period (rationing capital) as a way to increase their ability to take advantage of projects that they hope will appear in future periods but about which they currently do not have detailed information for formal evaluation.

In many small firms and especially young firms, the need to ration capital arises sometimes not from overriding policy considerations, but simply from the nonavailability of funds. In a world of imperfect information, a firm may not be able to get funds for projects it thinks are good ones. A small, young firm with good investment opportunities may have low current cash inflows, may have no access to the regular capital markets, and, at the same time, may be reluctant to bring in outsiders as equity partners. In such cases, there may be only limited sources of outside funds. Such sources offer debt funds only; with no access to outside equity funds, such a firm would have a definite limit on total external financing.

In addition, given complex organizational structures in a firm, forms of capital rationing may be implemented. For example, a division may be limited to a certain annual allotment of capital funds by top management at the corporate level. Given the complexities and costs of information, the top levels of management can never analyze each and every investment proposal in a large firm. Decision-making authorities are delegated. Top management may exercise some control over the general direction in which investments will go by allocating certain dollar amounts to different segments of the business. For a division manager facing such a limit, the challenge is to be effective in making decisions where capital is rationed.

Where the firm has more investment opportunities than it can accommodate within the financing limit, it must ration capital and rank its projects. The costs of doing so are the opportunities forgone.

Appendix 9D

The Effects of Inflation

Prior to the mid-1960s, the general price indexes increased at only about 1.5 to 2.0 percent per year, on an average. Although important to other decisions, inflation at such relatively low rates usually did not seriously distort the investment decisions of firms and individuals. Exceptions were decisions that involved investment or financing across international boundaries, when inflation rates in different countries might differ.

The high rates of inflation encountered in the United States and elsewhere in the 1970s and early 1980s were a different matter. When inflation reaches high levels, it can have a seriously adverse impact on returns to capital investment because of the nature of existing tax laws and rules for treating depreciation. While at least U.S. inflation rates dropped from the peaks of the early 1980s, some countries still have rampant inflation. We hope that inflation will not return as a major problem for the U.S. economy; nonetheless, it is important to understand its effects on investment incentives.

Suppose a firm is considering an investment of $300,000 that generates the cash flows shown in Table 9D–1.[1] The investment has a useful life of 5 years and generates net cash receipts (after cash expenses) of $100,000. Assume for simplicity a tax rate of 50 percent. As indicated in Table 9D–1, the internal rate of return of the investment is 10.4 percent (the rate that discounts $80,000 per year for 5 years back to equal the outlay of $300,000).

Now consider the impact of an inflation rate of, say, 5 percent per year. Table 9D–2 displays the resulting cash flows. Suppose revenues and expenses are affected equally so that net cash receipts grow 5 percent per year. Depreciation is based on historical cost and does not change, so taxable income is higher and taxes are higher. After-tax cash flow also is higher, and the nominal return, calculated by discounting the cash flows in column (4) of Table 9D–2, rises to 14.0 percent. But the real return, adjusted for inflation in column (5), falls to 8.5 percent.

---

[1]This example is from J. A. Tatom and J. E. Turley, "Inflation and Taxes: Disincentives for Capital Formation," *Monthly Review*, Federal Reserve Bank of St. Louis, January 1978. See also C. R. Nelson, "Inflation and Capital Budgeting," *Journal of Finance* 31 (June 1976): 923–31.

Table 9D–1
Return on a Hypothetical Investment with Zero Inflation (thousands of dollars)

Year	Receipts (1)	Depreciation (2)	Tax Paid* (3)	After-Tax Cash Flow (4)
1	100	60	20	80
2	100	60	20	80
3	100	60	20	80
4	100	60	20	80
5	100	60	20	80

Internal rate of return = 10.4 percent

*Tax paid is 50 percent of (receipts − depreciation) = 0.5 ($100,000 − $60,000).

A part of the higher returns achieved under inflation is necessary to compensate lenders and investors for the decline in the purchasing power of the dollar. This *inflation premium* is really a principal payment the purpose of which is to maintain the real (inflation-adjusted) value of the investor's claim. It is not income, but our current tax system treats it as if it were income.

One purpose of depreciation is to protect the principal from taxation, but the depreciation charge is fixed and does not provide complete protection in an inflationary environment. The net effect is that inflation causes the government's share of the real returns to rise and the investor's share to fall. Some projects that may have produced adequate returns under low rates of inflation produce returns considered inadequate by investors when inflation rises. As a result, the tax effects of inflation may reduce incentives for new investment.

The basic problem is that under current laws depreciation is based on historical cost rather than replacement cost. While forms of accelerated depreciation and shortened periods over which equipment can be depreciated may work to encourage investment,

Table 9D–2
Return on a Hypothetical Investment with a 5 Percent Inflation Rate

Year	Revenue (1)	Depreciation (2)	Tax Paid (3)	After-Tax Cash Flow (4)	Purchasing Power (5)
1	$105,000	$60,000	$22,500	$82,500	$78,571
2	$110,250	$60,000	$25,125	$85,125	$77,211
3	$115,763	$60,000	$27,882	$87,881	$75,915
4	$121,501	$60,000	$30,776	$90,775	$74,681
5	$127,628	$60,000	$33,814	$93,814	$73,506

*Purchasing power is the figure in column (4) divided by $(1 + 0.05)^n$ where n is the year.

they do not solve a basic problem introduced by inflation. In an inflationary world, historical costs are not a good basis for calculating depreciation.

Inflation should be recognized both in estimates of cash flows and in target rates of return. The best approach is to project cash flows in nominal (inflated) dollars and then to discount those flows at a rate that also includes an inflation premium. Different kinds of cash flows, however, may be affected differently by inflation. For some firms, costs may be inflating at 10 percent per year while sales prices are going up only 8 percent. The dollar value of depreciation, based on historical costs, is not affected by inflation after the purchase of the asset. Chapters 10 and 11 will return to the matter of how inflation is included in return targets.

Appendix 9E

Accelerated Depreciation

In Chapter 9, we used the straight-line depreciation method in working our examples to simplify the analysis. In practice, most firms use some form of accelerated depreciation for tax purposes. Such accelerated methods allow the firm to take a larger portion of total depreciation charges early rather than late and, therefore, increase the present value of tax benefits related to depreciation. The actual form of depreciation that the tax authorities will allow changes over time as Congress enacts changes in the tax code. The appendix at the end of this book discusses current developments in tax law.

As an example of the type of schedules that have been used in the past, let us look at the early 1980s. In 1981, there was a major change in laws affecting depreciation (cost recovery) in the United States. The accelerated cost-recovery system (ACRS) divided all assets acquired after 1980 into five categories with prescribed depreciation periods. The rules adopted in 1981, along with some revisions made in 1982, are shown in Table 9E–1.

Assets acquired prior to 1981 were still depreciated according to various other schedules; thus, a number of depreciation methods were actually in use. For new investments, however, the appropriate depreciation methods were those prescribed by the accelerated cost-recovery system, which provided for accelerated depreciation charges. ACRS rules are applied to the full purchase price of the asset, not the purchase price less salvage value.

Because tax laws may change in the future and because the details of the tax treatment of any capital asset can become quite complex, it is important for a financial manager to obtain the relevant tax information on a capital asset. The depreciation schedule that matters for cash-flow purposes is the one allowed by the Internal Revenue Service.

Table 9E–1

Prescribed Depreciation Periods for Various Types of Property under the Accelerated Cost-Recovery System

Type of Property (selected items)	Allowable Recovery Period for Depreciation (years)
Autos, light trucks, R&D equipment	3
Machinery and equipment not in other classes, agricultural structures	5
Railroad tank cars, selected public utility property	10
Selected public utility property with long lives	15
Some low-income housing	15
Real estate	18

10

Setting Target Rates of Return

In this chapter we will learn how companies and other organizations establish return targets for capital-investment projects. We will explore the relationship between return targets inside the firm and returns earned by investors in financial markets outside the firm. After learning how to calculate return targets, we will then discuss how the targets are actually used in evaluating projects.

A **return target** or **target return**—is the minimum acceptable expected return on an investment.

In Chapter 9, we discussed two important steps in analyzing investment opportunities: (1) choosing a decision criterion and (2) estimating cash flows. We settled on the discounted-cash-flow calculations of net present value *(NPV)* and internal rate of return *(IRR)* as the most useful criteria because they take into account the time value of money. We also discussed the calculation of incremental after-tax cash flows. Now we come to step (3): choosing an appropriate required rate of return. Such a return is sometimes referred to as a **target return** or, alternatively, a **return target**.

The **required rate of return**—is the minimum acceptable return on any investment and is the rate forgone on the next best alternative investment opportunity of comparable risk; it is an *opportunity rate*.

In using the *NPV* rule, what do we use for a required rate of return? If the expected internal rate of return is, say, 12 percent, is the investment acceptable? To answer this question, we must establish a return target. The return target, another name for **required rate of return,** is the minimum acceptable expected return on the investment. We use it as the discount rate in *NPV* calculations, or as the **hurdle rate** in evaluating the internal rate of return.

In this chapter, we will discuss the concept of return targets and develop our basic approach to setting targets. Refinements to the basic approach will be saved for the next chapter. The story about nuclear power plants in Finance in Practice 10–1 sets the stage for our discussion of return targets.

HOW THE RETURN TARGET IS DETERMINED IN MARKETS

Where does a firm get the funds to invest? When a firm invests, it uses capital funds supplied by others—namely, lenders and investors. Therefore, investments undertaken by a firm must earn a return sufficient to compensate suppliers of capital.

> **Because the funds used by a firm to make investments are supplied by others, the investments must earn a return sufficient to compensate these suppliers of capital.**

A **hurdle rate**—is the return target to which an investment project's internal rate of return is compared in determining whether or not the investment project is acceptable to the firm.

This proposition is basic to the operation of a market economy, but it is not always applied in practice. Firms sometimes find themselves pressed to put too much emphasis on profits and earnings per share in the short run, to the neglect of long-run return on investment. Such preoccupation with near-term profits can lead to a failure to earn an adequate return on invested capital.[1]

Systematic failure to earn the market required rate of return over an extended period can lead only to serious financial difficulty. A symptom of such a sustained shortfall in return is a decline in stock price below *book value,* often followed by excessive reliance on debt to obtain needed funds. Managers sometimes lay the blame on the capital markets for their inability to raise capital at reasonable rates when, in fact, the markets are performing exactly as they should be in disciplining firms that fail to earn the market rate of return.

---

[1]See S. Lohr, "Overhauling America's Business Management," *New York Times Magazine,* January 4, 1981; and R. H. Hayes and W. J. Abernathy, "Managing our Way to Economic Decline," *Harvard Business Review* 58 (July/August 1980): 57–77. For a discussion of the potential conflicts between earnings per share and return on investment, see F. W. Searby, "Return to Return on Investment," *Harvard Business Review* 53 (March/April 1975): 113–19.

An article in the *Wall Street Journal* in August 1985 raised the question of who should pay for power-plant duds in connection with electric-utility plants. The article was written by Alfred Kahn, a Cornell economist, former chairman of the Civil Aeronautics Board, champion of airline deregulation during the Carter Administration, and noted authority on regulated industries. The article began, "The New York Public Service Commission decided in June to disallow, on grounds of imprudence, the passing on to consumers of $1.35 billion of Long Island Lighting Company's $4.2 billion-plus investment in its Shoreham nuclear plant. This is only the latest and most dramatic of a series of similar decisions confronting utility commissions all over the country—what to do with the billions of dollars sunk in nuclear generating plants that have either been abandoned or threaten, upon coming into service, to require rate increases in the 20–60 percent range."

The struggle over who should pay for nuclear power plants that cost more than originally envisioned or that were never completed is peculiar to the electric-utility industry. But the dilemma illustrates one of the basic concepts of finance—namely, that capital investments must earn a return sufficient to compensate those who put up the funds to finance them.

Electric utilities are regulated, and electricity rates supposedly are set so that utility investors earn a fair rate of return on their investment—a fair rate being defined as a return roughly equal to that of other investments of com-

Return Targets as Opportunity Rates

When a firm invests, the funds are supplied by the company's creditors and shareholders. What return do they expect on their additional investment? It is reasonable to suppose that they expect a return at least equal to what they could earn on other alternative investments of comparable risk. When an investment decision is to be made, the investor—whether an individual or a manager acting on behalf of shareholders—always has alternative opportunities in which to invest the funds. If not, there is no decision to be made.

Consider the problem of an investor analyzing a new investment opportunity, called Project X. Project X requires an outlay of $10,000 now and promises cash inflows in the future. If the investor undertakes Project X, he or she must forgo the opportunity to do something else with the money. Hence, by undertaking Project X, the investor incurs an **opportunity cost**—namely, whatever could have been earned on an alternative investment.

The **opportunity cost**—is the return an investor could have earned on the next best alternative investment forgone.

The concept of opportunity cost is a general and very useful one. The true economic cost of any action includes all that one must give up in order to undertake the action. The $5 spent on a movie means $5 less available for something else. The money provided to a corporation is unavailable for other investments that might have returned more.

parable risk. Later this chapter will define this rate as the "market required rate of return." During the 1950s and 1960s, utilities consistently earned more than the market required rate of return. At the same time, because of falling costs, customer prices for electricity dropped by 12 percent from 1950 to 1970. Allowing for inflation, the drop in real terms was much greater. Through the rate-setting process, utility commissions saw to it that many cost reductions were passed along to customers. But in the 1970s the situation reversed, and utilities on average earned much less than the market required rate of return on nuclear plants opened during that period, partly because of cost overruns, delays in construction, and other factors related to public controversy over nuclear power.

With respect to these nuclear plants that have not paid their way, the question is: who foots the bill? Some utility commissions, such as New York in the above example, are saying that it must be the investors. But in taking this position, the regulators are trying to have it both ways—setting rates so that utility investors earn no more than the market required rate of return on successful projects and less than the required rate of return on failures. Consumers get the benefits of good investments, and investors foot the bill for bad ones. Such an arrangement will hardly be acceptable to those asked to supply the funds.

No one knows in advance which investments will turn out to be successful and which will not. One way to proceed would be to allow utilities to earn the market required rate of return on all investments, successes and failures alike. An alternative would be to allow more on successes, by allowing utilities to keep returns above the market rate, and less on failures, by forcing utilities to pay for them. This latter arrangement is essentially the situation in unregulated firms.

No matter how the problem of nuclear plants finally is resolved, the lesson pertinent to this chapter is clear: investments that fail to earn the market required rate of return are going to mean trouble for someone.

Source: Alfred E. Kahn, "Who Should Pay for Power Plant Duds?" *Wall Street Journal*, August 15, 1985.

In general, if by undertaking a given investment—say, Project X—one gives up an opportunity to earn R percent in an alternative investment, then R percent is the minimum that should be demanded of Project X. The required rate of return, K, on Project X is R percent.

Whose Targets?

For an individual, it is clear that the required return on a prospective investment should be set in relation to other opportunities available. What about the case of a professionally managed firm? Whose required rate of return is appropriate? Management's? The shareholders'?

An **agent**,—in economic terms, is an individual or organization that acts in behalf of and to promote the interests of another party, usually referred to as the *principal*.

Because value maximization is our decision criterion, and because value ultimately is determined in the financial marketplace by investors, the value of the investment to the shareholders is the value to maximize. To determine value to shareholders, we must use the *shareholders'* required rate of return in calculating the target. In evaluating investment opportunities, management acts as the **agent** of shareholders. In setting return targets, management should base decisions on shareholders' required returns—that is, on the rates the shareholders would use if they were performing the evaluation themselves.

Figure 10–1
The Market Risk/Return Schedule

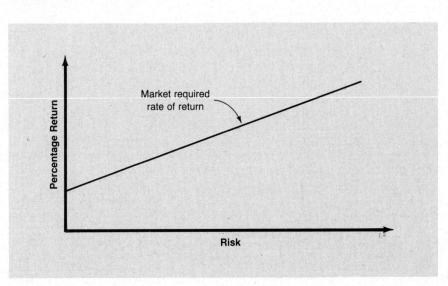

The Role of Markets

Suppose there are thousands of shareholders. Must management ask each for his or her required rate of return? Fortunately, the answer is no. *Financial markets* provide a solution to this problem. In financial markets, investors express their preferences by their own actions. From market data on stocks and bonds, we can infer the expectations of investors and lenders regarding returns.

Returns in organized public financial markets, such as the markets described in Chapter 2, are available at low transaction costs and relatively little effort (almost anyone can call a stockbroker or buy a mutual fund). Market returns, then, represent the minimum that an investor should accept on any investment opportunity. Organized markets, thus, establish the required rate of return for managers to use in evaluating investment opportunities. Since everyone faces essentially the same set of investment opportunities in markets, we need not worry about a different rate for each shareholder; opportunity rates are the same for everyone.

Setting return targets need not involve complex mathematics. The proper approach stems directly from the fundamental premise that management's job is to act as agent of shareholders in investing shareholder funds. In effect, suppliers of funds say to the management of any firm: "These are the rates we can expect to earn outside the firm in other investments. If you cannot equal or exceed these rates, pay the funds out to us and we will do the investing ourselves somewhere else."

> **Market opportunities available to investors *outside* the firm set the minimum standard for investment by management *inside* the firm.**

Required rates of return are not set by management, nor are they set by negotiation between management and suppliers of funds. Rather, they are set impersonally in the financial markets by the actions of investors and lenders competing against one another. Managers must examine market data to determine what those rates are and then use them as return targets.

Marginal Cost of Capital

The **marginal cost of capital**—is another name for the *return target* for an investment project.

The discussion so far has emphasized that a required rate of return for a project reflects opportunity costs of investors as the firm uses additional capital for investment. The flip side of this interpretation of the firm's return target is the interpretation of the return target as the cost of using capital. A return target is often referred to as the **marginal cost of capital.** The term *marginal* reflects the fact that the required return should be determined on *incremental* investment leading to incremental cash flows. Such incremental investment occurs now—not in the past—and has its own risk characteristics. The term *cost* reflects the fact that capital is not free. We will continue to use the term *required return* (rather than *marginal cost of capital*) in order to emphasize the links between return targets and risk/return trade-offs.

Return and Risk

The **risk premium**—is the difference between the required rate of return on a particular risky asset and the rate of return on a riskless asset with the same expected life.

In Chapters 4 and 5, we discussed the relationship between risk and risk aversion and concluded that risk-averse investors will expect a **risk premium** on risky investments. The greater is the risk, the higher is the required rate of return. Figure 10–1 diagrams a market risk/return schedule.

At the low end of the risk spectrum are savings accounts and, for those with sufficient funds, U.S. government securities. Money-market mutual funds offer low-cost investment in a diversified portfolio of very low-risk assets. Next in risk come corporate bonds followed by common stocks, which vary widely in risk from stable and well-established firms, such as telephone and electric companies, to new high-technology firms, such as Apple Computer. Commodity futures are generally considered to be of very high risk. Markets for all of these assets are public and highly organized; information is readily available to participants, and the cost of transacting is low. Other markets for investment assets, such as real estate, present additional opportunities on the risk/return spectrum but are less highly organized.

In setting return targets, managers are acting as agents of shareholders who are risk-averse. Those shareholders expect management to take risk into account and to set return targets that vary with risk.

> **Return targets should include a risk premium. The greater is the risk, the higher should be the target.**

Let us summarize our discussion to this point. Management acts as the agent of shareholders in analyzing investment opportunities and making investment decisions. A firm's investments must be expected to earn a return adequate to compensate suppliers of funds. Management must set return targets that ensure this result. Return targets are opportunity rates derived from data on market opportunities available to investors in financial markets. Targets should include a premium for risk.

REQUIRED RETURNS ON A FIRM'S SECURITIES

Our discussion of the required rate of return on risky assets and individual investments can be extended to the stocks and bonds that firms issue to finance their assets.

Required Returns on Equity and Debt

Consider a firm that has financed its assets by issuing common stock and debt. Given the firm's history and financial policies, the investments it has made in the past, and the nature of its business, the market will have a set of expectations regarding the magnitude and riskiness of the firm's future earnings. The market will require a return on the firm's stock commensurate with the perceived risk. We can represent the **required return on equity** as K_e. K_e varies with risk; the greater is the risk, the higher is K_e, and vice versa.

The **required return on equity**—equates the price of a stock to the present value of the expected future cash benefits of owning the stock; also known as the *cost of equity capital*.

Recall from Chapter 4 that K_e sometimes is called the **capitalization rate** of the firm's equity because K_e is the discount rate at which the market *capitalizes* the expected future cash flows to equity holders in order to determine the present value of its stock.

The **capitalization rate**—is another name for the *discount rate*.

Now consider the firm's debt financing. Suppose it issues some bonds with a 20-year maturity and an interest rate of 12 percent. Each $1,000 bond pays its holder $120 per year in interest. At the time of issue, 12 percent is the market required rate of return on the bonds because this rate is required in order to induce bondholders to buy. Bonds are only one type of debt. The firm also might borrow from a bank or an insurance company. If a bank charged the firm 15 percent interest, we can say that the bank's required return is 15 percent. We can represent the **required return on debt** as K_d.

The **required return on debt**—is the internal rate of return that equates the price of a bond (or debt instrument) to the present value of the expected future cash benefits of owning the bond (or debt instrument).

As we discussed in Chapter 4 and will discuss again in Part Five, we expect the required return on debt to be lower than the shareholders' required return for any firm because the debt owners bear less risk. In the event of financial difficulty, the debt owners have first claim. Shareholders, on the other hand, bear the residual risk. That is, shareholders bear financial risk introduced by the use of debt in addition to the firm's underlying operating risk.

> **Because equity is more risky than debt, for a given firm the required return on equity is greater than the required return on debt; that is, $K_e > K_d$.**

Variations Among Firms

What about variations in K_e from one firm to another? Apple Computer Inc., a company we mentioned earlier, is a manufacturer of microcomputers for personal and professional use. Apple is likely to be perceived by the market as relatively risky. The company was born in 1975 and is still young as companies go. It is part of a high-technology industry subject to rapid technical advances, rapid obsolescence, and fierce competition. It is true that the microcomputer industry is growing rapidly, but in a firm of Apple's size one big mistake can mean trouble, especially when competing against IBM. Thus, while the *expected return* on Apple stock is high because of the prospect of rapid growth, the *required return* also is high because of the high risk. Other high-risk companies include airlines and electronics firms.

Contrast Apple Computer with General Mills, the packaged-foods company with multibillion-dollar-per-year revenues. General Mills is able to count on cash flows generated by products such as Gold Medal flour (marketed for more than 100 years) and Wheaties, the "breakfast of champions." While the growth of General Mills is slower than that of Apple Computer, its revenues are subject to far less uncertainty than are Apple Computer's. Because the risk is lower, we would expect the General Mills K_e to be less than the Apple Computer K_e. Because investors are risk-averse, K_e is a function of risk and varies from one firm to another.[2]

How about required returns on debt? Required return on debt, K_d, also varies from one firm to another for exactly the same reasons. U.S. government bonds are generally considered to be the least risky debt of all. Corporate bonds are somewhat riskier. Although low in risk, the bonds of large corporations are by no means riskless. One need only point to the bankruptcy of the Penn Central railroad in 1970, to the difficulties of Lockheed in 1971, and to the troubles of Chrysler in 1980 to prove the point. Lockheed and Chrysler never formally declared bankruptcy, but both were unable to meet their contractual financial obligations at one time or another, and both required federal-government guarantees of their debt in order to induce banks and others to lend. In the absence of the guarantees, both Lockheed and Chrysler likely would have gone bankrupt.

Bonds of many large corporations are rated according to their degree of default risk by rating services, such as Moody's Investors Service and Standard & Poors. Moody's rates the very safest bonds as *Aaa*, the next category as *Aa*, the next as *A*, and the relatively risky bonds as *Baa*. Standard & Poors uses the ratings *AAA, AA, A,* and *BBB*. Both services have yet other ratings for even more risky debt. Table 10–1 gives the yields for some rating categories. The bonds in Table 10–1 are all of roughly the same maturity. The differences in yields result primarily from differences in perceived risk.

---

[2]Table 5–8 in Chapter 5 shows *beta values* of stocks in various industries. Beta is one measure of risk typically used in finance. The higher is the beta, the higher is the risk. According to the Value Line reports as of this writing, Apple has a beta of 1.70, and General Mills has a beta of 0.85. A beta of 1.0 represents average risk.

Table 10–1

Interest Rates by Category of Long-Term Bonds

	Yield to Maturity as of October 4, 1985 (percent)
U.S. government bonds	10.76
Corporate bonds:	
Aaa	11.09
Aa	11.53
A	12.01
Baa	12.45

Source: *Moody's Bond Survey.* (October 14, 1985).

Inflation

The **nominal rate of return**—is the contract or observed rate of return.

The **real rate of return**—is the difference between the nominal rate and the inflation rate.

An **inflation premium**—is an addition to the real rate of return required by investors to compensate them for the change in the value of the investment that results from anticipated inflation.

Table 10–1 shows a yield of 10.76 percent on U.S. government bonds. This rate may seem a bit high for a *default-free* investment, but the reason the rate is not lower has to do with market expectations of inflation.

Lenders who expect inflation in the coming year of, say, 6 percent are going to seek a return on a loan of more than 6 percent in order to protect themselves against inflation. If inflation is 6 percent, lenders will be repaid in dollars that will buy 6 percent less. Thus, if the **nominal rate of return** on the loan were set at 6 percent, the lender's **real rate of return,** net of inflation, would be zero. At a nominal return of 9 percent, the real return would be 9 percent $-$ 6 percent, or 3 percent. In general, the real return is the difference between the nominal return and the inflation rate.

In the absence of inflation, the yield on U.S. government bonds would be much lower than those presented in Table 10–1, as would yields on corporate Aaa bonds. So the yields in Table 10–1 all contain an **inflation premium.** Although our accounting and tax systems treat this inflation premium as income to the lender, in fact it is not income at all, but a principal payment to maintain the real value of the lender's claim.

Required rates of return on equities likewise contain an inflation premium. If the market required return (K_e) on the stock of General Mills Inc. were, say, 8 percent in

Table 10–2

Summary Balance Sheet for Mattari, Inc. (thousands of dollars)

Current assets	$2,000	Long-term debt	$1,500
Fixed assets	3,000	Equity	3,500
Total assets	5,000	**Total capital**	5,000

the absence of inflation, with an expected inflation rate of 8 percent, then the K_e for General Mills would be about 16 percent. Although this figure sounds high, half is the inflation premium.

> **All market required rates of return include an inflation premium approximately equal to the rate of inflation expected in the future.**

Return targets set by management, therefore, must include an inflation premium. We will explore ways to include this inflation premium in return targets shortly. *Future expectations of inflation,* not past inflation, are the determining factor in establishing an inflation premium. Of course, past inflation provides a basis for future estimates.[3]

THE WEIGHTED-AVERAGE REQUIRED RETURN *(WARR)*

The preceding section discussed the market required return on equity and debt. Consider the hypothetical case of Mattari, Inc., a manufacturer of electronic games. The market might require a return of, say, 17 percent on Mattari's equity and 11 percent on Mattari's debt. For the moment, we will just make up these required returns. Later on we will examine how to estimate values of K_e and K_d.

The **weighted-average required return** *(WARR)*—is the required return for an investment project based on an average of equity and debt returns, where the weights are the respective proportions of equity and of debt used by the firm.

Most firms, as does Mattari, finance their assets with some combination of equity and debt. For purposes of analyzing investment opportunities, it is often easier to use an *average* of the equity and debt returns rather than to apply the equity and debt required returns separately. In effect, we lump all suppliers of funds together and calculate a **weighted-average required return** *(WARR)*. The same concept is sometimes referred to as the *weighted-average cost of capital.* Later we will return to the term *cost of capital* and examine it more closely, after the required analytical tools have been provided. In addition to the values of K_e and K_d, we also need to know the proportion of equity and debt used by the firm in order to calculate the *WARR*.

The Mix of Equity and Debt

Flotation costs—are the cash costs associated with the issuance of a company's new long-term debt or stock.

Summary data from Mattari's balance sheet of December 31, 1986, are given in Table 10–2. The Mattari balance sheet is highly simplified to permit us to concentrate first on the basics. We will return later in this chapter to the question of how to deal with details such as accounts payable, accruals, capital stock, and retained earnings. Appendix 10A, which follows this chapter, discusses the effects of **flotation costs** on *WARR*.

---

[3]Just how inflation, and especially uncertain inflation, affects risk premiums and perceived risk is not well understood. See J. Lintner, "Inflation and Security Returns," *Journal of Finance* 30 (May 1975): 259–80; I. Friend, Y. Landskroner, and E. Losq, "The Demand for Risky Assets Under Uncertain Inflation," *Journal of Finance* 31 (December 1976): 1287–97; and B. M. Friedman, "Who Puts the Inflation Premium into Nominal Interest Rates?" *Journal of Finance* 33 (June 1978): 833–45. For a detailed discussion of how inflation affects investment decisions, see S. L. Hayes, III, "Capital Commitments and the High Cost of Money," *Harvard Business Review* 55 (May/June, 1977): 155–61.

Table 10–3
Relative Weight of Capital Items in Mattari's Balance Sheet

Capital Item	Amount (thousands of dollars)	Weight (proportion)
Long-term debt	$1,500	0.30
Equity	3,500	0.70
Total	5,000	1.00

As a first step in calculating the weighted-average required return, we must calculate the proportion of total financing provided by each source. Table 10–3 shows the proportion of total financing provided by each source as the amount of financing done by each source divided by the total amount of financing ($5,000,000).

Tax-Deductibility of Interest

An **interest tax shield**—is the tax saving a firm generates by using debt because interest on debt is tax-deductible. For example, if a firm has a marginal tax rate of 46 percent, each dollar of interest generates a tax shield of 46 cents.

If we know that 70 percent of Mattari's capital is supplied by equity investors requiring a 17 percent return and that the remaining 30 percent is supplied by debt holders requiring an 11 percent return, we should be able to calculate our weighted-average required return. Before making this calculation, however, we must first recognize a critical factor: taxes. Interest on debt is tax-deductible. If the corporate marginal tax rate is, say, 46 percent, then each dollar of interest generates a tax saving, or **interest tax shield**, of $0.46. Mattari pays interest of 11 percent annually on $1.5 million in long-term debt for a total of $165,000 in interest. Deducting this $165,000 from taxable income saves $165,000 × 0.46 = $75,900 in taxes. The net interest cost to Mattari, after taxes, is $89,100, or $165,000 minus tax savings of $75,900. In percentage terms, Mattari's after-tax interest cost is $89,100/$1,500,000, or 5.94 percent. We can calculate the after-tax cost of debt more simply by multiplying K_d times $(1 - T)$, where T is the tax rate. In the case of Mattari, this after-tax cost of debt would be $0.11 × (1 - 0.46) = 0.0594$, or 5.94 percent.[4] The figure of 5.94 percent represents the *after-tax equivalent* of the required return on debt, which is the cost of debt to the firm.

---

[4]Technically, the adjustment stated in the text is not always a precise way to get the after-tax cost of debt. It is an exact adjustment when new bonds are sold at face value and flotation (issue) costs are ignored or when a company is borrowing from a bank where interest costs are the only financial cost of borrowing. In most instances, companies do sell new bonds at approximately face value, so the above calculation is appropriate. Cases such as zero-coupon bonds sold at a substantial discount require more advanced treatment. See A. Silver, "Original Issue Deep Discount Bonds," *Federal Reserve Bank of New York Quarterly Review*, Winter 1981–82, pp. 18–28, for a discussion of the tax effects of zero-coupon bonds.

Table 10–4

Calculating the Weighted-Average Required Return (WARR) for Mattari, Inc.

	Required Return (1)	Weight (2)	Weighted Required Return (3) = (1) × (2)
Debt, K_d	0.0594	0.30	0.01782
Equity, K_e	0.1700	0.70	0.11900
Weighted average			0.13682

Mattari's WARR = 13.682 percent

Sample Problem 10–1

Calculating the Weighted-Average Required Return for Mattari, Inc.

Calculate the weighted-average required return for Mattari, Inc. from the data in Tables 10–2 and 10–3.

Solution

Equity holders supply 70 percent of Mattari's capital and require a return of 17 percent; debt holders supply 30 percent of the capital and require a return of 11 percent, which comes to 5.94 percent after taxes. We can calculate the weighted average as shown in Table 10–4. As the calculations show, Mattari's weighted-average required return is found by first multiplying the required returns on debt and equity by their respective weights in the firm's financing plan. The results are then added together to get Mattari's WARR of 0.01782 + 0.11900 = 0.13682, or 13.682 percent. ∃ll̄Ħ

Summary of *WARR* Calculations

Table 10–5 summarizes our procedure for calculating the WARR. In calculating the weighted-average required return, it is important to keep in mind the following points:

Table 10–5

Summary of Symbols Used in Calculating the Weighted-Average Required Return (WARR)

Symbol	Meaning
K_e	The rate of return required by equity holders
K_d	The rate of return required by debt holders
$K_d(1-T)$	The after-tax equivalent of the debt required return
T	The corporate marginal tax rate
K_w	The WARR on equity and debt
W_e	Target equity proportion, $E/(E+D)$
W_d	Target debt porportion, $D/(E+D)$

$$WARR = K_w = W_e K_e + W_d K_d (1 - T)$$

1. We ignore accounts payable, accruals, and other short-term liabilities arising out of the course of doing business because normally no interest is paid on these liabilities.
2. We include all sources of funds that require an explicit return. If the firm uses bank debt as a permanent part of its financing, it would be included and treated the same way as long-term debt. Likewise, preferred stock would be included also. Later in this chapter, we will consider an example that includes these two sources.
3. The required returns on sources of financing (K_d and K_e) are based on current financial-market conditions. For example, K_d is the interest rate on *new* borrowing, not the coupon rate on a company's existing debt that was issued in the past.
4. The weights in the *WARR* calculation are *targets*—that is, the planned proportions of debt and equity in the future.
5. In considering equity, we do not distinguish between new stock issues and retained earnings. Strictly speaking, equity obtained through stock issues is slightly more costly than retained earnings because of flotation (issue) costs, but this difference can be ignored in nearly all cases in practice.[5]
6. In theory, the weights (W_e and W_d) used to calculate the *WARR* should be based on market values of debt and equity rather than book values. In practice, however, book values are frequently used, mainly because market values can vary considerably from period to period.

The Weighted-Average Required Return as a Return Target

How can we use the *WARR* in evaluating investment opportunities? We can use it as the return target for evaluating average-risk investments.

The **operating return**—is the internal rate of return for an investment project calculated considering only operating cash flows.

Suppose Mattari is evaluating a prospective investment that has an expected **operating return**—the internal rate of return calculated considering only after-tax operating cash flows—of exactly 13.682 percent after taxes. Financing flows (interest, principal, and dividends) are excluded from the project flows and instead enter the analysis through the weighted-average required return.

Suppose the investment requires an outlay of $100,000. To keep our example simple, suppose the investment generates a *perpetuity*—that is, level cash flows indefinitely into the future. (Some projects in practice approximate this pattern as depreciation flows are reinvested). With an operating return of 13.682 percent, the project will generate a cash-flow stream of $13,682 annually.

Table 10–6 shows how this stream is divided up. Debt holders provide $30,000 at a rate of 11 percent, so they collect $3,300. Deducting the interest saves $1,518 in taxes (0.46 × $3,300), so there is left for equity holders $13,682 − $3,300 + $1,518 = $11,900. On the equity holders' investment of $70,000, a return of $11,900 represents 17 percent, exactly their required rate.

We find that if the investment has a return exactly equal to the *WARR* (13.682 percent in this case), it will exactly compensate all the suppliers of capital at their

---

[5] One exception is rate setting in utility companies. Utility regulatory commissions typically do consider flotation costs in connection with equity obtained through stock issues. Flotation costs are treated in Appendix 10A, which follows this chapter.

Table 10–6
Compensation of Capital Suppliers for a Hypothetical Investment

Operating cash flow	$13,682
minus	
Interest to debt holders	− 3,300
plus	
Interest tax shield	+ 1,518
equals	
Return available for equity holders	$11,900
Return to debt holders	$3,300/30,000 = 11 percent
Return to equity holders	$11,900/70,000 = 17 percent

respective required rates. Therefore, we can use the weighted-average required return as a target, either as the discount rate in calculating net present value or as the rate to beat in calculating internal rate of return. If the expected *IRR* exceeds the *WARR*, we would anticipate—if things work out as planned—that all suppliers of capital can be repaid at their required returns, with some left over. This excess normally accrues to the benefit of the equity holders. If the expected *IRR* falls short of the *WARR*, the project return is inadequate and someone—most likely the equity holders—will come up short because the project will have failed the economic test.

Now we can see more clearly why in Chapter 9 we included only operating flows in the project's cash-flow schedule: we incorporate financing requirements in the return target and evaluate the project to see whether it returns enough to compensate suppliers of funds.

> **The appropriate return target for evaluating projects of average risk is the weighted-average required return *(WARR)* on the firm's securities.**

What do we mean by *average-risk* projects? We mean projects whose risk is approximately equal to the overall risk of the firm—that is, projects at about the middle of the risk spectrum considering all of the firm's investments. Because the *WARR* represents the market required return on the firm as it now exists, it is appropriate for the current overall risk of the firm and is, thus, appropriate only for projects that have this same level of risk. Projects that are more risky than average should have a higher required return, and less risky projects should have a lower required return. Measuring risk and dealing with risk differences are difficult problems that we will defer to the next chapter. In this chapter, we will consider only projects of average risk. For average-risk projects, the *WARR* is the appropriate target.

Financing Mix and the Weights Used in Calculating the *WARR*

As stated earlier, theory suggests the use of market-value weights in calculating W_d and W_e to reflect the fact that it is the market value of the firm that managers are attempting to maximize. In addition, the required returns of shareholders and bond-holders are based on the market values of their claims on the company. Because market values of stock and debt can vary widely, however, managers in practice often set target ratios for financing that they monitor using book values. For example, management may have a target debt-to-equity ratio of 2. This ratio indicates that one third of funds would be raised by equity and two thirds by debt—that is, $W_e = 1/3$ and $W_d = 2/3$—and management would use its book-value debt-to-equity ratio to see if its financing were deviating from its target ratio. When new funds are raised, the market values of debt and equity funds obtained are often approximately equal to book values, so at least at the margin, for additional funding, book-value weights may represent how funds are being raised to finance projects. We must recognize that the use of book-value weights is only a pragmatic way to apply concepts based on market values and is one of the problems of attempting to apply theory in an imperfect world.

Note that the weights to be used in calculating *WARR* are long-run weights to reflect the mix of financing over a number of years. At any one time, the company may have just raised money by borrowing—it is understood that at some time additional equity financing will be used to keep the long-run mix of debt and equity in line with the weights W_e and W_d. (Choosing the appropriate mix of financing is a topic we will discuss in Part Five.)

THE COST OF CAPITAL

The **cost of capital**—is
another name for the
required rate of return.

Before we go further, we need to say a bit more about terminology. We have used the terms *return target* and *required return* to describe the minimum acceptable expected rate of return on a project. This concept is also referred to in financial circles as—the **cost of capital**. By now you may wonder why there are so many names for the same thing. Is it just a conspiracy against students? Not really, the different terms each emphasize a different aspect of the concept.

The cost of capital is the rate of return required by those who supply the capital. It is defined in the same way as the cost of anything else. If $0.50 is the price of a cup of coffee, then $0.50 is the amount required by the restauranteur in exchange for the coffee. Similarly, if 15 percent per year is the cost of capital to a firm, those with the capital are saying they require a return of 15 percent per year for the use of the capital. They set this requirement because, presumably, 15 percent is the rate they can earn elsewhere on other investments of comparable risk.

The term *cost of capital* was first used in connection with regulated industries, such as electric and gas utilities and telephone companies. In setting the rates (prices) that such companies are allowed to charge the public for services, the regulatory authorities are required by law to allow the company to cover its operating costs plus a "fair" rate of return on its invested capital. Although the original legislation was not explicit about how a fair rate should be defined, especially for equity capital, judicial decisions and regulatory practice provided some guidance. A fair rate should be comparable to rates earned in those unregulated sectors that have risks comparable to those of the regulated utility. The rate should be high enough to attract sufficient new capital for the utility to provide the services required by the public. In the rate-setting process, capital was an input, just as were labor, land, and materials, and was assigned a cost, just as the other inputs were. Out of this process emerged the term *cost of capital*.

The **weighted-average cost of capital** *(WACC)*—is another name for the *weighted-average required return (WARR)*.

The *cost of equity capital* is the required return on equity, K_e, and the *cost of debt capital* is the required return on debt, K_d. The **weighted-average cost of capital (WACC)** is simply the weighted average of K_e and K_d. Because interest is tax-deductible, on an after-tax basis, the weighted-average cost of capital is simply the weighted average of K_e and K_d multiplied by $(1 - T)$, and is equal to the *WARR, K_w*. The *WACC* and the *WARR* are, thus, one and the same—two labels for the same thing.

The terms *required rate of return* and *cost of capital* can be used interchangeably, provided one is careful. One difficulty with the term *cost of capital* is that it may imply to the unwary that there is some cost (rate) at which capital can be raised, and that this rate is independent of the way the capital is to be used. Such a view is incorrect. The capital being employed is provided by lenders and investors who expect management, acting as agent on their behalf, to take into account their opportunities to invest the capital elsewhere. Because suppliers of capital are risk-averse, the cost of capital depends on the way it is to be used—that is, on the riskiness of the investments it is to finance. It is important to remember that the *cost of capital*, when applied to investment decisions, is a marginal cost. It must reflect the costs of funds for the new investment proposal under consideration. The more risky is the investment, the higher must be the cost of capital.

While the term *cost of capital* is useful and widely used, it has the potential for confusion. To avoid this confusion and to emphasize the link between the required rate of return and investment risk, we will use the term *required rate of return* throughout this book.

APPLICATIONS OF TARGET RATES

The **yield to maturity**—is the internal rate of return that equates the price of a bond (or debt instrument) to the present value of the expected future cash benefits of owning the bond (or debt instrument); also known as the *required return on debt*.

A **capital gain**—is a gain that results from the increase in the value of an asset, or the difference between the purchase price and the sale price.

How do we determine the return expected by the market on a firm's equity and debt? For debt, the required return is the market rate of interest on new debt. For example, in the case of bonds, K_d is the **yield to maturity** the company would have to pay if it issued new debt selling it at face value.

Unfortunately, we can not directly observe a comparable figure for equity for two reasons: first, equity is not a contractual claim as debt is; second, equity has no maturity. Knowing the maturity of a bond, we can compute its yield to maturity, defined as the internal rate of return of an investment in the bond.

To make a comparable computation for equity requires that we make some assumptions. The return on an equity investment normally has two components, a dividend component and a capital-gain component. The **capital gain** is the difference between what we pay for the stock and what we sell it for. We know what the current dividend is, but we do not know what the capital gain is going to be. So, if we want to calculate an expected return on equity, we must assume sale of the stock at some future date and price.

Looking Ahead: The Required Returns on Equity

In principle, what we desire is the required return of equity owners in the firm. Unfortunately, it is not feasible to ask the shareholders directly, so we must infer such a required return. One method of doing so is to try to find what return shareholders seem

Table 10–7
Expected Dividends for Franklin Corporation, 1987–1991

	Dividend Expected at Year End (dollars per share)
1987	0.50
1988	0.75
1989	0.75
1990	0.75
1991	0.90

to expect given the current market price of the company's stock. If the market price is set in competitive financial markets, this expected return should be equal to the required return of shareholders. For example, if expected return exceeded required return, there would be increased demand for the stock, driving its price up and its expected return down. The process would continue until expected return and required return were equal.

Fortunately, the materials we covered in Chapters 3, 4, and 5 provide exactly the tools to calculate such a required return, K_e. One approach to measuring K_e is the dividend-valuation model explained in Chapter 4. This model says that at time 0 the current share price (P_0) is the present value of expected future dividends (D_t) and of the proceeds from the sale of the stock at a price (P_n) at some future date (n). Equation (1) is identical to Equation (2) in Chapter 4.

The Dividend-Valuation Model

The present value, P_0, of a share of stock can be calculated as

$$P_0 = \left[\sum_{t=1}^{n} \frac{D_t}{(1 + K_e)^t} \right] + \frac{P_n}{(1 + K_e)^n} \tag{1}$$

where D_t = dividend expected in period t, K_e = the rate of return required by the market on the firm's stock, and P_n = the price at which the share is expected to be sold at the end of the final period.

Note that the shareholders' required rate of return, K_e, is perfectly analogous to the yield to maturity on a bond. That is, K_e equates the price of the stock to the present value of the expected future cash benefits of owning the stock. If we could observe the current market price, estimate shareholder expectations of dividends for n periods, and estimate shareholders' expectation of the price at which the stock will sell, we could solve for K_e in Equation (1)—the shareholders' required return. K_e is simply an internal rate of return. Of course, the difficulty is estimating future dividends and share price.

**Sample Problem
10–2**

Calculating Shareholder Required Return for Franklin Corporation

Shareholders in Franklin Corporation expect dividends to grow in the next five years as shown in Table 10–7. In addition, at the end of the five years, Franklin stock is expected to have a price equal to 10 times earnings per share, which are then expected to be $1.15 (that is, Franklin will have a price/earnings (PE) ratio of 10). What is the shareholders' required rate of return on Franklin's stock if the current market price (year-end 1986) is $6.50?

Solution

The price in 1991, P_n, is expected to be $10 \times \$1.15 = \$11.50$, and the current price, P_0, is $6.50 Using these figures and the expected dividends in Table 10–7, we can substitute into Equation (1) and solve for K_e by trial and error (just as we did to find internal rates of return in Chapter 9):

$$\$6.50 = \frac{0.50}{(1 + K_e)} + \frac{0.75}{(1 + K_e)^2} + \frac{0.75}{(1 + K_e)^3}$$

$$+ \frac{0.75}{(1 + K_e)^4} + \frac{0.90}{(1 + K_e)^5} + \frac{11.50}{(1 + K_e)^5}$$

We find K_e to be 20.9 percent. ≡lıl╒

Sometimes the use of Equation (1) can be simplified if we expect dividends to grow at a constant rate, g, indefinitely. As we saw in Equations (4) and (5) of Chapter 4, in this constant-growth case, we can rewrite Equation (1) as shown in Equation (2).

The Dividend-Growth Model

The present value of a share of stock, assuming the dividend will grow at a constant rate, g, can be calculated as

$$P_0 = \frac{D_1}{K_e - g}.$$

The capitalization rate that equates the present value of a share of stock and the streams of all future benefits expected, assuming that the dividend will grow at a constant rate, can be calculated as

$$K_e = \frac{D_1}{P_0} + g \tag{2}$$

That is, the required return of equity holders can be thought of as a given dividend rate, D_1/P_0, plus a growth rate, g.

Sample Problem 10–3

Calculating Shareholder Required Return for Jefferson Company

Jefferson Company just paid its dividend of $1.00 per common share, each share of which sells for $10.00. Jefferson dividends per share are expected to grow at 12 percent per year indefinitely. What is the required rate of return on Jefferson Stock?

Solution

Before solving this problem, we must note that applying Equation (2) requires an estimate of D_1—the dividend expected to be paid one year hence. In this example, dividends are expected to grow at 12 percent annually, so $D_1 = \$1.00(1 + 0.12) = \$1.12$. Now using Equation (2), we can solve for K_e as $\$1.12/\$10.00 + 0.12 = 0.232$. Jefferson stockholders appear to have a required return of more than 23 percent. Investing in Jefferson Company is, thus. somewhat more risky than investing in Franklin Corporation in Sample Problem 10–2. ≡▮F

The primary difficulty in using Equation (2) is obtaining an estimate of g because this estimate should reflect market expectations of future performance. One source of such expectations are financial analysts' forecasts of corporate earnings and dividend performance. Financial analysts working for investment advisory services, such as Value Line, Merrill Lynch, and Goldman, regularly publish their own estimates of future corporate performance. In recent years, investor interest in such forecasts has lead to services that collect and publish such forecasts from hundreds of analysts on thousands of stocks. For example, IBES (Institutional Broker's Estimate System) provides clients with earnings-per-share estimates made by about 2,000 individual analysts from 100 brokerage firms on more than 2,000 corporations. Zacks provides a similar service. This sort of data allows one to estimate for a particular stock the type of average-growth figure that Equation (2) calls for. These data reflect the expectations of market participants about the future.[6]

Using the forecasts of financial analysts goes a long way in reducing the problems of applying the dividend-valuation model. Such forecasts are not, however, foolproof. In practice, growth estimates are typically available for horizons of about five years. People just don't often look into their crystal balls for longer periods. In addition, at least currently, the organized collections of analyst data cover earnings rather than dividend-growth forecasts. While these features do not exactly fit the requirements of the dividend-valuation model, for large groups of stocks they may not cause too many difficulties. In the long run, dividend growth is dependent on earnings growth. Furthermore, without compelling evidence to the contrary, there is no reason to believe that investors somehow feel that growth will dramatically change after five years. The virtue of analyst forecasts is that they are direct measures of the type of expectations that determine value in markets.

Table 10–8 shows the results of using an average of analysts' forecasts to estimate shareholder required returns and risk premia for stocks in general as proxied by the

---

[6]IBES is a product of Lynch, Jones and Ryan, a major brokerage firm. In recent years, a growing body of research has shown that market prices are related to analyst forecasts, thus strengthening the case for their use. For example, Carleton and Vander Weide (1985) show that IBES growth forecasts are superior to more than 40 variations of historical growth rates in explaining companies' price/earnings ratios. For a discussion of the use of analysts' forecasts in estimating required returns, see R. Harris, "Using Analysts' Growth Forecasts To Estimate Shareholder Required Returns," *Financial Management,* Spring 1986.

Table 10–8

Expected Required Returns and Risk Premia for Standard and Poor's (S&P) 500 Stocks, 1982–1984

Year	Quarter	Government Bond Yield (percent) (1)	S&P 500 Required Return (percent) (2)	S&P 500 Risk Premium (percent) (3) = (2) − (1)
1982	1	14.27	20.81	6.54
1982	2	13.74	20.68	6.94
1982	3	12.94	20.23	7.29
1982	4	10.72	18.58	7.86
1982 average		**12.92**	**20.08**	**7.16**
1983	1	10.87	18.07	7.20
1983	2	10.80	17.76	6.96
1983	3	11.79	17.90	6.11
1983	4	11.90	17.81	5.91
1983 average		**11.34**	**17.88**	**6.54**
1984	1	12.09	17.22	5.13
1984	2	13.21	17.42	4.21
1984	3	12.83	17.34	4.51
1984	4	11.78	17.05	5.27
1984 average		**12.48**	**17.26**	**4.78**
Average 1982–1984		**12.25**	**18.41**	**6.16**

Note: Government bond yield is the yield to maturity on U.S. Treasury obligations with a 20-year constant maturity. Required return is estimated using equation (2) of the text as the sum of dividend yield plus expected growth where expected growth is average of analysts' growth forecast (5-year earnings per share) from Institutional Brokers' Estimate System. Standard & Poors figures are market-value weighted averages of required returns for all dividend-paying stocks in the S&P 500. Quarterly values are averages of monthly figures.

Source: R. Harris, "Using Analysts' Growth Forecasts To Estimate Shareholder Required Returns," *Financial Management,* Spring 1986.

Standard & Poors 500 stock index, a widely followed index of stock performance in the United States. As the estimates show, shareholders do require a risk premium over returns on safer government bonds. For the 1982–84 period, the estimated risk premium has averaged slightly more than 6 percent. This risk premium also appears to change over time with changing conditions in financial markets. The figures in Table 10–8 are averages for the stock market. As such, they average together data for hundreds of stocks combining both low- and high-growth securities. At the same time, the data reflect the average risk of equity investments. For an individual stock, risks may well differ from average and as a result shareholder required returns will differ from average. In such a case, the dividend-valuation model could be applied to the individual stock or to a select group of stocks deemed to be of comparable risk. The difficulty when working with smaller groups of stocks is that the simplified version of the dividend-valuation model given in Equation (2) may not fit the pattern of expected growth. In such cases, the use of Equation (1) is appropriate.

Table 10–9
Past Returns in U.S. Financial Markets

Panel A: Basic Series, Investment Total Annual Returns,* 1926–1981

Series	Arithmetic Mean (percent)
1. Common stocks	11.4
2. Long-term corporate bonds	3.7
3. Long-term government bonds	3.1
4. U.S. treasury bills	3.1
5. Inflation	3.1

Panel B. Annual Risk Premia for Common Stocks

Series	Arithmetic Mean (percent)
6. Common stocks compared to long-term corporate bonds	7.7
7. Common stocks compared to long-term U.S. government bonds	8.3
8. Common stocks compared to U.S. Treasury bills	8.3

Source: R. Ibbotson and R. A. Sinquefield, *Stocks, Bonds, Bills and Inflation: The Past and the Future.* The Financial Analysts Research Foundation (1982).

In practice, obtaining estimates of dividend-growth rates or future share prices is quite difficult. Unfortunately, the process is still a very imprecise one. As companies and the economy change, dividend and share price expectations change. We should remember that estimates of K_e are only that—estimates. The result of using any model must be checked to see if it is at all reasonable. One way to check the reasonableness of estimated equity required returns is to compare them to similar estimates for stocks believed to be of similar risk. In efficient financial markets, investments of comparable risk will have similar required rates of return. Another check of reasonableness is to examine the past history of returns on financial securities.

Looking Back: Historical Data

To help gain some sense of the reasonableness of our calculated K_e, we can look back in time to see past returns on equity securities and past risk premia that equities have provided over and above returns on debt. While there is no assurance that future returns are expected to be like returns in the past, historical perspective provides at least something of a benchmark.

Table 10–9 presents the results of one study covering more than 50 years of U.S. financial history. Panel A shows the arithmetic mean (the average) of the annual returns over the 1926–1981 period. The returns on common stocks include both dividends and capital gains—that is, increases or decreases in the price of stocks.

Panel B shows the historical-average market risk premium on corporate equities—that is, the premium return to equities over and above rates of return on various forms of debt. From row (6), we see that stocks have on average returned about 7.7 percent more than bonds of the same firms. In row (7), we see that stocks have returned 8.3 percent more than long-term U.S. government bonds. Finally, in row (8) we see the risk premium on stocks relative to short-term Treasury bills also has been around 8.3 percent.

What do these data on historical returns tell us? They tell us that, on average, the market requires a higher return on equity than it does on bonds. They also tell us how large that premium has been for one long period in U.S. financial history.

Do these results necessarily mean that these risk premia will be demanded in the future? Unfortunately, the answer to that question involves predictions about which we can at best speculate—only time will tell. We can, however, use these past data as another way to estimate a required return on equity and to compare it to results we might obtain using, for example, a dividend-growth model.

To use these results for estimating required returns, we must assume that the average risk premia actually earned over very long periods in the past represent a good measure of the normal risk premia expected by investors. This assumption represents a "leap of faith," but making estimates of future dividends and growth rates in using a dividend-growth model are also such leaps. To obtain information for use in making decisions, we must often pay the price of adopting rather strong assumptions.

The **risk-premium approach**—bases estimates of required returns on risk-premium data.

To illustrate how we might use this **risk-premium approach** to estimating required returns, let us focus on calculating the required return on a typical common stock using the long-term U.S. government bond rate to gauge a risk premium. We can make our estimate of the market required return on an average common stock as shown in Equation (3).

The market required return on an average common stock can be estimated as

$$K_e = i + \text{Risk premium} \qquad (3)$$

where i = the current market required return on long-term government bonds.

We use the long-term U.S. government rate in Equation (3) because government bonds are one of the safest investments one can make over a relatively long time period. Incorporating the historical risk premium of 8.3 percent from row (7) of Table 10–9, Equation (3) becomes

$$K_e = i + 8.3 \text{ percent.}$$

That is, looking ahead, we could assume that the market requires a return on common stocks of average risk 8.3 percent higher than the current yield to maturity on U.S. government bonds. To illustrate, if at a particular time government bonds were yielding 10 percent, then one could say that the market required return on common stocks of average risk at that time was 18.3 percent. Appendix 10B, which follows this chapter, discusses how this risk-premium approach might be applied to account for differences in the riskiness of stocks.

We mentioned earlier that return targets must include an inflation premium. By using the government-bond rate, i, as the base for calculating K_e, we *automatically* include the market inflation premium because i includes the market's consensus judgment regarding the appropriate inflation premium. A government-bond rate of, say, 10 percent already includes an inflation premium. So when we add the risk premium to i to get K_e, an inflation premium has been built into K_e. To a large extent, this fact explains why current required returns on equity (in an inflationary environment) are much higher than the historical-average returns in row (1) of Table 10–9.

Adjusting for Time Horizon

There is, however, at least one further catch in our calculation of K_e. Investment projects in firms cover periods longer than one year—typically, 5 to 15 years or sometimes more. Furthermore, yields to maturity on long-term government bonds represent returns over a reasonably long time horizon. To be correct, as a basis for return targets on investment projects in firms, we need market returns measured over comparable time periods. For a project with a 10-year life, for example, we need a market return measured over 10 years.

If returns on stocks are measured and averaged over periods longer than one year, the results are returns and risk premia lower than those shown in Table 10–9. For example, the arithmetic-average annual return figure of stocks is given as 11.4 percent in Table 10–9 and is calculated by taking the 56 individual returns for the period 1926–81, adding them up, and dividing by 56. From this 11.4 percent figure, we derived our 8.3 percent risk premium. Suppose, however, we wanted to know what compound rate of return an investor in stocks actually earned over the entire 56-year period.

The **compound annual return**,—or *geometric-average return*, for a specific time period is calculated by multiplying together annual returns and applying discounted-cash-flow techniques.

Let us assume you could have invested $1 in 1926 and bought some of all the common stocks that went into the figuring of the 11.4 percent average annual return. Of course, this example is only hypothetical because with $1 you would have been buying miniscule fractions of shares. If you allowed your $1 to stay in stocks and cashed in on your investment in 1981, you would have about $131. This $131 figure is the result of multiplying together the actual annual returns earned for the 56-year period 1926–1981. Using the mathematics of discounted cash flow, we could calculate the **compound annual return,** also called the *geometric-average return, R,* as

$$\$1(1 + R)^{56} = \$131$$

$$(1 + R)^{56} = 131$$

$$R = 0.091 = 9.1 \text{ percent}$$

This 9.1 percent annual return on common stock[7] is substantially less than the

---

[7] See R. Ibbotson and R. A. Sinquefield, *Stocks, Bonds, Bills, and Inflation*, The Financial Analysts Research Foundation, 1982, for specific numbers used in the calculations. The figure of 9.1 percent is the geometric average of stock returns over the 1926–1981 period and can also be figured by multiplying the individual figures (1 + rate of return) together and taking the 56th root. The geometric average is less than the arithmetic average unless returns are the same in each year. Furthermore, the geometric average tends to be further away from the arithmetic average the more variability there is in the actual returns.

arithmetic average of 11.4 percent because of the nature of compounding when annual returns fluctuate up and down. The same is true for long-term government bonds. Over the 56-year period, the compound return on such bonds was 3.0 percent, or slightly less than the arithmetic-average return of 3.1 percent reported in Table 10–9.

An example will illustrate the difference between a *geometric average* and an **arithmetic average.** Suppose you had $100 to invest for two years. In the first year, you lost $50 (a -50 percent return on your $100), and in the second year you gained $50 (a 100 percent return on the $50 you had at the end of the first year). At the end of two years, you had the same $100 you started with. What was your annual rate of return? It was 0 percent—you neither gained nor lost. But let's see what the arithmetic and geometric averages are. The arithmetic average would be the simple average of the rates of return in the two years and is equal to $(-0.50 + 1.00)/2 = 0.25$, or 25 percent. But we know that this rate of return is wrong—you didn't earn a cent, much less 25 percent per year. On the other hand, we can calculate the geometric average as the rate, R, such that $\$100(1 + R)^2 = \$100$. When we solve for R, we find that $R = 0$, so the geometric-average return shows our true rate of return over the entire two-year period.

On balance then, the risk premium measured over a very long horizon—56 years in this case—is only about 6.1 percent (9.1 percent on stocks versus 3.0 percent on U.S. government bonds), which is substantially less than the 8.3 percent figure measured for a single year.[8] For investments that may have a time horizon of 5 to 15 years, the risk premium has been somewhere between 8.3 percent and 6.1 percent.

Remember that we have already made substantial leaps of faith in assuming that past risk premia are useful guides to estimating a forward-looking risk premium, so we can't become artificially precise about plugging in numbers for our risk premia. We can say that historical risk premia on average stocks have been around 6.1 percent to 8.3 percent, depending upon the time horizon involved. As a workable compromise, let us take an average of these two figures—7.2 percent. We cannot be much more precise than this.[9]

Using a figure of 7.2 percent as the estimated risk premium on average-risk equity investment over multiyear periods, we can apply Equation (3) to calculate a required return as

$$K_e = i + 7.2 \text{ percent.}$$

For stocks of other than average risk we would need to adjust this risk premium. Chapter 5 discussed one way to do this. We will return to risk adjustments in the next chapter.

---

[8]Technically, one could use the mathematics of compounding to calculate the risk premium as

$$(1 + rp)^{56} = \frac{(1 + 0.091)^{56}}{(1 + 0.03)^{56}},$$

or $rp = 5.9$ percent. The difference between the 6.1 percent calculated in the text and the 5.9 percent calculated here is not large enough to affect any of our conclusions.

[9]More advanced financial theory might allow us to deal with risk premia in a different form where there could be a different risk premium for each cash flow depending on its distance in the future and its underlying risk. Unfortunately, developments in this area have as yet not proved useful for applied capital budgeting.

**Sample Problem
10–4**

Calculating a Required Return and Weighted-Average Required Return for Largo Enterprises

Largo Enterprises is currently reevaluating its return target for analyzing investment proposals. Largo has already decided that its financing will be done 25 percent by debt and 75 percent by equity. In recent conversations with an investment banker, Largo has determined it can issue new bonds with a yield to maturity of 16 percent, which is 1 percent above the present long-term government-bond rate of 15 percent. Largo management feels comfortable that their current dividend (expected to be $2 per share in 1987) can grow at 12 percent per year in the forseeable future. In addition, they are quite pleased with a recent analyst forecast that Largo stock will increase in price from its current level of $20 (year-end 1986) to $50 in 1991. Largo management feels that all of these assumptions are consistent with shareholders' expectations and are in keeping with Largo's reputation as an aggressive but sound company. Largo is quite proud that, despite its success, its stock is viewed as no more risky than average by the financial community. Largo pays taxes at a rate of 46 percent. What is an appropriate figure to use for the required return, K_e, of Largo's shareholders? What is Largo's weighted-average required return?

Solution

To estimate K_e, we can apply three methods. We can (A) use the dividend-valuation model for a finite horizon, (B) use the dividend-valuation model assuming constant growth of dividends, and (C) use the historical risk premium on stocks.

A. The data we need to apply the dividend-valuation model are summarized in Table 10–10. Using equation (1), we can calculate

$$\$20.00 = \frac{2.00}{(1 + K_e)} + \frac{2.24}{(1 + K_e)^2} + \frac{2.51}{(1 + K_e)^3}$$

$$+ \frac{2.81}{(1 + K_e)^4} + \frac{3.15}{(1 + K_e)^5} + \frac{\$50.00}{(1 + K_e)^5}$$

Solving for K_e by trial and error, we find that K_e = 29 to 30 percent.

B. Applying the dividend-growth model, we can use Equation (2) to calculate K_e as

$$K_e = \frac{2.00}{20.00} + 0.12$$

$$= 0.22 = 22 \text{ percent.}$$

C. Using the historical risk premium, we can calculate K_e as

$$K_e = i + 7.2 \text{ percent}$$

$$= 15 \text{ percent} + 7.2 \text{ percent}$$

$$= 22.2 \text{ percent.}$$

Table 10–10
Expected Year-End Prices and Dividends for Largo Enterprises, 1986–1991

Year	Price at Year End	Dividend Expected at Year End Assuming Growth at 12 Percent
1986	$20.00	
1987		$2.00
1988		$2.24
1989		$2.51
1990		$2.81
1991	$50.00	$3.15

The three calculations of K_e all provide different answers. This inconsistency should not be surprising given the type of estimates and assumptions we have to make to use these models. At this stage, the problem of the financial manager is to make a reasonable judgment about K_e based on these three calculations and any other relevant information. Is 30 percent appropriate for K_e, or is a figure near 22 percent more appropriate? Given the data in the problem, a required return in the 22–23 percent range appears more appropriate. This figure is consistent with dividend-growth expectations and fits fairly well with the historical risk premium for average-risk common stocks. Does this mean the dividend-valuation model for a finite period is wrong? No, it simply means that in this case the estimates used may be in error. The $50 stock price for 1991 may just be too high. At a minimum, getting different answers using the different techniques should motivate managers to reevalaute their assumptions about the values to put into the models. In fact, most decisions that financial managers must make are judgment calls, and there is no way to make things neat and precise when in fact the world is an uncertain and sometimes ornery place.

If we adopt K_e = 22 percent as a working assumption, we can now calculate the weighted-average required return as

$$WARR = 0.75K_e + 0.25K_d(1 - 0.46)$$

$$= 0.75(0.22) + 0.25(0.16)(1 - 0.46)$$

$$= 0.187 = 18.7 \text{ percent.}$$

These figures, thus, suggest that Largo should use a return target of 18.7 percent on its average-risk investments. Note, however, the sorts of difficult judgments we must make in coming up with such a figure. ≡ⅢϜ

In practice, it is prudent to try a number of different techniques in estimating K_e, as we have done here. As Sample Problem 10–4 showed, estimating a required return is not a "black box" exercise. The financial manager must use judgment in the process.

Finance in Practice 10–2

How the Market Required Return Changes Over Time

This chapter has looked at financial market data. We used these data as the basis for deriving required rates of return on a firm's securities and also on capital-investment projects.

What we found is that all mar- ket required rates of return are scaled upward from the U.S. government bond rate as a base. The rates on government bonds are the base rate because they are almost default-free and, hence, represent the least-risk investment for any given maturity.

Suppose the government-bond rate changes over time. Do market required rates change also? The government bond rate *does* change over time, as do other market rates, including required rates on firms' stocks and bonds as well as return targets for capital-investment projects, as the data in the accompanying table show.

Earlier in the chapter, we calculated the weighted-average required return for Largo Enterprises as 18.7 percent. That calculation was based on required returns when the government-bond rate was 15 percent. Suppose the government rate was 8 percent instead, as it was in 1975. Had we calculated Largo's *WARR* at that time, following the procedure we used before, we would have obtained a very different answer. For example, if Largo could borrow at 1 percent above the government rate of 8 percent, its required return on debt (K_d) would be 9 percent. Requirements of equity holders would also be different. Using the historical-risk-premium approach, we would obtain a required return on equity (K_e) of 8 percent + 7.2 percent = 15.2 percent. In an environment of 8 percent government-bond rates, we would have expected stock prices and expected-

Sample Problem 10–5

Calculating the Weighted-Average Required Return for American Foods

Calculate the weighted-average required return for American Foods, Inc., the company described in Chapter 9. Balance-sheet data are given in Table 10–11.

Solution

We noted earlier in this chapter that, in calculating the *WARR*, we consider only those sources of financing on which a return actually must be paid. In the case of American Foods, such sources would include bank debt, preferred stock, long-term debt, and common stock. We would exclude from the calculation accounts payable and accruals on grounds that the firm does not have to pay an explicit return on these sources. (In fact, Appendix 9B showed that our cash flows would already be adjusted to reflect accounts payable and accruals through their effects on net working capital. Because they are handled in the cash flows, they do not need to be incorporated in our required return.) We can lump common stock and retained earnings together because both represent common stockholders' equity. The relevant sources and their proportions are shown in Table 10–12.

We can now calculate the *WARR* by following the five steps outlined below.

1. First, we must determine the target financing mix. American Foods management tells us that they plan to maintain the current capital structure in the future, so the

	Interest Rate of Long-Term U.S. Government Bonds (percent)	Interest Rate of Corporate AAA Bonds (percent)
1962	4.0	4.3
1972	6.0	7.2
1975	8.0	8.7
Feb. 1980	12.2	13.0
Aug. 1981	14.0	15.0
Nov. 1982	10.3	11.7
June 1983	11.0	11.7
June 1984	13.3	13.5
June 1985	10.7	11.1

dividend-growth rates to have adjusted, so that the use of dividend-growth models would produce a similar estimate (15 percent to 16 percent) of K_e. We would have calculated WARR to be 12.6 percent rather than 18.7 percent. (For simplicity, assume no changes in Largo's capital structure or tax rates.) The 7-percentage-point reduction in the government-bond rate (from 15 percent to 8 percent) reduced the WARR by more than 6 percent. In general, the drop in WARR is going to be less than the drop in government rates because of the tax deductibility of interest. If Largo's WARR had been figured in 1962 when the government-bond rate was 4 percent, the result would have been a WARR of around 9 percent.

So we see that market required rates of return rise and fall over time as conditions in the financial markets change—which is as it should be. Financial-market rates reflect investors' expectations about future inflation, risk, and other market conditions. When investors expect high inflation, they demand a high inflation premium to compensate for the loss of purchasing power in future returns. Managers, in setting return targets for use in evaluating capital-investment projects, must take those expectations into account.

Source: Table data from Federal Reserve Bank of St. Louis.

financing proportions in Table 10–12 are the targets that we use for weights in calculating the WARR.

2. Next, we must determine the required return on each financing component. Beginning with K_e, American Foods management estimates that dividends per share will be $4.20 next year and will grow at about 8 percent annually indefinitely. Management feels these figures are appropriately reflected in the current stock price of $50 per share. Using the dividend-growth model, we can estimate K_e as

$$K_e = \frac{\$4.20}{\$50.00} + 0.08 = 0.164 = 16.4 \text{ percent.}$$

In this example, we are using one technique—the dividend-growth model—of estimating K_e. In practice, other methods might also be used.

3. The interest rate on the long-term debt of American Foods currently is 10.7 percent. Preferred stock is *junior* to bonds, meaning that claims of bondholders come before those of preferred shareholders in the event of trouble. (Chapter 12 will discuss preferred stock in more detail.) So the preferred stock of a firm is more risky than its bonds and has a higher required return. The preferred stock of Amer-

Table 10–11

Balance Sheet, American Foods, Inc.

Category	Amount (thousands of dollars)
Cash	3,000
Accounts receivable	9,000
Inventories	13,000
Fixed assets	35,000
Total assets	60,000
Accounts payable	6,000
Accruals	4,000
Notes payable (bank)	5,000
Long-term debt	10,000
Preferred stock	5,000
Common stock	10,000
Retained earnings	20,000
Total liabilities and equity	60,000

ican Foods currently is yielding 11.5 percent, and management estimates that the interest rate on bank debt will average 12.0 percent. These required returns and their weights are summarized in Table 10–12.

4. We know that interest on bank loans and on long-term debt is tax deductible, so we must calculate their after-tax equivalents. Dividends on preferred and common stock are not tax deductible. The after-tax equivalents for required returns on loans and debt can be calculated as

$$\text{After-tax } K_l = K_l(1 - T) = 12.0 \ (1 - 0.46) = 6.5$$
$$\text{After-tax } K_d = K_d(1 - T) = 10.7 \ (1 - 0.46) = 5.8$$

Table 10–12

Financing Components' Required Rates, American Foods, Inc.

Source	Symbol	Amount (thousands of dollars)	Required Return (percent)	Weight
Bank debt	K_l	5,000	12.0	0.10
Long-term debt	K_d	10,000	10.7	0.20
Preferred stock	K_p	5,000	11.5	0.10
Common equity	K_e	30,000	16.4	0.60
Total sources		50,000		1.00

Table 10–13
Weighted-Average Required Return (WARR), American Foods, Inc.

Source	Symbol	Required Return (percent) (1)	Weight (2)	Weighted Required Return (percent) (3) = (1) × (2)
Bank debt	$K_i(1 - T)$	6.5	0.10	0.65
Long-term debt	$K_d(1 - T)$	5.8	0.20	1.16
Preferred stock	K_p	11.5	0.10	1.15
Common equity	K_e	16.4	0.60	9.84
			WARR = K_w =	12.80

5. Finally, we can calculate the *WARR* as shown in Table 10–13. The weighted-average required return for American Foods is 12.80 percent. This figure reflects the required returns of all the suppliers of capital to American Foods after adjusting for the tax deductibility of interest. ∃⫾⊩𝄘

Using Return Targets

Let us now tie our discussion back to that of Chapter 9 by asking ourselves what we do with the answer—the return target for an investment opportunity—once we have it. We can use it one of two basic ways: as the discount rate in a net present value *(NPV)* calculation or as the hurdle rate to which the project's internal rate of return *(IRR)* is compared. Sample Problem 10–6 illustrates the use of return targets with an example.

Sample Problem 10–6

Evaluating an Average-Risk Investment for Integrated Systems, Inc.

Integrated Systems, Inc. (ISI) is considering the possibility of expanding its production facilities for integrated-circuit boards, which are components used in the manufacturing of electronic equipment. The project involves expansion of an existing product, and management judges it to be of average risk compared to ISI's other projects. ISI follows a policy of financing with 35 percent long-term debt and 65 percent equity. The government-bond rate currently is 10 percent, and the yield to maturity of ISI's bonds currently outstanding is 11.2 percent. ISI estimates its cost of equity to be 18.76 percent, and the tax rate is 46 percent. Should the investment be undertaken?

Solution
Table 10–14 outlines the process for calculating the weighted-average required return for ISI. Rounding off the result in Table 10–14, we will take 14 percent as ISI's *WARR*. The project requires an immediate outlay of $350,000 and produces the cash flows shown in Table 10–15. Sales and profits from the product build in the early

Table 10–14

Calculating Integrated Systems' Weighted-Average Required Return (WARR)

	Required Return (percent) (1)	Weight (2)	Weighted Return (percent) (3) = (1) × (2)
Long-term debt, after taxes	6.05	0.35	2.12
Equity	18.76	0.65	12.19
			WARR = 14.31

Note: K_e = 18.76 percent; K_d = 11.2 percent; after-tax K_d = 11.2(1 − 0.46) = 6.05 percent

years, peak, and then begin to decline, reflecting the likelihood that new and better products will come along to replace this one. The cash inflow of $105,000 in year 10 reflects management's estimate of the salvage value of the plant and equipment in that year. The *NPV* calculation shown in Table 10–14 was calculated using ISI's *WARR* of 14 percent as the return target for discounting the cash flows.

We see the project has a negative *NPV* when evaluated at the company's *WARR* of 14 percent. Because *NPV* is negative at 14 percent, we know that the project's internal rate of return must lie below 14 percent, and in fact it turns out to be about 11.6 percent—well below the target. Thus, the project does not pass the economic test and cannot be said to constitute a wise use of capital funds. Unless there are compelling reasons for the project that are not reflected in the economic analysis, the project should be rejected. ∃⫿⊩

Using the *WARR* as a Target

In this chapter, we have developed an approach to calculate the weighted-average required return, and we have discussed its use in evaluating investment opportunities. We noted at several points that the *WARR* is the correct target for evaluating investment opportunities of average risk.[10]

Some firms use the *WARR* for evaluating all capital-investment projects. Such an approach is correct in principle only if all the firm's projects are equally risky—seldom the case in practice. Cost-reduction projects usually are subject to much less uncertainty than are new products and, hence, are much less risky. The introduction of Product 99 by American Foods, which we discussed in Chapter 9, is more risky than building a plant to produce parts or materials previously purchased outside. Cost savings in the latter case are less uncertain than are profits of Product 99.

---

[10]Approaches other than the weighted-average required return will be discussed in Chapter 11. For evaluating average-risk projects, the *WARR* has both theoretical and practical advantages over alternative methods and is the simplest to use. See D. R. Chambers, R. S. Harris, and J. J. Pringle, "Treatment of Financing Mix in Analyzing Investment Opportunities," *Financial Management,* Summer 1982, pp. 24–41.

Table 10–15

Net Present Value of Expansion Project at Integrated Systems, Inc.

Year	After-Tax Cash Flow (1)	Present-Value Factor at 14 Percent (2)	Present Value (3) = (1) × (2)
0	− $350,000	1.000	− $350,000
1	− 15,000	0.877	− 13,155
2	40,000	0.769	30,760
3	60,000	0.675	40,500
4	85,000	0.592	50,320
5	95,000	0.519	49,305
6	95,000	0.456	43,320
7	80,000	0.400	32,000
8	75,000	0.351	26,325
9	70,000	0.308	21,560
10	105,000	0.270	28,350

Net present value at 14 percent =   − $ 40,715

Most firms face investment opportunities that vary across the risk spectrum, and in such cases, the use of the *WARR* as a target for all projects is not correct theoretically. One might defend the use of the *WARR* as a single target for all projects on grounds that all projects should return at least the firm average. This argument may sound plausible, but it is not correct because suppliers of capital are risk-averse and demand higher rates of return for greater risk. Investors might expect a weighted-average return of, say, 15 percent on the securities of a given firm. But on funds for a particular project that has a risk greater than the firm's average risk, they would expect a higher return.

To set different targets for individual projects depending on their risk, however, brings us face to face with a problem of great difficulty: measuring risk *quantitatively* is not just being able to say that Project A is more risky than Project B, but *how much* more risky. As we will see in Chapter 11, measuring risk quantitatively is extremely difficult, and even when carefully done, the results may not always be credible to managers and investors.

Given the difficulty of measuring risk quantitatively, some firms adopt the approach of using the same target for all projects, and in effect treat all projects as equally risky. The single target most often used is the target appropriate for an average-risk project, the *WARR*. While not strictly correct in principle, this approach is a pragmatic and workable one that recognizes the great difficulty of measuring risk accurately. While many firms use the *WARR* as a general-purpose target, others go on to refine this basic approach by setting targets for individual projects or categories of projects. We will discuss these refinements in the next chapter.

Finance in Practice 10–3

Required Returns, Capital
Spending, and the Economy

Table A

	1982 Capital Spending Plans as a Percentage Change from 1981	
	November 1981	*March 1982*
All business	**9.6**	**6.9**
Mining	24.8	−3.1
Railroads	23.4	3.1
Rubber	21.2	11.5
Food and beverages	20.6	2.7
Nonferrous metals	18.2	−4.6
Petroleum	16.8	8.2
Communications and other	12.2	7.8
Electrical machinery	10.4	6.2
Autos, trucks and parts	10.2	2.6
Gas utilities	8.7	−3.5
Textiles	2.5	−0.9

In the early spring of 1982, many firms were cutting back on their capital-spending plans, much to the disappointment of the Reagan Administration and of others concerned about the economy. A survey of capital-spending plans of major business firms conducted by McGraw-Hill Inc. in November 1981 showed firms planning to increase their 1982 capital outlays by 9.6 percent over 1981. In March, 1982, a second survey found that plans had been cut back and now called for only a 6.9 percent increase over 1981. Once inflation was taken into account, the 6.9 percent increase projected for 1982 became hardly any increase at all. The accompanying Table A gives data for selected industry groups.

The Economic Recovery Act of 1981 had put in place substantial tax reductions for business on the premise that tax reductions would stimulate capital spending, yet just the opposite was taking place. Why? The answer is that business executives were expecting a weak economy in 1982. One executive stated that "It made sense to batten down the hatches and hold on to our cash." Said another: "Interest rates, excess capacity, and poor profits have more than offset the incentive provided by the tax bill."

Firms responded to the expectation of weak economic activity by cutting back capital expendi-

KEY CONCEPTS

1. Setting return targets is an important step in evaluating investment opportunities. Return targets should be set by management based on market required rates of return. These required rates of return can then be used in discounted-cash-flow analysis of the desirability of individual investment projects.

2. Required rates of return are opportunity rates that are determined in the financial markets by the competitive interactions of suppliers of funds. In effect, the required return of investors is the marginal cost of capital to the firm.

3. Management acts as the agent of shareholders in setting return targets.

4. Return targets must include both a risk premium and an inflation premium. The risk premium should depend on the risk of the incremental investment being made.

5. The weighted-average required return *(WARR)*, also called the *weighted-average cost of capital (WACC)*, is a weighted average of the return re-

Table B

Year	Expenditure for Nonresidential Plant and Equipment (billions of dollars)
1980	308.8
1981	352.2
1982	348.3
1983	352.9
1984	425.7

tures along with operating expenses. Halliburton Company, a Dallas-based supplier of oil-field equipment, planned to keep 1982 spending constant at the 1981 figure. Armco Steel Company delayed indefinitely plans to construct a new mill for $671 million. Champion International Corporation cut 1982 capital spending to $250 million from $600 million in 1981. Aggregate plant-and-equipment spending for the whole economy is given in the accompanying Table B.

Rather than increasing in response to the 1981 tax cuts, capital spending actually declined in 1982. As a percentage of gross national product (GNP), it declined in 1982 and again in 1983.

How can we interpret these reactions in light of financial theory? Our capital-budgeting model discussed in this and earlier chapters tells us to evaluate investment opportunities by discounting expected future cash flows to their present value using a market required return. What happens when the economy weakens or a recession begins? The answer is that estimates of future cash flows become lower. If a project that looked attractive in the fall of 1981 is reevaluated in the spring of 1982, and lower cash-flow estimates are the result, the project may no longer look attractive.

In 1981 and 1982, firms were also faced with extremely high interest rates. For example, in August 1981 the interest rate on corporate AAA bonds was 15 percent. As we have seen from our earlier calculations, such high interest rates increase required returns on projects, not only because of the higher interest costs themselves but also because higher interest rates mean higher required returns on equity as well.

As a result, in 1982 many U.S. firms faced a double whammy: lower estimated cash flows resulting from economic recession and higher required returns resulting from capital-market conditions. Both of these effects reduced net present values on projects and made investments look less attractive. While the 1982 cutbacks in capital spending may have surprised Reagan Administration tax planners at the time, the cutbacks can readily be interpreted in light of financial theory.

Source: "Capital Spending Takes a Dive," *Business Week*, March 22, 1982, p. 24, updated with subsequent data from the Federal Reserve *Bulletin*.

quired by the market on debt (K_d) and on equity (K_e), with K_d adjusted for the tax-deductibility of interest. For a given firm, K_e is greater than K_d.

6. The weighted-average required return is the appropriate return target for evaluating projects of average risk.

7. Market data are useful in estimating values for K_e and K_d. Estimates of K_e, however, are necessarily somewhat imprecise.

8. A weighted-average required return for individual firms can be calculated using market required returns on each future source of funds (K_e, K_d, plus returns on bank debt and preferred stock if used) along with data on future financing proportions (W_e, W_d).

9. Using the weighted-average required return as a return target for all projects is not correct theoretically but is a pragmatic approach that recognizes the great difficulty of measuring the risk of individual investment opportunities.

SUMMARY

The third step in evaluating investment opportunities, after estimating cash flows and choosing an investment criterion, such as the *NPV* rule or the *IRR* rule (Chapter 9), is to set a return target. The return target is the minimum acceptable return on the investment. It is an *opportunity rate*—the rate forgone on the next best alternative investment opportunity of comparable risk. In evaluating investments, management acts as the agent of shareholders, setting return targets based on the shareholders' required return.

The purpose of return targets is to impose an economic test to ensure that prospective investment opportunities constitute wise and efficient uses of shareholder capital funds. The economic analysis of a project is a second step in the overall planning process of the firm, the first step being a strategic test to make certain that a prospective investment is consistent with the firm's commercial strategy. Its commercial strategy tells the firm where to look for profitable investment opportunities; return targets tell which of those opportunities to select. In addition to these strategic and economic tests, the evaluation process must take into account the risk preferences of shareholders and managers, interactions among various parts of the firm, constraints on managerial and technical personnel, impact on local communities, environmental factors, and other qualitative considerations.

Although not sufficient by itself, an economic test is wise in nearly all cases because if a prospective investment is not likely to earn the market return, suppliers of capital will not wish it to be undertaken. Going ahead with a project that has little chance of earning a satisfactory return is likely to lead to shareholder unhappiness.

Required rates of return are *market-determined* by the actions of suppliers of capital competing against one another. These market rates represent opportunities available to investors outside the firm and, hence, the minimum return acceptable on investments inside the firm.

The simplest and most basic approach to setting return targets is to calculate a weighted-average required return for the firm individually. Such a *WARR* is a weighted average of the market required returns of all the suppliers of capital. The weights reflect the proportion of total financing coming from each source. In calculating the *WARR*, we must take care to use the after-tax cost of debt to take into account the tax deductibility of interest. Calculating required returns on equity can be a difficult task. A number of different methods can be used (for example, dividend-growth models or historical risk premia), but the process of estimating the required return on equity involves a number of educated guesses. Once estimated, the *WARR* is appropriate for evaluating projects whose risk is approximately equal to the overall risk of the firm.

The most refined approach is to set targets individually for projects or for categories of projects. This kind of specific target setting requires quantitative measures of project risk, a difficult thing to measure. Many firms stop short of attempting to measure project risk explicitly and instead use the *WARR* as a target for all projects. The next chapter will discuss refinements in target setting to measure project risk and set project targets.

QUESTIONS

1. Why can the required rate of return be viewed as an opportunity rate?
2. To what extent should management's own preferences enter into the establishment of required rates of return?
3. "The required rate of return of any investment opportunity is the rate that could be earned on the next best investment opportunity that must be forgone by the firm." Is this statement true or false? Explain.

4. Why does the required return of an investment opportunity depend on its riskiness?

5. What role is played by the financial markets in establishing required rates of return?

6. "The required rate of return on a firm's stock is always greater than that on its bonds or other debt." Is this statement true or false? Explain.

7. What is the effect of inflation on rates of return in the financial markets?

8. Why must inflation be taken into account in evaluating investment opportunities in a firm?

9. Under what circumstances would the required return on a new investment opportunity equal the weighted-average return required by the market on the firm's outstanding securities (stocks and bonds)?

10. Define the term *cost of capital* and explain its relationship to the market required rate of return.

11. What is the best source of information regarding returns required by investor?

12. How might an economywide required rate of return be used?

13. Explain the steps in calculating a firm's weighted-average required return.

14. What problems do you see in a firm using the *WARR* on its securities as the return target for evaluating all of its capital-investment projects?

15. What are some of the problems in calculating the required return on equity, K_e?

PROBLEMS

To work problems preceded by an asterisk (*) requires knowledge of material in Appendix 10A. To work problems preceded by the two asterisks(**) requires knowledge of material in Appendix 10B.

1. Assume that a firm can borrow from its bank at 14 percent annual interest, and it can issue long-term debt at an interest rate of 12.5 percent and preferred stock at 13.5 percent. Calculate the after-tax equivalent required return on each of these sources of funds, assuming a tax rate of 46 percent.

2. Alamance Corporation has a 1986 balance sheet as shown in Table A. The company can borrow new long-term funds at 12 percent. Preferred stock holders require a 13.5 percent return. The company's stock is presently selling for $10 a share based on next year's expected annual dividend of $1 per share and growth in dividends of 9 percent a year after that. Assuming a corporate tax rate of 46 percent, calculate Alamance's weighted average required return (WARR). Assume book-value weights are approximately equal to market-value weights.

3. During the past five years, the dividends of Delta Inc. have grown at an annual rate of 5 percent, leading to a current dividend per share of $.60. Delta's stock is presently selling for $10 a share.

Table A

Assets			Liabilities		
Current assets		$6,854,000	Current liabilities		$5,341,000
Fixed assets		7,336,000	Long-term debt		3,000,000
	Total	$14,190,000	Preferred stock		800,000
			Common stock		1,700,000
			Retained earnings		3,349,000
				Total	$14,190,000

Table B

Year	Dividend
1979	$1.25
80	$1.25
81	$1.35
82	$1.35
83	$1.35
84	$1.35
85	$1.50
86	$1.50

a. Suppose you assumed that past dividend growth was expected to continue indefinitely into the future. What would be your estimate of the required return of Delt's stock (K_e)?

b. If government long-term bond rates were 12 percent, how would you feel about the validity of your answers as calculated in part (a)?

4. Consider the data on Durham Industries (DI) in Table B, showing company dividends for the years 1979 through 1986. At year-end 1978, DI stock was quoted at $25.00, and at year-end 1986, $35.00.

a. Calculate the return realized by investors over the period 1979–86 assuming the stock was purchased at the end of 1978 and sold at the end of 1986 (the solution requires trial and error).

b. Discuss the use of these data as a basis for estimating K_e, the required return on DI's stock as of early 1987. Suppose the U.S. government bond rate was 11 percent.

5. Skeleton Enterprises has the balance sheet items listed in Table C. The company is paying 12 percent on borrowing from the bank (and expects that rate to continue). Skeleton can issue new long-term debt at 10.7 percent. Preferred stock, being more risky, has a higher required return. In Skeleton's case it is 11.5 percent. Skeleton plans to maintain its current capital structure (book and market values are approximately equal). Management is proud of the fact that Skeleton stock is currently selling for $20 per share based on an expected annual dividend growth rate of 6.4 percent,

Table C

Category	Amount (dollars)
Accounts payable	6,000
Accruals	4,000
Notes payable (bank)	8,000
Long-term debt	7,000
Preferred stock	4,000
Common stock	8,000
Retained earnings	25,000
Total liabilities and net worth	62,000

leading to a dividend for next year of $2 per share. Assuming a 46 percent tax rate, calculate Skeleton's *WARR*.

6. Rock Creek Enterprises is considering an investment opportunity that management judges to be of average risk, measured relative to the firm itself. Management has estimated the company's K_e to be 20 percent, yet the return on the project is estimated at only 17 percent. Hence, a net present value calculation shows a negative net present value (*NPV*), and the financial vice-president, Laura Perry, recommends against the proposal. The marketing manager, Julius Joseph, is deeply committed to the project and wants to convince top management to go ahead. The company historically has used no debt, and top management had shown no inclination to change that policy. Joseph argues that the Company could borrow 100 percent of the funds required to finance the project at an interest rate of 13 percent. He points out that the after-tax cost of these new funds (assuming a tax rate of 0.46) would be only $13(1 - 0.46) = 7.02$ percent. He states that it makes sense to borrow at 7.02 percent if the funds can be put to work to earn 17 percent and that doing so will increase the value of the firm. He produces a net present value calculation to support his contention. Joseph argues that the company is better off to borrow and undertake the project than to forgo it. Evaluate Joseph's argument, and state your reasons for agreeing or disagreeing. If you disagree, what in your opinion is the correct approach for evaluating the project?

Table D

Assets		Liabilities and Owner's Equity	
Cash	10	Accounts payable	20
Accounts receivable	10	Long-term debt (3 percent coupon)	20
Plant and equipment	60	Preferred stock (9 percent)	10
Other assets	20	Common stock	20
		Retained earnings	30
Total assets	100	**Total liabilities and owner's equity**	100

7. Show why market-value weights are theoretically correct for calculating the *WARR* for a firm and book-value weights (from the balance sheet) incorrect.

8. Jane Dixie of Shallow Vineyards, Inc. has taken a close look at her firm's required rate of return. It seems as if some aspiring finance student has convinced her that the financial complexity of her holdings makes the calculation of her "cost of capital" an intriguing project. Consequently, the balance sheet as of December 31, 1986, shown in Table D (with figures in millions of dollars) is being closely scrutinized. In addition to the balance sheet, you have learned that new long-term debt can be sold at face value ($1,000) if the coupon rate is 8 percent. This explains why the existing bonds (3 percent coupon) have a market value of only $16,014,000 as compared to their book value of $20 million. New preferred stock can be sold at par (100) if a 9 percent dividend payment is stipulated. Shallow Vineyards presently has one million shares of common stock outstanding. The market price of this stock has been roughly constant at $72 per share. Dixie feels that this is a fair price. The firm is expected to pay a dividend of $8 per share in 1987, and dividends (per share) and earnings (per share) of Shallow Vineyards are expected to grow at 4 percent per year for the foreseeable future. Assume that the corporate tax rate is 40 percent and that there are no flotation costs (for simplicity). Dixie views her capital structure as the best financial mix for Shallow Vineyards. She bases this upon market-value cal-

culations. Now that the hard work has been done—gathering the data and making estimates—Dixie requires a discount rate to use in evaluation of some small investment proposals. What rate would you suggest? Under what conditions might the rate that you calculate be an *improper* discount rate to use in net-present-value calculations?

*9. Recalculate Skeleton Enterprises' *WARR* as figured in problem (5), assuming flotation costs of 5 percent on stock ($1.00 flotation costs per share). What WARR should Skeleton use if it plans to do all of its equity financing through retention of earnings? Why?

*10. Recalculate Shallow Vineyards' *WARR* as figured in problem (8), assuming flotation costs of 10 percent on new stock issues.

*11. Table E gives earnings-per-share (EPS) figures for Carrboro Manufacturing during the years 1977–

Table E

Year	Earnings per Share
1977	$2.00
1978	$2.16
1979	$2.33
1980	$2.52
1981	$2.72
1982	$2.94
1983	$3.18
1984	$3.43
1985	$3.70
1986	$4.00

1986. The firm's common stock, 140,000 shares outstanding, is now selling for $50 a share, and the expected dividend for the current year is 50 percent of the 1986 EPS. Investors expect past trends to continue. New preferred stock paying a $5 dividend could be sold to the public at a price of $52.50, which includes a $2.50 flotation cost (that is, the net proceeds to Carrboro are $50). The current interest rate on new debt is 8 percent. The firm's marginal tax rate is 40 percent. The firm's capital structure, considered to be optimal, is as shown in Table F.

a. Calculate the after-tax cost of (i) new debt, K_d, (ii) new preferred stock, K_p, and (iii) common equity, K_e, assuming new equity comes only from retained earnings. Calculate the cost of equity using the dividend-growth model.

b. Find the weighted-average required return, again assuming no new common stock is sold.

c. How much can be spent for capital investments before external equity must be sold? (Assume that retained earnings available for 1987 investment are 50 percent of 1986 retained earnings.)

d. What is the weighted-average required return, if the firm can sell new common stock at $50 a share, at flotation costs of $5 a share? The cost of debt and of preferred stock is constant.

**12. Suppose that Dixie in problem (8) now hears about the capital-asset-pricing model (CAPM) and decides to abandon use of dividend-growth models

Table F

Source of Financing	Amount (dollars)
Debt (6 percent)	2,500,000
Preferred stock (7 percent)	500,000
Common equity	7,000,000
	10,000,000

to estimate K_e. Dixie has estimated that Shallow Vineyards stock has a beta of 1.2 and that the market risk premium is 7 percent. Assume that the long-term government bond rate is 6.5 percent.

a. Calculate Shallow Vineyards required return on equity, K_e, using the capital-asset-pricing model.

b. Calculate Shallow Vineyards WARR based on your estimate in part (a).

c. How do you interpret differences in your answers here compared to those in problem (8)?

13. The balance sheet as of December 31, 1986, (in millions of dollars) for the Greensboro Corporation appears in Table G. Greensboro is presently in the textile business and is contemplating the expansion of its textile-production facilities. The management of the firm considers its present debt-equity mix of long-term financing (at book value which is approximately equal to market value) to

Table G

Assets		Liabilities and Owner's Equity	
Cash	5	Current liabilities	20
Accounts receivable	20	Debt (16 percent coupon bonds)	40
Inventory	30	Common stock	5
Land and buildings	30	Retained earnings	35
Other assets	15		
Total assets	100	**Total liabilities and owner's equity**	100

Table H

Depreciation estimate for 1986	$10,000,000
Profits after taxes estimate for 1986	$10,000,000
Dividends expected for 1986 ($4 per share for 1,000,000 shares)	$4,000,000
Effective tax rate	40 percent
Market price of stock	$40 per share
Interest rate at which new bonds can be issued	16 percent
Expected growth in earnings and dividends (per year)	12 percent
Stock beta with the market rate of return (S&P 500)	1.5
Expected rate of return on the market (per year)	20 percent
Rate of return on long-term U.S. government bonds (per year)	14 percent

Note: Assume zero flotation costs.

be optimal and is interested in computing a weighted-average required return in order to evaluate the proposed expansion. You have been assigned the task and have gleaned financial data from various sources as shown in Table H. While this array of numbers represents merely rough estimates (albeit based on expert opinion), it represents the best that you can do.

a. Calculate Greensboro's *WARR* for 1986 using the dividend growth model.

**b. Calculate Greensboro's cost of equity capital, K_e, using the capital asset pricing model. If your answer differs from any calculations in part (a) of this problem, does this mean that the CAPM is not valid? What might lead to any differences?

c. Under what conditions is the *WARR* calculated in part (a) a legitimate discount rate with which to analyze the expansion of Greensboro's textile facilities?

REFERENCES

Bowsher, N. M. "The Rise and Fall of Interest Rates." Federal Reserve Bank of St. Louis *Review* 62, (August–September 1980): 16–23.

Brealey, R. *Security Prices in a Competitive Market.* Cambridge, Mass.: MIT Press, 1971.

Brigham, E. "Hurdle Rates for Screening Capital Expenditure Proposals." *Financial Management* 4 (Autumn 1975): 17–26.

Carter, E. E. "What Are the Risks in Risk Analysis?" *Harvard Business Review* 50 (July 1972): 72–76.

Chambers, D. R., R. S. Harris, and J. J. Pringle. "Treatment of Financing Mix in Analyzing Investment Opportunities." *Financial Management* (Summer 1982): 24–41.

Cooley, P. L., R. L. Roenfeldt, and I. Chew. "Capital Budgeting Procedures Under Inflation." *Financial Management* 4 (Winter 1975): 18–27.

Cooley, P. L., R. L. Roenfeldt, and N. K. Modani. "Interdependence of Market Risk Measures." *Journal of Business* 50 (July 1977): 356–363.

Crum, R. L., D. J. Laughunn, and J. W. Payne. "Risk Seeking Behavior and Its Implications for Financial Models." *Financial Management* 10 (Winter 1981): 20–27.

Donaldson, G. "Strategic Hurdle Rates for Capital Investment." *Harvard Business Review* 50 (Mar.–Apr. 1972): 50–55.

Friedman, B. M. "Who Put the Inflation Premium into Nominal Interest Rates?" *Journal of Finance* 33 (June 1978): 833–845.

Friend, I., and M. E. Blume. "The Demand for Risky Assets." *American Economic Review* 65 (Dec. 1975): 900–922.

Friend, I., Y. Landskroner, and E. Losq. "The Demand for Risky Assets under Uncertain Inflation." *Journal of Finance* 31 (Dec. 1976): 1287–1297.

Geske, R., and R. Roll. "The Fiscal and Monetary Linkage Between Stock Returns and Inflation." *Journal of Finance* 38 (Mar 1983): 1–34.

Haggerman, R. L. "Finance Theory in Rate Hearings." *Financial Management* 5 (Spring 1976): 18–21.

Harris, R. "Using Analysts' Growth Forecasts to Estimate Shareholder Required Returns," *Financial Management* (Spring 1986).

Harris, R. S., and J. J. Pringle. "A Note on the Implications of Miller's Argument for Capital Budgeting." *Journal of Financial Research.* (Spring 1983): 13–23.

Hastie, K. L. "One Businessman's View of Capital Budgeting." *Financial Management* 4 (Winter 1974): 36–44.

Hayes, R. H., and W. J. Abernathy. "Managing Our Way to Economic Decline." *Harvard Business Review* 58 (July–August 1980): 67–77.

Hayes, S. L., III. "Capital Commitments and the High Cost of Money." *Harvard Business Review* 55 (May–June 1977): 155–161.

Hertz, D. B. "Investment Policies that Pay Off." *Harvard Business Review* 46 (Jan.–Feb. 1968): 96–108.

Ibbotson, R., and R. A. Sinquefield. *Stocks, Bonds, Bills and Inflation: The Past and the Future.* The Financial Analysts Research Foundation, 1982.

Ibbotson, R. G., and R. A. Sinquefield. *Stocks, Bonds, Bills and Inflation: The Past (1926–1976) and the Future (1977–2000).* Charlottesville, Va.: Financial Analysts Research Foundation, 1977.

Lewellen, W. G. "Some Observations on Risk-Adjusted Discount Rates." *Journal of Finance* 32 (Sept. 1977): 1331–1338.

Lintner, J. "Inflation and Security Returns." *Journal of Finance* 30 (May 1975): 259–280.

Litzenberger, R. H., and A. Budd. "Corporate Investment Criteria and the Evaluation of Risk Assets." *Journal of Financial and Quantitative Analysis* 5 (Dec. 1970): 395–420.

Lohr, S. "Overvaluing America's Business Management." *New York Times Magazine* (January 4, 1981).

Martin, J. D., and D. F. Scott. "Debt Capacity and the Capital Budgeting Decision: A Revisitation." *Financial Management* 9 (Spring 1980): 23–26.

Miles, J. A., and J. R. Ezzell. "The Weighted Average Cost of Capital, Perfect Capital Markets and Project Life: A Clarification." *Journal of Financial and Quantitative Analysis* (September 1980).

Miller, M. H. "Debt and Taxes." *Journal of Finance* 32 (May 1977): 261–275.

Modigliani, F., and M. H. Miller. "Corporate Income Taxes and the Cost of Capital: A Correction." *American Economic Review* 53 (June 1963): 433–443.

Nelson, C. R. "Inflation and Capital Budgeting." *Journal of Finance* 31 (June 1976): 923–932.

Reilly, F. "Companies and Common Stocks as Inflation Hedges." *The Bulletin.* New York: New York University, 1975.

Reinhardt, U. E. "Break-Even Analysis of Lockheed's TriStar—An Application of Financial Theory." *Journal of Finance* 28 (Sept. 1973): 821–838.

Searby, F. W. "Return to Return on Investment." *Harvard Business Review* 53 (Mar.-Apr. 1975): 113–119.

Silver, A. "Original Issue Deep Discount Bonds." *Federal Reserve Bank of New York: Quarterly Review* (Winter 1981–82): 18–28.

Tuttle, D. L., and R. H. Litzenberger. "Leverage, Diversification, and Capital Market Effects on a Risk Adjusted Capital Budgeting Framework." Reprinted in S. H. Archer and C. D'Ambrosio (eds.), *The Theory of Business Finance.* 2d ed. New York: Macmillan, 1976.

Vander Weide, J., and W. T. Carleton. "Investor Growth Expectations and Stock Prices." Working paper Duke University and University of Arizona, July 1985.

Appendix 10A

Flotation Costs and the Weighted-Average Required Return

Chapter 10 ignored *flotation costs* that a company may pay when it raises new money. For example, when a company issues new long-term debt, it typically has cash costs associated with the bond issue, including fees paid to lawyers and investment bankers. When a company raises money, investment bankers typically keep a portion of the sale price of a bond or share of stock as part of their return for helping raise funds. For example, even though an investment banker might sell a company's bond for $1,000 face value to the public, only $990 might go to the company issuing the bonds—the remaining $10 going to the investment banker. This $10 would be part of the firm's flotation costs. Other flotation costs may be associated with other types of financing.

Table 10A–1 shows flotation costs associated with public issues of bonds, preferred stocks, and common stocks. Two trends are evident in the table. First, the larger is the size of the issue, the lower are the percentage flotation costs because certain flotation costs are fixed and have to be borne no matter how small the issue. As a result, smaller firms that would have smaller issues are subject to higher percentage flotation

Table 10A–1
Flotation Costs of Bonds, Preferred Stock and Common Stock

Size of Issue (millions of dollars)	Flotation Costs as a Percentage of Issue's Total Dollar Value		
	Bonds	*Preferred Stock*	*Common Stock*
Under 0.5		NA*	23.7
0.5–0.9	Average 13.3	NA*	20.9
1.0–1.9		11.8	16.9
2.0–4.9	6.2	NA*	12.4
5.0–9.9	3.2	2.6	8.1
10.0–19.9	1.9	1.8	5.9
20.0–49.9	1.4	1.7	4.6
50.0 and over	1.1	1.6	3.5

*Information is not available.
Source: Securities and Exchange Commission.

costs. Second, percentage flotation costs are typically lower for bond issues than for preferred-stock issues. Raising new common stock has the highest percentage flotation costs. Though there are no organized data to report on flotation costs of bank loans, they are lower than the percentage costs of bond issues.

In many cases, especially for large companies, flotation costs are a very small percentage of the value of the money raised. In the case of retained earnings, there are no flotation costs at all. The company simply keeps money it has earned.

As a result, flotation costs can often be ignored without having an important effect on the calculation of the weighted-average required return. Following this reasoning, we have ignored flotation costs in the body of Chapter 10.

Sometimes, however, flotation costs may be large. In such cases we need to know how to deal with them. As we will see, we can raise the *WARR* to incorporate these costs. In essence, we will require a higher return on projects with high flotation costs to ensure that the projects not only can provide the required returns of the suppliers of capital but can also cover the flotation costs of raising that capital. We adjust the return target rather than introducing flotation costs in the cash flows in keeping with our separation of operating and financial flows.

To illustrate the effects of flotation costs, let us consider a firm that is entirely equity financed and plans to sell new stock. First, we will assume zero flotation costs, then we will introduce these costs. Suppose the firm can sell new shares of stock for a price, P, of $40 per share. Shareholders expect next year's dividend, D_1, to be $3.60 per share and that dividends will grow at 7 percent thereafter ($g = 0.07$).

Without flotation costs, we proceed just as we did in the body of Chapter 10. We can use the dividend-growth model in Equation (2) of Chapter 10 to calculate the shareholders' required return, K_e, as

$$K_e = \frac{\$3.60}{\$40.00} + 0.07 = 0.09 + 0.07 = 0.16, \text{ or 16 percent.}$$

For an all-equity firm, 100 percent of the financing is by equity so $WARR = K_e = 0.16$. Thus, the firm must expect to earn at least 16 percent on its average-risk investment opportunities to satisfy shareholders' expectations.

Now let us introduce flotation costs. We will assume that the stock could be sold for $40.00 per share, just as before, but of this $40 the firm will get only $38.00 available for new investment. This $38.00 is the net proceeds, *NP*, of selling stock and is equal to the share price, P, minus flotation costs, F. In this case, flotation costs are $40.00 − $38.00 = $2.00 per share and represent 5 percent of the share price ($2.00/$40.00 = 0.05).

What rate of return must the firm expect to earn on its investments to both (1) cover these flotation costs and (2) just meet the dividend expectations of shareholders? Unless this rate (or more) is expected to be earned, the shareholders will be disappointed, and we would expect the value of the firm to fall. That is, unless this rate is earned, the project has a negative net present value. This rate is the *cost of equity capital* adjusted for flotation costs. We will call this K_e, as before, remembering that K_e now is adjusted for flotation costs.

To calculate this adjusted rate, K_e, let us look at the $38.00 net proceeds the firm will have for investment. We will already have covered the $2.00 flotation costs before investing ($40.00 − $38.00 = $2.00), but we still have to meet shareholders' dividend expectations. To do this, the net proceeds, NP, when invested, must earn a rate, K_e, such that the present value of the expected future dividend payments at K_e percent is precisely equal to NP, as expressed in Equation (A–1).

The required return on equity, K_e, adjusted for flotation costs, can be calculated by solving for K_e in the following equation:

$$NP = \sum_{t=1}^{t=\infty} \frac{D_t}{(1 + K_e)^t}$$

$$= \sum_{t=1}^{t=\infty} \frac{D_0(1 + g)^t}{(1 + K_e)^t}$$

(A–1)

where g = the expected constant growth rate in dividends per share (D_t) and NP = the net proceeds of the sale of a share of stock.

Equation (A–1) applies to a case of constant growth, so we know from our work in Part Two on the time value of money that we can rewrite Equation (A–1) as shown in Equation (A–2).

The required return on equity, K_e, adjusted for flotation costs can be calculated as

$$NP = \frac{D_0(1 + g)}{K_e - g} = \frac{D_1}{K_e - g}$$

$$K_e = \frac{D_1}{NP} + g$$

(A–2)

where NP = net proceeds, or share price (P) minus flotation costs (F), per share.

Note that Equation (A–2) is simply the dividend-growth model from Equation (2) in Chapter 10 with one adjustment. The net proceeds, NP, appear in Equation (A–2), while the price, P, appears in Chapter 10's Equation (2). This difference is no coincidence. Because net proceeds are less than price as a result of flotation costs, using Equation (A–2) is just like saying that the firm sold stock at a price less than the share price. This lower price is simply the dollar value *(NP)* the firm receives after flotation costs: $NP = P - F$. If there were no flotation costs, Equation (2) from Chapter 10 and Equation (A-2) would be identical. Note that if the firm were using only retained earnings (instead of new stock), there would be no flotation costs, and we could use Chapter 10's Equation (2) to determine the required return on equity, K_e.

Putting the figures in this example into Equation (A–2), we can calculate the return on equity for our hypothetical all-equity firm as

$$K_e = \frac{\$3.60}{\$38.00} + 0.07 = 0.0947 + 0.07 = 0.1647, \text{ or } 16.47 \text{ percent.}$$

This calculation shows that the cost of equity adjusted for flotation costs is 16.47 percent. For an all-equity firm, $WARR = K_e$, so for this firm, the weighted-average required return also equals 16.47 percent if it plans to issue new stock to finance investments.

Note the difference in the two calculations we have done. Without flotation costs, $WARR$ was calculated to be 16 percent. With flotation costs, $WARR$ was calculated to be 16.47 percent. The higher $WARR$ with flotation costs reflects the fact that cash flows from investments must not only meet the requirements of the suppliers of capital but also cover the flotation costs associated with raising that capital.

Although we have described only a very simple example of an all-equity firm, the same general procedures apply to more complex cases. First, we calculate the cost of an individual source of funds adjusted for flotation costs by finding the rate of return that makes the net proceeds of the financing (for example, a bond issue or a sale of stock) equal to the present value of the future cash flows expected by the suppliers of capital. This process was outlined in Equation (A–2). Note that these future cash flows should be after-tax cash flows to the corporation. In the case of stock, dividends are not tax-deductible, so in our example we did not make any tax adjustments. In the case of debt, future interest payments should be determined on an after-tax basis given the tax deductibility of interest.[1]

After the cost of each source of funding, adjusted for flotation costs, has been calculated, we then combine the separate costs to calculate the weighted-average required return.

Sample Problem 10A–1

Calculating the WARR Adjusted for Flotation Costs for American Foods

Recalculate the $WARR$ for American Foods (see Tables 10–12 and 10–13 in Chapter 10), assuming that American Foods will sell new shares of common stock and be subject to 5 percent flotation costs. That is, flotation costs will be $2.50 per share based on a share price of $50. Assume that flotation costs on debt and preferred stock are 0 percent. (Typically, percentage flotation costs on debt are much smaller than on equity.)

Solution

We begin by calculating the cost of equity, K_e, adjusted for flotation costs. From Chapter 10, we know that American Foods shareholders expect next year's dividend (D_1) to be $4.20 and dividend growth (g) to be 0.08. The net proceeds per share will be $50.00 − $2.50 = $47.50. Using Equation (A–2), we can calculate the cost of equity as

$$K_e = \$4.20/\$47.50 + 0.08 = 0.088 + 0.08 = 0.168.$$

All the other figures necessary to calculate the $WARR$ are the same as those in Table 10–12. Table 10A–2 shows the calculation of the weighted-average required return for American Foods, adjusted for flotation costs.

---

[1]In practice, the treatment of debt may require that numerous tax effects be considered. The effects depend on the details of tax laws. Note also that we have restricted our focus to the determination of return targets for investment projects and have not introduced more complicated issues that sometimes arise in the context of regulated firms.

Table 10A–2

Weighted-Average Required Return (WARR) for American Foods, Adjusted for Flotation Costs

	Required Return (percent) (1)	Weight (2)	Weighted Required Return (percent) (3) = (1) × (2)
Bank debt, after taxes	6.5	0.10	0.65
Long-term debt, after taxes	5.8	0.20	1.16
Preferred stock	11.5	0.10	1.15
Common equity	16.8	0.60	10.08
		WARR =	13.04

This 13.04 percent is slightly higher than the *WARR* of 12.80 calculated assuming no flotation costs. As a practical matter, the difference between the two numbers is so small that we should not give it too much significance. Given the imprecision of estimating shareholder required returns in the first place, the difference between a K_e of 16.4 (without flotation costs) and a K_e of 16.8 (with flotation costs) is small. This difference in K_e translates into an even smaller difference in *WARR*. In practice, flotation costs may be important, especially for smaller firms. In most situations, however, adjustments for flotation costs are not likely to produce large changes in the *WARR* appropriate for evaluating average-risk investments. ＥＩＩＦ

Appendix 10B

Using the Capital-Asset-Pricing Model to Calculate Required Returns on Equity

In Chapter 10, we focused on the historical-risk-premia approach and dividend-growth models to calculate the required return on equity, K_e. Another method sometimes used to estimate K_e is the capital-asset-pricing model (CAPM), discussed in Chapter 5. There we saw that, according to the CAPM, the required return on any asset (for example, a share of stock) could be calculated as shown in Equation (B–1).

> According to the capital-asset-pricing model (CAPM), the required return on any asset can be calculated as
>
> $$K_j = R_f + (K_m - R_f)\beta_j \qquad \text{(B–1)}$$
>
> where K_j = the required rate of return on asset j, R_f = the risk-free rate of return, K_m = the required rate of return on the market portfolio, and β_j = the beta coefficient of asset j (a measure of nondiversifiable risk).

If we think of the stock of a company as just another asset, we can use Equation (B–1) to estimate K_e. In Equation (B–1), K_j can stand for K_e.

The CAPM risk/return relationship states that the required return, K_j, on any asset, j, is equal to a least-risk rate, R_f, plus a risk premium. In theory, R_f is a risk-free rate of interest. In practice, the interest rate (yield to maturity) on long-term U.S. government bonds is often used as a value for R_f when looking at long-term rates of return. While U.S. government bonds are not risk-free, they are perhaps the least risky of long-term investments.

The risk premium of any asset is the result of taking the market risk premium ($K_m - R_f$) and multiplying it by a measure of the nondiversifiable risk of the asset relative to the risk of the market (β_j). The "market" is, in theory, the portfolio of all risky assets in the economy. In practice, a widely diversified portfolio, such as the Standard & Poors 500 stock index, is often used as a proxy for the market portfolio.

The most frequently used measure of nondiversifiable risk is the beta coefficient, β_j, shown in Equation (B–1). As we saw in Chapter 5, the beta coefficient is a measure of how returns on an asset move *relative* to returns on the market portfolio. A beta of 1.0 indicates an asset of average risk. A beta greater than 1.0 indicates an asset of above-average risk, whose returns tend to be more risky than the market. For example, the stocks of high-risk firms, such as airlines, typically have estimated beta coefficients well above 1.0.

The higher is the beta, the higher is the nondiversifiable risk of the firm and, as a result, the higher is the risk premium.

Sample Problem 10B–1

Estimating the Required Return on Equity for Malta Mining Company

Suppose that stock in Malta Mining Company has an estimated beta coefficient of 1.1 and that Malta Mining management thinks that the market risk premium $(K_m - R_f)$, given current financial-market conditions, is 7.5 percent. Assume that the long-term government-bond rate is 10 percent. Estimate the required return on equity, K_e, for Malta Mining using the capital-asset-pricing model.

Solution

Using Equation (B–1), we can calculate Malta Mining's required return on debt as

$$K_e = 0.10 + [(0.075)(1.1)]$$

$$= 0.10 + 0.0825 = 0.1825 = 18.25 \text{ percent}$$

Note that the capital-asset-pricing model adds a risk premium of 8.25 percent to calculate Malta Mining's K_e. This risk premium is larger than the market risk premium of 7.5 percent because Malta Mining is riskier than average (the beta coefficient of Malta Mining is greater than 1.0). This estimate of the required return on equity can now be used to calculate the weighted-average required return for Malta Mining. ▰▰▰

Chapter

11

Dealing with Risk in Capital Budgeting

In this chapter, we will learn how to deal with risk in capital budgeting. We will use sensitivity analysis to determine the impact of different cash-flow assumptions. Then we will discuss risk-adjusted discount rates and learn how to set the return target for a project on the basis of its risk. Finally, we will summarize the approach developed in Part Four of the book to analyzing capital investment opportunities.

Risk—is the degree of uncertainty about future events or outcomes and is very difficult to measure accurately or quantitatively.

In this chapter, we address the thorny problem of how to deal with **risk**—uncertainty about future events or outcomes.[1] In Chapter 10, we discussed the calculation of a weighted-average required return *(WARR)*, which is appropriate for evaluating projects of average risk for a firm. If we use the *WARR* for evaluating all projects, we are in effect treating all projects as if they are equally risky. For most firms, however, all projects are not equally risky. Some prospective investments may involve new products and untried technologies. In these cases, risks are likely to be high. On the other hand, when an existing machine wears out and is replaced by essentially the same type of equipment, risks are likely to be relatively small.

> **If we use the weighted-average required return, *WARR*, to evaluate all investment projects, we are treating all projects as if they are equally risky.**

From our earlier discussion, we know that there is a trade-off between risk and investors' required rate of return. This trade-off is just as applicable to investment projects considered by a firm as it is to individual investors' decisions about investments (stocks and bonds) in financial markets. The higher the risk, the higher should be the required rate of return. Remember that the firm is ultimately interested in creating value for shareholders. Consequently, managers must take into account investors' dislike of risk. The problem is finding practical ways to implement such risk adjustments.

Measuring risk accurately in a manner that has credibility with executives is so difficult, in fact, that some firms do not attempt it and simply use the weighted-average required return as the return target for all projects. Others adjust the *WARR* "up a bit" for high-risk projects and "down a bit" for low-risk projects. In many situations, it is desirable to deal more rigorously with risk. Ways of doing so are the topic of this chapter. Before grappling with techniques for dealing with risk, let us consider the problem of risk in connection with a very large and interesting project—the Alaska gas pipeline.

TECHNIQUES FOR DEALING WITH RISK

For the Alaska gas pipeline to be privately financed, prospective investors and lenders had to analyze it as an investment opportunity. This analysis required estimating future cash flows and dealing with uncertainties. The gas pipeline is by no means a typical project, but the same techniques used in analyzing it would be applicable to the more usual investments undertaken by firms.

---

[1]Some economists attach different meanings to the terms *risk* and *uncertainty*. Where this distinction is drawn, *risk* refers to situations in which the probabilities of future events are known objectively from prior experience over many trials—for example, as in a game of roulette. *Uncertainty* refers to situations in which the probabilities are not known but can only be estimated, as is true in virtually all business decisions. For a discussion of these concepts, see F. H. Knight, *Risk, Uncertainty and Profit* (New York: Houghton Mifflin, 1921). Throughout this book, this distinction is ignored and the terms *risk* and *uncertainty* are used interchangeably.

What are those techniques? The two techniques for dealing with risk that find the widest use are **sensitivity analysis** and the **risk-adjusted discount rate**. Equation (1) restates the basic formula for calculating net present value that we have used in analyzing investment opportunities, originally presented as Equation (2) in Chapter 9.

> The net present value (*NPV*) of an investment project can be determined, using discounted-cash-flow techniques, as
>
> $$NPV = \sum_{t=0}^{n} \frac{C_t}{(1 + K)^t} \qquad (1)$$
>
> where C_t = the expected cash flow in period t and K = the required rate of return.

A **risk-adjusted discount rate**—is a return target that reflects the risk of the investment being analyzed.

In sensitivity analysis, we focus on the cash flow, C_t—the *numerator* of the *NPV* calculation. We can ask ourselves *what if* cash flows turn out to be different from those anticipated—that is, what if cash flows do not turn out to be the most likely flows. In using risk-adjusted discount rates, we focus on the required return, K—the *denominator* of the *NPV* calculation. We incorporate the uncertainty surrounding the cash flows into the discount rate used to calculate present value. We will explore these two techniques in more depth.

> *Sensitivity analysis* **focuses on cash flows—the numerator in the net-present-value calculation. The** *risk-adjusted discount rate* **focuses on the required return—the denominator in the** *NPV* **calculation.**

SENSITIVITY ANALYSIS

Sensitivity analysis—is a technique for examining the impact on return and net present value of variations in underlying factors and can show the consequences of different possible outcomes.

There are as yet no publicly available data on the Alaska gas pipeline on which we could practice sensitivity analysis. To provide an example for which we have information, let us return to Product 99, the new dessert being contemplated by American Foods that we analyzed in Chapter 9. Data for the Product 99 project are repeated in Table 11–1.

The figures in Table 11–1 are all expected cash flows, but in most cases there is no assurance that these cash flows will actually materialize. No one knows for sure that sales of Product 99 in 1987 will turn out to be $250,000. Sales in any year will depend on many factors, including consumer acceptance of the product, the state of the economy, advertising effectiveness, and countermoves by competitors. Actual sales in 1987 may turn out to be lower than $250,000 or higher. So the sales figure for 1987 should be thought of as a *range* of possible outcomes. The single best guess for sales, according to American Foods management, is $250,000, so that figure appears in Table 11–1 and is used in our calculation of the internal rate of return on the project.

As we proceed farther out into the future, the uncertainties surrounding the sales

Table 11–1
Cash Flows for Product 99, 1986–1996 (thousands of dollars)

	1986	87	88	89	90	91	92	93	94	95	96
Sales	0	250	1,250	1,900	2,550	2,750	3,000	3,000	2,800	2,600	2,200
Cost of goods sold	0	137	687	1,045	1,402	1,512	1,650	1,650	1,540	1,430	1,210
Advertising expense	0	75	125	190	127	137	150	150	140	130	110
Selling expense	0	63	313	475	638	688	750	750	700	650	550
Depreciation	0	76	76	76	76	76	76	76	76	76	76
Profit before tax	0	− 101	49	114	307	337	374	374	344	314	254
Tax	0	− 46	23	52	141	155	172	172	158	144	117
Profit after tax	0	− 55	26	62	166	182	202	202	186	170	137
Add back depreciation	0	76	76	76	76	76	76	76	76	76	76
Operating cash flow	0	21	102	138	242	258	278	278	262	246	213
Capital outlay	− 325	− 389	− 25								
Total cash flow	− 325	− 368	77	138	242	258	278	278	262	246	213

Internal rate of return = 21.3 percent

estimates increase. The estimate of $2,200,000 for 1996 is very speculative; indeed, it is management's best guess as to the most likely outcome in that year, with a wide range of possibilities above and below.

The sales estimate is not the only figure in Table 11–1 that is subject to uncertainty. Raw-material costs, manufacturing costs, energy costs, selling and other marketing costs are all subject to uncertainty. As with sales, the figures in Table 11–1 are management's estimates of *most likely* figures.[2]

Thus, the final set of cash flows from which Product 99's internal rate of return is calculated, labeled "Total Cash Flow" in Table 11–1, is composed of the *most likely* figures from a range of possible outcomes. In a world characterized by unpredictability, no amount of analysis can eliminate entirely the uncertainty surrounding estimates of future cash flows. In the decade of the 1970s, crude-oil prices increased by a factor of 30, and inflation ran as high as 13 percent on an annual basis. Oil prices then did an abrupt turn-around in late 1985 and fell by two-thirds during the spring of 1986. Inflation dropped temporarily—essentially to zero—in the United States during early 1986, although most economists expected it to pick up again. The U.S. dollar also exhibited great volatility, rising to new highs against major foreign currencies during the mid-1980s and dramatically affecting the competitive balance in many import and export markets. Then, during 1985 and 1986, the dollar reversed course and fell by

---

[2]As we stated in Chapter 5, technically speaking there can be a difference between the *expected value* of an outcome and the *most likely single outcome*. We will not make that distinction here. In doing *NPV* and *IRR* analysis without sensitivity analysis, it would be appropriate to use expected cash flows.

Finance in Practice 11–1

The Alaska Gas Pipeline

In the summer of 1981, John McMillian, chairman of the Northwest Energy Company, a natural-gas-transmission company, faced a problem: how to raise $22 billion. Companies do not often set out to raise this kind of money, but McMillian's company needed it for an unusual purpose: to finance a pipeline across Alaska and Canada to carry natural gas from the Prudhoe Bay oil fields on Alaska's north slope to users in the United States. The idea for the gas pipeline grew out of the success of a similar pipeline built during the 1970s to carry oil from Prudhoe Bay south across Alaska to Valdez, where it was loaded onto tankers for shipment to other parts of the United States.

The gas-pipeline project was mind-boggling in its scope and complexity. When complete, the line was to carry 2.5 billion cubic feet of gas daily, about 5 percent of current U.S. consumption, south through part of Alaska and across western Canada to a point in southern Alberta. There the line was to split, with one leg running to Chicago and the other to San Francisco. The finished line was to involve a total of 4,800 miles of pipe and was expected, ultimately, to cost between $35 billion and $50 billion.

Some who studied the project concluded that it was so large and faced so many unknowns that private companies would not risk putting up the money and that only the federal government would be able to take the risk. Others, including McMillian, believed that private capital could do the job. McMillian's plan was to put together a consortium of 100 banks—50 domestic and 50 foreign—to put up about $9.5 billion in the form of loans. Insurance companies would be asked to lend $2.25 billion, and equipment and material suppliers would be asked for about $4.5 billion. The remainder of the initial $22 billion, which would finance the 745-mile segment across Alaska, would come from the sale of bonds. Later, after the Alaska segment was complete, financing would be arranged for the segments across Canada and the United States.

Consider the risks in the project, both from the standpoint of the 11 sponsoring firms putting up the equity capital (about 30 percent of the total) and the lenders putting up the balance. No one knew for certain how much the pipeline ultimately would cost or exactly how long it would take to build. Unforeseen problems might be encountered. Costs might run higher than anticipated because of technical problems, weather, or inflation. Before the pipeline was completed, alternative sources of energy, such as coal, solar, or nuclear power, might drive down the price of natural gas to the point where the pipeline was a losing proposition. To McMillian and others contemplating the Alaska gas pipeline in the summer of 1981, the word *risk* had real significance.

Source: Adapted from the *Wall Street Journal*, July 2, 1981.

35 percent. Few foresaw these and other events that had significant impact not only on economic activity in general, but also on the cash flows generated by thousands of capital-investment projects of individual firms, no matter how carefully planned.

What can management do to deal with such uncertainties? It can do little to control outside events, but it can prepare itself by anticipating outcomes other than the single most likely one. By using the technique of sensitivity analysis, management can examine the impact on return and net present value of variations in the underlying factors.[3]

---

[3]For a good discussion of the use of sensitivity analysis in capital-investment decisions, see K. L. Hastie, ''One Businessman's View of Capital Budgeting,'' *Financial Management*, Winter 1974, pp. 36–44.

Table 11–2
Sensitivity of Sales for Product 99

Sales as Percent of Most Likely *Value*	Internal Rate of Return (percent)
110	23.4
105	22.4
100	21.3
95	20.3
90	19.2

In a world of uncertainty, no amount of analysis can eliminate the uncertainty surrounding cash-flow estimates in the future. Analysis can, however, help one be prepared.

What If?

Sensitivity analysis is a "What if?" technique. What if the sales of Product 99 turn out lower than expected? What if manufacturing costs are higher? Perhaps by good fortune sales will be higher, or costs lower. Let us examine the impact of a shortfall in sales—say, 5 percent below the most likely figures in Table 11–1. To do so we multiply all the sales figures in Table 11–1 by 0.95 and recalculate profits, cash flows, and internal rate of return. We find that the internal rate of return falls to 20.3 percent from 21.3. If sales are 10 percent below the most likely level in each year, return drops to 19.2 percent. If, on the other hand, sales run 10 percent above the most likely level, return will be 23.4 percent. The results of these various assumptions about sales are displayed in Table 11–2.

We can also perform sensitivity analysis on costs. What if costs of production run 5 percent above the most likely level? Return drops from 21.3 to 16.9 percent. Results of sensitivity analysis on cost of goods sold are displayed in Table 11–3.

Table 11–3
Sensitivity of Cost of Goods Sold for Product 99

Cost of Goods Sold as Percent of Most Likely *Value*	Internal Rate of Return (percent)
110	11.9
105	16.9
100	21.3
95	25.4
90	29.3

Figure 11–1

Sensitivity Analysis for Product 99

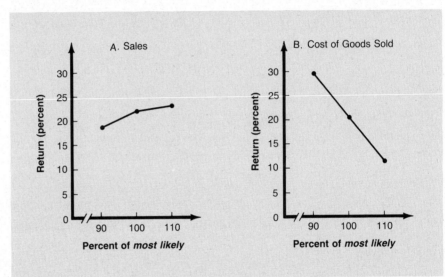

Sensitivity-analysis data also can be displayed in graph form, as shown in Figure 11–1.

What if sales are below the most likely and costs are above their most likely level? Sensitivity analysis is very valuable for **worst-case analysis**. If sales are 90 percent of the most likely level, and cost of goods sold are 105 percent, return falls to 15.0. What combination of sales shortfall and cost overrun would cause return to fall to, say, 12 percent? If sales dropped to 90 percent of the most likely level, costs could run as high as 108 percent and still not push return below 12 percent. If costs rose to 110 percent, sales would have to run at 101 percent to produce a return of 12 percent.

Return Target for Worst-Case Analysis

Worst-case analysis—tells management how low a return could fall under adverse circumstances by calculating net present value and internal rate of return under the worst conditions likely to be encountered, such as highest possible cost and lowest possible sales. The return target for evaluating the worst case should not include a risk premium for bearing risk.

In a worst-case analysis, we are dealing with uncertainty by looking at cash flows under adverse conditions. If we then compare the resulting return to a return target that includes a risk premium, we would "double count" with respect to risk. As a result, the return target for evaluating the worst case should not include a risk premium to compensate equity owners for bearing risk. If we have truly identified the worst case, we need not add a risk premium to the required return. Risk has already been taken into account by the fact that the cash flows we are analyzing (in the worst case) are typically much lower than the cash flows we expect.

Let us assume that, at the time American Foods management is analyzing Product 99, the long-term government-bond rate is 12 percent. For our purposes, this 12 percent figure can be taken as shareholders' required return without any added risk premium. As noted above, a shortfall in sales to 90 percent of the most likely level, coupled with costs of 108 percent of the most likely level, would produce a return of 12 percent. In this situation, the project would return just enough to satisfy shareholders even if the project were entirely financed by stock.[4] If this were the worst possible outcome, Product 99 would be an excellent investment. If, as seems more likely, management concluded that sales could fall below 90 percent and that, simultaneously, costs could go above 108 percent, the case would be less clear. In any event, the technique of worst-case analysis tells management just how low the return could fall under adverse circumstances.

Computer-Assisted Financial Modeling

Sensitivity analysis requires a large amount of calculation, a requirement that can inhibit the use of the technique. To examine the impact of a shortfall in sales to 95 percent of the most likely level, we must recalculate the entire income statement for each year, refigure cash flow, and recalculate the internal rate of return. These calculations can be done by hand using present value tables, but someone forced to do it this way will not perform many sensitivity analyses. An easier way is to use an electronic calculator equipped to do discounted cash flow.

Financial-modeling programs—are computer programs specially designed to do *What if?* analysis by calculating the consequences of changing assumptions.

Still a better way is to use a computer program especially designed to do *what if?* analysis. Programs of this type generally are referred to as **financial-modeling programs**. These programs first became available during the early 1970s but were limited initially to large main-frame computers and were generally accessible only to large companies. Rapid technological advances in computers during the early 1980s made quite powerful financial-modeling programs, the most popular of which were labeled *spreadsheet programs*, available on desktop microcomputers costing less than $2,000. This development has made financial-modeling technology available to the smallest firms and even to individuals. Financial-modeling programs permit analysts and executives to program the computer themselves without having to go through a specialist in the programming department. All the data in Tables 11–1 through 11–3 (and in fact many of the tables in this book) were developed using a spreadsheet program on a small desktop computer. We discussed financial modeling in Appendix 8A in connection with Aquatic Systems, Inc.

Once the model of the Product 99 cash flows is developed, it is a simple matter to ask the computer *what if* sales are only 95 percent of the most likely level. The computer then recalculates all the figures in the tables, including the internal rate of return, in a few seconds. Such computer models also make it easy to do sensitivity analysis using changes in many variables (such as sales, operating costs, or tax laws).

Using Sensitivity Analysis

Sensitivity analysis is a powerful planning technique useful in virtually any situation involving uncertain future events. Computer-based modeling programs take the drudgery out of the calculations so that sensitivity analysis now can be done quickly and inexpensively.

---

[4]In the general case where the company has a policy to finance W_d percentage of investment with debt and W_e percentage with equity, we would calculate a weighted-average required return as we did in Chapter 10 using the government-bond rate as our estimate of K_e (without a risk premium). This calculation would assure that we recognize the after-tax cost of debt, $K_d(1 - T)$, with shareholders evaluating their residual claim at a risk-free required rate of $K_e =$ the government-bond rate. Note that we should not add a risk premium to K_e because risk has already been taken into account in the cash flows when we do worst-case analysis.

Consider the uncertainties involved in planning the Alaska gas-pipeline venture. Given the long planning and construction period, inflation can have a major impact on costs and financing requirements. What if the inflation rate runs 1 or 2 percentage points higher than anticipated? Is the viability of the project threatened? Using sensitivity analysis, planners and executives can ascertain the financial impact of a wide range of inflation rates. Similarly, they can examine the impact of ranges of construction costs, prices for natural gas and competing fuels, or any other variable about which there is uncertainty.

It is a safe bet that, during the planning period of the gas-pipeline project, questions such as these were being examined carefully. Sensitivity analysis could not tell those responsible what would happen in the future, and it certainly could not make the decision for them, but it could show them the consequences of many possible outcomes and help them prepare by reducing surprises. Sensitivity analysis can show what key variables dramatically affect the success of the project and give managers guidance as to where they might best spend time in further analysis or planning.

FORMULATION OF RISK-ADJUSTED DISCOUNT RATES

We noted earlier that sensitivity analysis is one of two main techniques for dealing with risk in capital-investment analysis. Sensitivity analysis focuses on the impact of changes in cash flows—the *numerator* in the *NPV* and *IRR* calculation. The second approach is to formulate risk-adjusted discount rates. In formulating risk-adjusted discount rates, we use only the expected cash flows in the numerator of the *NPV* or *IRR* calculation and focus instead on the discount rate in the *denominator*. We can attempt to take into account the uncertainty surrounding the cash flows by adjusting the discount rate to reflect the degree of risk.

> The more uncertain (risky) the cash flows, the higher the required rate of return, *K*, that we use as the discount rate to calculate net present value or as the target against which to compare the internal rate of return. The lower the risk, the lower the required rate of return used in the *NPV* or *IRR* calculation.

For example, in Chapter 10 we calculated the weighted-average required return for American Foods to be 12.8 percent (see Table 10–13). This 12.8 percent required return would be appropriate as a discount rate to evaluate projects of average risk for American Foods. For projects of higher than average risk, American Foods should use a higher discount rate—say, 16 percent. One of our goals in this chapter is to see how we would go about determining such a 16 percent figure.

This risk-adjusted-discount-rate technique simply applies the risk/return trade-off concept (already discussed) to the analysis of investment proposals. An example can highlight the difference between the two techniques of *sensitivity analysis* and *formulating risk-adjusted discount rates*.

Look carefully at the flows in Table 11–4. In Period 1, Project A's flows will fall somewhere between $140 and $260, with a most likely value of $200. In the case of Project B, the range of possible outcomes is much wider, from −$250 to $550, but the most likely figure is the same, $200. Similarly, in each period the *range* of possible outcomes is much wider for Project B than for Project A.

Table 11–4

Uncertainty of Cash Flows Expected for Two Hypothetical Projects

	Cash Flows				
	Period 0	Period 1	Period 2	Period 3	Period 4
Project A					
Outlay	−$1,000				
Possible inflows					
Maximum value		$ 260	$500	$ 800	$ 800
Most likely value		$ 200	$400	$ 600	$ 600
Minimum value		$ 140	$300	$ 450	$ 450
Project B					
Outlay	−$1,000				
Possible inflows					
Maximum value		$ 550	$750	$1,050	$1,050
Most likely value		$ 200	$400	$ 600	$ 600
Minimum value		$− 250	$ 50	$ 200	$ 200

In Table 11–5, the data for Projects A and B are displayed the same way as in earlier chapters—that is, showing only the most likely cash flow in each year.

As Table 11–4 makes clear, Project B's flows are far more uncertain (risky) than are those of Project A. Yet the presentation in Table 11–5, looking only at most likely values, obscures the difference in uncertainty between the two projects. Sensitivity analysis, along lines outlined earlier in this chapter, would make clear the difference in uncertainty and permit us to deal with it.

The second approach, using risk-adjusted discount rates, deals only with the most likely cash flows (those listed in Table 11–5), but *discounts them at different rates*. The flows for Project B, being more risky, would be discounted at a higher rate. Low-risk and high-risk projects will have different discount rates—the rates adjusted for the risk of the project. Table 11–6 gives illustrative calculations of risk-adjusted discount rates for Projects A and B. Here, Project B is evaluated using a higher required return (assumed 18 percent) reflecting that it is more risky than Project A, which has an assumed required return of 10 percent. As the calculations show, Project B has a lower net present value ($131) than does Project A ($373) even though the two projects have the same expected cash flows. The lower net present value for Project B reflects the higher penalty for risk imposed on that project through a higher required return.

Table 11–5

Most Likely Cash Flows for Two Hypothetical Projects

	Cash Flows				
	Period 0	Period 1	Period 2	Period 3	Period 4
Project A	−$1,000	$200	$400	$600	$600
Project B	−$1,000	$200	$400	$600	$600

Table 11–6
Application of Risk-Adjusted Discount Rates

Project A: Low Risk Required Return, K, = 0.10	Project B: High Risk Required Return, K, = 0.18
$NPV = -1,000 + \dfrac{200}{(1.10)} + \dfrac{400}{(1.10)^2} + \dfrac{600}{(1.10)^3} + \dfrac{600}{(1.10)^4}$ $= -\$1,000 + \$1,373 = \$373$	$NPV = -1,000 + \dfrac{200}{(1.18)} + \dfrac{400}{(1.18)^2} + \dfrac{600}{(1.18)^3} + \dfrac{600}{(1.18)^4}$ $= -1,000 + \$1,131 = \$131$

Grouping Investments by Risk Category

Risk categories—are
groups of investment
projects of similar risk.

In principle, investment opportunities of a given firm will vary in risk over a wide range. In theory, this variation would require determining a separate required rate of return for each investment proposal. Such an attempt would, however, ignore the costs and difficulties in estimating required returns. One practical solution to this problem is to group investment opportunities into **risk categories**. For example, a company might divide projects into three possible risk categories: cost-reduction projects, expansion projects, and new products.

Cost-reduction projects might include a variety of investment opportunities, such as the substitution of equipment for labor, the substitution of a new machine for an older, less efficient one, or the substitution of a completely new manufacturing facility for an old, outmoded one. Cash flows attributable to such projects often, though not always, can be estimated with reasonable accuracy at least during their first several years.

A second project category might include projects that would expand existing product lines. Such projects might include expansion of existing facilities or addition of new facilities to manufacture existing products. Because expansion projects generate additional sales revenue, cash flows attributable to such projects usually are more uncertain and, hence, more risky than those of cost-reduction projects.

A third and still more risky project category includes the introduction of new products. Such projects may involve new technology for manufacturing, packaging, or marketing. Judgments may be required as to the likelihood that the firm will be able to solve complex engineering and manufacturing problems. The effects of inflation may be very uncertain. The possibility of shifts in consumer preferences, countermoves by competitors, and technological obsolescence must be taken into account. Because of these and other considerations, both the sales revenue and cost estimates associated with new products usually are subject to considerably greater uncertainty than are those associated with the expansion of existing products. Within the new-products category itself, there may be considerable variation in uncertainty.

As a practical approach to capital budgeting, a firm might establish investment categories along the above lines. Required rates of return then could be set by category rather than for each new project individually. Any number of risk categories might be established. For each category, a measure of risk would have to be estimated.

If expansion projects, for example, were considered to be of average risk for the firm as a whole, then the required return of expansion projects, K_{exp}, would be the firm's weighted-average required return that we calculated in the last chapter; that is,

Figure 11-2
Required Return by Risk Category

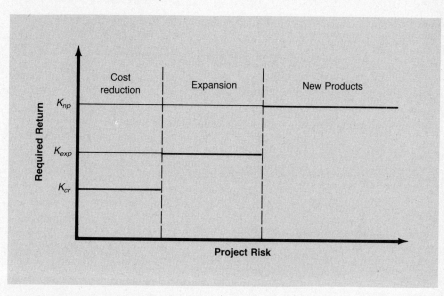

K_{exp} = *WARR*. Cost-reduction projects likely would be less risky, and projects involving new products would be more risky. The relationships might be represented as in Figure 11-2 where K symbolizes the required rate of return.

Because we are grouping projects into risk categories, Figure 11-2 shows only a crude risk adjustment. All cost-reduction projects would be treated as equally risky, and all would be evaluated using a required return of K_{cr}. All new products would be evaluated using a required return of K_{np}. In practice, we know that some new products may be more risky than others, but the risk adjustment shown in Figure 11-2 would not make this distinction. Figure 11-2 represents an improvement over using a single discount rate for all projects, but it is still a crude form of risk adjustment.

> **Grouping investment projects by risk categories is a practical response to the difficult problem of measuring risk.**

In practice, risk adjustments may use the *WARR* as a baseline for return targets, as demonstrated in Sample Problem 11-1.

Sample Problem 11-1

Setting Return Targets by Project Category for Menlo Corporation

Kim Park, the financial vice-president of Menlo Corporation, has decided to establish a system for setting return targets for capital-investment projects. The company regularly undertakes projects that involve installation of labor-saving machinery. The company operates 12 manufacturing plants located in the United States and frequently receives recommendations from division executives that manufacturing facilities be expanded. Over the past 5 years, the company has built three new plants and marketed

Table 11–7
Three Risk Categories Established for Menlo Corporation

Category	Risk Premium (percent)	Return Target (percent)
Cost reduction	2.5	10.5
Expansion	5.0	13.0
New products	12.5	20.5

a total of eight entirely new products. By gathering data on past investment projects, Park has determined that most cost-reduction projects are about half as risky as expansion projects. New products, on the other hand, are two to three times as risky.

Set up a system of return targets for Menlo Corporation, assuming that the U.S. government bond rate is 8 percent and that Menlo's weighted-average required return is 13 percent.

Solution

The simplest system for a firm such as Menlo is to establish several risk categories for capital-investment projects. In this case, three categories—cost reduction, expansion, and new products—seem to fit the situation. Taking expansion projects to be approximately average in risk, Park has decided to establish a target return of 13 percent for those projects—a target return that is equal to the company's *WARR*. The risk premium for this category would then be 5 percent—which is the weighted-average required return minus the U.S.-government-bond rate. Cost-reduction projects would be assigned a premium of $0.5 \times 5 = 2.5$ percent over the bond rate. Although new products vary somewhat in risk (two to three times as risky as expansion), it would be acceptable as a first approximation to establish a single category for new products with a risk premium of $2.5 \times 5 = 12.5$ percent. The complete system is shown in Table 11–7 where the risk premium is added to the 8 percent government-bond rate to get the return target. ∎

Multidivision Firms and Risk Adjustments

One particularly important application of risk-adjusted required rates of return occurs in multidivision firms. Consider R. J. Reynolds, the consumer-products giant with almost $20 billion worth of sales after its 1985 acquisition of Nabisco. In addition to its tobacco operations, R. J. Reynolds markets Kentucky Fried Chicken, Del Monte food products, and Nabisco brands, such as Oreo cookies. How should R. J. Reynolds allocate capital among its different divisions that produce quite different sorts of products? One mechanism is to use divisional required rates of return that reflect the differential risks of the different lines of business. The risks of investment in cigarette production are quite different from those in the fast-food business, for example. Required rates of return should reflect these differences in risk. It would not be appropriate to apply one single rate (the company's *WARR*) to all lines of business.

Table 11-8

Risk-Adjusted Discount Rates and Penalties for Risk

Year	Expected Cash Flow	Present Value at 10 Percent (1)	Present Value at 14 Percent (2)	Penalty for Risk (3) = (1) − (2)
1	$1,000	$909	$877	$32
2	$1,000	$826	$769	$57
3	$1,000	$751	$675	$76

Risk-Adjusted Discount Rates and Future Risks

In our calculation of a weighted-average required return and in formulating risk-adjusted discount rates, we have used a single rate that will then be applied to all future periods. We used this exact same procedure in our discussion of the time value of money. In using this method, we need to be aware of the implicit assumption it makes about the riskiness of future cash flows. Specifically, this method imposes a greater penalty for risk on cash flows the further they are in the future.

An example will illustrate. Suppose a project was expected to have a cash flow of $1,000 in each of the next three years. Assume further that, given the risk of the project, we have decided to use a required rate of return of 14 percent when U.S. government bonds are yielding only 10 percent. In other words, the risk premium on the project is 4 percent, using the government-bond yield as a proxy for a risk-free rate. Table 11-8 shows the present values of these future cash flows at both 10 percent and at 14 percent. We can interpret the present values at 10 percent as adjusting only for the time value of money (including a premium for expected inflation). The present values at 14 percent are lower, reflecting an extra penalty for the risk of the project.

The last column of Table 11-8 reports the differences between the present-value figures. These differences are the penalty for risk in dollar terms. For example, for the cash flow expected in year 1, the 4 percent risk premium in the discount rate translates into a $32 reduction in present value. As the figures in the last column show, the dollar penalty for risk gets larger the further the cash flow is in the future. The lesson from this example is that using the same discount rate for all future periods provides a larger and larger dollar penalty for risk the further in the future is the projected cash flow.

Is this a reasonable result? In many cases the answer is yes. The further in the future we have to project cash flows, the more likely we are to encounter uncertainties in making those estimates. It is typically easier to predict sales for the next year than for five years hence. In these cases, applying the same discount rate to all time periods is exactly what is needed. But we may sometimes encounter investments that don't fit this scenario. Perhaps the speed with which a new product can penetrate a market is highly uncertain, but the company is relatively confident that the product will ultimately be successful; the chief uncertainty is how long it will take. In this case, cash flows in the first few years might be more uncertain than those in later years. How could we handle such a situation? One way would be to establish different required rates of return for different phases of the project. During the early high-risk phase, we might require 15 percent; for cash flows after that phase, we might apply only 13 percent. The difficulty here, as with risk-adjusted discount rates in general, is coming up with specific ways to develop such rates. As a practical matter, it is usually appropriate to obtain a single required return for a project and then apply it to all future cash flows. We should, however, be aware of the implicit assumption this procedure makes about risk in case we find specific situations that do not fit this assumption.

Developing Specific Risk-Adjusted Discount Rates

How can we develop risk-adjusted required returns? The place to start is to recall our calculation of the weighted-average required return. As developed in Chapter 10, the *WARR* is a rate that reflects the average-risk investment for a firm. Firms with different risks will have different *WARR*s. For example, Apple Computer, a firm in the highly volatile personal computer industry, is more risky than Duke Power Company, a largely regulated provider of electricity in the southeastern United States. As a result, if we calculated *WARR*s for the two firms, we would expect a higher figure for Apple Computer. This higher figure for Apple Computer would reflect the market's distaste for risk. In other words, the market requires higher returns the higher the risk.

The difficulty is that we often need required returns for projects or divisions of companies that will not be traded separately in financial markets. Take the case of R. J. Reynolds, a tobacco company that has diversified into a variety of other activities. The debt and stock of R. J. Reynolds reflect the risk characteristics of its entire portfolio of activities. Thus, its traded securities do not have the same risk as one of its divisions. In fact, there is no separate set of securities that show ownership in just one of the R. J. Reynolds divisions. If there were, and we needed a required rate of return for one division, we could just treat these securities as a separate company and use the techniques discussed in Chapter 10 to calculate the weighted-average required return based on those securities. This division *WARR* would be the appropriate required return for that division.

If different divisions had different risks, we would get different required returns for each division. The market would do our risk adjusting for us. Unfortunately, life is not so easy. Divisions or projects are not traded as separate companies in financial markets. While this makes our job of risk adjustment more difficult, we still can use market information to help. The principle we will use is: *investments of equal risk should have the same required return.* One way to use this basic principle and take advantage of financial-market information is the **pure-play technique**.

The **pure-play technique**—calculates risk-adjusted discount rates by matching a particular investment to one or more publicly traded companies that have risks comparable to those of the investment.

The Pure-Play Technique

The pure-play technique calls for matching a particular investment proposal under consideration to some traded company (or group of companies) based on risk. The idea is to find two situations in which the risks are equal and calculate the required return *(WARR)* for the case where market data are available—that is, the company whose stock is publicly traded. This rate will also be appropriate for the investment proposal provided it has approximately the same risk.

To illustrate, take the case of the American Telephone & Telegraph (AT&T) divestiture in 1984, in which the parent company (AT&T) and its operating subsidiaries

Table 11–9
Selected Financial Data

Category	Rate (percent)
Long-term interest rate for government bonds	10.0
Market risk premium on stocks	7.2
Firms' interest rate on new debt	11.0
Tax rate	50.0

(the local telephone companies) were split up into separate corporations. After the divestiture, the new AT&T provided long-distance phone service, produced telecommunications equipment, and was entering new information-processing markets. This last entry involved introducing its own line of computers in direct competition with IBM. How might AT&T decide on an appropriate required return for investments in the computer business? The pure-play technique might be applied by finding a set of companies whose predominant activities were in the computer field.

Standard industrial codes (SICs)—are a system for classifying companies by their primary line of business.

A practical way of selecting such companies is to use the system of **standard industrial codes (SICs)** developed to classify companies by their primary line of business. According to these codes, the computer group would include IBM, Burroughs Corporation, Control Data Corporation, Hewlett-Packard, Apple Computer, Honeywell, NCR Corporation, and Sperry Corporation plus others. A weighted-average required return could be calculated for each of these companies and the resultant figures averaged to produce an *industry required return*. This industry figure would then serve as an estimate of the required return appropriate for investment in the computer business. AT&T would now have a risk-adjusted required return for its computer operations. This rate would be based on the risks of that business, as reflected in market required rates of return on companies in that business.

Using Entry into the Computer Industry as an Example. To see how this risk-adjusted required return could be formulated, we can attempt to find a required rate of return for AT&T's investments in the computer industry. The first step is to gather some data from financial markets. Table 11–9 shows data collected in November 1985. At that time, yields on long-term government bonds were slightly above 10 percent—we will round to 10 percent for this illustration. In addition, suppose that the market risk premium on stocks in general was 7.2 percent. This figure is based on historical risk premia on equity, as discussed in Chapter 10. Finally, assume for simplicity that all of the firms could issue new long-term debt at a yield to maturity of 11 percent. With extra effort, we could get borrowing costs for each of the individual companies based on the market's assessment of the risk of each company's debt. Assume a 50 percent tax rate for this example.

Company Data. For this illustration, we have limited ourselves to data on four companies, though in practice one might use more. In addition to AT&T, we have selected three firms who are classified by Value Line as being in the computer business. The beta coefficient and proportions of equity financing and debt financing are given in Table 11–10.

Table 11–10

Beta Coefficients and Financing Mix for Selected Firms

Firm	Beta Coefficient	Proportion of Financing Done with Equity, W_e	Proportion of Financing Done with Debt, W_d
AT&T	0.80	0.63	0.37
Apple	1.70	1.00	0.00
Amdahl	1.55	0.81	0.19
IBM	1.05	0.89	0.11

Source: Value Line Investment Survey.

Calculating the Weighted-Average Required Return.   First, let us calculate the *WARR* for AT&T. Using the capital-asset-pricing model, we can calculate AT&T's required return on equity as

$$K_e = R_f + (K_m - R_f) \text{ (Beta)}$$

$$= 0.10 + (0.072)(0.80) = 0.10 + 0.06 = 0.16.$$

Note that according to Value Line's estimate of the beta coefficient, stock in AT&T is less risky than the average stock, so it gets a risk premium of 6 percent, which is below the assumed market risk premium of 7.2 percent.

We can now calculate AT&T's weighted-average required return using our earlier assumptions and the data from Table 11–10 as

$$WARR = W_e K_e + W_d K_d (1 - T)$$

$$= (0.63)(0.16) + 0.37(0.11)(1 - 0.5) = 0.1212.$$

Based on this *WARR*, AT&T's average-risk project should have a required rate of return of approximately 12 percent. Is this rate appropriate for its computer investments? No. A look at the data for the three computer firms tells us that the computer business is more risky. Each of the computer stocks has a beta coefficient greater than 1.0, indicating that these stocks are more risky than AT&T's stock. The computer business is more risky even though the computer firms use very little debt financing compared to AT&T. Remember that the use of debt exposes shareholders to extra risks over and above the operating risks of the company. So if the operating risk of AT&T and the computer firms were the same, we would expect the computer stocks to be less risky than AT&T stock because AT&T uses more debt. The data show this is not the case: despite their lower use of debt, the computer stocks are more risky. Therefore, there are greater operating risks associated with the computer business compared to AT&T's average risk.

To estimate the required return associated with the computer business, we can calculate the weighted-average required return for each of the three computer firms. First, we use the capital-asset-pricing model to estimate the shareholders' required return. From these calculated required returns on equity, we can then calculate the weighted-average required return, as shown in Table 11–11.

Table 11–11

Calculating Required Return on Equity and Weighted-Average Required Returns for Three Firms in the Computer Industry

$R_f + (K_m - R_f)\, \beta = K_e$	$W_e K_e + W_d K_d\, (1 - T) = WARR$
Apple Computer $0.10 + (0.072)(1.7) = 0.2224$	$1.0\,(0.2224) + 0\,(0.11)(1 - 0.5) = 0.2224$
Amdahl Corp $\quad 0.10 + (0.072)(1.55) = 0.2116$	$0.81\,(0.2116) + 0.19\,(0.11)(1 - 0.5) = 0.1818$
IBM Corp $\quad\;\; 0.10 + (0.072)(1.05) = 0.1756$	$0.89\,(0.1756) + 0.11\,(0.11)(1 - 0.5) = 0.1623$
	Average $= 0.1888$

Interpreting the Results. In each case, the required return is substantially above AT&T's *WARR* of 12 percent. There are, however, variations even within the computer industry. For example, the relatively new entrant, Apple Computer, appears to have a higher *WARR* than does the computer giant, IBM. This higher *WARR* undoubtedly reflects the higher risks to Apple Computer as it tries to establish its long-term presence in the market.

What rate should AT&T use? One approach is to take an average for the three computer companies. Averaging the three *WARR* figures calculated above gives us an industry average of 0.1888, or approximately 19 percent. If AT&T felt it had risks comparable to this average for the industry then it could use a 19 percent required return for its computer investments. The 19 percent figure is higher than AT&T's *WARR* of 12 percent to reflect the extra risks of the computer business. We have adjusted for risk by using a higher required rate of return.

Before leaving this example, remember that we have made some very specific assumptions in deriving the figure of 19 percent. To test the reasonableness of our results we might do alternative calculations of K_e using the dividend-growth model, which we discussed in Chapter 4. In addition, the 19 percent is a simple average of three *WARR*s. If we thought AT&T was more like IBM in terms of its risk in the computer business, then we would give more weight to IBM's *WARR* in determining the average. One way to calculate such a weighted average would be to weight the *WARR*s by the market shares of the companies because IBM is much larger than either Apple or Amdahl. On the other hand, AT&T is a new entrant into the computer business, which might make it more risky than IBM and more like Apple Computer. As we can see, the process of risk adjustment is not easy. Often there are no simple answers, and a good deal of judgment is required.

The illustration above shows one way to apply the pure-play technique. Such an application would provide important insights into the relative risks of the computer business as compared to AT&T's overall risks. At least in the environment of the mid-1980s, the computer business is probably more risky than AT&T's long-distance phone operations. The above application of the pure-play technique would give an idea of how required rates of return should be adjusted to reflect such risk differences.

Problems in Obtaining Data. The pure-play technique does not solve all our problems, however. First, we have the difficulty of defining comparable risks. The industry classifications may be a useful start, but they may not capture all dimensions of risk. As an example, what, if any, additional risk would AT&T bear as a new entrant into

Finance in Practice 11—2

Methods for Dealing with Risk

As we have discussed, there are a number of different ways of dealing with risk in capital budgeting, such as sensitivity analysis and using risk-adjusted discount rates, which we have been discussing in this chapter. What methods do firms actually use in practice?

By looking at the results of a survey of 189 large U.S. firms conducted in the 1970s, we can get some idea of what many firms do. Of the 143 firms responding to questions about how they deal with risk, 90 percent of the firms assign a higher required rate of return on the project for higher risk. That is, they use risk-adjusted discount rates. About 10 percent of the firms used a short-

ened payback period as their only means of risk adjustment. About 31 percent of firms combine a shortening of the payback period with a raising of the required return.

While the firms often raise required returns, many of them do so based only on a subjective evaluation of risk. In the sample, more than 57 percent of the firms responded that they either assess project riskiness based only on a subjective evaluation or ignore risk differences altogether. Another 23 percent of the firms assigned projects to risk categories. About 35 percent of the firms used sensitivity analysis or some other method incorporating a probability distribution of cash flows rather than a single best guess at a projected cash flow.

Why aren't more firms making sophisticated risk adjustments? Don't managers know about the methods? Are the methods wrong? The answers lie in the standard logic of a cost/benefit

trade-off. It's not that the techniques for risk adjustment are wrong. Nor is it the case that the techniques are not widely known. The fact is that dealing with risk is extremely difficult. The information required to use many formal risk-adjustment techniques is sometimes very costly, if not impossible to come by. Facing such a situation, managers often must deal with risk subjectively.

The fact that there are problems of applying the techniques does not mean that studying risk-adjustment techniques is a fruitless exercise. In some cases, the techniques can be applied. In many more instances, the basic insights attained from studying risk-adjustment methods are extremely useful in improving a person's ability to deal subjectively with risk.

Source: Adapted from L. D. Schall, G. L. Sundem, and W. R. Geijsbeck, Jr., "Survey and Analysis of Capital Budgeting Methods," *Journal of Finance*, March 1978, pp. 281–87.

the computer field? It is possible to use other criteria for picking comparable-risk companies such as financial ratios, past variability of returns, or measures of nondiversifiable risk (such as beta coefficients). It may be difficult or impractical, however, to develop such measures for the investment proposal under consideration. Second, the pure-play approach relies on finding traded companies that have risks directly comparable to the investment in question. Sometimes such companies do not exist, possibly because all the firms producing a product are themselves significantly involved in other product lines. In other cases, the proposed investment may represent a completely new product or technology. As is usually the case, the manager's job is not an easy one. In practice, many difficult judgments must be made. The key is to make the best use of the information that is available.

Using Theoretical Models of the Risk/Return Trade-Off

The pure-play technique makes use of the basic principle that investments of equal risk should have the same required rate of return. It implements this principle by identifying traded companies with risks comparable to those of the investment in question. In the example above, we made direct use of theoretical models to carry out our risk adjustments. In particular, we used the capital-asset-pricing model (CAPM) in estimating the required return on the stocks of AT&T and of the three computer companies. The CAPM provided one way to quantify the risks of stock ownership in the individual companies.

> **A basic principle in determining risk-adjusted discount rates is that investments of the same risk should have the same required rate of return.**

Suppose, however, that we could not find traded companies with risks comparable to the investment under consideration. Can we apply the capital-asset-pricing model or other models directly to the project? In theory, the answer is yes. We can view the project as another asset. Given the risks of that asset, investors will have a particular required rate of return. The difficulty is that we typically have no independent financial market data on the project. We don't have a ''project'' share price or dividend, so we can't calculate a dividend yield to use a dividend-growth model tailored to the project. There is no such thing as stock in the project, so we can't use standard techniques to estimate a project beta coefficient. As a result, we must typically make subjective risk estimates.

After our discussion of the effects of financing on risks and value in the next two chapters, we will have more to say about how one might apply theoretical models directly to a project. For now the important message is that despite its difficulties, risk adjustment is critical to making sound investment decisions. Even when theory does not give explicit guidance on how to quantify risks, the insights about the risk/return trade-off can offer substantial benefits in adjusting for risk.

UNRESOLVED ISSUES

In this chapter, we have focused on ways to deal with risk. The two techniques we discussed were sensitivity analysis and the formulation of risk-adjusted discount rates. Before closing our discussion, we want to point out a number of key difficulties in doing risk adjustments.

Diversifiable Risk

Nondiversifiable risk—is market-related risk, the risk that cannot be eliminated by diversification. It depends on how a project's cash flows are related to changes in general economic and market conditions, such as interest rates, GNP growth, or inflation.

The first difficulty is conceptual in nature and goes back to the basic problem of measuring risk. For example, the capital-asset-pricing model (CAPM) says that the only type of risk that matters to investors is **nondiversifiable risk**—risk relative to the market. The rationale for looking only at nondiversifiable risk is that, in the CAPM, investors are well diversified, holding many stocks and bonds. The only risk such investors care about is the risk that a project will add to their total portfolio. That added risk is the only extra risk they have to bear as a result of the project. The nondiversifiable risk of the project is a measure of this extra risk. Such nondiversifiable risk depends on how the cash flows on the project are related to changes in general market conditions, such as interest rates, GNP growth, and inflation. Nondiversifiable risk does not depend on project-specific risk, such as whether there is a chance for the

Diversifiable risk—is project-specific risk, such as that deriving from uncertainty over entry of competitors, strikes, or technological advances.

unexpected entry of a new competitor, a strike, or a sudden technological development that affects a key product. These types of uncertainty would be examples of **diversifiable risk**.

What about diversifiable risk? The CAPM says diversifiable risk should not affect the risk premium because well diversified investors won't bear such diversifiable risks: they diversify them away.

In the real world, however, not all investors are well diversified. Suppose an individual has all of his or her wealth invested in one business. Clearly, such an individual's risk from owning this business is the total risk (nondiversifiable risk plus diversifiable risk) of the company because he or she is not diversified. The individual doesn't own other assets whose returns may offset returns on this company. As a result, the individual will be interested in how a project affects the total risk of this company, not just in how the project affects the market portfolio—that is, the person will not be interested solely in how the project affects nondiversifiable risk.

In such a situation, this individual may require an extra risk premium for both nondiversifiable (beta) risk and diversifiable risk.

Now we can see a potential problem. Can we distinguish between types of risk—nondiversifiable and diversifiable—associated with a project and the types of risks they pose to investors? Unfortunately, there is no easy answer. It is probably the case that nondiversifiable risk should be given more weight in determining a risk premium than diversifiable risk, but as yet we have no well developed theory that allows us to know what weights we should give to the two types of risk. It is probably safe to say that diversifiable risk would be much less important for large companies whose stock is held by well-diversified investors than it is for small firms owned by a few individuals.

While the capital-asset-pricing model focuses only on nondiversifiable risk, sensitivity analysis portrays total risk. It looks at the variability of outcomes, but in practice it does not try to distinguish between diversifiable and nondiversifiable risk. Sensitivity analysis has the virtue of focusing on specific events that may cause a project to succeed or fail—for example, changes in tax laws or energy prices. Such a focus makes financial managers think carefully about the project. Sensitivity analysis does not, however, distinguish between diversifiable and nondiversifiable risk and does not tell us what weights to assign to diversifiable risk versus nondiversifiable risk.

> **The capital-asset-pricing model gives no weight to diversifiable risk in determining risk adjustments, but diversifiable risk may be important to investors who are not well diversified. Sensitivity analysis, on the other hand, measures total risk, and does not distinguish between diversifiable and nondiversifiable risk.**

Quantification

A second major difficulty that we found in dealing with risk is coming up with the numbers to use to quantify risk adjustments. The costs and difficulties of developing information are not small ones, and these costs will affect the types of risk adjustments that firms decide to apply in practice. Just as is true in making any financial decision, firms must evaluate whether or not the benefits of adopting a particular form of risk adjustment outweigh the costs. As a result, it may be prudent for a firm to apply detailed risk adjustments to large projects while many smaller projects are placed in one of a number of risk categories with no further analysis of the project's risk.

Do these problems mean that we should not consider risk adjustments in making investment decisions? The answer is no. Investors in financial markets require extra returns for bearing risk and incorporate these requirements in determining the value of shares of stock in a company. If managers pursue the objective of value maximization, they must grapple with the problems of adjusting for risk, even though it is an extremely difficult task. The techniques we have discussed in this chapter provide some guidance in this difficult job.

SUMMARY OF PART FOUR

We have reached a point where we can summarize the basic approach to analyzing investment opportunities that has been developed in Chapters 9, 10, and 11. As we discussed in Chapter 9, we use discounted-cash-flow techniques to calculate the net present value and the internal rate of return for an investment project, as presented in Equation (2) and Equation (3) in Chapter 9.

A positive net present value signals that an investment opportunity passes the economic test. In the case of a positive *NPV*, the present value of the cash benefits of the project exceed the present value of the cash costs. In other words, the outputs are worth more than the inputs. As a result, projects with a positive net present value create value for the firm and for society as well. By accepting such projects, managers further the objective of value maximization. If forced to rank mutually exclusive projects, managers should pick the project with the highest net present value—that is, the project that adds the most value.

To use *NPV* analysis, we need to calculate expected cash flows, C_t, and an appropriate required rate of return, K, at which to discount these cash flows. We have taken the approach of looking at operating cash flows and letting the discount rate reflect the financing mix of the corporation. In Chapter 9, we saw that the cash flows appropriate to use in calculating net present value are the firm's *incremental after-tax operating cash flows* that result from adopting the project.

The required return, K, is based on the required returns of the suppliers of capital to the firm. As a result, we look to financial markets to determine required returns. In Chapter 10, we saw that, for a firm's average-risk project, the weighted-average required return could be used as a discount rate. The *WARR* is a weighted average of the required returns of the suppliers of capital to the firm. In the simple case where a firm uses only debt and common stock, we can calculate *WARR* as

$$WARR = K_w = W_d K_d (1 - T) + W_e K_e$$

Note that because of the tax deductibility of interest, we use the *after-tax* cost of debt, $K_d(1 - T)$, in calculating *WARR*.

In Chapter 11 we addressed the problems of adjusting our analysis for differences in project risk. Remember that the *WARR* is an appropriate discount rate only if the project is of average risk for the firm.

Because investors in financial markets require higher returns for bearing higher risk, it is important to adjust for risk. The two most widely used techniques for dealing with risk are (1) sensitivity analysis and (2) risk-adjusted discount rates. Sensitivity analysis focuses on the numerator of our *NPV* calculation and allows managers to ask: what if cash flows turn out different than expected? Techniques for adjusting discount rates to take risk into account focus on the denominator of the *NPV* calculation. Required returns are changed as risk changes. The higher the risk of a project, the higher is the required return used as a discount rate.

The three chapters of Part Four have developed the tools necessary to analyze investment projects. It is important to remember, however, that being successful at capital budgeting requires much more than applying the tools of finance. Someone has to come up with ideas for new investments. As we mentioned in Chapter 9, investment alternatives don't arrive in neat bundles for managers to evaluate—the alternatives must be thought up and defined. In addition, once an investment decision is made, it still must be implemented. That implementation involves the time and talents of many managers in addition to other corporate employees.

Chapters 9 through 11 have focused on the basic economic analysis of investment decisions—the tools of finance. It is important to remember that these tools are only part of the process of making investment decisions. No amount of sophistication with discounted-cash-flow techniques can salvage a company that never comes up with good investment alternatives to analyze. On the other hand, the tools we have developed can help improve decisions for all companies.

KEY CONCEPTS

1. The two main practical techniques for dealing with risk in capital-investment analysis are sensitivity analysis and risk-adjusted discount rates.

2. Sensitivity analysis is a *What if?* technique useful for examining the impact on net present value and internal rate of return of variations in underlying factors.

3. Risk-adjusted discount rates (required rates of return) can be used as return targets for projects that are not of average risk because they have been formulated to take risk into account. The higher the risk, the higher is the required rate of return.

4. Classifying projects by risk category is a useful way of simplifying the capital-budgeting process.

5. A basic principle in setting risk-adjusted discount rates is that investments of equal risk should have the same required return.

6. One way to estimate risk-adjusted discount rates is to use *WARR*s for companies that are similar in risk to the investment proposal under consideration.

SUMMARY

Dealing with risk is one of the most difficult problems a manager faces. Two techniques for dealing with risk in capital-investment analysis are sensitivity analysis and use of risk-adjusted discount rates. Using sensitivity analysis, the manager can ask *what if* important factors turn out different than expected. Using risk-adjusted discount rates, the manager can incorporate risk into the return target rather than in the cash-flow estimates.

Projects can be classified into risk categories—such as cost-reduction projects, expansion projects, and new products—as a way of simplifying the capital-budgeting process. Return targets can then be set by category rather than for each project individually. Return targets may also be determined at the division level to provide for effective allocation of capital in multidivision firms. A basic principle in estimating risk-adjusted discount rates is that investments of the same risk should have the same required rate of return.

Adjusting for risk is not an easy task. Each specific tool we have suggested for risk adjustment has its strengths and weaknesses. It is important to remember, however, that investors in financial markets require extra returns for bearing risk. The higher required returns affect the value of the stocks and bonds that are traded in financial markets.

To pursue the objective of maximizing the value of the firm, financial managers must deal with the problem of adjusting the risk in analyzing investment opportunities.

QUESTIONS

1. Explain the two general approaches to dealing with risk in capital budgeting.
2. How can sensitivity analysis be used in capital budgeting?
3. Discuss the considerations in setting the return target for a worst-case analysis.
4. Explain the basic differences between risk-adjusted discount rates and sensitivity analysis as techniques for dealing with risk.
5. Explain how the notion of risk categories can be used to simplify capital budgeting in a firm.
6. Describe the pure-play technique. How can it be used to determine risk-adjusted discount rates?
7. If a firm uses a single return target to evaluate projects of widely varying risk characteristics, what is the likely outcome over an extended period of time?
8. How can a firm undertake a high-risk investment opportunity without increasing overall risk to its shareholders?

PROBLEMS

1. The Community Hospital is planning to expand its facilities. Capacity for 50 new beds is needed immediately and for another 50 in 5 years. A contractor submits a bid to build the entire 100-bed facility for $500,000. Maintenance and utilities on the 100-bed facility will run $10,000 per year. As an alternative, the contractor is willing to build a 50-bed facility now for $300,000 and to agree to build the remaining 50-bed facility in 5 years for an additional $350,000 under a fixed-price contract. Maintenance and utilities on the 50-bed facility will run $5,000 per year. Assume that the yield to maturity on long-term United States government bonds is 10 percent and that the hospital is not subject to taxation. Which alternative should the hospital elect?

2. The Downtown Municipal Hospital is considering installing an automatic dishwashing facility as a labor-saving measure. The hospital is municipally owned and not subject to taxation. The dishwasher, conveyor system, and other ancillary equipment require an outlay of $45,000 and have an expected life of 8 years, at the end of which time they are expected to have zero salvage value. Electrical power, supplies, and maintenance are expected to cost $1,300 per year. Direct labor savings are expected to be $11,500 annually (one full-time employee). At the time the project is being considered, the yield to maturity on long-term United States government bonds is 11 percent. The rate on an issue of bonds sold recently by the city was 9 percent.

  a. Can discounted cash flow techniques be used to analyze the decision? If so, what discount rate should be used?

  b. What decision should the hospital make?

3. The Orion Company has decided to categorize its investment opportunities by degree of risk and to set return targets by risk category. Orion's management has conducted a study of past investment projects to measure their relative risk. A large amount of data has been gathered to permit calculation of relative risk ratios. Results of the study are given in Table A. Develop a system of return

Table A

Category	Relative Risk Ratio
Cost reduction	0.40
Expansion—existing product lines	1.00
New products—existing industries	1.75
New products—new industries	3.00

Table B

	Dividend Growth Rate (percent)	Current Dividend	Current Share Price	Proportion of Financing Done by Debt, W_d (percent)	Required Return on Debt, K_d (percent)
Imitations, Inc.	5	$4.40	$54.00	40	11
Images Corp.	8	$3.25	$42.00	55	14
Copy-Rite Co.	3	$6.30	$86.00	30	8

targets for Orion. Use a government bond rate of 10 percent. Assume Orion is an all-equity firm and the market risk premium is 7.2 percent.

4. The Saki Camera Company, manufacturer of high-quality cameras and photographic equipment, feels that the time is right to enter the photocopy business. After three years of research and development, company engineers have designed a copy machine that they feel will be able to compete effectively with three established manufacturers, for whom selected financial data are presented in Table B.

  a. Using the Dividend Valuation Model of Chapter 4, calculate the shareholders' required rate of return, K_e, for each of the photocopy companies listed in Table B.

  b. Calculate the weighted average required return (WARR) for each of these potential competitors, and suggest a WARR suitable for Saki to evaluate the manufacturing and marketing of photocopy machines. Assume that all of these firms are subject to a marginal tax rate of 40 percent.

5. McIntyre Industries is considering a plan to establish return targets for investment decisions in its various divisions. A study of past data indicates that projects in different categories are not uniformly risky from one division to another. For example, cost reduction projects in the Electric Motors Division were found to be generally less risky than cost reduction projects in the Microelectronics Division. These risk differences were due primarily to differences in technology among divisons. Data gathered on relative risk was as shown in Table C. Assume McIntyre is an all-equity firm and the market risk premium is 7.2 percent. Develop a system of return targets for each divison, assuming a government bond rate of 11 percent.

6. Consider the Neptune Company, in the business of installing swimming pools and manufacturing pool equipment. The management of Neptune has decided that the firm would do well to begin building tennis courts as part of its product offering. The problem is to develop a WARR appropriate for the tennis court line of business. Neptune has discovered four tennis-court builders listed on the New York Stock Exchange that are characterized by operating risks similar to those expected for the new tennis-court line. Selected data for these firms and Neptune are presented in Table D. The current

Table C

Division	Relative Risk in Various Project Categories		
	Cost Reduction	Expansion	New Products
Electric Motors	0.5	1.0	2.0
Electrical Components	0.3	1.0	1.5
Microelectronics	0.8	1.5	3.5

Table D

Firm	Beta Coefficient	Proportion of Financing Done with Equity, W_e (percent)	Proportion of Financing Done by Debt, W_d (percent)
Connors, Inc.	1.15	0.60	0.40
Borg and Co.	1.05	0.35	0.65
McEnroe Corp.	1.20	0.45	0.55
Evert-Lloyd Assoc.	1.10	0.40	0.60
Neptune Company	0.89	0.65	0.35

yield to maturity on long-term U.S. government bonds is 10 percent. The market risk premium on stocks in general is 7.2 percent. Each of these firms may issue long-term debt with a yield to maturity of 14 percent. The tax rate applicable to all of these firms is 40 percent.

a. Calculate K_e and the *WARR* for Neptune before the product line expansion. Is this rate appropriate for evaluating the proposed expansion into tennis courts?

b. Calculate K_e and the *WARR* for each of the tennis-court companies listed in Table D. What would you recommend to be a suitable required rate of return for Neptune's tennis-court line of business?

7. Atlantic Leasing Company is considering an investment opportunity involving the construction of a plant and the subsequent rental of the facility to a user, the Ajax Manufacturing Corporation. The total outlay for construction would be $1 million. The plant would be leased to Ajax for a period of 10 years. Atlantic would take the depreciation and pay for property taxes and insurance. The net after-tax operating cash inflow to Atlantic during years 1–10, including the lease payment, insurance, and all taxes, would be $115,000 per year. At the end of the 10 years, Atlantic would own the plant. Its market value at that time, net of all taxes, is estimated to be $1 million. Calculate the net present value *(NPV)* of the operating cash flows and the terminal value. Assume that, even though the lease payment from Ajax is contractual, it is not riskless because of the possibility, even though small, that Ajax might default. Given this risk, Atlantic has determined the required rate

of return for the operating cash flows ($115,000 per year) to be 13 percent. The terminal value is subject to greater uncertainty and is to be evaluated using an 18-percent required rate of return. What decision should Atlantic make?

8. Estimate the required rate of return on equity (K_e) for the stocks listed in Table E, assuming a government bond rate of 11 percent and a market risk premium of 7.2 percent. Are the rates appropriate as required rates of return to be used on the "typical project" in each firm? Explain.

9. An electronics firm is evaluating a proposal to manufacture and market light bulbs. The project is characterized by the estimated cash flows shown in Table F. Expected cash inflows are derived from the sales revenue associated with the project, which represents an entirely new business venture for the firm. The project is considered to be a natural extension for the company, however, in that light bulbs may be produced with existing equipment. The primary component of the expected cash outflows listed in Table F is the increment in operating expenses of this machinery associated with the manufacture of light bulbs. An extensive

Table E

Stock	Beta Coefficient
A	0.80
B	0.95
C	1.25
D	1.45

Table F

| | *Expected Cash Flows* | | | | |
	Year 1	Year 2	Year 3	Year 4	Year 5
Inflow	5,000	5,050	6,020	6,900	7,300
Outflow	3,000	3,500	4,000	4,500	5,000

marketing campaign is not believed to be necessary, so marketing expenses will be minimal. The market for light bulbs is excellent, but the firm will only be accepted as a reputable manufacturer of light bulbs after it has been in the business for a few years. The firm has a policy of grouping all investment projects into risk categories for purposes of evaluation. Because the proposed project is unrelated to the firm's existing product line, it will be evaluated at the standard rate applicable to new products: 16 percent which includes a 5 percent premium for risk.

a. What is the dollar risk penalty associated with each year's cash inflow for the project? Does this pattern seem reasonable?

b. What do you notice about the dollar risk premium associated with cash outflows? Does this pattern seem reasonable?

c. How would you go about deriving a discount rate suitable for this project?

10. Redo problem (28) from Chapter 9 assuming that National will have to pay $500,000 (instead of $400,000) for the equipment but that each package of Tasty can be sold for $0.50 (instead of $0.40).

11. Redo problem (29) from Chapter 9 assuming that a new model of tractor has been introduced. While it costs $50,000, it is expected to produce annual cash revenues of $16,000 (before taxes).

12. Refer to problem (25) from Chapter 9. Recall that the Allen Company, a manufacturer of perfumes and toiletries, is evaluating the potential of a new line of perfume, Jasper, to replace an existing line, Rosalyn. Company management has just learned of sensitivity analysis as a means of evaluating a new investment project. Assume that the company's beta is 1.25, the market risk premium

is 7.2 percent and that the company is 100 percent equity-financed.

a. What is the Allen Company's required return for evaluating "worst-case" cash flows using sensitivity analysis?

b. As a financial analyst with the Allen Company, you have been asked to examine the potential of the new project under the following "worst-case" scenarios: (i) The annual overhead maintenance and power expenses of the new packaging machine required to produce Jasper are twice the expected $1000; (ii) Actual sales (number of bottles) of Jasper turn out to be 10 percent below expected sales; (iii) The public is less receptive of Jasper than management hopes, forcing marketing expenses to be increased by 5 percent in year 2, 10 percent in year 3, and 5 percent in year 4.

13. Refer to problem (27) in Chapter 9. Assume that the Cartwright Company's 14 percent required return includes a risk premium of 5 percent.

a. Suppose that the new machine being considered by the Cartwright Company increases sales revenue by only $9,000 per year. This is considered by management to be the worst possible shortfall in revenue. By how much must annual operating costs be reduced from their present level in order for you to recommend the purchase of the new machine?

b. Suppose that, in the worst case, annual operating costs are reduced by only $10,000. How much increased sales revenue must occur in order for the new machine to be acceptable?

c. What are your recommendations for the project?

REFERENCES

Arditti, F. D., and H. Levy. "The Weighted Average Cost of Capital as a Cutoff Rate: A Critical Examination of the Classical Textbook Weighted Average." *Financial Management* XX (Fall 1977): 24–34.

Bower, R. S., and J. M. Jenks. "Divisional Screening Rates," *Financial Management* 4 (Autumn 1975): 42–49.

Bower, R. S., and D. R. Lessard. "An Operational Approach to Risk Screening." *Journal of Finance* 28 (May 1973): 321–328.

Bowsher, N. M. "The Rise and Fall of Interest Rates." Federal Reserve Bank of St. Louis *Review* 62 (August–September 1980): 16–23.

Brealey, R., and S. Myers. *Principles of Corporate Finance*. New York: McGraw Hill Book Company, 1981.

Brigham, E. "Hurdle Rates for Screening Capital Expenditure Proposals." *Financial Management* 4 (Autumn 1975): 17–26.

Carter, E. E. "What Are the Risks in Risk Analysis?" *Harvard Business Review* 50 (July 1972): 72–76.

Chambers, D. R., R. S. Harris, and J. J. Pringle. "Treatment of Financing Mix in Analyzing Investment Opportunities." *Financial Management* (Summer 1982): 24–41.

Cooley, P. L., R. L. Roenfeldt, and I. Chew. "Capital Budgeting Procedures Under Inflation." *Financial Management* 4 (Winter 1975): 18–27.

Crum, R. L., D. J. Laughhunn, and J. W. Payne. "Risk Seeking Behavior and Its Implications for Financial Models." *Financial Management* 10 (Winter 1981): 20–27.

Donaldson, G. "Strategic Hurdle Rates for Capital Investment." *Harvard Business Review* 50 (Mar.–Apr. 1972): 50–55.

Findlay, M. C., A. E. Gooding, and W. Q. Weaver. "On the Relevant Risk for Determining Capital Expenditure Hurdle Rates." *Financial Management* 5 (Winter 1976): 9–17.

Haley, C. W., and L. D. Schall. "Problems with the Concept of the Cost of Capital." *Journal of Financial and Quantitative Analysis* 13 (Dec. 1978): 847–871.

Harris, R. S., and J. J. Pringle. "A Note on the Implications of Miller's Argument for Capital Budgeting." *Journal of Financial Research* (Spring 1983): 13–23.

Hastie, K. L. "One Businessman's View of Capital Budgeting." *Financial Management* 4 (Winter 1974): 36–44.

Hayes, S. L., III. "Capital Commitments and the High Cost of Money." *Harvard Business Review* 55 (May–June 1977): 155–161.

Hertz, D. B. "Investment Policies that Pay Off." *Harvard Business Review* 46 (Jan.–Feb. 1968): 96–108.

Hertz, D. B. "Risk Analysis in Capital Investment." *Harvard Business Review* 42 (Jan.–Feb. 1964): 95–106.

Hong, H., and A. Rappaport. "Debt Capacity, Optimal Capital Structure, and Capital Budgeting Analysis." *Financial Management* 7 (Autumn 1978): 7–11.

Lewellen, W. G., "Some Observations on Risk-Adjusted Discount Rates." *Journal of Finance* 31 (Sept. 1977): 1331–1338.

Lintner, J. "The Evaluation of Risk Assets and the Selection of Risky Investments in Stock Portfolios and Capital Budgets." *Review of Economics and Statistics* 47 (Feb. 1965): 13–77.

Litzenberger, R. H., and A. Budd. "Corporate Investment Criteria and the Evaluation of Risk Assets." *Journal of Financial and Quantitative Analysis* 5 (Dec. 1970): 395–420.

Miles, J. A., and J. R. Ezzell. "The Weighted Average Cost of Capital, Perfect Capital Markets and Project Life: A Clarification." *Journal of Financial and Quantitative Analysis* XX (Sept. 1980): 719–730.

Myers, S. C., "Interaction of Corporate Financing and Investment Decisions—Implications for Capital Budgeting." *Journal of Finance* 29 (Mar. 1974): 1–25.

Myers, S. C., and S. M. Turnbull. "Capital Budgeting and the Capital Asset Pricing Model—Good News and Bad News." *Journal of Finance* 32 (May 1977): 321–333.

Nelson, C. R. "Inflation and Capital Budgeting." *Journal of Finance* 31 (June 1976): 923–932.

Reinhardt, U. E. "Break-Even Analysis of Lockheed's TriStar—An Application of Financial Theory." *Journal of Finance* 28 (Sept. 1973): 821–838.

Rubinstein, M. "A Mean-Variance Synthesis of Corporate Financial Theory." *Journal of Finance* 28 (Mar. 1973): 167–182.

Searby, F. W. "Return to Return on Investment." *Harvard Business Review* 53 (Mar.–Apr. 1975): 113–119.

Sharpe, W. F. "Capital Asset Prices: A Theory of Market Equilibrium Under Conditions of Risk." *Journal of Finance* 19, 3 (1964): 425–442.

Tuttle, D. L., and R. H. Litzenberg. "Leverage, Diversification, and Capital Market Effects on a Risk-Adjusted Capital Budgeting Framework." *Journal of Finance* 22 (June 1968): 427–443.

The Wall Street Journal (July 2, 1981).

Wallace, A. "Is Beta Dead?" *Institutional Investor* (July 1980): 23–30.

Weston, J. F. "Investment Decisions Using the Capital Asset Pricing Model." *Financial Management* 2 (Spring 1973): 25–33.

Part Five

Financing the Firm's Assets

In the last few chapters, we have discussed ways of analyzing investment decisions—perhaps the most critical set of decisions a financial manager has to make. We must realize, however, that all money that is spent has to come from somewhere. In other words, investment has to be financed. In this portion of the book, we analyze the sources of long-term financing available to corporations.

It is useful at this stage to look back at Figure 1–1 in Chapter 1, which gave an overview of the role of financial management. In each part of the book we have analyzed key topics necessary for fulfilling that role. In Part One, we provided background on the objectives of financial management and the nature of the financial environment. Basic tools of dealing with time and risk were developed in Part Two, while in Part Three we focused on developing information and used some principles of accounting. In Part Four, we applied these tools to the firm's investment decision—a *use* of corporate funds. We now focus on decisions about *sources* of funds. How can money be raised in financial markets? What are the best forms in which to raise money?

In addressing these questions we will discuss many of the numerous methods that corporations can use to obtain funds. In addition, we will discuss ways to analyze whether one means of financing is better than another and whether there is some best financing policy for the firm. Not surprisingly, we will find that we must give careful attention to the matter of risk. In an uncertain world, adverse things can happen and probably will. In almost every business decision, there is the opportunity to increase the potential return at the price of uncertainty, and financing decisions are no exception.

We will find many of the tools developed in Parts Two, Three, and Four useful. In Chapter 12, we will consider the main sources of long-term funds available to firms: debt, preferred stock, common stock, and specialized sources. We will also discuss the efficiency of the financial markets in which these funds are raised. In Chapter 13, we will begin a discussion of one of the major decisions facing financial managers—whether to borrow money (use debt) or to raise funds from shareholders (use equity). As we will see in Chapter 13, the use of debt (financial leverage) can affect the expected returns and risk to shareholders and ultimately the value of the firm. In Chapter 14 we will develop specific analytical tools for determining the appropriate level of debt for a firm, and in Chapter 15 we will examine dividend policy. The payment of dividends ultimately is a financing decision because funds used to pay dividends are unavailable for other uses in the firm. Specialized financing instruments, such as leases and convertible securities, are discussed in Chapter 16, and Chapter 17 focuses on the management of outstanding stock and bond issues.

In Part Six, we will give more attention to short-term financing. Our focus in this part (Part Five) will be on raising long-term funds. What are the best sources for the funds a corporation needs for investment? The following chapters will provide some answers to that question.

Chapter

12

Sources of Long-Term Financing

In this chapter, we will learn about the basic methods of raising long-term outside funds to finance investments. We will discuss the characteristics of the financing instruments that firms use to raise money, including basic instruments such as debt, preferred stock, and common stock as well as more specialized types. We also will discuss the efficiency of the financial markets in which these financing instruments are traded.

A glance at the balance sheet of most major corporations will show that corporations typically get money in a wide variety of ways. But no matter what the specific form of financing, the money is ultimately supplied by investors. In return for their money, these suppliers of funds (investors) expect future benefits of ownership. For example, shareholders expect dividends or increases in share price. We saw earlier how these shareholder expectations can be translated into a required rate of return using the dividend-growth model. This general feature is true for all forms of financing. Suppliers of capital require a return on their investment. These required returns ultimately affect the way a financial manager makes decisions. If the firm's investments can't earn returns high enough to meet the required returns of investors, the firm's market value will drop, and shareholder interests will not be served. This is why we used investor required rates of return in determining discount rates to evaluate capital-budgeting projects.

But why do companies use so many forms of financing? What are the relative advantages of each? To make some headway in answering these questions a working knowledge of the forms of financing available is needed. In fact, understanding all the financial channels available for obtaining funds is a never-ending challenge for a financial manager because new financing methods appear as financial markets change.

CORPORATE FINANCING OVERVIEW

Bonds—are long-term debt claims entitling the holder to periodic interest and full repayment of principal by the firm received in exchange for investment funds.

A **mortgage**—is a bond that has particular assets— usually buildings or equipment—pledged as security against default on interest or principal payments.

A **commercial loan**—is money borrowed by a business from a bank or lending institution in exchange for a promise to repay at a specified schedule and rate of interest.

Table 12–1 is a starting point for getting some idea of the major sorts of funding used by corporations. Table 12–1 gives a breakdown of the liabilities of nonfinancial corporations in the United States as of December 31, 1984. From these figures we can get a picture of the sources of financing—other than equity—used by the major producers of goods and services in our economy.

Of the total of $1,940 billion worth of financing broken down in Table 12–1, about 23 percent was derived from sources that arise spontaneously out of normal business operations—primarily trade credit and wage and tax accruals. The remaining 77 percent, about $1,486 billion, was derived from credit markets ($1,326 billion) and foreign sources ($160 billion).

Bonds accounted for about 43 percent of the funds raised through the credit markets and constituted the single largest source of debt funds for nonfinancial firms. The bond total includes funds raised through public issues and private placements. It also includes $102.4 billion worth of tax-exempt bonds. For particular socially desirable purposes, such as environmental-pollution control, the U.S. tax laws allow state and local governments to pass on their tax-exempt status to industrial bonds issued by profit-seeking enterprises.

Mortgages, another major form of long-term borrowing, provided $80 billion worth of the total in Table 12–1. In recent years, a growing part of corporate mortgage financing has been devoted to the construction and financing of homes, apartments, and residential developments. However, the bulk of mortgage borrowing by nonfinancial companies still finances industrial and commercial properties.

Commercial loans provided the third major source of funds for nonfinancial corporations. According to Table 12–1, bank loans financed about 36 percent of the total funds raised in the credit markets.

Table 12–1
Financial Liabilities of All Nonfinancial Corporations, December 31, 1984 (billions of dollars)

Credit market instruments		
Corporate bonds	$463.8	
Tax-exempt bonds	102.4	
Mortgages		
Residental	49.3	
Commercial	30.7	
Bank loans (other than mortgages)	479.1	
Commercial paper	58.5	
Bankers' acceptances	10.4	
Finance company loans	120.4	
United States government loans	11.6	
Total credit market		$1,326.2
Other sources		
Spontaneous sources		
Trade credit	$ 444.0	
Taxes payable	10.5	
Foreign direct investments in United States corporations	159.6	
Total other sources		$ 614.1
Total Financial Liabilities		$1,940.3

Source: Board of Governors, Federal Reserve System, *Flow of Funds Accounts* (October 1985).

Equity Versus Debt

Equity—is ownership in a firm—specifically, the claims of preferred and common stockholders.

Table 12–1 includes only sources of **debt** funds and excludes **equity**. Reliable figures on the value of equity are more difficult to obtain. The data on equity values in Table 12–2 are for all corporations, rather than only nonfinancial firms, and are not directly comparable to the debt figures in Table 12–1. They do, however, communicate a sense of the relative importance of debt and equity sources.

Sources of Long-Term Funds

Debt—is the contractual liability of a firm to lenders and consists of a promise to make periodic interest payments and to repay the principal according to an agreed-upon schedule.

Table 12–3 shows the sources of long-term funds to nonfinancial firms. The figures shown are amounts raised during 1979 and estimated figures for 1984. The figures show that pension funds have become important sources of long-term funds and that individuals were net sellers of equities rather than buyers. Over the past two decades, there has been an increasing trend toward institutional ownership of equities (insurance companies, pension funds, and the like), while individuals have reduced their holdings.

Table 12–2
Corporate Debt Versus Corporate Equity, 1950–1984

Year (as of December 31)	Total Liabilities of Nonfinancial Corporations (billions of dollars)	Total Market Value of Equities of All Corporations (billions of dollars)
1950	124	146
1955	174	317
1960	239	451
1965	351	749
1970	542	906
1975	771	893
1980	1,380	1,636
1981	1,533	1,569
1982	1,603	1,811
1983	1,711	2,152
1984	1,940	2,183

Source: Board of Governors, Federal Reserve System, *Flow of Funds, Assets and Liabilities Outstanding* (1957–1985, various issues).

Characteristics of Financing Instruments

Financing instruments—are claims against the firm's income and assets.

Having described recent trends in long-term financing in the aggregate, we turn now to a more detailed discussion of the principal types of claims issued by firms in order to acquire funds.

Financing instruments issued by a firm represent claims against the firm's income and assets. Suppliers of capital exchange their funds for these claims against the firm. The principal types of long-term claims issued by firms are debt, **preferred stock**, and **common stock**. In addition, firms may lease assets or issue convertible securities. We will describe each of these forms of financing.

Preferred stock—is long-term equity that pays a fixed dividend. Preferred stock is senior to common stock with respect to both income (preferred dividends come ahead of common) and assets.

It is useful to outline the different characteristics of financing instruments before describing how each of the major types of financing instruments differ with respect to these characteristics.

Common stock—is a perpetual ownership claim that has no maturity.

Maturity—is the time at which the principal amount of the claim is to be paid.

Maturity. First, financing instruments may differ with respect to **maturity**. Maturity refers to the time at which the principal amount of the claim is to be paid. If a loan requires payments of interest at the end of each year for three years and the principal amount repaid at the end of the third year, such a loan is said to have a three-year maturity. In the case of a mortgage loan, where equal payments are made over the life of the loan, each payment includes some interest and some principal. Here the term *maturity* is somewhat ambiguous; it might refer to the entire time span over which payments are made or to the average maturity of the payments. As we will see later, some claims—notably common stock and most preferred stock—have no maturity date; they are *perpetual claims.*

Table 12–3
Sources of Long-Term Funds, 1979 and 1984

| | Net Purchases (billions of dollars) | | | | | |
| | Bonds | | Equities | | Mortgages | |
	1979	1984	1979	1984	1979	1984
Thrifts	− $1.1	− $0.7	− $0.1	$0.2	$48.2	$90.6
Life insurance companies	11.6	21.5	0.6	0.4	12.6	9.4
Property liability companies	2.0	− 1.6	3.2	2.3	—	—
Private pension funds	12.8	1.7	9.3	7.0	0.3	0.6
Public pension funds	3.2	1.1	4.1	10.3	1.0	1.0
Foundations and endowments	.2	1.1	1.8	3.0	0.2	0.1
Real estate investment trusts	—	—	—	—	0.0	0.1
Mortgage corporations	—	—	—	—	0.8	1.2
Stock mutual funds	0.8	1.4	− 2.8	9.7	—	—
Commercial banks	− 0.1	2.6	—	—	30.7	40.7
Securities dealers and brokers	− 1.5	1.6	− 1.5	0.7	—	—
Households	5.1	15.0	− 18.2	− 123.9	19.2	5.0
Foreign	2.6	7.0	1.7	1.3	—	—
Total	**$35.7**	**$50.5**	**− $1.9**	**− 189.1**	**$113.1**	**$148.5**

Note: Figures for 1984 are projections.

Source: 1985 Prospects for Financial Markets, Salomon Brothers, Inc. Copyright © 1985 Salomon Brothers, Inc. Reprinted by permission.

Priority, or **seniority**,—is the order in which types of financial claims are satisfied.

A **contractual claim**—is a claim that is an enforceable contract, such as debt.

A **residual claim**—is a claim, such as common stock, to what is left after contractual claims are settled.

Seniority. In an uncertain world, there always is a chance that the income or assets of the firm will be inadequate to satisfy all claimants. Hence, there must be agreement in advance as to whose claim comes first. In short, the **priority**, or **seniority**, of the claims must be established.

To understand this priority characteristic of a financial instrument, one must understand the distinction between **contractual claims** and **residual claims**. Contractual claims are *debt* and involve an agreement by the obligor, firm or individual, to make certain payments of interest and principal at certain times. The agreement is an enforceable contract; if the obligor fails to make the specified payments, the claim holder can take legal action to enforce the claim. Such legal action includes forcing a company into bankruptcy. Residual claims, such as common stock, on the other hand, involve no enforceable agreement; rather, they entitle the claimant to what is left after higher-priority contractual claims are paid. Contractual claims are usually fixed in amount, and residual claims by their nature are variable. Hence, in any given firm, payments to residual claimants are inherently more uncertain than are payments to contractual claimants.

Priorities also may be established within major categories. Some contractual claims may be junior to others; such claims are often referred to as *subordinated claims.* Some residual claims may be senior to others; preferred stock is senior to common stock.

> **Debt represents a contractual claim and equity represents a residual claim against the firm's income and assets. Residual claimants get what is left after contractual claims have been paid.**

As we have noted, financial claims against firms represent claims against both income and assets. In many cases, the claim is against all income and all assets, subject to the priorities established. In some cases, however, specific assets are pledged as *collateral* to secure specific claims. We will discuss secured and unsecured debt in more detail shortly.

Tax Treatment.   Another important difference in claims of different types is tax treatment. Under present law, interest paid on contractual claims is deductible for income-tax purposes to the firm or individual paying it. Payments made on residual claims, normally called *dividends* rather than interest, are not deductible under present law.

Risk.   Different claims also vary with respect to the return required by the claimants. These differences result primarily from differences in risk, or the uncertainty about whether or not the agreed-upon payments will be made. Risk-averse investors require a higher return in exchange for a higher degree of risk. Hence, the more subordinated the claim on the firm, the higher is the required return on that claim.

A **voice in management**—
is the extent to which
various financial-claim
holders can influence the
policies of a firm.

Voice in Management.   A final important difference among claims of different types concerns the extent to which claim holders can influence the policies of the firm. We will refer to this influence as the **voice in management**. This right may include the right to choose the firm's board of directors and the right to vote on other matters of importance.

DEBT

Short-term debt—is debt
with a maturity of less
than 1 year.

Intermediate-term debt—
is debt with a maturity of
between 1 year and 5–7
years. Intermediate-term
financing usually is used to
finance part of a firm's
fixed assets or permanent
additions to working
capital.

Long-term debt—is debt
with a maturity of 8-10
years or longer.

Short-term debt generally refers to debt with a maturity shorter than 1 year. **Intermediate-term debt** has no generally agreed upon definition but usually refers to maturities between 1 and 5–7 years. **Long-term debt**, usually given the label *bonds*, refers to debt with maturities of 8–10 years or longer. Sources of short-term debt funds will be discussed in Chapter 18. In this chapter, we will consider primarily long-term debt and provide a brief look at intermediate-term debt.

A long-term debt contract is a loan of a specified principal amount made in exchange for a promise to make periodic interest payments and to repay the principal according to an agreed upon schedule. Repayment schedules are negotiable and may call for the principal to be repaid in one lump sum, in equal installments, or in amounts such that the sum of the interest and principal payment each period is constant. The latter type of schedule is typical of mortgage loans.

The agreement between lenders and borrowers, called the *indenture*, usually includes a number of provisions in addition to the interest rate and repayment schedule. The provisions typically encountered require the borrower to maintain certain financial standards with respect to liquidity and working capital. Restrictions may be placed on

Finance in Practice 12–1

Increased Use of Debt

Frequently during the 1980s, stories have appeared in the financial press about the rise in debt on corporate balance sheets in the United States. In 1960, total liabilities of the *Fortune* 500 industrial companies (the 500 largest industrial companies as identified each year by *Fortune* magazine) averaged 35 percent of assets, with the other 65 percent of assets financed by equity. By the end of 1984, liabilities of the *Fortune* 500 had risen to 55 percent of assets. Total debt of all nonfinancial firms was $1.3 trillion. Over the 1960–84 period, interest rose from about 8 percent of total cash flow to about 20 percent. The accompanying table shows the debt burden by industry for 15 industries.

Are these trends alarming? Certain factors suggest that they are less serious than they first appear. Many years of inflation have left assets, especially real property and inventories, undervalued on corporate balance sheets. Real property has increased greatly in value over the years, but in many cases the in-

Figure A

creases are not reflected on balance sheets. Under the LIFO (last in, first out) method of inventory accounting, inventories become progressively more understated over time relative to replacement value. Even measuring interest as a percentage of cash flow can be misleading because of the dramatic rise in interest rates during the 1970s and early 1980s, again under the influence of inflation. Much of that higher interest ex-

pense is attributable to the inflation premium, which is actually not a true expense, even though the accounting system treats it as such, but rather a payment to debtholders to maintain the purchasing power of the debt.

This is not to say that some companies didn't overdo it. Some that borrowed heavily and then went bankrupt were Baldwin-United, Charter Company, Lionel, Saxon Industries, Wickes,

---

Protective covenants—are restrictions, made as part of a loan agreement, that are placed on dividend payments, capital expenditures, or other firm actions, designed to protect the position of lenders.

the payment of dividends, capital expenditures, or repurchase of common or preferred stock. Such **protective covenants** are designed to protect the position of lenders by giving them certain rights (discussed further below) in the event the covenants are violated. In a way, the covenants act as an early warning system to signal trouble. Some covenants are relatively simple; others run into hundreds of pages.

Bondholders are represented by a *trustee* whose function is to administer the agreement and to see that the borrower lives up to its provisions. In the event of *default* on any provision, the trustee generally is required to report the violation to bondholders.

Table A

Liabilities as Percentage of Assets		
	1984	1974
Retailing	68.8	58.6
Utilities	64.3	62.6
Transportation	64.0	63.6
Metals	61.4	48.6
Aerospace	61.1	62.0
Petroleum refining	59.5	49.9
Drugs	58.6	41.7
Motor vehicles and parts	58.6	50.4
Food	56.4	56.0
Electronics	54.0	55.5
Forest products	52.6	51.6
Chemicals	52.2	50.3
Rubber	51.8	57.0
Textiles	45.9	50.5
Computers	44.9	42.9

Figure B

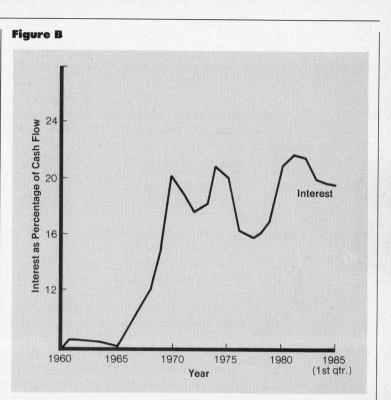

and Wheeling Pittsburgh Steel. Phelps Dodge, a copper producer, borrowed extensively during the 1970s and early 1980s to finance capital investment and subsequently had to sell parts of the business when it got into difficulty.

Mergers also account for an important share of the increase in debt. Chevron borrowed $12 billion to finance its acquisition of Gulf Oil. Martin Marietta borrowed heavily in a celebrated case during the early 1980s to escape a takeover attempt by Bendix Corporation. Phillips Petroleum and Unocal likewise used heavy borrowing to thwart takeover attempts by rearranging their capital structures. All in all, mergers during the late 1970s and early 1980s did contribute significantly to total corporate use of debt financing.

While not as alarming as they first appear, the figures in the accompanying table and diagrams nevertheless are not to be taken lightly. As Figure A shows, debt levels are higher than they were two decades ago, and Figure B shows that a higher proportion of corporate cash flow must be allocated to making interest payments.

Source: Adapted from K. Labich, "Is Business Taking On Too Much Debt?" *Fortune,* July 22, 1985.

The trustee usually is empowered to take legal action to force compliance. Where the firm is unable to comply, the trustee can force bankruptcy proceedings.

Bondholders normally do not have a direct voice in the affairs of the firm or in the voting for director. They indirectly may influence policies through the protective covenants in the indenture. In the event of default, bondholders come to have a much larger voice through the trustee. In the event of a bankruptcy proceeding, bondholders and other contractual claim holders are in virtually complete control, with common stockholders having little say in the settlement.

Claim on Income and Assets

The **coupon rate**—is the contractual rate of interest paid on a bond.

The rate of interest on a bond is fixed by contract and often is referred to as the **coupon rate**. Interest on most bonds is paid semiannually, although different schedules sometimes are encountered. In terms of seniority, bondholders have first claim on the firm's income. Interest always is paid on debt before dividends can be paid on preferred and common stock. Even where income is not sufficient to cover interest, firms go to great lengths to avoid defaulting on an interest payment.

> In general, if a firm remains a going concern, it is only the claim against income that is operative. The claim against assets comes into play only if the terms of the agreement are not met.

As in the case of the claim on income, the claim of bondholders against assets is senior to that of preferred and common shareholders. With respect to other contractual-claim holders, the seniority of a particular claim depends on the terms of the agreement. Where several debt issues are outstanding, there usually is a clearly specified priority.

Debentures—are unsecured bonds with no particular assets pledged as security.

Seniority also depends on whether the bonds are secured by particular assets. Mortgage bonds have specific assets, usually buildings or equipment, pledged as security against default on interest or principal payments. In the event of default, mortgage holders are entitled to liquidate the asset(s) to settle their claim, with any excess returned to settle claims of unsecured creditors. Unsecured bonds, having no particular assets pledged as security, are called **debentures**. In the event of trouble, debenture holders stand in line with other unsecured creditors, such as trade creditors and banks, behind secured creditors but ahead of shareholders. When the claims against a firm include both secured and unsecured creditors (and in the latter category, there may be both senior and subordinated creditors), the determination of how to divide funds received from liquidation of assets becomes a very complex matter.

As we can see, the type of bond—debenture, mortgage bond, subordinated bond—often is defined in terms of the nature of the claim against assets. Many specialized types of bonds exist that are not discussed in detail here. There are, for example, *collateral-trust bonds* secured by the stocks and bonds of other firms, and *equipment-trust certificates* used to finance certain types of equipment. Discussions of these more specialized financing vehicles may be found in the references at the end of this chapter.

Risk Associated with Bonds

Default Risk. Because debt is a contractual claim, debt obligations of a given firm are less risky than are the preferred or common stock of the same firm. In an uncertain world, however, default can and does occur. From the standpoint of lenders, debt obligations of firms are not riskless. From the firm's standpoint, on the other hand, interest and principal payments on debt can be viewed as certain if the firm is to remain in business.

Default risk—is the risk that the firm will not make specified contractual payments at the specified times.

Default risk is the risk that the firm will not make its specified contractual payments at the specified times. Bonds of many large corporations are rated according to default risk by rating services.

Table 12–4

Interest Rates on Long-Term Utility Bonds, 1965–1984

Year	Bond Rating Interest Rate (percent)			
	Aaa	*Aa*	*A*	*Baa*
1965	4.50	4.52	4.58	4.78
1966	5.19	5.25	5.39	5.60
1967	5.58	5.66	5.87	6.15
1968	6.22	6.35	6.51	6.87
1969	7.12	7.34	7.54	7.93
1970	8.31	8.52	8.69	9.18
1971	7.72	8.00	8.16	8.63
1972	7.46	7.60	7.72	8.17
1973	7.60	7.72	7.84	8.17
1974	8.71	9.04	9.50	9.84
1975	9.03	9.44	10.09	10.96
1976	8.63	8.92	9.29	9.82
1977	8.19	8.43	8.61	9.06
1978	8.87	9.10	9.29	9.62
1979	9.86	10.22	10.49	10.96
1980	12.30	13.00	13.34	13.95
1981	14.64	15.30	15.95	16.60
1982	14.22	14.79	15.86	16.45
1983	12.52	12.83	13.66	14.20
1984	12.72	13.66	14.03	14.53

Source: Moody's Public Utility Manual, vol. 1 (1985).

The two major bond-rating agencies are Moody's Investors Service and Standard & Poors Corporation (S&P). The former uses the rating of *Aaa* for the very best bonds, *Aa* for the next category, *A* for the next, and *Baa* for relatively risky bonds. Bonds rated below *Baa* are those with severe exposure to possible default. Standard & Poors uses *AAA*, *AA*, *A*, and *BBB* for its classifications. The two agencies do not always agree with each other, so dozens of bond issues are *split-rated*—that is, rated differently by the two agencies.

Prior to the onset of high inflation in the 1970s, bond rating was mainly an objective skill. It rested heavily on capital-structure analysis, the adequacy of operating income relative to fixed charges (known as the *fixed-charge-coverage ratio*), and the general trends and fluctuations in the company's earnings. This analysis employs many of the techniques we discussed in Part Three, such as ratio analysis and source-and-use-of-funds analysis. Over the past years of severe inflation (and the steep rise in the cost of energy), bond-rating agencies have had to move to broader measures and more subjective judgment. As a result, the number of split ratings has increased dramatically.

By and large, the yield on bonds is inversely related to their ratings. How much difference does a rating make as far as yield is concerned? The data in Table 12–4 reveal three important facts:

1. Long-term bond yields have risen sharply since inflation began in 1965. By 1975, they were twice as high as they had been in 1965. After a moderate decline in 1976, they rose again to reach a secondary peak in 1979, which was even higher than those reached in 1975. New highs were reached again in the early 1980s.
2. There is clearly a spread between upper and lower ranges of bond yields, which reflects quality differentials.
3. The spread rises during periods of general financial stress; for example, the spreads rose sharply in 1970, 1974–1975, and again in 1979. The spread has remained high throughout the early 1980s.

Interest-rate risk—is the risk arising because bond prices change as market interest rates change; the risk that a bond may have to be sold before maturity at a price lower than the price paid for it because of changing interest rates.

Interest-Rate Risk. Obligations of the U.S. government are considered default-free, because the payments are essentially certain to be made. However, government bonds are not totally riskless, for they are subject to a second type of risk: **interest-rate risk**, or uncertainty about future interest rates.

We showed the effects of interest-rate risk on bond prices earlier in Chapter 4. Suppose you buy a 20-year bond and sell it one year later. Your actual return over the year will depend on the price of the bond in one year; that price will depend on next year's interest rates—a rate that you can now only guess. Any time the *holding period* (the period over which the investor holds the bond) is shorter than the maturity of the bond, the holder is subject to interest-rate risk.

Purchasing-power risk— is the risk that a bond may not bring the expected *real* rate of return because unexpected inflation will have diminished the purchasing power of dollars received.

Purchasing-Power Risk. Still a third type of risk, to which holders of all assets are subject, is **purchasing-power risk**. Purchasing-power risk results from uncertainty about what the future rate of inflation will be. In the case of a government bond, if we know with certainty that we will hold the bond to maturity, there is no default risk and no interest-rate risk. If we are uncertain about the future rate of inflation, then we cannot be certain of the real rate of return on the bond.

Interest Cost to the Borrower

The yield to maturity (YTM)—on a bond is the internal rate of return on a bond earned by an investor if the bond is bought now and held to maturity.

In the case of long-term debt funds raised in competitive financial markets, the rate of return required by lenders is a *market-determined rate*. The required rate of return depends in part on the riskiness of the bond as perceived by the market. The required rate of return on a bond at any point in time often is called the **yield to maturity (YTM)**, which we discussed in Chapter 4. Using discounted-cash-flow techniques, the price of a bond can be expressed as shown in Equation (1).

The price, P_0, of a bond can be expressed as

$$P_0 = \frac{C_1}{1 + i} + \frac{C_2}{(1 + i)^2} + \cdots + \frac{C_n}{(1 + i)^n} + \frac{P_n}{(1 + i)^n} \qquad \textbf{(1)}$$

where C_n = the coupon payment to be made in period n, P_n = the principal amount due at maturity n years hence, and i = the yield to maturity (YTM).

The yield to maturity is the internal rate of return on the bond if the bond is bought at P_0 and held to maturity.

The **par value of a bond**—is the value that is equal to the principal amount.

The rate of return required by lenders, let us call it K_d, is the pretax cost of the debt funds to the firm. At the time a bond is issued, the cost to the firm, K_d, and the yield to maturity to the lender, i, are equal, if we exclude flotation costs. If the bonds are issued at par, i.e., at the **par value of the bond**, then the percentage coupon rate will equal K_d. Selling a bond at par value means selling it for a price, P_0, equal to the principal amount, P_n. The principal amount is sometimes referred to as the *par value*, or the *face value*. Subsequent to issue, the yield to maturity, i, will vary with the level of market rates, but the coupon rate, C, is fixed over the life of the bond.

As we noted earlier in Chapter 10, current tax laws permit deduction of interest for income-tax purposes. The after-tax equivalent of the interest cost, then, is $K_d(1 - T)$. Deductibility of interest is an important advantage of debt that we will discuss in more detail in Chapter 13.

> **The tax deductibility of interest is an important advantage of debt.**

Foreign Bonds and Eurobonds

A **foreign bond**—is a bond sold in a foreign country by a home-country borrower and is denominated in the currency of the foreign country.

Eurobonds—are bonds that are sold mainly in countries other than the country in whose currency the interest and principal payments are to be denominated.

With the increasingly international nature of business and financial activity, U.S. companies have also turned outside the United States to issue bonds. In the international bond market, bonds are sold outside the country of the borrower, often in many countries. A **foreign bond** is a bond sold in a foreign country by a home-country borrower and is denominated in the currency of that foreign country. For example, a U.S. company might borrow money in West Germany and promise to pay interest and principal in the West German currency, the mark.

Some companies also issue **Eurobonds**, or bonds that are sold mainly in countries other than the country in whose currency the interest and principal payments are denominated. For example, if a U.S. company borrowed money in West Germany but promised to make payments in U.S. dollars rather than German marks, the bond issue would be a Eurobond. If a Japanese company issued bonds in the United States denominated in yen, these bonds would also be Eurobonds because the term has been extended to cover this type of borrowing abroad independent of whether a European company or country is involved. In Chapter 21, we will discuss some of the important features of the international financial markets as they affect U.S. companies.

PREFERRED STOCK

The second of the three major types of claims issued by firms is preferred stock. Preferred shareholders are owners, not creditors. However, their claim differs in important respects from that of the residual claimants, the common shareholders.

Claim on Income and Assets

In terms of seniority, preferred claims stand behind all contractual claims of creditors and ahead of the common shareholders. Payments on preferred stock are usually called *dividends*. Such payments are fixed in amount, usually as a percentage of par value. A 12 percent preferred, for example, would pay a dividend of $12 per year if its par value were $100.

Although fixed in amount, preferred dividends are not contractual. Each time they are due to be paid, they must be declared by the board of directors. If for some reason a preferred dividend is not paid, preferred shareholders have no right to take legal action. The agreement between the firm and the preferred shareholders provides only that dividends will be paid in the agreed amounts prior to any payments to common shareholders. In a sense, preferred stock is a hybrid security. Like debt, payments are fixed in amount. Unlike debt, payments are not contractual, and failure to make a payment does not bring insolvency or bankruptcy. Because they are not contractual, preferred dividends are not deductible by the firm for income-tax purposes.

Nearly all preferred-stock issues are *cumulative* in that dividends passed without payment accumulate and must be cleared completely before any payments can be made to common shareholders. For example, suppose you owned a share of 12 percent preferred stock ($100 par value). If last year the company did not pay you the $12 preferred dividend, it would have to pay you $24 this year before making any payments to common shareholders.

Other protective covenants similar to those found in long-term-debt and term-loan contracts also are often included. For example, common dividends might be restricted to amounts that will maintain a specified current ratio or working-capital position. By restricting common dividends, the preferred shareholders, who have claims senior to common stock, reduce their risk. The claim of preferred shareholders against the assets of the firm, like that of common shareholders, is general rather than specific, with no particular assets set aside to settle preferred claims.

Voting rights of preferred shareholders are specified in the corporate charter. Such rights normally concern payment of common dividends and issuance of other classes of securities of equal or higher seniority. In addition, preferred agreements usually provide for election of a specified number of directors by preferred shareholders in the event that the provisions of the preferred agreement are not met.

Investors' Required Rate of Return

The cost of preferred stock to the firm is the rate of return required by the preferred shareholders to induce them to supply capital to the firm. As always, the rate of return required by preferred shareholders depends in part on the degree of risk perceived by investors. Risk depends, in turn, on the firm's operating risk, on the nature of its business, and on the extent to which there exist prior contractual claims senior to the preferred shareholders' claim.

Just as in the case of debt, we can use our discounted-cash-flow techniques to express the price of a share of preferred stock as shown in Equation (2).

The price, P_0, of a share of preferred stock can be expressed as

$$P_0 = \frac{DPF_1}{(1 + K_{PR})} + \frac{DPF_2}{(1 + K_{PR})^2} + \cdots$$

$$= \sum_{t=1}^{\infty} \frac{DPF_t}{(1 + K_{PR})^t}$$

(2)

where DPF_t = the expected preferred dividend per share in time period t, and K_{PR} = the required rate of return on preferred stock.

If the preferred dividend is to be the same indefinitely, the result is a perpetuity, and Equation (2) can be written as shown in Equation (3).

The price, P_0, of a share of preferred stock, when the preferred dividend is to be the same indefinitely, can be expressed as

$$P_0 = \frac{DPF}{K_{PR}}. \qquad (3)$$

The required return, K_{PR}, is the percentage cost of preferred stock to the firm. For example, suppose a firm could sell preferred stock with a dividend of $10 per share (to be paid indefinitely) and the preferred stock sold for $80 per share. Using Equation (3), we can calculate investors' required rate of return on preferred stock, K_{PR}, as

$$\$80 = \frac{\$10}{K_{PR}}$$

$$K_{PR} = \frac{\$10}{\$80} = 0.125 = 12.5 \text{ percent}$$

Note that because preferred dividends are not tax-deductible, the calculated rate K_{PR} is the after-tax cost of preferred stock to the firm. There is no tax adjustment.

Use of Preferred Stock

It was noted earlier that tax deductibility of interest is a major attraction of long-term debt. Preferred stock does not have this advantage. Relative to debt, an advantage of preferred stock is its flexibility. If earnings fall below expectations, or if the firm encounters difficulties for other reasons, the preferred dividend can be omitted without the threat of legal action, including bankruptcy. Contractual claims do not offer such flexibility.

While flexible relative to debt, preferred stock is less flexible than common stock. Protective convenants exist on preferred, and omission of a preferred dividend normally is viewed by the financial markets as a more serious matter than is omission of a common dividend. In addition, the payment of preferred dividends, just as in the case of dividends on common stock, does not lead to tax deductions. As a result, the use of preferred stock in addition to common stock is suitable only under special circumstances. Over the six-year period 1979–1984, new issues of preferred stock by U.S. corporations averaged only $3.9 billion a year compared to new bond issues (including private placements) of $36.0 billion a year and annual new common-stock offerings of $21.3 billion.[1]

Public utilities have been among the major issuers of preferred stock, at least partly in response to regulatory restrictions on the design of utility capital structures. Another specialized use has been in connection with mergers and acquisitions where tax considerations may make preferred stock advantageous as a vehicle for acquiring another firm. Finally, for some corporations, a combination of two circumstances may give

[1]Salomon Brothers, *1985 Prospects for Financial Markets*.

Table 12–5
Par Value in Accounting Records

Debit		Credit	
Cash	$1,000,000	Common stock $1 par	$100,000
		Paid-in surplus	900,000

preferred financing an edge over both bond financing and financing through a new issue of common stock. The first circumstance is a depressed market price for a firm's common stock relative to past and future expected levels, in which case a new common issue would dilute its per-share earnings—a development most managers would prefer to avoid and can avoid by issuing preferred stock. The second circumstance is the case in which a company's tax bracket is significantly below the normal percentage rate (as might be the case if it has a large investment tax credit or heavy investment outlays that can be expensed for tax purposes), in which case the fact that bond interest payments are tax-deductible may be a less important factor than the greater flexibility associated with preferred-stock financing.

We can gain a further insight into the use of preferred stock by looking at the *demand side* of the equation: who wants to buy preferred stock and why? As we noted in looking at the supply of this form of security, preferred stock is a hybrid that combines the fixity of return normally associated with a bond and the ownership feature normally associated with common stock. As such a hybrid, there is a demand for preferred stock only under special circumstances:

1. Some investors desire large and dependable amounts of current income, which are often not available from common stock whose returns may come largely from capital gains. Preferred stock typically offers higher *current yields* (dividends divided by price) than does common stock and, hence, would be more attractive than common stock to such investors. Preferred stock may also be more attractive than bonds because some types of preferred stock, such as *convertible preferred stock*, offer the potential for capital gains, in addition to current income. Convertible preferred stock is convertible into common stock on specified terms, and its price goes up if the common-stock price rises substantially. In recent years, many preferred-stock issues have been convertible.

2. Corporations receiving preferred-stock dividends (other than dividends paid by public utilities) are allowed under current law to exempt 85 percent of such receipts in computing their taxable income. (The exemption on public-utility preferred dividends is lower.) This feature increases the after-tax yield on preferred stock relative to the yield on bonds. As a consequence, for many fire- and casualty-insurance companies, which pay normal corporate tax rates on taxable investment income, preferred stock offers a better yield than do bonds.

These specialized and, hence, competing demands for preferred stocks *as investments* lead to a lowering of the gross yields that preferred-stock issuers have to pay when they raise funds through this instrument. As a result, such issuers may then find it worthwhile in some situations to use preferred-stock financing as opposed to other types of financing.

COMMON STOCK

In any commercial enterprise, some one or some group must have final responsibility for policy and a residual claim to income and assets. In a corporation, common shareholders play this role and are entitled only to what remains after creditors and preferred-stock owners are compensated. In an uncertain world, the residual claim is inherently uncertain as to amount. Sometimes residual returns are greater than anticipated; sometimes they are less.

Returns to common shareholders have two components: dividends and capital gains (or losses). Capital gains arise through changes in the price of the firm's stock. As a firm reinvests and grows, its value presumably increases, and the increase is reflected in a higher stock price. Dividends are declared by action of the board of directors and are not contractual; shareholders cannot take legal action to force payment. Because they are not contractual, dividends on common stock are not deductible for income-tax purposes under current law.

In this section, we will concentrate on the characteristics of common stock and the rights of its holders. We defer a discussion of the problems of issuing common stock to Chapter 17.

In the United States, common stockholders have limited liability; that is, their liability is limited to the amount of their investment. If the corporation's liabilities exceed its assets, the common stockholders cannot be held liable for the difference, as can a sole proprietor or a member of a partnership.

Common stock is a perpetual claim; it has no maturity. An individual shareholder can typically liquidate an investment in the firm only by selling shares to another investor. The value of a share at any point in time is, in the final analysis, a function of the dividends that all investors expect to receive, whether in the immediate or distant future.

A corporation's charter specifies the number of shares of common stock that the directors are authorized to issue. The number of authorized shares normally can be changed by a vote of the shareholders. **Issued shares** are those shares of stock that have been sold to investors. **Outstanding shares** are those shares of stock held at any point in time by the public. If a firm repurchases previously issued shares, such **treasury shares** are issued but not outstanding.

Stock can be issued with or without **par value**; this term has some historical, legal, and accounting significance, but little economic significance. In many states, shareholders are liable to creditors for the difference between the price at which the stock originally was issued and the par value, if the latter is greater. For that reason, par value normally is set at a figure lower than the price at which the stock is to be issued. To illustrate, consider the sale of 100,000 shares of $1 par value stock at an issue price to the public of $10 per share. The accounting entries, ignoring issue costs, are displayed in Table 12–5.

The **book value of stock** per share at any point in time is simply net assets available for common shareholders, after subtracting claims of creditors and preferred shareholders, divided by the number of shares. As noted earlier, **market value** for publicly traded stocks is the price at which transactions are taking place. Stocks are bought and sold on the *stock exchanges* and in the *over-the-counter (OTC) market*, about which we will have more to say in Chapter 17.

Issued shares—are those shares of stock that have been issued at one time or another by the firm to investors.

Outstanding shares—are those shares of stock held by investors at a given time.

Treasury shares—are previously issued shares of stock that a firm repurchases; they are issued but not outstanding shares.

The **par value of stock**—is the nominal or face value of the share of stock.

The **book value of stock**—is the total of book value of net assets available for common shareholders after subtracting claims of creditors and preferred shareholders.

The **market value of stock**—is the price at which stock is being traded in the marketplace.

Sometimes a firm will issue more than one *class* of common stock, often referred to as *Class A* and *Class B* stock. One of the classes usually has a larger voice in management and a junior claim to income. The senior class takes on some of the characteristics of preferred stock.

Roughly speaking, the term *equity* means "ownership," so it is correct to speak of *preferred equity* or *common equity*. Where a firm has no preferred stock outstanding, *equity* refers to the entire claim of the common stockholders, including retained earnings. Where preferred stock is involved, it is important to be clear as to which type of equity is meant.

Rights of Residual Owners

The rights of common shareholders are established by the laws of the state in which the corporation is chartered. Many of these rights are spelled out in the charter itself. Some rights belong to the shareholders as a group and usually are exercised by a vote. Such collective rights normally include: amending the corporation's charter (usually with the approval of designated state officials), adopting and amending bylaws, electing directors, entering into mergers with other firms, and authorizing the issuance of senior claims such as preferred stock and long-term debt. In addition, shareholders have a number of rights they may exercise as individuals, including the right to sell their shares to others and the right to inspect the records of the firm.

Shareholders normally exercise their collective rights by voting. Most corporations hold a regular annual meeting of shareholders, at which voting takes place on issues presented to the shareholders by the directors. Special meetings sometimes are held to vote on specific issues, such as approval for a merger. A shareholder unable to attend may vote by means of a *proxy*—that is, by giving written authorization to someone to represent him or her at the meeting. Election of directors is by majority vote in many states, but some states permit an alternative system called *cumulative voting*, which makes it easier for minority interests to gain representation on the board of directors. Cumulative voting permits multiple votes for a single director. For example, if you owned 100 shares of stock in a company that was electing five directors, you would get 500 votes and could cast all of them for a *single* candidate instead of spreading them out over five candidates.

The claim on the income and assets of the firm also is a right. We noted earlier that the residual owners are last in line with respect to both income and assets. Creditors and preferred shareholders must receive their interest and dividends before dividends are paid on common stock. In the event of serious difficulty leading to bankruptcy, claims of common shareholders are settled last. In the unhappy event of dissolution of a firm, common shareholders have claim to whatever assets remain after creditors and preferred shareholders are satisfied in full.

In connection with new issues of common stock, laws of many states give existing shareholders the *preemptive right* to maintain their current percentage claim on the income and assets of the firm. Under this provision, existing shareholders must be offered first refusal on any new offering of stock prior to sale to the general public. Each existing shareholder has the preemptive right to purchase new shares in the amount necessary to maintain his or her current share in the firm. For example, suppose that you owned 100 shares of the 1,000 presently outstanding shares of stock in a company. You currently own $100/1,000 = 10$ percent of the firm. If the firm issues 500 new shares (for a total of 1,500 total shares after the new issue), you would have to own 150 shares of stock to maintain your 10 percent share of ownership. This would require that you purchase 50 additional shares. A preemptive right would give you the privilege to buy these 50 shares prior to the sale of stock to the general public. *Rights offerings* are discussed in more detail in Chapter 17.

In principle, common stockholders control the policies of the firm by means of their rights to establish bylaws and to elect directors to represent them. Directors then appoint the executive officers of the firm, generally referred to as *management*. Management's job, therefore, is to act as agent of the firm and to work in the best interests of shareholders. This statement is a normative one—it describes the way things *should* be and the way professional managers *should* behave. In practice, it would be naive to suppose that all managers always act only in the interests of shareholders. There are many instances in corporations where the interests of managers and shareholders may diverge. Managerial behavior under such circumstances raises important moral, ethical, and perhaps even legal questions, but full discussion of these questions is beyond the scope of this book. The primary responsibility of professional managers is clear: manage the firm to serve the best interests of shareholders.

Investors' Required Rate of Return

Because common stock is a residual claim, its return is subject to greater uncertainty than is the return to preferred shareholders and creditors. Because investors as a group are risk-averse, we would expect common shareholders to require a higher rate of return than preferred shareholders and creditors, and, indeed, common shareholders do require a higher return. In terms of a probability distribution, the return to common stock has a higher expected value, but also higher dispersion.

Approaches to the problem of estimating the rate of return required by common stockholders were discussed in Parts Two and Four. One way to represent this required return is to define it as the rate that discounts future expected dividends to equal current market price, as shown in Equation (4).

The price, P_0, of a share of common stock can be expressed as

$$P_0 = \frac{D_1}{1 + K_e} + \frac{D_2}{(1 + K_e)^2} + \cdots$$

$$= \sum_{t=1}^{\infty} \frac{D_t}{(1 + K_e)^t}$$

(4)

where D_t = the expected dividend in period t and K_e = the market required rate of return, or the rate that discounts future expected dividends to equal current market price.

The discount rate, K_e, in Equation (4) is the market required rate of return on the firm's stock. Earlier, we noted that K_e also has two other commonly used labels: the *equity capitalization rate* and the *cost of equity capital*.

Convertible Securities

A **convertible security** is a claim that begins as a debenture or as preferred stock but that can later be *converted* at the holder's option (and at a specified rate) into shares of the issuing company's common stock. Convertible securities represent a specialized form of financing, so we defer a discussion of them to Chapter 16.

INTERMEDIATE-TERM FINANCING

A **convertible security**—is a claim that begins as a debenture or as preferred stock but that can later be converted *at the holder's option* and at a specified rate into shares of the issuing company's common stock.

Thus far in this chapter, we have discussed sources of long-term funds—debt usually involving maturities of 8–10 years or more and equity involving no maturity at all. In Chapter 18, we will discuss sources of short-term funds, usually involving maturities of 1 year or less. Let us now consider sources of financing over intermediate periods, usually defined as longer than 1 year but no more than 5–7 years.

Intermediate-term financing normally is used to finance fixed assets or permanent additions to working capital. Repayment usually must come from profits rather than from liquidation of the assets financed, as in the case of seasonal short-term loans. For this reason, intermediate-term lenders, along with long-term lenders, are more concerned with earning power than are short-term lenders.

Term Loans from Banks

Seasonal loans—are funds that are borrowed for use during a part of a year and that are repaid out of seasonal inflows of funds.

Term loans—are secured loans made by banks, insurance companies, or other lending institutions that must be repaid usually within 3 to 7 years.

Collateral—is property pledged by a borrower to protect the interests of the lender.

Historically, bankers have preferred short-term **seasonal loans** to **term loans**. Seasonal loans are to be used for only a few months to fund seasonal needs but generally have to be paid off in full during the course of a year. Terms loans, on the other hand, obligate the bank's funds for a longer period of time. In recent years, banks have expanded their term lending significantly. Maturities normally range from 3 to 7 years, seldom going beyond 10 years. Banks nearly always require security on term loans; the most commonly used **collateral** is equipment or real estate.

Since repayment is to come from operating profits, term loans nearly always are *amortized*, or repaid in installments. The amortization requirement encourages the borrower to earmark a portion of the firm's earnings for debt repayment and avoids leaving the lender dependent on the borrower's asset structure at the end of the loan's term. Home mortgages are amortized for precisely this same reason.

Interest rates on term loans usually run higher than on short-term loans of similar size and riskiness. Because of large shifts in the general level of interest rates during the last 10 years, many banks have moved to a variable-rate arrangement, whereby the rate on the term loan is tied to the prime rate. Compensating-balance requirements make the effective cost of both term loans and short-term loans higher than the stated rate of interest on the loan because the borrower gets to use only a portion of the money borrowed while paying interest on the full amount.

Term loans usually include restrictive covenants similar to those used in long-term debt agreements. To ensure that the borrower maintains an adequate degree of liquidity, restrictions may be included on minimum net working capital and current ratio.

Restrictions also may be placed on the payment of dividends and on the purchase and sale of fixed assets. Pledging assets to others often is prohibited by a *negative-pledge clause*. Additional borrowings senior to the term loan in question may also be prohibited. In smaller firms with less depth in management, insurance often is required on the lives of the principal officers. In all cases, periodic financial statements are required of the borrower.

Term Loans from Insurance Companies

Insurance companies also represent a source of intermediate-term financing to business. To the insurance company, the loan is simply an investment, rather than a part of a larger and continuing customer relationship, as it is to a bank. Insurance companies tend to prefer larger loans and often are unwilling to lend to smaller firms.

Because of the longer maturity of their liabilities, insurance companies prefer maturities of 10 years or longer and often are not interested in those shorter than 7 or 8 years. Prepayment penalties are more common on loans by insurance companies, though other restrictive covenants are similar to those imposed by banks.

Loans Against Equipment

A **chattel mortgage**—is a security claim against equipment (or anything other than land or buildings) used in providing collateral for a loan.

Equipment often is pledged as collateral against a term loan from a bank or insurance company. The proceeds of the loan may be used to purchase the equipment itself or for other purposes. Title to the equipment rests with the borrower, whose balance sheet will show both asset and loan. A security interest in the equipment is given to the lender by means of a **chattel mortgage**, which gives the lender the right to seize and sell the equipment in the event of default on the loan by the borrower. Public notice of this right, referred to as a *lien*, is filed in the state in which the equipment is located. The word *chattel* literally means "thing" and indicates that the lien is on something other than real property, such as land or a building.

Commercial finance companies also represent an important source of equipment financing. Two methods of equipment financing normally are used: conditional sales contracts and leasing.

Conditional Sales Contracts

A **conditional sales contract**—is an installment equipment-purchase contract under which title to the equipment remains with the lender until all payments are made.

A **conditional sales contract** is an installment purchase contract under which title to the equipment remains with the lender until all payments are made. Consummation of the contract by passage of title is conditioned on the borrower making all payments. A *down payment* is nearly always required, and the borrower signs a *promissory note* for the balance. Under present accounting guidelines, both equipment and loan appear on the borrower's balance sheet. For accounting and tax purposes, borrowers treat the equipment as if they own it, taking depreciation and deducting only the interest portion of the payment to the lender. The amount of the down payment and the maturity of the contract are set so that the unpaid balance always is below the resale value of the equipment. If the borrower defaults, the lender sells the equipment to satisfy the contract. Maturities usually range between 1 and 4 years.

Leasing

A **lease**—is a contractual arrangement for financing equipment under which the lessee (the firm) has the right to use the equipment in return for making periodic payments to the lessor (the owner of the equipment).

A second method of financing equipment is via a **lease**. A lease is a contractual arrangement under which the *lessee* has the right to use the equipment, and in return makes periodic payments to the owner, or *lessor*. The lessor retains title to the equipment. Accounting and tax treatment of leases is very complex, and the applicable rules have undergone significant change in recent years. Normally, the lessor carries the equipment on its balance sheet as an asset and takes the depreciation on it. The lessee shows nothing on the balance sheet and deducts the full amount of the lease payment as an expense. Thus, the party providing the financing, rather than the user, is treated as the owner for accounting and tax purposes, whereas it is the other way around in the case of the conditional sales contract. To qualify for this treatment, however, certain conditions must be met, and the Internal Revenue Service goes to great lengths to distinguish leases from conditional sales contracts. In recent years the accounting profession has tightened its guidelines regarding disclosure of lease contracts in financial statements. In some cases, a lessee is required to capitalize a lease and to show both asset and lease obligation on the balance sheet. Sometimes the accounting treatment may be handled one way for financial-reporting purposes and another way for tax purposes.

Lease contracts to finance equipment usually are written for periods of 1 to 5 years. Commercial banks and finance companies most often act as lessors. On longer-lived assets, such as building and land, lease contracts are written over longer time periods, with insurance companies and pension funds more often acting as lessors. Leases on real estate typically provide that maintenance, taxes, and insurance expenses are borne by the lessee rather than the lessor. In the case of equipment leases, the lessor often bears these maintenance, tax, and insurance costs.

Leasing is a very important means of both intermediate-term and long-term financing. We will discuss leasing in more depth in Chapter 16.

Borrowing Abroad

Just as U.S. companies can issue long-term bonds in other countries, intermediate-term financing can be arranged from sources outside the United States. In Chapter 21, we'll discuss international financial markets in more detail.

RECENT FINANCING INNOVATIONS

For most of the period since World War II, the nation's leading companies raised most of their capital by issuing straight equity and straight debt. Convertible securities, *warrants* (special contracts giving the buyer of a bond the right to buy stock), floating-rate notes, and other such features were used only in unusual circumstances. Beginning in the late 1970s, however, financing innovations arose primarily as a result of three main factors: a decade of high inflation, the greatly increased volatility of interest rates, and the deregulation of financial institutions. These changes produced a number of new and innovative financing instruments.

Response to Inflation

We have discussed the effects of inflation at a number of points earlier in the book. In the last 20 years, inflation was the single most important factor driving interest rates upward. The effects of this upward pressure can be seen in Figures 2–4 and 11–5 in earlier chapters. Not only did inflation drive rates upward, it increased the *uncertainty* about what future rates would be. High inflation and high interest rates gave rise to several innovations, including *original-issue, deep-discount bonds, zero-coupon bonds, convertibles*, and *exchangeables*.

Original-Issue, Deep-Discount Bonds.   For buyers who believed that rates would trend downward, there arose considerable interest in the **original-issue, deep-discount bond (OID)**. These securities typically are issued at 40 to 55 percent of face value, with very low coupon rates of interest—say, 6 to 7 percent at a time when standard issues carried rates of 14 to 16 percent. For example, in March 1981, Martin Marietta sold 30-year bonds with a total face value of $175 million, but with the bonds priced initially at $538.85 per $1,000 bond, yielding Martin Marietta a total of $92.2 million in proceeds. At a coupon rate of 7 percent of face value, this worked out to an effective interest cost to the company of 13.25 percent to maturity, less than Martin Marietta would have had to pay on a standard (nondiscounted) issue. The return to buyers consisted of the 7 percent interest ($70 per bond) plus a capital gain at maturity of $461.65 per bond. After the Martin Marietta issue, a dozen other companies quickly followed suit, and by June 1981 OID issues totaling $2.5 billion had been sold.

A major feature of OIDs is that much of the return comes in the form of the final principal payment—less of the return is in the form of coupon payments. As a result, owners of OIDs need not worry as much as owners of regular bonds about reinvesting coupon payments in future periods. Of course, the way to eliminate the reinvestment problem completely is to have a bond with *no* coupon payments, and just such bonds appeared in the financial markets of the early 1980s.

Zero-Coupon Bonds.   Taking the OID one step further, Pepsico placed privately a **zero-coupon bond**, that is, a bond paying no interest at all. Like a U.S. savings bond, the zero-coupon bond is bought at a discount and later redeemed at face value. J. C. Penney followed soon thereafter with a public issue of zero-coupon bonds. In Chapter 4, we discussed the General Mills zero-coupon money-multiplier notes issued in summer 1982.

OIDs and zero-coupon bonds also exploited a provision in the tax laws at that time that was favorable to the issuing firm. The 1982 tax bill changed the tax rules and spoiled the fun, and corporate issues of OIDs and zero-coupon bonds dropped sharply. Both types still find occasional use by corporations, and there is some activity in zero-coupon Eurodollar bonds (see Chapter 21 for a discussion of Eurodollars).

Convertibles and Exchangeables.   Financing by means of convertible bonds (discussed in detail in Chapter 16) increased in the mid-1980s, perhaps in part because of a perception by management in many companies that their common stock was undervalued in the stock market, making the issuance of ''debt now, stock later'' more

> **Original-issue, deep-discount bonds (OIDs)**— are bonds issued at prices well below face value with very low coupon rates and have appealed to buyers who believe that interest rates will trend downward.

> A **zero-coupon bond**—is a bond that pays no interest but that is issued at a large discount and later redeemed at face value.

An **exchangeable bond**—is a bond that can be exchanged for another type of security *at the option of the issuer*.

attractive. At the same time there was born a new security—the **exchangeable bond**—resulting primarily from the high-interest-rate environment of the late 1970s and early 1980s. Whereas convertibility is at the option of the *holder* of the bond, exchangeability is at the option of the *issuer*, giving the issuer the right to exchange the bond for another issue of securities. Exchangeability is an attractive option to management in the event of a decline in interest rates or a change in the firm's situation.

Response to Market Volatility

The second major factor resulting in financial innovation was a significant increase in the volatility of financial markets, especially in interest rates. Take a look back at Figure 2–3 and its text description in Chapter 2. The violent gyrations in interest rates during the 1970s and 1980s were unprecedented for most participants in the markets at that time. Both issuers and buyers of securities were scarred by that experience and sought protection from the ravages of interest-rate risk. The markets, true to form, brought forth new products to fill the need, including floating-rate notes, financial futures contracts, and interest-rate swaps.

Floating-rate notes (FRNs)—are debt instruments for which the interest rate is adjusted periodically with the rise and fall of interest rates generally.

Floating-Rate Notes.   **Floating-rate notes (FRNs)** have their interest rates adjusted periodically with the rise and fall of rates generally. Typically, FRNs have their rates tied to a widely representative market rate, such as the Treasury bill rate. FRNs appeal to investors who believe that rates will fluctuate and who do not wish to be exposed to changes in market value. Because the interest rate on the FRN is altered with market rates, its value does not rise and fall with changes in rates as does that of a fixed-rate instrument.

Citicorp pioneered the floating-rate note in 1974, and FRNs became increasingly popular as rates became more volatile later in the decade. Many of these issues had rates adjusted every six months and in some cases even less frequently. Such infrequent adjustment became inadequate in the super-volatile early 1980s as rates moved quickly through wide ranges. (During one 12-month period in 1981, the Treasury-bill rate went from 16 percent to 7 percent and back to 16 percent!)

To deal with such changes, more frequent adjustment of rates was needed, and in 1984 American Express responded with a new security called a *money-market preferred stock*, a $150 million preferred stock issue with a dividend rate that was reset every seven weeks. U.S. Steel issued $62.5 million worth of money-market preferred stock with a seven-week adjustment period in 1985, and American Express issued $100 million worth of money-market notes with a five-week reset also in 1985. Adjustable-rate mortgages have become very important also, accounting for 55–65 percent of new mortgages during 1984 and 1985. In 1983, Chemical Bank in New York even offered floating-rate automobile loans.

Financial Futures.   The **financial futures contract** represents another major innovation, resulting directly from the high volatility of the late 1970s and early 1980s. A **futures contract** is an agreement between a buyer and a seller to buy or sell something at some future date, with the price set at the present—that is, at the time of the contract. Futures contracts have been widely used in commodities markets, such as wheat, corn, or cocoa, for a long time, allowing a farmer, for example, to sell wheat

A **financial futures contract**—is an agreement between a buyer and seller to buy or sell a financial security at some future date but with the price set at the time of the contract.

A **futures contract**—is an agreement between a buyer and seller to buy or sell something, such as a commodity, at some future date but with the price set at the time of the contract.

in December for delivery in March at a price fixed in December. The farmer then worried about growing the wheat and let someone else worry about the risk of price changes. Producers (such as farmers) and consumers (such as flour or chocolate manufacturers) have used futures contracts for many years to hedge their risk.

Futures contracts came to the financial world in 1976 with the advent of Treasury-bill futures. Consider a company in December anticipating completion of a major contract the following March. Using T-bill futures, the company can invest in December the funds to be received in March *at a rate agreed-upon in December*. By appropriately buying or selling bill futures, both holders and issuers of financial obligations can hedge away the risk of fluctuations in interest rates.

Since 1976, futures contracts have been introduced on Treasury bonds, bank certificates of deposit, Eurodollars, several major international currencies, and even on the Standard & Poors 500 stock index and the New York Stock Exchange index. Some suspect that stock-index futures are being used more for speculating than for hedging risk, but that is another story. In 1985, a futures contract on the U.S. dollar was introduced, and for those worried about uncertain inflation rates, a contract on the consumer price index was introduced!

An **interest-rate swap**—is an agreement between two companies in which each takes on the obligation of paying interest on the debt of the other company.

Interest-Rate Swaps.   Another important innovation of the early 1980s growing out of interest-rate volatility is the **interest-rate swap**. Basically, two companies get together and agree to swap interest payments, A paying interest on B's debt and B paying interest on A's debt. What is the advantage? Consider a company that issued long-term debt but, after changes in market conditions, finds that it would prefer to have short-term debt. A savings-and-loan association has long-term mortgages financed by short-term deposits but would prefer to use long-term financing. Both can benefit by making each other's interest payments. In effect, each is adjusting the maturity of its liabilities to better fit changing circumstances.

Corporate Restructuring

The combination of a decade of inflation and high financial volatility also led to widespread corporate restructuring during the early and middle 1980s. Some of this activity took the form of multibillion dollar *leveraged buyouts*, in which venture capitalists often working with a firm's management bought out the public shareholders and took the firm private. There were many large and celebrated *takeovers* where a firm, or in some cases an individual, would buy another company, sometimes against the will of management. Chevron bought Gulf Oil for $13.2 billion. Mesa Petroleum, headed by T. Boone Pickens, a renowned corporate raider, attempted unsuccessfully to buy both the Gulf Oil Company and Phillips Petroleum, and succeeded in buying Cities Service. Texaco bought Getty Oil for $10.1 billion.

Junk bonds—are bonds with low credit ratings and high interest rates that play a role in corporate buyouts and takeovers.

We will discuss leveraged buyouts and takeovers in more depth in Chapter 22. We mention them briefly here because many of these and other acquisitions were financed by securities that came to be known as **junk bonds**, a reference to their low credit ratings and high interest rates. The corporate restructuring of this period also involved extensive repurchase of their own shares by some companies. We will discuss stock repurchase in Chapter 17.

MARKET EFFICIENCY

One issue that managers often face is the timing of new issues. Firms naturally prefer to sell new securities when prices are high. The real question is whether managers, or any investors for that matter, can identify when market prices are high or low relative to their true economic value. For investors an attractive path to a plush retirement is to buy low and sell high. Financial managers for companies want to make sure that they don't sell securities for too low a price. Doing so would deprive existing shareholders of funds that could be invested profitably.

What are the real benefits of timing? How easy is it to make money buying and selling securities? The answers depend on how good financial markets are at pricing securities. Can individuals do a better job of knowing an asset's true economic value than can financial markets, made up of thousands of presumably well-informed individuals?

An **efficient market**—is one in which market prices fully reflect all the information that is available about the assets being traded.

An **efficient market** is one in which market prices fully reflect all the information that is available about the assets being traded. In such a market, prices will reflect the cumulative wisdom of all market participants. Robert Higgins provides a graphic description of the forces that could lead to market efficiency: "The arrival of new information to a competitve market can be likened to the arrival of a lamb chop to a school of flesh-eating piranha, where investors are plausibly enough the piranha. The instant the lamb chop hits the water, there is turmoil as the fish devour the meat. Very soon the meat is gone, leaving only the worthless bone behind, and the water returns to normal. Similarly, when new information reaches a competitive market there is much turmoil as investors buy and sell securities in response to the news, causing prices to change. Once prices adjust, all that is left of the information is the worthless bone. No amount of gnawing on the bone will yield any more meat, and no further study of old information will yield any more valuable intelligence."[2]

In essence, a competitive financial market will incorporate information into prices very rapidly as a result of the competition among thousands of buyers and sellers. If the market is efficient, such information is fully reflected in prices, so no further study of the existing information will give us a better estimate of true economic value than the one already given by the market price.

Whether or not financial markets are efficient is one of the most controversial topics in finance, and a few preliminary comments are important before it is discussed further. First, some parts of the financial markets may be efficient while others are not. Highly organized and competitive markets for U.S. government securities may turn out to be reasonably efficient, whereas markets for the trading of stocks in new smaller companies may not. Second, efficiency is in the eye of the beholder and depends on the type of information available to a particular investor or manager. Market prices may reflect all the information known by an aspiring millionaire who doesn't yet know the difference between profits and cash flow. At the same time, the market can be inefficient to a corporate executive who happens to know about as-yet undisclosed merger plans.

---

[2]R.C. Higgins, *Analysis for Financial Management* (Homewood, Ill.: R.D. Irwin, 1984), p.133.

The Case of Sam Q. Public

To gain a better understanding of the processes that could lead to market efficiency, let's take a look at a hypothetical series of events. Rambo, Inc. recently had its stock begin to trade publicly. Based on the limited information available, Rambo's stock price was $10 per share at the beginning of trading one Monday morning. That afternoon, the U.S. government announced that it was awarding the company a highly lucrative contract. Monday afternoon the announcement was carried over the major news wires and by evening made all the network television newscasts. On Tuesday, the contract made headlines in the *Wall Street Journal*.

Sam Q. Public happened to hear about the contract as he lounged in front of the TV Monday night and went to bed with a smile on his face dreaming of a vacation to the Bahamas. Sam planned to finance the trip by buying Rambo stock first thing Tuesday morning and then cashing in later when Rambo's stock price went up. Sam called his broker Tuesday morning just as the market opened with instructions to buy 1,000 shares of Rambo, but first he asked about the price. His broker noted that Rambo was selling for only $5 a share two months ago but had gone up by $2 a share Monday to close at $12. Undaunted, Sam purchased the stock and waited for the big profit.

Weeks go by and Sam begins to frown. Rambo's price has moved up and down with general market conditions, but the big profit just hasn't materialized. Disappointed, Sam sells at $12.25 a share, and his vacation dreams fade. His profit turns out to be a meager rate of return considering the brokerage fees and the fact that he pulled the money out of an interest-bearing bank account to finance the stock purchase.

What went wrong for Sam? He was right in his conclusion that the government contract was a bonanza for Rambo, Inc. The trouble was that he was just too late to cash in. The stock price had already adjusted by the time Sam got the information because other investors got the information earlier and bid up the stock price. In Sam's case, on Tuesday morning the market was efficient in that Rambo's stock price fully reflected the information about the contract.

Now consider Sam's cousin Ernest who happened to work for the government-contract office. Ernest knew that Rambo was going to get the contract a full two months before the announcement. At that time, the stock was still selling for only $5 a share. Ernest also knew that the contract information had not yet leaked out. Could Ernest have made money? You bet. By purchasing at $5 per share based on his inside information, he could have profited from the price run-up to $12 a share, more than doubling his money in a couple of months. Two months before the announcement the market was not efficient with respect to Ernest's information. The stock price was too low because investors had yet to find out about the contract. As it turns out, Ernest, realizing his conflict of interest as a public servant, could not take advantage of his inside information. In fact, it would have been a violation of the law for him to have done so. So, like Sam, he doesn't have any big vacations planned either.

Forms of Market Efficiency

The above scenario illustrates an important point: efficiency depends on the nature of information available. Three forms of market efficiency can be defined, each making use of a different definition of available information.

Table 12-6

Type of Information and Market Efficiency

Type of Information Fully Reflected in Prices	Examples of Information	Form of Market Efficiency
Past prices and returns	Price of IBM stock last year Whether IBM stock price increased last month	Weak
All publicly available information, including past prices and returns	Article in *Wall Street Journal* Financial Statements Information on the CBS Evening News	Semistrong
All information, including all public information	Unannounced plan to acquire another company Quarterly earnings figure before it is announced	Strong

1. A market is *weak-form efficient* if current prices fully reflect all information about past security prices and returns.
2. A market is *semistrong-form efficient* if current prices fully reflect all publicly available information.
3. A market is *strong-form efficient* if current prices fully reflect *all* information, both public and private.

Table 12–6 defines the three types of market efficiency and gives examples of each type of information. Note that a market can be weak-form efficient but not efficient in the semistrong form. If this were the case, an investor might be able to find underpriced stocks by diligent research of material in a company's financial statements and in the financial press. If the investor has in truth identified such underpriced securities, he or she should be able to make lots of money by purchasing them while they are still cheap and profiting from sales at higher prices when the market finally does adjust to the information. On the other hand, no amount of studying past prices would yield such profitable investment opportunities if the market is weak-form efficient. If a market is weak-form efficient, all the information contained in past prices will already be reflected in the asset's market price, so it is already too late to use the information to pick underpriced stocks. For example, if the information found was good news about the company's future profitability, the stock price would have already gone up before an investor had a chance to purchase it.

Findings on Market Efficiency

Are financial markets actually efficient? An immense amount of research has been addressed at exactly this question, mostly focusing on the stock market. Most studies approach the problem by trying to see if you could make abnormally high returns (relative to returns generally available in the market) if you bought and sold stocks based on a particular type of information. Similar approaches have been used to study the efficiency of markets for assets other than stocks.

For example, suppose you followed Sam's strategy and bought stocks based on the TV evening news. If, based on such information, you could make abnormally high returns, this outcome would be evidence that the stock market was not semistrong-form efficient. TV news is public information, and semistrong-form efficiency requires that such public information already be reflected in stock prices. To control for getting lucky on a single day, it would be necessary to follow the results of applying the strategy based on a number of different news telecasts. If Sam's experience is typical and no abnormal returns are earned based on the TV information, then the market is truly characterized by semistrong-form efficiency.

While the evidence is not crystal clear, there are some useful lessons that emerge from the findings.[3] First, it is very difficult, if not impossible, to consistently find underpriced securities based solely on information about past prices or returns. There will always be the exception to the rule, but U.S. financial markets appear to satisfy the requirements for weak-form efficiency. If some weak-form inefficiencies can be found, they likely involve quite complicated patterns that have yet to be unearthed and tested rigorously.

Second, market prices adjust quite rapidly to new information that comes into the public domain. In fact, the market often anticipates many public announcements, such as a company's intention to raise its dividend or its announcement of a particularly good year in terms of earnings.

Third, the market is definitely not efficient with respect to types of inside information sometimes held by corporate managers. In our example about Rambo, Inc., the market was not efficient with respect to Ernest's inside information on the government contract. A number of studies have shown that managers acting on inside information could make substantial profits by buying and selling stock in the companies for which they work because managers sometimes have important information that has not yet been made available to the public. For example, a manager in the oil business might know that his or her company just made a major find of new oil reserves. If the manager bought stock in the company before the news became public, he or she would stand to reap a handsome profit as the stock price increased. As noted earlier, the use of such inside information is illegal, but there is evidence that it does occur.

Sources of Market Inefficiencies

The above discussion has stressed the relative efficiency of U.S. financial markets, especially with respect to public information, an emphasis that we believe is warranted. Corporate managers are likely to serve their shareholders best in the long run by focusing on the investments and commercial stategy of the company rather than investing large blocks of time trying to spot market inefficiencies. That conclusion does not imply, however, that financial markets are infallible. There are intriguing findings that reveal apparent inefficiencies, and more will probably be discovered in

---

[3]For a useful review and interpretation of much of the research on market efficiency, see B. Boldt and H. Arbit, ''Efficient Markets and the Professional Investor,'' *Financial Analysts Journal*, July-August 1984.

the future. One such finding concerns the reaction of a company's stock price to an announcement of higher-than-expected earnings. Stock prices go up as would be expected. The puzzling finding in terms of market efficiency is that the adjustment is relatively slow. This slow adjustment means that someone could consistently make money by buying stocks after the earnings announcement is public. Apparently, at least for a while, the market price does not fully reflect the "earnings surprise."

One difficulty with spotting a market inefficiency is that bringing it to investors' attention is likely to make it disappear. A quick way to get a stock price to stop being undervalued is for investors to think that it really is priced too low. The buy orders will hit the market in a hurry if people think there is money to be made. The message from studies of market efficiency is that there aren't many free lunches in financial markets.

Implications for Decisions

Relatively efficient markets have some important implications for both investors and managers. For investors, market efficiency means that earning above-average returns in the financial markets is not an easy business. Just looking at past price trends and reading the financial press is not likely to produce a highly profitable way to pick underpriced stocks. The key to amassing a fortune is getting information before it is already impounded in prices. This task isn't necessarily hopeless, but it is difficult—just the type of result you would expect in competitive financial markets. For the vast majority of individual investors who don't have the resources or time to uncover new information, the best prescription is probably to pick a preferred level of risk, invest in a well-diversified portfolio of assets that fit that risk profile, and be satisfied to earn the market (average) return. Instead of devoting considerable expense in trying to pick winners, most investors should diversify their portfolios and trust that market prices already reflect the information that they might uncover. This approach might be less glamorous than hunting for the next IBM, but it likely will turn out to be a more sound investment stategy in the long run.

Findings on market efficiency also have important lessons for managers. One of them is not, however, to trade for personal gain based on inside information. As noted above, such insider trading is illegal and for good reasons. The managers' charge is to work in the best interests of shareholders, not to take advantage of them based on inside information. A first lesson is that financial markets will react quickly to new information. One of the jobs of corporate management is to be sure that it communicates such information to the market in a careful and responsible manner. For a company's stock price to reflect the value of the investments managers have made, the market must have relevant and reliable information. We will have more to say on communications with the market when we discuss dividend policy in Chapter 15 and managing outstanding securities in Chapter 17.

A second lesson is that market prices already reflect a great deal of information. Unless a manager has some comparative advantage in gathering and processing information about a particular asset, he or she is unlikely to identify any pricing error made in the market. As a result, speculating in marketable securities or stocks is not a prudent course of action for corporate managers. After all, there are major banks, large brokerage firms, and savvy private investors already trading in those securities. For the same reasons, trying to time debt issues to outguess the market about interest-rate trends is usually unwarranted.

A third lesson is that markets are not strong-form efficient. As a result, managers may sometimes know inside information that the market does not. Usually it is best to go ahead and relay this information to the financial markets, but there are times—for example, when disclosure would give away a major competitive advantage—when relaying this information may not be possible. The last thing a company wants to do is let competitors know the details of a new technology that can't be protected by patent laws. The manager faces a dilemma in such a situation. The current stock price may not reflect the inside information, but releasing that information may destroy long-run value. If managers make decisions for the long run, ultimately that economic value will surface in the prices of the firms' securities.

In summary, a lesson of market efficiency is that managers should focus their efforts on making the company a sound profitable enterprise. If they succeed in this effort, stock prices will go up and shareholders will reap the economic rewards.

KEY CONCEPTS

1. Firms can choose from among a wide variety of long-term financing methods to raise money.

2. Three principal forms of financial instruments are debt, preferred stock, and common stock. These types of securities issued by firms are valued in financial markets.

3. Debt is the most senior claim on the firm and gives the owner the legal right to receive interest and principal payments.

4. Preferred stockholders, though junior to debtholders, have prior claim to common shareholders. Preferred stockholders receive preferred dividends.

5. Common stockholders are the residual owners of the corporation. They have the most risky claim on the corporation and, as a result, require a higher rate of return than do owners of the company's debt and preferred stock.

6. Firms use intermediate-term financing (maturities of 2–7 years) in addition to long-term (maturities of 8–10 years or longer) and short-term (maturities of less than 1 year) financing.

7. In recent years, firms have come to rely more on innovative financing schemes as financial markets have changed.

8. An efficient financial market is one in which current market prices fully reflect all available information.

9. The three forms of market efficiency are weak-form, semistrong-form, and strong-form efficiency.

10. U.S. financial markets are at least reasonably efficient with respect to publicly available information.

11. The research on market efficiency shows the importance of information in determining market values.

SUMMARY

The major types of long-term financing available to firms are debt, preferred stock, common stock, leases, and convertible securities. Financing instruments differ with respect to maturity, seniority, whether they are contractual or residual, the use of collateral, tax treatment, cost, and the right to a voice in management.

Long-term debt is a contractual claim that normally has a maturity of 8–10 years or longer. Protective covenants in the debt contract are designed primarily to protect lenders. The claim of bondholders against income and assets is senior to that of preferred and common stockholders. In addition to default risk, debt holders are subject to interest-rate risk and purchasing-power risk. Deductibility of interest lowers the effective cost of debt to the borrower.

Preferred stockholders are owners, not creditors. Preferred dividends are fixed in amount but are not contractual and are not deductible by the firm for tax purposes. In seniority, preferred claims come after those of bondholders but ahead of those of common stockholders.

Common stockholders have final responsibility for policy and residual claim to income and assets. Common stockholders bear the ultimate risks of commercial enterprise, receiving more return than bondholders and preferred stockholders in good times and less in bad times. The return to common stockholders is made up of two components: dividends and capital gains. Dividends are not deductible for tax purposes under present law. The liability of common stockholders is limited to the amount of their investment.

In addition to long-term and short-term sources of financing, firms can also obtain funds from intermediate-term sources with maturities of more than one year and up to 5–7 years. Term loans from banks and insurance companies, loans against equipment, condi-

tional sales agreements, leases, and foreign loans are all sources of intermediate-term financing.

Recent innovations in long-term financing include issuance of bonds with very low coupon rates (and in some cases no coupon payments at all) as well as floating-rate and adjustable-rate notes.

An efficient financial market is one in which market prices fully reflect all available information about the assets being traded. The three forms of market efficiency relate to different definitions of information. Weak-form efficiency requires only that prices fully reflect the information contained in past prices and returns. Semistrong-form efficiency means that all public information is fully refected in prices, while strong-form efficiency requires that all information (both public and private) be fully reflected in market prices.

Though not efficient in the strong-form sense, U.S. financial markets do seem to meet the basic requirements of weak-form efficiency. In addition, prices react quickly to the revelation of new public information. As a result, most investors and managers are not likely to be able to profit by trying to outguess the market and find mispriced assets.

QUESTIONS

1. In what important respects do the major types of financial claims issued by firms differ?

2. How is the cost of a particular source of funds to the firm related to the rate of return required by the financial markets?

3. In connection with debt claims, what is meant by the term *contractual*?

4. What is a *residual claim*?

5. What is a *subordinated claim*?

6. What is the purpose of protective covenants in a debt contract?

7. How does a mortgage bond differ from a debenture?

8. In general, a bondholder is exposed to three different types of risk. What are they, and how do they differ?

9. What determines the yield to maturity of a bond?

10. Contrast preferred stock with debt and common stock. What are the similarities and differences?

11. What are the key characteristics of common stock?

12. How do common stockholders receive their financial return?

13. How is book value of common stock related to market value?

14. What is meant by the term *preemptive rights*?

15. Define the three forms of market efficiency.

16. Suppose that, in response to quarterly earnings reports, the price of a company's stock increases dramatically within a few hours but levels off by the end of the trading day. What type of market efficiency does this represent?

17. Does semistrong-form efficiency imply weak-form efficiency? Does it imply strong-form efficiency?

REFERENCES

Brigham, E. F. "An Analysis of Convertible Debentures: Theory and Some Empirical Evidence." *Journal of Finance* 21 (Mar. 1966): 35–54.

Buse, A. "Expectations, Prices, Coupons and Yields." *Journal of Finance* 25 (Sept. 1970): 809–818.

Business Week (March 1, 1982).

Carson-Parker, J. "The Capital Cloud Over Smokestack America." *Fortune* (Feb. 23, 1981).

Cohan, A. B. *Yields on Corporate Debt Directly Placed.* (New York: National Bureau of Economic Research, 1967.

"The Creative New Look in Corporate Finance." *Dun's Review* (July 1981).

Donaldson, G. "In Defense of Preferred Stock." *Harvard Business Review* 40 (July–Aug. 1962): 123–136.

Friend, I., and M. E. Blume. "The Demand for Risky Assets." *American Economic Review,* 65, (Dec. 1975): 900–922.

Gritta, R. D. "The Impact of Lease Capitalization." *Financial Analysts Journal* 30 (Mar.–Apr. 1974): 47–52.

Hayes, S. L., III. "New Interest in Incentive Financing." *Harvard Business Review* 44 (July–Aug. 1966): 99–112.

Hayes, S. L., III, and H. B. Reiling. "Sophisticated Financing Tool: The Warrant." *Harvard Business Review* 47 (Jan.–Feb. 1969): 137–150.

Pinches, G. E. "Financing with Convertible Preferred Stock, 1960–67." *Journal of Finance* 25 (Mar. 1970): 53–64.

Pogue, T. F., and R. M. Soldofsky. "What's in a Bond Rating?" *Journal of Financial and Quantitative Analysis* 4 (July 1969): 201–228.

Werner, G. F., and J. J. Weygandt. "Convertible Debt and Earnings Per Share: Pragmatism vs. Good Theory." *Accounting Review* 40 (Apr. 1970): 280–289.

West, R. R. "An Alternative Approach to Predicting Corporate Bond Ratings." *Journal of Accounting Research* 8 (Spring 1970): 118–125.

Chapter

13

The Effects of Financial Leverage

In this chapter, we will investigate the effects of using debt (financial leverage) on the returns and risks to shareholders. We show that financial managers should attempt to maximize value when using debt. This value maximization requires trading off the benefits of debt, including the tax-deductibility of interest payments made by a corporation, against its costs, including agency costs and the costs of financial distress.

In the last chapter we discussed the many types of long-term and intermediate-term financing that a corporation can use. Now we can address the questions of what *mix* of these financing sources a firm should use to obtain funds. Just as the firm tries to increase its value by making good investment decisions, can the firm increase its value by making wise financing decisions? If so, how should financial managers go about making choices about the firm's financing mix?

Financial leverage—is the use of debt.

In this chapter, we focus on **financial leverage**—the use of debt. In Chapter 10, in which we calculated a weighted-average required return for use in analyzing investment projects, the weights we used assumed some financing mix for the firm—a certain percentage of debt and a certain percentage of equity. We now want to explore how this **financing mix** is determined.

The **financing mix**—is the proportion of debt and equity used to finance investments.

How should the managers make decisions about the appropriate *sources* of funds? In this chapter, we will discuss the effects of financial leverage on the value of the firm in order to provide qualitative guidance and a way of thinking about financing decisions. In the next chapter, we will discuss practical applications of these concepts.

LEVERAGE AND REQUIRED RETURNS

One way to evaluate the firm's financial choice is to look for the financing mix that will lower the firm's overall required rate of return, given the risk of its investments. This required return is what suppliers of capital require on their investment for any given level of risk. The lower this rate, the higher will be the *value* of the firm's future cash flows because the value of a given future cash flow increases as the discount rate drops.

To see the nature of the problem, let's suppose a firm currently does its financing with equal amounts of debt and equity and faces a 40 percent tax rate. Given the underlying operating risk of the company and its current financing mix, shareholders require a 16 percent return, and the firm can borrow long-term funds at an interest rate of 10 percent. Using these data and the techniques developed in Chapter 10, we can calculate the weighted-average required return *(WARR)* of suppliers of capital as

$$WARR = W_e K_e + W_d K_d (1 - T)$$

$$= 0.5(0.16) + 0.5(0.10) (1 - 0.4) = 0.11.$$

This 11 percent return requirement can be used as a discount rate to analyze projects that are of average risk for the firm.

Now suppose a new analyst for the company suggests: "Why don't we just do more financing with debt? Because it has a lower required rate of return, switching more of our financing to debt will lower our *WARR*. In essence, we can lower our cost of capital."

The Problem of Risk

The goal of lowering the *WARR* is a laudable one, but there is a major problem with the analyst's recommendation. The analyst has forgotten about the effects of financial leverage on the risks to shareholders. Remember that the shareholders' return requirement of 16 percent is based on the firm's current financing mix of 50 percent debt. If

Figure 13–1
Leverage and the Required Rate of Return

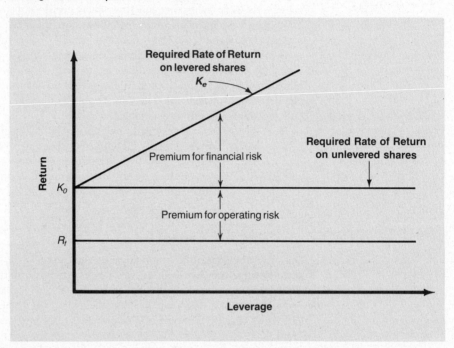

the firm tries to use more debt—say, raising the debt financing to 60 percent—shareholders will face higher risks and, as a result, will increase their required return to more than 16 percent. This extra risk to shareholders arises from the fact that, with higher borrowing, the firm will have to pay more in interest and principal before shareholders receive any returns. In addition, an increase in the firm's use of debt might push borrowing costs above a 10 percent interest rate if lenders perceived extra risks that the company might default on the promised (now higher) debt payments.

To illustrate these effects, let's use some hypothetical numbers. Suppose shareholders and lenders were told of the change in financing, and as a result increased their required returns to 18 percent and 11 percent, respectively. We can calculate the *WARR* at the proposed new financing mix of 60 percent debt and 40 percent equity as

$$WARR = 0.4(0.18) + 0.6(0.11)(1 - 0.4) = 0.1116.$$

The new *WARR* is 11.16 percent, which is actually *higher* than the original *WARR* of 11 percent. We can see the problem with the analyst's recommendation. Even though debt has a lower required return than equity, increasing the use of debt doesn't necessarily lower the *WARR*. Although in some instances the *WARR* might drop as more debt is used (we will return to this point later), in our example the *WARR* actually went up when the firm increased its use of debt. Changing the financing mix affects the risks borne by suppliers of capital and, in particular, affects risks to shareholders. In financial markets, shareholders will demand a **risk premium** for any ad-

A **risk premium**—is the difference between the required rate of return on a relatively riskless asset and that on a risky asset of the same expected life.

ditional risk. In choosing any financing mix, financial managers must be aware of these effects on risk.

> As financial leverage increases, risk also increases, and risk-averse investors demand a higher return as compensation for the higher level of risk. The required rate of return on the firm's shares rises with leverage, other things being equal.

To examine more carefully the relationship between required return and leverage, let us define K_o as the return that shareholders would require if the firm used no debt. In such a case, the firm uses no financial leverage, and its common shares are referred to as **unlevered shares**. We will let K_e represent the return required on equity at any given level of financial leverage, or the required return on **levered shares**. Now imagine what happens when leverage is increased, with everything else held constant. Such a controlled situation would be very difficult to achieve in practice, but for purposes of understanding the relationships, we can imagine that it is achieved by issuing debt and using the proceeds to repurchase equity.

As leverage increases, risk increases, and investors demand a higher return, so K_e rises. Equation (1) expresses this relationship symbolically and is diagrammed in Figure 13–1.[1]

Unlevered shares—are shares of stock in a company that uses no debt.

Levered shares—are shares of stock in a company that uses debt.

> The relationship between the required return on levered equity, K_e, and the required return on unlevered equity, K_0, can be expressed as
>
> $$K_e = K_0 + \text{risk premium for financial risk.} \qquad (1)$$

---

[1]The exact relationship between K_e and K_o depends on assumptions that one makes about the effects of the use of leverage on the value of the firm. For example, F. Modigliani and M. Miller determined that under certain assumptions the relationship would be expressed as:

$$K_e = K_o + \frac{D(1 - T)}{E} (K_o - R_f)$$

In this expression, D represents the market value of the firm's debt, E is the market value of its equity, T is the corporate tax rate, and R_f is the risk-free rate of interest. The term $(1 - T)$ accounts for the fact that interest is tax-deductible. Starting with no leverage ($D = 0$), we see that $K_e = K_o$. As leverage increases, D increases and E decreases, so K_e rises. The second term in the expression represents the premium for financial risk required by the market. This financial risk premium is equal to the premium for operating risk, $(K_o - R_f)$, multiplied by the leverage ratio. The original article was F. Modigliani and M. H. Miller, "The Cost of Capital, Corporation Finance, and the Theory of Investment," *American Economic Review* 48 (July 1958): 261–97. They subsequently clarified some of the tax issues in "Corporate Income Taxes and the Cost of Capital—a Correction," *American Economic Review* 53 (June 1963): 433–43. Their analysis included corporate taxes but not personal taxes. Personal taxes are included in the more recent work of M. H. Miller, "Debt and Taxes," *Journal of Finance* 32 (May 1977): 261–76. When personal taxes are included, the relationship between K_e and K_o is altered, but its basic form remains the same, with K_e rising as leverage increases. Miller's argument is discussed in a later section in this chapter. The key point for our discussion here is not the exact relationship between K_e and K_o; rather, the point is that K_e increases as leverage decreases.

Financial risk—is the increased risk to shareholders that arises from the use of debt.

Operating risk—is the uncertainty about future profitability that arises from the basic nature of the business and operation of a company, the business risk inherent in the firm's operations.

The **risk-free rate of interest**—is the interest rate on a relatively riskless asset.

The increased risk to shareholders that arises from the use of debt is **financial risk.** Because of the increased risk, investors demand a higher return.

Looking at Figure 13–1, a number of questions arise. What determines the risk premium for **operating risk**, where operating risk is the business risk inherent in the firm's operations? In the figure, operating risk is measured as the vertical distance between the **risk-free rate of interest**, R_f, and the required return on unlevered shares, K_o. What is the nature of the extra risk premium shareholders demand as the firm increases its use of financial leverage? What criteria can financial managers use to pick the best mix of financing given that shareholders require an additional risk premium when more financial leverage is used? As will be discussed later, the appropriate criterion for choosing the firm's financial mix is to make decisions to maximize the market value of the firm. This is the same criterion we used to analyze investment decisions.

Before we discuss the choice of financing mix further, however, let us explore more fully the nature of both operating risks and financial risks. Shareholders must bear both forms of risk, so it is not surprising that both play key roles in any decision about capital structure.

Operating Risk and Operating Leverage

Earnings before interest and taxes (EBIT)—is a measure of operating earnings.

Even if a firm used no debt financing, shareholders would require a risk premium to invest in the firm. In Figure 13–1, this risk premium is shown as the vertical distance between K_o and R_f and is the premium for operating risk. Operating risk is the uncertainty about future profitability that arises from the basic nature of the business, i.e., from the firm's commercial operations. Operating risk can be thought of in terms of variability of operating earnings, or **earnings before interest and taxes (EBIT)**.

In discussing operating risk, it is useful to consider revenues and expenses separately. Clearly, one major determinant of operating risk is the variability of sales revenue. In general, variability of sales depends on the nature of the business, specifically on industry characteristics, the effectiveness of marketing efforts, countermoves by competitors, technological developments, shifts in consumer preferences, and similar factors. In addition to industry and company factors, general economic conditions play a part.

Strictly speaking, *predictability* is a more important factor than variability. A manufacturer of garden tools may experience a highly seasonal sales pattern, but a good part of the variability may be predictable. A toy manufacturer also may experience seasonality, but sales may be much more uncertain because of the faddishness of toys. Although individual products may be highly variable, overall sales variability will depend on the degree of diversification of the firm's investments.

Operating leverage—is the relationship between fixed and variable operating expenses and measures the sensitivity of operating profit to changes in sales.

The variability of operating earnings also depends on the nature of operating expenses. The term *operating expenses* refers to expenses related to the firm's operations and includes all expenses except interest and taxes. One important factor in operating expenses is the firm's degree of **operating leverage**, which was defined in Chapter 7 as the relationship between fixed and variable operating expenses.

The higher a firm's ratio of fixed to variable operating costs, the higher is its operating leverage. An example of a firm with high operating leverage is an airline. In the short run, few of an airline's costs vary with the level of passenger traffic—perhaps little more than the cost of meals served in flight. Above its break-even passenger load, its operating profits rise very rapidly with increases in the number of passengers. Below this break-even load, the opposite occurs. Contrast this behavior with that of a wholesaler, the majority of whose operating costs are goods purchased for resale. A wholesaler has a low degree of operating leverage, and operating profits are much less sensitive to changes in revenues, up or down. The degree of operating leverage of a firm, thus, has a pronounced effect on the sensitivity of its operating profit to revenue changes.

Variations in expenses that result from factors other than volume changes also contribute to the variability of EBIT. Increases in supply prices of materials or labor represent factors of this sort.

A final factor that influences the variability of EBIT is asset structure. We discussed variability of operating revenues above. The firm also may derive revenues from such nonoperating sources as marketable securities held for liquidity purposes. The proportion of total revenues derived from relatively stable nonoperating sources would affect the overall variability of EBIT.

Financial Risk and Financial Leverage

Returning to Figure 13–1, we see that shareholders will require a particular required rate of return, K_o, even if the firm issues no debt. As debt is used, shareholders require yet higher returns because of the financial risks imposed on shareholders over and above the operating risks. Such risks occur because shareholders have the *residual claim*, meaning that they must wait until after debtholders have been paid before getting any financial rewards. Interest charges and principal payments on debt must be paid before shareholders receive anything. The more financial leverage is used by the firm, the higher are these contractual interest and principal payments.

Even with no financial leverage, shareholder returns move up and down because of operating risk. But as financial leverage increases, the firm incurs higher interest payments. Once these contractual payments to debt owners are covered, returns to shareholders increase dramatically with increases in operating results because there are relatively few shareholders over which the benefits have to be spread. The firm has used debt financing to replace funds that it otherwise would have to raise by issuing new shares of stock. But if operating results are poor, shareholders suffer because practically all the operating profits have to go toward interest payments.

In sum, financial leverage causes returns to shareholders to fluctuate more dramatically than do the underlying operating returns to the firm. As a result, the use of financial leverage increases risks to shareholders. Such risks are manifested by both higher variability in annual returns to shareholders and, in the extreme case, a higher chance of the firm going bankrupt and the shareholders losing their entire investment.

In Chapter 4, we analyzed this effect of financial leverage increasing risks to shareholders. Let us look at this effect once again, bringing together the effects of both operating and financial risks on shareholders. Remember, shareholders are affected by both operating risks (that arise from the underlying variability in sales and operating profits) and financial risks (that arise from the extra variability in shareholder returns resulting from the use of financial leverage).

RISKS TO SHAREHOLDERS: OPERATING PLUS FINANCIAL RISKS

Profit after taxes (PAT)—is a dollar measure of firm profit.

To illustrate the effects of operating and financial decisions on risks to shareholders, let us look at potential changes in earnings available to shareholders. For simplicity we will focus on **profits after taxes (PAT)** and **return on equity (ROE)** as measures of shareholder earnings, although other measures such as earnings per share (EPS) would serve just as well.[2] The larger the prospective variability in profit after taxes or return on equity, the larger are the risks faced by shareholders. These variables represent the dollar (PAT) and percentage (ROE) returns that shareholders receive in a year. Despite the shortcomings of such accounting variables, they illustrate risk effects well. To see what contributes to variability in profit after taxes, let us decompose the percentage change in PAT as shown in Equation (2).

A given percentage change (%Δ) in profit after taxes (PAT) can be broken down as

$$\%\Delta\ PAT = \frac{\%\Delta\ PAT}{\%\Delta\ EBIT} \times \frac{\%\Delta\ EBIT}{\%\Delta\ SALES} \times \%\Delta\ Sales$$

$$= DFL \times (DOL \times \%\Delta\ Sales) \qquad (2)$$

$$= Financial\ Risk \times Operating\ Risk$$

where %Δ = "percentage change in," EBIT = earnings before interest and taxes, DFL = degree of financial leverage, and DOL = degree of operating leverage.

Return on equity (ROE)—is a percentage measure of the rate of return on an investment and equals income available to common stockholders divided by common equity.

Equation (2) must always hold because when we multiply through on the right-hand side, terms cancel leaving us with just the percentage change in PAT. In essence, Equation (2) just provides a useful way to see the factors that ultimately determine changes in PAT. As it turns out, the three terms on the right-hand side of Equation (2) are direct representations of the operating and financial risks we have been discussing.

The last term—the percentage change in sales—responds to the underlying variability in sales revenue that we discussed as a major determinant of operating risk.

The degree of operating leverage (DOL)—is the percentage change in EBIT divided by the percentage change in sales.

The second term—the percentage change in EBIT divided by the percentage change in sales—represents the sensitivity of operating profits (EBIT) to changes in sales volume and was given in Chapter 7 as the definition for the **degree of operating leverage (DOL)**. The higher the degree of operating leverage, the higher will be the effects of changes in sales on changes in profit after taxes. As we discussed earlier,

---

[2]Note that unless a firm issues more shares of stock, the percentage change in PAT will be equal to the percentage change in EPS. Likewise, for a given level of equity on a company's balance sheet, the percentage change in PAT will also be equal to the percentage change in ROE because both EPS and ROE will be equal to PAT divided by a constant(number of shares and book value of equity, respectively). As a result, our analysis of percentage changes in PAT is directly applicable to changes in EPS and ROE.

the degree of operating leverage is determined by the amount of fixed operating costs the firm has. The higher the fixed costs as a proportion of total costs, the higher the degree of operating leverage.

Finally, the first term—the percentage change in PAT divided by the percentage change in EBIT—represents the sensitivity of shareholder performance (PAT) to changes in operating results (EBIT). This term depends on the financial leverage of the firm, and this ratio is sometimes referred to as the **degree of financial leverage (DFL)**.

The **degree of financial leverage (DFL)**—is the percentage change in PAT divided by the percentage change in EBIT and represents the extent to which changes in operating results affect shareholders.

To see how the relationships in Equation (2) apply, let us examine a stylized example. Suppose a firm has $500 in assets. During the upcoming year, sales are expected to be $200 but might drop to $100 or surge to $300, depending on industry and economic developments. Now the firm is facing two decisions. The first concerns its operating plans. One plan (Operating Plan A) calls for setting variable costs equal to 60 percent of sales and requires no fixed operating costs. The other plan (Operating Plan B) can cut variable costs to only 20 percent of sales but will require a commitment of $70 per year in fixed operating costs. The second major decision is how to finance the firm. The firm could use all-equity financing, or $500 of equity (Financing Plan X), or instead could raise only $300 of equity, borrowing the remaining $200 from the bank at 5 percent interest (Financing Plan Y). For simplicity, we assume a 50 percent tax rate.

Let's first examine the effects of the choice of operating plans. Table 13–1 summarizes the necessary calculations. Note that, at this stage, we are focusing entirely on operating profits (EBIT) and that no financing charges or taxes are entered in the calculations. The numbers in Table 13–1 show a number of important features. Part I shows that under normal conditions (sales of $200), Operating Plan B, which has higher operating leverage, provides a higher EBIT than does Operating Plan A ($90 for Plan B versus $80 for Plan A). This higher EBIT result would be an incentive to adopt the higher operating leverage represented by Plan B. Part I also shows that Plan B leads to wider swings in EBIT than does Plan A as the sales outcomes vary. Part II of Table 13–1 shows these changes in sales and EBIT in percentage terms. As sales go up by 50 percent from $200 to $300, EBIT also changes by 50 percent with Plan A. With Plan B, however, the same 50 percent change in sales raises EBIT by 89 percent (from $90 to $170). In effect, use of Operating Plan B has magnified a 50 percent change in sales into an 89 percent increase in EBIT. The magnification shows the effect of operating leverage. The DOL just expresses these results in ratio form to show that for every 1 percent change in sales, EBIT goes up by 1.78 percent with Operating Plan B (because 0.89/0.50 = 1.78). As long as sales go up, a high degree of operating leverage (resulting from a high proportion of fixed operating costs) is desirable. The trouble comes when sales drop below expectations. Operating leverage is a two-edged sword: it is advantageous if sales are favorable but turns into a burden when sales levels drop.

The message from Table 13–1 is that operating leverage, because of the nature of fixed costs, increases the uncertainty associated with a firm's operating results. Changes in EBIT depend on both the underlying variability in sales revenues as well as a firm's DOL. In making production decisions, managers should assess the effects of such operating leverage on shareholder risks. If sales variability is already high, a high DOL adds even more potential for variations in earnings performance.

Table 13–1 only tells part of the story for shareholders, however, because it shows

Table 13–1

Operating Leverage and Risks of Two Alternative Investments

Part I: Operating Profitability

	Operating Plan A: No Operating Leverage			Operating Plan B: Operating Leverage		
	Bad Outcome	*Normal Outcome*	*Good Outcome*	*Bad Outcome*	*Normal Outcome*	*Good Outcome*
Sales	$100	$200	$300	$100	$200	$300
minus						
Variable costs[a]	−60	−120	−180	−20	−40	−60
minus						
Fixed operating costs[b]	−0	−0	−0	−70	−70	−70
equals						
Earnings before interest and taxes (EBIT)	$ 40	$ 80	$120	$ 10	$ 90	$170

[a]For plan A, variable costs are calculated at 60 percent of sales. For plan B, they are calculated at 20 percent.
[b]Fixed operating costs do *not* include any financial costs such as interest payments.

Part II: Changes from a Normal Outcome

	Good Versus Normal Outcome (percentage difference)		Bad Versus Normal Outcome (percentage difference)	
Area of Change	*Operating Plan A*	*Operating Plan B*	*Operating Plan A*	*Operating Plan B*
Sales	50	50	−50	−50
EBIT	50	89	−50	−89

Part III: Degree of Operating Leverage (DOL)

Operating Plan	DOL
A	1.0
B	1.78

Note: DOL = percentage of change in EBIT ÷ percentage of change in sales.

only operating results. How do operating results translate into returns to shareholders? Table 13-2 carries the calculations further. Let's assume that our firm chooses to adopt Operating Plan B (hence, taking on some operating leverage). Part I of Table 13–2 shows the operating outcome of Operating Plan B under the three possible conditions. Now the choice is between two financial plans, Financial Plan X (which uses no debt) and Financial Plan Y (which uses some debt). Part II traces through the implications of the two financing plans for profit after taxes and return on equity. Part II shows that the use of debt introduces a fixed interest cost—in this case, $10 based on 5 percent interest on $200 debt. Table 13–2 shows that the use of financial leverage in Financing Plan Y increases the return on equity as long as normal conditions hold but

Table 13–2

Financial Leverage and Risk of Two Alternative Investments

Part I: Operating Outcome

	Operating Plan B: Operating Leverage		
	Bad Outcome	*Normal Outcome*	*Good Outcome*
Sales	$100	$200	$300
Earnings before interest and taxes (EBIT)	$ 10	$ 90	$170

Part II: Financing of a $500 Investment

	Financing Plan X: No Financial Leverage[a]			Financing Plan Y: Financial Leverage[b]		
	Bad Outcome	*Normal Outcome*	*Good Outcome*	*Bad Outcome*	*Normal Outcome*	*Good outcome*
EBIT	$10	$90	$170	$10	$90	$170
minus						
Interest	− 0	− 0	− 0	−10	−10	−10
equals						
Profit before tax	$10	$90	$170	$ 0	$80	$160
minus						
Tax	− 5	−45	−85	− 0	−40	−80
equals						
Profit after tax (PAT)	$ 5	$45	$85	$ 0	$40	$80
Return on equity (ROE)	1 percent	9 percent	17 percent	0 percent	13.3 percent	26.7 percent

[a]$500 equity + $0 debt = $500 invested.
[b]$200 debt at 5 percent interest + $300 equity = $500 invested.

Part III: Changes from a Normal Outcome

	Good Versus Normal Outcome (percentage difference)		Bad Versus Normal Outcome (percentage difference)	
Area of Change	*Financing Plan X*	*Financing Plan Y*	*Financing Plan X*	*Financing Plan Y*
EBIT	+89	+ 89	−89	− 89
PAT	+89	+100	−89	−100
ROE	+89	+100	−89	−100

Part IV: Degree of Financial Leverage (DFL)

Financing Plan	DFL
X	1.0
Y	1.12

Note: DFL = %Δ PAT ÷ %Δ EBIT.

that financial leverage increases the variability in both PAT and ROE, thereby increasing risks to shareholders. Part III converts the changes into percentage terms and shows that financial leverage (borrowing $200 under Financing Plan Y) magnifies an 89 percent change in EBIT into a full 100 percent change in PAT and ROE. The degree of financial leverage (DFL) expresses this result in ratio form showing that the plan to borrow $200 has a DFL of 1.12 (that is, 1.00/0.89 = 1.12).

We see that financial leverage can have a favorable impact on shareholder earnings. This favorable impact depends very much on the relationship between the firm's ability to earn, or its rate of return on assets, and the interest cost of debt. In the above example, under normal conditions the firm is earning 18 percent before interest and taxes on its assets (the firm has EBIT of $90 on assets of $500). As long as it can borrow money at 5 percent and put those funds to work to earn 18 percent, financial leverage will have a favorable impact on return on equity. This favorable impact showed up as an increase in ROE from 9 percent to 13.3 percent in Table 13–2 when financial leverage was used under normal operating conditions. In fact, the more debt the firm had used, the more favorable would have been the impact on return on equity (as long as the percentage interest cost was lower than the rate of return on assets). If, on the other hand, the firm could only earn 5 percent on assets, there would be no advantage to the use of debt. In Table 13–2, if EBIT were $25 (0.05 × $500), after-tax ROE would be 2.5 percent no matter how much debt were used. If the firm's return were less than the cost of debt, the effects of leverage would be unfavorable.

> **When the return on assets exceeds the interest cost of debt, financial leverage has a favorable impact on return on equity (ROE). The more the return on assets exceeds the cost of debt, the more pronounced is the favorable impact.**

Do we conclude that, when the return/cost relationship is favorable, the more debt the better? The reason for the favorable leverage effect is that debt represents a fixed, prior claim on income. When times are good, debt is advantageous, but what happens if times are not good? Suppose the return/cost relationship suddenly turns from favorable to unfavorable, and EBIT drops? The fixed claim is a two-edged sword.

> **Because debt is a fixed, prior claim on income, financial leverage may produce a favorable effect when times are good but an unfavorable one when times are bad.**

Now let's pull together the results from Tables 13–1 and 13–2 to see the ultimate effects of operating and financial risks on shareholders. Suppose our hypothetical firm adopted Operating Plan B for its operating strategy. In addition, suppose it committed itself to borrowing $200. As a result, the firm's shareholders are affected by both operating and financial leverage. Table 13–3 summarizes the results. Part I shows that a 50 percent sales increase from $200 to $300 results in an increase in profit after taxes from $40 to $80—an increase of 100 percent. Part II decomposes this 100 percent change in PAT using Equation (2). As the table shows, the 50 percent sales change is magnified by the two effects—the degree of operating leverage and the degree of

Table 13–3

The Combined Effect of Operating and Financial Leverage

Part I: Possible Outcomes of Investment

	Outcome		
	Bad	*Normal*	*Good*
Sales	$100	$200	$300
Earnings before interest and taxes—Plan B	$ 10	$ 90	$170
Profit after taxes (PAT)—Plan D	$ 0	$ 40	$ 80
Return on equity	0 percent	13.3 percent	26.7 percent

Part II: Results of a 50 Percent Change in Sales

Degree of operating leverage (DOL) = 1.78
Degree of financial leverage (DFL) = 1.12
Percentage of change in PAT = DFL $\times$ DOL $\times$ %Δ sales
$$= 1.12 \times 1.78 \times 0.50$$
$$= 2 \times 0.50$$
$$= 100 \text{ percent}$$

financial leverage. These two effects combine to double the effects of sales variability.

We can see from the preceding discussion that operating leverage determines the extent to which a change in sales revenue affects EBIT. On the other hand, financial leverage does not affect EBIT because interest payments on debt come *after* the calculation of EBIT on the income statement. This does not mean that financial leverage has no effect. Financial leverage determines the extent to which changes in EBIT affect shareholders. Interest charges on debt are fixed costs from the shareholders' perspective. The higher is the financial leverage, the more sensitive shareholder returns (for example, profits after taxes or return on equity) will be to changes in EBIT.

As a result, shareholders are affected by both operating leverage (determining the relationship between sales revenue and EBIT) and financial leverage (determining the relationship between EBIT and shareholder profits). Managers must be aware of the way both of these forms of leverage magnify risks to shareholders. The effects of this leverage can be dramatic.

A couple of final comments are in order. The preceding example implied that firms can choose their degree of operating leverage at will. We used the example to illustrate the effects of different degrees of operating leverage. It is true that firms in some lines of business can vary the degree of operating leverage to a degree, but in other cases DOL is dictated to a large extent by technology and the nature of the firm's business. Firms have more discretion with respect to financial leverage, and here the choice is a difficult one. The reason it is difficult is because the world is uncertain. We saw above that debt can have a favorable effect when times are good, but an unfavorable effect when times are bad. If we only knew what was going to happen in the future, the choice of financing plans would be easy. But we don't know the future, and if we are imprudent in using debt, and bad times come, the results can be unpleasant.

Sample Problem
13—1

Operating and Financial Leverage for Firms A and B

Firms A and B both produce the same final output but have chosen different operating plans. Firm A has low fixed costs but has managed to make most of its costs change-able with the level of sales by purchasing (rather than making) all key parts needed and by hiring temporary help that it is not reluctant to lay off in bad times. (Variable costs for Firm A are 70 percent of sales). Firm B, on the other hand, makes a large number of key parts and views its workforce as permanent; its personnel policy is to keep people on the payroll. Firm B's strategy tends to keep its costs per unit below those of firm A at expected levels of output but involves higher fixed operating costs. Table 13–4 gives data on sales revenues and costs for the two firms under normal sales conditions and if sales drop by 10 percent below normal.

A. What is the degree of operating leverage for each firm?
B. Suppose that each firm needs $2,000 in assets. (In practice, Firm A might need fewer assets because of its operating policies.) Also suppose that Firm B uses no debt financing but that Firm A borrows $1,000 at 10 percent. Assume a 40 percent tax rate. Calculate the degree of financial leverage for each firm.
C. Which firm has higher risks to shareholders in terms of variability of profit after taxes?

Solution
A. The degree of operating leverage (DOL), which is defined as the percentage change in EBIT divided by the percentage change in sales, can be calculated for Firms A and B as

$$DOL_A = \frac{230 - 260}{260} \div \frac{900 - 1,000}{1,000} = -0.115 \div -0.10 = 1.15$$

$$DOL_B = \frac{220 - 300}{300} \div \frac{900 - 1,000}{900} = -0.267 \div -0.10 = 2.67$$

Note that Firm B experiences a larger change in EBIT for the same change in sales because of its higher DOL.

Table 13—4
Revenues and Costs for Firms A and B

	Normal Sales		A Drop in Sales of 10 Percent	
	Firm A	Firm B	Firm A	Firm B
Sales	$1,000	$1,000	$900	$900
Fixed operating costs	− 40	− 500	− 40	− 500
Variable costs	− 700	− 200	− 630	− 180
Earnings before interest and taxes	$ 260	$ 300	$230	$220

Table 13-5

Return on Equity (ROE) and Profit After Taxes (PAT) for Firms A and B

	Firm A		*Firm B*	
Sales	$900	$1,000	$900	$1,000
Earnings before interest and taxes	$230	$ 260	$220	$ 300
Interest	100	100	0	0
Profit before taxes	$130	$ 160	$220	$ 300
Taxes at 40 percent	52	64	88	120
Profit after taxes	$ 78	$ 96	$132	$ 180
Return on equity	7.8 percent	9.6 percent	6.6 percent	9 percent

B. To calculate the degree of financial leverage, we must first calculate profit after taxes for the two firms at both sales levels used above. (See Table 13–5.) Interest for Firm A is $1,000(0.10) = $100. ROE is PAT/equity. Firm B has equity of $2,000, while Firm A requires equity of only $1,000 because it borrows another $1,000 to finance its assets. The degree of financial leverage, DFL, is calculated as the percentage change in PAT divided by the percentage change in EBIT, which for Firms A and B is

$$\text{DFL}_A = \frac{78 - 96}{96} \div -0.115 = -0.188 \div -0.115 = 1.63$$

$$\text{DFL}_B = \frac{132 - 180}{180} \div -0.267 = -0.267 \div -0.267 = 1.0$$

C. For a 10 percent sales decrease, the calculations above show that Firm A's PAT drops by 18.8 percent. For Firm B, the drop in PAT is 26.7 percent. Thus, for any given variability in sales, Firm B shareholders will experience a larger variation in PAT and ROE than will shareholders in Firm A. The ultimate changes in PAT can be decomposed using Equation (2), which states that the percentage change in PAT = DFL × DOL × percentage change in sales:

For Firm A, 1.63 × 1.15 × 0.10 = 0.188 = 18.8 percent

For Firm B, 1.0 × 2.67 × 0.10 = 0.267 = 26.7 percent

As the decomposition shows, the much higher operating leverage of Firm B more than offset its lack of financial leverage. In practice, Firm B's high DOL may well be a motive for using less debt. ∃⌐⌐₣

From our analysis thus far, we can see that managers make both operating and financial decisions that affect shareholder risks. The operating decisions and the resultant operating leverage are ultimately investment decisions that are best analyzed using capital-budgeting techniques, such as the ones covered in prior chapters. Such tech-

Finance in Practice 13—1

The Case of UAL, Inc.

UAL, Inc. is a holding company whose major operating unit is United Airlines. Airlines provide good illustrations of the effects of operating and financial leverage because they have relatively high fixed costs (high operating leverage), and they also tend to use debt financing extensively (high financial leverage).

From 1976 to 1978, UAL's revenue rose by 37 percent, while operating profit rose by a whopping 5 times (500 percent). This rise was due to the effect of operating leverage. During the same period, profits before taxes rose by more than 1100 percent—more than double the 500 percentage increase in operating profit. Financial leverage was at work.

Then, from 1978 to 1979, things went the other way. Revenue fell by 5 percent and yet operating profit and profit before tax both fell by much more than 100 percent. Unfortunately for UAL, operating and financial leverage magnify bad as well as good results. Such is life in the airline business: certainly exciting, but probably too exciting for some. The high degree of both operating and financial leverage in this business means that shareholders (if not customers) are often in for a bumpy ride.

UAL's revenues turned around again in 1980 and have risen every year since, reaching $6.9 million in 1984. The drop in revenues in 1979 is a good illustration of the effects of operating and financial leverage. UAL's shareholders undoubtedly prefer that they not see illustations like 1979 happening again.

Source: UAL Annual Reports, 1976–1984.

niques address the question of whether the proposed investment stategy is desirable given both its prospective returns and risks.

How should the decision about financial leverage be made? We can see that financial leverage increases the expected return on the firm's equity but at the expense of increased risk. Because of the increased risk, investors demand a higher return. How do we decide whether the terms of the risk/return trade-off are favorable—that is, whether to accept increased risk in order to gain increased expected return? As we confront this question, let us keep firmly in mind that expected return is not guaranteed; it is, in a rough sense, a most likely return in a range that can go much higher or much lower than the most likely figure.

We cannot make the risk/return trade-off decision simply by examining Tables such as Table 13–1 or graphs such as that in Figure 13–1. These provide insights, but to make the choice we need a decision criterion.

CRITERIA FOR FINANCING DECISIONS

To make a choice between alternative financial plans in the face of a risk/return trade-off, we need a criterion for determining whether gains in expected return to shareholders by using more leverage are sufficient to justify the extra risks. Our decision criterion must, thus, be able to incorporate the effects of changes in both risk and return.

Sometimes accounting measures of shareholder interest, such as return on equity (ROE) or earnings per share (EPS), are suggested as decision criteria for financial decisions. Unfortunately, they are not adequate for the job because they measure return but not risk. Projecting what ROE or EPS might be at future EBIT levels gives us a useful display of possible outcomes, but it doesn't resolve the risk/return trade-off. Picking a financing plan with the highest ROE or EPS at expected EBIT levels ignores the critical factor of extra risks if EBIT drops below the expected outcome. Often a firm can continue to improve *expected* earnings per share or return on equity by increasing debt, but this decision could lead to a decline in the market price of the firm's stock as investors become concerned about greater risks—clearly an undesirable outcome.

Another suggested decision criterion is to pick the source of financing with the lowest cost, where the cost of any source of funds is the rate of return required by those who supply the funds. While such a rule may sound appealing, it ignores the changes in risk that occur when a firm changes its financial leverage.

In the case of firms to whom both equity and debt are available, debt is always the cheaper of the two. This being so, why use any equity at all? Using cost as our only criterion always would lead to a choice of debt, right up to the point of going bankrupt! Here, as before, using cost as the criterion considers only half of the issue: it ignores risk. Equity costs more—that is, has a higher required rate of return—because it does more: it bears risk. A bicycle costs less than an automobile, and both provide transportation, but to choose the bicycle because it is cheaper ignores some rather obvious differences between the two. Likewise, it is misleading to compare the cost of debt to the cost of equity because the use of additional debt (increasing financial leverage) without adding more equity increases risks to shareholders, and shareholders demand compensation for this additional risk.

We have looked at a number of criteria and found serious shortcomings with each. What about market value? Is our general criterion for financial-management decisions—value maximization—applicable to financing decisions as well as to investment decisions? Indeed it is.

The best criterion for choosing a financing plan is to pick the financing alternative that maximizes the value of the firm.

Figure 13–2
Division of Earnings Before Interest and Taxes (EBIT)

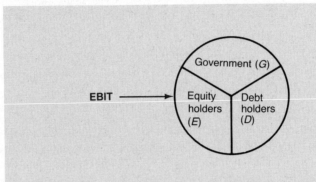

In principle, the use of value as our criterion solves our problems with respect to both time and risk. A value criterion can be used to compare the effects of alternative plans over many future periods rather than only near-term periods. A value criterion takes into account not only expected value, but also risk and variability. As a criterion, value recognizes the risk/return trade-off. Although a value criterion accomplishes these goals in principle, application of value as a criterion in practice is not easy. To develop valuation as a criterion for financing decisions, we need to know more about the way in which changes in leverage affect value.

HOW LEVERAGE AFFECTS FIRM VALUE

If we view a firm as a going concern, its value depends on the cash flows it can generate in the future. The firm's pretax operating profit, or EBIT, is divided among three principal claimants. Debt holders (D) receive their share in the form of interest, the government (G) receives its share in taxes, and equity holders (E) receive what is left. Thus, we can think of EBIT as a pie to be divided among the three claimants, as illustrated in Figure 13–2.

Investment decisions determine the size of the EBIT pie, while financing decisions determine the way it is to be sliced. The total value of the firm is its value to owners and creditors together and is determined by the combined slice going to equity holders and to debt holders in Figure 13–2. Investment decisions increase the value of the firm by increasing the size of the pie. Financing decisions can increase firm value by reducing the share of the pie going to the government—that is, by reducing the taxes paid by the firm.

> **Investment decisions determine the size of EBIT, while financing decisions determine how EBIT is to be divided among debt holders, equity holders, and the government (taxes).**

Table 13–6

Division of Earnings Before Interest and Taxes (EBIT) Among Claimants

		Claimant's Share When	
		Interest is Not Deductible	Interest is Deductible
EBIT (O) →	Debt holders	iD	iD
	Government	OT	$OT - iDT$
	Equity holders	$O - iD - OT$	$O - iD - OT + iDT$
Debt and equity together		$O(1 - T)$	$O(1 - T) + iDT$

Tax Effects

Financial friction—is the additional cost of financial transactions, such as commissions paid by investors to buy or sell securities, flotation costs of issuing new securities, information costs of financial decision making, and costs associated with financial distress.

Financing decisions affect the firm's tax liability because interest on debt is tax-deductible. To simplify the analysis, we will discuss tax effects as they would work in well developed financial markets without the **financial friction** that makes it more difficult or more costly to undertake financial transactions. Financial friction includes commissions paid by investors when they buy or sell stocks and bonds, the flotation costs of issuing new securities, and the information costs, in time and effort, required by investors to gather and analyze information in making financial decisions. Markets without friction would be efficient in the sense that market values would reflect all available information. By ignoring financial friction, we can focus on the tax effects of leverage without adding other complications (such as transactions or information costs). Even if some of these complications are added (as we do later), the same basic message remains: financing decisions affect the firm's tax liability because interest on debt is tax-deductible.

If interest were not deductible, a change in the firm's debt/equity mix would have no effect on taxes. Let us examine the slicing of the EBIT pie with and without deductibility of interest. In Table 13–6, the firm's EBIT each period is represented by the symbol O to emphasize that EBIT is a result of operations. Assume for simplicity that the firm pays interest at a rate, i, on total debt, D. Total interest payments each period are iD. With interest not deductible, the firm pays taxes of OT, where T is the tax rate. As leverage is increased, the share to debt holders increases, the share to equity holders decreases by a like amount, and the share to the government remains unchanged. Thus, the share to debt and equity holders together is fixed at $O(1 - T)$ and does not vary with changes in leverage.

The **interest tax shield**—is the reduction in taxes that results from the tax-deductibility of interest.

With interest tax-deductible, the government's share each period is lowered by iDT, sometimes called the **interest tax shield** on interest. The combined share to debt and equity together is higher by iDT. Table 13–7 illustrates this effect for a firm that has EBIT of $1,000, that faces a 40 percent tax rate, and that uses $3,000 of debt financing with an interest rate of 10 percent.

Table 13-7

Effect of Tax Deductibility of Interest on Cash Flows to Owners

	Earnings Before Interest and Taxes, O (1)	Interest on Debt, iD (2)	Pretax Profits (3) = (1) − (2)	Taxes, T (at 40 percent) (4)	Profits after Tax (5) = (3) − (4)	Debt and Equity (6) = (2) + (5)
Company having no debt	$1,000	$ 0	$1,000	$400	$600	$600
Company with debt of $3,000 at interest of 10 percent	$1,000	$300	$ 700	$280	$420	$720
		↓		↓	↓	
		Debtholders		Government	Equityholders	

As a comparison of the rows in Table 13–7 shows, the use of debt increases the combined share to debt and equity together from $600 to $720. This increase of $120 is exactly the amount of the tax shield on interest: $iDT = 0.10(\$3,000)(0.4) = \$120$. As shown in the table, the $120 increase to debt and equity owners comes at the expense of the government that sees its tax revenues reduced by $120, from $400 to $280.

From the analysis above, we can conclude that interest deductibility is an important benefit of debt financing. With interest not deductible, the use of debt financing in lieu of equity does not make the firm more valuable. The portion of the EBIT pie to be shared by debt and equity holders, $O(1 - T)$ in Table 13–6, is fixed in total, and leverage affects only the way the portion is sliced between debt and equity holders. An increase in the size of the slice to one group must come at the expense of the other. Hence, in frictionless, well developed financial markets, with interest not deductible, leverage cannot increase the combined value of debt and equity together.

To see this point more clearly, consider a firm whose debt and equity are entirely held by a single individual. With interest not deductible, for a given level of EBIT total payments to debt and equity are fixed, and changes in the split between the two cannot make the holder better or worse off. Given the existence of organized financial markets, the same conclusion holds if there are many holders of the firm's debt and equity.

Although (with interest not deductible) leverage does not increase the total value of the debt and equity, it does affect characteristics of the cash-flow streams going to the two groups. An increase in leverage increases the expected rate of return to equity in percentage terms but, as we found earlier in this chapter, simultaneously increases the riskiness of that return. As risk increases, risk-averse investors demand a higher return. The increase in risk offsets the increase in expected return, and the value of a share of stock remains unchanged. In other words, while leverage increases the expected return, because of the accompanying increase in risk the market does not place a higher valuation on that return.

When interest is tax-deductible, the picture changes. An increase in leverage decreases the share of EBIT going to the government and increases the share going to debt and equity.

> The firm's cash flows to owners increase with leverage because of the *interest tax shield* provided by the use of debt.

Value of the Tax Subsidy

What value does the market place on this tax subsidy? If the firm had no debt, it would provide to investors a cash-flow stream equal to $O(1 - T)$, from Table 13–6, in each period. This cash-flow stream has a value that we will label V_U, where the subscript U signifies "unlevered."

With debt present, the stream shared by debt and equity holders with interest deductible is $O(1 - T) + iDT$. The value of this stream, thus, is V_U plus the value of the tax shield, iDT. For simplicity, we will assume that the firm plans to borrow for the indefinite future so that iDT is a perpetuity. We can determine the present value of this tax shield by discounting. When this problem was first worked out in the early 1960s, it was argued that the tax shield is of approximately the same degree of risk as the interest payments themselves and should be discounted at the same rate, i. Thus, the present value of the tax shield of iDT per period was then calculated as $iDT/i = DT$, and the value of the firm with interest deductible was calculated as shown in Equation (3).[3]

> The value, V_L, of the cash flows of the levered firm, with interest tax-deductible, can be calculated as
>
> $$V_L = V_U + DT \qquad (3)$$
>
> where V_U = the value of the cash flows of the firm with no debt and DT = the present value of the tax shield.

Graphically, we can represent the relationship in Equation (3) as shown in Figure 13–3. Equation (3) states that the value of the levered firm, V_L, is larger than the value of the unlevered firm, V_U, by the present value of the tax shield, DT, provided by the interest payments made by the levered firm.

---

[3]Equation (3) was first worked out by Modigliani and Miller, "Corporate Income Taxes and the Cost of Capital—a Correction," *American Economic Review* 53 (June 1963): 433–43. This analysis did not consider the effects of personal taxes paid by stockholders and bondholders. Personal taxes are discussed in the next section. Note also that to take full advantage of the tax-deductibility of interest, the firm must have an EBIT level large enough so that it will be paying taxes after it makes its interest payments. This need for taxable income has led some to argue that the tax shield on interest is riskier than the interest payments themselves and, thus, that this tax shield should be discounted at a rate higher than i to reflect such extra risk. While this modifies the exact form of Equation (3), it does not change the basic message: the value of the levered firm exceeds the value of the unlevered firm because of the tax shield on interest. For a discussion of some additional aspects of this issue, see J. R. Ezzell and J. A. Miles, "Capital Project Analysis and the Debt Transaction Plan," *Journal of Financial Research* 6, 1 (Spring 1983): 25–31. Note that the specific relationship between V_L and V_U will also be reflected in the relationship between K_e and K_o discussed in footnote 1. A full elaboration of these issues is beyond the scope of this text.

Figure 13–3
Leverage and Value Considering Only Corporate Taxes

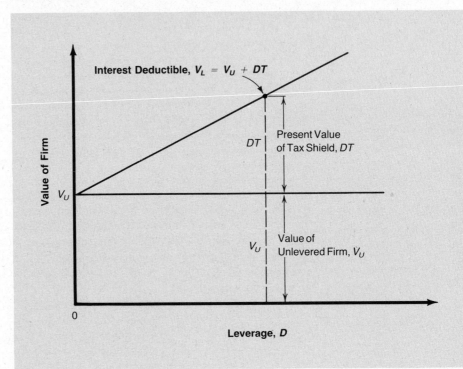

Sample Problem 13–2

The Effect of Corporate Taxes on Zetatronics, Inc.

Zetatronics, Inc. is financed entirely by equity that has a current market value of $16 million. The company is considering replacing some of its equity with debt by issuing bonds and using the proceeds to repurchase stock. Determine the theoretical value of the tax subsidy (considering corporate taxes only) if the amount of the swap were $4 million ($4 million in bonds replacing a like amount of stock). Assume a tax rate of 46 percent.

Solution
Assuming the change to be permanent and treating its cash flow as perpetuities, the value of the tax subsidy, from Equation (3), is

$$DT = \$4 \text{ million} \times 0.46 = \$1.84 \text{ million}$$

So, from Equation (3), the value of the firm after the transaction theoretically would be $16 million + $1.84 million = $17.84 million. ∃╟╠╞

To this point we have focused on the effects of leverage on value in light of the tax-deductibility of interest at the corporate level. We saw that leverage can increase value because of the tax shield on interest. But, as one would suspect, there is more to the story than this. Let us consider some complicating factors—personal taxes and financial distress.

Personal Taxes

The tax benefits considered in Figure 13–3 and Equation (3) take into account only taxes paid by the firm. It is clear that an increase in debt reduces the firm's tax liability and, thereby, increases total cash flows accruing to debt and equity holders together.

But corporate taxes are not the whole story. Bondholders and stockholders themselves must pay taxes on the returns they receive from the firm. These personal taxes act to offset part of the saving in the firm's taxes. Some economists argue that the offset is total and that, in general, there is no tax benefit to the use of debt at all.[4]

According to this view, the personal tax rate is effectively higher on returns to bondholders than on returns to shareholders because capital gains provide a large portion of a shareholder's return and are taxed at a lower rate than ordinary income, such as interest and dividends. Interest rates adjust to reflect the fact that bondholders must pay taxes on the interest they receive. The interest rate that the firm must pay on debt, thus, is higher by an amount sufficient to pay the bondholders' tax compared to what it would be if no taxes existed. This extra interest paid by the firm comes out of the stockholders' pockets. The net effect, so this argument goes, is that the taxes saved by shareholders due to deductibility of corporate interest are offset by the taxes paid by bondholders. An increase in debt by a firm would increase its after-tax cash flows, as indicated by Table 13–6. But this increase is offset by personal taxes paid by bondholders and stockholders (which are not shown in Table 13–6). In other words, while the *firm's* cash flows are altered by leverage, the net flows to *investors* are not. In the final analysis, when all taxes at all levels are taken into account, the use of debt by a firm provides no net tax benefit to its shareholders. The value of the firm, according to this argument, would be unaffected by changes in leverage, and V_L would always equal V_U. The elimination of the favorable treatment of capital gains, however, would reduce the personal tax disadvantage of equity.

The extent to which these various tax effects are offsetting is an unsettled issue at present. The weight of the evidence thus far suggests that there is, on balance, some tax benefit to the use of debt. It seems safe to bet, however, that the net benefit is less than that suggested by the corporate tax alone.[5] To the extent that personal taxes do offset the corporate tax saving, the upper line in Figure 13–3 would rise less steeply.

---

[4]The main proponent of this view is M. H. Miller, "Debt and Taxes," *Journal of Finance* 32 (May 1977): 261–75. Miller's argument recognizes that the tax-deductibility of interest does provide incentive for firms to issue debt and that some equilibrium level of debt will be issued by firms in the aggregate. The crux of his argument is that once this equilibrium is reached, interest rates and marginal tax rates are such that issuance of debt by an *individual firm* provides no net tax benefits to investors.

[5]For a good discussion of the tax issues and of literature on the subject, see R. H. Litzenberger and H. B. Sosin, "A Comparison of Capital Structure Decisions of Regulated and Nonregulated Firms," *Financial Management* 8 (Autumn 1979): 17–21. For a comprehensive analysis of alternative tax systems, see R. C. Stapleton and C. M. Burke, *Tax Systems and Corporate Financing Policy*, Monograph 1978–1 (New York University, Graduate School of Business Administration, 1978).

Financial Distress

Financial distress—occurs when a firm has difficulty meeting contractual obligations to its creditors.

Bankruptcy—is a legal procedure for reorganizing or liquidating a firm that is in financial difficulty, carried out under the supervision of the courts.

Figure 13–3 implies that the value of the firm continues to rise with leverage no matter how much is used and, therefore, that the firm should use as much debt as possible. We have considered the benefits of debt, but not the costs. Since EBIT is uncertain, there is always the possibility that it may drop too low to permit the firm to meet its contractual obligations. An increase in debt, thus, increases the probability of **financial distress**.

Financial distress usually is a matter of degree, with a declaration of **bankruptcy** the extreme form. Milder forms of financial distress occur when a firm's cash flows fall below expectations. In such a case, liquidity falls and the firm may have difficulty in meeting contractual obligations to its creditors. The costs of such financial distress are the modifications of investment and financing strategies made necessary by the distress condition. If a firm is forced to forgo desirable investments, significant opportunity costs may be incurred. Other costs may be incurred because of the inability of the distressed firm to negotiate effectively with suppliers, to ensure prompt delivery for customers, and to guarantee future availability of parts and service. During distress, creditors may restrict the firm's operations, thereby possibly reducing profitability. Dividend payments to shareholders also may be interrupted. Other kinds of opportunity costs may be incurred simply because of the diversion of management time from operating to financial matters.

Firms often encounter conditions of financial distress—sometimes mild, sometimes not so mild. Bankruptcy involves legal action and occurs much less often. Bankruptcy costs include costs of accountants, lawyers, judges, and lost time of managers in overseeing the bankruptcy proceedings. Even more important may be the opportunity costs of lost output resulting from underutilization of the firm's labor, management and physical plant during the bankruptcy proceedings. Losses may be incurred on sale of assets under distress conditions. There also may be psychological costs in the minds of investors, creditors, and managers. There has been little research on the magnitude of costs associated with bankruptcy, but it seems reasonable to suppose that they may be significant in relation to the value of the firm. Certainly the consequences of bankruptcy are significant in the minds of the firm's managers.[6]

In addition to costs incurred under conditions of distress, the use of debt may involve other opportunity costs that are more subtle but no less important. One of the important conclusions of this analysis is that the optimal amount of debt depends on the firm's operating risk and, therefore, on the nature of its business. Any use of debt, therefore, reduces a firm's flexibility to alter its commercial strategy in the direction

---

[6]Disagreement exists among financial economists as to the real significance of bankruptcy costs. For a view that bankruptcy costs are relatively small, see J. Warner, "Bankruptcy Costs: Some Evidence," *Journal of Finance* 32 (May 1977): 337–48. For a good discussion of the distinction between bankruptcy costs and liquidation costs, see R. A. Haugen and L. W. Senbet, "The Insignificance of Bankruptcy Costs to the Theory of Optimal Capital Structure," *Journal of Finance* 33 (May 1978): 383–94. Their argument that bankruptcy costs are insignificant rests on an assumption that bankruptcy is a matter of concern only to owners and creditors. They argue that bankruptcy is unimportant to all other parties and, therefore, will have no real effect on relationships between the firm and suppliers, between the firm and customers, on the morale of managers and employees, and, thus, on the commercial operations of the firm. A contrary view and another discussion of bankruptcy costs can be found in E. H. Kim, "A Mean-Variance Theory of Optimal Financial Structure and Corporate Debt Capacity," *Journal of Finance* 33 (March 1978): 45–64.

Figure 13–4
Leverage and Firm Value

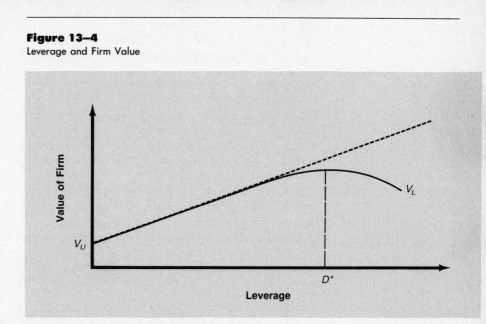

of higher risk. Consider, for example, a firm contemplating a new venture that promises high returns but also involves high risk. If the firm's preexisting capital structure included a level of debt that would be imprudent if the new venture were undertaken, three options would be available. The firm could:

1. alter the capital structure,
2. undertake the new venture and operate with too much debt, or
3. forgo the new venture.

Each of these options has its costs. Taking such costs into account is difficult because the need to alter the commercial strategy may not be foreseen at the time the debt policy must be set. Nevertheless, the reduction in the firm's commercial flexibility must be counted as a cost of using debt.

Leverage and Value

We can conclude that debt has both benefits and costs. The benefits arise from the deductibility of interest payments, and the costs arise from the possibility of financial distress and reduced commercial flexibility. Choosing the appropriate debt level, thus, involves a trade-off.

As leverage increases, the firm reaches a point where the expected costs of financial distress and reduced flexibility begin to outweigh the benefits of the tax subsidy. At that point, the value of the firm stops rising with leverage, and the optimal debt/equity ratio has been reached.

Pushing debt beyond the optimal point would result in a decline in value. We can represent the relationships graphically as in Figure 13–4, in which D^* represents the optimal debt level for the firm.[7] This debt level would correspond to an optimal debt/equity ratio, D/E^*, for financing the firm's operations.

Another important consideration is the possible loss of tax credits in bankruptcy. If a firm goes bankrupt, tax credits arising from losses normally cannot be recovered from the government, unless the firm merges with another firm or manages to carry the tax credits forward after bankruptcy. Thus, higher debt levels reduce the firm's tax liability during periods when profits are earned, but at the same time increase the likelihood of losing tax benefits during other periods if the firm goes bankrupt. These offsetting effects reduce the value of the tax subsidy below the theoretical maximum of DT in Equation (3) and cause the value of the firm to decline at high levels of debt, as depicted in Figure 13–4.[8]

From the foregoing discussion, we can conclude that theories explaining the relationship between leverage and firm value are not yet completely developed. A number of important factors have been identified, but their relative importance is not yet perfectly understood. The exact size of the tax subsidy is open to considerable question. Nevertheless, enough is known to suggest that the relationship between leverage and value is more or less as depicted in Figure 13–4. The value of the firm rises with leverage up to a point, and then begins to decline.

The value of a firm rises with leverage up to a point and then declines.

Figure 13–4 suggests that managers should, in practice, be careful in choosing their financial policies concerning financial leverage. By judicious use of debt, the firm may be able to create extra value for shareholders. Thought of another way, judicious choice of financing mix can lower investors' overall weighted-average required return *(WARR)* for supplying capital to the firm. For a given set of future operating cash flows, lower return requirements translate into higher values. Before talking about the practical aspects of using the insights from Figure 13–4, we need to discuss briefly some additional factors, other than tax effects and costs of financial distress, that also play roles in understanding debt policy.

---

[7]We are assuming that shareholders, as residual owners of the firm, will capture any increases in the value of the firm. As a result, maximizing the value of the firm will be in the shareholders' best interests. For an analysis of the conflicts between bondholders and stockholders and their implications for financing policy, see S. C. Myers, "The Determinants of Corporate Debt Capacity," *Journal of Financial Economics* 5 (November 1977): 147–75.

[8]For a discussion of these offsetting tax effects, see M. J. Brennan and E. F. Schwartz, "Corporate Income Taxes, Valuation, and the Problem of Optimal Capital Structure," *Journal of Business* 51 (January 1978): 103–14. Factors other than taxes and costs of financial distress also may affect the relationship between financial leverage and firm value. Secured debt (that is, debt secured by a pledge of assets) may reduce the firm's liability for future legal damages and, therefore, affect value differently than unsecured debt. See J. H. Scott, Jr., "Bankruptcy, Secured Debt, and Optimal Capital Structure," *Journal of Finance* 32 (March 1977): 1–20. Also important is the extent to which the firm's value rests on future growth opportunities requiring further discretionary expenditures by the firm. For a discussion of these issues, see S. C. Myers, "The Determinants of Corporate Debt Capacity," *Journal of Financial Economics* 5 (November 1977): 147–75. It is possible to view financial distress and agency costs (to be discussed shortly) as a form of financial friction constituting a fourth slice in the EBIT pie in Figure 13–2. As debt increases, the friction slice grows larger, while the government's slice grows smaller. The optimum occurs at the point where the government and friction slices combined are minimized.

OTHER CONSIDERATIONS IN USING DEBT

A full understanding of debt policies requires consideration of factors that are not fully reflected in the trade-off shown in Figure 13–4. These include issuance costs (especially for smaller firms), considerations of voting control, agency relationships, and possible differences in information. These factors in a sense all represent deviations from the ideal frictionless-market assumptions that we used earlier in discussing the tax benefits of debt financing.

Issuance and Financing Costs

In our discussion so far we have assumed that the corporation has easy and low-cost access to sources of debt and equity capital. Financing sources are considered low in cost if the cost of issuing the debt or equity is relatively minor in proportion to the funds raised. This assumption is usually valid in the case of larger firms raising large amounts of debt or equity. Debt may either be sold directly in public financial markets (as in the case of a bond issue) or may come in the form of a loan from a financial intermediary, such as a bank. New equity funds may come from the sale of new stock or the retention of profits.

For smaller firms, however, access to public markets for debt and equity is typically quite expensive. As an alternative, they rely more heavily on financial intermediaries as sources of funding. As we discussed in Chapter 2, such intermediaries include commercial banks, insurance companies, and savings-and-loan associations.

Consider what would happen if a small or little-known firm needed to raise $1 million worth of external funds. If it tried to issue stock or bonds for this amount in public financial markets, the process would likely be very expensive because it would require a substantial amount of information processing and credit analysis by hundreds or even thousands of different individuals. On the other hand, a commercial bank could perform this credit analysis and information-processing function—a major role of a financial intermediary—on behalf of all these individuals at much lower costs. By law, however, commercial banks can deal only in debt contracts. As a result, for smaller firms use of debt through a commercial bank may have added advantages over equity that are not captured in Figure 13–4. Commercial banks are primary suppliers of funds to smaller firms.

Larger firms also often find that debt obtained from financial intermediaries has certain advantages. By dealing with a financial intermediary, the firm raises the required funds conveniently in a single transaction and avoids some of the legal procedures, filings, and disclosure of information that come with public sales of securities. We will have more to say on these issues in Chapter 17.

Voting Control

In large, publicly held firms, stock ownership is typically dispersed among a wide array of individuals and institutions (such as pension funds). In such cases, no unified group of shareholders has voting control (50 percent or more) of the company and, hence, is in a position to dictate the future membership of the corporation's board of directors and its choice of management. In such instances, sale of new shares of stock typically has no appreciable effect on the concentration of voting control.

In some circumstances, however, issuance of new stock to raise funds may have important implications for control of the company. A prime example is the family-owned firm that is usually a relatively small enterprise, at least relative to major multibillion-dollar corporations. If such a firm were to raise large amounts of money by new equity sales, the original family owners (assuming they don't have the money to buy the newly issued stock too!) may eventually lose control of a majority of the voting shares. This dispersion of shares exposes them to the possibility that some other individual could buy up more than 50 percent of the stock and effectively take control of the company. This takeover could result in dramatic shifts in both corporate strategy and personnel. While such developments are not necessarily bad, the family owners may be reluctant to expose themselves to such prospects for change. Such a company would have a preference for issuing debt rather than equity if new funds are needed. Such debt does not give up any voting rights to its owners.

Agency Relationships

We have noted at many points throughout this book that management's job is to act as agent of the stockholders. Unfortunately, this agency relationship is not costless, for sometimes situations arise where the interests of managers and stockholders diverge. Conflicts can also arise between stockholders and bondholders. Sometimes these problems emerge because managers are unable to reveal full information to bondholders and stockholders regarding the firm's prospects without at the same time giving competitors an advantage. The limited liability of stockholders can motivate them to press for projects more risky than either the bondholders or the managers desire to undertake. Hired managers sometimes are known to allocate to themselves benefits in the form of salaries and *perquisites*, such as country-club memberships, travel, or company cars, over and above what they would allocate if they were the sole owners of the enterprise.

Agency costs—are the costs arising from the separation of ownership and management by the hiring of professional managers.

Collectively, these costs arising from the separation of ownership and management by the hiring of professional managers are known as **agency costs**. Some agency costs result from the use of debt in the capital structure, but others would exist whether debt were used or not. Because of the potential for conflict, stockholders and bondholders monitor and control the firm's activities by means of required reporting and covenants in agreements. All such arrangements involve some costs.

Competitive markets and innovative financing techniques help reduce agency costs but cannot eliminate them completely. Those agency costs that remain must be counted as another cost of doing business. Those related to the use of debt must be included along with the costs of financial distress in evaluating the wisdom of alternative debt policies.[9]

---

[9]Agency costs were first discussed rigorously by M. Jensen and W. Meckling, "Theory of the Firm: Managerial Behavior, Agency Costs, and Ownership Structure," *Journal of Financial Economics* 2 (October 1976): 305–60. For a good review of the subject, see A. Bernea, R. A. Haugen, and L. W. Senbet, "Market Imperfections, Agency Problems, and Capital Structure: A Review," *Financial Management* 10 (Summer 1981): 7–22.

Differences in Information

The discussion leading to Figure 13–4 assumes that financial markets are extremely efficient in digesting all the relevant information about the firm's future prospects. As a result, use of financial leverage creates value only to the extent that it generates a tax savings at the corporate level. In the real world, however, there is some controversy about whether financial markets actually are completely efficient in reflecting relevant information. In Chapter 12 we discussed three forms of market efficiency: weak-form, semistrong-form, and strong-form efficiency. There we argued that, at least as a first approximation, well developed U.S. financial markets do reflect information about past security prices and, hence, are weak-form efficient. Financial markets also respond rather quickly to major public disclosures of new information about a company, such as news of a corporate merger. As a result, markets at least approach the requirements of semistrong-form efficiency. But financial markets do not yet reflect inside (nonpublic) information and are, thus, not strong-form efficient.

The relevance of this type of market inefficiency for debt policy is that managers who are making the financial decisions may well possess some inside knowledge about the firm's prospects—information not yet reflected in market prices. In such a case, a manager may well feel that the company's stock is not properly priced in the market. For example, if the manager knows about a new technology the company has developed, but the news has not yet become public, he or she may feel the current stock price is undervalued because the financial market has not yet placed a value on the technology. The manager may be reluctant to issue stock because it will allow new shareholders to buy into the company at a relatively low price, thus depriving existing shareholders of the full-value gains when the market finally does give value to the technology. What is a manager to do in such a situation?

Our first advice is that, whenever possible, managers should communicate information to financial-market participants so that their firm's securities will be fairly valued. In Chapter 17, we will discuss such communication policy in detail. But suppose for competitive reasons such information cannot be disclosed fully. One solution is for managers to avoid equity financing and use debt. Thus, one motive for using debt is simply to gain the advantage of financial leverage that accrues to shareholders if things turn out well. If management is convinced that operating returns on assets in the future will exceed the interest rate on debt, the use of debt makes sense. In addition, management's willingness to take on debt may actually signal to the market that the firm does have a bright future. Such a signal through use of debt may, thus, increase firm value.[10]

The wisdom of this kind of "betting on the future" must be considered carefully. Any time debt is used, there is the prospect for higher returns to shareholders if operating results are good. But if operating results are not good, shareholders will suffer. Managers who bet on the future should do so only if they have a much better idea of

---

[10]See S. A. Ross, "The Determination of Financial Structure: The Incentive Signaling Approach," *Bell Journal of Economics* 8 (Spring 1977): 23–40.

the odds of winning than does the market. While this knowledge of odds may come with inside information, managers must be careful not to underestimate the potential risks to shareholders. Large doses of debt can threaten the very existence of the company if economic conditions turn sour.

Book Value

Before we leave our discussion of motives for using debt, let us consider an argument that is sometimes stated as a reason not to sell stock. Sometimes it is argued that a firm should never sell stock below *book value*. Book value usually is defined as tangible net worth per share. Leaving aside inflation effects, book value reflects in a rough way the cost of the firm's assets. Book value may be important for regulated firms that are allowed a "fair return" on book value. But for other firms, is book value a relevant consideration in making financing decisions?

The market price of a firm's shares reflects the consensus view of investors of the present value of the cash flows that the firm's investments are expected to generate. To say that an investment has a positive net present value *(NPV)* indicates that the cash flows it is expected to generate have a value greater than the cost of the assets required to generate those flows. If a firm undertakes only investments having a positive net present value—as it should—then in theory its stock price should rise above book value.

If a firm's stock is selling below book value, something has gone wrong. Some of its investments have not worked out as planned, and the market judges the value of future cash flows to be less than the cost of the assets required to generate those cash flows (inflation aside). A market price below book value, thus, represents a bad report for the firm. It may be that the poor performance resulted from factors beyond the control of management—general economic conditions, unforeseen cost increases, foreign competition, or any of a number of factors. Sometimes conditions in the world change so rapidly that many firms are adversely affected. In other cases, management error may be the cause.

Suppose a firm decides against selling stock because market price is below book value. If, as a result, it must forgo an attractive investment, shareholders are worse off. In this case, their position is diluted by *not* selling stock.

We can conclude that, in general, book value is not relevant to financing decisions. If funds are needed for attractive investments and equity is the right choice, stock should be sold regardless of the relationship between market price and book value. Here again, careful communication to investors of the reasons for the stock issue is very important and may alleviate any fears about dilution. We might recognize here a possibility that management might be reluctant to recommend sale of stock at a price below book value, because to do so draws attention to the price relationship and might require explanations (perhaps perceived as potentially embarrassing) as to why the price fell below book value in the first place. Such reluctance is understandable, but to argue that sale of stock below book value is counter to shareholder interests is a red herring. In such situations, the interests of managers must be separated from those of shareholders to make sure that concern is being focused only on the interests of the shareholders.

PRACTICAL IMPLICATIONS

As we have seen, there are a number of motives for borrowing by firms. One motive is to capture the tax benefits of deductibility of interest. Just how large these benefits are to shareholders after personal taxes is open to some question. Firms may also use debt when the sale of stock may dilute existing control of the firm or involve large issuance costs.

Even if there were no tax benefit at all, many firms would borrow for one of the other reasons. Firms with access to either debt or equity through the public markets might choose to borrow in order to exploit the effects of financial leverage. Firms that cannot raise equity economically choose debt because it is the only economical source of external funds.

Much of the material in this chapter is conceptual and theoretical. What guidance can it provide to decision makers in practice? Does an understanding of the effects of leverage on returns, risk, and value tell managers whether to use debt and, if so, how much? The answer is no, for our understanding of many of the key relationships is not sufficiently developed to permit exact quantitative application. The theory does, however, provide a useful way of thinking about the relationships and yields insights and qualitative guidance that is valuable.

One conclusion that emerges is that it is useful to consider debt in terms of its impact on firm value rather than only on earnings. By using value as the framework, we focus on what counts most to shareholders. Shareholders receive their return in the form of dividends and stock-price appreciation, not earnings per share. The valuation framework makes clear the fact that excessive use of debt can lower stock price and, thereby, reduce returns to shareholders, even though expected earnings per share may increase.

Should the effects of leverage on earnings be ignored? They should not, because earnings figures, such as EPS, are important and closely watched indicators of performance. Investors usually do not have access to projections of future earnings and cash flows and must rely heavily on historical data. In evaluating financing alternatives, management should analyze carefully the impact of each alternative on EPS and on *coverage* (how large the company's earnings are relative to fixed charges, such as interest payments). Useful techniques for such analysis are the EBIT/EPS chart and coverage ratios that we will discuss in the next chapter. If the alternative to be picked has an adverse impact on near-term EPS, management should communicate carefully and completely to investors the reasons why a plan that adversely affects near-term earnings is nonetheless best in the long run.

The valuation analysis indicates that the optimal financing mix depends on the risk of bankruptcy and financial distress. The risk of bankruptcy and financial distress depends to an important extent on the *operating risk*, or business risk, of the firm. Thus, the optimal debt/equity mix depends on the nature of the business and, therefore, on the kinds of investments that the firm makes. The more risky the firm's investments—that is, the higher is its operating risk—the less debt it should use.[11]

---

[11]For theoretical development of this point, see M. J. Brennan and E. F. Schwartz, "Corporate Income Taxes, Valuation, and the Problem of Optimal Capital Structure," *Journal of Business* 51 (January 1978) 103–14.

> **The optimal debt/equity mix depends on the nature of the business and, therefore, on the kinds of investments that the firm makes.**

When the firm maintains a more or less stable commercial strategy and remains in the industry in which it historically has operated, it likely will routinely invest in projects covering a wide spectrum of risk. In such cases, high-risk and low-risk projects may average out over time and leave the overall operating risk of the firm and, therefore, its optimal debt/equity mix, unchanged. Where a series of investments do have a cumulative effect on the firm's overall operating risk, the optimal debt/equity mix may change enough so that a revision in the actual debt/equity mix may become desirable.

Because the optimal debt/equity mix depends critically on operating risk, it is clear that the optimal mix is not static but is likely to vary, perhaps widely, over time. A debt level considered prudent one day may suddenly become too high.

Market value is the appropriate criterion for financing decisions, as it is for investment decisions. In this chapter, we have used the valuation criterion to provide qualitative guidance and a way of thinking about capital-structure decisions. We will turn to the difficult task of applying these concepts in the next chapter.

KEY CONCEPTS

1. Financial leverage increases the return to equity if return on assets exceeds the interest rate.

2. Financial leverage magnifies the variability of operating income and, thereby, increases the riskiness of the return to equity.

3. As financial leverage increases, risk increases, and the return required by equity holders increases.

4. Earnings per share is useful as a performance measure but not as a criterion for financing decisions because it does not take risk into account.

5. Return on equity, cost, and book value likewise are deficient as criteria for financing decisions. Market value is the theoretically valid criterion.

6. Financial leverage affects the value of the firm because the tax-deductibility of interest acts as a subsidy to the firm.

7. Offsetting the tax benefits of debt are the costs of financial distress, agency problems, and reduced flexibility. In principle, an optimal debt level exists beyond which the tax benefits of additional debt are outweighed by its costs.

SUMMARY

Financial leverage refers to the mix of debt and equity funds used to finance a firm's activities. Financial leverage affects both the magnitude and the variability of earnings per share (EPS) and return on equity (ROE). For any given level of operating return (EBIT), the effect of an increase in leverage is favorable if the percentage rate of operating return on assets is greater than the interest cost of debt and is unfavorable if the rate of operating return is less than the interest cost of debt. When EBIT varies over time, financial leverage magnifies the variation in EPS and ROE. Variability of EPS and ROE, thus, stems from two factors: variability of EBIT (operating risk) and the degree of financial leverage employed (financial risk). Thus, in general, the use of financial leverage increases both the expected return to shareholders and the variability of that return and presents the financial manager with the fundamental trade-off between return and risk: more return if things go well, less return if things go poorly.

To analyze financing alternatives, a decision criterion is needed that takes into account both sides of the risk/return trade-off. Earnings per share, while very useful as a performance measure, is not satisfactory as a decision criterion because it considers only return and ignores risk. Strict application of the EPS criterion would lead in the majority of cases to the use of too much debt and in some cases would lead to the use of too little. In no case does the EPS criterion systematically balance return against risk. As decision criteria, ROE and cost suffer from the same shortcoming. The criterion that does deal with the future and with both sides of the risk/return trade-off is the market-value criterion.

Financial leverage affects the value of the firm in several ways. Because interest on debt is tax-deductible, an increase in leverage reduces the firm's tax liability and, thereby, increases the share of EBIT going to debt and equity owners. At the same time, increased leverage reduces commercial flexibility and increases the probability of financial distress. Choosing the appropriate level of debt requires a trade-off among these opposing factors. The optimal debt level is that which maximizes the total value of the firm, equity and debt together. A critical determinant of the optimal debt level is the degree of operating risk inherent in the firm's commercial strategy.

The effect of personal taxes may negate some of the benefit of the tax-deductibility of interest to the firm. Motives for borrowing—other than tax benefits—include exploiting the favorable effect of financial leverage and reducing total financing costs by using debt supplied by financial intermediaries.

QUESTIONS

1. Explain the distinction between financial leverage and operating leverage.

2. How does financial leverage affect earnings after taxes, earnings per share, and percentage return on equity?

3. How does financial leverage affect the variability of dollar returns?

4. Why does the presence of financial leverage result in lower earnings per share and return on equity when EBIT falls to low levels?

5. Why is earnings per share unsuitable as a criterion for financing decisions?

6. Why does the use of earnings per share as a criterion for financing decisions result in a bias toward the use of debt?

7. Distinguish between accounting return on equity and return to shareholders. Can you think of an action that increases return on equity but simultaneously reduces return to shareholders?

8. What is the cost of debt funds? What is the cost of equity funds? How are the costs of debt and equity funds related for a given firm?

9. Discuss the use of cost as a criterion for financing decisions.

10. In choosing between debt and equity, how should the relationship between the market value and the book value of a firm's stock be taken into account?

11. How does market value as a criterion deal with the risk/return trade-off in financing decisions?

12. How do financing decisions affect the division of EBIT among its various claimants?

13. What effect does the tax-deductibility of interest have on the shares of EBIT going to the various claimants?

14. How can the use of debt increase the value of the firm?

15. If interest were not tax-deductible, what advantage would there be in using debt?

16. How is a firm's optimal debt/equity ratio related to its operating risk?

PROBLEMS

1. Assume that a firm is considering expanding assets by $5 million and has determined that it can finance the expansion either through a bond issue carrying a 10 percent interest rate or through a new issue of common stock which can be sold to net the company $20 per share. The firm currently has 400,000 shares of stock outstanding and $6 million of bonds with an 8 percent coupon. The tax rate is 48 percent.

   a. Calculate the earnings per share (EPS) for each alternative at EBIT levels of $1 million, $2 million, $3 million, and $4 million.

   b. What can be said from this analysis regarding the choice between bonds and stock?

2. Assume that an individual has $1,000 to invest and is faced with two potential investments. She could invest in a portfolio of common stocks with the three possible outcomes shown in Table A or she could buy risk-free U.S. Treasury bills yielding 10 percent. Assume that interest is tax-deductible, all returns are fully taxable as ordinary income, and that the marginal tax rate is 50 percent. Also assume that all losses lead to tax savings of $.50 for each dollar loss. Calculate the terminal value in each of three possible outcomes (after 1 year) of the $1,000 investment for three possible investment strategies: levering the investment through borrowing $500 at 12 percent and investing $1,500 in the stock portfolio; investing the $1,000 in the stock portfolio; investing $500 in the stock portfolio and $500 in risk-free United States Treasury bills.

3. Utilize the information in problem (2) to calculate the expected value and standard deviation of the terminal value of the portfolio for each of the three degrees of leverage. What can be said about the risk/return tradeoff?

4. Assume that a firm has a market value of $10 million if financed entirely with equity. Calculate the value of the firm if $1 million, $3 million, and $5 million in debt are used to replace equal amounts of equity. Assume a tax rate of 40 percent, and ignore the effects of personal taxes. Would the value of the firm continue to increase as more debt is used to replace equity? Why or why not?

5. Suppose a firm used no debt and its value was $1,000. Now suppose the same firm issued $300 of debt with an interest rate of 10 percent. Assume this debt is perpetual, so it pays interest payments for the indefinite future. Also assume that interest is tax deductible and the corporate tax rate is 40 percent.

   a. What would be the value (debt plus equity) of the firm after the debt was issued if both personal taxes and any costs of financial distress were ignored? Explain.

   b. What would be the value of the stock after the debt was issued?

   c. Suppose the beta of the unlevered (no debt) firm's stock was 1.0. What would you expect to be true about the beta of the stock after the debt was issued? Give a written explanation.

Table A

Possible Portfolio Outcomes	Probability (percentage of whole)	Return (percentage of investment)
Good	25	30
Normal	50	15
Bad	25	0
	100	

REFERENCES

Asquith, P., and D. W. Mullins, Jr. "Equity Issues and Stock Price Dilution." Working paper, Harvard Business School (May 1983).

Beaver, W., and D. Morse. "What Determines Price-Earnings Ratios." *Financial Analysts Journal* (July–Aug. 1978): 65–76.

Bernea, A., R. A. Haugen, and L. W. Senbet. "Market Imperfections, Agency Problems and Capital Structure: A Review." *Financial Management* 10 (Summer 1981): 7–22.

Brennan, M. J., and E. F. Schwartz. "Corporate Income Taxes, Valuation and the Problem of Optimal Capital Structure." *Journal of Business* 51 (Jan. 1978): 103–114.

Campbell, T. S. "Optimal Investment Financing Decisions and the Value of Confidentiality." *Journal of Financial and Quantitative Analysis* 14 (December 1979): 913–924.

Cordes, J. J., and S. M. Sheffrin. "Estimating the Tax Advantage of Corporate Debt." *Journal of Finance* 38 (Mar. 83): 95–105.

Dearborn, D. C., and R. I. Levin. "Error Visibility as a Factor in Executive Performance." *Southern Journal of Business* 6 (Jan. 1972): 65–70.

Ezzell, J. R., and J. A. Miles. "Capital Project Analysis and the Debt Transaction Plan." *Journal of Financial Research* VI, no. 1, 25–31 (Spring 1983).

Fama, E. F. "Efficient Capital Markets: A Review of Theory and Empirical Work." *Journal of Finance* 25 (May 1970): 383–417.

Flath, D., and C. R. Knoeber. "Taxes, Failure Costs and Optimal Capital Structure: An Empirical Test." *Journal of Finance* 35 (March 1980): 99–118.

Gritta, R. D. "The Effect of Financial Leverage on Air Carrier Earnings: A Break-Even Analysis." *Financial Management* 8 (Summer 1979): 53–60.

Hamada, R. S. "Portfolio Analysis, Market Equilibrium and Corporation Finance." *Journal of Finance* 24 (Mar. 1969): 13–31.

Haugen, R. A., and L. W. Senbet. "The Insignificance of Bankruptcy Costs to the Theory of Optimal Capital Structure." *Journal of Finance* 33 (May 1978): 383–394.

Higgins, R. C., and L. D. Schall. "Corporate Bankruptcy and Conglomerate Merger." *Journal of Finance* 30 (Mar. 1975): 93–114.

Hong, H. "Inflation and the Market Value of the Firm: Theory and Tests." *Journal of Finance* 32 (Sept. 1977): 1031–1048.

Jensen, M., and W. Meckling. "Theory of the Firm: Managerial Behavior, Agency Costs, and Ownership Structure." *Journal of Financial Economics* 2 (October 1976): 305–360.

Kim, E. H. "A Mean-Variance Theory of Optimal Financial Structure and Corporate Debt Capacity." *Journal of Finance* 33 (Mar. 1978): 45–64.

Kim, E. H., W. G. Lewellen, and J. J. McConnell. "Financial Leverage Clienteles: Theory and Evidence." *Journal of Financial Economics* (March 1979): 83–110.

Krainer, R. E. "Interest Rates, Leverage and Investor Rationality." *Journal of Financial and Quantitative Analysis* 12 (Mar. 1977): 1–16.

Kraus, A., and R. Litzenberger. "A State-Preference Model of Optimal Financial Leverage." *Journal of Finance* 28 (Sept. 1973): 911–922.

Litzenberger, R. H., and H. B. Sosin. "A Comparison of Capital Structure Decisions of Regulated and Non-Regulated Firms." *Financial Management* 8 (Autumn 1979): 17–21.

Litzenberger, R. H., and J. C. Van Horne. "Elimination of Double Taxation of Dividends and Corporate Financial Policy." *Journal of Finance* 33 (June 1978): 737–749.

Miller, M. H. "Debt and Taxes." *Journal of Finance* 32 (May 1977): 261–276.

Modigliani, F., and M. H. Miller. "Corporate Income Taxes and the Cost of Capital: A Correction." *American Economic Review* 53 (June 1963): 433–443.

Modigliani, F., and M. H. Miller. "The Cost of Capital, Corporation Finance, and the Theory of Investment." *American Economic Review* 48 (July 1958): 261–297.

Moyer, R. C. "Forecasting Financial Failure: A Reexamination." *Financial Management* 6 (Spring 1977): 9–17.

Myers, S. C. "The Determinants of Corporate Debt Capacity." *Journal of Financial Economics* 5 (Nov. 1977): 146–175.

Pringle, J. J. "Price/Earnings Ratios, Earnings per Share, and Financial Management." *Financial Management* 2 (Spring, 1973): 34–40.

Roberts, G. S., and J. A. Viscione. "Captive Finance Subsidiaries: The Manger's View." *Financial Management* 10 (Spring 1981): 36–42.

Ross, S. A. "The Determination of Financial Structure." *Bell Journal of Economics* 8 (Spring 1977): 23–40.

Schall, L. "Taxes, Inflation and Corporate Financial Policy." *Journal of Finance* 38 (March 1984): 105–126.

Scott, J. H., Jr. "Bankruptcy, Secured Debt and Optimal Capital Structure." *Journal of Finance* 32 (Mar. 1977): 1–20.

Scott, J. H., Jr. "On the Theory of Conglomerate Mergers." *Journal of Finance* 32 (Sept. 1977): 1235–1250.

Scott, J. H., Jr. "A Theory of Optimal Capital Structure." *Bell Journal of Economics* 7 (Spring 1976): 33–54.

Stapleton, R. C., and C. M. Burke. *Tax Systems and Corporate Financing Policy*. Monograph 1978–1, New York University, Graduate School of Business Administration, 1978.

Stiglitz, J. E. "A Re-examination of the Modigliani-Miller Theorem." *American Economic Review* 59 (Dec. 1969): 784–793.

Stiglitz, J. E. "Some Aspects of the Pure Theory of Corporate Finance: Bankruptcies and Take-overs." *Bell Journal of Economics and Management Science* 3 (Autumn 1972): 458–482.

Trzcinka, C. "The Pricing of Tax-Exempt Bonds and the Miller Hypothesis." *Journal of Finance* 37 (Sept. 1982): 907–923.

Von Furstenberg, G. M., and B. G. Malkiel. "Financial Analysis in an Inflationary Environment." *Journal of Finance* 32 (May 1977): 575–588.

Warner, J. "Bankruptcy Costs: Some Evidence." *Journal of Finance* 32 (May 1977): 337–348.

Chapter

14

Choosing the Appropriate Debt Level

In this chapter, we will examine the choice of an appropriate debt level for the firm. We will first discuss key qualitative factors in setting debt policy before learning how to analyze alternative financing plans. We will explore the use of EBIT/EPS analysis, interest coverage ratios, and cash-flow analysis under recession conditions. Finally, we will tie our discussion to the firm's overall policy and commercial strategy.

In Chapter 13, we analyzed the effect of financial leverage on return and risk. We concluded that leverage has costs as well as benefits, and we, therefore, found ourselves face to face with the basic question of the trade-off between risk and return. We turned to valuation as a criterion for resolving the trade-off question and found that it provided some useful insights and guidance. In particular, we identified certain factors as relevant to the leverage decision and eliminated some that are not. However, the guidance that we found was entirely qualitative, and we did not develop an approach to actually determining how much debt a firm should use.

Now it is time to apply the theory. Our problem is to determine the appropriate mix of debt and equity that the firm should use. Let us keep in mind the motives for using debt. Some firms may find debt advantageous because of its tax benefits. Others may use debt to increase prospective returns to shareholders, recognizing that the price for the increase in prospective returns is increased risk. Still others may find debt obtained through financial intermediaries, such as banks, to be a less expensive and more convenient way to satisfy investment requirements. Some firms do not have access to equity markets, and, for them, debt is the only available source of outside capital. Whatever the motive, users of debt need a way to decide how much debt to use.

TAILORING FINANCING MIX TO COMMERCIAL STRATEGY

We found in Chapter 13 that a firm's total risk, as measured by variability of earnings, depends partly on its operating risk and partly on the amount of financial leverage used. Operating risk can be measured in terms of variability of earnings before interest and taxes (EBIT). For any given operating risk, an increase in financial leverage increases the variability of net earnings. We concluded that the appropriate degree of financial leverage for a firm depends on its operating risk. The higher is the operating risk, the less debt the firm should use. The same reasoning applies to individuals: the more variable or uncertain is one's income, the more risky it is to use debt.

> **The appropriate degree of financial leverage for a firm depends on its operating risk.**

Understanding the relationship between leverage and variability still does not tell us how much leverage to use. At what point do the terms of the risk/return trade-off become unfavorable? To help resolve this question, we turned in Chapter 13 to our general criterion of value maximization. Because investors are risk-averse, value depends on both expected return and risk. Hence, in principle, we resolve the risk/return trade-off by pushing leverage to the point where the value of the firm is maximized.

We found that finding the optimal debt ratio requires trading off the benefits of debt (including tax-deductibility of interest and leverage effects) against the expected costs of financial distress, which includes a broad spectrum of problems ranging from relatively minor liquidity shortages all the way to the extreme case of bankruptcy. All these problems are assumed to involve some costs to the firm—the more serious is the problem, the higher is the cost. Such costs are borne by the shareholders up to the full

Finance in Practice 14—1

Debt Policies of Eastern and Braniff

In mid-December of 1980, Eastern Air Lines and Braniff International Corporation announced that they were exploring the possibility of a merger. From an operating standpoint, the merger had a number of pluses. In particular, it was believed that Braniff's routes across the sunbelt of the southern United States would complement nicely Eastern's heavy concentration in the east. Braniff's routes to South America also were an attraction.

Late in January 1981, the two companies announced that the merger talks had been halted. The reasons given in a joint statement issued by the two companies were primarily personnel considerations—that union contracts and seniority systems were conflicting and that layoffs and reassignments would be difficult.

But analysts contacted by the *Wall Street Journal* gave a different reason: too much debt. A source at Braniff was quoted as saying that "the debt at Braniff was too much for Eastern to take on."

Both companies had sizable debt loads. As of September 30, 1980, Braniff had long-term debt of $616 million plus $84 million owed on long-term leases. (Long-term leases used to acquire capital equipment, such as aircraft, normally are capitalized and shown on the balance sheet as a long-term liability. We will discuss the rules for capitalizing leases in Chapter 16.) Eastern's long-term debt was $709 million plus another $564 million in leases.

The lesson is that financing matters. Even though Eastern and Braniff may have had a good operating fit, the merger did not go through. Did Eastern and Braniff have too much debt? We explore ways to answer this question in this chapter.

Source: Wall Street Journal, January 28, 1981.

---

amount of their investment; above that point, costs are borne by creditors. The expected cost of financial distress can be thought of as the magnitude of the cost times the likelihood (probability) of its being incurred.

> **The optimal debt ratio is achieved by trading off the benefits of debt against the expected costs of financial distress and reduced commercial flexibility.**

Using valuation as a criterion for leverage policy clarifies the relationship between leverage and operating risk. At zero leverage, we start with some probability of encountering financial distress of one form or another. Increasing leverage increases that probability. Starting from zero leverage, the use of the first dollars of debt adds less to the expected costs of financial distress than it adds to benefits. Use of such debt provides a net benefit and increases the value of the firm. There comes a point, however, where the use of any additional debt will increase the expected costs of financial distress by *more* than it will increase the expected benefits of using this extra debt. At that point, the debt ratio is optimal. We can see that the extent to which leverage should be used depends on how high the firm's operating risk was to begin with.

Theory tells us that the optimal debt ratio for a firm depends on its operating risk.

> **The appropriate debt ratio for a firm depends on the nature of its business. In other words, the financing mix and commercial strategy of a firm must support one another.**

Although, in general, firms make their investment and financing plans jointly, in this chapter, for simplicity, we will take the firm's investment policy as given. The question is: given a set of investments, what is the appropriate mix of debt and equity for financing them? Financial theory gives valuable qualitative quidance but is quite difficult to apply quantitatively.

In this chapter, we will focus only on the appropriate mix of debt and equity. For now, we will draw no distinction between long-term and short-term debt; in order to determine the appropriate debt ratio, we will view all debt as the same.

ANALYZING FINANCING PLANS USING ACCOUNTING DATA

EBIT/EPS analysis—is an examination of the impact on earnings per share of a given financing alternative at different levels of earnings before interest and taxes.

Suppose a firm has decided to raise a given amount of money by issuing either common stock or bonds. How does it make the choice? We know from our earlier discussion that market value is the appropriate decision criterion so our job is to find methods of analysis that will give some insights into effects on market value. Because investors often analyze the firm in terms of accounting data, we begin with an examination of the impact of alternative financing plans on earnings and other key indicators, such as interest coverage.

EBIT/EPS Analysis

Given the importance of earnings per share (EPS) as a measure of a firm's performance, analysis of the impact of financing alternatives on EPS is an important first step in analyzing financing plans. Because earnings before interest and taxes (EBIT) is uncertain, it is useful to examine the impact of financing alternatives at different levels of EBIT. One technique for doing so is to perform an **EBIT/EPS analysis** and to diagram the results.

An EBIT/EPS chart—is a graph of the relationship between operating outcomes (as measured by earnings before interest and taxes) and financial results to shareholders (as measured by earnings per share) for a given financing alternative.

An **EBIT/EPS chart** is a graph of the relationship between operating outcomes (as measured by EBIT) and financial results to shareholders (as measured by EPS) for a given financing plan. Such a chart provides a clear display of some of the merits of alternative financing plans. Before proceeding further with the EBIT/EPS chart, let us consider more specifically the effects of financial leverage on return and risk.

The Effects of Financial Leverage on Return and Risk. Suppose that a firm wishes to invest in assets of $1,000 and that this investment can be financed one of two ways: Plan A is to finance the investment entirely by equity (common stock); Plan B is to finance 60 percent by debt and 40 percent by equity. Assume that debt requires an interest rate of 8 percent and that equity has a market price of $10 per share.

Table 14–1

Effects of Leverage on Earnings per Share (EPS)

	Leverage	
	Plan A	Plan B
Assets	$1,000	$1,000
Debt	$ 0	$ 600
Equity	$1,000	$ 400
Leverage ratio (percent of debt)	0	60
Earnings before interest and taxes (EBIT)	$ 240	$ 240
Interest at 8 percent	0	48
Profit before taxes	$ 240	$ 192
Tax at 50 percent	120	96
Profit after taxes	$ 120	$ 96
Shares	100	40
Earnings per share (EPS)	$ 1.20	$ 2.40
Return on equity (ROE, shown as a percent)	12.0	24.0

Assume also that the $1,000 in assets generates EBIT (earnings before interest and taxes) of $240. The two leverage plans are summarized in Table 14–1. A 50 percent tax rate is used for simplicity.

As Table 14–1 shows, the effect of leverage is significant. When financed 60 percent by debt (Plan B), the firm earns $2.40 per share, twice as much as the $1.20 per share earned with no leverage. Return on equity (ROE) is greater by the same percentage.

When the firm borrows at an interest rate of 8 percent, leverage has a favorable effect. But what happens if EBIT is not $240? Because every company bears a certain operating risk, EBIT will vary.

Let us simplify matters by assuming that a firm's operations can have three possible outcomes: a normal year for EBIT, a good year, or a bad year. In reality, many more than three outcomes are possible, but these three will serve to illustrate the effect of leverage when EBIT varies. Let us assume that EBIT will be $240 in a normal year, $60 in a bad year, and $400 in a good year. Table 14–2 shows the effect on earnings per share (EPS) at each level of leverage. Figure 14–1 displays the results graphically by plotting EPS against EBIT for the two plans. Figure 14–1 is an EBIT/EPS chart.

In Figure 14–1, we see that when leverage is used, EPS rises more in good years and falls more in bad years. When EBIT is rising, the more leverage we use the faster EPS rises. When EBIT is falling, greater leverage causes EPS to fall faster.

The EBIT/EPS chart displays the risk/return trade-off inherent in the use of debt. The benefit of using this framework is that we can obtain further insights about decisions, as we can demonstrate by considering a slightly more complicated example.

Analyzing a Financing Alternative.   Suppose a firm has decided to finance a $10 million expansion of its manufacturing facilities by issuing either common stock or bonds. Currently, the firm's stock is selling at $20 per share, and it has 2.5 million shares outstanding. Ignoring issue costs, the firm would have to issue 500,000 new

Table 14–2
Leverage Effects with Variable Earnings Before Interest and Taxes (EBIT)

		EBIT Outcome	
	Bad = $60	Normal = $240	Good = $400
Plan A: No Leverage			
EBIT	$ 60	$240	$400
Interest at 8 percent	0	0	0
Profit before taxes	$ 60	$240	$400
Tax at 50 percent	30	120	200
Profit after taxes	$ 30	$120	$200
Shares	100	100	100
Earnings per share (EPS)	$ 0.30	$ 1.20	$ 2.00
Return on equity (ROE, shown as a percent)	3.0	12.0	20.0
Plan B: 60 percent debt			
EBIT	$ 60	$240	$400
Interest at 8 percent	48	48	48
Profit before taxes	$ 12	$192	$352
Tax at 50 percent	6	96	176
Profit after taxes	$ 6	$ 96	$176
Shares	40	40	40
Earnings per share (EPS)	$ 0.15	$ 2.40	$ 4.40
Return on equity (ROE, shown as a percent)	1.5	24.0	44.0

Table 14–3
Earnings Per Share (EPS) at the Expected Level of Earnings Before Interest and Taxes (EBIT) for Two Financing Alternatives

	Stock Plan	Bond Plan
EBIT	$6,000	$6,000
Interest	0	800
Profit before taxes	$6,000	$5,200
Tax at 50 percent	3,000	2,600
Profit after taxes	$3,000	$2,600
Shares	3,000	2,500
EPS	$ 1.00	$ 1.04
Sinking fund	$ 0	$ 350
Uncommitted earnings	$3,000	$2,250
Uncommitted EPS (UEPS)	$ 1.00	$ 0.90

Figure 14–1

The Effects of Changes in Earnings Before Interest and Taxes (EBIT) on Earnings per Share (EPS)

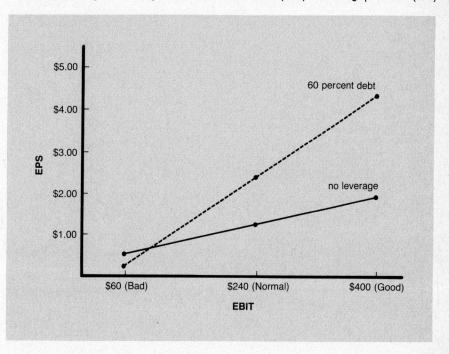

shares if it raises the needed funds by means of a stock issue. The firm has no existing debt.

Alternatively, the firm could issue 20-year bonds at 8 percent interest. **Sinking-fund payments** of $350,000 are required each year to retire $6.65 million by the end of the 19th year, with the final $3.35 million due at the end of the 20th year.

Let us assume that EBIT in the upcoming year is expected to be $6 million, including the earnings from the expanded facilities. However, EBIT in past years has been highly variable and could turn out to be considerably above or below the most likely level. Following the procedure used in the last chapter, we can calculate EPS at an EBIT of $6 million as in Table 14–3. In this table, **uncommitted earnings per share (UEPS)** refer to earnings remaining after the required sinking-fund payment of $350,000. Uncommitted earnings (UEPS) are available for payment of dividends and reinvestment to further expand facilities.

Our objective is to develop a chart that shows the behavior of EPS in response to variations in EBIT—that is, a chart that graphs EPS as a function of EBIT. Because EPS is PAT (profit after taxes) divided by the number of common shares, and because PAT is EBIT less interest and taxes (at a constant tax rate for practical purposes), EPS is a linear function of EBIT. There is one point on an EBIT/EPS line for each financing plan from Table 14–3. One more point on each line is all we need to draw the EBIT/EPS line. Often, it is convenient to pick as the second point the intercept of the EPS line and the EBIT axis. This point corresponds to the EBIT level required to

A **sinking-fund payment**—is the scheduled, periodic payment of principal to the trustee of a bond issue for the purpose of retiring a specific number of bonds by open-market purchase or by calling certain bonds at a previously agreed-upon price.

Uncommitted earnings per share (UEPS)—are earnings remaining after the required sinking-fund payment for a bond issue.

Figure 14–2
EBIT/EPS Analysis

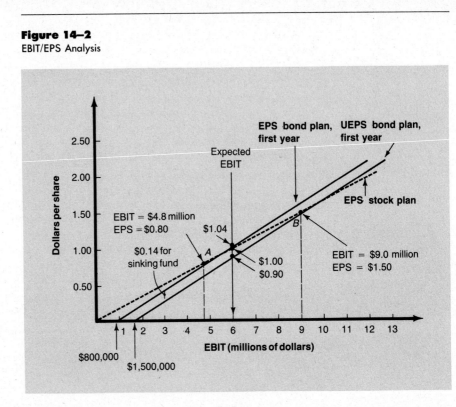

produce EPS of zero. For the stock plan, EPS of zero requires that EBIT = 0. For the bond plan, EBIT of $800,000 is required to cover interest and, hence, produce EPS = 0. Now we have two points on each EBIT/EPS line and can plot the lines in Figure 14–2.

In Figure 14–2, we see that the break-even EBIT (point A) is just under $5 million (we will calculate it exactly as $4.8 million below). At that point, EPS is equal under the two plans. If EBIT turns out to be above $5 million, EPS will be higher under the bond plan. If EBIT turns out to be below $5 million, the stock plan produces higher EPS. The expected EBIT level of $6 million is above the break-even point. Note that break-even EBIT from uncommitted EPS is much higher at an EBIT of $9 million (point B). Note also that the lines for the bond plan are graphed only for the first year. Because a sinking-fund payment is made each year, interest due will decline slightly each year, and the bond line will shift slightly to the left.

Here we see in graphic form the effects of leverage that we found earlier. The slope of the bond line is steeper than that of the stock line, indicating that, with leverage, EPS is more sensitive to changes in EBIT. The steeper slope is advantageous if EBIT rises and disadvantageous if EBIT falls.

We might ask here which earnings line in Figure 14–2 is appropriate for our analysis: the EPS line or the UEPS line? Which should we use in making a decision? Both are appropriate to use—and both should be used—because each answers a different question.

The **EPS break-even level of EBIT**—is the level of earnings before interest and taxes that equates earnings per share for two financing alternatives.

In our example above, we assumed for simplicity that the firm had no other debt outstanding. Often, this is not the case. Where other debt is outstanding, the interest and sinking-fund payments from that debt, if any, must be included. The old interest and sinking-fund payments are added to the new, and the total is used to calculate the points necessary to plot the graphs. Note that old interest and sinking-fund payments are made under both the stock financing and the bond financing alternatives now under consideration.

We also assumed that the firm had no preferred stock outstanding. The term *earnings per share* is interpreted as *earnings available to common stock* per share. If a firm did use preferred stock, in calculating EPS we would subtract any preferred-dividend requirement before dividing by the number of common shares.

The **UEPS break-even level of EBIT**—is the level of earnings before interest and taxes that equates uncommitted earnings per share for two financing alternatives.

Calculating Break-Even Points.   Sometimes it is useful to calculate EPS and UEPS break-even points algebraically. We know that EPS for the two plans are equal to each other at the break-even level of EBIT. To determine the **EPS break-even level of EBIT** under each plan, we set the EPS expressions equal to each other and solve for EBIT, as shown in Equation (1). Similarly, to determine the **UEPS break-even level of EBIT**, we set the UEPS expressions equal to each other and solve for EBIT, as shown in Equation (2). If the firm has no existing debt prior to the financing plans being analyzed, under the stock plan both interest payments and sinking-fund payments will be zero.

The EPS break-even level of EBIT can be determined, by setting EPS under the bond plan, EPS_B, equal to EPS under the stock plan, EPS_S, as

$$EPS_B = EPS_S$$

$$\frac{(EBIT - I_B)(1 - T)}{N_B} = \frac{(EBIT - I_S(1 - T)}{N_S}$$

(1)

where N_B = the number of shares of stock outstanding under the bond plan, N_S = the number of shares of stock outstanding under the stock plan, I_B = the firm's total interest payment under the bond plan, I_S = the interest payment under the stock plan, and T = the tax rate.

The UEPS break-even level of EBIT can be determined, by setting UEPS under the bond plan, $UEPS_B$, equal to UEPS under the stock plan, $UEPS_S$, as

$$UEPS_B = UEPS_S$$

$$\frac{[(EBIT - I_B)(1 - T)] - SF_B}{N_B} = \frac{(EBIT - I_S)(1 - T) - SF_S}{N_S}$$

(2)

where N_B = the number of shares of stock outstanding under the bond plan, N_S = the number of shares of stock outstanding under the stock plan, SF_B = the total sinking-fund payment under the bond plan, SF_S = the total sinking-fund payment under the stock plan, I_B = the total interest payment under the bond plan, I_S = the total interest payment under the stock plan, and T = the tax rate.

For our example, using a 50 percent tax rate, we can calculate the EPS break-even level of EBIT as

$$\frac{(\text{EBIT} - \$800{,}000)(1 - 0.5)}{2{,}500{,}000} = \frac{(\text{EBIT} - 0)(1 - 0.5)}{3{,}000{,}000}$$

$$\text{EBIT} = \$4.8 \text{ million}$$

Thus, at a level of EBIT of $4.8 million, EPS for the two plans are equal at $0.80 per share.

Similarly, we can calculate the UEPS break-even level of EBIT as

$$\frac{[(\text{EBIT} - \$800{,}000)(1 - 0.5)] - \$350{,}000}{2{,}500{,}000} = \frac{(\text{EBIT} - 0)(1 - 0.5) - 0}{3{,}000{,}000}$$

$$\text{EBIT} = \$9 \text{ million}$$

Thus, at an EBIT level of $9 million, UEPS for the two plans are equal at $1.50 per share.

We should note again that if the firm had had other debt issues outstanding, interest and principal (sinking-fund) payments on those issues should be considered in calculating break-even points. In calculating the EPS break-even level of EBIT, old interest payments would be figured in on both sides of Equation (1); likewise, old sinking-fund payments would be figured in on both sides of Equation (2). In addition, to simplify matters we did not incorporate preferred stock in the equations. If preferred stock were outstanding, its dividend requirements (and sinking-fund requirements, if any) would be subtracted before dividing by N_B and N_S.

Sample Problem 14-1

EBIT/EPS Analysis for the Franklin Corporation

The Franklin Corporation has decided to finance a $4 million expansion program by issuing either common stock or bonds. Currently, the firm has 200,000 shares outstanding and no long-term debt. Common stock can be sold to net $40 per share. The bond issue will be a 25-year issue at 12 percent interest with sinking-fund payments of $200,000 per year starting in year 5. Franklin's tax rate is 50 percent.

A. Assume that Franklin's EBIT next year is expected to be $1.5 million. Calculate the expected EPS next year for the two alternative financing plans.

B. Determine the EPS break-even EBIT level.

Solution

A. This type of problem is best attacked by constructing a table similar to Table 14–4, which shows the derivation of EPS for each alternative.

B. To determine the EPS break-even EBIT level, we can use Equation (1), after determining that $I_B = (0.12)(\$4{,}000{,}000) = \$480{,}000$, $N_B = 200{,}000$, $I_S = 0$, and $N_S = 200{,}000 + (\$4{,}000{,}000/\$40) = 200{,}000 + 100{,}000 = 300{,}000$ shares.

Table 14–4

Derivation of Expected Earnings per Share (EPS) for Two Financing Alternatives Available to the Franklin Corporation

	Stock Plan	Debt Plan
Earnings before interest and taxes (EBIT)	$1,500,000	$1,500,000
Interest	—	480,000
Profit before tax	$1,500,000	$1,020,000
Tax at 50 percent	750,000	510,000
Profit after tax	$ 750,000	$ 510,000
Shares	300,000	200,000
EPS	$2.50	$2.55

$$\frac{(\text{EBIT} - \$480,000)(1 - 0.5)}{200,000} = \frac{(\text{EBIT} - 0)(0.5)}{300,000}$$

$$\text{EBIT} = \$1,440,000$$

Thus, the EPS break-even level of EBIT is $1,440,000. ∃▮𝄐

Coverage Ratios

Another useful analytical technique for comparing financing alternatives is to calculate **interest coverage ratios**. The interest coverage ratio is the number of times interest payments are covered by EBIT and is calculated as shown in Equation (3).

> The interest coverage ratio, or the number of times interest payments are covered by EBIT, can be calculated as
>
> $$\text{Interest coverage ratio} = \frac{\text{EBIT}}{I} \qquad (3)$$
>
> where I = the pretax interest payment.

We also can calculate the **sinking-fund coverage ratio**, as shown in Equation (4).

> The sinking-fund (SF) coverage ratio can be calculated as
>
> $$\text{SF coverage ratio} = \frac{\text{EBIT}}{I + [\text{SF}/(1 - T)]} \qquad (4)$$
>
> where I = the pretax interest payment, SF = the sinking-fund payment, and T = the tax rate.

For the bond alternative graphed in Figure 14-2, we can calculate coverage as

$$\text{Interest coverage ratio} = \frac{\$6,000,000}{\$800,000} = 7.5.$$

$$\text{SF coverage ratio} = \frac{\$6,000,000}{\$800,000 + (\$350,000/0.5)} = 4.0.$$

The **interest coverage ratio**—is the number of times interest payments are covered by EBIT and is calculated as EBIT divided by pretax interest.

The **sinking-fund coverage ratio**—is the number of times interest-plus-sinking-fund payments are covered by EBIT.

Note that to calculate coverage of interest plus sinking fund, the latter must be converted to a pretax basis by dividing by $(1 - T)$. Thus, to make a sinking-fund payment (not tax-deductible) of $350,000 requires EBIT of $700,000, which when added to the interest requirement gives a total burden to be covered of $1,500,000. As before, any interest and sinking-fund payments on old bonds should be included.

Suppose that the firm wished to pay a dividend on its common stock of $0.70 per share. We could calculate a third coverage ratio—the number of times that EBIT covers both debt service and dividend requirements. On 2.5 million shares, the total dividend would be 2.5 million × $0.70 = $1.75 million, or $3.5 million on a pretax basis. Added to the $1.5 million for debt service, we would have a total of $5 million, which would be covered 1.2 times by EBIT of $6 million. In a similar manner, we could calculate coverage of preferred dividends if applicable.

What do coverage ratios tell us? They provide a measure of the safety of the interest payment or of whatever specific commitment is being considered. The greater is the coverage, the more secure is the payment. Thus, an interest coverage ratio of 7.5 tells us that EBIT must fall well short of its expected level of $6 million before the interest payment is in jeopardy.

The interest coverage ratio simply measures the size of the interest payment relative to EBIT. The reciprocal of this ratio—$I/EBIT$—measures the proportion of EBIT devoted to interest. In our example, we then have $800,000/$6,000,000 = 0.13, which tells us that 13 percent of the firm's EBIT must go to interest. Here we have a measure of the firm's debt ratio in flow terms, which may give a more accurate representation of leverage than do debt ratios calculated from balance-sheet relationships. After all, interest payments typically must be paid from flows to the company, whereas balance-sheet debt may not be due for a number of years to come. One obvious drawback of viewing $I/EBIT$ as a measure of leverage is that EBIT often is highly variable, and we get a different leverage ratio for each value of EBIT.

The variability of EBIT points up a major shortcoming of coverage ratios in general. Which EBIT do we use to calculate coverage? In the example above, we calculated coverage at the expected (most likely) level of EBIT. To draw meaningful conclusions regarding the safety of various payments that the firm is committed to make would require some knowledge of the likelihood of a decline in EBIT to levels at which the payments are threatened. We can calculate coverage at several different levels of EBIT. If we could construct a probability distribution over all possible values of EBIT, we then would have a better sense of the adequacy of various coverage levels.

Sample Problem 14–2

Coverage Ratios for the Franklin Corporation

Calculate coverage ratios for the debt financing being contemplated by Franklin Corporation in Sample Problem 14–1.

Solution

Using the data from Sample Problem 14-1 and Equation (3), we can calculate interest coverage as

$$EBIT/I = \$1,500,000/\$480,000 = 3.125 \text{ times.}$$

Using Equation (4), we can calculate interest-plus-sinking-fund coverage as

$$EBIT/(I + SF/0.5) = \$1,500,000/(\$480,000 + \$200,000/0.5)$$

$$= 1.70 \text{ times.}$$

Note that we have used Franklin's expected EBIT level of $1,500,000. As a result, these are coverage ratios Franklin would expect to experience. Actual results could differ. Also note that, for purposes of illustration, we have calculated an interest-plus-sinking-fund coverage even though the sinking-fund payments do not begin until year 5. By that time, Franklin may anticipate a higher EBIT level. ▰▮▮▰

SETTING DEBT POLICY AND DEFINING DEBT CAPACITY

Now let us return to the policy question of choosing an appropriate debt policy. Our analysis of earnings and coverage outlined the nature of the risk/return trade-off facing the firm. If investors believe the firm has gone too far in its use of debt, they will judge that the prospective return was not enough to compensate for the added risk, and we would expect the market value of the firm to fall. While useful, our analysis so far still leaves unanswered questions. Even if we had a probability distribution over all possible EBIT levels, could we say how much coverage is enough? Can we examine the EBIT/EPS chart in Figure 14–2 and decide which plan is best? We cannot, because to say that one plan is best requires an unambiguous criterion on which to make the comparison. EBIT/EPS analysis and coverage ratios are very useful in making explicit the impact of leverage on EPS and on the firm's ability to meet its commitments at various levels of EBIT. However, we still face the risk/return trade-off: should we accept greater risk in order to gain a higher expected return?

One approach to the problem of setting debt policy is to rely on industry standards. ABC Corporation might calculate the equity or debt ratios for other firms in its industry and set its own ratio equal to the industry average. The logic of the use of industry standards is that debt ratios appropriate for other firms in a similar line of business should be appropriate for ABC Corporation as well. Also, this approach ensures that ABC Corporation appears to lenders and investors to be right in line with industry averages.

To illustrate, suppose ABC Corporation were an integrated oil company. ABC Corporation management might gather the data listed in Table 14–5. The difficulty with the use of industry standards in this way is that it relies on the judgment of others. Can we be sure that the managements of the other firms in the industry will not err? Also, in many cases, there may be no well-defined industry—that is, no group of firms whose structure and commercial strategy are similar enough to provide a good comparison. Industry standards, when available, certainly provide a useful benchmark. If a firm is out of line, it should know the reasons why and be satisfied that they are

Table 14–5
Ratio of Equity to Total Assets for Selected Oil Companies, December 31, 1985

	Total Assets (millions of dollars)	Stockholders Equity (million of dollars)	Equity Ratio (percent)
Exxon	69,160	36,238	52.40
Mobil Oil	41,752	14,689	33.74
Texaco	37,703	15,253	40.46
Chevron	38,899	15,554	39.99
Sunoco	12,923	6,065	46.93
		Average	42.70

Source: Moody's Industrial Manual, 1986.

good reasons. But a comparison with industry standards should be the final step, not the beginning point in the analysis.

Another approach to setting debt policy is to seek the opinion of lenders and investment bankers. ABC Corporation might ask the advice of investment-banking firms, who regularly participate in marketing debt issues, and of institutional buyers of debt issues, such as insurance companies. Commercial banks may provide useful advice. Investment rating services, such as Moody's Investors Service or Standard & Poors Corporation also might be helpful. A firm whose debt already has been rated by such services might be able to draw some inferences from the ratings themselves. If more recent debt issues were rated lower than older issues, indicating a rise in risk, the firm might view this trend as an indication of having pushed its debt far enough.

The opinions of prospective lenders are likely to be very useful, but to rely on them too heavily runs the risk of answering the wrong question. The firm may learn how much the lenders would like to lend—or the maximum that the lenders would be willing to lend. But just because lenders are willing to lend does not mean that the firm should take them up on it. Lenders err also—many firms have encountered serious difficulties because of using too much debt, with once-willing lenders a party to the arrangement. The responsibility for debt policy belongs to management, and the central question is how much debt should be used, not how much the lenders are willing to lend.[1]

The notion that there is some absolute dollar ceiling on the amount that lenders will lend is vague. In practice, such a ceiling may exist. In principle, the amount that lenders will lend should depend on the interest rate that the firm is prepared to pay. By paying a sufficiently high rate, a firm should be able to induce lenders to lend well beyond the debt ratio that is optimal for shareholders.

---

[1]For theoretical proof that the optimal debt level for shareholders is less than the maximum amount of debt the financial markets will supply, see S. M. Turnbull, "Debt Capacity," *Journal of Finance* 34 (September 1979): 931–40. See also E. H. Kim, "A Mean-Variance Theory of Optimal Financial Structure and Corporate Debt Capacity," *Journal of Finance* 33 (March 1978): 45–64.

Debt Capacity and Cash Flows

A firm's **debt capacity**, then, should be defined as the optimal amount of debt from the standpoint of shareholders, which is the amount of debt the firm should use and not necessarily the maximum that lenders will lend.

Defining debt capacity as optimal debt provides a useful framework for analyzing policy options. For example, sometimes it is suggested that the use of leases to finance assets increases the firm's total debt capacity because the leases do not appear on the balance sheet. Here, debt capacity refers to the willingness of lenders to lend. Even if lenders were fooled by the leases, which is doubtful, should the firm borrow more just because the lenders are willing? In many cases, it should not. If we analyze the leasing decision in the context of the theory of optimal financial leverage, we will conclude that leases are quite similar to debt. Therefore, the use of leases does not necessarily increase the optimal debt ratio—the total that the firm should use. Hence, by viewing debt capacity and optimal debt as one and the same, we are able to analyze the leasing decision more effectively.

To determine a firm's debt capacity, then, requires a method of evaluating the effect of different debt policies on the firm's risk of financial distress. This evaluation will provide an operational way to link our debt-policy decisions to the valuation framework we outlined in the last chapter. There we saw how the benefits of debt were traded off against the costs of financial distress. We can develop such a method for looking at the risk of financial distress by looking at cash flows. As we explain below, for purposes of understanding the risks of financial distress, the use of cash-flow analysis has major advantages over analysis of accounting numbers, such as earnings or coverage ratios.

To simplify matters, let us ignore milder financial difficulties for the moment and consider only the risk of bankruptcy. The principal factor in avoiding bankruptcy is maintaining the ability to meet contractual interest and principal payments that must be made in cash. Hence, it is more useful to view debt capacity in terms of cash flows than in terms of balance-sheet ratios of debt to equity or accrual-accounting estimates of earnings per share. This point becomes all the more clear when we consider that just knowing the principal amount of debt tells us nothing about the repayment schedule and the firm's ability to meet it.

For example, suppose we see that a firm has $1 million in long-term debt outstanding and an equity base of $4 million. The debt/equity ratio is 0.25—not an alarming figure at first glance. But the principal may be due in 2 years or in 20 years. Clearly, maturity makes a big difference to the firm's ability to meet the payments.

Suppose we find that repayment is to be made over 4 years. We now know a good deal more than before but still not everything we need. Consider the repayment schedules listed in Table 14–6, assuming interest at 12 percent. From this table, we see that even knowing the amount of debt and the maturity does not tell us whether the firm can meet the payments. The firm's ability to meet its payments depends on the total payments required—interest and principal—in relation to the cash flow available to meet them. In Table 14–6, we see only three of an infinite number of possible repayment schedules. It is clear that the cash flow required to service a given amount of debt can cover a wide range. Conversely, a given cash flow can service widely varying principal amounts of debt, depending on the repayment schedule.

Table 14—6
Alternative Repayment Schedules for $1 Million over 4 Years at 12 Percent (thousands of dollars)

Year	A: *Principal at Maturity*			B: *Equal Annual Payments*			C: *Principal in Equal Installments*		
	Interest	*Principal*	*Total*	*Interest*	*Principal*	*Total*	*Interest*	*Principal*	*Total*
1	120	—	120	120	209	329	120	250	370
2	120	—	120	95	234	329	90	250	340
3	120	—	120	67	262	329	60	250	310
4	120	1,000	1,120	35	294	329	30	250	280

The repayment schedule on the firm's debt is only half of the picture. We also must examine the firm's ability to meet the schedule. Normally, principal and interest payments are met out of cash flows from operations. During emergencies, however, other sources are available. Marketable securities held for liquidity purposes might be sold, or cash may be drawn down. Other current assets, such as inventories and receivables, might be reduced, and current liabilities might be increased. Certain discretionary expenditures might be reduced or postponed, such as those for capital improvements, dividends, or research and development.

Cash-flow analysis—of debt capacity is the comparison of cash-flow patterns under adverse, or recession, conditions at various levels of leverage in order to determine the level of debt that will allow the firm to meet its contractual obligations in a recession (or other set of adverse circumstances).

> **To determine the impact of alternative debt policies on the risk of bankruptcy requires a careful analysis of how the firm's cash flows might be affected by adverse developments in the future.**

The best way to explain how **cash-flow analysis** works is to examine a specific example. Because many variables are involved, cash-flow projections can be tedious, but the procedures are essential to good financial planning.

In the following section, the effects of alternative debt policies on the risk of bankruptcy are analyzed in terms of specific numbers. The risk of bankruptcy, however, is not the only consideration in setting debt policy. The optimal debt policy also provides for a reserve for contingencies and commercial flexibility. We will consider these later factors in a separate section following the basic cash-flow analysis.

Analyzing Cash Flows

To illustrate the approach of using cash-flow analysis to determine debt capacity, let us consider a specific situation in detail. The time is late 1984, and Omega Manufacturing Corporation is planning its financial structure. The question at issue is the appropriate amount of debt that Omega should use in its capital structure. Currently, Omega's ratio of debt to total capital is 20 percent. Omega management must decide whether to continue the present policy, use more debt, or use less debt.

The objective of the analysis is to determine Omega's debt capacity. During good times, meeting contractual obligations usually is no problem. When times are bad, difficulties do occur. Thus, we are interested in Omega's ability to make contractual

Table 14-7

Actual Cash Flows at Omega Manufacturing Corporation, 1980-1983 (millions of dollars)

	1980	1981	1982	1983
Sales	116.6	121.1	112.0	$126.5
Profit after taxes	5.8	7.7	6.7	6.5
Sources of funds				
Operations	21.2	23.1	22.4	22.4
Working capital	3.0	(0.6)	3.1	(1.2)
Total sources	24.2	22.5	25.5	21.2
Uses of funds				
Plant and equipment	(6.8)	(8.2)	(13.2)	(14.5)
Taxes	(3.8)	(3.7)	(3.4)	(3.2)
Lease payments	(1.9)	(2.0)	(2.1)	(2.1)
Interest on debt	(2.0)	(1.8)	(1.7)	(1.6)
Principal on debt	(1.4)	(1.4)	(1.4)	(1.4)
Dividends on common stock	(2.8)	(2.8)	(2.8)	(3.0)
Miscellaneous	(0.1)	(0.2)	(0.7)	(0.3)
Total uses	(18.8)	(20.1)	(25.3)	(26.1)
Change in cash balance	5.4	2.4	0.2	(4.9)

payments under adverse conditions. The essence of the approach is to analyze cash-flow patterns under conditions of recession.

Omega manufactures a variety of industrial products. Its sales are moderately sensitive to the business cycle. During the early 1980s, Omega had a very good year in 1981, then suffered a decline in sales in the 1982 recession, and experienced a sharp recovery in 1983. Sales and cash-flow data for 1980-1983 are given in Table 14-7. This table shows that cash declined by $4.9 million in 1983 even though the firm earned a profit of $6.5 million. A significant factor in explaining the cash decline was the large increase in capital outlays in 1982 and 1983 to establish facilities to manufacture a new product.

Recession Behavior.   Omega management did not consider the behavior of company sales during the 1982 recession to be typical. A study of company data back to 1950 revealed that, in previous recessions, sales volume usually declined for 2 years in a row, then recovered in the third year. Total declines ranged from 12 percent to 16 percent. For purposes of establishing debt capacity, management decided to err on the side of conservatism and to assume that the effect of a recession on sales could last a year longer, with recovery only in the fourth year, and that the total decline could reach 20 percent. Thus, the pattern of sales during future recessions was assumed to be as given in Table 14-8.

In prior recessions, prices of some of Omega's products had fallen somewhat, but the declines had not been significant. To be conservative, however, management decided to assume that prices of products would decline by 3 percent and recover in year 4. Prices of all cost elements were assumed to remain constant.

Table 14–8
Assumed Pattern of Sales During Future Recessions for Omega Manufacturing Corporation

Sales Year Prior to Recession (percent)	Recession-Year Sales as a Percentage of Nonrecession-Year Sales			
	Year 1	Year 2	Year 3	Year 4
100	90	80	80	100

In some cases, an assumption of constant prices for cost elements during a recession may not be appropriate, because prices in general have continued to rise during recent recessions. The objective should be the best possible estimate of all cash flows—revenues as well as expenses—in nominal terms, with the effects of inflation included.

Omega management was now ready to prepare forecasts of the cash flows under recession conditions. It was decided to group cash flows into three categories: operating cash flows, investment cash flows, and financing cash flows.

Cash Flows from Operations.   Using the relatively pessimistic, or adverse, assumptions regarding sales volume and price discussed above, operating cash flows over a future recession would be those listed in Table 14–9.

Investment Cash Flows.   Major investment cash flows include capital outlays for plant and equipment and changes in working capital. These cash flows were projected by Omega management to be those listed in Table 14–10 under recession conditions.

During 1982 and 1983, Omega had made exceptionally large capital outlays, a major part of which were attributable to facilities for a new product. During 1985, outlays of $10 million were planned, which management viewed as approximately the normal level to be expected for about 5 years beyond 1984 if business conditions remained normal. In a recession, however, a portion of such outlays could be deferred.

Table 14–9
Projected Operating Cash Flows at Omega Manufacturing Corporation under Future Recession Conditions (millions of dollars)

	Year Prior to Recession, 0[a]	Recession Year			
		1	2	3	4
Sales at stable prices	126.5	113.9	101.2	101.2	126.5
As percent of year 0 sales	100	90	80	80	100
Sales reflecting a 3 percent price decline	126.5	110.5	98.2	98.2	126.5
Cash operating expenses[b]	101.6	90.7	84.4	82.6	101.6
Net cash inflow from operations	24.9	19.8	13.8	15.6	24.9

[a]The expected figures for 1984 are used as benchmark figures for the hypothetical year 0.
[b]These exclude nonoperating and financial flows discussed later in Tables 14–11 and 14–12.

Table 14—10

Projected Investment Cash Flows for Omega Manufacturing Corporation under Recession Conditions (millions of dollars)

	Year prior to Recession, 0	Recession Year			
		1	2	3	4
Plant and equipment expenditures	(10.0)	(10.0)	(5.0)	(3.0)	(7.0)
Expenditures for working capital					
Cash	(0.2)	0.3	—	—	(0.4)
Marketable securities	—	0.4	—	—	—
Accounts receivable	(1.2)	(1.6)	2.4	(1.1)	(3.6)
Inventories	(1.7)	2.6	0.4	(1.2)	(3.4)
Accounts payable	1.6	(2.1)	(2.0)	0.8	1.0
Total working capital expenditures	(1.5)	(0.4)	0.8	(1.5)	(6.4)
Total nonoperating cash outflow	(11.5)	(10.4)	(4.2)	(4.5)	(13.4)

Nonetheless, management considered some portions of the capital budget to be essential and, therefore, gave these a higher priority than maintaining the dividend on common stock. These outlays were estimated to be $3 million per year. The remaining $7 million was viewed as postponable and of lower priority than the dividend. Management's recession plan for plant-and-equipment outlays, therefore, was to cut expenditures as rapidly as possible to the irreducible minimum of $3 million and then to restore the budget to $7 million in the year of full sales recovery and to the full amount the following year. Because of the nature of construction and equipment contracts, however, a time lag of at least one year was anticipated in implementing the cuts. The final projected plant and equipment budget appears in Table 14–10.

Omega management anticipated that cash could be drawn down by about $0.3 million during a recession—the reduction coming mainly in compensating balances normally held at commercial banks. Marketable securities worth $0.4 million and held for liquidity purposes would be sold during the first year of the recession. Accounts receivable were expected to rise and require funds during the first year as customers stretched their payments and were then expected to fall with sales and, as a result, release funds. Inventories were projected to change proportionally with sales.

Financial Flows. Financial flows include lease payments, interest and principal on debt, and dividends on common stock. Lease payments and debt service are contractual and must be maintained, whereas dividends are discretionary. Although discretionary, dividends were viewed as of very high priority by Omega management. Financing flows under Omega's present capital structure were, therefore, projected as shown in Table 14–11.

Alternative Debt Policies. Omega management was considering two alternative debt policies: Policy A involved a debt ratio of 35 percent (debt to total capital) versus 20 percent at present, and Policy B involved a debt ratio of 50 percent debt. In Table 14–12, cash flows are presented for each of these alternatives as if they had been imple-

Table 14–11

Projected Financial Flows under Present Capital Structure at Omega Manufacturing Corporation (millions of dollars)

	Year prior to Recession, 0	Recession Year			
		1	2	3	4
Lease payments	(2.1)	(2.1)	(2.1)	(2.1)	(2.1)
Interest on debt[a]	(1.6)	(1.4)	(1.3)	(1.1)	(0.9)
Principal on debt	(1.4)	(1.4)	(1.4)	(1.4)	(1.4)
Common dividend[b]	(3.0)	(3.0)	(3.0)	(3.0)	(3.0)
Taxes	(3.2)	(2.6)	(2.1)	(2.6)	(3.2)
Total financial flows	(11.3)	(10.5)	(9.9)	(10.2)	(10.6)

[a]Principal due was $12.5 million at year-end 1983. Interest rate is 13 percent. Interest shown for year 0 is that due in 1984. Sinking-fund payments are $1.4 million per year.

[b]Dividend is $2.00 per year on 1.5 million shares outstanding.

Table 14–12

Alternative Debt Policies for Omega Manufacturing Corporation (millions of dollars)

	Year prior to Recession, 0	Recession Year			
		1	2	3	4
Current Capital Structure					
1. Nonfinancial flows (see Tables 14–10 and 14–11)[a]	13.4	9.4	9.6	11.1	11.5
2. Financial flows (see Table 14–8)	(11.3)	(10.5)	(9.9)	(10.2)	(10.6)
3. Change in cash balance	2.1	(1.1)	(0.3)	0.9	0.9
4. Cumulative change	2.1	1.0	0.7	1.6	2.5
5. Change in cash with dividend eliminated in year 1[b]	2.1	1.9	2.7	3.9	3.9
6. Cumulative change	2.1	4.0	6.7	10.6	14.5
Policy A: 35 Percent Debt					
7. Financial flows	(12.3)	(11.5)	(10.8)	(11.1)	(11.5)
8. Change in cash balance	1.1	(2.1)	(1.2)	0.0	0.0
9. Cumulative change	1.1	(1.0)	(2.2)	(2.2)	(2.2)
10. Change in cash with dividend eliminated in year 1[c]	1.1	0.3	1.2	2.4	2.4
11. Cumulative change	1.1	1.4	2.6	5.0	7.4
Policy B: 50 Percent Debt					
12. Financial flows	(13.3)	(12.4)	(11.8)	(12.0)	(12.4)
13. Change in cash balance	0.1	(3.0)	(2.2)	(0.9)	(0.9)
14. Cumulative change	0.1	(2.9)	(5.1)	(6.0)	(6.9)
15. Change in cash with dividend eliminated in year 1[d]	0.1	(1.1)	(0.3)	1.0	1.0
16. Cumulative change	0.1	(1.0)	(1.3)	(0.3)	0.7

[a]The nonfinancial flow is the sum of cash flows in Tables 14–10 and 14–11.

[b]The dividend referred to is $3.0 million per year. Line 5 assumes that the dividend is eliminated completely in year 1 and no dividend at all is paid in years 1–4.

[c]The dividend referred to is $2.4 million per year, with less equity and more debt in capital structure. The same assumption regarding elimination of dividend payment in year 1 that is made in line 5 is made here.

[d]The dividend referred to is $1.9 million per year, with the same assumption made here regarding the elimination of dividend payment that is made in line 5.

mented. In other words, Policy A presents cash flows as if Omega's debt ratio presently were 35 percent, all other factors unchanged. Interest on incremental debt is 13 percent a year. Dividends on common stock, principal payments, and tax payments are altered commensurately.

Table 14–12 traces out the changes in cash that are projected if a recession occurs. For example, given the current capital structure, in the first year of a recession cash outflows for financing—$10.5 million in row (2)—will exceed nonfinancial cash inflows—$9.4 million in row (1)—leading to a reduction in the cash balance of $1.1 million, as shown in row (3). On top of a $2.1 million increase in cash in year 0, this $1.1 million reduction in year 1 means that the cumulative change in cash through year 1 is $2.1 million − $1.1 million = $1.0 million, and this figure is shown in row (4). If this reduction in cash had been viewed as too large, Omega might have eliminated its cash dividend of $3.00 per year to reduce the financial outflows in year 1 to $10.5 million − $3.0 million = $7.5 million. As a result, in year 1, financial outflows would be less than the nonfinancial inflows by $9.4 million − $7.5 million = $1.9 million, and there would be a $1.9 million *increase* in cash in row (5). This $1.9 million could alternatively be calculated by adding the $3.00 dividend to the reduction in cash, in row (3), that would have taken place if the dividend were paid as -$1.1 million + $3.0 million = $1.9 million. Row (6) keeps a running total of the figures in row (5).

Conclusions of the Cash-Flow Analysis.   Recessions sometimes are difficult to diagnose in their very early stages and are even more difficult to forecast. Omega management likely would not have sufficient evidence to implement their recession plan until well into year 1. At that point, sales would be declining and action would be taken to cut back expenses. Action also would be taken to cut back the capital-expenditure program in the manner described earlier.

Omega management had established a dividend policy that treats dividends as a long-run residual and sets the dollar payout to be nondecreasing.[2] The dollar payout was set at a level that was thought to give a high probability of avoiding subsequent cuts, although it was recognized that circumstances could arise in which cuts clearly might become necessary. During temporary difficulties, management was willing to postpone, though not to forgo, certain types of capital-investment projects. Management had decided not to rely on temporary short-term borrowing to maintain either the capital-investment program or the dividend during adverse financial circumstances. While management had no objection to such a policy, there was always a possibility that short-term funds would not be available during a recession. Basing policy on an assumption that short-term borrowing would be possible, therefore, seemed unwise.

The three alternative debt policies then were evaluated in light of these and other policies. With the current capital structure of 20 percent debt, we can see from row (3) of Table 14–11 that Omega runs a cash deficit in years 1 and 2, assuming no cut in the dividend. However, these deficits are financed by the surplus in year 0, the year prior to the onset of the recession. Row (4) shows that on a cumulative basis, with the current capital structure, Omega could survive the recession without cutting the dividend on common stock.

If debt were increased to 35 percent according to Policy A, row (8) indicates that

---

[2]The concept of treating dividends as a long-run residual is discussed in Chapter 15.

Finance in Practice 14–2

A Survey of Financing Policies

How do managers actually go about setting financial policies? How is financial leverage measured? How do managers choose the right amount of financial leverage?

In response to a survey, 212 large U.S. corporations provided some answers to these questions. To measure financial leverage, most financial managers look at balance-sheet figures (for example, debt/equity ratios) and income-statement figures (for example, times-interest-earned ratios). The accompanying Table A shows the basic types of leverage measures used by the companies responding to the survey.

Perhaps more interesting were the managers' perceptions of the benefits of using financial leverage and the factors that shape their financing policies. The vast majority of managers (well over 90 percent) thought that the value of the firm could be increased by using leverage but that, after some point, using too much lever-

age would reduce the value of the firm. As a result, managers think that it is important to pick an appropriate amount of debt. In selecting the amount, about 87 percent of the respondents explicitly stated that their firm used the notion of a debt capacity of the firm—a maximum amount of borrowing. The firms wanted to use financial leverage, but not too much.

The firms also revealed the types of influences that shaped their financial policies. The accompanying Table B shows the rankings given by managers of various influences on their choice of a target financial structure.

As the responses show, man-

Table A

Type of Measure	Companies (percent)
Balance sheet only	17
Income statement only	0
Both types of measures	80
Other	2
Total	100

agers are actively engaged in choosing target financial policies and subscribe to the concept of an optimal capital structure.

Source: Adapted from D. F. Scott and D. J. Johnson, "Financing Policies and Practices in Large Corporations," *Financial Management*, Summer 1982, pp. 51–58.

Table B

Type of Influence	Ranked as Most Important Influence (percent)	Ranked as Second Most Important Influence (percent)
Internal management and staff analysts	85	7
Investment bankers	3	39
Commercial bankers	0	9
Trade creditors	1	0
Security analysts	1	4
Comparative industry ratios	3	23
Other	7	18
Total	100	100

somewhat larger cash deficits would be run in years 1 and 2. In this case, the surplus of $1.1 million in year 0 is not sufficient to finance the subsequent deficits, and a deficit is incurred on a cumulative basis, as reflected in row (9). If the dividend is cut in year 1, so that the dividend in years 1–4 is 0, the cash deficits are eliminated. We can conclude that under Policy A, Omega can survive the recession provided dividends are cut. With a little additional arithmetic, we can see that the dividend could be partially restored in year 2 and fully restored in year 3.

Under Policy B—a debt ratio of 50 percent—row (13) shows that cash deficits are run in each year of the recession. With the dividend eliminated, Omega still runs a cash deficit in years 1–3, even on a cumulative basis, as indicated in row (16). Thus, Policy B appears to be an unsustainable policy in a recession, even with a cut in dividends.

What can we conclude from the analysis? Which policies are safe and which are not? By asking this question, we can see some of the limitations of financial theory when the practical realities of the world are considered. Policy A permits Omega to survive the recession, but with at least some possibility of having to cut the dividend if the recession is severe. Are the additional benefits of policy A, compared to the present policy, worth the risk of a dividend cut in a severe recession? Perhaps so, but we can see that the cash-flow analysis does not give us a precise answer to the question of the effect of debt policy on bankruptcy risk.

Perhaps it is best to think in terms of a range of debt ratios. In this case, Policy A appears to exploit the benefits of leverage about as fully as is prudent. We might, therefore, conclude that, considering only the risk of bankruptcy, Omega could operate safely with a debt ratio of 30–35 percent.

Probabilities.   An extension and refinement of the basic cash-flow procedure illustrated above can be obtained by introducing probabilities. Probability distributions would be required for revenues and other uncertain cash flows. Probability distributions then could be estimated for the changes in cash balances shown in Table 14–12.

A complete analysis would yield a probability distribution for each cash-balance figure in each year. Clearly, such a procedure would greatly increase the complexity of the analysis and the time and effort necessary to carry it out. As a compromise, it would be possible to develop probability distributions for the most promising policy only for the most critical years. Where the additional effort seemed justified, the use of probability analysis would yield additional insights into the degree of risk that management considered appropriate to assume—for example, with respect to the probability of having to cut the dividend.

Advantages of Cash-Flow Analysis.   Compared to EBIT/EPS analysis and coverage ratios, cash-flow analysis provides a number of additional insights for the critical task of setting debt policy.

Solvency—is the ability to pay all legal debts.

First, the cash-flow analysis focuses on the **solvency** of the firm during *adverse* circumstances rather than on the effects of leverage under *normal* circumstances. Cash-flow analysis also considers balance-sheet changes and other cash flows that do not appear in the income statement (such as capital expenditures), whereas EBIT/EPS and coverage analysis do not. Cash-flow analysis also gives an *inventory of financial reserves* available in the event of recession.

Cash-flow analysis identifies discretionary cash flows and develops a plan of action in advance. Nothing precludes the development of such a plan in connection with EBIT/EPS analysis, but cash-flow analysis views the problem in a dynamic context over time, whereas EBIT/EPS and coverage analysis normally consider only a single year.

Cash-flow analysis is consistent with financial theory. The theory of optimal financial leverage tells us that debt should be used up to the point at which its benefits are outweighed by the expected cost of financial distress and reduced commercial flexibil-

Finance in Practice 14–3

Notable Examples of Leveraged Buyouts

During the early 1980s, one of the most interesting of a number of new developments in finance was the *leveraged buyout*—a transaction in which a firm is purchased using borrowed funds, with the firm's own assets or stock pledged as collateral to secure the loan and with the firm's own cash flows used to pay it off. The buyers often are the firm's own top management, sometimes acting in concert with venture capitalists. The technique has been used to purchase privately held companies from their former owner(s) as well as to purchase publicly held companies and thereby "take them private." Using the leveraged buyout, a group of individuals can purchase a sizable company without putting up very much of their own capital, sometimes none at all. The trick

is to use the firm itself to secure the debt.

For example, suppose four members of the top management of a manufacturer of desk calendars decided to purchase the company from its long-time owner. The owner had decided to retire and sell the company, and rather than see it sold to outsiders, members of management decided to purchase it themselves. The owner was asking $10 million, with at least $8 million in cash. The four prospective buyers, all of whom had been with the company for many years as members of management, between them raised $250,000 of their own money. Where was the remaining $9.75 million to come from?

The answer, as the term *leveraged buyout* implies, was debt. The former owner agreed to take a *seller's note* for $2 million. A large bank agreed to lend $3 million in the form of a term loan. The remainder came from a venture capitalist, who agreed to put up the $4.75 million in the form of debt, with part of it convertible into common stock.

Working out all the details of the seniority and other arrange-

ments among the various suppliers of funds was very complicated. For purposes of our present discussion of financial leverage, the main point is that a small group of people bought a $10 million company with $250,000 in equity and $9.75 million in debt.

The company described above was privately owned. A recent example of a buyout of a public company is the buyout of the Beatrice Company, a large food and consumer-products company based in Chicago. The total purchase price was $6.2 billion, making it at the time the largest leveraged buyout ever proposed. This time the buyers were former members of Beatrice management, acting in concert with the firm of Kohlberg Kravis Roberts & Company, a New York investment partnership that specializes in leveraged buyouts. Kohlberg Kravis played the role of the investment venture capitalist in this transaction. Beatrice was a public company that was taken private by means of a leveraged buyout. During 1985, there were a number of other well-known firms taken private, among them Storer Communications, Levi Strauss &

ity. Cash-flow analysis evaluates the risk of financial distress. We will consider the factors omitted by cash-flow analysis in the next section.

Cash-flow analysis also has its weaknesses. The analysis may give an illusion of precision that is not justified on the basis of the underlying information. In an uncertain world, the numbers may not capture all the relevant factors. Cash-flow analysis, as we have described it here, considers an economic recession as the main source of uncertainty. What about technological developments, or shifts in consumer preferences, or political changes? The cash-flow procedure can be adapted to include factors of this sort. The main point is that recessions are not the only source of economic unhappiness.

Company, Northwest Industries, Uniroyal, Inc., and Scovill, Inc. A name familiar to many is that of R. H. Macy & Company, the nation's tenth largest retailer and sponsor of the annual New York Thanksgiving Day parade. A group of Macy executives proposed in October 1985 to buy the firm in a transaction valued at $3.58 million.

The buyouts discussed above involve members of management and venture capitalists as buyers. Another interesting class of leveraged buyout during the early 1980s were buyouts by employees. These nearly always involved the use of Employee Stock Ownership Plans (ESOPs), under which substantial tax incentives are made available to encourage employee ownership of stock. ESOPs have been encouraged by legislation beginning in the early 1970s as a way to improve worker morale, increase productivity, and improve labor/management relations. The largest employee buyout as of 1985 was that of Blue Bell, Inc., a North Carolina textile manufacturer with sales of $1.2 billion and 25,000 employees. Other well-known companies purchased by their employees were Rath Packing in 1982 and Weirton Steel, a division of National Steel, in 1982.

Leveraged buyouts are very interesting and exciting transactions, expecially to the buyers. Some of the numbers are very large. Very large companies can be bought with relatively small equity bases, and therein lies the focus of our interest in this chapter that discusses how far to go with the use of financial leverage. Most leveraged buyouts appear to go *much* farther than would seem prudent following the guidelines discussed in this chapter. In explanation, two points are important: first, leveraged buyouts are attempted only with companies that meet special criteria, such as low debt to begin with, very stable operating cash flows, profit margins sufficient to finance growth internally with funds left over to service the new debt, and assets for use as collateral. It is very unlikely that anyone could get financing to do a leveraged buyout of a high-growth, high-risk company. Second, the fact is that the transactions indeed are risky and go well beyond the risk levels that would be acceptable in typical situations. The operating risk of the firms is low, but once all the new debt is put in place, the residual cash flow available for equity holders is very risky indeed. The new owners in fact are taking a big gamble.

Leveraged buyouts on the scale of the early 1980s are a new phenomenon. Have they exceeded the bounds of prudence and gone too far in the use of debt? Some would say yes, and as noted above, they go much farther in the use of debt than conventional wisdom suggests is prudent. Time will tell, and as of the time of this writing, the test—namely the next recession—has not yet come. One can only wish the owners and lenders good fortune and recommend hard work to keep those operating cash flows coming in.

Sources: J. K. Butters *et al,* "Harrington Corporation," *Case Problems in Finance,* 8th ed. (Homewood, Ill.: R. D. Irwin, 1981); articles on Beatrice Corporation buyout, *Wall Street Journal,* November 15, October 17, October 18, October 21, and October 22, 1985; "Firms Have Two Avenues for Going Private," *Wall Street Journal,* August 12, 1985.

Allowing for Reserve Borrowing Capacity

As noted earlier, the theory developed in Chapter 13 tells us that the optimal debt level includes a reserve for contingencies and commercial flexibility. The cash-flow analysis outlined above does not include these factors, mainly because they are very difficult to quantify.

Reserve for Contingencies. Cash-flow analysis tells us approximately how much debt a firm can use without running a significant risk of bankruptcy. Should we assume that the risk of bankruptcy is constant through time? We should not. We noted earlier that, in an uncertain world, there are factors in addition to investment policy that can change a firm's operating risk.

A good case can be made, therefore, for backing away from the maximum safe debt level indicated by the cash-flow analysis. By such a reduction, the firm obtains a margin to allow for error and for changes over time and a cushion to provide flexibility to deal with problems that cannot be foreseen.

Inflation provides further reason for caution. In the cash-flow analysis, cash flows are estimated in nominal terms, with the effects of inflation included. Considerable uncertainty may exist, however, about the future rate of inflation. Even though the earlier cash-flow estimate is a best guess, uncertainty regarding the rate of inflation suggests that we back away still further from the point of maximum debt indicated by the cash-flow analysis.

Maintaining Flexibility for Commercial Strategy.   Another reason for operating below the maximum safe debt level is to preserve operating flexibility. A debt policy that might force a firm subsequently to make an undesirable change in its commercial strategy or to forgo a desirable change would be costly. An aggressive debt policy might look good at one point, but later—because of changes in technology that make products obsolete or because of rapid increases in the prices of key inputs—that same policy might threaten the firm's existence. Faced with such a situation, a firm might find it necessary to forgo investments that it otherwise would have made or to alter its strategy in other important ways. Similarly, a firm faced with unexpected and attractive new opportunities might wish to alter its commercial strategy to take advantage of them. If it is unable to do so because of a debt policy adopted earlier, the opportunity cost could be high.

Considerations such as these suggest a cautious approach to debt policy that leaves room for operating flexibility. In the long run, firms succeed primarily because of their commercial strategies rather than because of debt/equity or dividend policies. Management should avoid too much emphasis on the right-hand side of the balance sheet and not lose sight of the fact that successful commercial strategy comes first and that financing policies play a supporting role.

> **In the long run, firms succeed primarily because of their commercial strategies rather than because of debt/equity or dividend policies.**

CHOOSING THE APPROPRIATE DEBT POLICY

How much should a firm back away from the maximum safe debt level indicated by cash-flow analysis because of factors discussed above? We cannot be precise in answering this question, because the answer requires far more knowledge of the costs of financial distress and reduced flexibility than we have at present. Our theories provide qualitative guidance, and we can answer some questions with cash-flow analysis, but the final decision is a subjective one.

The concept of a reserve for contingencies is especially relevant to firms whose

A **leveraged buyout**—is a transaction in which a firm is purchased using borrowed funds, with the firm's own assets or stock pledged as collateral to secure the loan and with the firm's own cash flows used to pay off the loan.

operating risk is especially high because of size or technology or length of experience. In many cases, the optimal debt ratio may well be zero.

Finance in Practice 14–2 looks at how financial managers of 212 firms make their decisions about debt policy. Finance in Practice 14–3 examines the 1980s phenomenon of the **leveraged buyout** and its relationship to setting debt policy. When a firm uses debt, it takes more risk in hopes of earning higher future returns. Debt has advantages, but to go too far in exploiting them can be costly. The use of debt represents essentially a gamble that the benefits of debt will exceed the costs. Such bets should be placed with caution.

KEY CONCEPTS

1. Financing mix should be tailored to commercial strategy. The higher is the operating risk, the less debt the firm should use.
2. EBIT/EPS analysis is very useful for analyzing the impact of alternative financing plans on earnings.
3. Coverage ratios, which measure the margin of safety by which earnings and cash flows cover debt service, are useful in measuring risk.
4. Debt capacity is best defined as the optimal level of debt for the firm from the perspective of shareholders and not as how much lenders are willing to lend.
5. A useful approach to determining the appropriate debt level in practice is to analyze the firm's cash flows under conditions of recession.
6. Good financial planning requires that some reserve borrowing capacity be maintained to allow for contingencies and to provide operating flexibility.

SUMMARY

In planning its financial structure, the first major policy decision facing the firm is that of determining the appropriate level of debt. For some firms, the decision involves a choice between long-term debt and equity. Firms without access to the public equity markets also must decide how much debt they prudently should use.

The choice of an appropriate debt policy involves a trade-off between benefits and costs of financial leverage. The optimal debt level depends to an important extent on the firm's operating risk. The greater is the operating risk, the less debt the firm should use. Therefore, a firm's financing policy should be tailored to its commercial strategy.

Alternative financing plans should be analyzed along several dimensions. EBIT/EPS analysis is useful for evaluating the sensitivity of earnings per share (EPS) and uncommitted earnings per share (UEPS) to changes in EBIT under alternative financing plans. EPS and UEPS break-even levels of EBIT can be calculated to determine the EBIT level at which EPS (or UEPS) for two alternative plans are equal. Coverage ratios provide a measure of the security of interest payments. None of these measures, however, tells the firm how far it should go in using debt. The firm's debt capacity is best defined, not as the maximum amount that lenders are willing to lend, but as the amount of debt that is optimal for shareholders.

A determination of debt capacity requires an analysis of the likelihood of financial distress, which depends on the firm's ability to meet its financial obligations. Analysis of cash flows expected under adverse conditions (for example, recession or loss of market due to a change in technology) provides information about the effects of alternative financing plans on the risk of insolvency. Cash-flow analysis considers balance-sheet changes as well as operating flows, provides an inventory of financial reserves, and outlines a plan of action in the event of recession. However, cash-flow analysis does not automatically provide a reserve for contingencies and commercial flexibility. In setting debt policy, a firm should allow for these factors by backing away from the maximum safe debt level indicated by cash-flow analysis. The appropriate amount of such reserve borrowing capacity is largely a matter of subjective judgment.

QUESTIONS

1. What are the principal determinants of a firm's operating risk?

2. Discuss the relationship between the optimal financial structure of a firm and its commercial strategy.

3. Should short-term debt be considered in determining the optimal level of debt?

4. How should a firm's debt capacity be defined?

5. What can be said about a firm's exposure to the risk of financial distress, knowing only the total level of debt (principal amount) in its financial structure?

6. What information is provided by a complete analysis of cash flows that normally is not provided by EBIT/EPS or coverage analysis?

7. Should a firm extend its debt level to the point indicated as safe by a cash-flow analysis?

PROBLEMS

1. Utilize the information given in problem (1) in Chapter 13 to construct an EBIT/EPS chart. Which financing alternative would you recommend? Why?

2. Utilize the information given in problem (1) in Chapter 13 to calculate the EPS break-even point using Equation (1) of this chapter. (*Hint:* Be sure to include old interest payments.)

3. Assume that the firm in problem (1) in Chapter 13 has a third financing alternative, that of selling 100,000 shares of 11 percent preferred stock to net $50 per share. Beginning in the fifth year after issuance, the firm would make annual sinking-fund payments of $500,000 for retirement of the preferred stock over a 10-year period.

   a. Add to the EBIT/EPS chart in problem (1) lines representing the preferred stock alternative in years 1 and 5. (*Note:* Show both EPS and UEPS in year 5.)

   b. Calculate EPS and UEPS break-even points for the preferred stock plan compared with the common stock plan.

   c. How attractive is the preferred stock plan? Under what circumstances might the preferred stock plan be attractive?

4. Steven Lock, president of Lock Enterprises, had recently attended a seminar on the benefits of financial leverage. Lock Enterprises has assets of $2 million financed entirely with 100,000 shares of common stock currently selling at $20 per share. Lock is considering retiring some of the stock with borrowed funds, which he can obtain at an interest rate of 14 percent. He expects the company to earn $440,000 next year before interest and taxes. The company's tax is 50 percent.

   a. What will be the expected earnings per share (EPS) and return on equity (ROE) at next year's expected level of earnings before interest and taxes (EBIT), given all equity financing?

   b. What would be the effect of increased leverage on expected EPS and ROE? Why?

   c. Lock is considering two alternative leverage ratios, 25 percent debt and 50 percent debt (percent debt to total assets). Calculate expected EPS and ROE for each of these debt ratios at next year's expected EBIT.

   d. Lock thought that, in a bad year, Lock Enterprises' EBIT could fall as low as $100,000 and in a good year could rise as high as $750,000. He wondered what effect this might have at the leverage ratios he was considering. Calculate expected EPS and ROE at the low and high EBIT levels for debt ratios of 0 percent, 25 percent, and 50 percent, and compare the results with those of part (c).

5. The current balance sheet for Rafferty Corporation shows $10 million of 8 percent bonds and $7.2 million of $4.00 par value common stock. Total current sales of $45.5 million per year are to the United States Navy on a 10-year contract. The United States Air Force has offered a similar 10-year contract for $13.0 million per year. The company has accepted the new contract and now must raise $7.5 million from external sources in order to expand its production facilities. The financing could be accomplished through a debt issue carrying a 13 percent coupon rate or by selling shares of common stock to net the company $6.25 per share. EBIT is 3.3 percent of sales and the tax rate is 45 percent.

Table A

Policy	Debt (percent)	Equity (percent)
A	0	100
B	20	80
C	50	50

Table B

Sales Year Prior to Recession	Recession-Year Sales as a Percentage of Nonrecession-Year Sales			
	Year 1	Year 2	Year 3	Year 4
100	90	75	70	90

a. Calculate the EPS break-even level of EBIT, that is, the level of EBIT at which the EPS figures for the two financing alternatives are equal.

b. Assuming that a $500,000 per year sinking-fund payment would be required on the new debt issue, calculate the UEPS break-even level of EBIT.

c. Analyze the coverage ratios for Rafferty Corporation under each of the two financing alternatives. What conclusions can you draw?

6. The Osgood Company has assets of $4 million that are expected to generate $800,000 next year before interest and taxes.

a. Assume that Osgood's assets could be financed in one of the three ways shown in Table A. Also assume that debt requires an interest rate of 10 percent, that equity has a market price of $20 per share, that the market price per share of stock is equal to the book (balance-sheet) value per share under each of the alternatives, and that the firm's tax rate is 50 percent. What will be the expected earnings per share and return on equity under each of these plans at next year's expected level of EBIT?

b. In a bad year Osgood's EBIT may fall as low as $400,000, and in a good year EBIT may rise to $1,000,000. Calculate the expected earnings per share and return on equity for the high and low EBIT for the financing plans discussed in part (a) of this problem.

7. Omega Manufacturing Corporation, which was described in the text of this chapter, wishes to reevaluate its cash-flow forecasts on the expectation of a more severe recession than the one previously anticipated.

a. Revise Tables 14–9 and 14–12 in the text, assuming the sales pattern shown in Table B. As-

sume cash operating expenses to be the same as forecasted in Table 14–9 and the 3 percent price decline to continue through year 4.

b. What conclusions can be reached from this revised analysis? How do these conclusions compare with those in the text based on a less severe recession?

8. The Bengston Corporation has undertaken a 5-year plant expansion program, which will require $5 million in external capital in year 1 and $6 million in year 2. The company has several alternative financing plans available to it to meet its financing needs. Plan A is to issue $11 million in new common stock in year 1. Plan B is to issue $5 million in new common stock in year 1 and $6 million in 25-year bonds in year 2. Plan C is to issue $5 million in 20-year bonds in year 1 and $6 million in stock in year 2. Currently, the firm has 500,000 shares of stock outstanding and $3 million of 6 percent bonds. Beginning in year 1, sinking-fund payments of $300,000 on the existing debt will be required to retire the debt in 10 years. The new bond issues in year 1 or year 2 will carry 12 percent interest. If a $5 million bond issue occurs in year 1, annual sinking-fund payments of $250,000 will be required starting in year 5. The $6 million bond issue in year 2 will require annual sinking-fund payments of $300,000 starting in year 6. Bengston's EBIT this year (year 0) was $3.5 million. Management expects EBIT to grow 10 percent annually over the next 10 years. New common stock can be issued now to net $50 per share.

a. Calculate the EPS and UEPS at the end of year 2 and at the end of year 6 for each of the financing alternatives. Assume that stock can be issued at the beginning of year 2 to net $50 per share. Also assume a 50 percent tax rate.

Table C

Hills Brothers, Balance Sheet, December 31, 1986 (Thousands of Dollars)			
Current assets	3,200	Current liabilities	2,850
Net plant and equipment	5,320	Long-term debt*	2,000
Other	480	Total liabilities	4,850
		Equity	
		Common stock—200,000 shares at $1 par	200
		Additional paid-in capital	2,800
		Retained earnings	1,150
Total assets	9,000	**Total liabilities and equity**	9,000

*This is the balance of an 8 percent 20-year bond issue with annual sinking-fund payments of $125,000.

b. Calculate the EPS break-even point for plan A compared with plan B for the end of year 2.

c. Analyze the coverage ratios under each of the three plans at the end of year 2.

d. Which alternative would you recommend? What factors do you consider important in making these recommendations?

9. As a new financial analyst for Hill Brothers, Inc., you have been asked to help evaluate the alternative financing plans for the corporation's expansion program. The firm's balance sheet and income statement as of December 31, 1986, (in thousands of dollars) are summarized in Tables C and D.

One alternative financing plan is a new stock issue of $4 million. Stock can be issued to net $25 per share. The other alternative is a 20-year, 9 percent, $4 million bond issue with annual sinking-fund payments of $200,000 beginning in the first year.

a. The company has maintained a 50¢ annual dividend in the past and wishes to continue this annual dividend payment regardless of the financing plan chosen. What level of EBIT would be required in the first year in order to cover interest, sinking funds, and dividend payments?

b. Calculate EPS break-even points for the bond plan compared with the stock plan for year 1.

c. Suppose Hill Brothers expects the EBIT level in year 1 to be $1,033,000 with a two-thirds probability that it will be between $833,000

and $1,233,000. Which financing alternative would you recommend and why?

d. Calculate the UEPS break-even point for the two plans. Does this change your recommendation in part (c)?

10. The A. M. Thomas Corporation is planning to raise $6 million for financing plant additions and working capital. Two alternative financing plans are available to the firm: a new issue of common stock that can be sold to net $30 per share or a bond issue carrying a 12 percent interest rate. Balance sheet and income statements as of December 31, 1986, (in thousands of dollars) for Thomas Corporation are summarized in Tables E and F. If the economy experiences continued growth the next year (1987), the plant addition is expected to increase sales by 20 percent. If the economy slows

Table D

Sales	2,030
Cost of goods sold	1,624
Gross margin	406
Interest*	165
Profit before tax	281
Tax at 48 percent	135
Profit after tax	146

*Long-term debt was $2,125,000 at the beginning of 1986. A sinking-fund payment of $125,000 was made on June 30, 1986. Interest for the year, therefore, is [($2,125,000 + 2,000,000) ÷ 2] × 0.08 = $165,000.

Table E

Current assets	50,000		Current liabilities	46,000
Net plant and equipment	80,000		Long-term debt	1,000
Other	1,000		Total liabilities	47,000
			Equity	
			Stock—500,000 shares	
			at $2 par	1,000
			Additional paid-in capital	42,000
			Retained earnings	41,000
Total assets	131,000		**Total liabilities and equity**	131,000

down, a 15 percent decrease in sales will be experienced. Variable costs are expected to remain at 60 percent of sales and fixed costs are expected to increase by $800,000.

a. Calculate the EPS and ROE for each financing alternative at the sales levels expected under continued economic growth and under an economic slowdown. Assume the interest expense on the existing debt will remain at $100,000.

b. Thomas' staff economist has provided the forecast for next year's economy which appears in Table G. Using this information, calculate the expected value and standard deviation of EPS for each of the two alternative financing plans.

11. Suppose that in problem (10), the Thomas Corporation's variable costs were 40 percent of sales instead of 60 percent and that fixed costs were $9,000,000 instead of $5,000,000. These changes are shown in the income statement as of December 31, 1986, (in thousands of dollars) appearing in Table H. What can you say about the degree of operating leverage under this cost structure relative to the cost structure in problem (10)? How does this change in the cost structure affect your answers to part (a) in problem (10)? (Assume that variable costs remain at 40 percent of sales and that fixed costs increase by $800,000 with the plant expansion.) What implications do you see with regard to operating leverage and financing decisions?

Table G

Outcome	Probability (percent)
Continued growth	0.75
Slowdown	0.25

Table F

Sales	20,000
Variable operating expenses	12,000
Fixed operating expenses	5,000
Earnings before interest and taxes	3,000
Interest	100
Profit before tax	2,900
Tax at 50 percent	1,450
Profit after tax	1,450
Earnings per share	$2.90
Return on equity (percent)	1.73

Table H

Sales	20,000
Variable operating expenses	8,000
Fixed operating expenses	9,000
Earnings before interest and taxes	3,000
Interest	100
Profit before tax	2,900
Tax at 50 percent	1,450
Profit after tax	1,450
Earnings per share	$2.90
Return on equity (percent)	1.73

REFERENCES

Donaldson, G. *Corporate Debt Capacity*. Boston, Mass.: Division of Research, Harvard Business School, 1961.

Donaldson, G. *Strategy for Financial Mobility*. Homewood, Ill.: Richard D. Irwin, 1971.

Higgins, R. C., and L. D. Schall. "Corporate Bankruptcy and Conglomerate Merger." *Journal of Finance* 30 (Mar. 1975): 93–114.

Kim, E. H. "A Mean-Variance Theory of Optimal Financial Structure and Corporate Debt Capacity." *Journal of Finance* 33 (Mar. 1978): 45–64.

Krainer, R. E. "Interest Rates, Leverage and Investor Rationality." *Journal of Financial and Quantitative Analysis* 12 (Mar. 1977): 1–16.

Moyer, R. C. "Forecasting Financial Failure: A Reexamination." *Financial Management* 6 (Spring 1977): 9–17.

Pringle, J. J. "Price/Earnings Ratios, Earnings per Share, and Financial Management. *Financial Management* 2 (Spring 1973): 34–40.

Roberts, G. S., and J. A. Viscione. "Captive Finance Subsidiaries: The Manager's Views." *Financial Management* 10 (Spring 1981): 36–42.

Turnbull, S. M. "Debt Capacity." *Journal of Finance* 34 (Sept. 1979): 931–940.

Von Furstenberg, G. M., and B. G. Malkiel. "Financial Analysis in an Inflationary Environment." *Journal of Finance* 32 (May 1977): 575–588.

Appendix 14A

Return Targets and Financing Mix

In Chapters 13 and 14, we addressed the issue of financing decisions—choosing the appropriate mix of debt and equity for financing the firm's assets. We took the firm's investments and assets as given and tailored the financing plan to fit. In this appendix, we return to a topic that we adressed earlier in Chapters 10 and 11—namely, setting return targets for capital-investment projects. Here we will explain how to determine risk-adjusted discount rates for individual projects that vary in riskiness, at the same time taking into account the way the projects are financed.

In our earlier discussion in Chapters 10 and 11, we saw some of the difficulties of setting return targets when projects have different risk characteristics. Risk also played a key role in our discussion of the firm's choice of debt or equity financing in Chapters 13 and 14. In this appendix, let us return to the problem of estimating return targets armed with the material we have covered on capital structure. At the outset we should stress that this material is one of the most difficult areas facing financial managers in practice.

First, let us see how the tax advantages of debt affected our calculation of return targets. Recall that the weighted-average required return, *WARR*, that we developed in Chapter 10 is an appropriate discount rate for evaluating an average-risk project, where average means average for the firm itself.

We saw in Chapter 10 that the *WARR* is calculated as the weighted average of the required returns of the suppliers of capital, including a tax adjustment for the tax-deductibility of interest. In equation form, *WARR* is expressed as shown in Equation (A-1).

> The weighted-average required return (*WARR*) for a firm can be expressed as
>
> $$WARR = K_w = W_d K_d (1 - T) + W_e K_e \qquad \textbf{(A–1)}$$
>
> where W_d and W_e are the proportions of financing done by debt and equity, respectively; K_d and K_e are the required returns on debt and equity, respectively; and T = the corporate tax rate.

For the firm's *WARR* to be an appropriate return target for a *project*, there are two conditions that must be met: (1) the project's operating risk must be approximately equal to that of the firm's overall average risk, and (2) the project must be financed with the firm's standard mix of debt and equity.

What do we do when a project is not of average risk? We know that investors require higher returns on high-risk projects. In addition, as we saw in Chapters 13 and

14, the riskiness of the firm's investments should affect the firm's debt policy. High-risk investments should be financed with less debt than low-risk investments. If one project can be financed with more debt than another, then because the interest tax shield on debt has value, the difference in financing mix should be taken into account in evaluating the desirability of the two projects.

A project adds value to the firm through two separate channels. First, even if the project were entirely financed with equity, it could have a positive net present value. Second, the project may add to the firm's debt capacity and, thereby, allow the firm to borrow more money. The use of such additional debt may also create value. What we need is a way to estimate the total value a project adds. The *WARR* does this for average-risk projects because it incorporates the firm's overall financing mix, but it is appropriate only for average-risk projects. Here we will extend the basic concept of *WARR* allowing for projects of differing risks. In effect, we will determine a *project WARR*, adjusted for the project's risks and the project's effect on the firm's use of debt.

THE WEIGHTED-AVERAGE REQUIRED RETURN AND THE VALUE OF DEBT FINANCING

The first step is to break *WARR* into two parts, one of which shows the value of debt financing. Rearranging Equation (A–1), we can write the *WARR* as shown in Equation (A–2).

Alternatively, the weighted-average required return (*WARR*) for a firm can be expressed in two components, to separate out the value of debt financing, as

$$WARR = (W_d K_d + W_e K_e) - W_d K_d T \qquad \text{(A–2)}$$

where $(W_d K_d + W_e K_e)$ reflects the required return on the project due to its risk before tax-deductibility of interest payment and $W_d K_d T$ reflects tax savings due to tax-deductibility of interest paid on debt used to finance the project.

Thus, K_w can be viewed as having two components: the basic return required by equity and debt holders, adjusted downward by an amount that reflects the tax shield on interest.

Let us now focus on the term $(W_d K_d + W_e K_e)$ in Equation (A–2). This term represents a weighted average of the returns on debt and equity and is what an investor would receive if he or she held the bonds and the stock of the firm in exactly the proportions W_d and W_e. By holding both the bonds and stock in exactly the same proportions as they are issued by the firm, W_d and W_e, the investor in effect negates the financial leverage. The average risk of the combination of debt and equity in exactly those proportions is the same as the firm's overall operating risk. Hence, the term $(W_d K_d + W_e K_e)$ gives us a measure of the firm's *unlevered* equity return, K_o, and allows us to rewrite Equation (A–2) as shown in Equation (A–3).[1]

---

[1]For a discussion of the assumptions underlying this argument, see R. Harris and J. Pringle, "Risk-Adjusted Discount Rates—Extensions from the Average-Risk Case," *Journal of Financial Research*, 1985. In particular, we assume that interest tax shields are capitalized at the firm's unlevered equity rate, K_o.

> The weighted-average required return for a firm can be expressed as the sum of a firm's return on unlevered equity plus an adjustment for the tax-deductibility of interest, or as
>
> $$WARR = K_w = K_o - W_d K_d T \qquad \text{(A–3)}$$
>
> where K_o = the firm's return on unlevered equity.

Equation (A–3) tells us that the firm's *WARR* can be thought of as having two components: the unlevered required return, which depends on the firm's operating risk, and an adjustment for the tax-deductibility of interest.

THE PROJECT WEIGHTED-AVERAGE REQUIRED RETURN

We can represent the *WARR* for a project in the same way as for a firm. We calculated the *WARR* for a project in Chapter 11 using the pure-play technique—that is, by using data on other companies. Here we are going to calculate a project *WARR* using the project's own risk characteristics. For a project j, we can rewrite Equation (A–3) as shown in Equation (A–4).

> The project weighted-average required return, K_{wj}, on project j can be expressed as
>
> $$K_{wj} = K_{oj} - W_j K_d T \qquad \text{(A–4)}$$
>
> where K_{oj} = the unlevered required return for project j and W_j = the project's debt ratio.

K_{oj} is to the project as K_o is to the firm; it is the required rate of return for the project if the project were unlevered—that is, financed entirely by equity. W_j, the project debt ratio, is the proportion of debt to be used to finance the project, just as W_d is the firm's debt ratio. So the project *WARR* can be thought of as having the same two components as the firm *WARR*, an unlevered required return that depends on the project's operating risk and an adjustment for the tax-deductibility of interest on the debt to be used to finance the project.

For the firm, we can estimate K_o by calculating the weighted average, but to determine K_{oj} for the project we can apply the capital-asset-pricing model.

RISK ADJUSTMENT USING THE CAPITAL-ASSET-PRICING MODEL

The basic risk/return relationship given by the capital-asset-pricing model (CAPM) in Chapter 5 is restated in Equation (A–5).

According to the capital-asset-pricing model, the required return for any risky asset or project can be expressed as

$$K_j = R_f + (K_m - R_f)\beta_j \qquad \text{(A–5)}$$

where R_f = the risk-free rate of return, K_m = the required return on the market portfolio, and β_j = the beta coefficient of asset or project j, which is a measure of nondiversifiable risk.

The CAPM is a general model that can be used to estimate return targets on any types of risky assets, including projects as well as firms. We can use the CAPM to estimate K_{oj}, the unlevered required rate of return on a project, in Equation (A–4).

Let us examine the terms in Equation (A–5) more carefully. In theory, R_f is the risk-free return rate. In practice, the interest rate (yield to maturity) on long-term U.S. government bonds is often used as a value for R_f when analyzing long-term capital-investment projects. While U.S. government bonds are not risk-free (they are free of default risk but not interest-rate or purchasing-power risk), they are perhaps the least risky of long-term investments. The problems become stickier in the choice of $(K_m - R_f)$ and β_j, the market risk premium and the project's beta.

Recall that K_m is the required rate of return on the market portfolio, which in theory is the portfolio of *all* risky assets held by investors—including stocks, bonds, gold, real estate, commodities, and any other assets. In practical applications of the CAPM, it is usually necessary to select only a portion of these assets as the reference portfolio to be used for estimating returns; it is hard to obtain meaningful data on returns for some of the asset types mentioned above that normally are not traded actively in financial markets.

The most typical practice in applying the CAPM is to take some portfolio of corporate stocks as the market portfolio and to measure both expected return and risk relative to that portfolio. For the present discussion, however, there is an advantage in using as the *reference portfolio* (our proxy for the market) a portfolio composed of both corporate stocks and corporate bonds. If we look at a market portfolio containing only stocks, we have a portfolio that overstates the risks and required returns of suppliers of capital to U.S. corporations that use both stock and debt financing. Because debtholders have prior claim, returns to shareholders are more risky. To compensate for this extra risk, higher returns are required. Therefore, a portfolio that included only stocks would not take into consideration the lower risk faced by debtholders.

We can find a K_m that reflects required returns to both equity and debt by calculating a weighted average of returns to equity and debt.

Measuring the Unlevered Market Risk Premium

On a portfolio combining both corporate stocks and corporate bonds, investors would require a risk premium that is a weighted average of the risk premiums on corporate bonds and stocks, where the weights depend on the amounts of bonds and stock in the portfolio. To get this average, we need forecasts of the risk premia on bonds and stocks. The risk premium on bonds can be estimated by observing the difference between yields to maturity on corporate bonds and U.S. government bonds. For example, suppose that long-term U.S. government bonds had a yield to maturity of 12 percent, while at the same time long-term corporate bonds had an average yield of 13.5 percent. The risk premium on corporate bonds would, therefore, be 1.5 percent. Note that this risk premium might be different as financial-market conditions changed.

Estimating a risk premium on equities is a more difficult challenge, as we saw in Chapter 10. There we concluded that one useful gauge was to observe that over a relatively long period of U.S. financial history, the risk premium on equities appears to have averaged about 7.2 percent. Remember that this 7.2 percent is for investments with a relatively long holding period, as would be appropriate for investment projects. If we think there is no convincing evidence that future risk premia on equities will differ from those earned in the past, we can use this 7.2 percent figure. Another way to determine a risk premium on equities would be to use financial analysts' forecasts as outlined in Chapter 10.

Next, we need figures for the proportions of bonds and stocks for firms in general— that is, firms making up the market portfolio. Debt ratios of U.S. corporations have varied quite a bit over the past two decades. They averaged 25 to 30 percent during the late 1970s. As a typical figure for the remainder of the 1980s, let us use 30 percent as our estimate of the average debt ratio for U.S. corporations and 70 percent for equity. Using these estimates, we can calculate a weighted-average market risk premium as

$$\text{weighted-average market risk premium} = (0.70)0.072 + (0.30)0.015$$

$$= 0.0549 = 5.49 \text{ percent}$$

This weighted-average risk premium on the market of 5.49 percent becomes our estimate of $(K_m - R_f)$ in Equation (A–5). Just as in the case of the firm and the project, calculating the weighted average in this way gives us the *unlevered* risk premium on the market—which is exactly what we need to use Equation (A–5) to calculate *unlevered* required rates of return for projects.

Measuring Project Risk

Having obtained an estimate of the risk-free rate and the market risk premium, we now must obtain estimates of the risk measure, β_j, in Equation (A–5). The beta coefficient is the project's risk ratio—that is, its risk relative to that of the market. Given our definition of the market (containing both corporate bonds and stocks), we can think of the market's risk as depending primarily on the risk of a *typical project* for the economy as a whole. This typical project is what, on average, the bondholders and stockholders own. Our problem is to measure the risk of the project under evaluation— Project *j*—relative to that of a typical project for the economy as a whole.[2] These project risk ratios, or beta coefficients, are perfectly analogous to the beta coefficients for stocks that we used to find required returns on stocks. Estimates of beta coefficients on stocks are widely published by services, such as the *Value Line Investment Survey*. Such beta coefficients are typically derived from looking at past stock returns and assuming that these patterns hold in the future.

---

[2]Measuring risk in this way was first suggested by R.S. Bower and D.L. Lessard, "An Operational Approach to Risk Screening," *Journal of Finance* 28 (May 1973): 321–28. As Bower and Lessard show, defining market risk as the risk of a typical project for the economy as a whole ensures that project and market risk are measured in a consistent manner and avoids some difficult problems of measurement. The risk of both the project under evaluation and the benchmark (typical) project should be defined as nondiversifiable risk.

For *projects*, however, there are not such easily available estimates of risk measures. The measure of project risk required by the CAPM depends on the life of the project, the growth trend in expected project cash flows, the time pattern of those cash flows, growth opportunities of the firm, and the relationship of project *j* to other projects in the economy. In reality, we cannot measure beta coefficients for projects as required by the CAPM except in unusual circumstances and with considerable effort and expense. So, to use the CAPM for estimating project return targets, we must make some compromises.

As an approximation, suppose management can make an "informed judgment" regarding the value of β_j for a project. Some may object that an informed judgment is not sufficiently rigorous, but to estimate beta coefficients quantitatively also requires informed judgments regarding many inputs, no matter how sophisticated is the computational procedure for manipulating the data. So it is difficult to say that an informed judgment regarding the value of the ratio itself produces a result any less accurate than explicit attempts at quantitative estimation. A typical project (that is, a project of average risk for the economy) has a risk ratio (beta coefficient) of 1.0; projects of above-average risk have beta coefficients greater than 1.0; projects of below-average risk have beta coefficients less than 1.0. Thus, the beta coefficient is simply a *relative-risk ratio*, where we measure the project relative to a typical (average-risk) project for the whole economy.

With this idea in mind, we can rewrite Equation (A–5) as shown in Equation (A–6).

The required return K_{oj} for a risky project can be expressed as

$$K_{oj} = R_f + [(K_m - R_f) \times (\text{project risk ratio})] \tag{A–6}$$

$$= R_f + [(\text{unlevered market risk premium}) \times (\text{project risk ratio})]$$

where the project risk ratio measures the risk of project *j* relative to the risk of the typical project in the economy.

Equation (A–6) is simply an application of the CAPM risk/return relationship from Equation (A–5) and gives us a means to adjust for risk the required returns on projects.

Sample Problem 14A–1

Applying Relative Risk Measurement to Three Projects

Determine the required rate of return, K_{oj}, for each of the following projects: (a) a typical project of average risk for the economy; (b) a project judged half as risky as the typical project; (c) a project judged twice as risky as the typical project. Assume that the long-term government bond rate is 12 percent, that average long-term corporate bond rates are 13.5 percent, and that the risk premium on stocks is 7.2 percent (its long-term historical average).

Solution

Assuming that 70 percent of the market portfolio is stock and that 30 percent is corporate bonds, we can calculate the unlevered market risk premium as

$$K_m - R_f = 0.70 \, (7.2) + 0.30 \, (13.5 - 12) = 5.49 \text{ (percent)}.$$

Applying Equation (A–6) to (a) the average-risk project yields $K_{oj} = 12 + 5.49(1.0) = 17.49$ percent; (b) the half-as-risky project yields $K_{oj} = 12 + 5.49(0.5) = 14.75$ percent; (c) the twice-as-risky project yields $K_{oj} = 12 + 5.49(2.0) = 22.98$ percent.

≡Ⅲ⫶

TAKING PROJECT FINANCING INTO ACCOUNT

We have one major step remaining to complete our estimate of a project *WARR*. We have used the CAPM to estimate the unlevered required rate of return, K_{oj}, in Equation (A–4). Now we must take project financing into account, which we do by means of the second term in Equation (A–4). (As noted in Chapters 13 and 14, project financing could affect the value of the firm through channels other than the tax-deductibility of interest. We ignore those effects in our discussion in this appendix.) To summarize our overall approach, we can restate Equation (A–4) as shown in Equation (A–7).

The required return, K_{wj}, for a project can be calculated as

$$K_{wj} = K_{oj} - W_j K_d T \qquad \text{(A–7)}$$

where K_{oj} is calculated as shown in Equation (A–6), W_j is the debt ratio for the project, K_d is the firm's interest rate, and T is the tax rate.

In Equation (A–7), K_{oj} is the required rate of return that we would use if the project were to be financed entirely by equity. We can derive K_{oj} using the CAPM by applying Equation (A–6). K_d is the interest rate on the firm's debt, and W_j is the *debt ratio* for the project—that is, the proportion of debt that will be used to finance the project. For example, if the initial outlay for the project were $1,000 and $300 of that was to come from debt, W_j would be 0.30. T in Equation (A–5) is the corporate tax rate. The result, K_{wj}, is the appropriate required return for evaluating the project, taking into account the effects of debt financing.

The rate K_{wj} calculated for an individual project as above is exactly comparable to the rate K_w calculated for the firm in Chapter 10. The K_{wj} calculated using Equation (A–7) is a *WARR* for the *project*. Like all return targets, K_{wj} is the return the project must provide if it is to compensate the suppliers of capital (equity and debt) at their respective required rates, after payment of all taxes. Just as we did with all return targets in Chapters 10 and 11, we use K_{wj} to discount the after-tax operating flows of the project to compute net present value or as a target against which to compare the project's internal rate of return.

Where do we get W_j, the project's debt ratio? In theory, we want to know the contribution that the project makes to the firm's debt capacity, as defined in Chapter 14. By virtue of undertaking the project, how much more debt should the firm add to its total debt given the objective of maximizing the value of the firm? In some cases, the financing associated with an investment can be directly identified, as in the case of a mortgage loan to finance a real-estate project. In the case of many investments typically made by firms, however, identifying the amount of debt to be associated with the project is not so easy. Firms normally undertake investments more or less continually over time, while funds typically are raised from banks and the financial markets in large blocks rather than for each investment individually. Usually it is very difficult to tell exactly how the project affects the firm's overall financing mix.

One solution is to define W_j for the project as equal to the firm's overall target financing ratio. If, for example, the firm plans as a matter of general policy to finance its operations with 25 percent debt and 75 percent equity, we might define W_j for any particular project as 0.25. This approach is not strictly correct theoretically, but it is often a reasonable first approximation.[3] Suppose, however, that an extremely safe project is under consideration. Perhaps adopting this project will enable the firm to use a larger amount of debt financing than if it adopts a project of average risk. For a high-risk project, the percentage of debt financing may be less than the firm's average debt ratio. In Chapters 13 and 14, we discussed the choice of financing mix in more detail. What is important here is that low-risk and high-risk projects can affect the firm's financing plans in different ways.

One possible approach would be to use the firm's debt ratio for all projects that have equal or less risk than the firm's overall average risk. For projects of risk greater than the firm's average, we might define W_j as one-half the firm's debt ratio. For very high-risk projects, we might define W_j as zero. Such an approach would be conservative in that it would tend to understate rather than overstate the reduction in K_{wj} due to financial leverage. This understatement would occur because projects with less risk than average for the firm are likely to have a debt ratio greater than the firm's debt ratio.

Sample Problem 14A–2

Calculating K_{wj} for a Jefferson Industries Project

Jefferson Industries has a target debt ratio of 0.30; that is, the company plans as a matter of long-term policy to finance its operating assets with a mix of 30 percent debt and 70 percent equity. Jefferson's controller is evaluating a prospective investment opportunity that the firm's capital-budgeting staff analysts have judged to have a "project beta" of 1.5—that is, to be 1.5 times as risky as the average project for the economy as a whole. Jefferson's typical project, on the other hand, has a project beta of only 1.2. The government bond rate at the time is 11.5 percent, the interest rate on Jefferson's debt is 13.5 percent, and the tax rate is 0.46. Jefferson has concluded that the market risk premium $(K_m - R_f)$ is 5 percent. Determine the appropriate required return for evaluating the project. Assume that Jefferson will use a debt ratio of 0.15 in evaluating this project because the project is considered to be riskier than Jefferson's typical project.

Solution

Applying Equation (A–6), we can calculate the unlevered required return as

$$K_{oj} = 11.5 + (5 \times 1.5) = 11.5 + 7.5 = 19.0 \text{ percent.}$$

Now we use Equation (A–7) to calculate K_{wj} using the debt ratio of 0.15 for the project:

$$K_{wj} = 19.0 - (0.15)(13.5)(0.46) = 18.1 \text{ percent.}$$

---

[3] For a discussion of some issues involved in choosing levels of project debt, see J.D. Martin and D.F. Scott, Jr., "Debt Capacity and the Capital-Budgeting Decision," *Financial Management* 5 (Summer 1976): 7–14.

To evaluate the project, we discount its after tax operating cash flows at 18.1 percent to compute net present value. Alternatively, we could compare its expected internal rate of return to 18.1 percent. ▪▮▮

WORDS OF CAUTION

We have developed a means to find project-specific required returns. As we saw, however, the job requires a number of difficult judgments. First, we need to be careful when we use a phrase such as the "risk of a company" or "average risk." When we applied the *WARR* in Chapter 10, an average-risk project meant average risk for the firm. In applying the CAPM, average-risk project meant average risk for the whole economy. There is no contradiction between the two meanings of *average risk* as long as we are careful. For example, if a firm in a risky industry finds that its typical project is riskier than projects in the economy generally, then the CAPM would assign a project risk ratio of greater than 1.0 for the firm's average-risk project.

Second, the approach we have outlined for developing unlevered risk-adjusted discount rates uses the CAPM as its foundation. This foundation has some weak spots of which we need to be aware. Critics of the CAPM point out that assumptions of the CAPM—for example, that all investors hold identical beliefs about the future and that investors can borrow and lend at a risk-free rate of interest—do not hold in practice. They argue also that the CAPM does not fully explain relationships between return and risk in financial markets.

The critics are right. But in defense of the CAPM, several points can be made. First, the model is useful for its *qualitative* insights, quite apart from its use in generating numerical answers. It gives us a useful frame of reference, or way of thinking, about the risk/return trade-off in financial markets and about how risk ought to be measured. Perhaps the greatest contribution of the CAPM has been in helping us to gain additional insights into the nature of risk and the risk/return trade-off.

Third, the difficulty of estimating a project's contribution to debt capacity should not be underestimated. Nor should we forget that there is controversy about exactly how such debt adds to the value of the firm. Our approach assumes that interest tax shields do add value to the firm, but as we discussed in Chapter 13, the effects of debt on firm value can be complex.

Despite all these difficulties, the approach offers a useful framework for calculating risk-adjusted discount rates. Although it is not the ultimate solution to establishing risk-adjusted discount rates, setting return targets allowing for differences in project risk is in most cases superior to using a single target return for all projects regardless of risk. This technique can give financial managers another way to tackle difficult problems.

Chapter

Dividend Policy

In this chapter we address the important issue of dividend policy. We will first discuss the underlying theories and concepts of dividend policy to learn how dividends affect the value of the firm. We will explore the effects of taxes, financial friction, and information, followed by a discussion of the linkages between dividends, investment decisions, debt levels, and external financing. We will learn how to actually set a firm's dividend payout ratio in practice. Finally, we will explore some of the procedural and legal questions in connection with the paying of dividends.

In the last two chapters, we examined financial-leverage policy—the choice of debt versus equity in financing a corporation. There we saw that, used prudently, some debt financing can increase the value of the firm and that managers should strive to pick the amount of leverage that will maximize the value of the firm. Now we focus our attention on the equity financing of a corporation from internal sources, with particular emphasis on the issue of dividend policy.

The **dividend decision**—is the choice between retention and investment of earnings on the one hand and the payout of earnings to shareholders as dividends on the other hand.

In addition to making investment decisions and planning the firm's financial structure, a firm's management has a decision to make about dividend policy—whether the earnings of the firm should be retained for reinvestment in the firm or paid out to shareholders. The earnings belong 100 percent to the owners, but if retained they can be invested in future projects. If paid out in dividends, the funds are unavailable for investment inside the firm. If paid out immediately, the current return or yield to investors is increased; if retained and invested profitably, future returns to stockholders are increased. The **dividend decision** basically is a decision between return now versus larger expected returns later. In public corporations, stockholders hire managers to make this decision in their behalf. In this chapter, we will consider only dividends on common stock because preferred dividends are stipulated and fixed in amount.

> The dividend decision is a choice between return now versus larger expected returns later. Dividends are not necessary for high returns to shareholders, and dividend increases do not ensure high returns.

HOW DIVIDENDS AFFECT FIRM VALUE

Financial friction—is the cost of financial transactions, such as commissions on trading stocks and bonds, flotation costs, and the time and effort spent to analyze information concerning investment decisions.

Throughout this book our basic organizing framework has been *valuation*. We use the value of the firm as the criterion for financial-management decisions as well as the yardstick against which we judge those decisions. We found in our earlier discussion that investment decisions affect value; indeed, it is through its investment decisions that a firm creates value and, thus, benefits its shareholders. We found that financing (debt versus equity) decisions also affect value, primarily because of the tax-deductibility of interest payments on debt.

What about dividend decisions? Can a firm be made more valuable by manipulating the proportion of earnings paid out? Because this question is a complex one, let us attack it by first assuming away many of the complexities in order to understand the underlying relationships. Later, we will add back the complexities.

Assumptions that Simplify the Analysis

Information effects—are the change in stock price that results from the market's knowledge that the dividend is to change.

Taxes complicate matters, so we will begin by assuming them away. We will assume there is no **financial friction**—costs involved in financial transactions, such as commissions on the trading of stocks and bonds by investors, flotation (issue) costs on new issues of stocks and bonds by firms, and the time and effort by investors to gather and analyze information necessary to make decisions regarding their investments. Let us also assume that dividend decisions have no **information effects**; that is, the investors draw no inferences from dividend decisions regarding the firm's earning prospects, investment opportunities, or debt/equity policy. We will come back to information effects shortly.

Finance in Practice 15–1

How Important Are Dividends?

Financial managers attempt to maximize the value of the firm to shareholders. Such shareholder value is determined in financial markets and is based on shareholder expectations of future dividends and of increases in share price (capital gains). Basic questions for financial managers are: How do stock prices react to dividends? If increasing current dividends will reduce the dividends per share that shareholders expect to receive in the future, how should financial managers evaluate whether such an increase in dividends is good or bad?

In fact, one of the most controversial topics in finance is the issue of the effect of dividends on stock prices. Many argue that most investors prefer the security of dividends to the vague prospect of future capital gains. Many corporations seem to feel that the best way to win favor with the financial markets is to increase dividends every year.

Some companies go to great lengths to avoid skipping or even cutting a dividend. Both Ford and General Motors, for example, continued to pay dividends in 1980 despite record losses. Ford subsequently changed this policy in early 1982, as we will see shortly. A number of other companies on *Fortune*'s list of the 500 largest U.S. firms, including Republic Steel and Weyerhaeuser Corporation, also continued to pay dividends during 1980 while incurring losses.

Over recent years a number of studies by financial economists have raised questions about the wisdom of the apparent preoccupation with dividends on the part of corporate treasurers. With the tax rate on ordinary income higher than that on capital gains, investors should prefer greater capital gains to dividends if given a choice. As long as a firm can reinvest internally at rates of return higher than those available to investors outside in the financial markets, the firm should retain the funds and reinvest them—or so goes the argument.

Data from the 1981 *Fortune* 500 (*Fortune* magazine's list of

Table A

Firms That Paid No Dividends, 1971–1980	Total Return to Investors, 1971–80	
	Annual Average, Compounded (percent)	Rank among Other Fortune 500 Firms
NVE	41.7	2
National Semiconductor*	33.3	7
Teledyne*	32.2	9
Tosco*	28.9	17
Data General*	25.3	34
Penn Central	19.9	78
Digital Equipment*	17.4	98
Lockheed	13.9	143
Median for 500	9.4	
LTV	6.9	284
Crown Cork & Seal	4.6	342
DPF*	(5.7)	451
Memorex*	(13.9)	463

*Company has never paid a cash dividend.

the 500 largest firms) provide some ammunition to those who argue that some firms give too much emphasis to dividends. The accompanying Table A gives total-return figures for 12 firms from the *Fortune* list that paid no dividends during the period 1971–1980. Out of these 12 firms, 4 rank in the top 20 in terms of total return to shareholders, and 8 were above the median.

The accompanying Table B lists 19 companies from the 1981 *Fortune 500* that had the opposite experience: they increased their dividends every year during the period 1971–1980, yet still experienced a decline in stock price over the period. To take one example, Avon Products increased its dividend at an average rate of

Table B

Firms That Increased Their Dividends, 1971–1980	Average Annual Rate of Growth in Cash Dividends Compounded, 1971–80 (percent)	Decline in Stock Price, 1970–80 (percent)	Total Return to Investors, 1970–80	
			Annual Average, Compounded (percent)	Rank among Other Fortune 500 Firms
Burroughs	26.6	(1.4)	1.2	398
Brunswick	24.7	(17.3)	1.3	396
Economics Laboratory	16.7	(13.2)	0.8	404
Jim Walter	16.3	(16.4)	1.9	386
Georgia-Pacific	14.0	(4.1)	2.4	381
Nashua	13.5	(16.8)	1.5	392
Coca-Cola	11.8	(21.2)	1.0	402
Brockway Glass	10.4	(36.4)	0.7	411
Avon Products	10.0	(61.4)	(5.2)	449
Colgate-Palmolive	9.9	(8.1)	3.0	375
Quaker Oats	9.0	(6.4)	2.9	376
Warner-Lambert	8.7	(41.2)	(1.8)	432
ITT	8.5	(40.7)	0.5	413
Owens-Illinois	8.4	(10.5)	3.3	370
Champion Spark Plug	8.0	(11.5)	4.2	350
Heublein	7.7	(38.3)	(1.3)	428
National Service Industries	7.3	(9.3)	5.0	324
Sybron	6.8	(45.4)	(1.7)	431
Squibb	4.9	(17.9)	0.8	405

10 percent per year over the period, yet its stock price fell more than 60 percent. Coca-Cola's dividends grew at 11.8 percent per year, but its stock price fell 21 percent. The median return for the group of 19 firms in Table B was 1.2 percent, versus 9.4 percent for the *Fortune* 500 as a whole. These 19 firms represent the extreme cases among the group of companies that followed a policy of steady dividend increases. Of the 500 companies on the *Fortune* list, a total of 115 raised their dividends each year during 1971–1980; the median return of this group of 115 was 10.7 percent, slightly above that of the *Fortune* 500 as a whole. As the experience over the decade of the 1970s shows, increases in dividends certainly do not guarantee good returns for shareholders.

There are signs that attitudes toward paying high dividends are changing. The median dividend-payout ratio of the 400 companies in the Standard & Poors industrial stock index has fallen from 59.2 percent of earnings in 1970 to 40 percent in 1980. In 1984, this median payout ratio averaged 43 percent. The reason for this decline is not that corporate treasurers have come to believe that dividends do not matter. Among the other significant forces at work producing pressures for lower payouts is inflation, which increases a firm's reliance on external financing and makes increased retention attractive. But the academic studies of the topic, along with data such as that from *Fortune*, do raise the question of whether dividends are as important a factor in stock prices as some believe. Certainly the data in Tables A and B demonstrate that dividends are not necessary for high returns to shareholders.

Source: "Fresh Evidence that Dividends Don't Matter," *Fortune*, May 4, 1981, pp. 351–54. Copyright © 1981 by *Fortune* Magazine. Reprinted by permission.

In our simplified world of no taxes, friction, or information effects, shareholders would be indifferent between dividends and capital gains. Shareholders would wish the firm to undertake all attractive investment opportunities—defined as projects with positive net present values. Such attractive opportunities promise returns greater than those available to investors outside the firm. Hence, the shareholder prefers to forgo a dividend now in order to receive a larger dividend in the future, larger by more than enough to compensate for time and risk.

If internal funds were insufficient to finance all attractive projects, the firm would issue new securities, incurring no issue costs in the process. In the opposite case, when internal funds were more than adequate to undertake all attractive projects, the excess would be paid out to shareholders as dividends. In this case, payout would be preferable to retention because the firm, having exhausted all attractive investment opportunities, could invest the remaining funds only at rates below what shareholders themselves could earn outside. Note that under our assumptions, no costs are incurred in paying the dividend. If the firm erred and paid out too much, it would simply issue new securities to get the funds back. It would incur no costs in this process either.

A **residual**—in earnings is the amount of earnings available for retention or distribution as dividends after all desirable investment opportunities are undertaken and after a target debt/equity ratio has been reached.

In our simple taxless and frictionless world, the firm treats dividends as a **residual**. Investment policy is king because the firm creates value through its investment decisions. Each year, the firm undertakes all attractive investments, issuing new securities if necessary in order to finance them. Where earnings and investment opportunities vary from year to year, as they do in practice, the firm's dividend would also be highly variable from year to year. Such variations would cause no discomfort to investors in our hypothetical world, because they could alter their investment portfolios as often as they wish at no cost to themselves either in time or money. If they were dissatisfied with a particular firm's dividend payout, they would simply sell its shares and buy those of another firm whose policy is more to their liking.

> **In a simplified world of no taxes, friction, or information effects, shareholders would be indifferent between dividends and capital gains, and the firm would treat dividends as a residual.**

Dividend policy in a simplified world is straightforward: pay out what funds are left after making all attractive investments. In practice, taxes, friction, and information effects do exist. The purpose of trying to analyze the problem in the absence of factors known to exist is to isolate these factors as the ones that matter.

Before leaving our hypothetical world, let us point out that at the time a dividend is paid, we would expect the price of a share to fall by exactly the amount of the dividend. For example, suppose a shareholder pays $60 for a share of stock that is going to pay a $10 per share dividend immediately. In essence, the shareholder is paying $50 for any ownership benefits that the stock will produce after the $10 dividend payment, and paying $10 for the dividend. Immediately after the dividend payment, the shareholder has a stock worth only $50—the value of the future benefits of stock ownership. The shareholder still has $60 of value ($10 in hand from the dividend and $50 worth of stock), but the stock price has dropped from $60 to $50. Hence, when we say that dividend policy does not affect firm value in our hypothetical world, strictly speaking we mean that it does not affect shareholder wealth. We will have more to say later in this chapter about the price behavior of common stock upon payment of a dividend.

Tax Effects

Let us now reintroduce taxes in our analysis of dividend policy. Here, we will focus on the *personal* taxes paid by investors, and not on taxes paid by the firm. Investors pay taxes both on dividends and on capital gains resulting from appreciation in market price. If both were taxed at the same rate, personal taxes would introduce no bias. Other factors being equal, shareholders would wish management to undertake all attractive investments and to pay out any funds left over.

In practice, dividends and capital gains are not taxed at the same rates. Under present tax laws, the capital-gains tax rate for most individuals is much lower than the rate on ordinary income, which is the rate applicable to dividends. This *differential* in personal tax rates induces a strong bias in favor of retention as opposed to the payment of dividends. In addition, capital-gains taxes are paid only upon sale of the stock and, thus, may be deferred, whereas taxes on dividends accrue in the year that the dividend is received.

> **The difference between the tax treatment of capital gains and the tax treatment of income results in a bias on the part of shareholders toward retention of earnings for reinvestment as opposed to payment of dividends.**

Consider, for example, a firm having investment opportunities with expected returns exactly equal to the required rates—that is, equal to shareholders' opportunity rates outside the firm. With no tax differential between capital gains and ordinary income, investors would be indifferent between retention and payout (still assuming no transaction costs). With capital gains taxed at a lower rate, investors would be better off under retention, taking all their return in the form of price appreciation. Those shareholders needing current income simply would sell a portion of their holdings periodically, incurring no transaction costs.

For shareholders who pay taxes—as most *individual* shareholders do—the tax differential creates a preference for retention when other factors are equal. However, not all shareholders pay taxes. Pension trusts, tax-exempt foundations, and some individuals pay no taxes at all. Present tax laws permit shareholders to exclude from taxation the first $100 in dividends. Corporations, such as insurance companies, pay federal income taxes on only 15 percent of their dividend income. For these firms, there is a tax bias in the opposite direction, for they are taxed on all capital gains.

Although individual shareholders outnumber institutional holders, the proportion of total market value owned by institutions has increased markedly in recent years. Although fewer in number, institutional holders may exert more influence on market prices because they have greater analytical resources and do more trading.

Overall, it is difficult to determine the net effect of the bias resulting from the differential tax rates on ordinary income and capital gains. The effect likely varies from firm to firm, depending on the makeup of shareholder groups. We can conclude that the tax bias is potentially significant and should be taken into account by management in setting policy for its firm.

Tax laws change. There were major changes in the tax code in 1981, 1982, and 1984, and subsequently Congress has been considering even more radical changes. One major area of discussion has been the possible elimination of the favorable tax treatment of capital gains. If tax regulations do change significantly the relationship

between taxation of ordinary income and capital gains, the tax bias in dividend decisions will be affected.

Financial-Friction Effects

Having reintroduced taxes, let us now reintroduce financial friction. One element of
friction is commissions on purchases and sales of securities. Such commissions are
paid to brokers for executing the transactions and handling related bookkeeping. In
percentage terms, commissions vary inversely with the size of the transaction, from 1
percent to 1.5 percent on a transaction of several thousand dollars up to 10 percent or
more on transactions of less than $100.

Such commissions tend to exert a bias in favor of payout rather than retention for
some shareholders. Shareholders can no longer sell a portion of their holdings without
cost when they need cash. In addition to commissions, the necessity of selling small
amounts of stock periodically is inconvenient and involves time and effort. Reevalua-
tion of holdings made necessary by periodic sales also involves effort. Taken together,
commissions and these inconvenience costs may be significant on small periodic sales.
In such cases, other factors being equal, shareholders needing income would prefer
the payment of at least some dividend.

These same commissions may exert a bias in favor of retention rather than payout
for other shareholders who do not desire current income. For example, individuals
with high salaries may be investing in stocks to accumulate wealth for future retirement because their current salaries provide more than enough money for their current
needs. In such a case, individuals may prefer the company to retain funds rather than
pay out dividends that individuals will then have to reinvest (with the resultant transactions costs and payment of further tax on the dividends).

Flotation costs—are the
cash costs associated with
the issuance of a
company's new long-term
debt or stock issue.

A second type of transaction cost is incurred in the issuance of new securities.
Flotation costs, which are the compensation of investment bankers for assisting in
issuing the securities, can be significant. Given such costs, a firm no longer can err in
calculating funds available for dividends and expect to get the money back later at no
cost by selling securities.

> Some elements of friction exert a bias in favor of higher payout, while other
> frictions bias toward retention and lower payout.

Given taxes and friction, we see that a firm's dividend policy does matter and that
shareholders are not likely to be indifferent toward it. The existence of transaction
costs to shareholders—commissions as well as inconvenience costs—suggests the desirability of minimizing the transactions shareholders must make. The existence of
flotation costs on new issues suggests the need to avoid overpaying in one year and
selling securities the next. When friction costs are incurred unnecessarily, shareholder
wealth is adversely affected. We will come back to these points again later.

Information Effects

In practice, there is ample evidence that announcements of dividend actions by firms
affect the market prices of their shares. Often, the magnitude of the effect goes beyond

what can be attributed to friction costs. In the second quarter of 1974, for example, Consolidated Edison, an electric utility serving New York City, omitted its regular quarterly dividend of $0.45 per share. The price of its stock immediately dropped from $18 to about $12 and declined to $8 within two weeks. How can we explain this behavior? In terms of information effects, the dividend action sent a message to investors that motivated them to revise sharply downward their estimate of the value of Consolidated Edison common stock.

What was the nature of the message? For some time prior to its dividend cut, Consolidated Edison and other electric utilities had been encountering increasing financial difficulties because of the impact of inflation on costs, the reluctance of regulatory officials to grant rate increases, and pressures to take expensive measures to protect the environment. Share prices had been declining as the outlook for utility earnings worsened. The omission of the first-quarter (1974) dividend was taken by investors to mean that the board of directors and management expected things to get even worse. In short, investors thought that those in the best position to know were saying that things did not look good. The impact on share prices was immediate and dramatic.

A similar thing happened to ITT Corporation in July 1984. Late on the afternoon of July 10, ITT's chairman, Rand Araskog, stunned Wall Street by announcing a cut in the company's dividend by nearly two thirds, from $2.76 per share to $1.00 annually. The next morning, the opening of trading in ITT stock was delayed for more than an hour, and by the end of the day ITT stock had lost nearly a third of its value. As in the Consolidated Edison case, the dividend cut sent a message to the market that things did not look good, and ITT's stock reacted immediately.[1]

Contrast the above examples with the experience of RCA Corporation in the spring of 1982. On March 3, RCA announced a cut in its quarterly dividend from $0.50 per share to $0.225. RCA had been paying a dividend regularly since 1937, and this was the first time in the company's history that its board of directors had reduced it. While the dividend was cut in half, RCA's stock fell only $1 per share on the announcement, from $18 to $17. Why was the reaction in RCA's stock price so much milder than that in the cases of ITT or Consolidated Edison? The answer is that the RCA cut was not a surprise. Financial analysts familiar with the RCA situation had anticipated the cut, and the effects of a prospective cut already had been reflected in RCA's stock price prior to the announcement. One analyst commented that the cut was a "sound management decision."[2]

While RCA cut its dividend in half during early 1982, the Ford Motor Company omitted its first quarter 1982 dividend entirely. In July of 1980, Ford's directors had cut the quarterly payment from $1 to $0.30, but the 1982 action constituted the first time the dividend had been omitted since Ford had become a public company in 1956. Following a temporary halt in trading, Ford's shares the day of the announcement closed down $0.50. As in the RCA case, the reaction was mild in relation to the change in the dividend, which was cut by 100 percent. The reason for the mild reaction was the same—the market had already anticipated the action. One analyst commented that the action "shows some good hard realism by Ford management."[3]

---

[1]"The Troubles That Led To ITT's Dividend Shocker," *Business Week*, July 23, 1984.

[2]The RCA dividend cut was reported in the *Wall Street Journal* of March 4, 1982.

[3]*Wall Street Journal*, January 15, 1982.

Let us consider a different, and this time hypothetical, situation. Consider a firm, ABC Corporation, that historically has paid out a significant portion of earnings and has increased its dividend payment as earnings have grown. ABC is known to have under development a new family of products that appear quite promising but that will require considerable capital investment. Suddenly ABC's directors announce that, in order to conserve cash, dividends no longer will be increased each quarter and may even be reduced. What impact might be expected on the firm's stock price? It is possible that investors would interpret the announcement as evidence that investment opportunities did indeed look very attractive. Its stock price might well rise upon the announcement that dividends no longer will be increased each quarter.

Contrast ABC's situation with that of Consolidated Edison. Both firms announced a dividend lower than that previously expected by investors. In both cases conserving cash was the immediate objective. Why did the stock prices in the two cases behave in exactly opposite ways? *Investors drew different inferences* regarding the firms' respective investment opportunities. In Consolidated Edison's case, the dividend action signaled a situation worse than previously envisioned; in ABC's case, the dividend action signaled a better situation.

Consider another hypothetical case, that of DEF Corporation. DEF has a history of above-average return on investment and above-average earnings growth, coupled with a very low dividend payout averaging about 5 percent of earnings. Suddenly DEF's board of directors announces that the payout will be increased to approximately 25 percent of earnings. How might the stock price react? It might well fall if investors inferred from the dividend action that DEF's management believed it was running out of high-return investment opportunities.

In the ABC and DEF cases described above as well as in the ITT and Consolidated Edison cases, a common element is that the dividend action was unexpected; that is, the change in policy was a surprise. A change in policy that had been anticipated—as in the cases of RCA and Ford—likely would have had little or no impact on price, because such impact would have already been felt. Where the action is unexpected, investors draw an inference from the dividend action about the firm's investment and earnings prospects. As a result, investors revise their estimates of the value of the firm's stock, and stock price moves quickly to a new equilibrium level.

> **A decision to cut dividends can have different effects on share price, depending on the inference drawn by investors concerning the firm's investment opportunities. A surprise change in dividend policy tends to have a greater effect than an anticipated change.**

Such a role for the information effects of dividend announcements suggests that managers possess inside information which is signaled to the market by means of dividends.[4]

What conclusions can we draw about the information effects of dividend actions? We can say that the magnitude of the information effect can be quite large, but what

---

[4]There is a developing financial literature on dividends as signals. Recently work in this area has begun to integrate theoretically both the information and tax effects of dividends. See K. John and J. Williams, "Dividends, Dilution, and Taxes: A Signaling Equilibrium," *Journal of Finance*, September 1985, pp. 1053–70.

about the direction? Do dividend increases always lead to an increase in stock price? Not always. In one of the examples above, a dividend increase led to a drop in stock price, and in another case a dividend reduction led to a price increase. We can make no general statement at all regarding the direction of the information effect of a dividend decision. It depends on the inferences drawn by investors, and many different inferences are possible.

The empirical evidence regarding the effects of dividend actions on stock price is mixed. Most recent studies find a relationship between dividends and value, but expert opinions differ as to the reasons. Some researchers have concluded that the effect is primarily tax-related—that is, resulting from the difference between ordinary income and capital-gains tax rates. These studies conclude that "tax clienteles" exist—that high-payout firms tend to attract low-tax-bracket investors, and vice versa. They conclude further that payment of dividends in lieu of capital gains through retention of earnings has a negative effect on firm value.

A **tax shelter**—is an investment opportunity that protects the investor from paying some or all of the taxes the investor would otherwise have to pay on the funds invested.

Other researchers believe that the relationship between dividends and stock value can be explained almost entirely in terms of information effects. This argument rests on the proposition that investors can avoid taxes on dividend income by means of various **tax shelters** permitted under the tax code. If the effective tax rate on dividends really is low, then the observed impact of dividends on stock values must operate through information effects.[5]

HOW INVESTMENT, FINANCING, AND DIVIDEND DECISIONS ARE INTERRELATED

It is apparent from our earlier discussion that dividend, investment, and financing decisions are interdependent.[6] Funds paid out in dividends are unavailable for investment, unless replaced through external financing. We will explore these interdependencies in more depth with an example.

> **Dividend, investment, and financing decisions are interdependent. Changes in one of these policy variables cannot be made without affecting the other policy variables.**

[5]For research that concludes that the effect of dividends on value is primarily by means of taxes, see R. H. Litzenberger and K. Ramaswamy, "Dividends, Short-Selling Restrictions, Tax-Induced Investor Clienteles, and Market Equilibrium," *Journal of Finance* 35 (May 1980): 469–82. For an opposing argument—namely, that tax effects are minimal and that the dividend impact operates primarily by means of information effects, see M. Miller and M. Scholes, "Dividends and Taxes," *Journal of Financial Economics* 6 (December 1978): 333–64 and "Dividends and Taxes: Some Empirical Evidence," *Journal of Political Economy*, December 1982, pp. 1118–41.

[6]Here we discuss basic interdependencies introduced because the uses of funds must always be equal to the sources of funds; that is, investment must be financed. There are also fundamental economic interdependencies that may exist among decisions. For example, a particular investment may have a special effect on a firm's debt capacity, which may affect the value of the investment proposal itself. In Appendix 14A, we discussed one way of taking financing mix into account in dealing with investment decisions. For a further discussion, see S. C. Myers, "Interactions of Corporate Financing and Investment Decisions—Implications for Capital Budgeting," *Journal of Finance*, March 1974, pp. 433–43.

Table 15–1

The Interdependence of Dividend, Investment, and Financing Decisions at a Hypothetical Firm (million of dollars)

	No Residual Policy 1	No External Equity Investment Residual Policy 2	Debt/Equity Residual Policy 3	Dividend Residual Policy 4
Before external financing				
Debt	$ 300	$ 300	$ 300	$ 300
Equity	$1,000	$1,000	$1,000	$1,000
Debt/equity ratio	0.30	0.30	0.30	0.30
Investment opportunities (Net Present Value > 0)[a]	**$ 100**	**$ 62**	**$ 100**	**$ 100**
Earnings	$ 120	$ 120	$ 120	$ 120
Dividend-Payout ratio[a]	**0.60**	**0.60**	**0.60**	**0.36**
Dividends	$ 72	$ 72	$ 72	$ 43
Earnings retained	$ 48	$ 48	$ 48	$ 77
External financing				
Debt	$ 23	$ 14*	$ 52	$ 23
Equity	$ 29	$ 0	$ 0	$ 0
After external financing				
Debt	$ 323	$ 314	$ 352	$ 323
Equity	$1,077	$1,048	$1,048	$1,077
Debt/equity ratio (optimum = 0.30)[a]	**0.30**	**0.30**	**0.34**	**0.30**

*Since $48 million of new equity is available (retained), the firm issues 0.3 ($48 million) = $14 million (rounded) of new debt to maintain its debt/equity ratio of 0.3.
Note: Policy variables appear in bold type.

The dividend-payout ratio—is the percentage of earnings a firm pays out as dividends.

Suppose a firm has attractive new investment opportunities—defined as opportunities having a positive net present value—requiring an aggregate outlay of $100 million. These opportunities are in addition to replacement projects, which we will assume exactly equal depreciation charges. The firm has decided that the appropriate debt/equity ratio, given the nature of its business and its operating risk, is 0.30. This ratio implies that 23 percent of financing is done by debt and 77 percent by equity (23 percent/77 percent = 0.30). Historically, it has paid out 60 percent of its earnings in dividends. Its earnings for the period just ended were $120 million.

The firm, thus, has three policy variables: the amount of new investment, the debt/equity ratio, and the **dividend-payout ratio**. The data are listed in Table 15–1. In column (1), the firm treats all three decisions as active; that is, it sets each at the desired level. To meet its goal of paying out 60 percent of earnings in the form of dividends, the firm must pay dividends of 0.6($120 million) = $72 million, leaving $120 million − $72 million = $48 million of internally generated equity funds for investment. The remaining $52 million for investment ($100 million − $48 million = $52 million) must be raised by issuing new securities. To maintain its policy of financing investments with 23 percent debt, (0.23)$100 million = $23 million of these securities must be debt. The remaining $29 million will be equity. Note that the internal equity funds of $48 million plus the newly issued equity of $29 million provides a total of $77 million of equity. Thus, by raising $52 million in new funds by issuing securities—$23 million in debt and $29 million in equity—the firm is able to undertake investments totaling $100 million, pay dividends of $72 million, and reach its target debt/equity ratio of 0.30.

What if the firm decides it does not want to sell new stock? It can do so by adopting one of three policies. It can forgo some of its investment opportunities, as shown in column (2) and thereby maintain its dividend at $72 million and its target debt/equity ratio at 0.30. Alternatively, it can increase its debt ratio to 0.34, as shown in column (3), and thereby maintain its dividend at $72 million and its investment level of $100 million. Or, finally, it can cut its dividend from $72 million to $43 million, as shown in column (4), and reduce its payout ratio to 36 percent.

Which should the firm do? Our theories tell us that forgoing profitable investments is a poor choice. Through its investments, a firm implements its commercial strategy, the pursuit of which is the reason for its existence. When a firm passes up an investment opportunity having a net present value of X, shareholders in principle are poorer by X.

Suppose we allow the debt/equity mix to be the slack variable. In principle, an optimal debt/equity ratio exists. In practice, finding it is difficult, and operating a few percentage points on either side may not make much difference. However, if the optimal ratio is thought to be 0.30, then operating at a different ratio is the result of a conscious decision to follow a less than optimal debt policy.

If investment and debt/equity decisions both affect firm value, a case exists for treating both as active variables rather than as residuals. In order to do so, we must either cut the dividend or sell stock. Put another way, to avoid cutting the dividend, we must finance a part of it—that is, $29 million of the total desired dividend of $72 million—by selling stock. In effect, we sell stock and use the proceeds to pay dividends.[7] Let us examine this option in more detail.

Another way to describe this option is to pay a dividend and then sell stock in order to maintain the desired level of investment. Either way, the firm is paying equity money out at the same time it is raising it through sale of new stock.

One argument against this option is that it incurs flotation costs in connection with selling stock. If the dividend were reduced and the stock not sold, the flotation costs would not be incurred.

Another argument involves taxes. Suppose a firm sells common stock to existing shareholders and uses the proceeds to pay dividends to those same shareholders. The shareholders pay income taxes on the dividend, but because of their additional capital contribution, their capital-gain tax liability is reduced. If capital-gain and ordinary-income tax rates were the same, the transaction would not increase the shareholders' total tax liability. However, the timing of the tax payments would differ, because the tax on a dividend would be due in the year paid, whereas the capital-gains tax is deferred until the stock is sold.

---

[7]For a good discussion of interdependencies and problems of conflicting management policies regarding growth, capital structure, dividends, and new equity issues, see R. C. Higgins, "How Much Growth Can a Firm Afford?" *Financial Management* 6 (Fall 1977): 7–16. For an analysis of the impact of inflation on growth, see R. Higgins, "Sustainable Growth Under Inflation," *Financial Management* 10 (Autumn 1981): 36–40.

Finance in Practice 15–2

Interdependencies of Financing and Investment

Ford Motor Company's actions during 1980 and 1981 provide a good example of the dilemma posed by the interactions of major policy decisions. In the face of a seriously deteriorating market share, Ford planned capital outlays totaling $16 billion over the period 1981–85. Issuing common stock was not attractive to Ford's management because the company had lost more than $1 billion during the first three quarters of 1980, and taking such a record to the financial markets would not be easy. Debt also looked unpromising because Ford's bonds had been downgraded twice during 1980 by the Standard & Poors rating service. In the face of these constraints, Ford chose to do three things: reduce its dividend,

reduce its liquidity, and borrow heavily short-term. During the period September 1979 to May 1981, Ford borrowed nearly $2 billion at rates in the neighborhood of 20 percent. Thus, Ford resolved the dilemma in favor of its capital-investment program, but it did opt to maintain some dividend payout during 1981 even at the expense of higher borrowing. Ford subsequently cut out its dividend entirely in January 1982, as noted in the chapter.

General Motors resolved a similar dilemma in the spring of 1981 by postponing parts of its investment plan. GM announced in May of that year that it was deferring for at least a year construction of a $500 million automobile-assembly plant in Kansas City, Missouri, and putting off for a year a decision on whether to build a plant at Flint, Michigan. The company explained that these plans were part of an overall $40 billion, 5-year capital-spend-

ing program and that all of the spending eventually would take place, although portions would be delayed.

GM's decision to postpone parts of its capital program was made against a backdrop of its first full-year loss in nearly 6 decades, a loss of $763 million in 1980. At the same time that the postponement of spending plans was announced, in May 1981, GM's board of directors voted to pay the regular quarterly dividend of $0.60 per share. GM's board and management evidently concluded that in the face of the cash shortage caused by the 1980 loss, maintaining the regular dividend had a higher priority than keeping the capital-investment program on schedule.

Sources: J. Carson-Parker, ''The Capital Cloud Over Smoke-Stack America,'' *Fortune*, February 23, 1981, pp. 70–80; ''GM Says Cash Crunch Is Forcing Delay In Parts of $40 Billion, 5-Year Outlay Plan,'' *Wall Street Journal*, May 5, 1981.

Because (at least at present) the capital-gains tax rate is lower, shareholders wind up paying more tax if stock is sold and dividends paid than they would if neither action were taken. If dividends are paid first and then stock sold to replace the funds, the effect is the same. Selling the stock to new shareholders also produces the same outcome. In all cases, the dividend-plus-stock-sale alternative, as compared to doing neither, leaves existing shareholders worse off by an amount equal to the dividend times the difference between the capital-gain and ordinary-income tax rates. Note that the firm's investment level is the same under both alternatives, so the tax and cost issues are the only differences. As noted earlier, many shareholders pay no taxes, and for them the tax effect does not apply. Others may be in low marginal tax brackets or may be protected by the $100 exclusion. However, to the extent that shareholders do pay taxes, they clearly are hurt by a policy of payout and offsetting sale of stock.

Given the effects of taxes and flotation costs, why would a firm engage in such a policy? Sometimes a change in commercial strategy may call for a much higher level of investment. The firm may be reluctant to cut its dividend abruptly enough to avoid some sales of stock.

Another class of companies that regularly engage in the payout/stock sale policy are utilities. However, utilities are a special case because they are regulated monopolies. It may be that the payout/stock sale policy follows from the desire of regulators to regularly subject utility management to the scrutiny and discipline of the financial markets as a way of promoting efficiency. To this end, regulators may encourage payout of a substantial portion of earnings and simultaneous financing of new investment through issues of new securities.

Clearly, certain factors may justify a payout/stock sale policy. In the case of utilities, management and regulators may feel that the extra costs of taxes and flotation are justified. For other types of firms, the costs and benefits of such a practice should be examined carefully.

SETTING DIVIDEND POLICY

We have laid the groundwork for our analysis of dividend policy with our discussion of theory and interdependence. Let us now turn to specific factors that a firm should consider in establishing dividend policy.[8]

Internal Investment Opportunities

From our earlier discussions, it is apparent that opportunities to invest are a major consideration in setting dividend policy. Other considerations aside, when the firm has opportunities to earn returns greater than those available to shareholders outside the firm, retention and reinvestment are appropriate.

Earnings, Cash Flow, and Liquidity

The firm's ability to generate earnings and cash flow also is a factor in determining dividend policy. When other factors are equal, the more profitable is the firm, the more earnings are available for payout. Dividends are paid with cash, so at any given moment a firm's ability to pay a dividend depends on its cash and liquid-asset position and its capacity for short-term borrowing.

External Financing Needs

In a world with taxes, inflation effects, and transaction costs, a firm must plan its program of external financing. For any firm there exists an optimal debt/equity ratio that depends in part on the nature of its business and its operating risk. That ratio should be established as a target. When not at its target debt/equity mix, the firm should take steps to reach it. In our example in Table 15–1, we found dividend payout to be interdependent with the target debt/equity ratio, actual debt/equity ratio, and

---

[8]For an analysis of industry influence on dividend policy and a comparison of dividend policy in various industries, see A. Michel, "Industry Influence on Dividend Policy," *Financial Management* 8 (Autumn 1979): 22–26.

Table 15–2

Patterns Likely to Influence the Credibility of Dividend Policies for Two Firms Over a 5-Year Period

	Firm A			Firm B		
Year	Earnings per Share	Dividend	Payout Ratio (percent)	Earnings per Share	Dividend	Payout Ratio (percent)
1	$1.38	$0.72	0.52	$1.26	$0.72	0.57
2	$1.62	$0.72	0.44	$1.10	$0.72	0.65
3	$1.92	$0.96	0.50	$1.32	$0.96	0.73
4	$2.08	$0.96	0.46	$1.12	$0.96	0.86
5	$2.46	$1.20	0.49	$1.20	$1.20	1.00

external financing requirements. As a result, changes in dividend policy are one means of altering (or maintaining) a firm's debt/equity ratio.

Earnings Record and Prospects

Of major importance to dividend policy is the firm's earnings record, its prospects for future earnings, and the market's perceptions of those prospects. Both the growth trend and the stability of earnings are also important. To be credible the dividend pattern must be consistent with the earnings pattern. Consider the data for the two firms listed in Table 15–2. Firm A's earnings have shown steady growth, and its dividend policy has been in line with that growth. Investors are likely to feel confident that the historical dividend pattern will be continued—subject, of course, to firm A's ability to continue its growth in earnings. Firm B's earnings, on the other hand, have been erratic around a flat trend, while the dividend has been steadily increased. In view of the earnings record, investors are likely to doubt B's ability to continue the historical pattern of steady dividend increases. Firm B's dividend pattern does not appear to be sustainable. The actual dividend payments in the two cases are identical, but A's pattern is more credible.

Clientele

An **investor clientele**—is a group of investors who are attracted to a certain stock investment because of a particular characteristic, such as the company's dividend policy.

There is some evidence that different dividend policies attract different types of investors, or different **investor clienteles**. This argument suggests that firms with high and stable payouts attract investors who prefer a large proportion of their total return in current income. Such investors may well depend on dividends for current consumption and, therefore, may prefer a dividend that is stable and predictable. On the other hand, because of the differential in tax rates on capital gains and dividends, low-payout growth companies might attract investors interested mainly in capital gains. In short, investors attempt to match their own income needs and tax brackets with the magnitude and stability of the firm's payout, with the capital-gains tax differential an extra incentive. The clientele argument is plausible and consistent with much of the available evidence.

Of what significance is the clientele argument? One might argue that if the firm's clientele were used to a particular dividend policy, that policy should not be changed. Most firms for which dividend policy is important are publicly traded. If the firm wished to change its dividend policy, those shareholders not satisfied with the new policy could simply sell their shares and buy those of another firm with a policy suited to their needs. The firm would lose one clientele and attract another.[9] However, in making portfolio shifts, shareholders incur transaction costs and also costs in time and effort to gather and analyze information and make decisions. Thus, because of friction in the markets, a change in dividend policy can impose costs on shareholders that are real and potentially significant in magnitude, especially to small shareholders. As a result, companies should consider carefully changes in dividend policy.

Legal and Regulatory Restrictions

Certain institutional investors, in particular insurance companies, are subject to a variety of legal and regulatory restrictions with respect to their investment policies. In some states, laws or regulations stipulate that for a firm's stock to qualify for certain institutional portfolios, an uninterrupted dividend record is required over some minimum number of years. Some states prohibit certain institutions, such as savings banks and certain trustees, from holding the bonds of a corporation unless there exists an uninterrupted dividend record on the underlying common stock over some minimum period. Omission of a dividend by a firm, thus, might result in removal of its stock or bonds or both from the legal list of investments of some institutions. It is difficult to judge the true significance of such a development, but it is plausible that institutional interest in a firm's securities may give it a broader, more liquid market and facilitate new issues of securities.

Universities and other endowed educational institutions sometimes are restricted in their use of capital gains on their securities. Since such institutions are generally not taxed, they might have a preference for stocks with a high payout.

Control

In some cases, control of the firm may be a factor in setting dividend policy. Suppose an individual or group owns a significant interest in a firm, the remainder of the stock being publicly held. The higher is the payout, the greater is the chance that a subsequent issue of common stock might be required—perhaps because of a change in commercial strategy requiring greater investment. Those in control might prefer to minimize the likelihood of a requirement for new outside capital by opting for low payout and a high liquid-asset position.

This argument applies also to firms that, because of size or reputation or other factors, might find their access to public equity markets limited. The lower is the payout, the less likely it is that outside capital will be needed.

---

[9]Evidence of a clientele effect is given by E. J. Elton and M. J. Gruber, "Marginal Stockholder Tax Rates and the Clientele Effect," *Review of Economics and Statistics* 52 (February 1970): 68–74; and R. R. Pettit, "Taxes, Transactions Costs and the Clientele Effect of Dividends," *Journal of Finance* 5 (December 1977): 419–36. Much weaker evidence is found by W. G. Lewellen *et al.*, "Some Direct Evidence on the Dividend Clientele Phenomenon," *Journal of Finance* 33 (December 1978): 1385–1400.

DIVIDEND-POLICY GOALS

We now have developed a basic framework of analysis and have discussed the major factors pertinent to setting dividend policy. No two firms are exactly alike, and the policy for a firm must be tailored to its own unique circumstances. Let us attempt, however, to set down some general policy goals that are applicable to most firms.

A Long-Run Residual

It is apparent that dividend policy depends on many factors that are often confusing and sometimes conflicting. In such situations, we must look to basic principles for guidance. What are those basic principles?

1. We know that valuation is the central organizing framework and that financial management decisions should be analyzed in terms of their effect on the value of the firm rather than on earnings or other yardsticks.
2. We know that it is through its investments that the firm executes its commercial strategy. Investments create value, and when a firm forgoes an attractive investment, shareholders incur an opportunity loss.
3. We know that the debt/equity mix also affects the value of the firm.
4. We know that friction exists in the system and that real costs are incurred when the firm issues securities and when shareholders make changes in their holdings.
5. We know that dividend, investment, and financing decisions are interdependent, and that tradeoffs must be made.

We found in our discussion of interdependence earlier in this chapter that the firm must either treat one of the three basic decisions as a residual or adopt a policy of offsetting dividend payments by selling new common stock. Put another way, the firm cannot actively manage all three policy variables unless it is willing to pay dividends and sell stock simultaneously.

Let us examine these trade-offs in a long-run setting. As a matter of *long-run policy*, does it make sense for the firm to plan consciously to forgo attractive investments or to operate at a nonoptimal debt/equity ratio or to finance dividend payments by selling stock? We conclude that none of these options is sensible as a long-run policy. The policy that avoids all of the above choices is to treat dividends as a *long-run residual*.

> **Treating dividends as a long-run residual allows the firm to avoid forgoing attractive investments or adopting unsound financing plans.**

Short-Run Constraints

In the short run, however, the firm faces a number of constraints that make a strictly residual dividend policy not feasible. Since investment requirements and earnings in most firms vary from year to year, treating dividends as a residual each year is likely to lead to a highly variable dividend that may even fall to zero in some years. From our earlier discussion, we know that a variable dividend is undesirable. Investors would have a difficult time interpreting the frequent changes in the dividend, and information effects likely would lead to wide fluctuations in stock price. Even if they averaged out over time, such fluctuations would benefit some shareholders at the expense of others who would be forced to sell at low points; therefore, it would be a highly unfair policy. In addition, fluctuations in price and dividends would cause shifts in the shareholder group, or clientele, that could impose significant costs on those shareholders who are induced by that policy to alter their holdings. If the residual policy dictated a dividend of zero in any year, the firm's dividend record would be broken and regulatory restrictions might force removal of the firm's securities from the approved buy lists of some institutions.

A Long-Run Residual Managed in the Short Run

Although a policy of treating dividends as a residual in the short run is unworkable, a workable compromise is to treat dividends as a long-run residual, but to constrain it in the short run in order to avoid undesirable variations in payout. To implement such an approach requires financial planning over a fairly long time horizon—probably 5 years.[10]

First, investment requirements must be estimated, with the estimate providing for all attractive opportunities that the firm expects to face. Next, funds expected to be available internally from earnings and depreciation should be estimated. A target debt/equity ratio then should be set based on the firm's operating risk and other relevant considerations. Given investment requirements, funds from internal sources, and a target debt/equity ratio, the firm can then determine whether, over the planning horizon, residual funds will be available for payout. If so, the ratio of residual funds to total earnings after taxes becomes the firm's **long-run target payout ratio**.

If no residual earnings remain after financing is provided for all attractive investment opportunities, the above approach suggests a policy of no dividend at all. External equity financing would be required to make up any shortfall in internal funds. Where institutional ownership of the firm's securities seems desirable, the firm might wish to compromise by paying a small token dividend with the intention of leaving it fixed over the planning horizon. Where the long-run analysis shows that residual funds will be available, the plan would prescribe dividends and no external equity financing.

The long planning horizon is necessary because the world is uncertain and not frictionless. Investment opportunities cannot be foreseen with complete accuracy each year, nor can earnings be accurately forecast each year. In effect, we plan the long-run dividend payout target based on *trend* values. Needed external financing can be planned in more economical amounts to avoid high issue costs associated with small financings. Also, the long horizon permits time to anticipate changes in commercial strategy or debt/equity policy.

The long-run target is stated in percentage terms—that is, dividends to be paid as a percentage of earnings. The short-run variability is in the *dollar* payout. Hence, our objective should be to set the dollar payout so as to average out to the target percentage over the planning horizon. As earnings fluctuate from period to period, the percentage payout will fluctuate. In some years, the percentage payout will be below the target,

A firm's **long-run target payout ratio**—is the ratio of residual funds to total earnings after taxes over a relatively long planning horizon.

---

[10]The approach suggested here draws on the work of Robert C. Higgins, "The Corporate Dividend-Saving Decision," *Journal of Financial and Quantitative Analysis* 7 (March 1972): 1527–42.

Table 15–3

Plan for Treating Dividends as a Long-Run Residual at the ABC Corporation (millions of dollars)

			Year				5-Year
	0	1	2	3	4	5	Total
Earnings	—	$ 7.00	$ 5.00	$ 3.00	$ 6.50	$ 3.50	$25.00
Dividends	—	$ 1.92	$ 1.92	$ 1.92	1 1.92	$ 1.92	$ 9.60
Earnings retained	—	$ 5.08	$ 3.08	$ 1.08	$ 4.58	$ 1.58	$15.40
Total equity	$200.00	$205.08	$208.16	$209.24	$213.82	$215.40	—
New debt	—	—	—	$ 4.60	—	—	$ 4.60
Total debt	$ 60.00	$ 60.00	$ 60.00	$ 64.60	$ 64.60	$ 64.60	—
Debt/equity ratio	0.30	0.29	0.29	0.31	0.30	0.30	—
Dividend-payout ratio	—	0.27	0.38	0.64	0.30	0.55	0.38
Funds available for investment							
Retained earnings		$ 5.08	$ 3.08	$ 1.08	$ 4.58	$ 1.58	$15.40
New debt		—	—	$ 4.60	—	—	$ 4.60
Cumulative total		$ 5.08	$ 8.16	$ 13.84	$ 18.42	$ 20.00	$20.00
Cumulative investment requirements		$ 4.00	$ 8.00	$ 12.00	$ 16.00	$ 20.00	$20.00

and in other years this percentage will be above the target. In effect, the firm saves during fat years in order to maintain the dividend during lean years.

Let us illustrate the approach with an example. We will assume that ABC Corporation, over a 5-year planning horizon, foresees investment opportunities requiring net new investment, over and above depreciation charges, of $4 million per year—or $20 million over the 5 years. This investment requirement includes plant and equipment plus additions to working capital. Aggregate earnings after taxes over the period are expected to be $25 million. We will assume that ABC Corporation is currently meeting its target debt/equity ratio of 0.30.

To finance the new investment requires that retained earnings (RE) plus new debt equal $20 million. In other words,

$$\$20 \text{ million} = \text{new debt} + RE$$

To maintain the target debt/equity ratio requires that new debt equal 30 percent of retained earnings. In other words,

$$\text{New debt} = (0.30)RE$$

Substituting the second equation into the first gives us

$$1.30 \, RE = \$20 \text{ million}$$

$$RE = \$20/1.30 = \$15.40 \text{ million,}$$

which tells us that RE over the 5 years must total $15.40 million. Subtracting this figure from total expected earnings of $25 million indicates that a total of $9.60 million can be paid in dividends over the 5 years, which is 38 percent of aggregate earnings. Spreading this total over 5 years amounts to $1.92 million per year. New debt of 0.30 × $15.40 million = $4.60 million must be raised during the period. We will assume that this debt is raised in year 3. Combining the new debt funds of $4.60 million with the retained earnings of $15 40 million gives us the $20 million that we need for new investment. Assuming that earnings vary from year to year as indicated, we can create the 5-year plan outlined in Table 15–3.

For example, in year 2 ABC Corporation expects earnings of $5 million. After paying the long-run target dividend of $1.92 million, ABC has $3.08 million of earnings retained for new investment. Adding this $3.08 million of new retained earnings to year 1's equity of $205.00 million, the total equity in year 2 is $208.16 million. Total debt is still $60 million (remember we assumed new debt would not be issued until year 3), so the debt/equity ratio has dropped to $60 million/$208.16 million = 0.29, which is slightly below the target debt/equity ratio. The dividend-payout ratio, on the other hand, is $1.92 million/$5.00 million = 0.38. In year 2, total new financing is just the $3.08 million of retained earnings (no debt was issued), which, when added to year 1's financing of $5.08 million, yields a cumulative total of $8.16 million of financing (funds available for investment) over the two-year period. This $8.16 million is sufficient to cover the cumulative investment needs of $8.00 million.

In this example, we assumed for simplicity that the firm expected a flat earnings trend, with earnings varying each year about that trend. We, therefore, held the dollar dividend constant each year. If earnings were expected to grow over time, as often would be the case, it would be desirable to modify the approach to permit a gradual increase in the dollar amount of the dividend payout over time. Given information effects, friction, and the existence of a clientele, cuts in the dollar payout are undesirable and should be avoided if at all possible. The best policy, therefore, would be a dividend that is nondecreasing in dollar terms. As earnings grow, the dividend would be raised in small steps; each step would be taken only when the probability appeared high that the dividend would not have to be cut subsequently.

Communicating the Policy

Whatever specific policies the firm adopts, it is desirable that the policy be communicated clearly to investors. Investors should not have to guess what policy management intends to follow. Investors then are better prepared to decide whether the policy suits their own preferences and needs. Good communication also reduces the chances of misinterpretation.

Changing the Dividend Policy

Given information effects, friction, and a clientele, consistency in policy is important. Erratic changes are costly and should be avoided. Sometimes, however, a policy change will become necessary—perhaps because of a change in commercial strategy, investment opportunities, or debt/equity policy. Changes in general economic conditions might also necessitate a change in policy. Or management simply might find that it had wrongly estimated one or more of the determinants of dividend policy, which in an uncertain world can happen to even the most capable and farsighted managers.

When a policy change is indicated, management should not shrink from the task. Dividend reductions are painful, but if a reduction is in the shareholders' best interests, it should be made. In such cases, communication becomes all the more important. If the reasons are sensible, investors will understand them. A dividend cut may well lead to a fall in stock price, but careful communications will increase the likelihood that stock price will adjust to the underlying economic realities.[11]

If a lower average payout became necessary, it might be possible to move to the new target gradually. Where a firm's earnings are growing, the dollar payout could be held constant and the average payout ratio allowed to decline over time. Such an approach would avoid a reduction in dollar payout, which could be inconvenient or costly to some shareholders. The policy change and the reasons for it should also be communicated to shareholders.

PROCEDURAL AND LEGAL CONSIDERATIONS IN PAYING DIVIDENDS

Each dividend payment must be declared by a vote of the board of directors. Suppose the directors of XYZ Corporation meet on Tuesday, January 21, and declare that the regular first-quarter dividend of $0.25 per share is to be paid on March 12 to all investors who hold the firm's stock on Wednesday, February 12. February 12 becomes the *record date*, and holders on that date become *holders of record*.

To account for the time required to record transfer of ownership, the major stock exchanges subtract four business days from the record date to establish the *ex-dividend date*—in this case, Thursday, February 6. Any investor purchasing XYZ stock on or before February 5 would become a holder of record on February 12 and would, therefore, receive the first-quarter dividend. Investors purchasing on February 6 and thereafter would not receive the dividend. On February 6, the stock, thus, sells *ex-dividend*. We would expect its price to drop on that date by the amount of the dividend to show that buyers that day will not receive the dividend. Testing this proposition is difficult because of the many factors, other than dividends, that affect prices. Carefully controlled empirical studies indicate that price does adjust on the ex-dividend date, but by something less than the full amount. The difference is at least in part due to the difference in tax rates on dividends and capital gains.

Once declared by the board, dividends payable become a current liability of the firm. If XYZ had 1 million shares outstanding, the accounting entries on the day of declaration would be a $250,000 credit (increase) in current liabilities and a $250,000 debit (decrease) in retained earnings. When the checks are paid, the current liability is eliminated and cash declines by $250,000. The net effect of paying the dividend is a reduction in cash and an offsetting reduction in retained earnings.

In many cases, long-term-debt and preferred-stock agreements contain restrictions on the maximum common-stock dividend that can be paid by a firm. Such covenants are designed to protect senior claim holders from excessive withdrawals by residual

---

[11]For an analysis of management attitudes about changes in dividend policy, see E. F. Fama and H. Babiak, "Dividend Policy: An Empirical Analysis," *Journal of the American Statistical Association* 63 (December 1968): 1132–61. Fama and Babiak conclude that managers generally believe that investors prefer a stable dividend policy. See also R. W. Kolb, "Predicting Dividend Changes," unpublished doctoral dissertation, School of Business Administration, University of North Carolina at Chapel Hill, 1978. Kolb found a marked reluctance among managers to cut dividends. When cuts finally were made, they tended to be large. Increases, on the other hand, tended to be small—the average increase being about 3 percent. This finding supports the notion that managers make dividend increases only when they are reasonably sure they can be sustained.

Finance in Practice 15–3

What Managers Consider in
Setting Dividend Policy

In 1983, three business-school
professors surveyed a group of
firms to find out what they con-
sidered important in setting divi-dend policy. They sent question-
naires to the chief financial
officers of 562 firms listed on the
New York Stock Exchange asking
them to rank the factors they considered most important. They divided the firms into three categories: manufacturing, wholesale/
retail, and utilities. The survey
yielded 318 usable responses, and
the results are summarized in the
accompanying table.

The results produced no surprises, but the differences in rankings are interesting. After what
happened to Consolidated Edison,
it is not surprising that utility executives think a lot about stock
price.

Source: H. K. Baker, G. E. Farrelly,
and R. B. Edelman, ''A Survey of
Management Views on Dividend Policy,'' *Financial Management*, Autumn
1985, pp. 78–84.

Factor	*Rank of Factor*		
	Manufacturing	*Wholesale/Retail*	*Utilities*
Anticipated level of future earnings	1	1	1
Pattern of past dividends	2	2	3
Availability of cash	3	4	4
Concern about maintaining or increasing stock price	4	3	2

owners. While frequently encountered, restrictions usually are not troublesome during normal times because they are consistent with what good financial management would require anyway.

In addition to covenants in debt and preferred-stock agreements, many state laws place restrictions on dividend payments designed to give further protection to senior claim holders. Many states require that dividends be paid only out of retained earnings. The effect of such a restriction is to permit dividend payments only when retained earnings is a positive figure. The intent of the provision is to permit withdrawal of earnings but not the withdrawal of the original capital contribution. Some states define the original capital contribution as including only the par value of the stock, while others include paid-in capital as well. A few states permit dividends if current earnings, usually over the most recent 12 months, are positive, even if total cumulative retained earnings is negative.

DIVIDENDS IN CLOSELY HELD FIRMS

The discussion to this point has concentrated on the formulation of dividend policy in publicly held corporations. Much of the discussion does not apply to firms that are not publicly held. In privately held firms, there are no problems with information effects, issue costs, or clientele.

Taxes, however, are a factor, and tax considerations are of major importance in establishing policy in private companies with respect to withdrawals by owners. The form of organization—whether proprietorship, partnership, or corporation—signifi-

Table 15–4
Another Example of the Interdependence of Decisions at a Hypothetical Firm (millions of dollars)

		No External Equity		
	No Residual Policy 1	*Investment Residual Policy 2*	*Debt/Equity Residual Policy 3*	*Dividend Residual Policy 4*
Before external financing				
Debt	$ 300	$ 300	$ 300	$ 300
Equity	$1,000	$1,000	$1,000	$1,000
Debt/equity ratio	0.30	0.30	0.30	0.30
Investment opportunities	**$ 150**	**$ 62.4**	**$ 150**	**$ 150**
Earnings	$ 120	$ 120	$ 120	$ 120
Dividend-payout ratio	**0.60**	**0.60**	**0.60**	**0.038**
Dividends	$ 72	$ 72	$ 72	4.6
Earnings retained	$ 48	$ 48	$ 48	$115.4
External financing				
Debt	$ 34.6	$ 14.4	$ 102	$ 34.6
Equity	$ 67.4	$ 0	$ 0	$ 0
After external financing				
Debt	$ 334.6	$ 314.4	$ 402	$ 334.6
Equity	$1,115.4	$1,048	$1,048	$1,115.4
Debt/equity ratio	**0.30**	**0.30**	**0.38**	**0.30**

cantly affects the firm's tax status. If certain conditions are met, a corporation having a small number of shareholders may be taxed as a partnership. If the firm is taxed as a corporation, long-range planning of investment and financing needs becomes essential. If funds are paid out and later returned, taxes would have been paid unnecessarily. The long-range residual approach to planning withdrawals would be appropriate. In many cases, the appropriate policy depends heavily on the income needs and tax brackets of the principals. In some cases, a policy of total retention may be best, but Internal Revenue Service regulations prohibit excessive retention as a means of avoiding income taxes. Given the complexity of the applicable tax laws, expert accounting and legal advice is necessary in most cases.

Sample Problem 15–1

Treating Dividends as a Long-Run Residual at ABC Corporation

Rework the plan for treating dividends as a long-run residual in Table 15–1, assuming that the firm has attractive new investment opportunities that require an investment of $150 million rather than $100 million.

Solution

Under Policy 1, $102 million is required in external financing ($150 million − $48 million). The mix of new financing should result in a final debt/equity ratio of 0.30.

In other words, total debt (new debt plus old debt) divided by total equity (new equity sold plus old equity plus earnings retained) should equal 0.30. Therefore, the amount of new equity to be sold can be calculated as

$$\frac{\text{New debt} + \$300 \text{ million}}{\text{New equity sold} + \$1{,}000 \text{ million} + \$48 \text{ million}} = 0.3.$$

$$\text{New debt} = 0.3 \text{ New equity} + \$14.4 \text{ million}$$

Because we know that new debt plus new equity must add up to the total $102 million needed in external financing, we know that new debt = $102 million − new equity sold, and we can substitute this expression for new debt in the above equation, which results in the following expression:

$$\$102 \text{ million} - \text{New equity sold} = 0.3 \text{ New equity sold} + \$14.4 \text{ million}$$

$$\text{New equity sold} \qquad\qquad = \$67.4 \text{ million}$$

Once we know the amount of new equity sold, we can determine the amount of new debt as

$$\text{New debt} = \$102 \text{ million} - \$67.4 \text{ million} = \$34.6 \text{ million}.$$

Under Policy 2, only $14.4 million can be raised in new debt if no new equity is issued and if the debt/equity and payout ratios are to remain constant. This policy leaves only $62.4 available for investment ($48 million + $14.4 million). Under Policy 3, the entire $102 million is raised through new debt, raising the final debt/equity ratio to 0.38. Under Policy 4, $34.6 million of the required $150 million comes from debt, leaving $115.4 million to come from retained earnings. This policy leaves $4.6 million for dividends ($120 million in earnings less $115.4 million retained), which represents a dividend-payout ratio of 0.038. The results of the four policies are summarized in Table 15–4. ∃ⅢϜ

KEY CONCEPTS

1. In the absence of financial friction and differential tax rates, dividend policy would not affect firm value.

2. Differential tax rates (ordinary-income rates higher than capital-gain rates) induce a bias on the part of shareholders in favor of retention, or lower dividends.

3. Commissions on stock trades exert a bias in favor of higher payouts on the part of some investors and a bias in favor of lower payouts on the part of other investors. Issue costs exert a bias in favor of lower payouts.

4. Information effects on the price of stock resulting from dividend actions can be quite pronounced, but there is no general rule regarding the direction of the effect.

5. Investment, financing, and dividend decisions are interdependent. It is not possible to set policies in all three areas independently.

6. Dividend policy is best set as a long-run residual managed in the short run.

SUMMARY

In analyzing dividend policy from the standpoint of firm value and shareholder interests, attention should focus on taxes, financial friction, and information effects. Ordinary income and capital gains are taxed at different rates. Friction costs include commissions, issue costs, and costs of analysis by investors. Information effects occur when, on the basis of dividend decisions by the firm, investors draw inferences regarding other important events or policies, such as investment opportunities in the future, earnings prospects, or changes in financing policy. Information effects result from unexpected dividend actions and can have a significant impact on stock price in either direction. The potential for undesirable information effects emphasizes the need for careful communication by management to the financial markets.

In setting its dividend policy, a firm must consider many factors in addition to taxes, friction costs, and information effects. It must consider interdependencies among investment, financing, and dividend policies; earnings prospects; liquidity requirements; the makeup of the stockholder group; and legal and regulatory restrictions.

When dividend policy is analyzed in a valuation framework, it becomes clear that, in general, dividends should be treated as a long-run residual. Although they can be treated as a residual in the long run, dividends must be managed carefully in the short run to avoid undesirable variations in payout that impose real costs on shareholders. In setting policy, consistency and careful communication are important.

In closely held firms, tax considerations usually are a central factor in determining a payout or withdrawal policy that best serves the interests of owners.

QUESTIONS

1. "In a world of no taxes and no financial friction, a firm cannot be made more valuable by manipulating the dividend-payout ratio." Is this statement true or false? Explain.

2. Discuss the implications of personal income taxes for dividend policy.

3. What types of transaction costs must be considered in setting dividend policy?

4. Describe the information effects that can be induced by dividend actions.

5. Why are investment, financing, and dividend decisions interdependent?

6. What are the principal factors that a firm should consider in setting its dividend policy?

7. Over the long run, which of the three major financial policy variables—investment policy, debt/equity policy, or dividend policy—should be treated as residual?

8. In practice, what constraints operate to prevent a firm from treating dividends as a residual in the short run?

9. Why must dividend policies be planned over a relatively long time horizon?

PROBLEMS

Note: To work problems preceded by an asterisk(*) requires knowledge of material in Appendix 15A.

1. Suppose that the board of directors of Orange Computer Company meets on April 16, 1987, and decides that the regular quarterly dividend of $4.00 per share will be raised to $5.00 per share beginning with the second quarter 1987 dividend. At the same meeting, the board declares that the second quarter dividend will be paid on Thursday, June 18, 1987, to holders of record on Monday, May 18, 1987. The results of this meeting, including the dividend-policy revision and the declaration of the second quarter dividend, appear in an article in the *Wall Street Journal* on April 17, 1987. Orange's stock price is observed to fluctuate as shown in Table A.

Table A

Date	Stock Price
April 10, 1987	$439.50
April 16, 1987	440.50
April 17, 1987	442.00
April 30, 1987	441.80
May 6, 1987	442.30
May 11, 1987	441.65
May 12, 1987	436.85
May 28, 1987	436.90
June 10, 1987	439.10
June 15, 1987	436.30
June 19, 1987	436.20

a. In the context of this dividend decision, when is the declaration date, the record date, the ex-dividend date, and the payment date?

b. Please refer to the stock prices listed in Table A. How might you explain the increases in stock price observed on April 16 and April 17? Why did the stock price drop on May 12? What can you say about the magnitude of the decline? Given the second quarter dividend, what sort of stock price movement would you have expected in June? Do your observations of a decline in price around the middle of June coincide with your expectations? Can this decline be explained in relation to the dividend payment?

2. Suppose that an individual stockholder of Payton Plastics, Inc., is taxed at a rate of 30 percent. The McMahon Metals Company also holds stock in Payton; the income of McMahon is taxed at a rate of 40 percent. Assume that the individual is permitted by the Internal Revenue Service to exclude the first $100 of dividend income, and that McMahon is taxed on only 15 percent of its dividend income.

a. Assuming that this is the only stock owned by an individual, how much would he or she have on an after-tax basis of pretax dividends from Payton totaling $1,000?

b. Assuming that the individual has already received dividends of $500 from another investment, how much of the $1,000 in dividends would he or she have on an after-tax basis?

c. On an after-tax basis, how much would the same $1,000 in dividends be worth to McMahon Metals?

Table B

Debt	14,000
Equity: 4,000,000 shares of common stock at $1 par	4,000
Additional paid-in capital	6,000
Retained earnings	30,000

d. Does the individual or the corporation face a larger tax disincentive on dividend income?

3. Troxler Manufacturing Company produces components for heavy machine tools. For the past 15 years, Troxler has experienced moderate sales and earnings growth. Currently, Troxler is considering expanding its production facilities and product line to include components for sensitive testing equipment. This is a new area of component manufacturing with no dominant firm in the market. Expansion into this line has met Troxler's economic and qualitative criteria for acceptance. The expansion program will require an investment of $30 million in the next year to set up operations. Troxler has 4 million shares of common stock outstanding and has maintained a stable annual dollar dividend of $2.50 per share. Troxler's board of directors is reluctant to have any sudden changes in this dividend level. The firm has a target debt/equity ratio of 0.35. Total earnings after taxes for the past year were $25 million. Earnings are expected to remain constant over the next year. Troxler's balance sheet for the past year indicates the capital structure (in thousands of dollars) shown in Table B.

a. What is Troxler's current dividend-payment ratio?

b. If Troxler undertakes the new investment and maintains its current dividend-payout ratio, how much external financing will be required? To maintain its target debt/equity ratio, how much must be raised in new equity? If new common stock can be issued to net $40 per share, how many new shares must be issued and what will be the effect of this issue on the dollar dividend per share if the current dividend-payout ratio is maintained?

c. Suppose the directors of Troxler are unwilling to undertake a new common stock issue at this time to finance the new investment. What poli-

Table C

Year	Expected Earnings
1	$7,000,000
2	$8,000,000
3	$6,000,000
4	$5,000,000
5	$6,000,000

cies could you suggest to the directors so that the new investment can be made? Discuss the advantages and disadvantages of each of your policies.

4. You are the president of a large manufacturing corporation that views dividends as a long-run residual. Currently, the dividend-payout ratio is 35 percent. The debt/equity ratio of 40 percent is considered to be optimal. You are reviewing the five year strategic plan in order to decide whether the current dividend-payout ratio of 35 percent should be revised. The plan anticipates investment opportunities of $5 million per year for five years, including plant and equipment plus additions to working capital. In keeping with the target debt/equity ratio, new debt will be issued in year 4. Assume that earnings over the five years are expected to vary as shown in Table C.

a. How much debt must be issued over the five years in order that the target debt/equity ratio of 40 percent is maintained?

b. If the firm did not view dividends as a long-run residual, what would dividend payments be in each of the next five years? What are the potential problems with such a policy?

Table E

Profit after tax	$10 million
Shares	5 million
Earnings per share (EPS)	$ 2.00
Dividend per share	$ 0.70
Total dividends	$ 3.5 million
Retained earnings	$ 6.5 million

c. Given that the firm does set dividend policy as a long-run residual, what annual dividends are indicated by the five-year plan?

d. If a change in the dividend-payout ratio is indicated, what issues should be considered before such a change is enacted?

5. The Wingo Manufacturing Company uses a 5-year time horizon for financial planning. After several months of study and discussion, management has developed certain estimates for the firm's financial performance over the next 5 years. Earnings after tax are expected to grow at 5 percent per year for the next 5 years. Wingo's earnings after tax last year were $10 million. Total new investments over the next 5 years are estimated to be $45 million. There will be stable or growing dollar dividends over the next 5 years. Ms. Howes, Wingo's president, believes the firm's current debt/equity ratio of 0.4 is too high, and she wants this ratio to be lowered to 0.35 during the next 5 years. The firm does not plan to issue any new stock over the next 5 years. Wingo's balance sheet (in millions of dollars) and other financial data for the past year are summarized in Tables D and E. Using the approach outlined in Table 15–3, devise a plan that will en-

Table D

Current assets	56	Current liabilities	49
Net plant and equipment	108	Long-term debt	34
Other	5	Equity	
		5,000,000 shares at $1 par value	5
		Additional paid in	25
		Retained earnings	56
Total assets	169	**Total liabilities and equity**	169

Table F

	Year					5-Year
	1	*2*	*3*	*4*	*5*	*Total*
Investment requirement by year	4	5	4	5	4	22
Cumulative investment requirement	4	9	13	18	22	22

able Wingo to meet its projected financial needs and to attain the president's desired dividend and debt/equity levels. What minimum aggregate level of earnings after tax is required over the 5-year period to meet these financial and policy demands?

6. Rework Table 15–1 in the text for a target dividend-payout ratio of 0.65 rather than 0.60. Determine for each of the four policy alternatives the external financing requirements (debt and equity) and the debt and equity levels after external financing is completed.

7. a. Rework Table 15–3 in the text to provide for an aggregate investment requirement of $22 million rather than $20 million, timed as shown in Table F (in millions of dollars).

   b. Suppose now that the firm currently has a debt/equity ratio of 0.35 (rather than 0.30 as in Table 15–3) and wishes to maintain that ratio. Total equity is $200 million. The investment requirement remains at $22 million. Rework the table a second time.

*8. The stockholders' equity account of the Stevens Manufacturing Company is given in Table G. The firm's common stock has a current market price of $45 per share.

   a. Show the results of a 10 percent stock dividend.
   b. Show the results of a 20 percent stock dividend.
   c. Show the results of a two-for-one stock split.
   d. Given your answers to the above analyses, explain the effects of stock dividends and stock splits on net worth.

Table G

Common stock	
(2,000,000 shares at $2 par value)	$ 4,000,000
Paid-in surplus	16,000,000
Retained earnings	28,000,000
Net worth	**$48,000,000**

REFERENCES

Bhattacharya, S. "Imperfect Information, Dividend Policy, and the Bird-in-the-Hand Fallacy." *Bell Journal of Economics* 10 (Spring 1979): 259–270.

Black, F., and M. Scholes. "The Effects of Dividend Yield and Dividend Policy on Common Stock Prices and Returns." *Journal of Financial Economics* 1 (1974): 1–22.

Brealey, R. A. *Security Prices in a Competitive Market.* Cambridge, Mass.: MIT Press, 1971.

Carson-Parker, J. "The Capital Cloud over Smoke-Stack America." *Fortune* (Feb. 23, 1981): 70–80.

Eiseman, P.C., and E. A. Moses. "Stock Dividends: Managements' Views." *Financial Analysts Journal* (July–Aug. 1978): 77–85.

Elton, E. J., and M. J. Bruger. "Marginal Stockholder Tax Rates and the Clientele Effect." *Review of Economics and Statistics* 52 (Feb. 1970): 68–74.

Fama, E. F., and H. Babiak. "Dividend Policy: An Empirical Analysis." *Journal of the American Statistical Association* 63 (Dec. 1968): 1132–1161.

Finnerty, J. E. "Corporate Stock Issue and Repurchase." *Financial Management* 4 (Oct. 1975): 62–66.

"Fresh Evidence that Dividends Don't Matter." *Fortune* (May 4, 1981): 351–354.

Friend, I., and M. Puckett. "Dividends and Stock Prices." *American Economic Review* 54 (Sept. 1964): 656–682.

"GM Says Cash Crunch Is Forcing Delay In Parts of $40 Billion, 5-Year Outlay Plan." *Wall Street Journal* (May 5, 1981).

Higgins, R. C. "The Corporate Dividend-Saving Decision." *Journal of Financial and Quantitative Analysis* 7 (Mar. 1972): 1527–1541.

Higgins, R. C. "Dividend Policy and Increasing Discount Rates: A Clarification." *Journal of Financial and Quantitative Analysis* 7 (June 1972): 1757–1762.

Higgins, R. C. "Growth, Dividend Policy and Capital Costs in the Electric Utility Industry." *Journal of Finance* 29 (Sept. 1974): 1189–1202.

Higgins, R. C. "How Much Growth Can a Firm Afford?" *Financial Management* 6 (Fall 1977): 7–16.

Higgins, R. "Sustainable Growth Under Inflation." *Financial Management* 10 (Autumn 1981): 36–40.

John, K., and J. Williams. "Dividends, Dilution and Taxes: A Signalling Equilibrium." *Journal of Finance* (September 1985): 1053–1070.

Kolb, R. W. "Predicting Dividend Changes." Unpublished doctoral dissertation, Graduate School of Business Administration, University of North Carolina at Chapel Hill, 1978.

Krainer, R. E. "A Pedagogic Note on Dividend Policy." *Journal of Financial and Quantitative Analysis* 6 (Sept. 1971): 1147–1154.

Lewellen, W. G., et al. "Some Direct Evidence on the Dividend Clientele Phenomenon." *Journal of Finance* 33 (Dec. 1978): 1385–1400.

Litzenberger, R. H., and K. Ramaswamy. "Dividends, Short Selling Restrictions, Tax-Induced Investor Clienteles and Market Equilibrium." *Journal of Finance* 35 (May 1980): 469–482.

Litzenberger, R. H., and K. Ramaswamy. "The Effect of Personal Taxes and Dividends on Capital Asset Prices." *Journal of Financial Economics* 7 (1979): 163–195.

Litzenberger, R. H., and J. C. Van Horne. "Elimination of the Double Taxation of Dividends and Corporate Financial Policy." *Journal of Finance* 33 (June 1978): 737–749.

Michel, A. "Industry Influence on Dividend Policy." *Financial Management* 8 (Autumn 1979): 22–26.

Miller, M. H., and F. Modigliani. "Dividend Policy, Growth, and the Valuation of Shares." *Journal of Business* 34 (October 1961): 411–433.

Miller, M., and M. Scholes. "Dividends and Taxes." *Journal of Financial Economics* 6 (1978): 333–364.

Miller, M., and M. Scholes. "Dividends and Taxes: Some Empirical Evidence." Working Paper no. 55, Center for Research in Security Prices, Graduate School of Business, University of Chicago.

Myers, S. C. "Interactions of Corporate Financing and Investment Decisions—Implications for Capital Budgeting." *Journal of Finance* (March 1974): 433–443.

Pettit, R. R. "Dividend Announcements, Security Performance, and Market Efficiency." *Journal of Finance* 27 (Dec. 1972): 993–1007.

Pettit, R. R. "Taxes, Transactions Costs and the Clientele Effect of Dividends." *Journal of Finance* 5 (Dec. 1977): 419–436.

Ross, S. A. "The Determination of Financial Structure: The Incentive-Signalling Approach." *Bell Journal of Economics* 8 (1977): 23–40.

Van Horne, J. C., and J. G. McDonald. "Dividend Policy and New Equity Financing. *Journal of Finance* 26 (May 1971): 507–519.

Walter, J. E. "Dividend Policy: Its Influence on the Value of Enterprise." *Journal of Finance* 18 (May 1963): 380–391.

Watts, R. "The Information Content of Dividends." *Journal of Business* 46 (Apr. 1973): 191–211.

Appendix 15A

Stock Dividends and Stock Splits

This appendix discusses two topics—stock dividends and stock splits—that do not involve a distribution of earnings and, therefore, are not dividends. Each is more properly considered a recapitalization, or a restructuring, of capital accounts of the firm. We discuss these topics here because the motives for paying stock dividends are related to those of distributing cash dividends. We include a discussion of stock splits because they are very similar in effect to stock dividends. In Chapter 17, we will discuss yet another related topic—the repurchase of shares of stock as an alternative to paying such dividends.

STOCK DIVIDENDS

Some firms pay a *stock dividend* in lieu of, or in combination with, a cash dividend. Stock dividends usually take the form of shares of common stock. Consider a firm whose stock has a par value at $1, was originally sold at $10 per share, and now has a market price of $20. When a 10 percent stock dividend is paid, the balance sheet, before and after the stock dividend is paid, would appear as shown in Table 15A–1.

The number of shares outstanding increases by 100,000 (10 percent) to 1,100,000. However, net worth remains the same and no cash has been paid out. The issue of the additional shares has been accompanied by a restructuring—or a relabeling—of accounting entries in the net-worth section of the balance sheet. Retained earnings has

Table 15A–1
Balance Sheets, Both Before and After the Payment of Stock Dividends, for a Hypothetical Firm

	Before	
Cash $1,000,000	Common stock (1,000,000 shares at $1 par value)	$ 1,000,000
	Paid-in surplus	9,000,000
	Retained earnings	15,000,000
	Net worth	$25,000,000

	After	
Cash $1,000,000	Common stock (1,100,000 shares at $1 par value)	$ 1,100,000
	Paid-in surplus	10,900,000
	Retained earnings	13,000,000
	Net worth	$25,000,000

Table 15A–2

Changes for an Individual Shareholder after a Firm's Payment of a Stock Dividend

	Shares Owned	Earnings per Share	Total Claim on Earnings
Before	100	$2.00	$200
After	110	$1.82	$200

been reduced by $2,000,000 (100,000 shares times the market price of $20), with $1,900,000 transferred to paid-in surplus and $100,000 transferred to common stock (based on par value).

Each shareholder now has 10 percent more shares than before. Is the shareholder better off? One firm justified a stock dividend on grounds that it "should enable stockholders to benefit from the improving earnings outlook." However, total earnings are unchanged, so earnings per share decline by 10 percent, and each shareholder's proportional share in earnings is the same as before.

To illustrate, consider a shareholder who owned 100 shares before the stock dividend, and assume that total earnings after taxes were $2,000,000, or $2.00 per share before the stock dividend, as shown in Table 15A–2. Because the claim on earnings is unchanged, if the shareholders are better off, it must be because the firm is worth more. Such would be the case if market price per share declined by less than 10 percent. Empirical evidence suggests, however, that prices on average do adjust by the same amount as the stock dividend. A direct analogy is that of two pies, both the same size, with one sliced 10 ways and the other sliced 11 ways. It seems doubtful that the pie with 11 slices would command a higher price in the market place. Likewise, to argue that a stock dividend alone can permanently affect the value of a firm requires an assumption of irrationality on the part of investors, not a very comfortable basis for making financial policy. As a final bit of evidence on the true value of stock dividends, we might note that the Internal Revenue Service views them as nontaxable.[1]

With the economic benefits of stock dividends in doubt, what about their cost? The firm incurs costs in connection with issuing the new stock certificates. In addition, owners of small amounts of stock receive fractional shares and must either sell the fractional shares or *round up* by buying more fractional shares to obtain full shares. The cost to the firm of handling these transactions may be significant. There also are costs to shareholders in terms of inconvenience and additional recordkeeping.

Occasionally, a firm may use a stock dividend as a mechanism for increasing cash-dividend payout. If the dollar dividend per share is held constant, a stock dividend has the effect of increasing the aggregate cash-dividend payout by the firm. Chapter 15 discussed the effects of such an increase in cash dividends.

---

[1]For a survey of management attitudes toward stock dividends, see P. C. Eisemann and E. A. Moses, "Stock Dividends: Management's View," *Financial Analysts Journal*, July/August 1978, pp. 77–85.

Table 15A–3

Changes Occurring When a Hypothetical Firm Recapitalizes with a Two-for-One Stock Split

	Before	
Cash $1,000,000	Common stock (1,000,000 shares at $1 par value)	$ 1,000,000
	Paid-in surplus	9,000,000
	Retained earnings	15,000,000
	Net worth	$25,000,000

	After	
Cash $1,000,000	Common stock (2,000,000 shares at $0.50 par value)	$ 1,000,000
	Paid-in surplus	9,000,000
	Retained earnings	15,000,000
	Net worth	$25,000,000

STOCK SPLITS

We noted above that a stock dividend is not a distribution of earnings, but a recapitalization of sorts. A closely related type of recapitalization is the *stock split*. A stock split involves different accounting entries from a stock dividend and usually can be accomplished at lower cost because fractional shares can be avoided. Consider the illustration given in Table 15A–3 of a two-for-one split, using the same firm described earlier as an example.

In this case, 1 million new shares are issued, and the par value is cut in half. No transfer is made from the retained-earnings account. Earnings per share are cut in half. We would expect market price also to be cut in half, and evidence shows that this is what occurs.

One motive for a stock split is to increase the number of shares outstanding and, thereby, broaden the market for the stock. Another motive is to reduce the price to a more favorable trading range. Reducing the price, therefore, may increase the stock's appeal to investors with small amounts to invest. There is no evidence, however, that a broadening of the market, if it does occur, has any lasting impact on the total value of the firm. For example, in a two-for-one split, the number of shares doubles, but share price is cut in half; total value remains unchanged. For reasons cited earlier in discussing stock dividends, any such value impact is doubtful.

Chapter

16

Specialized Financing Methods: Leases, Convertible Securities, and Warrants

In this chapter, we examine specialized forms of financing. We explain the motivations for obtaining leases as well as how to use discounted-cash-flow analysis to evaluate whether leasing is desirable for the firm. We also discuss how to determine the value of convertible securities and warrants and under what conditions they might be useful forms of financing.

In Chapters 12 through 15, we considered the basics of financing decisions—the impact of leverage on return and risk, the theory of capital structure, techniques for determining the appropriate mix of debt and equity, and issues in setting dividend policy.

In this chapter, we will consider some specialized but no less important topics in financing. Leasing has grown in importance over the least two decades to become an important item in the financial manager's kit of financing tools. Convertible securities can provide a company with a financing vehicle that has characteristics of both debt and equity securities. Warrants likewise are useful in the right situations.

LEASING

Leasing—is a specialized means of acquiring the use of assets without owning the assets.

A lease—is a contractual arrangement where the *lessee* has the right to use the asset in return for making periodic payments to the owner, or *lessor*.

Firms obtain funds in order to acquire income-producing assets. In the case of physical (nonfinancial) assets, firms that are in business to produce goods and services usually are more interested in *using* the asset than in *owning* it *per se*. A specialized means of acquiring the use of assets without ownership is **leasing**. Because it represents an alternative to ownership, leasing can be viewed as a specialized means of obtaining funds—one of a number of financing alternatives open to a firm.

A **lease** is a contractual arrangement under which the *lessee* has the right to use the equipment and, in return, makes periodic payments to the owner, or *lessor*. The lessor retains title to the equipment. Figure 16–1 diagrams the difference between leasing and ownership for Firm X. Firm X wants to use a particular asset. One alternative, displayed in Panel A, is to purchase the asset from the manufacturer and obtain the necessary funds by using debt or equity financing. For example, Firm X might borrow money from a bank.

Another alternative, shown in Panel B, is to lease the asset from a lessor who has bought the asset from the manufacturer. As a lessee, Firm X uses the asset even though the lessor owns the asset. In essence, the lessor performs the role of a financial intermediary. The lessor raises the funds for purchasing the asset and then provides the asset to the lessee in exchange for lease payments.

A specific example of the situation shown in Figure 16–1 often occurs in the airline

Figure 16–1
Leasing Versus Owning an Asset

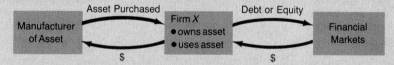
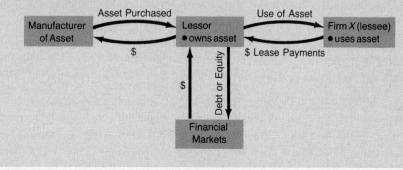

industry. Firm X could be an airline company that flies the plane, but the lessor may be a large bank that actually owns the plane that was manufactured by yet another company.

Leasing grew rapidly in popularity during the 1960s and 1970s. During this period, many new firms, including a large number of commercial banks, entered the leasing field as lessors. It is clear that during the 1980s, leasing has become an important means of asset financing. A firm can issue a claim against its future cash flows by means of long-term debt, equity, or a lease obligation. Each of these claims would allow the firm to obtain use of an asset. Issuing debt or equity provides funds to purchase the asset. The lease provides an alternative way for the lessee to use the asset even though the lessor retains ownership.

Types of Leases

An **operating lease**—is a contract covering intermediate to short terms where the lessor (owner) typically is responsible for maintenance, insurance, and property taxes; also known as a *maintenance lease* or *service lease*.

A **financial lease**—is a noncancelable, fully amortized contract typically covering intermediate to long terms where the lessee (user) normally is responsible for maintenance, insurance, and taxes; also known as a *net lease*.

Figure 16–1 shows a simple type of lease arrangement. In practice, there are many types of leases, some of which become quite complicated. The two most frequently encountered types of leases are the **operating lease** and the **financial lease**. Under an operating lease, sometimes called a *maintenance,* or *service, lease*, the lessor (owner) typically is responsible for maintenance, insurance, and property taxes. Compensation for providing these services is included in the lease payment. Assets leased under operating leases include computers, office equipment, automobiles, trucks, and a wide variety of other types of equipment. Contracts typically are intermediate- to short-term. Computers, for example, typically are leased for 3–5 years, and automobiles are leased for 1–3 years. Other types of equipment may be leased or rented on a daily or even an hourly basis. Contracts covering intermediate periods usually are cancelable. Because they usually cover a period considerably shorter than the usable life of the asset, operating leases normally do not fully amortize the original cost of the asset. Rather, the lessor expects either to lease the asset again or to sell it at the expiration of the original contract. Because contracts are short- to intermediate-term and cancelable, the lessor bears the risk of technological obsolescence of the asset.

Financial leases are noncancelable contracts typically covering intermediate to long terms. Provision often is made for renewal or purchase of the asset at expiration. The lessee (user) normally is responsible for maintenance, insurance, and taxes, and for this reason financial leases often are called *net leases*. Types of assets leased under financial leases include aircraft, rail cars, land, and buildings. Normally, the payments under a financial lease fully amortize the original cost of the asset over the term of the lease, which usually approximates the useful life of the asset. Full amortization and noncancelability are the key features that distinguish financial leases from operating leases. Noncancelability implies that lessees are legally obligated to make all the lease payments regardless of whether they continue to use the asset and, thus, can cancel only by paying off the entire contract. Default by the lessee can lead to bankruptcy, just as in the case of a debt contract.

As shown in Figure 16–1, the asset may be acquired from the manufacturer by a lessor who then leases it to the user. Lessors entering into such transactions include finance companies, commercial banks, specialized leasing companies, and individuals. Individual lessors usually are high-tax-bracket investors who can receive large tax benefits from being the owner of the asset for tax purposes (depreciation tax shields and investment tax credits). We will discuss these tax benefits shortly. Alternatively, the

A **sale-and-leaseback agreement**—is an arrangement in which a firm or individual owning an asset sells it to another party and then leases it back.

manufacturer may itself serve as the lessor as is often done in the case of computers and office equipment.

Yet another variation on leasing is the **sale-and-leaseback agreement**. Under a sale-and-leaseback agreement, a firm or individual owning an asset sells it to another party and then leases it back. The seller gives up title to the asset but retains its use. The selling price usually approximates the fair market value of the asset, and the lease contract is nearly always written as a financial lease. In essence, the sale-and-leaseback agreement allows a firm to obtain cash by selling an asset but to retain use of the asset by becoming a lessee.

A **leveraged lease**—is a lease agreement in which the lessor borrows a substantial part of the purchase price of the asset to be leased.

A **leveraged lease** is a lease in which the lessor borrows a substantial part of the purchase price of the asset to be leased. The lessor has used financial leverage (debt) to obtain the asset to be leased. The lender—often an insurance company or pension fund—typically takes a mortgage on the asset for security. The lender also may require that the lessors assign their interests in the lease. Under this arrangement lease payments would go directly to the lender, who would deduct principal and interest payments due on the loan and then send the balance to the lessor. Risk to the lender, therefore, is the risk of default by the lessee, even though the loan was made to the lessor.[1]

An **investment tax credit**—is the deduction of a percentage of money spent on certain types of investments from a firm's tax liability.

As the above discussion shows, leases can take on many forms. A basic question is, what advantages do such leases have over direct ownership? Before we can address that question, however, we need to look at the accounting and tax treatment of lease arrangements. As it turns out, this treatment has direct bearing on the decision to lease an asset rather than to purchase it directly.

Tax and Accounting Treatment of Leases

A **depreciation tax shield**—is the tax saving a firm generates as a result of deducting depreciation costs.

Accounting and tax treatment of leases can become quite complex, and the applicable rules have undergone significant change in recent years. For tax purposes, the lessor is typically designated as the owner of the asset. As the owner, the lessor is entitled to the tax benefits of ownership, including any **investment tax credit** and **depreciation tax shield** associated with the purchase of the asset. The lessee is allowed to deduct lease payments as tax-deductible expenses. In determining the tax treatment of a lease, the Internal Revenue Service goes to great lengths to distinguish between a lease and a **conditional sales agreement**, which details the sale of an asset. If a transaction is declared a conditional sale by the IRS, payments for use of the assets will not be allowed as tax-deductible items but will be treated as payments toward the purchase of the asset. The details of the tax treatment of specific leases are beyond the scope of our present discussion. In practice, tax experts scrutinize leases to make sure of the treatment of the transaction by the IRS. For our present purposes, the important tax implication is that the owner-lessor for tax purposes will get the tax benefits of

A **conditional sales contract**—is an installment contract for the purchase of equipment in which title to the equipment remains with the lender until all payments are made.

---

[1]Under current accounting rules, it is possible for lessors to record on their balance sheets only their equity investment in the lease, rather than the full purchase price of the asset. Even though only the equity interest is shown, the lessor still will receive 100 percent of the investment tax credit, depreciation, and residual values. These features will be discussed later in this chapter. For a discussion of leveraged leases, see P. J. Athanasopoulos and P. W. Bacon, "The Evaluation of Leveraged Leases," *Financial Management* 9 (Spring 1980): 76–80.

ownership (investment tax credits and depreciation tax shields), whereas the lessee will be allowed to treat lease payments as tax-deductible expenses. Before analyzing any lease, financial managers should check carefully to see exactly what the tax treatment of a specific lease will be.

The accounting treatment of leases has been the subject of considerable debate. As a lessee, a firm does not own an asset. Hence, one could argue that the asset should not appear on the company's balance sheet as an asset and that lease payments, just like other costs of doing business, should be deducted as expenses on the income statement. For most operating leases, which cover a period considerably shorter than the usable life of the asset, the accounting is done in this way. Lessees show nothing on their balance sheets and deduct the full amount of the lease payment as an expense.

In the case of long-term financial leases, matters are not so clear-cut. If a lease lasts for the effective life of the asset, one could argue that the company ought to show the asset on its balance sheet and at the same time somehow recognize future lease payments as an obligation reflected in a liability on the balance sheet. The accounting profession has established rules, detailed by the Financial Accounting Standards Board in Financial Accounting Standard No.13, whereby certain leases are classified as **capital leases**. If a lease is a capital lease, it must be capitalized by the lessee on its balance sheet as an asset and as an obligation. In essence, a lease will be classified as a capital lease if the terms of the lease last for more than 75 percent of the estimated uselife of the asset or involve any provisions that effectively transfer ownership of the asset to the lessee by the end of the lease term.[2]

> A **capital lease**—is a lease that, for accounting purposes, must be capitalized on the lessee's balance sheet as an asset and as an obligation.

Just as the tax laws affecting leases can become complicated, so can the accounting treatment. And to make matters more complex, sometimes the accounting may be handled one way for financial-reporting purposes and another way for tax purposes. The important point to note is that for short-term operating leases, the leased asset typically will not appear on the lessee's balance sheet, whereas with long-term financial leases, the lessee will show the lease on the balance sheet as both a leased asset and a lease obligation. Whether leases are on the balance sheets of lessees or not, lease payments constitute a fixed, contractual claim against a firm's cash flows and, hence, affect risk in much the same way as debt does.

Motives for Leasing

Now we turn to the question of what motivates firms to lease assets rather than buy them directly. Leases have both advantages and disadvantages to both lessee and lessor.

The major motive for many leases is tax treatment. When a company buys an asset, it can receive two major tax benefits: an investment tax credit and a depreciation tax shield. Normally both of these tax features reduce a firm's tax bill. But if a firm has suffered losses and isn't paying taxes in the first place, investment tax credits and

---

[2]The details of FASB 13 classify a lease as a capital lease if a lease has any one of the following four elements: (1) the lease transfers ownership of the property to the lessee by the end of the lease term, (2) the lease contains an option to buy the property at a bargain price, (3) the lease term is equal to 75 percent or more of the estimated economic life of the property, or (4) the present value of the rentals and other minimum lease payments is equal to 90 percent or more of the fair value of the leased property less any related investment tax credit retained by the lessor.

depreciation tax shields are of little immediate value.[3] Certainly the tax benefits of ownership would be worth more to a profitable firm that has a large taxable income or to a private individual with a high tax rate.

The lease offers a made-to-order financial arrangement. Suppose an airline needed a new plane but currently had losses for tax purposes. The airline itself could gain little or no immediate tax benefit from any investment tax credit or depreciation on the plane. Enter a highly profitable bank, which could use those tax benefits of ownership. The bank buys the plane and acts as a lessor. The airline—the lessee—uses the plane but the bank gets the tax benefits of ownership. In the process of the lease arrangement, there has been a tax savings. Tax benefits that might have gone unused by the airline are utilized by the bank. The airline shares in the tax savings to the extent that the bank requires lower lease payments for use of the asset because of the tax benefits it reaps. In effect, the lease arrangement allows the tax savings related to owning an asset to be used by the entity that can benefit most from those savings. It, thus, comes as no surprise that many lessors are profitable firms or wealthy individuals in high tax brackets.

> **In effect, the lease arrangement allows the tax savings related to owning an asset to be used by the entity that can benefit most from those savings.**

One often-cited advantage of leasing is that it may provide 100 percent financing. Elimination of the requirement for a down payment may indeed be a real advantage to a lessee who has no cash. However, we should not lose sight of the fact that lease payments are contractual, and the lease, therefore, provides the equivalent of debt financing. The financing is not free. Furthermore, for practically all firms, cash to purchase an asset can be obtained from financial markets—for example, by borrowing money.

Operating leases may give a firm greater flexibility than ownership by shifting the risk of obsolescence to the lessor. The same is not true of financial leases, because they are noncancelable and normally cover the useful life of the asset. Where the risk is shifted, we can expect the lessor to require compensation for bearing it, usually incorporating the compensation directly in the lease payment. Taking such risks into account is central to the leasing business, and in general lessors are likely to be more expert at judging the risks than are lessees. While flexibility with respect to obsolescence is indeed an advantage of the operating lease, it is one for which the lessee pays. In effect, the lessee buys insurance against obsolescence.

In situations of bankruptcy or reorganization, whether a lease contract is advantageous as compared to ownership depends on circumstances. Under ownership with a mortgage, in the event of default, the mortgagee (lender) is entitled to seize the asset and sell it to satisfy the debt. Any excess accrues to the firm, and any deficiency usually becomes an unsecured general obligation of the firm. Under a lease, the owner may repossess the asset and file a claim for lost rent against the lessee, with the maximum allowable claim depending on the type of asset and the nature of the pro-

---

[3]Using the provisions of the tax laws, such tax benefits might be used in future periods if and when the firm had taxable income. Because of the time value of money, however, tax savings in the future are worth less than tax savings taken today.

Table 16–1
The Leasing-Versus-Purchase Decision: A Comparison of Balance Sheets

*Panel A. **Existing Balance Sheet:** Assume the firm finances half of its assets with equity.*

Assets	Liabilities plus Owner Equity
Asset $1,000	Debt $ 500
	Equity $ 500
Total $1,000	Total $1,000

*Panel B. **Balance Sheet:** Purchase new asset for $200, financed by $100 of new debt and $100 of new equity.*

Assets	Liabilities plus Owner Equity
Assets $1,200	Debt $ 600
	Equity $ 600
Total $1,200	Total $1,200

*Panel C. **Balance Sheet:** Lease the same asset. Note that debt is reduced in order to maintain the desired financing mix.*

Assets	Liabilities plus Owner Equity	
Assets $1,000	Lease obligation $ 200	Contractual
Leased Asset $ 200	Debt $ 400	obligations
	Equity $ 600	
Total $1,200	Total $1,200	

ceeding. For example, in the case of real property, a claim for lost rent in bankruptcy is limited to a maximum of one year's rent. Whether the lessee is better off leasing or owning in the event of distress, thus, depends on the relationship between the current market value of the asset at the time and the remaining lease or debt obligation, and also on the ability of the lessor to find a new lessee. Because these considerations regarding bankruptcy and reorganization mean nothing as long as the firm remains a going concern, they usually are of secondary importance in leasing decisions.

Residual value—is the value of leased property at the close of the lease term.

A major consideration in many leasing decisions concerns the **residual value** of the asset at the end of the lease period. By opting for leasing rather than owning, the lessee gives up any claim to residual value. The lessor, on the other hand, benefits from any residual value. If residual values are correctly taken into account and markets for leasing are reasonably competitive, the anticipated residual value should be reflected in lower lease payments. Where residual values are significant, as in real-estate projects, they can significantly affect the return to the lessor and the cost to the lessee. We will deal explicitly with residual values in developing an approach to lease analysis later in this chapter.

In summary, being a lessee and leasing an asset has certain advantages (often tax-related) and disadvantages (for example, loss of residual value) relative to owning the asset directly. To make the decision about whether or not to lease requires an economic evaluation of whether the advantages of leasing outweigh the disadvantages.

Economic Evaluation of Leases

In its most general form, we can view the leasing decision as choosing among three mutually exclusive alternatives: (1) leasing the asset, (2) purchasing the asset, or (3) not using the asset at all. The economic analysis must examine the effect of the leasing decision on both the risk to firm shareholders and the return to firm shareholders.

Effects of the Leasing-Versus-Debt Decision on Risks to Shareholders.   If we assume that the decision has already been made to use the asset, our decision about leasing can be usefully simplified by viewing the problem as leasing versus borrowing.[4] That is, we view leasing as a means of financing to be compared to debt financing. The reason for comparing leasing to debt financing is that a lease is a contractual arrangement under which the owner of an asset (the lessor) permits another party (the lessee) to use the asset for a specified period of time in return for a specified payment. Lease payments are fixed and contractual, just as are payments on debt. Thus, a lease can be viewed as a specialized form of debt financing. Here we will consider only financial leases, which are noncancelable and, therefore, essentially equivalent to debt as far as effect on firm risk is concerned.

In comparing leasing to debt financing, we are implicitly assuming that a lease obligation will reduce the firm's ability to borrow funds on a dollar-for-dollar basis—leases displace debt financing. Table 16–1 illustrates this debt displacement caused by leasing for a firm that presently has $1,000 worth of assets financed half with debt and half with equity. The balance sheet in Panel A summarizes the firm's existing financial position.

Now suppose the firm plans to use a new asset. The firm can either purchase the asset for $200 or lease it. If purchased, the firm plans to maintain its existing debt/equity mix. In Table 16–1, the balance sheet in Panel B shows the firm after having purchased the asset. The $200 purchase has been financed with $100 of new debt and $100 of new equity.

Now consider what happens if the firm instead leases the asset and still tries to do half of its financing with equity and half with debt or debtlike financing, such as a lease. The balance sheet in Panel C illustrates the situation and shows the firm after leasing the asset. This balance sheet portrays the underlying economics and simplifies rather complicated accounting rules. The left-hand side of the balance sheet in Panel C shows $1,200 of assets: $1,000 of existing assets plus the new leased asset. The right-hand side of the balance sheet shows the important result for financing. To finance $1,200 of assets and keep half of the financing from equity sources, the firm must use $0.5($1,200) = $600 of equity. This leaves $600 to be financed. Of that, $200 is represented by the lease, leaving $400 of debt.

Now let us compare the balance sheets in Panels B and C to see what leasing has really done relative to purchasing the asset. In Panel B's balance sheet (purchase), the

---

[4]In practice, this is often the case. For example, if a company needs a new truck to continue its delivery operation, the question is whether to lease the truck or to purchase it. In theory, one must consider all three alternatives including the do-not-use option. See R. Brealey and S. Myers, *Principles of Corporate Finance* (New York: McGraw-Hill, 1984) for further discussion of these issues.

Finance in Practice 16–1

The Anaconda Company's Leasing Decision

In 1973, the Anaconda Company entered into an agreement to lease a new aluminum-reduction mill from a consortium of five banks and one commercial finance company. The mill cost $110.7 million. Anaconda agreed to make 40 semiannual payments over a 20-year period. The first 21 payments were to be $3.985 million each, and the last 19 payments $5.460 million each. The lessors were to have title to the mill at the end of the lease in 1993 and also would get the investment tax credit and the depreciation tax shield. Anaconda was to be responsible for all operating cash flows, including maintenance and insurance.

The Anaconda lease illustrates the central importance of taxes in lease financing. The lease turned out to be advantageous to both lessor and lessee at the same time because of taxes. Because the Chilean government had expropriated some of Anaconda's properties in Chile, Anaconda had a large tax loss to carry forward and, therefore, a very low marginal tax rate for a period several years beyond 1973. If Anaconda had purchased the aluminum-reduction mill, it could not have used the depreciation tax shield to full advantage nor the investment tax credit. By means of the lease, Anaconda transferred the tax shields that it could not use to the lessors, who could use them. By properly designing the lease terms, Anaconda and the lessors reduced their combined tax liability. So, the lease left both Anaconda and the lessors better off, with the tax collector footing the bill. Although now dated, the Anaconda lease remains a classic example of a lease designed around tax factors.

Sources: P. Vanderwicken, "The Powerful Logic of the Leasing Boom," *Fortune* 88 (November 1973): 132–36; S. C. Myers, D. A. Dill, and J. A. Bautista, "Valuation of Financial Lease Contracts," *Journal of Finance* 31 (June 1976): 799–820; and J. R. Franks and S. C. Hodges, "Valuation of Financial Lease Contracts: A Note," *Journal of Finance* 33 (May 1978): 657–69.

firm uses $600 of debt. In Panel C's balance sheet (leasing), the firm has only $400 of debt—a net reduction of debt of $600 − $400 = $200. The lease has displaced $200 of debt, which is equivalent to displacing enough debt to purchase the asset.

Has the debt reduction made the shareholders subject to less risk? The answer is no. While debt has been reduced by $200 (comparing Panels B and C), the firm has a binding lease obligation. As a first approximation, shareholders face the same risk whether the firm chooses the balance sheet in Panel A or the one in Panel C—in both cases, there are $600 worth of contractual debtlike claims on the firm.

The results from Table 16–1 show that leasing the asset displaces $200 of debt. In other words, leasing is equivalent to borrowing enough money to actually buy the entire $200 asset. In effect, we compare leasing to 100 percent debt financing.[5] If either leasing or debt subjects the shareholders to the same risk, the remaining question is whether leasing or debt has a lower cost. To answer this question, we will use discounted-cash-flow techniques to calculate the effective interest costs of both debt financing and leasing.

---

[5]We have assumed that leases will typically displace debt dollar for dollar and, hence, that leasing can be compared to 100 percent debt financing. In practice, this assumption is likely to hold if sophisticated creditors analyze the firm. In situations where leasing displaces debt less than dollar for dollar, we would have to compare leasing to whatever financing package it did displace. See R. Brealey and S. Myers, *Principles of Corporate Finance* (New York: McGraw-Hill, 1984).

Table 16–2

Calculating the Equivalent Interest Cost (EIC) of a Hypothetical Loan

Year	Loan Proceeds	Principal Payment	Interest		Total Cash Flow	
			Pretax	After Tax	Pretax	After Tax
0	$1,000,000				$1,000,000	$1,000,000
1		−$250,000	−$120,000	−$64,800	−$370,000	−$314,800
2		−$250,000	−$ 90,000	−$48,600	−$340,000	−$298,600
3		−$250,000	−$ 60,000	−$32,400	−$310,000	−$282,400
4		−$250,000	−$ 30,000	−$16,200	−$280,000	−$266,200
		Rate that discounts cash flows to zero			**12.00 percent**	**6.48 percent**

Using DCF Techniques to Evaluate Leasing Costs. Sometimes it is useful to use discounted-cash-flow techniques to evaluate financing alternatives. A financing plan is, after all, a series of cash flows over time. DCF techniques are designed to analyze complex cash-flow patterns.

The **equivalent interest cost (EIC)**—is the rate that discounts all cash flows of any financing plan such that their present values sum to exactly zero.

Suppose a firm faces two financing alternatives, each involving cash inflow (the proceeds) followed by a series of outflows (the payments). The general cash-flow pattern (inflow, then outflows) is the opposite of that associated with an investment (outflow, then inflows). The **equivalent interest cost (EIC)** of any financing plan is the rate that discounts all cash flows of the plan such that their present values sum to exactly zero. Hence, the *EIC* is the direct analog of the internal rate of return of an investment and is calculated in exactly the same way, as shown in Equation (1).

> The equivalent interest cost *(EIC)* of a lease is the rate that discounts all the cash flows associated with a lease to exactly zero and can be calculated by solving for R in the equation:
>
> $$0 = \sum_{t=0}^{n} \frac{C_t}{(1 + R)^t} \qquad (1)$$
>
> where *EIC* is the rate, R.

In the case of bonds, the equivalent interest cost is called the *yield to maturity*. In the case of standard loan plans, relevant cash flows are easy to identify, and the calculation of the *EIC* is straightforward. The result is what we would expect: the *EIC* works out to be the interest rate on the loan. To illustrate, consider a $1 million loan at 12 percent to be repaid in equal installments of $250,000 over 4 years. The cash flows are listed in Table 16–2, assuming a tax rate of 46 percent.

As expected, the rate that discounts the pretax cash flows to equal zero is 12 percent, the interest rate on the loan. The above procedure verifies the fact that the after-tax *EIC* is the pretax *EIC* multiplied by $(1 - T)$, where T is the tax rate. In this case, $12(1 - 0.46) = 6.48$ percent.

One might wonder why we went to such lengths to calculate something whose value we already knew—namely, the interest rate on the loan. We did so to demonstrate the *EIC* approach in a simple case and to lay the groundwork for applying it to more complex financing plans, such as leases.

The most direct way to compare leasing and debt financing is to calculate the after-tax equivalent interest cost of the lease and compare it to the after-tax interest rate that the firm would have to pay on debt.[6]

To calculate the equivalent interest cost, we apply the incremental-cash-flow rule to identify all cash flows attributable to leasing—that is, those cash flows that will be different if leasing is selected rather than owning. By leasing, the firm avoids the cash outlay required to purchase the asset, forgoes the investment tax credit received by the lessor, incurs an obligation to make lease payments, forgoes the depreciation tax shield, and forgoes the residual (salvage) value of the asset at the expiration of the lease. Costs of operation, maintenance, insurance, property taxes, and the like often are the same under leasing, but if they were different, the difference would represent an incremental cash flow. In the case of all cash flows, associated tax effects must be taken into account.

Some of the incremental cash flows attributable to leasing are inflows (the outlay avoided), and some are outflows (the investment tax credit forgone, the lease payment, depreciation tax shield forgone, and terminal value forgone). The cash-flow pattern, thus, is analogous to that of a loan—an inflow followed by a series of outflows. Once the incremental cash flows have been identified, we find the discount rate that causes their present values to sum to exactly zero. That rate is the after-tax *EIC* of the lease.

Our first task, then, is to identify the incremental cash flows attributable to leasing. Generally, five categories of cash flows are involved:

1. the acquisition cost of the asset (adjusted for any investment tax credit),
2. the lease payment,
3. the depreciation tax shield,
4. the operating and maintenance costs, and
5. the residual (salvage) value.

The first item above—the acquisition cost of the asset—is the outlay that will be avoided if the asset is leased rather than purchased. Because it is an outlay avoided, it is treated as a net cash inflow attributable to the lease. The timing of the inflow is the point at which the outlay would have been made. The outlay avoided is usually the purchase price of the asset reduced by any investment tax credit.

The lease payment is the cash payment that will be made to the lessor in each period over the term of the lease, net of taxes. Assuming that the lessee will make a profit in each period, its after-tax lease payment is the pretax payment times (1 − the marginal tax rate).

The depreciation tax shield is the tax saving forgone by the lessee because of the fact that depreciation cannot be taken for tax purposes (but is taken by the lessor

---

[6]The approach described below draws on Rodney L. Roenfeldt and Jerome S. Osteryoung, "Analysis of Financial Leases," *Financial Management* 2,1 (Spring 1973): 34–40.

instead). The tax shield in each period is a cash outflow and is calculated as the depreciation in each period times the marginal tax rate.

In some cases, certain costs of operation, maintenance, insurance, property taxes, or similar items may be different if the asset is leased rather than owned. If these costs are greater under leasing, they should be treated as a cash outflow; if they are less, they should be treated as inflow. Tax effects should be included. If the amounts are uncertain, strictly speaking, they should be adjusted for uncertainty. We will ignore this problem in our discussion here.

When an asset is leased rather than purchased, the lessor has title to it at the expiration of the lease. Hence, as compared to owning, the lessee forgoes the benefit of whatever value the asset might have at expiration. This residual value must be treated as a cash outflow attributable to the decision to lease. In many cases, it may be small enough to ignore. In others—notably in connection with leases involving real estate—residual values may be very significant and may have a significant impact on the cost of leasing as compared to owning. The higher is the residual value forgone, the higher is the cost of leasing relative to owning.

We have two remaining problems to address: tax effects and uncertainty. The residual value of the asset is likely to be more uncertain than other elements of the cash-flow stream and must be adjusted if the *EIC* calculation is to give valid results. One method of adjusting for uncertainty is to estimate the minimum residual value that reasonably can be anticipated, rather than the most likely. This **risk-adjusted residual value** should be a figure such that there is a low probability of realizing less.[7]

Risk-adjusted residual value—is the minimum residual value that reasonably can be anticipated.

Having estimated the incremental cash flows of leasing relative to owning, we now can calculate the equivalent interest cost of the lease, following the procedure outlined earlier in this chapter and given by Equation (1). The *EIC* is the discount rate that sums the present values of all the cash flows to zero and is exactly analogous to the internal rate of return *(IRR)* of an investment. As a measure of cost, the *EIC* suffers from the same technical shortcoming as does the *IRR*; it does not take into account the firm's reinvestment rate (see Chapter 9 for a discussion of this problem). For this reason, to be strictly correct, we should refer to the result of this calculation as the *approximate EIC*. In many cases, it is sufficiently accurate. Where it is not, methods exist to calculate the *true EIC*, but we will not consider them here. Let us now illustrate the calculation of the *EIC* with a simplified example.

Suppose a firm has decided that it needs a particular machine. The machine can be purchased for $50,000 or leased from the manufacturer for $11,850 per year under a 5-year noncancelable lease. Lease payments would be due at year end. If purchased, the firm would receive an investment tax credit of 10 percent. The firm uses straight-line depreciation, and Internal Revenue Service regulations permit depreciation of the machine over 5 years. The combined federal and state tax rate is assumed to be 46 percent. The firm's interest rate on 5-year debt is 13 percent, before taxes. The operating, maintenance, and insurance costs of the financial lease are the same as under ownership.

Table 16–3 outlines the incremental cash flows attributable to leasing. By leasing, the firm avoids an immediate outlay of $50,000, but forgoes the tax credit of $5,000,

---

[7]Technically, the appropriate figure to use for the residual value is a cash flow that has the same amount of risk as the other cash flows in the lease analysis.

Table 16–3

Incremental Cash Flows Attributable to a Hypothetical Lease (dollars)

Year	Acquisition Cost*	After-Tax Lease Payments	Depreciation Tax Shield	Residual Value After Tax	Total Cash Flow
0	45,000				45,000
1		−6,399	−4,600		−10,999
2		−6,399	−4,600		−10,999
3		−6,399	−4,600		−10,999
4		−6,399	−4,600		−10,999
5		−6,399	−4,600	−2,700	−13,699

Lease: Equivalent interest cost *(EIC)* after taxes = 8.62 percent
Debt: *EIC* after taxes = 13 (1 − 0.46) = 7.02 percent

*Adjusted for investment tax credit.

which we will assume to be available immediately. The lease, thus, provides an inflow of $45,000 in period 0. The annual lease payment net of taxes is $11,850(1 − 0.46) = $6,339 due at the end of each year 1–5.[8] Depreciation forgone is $50,000/5 = $10,000 per year, so the tax shield forgone is $10,000(0.46) = $4,600 per year. This depreciation tax shield that we lose is precisely the tax savings that depreciation would have provided had the asset been purchased. We discussed such tax shields earlier in Chapter 9.

The firm's best guess of the market value of the machine at the end of year 5 is $10,000. It is considered highly unlikely that the value will be less than $5,000. Let us, therefore, use $5,000 as our estimate of the risk-adjusted residual value. Because book value at year 5 will be zero, if the firm owns the machine, it will have a tax liability against the market value of ($5,000 − 0)(0.46) = $2,300. The adjusted residual value at the end of year 5, net of the tax liability, is $2,700.

Our task now is to find the rate that discounts the total cash-flow stream to zero. Using present-value tables in the Appendixes at the end of this book, we find that the rate is between 8 and 9 percent.

By interpolating, we can determine that the rate is about 8.6 percent. With a calculator equipped to do discounted-cash-flow analyses, we can determine it to be exactly 8.62 percent.

How do we interpret the equivalent interest cost calculated above? What exactly does it tell us? It tells us that the lease, with an *EIC* of 8.62 percent, is more expensive than borrowing, which the firm can do at an after-tax equivalent rate of 7.02 percent.[9]

---

[8]Leases often have payments due at the beginning of each period. Year-end flows are assumed here to simplify the analysis.

[9]For an approach to lease analysis that calculates benefits in dollar terms rather than as a percentage rate, see S. C. Myers, D. A. Dill, and A. J. Bautista, "Valuation of Financial Lease Contracts," *Journal of Finance* 31 (June 1976): 799–820. The present-value analysis has the additional advantage of indicating the dollar contribution to firm value of a given lease proposal. The *EIC* technique, on the other hand, yields a percentage rate that is easy to interpret and can be compared directly to the cost of borrowing.

In practice, leases often turn out to be more expensive than debt, unless the tax advantages to the lessor are sufficient to permit a lease payment that is low enough to reduce the equivalent interest cost below the borrowing rate.[10] Finance in Practice 16–1 describes such a lease in the case of the Anaconda Company. An *EIC* above the borrowing rate does not necessarily mean that the lease should be rejected. The qualitative advantages of the lease may be worth the additional cost, but the *EIC* tells management just how large a premium it really is paying.

A little additional arithmetic shows how important are some of the key elements in the analysis, such as taxes. The investment tax credit turns out to have a significant impact on the *EIC*. If, for example, the investment tax credit were 7 percent rather than 10 as assumed above, the *EIC* would be 7.4 percent rather than 8.6 percent. If there were no investment tax credit at all, the *EIC* would drop to 4.8 percent. The higher is the investment tax credit, the smaller is the outlay the firm avoids by leasing, and the higher is the cost of leasing. So a higher investment tax credit favors ownership.

We illustrated the calculation of the EIC using a simple example. In practice, leasing decisions often involve a more complex set of cash flows, longer time periods, accelerated depreciation, purchase and renewal options at the expiration of the lease, and so on. Occasionally, situations may be encountered in which an asset can be used only if it is leased because no option to purchase exists. In such cases, the investment and financing decisions are made together.

All these complications can be handled using DCF techniques. The computations are more tedious, but the logic is the same.

Sample Problem 16–1

Evaluating the Leasing Alternative for Ozark Printing Company

The Ozark Printing Company has decided to acquire a new printing press and is trying to decide between leasing and buying the machine. The press can be purchased from the manfacturer for $50,000 (delivered). The investment tax credit is 8 percent. The machine will be depreciated over a 5-year life, using straight-line depreciation to a zero salvage value. Ozark could lease the machine from the manufacturer for $12,000 per year for 5 years. All operating, maintenance, and insurance costs for the new machine will be borne by Ozark. Ozark has a 46 percent tax rate and a before-tax interest rate on long-term debt of 14 percent. Which financing alternative do you recommend (assuming there is no residual value of the machine in year 5)?

Solution

This problem can be approached by examining the incremental cash flow associated with leasing rather than purchasing. Table 16–4, which is similar to Table 16–3, can be used to trace the cash-flow patterns. The investment tax credit is 0.08 × $50,000 = $4,000. By leasing rather than purchasing, Ozark saves $46,000, an incremental cash inflow in year 0. The after-tax lease payments equal ($12,000)(1 − 0.46) = $6,480 per year, representing incremental cash outflows in years 1–5. The depreciation tax shield forgone by leasing equals ($50,000/5)(0.46) = $4,600 per year. We have assumed there is no residual or salvage value. Because we have a series of equal

---

[10]For evidence that most lease contracts have equivalent interest costs in excess of the cost of debt, see I. W. Sorensen and R. E. Johnson, "Equipment Financial Leasing Practices and Costs: An Empirical Study," *Financial Management* 6 (Spring 1977): 33–40.

Table 16–4

Cash Flows Attributable to Lease of Printing Press at Ozark Printing Company

Year	Acquisition Cost*	After-Tax Lease Payments	Depreciation Tax Shield	Residual Value After Tax	Total Cash Flow
0	$46,000				$46,000
1		−$6,480	−$4,600		−$11,080
2		−$6,480	−$4,600		−$11,080
3		−$6,480	−$4,600		−$11,080
4		−$6,480	−$4,600		−$11,080
5		−$6,480	−$4,600	0	−$11,080

*Adjusted for investment tax credit.

cash outflows (an annuity), we can solve for the *EIC* by determining that discount rate, x, for which the present-value annuity factor (from Appendix Table II at the end of the book) multiplied by the annuity amount of $11,080 would equal the $46,000 saving from leasing:

$46,000 = $11,080 \times$ present-value annuity factor for 5 years at x percent.

Solving the above equation, we see that the present-value annuity factor for 5 years at x percent must equal 4.152. This number lies between the numbers that can be found in the row for 5 years and the columns for 6 and 7 percent in Appendix Table II. Interpolating, we determine the equivalent interest cost to be:

$$EIC = 6 \text{ percent} + \frac{4.152 - 4.100}{4.212 - 4.100} = 6 \text{ percent} + 0.46 = 6.5 \text{ percent}$$

The after-tax equivalent rate for debt equals $(1 - 0.46)(0.14) = 0.076$, or 7.6 percent. Comparing the after-tax rate for debt to the equivalent interest cost for leasing, we see that it is cheaper to lease rather than purchase the machine. ▪▥▦

Leasing and the Tax Laws

As discussed earlier, a lease is often a way for a company effectively to sell tax benefits to another company. This exchange can be advantageous when the lessor can make better use of the tax benefits of ownership than can the lessee. By shifting tax benefits from the lessee to the lessor, the lease lowers the total taxes paid by the corporations to the government.

This tax effect of leasing has not gone unnoticed by Congress. In fact, in the Economic Recovery Act of 1981, Congress actually encouraged the use of leasing to save taxes as part of a series of measures (primarily shortening of periods over which capital equipment could be depreciated) to reduce corporate taxes and spur investment. Prior to the 1981 Tax Act, any lease that appeared to be designed to pass tax credits from one firm to another was resisted by the Internal Revenue Service, usually successfully. The new law actually encouraged this practice, and the mechanism was simple: the lessee was a firm with low or negative profits and, therefore, low taxes. The lessor was paying taxes. The lessor purchased the equipment needed by the lessee, took advantage of the new short depreciation periods, and passed most of the tax savings along to the lessee in the form of lower lease payments. Competition forced this outcome, for if the lessor tried to retain too large a share of the tax savings, another lessor would offer the lessee a lower lease rate.

Firms, along with their investment bankers, lawyers, and accountants, jumped to take advantage of the new law. By means of a lease, Ford Motor Company sold the tax credits on virtually its entire 1981 domestic capital-spending program to IBM for a price reported to be between $100 million to $200 million. B. F. Goodrich sold tax credits to IBM for $60 million, and Chrysler raised $26 million this way from General Electric Credit Corporation. During the first 90 days after passage of the 1981 law, some $2 billion in tax credits, involving equipment worth $15 billion, changed hands by means of the new leasing mechanism. The 1981 Tax Act was the biggest development in leasing in some time.

In fact, the use of these leases to avoid taxes became a prime target for criticism in times of large federal deficits. In 1982, Congress passed legislation restricting the generous lease treatment in the 1981 act. Leasing still remained a way to shift tax benefits but was subject to tighter regulations. What will be the tax treatment of leases in the future? Only time and the actions of tax authorities will tell. Financial managers must continually monitor the tax treatment of leases because tax benefits often play a key role. Changes in laws governing investment tax credits and depreciation schedules can dramatically affect incentives for leasing.

CONVERTIBLE SECURITIES

A **convertible security**—is a security that can be converted at the option of the holder into a security of the same firm but of another type.

In Chapter 12, convertible securities and warrants were described as potential sources of funds. A **convertible security** is one that can be converted at the option of the holder into a security of the same firm but of another type. Both bonds and preferred stock are issued as convertible securities and in nearly all cases are convertible into shares of common stock. Once converted into common stock, the process cannot be reversed. Holders of convertible bonds, thus, give up their position as creditors to become owners.

The use of convertible securities has varied over time. During the period 1960–1981, about 10 percent of all new corporate-bond offerings were convertible, and more than 20 percent of preferred-stock issues were convertible. In the late 1960s, convertible securities saw their largest use when many were used to finance corporate acquisitions. In the three-year period 1966–1968, about 25 percent of all corporate-bond issues were convertible, and the comparable figure for convertible preferred stock was almost 50 percent.[11]

The terms of the conversion privilege can be stated in terms of either a conversion price or a conversion ratio. For example, in August 1981, MCI Telecommunications

---

[11]Data on the use of convertible securities are from J. Hannum, *Convertible Bond Financing*, unpublished dissertation, University of North Carolina at Chapel Hill, 1983. The data describe new convertible financing as a proportion of underwritten public offerings. The numbers reported are averages of annual percentages.

Corporation, a competitor of AT&T in offering long-distance telephone service, issued $100 million worth of 20-year convertible subordinated debentures at an interest rate of 10.25 percent. The debentures were convertible into MCI common stock at $25.65 per share (the conversion price); that is, each $1,000 bond could be exchanged, at the holder's option, into $1,000/$25.65 = 38.986 shares of common stock (the conversion ratio). At the time of the debenture issue, MCI stock was selling at $21.75 per share. Thus, the conversion price was set about 18 percent above the then market price of the common stock.

Convertible securities nearly always include a *call feature* whereby the issuer, at its option, can call the issue for redemption. However, the purpose of the call feature usually is not to force redemption but to force conversion. When the value of the common shares into which the security is convertible exceeds the call price, holders would opt to convert rather than to redeem. Convertible securities usually are issued with the expectation that they will convert. The call feature provides the issuer some control over the timing of the conversion. We will return to the matter of forced conversion later.

Valuation of Convertible Securities

A convertible security derives value from two sources: its value as a bond or preferred stock and its potential value as common stock if converted.[12] The same general valuation principles apply in the case of both convertible bonds and convertible preferred stock. In the case of a convertible bond, we can label the two components of value the *bond value* and the *conversion value*. The convertible bond can be thought of as a combination of a bond plus an option to buy the firm's common stock. If the value of the common stock rises, the value of the option and, hence, that of the convertible bond will rise. If the value of the stock falls, the value of the convertible as a bond provides a floor below which the price of the convertible will not fall. The **bond value of a convertible bond** can be thought of as the present value of future interest and principal payments and can be expressed as shown in Equation (2).

The **bond value of a convertible bond**—is the present value of future interest and principal payments.

> The bond value of a convertible bond (V_B) can be determined, by calculating the present value of future interest and principal payments, as
>
> $$V_B = \left[\sum_{t=1}^{n} \frac{I}{(1 + K_d)^t} \right] + \frac{P}{(1 + K_d)^n} \qquad (2)$$
>
> where I = the annual interest payment, P = the principal amount due at maturity, n = number of years to maturity, and K_d = the yield to maturity on a nonconvertible bond of the same company or same risk class.

---

[12]Recent advances in finance theory that are beyond the scope of this text provide an alternative means to value convertible securities using options pricing theory. Such theory places a value on the ability to convert the bond to stock if the owner desires (the owner's option) and adds this value to the bond value. For a discussion of this valuation approach see R. Brealey and S. C. Myers, *Principles of Corporate Finance* (New York: McGraw-Hill, 1984).

Equation (2) represents the standard valuation equation for a bond. For simplicity, the expression assumes annual interest payments rather than the semiannual payments more often encountered in practice.

Consider the MCI convertible debenture mentioned earlier. It offered a 10.25 percent interest rate, or $102.50 a year per $1,000 bond at a time when the market interest rate on a straight (nonconvertible) bond for this company, according to company officials, would have been around 18 percent.[13] Applying Equation (2), we find the bond value of such a convertible bond to be

$$V_B = \left[\sum_{t=1}^{20} \frac{\$102.50}{(1.18)^t} \right] + \frac{\$1,000}{(1.18)^{20}}$$

$$= \$548.66 + \$36.51$$

$$= \$585.17$$

The **conversion value of a convertible bond**—is the market value of the common stock into which the bond is convertible.

The **conversion value of a convertible bond** is the market value of the common stock into which the bond is convertible. The bond described above is convertible into 38.986 shares of common stock, and the market price per share of stock was $21.75. The conversion value of each bond was, therefore, (38.986)($21.75) = $847.95.

> **The value of a convertible bond depends on both its bond value and its conversion value.**

Because the convertible security has value as a bond (or as preferred stock), its market price will not fall below its bond value. Because of the value of this downside protection, a convertible security nearly always sells at a premium over its exact conversion value. For example, if the MCI convertible debenture were sold for $1,000, the premium over its exact conversion value would be $1,000 − $847.95 = $152.05. The magnitude of this premium depends on the likelihood that conversion value will drop below bond value.

The **conversion premium**—is the amount by which a convertible bond's market price exceeds the higher of its bond value or its conversion value.

The **conversion premium**, therefore, is a function of the difference between conversion value and bond value and also of the volatility of the conversion value, which depends on the volatility of the price of the underlying stock. As noted earlier, the bond value of a convertible bond provides a floor below which its price will not fall. A convertible bond usually sells at a premium over bond value because of the value of the conversion privilege. Thus, the conversion premium of the bond is the amount by which its market price exceeds the higher of its bond value or its conversion value. Figure 16–2 diagrams these price relationships.

When the conversion value of the bond is below bond value, the conversion premium over bond value can be ascribed to the value of the conversion privilege. When conversion value exceeds bond value, the premium over conversion value can be as-

---

[13]See "Funding Fast Growth at MCI," *Business Week*, October 5, 1981. The MCI bonds were sold in August 1981, a time of unusually high interest rates in the long-term bond market. At the time, the rate on AAA corporate bonds was about 15.2 percent.

Figure 16–2
Relationship of Convertible-Bond Price to Common-Stock Price

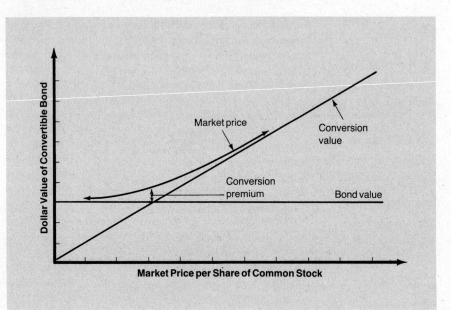

cribed to the downside protection of the floor. As the stock price rises, the conversion value rises, and the value of the downside protection declines. Also, the probability of a call of the issue increases, and if called, the bond is worth only its conversion value. On the other side, the farther conversion value falls below bond value, the less the conversion privilege is worth. Consequently, as indicated in Figure 16–2, the conversion premium narrows at both ends of the spectrum of stock prices.

The diagram in Figure 16–2 assumes that the bond value is constant. In fact, the floor provided by the bond value is not fixed, and in practice it may vary because of the same factors that affect stock price. The element K_d in Equation (2) represents the rate of return required by the market on a straight debt issue of the firm in question. This required rate of return may change either in response to a change in the general level of interest rates or to a change in the perceived riskiness of the particular firm's cash flows. For example, an increase in the required rate of return on the firm's debt from 18 to 19 percent would cause the bond value in the example cited earlier to drop from \$585.17 to \$553.68. Thus, a decline in the firm's prospects might give rise to a decline in the bond value of its convertible bonds just at the time when the bond value is most needed as downside protection against a stock price that is also declining for the same reason. The floor provided by the bond value is not a fixed floor, but one that can vary.

Accounting Treatment

Conversion of a convertible security into common stock affects earnings per share for two reasons: first, the requirement to pay interest (or dividends, in the case of preferred

Table 16–5

Effect of Conversion on Earnings per Share at a Hypothetical Firm (thousands of dollars)

	Before Conversion	After Conversion
Expected earnings before interest and taxes (EBIT)	$5,000	$5,000
Interest on bonds at 9 percent	540	—
Profit before taxes	$4,460	$5,000
Taxes at 50 percent	2,230	2,500
Profit after taxes	$2,230	$2,500
Common shares outstanding	500	620
Expected earnings per share	$ 4.46	$ 4.03

stock) is eliminated, and second, the number of common shares is increased. For example, assume a company issues $6 million of 9 percent convertible bonds and that each bond is convertible into 20 shares of stock. Assume further that expected earnings before interest and taxes (EBIT) is $5 million, that the tax rate is 50 percent, and that 500,000 shares of common stock are outstanding before conversion. Earnings per share before and after conversion are shown in Table 16–5.

As indicated, conversion causes the firm's earnings per share to decline. Whether the stock price also will decline depends on circumstances. Conversion reduced expected earnings per share from $4.46 to $4.03 (that is, by 9.6 percent), but at the same time it also reduced the firm's debt/equity ratio, thereby reducing the riskiness of earnings per share (EPS). The reduction in risk offsets at least in part the reduction in expected EPS. Applying the theory of financial leverage developed in Chapter 13, the effect on the value of the firm's shares should depend on the effect of the conversion on taxes and bankruptcy risk. If the firm were significantly below its optimal debt ratio, conversion would reduce the total value of the firm by the amount of the net tax benefits forgone, considering both corporate and personal taxes of investors (see discussion in Chapter 13). If the firm were above its optimal debt ratio, conversion theoretically should increase firm value. In the latter case, the reduction in risk would more than offset the reduction in expected EPS.

To assist investors in evaluating the impact of convertible securities, current accounting guidelines require reporting of two EPS figures: primary EPS and fully diluted EPS. The fully diluted figure shows on a pro-forma basis what EPS would be if all outstanding convertible securities were converted to common stock.

Financing with Convertible Securities

Convertible securities usually are issued at a premium over current conversion value. Consider a 9 percent convertible bond issued by ABC Corporation at $1,000 with a conversion price of $50 (conversion ratio is 20 shares of common stock per bond) and a call price of $1,090. If the market price of the common stock at the time the bonds are issued is $44 per share, the conversion value of the bonds is 20 × $44 = $880. The issue price of $1,000, thus, represents a premium of 13.6 percent over the conversion value. The premium also can be calculated by comparing the conversion price,

$50, to the market price at the time of issue, $44—a premium of ($50 − $44)/$44 = 13.6 percent.

The conversion premium set at time of issue varies from one issue to another but usually lies between 10 percent and 20 percent. The premium is set by adjusting the conversion ratio. In general, the faster the firm is growing, the higher the premium is set. Most convertible securities are issued with the expectation that they will convert in the not too distant future—say, a period of a few years. A convertible issue, thus, can be viewed as a deferred common-stock issue, with the stock sold for future delivery at a price above current market price. Compared to a sale of common stock now, the firm obtains a higher price for the stock, issues fewer shares, and subjects existing shareholders to less earnings dilution. As compared to a straight-debt issue, the convertible issue can be sold at a lower interest rate—sometimes substantially lower, as in the MCI case. Similarly, convertible preferred stock can be sold at a lower dividend rate than can straight preferred stock.

In order to induce complete conversion, the issue usually must be called by the issuing firm. Calling the issue would force conversion provided the conversion value of the bonds were sufficiently above the call price. If ABC Corporation called its convertible bonds at $1,090 at a time when its stock was selling for $60, holders would be forced to choose between $1,090 in cash or stock worth $1,200. Most, undoubtedly, would convert. Because some reasonable period must be allowed for the transaction to be consummated, firms usually find it wise to wait until conversion value is 10 percent to 20 percent above the call price before calling the issue. Such a margin gives some protection against unexpected drops in the stock price during the conversion period.

On June 3, 1981, Wang Laboratories, a manufacturer of computer equipment based in Massachusetts, announced the call of its 9 percent convertible subordinated debentures due in 2005. The debentures were convertible into Wang Class B common stock at a conversion price of $32, so each $1,000 debenture could be exchanged for 31.25 shares of common stock. At the time the debentures were called, Wang Class B common stock was selling for $40.625 per share. Wang wanted the bondholders to convert, but they would not do so voluntarily even though they could exchange a bond with a face value of $1,000 for 31.25 shares of stock worth $1269.53. Why wouldn't the bondholders convert? The dividend on Wang Class B common stock was only $0.12 per share at that time. Thus, a bondholder would give up a bond paying $90 per year in interest for stock paying only $0.12 × 31.25 = $3.75—not a good bargain. So Wang had to *force* bondholders to convert. According to the original terms of issue, each bond was callable at *Wang's* option at a price of $1,090 (a premium of one year's interest) plus accrued interest to the date of the call—a total of $1,124.25 per bond. Thus, by calling the issue, the company forced holders of a bond to choose either $1,124.25 in cash or stock worth $1,269.53. One would anticipate that all would choose to convert into stock, as desired by the company.

When a firm that has issued convertible securities does not perform as well as had been expected, its stock price may not rise sufficiently to permit a forced conversion. If this situation persists, the convertible issue is said to be *hung*, or *overhanging*. The existence of a hung convertible issue in a firm's capital structure usually is taken as evidence that things have not gone as planned. Often the firm's flexibility with respect to external financing is reduced considerably, because any new issue may be difficult as long as the uncertainty over the convertible issue is unresolved. If the financing constraint motivates the firm to alter its commercial strategy—perhaps by forgoing

Finance in Practice 16–2

Why Investors Like Convertibles

Convertibles are hybrid securities, offering to investors some of the advantages of fixed-income securities, while at the same time providing an opportunity to participate in rising stock prices. If the market advances, holders of convertible securities can convert their bonds or preferred stock into common stock and reap the rewards of the appreciation in the common stock. As noted earlier, they actually do not even have to convert because the price of the convertible security (assuming that it is publicly traded) will rise right along with the common-stock price. The investor can simply sell the convertible security. If, on the other hand, common-stock prices fall, investors can hold onto their convertible securities and remain protected on the downside.

For example, on February 4, 1985, the common stock of Computervision Corporation hit a high of $44.25 a share. On April 8, it closed at $15.65, a drop of 65 percent. But Computervision's 8 percent convertible bonds due in 2009 fell only 39 percent, from $1,162.50 in February to $705 in April. A fall of 39 percent isn't good, but it is better than 65 percent. The convertible, thus, did provide some downside protection.

Westinghouse Electric Corporation provides a happier example. Westinghouse sold an issue of 9 percent convertible bonds at par ($1,000 per bond) in August of 1984. The common stock was selling at $26.625 at the time, and the bonds were convertible at $31. On April 8, 1985, the stock had risen to $29.125, an increase of 9.4 percent. During that time the convertible bonds appreciated 12.5 percent to $1,125. They also provided a higher current yield of 9 percent versus about 3.7 percent for the common stock.

The importance of convertible securities to firms as financing instruments depends on their popularity with investors. Just how great the benefits of convertible securities to firms really are is a matter of some dispute, but we can be sure that as long as convertible securities appeal to some investors, firms will continue to find them useful as financing vehicles.

Source: Adapted from "When the Stock Market is Stuck in a Rut, Convertible Securities May Be a Good Play," *Wall Street Journal*, April 9, 1985.

---

investments that it otherwise would have made—the cost of a hung convertible issue to the shareholders may be very high. Such potential complications in the event of unfavorable developments constitute an important disadvantage of convertible securities. A firm issuing convertible securities, therefore, must be prepared to see the issue remain as debt or preferred stock for an indefinite period.

A firm may issue convertible securities as a means of obtaining a lower interest rate on debt or a lower dividend on preferred stock than would be possible with a nonconvertible issue. Another motive might arise in a situation in which management felt that its prospects were not being fairly evaluated by the stock market. A convertible issue offers an opportunity to sell common stock at a premium over current market rates, assuming that conversion eventually takes place. Rapidly growing firms might find this possibility especially appealing.

Convertible securities also might be attractive in more specialized financing situations. Consider, for example, a relatively young firm with no track record that is attempting to raise outside capital. In such high-risk situations, investors might wish to participate provided that they share in the firm's good fortunes as equity investors, should the outcome be favorable. A convertible bond gives them an option on an equity position but at the same time provides a senior debt claim against assets during the early, more uncertain, period. Other specialized situations in which convertible securities might be attractive include mergers and acquisitions. In such cases, tax considerations might make a convertible security attractive to both buyers and sellers.

WARRANTS

A **warrant**—is an option to purchase a specified number of shares of common stock at a specified price for a specified period of time, is typically issued in connection with bonds, and is usually detachable.

A **warrant** is an option to purchase a specified number of shares of common stock at a specified price for a specified period of time. Warrants typically are issued in connection with bonds and usually are detachable, but not always. If detachable, the warrants can be detached from the bonds and sold separately. Markets exist for detachable warrants; many are listed on the American Stock Exchange, and a few are listed on the New York Stock Exchange.

The warrant itself sets forth the terms of the option, which include the number of shares that can be purchased with each warrant, the exercise price, and the time period over which the warrant can be exercised. Most warrants can be exercised over a number of years, and most have a stated expiration date. Sometimes the terms—either the exercise price or the shares per warrant—may change over time. When the warrant is exercised, it is exchanged along with an appropriate sum of money for the specified number of shares of common stock.

Besides providing an option that is detachable, warrants differ from convertible securities in other respects. First, the firm receives additional funds when warrants are exercised, whereas it does not when convertibles convert. Accounting entries in the capital section of the balance sheet differ accordingly. Second, the combination of warrant and bond is more flexible from the holder's standpoint than a convertible bond, because there are two separate claims with different characteristics both of which have value. From the firm's standpoint, warrants may provide less control than convertible securities, because the firm cannot force holders of warrants to exercise them. Warrants, like convertible securities, are taken into account in calculating fully diluted EPS.

> **A firm receives additional funds when warrants are exercised but receives no additional funds when convertibles convert.**

If a warrant were about to expire, the value of the warrant, W, could be determined as shown in Equation (3).

The value of a warrant (W), can be determined, depending on whether market price (P) or exercise price (E) of the common stock per share is greater, as

$$W = N(P - E) \qquad \text{if } P > E$$

or (3)

$$W = 0 \qquad\qquad \text{if } P \leq E$$

where N = the number of shares of common stock that can be purchased with one warrant, P = the market price of the common stock per share, and E = the *exercise price* of the common stock per share that has been stipulated in the warrant.

Figure 16—3
Valuation of a Warrant

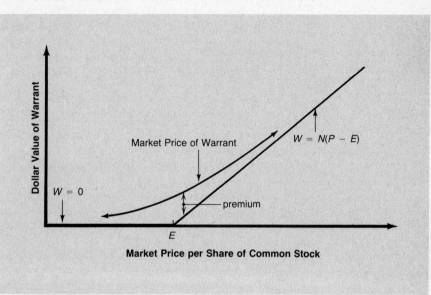

Equation (3) states that if the stock is selling for more than the exercise price (if P is greater than E), the warrant has a value equal to the difference between the market price and exercise price of the stock times the number of shares of stock the warrant allows you to buy at the exercise price. For example, if $P = \$5$, $E = \$3$, and $N = 100$, Equation (3) indicates that the value of the warrant = $\$100(\$5 - \$3) = \$200$. The warrant would be worth $200 because the holder could immediately make a $200 profit by purchasing 100 shares of stock for $3 a share and selling it in the market at $5 a share. Equation (3) also indicates, however, that if the market price is less than or equal to the exercise price the warrant is worthless.

Note that Equation (3) was developed assuming the warrant was about to expire, so that an owner could either exercise the warrant by buying stock at the lower price and selling this stock at the prevailing market price or see the warrant expire and become worthless.

In fact, as long as a warrant has an extended time period left before expiration, there is some chance that the stock's market price will go higher and that the warrant will be worth even more than indicated by Equation (3). As a result, warrants normally sell for more than the theoretical value given in Equation (3). Figure 16-3 displays the situation graphically. The magnitude of the premium over theoretical value depends primarily on the time remaining to expiration, the volatility of the common stock, and the opportunity cost of funds to investors.

Like convertible securities, warrants give the holder an option on an equity claim and, therefore, a chance to share in a firm's good fortunes. Warrants usually are issued in connection with debt securities and can be sold privately or publicly, but sometimes they may be issued by themselves. When issued in connection with debt securities, the motive usually is to sweeten the deal and, thereby, to make the issue easier to sell or salable at a lower rate of interest. In exchange for the option, the buyer accepts the lower rate. A firm with a marginal credit rating faced with an embarrassingly high interest rate might use warrants to lower the rate. A firm unable to sell a debt issue at any rate, presumably because of risk or the lack of a track record, might find that warrants would make the issue salable. Venture capitalists might find warrants an alternative to convertible securities as a means of providing funds to a fledgling firm, with the security of a debt claim and also an option on the equity.

FINANCING IN COMPETITIVE MARKETS

The use of convertible securities and warrants does indeed lower the rate of interest (or preferred dividends) to the firm, but at a price. In return for the lower rate, the buyers of convertible securities or warrants obtain a claim against the firm's equity. If things turn out favorably, they later will be able to buy the firm's stock at a bargain price. In the case of firms with marginal credit ratings or unproven records, convertible securities and warrants may provide sources of financing not available otherwise. Here again, the firm pays for the accommodation with a claim on its equity.

> The use of convertible securities and warrants lowers the rate of interest (or preferred dividends) to the firm, but at the price of granting a claim against the firm's equity.

If a firm issuing convertible securities or warrants fully discloses all material information, as it should, we would expect a competitive market to evaluate the firm's prospects in an unbiased manner. The market is likely to value the option on the common stock properly, meaning that overvaluation and undervaluation are about equally likely. In a competitive market, we would expect investors to reduce the dividend or interest rate on the securities by an amount that correctly reflects the value of the option to buy the firm's stock. Thus, the firm pays for the lower interest or dividend rate approximately what it is worth.[14]

What of the argument that convertible securities permit sale of common stock at a premium price at a time when a sale of straight equity may be disadvantageous because of depressed prices? The use of convertible securities can offer advantages. However, if the market were placing an unfairly low value on the firm's stock, it likely would place a correspondingly low value on the conversion privilege.

What, then, do we conclude with respect to the use of convertible securities and warrants? For reasons discussed above, convertible securities and warrants are unlikely to offer advantages for which the firm does not pay full price. Both are complex securities requiring considerable expertise to market. Convertible securities have the additional disadvantage of exposing the firm to potentially serious complications if they do not convert as planned. As noted earlier, a hung convertible issue can constrain a firm's future financing and operating flexibility. The uncertainty regarding

---

[14]For a theoretical development of this argument in the case of convertible debt, see Wilbur G. Lewellen and George A. Racette, "Convertible Debt Financing," *Journal of Financial and Quantitative Analysis* 8,5 (December 1973): 777–92.

future conversion in and of itself may be a drawback. The possibility of complications serious enough to require an alteration of commercial strategy is not a prospect to be taken lightly.

We can conclude that convertible securities and warrants find their main application in specialized financing situations. Besides providing a source of funds to firms unable to use conventional securities, convertible securities and warrants also may be useful in mergers and acquisitions and in regulated industries, such as utilities. Thus, convertible securities and warrants are specialized securities that provide varying combinations of contractual claims with options on equity. Where the need is specialized, they can be used to advantage.

KEY CONCEPTS

1. By leasing, a firm can obtain use of an asset without owning the asset.

2. Leases are forms of financing that are similar to debt financing. Much of the motivation for leases arises from tax considerations.

3. To analyze the desirability of leasing, one can estimate the incremental cash flows associated with a lease and determine the effective interest cost of a lease. If this cost is lower than the cost of alternative financing, the lease is a desirable choice of financing.

4. Convertible securities and warrants are specialized securities that provide varying combinations of contractual claims with options on equity.

5. Convertible bonds have two sources of value: bond value and conversion value.

6. Warrants can be used as an extra incentive to lenders for debt issues.

7. While the use of convertible bonds or warrants can lower the rate of interest to the firm, this lower interest rate comes at a cost—the cost of giving up a claim on the firm's equity. In competitive financial markets, the firm pays for the lower interest rate approximately what it is worth. As a result, the lower interest rate does not necessarily mean that existing shareholders will obtain a net benefit (increase in value) as the result of the firm's use of convertible securities or warrants.

SUMMARY

Leasing has become an important means of financing in special situations. Leasing allows a lessee to use an asset even though the asset is owned by the lessor.

Discounted-cash-flow techniques can be used to calculate the equivalent interest cost *(EIC)* of any financing plan. The *EIC* technique is especially useful in analyzing leases. A noncancelable (financial) lease is the functional equivalent of debt and has the same effect on firm risk. Therefore, the *EIC* of a financial lease can be compared directly to the cost of borrowing.

To calculate the equivalent interest cost of a lease, the incremental-cash-flow rule is applied in order to identify the cash flows attributable to the lease. Such cash flows normally include the avoided outlay for the asset, the lost investment tax credit, the lease payment,

the depreciation tax shield, and the residual value of the asset. Given estimates of these cash flows, the equivalent interest cost of the lease can be calculated to determine whether the lease is more or less expensive than borrowing.

Convertible securities (bonds and preferred stock) and warrants represent additional financing options open to a firm. A convertible security derives its value from two sources: its value as a bond or preferred stock and its value as common stock if converted. Convertible securities normally carry a lower interest or dividend rate than would nonconvertible securities of the same firm, reflecting the value of the option to convert the security into common stock.

Warrants are options to buy common stock at a

specified price. Warrants normally are issued in combination with debt securities for the purpose of improving the marketability of the debt or obtaining a lower rate of interest. Like convertible securities, warrants find their main application in specialized financing situations.

QUESTIONS

1. How can discounted-cash-flow techniques be used to evaluate financing alternatives?
2. In what sense can a lease be viewed as a specialized form of debt financing?
3. How can discounted-cash-flow techniques be used to evaluate leases?
4. What is a convertible security?
5. What is the function of the call feature of a convertible security?
6. What is the *conversion premium* of a convertible-bond or preferred-stock issue?
7. What consequences do you foresee if a convertible security fails to convert as originally planned?
8. Under what circumstances might warrants be used to advantage in financing?
9. What are the implications of highly competitive financial markets for the use of convertible securities and warrants?

PROBLEMS

1. Find the equivalent interest cost of each of the following loans:
   a. A $1,000 loan repaid in one payment of $1,080 at the end of 1 year.
   b. A $1,000 loan repaid in four annual payments of $80 each and one final payment of $1,080 at the end of the fifth year.
   c. A $1,000 loan repaid in five annual payments of $250.44.
   d. A $1,000 loan repaid in five annual payments of $280, $264, $248, $232, and $216, respectively.
2. Queens Manufacturing Company has decided to acquire a new pressing machine and is trying to decide between the leasing and buying alternatives. The machine can be purchased from the manufacturer for a delivered price of $85,000. The machine will be depreciated over a 10-year period to a zero salvage value although the firm estimates that it could be sold for a minimum of $5,000 at the end of the 10 years. Alternatively, the manufacturer has offered a financial lease at $11,000 per year for the 10 years with all operating, maintenance, and insurance expense to be borne by the lessee. The firm's before-tax interest rate on long-term debt is 10 percent, all depreciation is straight-line, and the tax rate is 45 percent. Which financing alternative would you recommend?

3. The Mudville public school system plans to install a computer to cut expenses for record-keeping, payroll, and other clerical functions. The manufacturer offers two options: purchase or a noncancelable lease. Outright purchase would require an outlay of $150,000. If purchased, maintenance and insurance would run $1,000 per month. Alternatively, Mudville could lease the computer for an initial term of 4 years at $4,000 per month, maintenance and insurance included. At the end of 4 years, Mudville would have the option of purchasing the computer for $40,000 (the estimated fair market value at that time), leasing for a second 4-year term for $2,500 per month, or terminating the arrangement. At the end of year 8, the computer is expected to have zero salvage value. Lease contracts would be noncancelable in both years 1–4 and 5–8. Operating costs other than maintenance and insurance would be the same under either purchase or lease. The interest rate on long-term U.S. government bonds is 10 percent, and Mudville's borrowing rate (on tax-free municipal bonds) is 9 percent. How should Mudville finance the computer?

4. Levy Industries has determined that holders of the company's convertible bonds would convert the issue if it were called. The company therefore has decided to force the conversion of the 10,000 outstanding bonds in order to increase its equity base

in preparation for future bond issues. The $1,000 par bonds mature in 20 years and carry an 11 percent coupon. Each bond is convertible into 50 shares of common stock. The firm currently has 1.7 million shares of stock outstanding. The tax rate is 46 percent.

a. Assuming that the market rate of interest on nonconvertible bonds of comparable risk is 13 percent, calculate the bond value of Levy's convertible issue.

b. Levy's stock currently is selling for $22 per share. Calculate the conversion value of the convertible bonds.

c. Calculate the effect of conversion on earnings per share (EPS) at an expected earnings before interest and taxes (EBIT) of $8 million.

5. The Schlotterbeck Manufacturing Company has decided to acquire a new automated drilling machine for its plant in Portland, Maine. The firm can purchase the machine from the manufacturer for a delivered price of $125,000. If purchased, the machine qualifies for an investment tax credit of 10 percent. The incremental servicing and maintenance costs of the new machine are estimated to be $5,000 annually. These costs would not be incurred if the machine is leased. If purchased, the machine will be depreciated over a 10-year period to a zero salvage value using the straight-line method. Even though depreciation will be based on a zero salvage value, the company anticipates being able to sell the machine for a minimum of $6,000 at the end of the 10 years. Alternatively, Schlotterbeck could lease the machine for an initial term of 5 years at $3,000 per month with the option of purchasing the machine at the end of year 5 for $50,000 (the estimated fair market value at that time) or renew the lease for another 5-year term for $2,000 per month. At the end of year 10, all rights to the machine would revert back to the leasing company and Schlotterbeck would not be given a purchase option. The monthly lease payments include all servicing and maintenance costs for the machine. The firm's tax rate is 46 percent, and its before-tax interest rate on long-term debt is 12 percent.

a. Which plan would you recommend? (For simplicity, in your calculations use annual year-end lease payments of $36,000 (years 1–5) and $24,000 (years 6–10) rather than the monthly payments.)

b. If the firm used the sum of the years' digits rather than straight-line depreciation, how would the cash-flow pattern change? (Give a general answer rather than detailed calculations.)

c. Suppose this industry is subject to rapid technological changes in production methods which makes existing equipment obsolete relatively quickly. Would this change your recommendation in part (a)?

6. Two years ago, Peterson and Peterson, Inc., sold $5 million in 10 percent, 20-year convertible bonds. The $1,000 par bonds are convertible into 25 shares of common stock each and are callable after 2 years at a price of $1,100. The firm currently has 1.4 million shares of stock outstanding. The stock is currently trading at $45 per share. The marginal tax rate of the firm is 46 percent.

a. At the time of the bond issue, Peterson stock was selling for $35 a share. What was the initial conversion premium of the convertible issue?

b. If the interest rate on nonconvertible bonds of comparable risk currently is 12 percent, what is the bond value of Peterson's convertible issue?

c. What is the current conversion value of Peterson's convertible bonds? What is the minimum price at which you would expect to see the convertible bonds selling? If Peterson's stock price fell to $30 per share, what would be the bonds' minimum price?

7. Suppose you are considering purchasing a call option on 100 shares of Robinson Industries common stock at a price of $43.50 per share. The option expires three months from today. The stock is currently selling for $36.125 per share.

a. Does this call have any value? Why or why not?

b. In order for this to be an attractive investment for you how would you expect the stock price to behave in the future (rise or fall)?

c. Suppose that you decide to purchase the contract. One month later, you need cash and would like to sell the contract to another investor. At that time, the stock price happens to be $36.125 per share. Would there be a market for the contract? If so, what would you expect the price of the contract to be relative to the price that you paid for the contract one month ago?

d. Now suppose that you still hold the call, and it is due to expire in one week. The stock price has jumped around considerably and is now $42.00. If you decide to sell the contract at this time, would anyone be willing to buy it? If so, what considerations would be important in determining a fair price for the call-option contract?

e. Suppose that on the expiration date of the call, the stock price is $45.25 per share. What is the value of the contract?

f. Now suppose that on the expiration date of the contract, the stock price is $39.75 per share. What is the value of the contract?

REFERENCES

Andersen, P. F., and J. D. Martin. "Lease Versus Purchase Decisions: A Survey of Current Practice." *Financial Management* 6 (Sept. 1977): 41–47.

Athanasopoulos, P. J., and P. W. Bacon. "The Evaluation of Leveraged Leases." *Financial Management* 9 (Spring 1980): 76–80.

Bacon, P. W., and E. L. Winn, Jr. "The Impact of Forced Conversion of Stock Prices." *Journal of Finance* 24 (Dec. 1969): 871–874.

Baumol, W. J., B. G. Malkiel, and R. E. Quandt. "The Evaluation of Convertible Securities." *Quarterly Journal of Economics* 80 (Feb. 1966): 48–59.

Bierman, H. *The Lease Versus Buy Decision.* Englewood Cliffs, New Jersey: Prentice Hall, Inc., 1982.

Black, F., and M. Scholes. "The Pricing of Options and Corporate Liabilities." *Journal of Political Economy* (May–June 1973): 637–654.

Bower, R. S. "Issues in Lease Financing." *Financial Management* 2 (Winter 1973): 25–34.

Bowlin, O. D. "The Refunding Decision: Another Special Case in Capital Budgeting." *Journal of Finance* 21 (Mar. 1966): 55–68.

Bradford, W. D. "Monetary Position, Unanticipated Inflation and Changes in the Value of the Firm." *Quarterly Review of Economics and Business* 16: 47–53.

Brealey, R. A. *Security Prices in a Competitive Market.* Cambridge, Mass.: MIT Press, 1971.

Brealey, R., and S. Myers. *Principles of Corporate Finance.* New York: McGraw Hill, Inc., 1981.

Brigham, E. F. "An Analysis of Convertible Debentures: Theory and Some Empirical Evidence." *Journal of Finance* 21 (Mar. 1966): 35–54.

Buse, A. "Expectations, Coupons, and Yields." *Journal of Finance* 25 (Sept. 1970): 809–818.

Cooper, K., and R. H. Strawser. "Evaluation of Capital Investment Projects Involving Asset Leases." *Financial Management* 4 (Spring 1975): 44–49.

Cretein, P. D., Jr. "Convertible Premium vs. Stock Prices." *Financial Analysts Journal* 25 (Nov.–Dec. 1969): 90–96.

Franks, J. R., and S. C. Hodges. "Valuation of Financial Lease Contracts: A Note." *Journal of Finance* 33 (May 1978): 657–669.

"Funding Fast Growth at MCI." *Business Week* (October 5, 1981).

Gritta, R. D. "The Impact of Lease Capitalization." *Financial Analysts Journal* 30 (Mar.–Apr. 1974): 47–52.

Jen, F. C., and J. E. Wert. "The Deferred Call Provision and Corporate Bond Yields." *Journal of Financial and Quantitative Analysis* 3 (June 1968): 157–170.

Jen, F. C., and J. E. Wert. "The Effect of Call Risk Upon Corporate Bond Yields." *Journal of Finance* 22 (Dec. 1967): 637–652.

Kalotay, A. J. "Innovations in Corporate Finance: Deep Discount Private Placements." *Financial Management* 11 (Spring 1982): 55–57.

Katzin, J. S. "Financial and Legal Problems in the Use of Convertible Securities." *Business Lawyer* 24 (Jan. 1969): 359–373.

Kirkland, R. I., Jr. "The Trade in Tax Breaks Takes Off." *Fortune* (September 21, 1981).

Lewellen, W. G., and G. A. Racette. "Convertible Debt Financing." *Journal of Financial and Quantitative Analysis* 8 (Dec. 1973): 777–792.

Miller, A. B. "How to Call Your Convertible." *Harvard Business Review* 49 (May–June 1971): 66–70.

Miller, M., and C. W. Upton. "Leasing, Buying and the Cost of Capital Services." *Journal of Finance* 31 (June 1976): 761–786.

Meyers, S. C., D. A. Dill, and J. A. Bautista. "Valuation of Financial Lease Contracts." *Journal of Finance* 31 (June 1976): 799–820.

Nantell, T. J. "Equivalence of Leases vs. Buy Analysis." *Financial Management* 2 (Autumn 1973): 61–65.

Pinches, G. E. "Financing With Convertible Preferred Stock, 1960–1967." *Journal of Finance* 25 (Mar. 1970): 53–64.

Pye, G. "The Value of Call Deferment on a Bond: Some

Empirical Results.'' *Journal of Finance* 22 (Dec. 1967): 623–636.

Roenfeldt, R. L., and J. S. Osteryoung. ''Analysis of Financial Leases.'' *Financial Management* 2 (Spring 1973): 34–40.

Schachner, L. ''The New Accounting for Leases.'' *Financial Executive* (Feb. 1978).

Scott, J. H., Jr., ''Bankruptcy, Secured Debt, and Optimal Capital Structure.'' *Journal of Finance* 32 (Mar. 1977): 1–20.

Shelton, J. P. ''The Relation of the Price of a Warrant to the Price of Its Associated Stock.'' *Financial Analysts Journal* 23 (May–June, 1967): 143–151.

Soldofsky, R. M. ''Yield-Risk Performance of Convertible Securities.'' *Financial Analysts Journal* 39 (Mar.–Apr. 1971): 61–65.

Sorensen, I. W., and R. E. Johnson. ''Equipment, Financial Leasing and Costs: An Empirical Study.'' *Financial Management* 6 (Sept. 1977): 33–40.

Stevenson, R. A., and J. Lavely. ''Why a Bond Warrant Issue?'' *Financial Executive* 38 (June 1970): 16–21.

''The Tax-Credit Trade Soars.'' *Fortune* (December 14, 1981).

Vanderwicken, P. ''The Powerful Logic of the Leasing Boom'' *Fortune* 88 (Nov. 1973) 132–136.

Van Horne, J. C. ''Warrant Valuation in Relation to Volatility and Opportunity Cost.'' *Industrial Management Review* 10 (Spring 1969): 19–32.

Weil, R. L., Jr., J. E. Segall, and D. Greene, Jr. ''Premiums on Convertible Bonds.'' *Journal of Finance* 23 (June 1968): 445–463.

Appendix 16A

Options and Futures

Two types of specialized financial contracts have become increasingly important—options and futures contracts. Both types of contracts have specialized uses for both individual investors and corporate managers.

OPTIONS

As we have discussed in Chapter 16, warrants are sold (typically attached to bonds) by the company to raise new funds and give the owner an option to buy the company's stock at a certain price for a specified period of time. If the warrant's owner exercises the option, he or she will purchase stock from the company.

In fact, warrants are just one type of *option* contract. An option is a contract conveying the right to buy or sell designated securities or commodities at a specified price during a stipulated period of time. Such a contract is an agreement between two parties. The option buyer has the right to exercise the option but does not have an obligation to buy or sell the security. The option seller, sometimes referred to as the *writer* of the option, must stand ready to honor the buyer's choice. A warrant is, thus, an option on the common stock of a company where the company is the option seller.

In recent years, the variety of options on financial securities has increased tremendously, as have their uses. Now there are options on stocks, interest rates, stock indexes and foreign currrencies, to name a few examples. All options have the same basic elements: (1) the option buyer has a right, not an obligation; (2) the price of the underlying security is specified when the option is originally sold; (3) there is a time frame in which the option must be exercised. There are, however, many important differences among options. *European options*, for example, may be exercised only at maturity. *American options* can be exercised at any time up through the expiration date.

Options on Common Stock

There are three basic categories of options allowing investors to purchase stock: (1) warrants, (2) stock options given to employees, and (3) call and put options. Warrants, as discussed in Chapter 16, are sold by the company to outside investors. *Stock options* are similar to warrants but are granted by the company to selected managers as part of the managers' compensation to allow the managers to share in the company's good fortune if share prices go up. The last category, call and put options, are traded between outside investors on organized exchanges.

A *call option* gives the owner the right to buy a specified number of shares of stock for a specified price for a specified period of time. Call options differ from warrants and stock options given to managers in that the call option is sold by another investor (not the corporation), so that if the call option is exercised its owner does not purchase new stock from the company. Rather there would be a financial transaction between two investors with no cash flow to the company. Call options typically cover a shorter time period for exercise (up to nine months) than do warrants or stock options. Call options are attractive investments to individuals who are betting on large increases in stock prices. Similarly, a *put option* gives the owner of the option the right to *sell* at a specified price for a specified period of time. Thus, a put option might be an attractive investment for someone who thinks the stock price is likely to fall. Trading in put and call options has received considerable interest in the financial community.

The valuation of stock options and call options is based on the same fundamentals as described for warrants. The key is that increases in the stock price make the call option more valuable. Valuation of put options is similar except that share-price *drops* create value to the option owner.[1]

Call and put options have existed for years, but only in the last decade has there been large-scale trading activity. In April 1973 the Chicago Board Options Exchange (CBOE) began trading call options on stocks. With the advent of standardized contracts and published prices, the markets for options on common stock have flourished. Now calls and puts are a standard part of the investment menu in U.S. financial markets.

Other Types of Options

Thus far we have discussed options where the underlying asset is the common stock of a particular company. For example, an investor anticipating a large rise in IBM's stock price might buy a call option on IBM stock. Not all options are based on stock of individual companies, however.

Foreign-Currency Options. Each day in the financial press (for example, in the *Wall Street Journal*), you can find price quotations to buy options on various foreign currencies, such as the British pound or Japanese yen. These foreign-currency options are similar to stock options but the underlying asset is a specified currency. A buyer of a foreign-currency option can "lock in" the right to buy the foreign currency for a specified price in dollars. Such options might be quite useful to a financial manager whose company was considering doing business abroad but did not know whether the business would actually materialize. (In Chapter 21, we will discuss other ways of dealing with exchange-rate fluctuations between currencies.)

Stock-Index Options. In addition to options on individual stocks, there are now *index options* that are based on the level of a particular stock-price index. Though the technical details are more complicated, index options are essentially ways to take advantage of movements in a stock index rather than movements in just a single stock.

---

[1] A considerable literature has been developed on valuing put options, call options, stock options, and warrants. A more elaborate valuation framework than that given in Figure 16–3 of Chapter 16 is the option-pricing formula developed by F. Black and M. Scholes, in ''The Pricing of Options and Corporate Liabilities,'' *Journal of Political Economy*, May/June 1973, pp. 637–54. Although its detail is beyond the scope of this book, the Black-Scholes formula (and variations) for valuing options is widely used in the investment community. For a readable development of options pricing, see W. Sharpe, *Investments*, latest edition.

Some index options are based on broad stock-market aggregates, while others are related to particular industries. Index options have been offered on the Standard and Poors 500 Stock Index, the New York Stock Exchange Composite Index (which is based on approximately 1500 stocks), and the American Stock Exchange Major Market Value Index (which is based on about 800 stocks)—to name only a few.

Interest-Rate Options.   Options are available on debt securities, including bills, notes, and bonds issued by the U.S. Treasury. Because the prices of such debt securities change with changes in prevailing market interest rates, these options are referred to as *interest-rate options*. Such options give individuals and corporate managers ways to take advantage of swings in interest rates.

As the preceding discussion shows, there are many types of options already traded in financial markets, and we have covered only a subset of those. In theory, one can create options on almost any underlying asset. If investors find such options attractive, innovators in financial markets will design and trade them. The options markets will become an increasingly important part of the environment facing financial managers.

FUTURES

A *financial futures contract* is a contract to buy or sell a stated financial claim (such as a U.S. Treasury bond) at a specified price at a specified time. Unlike an option, a futures contract *requires* the holder to buy or sell the asset at a specified date; the holder doesn't have an option.[2] Just as in the case of options, it is possible to trade futures contracts on many different types of underlying assets. Financial futures are simply futures where the underlying asset is some type of financial security.

For decades, there had been futures contracts on commodities, such as wheat, corn, and cocoa, but not until the 1970s and early 1980s did financial futures became an integral part of financial markets. Trading in financial futures contracts has skyrocketed in recent years. As an example, in 1984 daily trading in U.S. Treasury-bond futures represented claims on about $15 billion in securities—more than twice the trading volume in Treasury bonds themselves. Other financial futures cover foreign currencies, Treasury bills, and stock-market indices. In 1985, a futures contract on the U.S. dollar was introduced, and for those worried about uncertain inflation rates, a contract on the consumer price index was introduced!

One use of financial futures by financial managers is to protect against changing and uncertain interest rates through the process of hedging. *Hedging* is the process of reducing risk by taking more than a single bet on an outcome. Suppose, for example, that you bet $5.00 that a particular college basketball team would win the national championship, but afterwards felt unhappy about the bet.[3] If you could put down an additional $5.00 bet that the same team would *not* win the championship, you would have created a hedge. No matter what happens you'll break even—not very exciting but at least there is no risk. Hedging interest-rate risks works in the same way. Sup-

---

[2]Actually, futures contracts often involve a cash settlement equivalent to the profit or loss that you would make if you actually bought the asset.

[3]Our recommendation is to put your money on the UNC Tarheels.

pose you are a corporate manager with a temporary surplus of funds and have used them to purchase a long-term U.S. Treasury bond. You will need to sell the bond in six months, however, to obtain cash. Your problem is that if interest rates go up the value of your bond will drop. You are exposed to interest-rate risk, as we discussed in Chapter 4. To hedge this risk you may take a position in Treasury bond futures and agree to sell Treasury bonds in six months at a specified price. In effect, your position in the Treasury bond future gains money whenever interest rates go up unexpectedly. You have locked in a selling price even though the market value of the Treasury bond may drop as interest rates rise. The two positions, owning a Treasury bond and effectively selling in the futures market, create a hedge. One position makes money whenever the other loses money.

In practice, the details of hedging become more complicated, but the potential benefits can be large. Hedging can be used to reduce risks about borrowing costs as well as returns on investments. Hedging interest-rate risks with financial futures has become another tool for sophisticated financial management.[4]

---

[4]For an account of the growth in the use of financial futures see ''Big Players in Financial Futures,'' *Fortune*, September 17, 1984. For a useful introduction to the topic see R. Kolb, *Understanding Futures Markets* (Glenview, Ill.: Scott, Foresman, 1985).

Chapter

17

Issuing and Managing Long-Term Securities

In this chapter, we discuss two main topics: first, the policies and procedures that firms follow in actually issuing new equity and debt securities to investors and, second, the responsibilities of the firm in managing its outstanding securities after they have been issued. We will learn about public offerings versus private placements, the use of privileged subscriptions, disclosure requirements in connection with new issues, and considerations in deciding the exact timing of new issues. We will then discuss the unhappy matter of financial distress and failure, including reorganization and liquidation under the bankruptcy laws.

In Chapters 12–16, we focused on problems of making decisions about capital structure—analyzing debt/equity decisions, deciding how much debt to use, formulating dividend policy, and contemplating the use of specialized forms of financing. In this chapter, we will discuss the practical problems of actually issuing securities to buyers and of managing these securities after they are issued. We will distinguish between public offerings in which securities are sold directly to the investing public, and private placements, in which securities are sold to one or a small number of buyers, generally insurance companies.

Financial securities—are financial claims, such as bonds and stocks.

The material in this chapter, for the most part, is applicable to firms that have reached a stage in their development that permits access to the public capital markets. The financial claims that we shall discuss usually are referred to as **financial securities**. Firms that are too small or too new to have their securities accepted by the capital markets usually acquire their external funds by means of *loans*, the label normally given to debt contracts negotiated with financial intermediaries, such as commercial banks, finance companies, and insurance companies.

ISSUING LONG-TERM SECURITIES

Firms normally issue debt and equity securities to the public using one of three methods: public offerings through investment bankers, public offerings through privileged subscription, and private placements. We will discuss each of these methods below. We then will discuss government regulation of securities issues, especially requirements for disclosure of information. Finally, we will take up considerations such as issue costs and timing that are pertinent to all types of issues.

Methods of Issuing Securities

Firms that sell securities directly to the public tend to be large companies. For example, on June 27, 1985, Eastern Airlines sold stock worth $88 million to the public. Only a few weeks later Beatrice Companies sold more than $400 million worth of stock. While large, these stock offerings are not close to record sizes. In the early 1980s, American Telephone and Telegraph Company (AT&T) had three separate stock issues, each of which was about $1 billion in size. These issues predated the breakup of AT&T into eight smaller companies in January 1984.

Public offerings—are security offerings in which securities are made available to the public and are sold to large numbers of buyers.

Single buyers, such as insurance companies or banks, usually are unable to supply such large sums, and are unwilling to concentrate their investments to such an extent because of risk considerations. Large amounts, therefore, usually are sold to large numbers of buyers in **public offerings**. To assist firms in public sales of securities, the specialized institution of investment banking has developed.

Public Offerings Through Investment Bankers. Investment bankers are essentially intermediaries who bring together the seller of securities—namely, the firm—and the buyers—namely, the public. The largest investment banking firms, such as Morgan Stanley, Salomon Brothers, and Goldman Sachs, are found in New York City, but many regional firms also exist. The specialized function performed by the investment banker is directly analogous to that of the retailer of goods. The investment banker has the expertise and specialized sales organization to do an effective marketing job. Because of this specialization, the investment banker generally can perform the distribution job at lower cost than can the firm itself, which normally would issue securities relatively infrequently.

One of the most important functions of the investment banker is to *underwrite* the issue. The underwriter actually buys the securities from the selling firm and resells them to the public. Thus, a good part of the risk of issuing the securities—for example, the risk of adverse reception because of overpricing or adverse general market fluctuations during the distribution period—is borne by the underwriter. In large issues, a number of underwriters often will join together in a *syndicate* to spread the risk.

The second major function of the investment banker is that of *selling* the securities to investors. The selling and risk-bearing functions are separable, and the investment banker is compensated for both. The total compensation to the investment banker is the difference between the price paid to the issuing firm and the resale price to the public. The total spread usually is divided into an *underwriting profit*, which compensates for risk-bearing, and the *selling concession*, which compensates for the service function of selling.

Not all securities sold through investment bankers are underwritten. Sometimes an issue is sold on a *best-efforts basis*, an arrangement under which the investment banker acts as *agent* of the seller and sells as many securities as possible at an agreed-upon price. In this situation, the investment banker has no responsibility for unsold securities and, thus, bears no risk. Compensation to the investment banker includes only the selling concession.

Another major function of the investment banker is to advise the issuing firm with respect to *pricing* the issue. When the firm has securities of the same class already outstanding, the issue price is likely to be set slightly below the market price of the then outstanding securities. Pricing is most critical in connection with **new issues**— the initial public offering of securities of a given class. For example, when a firm issues common stock for the first time, there is no established market price to serve as a benchmark.

In pricing a new issue, it is in the interests of all parties that the securities be priced fairly—neither too high nor too low. Too high an offering price benefits existing holders at the expense of new holders, whose interests are soon to become a responsibility of the management by virtue of the transaction. Likewise, too low a price damages existing holders. Pricing a new issue is part art and part science, and the judgment of the investment banker, a feel for the market, and experience with similar firms in the past play a key role.

An offering that is underwritten may be sold either on a negotiated or a competitive-bid basis. In the former case, the seller and the underwriter mutually agree on the price to be paid for the securities by the underwriter. Under competitive bidding, the seller invites bids from several firms and awards the issue to the highest bidder. Bids are based on the anticipated resale price to the public and the desired spread.

Another important function of the investment banker is to assist the seller and its lawyers in preparing the offering circular or **prospectus**, which provides important information about the securities to potential buyers. We will discuss the prospectus in more detail below in connection with government regulation.

Public Offerings Through Privileged Subscription.   When new common shares are sold to the general public, the proportionate ownership share of existing shareholders is reduced. For this reason, when new common stock or securities convertible into common stock are to be issued, many firms follow a practice of first offering the new securities to existing shareholders on the basis of **privileged subscription**. The right of shareholders to have first chance at purchasing new shares is called a **preemptive right** and is supported by some state laws as well as by the corporate charters of many firms.

New issues—are the initial public offering of a security of a given class.

Privileged subscription—is the practice of offering new securities to existing shareholders first, before any public offering is made.

A **preemptive right**—is a provision in corporate bylaws and charters giving existing common stockholders the right to purchase new issues of common or convertible securities on a prorated basis.

Finance in Practice 17—1

Going Public

One way for entrepreneurs to cash in on their success is to sell shares to the public after their company establishes itself. In the five years ending mid-1986, more than 1500 U.S. companies "went public" by making their first public sale of shares. In the process, quite a few fortunes took shape. Take the case of Bill Gates, a computer-software prodigy who helped found Microsoft.

Founded in 1975, Microsoft emerged as a leader in producing software for personal computers. The company's major successes included operating systems that run millions of personal computers and fast-selling applications programs that could be used on those same computers. By Spring 1986, revenues were approaching $200 million a year. In addition, Microsoft's pretax profits were running as high as 34 percent of revenues. Unlike many companies, Microsoft generated sufficient cash flow to finance its growth without needing external financing.

To attract top managers and programmers, Gates had been offering them shares in Microsoft as well as stock options. These provided a powerful incentive for these employees to work in the interest of the firm. As the firm grew, the number of shareholders grew until it was expected to hit 500 by 1987. This 500 level would require Microsoft to register with the Securities and Exchange Commission. Furthermore, to give employees a chance to cash in on Microsoft's success, a public market for the stock would be desirable.

The stage was set for going public and in March 1986 Microsoft offered shares to the public at $21 per share. Traded in the over-the-counter market, the price shot to more than $30, representing a price/earnings ratio of well over 20 times. It was apparent that the market anticipated a bright future for Microsoft, and the company raised more than $60 million even though employees still retained the vast majority of shares.

How did Bill Gates make out? He got $1.6 million from the shares he sold personally, but that was only the tip of the iceberg. He retained 45 percent ownership of the company. At the going market price, this holding had a market value of $350 million making Gates, at age 30, probably one of the 100 richest Americans. Despite his immense personal gain, Gates still had concerns that too much emphasis on the firm's share price might distract managers and programmers from doing what made Microsoft a success in the first place: excelling in the computer-software business. A few weeks after the offering, Gates noticed a chart of Microsoft's stock price on a programmer's door. Gates queried the programmer, "Is this a distraction?"

Source: Adapted from B. Uttal, "Inside the Deal that Made Bill Gates $350,000,000," *Fortune*, July 21, 1986, pp.23–33.

A **rights offering**—is the offering of new securities on the basis of privileged subscription.

When a firm undertakes a **rights offering**, as privileged subscriptions often are called, it mails directly to shareholders one right for each share held. The terms of the offering specify the subscription price and number of rights required to purchase an additional share. For example, if a firm had 1 million shares outstanding and wished to offer 100,000 new shares, it would mail out 1 million rights and require 10 rights to purchase an additional share.

The subscription period during which the rights can be exercised generally runs 20–30 days. During that period, the rights have value because the subscription price is set below the current market price of the stock at the beginning of the subscription period. Shareholders, therefore, have several options: they can exercise their rights and purchase their prorated share of the new securities; they can sell their rights; they can buy additional rights from others not wishing to exercise them and subscribe to more than their prorated share; they can do nothing. One of these alternatives must be selected prior to the end of the subscription period, because at that point the rights become valueless.

When a rights offering is announced, the firm establishes a *date of record*. Owners of the stock on that date will receive rights to subscribe to the new offering. Prior to the record date, the stock sells *rights on*, which means that a purchaser of existing shares in the market prior to the record date will receive rights to the new offering. On the record date, the price of existing shares drops and the stock sells *ex rights*, meaning that purchasers of the stock after the record date do not receive rights to subscribe to the new offering. By the end of the subscription period, the firm has collected the rights and the subscription proceeds, and any unexercised rights become worthless. Certificates for the new shares are issued at some later date.

Let us explore these price relationships in more detail. To simplify our discussion, we will assume that the market price would remain constant at P_0 without the rights offering, and we will ignore the time value of money for the short time period surrounding the rights offering. Suppose a firm has Y shares of stock outstanding selling at a price of P_0. A rights offering of X new shares is planned. Thus, a total of Y rights will be issued to shareholders, and the number of rights, N, required to purchase one new share is Y/X. The subscription price is set at S, so the shareholder will exchange N rights plus $\$S$ for one new share.

Let us assume that the total value of the firm is unchanged by the announcement of the offering; in other words, we will assume that there are no *information effects*. When the new shares actually are issued, total value will increase by the amount of new funds obtained, SX. Total value after the offering is completed, thus, will be value before the offering plus SX, as indicated in Equation (1).

The value of the firm, V_1, after a rights offering is completed can be calculated as

$$V_1 = P_0 Y + SX \tag{1}$$

where P_0 = the market price of the firm's stock before the rights offering, Y = the number of shares of stock outstanding before the rights offering, X = the number of shares of stock being offered on a privileged-subscription basis, and S = the subscription price for shares offered on a privileged-subscription basis.

Value per share after the offering, P_1, will be the total value, V_1, divided by the total number of shares $(Y + X)$, as shown in Equation (2). Note that in the last step of Equation (2), we divide through by X.

Value per share, P_1, after a rights offering can be calculated as

$$P_1 = \frac{V_1}{Y + X} = \frac{P_0Y + SX}{Y + X} = \frac{P_0 N + S}{N + 1} \qquad (2)$$

where V_1 = the value of the firm after the rights offering, N = the number of rights required to purchase one new share = Y/X, and Y, S, and X are as defined in Equation (1).

Equation (2) establishes the price per share after the offering. Now let us move back in time from a point after the offering to the period before the issue date but after the record date. Because the stock sells *ex rights* during this period, purchasing one share of the stock entitles the buyer to that share of the stock only after the rights offering is completed. As a result, when the stock sells *ex rights*, the buyer will pay only P_1 for a share of the stock. P_1 represents the value of the one share that will be owned after the offering. Thus, we expect the market price of the stock to change from P_0 to P_1 when the stock goes *ex rights* (even before the offering). Thus, P_1 is the price during the *ex rights* period as well as after the offering.

Continuing back in time, the record date is the date on which the rights take on value independently of the stock. Investors know that on the issue date they will be able to purchase a share of stock for $\$S + N$ rights. During the subscription period, the value of one right, therefore, can be determined as shown in Equation (3).

The value of one privileged-subscription right, R, during the subscription period, can be calculated as

$$R = \frac{P_1 - S}{N} \qquad (3)$$

where P_1 = the value per share after the rights offering, S = the subscription price for shares offered on a privileged-subscription basis, and N = the number of rights required to purchase one new share = Y/X.

While the stock is selling ex rights, the total value of the firm is the value of the stock plus the value of the rights, or $P_1Y + RY$. Prior to the record date, total value was P_0Y. Because the total value of the firm remains unchanged on the record date, we see that

$$P_1Y + RY = P_0Y$$

and that the market price of the stock on the record date can be calculated as shown in Equation (4).

Figure 17–1
Chronology of a Rights Offering

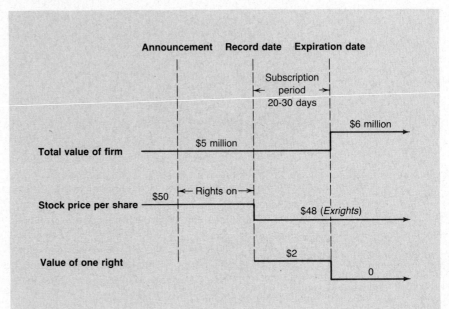

The market price of a share of stock, P_1, on the record date of a rights offering can be expressed as

$$P_1 = P_0 - R \tag{4}$$

where P_0 = the market price of the firm's stock before the rights offering, and R = the value of one right during the subscription period.

The market price of the stock, thus, drops on the record date by the amount of the value of one right.

Let us illustrate these relationships with an example. ABC Corporation has 100,000 shares outstanding at $50 per share and plans a rights offering of 25,000 shares. The subscription price is set at $40, and 100,000 rights are to be issued. Purchase of one new share, thus, will require $40 + 4 rights. Applying Equation (2), we find that the value per share after the rights offering is

$$P_1 = [(50 \times 4) + 40]/(4 + 1) = \$48.$$

Applying Equation (3), we find that the value of one right during the subscription period is

$$R = (48 - 40)/4 = \$2.$$

On the record date, the price of ABC stock drops from $50 to $48, and the rights take on an independent value of $2. A holder of a share previously worth $50 now holds a share worth $48 and a right worth $2. On the issue date, 25,000 new shares are issued at $40. The total value of the firm becomes ($50 × 100,000) + ($40 × 25,000), or $6 million. With 125,000 shares outstanding, price per share is $48. These various price and value relationships are illustrated in Figure 17–1.

The value given by Equation (3) is the theoretical value of one right. In practice, the value of rights during the subscription period may deviate somewhat from the theoretical figure because of transaction costs and speculative pressures. Also, the value of both stock and rights may fluctuate because of changes in investor expectations regarding the firm or the economy.

It is important to note that, even though rights have value, the net worth of a shareholder is unchanged by a rights offering as long as the shareholder exercises or sells the rights. Consider an individual holding four shares of ABC Corporation stock (worth $200) and $40 in cash prior to the offering. If the rights are exercised, the shareholder winds up with five shares worth $48 each, a total of $240. If the four rights are sold, the shareholder winds up with four shares worth $48 each plus $48 in cash, again $240. Note also that to purchase one of the new shares, a nonshareholder must buy four rights at $2 each and put up $40 in addition for a total of $48.

Because the offering itself does not affect shareholder wealth, the subscription price can be set at any figure, provided that it is less than the current market price. The lower subscription price does not permit outsiders to buy in at a lower figure because outsiders must purchase the rights.

To ensure a successful offering, it is important that the market price of the stock not fall below the subscription price. If market price were below subscription price, no one would buy the new shares because old shares could be bought at a lower price in the open market. Because the subscription price does not affect the net worth of existing shareholders, it can be set low in relation to current market price in order to reduce the likelihood that the rights would not be exercised. The more volatile is the market price, the greater the discount should be. The lower the subscription price is set, however, the greater is the number of new shares that must be issued to raise a given amount of money. In deciding this question, the implications for dividend policy must be taken into account. For example, if a firm desires to maintain a given level of dividends per share, a larger total dollar payment of dividends will be required as the firm issues more shares.

Some rights offerings are undertaken by the issuing firm without the assistance of an investment banker. The success of such offerings depends in part on factors under the control of management, such as the relationship between subscription price and market price and the size of the issue, and also on factors that management cannot control, such as general economic and market developments. To protect against unfavorable developments that might jeopardize the success of an offering, many firms find it wise to obtain a *standby* commitment from an investment banker, or group of investment bankers, to underwrite any unsubscribed portion of the issue. In this way, the firm ensures that it will receive the funds. For this insurance, the firm pays a fee to the investment banker.

In recent years, the use of rights offerings has fallen off markedly. Many corporations have changed their charters to eliminate the preemptive right previously given to shareholders. They are, thus, free to go directly to the market.

Private placements—are offerings of new securities in which firms sell securities directly to one investor or to a small group of investors rather than to the public.

Private Placements.   Firms often sell securities directly to one investor or to a small group of investors rather than to the public through **private placements**. The great majority of private placements are debt issues; common stock is placed privately rather infrequently. Buyers of private placements are nearly always financial intermediaries, such as insurance companies and pension funds.

A firm may opt for a private placement rather than a public offering for any of several reasons. Firms that have not yet reached a sufficient size or established a sufficient track record to permit a public offering may find a private placement feasible. In fact, a major function of the private-placement market is to serve as a source of long-term debt financing for smaller, less financially secure firms. In a private placement, a financial intermediary (say, an insurance company) performs the necessary tasks of information gathering and analysis at much less expense than would be the case in a public offering. Smaller amounts of funds—say, in the range of several hundred thousand to several million dollars—can be raised through private placement, whereas such amounts usually would be judged too small for a public offering. Registration by the Securities and Exchange Commission is not required, so private placements generally can be consummated more quickly than can public offerings. Terms can be negotiated directly by lender and borrower without the involvement of an investment banker, although the latter often plays a role both in bringing borrower and lender together and in the negotiations. Because terms are negotiated and the time frame usually is shorter, timing problems arising from market fluctuations are less troublesome than in the case of public offerings. Another advantage of a private placement is that the borrower can obtain a forward commitment by the lender to deliver funds in the future at a known rate.

Because registration is not required and because no underwriting and selling expenses are involved, the direct expenses of private placements tend to be lower than those of public offerings, thereby reducing effective borrowing costs as much as 1 percentage point for small offerings ($1 million or less) to 0.10 percentage point for large offerings. Interest costs, on the other hand, tend to be slightly higher on private placements. The rate differential depends on the financial strength of the borrower, ranging from essentially no differential for stronger firms to 0.30 percentage point for less secure firms.[1]

The major borrower categories—public utilities, finance companies, and industrial companies—have exhibited markedly different patterns of reliance on the private-placement market. Public utilities have sold their debt almost entirely in the public markets. Large finance companies have sold a majority of their debt in the public markets. Small finance companies have sold most of their debt in the private markets.

Other Methods of Security Issuance

Dividend-Reinvestment Plans.   One method corporations have devised to ensure a steady inflow of new equity capital is to allow shareholders to apply their periodic dividend receipts automatically to the purchase of new shares. Under this procedure, dividend payments never actually go to the shareholder but rather are applied directly

---

[1]See Eli Shapiro and Charles R. Wolf, *The Role of Private Placements in Corporate Finance* (Cambridge, Mass.: Graduate School of Business Administration, Harvard University, 1972).

by the company to a purchase of new shares. One unfortunate disadvantage of such plans is that the Internal Revenue Service taxes the dividend as usual, even though the shareholder never actually receives the cash. In spite of this drawback, **dividend-reinvestment plans** have grown in popularity, especially among utility companies during periods when they face large needs for new capital.

Direct Sales to the Public.   Yet another innovation in financial markets is direct sale of securities to the public without the use of an investment-banker intermediary. The innovator was Exxon Corporation, which bypassed Wall Street in late 1976 by offering a $50 million issue of new debt securities to the public. In order to bring in small as well as large investors, Exxon used the so-called *Dutch auction method*. Under this system, prospective investors submitted individual bids (prices) to purchase selected amounts of the issue, but every successful bidder eventually paid the *same price*—which was the lowest price that Exxon had to accept in order to sell the stated $50 million amount of the issue.

A **dividend-reinvestment plan**—is the policy of allowing shareholders to apply their periodic dividend receipts automatically to the purchase of new shares.

Disclosure Requirements

Both the federal and state governments regulate the sale of securities to the public. The principal objective of such regulation is to ensure that adequate information is provided to prospective buyers of the securities and to protect buyers against misinformation and fraud.

The Securities Act of 1933, passed in the aftermath of the Great Depression and in response to stock-market abuses of earlier years, sets forth federal regulatory requirements for new security issues. The Securities Exchange Act of 1934 regulates securities already outstanding. The Securities and Exchange Commission (SEC) administers both sets of requirements.

Under the provisions of the 1933 act as administered by the SEC, a firm wishing to sell securities to the public must register the issue with the SEC. Smaller issues are subject to considerably less detailed disclosure requirements. Certain specialized types of firms, such as railroads, are exempt from SEC registration requirements because they are regulated by other government agencies.

The *registration statement* filed with the SEC contains information on the firm's history, its management, financial data, a description of the securities to be offered, uses to which proceeds will be put, and legal and accounting opinions. The firm also must file a *prospectus*, a summary of the information provided in the registration statement. A copy of the first page of the prospectus for an issue of System Associates common stock is shown in Figure 17–2. The prospectus is the primary vehicle by which information is communicated to prospective investors. The prospectus is made available to investors by the investment banker or by the issuing firm if no investment banker is involved.

All parties to a securities offering have an interest in full disclosure of relevant information. The evidence indicates that the securities markets in general do an effective job of processing information and incorporating it into security prices. One of the most important objectives in a new issue is to see that it is priced so that neither new buyers nor existing holders are treated unfairly. Given the evidence regarding market efficiency, a firm's management can rely on the impersonal action of the marketplace to see that the information is evaluated in an unbiased manner. A policy of full disclo-

Figure 17–2
An Example of a Prospectus

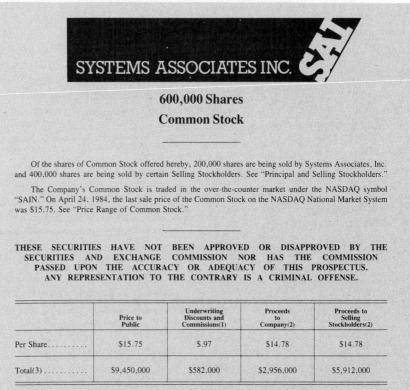

sure coupled with the market's efficiency is management's best guarantee that new securities will be issued at fair prices.

Beginning in 1982 the SEC authorized a type of registration statement that allows a firm, if it desires, to prepare all the registration and legal documents for a financing and then "put it on the shelf" to await favorable market conditions. When conditions were favorable, the firm could proceed with the offering in a matter of days without having to repeat the steps in the registration process. After a successful trial period, in late 1983 *shelf registration* was permanently authorized under Rule 415 for large firms. Rule 415 allows a firm to register all securities it expects to sell over the upcoming 24 months and then sell them over that period whenever it chooses.[2]

Costs of Issuing Securities

The two major costs of issuing securities are direct flotation expenses and interest costs. Direct expenses include underwriting commissions, selling expenses, legal fees, printing expenses, and mailing expenses. Another significant expense is the management time that must be devoted to planning and negotiating an issue. The interest cost of a debt issue represents the return required by lenders. The return required by suppliers of equity funds is paid in the form of dividends and growth in capital values.

Some of these issue costs vary with the size of the issue, and some are fixed. Consequently, issue costs as a percentage of funds raised vary inversely with the size of the issue. Raising small amounts of money, therefore, is uneconomical, and firms generally attempt to limit the frequency of trips to the markets and to finance in blocks. This lumpiness imposes short-run constraints on firms' investment policy, as we have noted in earlier chapters. Appendix 10A details the flotation costs associated with security issues.

Dealing With Variable Interest Rates

A major problem for both borrowers and lenders is high and variable interest rates. Many long-term lenders, such as insurance companies, suffered heavy losses during the late 1970s when, believing that interest rate were near their peaks, they placed long-term debt issues in their portfolios only to see rates go higher still. When rates rose, bond prices dropped; losses ran into hundreds of millions of dollars.

In the face of these losses lenders became increasingly reluctant to purchase long-term issues. At the same time, borrowers worried about issuing long-term bonds at historically high rates when lower rates might be just ahead. To resolve these problems, some lenders and borrowers turned to issues with variable interest rates (variable-rate notes were discussed in Chapter 12). The technique gained popularity at the beginning of the 1980s. In November 1980, General Motors Acceptance Corporation sold publicly a 10-year $250 million issue with an adjustable rate tied to the rate on 10-year Treasury bonds. Chemical New York Corporation and Citicorp followed shortly thereafter with private placements totaling $150 million worth of adjustable-rate preferred stock and notes. Variable-rate financing is now one of the financing tools available for corporate managers. Another techique for dealing with unanticipated swings in interest rates is hedging with financial futures contracts as discussed in Appendix 16A.

---

[2]For studies of the effects of shelf registration, see D. Kidwell, M. Marr, and G. Thompson, "SEC Rule 415: The Ultimate Competitive Bid," *Journal of Financial and Quantitative Analysis*, June 1984, pp. 183–95; and S. Bhagat, M. Marr, and G. Thompson, "The Rule 415 Experiment: Equity Markets," *Journal of Finance*, December 1985, pp. 1385–1401.

Timing of New Issues of Securities

From the standpoint of existing shareholders, it would be desirable to issue new stock when stock prices are relatively high and to issue new bonds when long-term interest rates are relatively low. Should managers devote significant effort to an attempt to time new issues for stock-price highs and interest-rate lows? The timing issue is a controversial one.

As discussed earlier in Chapter 12, the benefits of timing depend on the efficiency of financial markets. The theory of market efficiency holds that prices and interest rates reflect all public information in an unbiased manner. In such an efficient market, current prices and rates would reflect a consensus forecast of future prices and rates by the best-informed and best-financed investors. Everyone knows that the consensus forecast could be inaccurate and that the future might well be different from the expectation. But the error is about as likely to be in one direction as the other, and most attempts to outguess the market will have only about a 50/50 chance of success. If managers operate in efficient financial markets and face such odds, firms should not attempt to time issues, but rather should adopt a general policy of raising funds when needed.

What is the evidence? Research on the subject, mostly by academic researchers, suggests that financial markets are reasonably efficient.[3] This finding suggests that consistently superior timing is very difficult—so difficult that most firms should not waste effort trying. Frequently, conditions that appear to be depressed will turn out, in retrospect, to be not so depressed after all. Deferral of security issues is likely to mean deferral of investment decisions and interference with the firm's commercial strategy. Given the odds of success, a policy of attempting to exploit market movements is unlikely to provide gains that consistently outweigh the costs of interruptions in investment plans. The best policy is, thus, to let the commercial strategy dictate the timing of external financings and to rely on full disclosure and market efficiency to ensure fair pricing of these financings.

> **Because it is difficult to consistently time the issuance of new securities to capture stock-price highs or interest-rate lows, the best policy is to let the commercial strategy dictate the timing of external financings and to let market efficiency ensure fair pricing.**

Many practicing managers reject the suggestion that timing is too difficult to be worthwhile. Data on new issues of securities indicate that the volume of new stock issues increases after a significant rise in stock prices and falls after a decline.[4]

---

[3] See Chapter 12 for a discussion of evidence on market efficiency. There we also distinguish between three forms of market efficiency.

[4] See R. A. Taggart, "A Model of Corporate Financing Decisions," *Journal of Finance*, December 1977, pp. 1467–84. For further evidence that companies time security issues, see A. Jalilvand and R. Harris, "Corporate Behavior in Adjusting to Capital Structure and Dividend Targets," *Journal of Finance*, March 1984, pp. 127–45.

It is not hard to imagine why a manager would attempt to time new security issues. A new stock issue at a market low does not look good to the existing shareholders— that is, those who were shareholders prior to the new issue. They feel that newcomers will capture a part of an increase in value that is rightfully theirs. Much better, they would say, to wait until *after* the price rise to issue the new stock. Then fewer new shares must be issued to raise a given amount of money, and the position of the old shareholders is diluted less. The same would hold for new bond issues. A manager looks much better if he or she issues new bonds *before* a rise in interest rates rather than after.

A new stock issue after an increase in stock prices reduces the risk of appearing to misjudge the market. If prices go back down, the manager is a hero for catching the peak. Even if prices continue to rise, he or she has captured at least part of the increase for the old shareholders. If, on the other hand, a manager issues stock when the market is low relative to the recent past or issues bonds when interest rates are high, he or she runs the risk of appearing to be imprudent.

There also are situations in which managers have important information about a company's future earnings prospects that they do not wish to make public for competitive reasons. Issuing stock before the new information is released could be disadvantageous to existing shareholders because they would not capture for themselves the resulting increase in the value of the firm. In this case, the firm may choose to issue debt to raise needed new funds and wait until the information can be made public at an advantageous time before issuing new stock.[5]

In sum, managers have good reason to attempt to time new issues of stocks and bonds to take advantage of market conditions. The question is not over the wisdom of doing so, but rather over the chances of success. The weight of the research evidence suggests that the odds of *consistently* timing new issues to advantage are not good, and that managers' time is better spent concentrating on other matters. Most likely, however, managers will continue to try.

Other Considerations in Issuing Securities

At this point, it is appropriate to remind ourselves of several other considerations that we have discussed at other points in this book. One such consideration is *control*. Maintenance of control usually is a major consideration in closely held firms when external financing is contemplated. In order to maintain control, a firm may impose restrictions on financing alternatives, which in turn may constrain its investment policy. Control is very important in some situations, but maintaining it is likely to entail costs in terms of reduced access to the financial markets and constraints on commercial strategy.

Another important consideration is the *sequencing* of issues when a series of external financings is in prospect. A major objective in planning sequential issues is to maintain flexibility with respect to alternative sources.

---

[5]In this situation the financial market is not efficient in the strong form because it does not reflect inside information (see Chapter 12 for discussion) known by the manager. In practice, markets are not strong-form efficient, so such situations may arise.

Some financial economists have argued that new stock and bond issues have the potential for inducing significant information effects of the sort discussed in connection with dividend policy in Chapter 15. The potential for information effects could exist when managers have inside information not yet reflected in market prices. Suppose a firm's management has significant and favorable information about its firm's future prospects that investors do not have. In order to preserve the benefits for existing shareholders, the management issues debt instead of equity, planning to issue equity later after the good news has been reflected in the stock price. If investors begin to see such actions as a typical pattern, they may interpret a decision *not to issue* stock as evidence of good news. A decision *to issue* stock might imply that there existed no future prospects sufficiently favorable to justify preserving them for existing shareholders by issuing debt. Hence, a debt issue might signal good news, and a stock issue might signal bad news, or at least news that is less good. Such reasoning might explain why stock prices often fall upon the announcement of a stock issue.[6]

Managers should be conscious of any such information effects that new security issues might have. As our discussion has indicated, the manager's job is not simply to choose whether to issue one type of security or another. The actual process of issuing the securities requires management time and consideration.

MANAGING SECURITIES AFTER ISSUANCE

Stock exchanges—are formal organizations that act as auction markets in the trading of financial securities.

Once a firm has issued securities to the public, it incurs some responsibilities for managing the securities after issuance. The discussion in this section pertains primarily to publicly traded issues, although parts of the discussion, such as that pertaining to communications, are pertinent to privately held issues as well.

Trading of Securities After Issuance

Over-the-counter (OTC) markets—are facilities, such as investment firms, that trade in securities not listed on organized security exchanges.

An auction market—is a market in which buyers and sellers state their terms and intermediaries act to bring the buyers and sellers together.

If holders of the bonds or stock of a firm wish to liquidate their investment, they must sell their securities to someone else. They cannot return them to the issuing firm for redemption. In the case of closely held firms, finding an interested buyer may be difficult. In the case of more widely held firms, public markets exist in which shares can be freely bought and sold. Public markets in the United States are of two general types: the organized **stock exchanges** and the **over-the-counter (OTC) market**.

The best known stock exchanges are the New York Stock Exchange and the American Stock Exchange, both located in New York City. There also exist a number of regional exchanges elsewhere in the United States. The exchanges are an **auction market** where buyers and sellers state their terms. Specialists act as brokers to bring buyers and sellers together, sometimes buying and selling for their own account.

The over-the-counter market is made up of a larger number of investment firms that act as dealers. Dealers *make a market* in the shares of a particular firm by quoting *bid*

---

[6]For an analysis of this argument, see S. C. Myers and N. J. Majluf, "Stock Issues and Investment Policy When Firms Have Information that Investors Do Not Have," *Journal of Financial Economics* 13 (1984): 187–221.

and *asked* prices at which they stand ready to buy or sell. The dealer is compensated by the spread between the bid and asked prices.

Communication with the Markets

Heading the list of important responsibilities in connection with outstanding issues is *communication*. Earlier in this chapter we discussed the importance of full disclosure of all pertinent information to prospective buyers of new issues. Here we focus on communication with holders of existing issues.

Regular Financial Reporting. Because management acts as agent of the owners of the firm, keeping those owners informed clearly is an important management responsibility. In the case of publicly held firms, SEC regulations require regular reporting, at least annually, to shareholders. Larger firms also are required to report to shareholders quarterly. The New York Stock Exchange requires both annual and quarterly reports by firms whose stock is traded on the exchange.

The format and content of such published financial reports are prescribed by the SEC in cooperation with the accounting profession. Quarterly reports generally are brief and cover the most recent quarterly and year-to-date informaton. Annual reports usually are much more comprehensive; they often include extensive historical statistical data as well as narrative information on the firm's operations and plans. Financial statements in annual reports are audited by a certified-public-accounting firm.

Besides the above published reports, firms also are required to file certain regular reports directly with the SEC. These reports include standard financial information and also reports of special events such as changes in directors and principal officers, mergers and acquisitions, lawsuits, large losses, and the like. Information of this sort also should be reported to shareholders and the investing public, and most firms follow a policy of doing so.

Firms also are required to hold a general meeting of shareholders at least annually, at which time directors are elected and other business is conducted. In addition to regularly scheduled communications through meetings and reports, firms typically communicate a variety of routine information through press releases.

In addition to reporting historical information, firms should keep investors fully informed with respect to strategy and policy. Owners and potential investors are entitled to know what basic goals management has set, the general outline of the commercial strategy, and the major policies that will be followed. With respect to financial management specifically, investors are entitled to know what management's target debt/equity ratio is, what policies will be followed with respect to debt maturity, and what the target dividend-payout ratio is. To the extent that competitive considerations permit, future investment opportunities and plans also should be communicated. With respect to all such policies, the objective is to tell investors what is going on rather than force them to guess. Complete disclosure is good practice not only because owners are entitled to the information, but also because better disclosure promotes fairer pricing of securities. In general, comprehensive disclosure on a regular basis contributes to smaller price fluctuations and avoids surprises.

Regular reporting also lays the groundwork for future securities issues. Where a firm has publicly traded securities, their market price is a major factor in setting the price of a new issue. Hence, the price at which new securities are offered is largely determined by holders of existing securities. For this reason, comprehensive disclosure on a regular basis provides the best assurance of fair prices for new issues.

Reporting in Connection with Extraordinary Events. Even with a comprehensive program of disclosure on a regular basis, special effort is required in connection with extraordinary events such as new security offerings or major new investment plans. Security prices are determined by future-oriented factors: future cash flows and the riskiness of those cash flows. When only historical information is reported, the market is forced to draw inferences from management actions and whatever data are reported. The announcement of investment, financing, and dividend decisions, thus, can produce significant and possibly undesirable information effects as the market attempts to draw inferences regarding the future.

For example, announcement of a financing decision may convey information regarding investment opportunities. If the market interprets the announcement of a new financing as a signal that management sees more attractive investment opportunities ahead than previously had been anticipated, the stock price may rise. If the market sees no such attractive opportunities, the price may fall. In either case, the market is using the financing decision as the basis for drawing an inference about investment opportunities. Rather than relying on the market to draw the proper inference, it is better to communicate the facts directly.

A similar situation might arise in connection with a change in dividend policy. A cut in dividends, for example, might indicate that management sees attractive investment opportunities ahead and is conserving funds for investment. Alternatively, the market might infer that management sees bad times ahead and is conserving cash for emergency use. The first inference is likely to cause a rise in stock price; the second is likely to cause a fall in stock price. To avoid the possibility of incorrect interpretations, management should communicate the reasons for the change carefully and clearly. If the news is bad, owners and prospective investors are entitled to know it.

The preceding examples illustrate situations in which the market draws inferences from management actions. It is clear that straightforward communication is desirable so that the market bases its actions on facts rather than inferences. A related situation can occur when a firm's management is contemplating an action that is believed to be in the shareholders' interests, but that may be misinterpreted by the market. If funds are needed for investment and the firm is at or near its debt capacity, equity may be the right choice. Will the resulting dilution of earnings per share reduce stock price? Suppose equity is needed at a time when market price is below book value. Will a sale of equity at a price below book value be viewed negatively by the market? A third situation can occur in the case of an investment opportunity with a very high rate of return but low cash flows in early years and, therefore, adverse implications for near-term accounting profits. Fear of misinterpretation and an adverse reception by the market may lead a firm's management to forgo actions that in fact are in the shareholders' interests.

Problems of the above sort usually can be minimized by careful communication. Investors are rational and entirely capable of understanding their own self-interests. If a particular decision is in the interests of shareholders, it is likely that they will agree.

If a dividend cut really is needed, it should be made and the reasons carefully communicated. If an investment really does have attractive long-run returns, investors will be quite prepared to ignore an adverse impact on near-term profits. Forgoing such investments does shareholders no favor. If an equity issue is needed, investors can be persuaded. In fact, firms that issue debt instead of equity for fear of earnings dilution and, thereby, exceed their debt capacity ultimately will receive a message of disapproval from the market in the form of a low price/earnings (PE) ratio.

Communication Policy.   From the foregoing discussion of communications, what can we conclude with respect to appropriate policies? In general, firms should make financial-management decisions using value maximization as their criterion. Insofar as is possible in an uncertain world, a firm's management can be confident that decisions reached in this way are in the shareholders' interests. Once the appropriate action has been chosen, the reasoning behind it should be communicated as completely as possible. Often competitive considerations will make complete disclosure unwise. In such cases, the benefits of disclosure have to be weighed against loss of competitive advantages, with the interests of existing shareholders the guiding criterion. Difficulties with controversial decisions often center on adverse near-term impact on earnings per share. Communications should deal with this problem by explaining long-run implications. Good communication helps management take a long view, which, after all, is management's job.

> **Because management's role is to act as the agent of the firm's owners, managers have the responsibility of keeping owners and investors fully informed about the firm's strategy and policy. In the long run, full disclosure promotes the fair pricing of securities.**

Listing of Shares

Shares that trade on an exchange, such as the New York or the American Stock Exchange, are said to be *listed* on the exchange. Exchanges have certain requirements with respect to size, years in business, number of shares outstanding, trading volume, market value, and earnings record that must be met before a firm will be accepted for listing. The reporting requirements of the exchanges over and above those already imposed by the SEC are not great in the case of nonfinancial firms, although there historically have been differences in the case of banks.

Most firms, therefore, begin their existence as public companies in the over-the-counter market and graduate to an exchange at a later state in their development. Listed firms make up only a small percentage of the total number of business firms in the United States, but include the great majority of the larger nonfinancial firms. Banks and insurance companies historically have had their shares traded on an over-the-counter basis, but recently there has been a strong trend toward listing of bank holding company shares.

Advantages of exchange listing that typically are cited include a better market for shareholders wishing to buy and sell, better accommodation of large transactions, facilitation of future financings, and an improvement in the firm's status. While these indeed may be real advantages, studies of listing have found no evidence that exchange listing itself adds permanently to a firm's value.[7]

Retiring Outstanding Securities

Long-term debt issues of firms almost without exception have a final maturity date by which the principal must be repaid.[8] Maturities range from a few years to about 25 years. Maturities beyond about 25 years are rare, because over longer periods the nature of a business and its environment can change radically, and lenders usually want an opportunity to reevaluate the risk from time to time.

Unlike debt, common stock is a perpetual claim with no provision for retirement, although retirement can be accomplished by means of repurchase. Preferred stock usually carries a provision for retirement but sometimes does not.

A sinking fund—is an arrangement in which firms make periodic repayments of principal to the trustees of a bond issue, who retire a specified number of bonds by open-market purchases or by calling certain bonds at a previously agreed-upon price.

Serial redemption—is the retirement each year as they mature of bonds that have been issued with serial maturity dates.

Retirement of Long-Term Debt. Long-term debt can be retired in a number of ways. One way is simply to repay the entire principal at maturity. Most issues, however, require periodic repayment either by means of a **sinking fund** or through **serial redemption**. Some bond issues can be called at the option of the issuer. Convertible bonds are retired by conversion into common stock.

Under a sinking-fund arrangement, the terms of which are set forth in the bond indenture, the firm makes periodic payments, usually annually or semiannually, to the trustee of the bond issue. The trustee uses the funds to retire a specified number of bonds in one of two ways: by open-market purchases or by calling certain bonds at a previously agreed upon price. The trustee will purchase in the open market as long as the market price is less than the call price. When market price is above the call price, the call provision will be exercised. Bonds to be called usually are selected on a lottery basis using their serial numbers to identify them.[9]

The proportion of the total issue to be retired at each sinking-fund payment date is set forth in the indenture. The amount of the periodic sinking-fund payment usually is fixed so that the same number of bonds is retired each time. Some issues provide for retirement of the entire issue by the final maturity date, whereas others may provide for only partial retirement with a *balloon payment* at maturity.

Sinking-fund bonds all have the same maturity date, although a portion of the bonds are retired in advance of maturity under procedures described above. *Serial bonds*, on the other hand, have sequential maturity dates. A $50 million issue, for example, may have $2.5 million in bonds maturing each year for 20 years. Over the life of the issue, bonds are redeemed each year as they mature.

Under a sinking-fund arrangement, the trustee is empowered to call a portion of the bonds each year. Most corporate-bond issues also provide for calling the entire issue

---

[7]See James C. Van Horne, "New Listings and Their Price Behavior," *Journal of Finance* 25 (September 1970): 783–94. See also Susan M. Phillips and J. Richard Zecher, "Exchange Listing and the Cost of Equity Capital," Capital Market Working Paper 8 (U.S. Securities and Exchange Commission, March 1982).

[8]An exception is the Canadian Pacific 4 percent perpetual bonds, which are consoles having no maturity.

[9]For a theoretical analysis of callable bonds, see J. E. Ingersoll, "A Contingent-Claims Valuation of Convertible Securities," *Journal of Financial Economics* 2 (May 1977): 289–322.

at the option of the issuer. Some issues permit call at any time, although more typically the call privilege is not effective for 5-10 years after issuance.

Retirement by means of a sinking fund or through serial redemption usually is a provision sought by lenders. The option to call the entire issue is a provision sought by the borrower. Call of an entire issue might be advantageous to a firm either to permit changes in capital structure or to permit refunding of the issue at a lower interest rate. The latter reason probably is more often the principal motive for the call provision from the borrowers' standpoint. In an uncertain world in which interest rates vary, having the option to retire a bond issue and reborrow at a lower rate clearly is advantageous. The advantage accrues to the shareholders, who would benefit from the reduction in interest costs. To the extent that the call privilege is advantageous to shareholders, it is usually disadvantageous to holders of the bonds, for in the event that the privilege is exercised, bondholders must give up a security paying an interest rate above the prevailing market rate.[10] As one would expect in a competitive market, bondholders insist on being compensated for the call privilege. Other factors being equal, the interest rate on a callable issue will be higher. Also, the price at which the bonds are callable is set above par value. In short, the shareholders must pay for the flexibility afforded by the call privilege.

As noted above, the most frequent motive for calling an issue is to refund it—that is, to issue a new set of bonds in its place. The usual motive is to refund at a lower interest rate, although sometimes renegotiation of restrictive covenants also is a consideration. Considering only the interest-rate motive, the decision of whether to refund can be analyzed using discounted-cash-flow techniques. To identify the relevant cash flows, we apply the incremental-cash-flow rule. The firm makes an outlay—essentially, the difference between the amount required to call the old issue and the proceeds of the new issue—and receives a stream of inflows consisting mainly of the annual interest savings. Other incremental cash flows include expenses of the transaction and tax effects. Because the interest savings are known with certainty and the expenses and tax effects are subject to little uncertainty, the appropriate discount rate is the after-tax equivalent of the interest rate on the new bonds.[11]

Sample Problem 17—1

Bond Refunding for Geoffrey Enterprises

Geoffrey Enterprises is considering the refunding of an issue of 12 percent coupon, 25-year bonds issued 5 years ago. The bonds have a call price of $1,120 (per $1,000 of face value) and were originally sold at face value for $50 million. The initial flotation costs were $500,000. Interest rates have gone down, and Geoffrey can now issue $50 million of new 20-year bonds with a coupon rate of 10 percent and sell them at face value. There will also be a $500,000 flotation cost involved in issuing the new bonds. Geoffrey faces a 40 percent corporate tax rate. Flotation costs must be amortized over the life of the bond for tax purposes. Should the bond be refunded?

---

[10]Differential tax rates between lenders and borrowers sometimes can create an economic incentive for a call feature beneficial to both borrower and lender. For an analysis of tax incentives for call features, see W. M. Boyce and A. J. Kalotay, "Tax Differentials and Callable Bonds," *Journal of Finance* 34 (September 1979): 825–38. The tax-incentive argument sheds light on why corporate bonds nearly always have a call feature and on why Treasury bonds almost never have one.

[11]Use of the after-tax equivalent of the interest rate on the new bond is one method of analyzing refundings. For an analysis of the assumptions of this method, see Aharon R. Offer and R. A. Taggart, "Bond Refunding: A Clarifying Analysis," *Journal of Finance*, March 1977, pp. 21–30.

Table 17–1
Cash Flows Associated with Bond Refunding at Geoffrey Enterprises

Initial outlay:

Cost of calling old bonds (50,000 bonds at $1,120 each)	$-$56,000,000
Receipts from new bond issue	$+$ 50,000,000
(1) Net outlay	$-$$ 6,000,000
Expenses	
(2) Flotation cost on new bonds	$-$ 500,000
Tax Savings*	
(3) Unamortized flotation cost on old bonds, 0.4($400,000)	$+$ 160,000
Net cash flow, (1) + (2) + (3)	$-$$ 6,340,000

Annual cash flows (for 20 years):

(4) After tax interest expense on new bonds (10 percent),	
0.10(1 − 0.4)($50,000,000)	$-$$ 3,000,000
(5) After tax interest savings having retired old bonds (12 percent),	
0.12(1 − 0.4)($50,000,000)	$+$ 3,600,000
(6) Net after tax interest savings, (4) + (5)	$+$$ 600,000
Tax effects of flotation costs*	
(7) Loss of tax shield on amortization of old bond, 0.4($20,000)	$-$$ 8,000
(8) Tax Shield on amortization of flotation costs on new bond,	
0.4($25,000)	$+$ 10,000
(9) Net savings, (7) + (8)	$+$$ 2,000
Total annual cash flow, (6) + (9)	$+$$ 602,000

*See text for explanation of the treatment of flotation costs.

Solution

The task is to estimate the relevant cash flows and then determine if they have a positive net present value. Do interest savings outweigh the costs of the refunding operation? The cash flows associated with the refunding are shown in Table 17–1. The flotation costs are assumed to be amortized straight-line over the life of the bond. For example, when the old bond was issued 5 years ago, the flotation cost of $500,000 would have been spread over the 25-year life of the bond for an annual tax-deductible noncash expense of $500,000/25 = $20,000. After 5 years, only $100,000 of the expense would have been taken, so the company could deduct the remaining $400,000 for tax purposes when the bond was refunded. This deduction would produce a tax savings of 0.4($400,000) = $160,000 as shown in row (3) of Table 17–1. On the new bond, flotation costs would be amortized over the 20-year life of the bond to be $500,000/20 = $25,000 per year. Note that these amortized charges are *noncash* charges, which give rise to tax shields perfectly analogous to tax shields created by depreciation charges, as we discussed in Chapter 9.

Looking at the data in Table 17–1, we see that for an initial outlay of $6,340,000, the company can obtain an annual after-tax cash flow of $602,000 for 20 years. The after-tax cost of new debt is 6 percent: $K_d(1 - T) = 0.10(1 - 0.4) = 0.06$. Using this discount rate and Appendix Table II at the end of the book, we can calculate the net present value of the refunding as

$$NPV = -\$6,340,000 + \left[\sum_{t=1}^{t=20} \frac{\$602,000}{(1 + 0.06)^t}\right]$$

$$= -\$6,340,000 + [\$602,000 \, (11.47)]$$

$$= \$564,940.$$

The positive net present value suggests that the old bond should be refunded. ∃Ⅲ⊩

Bond-refunding problems can become much more complicated than the one worked out in Sample Problem 17–1. For simplicity, we assumed that the new bonds had maturity equal to the remaining maturity of the old bond. In addition, we assumed away any bond discounts (selling a bond at less than face value) that add additional tax complications. Perhaps more fundamentally, we have not considered whether it is best to refund now or wait a few more months to refund if interest rates are expected to decline further.[12] Despite all these qualifications, however, we have shown the basic nature of the refunding problem: are the costs of refunding justified by future cash savings?

Retirement of Preferred Stock.   Although preferred stock has no maturity date and the preferred shareholders' investment is considered permanent, preferred issues nearly always include some provision for retirement. Some issues provide for periodic retirement by means of a sinking fund, although many do not. Where used, the procedure is essentially the same as that in the case of bond sinking funds.

Nearly all preferred issues include a call privilege. As in the case of callable debt issues, the call price is above par value. Buyers of preferred issues charge for the call privilege by demanding a higher dividend rate. The usual motives for calling a preferred issue are to refinance at a lower dividend rate, to alter the firm's capital structure, or to renegotiate restrictive covenants.

Many preferred issues are convertible into common stock and are subject to retirement in that manner.

Repurchase of Common Stock.   Common stock has no maturity and never includes provisions either for periodic retirement or for call. The only means by which common stock can be retired is by repurchase of outstanding shares—either through open-market purchases or through an *invitation to tender*. In the latter case, a firm invites shareholders to offer, or tender, their shares to the firm at a specified price. Usually, the firm specifies a minimum and maximum number of shares that will be repurchased.

> **Common stock can be retired only by repurchase of outstanding shares, either through open-market purchases or an invitation to tender.**

The incidence of repurchasing by firms of their own shares seems to ebb and flow, becoming more prevalent in some periods and then declining again in other periods.

---

[12]See E. J. Elton and M. J. Gruber, *Finance As A Dynamic Process* (Englewood Cliffs, N.J.: Prentice-Hall, 1975), Chapter 2, for a more thorough discussion of the analysis of bond refundings considering the set of possible future decisions on capital structure.

Finance in Practice 17–2

How Stock Repurchase Affects Return to Investors

During the early 1980s, companies began to be more and more interested in buying back their own shares, and repurchase activity increased significantly. According to Merrill Lynch, a major New York investment banking firm, in 1984 some 600 companies announced programs to repurchase their own shares, a new record. A total of about $26 billion went into repurchases.

How does repurchase affect investors? To shed some light on this issue, *Fortune* magazine conducted a study using the 1,660 firms in the *Value Line Investment Survey*. *Fortune* identified those companies in the Value Line list that had engaged in significant repurchase activity during the 10-year period from 1974 through 1983. They then calculated the total annual return to shareholders (dividends plus capital gains) for

companies in this group, and compared them to returns on the Standard & Poors 500 Stock Index, a widely followed index of general stock-market performance. They found that return on the buy-back companies averaged 22.6 percent per year compounded over the 10 years, while the S&P 500 companies averaged only 14.1 percent—a big difference.

Critics of stock repurchase feel that repurchase programs accomplish little of value. A repurchase of stock is not an investment, but rather a stock issue in reverse. In and of itself it cannot create value. Can repurchase make a firm's shareholders better off? For some shareholders, the answer is yes. If a firm's stock is undervalued at the time of the repurchase, those who hold their shares and do not sell back to the firm defi-

Several motives may be cited by a firm for repurchasing, one of which is as an alternative to paying dividends. If a firm wishes to distribute a given amount of cash to its shareholders, in lieu of a cash dividend it can simply repurchase an appropriate number of its own shares. Cash received by shareholders upon sale of stock normally would be taxed at capital-gain rates, whereas a dividend would have been taxed at a higher ordinary-income rate. In effect, repurchase has the potential to transform ordinary income into a capital gain and save the shareholders some taxes. However, the Internal Revenue Service (IRS) has long since noticed the tax advantage to shareholders and has ruled against it. Any repurchase deemed to be in lieu of a dividend is likely to be treated as such by the IRS.

Repurchase, therefore, usually is justified on grounds other than as an alternative to a dividend. Sometimes repurchase is justified as an investment, or a means of improving earnings per share. However, it is improper to view repurchase as a new investment. In fact, it is nothing more nor less than a stock issue in reverse. It is true that earnings per share rise, but only in proportion to the reduction in the number of shares. If the shares are repurchased at less than their true value, those shareholders who do not sell realize a gain, but it represents a transfer of wealth from selling shareholders, not new value created, and raises serious questions of ethics.

Sometimes repurchase is justified as a means of accumulating shares for use in

nitely are made better off, because they have "bought out" other shareholders at less than true value. But those who sell are worse off then they would have been had they not sold. Hence, benefits to shareholders who don't sell come at the expense of those who do. It is a wealth transfer, not new value created. This situation presents a problem, because management is benefiting some shareholders at the expense of others. Proponents of repurchase point out that selling shareholders do so willingly and that the choice of whether or not to sell back lies entirely with them. Nevertheless, repurchase does put management in the position potentially of favoring one group of shareholders over another.

Another problem with repurchase is that it diverts management time from activities that truly do create new value. One critic stated that it is regrettable to see managers spending so much time worrying about the stock market "instead of finding good business opportunities, competing against the Japanese, and minding the store." Some feel that the market should regard repurchase as a negative signal, indicating that the firm has run out of profitable investment opportunities. Indeed, firms sell stock when they need money, and because repurchase is a stock issue in reverse, presumably they would repurchase when they have excess cash.

In spite of questions about repurchase, it has become an important phenomenon in the 1980s, and companies continue to announce repurchase programs. Ford Motor Company, for example, completed a 10-million-share buy-back program in the fall of 1985. In November of that year, the company announced a second repurchase program even bigger than the first, involving 20 million shares and $1 billion. Repurchases under the two programs, when completed, would account for approximately 15 percent of Ford's common-stock capitalization.

Many analysts attribute much of the buy-back activity in the early 1980s to a perception on the part of managers that their stocks were undervalued. If so, a major upward move in stock prices should reduce the repurchase activity.

Source: Adapted from C. J. Loomis, "Beating the Market by Buying Back Stock," *Fortune*, April 29, 1985; "Ford Plans $1 Billion Stock Buy-Back," *Wall Street Journal*, November 15, 1985.

future acquisitions or for employee stock options. Here, too, the advantage is illusory, for the purpose is served equally well by issuing new shares.

One motive for repurchase that does make economic sense is to return capital—that is, to achieve a partial liquidation of the firm. If a firm's markets have eroded and a reduction in scale is appropriate, a part of the shareholders' investment can be returned through repurchase. This reason for repurchase is not often used, however, because the managers of most firms prefer the alternative of seeking other investments to a partial liquidation. Another motive for repurchase that is defensible is to effect a change in the firm's debt/equity ratio. If a firm wishes to increase its debt ratio quickly, it can issue new debt and use the proceeds to retire common stock. Again, this motive is not often used in practice.

Whatever the motive for repurchase, management should be especially careful to communicate fully to investors its reasons for the repurchase. Because some shareholders give up all or a part of their interest in the firm, it is especially important as a matter of fairness and ethics that all shareholders have all pertinent information on which to base their decisions, including information regarding the firm's future prospects. As a practical matter, it is essentially impossible for a management to communicate all relevant information. Therefore, being entirely fair to both selling and nonselling shareholders is difficult indeed.

Of the motives usually given for repurchase discussed above, one motive (repurchase in lieu of a dividend) is not permitted under IRS regulations. Two others (repurchase as an investment and repurchase to obtain shares for other purposes) rest on questionable economic logic. The two that do make economic sense (repurchase as partial liquidation and repurchase to increase the debt ratio) are applicable in situations that do not often occur. In view of the potential ethical questions involved in repurchase, a management contemplating repurchase should consider carefully the benefits and costs and make certain that repurchase is the best vehicle for accomplishing the objectives at hand.

BUSINESS FAILURE AND REORGANIZATION

Thus far we have discussed issuing and managing securities under more or less normal circumstances. Unhappily, firms are not always as successful as their owners, managers, and creditors hope. Many firms encounter financial difficulty of one degree or another during their lives, and some fail. Here we consider failure and reorganization as a special case of managing relationships with suppliers of funds.

The reasons that firms encounter distress are varied. Sometimes distress is caused by external factors, such as changes in technology or markets. In an uncertain world, even the most capably managed firm is not immune to unexpected difficulties.

A more frequent reason for serious financial difficulty is poor management. A good example is W. T. Grant and Co., a giant retailing chain of over 1,000 stores that went into bankruptcy proceedings in 1975. As the court-appointed trustees explored the reasons for Grant's failure, the evidence clearly pointed to one overriding cause—bad management, exemplified by totally inadequate budgetary, inventory, and credit controls.[13]

In still other cases, financial difficulty may represent a signal that society wishes a reduction in the resources allocated to the activity in question. In a market economy, profits are the ultimate measure of whether resources are being allocated appropriately and managed efficiently.

Financial difficulties vary widely in severity, from relatively minor liquidity problems to complete failure. The number of firms having difficulties severe enough to file bankruptcy petitions is relatively small. The number encountering less severe forms of financial distress is much larger. The more severe is the difficulty, the more drastic is the remedy required and usually the more formal is the procedure for adjustment. In all cases, the rights of creditors and owners and their claims against the assets and earnings of the firm must be spelled out clearly. To begin our discussion, let us attempt to define business failure more clearly.

Business Failure

Under what conditions should a firm be considered to have failed? We must distinguish between two different situations of **business failure**. In the first situation, the value of

---

[13]For a discussion of the application of standard ratio analysis to the Grant case, see "Cash Flows, Ratio Analysis, and the W. T. Grant Bankruptcy," *Financial Analysts Journal* July/August 1980, pp. 51–54.

Business failure—is the situation that results (1) when the firm is unable to meet its contractual financial obligations even though the value of the firm's assets exceeds its liabilities (also known as *technical insolvency*) or (2) when the firm's liabilities exceed the value of its assets as a going concern.

the firm's assets exceeds its liabilities; that is, its net worth is greater than zero, but it is unable to meet its contractual financial obligations. These obligations might include interest or principal payments on debt, lease payments, or payments on installment sales contracts. The firm's cash flows are not sufficient to meet the contractual payments. Essentially, the problem is one of maturity; the firm's liabilities are maturing faster than its assets.

Such situations involving a shortage of liquidity sometimes are referred to as *technical insolvency*. Where the firm's prospects remain favorable, as implied by a positive net worth, the difficulties often can be resolved by means short of legal bankruptcy. Such adjustments are worked out voluntarily by the firm and its creditors. Where the difficulties are so resolved, the term *failure* probably overstates the case a bit, even though the situation initially involved a default on a financial obligation.

The second type of failure is one in which the firm's liabilities exceed the value of its assets as a going concern; that is, its net worth is zero. Often this type of failure is accompanied by the first type (a liquidity crisis), but the two are separable. In some cases, there may be uncertainty about the eventual value of the assets if the firm is liquidated, and the market price of the firm's stock may not fall entirely to zero. Where it is clear that liabilities exceed the firm's going-concern value, the ultimate outcome is likely to be bankruptcy, unless action can be taken to improve the firm's earnings prospects.

Voluntary Adjustments

In a crisis of the first type above—where the difficulty is one of cash flow and liquidity—the firm's value as a going concern exceeds its liabilities. In such situations, creditors usually are better off if they accommodate the firm's short-run difficulties and allow it to remain in operation, especially if the costs associated with bankruptcy are significant. In some cases, the firm may be able to adjust its cash flows to meet its financial obligations, with no changes in the terms of the latter. Adjustments of this sort usually involve a sale of assets. For example, accounts receivable or a part of the firm's plant and equipment might be sold. Such sales of assets are likely to be painful, but perhaps less so than the available alternatives.

Where cash-flow adjustments are not feasible or are inadequate, a second alternative is to adjust the financial obligations to fit the available cash flow. Often such adjustments are worked out between firm and creditors without recourse to the bankruptcy statutes and without the involvement of the courts. One possible adjustment is called an *extension*, whereby the maturity of one or more obligations is extended to give the firm more time to meet it. Another is called a *composition*, under which all creditors agree to accept a partial payment. Where the basic difficulty results from a liquidity shortage, an extension usually is the appropriate remedy.

The International Harvester Company is an example of the use of *voluntary adjustments*. Harvester lost $393 million during fiscal 1981 (with its fiscal year ending October 31, 1981). The loss from continuing operations actually was much higher, totaling $635 million, but was offset in part by a special nonrecurring gain, mainly on the sale of its solar turbines division. Late in 1981 International Harvester concluded a $4.2 billion debt restructuring plan with its creditors requiring that net worth be maintained above $1 billion. At that point, all parties seemed to agree that voluntary adjustments were preferable to bankruptcy proceedings. By 1986 the company had sold off some of its businesses and changed its name to Narvistar.

Braniff Airways provides another case in point. Braniff lost $128 million during 1980, a bad year for nearly all airline companies. By July 1981, Braniff was in such difficulty that it could not meet payments coming due on its debt, which totaled about $540 million. Braniff's lenders agreed to accept a deferral of some $45 million in interest charges and to negotiate a complete restructuring of the company's debt. Unfortunately for Braniff, even this arrangement was not enough. Within a year, Braniff was bankrupt.[14]

Bankruptcy

Bankruptcy—is the failure to meet contractual obligations that results in court action to have the firm administered for the benefit of the firm's creditors.

Where the appropriate remedy cannot be agreed upon informally, relief can be sought by either the firm or its creditors in the courts in **bankruptcy** proceedings. Bankruptcies are governed by federal law. Federal bankruptcy laws were first enacted in the late 19th century and most recently were changed by the Bankruptcy Reform Act of 1978. Under the act, a debtor may petition the court for reorganization. Alternatively, under certain circumstances, creditors may petition to have a firm adjudged bankrupt. Under either case, a basic purpose of the Bankruptcy Reform Act is to maintain the status quo so that no one group of creditors can gain at the expense of another. Time, thus, is made available to study the situation and determine the appropriate remedy.

When a bankruptcy petition is filed, it usually means that the firm's liabilities exceed its value as a going concern, at least in the eyes of creditors or owners, or both. The question of whether the firm should be reorganized and allowed to continue in operation, or liquidated, still remains.

Reorganization—is the restructuring of liabilities so that a firm's anticipated cash flows are sufficient to meet them.

Most **reorganizations** take place under Chapter 11 of the Bankruptcy Reform Act. The objective of the reorganization is to restructure the liabilities so that the firm's anticipated cash flows are sufficient to meet them. Reorganization may involve extension or composition of debt obligations or creation of new classes of securities. During the reorganization, the firm continues to operate, either under its old management or a receiver appointed by the court.

Liquidation—is the dissolution of a firm by selling its assets and distributing the proceeds to creditors and shareholders on the basis of seniority.

If the liquidation value of the firm is greater than its going-concern value, then **liquidation** of the firm's assets is probably the best remedy. Liquidation is conducted under procedures spelled out in Chapter 7 of the Bankruptcy Reform Act. Such liquidation may take place if no reorganization can be worked out under Chapter 11. Assets are converted to cash, and the proceeds are distributed to claimholders. Liquidation usually is lengthy and costly.

No matter what the outcome of bankruptcy, there are often large costs involved, including explicit costs, such as lawyers' fees, and indirect costs, such as forgone business opportunities.

---

[14]For International Harvester, see the *Wall Street Journal*, February 25, 1982. For Braniff, see the *Wall Street Journal*, July 2, 1981.

KEY CONCEPTS

1. Firms normally issue debt and equity securities to the public using one of three methods: public offerings through investment bankers, public offerings through privileged subscriptions, and private placements.

2. Investment bankers serve as intermediaries who bring together the seller of securities (namely, the firm) and the buyers (namely, the public).

3. Both the federal and state governments regulate the sale of securities to the public and require that the seller of the securities disclose certain types of information.

4. Firms incur flotation costs when new securities are issued.

5. While there are understandable motives for timing the issuance of securities to take advantage of capital-market conditions, the odds of *consistently* timing new issues to advantage are not good.

6. Keeping the owners of a firm's securities informed about the firm is an important management responsibility. It is important to have a good communications policy with the owners of a firm.

7. Sometimes firms retire long-term securities before the securities actually become due, as in the case of bond refunding.

8. Stock repurchases must be analyzed carefully to make sure that the stated objectives of the repurchase actually have sound economic foundations.

9. Business failure, often induced by poor management, can lead to bankruptcy.

SUMMARY

Firms have important responsibilities to their suppliers of funds, both creditors and investors. These responsibilities begin with the issuance of new securities and continue as long as the securities remain outstanding.

Firms normally issue new debt and equity securities to the public using one of three methods: public offerings through investment bankers, public offerings by means of privileged subscription, and private placements. Investment bankers are intermediaries who perform a number of important functions in the issuance of new securities, including underwriting, pricing, and selling. Some firms follow a practice of offering new common stock to existing shareholders by means of privileged subscription before offering it to the public at large. All public offerings are subject to government regulation, especially with respect to disclosure of pertinent information.

An alternative to a public offering, normally used only for debt issues, is a private placement with one or a small group of investors—usually insurance companies or pension funds. Private placements usually are simpler and quicker than public offerings and represent an important source of long-term financing to smaller, less financially secure firms.

In developing financing plans, the timing of new issues is an important consideration, especially when a sequence of issues is in prospect. Market conditions must be taken into account even though forecasting changes in conditions is very difficult.

One of the most important of the firm's continuing responsibilities after issuance of securities is communication. Comprehensive disclosure of developments within the firm and of management policies facilitates relations with the financial markets. Especially important is careful communication in connection with extraordinary events or changes in major policies so that investors and creditors can base decisions on facts rather than on inferences.

Long-term debt issues nearly always provide for gradual retirement (repayment) prior to maturity, either through a sinking-fund arrangement or by means of serial redemption. Many bond issues also include provisions for calling the issue at the option of management. Some preferred-stock issues include a sinking-fund provision, and nearly all include a call privilege. Common stock does not include provision for periodic retirement or for call and can be retired only through repurchase by the firm. Because of the potential for conflict between different groups of shareholders, re-purchase should be considered only when it can accomplish clear economic objectives equitably.

The responsibility of a firm to investors and credi-tors includes provisions for dealing with financial distress. Liquidation of assets is appropriate only if liquidation value exceeds the value of the firm as a going concern.

QUESTIONS

1. What are the three principal methods of issuing securities to the public?

2. What are the major functions of investment bankers?

3. What is a *privileged-subscription,* or *rights offering*?

4. In a rights offering, how does the subscription price of the offering affect the net worth of shareholders?

5. What is the purpose of federal and state regulation of the securities markets?

6. What is a *private placement* of securities? What are the advantages of private placements?

7. Why do issue costs affect the size and frequency of financing?

8. What responsibilities do firms have to provide information to investors and other participants in the financial markets?

9. Why is it desirable for firms to keep investors informed regarding future plans to the greatest extent possible? How does such information affect the price of the firm's securities?

10. How are long-term debt issues retired?

11. What is a *sinking fund* in connection with bonds or preferred stock?

12. How do *serial bonds* differ from sinking-fund bonds?

13. Why do borrowers normally wish to have the option to call a bond issue before maturity?

14. How can common stock be retired?

15. What motives exist for the repurchase by a firm of its own common stock?

16. What potential ethical questions do you see in a decision to repurchase stock?

17. In what way does financial difficulty represent a judgment by society regarding a firm's performance?

18. What is *technical insolvency*?

19. What steps are required when a firm encounters financial difficulty?

PROBLEMS

1. Head Over Heels, Inc., plans to raise $10,000,000 in new equity by means of a rights offering with a subscription price of $80 per share. The stock currently sells for $100 per share and there are 1 million shares outstanding.

   a. How many new shares will Head issue?

   b. How many rights will be required to buy one share?

   c. At what price will the stock sell when it goes *ex rights* if the total value of all stock increases by the amount of the new funds?

   d. What is the theoretical value of one right?

2. Suppose you have the income information shown in Table A for the firm in problem (1) before the rights offering. Suppose the market price does fall to the level determined in part (d) of the preceding problem when the stock goes *ex rights*.

   a. If the firm's total earnings remain at $10,000,000, what will be the new earnings per share (EPS)?

Table A

Total earnings	$10,000,000
Interest on debt	2,000,000
Income before taxes	$ 8,000,000
Taxes at 46 percent	3,680,000
Earnings after taxes	$ 4,320,000
Earnings per share	$4.32

b. What will happen to the *P/E ratio* (price per share divided by earnings per share)?

c. By how much must total earnings rise so that EPS remains the same before and after the rights offering?

3. Fan Attics Corporation has an outstanding issue of 16 percent 25-year bonds which have 15 years left to maturity. They have a call price of $1,160 (per $1,000 of face value) and were sold at face value

for $40 million dollars. Fan feels it could issue new bonds for $40 million at face value, with a 15-year life and a coupon of 12 percent. The flotation costs on the old issue were $500,000, which have been partially amortized on a straight-line basis. Flotation costs on the new issue would be $450,000 and would be amortized over the life of the bond. The corporate tax rate is 46 percent. Should the bond be refunded?

REFERENCES

Bacon, P. W. "The Subscription Price in Rights Offerings." *Financial Management* 1 (Summer 1972): 59–64.

Bhagat, S., M. Marr, and G. Thompson. "The Rule 415 Experiment: Equity Markets." *Journal of Finance* (December 1985): 1385–1401.

"Big Players in Financial Futures." *Fortune* (September 17, 1984).

Boyce, W. M., and A. J. Kalotay. "Tax Differentials and Callable Bonds." *Journal of Finance* 34 (Sep. 1979): 825–838.

"Cash Flows, Ratio Analysis, and W. T. Grant Bankruptcy." *Financial Analysts Journal* (July–Aug. 1980): 51–54.

Dyl, E. A., and M. D. Joehnk. "Competitive versus Negotiated Underwriting of Public Utility Debt." *Bell Journal of Economics* 7 (Autumn 1976): 680–689.

Elton, E. J. and M. J. Gruber. "The Effect of Share Repurchase on the Value of the Firm." *Journal of Finance* 23 (Mar. 1968): 135–150.

Hayes, S. L., III. "Investment Banking: Power Structure in Flux." *Harvard Business Review* 49 (Mar.–Apr. 1971): 136–152.

Ingersoll, J. E. "A Contingent Claims Valuation of Convertible Securities." *Journal of Financial Economics* 2 (May 1977): 289–322.

Jalilvand, A., and R. Harris. "Corporate Behavior in Adjusting to Capital Structure and Dividend Targets." *Journal of Finance* (March 1984): 127–145.

Jensen, M. C. "Capital Markets: Theory and Evidence." *The Bell Journal of Economics and Management Science* 3 (Autumn 1972): 357–398.

Johnson, K. B., T. G. Morton, and M. C. Findlay, III. "An Empirical Analysis of the Flotation Cost of Corporate Securities." *Journal of Finance* 30 (Sept. 1975): 1129–1134.

Kolb, R. *Understanding Futures Markets*. Glenview, Ill.: Scott, Foresman, 1987.

Kalotay, A. J. "Sinking Funds and the Realized Cost of Debt." *Financial Management* 11 (Spring 1982): 43–54.

Kidwell, D., M. Marr, and G. Thompson, "SEC Rule 415: The Ultimate Competitive Bid." *Journal of Financial and Quantitative Analysis,* June 1984, pp. 183–195.

Laffer, A. B., and R. D. Renson. "Some Practical Applications of the Efficient Market Concept." *Financial Management* 7 (Summer 1978): 63–75.

McDonald, J. G., and A. K. Fisher. "New Issue Stock Price Behavior." *Journal of Finance* 27 (Mar. 1972): 97–102.

Marks, K. R. *The Stock Price Performance of Firms Repurchasing Their Own Shares*. New York: Graduate School of Business Administration, New York University, Bulletin 1976–1.

Miller, E. "Risk, Uncertainty and Divergence of Opinion." *Journal of Finance* 32 (Sept. 1977): 1151–1168.

Myers, S. C., and N. J. Majluf. "Stock Issues and Investment Policy when Firms have Information that Investors Do Not Have." *Journal of Financial Economics* 13 (1984):187–221.

Norgaard, R., and C. Norgaard. "A Critical Examination of Share Repurchases." *Financial Management* 3 (Spring 1974): 44–51.

Offer, A. R., and R. A. Taggart. "Bond Refunding: A Clarifying Analysis." *Journal of Finance* (March 1977): 21–30.

Phillips, S. M., and J. R. Zecher. "Exchange Listing and the Cost of Equity Capital." U.S. Securities and Exchange Commission—Capital Market Working Paper #8 (March 1982).

Securities and Exchange Commission, *Annual Reports*. Washington, D.C.: U.S. Government Printing Office.

Shapiro, E., and C. R. Wolf. *The Role of Private Placements in Corporate Finance*. Boston: Graduate School of Business Administration, Harvard University, 1972.

Stanga, K. G. "Disclosure in Published Annual Reports." *Financial Management* 5 (Winter 1976): 42–52.

Part Six

Managing Working Capital

In Part Five, we discussed some basic long-term financing decisions facing a firm: What is the appropriate amount of debt financing? What is the best dividend policy for a firm to choose? In that discussion, we focused on long-term sources of funds.

In addition to these long-term financing decisions, corporations face many decisions involving short-term financing and short-term asset management. Short-term assets and liabilities are those that last less than one year. For example, firms have many current assets (such as cash, marketable securities, and inventories) that are usually replaced within a year. Similarly, there are many current liabilities (primarily accounts payable, accruals of various types, and short-term borrowing) that represent short-term financing for the corporation.

We turn our attention to a firm's decisions about managing its short-term assets and liabilities. Conceptually, the problems are the same as those we considered in discussing long-term investment and financing decisions. A current asset represents a type of investment and as such should provide a return to justify the investment. These assets consume cash that has been left in the business. For example, many large companies have substantial investments in inventories. In fact, any long-term project, such as the introduction of a new product, typically involves a buildup of inventory in the early phases of the project and is likely to cause a buildup of accounts receivable as sales increase.

Short-term liabilities are sources of funds, just as long-term debt and equity are. They often have explicit (or implicit) interest costs and involve risks. Financial managers must decide what mix of short-term and long-term financing should be used, and this decision requires analyzing the costs and risks of each funding source.

In Chapter 18, we will focus on short-term sources of finance and the general issues involved in choosing short-term versus long-term financing. In Chapters 19 and 20, we will turn our attention to short-term assets. In Chapter 19, we will focus on the important topic of cash management, while in Chapter 20, we will consider management of accounts receivable and inventory.

Working capital refers to the firm's current assets. *Net working capital* is current assets minus current liabilities. Current assets are called *working capital* because most of these assets vary closely with the level of the firm's operations—that is, with the level of production and sales. Most decisions with respect to working capital and its components have their impact over weeks and months rather than years. For this reason, short-term finance is often referred to as *working-capital management*.

The topics covered in Part Six are important to the management of any firm. Short-term finance is especially important to the small or new firm, where survival and growth are matters of continuous concern. In any growing firm, we will find that financing a growing working-capital requirement is a major problem. Short-term finance is especially important in retail and wholesale businesses and in many service businesses where the major investment is in short-term rather than long-term assets.

Chapter

18

Short-Term Financing

In this chapter, we will explore methods of providing short-term funds to the firm. First, we will explore the two main alternative approaches to financing fluctuating levels of assets—the use of liquid assets to cushion the fluctuations versus the use of short-term financing, including trade credit, loans from various types of financial institutions, and commercial paper issued by the borrower directly to investors.

To obtain funds, a firm issues claims against its income and assets. Liabilities are contractual claims; equities are ownership claims. Liabilities are obligations, but they also represent sources of funds. Some liabilities, such as accounts payable and accrual accounts of various kinds, arise naturally out of the firm's operations because of the lag between the time the liability is incurred and the time it is discharged or paid. Other liabilities, such as loans, are incurred at management's discretion.

Short-term funds—are funds borrowed for less than one year.

Intermediate-term funds—are funds borrowed for periods between 1 and perhaps 8 or 10 years.

Earlier, in Part Five, we discussed the major sources of long-term funds. Here we turn to **short-term funds** and **intermediate-term funds**. The words *short-term* and *intermediate-term* refer to the maturity of the claim against the firm—that is, the time horizon over which the principal amount remains outstanding. The short term is usually a period of less than a year; the intermediate term is usually a period between 1 and perhaps 8 or 10 years. These definitions are more or less arbitrary, and there often is no clear distinction between a short-term and an intermediate-term loan. A loan that begins as short-term may become intermediate-term if the borrower is unable to repay on schedule or renews it for other reasons.

Perhaps more useful distinctions can be drawn with respect to the purpose of the loan and the means of repaying it. Short-term loans often are made to finance seasonal working-capital requirements, such as the buildup of inventories that might occur for a company that stockpiled goods for sale at Christmas. Such seasonal loans might be repaid with the cash generated from sale of the goods and the resultant reduction of inventory. Intermediate-term loans, on the other hand, usually are made to finance permanent additions to working capital or fixed assets. Funds to repay such loans usually come from profits or cash flows generated from operations over a period of several years and not from liquidation of the assets being financed, as in the case of a seasonal working-capital loan. Short-term lenders, thus, are concerned mainly with the strength of the firm's balance sheet, the quality of assets, and other claims against the assets. Intermediate-term and long-term lenders are concerned more with the income statement, looking for their security to the firm's earning power over sustained periods of time.

> Short-term loans often are made to finance seasonal working-capital requirements, while intermediate-term loans usually are made to finance permanent additions to working capital or to fixed assets.

We discussed the financial environment in chapter 2. Finance in Practice 18-1 describes in more detail some recent developments in the interest-rate environment in which managers must operate.

ALTERNATIVE FINANCING STRATEGIES

As we discussed earlier in Chapters 13 and 14, a firm faces a basic choice about how much debt to use. In that earlier discussion, we did not concern ourselves with whether such debt was short-term or long-term; here, we will examine this choice between long-term and short-term financing.

Consider a firm whose earnings are stable from period to period. Let us assume that the firm reinvests a portion of its earnings each year and that its total assets grow

Figure 18–1
A Stable Financing Requirement

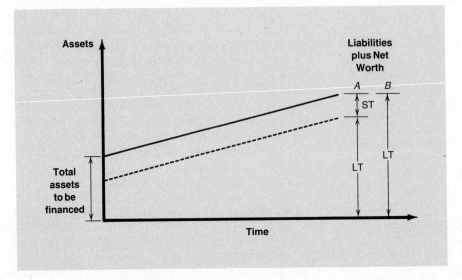

at a steady rate. Under such circumstances, the total financing requirement also will grow at a steady rate. If we assume that the use of at least some debt is appropriate for this firm, we have the option of using either short-term or long-term debt. Graphically, we can represent the situation as in Figure 18–1. Figure 18–1 shows that the assets (on the left-hand side of a balance sheet) must ultimately be financed by liabilities plus net worth (the right-hand side of a balance sheet).

Growing assets require growing sources of funds.

Accounts payable—are amounts of money owed by the firm to its trade creditors and listed under current liabilities on the balance sheet.

Accrual accounts—are accounts, such as those for the payment of wages or taxes, in which money accumulates over short, regular periods to be paid out at regular intervals.

In Figure 18–1 we represent the two policy alternatives as A and B. Under Policy A, the firm finances a part of the total requirement using long-term (LT) funds and part using short-term (ST) funds. Under Policy B, only long-term funds are used. Long-term funds might consist of equity or a combination of equity and long-term debt. Short-term sources might consist of bank loans or, if the firm were sufficiently large and well-known, *commercial paper* issued directly to lenders. (We will discuss commercial paper later in this chapter.)

In Figure 18–1, we are ignoring short-term liabilities that arise spontaneously and directly from the firm's operations, such as **accounts payable** and various **accrual accounts**. We can view these as having been subtracted from assets to reduce the total financing requirement. For example, suppose a firm purchased $1,000 worth of raw materials and created a raw-materials inventory account (current asset) in the amount of $1,000. If the purchase were on credit, there would be an account payable of

Figure 18–2
A Variable Financing Requirement

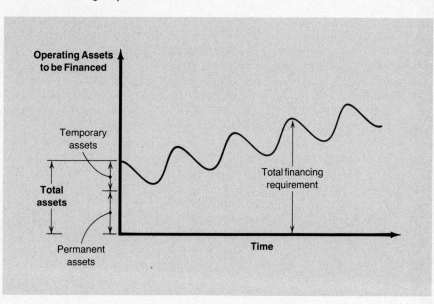

$1,000 (current liability). The net need for new financing would be zero until the firm paid its account payable.

Variable Financing Requirement

Now consider the more realistic case of a variable financing requirement, where current assets ebb and flow with sales and production. Such is the case for most firms. In Chapter 8, we looked at a particular example of this case, Aquatic Systems. We can represent this variable-financing situation as shown in Figure 18–2. The variable component of the requirement in Figure 18–2 can be financed in two basic ways: (1) by using reserve borrowing power or (2) by using holdings of liquid assets.

Liquid assets—are assets, such as marketable securities, that can be converted to cash almost immediately without having to sell at a price well below their value.

    Liquid assets are assets, such as marketable securities, that can be converted to cash almost immediately without having to sell at a price well below their value. For example, there are well-developed markets for U.S. Treasury bills in which they can be sold almost immediately at the going market price. On the other hand, it might be almost impossible to sell a manufacturing plant on short notice, and attempts to do so might require selling at a distress price well below the plant's true value.

    If the firm relies on reserve borrowing power, it simply borrows short-term funds, probably from a bank, as needed. Both sides of the balance sheet expand and contract in step. On the liability side, it is short-term debt that varies. If the firm also has access to long-term sources, it can finance the fixed portion of its requirement with

Figure 18–3
Using Short-Term Borrowing to Finance Variable Requirements

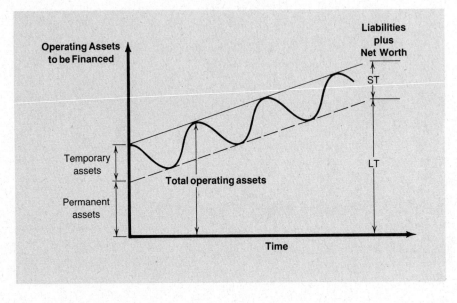

Figure 18–4
Using Liquid Assets to Finance Variable Requirements

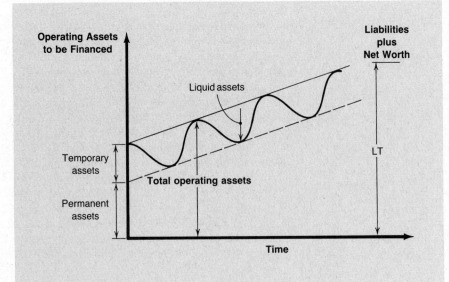

Figure 18-5

Choosing a Liquidity Policy

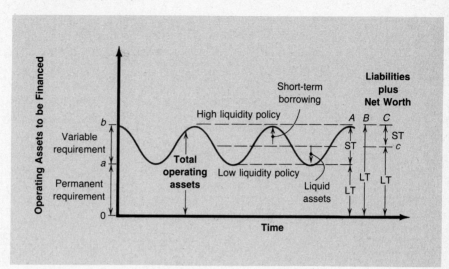

long-term sources and the variable portion with short-term sources. This approach is represented graphically in Figure 18–3.

Alternatively, if the firm relies on the second alternative—liquid assets—it finances entirely with long-term sources. Sufficient long-term funds are raised to finance both the permanent requirement and the liquid-asset buffer. Graphically, we can represent this approach as shown in Figure 18–4.

> **If the firm relies on reserve borrowing power to deal with a variable financing requirement, it simply borrows short-term funds as needed. Alternatively, if it relies on liquid assets, it finances entirely with long-term sources. Many firms find it wise to use a combination of liquid assets and reserve borrowing to deal with variable financing requirements.**

Following the policy represented in Figure 18–4, total assets and total liabilities plus net worth grow at a steady rate over time. All of the short-term variability is taken up within the current-asset section of the balance sheet, with liquid assets expanding and contracting in exact opposition to operating assets—mainly inventories and **accounts receivable**. When funds are needed for operating assets, liquid assets are sold.

Accounts receivable—are amounts of money owed to the firm by customers and listed under current assets on the balance sheet.

A Combination Policy

It is not necessary to select one or the other of the two alternatives described above. Many firms find it wise to choose a policy lying somewhere between the two.

This middle position is represented in Figure 18–5. In Figure 18–5, we simplify

Table 18–1
Pro Forma Balance Sheets for Aquatic Systems, Incorporated, 1987 (thousands of dollars)

	Actual 12/31/86	Jan.	Feb.	March
Cash	$ 50	$ 50	$ 50	$ 50
Marketable securities	94	0	0	0
Accounts receivable	353	345	385	523
Inventories	1,080	1,204	1,293	1,314
Total current assets	$1,577	$1,599	$1,728	$1,887
Gross plant and equipment	$4,960	$5,210	$5,460	$5,460
Less accumulated depreciation	− 1,850	− 1,875	− 1,900	− 1,925
Net plant	$3,110	$3,335	$3,560	$3,535
Total assets	$4,687	$4,934	$5,288	$5,422
Bank notes payable	$ 0	$ 291	$ 646	$ 799
Accounts payable	148	125	125	125
Taxes payable[a]	40	34	34	46
Other accruals	50	50	50	50
Total current liabilities	$ 238	$ 500	$ 855	$1,020
Mortgage payable[b]	960	960	960	960
Common stock	1,500	1,500	1,500	1,500
Retained earnings	1,989	1,974	1,973	1,942
Total liabilities and net worth	$4,687	$4,934	$5,288	$5,422

[a]The December 31, 1986, figure of $40,000 is the amount remaining on 1986 tax and is payable on April 15, 1987. The 1987 estimated
   tax is payable in equal installments in April, June, September, and December. The negative figure in April represents prepaid taxes
[b]$100,000 per year payable in June and December.

matters by looking at an example with no growth in its permanent requirement for operating assets. Lines A and B represent, as before, the two policy extremes. If the firm adopts Policy A, it uses long-term funds of amount a and finances the entire variable portion by borrowing short-term funds as needed. If it adopts Policy B, it finances entirely with long-term funds (amount b), using no short-term borrowing at all and taking up the variations in the liquid-asset buffer. Policy A, thus, represents a low-liquidity policy, and Policy B represents a high-liquidity policy.

Policy C represents a middle position. When total assets rise above c, the peaks are financed with short-term borrowing. During low points, the firm holds excess funds in liquid assets. Note that under Policy C, the firm at any point in time is *either* holding liquid assets *or* borrowing short-term funds, but never both simultaneously.

Aquatic Systems, Inc., the subject of our attention in Chapter 8, is an example of a firm that pursues a type C policy. Table 18–1 reproduces the Aquatic Systems pro-forma balance sheets from Table 8–6 in Chapter 8. During the period January through August, Aquatic Systems is borrowing. As inventories and receivables decline during the summer, the loan declines. Finally, in September, cash begins to build up above $50,000, and the excess is held in marketable securities. Then the cycle begins again.

April	May	June	July	Aug.	Sep.	Oct.	Nov.	Dec.
$ 50	$ 50	$ 50	$ 50	$ 50	$ 50	$ 50	$ 50	$ 50
0	0	0	0	0	172	382	482	301
688	853	1,073	1,100	963	798	633	468	413
1,267	1,152	935	752	637	590	611	700	789
$2,005	$2,055	$2,058	$1,902	$1,650	$1,610	$1,676	$1,700	$1,553
$5,460	$5,460	$5,460	$5,460	$5,460	$5,460	$5,460	$5,460	$5,460
−1,950	−1,975	−2,000	−2,025	−2,050	−2,075	−2,100	−2,125	−2,150
$3,510	$3,485	$3,460	$3,435	$3,410	$3,385	$3,360	$3,335	$3,310
$5,515	$5,540	$5,518	$5,337	$5,060	$4,995	$5,036	$5,035	$4,863
$ 912	$ 812	$ 775	$ 427	$ 25	$ 0	$ 0	$ 0	$ 0
125	125	125	125	125	125	125	125	125
(32)	6	(1)	49	87	49	61	61	0
50	50	50	50	50	50	50	50	50
$1,055	$ 993	$ 949	$ 651	$ 287	$ 224	$ 236	$ 236	$ 175
960	960	910	910	910	910	910	910	860
1,500	1,500	1,500	1,500	1,500	1,500	1,500	1,500	1,500
2,000	2,087	2,159	2,276	2,363	2,361	2,390	2,389	2,328
$5,515	$5,540	$5,518	$5,337	$5,060	$4,995	$5,036	$5,035	$4,863

Securities are liquidated in December and January to finance the seasonal buildup of inventories and receivables. When marketable securities fall to zero, Aquatic Systems begins to borrow.

Risk and Cost Considerations

The policy issue for management is where to draw the line. A low-liquidity policy may expose the firm to opportunity costs because in future periods the firm might have to forgo good investment opportunities. If bank credit is used, the loan must be renewed continually. Suppose at some maturity date the bank is unable or unwilling to renew the loan or will renew the loan only at a significantly higher interest rate. Such a circumstance might arise under conditions of tight money when commercial banks are forced to ration credit. Or the firm's prospects might deteriorate to the point where the bank becomes unwilling to renew. Commercial activities might have to be constrained, and attractive opportunities might have to be forgone. Flexibility during periods of tight money represents one of the major benefits of liquidity.

An even worse prospect during periods of credit rationing would be an unexpected

Finance in Practice 18—1

Roller-Coaster Interest Rates

In April 1980, the prime rate—the benchmark rate used in banking as the rate for the most creditworthy customers—reached 20 percent, the highest rate in more than 60 years. It had risen irregularly over the preceding 8 months from 11.5 percent in July 1979 to the April high. After peaking at 20 percent, the prime rate then fell 9 percentage points over the next 4 months to 11 percent in August. Most observers of the economy thought that the economy was slowing down and that interest rates would follow the classic pattern of climbing irregularly from the August low back to high levels over a period roughly corresponding to a typical business cycle—that is, 2 to 4 years. That was the pattern that interest-rate cycles historically had followed.

It was not to be. After bottoming out in August, rates began climbing again, but very rapidly, not slowly. By late December, only *four months* after the August low, rates had surpassed even the peak of the previous April. After topping out at 21.5 percent in early January of 1981, the prime bank rate again fell rapidly and by April was back down to 17 percent.

In a space of less than a year, short-term rates had risen rapidly to a peak and then declined not once but twice. In April 1981, most observers expected the decline to continue, but instead more gyrations were to come. Rates climbed very rapidly again in May, and by the end of that month the prime rate was back at 20 percent! It stayed at the 20 percent level until September and then declined rapidly to 15.75 percent by December 1981.

Long-term bond rates, while not nearly so volatile as short-term rates, nevertheless had gyrated over the preceding 18 months to an extent unknown in recent memory. Over a period of 20 months, the AAA corporate bond rate went from 9.5 percent up to 13 percent, back down to 10.5 percent, and up again to 15.5 percent. Movements of this magnitude produced very large changes in the price of long-term bonds. The initial move from 9.5 percent to 13 percent, for example, produced a drop of as much

increase in cash requirements. In an uncertain world, many things can happen that cannot be foreseen. Strikes occur, technology changes, new products fail to meet expectations, oil prices rise rapidly and then fall just as rapidly, and so on. If short-term credit is not available because of credit rationing or perhaps because creditors do not like the firm's prospects, the firm has no choice but to reduce operating assets. If the period of negative cash flow is prolonged, the potential exists for serious financial difficulty.

A celebrated case in point is that of Chrysler Corporation. Chrysler began having difficulties in the late 1970s. These difficulties were variously attributed to foreign competition, government regulation, and (by the company's critics) bad management. In 1979, Chrysler was able to stave off bankruptcy by persuading the U.S. Congress to guarantee its debt obligations, citing as precedent similar bail-outs of Lockheed Aircraft Corporation in 1971 and of New York City in 1975. Chrysler's problems culminated in 1980 with a loss of $1.71 billion, the largest annual loss ever recorded by a U.S. company.[1]

---

[1]*Wall Street Journal*, March 2, 1981.

as 25 percent in the prices of 20-year bonds over a 6-month period. Between June 1979 and the peak in October 1981, long-term bonds lost more than a third of their market value.

The financial markets were in a state of shock. Corporate treasurers responsible for raising funds threw up their hands at the thought of trying to forecast interest rates. Insurance companies and banks owning hundreds of millions of dollars worth of long-term bonds saw the market value of their holdings fluctuate by tens of millions of dollars over periods of several weeks. The bond markets in 1981–82 were dominated by a pervasive sense of gloom.

After declining throughout 1982, rates bottomed out in the spring of 1983 and then climbed slowly but steadily to mid-1984. They then began gradually drop-ping again in July 1984, and by mid-1985 the AAA corporate rate was about 11 percent and the prime bank rate was about 9.5 percent. The rate declines continued into 1986, and by mid-1986, the prime rate was at 8 percent and the AAA corporate rate was around 9 percent. The peaks of 1981 have not been reached again since, and most market participants hope that such days will not return.

The financial markets have been much less volatile during 1983–86 than during 1980–82. Some economists attribute much of the increased volatility during the earlier period to a change in the operating procedure of the Federal Reserve late in 1979 that placed greater emphasis on growth rates of the money supply and less emphasis on interest rates themselves. The particularly sharp drop in short-term rates from April to August of 1980 is attributed by some to the imposition of credit controls on commercial-bank lending by the Federal Reserve from March to July of that year (cynics don't miss the opportunity to note that 1980 was a presidential election year).

For the current generation of managers and participants in the financial markets, the experience of 1980–1981 was unprecedented in both the magnitude and frequency of the variations in interest rates. Figure 2–1 in Chapter 2 showed the pattern of rates over this period. The financial officer's job in such an environment is difficult, to put it mildly. One problem from which financial officers have not suffered in the 1980s is boredom.

Source: Wall Street Journal, December 11 and 17, 1980.

One set of lessons for managers from the Chrysler case comes from examining the company's actions during the crisis. Among other actions, the company closed plants temporarily, reduced inventories, reduced its workforce, cut wages and salaries, and entered into an extensive program of cash rebates to induce people to buy Chrysler cars. These are all *operating* decisions forced by a financial crisis—decisions that might well have been made differently in the absence of the financial crisis. Decisions with long-term effects were made to solve a short-term, though obviously critical, problem. More conservative financial policies—low debt and high liquidity—in the 1960s and early 1970s would not have prevented Chrysler's problems, but they would have made the crisis more manageable and permitted Chrysler management to decide operating issues on their merits rather than under pressure from creditors.

One of the principal benefits of liquidity is flexibility during times of financial stress.

Aside from risk considerations, in choosing between long-term and short-term funds a firm must consider the relative costs of the two. Generally, short-term rates

A **compensating balance**—is a minimum checking-account balance required by a bank as a condition for granting a loan to a firm.

tend to fluctuate more widely than do long-term rates but, at the same time, tend to average less over long periods. Straight comparisons of market rates, however, such as those on Treasury bills versus long-term government bonds, do not tell the whole story. When a firm uses bank credit, other costs are involved. Banks usually require **compensating balances** and often impose fees in addition to the nominal interest charge. We will discuss these arrangements and their effect on the cost of bank financing when we take up bank credit in more detail later in this chapter. For present purposes, the point is that the relative costs of short-term and long-term funds can be an important consideration.

The practice of holding liquid assets also can be analyzed in terms of the *asymmetric information hypothesis*. Normally shareholders and investors do not know all that a firm's management knows (information is ''asymmetric'') and must try to guess the outlook for the firm from its current actions. Major actions such as issuing securities convey lots of information to the markets, or at least the markets try to infer from such actions what is going on. We discussed this situation in Chapter 17. The markets often interpret securities issues as conveying unfavorable news, so managements tend to avoid issuing securities where possible, and instead finance operations and investment projects using internal funds.

This preference for internal finance leads firms to want to accumulate and ''store'' excess funds rather than pay them out in dividends so that, when unforseen opportunities or contingencies arise, they can finance them without having to issue new securities. We see these stored funds on corporate balance sheets as liquid assets.[2]

Setting Liquidity Policy

In practice, a combination policy, represented by line *C* in Figure 18–5, probably is best for most firms in most circumstances. To make its choice, a firm might project its operating assets and determine the range of variation within some confidence limits—say, 5 percent. It could interpret these upper and lower limits as points *a* and *b* in Figure 18–5. Having estimated *a* and *b*, the firm could aim for a point halfway in between or closer to one than the other. In choosing the appropriate policy, the degree of operating risk of the firm is a key consideration. The higher the operating risk, the more liquid the firm should be. The final choice is a judgment call, as are most management decisions.

> **The liquidity decision in a firm involves a choice between the costs of too much liquidity versus the costs of too little.**

Timing Debt Issues

In Chapter 17, we considered the matter of trying to time new issues of equity and debt so as to take advantage of favorable market conditions. Let us now consider

---

[2]For a discussion of the asymmetric-information hypothesis, see S. C. Myers and N. J. Majluf, ''Corporate Financing and Investment Decisions When Firms Have Information Investors Do Not Have,'' *Journal of Financial Economics* 13, 187–221; and S. C. Myers, ''The Capital Structure Puzzle,'' *Journal of Finance* 39(July 1984):575–92.

another aspect of the timing problem. Suppose a company could borrow money for six months from a bank at an interest rate of 16 percent per year (8 percent for six months) or could issue 20-year bonds that paid interest of 14 percent per year (rates actually were this high in the early 1980s). While the long-term interest rate in this case is lower than the short-term interest rate, these rates refer to very different time horizons. If you borrow short-term, you will know your interest costs for six months but then be faced with borrowing again (six months hence) at the interest rate then in effect. On the other hand, if you issue 20-year bonds, their interest costs will be set for a full 20 years.[3] Is short-term or long-term borrowing better in this case? As is often the situation, the answer depends on what you expect the future to hold. If you thought interest rates were going down substantially, it might pay to borrow short-term now and in six months obtain long-term financing at the then even lower interest rates (less than 14 percent). If your guess about interest rates is correct, this strategy of waiting might lower your interest costs over the life of the borrowing as compared to issuing long-term bonds now. On the other hand, if you thought both long-term and short-term rates were going to go up substantially, borrowing long-term now and locking in the interest rate might be advisable.

As the above discussion shows, attempts to time the issuance of debt involves making guesses about future interest rates. To make such timing profitable, the manager needs to outguess financial markets. But, as we discussed in Chapter 17, in relatively efficient financial markets, the prospects for consistently superior forecasting are not encouraging. Current interest rates reflect a consensus forecast of future interest rates by the best-informed investors. And in such a world, if interest rates are expected to go up or down, that expectation will already be incorporated in the current set of interest rates. For example, if the market expects short-term and long-term rates to go down in the future, it is likely that the strategy of borrowing short-term now to wait for new lower-cost financing in the future will not benefit the firm. The reason will be that the interest rate on the short-term borrowing will be sufficiently high to offset the future interest savings from financing at the lower rate next period—because other firms will also be trying to time their debt financing by borrowing short-term. The increased demand for short-term borrowing will drive up the short-term interest rate until there are no longer any benefits to timing the debt issue. Table 18–2 provides an illustration of this effect for a corporation that is borrowing $100 now, needs the funds for two years, and is considering two possible strategies. First, with Strategy Short, it could borrow for one year at the current one-year interest rate of 16 percent, hoping to refinance at the end of one year at 10 percent (its expectation of the interest rate that will prevail in one year). Strategy Long involves borrowing money now and locking in a two-year interest rate of 12.96 percent.[4]

---

[3]Many bonds are callable. This provision allows the corporation to retire the bond prior to maturity, often to refinance at lower costs. To call the bond, however, the corporation must usually wait a number of years after issuance and also pay an extra dollar amount (call premium) to bondholders over and above the bond's face value. See Chapter 17 for a discussion of bond refunding.

[4]This example is overly simplified. It assumes that in Strategy Short, the firm borrows money at the beginning of year 2 to pay off the entire loan (plus interest) due from year 1. In Strategy Long, it is assumed that the 2-year loan allows the firm to delay interest payments as long as it pays interest at 12.96 percent on these payments during year 2. In practice, the firm might well make interest payments quarterly or even more frequently. The addition of these factors complicates the example. The basic message, however, remains: a choice between short-term and long-term financing can't be made simply by comparing current interest rates.

Table 18–2

Comparison of Long-Term and Short-Term Financing in a Hypothetical Borrowing Situation

	Amount Owed at End of Year	
	With Strategy Short	*With Strategy Long*
Principal—year 1	$100.00	$100.00
plus		
Interest—year 1	+ 16.00 (at 16 percent)	+ 12.96 (at 12.96 percent)
equals		
Total amount owed for 1 year	$ 116.00	$ 112.96
plus		
Interest—year 2	+ 11.60 (at 10 percent, expected)	+ 14.64 (at 12.96 percent)
Total amount owed for 2 years	$127.60	$127.60

As Table 18–2 shows, at these interest rates, the total cost of borrowing for two years is expected to be the same, $127.60 at the end of the second year, no matter which strategy is tried.

Even though Strategy Short allowed the firm to wait for the low-cost financing expected to be available at 10 percent, it required paying a higher rate in the first year. On balance, given these interest rates, there are no interest savings from timing.[5]

In our uncertain world, forecasts often turn out wrong. So it is possible—even likely—that one alternative strategy will produce lower costs than the other. The problem for the manager is to figure out which one will be superior *before the fact*. In an efficient market, interest rates are set so that the odds are about 50/50 that any given strategy will turn out to be superior.

As we saw at the beginning of this chapter, investors and financial managers have faced highly variable and unpredictable interest rates in recent years. As a result, many lenders have become less willing to offer loans at fixed interest rates. Instead, even some forms of long-term financing have interest rates that change as market interest rates change. We discussed such forms of financing, such as floating-rate notes, in Chapter 12. If the interest rate on long-term debt varies with market interest rates, the potential gains from timing may not be very important. In fact, however, financial managers still have the option of issuing long-term debt at a fixed interest rate and are, thus, faced with issues similar to those in the situation represented by Table 18–2.

---

[5]Table 18–2 is based on the expectations theory of the term structure of interest rates, according to which the interest costs over any length of time are expected to be the same. In general, this theory requires that long-term interest rates be an average of expected short-term interest rates. Specifically, it requires long-term rates to be a geometric average of short-term rates. In the example in the text, it turns out that $(1 + 0.16)(1 + 0.10) = (1 + 0.1296)^2$, or 0.1296 equals the square root of $[(1 + 0.16)(1 + 0.10)] - 1$. That is, 1.1296 is a geometric average of 1.16 and 1.10. For a treatment of this topic, see R. Brealey and S. Myers, *Principles of Corporate Finance* (New York: McGraw-Hill, 1984).

SUPPLIERS OF SHORT-TERM AND INTERMEDIATE-TERM FUNDS

Trade credit—is short-term credit extended by a supplier in connection with goods purchased for ultimate resale; used by nearly all firms to some extent as a source of short-term funds

Business firms obtain funds from a variety of sources—from other business firms, from banks, and from the money market. Nearly all firms rely to some extent on **trade credit** as a source of short-term funds. Trade credit is short-term credit extended by a supplier in connection with goods purchased for ultimate resale. The credit appears on the supplier's balance sheet as an account receivable. Thus, although the trade creditor is the direct supplier of funds, ultimately the funds come from those who finance the trade creditor.

Wage and tax accruals provide another source of short-term financing, although one over which management has little control. Such accruals represent expenses incurred but not yet paid. For example, if a company pays its workers every two weeks, a balance sheet prepared the day before payday would show accrued wages owed to workers. Since any liability is a source of funds, workers are providing part of the firm's financing by agreeing to be paid every two weeks rather than every day. Likewise, accrued taxes constitute a source of financing. While accruals must be taken into account in financial planning, they are not usually the subject of decision making because their amounts are determined by the timing of wage and tax payments and, hence, are not subject to management control.

Bank loans provide a major source of short-term and intermediate-term financing. Although commercial banks are the most important of the intermediaries that finance business firms, other financial institutions also supply short-term and intermediate-term funds. Finance companies make specialized loans to finance working capital and equipment, and insurance companies make intermediate-term and long-term loans to business firms.

Commercial paper—is unsecured short-term promissory notes issued by firms with the highest credit ratings.

Firms, especially the larger more credit-worthy corporations, also obtain short-term funds by issuing interest-bearing unsecured promissory notes—known as **commercial paper**—in the open money market. Thus, the immediate suppliers of short-term and intermediate-term funds to business firms are other business firms, commercial banks, finance companies, insurance companies, and pension funds. However, it is important to note that all these suppliers of funds are themselves only intermediaries in the chain of finance, because they require financing also.

A portion of total investment capital is provided by individuals who have excess funds to save and invest. Firms themselves also provide investment funds via their own earnings retention and depreciation charges, but ultimately firms are owned by individuals, or by financial intermediaries (e.g., pension funds) that are owned by individuals. Thus, in the final analysis, the suppliers of all business funds are individuals, who, by consuming less than they earn, provide the savings necessary to finance investment. These funds are channeled from savers to firms and other investors through the specialized financial markets and financial intermediaries in our system.

> The immediate suppliers of short-term and intermediate-term funds to business firms include other business firms, commercial banks, finance companies, insurance companies, and pension funds. In the final analysis, the ultimate suppliers of all business funds are individuals who save.

Some of the direct suppliers of funds make more than one type of loan. Business firms supply trade credit and are major purchasers of commercial paper. Commercial banks make both unsecured and secured short-term loans as well as *term loans* with maturities of up to 7–10 years. Finance companies make short-term working-capital loans and intermediate-term loans to finance equipment. The financing instruments discussed below are organized according to the type of maturity and collateral, rather than by source.

TRADE CREDIT

Earlier, we defined trade credit extended in connection with goods purchased for resale. This qualification—that goods be purchased for resale—distinguishes trade credit from other related forms. Machinery and equipment, for example, may be purchased on credit by means of an installment-purchase contract of some sort. But if the equipment is used by the firm in its production process rather than resold to others, then the financing usually is not called trade credit. Trade credit is credit extended in connection with goods purchased for resale by a retailer or wholesaler or with raw materials purchased by a manufacturer for producing its products. Thus, we exclude also *consumer credit*, which is credit extended to individuals for purchase of goods for ultimate use rather than for resale.

Trade credit arises from the firm's normal operations, specifically from the time lag between receipt of goods and payment for them. The sum total of a firm's obligations to its trade creditors at any point in time normally is listed as *accounts payable* on the balance sheet. As we found in Chapter 6, an increase in accounts payable represents a source of funds to the firm; a decrease in accounts payable is a use of funds.

The extent to which trade credit is used as a source of funds varies widely among firms. In general, manufacturers, retailers, and wholesalers make extensive use of trade credit. Service firms purchase less and, therefore, rely less on trade credit. There is considerable variation also with respect to firm size; small firms generally use trade credit more extensively than large firms. When monetary policy is tight and credit is difficult to obtain, small firms tend to increase their reliance on trade credit. Large firms often have better access to financial markets and more bargaining power relative to commercial banks and other intermediaries than do small firms. During periods of tight money, small firms that are unable to obtain sufficient funds through normal channels may obtain financing indirectly from large suppliers by stretching their payment periods and expanding accounts payable. Large firms often are willing to finance their smaller customers in this manner in order to preserve their markets.

An **open account**—is a credit arrangement under which no promissory note is normally given, and the purchaser agrees to make payment at a later date under terms specified in the agreement.

Within certain limits, a firm has discretion with respect to the extent to which it uses trade credit as a source of funds. By altering its payment period, a firm can expand or contract its accounts payable. In theory, a firm could reduce accounts payable to zero and not use trade credit simply by paying each invoice on the day received. However, because trade credit is not interest-bearing, it represents a desirable source of financing; if used beyond certain limits, however, it can entail significant costs. Our concern here is with the use of trade credit extended by suppliers. In Chapter 20, we will discuss the other side of the coin—that is, the granting of trade credit to customers.

Forms of Trade Credit

Most trade is extended by means of an **open account**. Under this arrangement, goods are shipped and an invoice is sent to the purchaser, but the purchaser normally does not acknowledge the debt in writing. Payment is made later according to the terms of the agreement (discussed below). The major advantage of the open account is its simplicity and low administrative cost. Before granting credit through an open account, most suppliers perform a credit check.

A less common form of trade credit is the **promissory note**, usually listed as *note(s) payable, trade* on the balance sheet. The note is a written promise to pay that must be signed by the purchaser. Such notes usually bear interest and have specific maturity dates. They are used most often in situations in which the purchaser has failed to meet the terms of an open credit agreement, and the supplier wishes a formal acknowledgement of the debt and a specific agreement regarding payment date.

A **promissory note**—is a document specifying the conditions of a loan, including amount, interest rate, and repayment schedule. It is a legally enforceable "promise to pay."

Terms of Payment

Because the open account is by far the most common, we will restrict our discussion of payment terms to this form. A common arrangement is to specify a **net period** within which the invoice is to be paid. Terms of *net 30* indicate that the payment is due within 30 days of the date of the invoice.

Suppliers often give cash discounts for payment within a specified period. Terms of *2/10, net 30* indicate that a discount of 2 percent may be taken if the invoice is paid within 10 days of the invoice date; otherwise, the net (full) amount is due within 30 days. Such **prompt-payment discounts** are to be distinguished from *quantity discounts* given for purchase in large quantities and also from *trade discounts* given at different points in the distribution chain (such as wholesale versus retail). Prompt-payment discounts are very common.

The **net period**—is the period within which an invoice is to be paid.

Prompt-payment discounts—are discounts given for prompt payment of an invoice, within a specified time period.

Cost of Trade Credit as a Source of Funds

In the final analysis, the principal consideration in the use of trade credit is cost. Trade credit on open account normally bears no interest, but its use does involve costs. If prompt-payment discounts are allowed by the supplier, a cost is incurred if the discount is not taken. For example, suppose a firm purchases goods on terms of 2/10, net 30. If the invoice is for $1,000, the firm can take a discount of $20 and pay only $980 if payment is made within 10 days. If the firm forgoes the discount, it pays $1,000 by day 30, assuming it maintains its accounts on a current basis, as it should. By forgoing the discount, the firm has the use of $980 for 20 days, for which it pays interest of $20. This interest rate is $20/$980 = 2.05 percent for a 20-day period. Annualized, the **effective interest rate** is

The **effective interest rate**—is the rate compounded once per interest period (usually per year) that provides the same dollar payoff as the stated rate.

$$\frac{\$20}{\$980} \times \frac{365 \text{ days}}{20 \text{ days}} = 0.372 = 37.2 \text{ percent}$$

We find that in this case, not taking the discount is equivalent to borrowing at 37.2

percent per year, a rather expensive financing arrangement.[6] Equation (1) shows how to calculate the approximate cost of forgoing cash discounts.

> The approximate cost of forgoing a prompt-payment cash discount can be calculated as
>
> $$\text{Cost} = \frac{\text{Percentage Discount}}{100 \text{ percent} - \text{Percentage Discount}}$$
>
> $$\times \frac{365 \text{ days}}{\text{Net Period} - \text{Discount Period}} \quad (1)$$

Applying Equation (1) to our example, we can calculate the cost to be

$$\text{Cost} = \frac{2 \text{ percent}}{100 \text{ percent} - 2 \text{ percent}} \times \frac{365 \text{ days}}{30 \text{ days} - 10 \text{ days}}$$

$$= 0.372 = 37.2 \text{ percent}$$

Sample Problem 18–1

Calculating the Cost of Trade Credit

Calculate the cost of trade credit for the following discount periods:

A. 1/10, net 30;
B. 2/10, net 20;
C. 2/20, net 45.

Solution

A. Applying Equation (1) to the terms 1/10, net 30, we find that

$$\text{Cost} = \frac{1 \text{ percent}}{100 \text{ percent} - 1 \text{ percent}} \times \frac{365 \text{ days}}{30 \text{ days} - 10 \text{ days}} = 0.184 = 18.4 \text{ percent}$$

B. Using this procedure for terms of 2/10, net 20, we find that cost equals 74.5 percent.

---

[6]Note that the calculation in the text assumes only annual compounding. In fact, allowing for compounding every 20 days, the effective annualized interest cost, r_a would be calculated as

$$1 + r_a = (1 + \$20/\$980)^{365/20}$$

$$r_a = (1 + 0.0205)^{18.25} - 1 = 44.82 \text{ percent.}$$

In Chapter 3, we cover the effects of compounding many times during the year. The 44.82 percent figure is in fact the true effective annual cost of the trade credit.

C. Similarly, applying Equation (1) to terms of 2/20, net 45, we see that cost equals 29.8 percent.

The costs indicated represent the equivalent financing cost of forgoing cash discounts and then paying the full amount on the due date. In the case of 1/10, net 30, the above calculation assumes that the full amount of the invoice is paid on day 30.

≣lıl⁼

Other Considerations in Using Trade Credit

If there is no discount offered and if the firm pays during the net period, trade credit still is not free. The supplier must operate a credit department to conduct credit analysis, maintain records, and proceed against overdue accounts. The accounts receivable on the supplier's books must be financed. These administrative and financing costs, like all costs of doing business, in the long run are borne by the buyers of the supplier's output. We should note, however, that the purchaser is bearing these costs whether credit granted by the supplier is used or not.

Another element of cost is incurred if the firm delays payment beyond the net period. When a firm becomes overdue in its payments, its relationships with suppliers are bound to suffer. Some suppliers can be stretched more than others, and a given supplier may be more tolerant of late payment at some times than at others. Just how a far a firm can push its suppliers depends on circumstances. A policy of late payment, however, is bad business practice, and in the long run is likely to be costly. At the least, late payment damages a firm's credit reputation, which is a valuable asset and, once lost, is difficult to regain. At worst, late payment can cost a firm its sources of supply. During times of severe financial difficulty, a firm may be unable to avoid late payment. As a matter of long-run policy, however, obligations to suppliers should be discharged on schedule.

While late payment is dangerous and costly in the long run, early payment is uneconomical. Where prompt-payment discounts are offered, they should be taken if attractive, as they nearly always are. Otherwise, payment should be made within the net period. In either case, the full extent of the credit period should be utilized.

Sample Problem 18–2

Effect of Trade Credit on Financial Statements for the Perry Company

Table 18–3 shows the balance sheet of the Perry Company. Perry currently purchases a total of $120,000 per month on terms of 2/10, net 30, and is forgoing all cash discounts and paying invoices at face amount on day 30. Calculate the effect on Perry's financial statements of a change in policy to begin taking cash discounts.

Solution

Perry is purchasing $120,000 of materials per month, or $4,000 per day. Because the company is taking the full 30 days to pay each invoice, it has at any point in time 30 *days purchases outstanding* (DPO) in the form of accounts payable—a total of 30 × $4,000 = $120,000. To take cash discounts, Perry must pay within 10 days. Under this policy, accounts payable would amount to 10 days purchases outstanding, or 10 × $4,000 = $40,000.

Table 18–3
Year-End Balance Sheet for the Perry Company (thousands of dollars)

Cash	$ 40	Accounts Payable	$ 120
Receivables	300	Bank loan	0
Inventory	450	Accruals	50
Fixed assets	400	Mortgage loan	300
Other assets	50	Common Stock	770
Total assets	$1,240	**Total liabilities and net worth**	$1,240

If accounts payable were reduced from $120,000 to $40,000, what would make up the difference? Balance sheets, after all, must balance. One answer is bank credit. Something must replace the $80,000 in accounts payable, and if a bank loan were used, the balance sheet would show accounts payable of $40,000 and bank loans of $80,000.

What about the effect on the income statement? Perry now takes a total of $28,800 in cash discounts: $120,000/month × 12 months × 2 percent = $28,800. Offsetting this amount is interest on the bank loan, let's say at 12 percent: $80,000 × 12 percent = $9,600.

So Perry takes in an additional $28,800 per year in cash discounts and pays out an additional $9,600 to the bank, a gain in pretax profit of $19,200 per year. The gain arises from the fact that the cost of the bank loan is only 12 percent, while the cost of forgoing the cash discount was 37.2 percent on an annual basis. Given this effect on profits, firms should think carefully about a policy of forgoing cash discounts. ▄▊▐▀

Forgoing cash discounts is an expensive form of financing.

UNSECURED SHORT-TERM LOANS

An **unsecured loan**—is a loan against which no specific assets are pledged as collateral.

An **unsecured loan** is one against which no specific assets are pledged as collateral. Secured loans will be discussed in a later section. Commercial banks are by far the largest suppliers of unsecured loans to business firms, so in this section we will restrict our discussion to bank loans.

Whereas nearly all firms use trade credit to some extent as a source of funds, not all firms use bank credit. Bank credit is, however, a very important source of credit for many businesses. At the end of 1984, aggregate trade credit outstanding was $548 billion; commercial and industrial loans by banks totaled $479 billion.[7]

---

[7]Board of Governors, Federal Reserve System, *Flow of Funds Accounts: Second Quarter 1985*, September 1985.

Arranging Bank Financing

Most commercial banks view a relationship with a customer as involving more than just a loan. A loan is only one of a number of services that a bank normally will attempt to sell a business customer. Others are a checking account, time certificates of deposit, payroll and other accounting services, cash-flow analysis, lock-box services (discussed in Chapter 19) for speeding collections, investment services, pension and profit-sharing services, and corporate trust services pertaining to shareholder records and payment of dividends. The bank, in short, thinks in terms of a total customer relationship, not just a loan.

Before approving a loan, the bank also will want detailed information regarding the nature of the financing requirement, the amounts and timing of the need, the uses to which the funds will be put, and when and how the bank will be repaid. Here is where the financial plan, developed along lines that we discussed in Chapter 8, comes in. A comprehensive plan, including a pro-forma income statement and balance sheet and perhaps a cash budget, will prove very valuable to any firm's management when it is negotiating a bank loan. The financial plan not only communicates the information sought by the bank regarding the financing requirement; the mere fact that a plan has been prepared tells the bank that the firm's management is competent and knows its business.

Good communications are also important after the loan is made. Few financial plans are executed exactly as planned. In an uncertain world, we would be surprised if deviations did not occur. When deviations do occur that affect the financing requirement or the firm's overall financial condition, the bank should be informed. By this approach, the firm shares the problems with the bank and gives the bank an opportunity to respond. Banks expect their customers to have problems (banks have problems, too) and usually are pleased to learn that the problems have been recognized and are being acted upon even if the banks prefer (as does the firm) that the problems never arise.

Types of Bank Loans

A **line of credit**—is a noncontractual loan agreement between a bank or other lender and a firm in which the firm can borrow up to an agreed-upon maximum at any time during a specified period.

Short-term unsecured bank loans usually take one of three forms: a line of credit, a revolving-credit agreement, or a simple single-transaction loan. A **line of credit** is an agreement under which a firm can borrow up to an agreed-upon maximum amount at any time during an agreed-upon period—often one year. Lines of credit are not contractual and are not legally binding upon the bank, but they are nearly always honored. A major advantage of the line of credit is its convenience and administrative simplicity.

A line of credit often is used to finance seasonal working-capital requirements or other temporary needs. Banks typically require an annual paying up of the loan—a period usually of 1 or 2 months during which the loan is completely paid off, or "off the books." If a firm is unable to pay up, the bank will be alerted that the financing requirement may not be entirely seasonal. Lines of credit are renegotiated periodically, often annually, at which time the bank conducts a full review of the customer relationship, the financing requirement, and the firm's plans for the coming year.

A **revolving-credit agreement**—is a contractual agreement by the bank to provide funds

A **revolving-credit agreement**, unlike the line of credit, involves a contractual and binding commitment by the bank to provide funds. In return for this commitment, the borrower usually pays a fee of 0.25 to 0.5 percent per year on the average unused portion of the commitment. The size of the fee depends on credit conditions at the time—that is, the availability of funds in the banking system—and on the relative bargaining power of the bank and the borrower. Like the line of credit, the revolving-credit agreement permits the borrower to borrow any amount up to some maximum at any time. Revolving credit often is negotiated for periods longer than a year, and during the period of the contract are not subject to pay-up provisions or to renegotiation or cancelation by the bank because of tight credit conditions.

The line of credit and revolving-credit agreement are well suited to firms that need financing frequently and in varying amounts. Where a firm needs financing only occasionally for specific purposes, banks typically treat each request individually.

Interest Rates on Bank Loans

The **prime rate**—is the benchmark rate set by the banking industry as the rate for the class of borrowers deemed most credit-worthy.

Interest rates on bank loans to firms typically are scaled upward from the **prime rate**, the benchmark rate set by the banking industry for borrowers with the highest credit rating. Rates for other than prime borrowers may exceed the prime rate by several percentage points. On the other hand, some borrowers may be able to obtain bank loans at below the prevailing prime rate. Although banks continue to refer to the prime rate as the best short-term rate, it became increasingly evident during the early 1980s that some bank customers were able to negotiate loan rates below prime.

Interest rates vary from loan to loan and from borrower to borrower for a number of reasons. Slight variations occur from region to region and from state to state, the latter depending to some extent on statutory rate ceilings. Rates vary with the riskiness of the loan, the size of the loan, and often the size of the borrower. The size of the borrower often is related to risk, and the size of the loan is a factor in the bank's administrative costs. For example, it does not take 100 times as much work to negotiate and administer a $1,000,000 loan as a $10,000 loan; in fact, the large loan may even take less work if the borrower is well-known and an established customer.

When a lender quotes the nominal or stated interest rate on a loan, we still cannot be sure how much interest we will pay. There are several methods of computing the interest charge; each gives a different *effective interest rate*. Suppose we want to borrow $1,000 for 1 year. The lender quotes a rate of 8 percent. If we pay *interest in arrears on the unpaid balance*, we pay the lender $1,080 in 1 year—$1,000 principal and $80 interest.[8] The effective interest rate is $80/$1,000, or 8 percent.

If interest is computed using the *discount method*, the lender advances us $1,000 − $80 = $920, and we repay $1,000 in 1 year. We pay interest of $80 for the use of $920 for 1 year. The effective rate is $80/$920 or 8.70 percent.

Suppose now that the loan must be repaid in *monthly installments*. Interest on consumer installment loans often is computed using the *add-on method*. Using this

---

[8]The term *in arrears* in this context does not imply that the borrower is delinquent, only that interest is paid at the end of the period on the balance outstanding during the period.

Finance in Practice 18–2

Innovations in the Financial Industry

Recent years have brought major changes not only in banking and the type of products banks offer but in other financial institutions as well. Cash management has grown in importance to the point at which it has become the topic of books and of courses in schools of business. Banks now offer specialized cash-management services and highly sophisticated cash-collection systems (we will discuss this topic in detail in Chapter 19). Electronic banking is growing rapidly as technology develops, permitting banks to clear checks electronically, permitting firms to meet their payrolls and pay other bills electronically, and permitting consumers to dial their banks and conduct business from their homes using personal computers.

Deregulation of banking and finance is proceeding rapidly, begun with the Hunt Commission report in the 1970s and spurred on by Congress in 1980 with the Depository Institutions Deregulation and Monetary Control Act. Although bank mergers across state lines were not unheard of earlier, before 1984 they were seen mostly in very special situations involving failures and subsequent rescues by an out-of-state bank. In 1985, however, regional mergers across state lines began in earnest, and the trend appeared to be accelerating. Deregulation also has brought interest on checking accounts and a relaxation of ceilings on interest on savings deposits.

Firms other than banks also are entering the banking business. Merrill Lynch, the nationwide brokerage house, began offering a highly successful account, called appropriately the "cash-management account," which paid interest on excess funds at market rates and permitted automatic overdrafts, with interest charged at competitive rates. Because of regulatory constraints, similar products offered by banks were less convenient for many customers. Sears has moved strongly into financial services, as has American Express. Prudential Insurance Company acquired Donaldson Lufkin and Jenrette, a Wall Street investment banking firm, thus signalling its intentions to enter new territory. Throughout the entire financial-services industry, the decade of the 1980s is living up to expectations that it will bring big changes.

method, 1 year's interest of $80 is added on to the principal, and the result—$1,080—is divided by 12 to get the monthly payment of $90.00. Here, the effective rate is considerably higher than 8 percent because we are paying off the loan over the year. In effect, over the year we have the use on average of only about half the principal, for which we pay interest of $80. Thus, the effective rate is almost double the stated rate. To compute the effective rate exactly (which, in this case, is 14.44 percent) requires the use of discounted-cash-flow techniques, which we discussed in Chapter 3.[9]

Compensating Balances

In addition to the interest rate, banks often impose other conditions for obtaining a loan. A condition nearly always encountered is that the firm maintain a *compensating balance*, which is the agreed-upon minimum balance to be maintained in the checking account.[10] The minimum balance compensates the bank for clearing checks and other services and for any standby commitment to lend under a line of credit. The amount of the compensating balance usually is determined as a percentage, normally between 10 and 20 percent, of either the amount of the bank's commitment or of the loan outstanding. Under a $1 million line of credit, for example, a firm might be required to maintain a minimum deposit balance of $150,000 (15 percent of the line) at all times. An additional requirement might be imposed to compensate for other services.

From the bank's standpoint, the compensating balance, if in addition to balances otherwise maintained, has the effect of increasing the rate of return on the price of credit without changing nominal interest rates. This effect is sometimes an important consideration in the face of interest-rate ceilings or political pressures for lower rates. From the firm's standpoint, the compensating balance increases the effective interest rate.

----

[9]Specifically, we could calculate the effective annual interest rate, r_a, by seeing what interest rate would make the present value of the twelve $90 monthly payments equal to the amount of the loan ($1,000). First, we could find a monthly interest rate r_m such that

$$\$1,000 = PV \text{ of } \$90/\text{month for 12 months at } r_m$$

$$\$1,000 = \$90 \times PV \text{ annuity factor at } r_m \text{ for 12 periods}$$

$$\$1,000/90 = PV \text{ annuity factor at } r_m \text{ for 12 periods}$$

$$r_m = 0.0113 \text{ (approximating from Appendix Table II)}$$

Finally, we could annualize r_m to obtain

$$r_a = (1 + r_m)^{12} - 1$$

$$= (1 + 0.0113)^{12} - 1$$

$$= 0.1444 = 14.44 \text{ percent}$$

Rounding errors may change results substantially. For precise calculations, it is best to have a calculator or computer do the detail work.

[10]The terms of this minimum balance would be stipulated by the bank. For example, the minimum might be defined as an absolute dollar amount below which the account could not fall. Alternatively, the minimum might be defined as a minimum average balance over some time period.

**Sample Problem
18—3**

Effective Interest Cost for the Boyd Machinery Company

A. The Boyd Machinery Company needs $100,000 and plans to borrow the funds from a bank. The bank requires a compensating balance of 15 percent. How much will Boyd have to borrow? If the stated interest rate is 12 percent, what will be the effective rate?

B. Rework the problem described in part (A) assuming that the bank pays 10 percent annual interest on the compensating balance.

Solution

A. The amount to be borrowed, X, must be such that X minus the 15 percent compensating balance equals $100,000. Algebraically, we can write this relationship as

$$X - 0.15X = \$100,000$$

$$X(1 - 0.15) = \$100,000$$

$$X = \frac{\$100,000}{1 - 0.15} = \frac{\$100,000}{0.85}$$

$$= \$117,647$$

The net funds available are $117,647 - 0.15(\$117,647) = \$100,000$. On this loan of $117,647, interest will be calculated as $0.12 \times \$117,647 = \$14,118$.

Because the company has only $100,000 available for use (the loan minus the compensating balance), the $14,118 of interest represents an effective interest rate of $14,118/\$100,000 = 14.1$ percent. Thus, the compensating-balance requirement requires that Boyd borrow $17,647 more than actually needed and increases the effective interest rate on the loan to 14.1 percent versus the stated rate of 12 percent.

B. Here we need to calculate the *net* interest charge the bank makes. As we calculated in part (A), there is an interest charge of $14,118 on the loan. On the other hand, the bank will pay interest of $0.10(\$17,647) = \$1764.70$ on the compensating balance. The *net* interest charge would be $14,118 - \$1764.70 = \$12,353.30$. That is, the firm would owe the bank $12,353.30 over and above the interest the bank paid the firm on the compensating balance. The firm, thus, pays net interest of $12,353.30 to use $100,000 for a year. The effective interest rate is calculated as $12,353.30/\$100,000 = 0.124 = 12.4$ percent.

Although the 12.4 percent is still higher than the stated 12 percent on the loan, it is substantially lower than the 14.1 percent effective interest rate we calculated when the bank paid no interest on the compensating balance.

When the bank does pay such interest, the effective interest cost of the loan is reduced. Because the interest paid by the bank on the compensating balance will typically be less than the interest charged on the loan, however, the effective interest rate on the loan is still higher than the stated interest rate. ▤▮▰

Requiring collateral by no means provides complete security to lenders. The Great Salad-Oil Swindle of the early 1960s provides a classic, if extreme, case of what can go wrong if the borrower is determined, ingenious, and dishonest.

In the late 1950s, a man named Anthony De Angelis established the Allied Crude Oil Vegetable Refining Corporation. Allied was in the business of processing crude vegetable oil, mainly soybean and cottonseed oils, into salad oil.

The oil was stored in large tanks at Bayonne, New Jersey. A number of well-known banks, exporters, and Wall Street investment banking firms lent money to

Allied against the oil as collateral. The oil was controlled under a field warehousing arrangement supervised by the American Express Field Warehousing Corporation, a subsidiary of the American Express Company.

The job of the Field Warehousing Company was to supervise the storage of oil and certify that it was indeed on hand in the amounts specified (see Appendix 18A for a discussion of field warehousing). American Express issued field-warehouse receipts, which Allied then used as collateral for loans.

Over the period of 1957–1963, Allied managed to steal hundreds of millions of dollars worth of oil without the Field Warehousing

---

SECURED SHORT-TERM LOANS

Borrowers and lenders alike would prefer to do business on an unsecured basis. An unsecured loan provides maximum flexibility for the borrower and is less expensive to administer than a secured loan. However, in many situations the risk of default is sufficiently high that lenders are unwilling to lend on an unsecured basis.

A **secured loan**—is a loan against which specific assets are pledged as collateral by the borrower.

A **secured loan** is one against which specific assets are pledged as collateral by the borrower. In the case of short-term loans, lenders usually insist on **collateral** that is reasonably liquid—that is, assets that can be sold and, thereby, converted to cash without great difficulty. Inventory and accounts receivable are most often used. Marketable securities would serve nicely as collateral but seldom are available to firms needing secured loans. Fixed assets, such as equipment and buildings, sometimes are pledged against short-term loans but are more often pledged to obtain long-term funds. Since accounts receivable and inventory are the most common collateral for short-term loans, we will discuss these in more detail.

Collateral—is any asset pledged as security for a loan.

Commercial banks often require collateral under any of the lending arrangements discussed above. In addition to banks, commercial finance companies also make secured loans to business firms, with accounts receivable and inventories usually providing the collateral. The procedure for securing a loan is covered by the Uniform Commercial Code, adopted by all states during the 1960s. An agreement between lender and borrower identifying the collateral is filed in the public records. If the borrower

Company's knowledge. The tanks were connected by a complex system of pipes and valves. Allied personnel would pump out the oil in a tank and pump in sea water, leaving a foot or two of oil floating on top of perhaps 40 feet of sea water. Inspectors of the Field Warehousing Company would look into the tank and see only oil. Special devices lowered through ports in the tops of the tanks verified that oil extended to the bottom. Indeed, the oil did extend to the bottom, but only inside special narrow cylindrical chambers installed directly under the ports by Allied personnel. The sea water remained undetected.

When the swindle was finally uncovered, warehouse receipts were outstanding for 1.988 billion pounds of oil. Only 134 million pounds were actually on hand in the Bayonne tanks. The rest had either disappeared over the period 1957–1963 or never had existed in the first place. The amount of soybean oil certified to be in the Bayonne tanks by the warehouse receipts actually exceeded the total soybean-oil stocks in the entire United States in 1963 as reported by the U.S. government! The total shortage was 1.854 billion pounds, valued at about $175 million.

A total of 51 companies and banks that had loaned money to Allied using warehouse receipts as collateral suffered losses totaling $175 million. Two Wall Street investment banking firms went bankrupt, as did the American Express Field Warehousing subsidiary. The list of banks that lost money included nearly every major bank in New York City, as well as major banks in Chicago, on the West Coast, and abroad. The parent American Express Company incurred large losses in making good a portion of the claims.

De Angelis eventually went to prison for masterminding the swindle. Little of the $175 million was ever recovered, and just where it all went remains a mystery to this day. The salad-oil case remains the classic object lesson in making loans against inventory.

Source: N. C. Miller, *The Great Salad Oil Swindle* (Baltimore: Penguin Books, 1965).

defaults on the terms of the agreement, the lender may seize the collateral and sell it to satisfy the claim. Any excess proceeds are returned to the borrowing firm. If the proceeds are insufficient to satisfy the claim, the lender must share the remaining assets of the firm with unsecured creditors.

It is important to understand the function of collateral from the lender's standpoint. Collateral protects the lender in the event of default, but it does not lead to indifference to the prospect of default. There comes a point on the risk spectrum where lenders refuse the loan even with collateral. Lenders are in business to provide funds, not to liquidate inventories of electronic parts or fashion garments or to collect accounts receivable. The real function of collateral is to induce the lender to make a loan that, if unsecured, is too risky in relation to the rate that can be charged and yet still has reasonable prospects of being repaid.

In considering secured financing, we should not lose sight of the effect of pledging a firm's assets on its other creditors. Trade creditors and other general creditors look to the firm's assets for protection in the event of financial difficulty. If particular assets suddenly are pledged, the position of these unsecured creditors is weakened. Such changes are not likely to go unnoticed and may be taken into account by the affected parties in future transactions.

We will consider security arrangements in more detail in Appendix 18A, which follows this chapter. Finance in Practice 18–3 relates an example of the hazards to which a lender can be exposed, even when security is provided for a loan.

COMMERCIAL PAPER

Commercial paper is unsecured short-term promissory notes issued by borrowers to investors. Commercial paper distributed through organized financial markets is known as a *money-market instrument* (along with other short-term highly-liquid securities, such as U.S. Treasury bills and bank certificates of deposit).

Because commercial paper is unsecured, it can be issued only by firms with the highest credit ratings, which usually means only relatively large firms. Although a wide variety of firms use the commercial-paper market as a source of funds, the big borrowers are finance companies, financing subsidiaries of large manufacturers such as General Motors Acceptance Corporation and Chrysler Financial Corporation, and commercial banks and bank-holding companies who jointly account for 75 percent of the funds borrowed in this form. Major buyers of commercial paper include nonbank financial institutions, such as insurance companies, pension funds and mutual funds, and business firms with temporary excess cash.

Commercial-Paper Market

The commercial-paper market has grown rapidly since the 1960s, and as of October 31, 1985 some $281 billion worth was outstanding.[11] The minimum denomination is $25,000, although denominations of $100,000 up to several million dollars are much more common. Maturities usually range from 30 to 180 days but may go up to 270 days. Under current regulations, an issue of maturity longer than 270 days would have to be registered with the Securities and Exchange Commission.

The commercial-paper market is highly organized, with paper sold both directly and through dealers. Dealers typically charge a commission of 0.12 to 0.25 percent. The interest rate on commercial paper usually runs about 1 percent less than the prime lending rate at commercial banks, although in recent years this spread sometimes has widened to around 1.5 percent.

Commercial Paper as a Source of Funds

We noted above that only large firms with the highest credit ratings have access to the commercial-paper market. For such firms, the principal advantage of commercial paper is its lower cost relative to the cost of alternative sources, such as bank loans. Offsetting this cost advantage somewhat is the fact that borrowers in the commercial-paper market have to maintain backup lines of credit or revolving-credit agreements at commercial banks.

For lending agreements to backstop commercial paper, banks typically charge a commitment fee of between 0.25 to 0.5 percent. Even with this cost included, commercial paper usually is less expensive than bank loans because the commercial-paper market generally is more price-competitive than are bank-loan markets. The more competitive the market, the lower is the price to the buyer—in this case the buyer of funds.

---

[11]Federal Reserve *Bulletin*, February 1986. For a good discussion of the commercial-paper market, see E. M. Hurley, "The Commercial Paper Market," *Federal Reserve Bulletin*, June 1977.

KEY CONCEPTS

1. There are two basic approaches to the problem of financing a variable asset requirement: use of reserve borrowing power and use of holdings of liquid assets.

2. The liquidity decision in a firm involves a choice between the costs of too much liquidity versus the costs of too little.

3. The ultimate suppliers of funds are individuals who save and invest.

4. The principal factor determining the appropriate use of trade credit is cost.

5. The true interest cost of a bank loan depends on the timing and pattern of interest payments.

6. Compensating balances have the effect of increasing the effective interest rate on bank loans.

SUMMARY

To obtain funds, a firm issues claims against its assets and future income. Liabilities are contractual claims; equities are ownership claims. Some liabilities (for example, accounts payable) arise naturally as a consequence of the firm's operations, while others are discretionary (for example, bank loans).

The two basic approaches to the matter of financing a variable requirement, use of reserve borrowing power versus holding liquid assets, present the firm with an important policy decision regarding liquidity and the maturity structure of its liabilities. The decision in the final analysis is a judgment call involving considerations of risk and cost.

The direct suppliers of short-term and intermediate-term funds to business firms are other business firms, commercial banks, finance companies, insurance companies, and pension funds. These suppliers are themselves only intermediaries in the chain of finance. Ultimately, the suppliers of all business funds are individuals with funds to save and invest.

Trade credit is credit extended in connection with goods purchased for resale. Nearly all firms rely on trade credit to provide some financing, although the extent of its use varies widely among industries. Although trade credit is interest-free, its use does involve costs. In general, firms should take prompt-payment discounts when offered and otherwise pay within the specified credit period.

Commercial banks are the largest suppliers of unsecured short-term loans to business firms. A comprehensive financial plan is very useful during the process of negotiating bank financing. In addition to the contracted interest rate, the effective cost of bank credit includes the cost of compensating-balance requirements and any fees that are charged.

A secured loan is one against which specific assets are pledged as collateral by the borrower. Commercial banks and commercial finance companies make the majority of secured loans to business firms. Accounts receivable and inventory are the most commonly used collateral.

Commercial paper is unsecured short-term promissory notes issued by a borrowing firm directly to a lender. Because it is unsecured and marketable, commercial paper normally can be issued by only the largest and most credit-worthy firms.

QUESTIONS

1. Why is it risky to finance permanent asset requirements with short-term funds?

2. How do the costs of short-term sources of funds compare with those of long-term sources?

3. What are the two major alternative methods of financing asset requirements that vary over time?

4. What is a liquid asset?

5. How is the liquidity of a firm related to the maturity structure of its assets and liabilities?

6. What risks do you see in adopting a policy of low liquidity?

7. Who are the major suppliers of short-term and intermediate-term funds to business firms?

8. What are the costs of using trade credit as a source of funds?

9. How is the financial plan used in arranging bank financing?

10. Describe the major types of short-term unsecured bank loans.

11. What is the purpose of collateral, from the lender's standpoint?

12. How might the standards of credit-worthiness applied by a bank differ from those applied by a trade creditor?

13. Why might short-term lenders be less concerned with earning power than intermediate-term lenders?

14. Why do secured loans often carry higher rates of interest than unsecured loans?

PROBLEMS

1. Calculate for the following credit situations the effective annual interest rate that would be lost if a firm paid on the final due date rather than taking the cash discount. Assume a 365-day year and compounding once per year. (See footnote 6 of this chapter.)

   a. 2/15, net 45.

   b. 3/10, net 30.

   c. 1/15, net 40.

   d. 2/10, net 40.

2. Repeat problem (1) allowing for multiple compoundings per year (see footnote 6).

3. Suppose a firm faced credit terms of 2/15, net 45. Since it was running short of cash, the firm passed up the trade discount. In fact, it stretched its credit and paid the bill ten days late (on day 55 rather than day 45). Fortunately, the creditor was lenient and imposed no penalties for the late payment.

   a. What was the effective annual interest rate on the credit, given that the firm paid late? (Assume a 365-day year and compounding once per year.)

   b. How does the rate in part (a) compare to the effective annual interest cost if the bill were paid on time?

4. Calculate the effective annual interest rate on the following discount loans: (*Hint:* Calculate the interest using the discount method.)

   a. a $100,000 loan at 14 percent.

   b. a $50,000 loan at 14½ percent.

   c. a $25,000 loan at 15 percent.

5. Calculate the effective annual interest rate for the following loans.

   a. The firm needs $10,000, and the lending bank charges 15 percent and requires a 10 percent compensating balance.

   b. The firm needs $250,000, and the lending bank charges 16 percent and requires a 15 percent compensating balance.

6. Repeat problem (5) assuming that the bank pays 8 percent interest on money which is left in the bank as a compensating balance.

7. MSM, Incorporated, has been paying its major supplier approximately 20 days after the materials are received. The supplier offers terms of 1/10, net 45, on all open accounts. (For simplicity, assume compounding once per year.)

   a. What is the effective annual rate that MSM is giving up by not paying by the tenth day?

   b. Assuming that a local bank has offered to lend MSM the funds needed to purchase these materials at an effective annual rate of 16 percent, what strategy do you see as optimal for MSM?

8. Bland Corporation needs an immediate increase in short-term funds and has determined that four sources are available for the required $1,500,000:

   a. a 14 percent discount loan from the bank with a required compensating balance of 10 percent,

   b. commercial paper at 15 percent with a placement fee of $20,000 per year payable at the start of the year,

   c. foregoing discounts from suppliers at terms of 1/15, net 35, and

d. a bank loan quoted at an effective annual rate of 15 percent but requiring the pledging of accounts receivable.

Calculate the effective annual interest cost of each alternative. Which alternative should Bland choose? (Assume a 365-day year and, for simplicity, compounding once per year.)

9. DLM Enterprises needs to increase its short-term funds by $2,000,000 and has found two possible loan arrangements: Loan A is a 16 percent discount loan with no compensating balance. Loan B is a 16 percent nondiscount loan with a 10 percent compensating balance. Which loan should DLM choose?

10. Refer to problem (9) to calculate:

a. the nominal interest rate (discount basis) on loan A that would make its effective interest rate equal to loan B's effective interest rate, and

b. the nominal interest rate on loan B that would make its effective interest rate equal 16 percent.

REFERENCES

Abraham, A. B. "Factoring—the New Frontier for Commercial Banks." *Journal of Commercial Bank Lending* 53 (April 1971): 32–43.

Board of Governors. Federal Reserve System. *Flow of Funds Accounts: Second Quarter 1985*. Washington, D.C., September 1985.

Brealey, R., and S. Myers. *Principles of Corporate Finance*. New York: McGraw-Hill, 1981.

"The Commercial Paper Market." *Federal Reserve Bulletin* 63 (June 1977): 525–536.

Crane, D. B., and W. L. White. "Who Benefits from a Floating Prime Rate?" *Harvard Business Review* 50 (Jan.–Feb. 1972): 121–129.

Gibson, W. E. "Compensating Balance Requirement." *National Banking Review* 2 (Mar. 1965): 298–311.

Harris, D. G. "Rationing Credit to Business: More Than Just Interest Rates." *Business Review* (Aug. 1970): 3–14.

Hurley, E. M. "The Commercial Paper Market." *Federal Reserve Bulletin* (June 1977).

Jaffee, D. M., and F. Modigliani. "A Theory and Test of Credit Rationing." *American Economic Review* 59 (Dec. 1969): 850–762.

Lazere, M. R., ed. *Commercial Financing*. New York: Ronald Press, 1968.

Miller, N. C. *The Great Salad Oil Swindle*. Baltimore: Penguin Books, 1965.

Nadler, P. S. "Compensating Balances and the Prime at Twilight." *Harvard Business Review* 50 (Jan.–Feb. 1972): 112–120.

Small Business Administration. *Annual Reports*.

Appendix 18A

Secured Loans

LOANS AGAINST ACCOUNTS RECEIVABLE

Both banks and commercial-finance companies regularly make loans against accounts receivable as collateral. All or part of a firm's receivables may be pledged. Those pledged constitute a *pool* of collateral, with new receivables continuously feeding into the pool and payments made by customers reducing it.

Typically, the borrower retains responsibility for credit analysis of its customers and certifies to the lender that customers whose accounts are pledged are solvent. The lender judges the quality of the receivables and often has the option of rejecting any individual accounts. Because the borrower retains title to the receivables, defaults are the borrower's responsibility.

The lender and borrower agree upon a fixed percentage that will be advanced against the receivables. The percentage may vary from 60 to 90 percent, depending on the lender, an evaluation of the riskiness of the receivables, and the administrative costs of the arrangement. Commercial-finance companies usually are willing to advance somewhat more than banks.

As the borrowing firm makes sales, the new receivables are assigned to the lender, who advances the agreed upon percentage of the face amount to the borrower. The customers usually are not notified that the account has been assigned and make their payments to the borrowing firm. Many agreements specify that the full amount of payments be sent immediately to the lender to be applied against the loan balance. If the assigned receivables and the loan are in the agreed-upon-percentage relationship, the lender usually deducts the loan percentage and returns the balance to the borrower.

Loans secured by receivables usually involve high administrative costs to the lender. Charges sometimes are separated into two components, a service charge and an interest rate. The total of these charges varies from a minimum of 2 to 3 percent above the prime rate to figures considerably higher for small or marginal customers, depending on risk and administrative costs.

A major advantage of receivables financing to the borrowing firm is the link between the loan and the assets to be financed. If sales and receivables are seasonal, the loan varies automatically. Besides the relatively high cost, a disadvantage of receivables financing is its administrative complexity.

FACTORING

When a firm *factors* its accounts receivable, it sells them to another party—a factor—for cash. Title to the receivables passes to the factor, and the receivables are replaced by cash on the firm's balance sheet. In contrast, when a firm borrows against its receivables as collateral, it retains title, and both receivables and the loan appear on the balance sheet. Many commercial-finance companies, along with some commercial banks, engage in factoring, although banks usually conduct their factoring operations as separate subsidiaries of the bank or of a parent holding company.

Sale of the receivables to the factor normally is *without recourse*—meaning that the factor absorbs bad debt losses and cannot look to the seller in the event of default. Occasionally, receivables are sold *with recourse*, in which case uncollectable receivables are returned to the seller, who absorbs the bad debt expense.

The factor normally approves each order and reserves the right to reject individual accounts or orders. Once the order is approved by the factor, the goods are shipped, and the firm's customer is notified to remit directly to the factor. Because the customer is notified that the account has been sold to a factor, some firms may be inhibited from using factoring. In industries in which factoring is widely used—notably textiles, shoes, and furniture—there is no stigma attached.

Services performed by the factor include credit analysis, collection, and absorption of bad debts. The fee charged varies with the specific services and ranges between 1 and 3 percent of the face amount of the receivables purchased. If funds are advanced to the seller before the receivables are collected by the factor, an additional interest charge is levied that is normally tied to, and above, the prime bank rate.

In some situations, factoring offers significant advantages. With a factoring arrangement, a firm avoids the expense of bad debts and also may avoid the necessity of operating a credit department for analysis and collection. Firms that are small or have seasonal sales patterns may realize substantial savings. Costs avoided by the firm are borne by the factor, but because the factor serves many customers, the aggregate cost may be lower. By serving firms with different seasonal patterns, the credit analysis and collection workload may be spread more evenly over the year. By serving a large number of accounts, the factor can realize economies of scale and also can achieve better diversification with respect to default risk. For these reasons, in some industries, a factor can perform the services in question more economically than can firms individually.

To evaluate factoring as a financing arrangement requires a careful analysis of activities and costs and a comparison of the resulting savings with the fee charged by the factor.

LOANS AGAINST INVENTORY

Inventory also often is used as collateral for loans by both banks and commercial-finance companies. The nature of the inventory is an important factor in determining the attractiveness of the loan to a lender and the percentage to be advanced. The more readily salable the inventory, the higher is the loan percentage. A lumber wholesaler's inventory, for example, readily salable as is, likely would justify a higher loan percentage than would an inventory of specialized electronic parts or half-completed electronic instruments. Loan percentages against inventory typically vary from 50 to 90 percent.

The security arrangement is a critical factor in inventory loans and greatly affects the administrative costs. A number of methods are in common use; some leave the inventory in the possession of the borrower, and some place it under the control of a third party.

The simplest arrangement by which a borrower can retain control of the inventory is a *blanket*, or *floating, lien*. The Uniform Commercial Code includes a provision whereby a borrower may pledge inventory ''in general,'' without specifying the exact items involved. The floating lien is inexpensive to administer but difficult to police.

Considerably more security is afforded the lender under a *trust-receipt loan*. This arrangement often is used to finance automobiles, consumer durable goods, and certain types of equipment. In these applications, the arrangement is referred to as *floor planning*. Under such an arrangement, the lender advances the funds to purchase the inventory. The borrower signs a trust receipt, and each item is identified individually by serial number. Usually, title to the goods rests with the lender until sold. After sale, the proceeds belong to the lender and are forwarded immediately by the borrower. As inventory is sold, new inventory is entered into the arrangement and is controlled individually by serial numbers. Lenders usually audit the inventory periodically to insure that items that are supposed to be in the inventory, identified by serial number, in fact are there.

With goods in the hands of the borrower, the lender is not protected against fraud or misapplication. To gain complete protection, the goods may be placed under the control of a third party, or *warehouser*. The *warehouser* is given physical control of the inventory and issues a warehouse receipt assigning the security interest to the lender. The warehouser releases the inventory to the borrowing firm upon authorization of the lender, which usually requires that some portion of the loan be repaid.

There are two principal types of warehouse arrangements. A *terminal warehouse* is a public warehouse facility to and from which the inventory must be physically transported. Often a more convenient arrangement is the *field warehouse*, operated by the warehouse company on the premises of the borrower. Under this arrangement, a suitable facility is established providing storage under lock and key with direct control by the warehouser. The arrangement between Allied Crude Oil Company and American Express described in Finance in Practice 18–3 is a good example of a field-warehousing arrangement—albeit one that ultimately did not perform its function.

Because inventory must be controlled item by item, administrative costs are high under a warehouse arrangement. Floor-planning arrangements usually are somewhat less costly but provide less security and are not suitable for all types of goods. On warehouse loans, interest and service charges usually are listed separately. Interest charges are imposed by the lender and depend on the credit-worthiness of the borrower, the nature of the inventory, the loan percentage, and the amount of the loan. Service charges are levied by the warehouse company and depend on the nature of the inventory, the handling required, and the rate of turnover of the goods under control. Warehouse-receipt loans are an expensive method of financing, but in some cases involving firms in financial difficulty, with no established credit record, or in risky lines of business, they may be the only source available.

Chapter

19

Managing Cash

In this chapter, we will focus on how firms can keep their investment in cash to a minimum while still operating the firm effectively. The overall problem of cash management can be divided into three steps: (1) collecting and disbursing funds efficiently, (2) determining the appropriate working-cash balance, and (3) investing the remaining excess cash. As we will see, subject to the constraint of honoring its commitments to customers and suppliers, a firm's policy should be to collect early and pay late because money has a time value. Because of the high costs of financing and the attractive interest rates on investments in marketable securities, many firms are actively engaged in sophisticated cash management to reduce their investment in working-cash balances.

Figure 19–1
Overview of The Cash Cycle

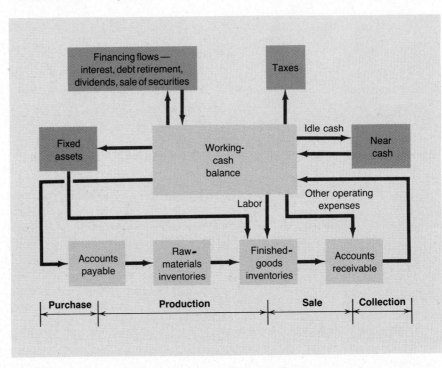

In the last chapter, we focused on sources of short-term and intermediate-term financing. Obtaining such financing is costly to the firm because the suppliers of funds must be compensated. For example, the firm makes interest payments when it borrows from a bank. One way to reduce these costs is to keep the amount of financing needed as low as is possible while still operating the firm effectively. Managers can reduce financing needs by reducing the assets that the firm uses.

Current assets—are assets with a maturity of less than one year and include a firm's holdings of cash, accounts receivable, and inventories.

In this chapter and in the next, we will focus on the **current assets** of the firm—such as cash, inventories, and accounts receivable. For many firms, current assets represent a large portion of total investment, and, like long-term assets, current assets must be financed. As an example, in 1984 Xerox Corporation had over $3.7 billion in current assets out of total assets of about $9.5 billion. That $3.7 billion dollar investment in current assets had to be financed by Xerox. In this chapter, we will focus on one major current asset—cash—then move on to accounts receivable and inventories in the next chapter.

Cash—for purposes of cash management is total liquid assets: cash plus near-cash.

Many firms actively try to keep cash to a minimum. It is not that firms do not want cash flow. In fact, getting large positive cash flows is what undertaking good investment opportunities is all about. But once cash comes in, there is good reason not to leave it idle in a cash account. Interest in cash management has risen to the extent that there now exists a national organization called the National Corporate Cash Managers' Association, which sponsors a journal and holds annual meetings devoted to topics in working-capital management.

Liquid assets—are assets that can easily be converted to cash on short notice.

The term **cash** sometimes refers to currency plus checking-account balances held at commercial banks and sometimes also includes *near-cash assets*, such as marketable securities or bank time deposits. Earlier, we used the term **liquid assets** to refer to the total of cash plus near-cash. In this chapter, however, we will use the term *cash* in its broader sense—that is, as total liquid assets. We will use the term **working-cash balances** to refer to the subset of liquid assets that includes only currency plus checking-account balances. We will not distinguish between currency and checking-account balances because for most firms the checking account is far more important than currency as a working balance.

Working-cash balance—is currency plus checking-account balances.

MOTIVES FOR HOLDING CASH

The **transactions motive**—for holding cash concerns the use of cash to pay bills.

Firms have two main motives for holding cash, or liquid assets: a **transactions motive**, and a **precautionary motive**. The transactions motive refers to cash balances required in the ordinary course of business—a pool from which the firm makes payments to suppliers, employees, and creditors and into which it places payments received from customers. These receipts and disbursements constitute a continuous flow through the firm's working-cash balance. The precautionary motive refers to cash held for unexpected problems or opportunities requiring funds on short notice. Precautionary cash balances usually are held in liquid assets that earn interest. In seasonal firms, a part of the transaction balance also may be stored temporarily in near-cash form—such as in marketable securities—during parts of the year. In addition to the transactions and precautionary motives, firms may sometimes build up liquid assets because of a *speculative motive* while they are waiting to decide on the long-term use of funds. For example, a buildup of liquid assets might provide some of the resources necessary to acquire another firm in the future. We will not discuss the speculative motive further in this chapter. In Chapter 22, we discuss mergers in detail.

The **precautionary motive**—for holding cash concerns the use of liquid assets as a reserve for contingencies in an uncertain world.

Cash-management policy—is the set of decisions related to (1) managing collections and disbursements of cash, (2) determining the appropriate working-cash balance, and (3) investing idle cash.

In order to concentrate on cash management, we will take as given all aspects of the firm's operating plan except those that directly affect its cash position. Inventory levels, for example, will be assumed to be already determined, as will trade credit policy and the level of accounts receivable.

Cash-management policy addresses three basic questions:

1. How should working-cash balances be stored, collected, and disbursed?
2. Given a total pool of cash, how should the appropriate working balance be determined?
3. How should any temporarily idle funds be invested in interest-bearing assets?

MANAGING COLLECTIONS AND DISBURSEMENTS

The **cash cycle**—is the process whereby cash is used to purchase materials from which are produced goods that are then sold to customers, who later pay their bills.

To size up our problem of cash management, let us examine the flow of cash through a firm's accounts. It is useful to think of the process as a **cash cycle** in which cash is used to purchase materials from which are produced goods, which are then sold to customers, who later pay their bills. The firm receives cash from its customers, and the cycle repeats. We can represent the cash cycle as shown in Figure 19–1.

Opportunities to improve efficiency in collecting and disbursing funds center on flows through the current section of the balance sheet, depicted in the bottom part of

Figure 19–2
Details of the Cash Cycle

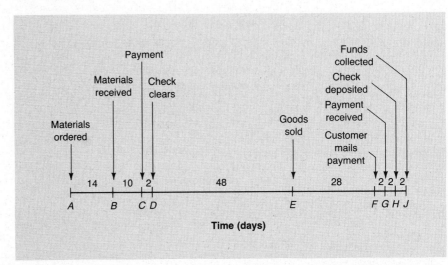

Figure 19–1. We diagram these flows in more detail in Figure 19–2, which shows the steps along the way as funds flow through the firm's accounts. Let us assume that XYZ corporation orders raw materials at point A in Figure 19–2 and receives them 14 days later at point B. Terms of 2/10, net 30 are offered, so the firm pays the invoice in time for the check to get to the supplier 10 days later at point C. However, it takes 2 days for the check to clear, and XYZ's bank account is not charged until point D. XYZ turns over its inventory six times per year, so 60 days after the materials are received, the product is sold and the customer is billed. The collection period is 30 days—28 days for the customer to pay and 2 days for the check to arrive by mail, bringing us to point G. XYZ processes the payment and deposits it 2 days later at point H. Another 2 days elapse while XYZ's bank collects the funds from the customer's bank, bringing us to point J.

In viewing Figure 19–2, the manager sees cash effectively leaving the firm's bank account at D and entering the account at J. Because money has a time value, it would benefit the firm to speed up the collection of funds (move J forward) and slow down the disbursement of funds (move D later). Such steps would reduce the firm's costs—either the direct interest cost of having to borrow funds to bridge the gap between D and J or the opportunity costs of not being able to earn interest by investing surplus cash. In short, subject to the constraint of honoring its commitments to customers and suppliers, the company's policy should be to collect early and pay late.

By speeding collections and controlling disbursements, firms can reduce their requirements for working-cash balances.

Another way to view this process is to note that the firm's total financing requirement is affected by the total time lag from point B to point J. The firm itself can control some factors that determine the various lags, but some factors it cannot control. Some of the lags affect the cash balance, while others affect other components of working capital, such as accounts receivable and inventory. In addressing ourselves to cash management, we are concerned with time periods *BCD* and *FGHJ*. Time period *AB* is beyond the firm's control and does not directly affect its financial statements, although it may affect production schedules. Time period *DE* is determined by the firm's production process and inventory policy and affects the total investment in inventory. Time period *EF* is determined by the firm's credit terms and the payment policies of its customers and affects the total investment in accounts receivable. We will examine the management of inventory and accounts receivable in the next chapter. Our present task is to examine what can be done to improve the efficiency of a firm's cash management. We will focus on three areas: concentrating working balances, speeding collections, and controlling disbursements. In each case, we will examine policies that reduce the amount of cash that a firm has to maintain.

One bank described the objectives of cash management in these terms: "Companies use cash-management services basically for two reasons—to maximize earnings from the investment of idle cash and to reduce the need for borrowing to finance daily operations. In addition, our cash-management services provide companies greater control through improved information, while helping to feed internal accounting and information systems."[1]

Speeding Collections

One important way that firms conserve cash is by reducing the lag between the time the customer mails the check and the time the funds become collected—that is, from points *F* to *J* in Figure 19–2. Of the 6-day lag in Figure 19–2, 2 days are mail time, 2 days are processing time within XYZ Corporation, and 2 days are collection time within the banking system.

Float—is the product of the time delay in collecting funds and the dollars collected.

These delays in collection create **float**, which is the product of the time delay and the dollars collected. For example, a firm that collects $1.5 million per day and experiences a 6-day lag in collecting the funds would have total float of $1.5 million per day × 6 days = $9 million. Reducing collection time by 2 days would reduce float by $3 million, and each dollar so released is available for investment. If the firm could earn, say, 10 percent on such an investment, it would have $300,000 per year in additional earnings. It's easy to see why firms work hard to reduce collection float.

Total float can be broken down into mail float, processing float, and availability float. Availability float refers to collection time in the banking system, to which we will return later. For now, let's focus on mail and processing float caused by the 4-day lag from *F* to *H* in Figure 19–2.

Small firms that operate in limited geographical areas can do little to reduce mail time. However, improvements often can be made in processing time within the firm. Suppose XYZ Corporation has credit sales of $5 million per year. With approximately 250 working days per year, XYZ's collections average $20,000 per working day. If XYZ could reduce its processing time from 2 days to 1 day and thereby get the checks to the bank 1 day sooner, its accounts receivable balance would be reduced by $20,000. XYZ's financing requirements would, therefore, be reduced by $20,000. If

---

[1]NCNB Corporation, *First Quarter Report to Shareholders*, 1985.

XYZ's borrowing costs were 9 percent, savings of about $1,800 per year would be realized. These potential savings could be compared to the cost of faster processing to determine whether the change in processing should be made. We can conclude that internal processing should be speeded up to the point at which the costs of further improvement exceed the additional savings.

Now let us consider a larger firm that receives remittances from customers over a wide geographical area. Opportunities may exist to reduce both mail time and processing time. One way to reduce mail time is by operating a number of strategically located collection centers to which customer payments are mailed.

Lock-Box Systems.   Many firms find it advantageous to engage the services of commercial banks to operate collection centers for them as part of a **lock-box system**. The firm first establishes a number of collection points, taking into account customer locations and mail schedules. Often the bank provides technical assistance in selecting the most advantageous locations for collection centers.[2] At each location, the firm rents a post-office box and instructs its customers to remit to the box. The firm's local bank is authorized to pick up mail directly from the box. The bank does so, perhaps several times a day, and deposits the checks in the firm's account. The bank makes a record of names and amounts and other data needed by the firm for internal accounting purposes and immediately enters the checks for collection.

The lock-box system results in two benefits to the firm. First, the bank performs the clerical tasks of handling the remittances prior to deposit, services that the bank may be able to perform at lower cost. Second, and often more important, the process of collection through the banking system begins immediately upon receipt of the remittance and does not have to wait until the firm completes its processing for internal accounting purposes. In terms of the activities in Figure 19–2, the activity represented by *HJ* now takes place simultaneously with *GH*. The firm processes remittances for internal accounting purposes using data supplied by the bank and can schedule this processing at any time without delaying collection. Using a lock-box system saves as much as 4 days in mailing and processing time. The cost saving to the firm from such a system can be significant.

For example, assume Ajax Manufacturing Company handles collections of $10 million a year and has an opportunity to use a bank lock-box system that offers to save 2 days of processing time on each check received. If the company's cost of short-term funds is 10 percent per annum, its *gross* saving would be the product of annual remittances times number of days saved times cost of funds times 1/365, or

$$\$10 \text{ million} \times 2 \text{ days} \times 10 \text{ percent per year} \times 1/365 = \$5,479 \text{ per year}.$$

The first lock-box system was set up in 1947 by RCA with the help of the First National Bank of Chicago and Bankers Trust Company. Since that time the use of lock-box systems has become commonplace. However, the use of a lock-box system is not without cost. The bank will either charge a flat amount for its services or ask that the firm maintain a compensating balance at the bank in exchange for the service. In the case of Ajax Company above, as long as these costs are less than $5,479 a

A **lock-box system**—a collection system in which payments are mailed to a post-office box, which is emptied several times a day by a bank, which then deposits the payments and updates accounting records.

---

[2]Determining optimal locations for collection points in a large lock-box system is highly technical and can be formulated and solved as a linear-programming problem. See J. Vander Weide and S. F. Maier, *Managing Corporate Liquidity* (New York: John Wiley and Sons, 1985), Chapter 3.

year, the system produces a net gain to the company. Whether the savings will out-weigh the costs for a particular company depends mainly on the geographical disper-sion of customers, the dollar amount of the average remittance, and the firm's cost of financing.

We see that a major advantage of speeding collections is to free cash and thereby reduce the firm's total financing requirement. There are other advantages as well. By transfering clerical functions to the bank, the firm may reduce its costs, improve inter-nal control, and reduce the possibility of fraud. By getting checks sooner to the banks on which they are written, the incidence of checks dishonored for insufficient funds may be reduced.

Collection Time in the Banking System.   The time required to collect a check through the banking system is represented by *HJ* in Figure 19–2). Suppose a customer in Chapel Hill, North Carolina, purchases electronics equipment from a firm in Palo Alto, California, and remits with a check drawn on a Chapel Hill bank. The seller deposits the check in a bank in Palo Alto, but the funds are not available for use until the check has been presented physically to the Chapel Hill bank, a process that de-pends on mail service between the two cities and may take several days. A very extensive clearing network has been established in the United States that involves the commercial banks and the Federal Reserve System. In the majority of cases, clearing times have been reduced to 2 days or less using the facilities of the Fed or direct interbank clearings. In the matter of check clearing, the banks are the experts, and firms usually can rely on their banks to minimize the time requirements.

Controlling Disbursements

Just as speeding collections turns accounts receivable into cash and thereby reduces the firm's financing requirements, slowing disbursements does the same. In Chapter 18, we discussed trade credit as a source of funds. There we concluded that the proper policy was to pay within the terms agreed upon, taking cash discounts when the terms offered were favorable. We concluded also that there is no point in paying sooner than agreed. By waiting as long as possible, the firm maximizes the extent to which ac-counts payable are used as a source of funds, a source which requires no interest payment.

Consider the effect of a 1-day change in payment period. Aquatic Systems, Inc. (see Table 18–1) planned to purchase about $1.5 million worth of raw materials in 1987 and followed a policy of paying within credit terms offered by suppliers. Suppose Aquatic paid 1 day earlier than necessary. Accounts payable would decline by 1 day's purchases, or by about $4,100. At an interest rate of 9 percent, Aquatic's interest costs would rise by $370 per year.

Firms with expense-generating activities that cover a wide area often find it advan-tageous to make disbursements from a single central account. In that way, schedules can be tightly controlled and disbursements can be made on exactly the right day. An alternative arrangement is to disburse from decentralized locations, but to wire transfer the exact amount needed in each local account for all disbursements scheduled that day.

Some firms find it advantageous to exploit the *checkbook float*, or *disbursement float*, which is the time between the writing of a check and its presentation for collection, represented by segment *CD* in Figure 19–2. If this lag can be exploited, it offsets at least partially the lag in the other direction in collecting checks from customers (*HJ*). Because of lag *CD*, a firm's balance on the bank's books is higher than that in its own checkbook. Knowing this, a firm may be able to reduce its working-cash requirements. Banks understand checkbook float also and can be expected to set compensating balances and fees based on balances on their (the banks') books. If a firm exploits checkbook float too far, it increases the likelihood of checks being dishonored for insufficient funds and the accompanying displeasure of both bank and payee.

Going beyond merely taking into account disbursement float, it has become common practice in recent years for aggressively managed firms to actually increase disbursement float by extending the lag from *C* to *D* in Figure 19–2. Mail time can be increased by mailing the check from a distant office; presentation time can be extended by drawing the check on a distant bank. In recent years, the matter of selecting disbursement centers to accomplish these aims has received as much attention as has selection of the collection centers discussed earlier.[3] The Federal Reserve, however, discourages such practices because it sees its own mission as that of reducing, not increasing, collection time. Vendors, likewise, disapprove of aggressive disbursement practices because the payer's disbursement float is the payee's collection float. Firms that go too far in extending disbursement float are simply taking advantage of their suppliers, and such practices are not conducive to good business relationships.

Concentration Banking

Many firms need only a single checking account. Larger firms that operate over wide geographical areas usually need more than one, sometimes dozens. Where many accounts are needed, **concentration accounts** can be used to minimize the total requirement for working balances.

Suppose a company has a number of branch offices, each with a local bank account. Branches collect accounts receivable and make deposits in their local accounts. Each day, funds above a certain predetermined minimum are transferred to a central concentration account, usually at the firm's headquarters. For example, a fast-food chain with 200 locations might make deposits of $2,000 per day on average per store and might have collected balances of $5,000 in each store's local bank account. Such a small amount could not be invested advantageously, especially on an overnight basis. On the other hand, if the franchise concentrates its funds at the close of business each day by transferring collected balances from all 200 local accounts to a single central account, it will have a pool of $1 million available for investing. Thus, the motivation for concentration banking is to maximize the amount of investable funds.

A **concentration account**—is a centralized bank account in which disbursement funds from different branches, divisions, or franchises of a company can be pooled so that the firm's aggregate working-balance requirement is lower than it would be if balances were maintained at each branch.

Methods of Funds Transfer. The daily transfer of funds can be made by one of three methods: by *depository transfer check (DTC)*, by *wire transfer*, or by an *automated clearinghouse (ACH)*. The DTC is the most widely used and least expensive but usually the slowest because it is performed with a piece of paper. Wire transfer is virtually instantaneous but is expensive.

The automated clearinghouse has grown over recent years out of the universal desire of banks and their customers to reduce the avalanche of paper required to execute

---

[3]See Vander Weide and Maier, *Managing Corporate Liquidity*, Chapter 4.

Finance in Practice 19–1

Integrated Cash-Management Systems

Many banks offer integrated cash-management systems designed especially for large firms with extensive collection and disbursement activities. Such systems rely heavily on the technology of computers and high-speed data transmission. A system offered by many banks features lock boxes and remote *zero-balance accounts* linked by wire to a centralized master-control account where working balances are pooled. The zero-balance accounts are used for decentralized collection and disbursement, with funds transferred in and out each day to achieve a zero balance at the day's end. Extensive reports are generated to provide data to the firm for control purposes. Such systems are costly but provide substantial benefits for firms that can utilize them. One major regional bank includes the following services in its cash-management program:

1. cash-management consulting that uses computer models to help identify ways in which companies can increase income from investments and reduce borrowing;

2. a lock box to speed the collection of payments by having a company's receipts mailed directly to the bank;

3. a controlled-disbursing service that allows firms to identify daily cash requirements precisely, enabling them to make timely, accurate investment and borrowing decisions;

4. account-reconciliation services, ranging from a paid-item listing to full reconciliation reports;

5. automated-clearinghouse capabilities, including electronic transfer of funds, direct debit and credit, corporate trade payments (which is the electronic payment of suppliers), and direct deposit of payroll;

6. concentration of receipts from regional locations in a single bank account for greater investment potential and better cash control;

7. a treasury-management system that enables corporate treasurers to use personal computers to receive and process information for improved management of cash flow, debts, and investments;

8. a freight-payment plan that handles the administrative details of paying bills for freight shipments through preauthorized withdrawals from a company's account; and

9. information services, including the sending and receiving of balance and related financial information worldwide through electronic networks.

Source: NCNB Corporation, *Report to Shareholders*, 1985.

---

payment transactions in the United States. The ACH system today, with the exception of that in New York City, is run by the Federal Reserve. Its basis is computer-to-computer transmission of payment instructions without paper ever being created. ACH, unlike wire transfer, is not intended for immediate transfer of funds, but normally involves a 1-day delay.[4]

Regardless of the transfer method used, the funds transferred to the concentration account are available for disbursement for other purposes. As we will see later, the more variable are a firm's cash flows, the higher is the requirement for working-cash balances. By pooling its funds for disbursement in a single account, the aggregate requirement for working balances is lower than it would be if balances were maintained at each branch office. Concentration, in short, permits the firm to store its cash

---

[4]For a discussion of the automated clearinghouse and of concentration banking in general, see Vander Weide and Maier, *Managing Corporate Liquidity*, Chapter 5.

more efficiently. Concentration banking has become widely used by firms with many retail outlets, such as fast-food franchises or department stores.

Electronic Banking.   The automated clearinghouse is a form of electronic banking because payments are transfered electronically, with no paper involved. Banks also are experimenting with other forms of electronic funds transfer, among them:

1. *point-of-sale terminals* located on a merchant's premises that permit direct transfer of funds from a customer's account to that of the merchant;
2. *automatic teller machines (ATMs)* that permit bank customers to execute a number of typical banking transactions at convenient locations on a 24-hour-per-day basis;
3. *telephone-instructed transactions* performed with a personal computer or terminal from the home or office of a customer to the bank.[5]

Although the venerable check remains the preferred means of payment for the majority of transactions, we can expect electronic banking to grow rapidly during the 1980s as technology advances. The impetus toward electronic banking is being stimulated also by the drive of the Federal Reserve to reduce float, specifically the availability float resulting from collection time within the banking system. In 1980 the Fed began charging banks for excess float, and in response to this change and to improved operating procedures total availability float in the banking system declined from a daily average of $6.3 billion in 1979 to $1.8 billion in early 1983.[6] The increased pressure by the Fed to reduce float is making electronic funds transfer relatively more attractive.

Sample Problem 19–1

Collecting Cash Quickly in the Omark Corporation

The Omark Corporation has a centralized billing system at its headquarters in Chicago to handle average daily collections of $200,000. The collection float for Omark averages 6 days.

A. How much money does Omark have tied up in collection float?
B. If Omark's opportunity cost on short-term funds is 6 percent, how much does this float cost the company?
C. Omark's treasurer is considering a concentration banking system, which, she estimates, will reduce float by 2 days. What is the largest total amount of required compensating balances Omark should be willing to accept with the concentration system? (Assume there are no cost savings from the system other than the reduced collection float.)

Solution

A. The total amount of funds tied up in collection float is equal to the firm's average daily collections times the number of days required for collection. For Omark, average daily collections are $200,000, and float is 6 days, so the total amount of funds tied up is:

$$\$200,000 \text{ per day} \times 6 \text{ days} = \$1,200,000.$$

---

[5]See Vander Weide and Maier, *Managing Corporate Liquidity*, Chapter 2.
[6]"Companies Learn to Live Without the Float," *Business Week*, September 26, 1983, p. 134.

B. The cost of float to the firm equals the amount of funds tied up in float times the opportunity rate at which these funds could be invested. Because Omark can invest the short-term funds to yield 6 percent, the opportunity cost of having $1,200,000 tied up in float is:

$$\$1,200,000 \times 6 \text{ percent} = \$72,000 \text{ per year.}$$

C. The concentration-banking system would reduce Omark's cost by reducing the opportunity cost of float. The system will reduce Omark's float by $200,000/day $\times$ 2 days = $400,000, reducing Omark's float costs by

$$\$400,000 \times 6 \text{ percent} = \$24,000 \text{ per year.}$$

The opportunity cost to Omark of compensating balances equals the required compensating balance times the opportunity cost of short-term funds. The maximum acceptable required compensating balance for Omark is found by equating the opportunity cost of the compensating balance to the savings from the concentration banking system, which we found to be $24,000.

$$\text{Compensating balance} \times 6 \text{ percent} = \$24,000.$$

Therefore,

$$\text{Compensating balance} = \$24,000/0.06 = \$400,000.$$

Note that if Omark maintained a $400,000 compensating balance, this would exactly offset the $400,000 of reduced float provided by the concentration-banking system. ∎

DETERMINING THE APPROPRIATE WORKING-CASH BALANCE

Let us assume the firm now is collecting, storing, and disbursing its cash as efficiently as possible. Given its long-term financial structure—fixed assets, long-term liabilities, and equity—its total cash position at any time is determined by its operating plan. Suppose total cash is more than the firm needs for operating purposes, if disbursements are made according to plan. Should all these funds be kept in the firm's checking account? No. Because checking accounts earn interest at lower rates than various interest-bearing liquid assets, such as marketable securities, it is to the firm's advantage to leave in the checking account only the amount necessary to operate and invest the remainder temporarily elsewhere until needed.

Our problem, then, is to determine how much cash a firm should maintain in its checking account as a working balance. We will address this question here, and in the next section we will discuss the investment of amounts above the working balance.

The working balance is maintained for *transactions purposes*—for paying bills and collecting payments on accounts receivable. If the firm maintains too small a working balance, it runs out of cash. It then must liquidate marketable securities, if available, or borrow. Liquidating marketable securities and borrowing both involve transaction costs. If, on the other hand, the firm maintains too high a working balance, it forgoes the opportunity to earn higher interest rates on marketable securities—that is, it incurs an opportunity cost. Thus, we are seeking the *optimal* working balance, rather than the minimum working balance. The optimal working balance occurs when total costs—that is, the sum of the transaction costs and the opportunity costs—are at a minimum. Finding the optimum involves a trade-off between falling transaction costs and rising opportunity costs. Figure 19–3 depicts the problem graphically. If a firm tries to keep its working balances low, it will find itself selling securities (and later repurchasing securities) more often than if it aims at a higher level of working balances. That is, transaction costs fall as the working-balance level rises. Opportunity costs, on the other hand, rise as the level of working balances rises. There is one level of working-cash balance, denoted by $C*$ in Figure 19–3, where the *sum* of the two costs, shown as the total-cost curve, is at a minimum. This level is the point efficient management should try to find.

> **The optimal working balance occurs when total costs (transaction costs plus opportunity costs) are at a minimum.**

The problem with the approach in Figure 19–3 is that, while it provides a useful way of looking at the problem and some useful insights, it cannot be directly applied in practice. That is, Figure 19–3 does not tell the manager in concrete dollar terms how much cash he or she should keep in the firm's checking account. One very important practical consideration not included in Figure 19–3 is compensating-balance requirements imposed by banks.

Compensating-Balance Requirements

If a firm uses bank credit as a source of financing, the question of the optimal checking-account balance may have a very simple answer: it may be dictated by compensating-balance requirements imposed by the bank. As we found in Chapter 18, banks typically impose minimum-balance requirements to compensate for various services, such as processing checks and standby commitments to lend. The amount of the compensating balance may be determined as a percentage of the loan outstanding or of the line of credit. Alternatively, if there is no loan involved and the balance requirement is strictly to compensate the bank for services rendered, such as clearing of checks, the amount may simply be some minimum dollar balance. The bank might require, for example, that the firm's balance not fall below $100,000, and in return, the bank agrees to process a certain number of transactions each month without charge. The bank, of course, is compensated in the form of what it can earn by lending or investing the minimum balance.

In some cases, a firm may determine with very little analysis that its optimal working balance is below the bank's compensating-balance requirement. In such cases, the latter figure becomes the firm's minimum checking-account balance. In other cases, where the answer is not so clear or where compensating balances are not required, we must put pencil to paper to determine the appropriate working balance.

Finding the Optimal Working Balance

Having done all we can to improve our collection and disbursement procedures, let us now take the pattern of receipts and disbursements as given. Over any time period, a firm's beginning and ending cash balances are related as follows:

Figure 19–3
The Optimal Working-Cash Balance

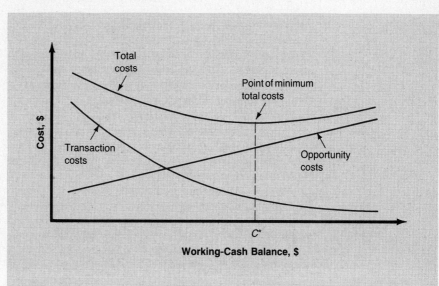

$$\text{Ending balance} = \text{Beginning balance} + \text{Receipts} - \text{Disbursements}$$

If receipts and disbursements were constant each day, we would know with certainty what each would be each day and our problem would be simple. Supposing that each day receipts exceeded disbursements by the same amount, we could withdraw the ending balance each day and use it for other purposes. In practice, we have two problems: variability and uncertainty. In most firms, receipts and disbursements vary both over the month and over the year. Over a month, receipts and disbursements for current operating expenses are likely to show some variation, perhaps in a regular pattern. In seasonal firms, the amounts also will vary over the year. Less frequent outlays, such as those for capital expenditures, taxes, and dividends, introduce still more variability. Some of this variability may be predictable, but some probably is not. Let us examine these two problems—variability and uncertainty—separately.

Variability.   Suppose receipts and disbursements both vary and are not synchronized, but the variations are completely predictable. Determining the appropriate working balance in the face of nonsynchronous but predictable cash flows is a problem of minimizing total costs. If we set the balance too low, we incur high transaction costs; one might say we make too many trips to the bank. If we set the balance too high, we lose too much interest on marketable securities.

The determination of the optimal working balance under conditions of certainty can be viewed as an *inventory problem* in which we balance the costs of too little cash (transaction costs) against the costs of too much cash (opportunity costs).[7] Figure 19–3 views the problem in this way. If the cash shortage becomes severe enough, we may begin to forgo cash discounts on purchases, adding another element to opportunity cost.

Formal models of the cash-balance problem have been developed using *inventory theory*. Inputs to such a model are the total net cash outflow over the period of time in question, the transaction costs of replenishing the cash balance by selling securities or borrowing, and the interest rate that can be earned on securities. The answer given by the model tells us how often and in what amounts funds should be transferred to the checking account from other sources.

Uncertainty.   Receipts and disbursements are very seldom completely predictable. If we go to the opposite extreme and assume receipts and disbursements (or the difference between them) to be completely random, a different kind of model can be developed using the technique of *control theory*. In addition to information on transaction costs and interest rates on securities, we need a measure of the variability of net cash flows. Using these data, we can determine the optimal maximum and minimum balances in the firm's checking account, denoted by levels Y and X in Figure 19–4.[8]

In Figure 19–4, the firm's working-cash balance fluctuates randomly in response to random inflows and outflows. At time t_1, the balance reaches the upper control limit, Y. At that point, $(Y - X)$ dollars are transferred out of the cash account and into marketable securities. The balance continues to fluctuate, falling to zero at t_2, at which time X dollars of marketable securities are sold and the proceeds transferred to the working balance. The control-limit model, thus, gives an answer in terms of maximum and minimum balances and provides a decision rule rather than a fixed schedule of transfers, as did the simple inventory model. One of the important insights of the control-limit model is that, where cash flows are uncertain, the greater the variability, the higher is the minimum balance (X in Figure 19–4).

> **Two factors complicate the determination of the optimal working-cash balance: variability and uncertainty.**

Using Mathematical Models

Formal mathematical models such as those mentioned above are useful for increasing our understanding of the cash-management problem and providing insights and *qualitative* guidance. The models tell us which factors are important and make the trade-offs explicit. We see, for example, that transaction costs play a central role. If transaction costs were zero, the firm would require no working-cash balance at all; it simply would sell securities or borrow to pay every bill.

---

[7]Inventory theory was first applied to the cash-balance problem by William J. Baumol, "The Transactions Demand for Cash: An Inventory Theoretic Approach," *Quarterly Journal of Economics* 66 (November 1952): 545-56. The model since has been further developed by other writers.

[8]The control-limit model discussed here was developed by Merton H. Miller and Daniel Orr, "A Model of the Demand for Money by Firms," *Quarterly Journal of Economics* 80 (August 1966): 413–35. Other writers also have applied control-limit theory to the cash-balance problem.

Figure 19–4
Cash-Balance Control Limits

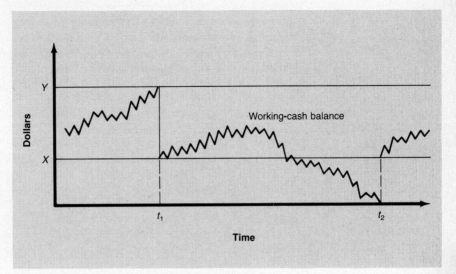

Source: Adapted from Merton H. Miller and Daniel Orr, ''A Model of the Demand for Money by Firms,'' *Quarterly Journal of Economics* 80 (August 1966): 413–35.

Are formal mathematical models also useful for *quantitative* applications? In practice, the cash-flow patterns of most firms are partly predictable and partly random. Neither the inventory model nor the control-limit model is strictly applicable. By combining the insights from formal models with the techniques of cash budgeting and proforma analysis, many firms can arrive at reasonable answers by experience and experiment. In deciding how far to go in analyzing the problem, we must consider the cost of the analysis. Except in the case of very large firms, quantitative solutions to the cash-balance problem using formal mathematical models are likely to be uneconomical. Often, the cost of obtaining the necessary input data and operating the model exceeds the savings over solutions that can be attained by experience and experiment.[9] As always, we must keep an eye on the cost of our analytical techniques as well as on the benefits.

Planning Cash Requirements

In most cases, to search for the optimal working-cash balance probably overstates our capabilities; we must be content to get reasonably close. Perhaps we should substitute the word *appropriate* for *optimal*.

---

[9]For a discussion of the usefulness of formal cash-management models, see Hans E. Daellenbach, ''Are Cash-Management Models Worthwhile?'' *Journal of Financial and Quantitative Analysis* 9,4 (September 1974): 607–26. For a description of a cash-management model that can be used in practice, see S. F. Maier and J. H. Vander Weide, ''A Practical Approach to Short-Run Financial Planning,'' *Financial Management* 7 (Winter 1978): 10–16.

The checking-account balance that the firm should maintain is the compensating-balance requirement or the optimal working balance—whichever is greater. Some firms, especially those with seasonal sales patterns, may find that the appropriate working balance varies somewhat over the year. As a firm grows, the appropriate working-cash balance also will grow, although probably not proportionally.

Once we have settled on the appropriate balance to be maintained in the checking account, we can integrate cash management into the financial-planning process. The projected checking-account balance goes into the pro-forma balance sheet. Any excess cash over that figure then may be invested in interest-bearing assets.

INVESTING IDLE CASH

Cash in excess of requirements for working balances normally is invested in interest-bearing assets that can be converted readily to cash. A firm might hold excess cash for two principal reasons. First, the firm's working-capital requirements may vary over the year, perhaps in a fairly predictable manner if the variation is the result of recurring seasonal factors. Variation of this type characterized Aquatic Systems, Inc., which was discussed in Chapter 8. From the pro-forma balance sheet, it was apparent that excess cash would build up during seasonal lows in accounts receivable and inventory and would be needed later to finance a reexpansion of receivables and inventory during the next seasonal high. We can view the excess cash as a part of the firm's transaction balances. Even though the cash is temporarily idle, there is a predictable requirement for it later.

> **Excess cash normally is invested in interest-bearing assets readily convertible to cash.**

Second, excess cash may be held to cover unpredictable financing requirements. In a world of uncertainty, cash flows can never be predicted with complete accuracy. Competitors act, technology changes, products fail, strikes occur, and economic conditions vary. On the positive side, attractive investment opportunities may suddenly appear. A firm may choose to hold excess cash to finance such needs if and when they occur. We noted earlier that cash held for such purposes is referred to as a *precautionary balance* and usually is invested in interest-bearing assets until needed.

An alternative exists to the holding of excess cash for either of the two purposes described above. The firm can simply borrow short-term funds to finance variable requirements as they arise. Under such a policy, the firm would never hold excess cash. A firm's choice between short-term borrowing versus liquid assets as a means of financing variable requirements will depend on policy decisions with respect to the firm's long-term financial structure, particularly the mix of short-term and long-term funds. Here, we take as given the long-term structure and the amount available for investment in interest-bearing assets. In Chapter 18, we discussed a firm's decisions about the mix of short-term and long-term funds.

For many companies, especially larger ones, investing idle cash is a very important matter indeed. Table 19–1 shows the holdings of cash and marketable securities of some major companies as of December 31, 1984. These numbers are very big. General

Table 19—1
Cash Positions of Selected Companies, Year-End 1984

Company	Cash and Short-Term Securities Year-end 1984 (millions of dollars)
GM	8,567
American Express	7,490
Ford	5,943
IBM	4,362
Exxon	3,290
GE	2,373
Phillips Petroleum	1,894
Boeing	1,595
Texaco	1,401
Reynolds Industries	1,323
Eastman Kodak	1,011
DuPont	674
Westinghouse	612
GTE Corporation	521
U.S. Steel	355
Standard Oil, Ohio	337
Xerox	227

Source: Value Line Investment Survey.

Motors alone held more than $8.5 billion, an impressive sum for a single company. On a portfolio of this size, an increase of half a percentage point in yield could add more than $42.5 million to the firm's pretax profits! Companies with much more modest holdings of cash and marketable securities find that the potential from careful management can be very attractive.

Investment Criteria

A firm might invest excess cash in many types of interest-bearing assets. To choose among the alternatives, we must establish criteria based on our reasons for investing excess cash in the first place. We are investing either temporary transaction balances or precautionary balances or both. When we need the cash, we want to be able to obtain it—all of it—quickly. Given these objectives, we can rule out common stocks and other investments with returns that are not contractual and with prices that often vary widely. Debt securities, with a contractual obligation to pay, are our best candidates. In selecting among debt securities, there are three principal characteristics we should examine: default risk, maturity, and marketability.

Default risk refers to the possibility that interest or principal might not be paid on time and in the amount promised. If the financial markets suddenly perceive a significant risk of default on a particular security, the price of the security is likely to fall substantially, even though default may not actually have occurred. Because investors

Default risk—is the possibility that interest or principal might not be paid on time and in the amount promised.

in general are averse to risk, even the possibility of default is sufficient to depress the price. Given our purposes in investing excess cash, we want to steer clear of securities that stand any significant chance of defaulting. In an uncertain world, there is no guarantee that is absolutely certain—except perhaps that of the U.S. government, with its capacity to create money. However, the default risk on some securities is sufficiently low to be almost negligible. In selecting securities, we must keep in mind that risk and return are related and that low-risk securities provide the lowest returns. We must give up some return in order to purchase safety.

Maturity—is the time period over which interest and principal payments are to be made.

Maturity refers to the time period over which interest and principal payments are to be made. A 20-year bond might promise interest semiannually and principal at the end of the 20th year. A 6-month bank **certificate of deposit** would promise interest and principal at the end of the sixth month.

A **certificate of deposit (CD)**—is a fixed-maturity time deposit.

When interest rates vary, the prices of fixed-income securities vary. A rise in market rates produces a fall in price, and vice versa. Because of this relationship, debt securities are subject to a second type of risk—**interest-rate risk**—in addition to default risk. A U.S. government bond, though free of default risk, is not immune to interest-rate risk. The longer the maturity of a security, the more sensitive will be its price to interest-rate changes and the greater will be its exposure to interest-rate risk. For this reason, short maturities are generally best for investing excess cash.

Interest-rate risk—is the risk that the price of a security may fall due to a rise in the level of interest rates.

Marketability refers to the ease with which an asset can be converted to cash. With reference to financial assets, the terms *marketability* and *liquidity* often are used synonymously. Marketability has two principal, and interrelated, dimensions: price and time. If an asset can be sold quickly in large amounts at a price that can be determined in advance within narrow limits, the asset is said to be highly marketable or highly liquid. Perhaps the most liquid of all financial assets are U.S. Treasury bills (discussed below). On the other hand, if the price that can be realized depends significantly on the time available to sell the asset, the asset is said to be *illiquid*. The more independent the price is of time, the more liquid is the asset. A Van Gogh painting appraised at $100,000 likely would fetch far less if the owner were forced to sell it quickly on short notice. Besides price and time, a third attribute of marketability is low transaction costs.

Marketability—refers to the ease with which an asset can be converted to cash on short notice (also known as *liquidity*).

> **Criteria for selecting the best vehicle for investing idle cash include the amount of money available and the default risk, maturity, and marketability of the investment.**

Investment Alternatives

Here we discuss briefly the principal types of interest-bearing assets that meet the criteria of low-default risk, short maturity, and ready marketability. Such securities often are referred to as **money-market securities**.

Money-market securities—are interest-bearing assets that have low default risk, short maturity, and ready marketability.

U.S. Treasury bills and notes are obligations of the U.S. government. Treasury bills are one of the most widely used mediums for the temporary investment of excess cash. Bills are issued weekly by the government, are readily marketable, and have maturities at issue ranging from 91 to 360 days. Treasury notes have initial maturities of 1–5 years. Because Treasury securities are default-free, they have somewhat lower yields than do other marketable securities.

U.S. Treasury bills and notes—are short-term obligations of the U.S. government.

Federal-agency issues—are short-term obligations of agencies of the federal government.

Federal-agency issues are obligations of agencies of the federal government rather than the U.S. Treasury. Such agencies include the Federal Home Loan Bank, the Federal Land Bank, the Federal National Mortgage Association, and several others. These agencies are closely associated in the minds of investors with the federal government—although their obligations, strictly speaking, are not guaranteed by the government. Yields normally are slightly higher than those on Treasury securities, and maturities range from 1 month to more than 10 years.

Bank *certificates of deposit (CDs)* are fixed-maturity time deposits placed with leading commercial banks. CDs in denominations over $100,000 usually are negotiable, meaning they can be sold in a secondary market prior to maturity. Maturities generally range from 90 to 360 days. CDs of the largest banks generally are considered to be money-market instruments and are marketable. Many banks issue CDs in denominations less than $100,000, although such certificates usually are not negotiable, and penalties are imposed if they are not held to maturity. Default risk is quite low, but not zero, as evidenced by the failures of some large banks in recent years. Yields are higher than those on Treasury securities and usually about equal to those on commercial paper (discussed below). Certificates of deposit have become the most widely used vehicle for temporarily storing idle cash funds.

Commercial paper—is short-term unsecured promissory notes of large corporations.

Commercial paper is short-term unsecured promissory notes of large corporations. We discussed commercial paper as a source of funds in Chapter 18. As an investment medium, we are interested in the commercial paper of other firms. Commercial paper is regularly issued by major finance companies, banks and bank-holding companies, and some nonfinancial firms. Denominations are usually larger than $100,000, and maturities range up to 270 days. Commercial paper is usually held to maturity because the secondary market is not well-developed.

Besides the principal alternatives discussed above, there are several others that meet our criteria but are less widely used. *Banker's acceptances* are drafts drawn against deposits in commercial banks. They are used as financing instruments in certain specialized lines of domestic and foreign trade. The draft has a specific payment date and, once accepted by the bank, becomes an obligation of the bank rather than of the initiating firm. By accepting the draft, the bank has guaranteed its payment at maturity. Yields are comparable to those on bank CDs, and maturities are usually less than 180 days.

Repurchase agreements are contracts whereby a firm lends by purchasing marketable securities (usually Treasury bills) from a borrower (often a bond dealer), with the agreement that the borrower will repurchase the securities at a specified price and time. The price difference represents interest earned by the lender. The arrangement provides great flexibility with respect to maturity, which usually is for periods of a few days to a week. Yields are comparable to those on Treasury bills.

State and local governments also issue debt securities that often meet our requirements. Income from such securities under present law is not taxable by the federal government. Yields are lower to reflect the tax advantage but often are higher on an after-tax basis than those on taxable securities. For example, suppose a firm was paying taxes at a 40 percent tax rate. If the firm bought a security paying 10 percent interest that was taxed, the firm would receive only $0.10(1 - 0.4) = 0.06$, or 6 percent, on an after-tax basis. A local-government debt security that was tax-exempt would have to pay only 6 percent to provide this same after-tax yield to the firm.

Eurodollar deposits are deposits (CDs of various maturities) denominated in dollars but held at branches of U.S. banks or other banks located *outside* the United States, principally in London but also in other European financial centers, the Caribbean, and Singapore. These deposits yield rates slightly above domestic U.S. CD rates; thus, this market is widely used by multinational corporations as a medium for placing temporarily idle funds. The principal reasons for the higher rate on Eurodollar deposits are that the depository banks face fewer regulations and restrictions on these deposits than on deposits in the United States. In short, their costs are lower, which allows them to offer depositors somewhat higher rates than can domestic U.S. banks. On the other hand, depositors require a slightly higher rate because the potential risks are also slightly higher. Among these risks are: (1) there is no federal insurance on funds deposited outside the United States; (2) there is no *legal* requirement for a U.S. parent bank to come to the aid of an overseas branch that may get into trouble; (3) no central bank is obligated to function as a lender of last resort should many Eurobanks get into trouble during periods of credit stringency or panic.

Money-market mutual funds—are funds set up to allow small investors to pool their funds to invest in money-market instruments in the required large denominations.

The **money-market mutual fund** is an important development in recent years. Money placed in such funds by shareholders is invested in money-market instruments of just the sort we are discussing here—U.S. Treasury bills, bank certificates of deposit, and commercial paper. Before the availability of the money-market funds, investments in high-yield money-market instruments were not available to small investors. The minimum denomination available in Treasury bills is $10,000 and in commercial paper is $100,000. Bank CDs are available in smaller denominations, but to get a true money-market yield requires a minimum purchase of $100,000—well beyond the means of most private individuals and small firms.

By means of the money-market fund, however, small investors can pool their funds and buy in the required large denominations. The funds also give the investor good diversification by holding a large number of different instruments.

The success of the money-market funds is evident from their dramatic growth. Starting at essentially zero in early 1978, the money-market funds grew to about $10 billion in assets by the end of that year, to $47 billion by the end of 1979, and to more than $230 billion by December 1982. At that time federally insured banks and thrift institutions first began to pay interest on demand deposits, and many experts predicted that money-market funds would no longer serve a purpose and would vanish. They did decline by 20 percent in 1983 but staged a comeback in 1984. In July 1985, money-market fund assets stood at $210 billion.[10]

Yields

All the characteristics we discussed above—default risk, maturity, and marketability—affect yields. In general, the lower the default risk and the better the marketability, the lower is the yield. Securities with these desirable characteristics have higher prices and (because price and yield are inversely related) lower yields.

The relationship between maturity and yield is more complex and changes over time. On an average, short maturities yield less, other factors being equal, because they are subject to less interest-rate risk. Rates on short maturities, however, are more volatile than those on longer maturities and at times exceed the latter.

---

[10]*Wall Street Journal*, March 13, 1981, April 22, 1983, and July 26, 1985; *Business Week*, July 29, 1985.

Finance in Practice 19—2

E. F. Hutton: Taking Cash Management Too Far

In May of 1985, E. F. Hutton, known to many as the stock brokerage firm "to whom people listen," pleaded guilty to 2,000 counts of mail and wire fraud involving overdrafts at as many as 400 banks where the firm had accounts between July 1980 and February 1982. Hutton's customers, employees, and many members of the investment community and the public at large were shocked. Fraud? E. F. Hutton?

The story made big news in both the general and financial press over the next several months. At first it appeared that the practices, while widespread at many Hutton branch offices, were carried out by overzealous local branch controllers and didn't have the sanction of top management. As the facts continued to unfold, however, allegations began to surface in the press that members of Hutton's top management indeed had known of the practices.

Many firms use zero-balance accounts, which are checking accounts at branch locations that are drawn to zero at the close of business each day. Hutton, according to press reports, was going much further and systematically *overdrawing* its bank accounts as part of its everyday operating procedure. The drawdown formula was intended to increase daily withdrawals in order to compensate Hutton for weekends and other times when it didn't have access to certain deposits. Such a practice might not be illegal, but Hutton apparently went even further by withdrawing from local accounts amounts it *expected* local customers to deposit during the next few days. Further, according to Hutton's plea filed with the Justice Department, company officials illegally transfered funds between branch offices by using some 50 elaborate chains around the country with the aim of delaying clearing of checks and increasing float. The objective of both the drawdown formula and the chaining, according to prosecutors, was to obtain interest-free loans amounting to hundreds of millions of dollars.

By mid-1985, the case still had not been settled, and new facts continued to emerge. It appeared, however, that a large number of U.S. banks had been defrauded of large amounts of money, perhaps totaling in the millions. Hutton set up a reserve of $8 million to pay claims filed by banks. Of the 400 banks involved, only about 50 actually filed claims. Some that did not file commented that reconstructing the exact amounts lost was too difficult. It may also be that some of the banks did not wish to admit that such practices could go on without their detecting them.

Regardless of how the case finally turns out, it is clear that Hutton was badly damaged by the scandal. Its reputation for honesty was sullied, and the judgment of its top officers was called into question. Hutton clearly had taken cash management well beyond the limits of proper business practice and had paid a heavy penalty for its transgression.

Source: The *Wall Street Journal*, July 5, 1985, p. 3, and July 25, 1985, p. 6.

At any point in time, rates on the major types of money-market securities discussed above are fairly close to one another. For equal maturities, the differentials usually are small and are due to small differences in default risk and marketability.

Over time, the entire structure of short-term rates varies significantly. Such variations are related to the business and monetary cycles, the demand for funds by individuals and firms, and the credit policies of the Federal Reserve, but the single most important factor is the rate of inflation. At the peak of the interest-rate cycle reached in 1974, money-market rates for business borrowers were close to 12 percent. Thereafter, rates fell rapidly to just under 5 percent at the end of 1976. After that, rates

Figure 19–5

Inflation and Nominal Interest Rates

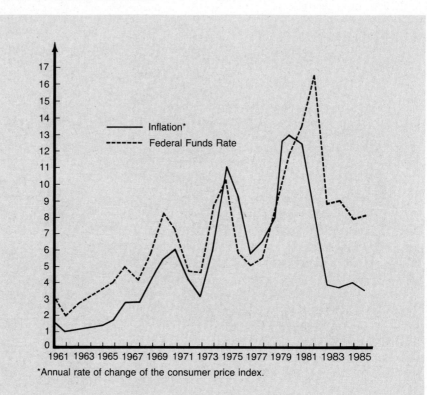

*Annual rate of change of the consumer price index.

Note: Inflation is measured as the annual rate of change of the Consumer Price Index.
Source: Salomon Brothers, *Comments on Credit* August 17, 1979; and Federal Reserve Bank of St. Louis.

An **interest-rate futures contract**—is an agreement to buy or sell a financial security in the future at an agreed-upon price and allows a manager to hedge against the risk of future rises or falls in interest rates by locking in today the price that must be paid in the future.

again rose, and during 1980 and 1981 the federal-funds rate was well into double-digit figures. Since that time, rates have declined substantially, and by mid 1986, money-market rates were down in the 6–7 percent range. It is clear that rising inflation rates played a key role in the rise of interest rates generally throughout the 1960s and 1970s, as indicated by Figure 19–5. Similarly, the relatively low level of inflation observed in recent years has been accompanied by declining interest rates.

Yields on money-market instruments tend to move together with a high degree of correlation for like maturities. Table 19–2 presents yield data as of one particular date—December 27, 1985. On other dates, the general level of rates would differ, but yields on these money-market securities would be quite close together.

As we have seen, the late 1970s and early 1980s brought significantly greater volatility to financial markets. Interest rates rose and fell with a frequency and magnitude not seen in recent history. Many managers of short-term funds began to see a need to protect themselves against changes in interest rates. A new tool appeared to serve this need: the **interest-rate futures contract**. Basically, the interest-rate futures contract

Table 19–2

Yields on Selected Money Market Instruments, December 27, 1985

Money Market Instruments	Yield on December 27, 1985 (percent)
90-day CDs	7.80
Prime commercial paper	7.86
Bankers acceptances	7.70
Federal funds	8.02
3-month Treasury bills	7.02
6-month Treasury bills	7.05
1-year Treasury bills	7.09

Source: Federal Reserve Bank of St. Louis, *U. S. Financial Data.*

gives a manager a way to contract to buy or sell debt instruments in the present at agreed-upon interest rates for future settlement. By using interest-rate futures, managers can hedge against the uncertainty of future changes in rates. We discussed financial futures in detail in Appendix 16A.

KEY CONCEPTS

1. Firms have two primary motives for holding cash and liquid assets: a transaction motive and a precautionary motive.

2. By speeding collections and controlling disbursements, firms can reduce their investment in working-cash balances. Such a reduction in working-cash balances allows the firm either to invest in interest-bearing marketable securities or to reduce its total financing needs and, hence, to save on financing costs.

3. The optimal working-cash balance is determined by trading off the transaction costs of holding too little cash against the opportunity costs of holding too much.

4. Two factors complicate the determination of the optimal working-cash balance: variability and uncertainty.

5. Criteria for selecting the best vehicle for investing idle cash include the amount of money available and the default risk, maturity, and marketability of the investment.

6. Yields on most short-term money-market instruments move together. The most important factor affecting the level of yields generally is inflation.

SUMMARY

The term *cash* in this chapter refers to total liquid assets, made up of working-cash balances plus interest-bearing marketable securities and deposits. Firms hold cash (liquid assets) for two primary reasons: to execute financial transactions and for precautionary purposes. The overall task of cash management comprises three steps: (1) collecting and disbursing funds efficiently,

(2) determining the appropriate working-cash balance, and (3) investing the remaining excess cash.

Steps to improve the efficiency of collection and disbursement must focus on the cash cycle of the firm. Concentration accounts can be used to reduce the requirement for working balances. Collection time can be reduced by the use of a lock-box system. Disbursements should be made within credit terms but no sooner than required.

A working-cash balance is required for transaction purposes. In some cases, bank compensating-balance requirements may determine the minimum working balance. Where this is not the case, finding the optimal balance involves a trade-off between transaction costs (high for low working balances) and opportunity costs (high for high working balances). By combining the qualitative insights from theoretical models with techniques such as cash budgeting and pro-forma analysis, most firms can arrive at reasonable answers with some experimentation.

Firms hold liquid assets over and above working-balance requirements for two main reasons: as temporarily idle transaction balances and as precautionary balances. Vehicles for investing such cash reserves should be evaluated on the basis of default risk, maturity, and marketability. Many alternatives exist, including U.S. Treasury bills, federal-agency issues, bank certificates of deposit, and commercial paper. Yields on such short-term money-market instruments vary over the business cycle and tend to average slightly less than those of longer-maturity issues.

QUESTIONS

1. What are the principal motives for holding cash and liquid assets?
2. From the standpoint of cash management, on what parts of the cash cycle (diagrammed in Figures 19–1 and 19–2) should attention focus?
3. What are the advantages of concentration banking?
4. How can a firm speed the collection of cash?
5. Suppose a firm's cash inflows and outflows are variable but completely predictable. How are the con-

cepts of inventory theory applicable to such a problem?
6. Suppose a firm's cash inflows and outflows are completely random. What approach might a firm use to set its minimum working balance?
7. Why might a firm have idle cash?
8. Discuss the criteria that a firm should use in choosing assets in which to invest idle cash.

PROBLEMS

1. The Uptown Supply Company has credit sales of $2 million per year. Collections average $8,000 per day with 250 working days assumed per year. Suppose Uptown could reduce its internal processing time by one day. What would be its annual savings, assuming a cost of funds of 12 percent?
2. The Monogram Company is a national retailing concern that sells primarily on a credit basis. Collections from the southern region average $100,000 a day, and the total *float* (amount of time it takes from payment mailing to the time when Monogram obtains the use of the funds) is averaging 5 days for customers in this area. The opportunity cost on short-term funds is considered to be 10 percent.
   a. An Atlanta bank has offered to set up a lock-box system which will reduce float by 3 days

but requires a compensating balance of $200,000. Would you recommend that Monogram accept the offer?
   b. The bank also proposes an alternative to the compensating-balance requirement of a flat annual fee of $10,000. Which option should Monogram prefer?
3. The Celec Company purchases $3 million of raw materials each year on terms of net 30. The purchasing agent currently is paying each invoice 20 working days after its date to make sure that payment is received by suppliers in 30 days. A study shows that payment could be delayed until the 25th working day and still leave enough time for receipt by the 30th day. How much would the company save annually by making this change, assuming an 11 percent cost of funds?

4. The MHF Company currently maintains an account with a Washington, D.C., bank for collections in the southeastern marketing area. The bank handles collections of $500,000 per day in return for a compensating balance of $300,000. The company is considering an alternative of opening two separate accounts in the southeastern area. It has been projected that total processing time could be reduced by 1½ days if accounts are maintained in a Richmond bank and an Atlanta bank, each requiring a $300,000 compensating balance. Would you recommend the two-bank system to MHF Company?

5. The Rice Company currently maintains a centralized billing system at its home office to handle average daily collections of $300,000. The total time for mailing, processing, and clearing has been estimated at 5 days.

a. If the firm's opportunity cost on short-term funds is 12 percent, how much is this time lag of 5 days costing the company?

b. If management has designed a system of lockboxes with regional banks that would reduce float by 2½ days and home office credit department expense by $30,000 annually, what is the largest total amount of required compensating balances that the firm should be willing to accept with the lockbox arrangement?

6. Creative Papers Inc., a nationwide wholesaler of paper supplies, currently has a centralized billing system costing $70,000 annually in record-keeping expenses with a collection float of 7 days. As the new treasurer of Creative Papers, you have been asked to evaluate two proposed cash-management systems. The concentration banking system would establish five regional banks to handle Creative's accounts and would require a minimum total compensating balance of $2 million. Collection float for this system is estimated to be 5 days. The lockbox system would establish 10 lockboxes throughout the country with collection float of 3 days. This system would require $3.5 million in compensating balances plus a $0.02 charge per check processed. Your assistant reports the average check from your customers is for $500, and the firm's opportunity costs on short-term funds is 8 percent. All sales are on credit. Assume 250 working days per year.

a. If average daily collections are $200,000, what is the annual cost of Creative's current system?

b. What must Creative's average daily collections be for the concentration system to be preferred to the current system? For the lockbox system to be preferred to the current system?

7. The Flyer Manufacturing Company has an account with a Philadelphia bank for collections in Flyer's northeast sales region. The bank charges the firm a flat annual fee of $20,000 plus a charge of $0.05 per check processed. Presently, annual credit sales are $50 million, and the typical check from customers is for $1,000. Flyer's opportunity cost on short-term funds is 11 percent. The Philadelphia bank has offered to set up a system of four lockboxes in return for $300,000 in compensating balances plus a charge of $0.03 per check processed. The boxes would be emptied three times daily and would reduce collection float by two days.

a. Would you recommend that Flyer accept the bank's offer? (Assume 250 working days per year.)

b. What is the largest total amount of required compensating balances that Flyer should be willing to accept for this new arrangement?

REFERENCES

Andrews, V. L. "Cash Management: An Overview for the Corporate Treasurer." *The First Report.* Atlanta, Ga.: First National Bank of Atlanta, undated.

Baumol, W. J. "The Transactions Demand for Cash: An Inventory Theoretic Approach." *Quarterly Journal of Economics* 66 (Nov. 1952): 545–556.

"Companies Learn to Live Without the Float." *Business Week* (September 26, 1983): 134.

Daellenbach, E. "Are Cash Management Models Worthwhile?" *Journal of Financial and Quantitative Analysis* 9 (Sept. 1974): 607–626.

Donaldson, G. *Strategy for Financial Mobility.* Homewood, Ill.: Richard D. Irwin. 1969.

Donoghue, W. E. *The Cash Management Manual.* Holliston, Mass.: Cash Management Institute, 1978.

Dufey, G., and I. H. Giddy. *The International Money Market.* Englewood Cliffs, N.J.: Prentice-Hall, 1978.

Gitman, L. J., D. K. Forrester, and J. R. Forrester. "Managing Cash Disbursement Float." *Financial Management* 5 (Summer 1976): 15–24.

Gitman, L. J., E. A. Moses, and I. T. White. "An Assessment of Corporate Cash Management Practices." *Financial Management* 8 (Spring 1979): 32–41.

Kolb, R. W. *Interest Rate Futures*. Richmond, Virginia: Robert F. Dame, Inc., 1982.

Kolb, R. W. *Understanding Futures Markets*. Chapter 5. Glenview, Illinois: Scott, Foresman and Company, 1985.

Maier, S. F., and J. F. Vander Weide. "A Practical Approach to Short-Run Financial Planning." *Financial Management* 7 (Winter 1978): 10–16.

Malkiel, B. G. *The Term Structure of Interest Rates*. Princeton, N.J.: Princeton University Press, 1966.

Mehta, D. R. *Working Capital Management*. Englewood Cliffs, N.J.: Prentice-Hall, 1974.

Miller, M. H., and D. Orr. "A Model of the Demand for Money by Firms." *Quarterly Journal of Economics* 80 (Aug. 1966): 413–435.

Nouss, R. M., and R. E. Markland. "Solving Lock-Box Location Problems." *Financial Management* 8 (Spring 1979): 21–31.

Orgler, Y. E. *Cash Management*. Belmont, Ca.: Wadsworth, 1970.

Vander Weide, J., and S. F. Maier. *Managing Corporate Liquidity*. New York: John Wiley and Sons, 1985.

20

Managing Accounts Receivable and Inventory

In this chapter we will learn how to apply the perspective of the financial manager to the task of managing two categories of assets that are vital to many firms: accounts receivable and inventories. We will learn how to calculate the expected return on the firm's investment in receivables and how changes in credit policy affect that return. We will apply this same technique to an individual account. Turning to inventory, we first will discuss the functions of inventory and explore relationships between key variables that determine optimal inventory levels. We then will calculate expected return on the investment in inventory and see how return varies with changes in the inventory level. Finally, we will discuss the relationship between expected return and required return for both accounts receivable and inventory.

In the last chapter we discussed a firm's cash-management policy. Two other important current assets for many firms are inventories and accounts receivable. The stock of inventories held by a firm and the amount of trade credit extended by a firm are *investments* in the sense that each represents a commitment of corporate funds (either of the firm's own capital or of borrowed funds) that the firm can expect to liquidate only at some later point or points in time. These working-capital investments differ from a firm's investment in fixed assets, such as plant and equipment, in only one respect: the average time lag between investment in working capital and its later recoupment is fairly short—a year or less—whereas the corresponding time lag for investment in fixed assets is considerably longer. In spite of this difference, funds committed to working-capital assets are investments, and financial management, therefore, has a responsibility to analyze these investments as carefully as it analyzes longer-term commitments to fixed assets. The benefits expected from any proposed increase in working-capital assets must be weighed against the cost to the firm of holding extra assets, including an allowance for the cost of any additional capital required. As a result, we can apply the principles developed in Part Four for analyzing these investments in working capital.

> **Inventories and accounts receivable are investments because both represent a commitment of funds that the firm can expect to liquidate only at some later periods in time.**

In many situations working-capital decisions are a source of potential conflict between financial managers and operating managers who are in charge of a firm's purchasing, production, and marketing departments. Consider a situation in which the marketing manager believes that the level of sales can be increased if the firm's credit policy is loosened—that is, if the firm extends credit to a wider range of customers or if it permits an easier collection policy for whatever credit it does extend. Even if the assumption is correct that such a change in credit policy will lead to an increase in sales volume, it does not necessarily follow that the firm should do what the marketing manager believes. For a marketing department, the maximization of sales volume is a natural and legitimate objective; for the firm, sales maximization is only a means to an end, and that end, as we saw in Chapter 1, is value maximization.

The loosening of credit terms may increase sales and, thus, provide gross benefits to the firm, but this loosening of credit is not costless. A likely consequence of the suggested change in credit policy is that accounts receivable will rise, and this rise imposes several kinds of cost:

1. As the firm's credit is extended to a wider group of buyers, the cost of credit analysis will rise, as will the cost of collecting, and most likely the cost of bad debts (credit that cannot be collected) will also rise.
2. The increase in accounts receivable has to be financed somehow. If the firm borrows the funds required, there is the out-of-pocket cost of the extra interest payments incurred.
3. If the firm finances the increase in accounts receivable out of its own funds, there is the opportunity cost that arises because funds used for this purpose cannot also be used in some other possibly lucrative way. Thus, the opportunity cost of using one extra dollar to fund an increase in accounts receivable would be the rate of return that the firm has to forgo on the best alternative use available for this dollar.

If it is estimated that the three costs together will exceed the benefits to be derived from increased sales, the suggested change in credit policy would not be a wise move. On the other hand, if benefits promise to exceed costs, the change would increase the firm's net wealth and should be pursued. The important point is that someone within the firm should be there to press the case for the firm's overall objective as opposed to subordinate objectives, such as sales maximization. Usually this function belongs to the financial manager. In this particular situation, it is his or her duty to see that credit policy and, hence, the level of trade credit extended (or the level of accounts receivable) is expanded as long as such an expansion contributes *net benefits* to the firm. It is also his or her duty to see that credit expansion does not proceed beyond this point. Thus, the financial manager's function is to ensure that the firm's investment in accounts receivable is at its optimum level. As we will see later, the same objective holds for the firm's investment in inventories.

> **The financial manager's function is to ensure that the firm's investment in accounts receivable and inventory is at its optimum level—the level that maximizes the value of the firm.**

Credit policy—is the set of decisions made about credit standards, credit terms, and collection policy.

Taking the viewpoint of the financial manager, we will analyze changes in the level of accounts receivable and inventory as *investment decisions* using wealth maximization for the firm as a whole as our decision criterion. Increases in inventory or accounts receivable are investments that should be undertaken only if the expected rate of return on such new investment exceeds the required rate of return.

INVESTING IN ACCOUNTS RECEIVABLE

A firm's **credit policy** consists of the set of decisions it makes about credit standards, credit terms, and collection policy.

Credit Policy

Credit standards—are criteria and guidelines used by a firm to decide to which accounts it will extend credit.

Credit standards are the criteria and guidelines used by a firm to decide to which accounts it will or will not extend credit. When the standards are applied to a credit applicant, a yes or no decision can be made.

Credit terms include both the length of the credit period and the discount offered. The *credit period* is the period over which credit is granted, usually measured in days from the date of the invoice. Terms of *net 30*, for example, mean that payment is due 30 days from the date of the invoice. If a *prompt-payment discount* is offered, both the amount and the discount period must be specified. Terms of *2/10, net 30* indicate that a 2 percent cash discount may be taken if payment is made within 10 days of the invoice date; otherwise the net (full) amount is due in 30 days.

Credit terms—include the length of the credit period and the discount offered.

Collection policy refers to procedures undertaken to collect accounts that have not been paid within the specified period. Included might be letters, telephone calls, personal visits, and legal action. These procedures normally are the province of the credit manager and concern the financial manager only to the extent that they affect the volume of accounts receivable.

Collection policy—is the set of procedures undertaken to collect accounts that have not been paid within the specified period.

We will refer to credit standards, credit terms, and collection policy collectively as the *credit policy* of the firm. A *loosening* of credit policy is a change toward less rigorous standards in granting credit, more liberal credit terms, or less vigorous collection policies. A *tightening* of credit policy is a change in the opposite direction.

Credit Policy and Return on Investment

Bad-debt expense—is the cost associated with customers who default on their payments.

Taken together, the elements of credit policy are key factors in determining the magnitude of the firm's investment in accounts receivable and the return on that investment. To examine this relationship, consider a firm pursuing a particular credit policy—Policy A. As the policy is applied, certain accounts are accepted, and others are rejected. Of those accepted, some will pay regularly on time, some will pay late, and some will default, giving rise to **bad-debt expense**. Of those rejected, some might have been good accounts if credit had been granted. Thus, any given credit policy results in many correct decisions but also is likely to result in two types of errors: (1) accepting some bad accounts that should have been rejected, and (2) rejecting some accounts that would have been good. Changing credit policy alters the mix of the two kinds of errors: loosening the policy increases type (1) errors and reduces type (2) errors; tightening credit policy does the opposite.

> **Any given credit policy will result in accepting some accounts that should have been rejected and rejecting some that should have been accepted.**

Each type of error has costs associated with it: type (1) errors incur bad-debt and related expenses, and type (2) errors incur the opportunity cost of contribution forgone. Thus, associated with Policy A is a particular level of bad-debt expense and a particular level of opportunity loss arising from the contribution forgone on good accounts that were rejected. Also associated with Policy A is some level of expense for credit analysis and collection.

Now suppose that credit policy is loosened, and a new policy—Policy B—is adopted. Some accounts now are granted credit that did not qualify under Policy A. Because these accounts lie outside previously established guidelines for credit extension, each new extension requires more careful credit analysis. Thus, the new accounts presumably have a higher default rate, so bad-debt expense rises, as do expenses of analysis and collection. Lost contribution, however, declines. Figure 20–1 represents these relationships graphically and shows credit policy as a continuum, ranging from tight to loose. As policy becomes progressively looser, accounts receivable expand. Each increment of new accounts to which credit is granted contains fewer good accounts and more bad accounts. Expenses of analysis, collection, and bad debts, therefore, rise at an increasing rate, and lost contribution declines at a decreasing rate. The sum of these costs is the total operating cost of having a particular credit policy and is shown in Figure 20–1 as the U-shaped curve labeled *total operating cost*. A point is reached, at C^*, where the sum of total operating costs is minimized. If the firm loosens credit policy beyond C^*, the additional contribution from the new accounts is less than the additional expense of analysis, collection, and bad debts. Hence, at C^*, operating profit is maximized.

> **A looser credit policy increases costs of analysis, collection, and bad debts and reduces the opportunity cost of lost contribution.**

Figure 20–1
Credit Policy and Costs

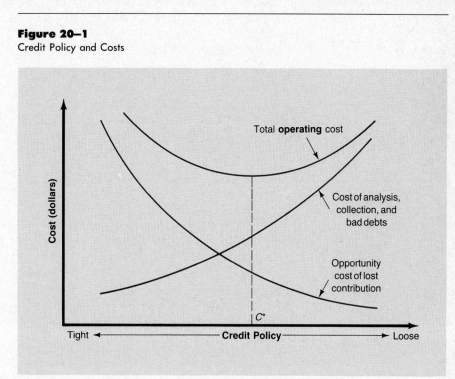

Does C^* in Figure 20–1 represent the optimal credit policy? It does not, for two reasons. First, the profits to be earned at C^* are *expected* profits. The figure is subject to uncertainty and may turn out higher or lower than expected. The analysis of Figure 20–1, thus, takes us to the point of maximum expected profits, but does not take *risk* into account. Second, at C^*, we maximize expected *operating* profit. We have given no consideration to the *investment* necessary to generate those operating profits and to the return required by those who finance the investment. Suppose, for example, that a firm can increase its operating profit by $1 if it invests $1 million of its own funds to finance an additional $1 million worth of accounts receivable. Obviously, this investment would not be optimal even though it leads to an increase in operating profit! We can remedy both of these difficulties by expanding the analysis to consider *return on investment*. When we do so, we will find that the optimal policy is to the left of C^*— that is, somewhat tighter.

As we noted in Chapter 7, return on investment can be measured in many ways. The measure we will use in this chapter is consistent with that used in our discussion of investment decisions in Part Four. The abbreviation *ROI* sometimes is used to refer to the *accounting rate of return*, which is useful as a performance measure, but not as a decision criterion. To avoid confusion with the accounting rate of return and to be consistent with terminology used elsewhere in this book, we will avoid the symbol *ROI* and refer to return on investment as the **expected rate of return**, or $E(R)$.

The **expected rate of return**—is the rate of return an investor expects to gain from an investment; the mean value of the probability distribution of expected returns.

Table 20–1

Fixed and Variable Costs for Delta Electric Company (percent of sales)

	Total Costs	Fixed Costs	Variable Costs
Cost of goods sold	87.0	—	87.0
Warehousing	5.1	2.9	2.2
Selling	4.4	0.3	4.1
Administration	1.1	1.0	0.1
Bad debts	0.13	—	0.13
Collection	0.04	—	0.04
Total costs	97.77	4.2	93.57
Operating profit	2.23		

Calculating Expected Return

Let us illustrate the calculation of expected return on investment in accounts receivable with an example. In this section we will focus on after-tax profits. In a later section, we will analyze the same problem using the discounted-cash-flow techniques developed in Parts Two and Four.

The Delta Electric Company is a large distributor of electrical parts and equipment with facilities in 14 states. In 1986, Delta Electric's sales totaled $46 million, and after-tax profits totaled slightly more than $1 million. Delta Electric's profit margins had declined over 1985 and 1986, and the credit manager believed that one reason was that credit policy was too loose. The manager identified a group of accounts that might have been considered marginal prospects and recommended that policy be tightened to eliminate them. Sales to this group of marginal accounts amounted to about 10 percent of Delta Electric's total sales, or about $4,600,000. Sales to the remaining good accounts made up the remainder, $41,400,000.

The financial manager decided to calculate the return on investment in these accounts. The first step was to examine the behavior of Delta Electric's costs if the accounts were to be eliminated entirely, in order to get a clear comparison between a tighter credit policy and existing policies. Using historical data on costs and past knowledge of the business, the financial manager developed the data in Table 20–1.

The financial manager believed that if some of the marginal accounts were eliminated, fixed costs would remain unchanged and, hence, that only the costs identifiable as variable would decline. The financial manager believed further that bad debt and collection expense were almost entirely attributable to the marginal accounts. Using this information, the manager allocated Delta Electric's income and expense between marginal accounts and good accounts as shown in Table 20–2.

As shown in Table 20–1, cost of goods sold is entirely variable. Hence, in Table 20–2 both good and marginal accounts have cost of goods sold of 0.87 times sales. Warehousing, on the other hand, is part fixed and part variable. The fixed portion amounts to 2.9 percent of sales (from Table 20–1), or $0.029 \times \$46,000,000 =$

Table 20–2

Comparison of Good with Marginal Accounts at Delta Electric Company, 1986

	Fraction of Sales	All Accounts (thousands of dollars)	Good Accounts (thousands of dollars)	Marginal Accounts (thousands of dollars)
Sales		46,000	41,400	4,600
Cost of goods sold	0.87	40,020	36,018	4,002
Gross profit		5,980	5,382	598
Warehousing expense				
Fixed	0.029	1,334	1,334	—
Variable	0.022	1,012	911	101
Selling expense				
Fixed	0.003	138	138	—
Variable	0.041	1,886	1,697	189
Administration expense				
Fixed	0.01	460	460	—
Variable	0.001	46	41	5
Bad debts	0.0013	60	—	60
Collection	0.0004	20	—	20
Total operating expense		4,956	4,581	375
Operating profit		1,024	801	223

$1,334,000. This fixed cost presumably would not disappear if the marginal accounts were dropped, so the $1,334,000 is allocated in Table 20–2 entirely to good accounts. Variable warehousing costs of 2.2 percent are allocated to both categories. This variable cost, then, is $0.022 \times \$41,400,000 = \$910,800$ in the case of good accounts and is $0.022 \times \$4,600,000 = \$101,200$ in the case of marginal accounts. This allocation assumes that, if the marginal accounts were dropped, costs would decline by $101,200, but $910,800 of the variable costs would continue. In Table 20–2, these figures are rounded to the nearest thousand.

Selling and administrative expenses are allocated in a similar manner, with the entire fixed portion allocated to good accounts, and the variable portion allocated to both categories. Bad-debt and collection expenses are assumed entirely attributable to marginal accounts. Adding up the figures shows that, of the total operating expense of $4,956,000, $4,581,000 is identified with the good accounts, and $375,000 is associated with the marginal accounts.

Assuming that the allocations shown in Table 20–2 are approximately correct, what conclusions should the financial manager draw from these figures? The profit margin from the two sets of accounts can be calculated from the sales and operating-profit data as shown in Table 20–3.

In other words, the marginal clients accounted for only 10 percent of sales, but they provided about 22 percent of total operating profit (from Table 20–2, $223,000/1,024,000 = 0.218$). Because most of Delta Electric's credit-management costs are incurred anyway in order to service the good accounts, the *incremental* profits contributed by the marginal accounts provided a significant addition to the company's total operating profits.

Table 20–3

The Profit Margin on Delta Electric Company's Good Accounts and Marginal Accounts

Accounts	Sales Volume (thousands of dollars)	Operating Profit (thousands of dollars)	Profit Margin (percent)
Good	41,400	801	1.94
Marginal	4,600	223	4.85

Calculating the Investment in Receivables

In order to complete the preliminary analysis, it is necessary to estimate the level of additional *investment* the firm had to make to sell and service the so-called marginal accounts. Delta Electric's credit files indicated that the receivables balance on marginal accounts averaged $567,000 during 1986. However, this figure overstates the amount the firm had to invest in accounts receivable in order to achieve its sales to the marginal accounts because this $567,000 figure includes a profit margin on sales, which does not constitute funds actually invested by Delta Electric. Only the *variable-cost* component of accounts receivable on the marginal accounts represents funds actually invested, or put at risk, by Delta Electric in order to sell to the marginal accounts.

From our discussion above, we see that marginal accounts generated pretax profits of $223,000 on sales of $4,600,000—a profit margin of 4.85 percent. Thus, 4.85 percent of the earnings on marginal accounts is profit, and the remaining 95.2 percent is variable cost. Hence, about 95.2 percent of $567,000 (about $540,000) represents the average amount the firm had to risk in order to sell to its marginal accounts, or the amount Delta Electric had *invested* in the marginal accounts.

The pretax return per dollar of investment, then, is annual pretax operating profit divided by total investment, or

$$\$223,000/\$540,000 = 41.3 \text{ percent.}$$

To determine the after-tax return on investment, we can multiply this 41.3 percent times $(1 - T)$, which is

$$0.413 \times (1 - 0.46) = 0.223, \text{ or } 22.3 \text{ percent.}$$

Our calculations show that the after-tax return on the marginal accounts was 22.3 percent per year. If Delta Electric made future sales to these marginal accounts and had no reason to expect changes from past experience, the expected rate of return, $E(R)$, on such new sales would also be 22.3 percent. If Delta Electric's management views a 22.3 percent return as attractive, the preliminary analysis above indicates that the financial manager might consider a move to loosen credit policy still further rather than a move toward a tighter policy.

Refining the Analysis

Before making a decision about Delta Electric's credit policy, further refinements of the analysis are possible, and in many situations such refinements are necessary.

First, the above calculation of the required investment included only accounts receivable. In practice, expanding the level of sales to include the marginal accounts would probably require some increase in the level of inventories held as well as some increase in operating cash balances, and these increases are also relevant elements in estimating the total investment required. Of course, any increase in accounts payable or other accruals would provide an offset.

Second, we have also assumed that the fixed costs shown in Table 20—1 would, in fact, remain fixed even if sales to marginal accounts are expanded. (Recall that the manager had determined that they were fixed with respect to a decline in sales, but he had not explicitly considered an increase in sales.)

Refining our estimates to include these two considerations would probably give us a figure somewhat below 22.3 percent per annum for the expected after-tax operating rate of return from our incremental sales to more marginal accounts. Our final step would be to ask the critical question: Given the riskiness of the marginal accounts, is the prospective after-tax return adequate to justify the investment? Is the expected return sufficient to compensate for the risks? After all, 22.3 percent (or whatever the adjusted rate might be) is the expected, or most likely, return, but it is not guaranteed. This final issue leads us directly to the central question: How should the proper goal of credit policy be defined?

Goal of Credit Policy

The **marginal expected return**—is the expected rate of return on incremental investment.

We noted earlier that expenses of analysis, collection, and bad debts rise at an increasing rate as credit policy is loosened. If Delta Electric were to loosen its policy, these expenses would rise relative to the new sales generated, and the expected rate of return, $E(R)$, on the newly made investment in accounts receivable accompanying the new sales would be lower than the expected return on previous investments in accounts receivable. The expected return on the *new*, or incremental, investment is the **marginal expected return**. In general, we would expect the marginal expected return to become lower and lower as the firm loosened its credit policy. Figure 20–2 illustrates this fall in marginal expected return. With a relatively tight credit policy—say, at point A in Figure 20–2—the expected return on new sales created by looser credit policy might be quite high. Having relaxed credit policy somewhat—say, by moving from A to B in the graph, any further relaxation of credit policy by moving to the right of B would bring in accounts with higher expenses of analysis, collection, and bad debts. As a result, at B, the marginal expected return on new investment in accounts receivable would be lower than the marginal expected return at point A.

How far should credit policy be pushed? At this point, we can give only a qualitative answer: credit policy should be set at the point where the marginal expected return on additional investment in receivables just equals the return required by those who supply the firm's funds—the lenders and investors. At that point, the value of the firm is maximized. We will come back to the question of the required rate of return later in this chapter after we discuss investment in inventory.

Credit policy often is viewed as a marketing tool with the purpose of expanding sales. The objective of credit policy is to maximize the value of the firm. Clearly, the goal is not to maximize sales, and just as clearly it is not to minimize bad-debt expense. To maximize sales, the firm would sell to anyone on credit; to minimize bad-debt expense, it would sell to no one. Nor does the optimum occur at the point where

Figure 20–2
Credit Policy and Expected Rate of Return

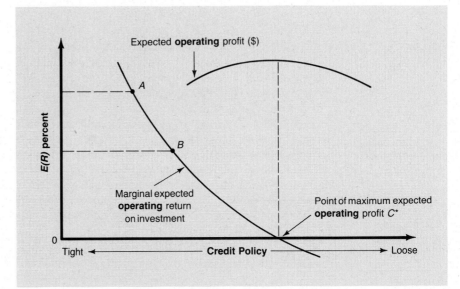

expected operating profits are maximized—point C^* in Figure 20–1. Figure 20–2 shows that when policy is loosened, operating profits increase continuously up to a point as new accounts are added. Before the point of maximum profit is reached, the incremental profit, though still positive, has fallen below that necessary to compensate those who finance the additional investment. In other words, expected return falls below the required rate at a point to the left of C^* both in Figure 20–1 and in Figure 20–2. At the point of maximum expected operating profit, C^*, the marginal expected operating rate of return has dropped to zero, providing no return to the extra investment in accounts receivable.

> **The goal of credit policy is to maximize the value of the firm. The optimal policy is the one at which the marginal expected return on incremental investment in receivables equals the required rate.**

To use a rate-of-return approach to establish credit policy, we must be able to define specific policy alternatives. We then must identify specific accounts or categories of accounts that would be sold under one policy but not under another. Costs must be separated into fixed and variable components. Incremental earnings and investment under various policy alternatives then can be calculated.

Applying Discounted-Cash-Flow Techniques to Credit Policy

In the foregoing analysis, we looked at after-tax profitability as a result of credit-policy decisions. Alternatively, we could analyze the example presented in Tables 20–1 and

Table 20–4

Discounted-Cash-Flow Analysis of Delta Electric Company's Credit Policy (thousands of dollars)

Cash Flows on Day 0 of 45-Day Period	Cash Flows on Day 45 of 45-Day Period
− $4,002 Cost of goods sold	+ $4,600.00
− 101 Warehousing expense	− 60.00 Bad debts
− 189 Selling expense	$4,540.00 Accounts collected
− 5 Administrative expense	− 20.00 Collection costs
− $4,297 Net cash outlay	+ $4,520.00 Net collections
	− 102.58 Taxes, 0.46($223)*
	$4,417.42 Net cash inflow

*Note that taxes are levied on the operating profit of $223,000 from Table 20–2.

20–2 using discounted-cash-flow (DCF) techniques.[1] In this case, the time period is short, and there are few (if any) noncash charges, so the results will not differ substantially from the prior calculations.

To use DCF techniques, we must isolate the after-tax cash flows associated with marginal accounts. To simplify matters, let us assume that for the marginal accounts, all expenditures for cost of goods sold, warehousing, selling, and administration are cash expenses incurred at one point in time. At the end of a waiting period, the accounts are collected less any bad debts, collection costs, and taxes—all assumed to occur at the end of the period. We'll assume that the marginal accounts remained outstanding for 45 days on average. We use 45 days because Delta Electric had receivables on marginal accounts averaging $567,000 during 1986 when sales due to these accounts were $4,600,000 per year, and $4,600,000/365 = $12,602 per day. The receivables, thus, represented 45 days of sales ($567,000/$12,602 per day = 45 days).

With these assumptions, we can calculate the after-tax cash flows on the marginal accounts as presented in Table 20–4. We have assumed that there are no noncash expenses attributable to these accounts. For example, there are no new depreciation charges as a result of these accounts.

We see that Delta Electric spends $4,297,000 at time 0 to receive $4,417,420 45 days later. This credit policy represents a one-period investment project with an internal rate of return, r, for 45 days that we can calculate as

$$-\$4,297,000 + \frac{\$4,417,420}{(1 + r)} = 0$$

$$r = \frac{\$4,417,420}{\$4,297,000} - 1$$

$$= 0.028 = 2.8 \text{ percent}$$

---

[1]This section on applying discounted-cash-flow techniques may be skipped if the reader has not yet covered Parts Two and Four of the text.

To put this rate on an annual basis, we can assume that this process repeats itself every 45 days, or about 8 times a year, because $365/45 = 8.1$. The annualized internal rate of return *(IRR)* can be calculated as

$$(1 + 0.028)^8 = (1 + IRR)$$

$$IRR = (1 + 0.028)^8 - 1$$

$$= 0.247 = 24.7 \text{ percent}$$

The 24.7 percent per year is the after-tax internal rate of return on Delta Electric's marginal accounts. Note that this rate is quite close to the 22.3 percent figure we calculated earlier using after-tax profits divided by investment in inventory. In fact, the only reason for differences involves slightly different assumptions about the timing of cash flows and the treatment of compounding. Remember, however, that we chose an example in which there were no major noncash expenses or long time periods between expenses and revenues.

The question that still remains is whether the internal rate of return alone is sufficient to justify the credit decision. This *IRR* is the expected return on the investment in receivables. A final step is the comparison of the expected return to the required return, which we will discuss later in this chapter.

IMPLEMENTING CREDIT POLICY

Once credit policy has been formulated, it must be translated into operational guidelines for use by the sales and credit departments. Of particular importance are credit standards for selecting individual accounts, because it is through individual decisions, account by account, that policy is implemented.

Selecting Individual Accounts

In principle, the correct approach to selecting accounts is to calculate expected return on each and make a judgment as to whether this expected return is above the required rate. Calculated expected return on an individual account follows the same general procedure as that discussed above for groups of accounts. Expected earnings are estimated over some convenient period, usually a year, and the investment necessary to generate those earnings is determined. Here again, the relevant investment amount is the out-of-pocket cash investment that the firm actually will have at risk at any point in time.

Sample Problem 20–1

Analyzing the Tarheel Industries Account for Chatham Supply Company

Suppose Tarheel Industries requests open-account credit of $2,500 from Chatham Supply Company for purchase of parts. Chatham estimates that the account will turn over four times per year; that is, it will generate $10,000 per year in sales volume. Chatham's gross margin on the parts to be sold is 20 percent, and commissions to sales representatives are 2 percent. There are no other variable costs associated with taking on the account. What would be the pretax rate of return on the account? What would be the after-tax rate of return on the account?

Solution

We begin by estimating the profit Chatham would earn over a year's time. Gross profit is 20 percent of sales, or $2,000; subtracting the 2 percent sales commissions leaves a profit before tax of $2,000 − $200 = $1,800. To simplify things, let us assume that Tarheel Industries orders $2,500 worth of parts, pays for them 45 days later, and then in another 45 days places another order, repeating this process four times per year. While credit is outstanding, Chatham's investment would be determined by subtracting profit of 20 percent (0.2 × $2,500 = $500) from the $2,500 order and adding sales commissions of 2 percent (0.02 × $2,500 = $50). Thus, $2,500 − $500 + $50 = $2,050.

During the periods when Tarheel Industries has purchased goods but has not yet paid for them, Chatham has out-of-pocket investment at risk of $2,050. But during 45 days of each 90-day period, Tarheel Industries owes nothing. So the *average* investment over the year is only $2,050/2 = $1,025. The expected rate of return on investment, then, is $1,800/$1,025 = 175 percent before taxes. Not bad, and probably good enough to induce Chatham to do business with Tarheel. Even if taxes are 46 percent, this return is 175(1 − 46) = 94.5 percent after taxes.

The figure of 175 percent, of course, assumes that Tarheel stays in business for a year and pays its bills. Thus, 175 percent, or 94.5 percent after taxes, is the *prospective* return if everything works out as planned. If all of Chatham's accounts actually returned this much, Chatham's owners would get very rich. The problem, of course, is that some accounts will not pay on time or perhaps at all. ∃⫿⊏

Discriminant analysis—is a technique for discriminating between good and bad accounts based on certain readily available financial data, such as firm size, acid-test ratio, or accounts-payable payment period.

Calculating expected return on individual accounts is expensive and often cannot be justified on every account. If groups of accounts with similar characteristics can be identified in terms of the product mix sold to the accounts and the rate of sales, shortcuts may be possible. For example, it may be found that in a particular group of accounts, the only major difference among accounts is in probability of default. It might be possible to calculate a target default probability at which point the expected return falls below the required rate. Accounts then would be analyzed only to estimate default probability, with those above the target rejected and those below accepted.

> **Although credit policy is implemented by making decisions on individual accounts, sometimes it is advisable to set standards and targets for categories of accounts.**

Credit scoring—is a technique for discriminating between good and bad accounts in which selection criteria are developed by relating past default experience to certain characteristics of the applicant, applicants are scored, and a decision is made based on a predetermined cutoff point.

Other more sophisticated techniques are available. **Discriminant analysis** is a technique for discriminating between good and bad accounts based on certain readily available financial data such as firm size, acid-test ratio, or accounts-payable payment period. The development of a model based on discriminant analysis involves complex statistical techniques but may be worthwhile for large firms that can justify the development expense.

A similar technique, known as **credit scoring**, has been employed with some success in consumer credit. In this approach, selection criteria are developed by relating past default experience to certain characteristics of the applicant, such as age, marital status, income, net worth, house ownership, and so on. New applicants then are scored, and a decision is made based on a predetermined cutoff point. Like discriminant analysis, the objective of credit scoring is to reduce the expense of selecting accounts that have a high likelihood of meeting the return criterion.

Monitoring Payment Patterns

Payment patterns by customers affect both the investment in accounts receivable and the return on that investment. It is, therefore, necessary to monitor payment patterns closely to detect any changes that might be occurring because of a recession, a change in the application of credit policy, or for other reasons.

In Chapter 7, we discussed two measures for use in evaluating a firm's collection of receivables: **days sales outstanding (DSO)** and the accounts-receivable **aging schedule**. These two measures are widely used and are perfectly adequate in many situations, but in some they are not.

Days sales outstanding is calculated by dividing the accounts-receivable balance at any point in time by credit sales per day. The DSO figure, thus, depends on three main factors: sales rate, averaging period (whether the most recent month, quarter, or year), and underlying pattern of payment by customers. This third factor is the one we wish to monitor, but changes in the sales rate or averaging period can produce widely varying DSO figures even when the underlying payment pattern remains stable.[2] In a firm with a seasonal sales pattern, for example, DSO figures will vary over the year even when the payment pattern remains unchanged.

The aging schedule suffers from the same difficulty. For example, the percentage of accounts less than, say, 30 days old will increase during periods when the sales rate rises and decrease when the sales rate declines. An aging schedule in a seasonal firm, thus, will be different at different times during the year, even when payment patterns are stable.

In many applications, DSO and the aging schedule are adequate measures of payment patterns. Where a more refined technique is needed, a useful approach is to identify receivables as to the month of origination—that is, the month in which the sale was made. In this way, the proportion of receivables arising from each prior month can be monitored. One way to organize the data is shown in Table 20–5.[3] The left-hand column of the table lists the month in which the original sales were made, and the column heads indicate the calendar month in which the receivables remain outstanding. Thus, for example, the figure of 19 percent in the bottom of the January column tells us that 19 percent of the sales made in November (2 months before January) were still outstanding and uncollected at the end of January. An increase in the fraction of receivables outstanding implies a corresponding *decrease* in payments received. These data indicate that Delta Electric's customers slowed their payments somewhat in February and March and then accelerated again in April. By identifying receivables balances by month of origination, changes in payment pattern can be detected.

Days sales outstanding (DSO)—is the ratio of accounts receivable to credit sales per day.

An **aging schedule**—is a technique for analyzing accounts receivable by cataloging receivables outstanding according to due dates.

---

[2]For a good discussion of this problem, see Wilber G. Lewellen and Robert W. Johnson, "Better Way to Monitor Accounts Receivable," *Harvard Business Review* 50,3 (May/June 1972): 101–109.

[3]The approach discussed here is that recommnded by Lewellen and Johnson, "Better Way to Monitor Accounts Receivable." See also B. K. Stone, "The Payments Approach to the Forecasting and Control of Accounts Receivable," *Financial Management* 5 (Autumn 1976): 65–82. Stone provides a good discussion of the relationship between the receivables-balance fraction outstanding (as in Table 20–5) and the payment proportion—the fraction of an account paid in each month following a sale.

Table 20–5
Receivables as a Percent of Original Sales for Delta Electric Company

Period Used as Sales Base	Receivables Outstanding as of Month End (percent of sales base)				
	January	February	March	April · · · December
Same month	89	91	93	90	90
One month before	62	65	67	61	63
Two months before	19	23	27	22	21

Measures such as days sales outstanding and aging schedules must be used with caution, especially in firms with seasonal sales patterns.

Credit-Department Procedures

Credit-department procedures are the province of the credit manager, but because the credit function often is under the overall supervision of the financial manager, we will touch briefly on these procedures.

Activities of the credit department fall into two main categories: credit analysis and collection. Credit analysis determines the selection of accounts—that is, the decision of whether or not to grant credit. In establishing procedures, a benefit/cost point of view must be maintained. Analysis is expensive, and care must be taken to see that the costs of the analysis and selection procedure do not exceed the potential earnings. The extent of the effort devoted to individual accounts must be related to the size of the account or the order and to its riskiness—although the latter cannot be determined until some analysis is performed. Ideally, we would like to devote little effort to accounts of very low and very high risk, and concentrate on those in the middle. The performance measures discussed in Part Three often are useful for making preliminary judgments as to whether further analysis is justified. Where detailed analysis is appropriate, the approaches discussed earlier in this chapter are applicable.

Analysis must begin with information, and the starting point usually is the applicant's own financial statements. Also very useful are specialized sources, such as Dun and Bradstreet, who provide a *credit-reference book* containing basic data on line of business, net worth, and credit rating for a large number of firms. Dun and Bradstreet *credit reports* then provide much more detailed data on individual firms. Other sources of credit information include local credit bureaus, banks, and other firms.

Collection procedures also are an important area of concern to the credit manager. Collection normally becomes an issue only after an account is past due. A basic question, therefore, is how long an account should be allowed to go past due before collection procedures are initiated. Many techniques then can be applied, including letters, telephone calls, personal visits, and finally a collection agency or legal action. The guiding principle in deciding how far to go to collect an account is benefits versus costs. Collection is expensive, and we do not want to spend $200 to collect a $100 account.

Evaluating the Credit Function

Evaluating the credit function in a firm is an important responsibility of the financial manager. The responsibility includes both the evaluation of credit policy and the performance of the credit department itself in executing the policy.

From our earlier discussion, it is apparent that neither sales nor bad-debt expense can be used as a guide in evaluating credit policy. The proper criterion is expected return on investment, and the firm's investment in receivables must be analyzed periodically to ensure that expected-return guidelines are being met. In evaluating rate of return, the costs of the credit department itself must be taken into account.

INVESTING IN INVENTORY

Inventories represent another important use of a firm's funds and are, therefore, an important concern of the financial manager. At any point in time, a firm has a given investment in inventory. For example, if a merchandising firm purchases $1 million worth of goods for later resale at a profit, that holding of goods should be viewed as an investment—that is, a commitment of funds now in the expectation of subsequent recoupment. As in the case of accounts receivable, we will view a decision to expand inventories as an investment decision. Again, we will use valuation as our basic conceptual framework and will define the financial manager's responsibility as making sure that inventories are set at the level that maximizes the value of the firm. As with receivables, we will find that the marginal expected return on investment in inventory declines as inventory is increased and that the optimum lies at the point at which marginal expected return equals the rate required by suppliers of funds.

Functions of Inventory

Raw materials—are materials, parts, and subassemblies that are purchased from others and that become part of the final product a firm produces.

Work in process—is goods in various stages of production.

Finished goods—are completed products awaiting sale.

Inventories of manufacturing firms can usefully be classified in three categories: raw materials, work in process, and finished goods. **Raw materials** are materials, parts, and subassemblies that are purchased from others and that become a part of the final product. Usually excluded from raw materials are supplies, such as pencils and paper clips, that are consumed but not in the manufacturing process. **Work in process** is goods in various stages of production. **Finished goods** are completed products awaiting sale.

The inventory of a wholesaler or retailer, as opposed to a manufacturer, normally would consist of only a single category—goods purchased from others for resale. Among manufacturers, the mix of the three types of inventory varies with the nature of the business. Proximity of raw-material supplies, length of the manufacturing process, and durability or perishability of the final product are all determinants. Manufacturers of machine tools or aircraft produced to customer order have large work-in-process inventories and relatively small finished-goods inventories. Manufacturers of off-the-shelf hardware items, such as hammers and screwdrivers, with short production times and low perishability and obsolescence are likely to maintain larger finished-goods inventories.

Each of the three types of inventory performs a different function. Work in process (WIP) inventory is necessary because production processes are not instantaneous. The total WIP inventory that a firm carries depends on the technology of the business and the firm's efficiency of production.

Raw-material and finished-goods inventories act as *buffers* to *decouple* the various activities of the firm so that all do not have to proceed at exactly the same rate. Raw-material inventories serve to decouple purchasing and production. If no raw-material stocks were maintained, purchases would have to be made continuously at exactly the rate of usage in production. Not only would ordering costs be quite high under such a system, but the firm would be unable to take advantage of quantity discounts on purchases.

Finished-goods inventories serve to decouple production and sales. When the most efficient production rate is faster than the sales rate, it is advantageous to produce for a period of time, letting finished-goods inventories build, and then to shut down production for a time. A firm with a seasonal sales pattern may find level production advantageous. Finished-goods inventories absorb unexpected changes in either sales or production rates resulting from recession, unexpected demand, strikes, or production delays.

> **The basic function of inventory is to decouple the major activities of the firm—purchasing, production, and sales—so that all do not have to proceed at the same rate.**

When friction exists in the form of ordering and setup costs, holding inventories becomes advantageous, even in a world of certainty. When we add uncertainty, the optimal level of inventory increases. Again and again in many areas of decision making within the firm—and not just in areas related to financial management—we find that friction and uncertainty are of central importance.

Costs of Holding Inventories

In discussing the functions of inventories, we have identified the major benefits of holding them. What about costs? As we saw before in discussing accounts receivable, looking only at operating costs associated with inventories will not be sufficient because having inventories also means that these inventories must be financed, and this financing has costs in addition to operating costs—namely, the required returns of the suppliers of capital. As a result, we will look at the total costs of inventory, both operating and financing. Inventory costs can be grouped into two categories: those that rise as inventory increases and those that fall as inventory increases.

Carrying costs—rise as inventories increase and include the costs of financing, storage, servicing, and the risk of loss in value.

Those costs that rise with increases in inventory often are referred to as **carrying costs**, which include costs of financing, storage, servicing, and risk of loss in value. Financing costs include the interest on borrowing necessary to finance the inventory as well as the required returns of any other capital supplied to finance inventories. Later, we will comment further on financing costs. Storage costs include rent on facilities and equipment (or the firm's cost of having its own facilities and equipment), property taxes, insurance, and utilities. Servicing costs include labor for handling the inventory, clerical and accounting costs for record keeping, and taxes on the inventory itself.

Decline in value may take place because of pilferage, fire, deterioration, technological obsolescence, style obsolescence, or price decline. Some of these risks can be insured, in which case the cost of insurance becomes a component of carrying cost. Not all these costs will be incurred by every firm in every situation, and the total cost of carrying inventory varies widely from one situation to another.

Ordering costs—decline as inventories increase and include the costs of placing orders and unit purchase costs.

Costs that decline as inventory increases are **ordering costs** (including unit purchase costs), production costs, and opportunity costs of lost sales. Ordering costs often are a fixed amount per order placed, without regard to the amount ordered. By ordering less frequently in larger quantities, total ordering costs are reduced, but average inventories are larger. Unit costs of materials purchased may be reduced if quantity discounts can be obtained by purchasing in larger quantities. With larger stocks of raw materials and work in process, longer production runs can be made with less frequent setup, lower total setup costs, and fewer delays. Finally, larger finished-goods inventories will reduce **stockouts** (running out of inventory) and lost contribution resulting from sales forgone. This latter cost is an opportunity cost, but an important element in determining the optimal inventory level.

A **stockout**—occurs when there is insufficient inventory to fill orders.

> **Some costs (carrying costs) rise as inventories are increased, while others (ordering costs, production costs, and opportunity costs of lost sales) fall as inventories are increased.**

Inventory-Decision Models

The use of inventories as buffer stocks has been studied extensively, and a large body of inventory theory has been developed. Inventory theory has been found useful for studying a broad class of problems in addition to the problems of stocking raw materials and finished goods in a firm. Cash and liquidity, for example, can be viewed as inventories and analyzed using inventory theory.[4]

Inventory theory—is the theory of how much should be ordered and when it should be ordered.

Inventory theory addresses two basic questions: (1) *How much* should be ordered? (2) *When* should it be ordered?

The first question—how much to order—arises because of "friction" in the form of ordering costs, setup costs, and the like. The second question—when to order—arises because the world is uncertain.

The Economic Order Quantity

The **economic order quantity (EOQ)**—is the optimal quantity of goods to be ordered and is determined by trading off ordering costs (or setup costs) against carrying costs.

Taking these two questions one at a time, we will deal with friction first and assume for the moment that no uncertainty exists with respect to the future. Inventory models deal with the question of how much to order by defining an **economic order quantity (EOQ)**. The EOQ is determined by trading off ordering costs (or setup costs) against carrying costs. A larger order quantity reduces the frequency of ordering and, therefore, total ordering costs but increases the average inventory level and, therefore, car-

---

[4]See William J. Baumol, "The Transactions Demand for Cash—An Inventory-Theoretic Approach," *Quarterly Journal of Economics* 65 (November 1952): 545–56; Merton H. Miller and Daniel Orr, "A Model of the Demand for Money by Firms," *Quarterly Journal of Economics* 80 (August 1966): 413–35; and Yair E. Orgler, *Cash Management* (Belmont, Calif.: Wadsworth, 1970).

Figure 20-3
The Economic-Order-Quantity Model

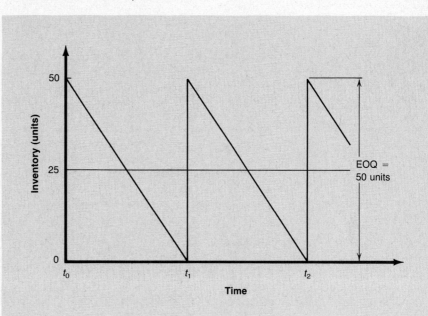

rying costs. The optimal order quantity can be defined as shown in Equation (1). Appendix 20A at the end of this chapter gives the derivation of Equation (1).[5]

The *economic order quantity (EOQ)*, can be expressed as

$$EOQ = \sqrt{\frac{2RO}{C}} \qquad (1)$$

where R = the usage per period in units, O = the ordering cost per order, and C = the carrying cost per unit per period.

To illustrate the use of the EOQ formula, consider an item that is used at the rate of 100 units per year. Ordering costs are $25 per order, and carrying costs are $20 per unit per year. The EOQ can then be calculated as

$$EOQ = \sqrt{\frac{2(1,000)(25)}{20}} = 50 \text{ units}$$

Assuming that the usage rate is uniform, we can illustrate the ordering and usage process as shown in Figure 20-3. At time t_0, 50 units are received and consumed over

---

[5]For a detailed development and discussion of the EOQ model, see Richard I. Levin and Charles A. Kirkpatrick, *Quantitative Approaches to Management*, 3rd ed. (New York: McGraw-Hill, 1975).

the period t_0 to t_1. At t_1, another 50 units are ordered. We can see that the average inventory level is 25 units, so that total carrying costs for the year are 25 units $\times$ \$20 per unit = \$500. We must place a total of 1,000/50 = 20 orders per year, so total ordering costs also are \$500 per year. The sum of ordering and carrying costs is \$1,000 per year. With a little arithmetic, we can verify that total costs are higher at any order quantity other than 50 units.

The EOQ formula is widely used in inventory control to determine optimal order quantities. To use the EOQ formula in quantitative applications, the cost of financing must be included as a component of carrying cost. Often, this cost is approximated using the interest cost of debt. Investment in inventory is not riskless, however, so the interest rate may understate the real cost of financing, which is the return required by lenders and investors. The use of the interest rate may be a satisfactory approximation for the production manager in calculating order quantities for individual items. When financial managers view inventory as an investment decision, they must take risk into account and require a return higher than the interest rate on debt.

In addition to its usefulness in quantitative applications, the EOQ model yields several useful qualitative insights. We see the importance of friction costs; if ordering costs were zero, the EOQ would be zero. The firm would order continuously at the usage rate, holding no inventory at all. We see also that the EOQ and, therefore, the average inventory level varies with the square root of usage. Thus, a doubling of usage does not double the optimal inventory level, but increases it by the square root of 2, or by about 1.4 times.

The basic EOQ model discussed above assumes that delivery is instantaneous when an order is placed. If delivery lead time is known with certainty, the EOQ is unchanged. We simply place the order earlier by the number of days required for delivery. We will discuss the effects of uncertain delivery times in the next section. The availability of quantity discounts does alter the EOQ and can be handled by modifying the analysis. However, because quantity discounts are of secondary importance to our discussion here, we will not deal with them.[6]

> **The economic order quantity takes into account usage rate, ordering costs, and carrying costs.**

Sample Problem 20–2

Determining the Economic Order Quantity for Tampa Building Company

Tampa Building Company sells 5,000 three-speed drills a year. The cost of holding inventory is \$20 per drill per year, and ordering costs are \$80 per order.

A. Determine Tampa's economic order quantity for three-speed drills, ignoring any potential stockout costs.
B. Determine the total annual inventory costs associated with this economic order quantity.

---

[6]For a treatment of the quantity discount in EOQ models, see Richard I. Levin and Charles A. Kirkpatrick, *Quantitative Approaches to Management*, 3rd ed. (New York: McGraw-Hill, 1975), Chapter 7.

Solution

A. The economic order quantity (EOQ) can be found by applying Equation (1) as

$$EOQ = \sqrt{\frac{2(5,000)(80)}{20}} = 200 \text{ drills}$$

B. The total inventory costs are composed of ordering and carrying costs. The total ordering cost is equal to the number of orders placed times the cost per order. The total carrying cost is equal to the average number of units in inventory times the carrying cost per unit. For Tampa, the number of orders placed = 5,000 drills/ 200 drills per order = 25 orders. Total ordering costs, then, are 25 orders × $80 per order = $2,000. The average inventory is 200 drills per order/2 = 100 drills. The total carrying costs are 100 drills × $20 per drill = $2,000, and the total annual inventory costs are $2,000 total ordering costs plus $2,000 total carrying costs, or $4,000. ▪▐▌▜

Safety Stocks

Now let us reintroduce uncertainty. In practice, uncertainty is likely to exist with respect to delivery times, production rates, and sales rates. Strikes occur, suppliers fail to deliver, and unexpected surges in demand appear. When delivery is delayed or usage unexpectedly increases, a *stockout* is likely to occur. To reduce the likelihood of stockouts, firms hold **safety stocks**, additional inventory over and above that prescribed by the EOQ formula.

A **safety stock**—is additional inventory over and above that prescribed by the EOQ formula.

Finding the optimal level of safety stock involves a tradeoff between stockout costs and carrying costs. When a stockout occurs, several kinds of costs may be incurred, some that are out-of-pocket costs and some that are opportunity costs. A stockout in raw materials may cause production delays or stoppages and higher costs of scheduling and setup. In continuous-process industries, such as paper or synthetic fibers, a production stoppage would be very costly indeed. A stockout in finished goods likely means that sales were lost or, at a minimum, customers inconvenienced. The relationship between on-time delivery and inventory level is not linear, and in most cases resembles the graph in Figure 20–4. The lower the level of inventories held, the larger is the volume of delayed deliveries on orders received.

The cost of stockouts includes lost contribution as well as damage to the firm's reputation. Calculating stockout costs is a difficult problem and one about which not much can be said of a general nature. In each situation, it is necessary to identify out-of-pocket and opportunity costs incurred because of the stockout.

The optimal size of the safety stock depends on stockout costs, carrying costs, and the probability that stockouts will occur. The optimal level of safety stock, thus, varies *directly* with:

1. stockout costs, either in lost contribution or production inefficiency,
2. uncertainty of usage or sales rates, and
3. uncertainty of delivery times.

Figure 20–4
Inventories and On-Time Deliveries

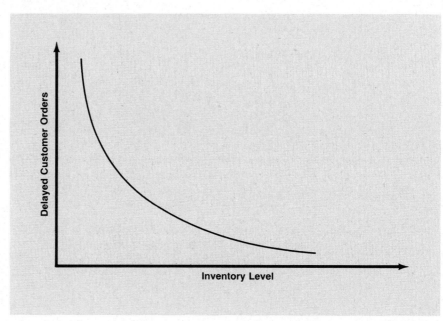

The optimal safety stock varies *inversely* with

4. inventory carrying costs.

Models incorporating safety stocks can also address the question of the appropriate *reorder point*, which is the level of inventory at which the firm should reorder new units for inventory. Such a reorder point can incorporate many factors, including the delivery time to receive the new inventory units after they have been ordered.[7]

Quantitative models for calculating reorder points and safety stocks are widely used in inventory-control systems. Having a safety stock, however, still does not eliminate the possibility of a stockout. The safety stock is intended to give a *known probability* of a stockout such that the expected cost of a stockout (cost times probability) is balanced against the inventory carrying cost. The quantitative models show us the important effect of uncertainty—the greater the uncertainty, the higher is the optimal level of inventory.

> **Safety stocks are held to protect against uncertainty in usage rates and delivery times.**

[7]For an excellent discussion of inventory models under conditions of uncertainty, see Richard I. Levin and Charles A. Kirkpatrick, *Quantitative Approaches to Management*, 3rd ed. (New York: McGraw-Hill, 1975), Chapter 8.

Figure 20–5
Minimizing Inventory Costs

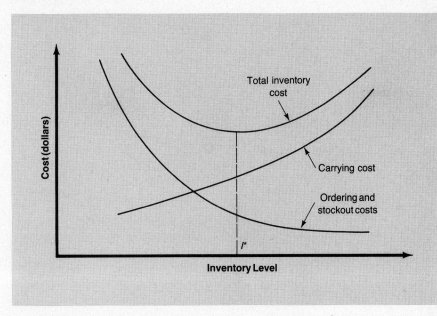

Total Inventory Costs

If we apply inventory theory as described above, we will be led to minimize the total costs of inventory, including opportunity costs of stockouts. Diagrammatically, we can view the relationships as shown in Figure 20–5. At inventory level I^*, the total out-of-pocket and opportunity costs of inventory are minimized. If another increment of inventory is added, carrying costs exceed the ordering and stockout costs that are saved. Thus, at point I^*, the firm has chosen its optimal level of inventory.

While Figure 20–5 looks quite similar to Figure 20–1, which showed trade-offs faced in credit-policy decisions, there is one important difference. In Figure 20–5, we have included financing charges in the inventory carrying costs. As a result, I^* minimizes total inventory cost and, hence, is the optimal inventory level. In Figure 20–1, we incorporated only operating costs.

While Figure 20–5 shows the trade-offs involved in inventory decisions, some extra insights into the problem can be gained by showing an alternative analysis of inventory decisions—that is, an alternative way to locate I^*. This analysis will allow us to focus on the risks involved. Although certain storage, handling, and ordering costs can be estimated fairly accurately, stockout costs may be subject to considerable uncertainty. Implicitly, our previous analysis has handled such risk by lumping the required returns of financing into the carrying costs of inventory, and these required returns will be higher the higher are the risks that are being considered.

Table 20—6

Lost Sales Estimated at Four Alternative Finished Goods Inventory Levels at Southeastern Motors, Inc. (thousands of dollars)

Policy	Inventory Level[a]	Lost Sales	Lost Contribution[b]	Incremental Contribution
Current	200	625	250	—
A	278	475	190	60
B	414	303	121	69
C	620	153	61	60
D	868	63	25	36

[a]Finished-goods inventory only.
[b]Variable costs equal 60 percent of sales. Thus, contribution is 40 percent of sales.

Now let us separate the cost of inventory into operating costs and the required return on financing. As in the case of accounts receivable, we can first calculate the expected operating rate of return on the investment in inventory and then compare this expected rate to the required rate of return. This required rate of return will reflect risk.

> The optimal inventory level is determined by trading off carrying costs against ordering and stockout costs.

Calculating Expected Return

As in the case of accounts receivable, we will illustrate the calculation of expected return on inventory investment with an example. Southeastern Motors, Inc. is a manufacturer of fractional-horsepower electric motors used in hand tools, electric fans, appliances, and other similar applications. The product line includes about 60 different models. All models are produced for stock according to a schedule jointly planned by the sales and production departments.

Southeastern Motors's sales totaled $7.8 million in 1986. In the past, inventories had been tightly controlled and were dictated to a considerable extent by production considerations. Inventory turnover in 1986 was 6.3 times, a figure considered quite good by industry standards. However, Southeastern management had become increasingly concerned over sales lost due to stockouts of finished-goods inventories. At year-end 1986, total inventories were $800,000, of which $200,000 was in finished goods.

Motivated by the problem of stockouts, management initiated a study to determine whether finished-goods inventories should be increased. From historical records of orders received and filled, management estimated that, at the present inventory level, lost sales due to stockouts were running at an annual rate of $625,000. Recall from the earlier discussion in this chapter that contribution to operating profits is equal to sales *less* variable costs. In this case, because variable costs totaled about 60 percent of sales, or $375,000, lost contribution amounted to $625,000 *less* $375,000, or about $250,000.

Table 20-7
Estimated Incremental Operating Profit at Four Alternative Inventory Levels at Southeastern Motors, Inc. (thousands of dollars)

Policy	Inventory Level	Carrying Cost[a]	Incremental Carrying Cost	Incremental Contribution[b]	Incremental Operating Profit Before Tax	Incremental Operating Profit After Tax[c]
Current	200	10	—	—	—	—
A	278	14	4	60	56	28
B	414	21	7	69	62	31
C	620	31	10	60	50	25
D	868	43	12	36	24	12

[a]5 percent of inventory level, exclusive of financing costs.
[b]From Table 20–6.
[c]Taxes at 50 percent.

The magnitude of the lost-contribution figure convinced management that further study was necessary. Lost sales were estimated at four alternative levels of finished-goods inventories associated with inventory policies A, B, C, and D, each of which represented an incremental increase over current levels. The results are listed in Table 20–6. The analysis shows that if finished-goods inventories were increased from the current level of $200,000 to $278,000, lost sales would decline from $625,000 to $475,000, and an additional contribution of $60,000 (from the last column in Table 20–6) would be realized. Similarly, the additional contributions at inventory levels B, C, and D also were determined.

The next step in the analysis of operating profit was to determine carrying costs (exclusive of financing costs) at each inventory level. These costs included warehousing, servicing, taxes, insurance, and record keeping, and amounted to about 5 percent of the value of the inventory. Incremental operating profit then was estimated as shown in Table 20–7. By moving to the inventory level associated with Policy A, carrying costs (excluding financing costs) would increase by $4,000. Subtracting this figure from an incremental contribution of $60,000 gives a pretax increase in operating profit of $56,000, or $28,000 after taxes (assuming a 50 percent tax rate for simplicity).

From the data in Tables 20–6 and 20–7, expected return on investment was calculated as shown in Table 20–8.

To move from the current policy to Policy A, Southeastern must invest an additional $78,000 in finished-goods inventory. This additional investment is expected to generate additional operating profit of $28,000 per year after taxes, yielding an expected return on investment of 35.9 percent after taxes.

An important feature of the analysis above is that it examines the *incremental* return on successive *increments* of inventory. We see in Table 20–8 that, for each successive increment of inventory, the incremental, or marginal, expected return declines. As finished-goods inventories are increased, each successive increment recaptures less lost sales and, therefore, less lost contribution, as shown in the last column of Table 20–8.

There is an advantage to looking at inventory policy in terms of increments. South-

Table 20–8
Expected Rate of Return, E(R), on Investment in Additional Inventory for Southeastern Motors, Inc.

Policy	Inventory Level (thousands of dollars)	Incremental Investment[a] (thousands of dollars)	Incremental After-Tax Operating Profit[b] (thousands of dollars)	Incremental After-Tax E(R) on Investment (percent)
Current	200			
A	278	78	28	35.9
B	414	136	31	22.8
C	620	206	25	12.1
D	868	248	12	4.8

[a]Out-of-pocket outlay.
[b]From Table 20–7.

eastern could have examined a single option—a major expansion of inventory from the current policy all the way to Policy D. From Table 20–8, we can see that this change would require a total investment of $868,000 − $200,000 = $668,000 and would generate additional operating profit of $96,000 (found by summing the incremental operating profits in Table 20–8). The expected return of this policy change from the current policy to Policy D would be $96,000/$668,000 = 14.4 percent—not bad. The expected return on the last increment from Policy C to Policy D, however, is only 4.8 percent.

Thus, by looking at several increments, we can better determine the point at which marginal expected return falls below the required rate. At inventory levels associated with Policies A and B, expected return appears to be quite attractive. Policy D, returning only 4.8 percent after taxes compared to Policy C, does not seem attractive. Even within increments, the figures in Table 20–8 represent averages. The marginal expected return on the last dollar of investment in increment B is quite a bit lower than the average expected return, 22.8 percent, on increment B as a whole.

Which policy should Southeastern Motors adopt? The answer depends on the target or required rate of return on investment in inventories that reflects financing costs and risks. We will return to this topic in the final section in this chapter.

In interpreting analyses of this sort, let us keep in mind the critical assumption that we are making with respect to the behavior of costs. We have identified the costs that vary and those that remain fixed as sales expand as a result of the recovery of lost sales. The validity of the analysis depends on our ability correctly to identify fixed and variable costs in the range of sales in question.

Inventory Policy in Seasonal Firms

Inventory policy in a firm with a pronounced seasonal sales pattern usually involves some additional complicating factors. A major policy question in manufacturing firms with seasonal sales is whether to adopt a level production policy or a seasonal production policy. Where level production is adopted, as in the case of Aquatic Systems, Inc. from Chapter 8, inventory levels vary over the year.

In such situations, production and inventory policy must be considered jointly. Level production results in savings in costs of setup, hiring, training, morale, productivity, and related factors. Savings in these areas must be traded off against higher carrying costs resulting from the higher average inventory level under level production. In some situations, risk of obsolescence or deterioration may represent an important component of total carrying costs.

The return-on-investment approach is applicable to inventory decisions in seasonal firms, but the analysis is more complex. The general approach is to analyze production and inventory costs under each policy alternative. Annual expected return then can be computed using the average investment in inventory over the year.

MANAGING INVENTORY

Establishing the appropriate overall level of inventory investment usually is the primary responsibility of the financial manager. Day-to-day management of inventory usually is the responsibility of the production manager in large manufacturing firms, or of someone with operating responsibilities in smaller firms or non-manufacturing firms. Included in the production manager's responsibility is the determination of economic order quantities, safety stocks, and reorder points for every individual item stocked. In the case of finished goods, the sales department is likely to take a strong interest in levels of safety stocks. The production manager also is responsible for ordering, receiving, handling, storing, protecting, and issuing inventory. In most firms, inventory management comprises an important set of responsibilities indeed and is a topic on which volumes have been written.[8]

Inventory control—is the determination of economic order quantities, safety stocks, and reorder points for every individual item stocked along with ordering, receiving, handling, storing, protecting, and issuing inventory.

Inventory control is the set of responsibilities that falls to the production manager (or other operating manager) with respect to inventories. Over the past two decades, the application of computers has brought major advances to inventory management. Sophisticated automated inventory-control systems are now available that integrate many of the necessary functions including determination of EOQs and reorder points, automatic preparation of orders, generation of accounting entries, and compilation of management information.

In most firms, policy formulation and inventory management involve an iterative process that goes on in a more or less continuous manner. Application of EOQ and order-point models item by item is not likely the first time around to lead to optimal aggregate inventory levels. Close cooperation is necessary between the financial manager and operating (sales and/or production) managers. The financial manager has the continuing responsibility of evaluating and reevaluating the firm's aggregate investment in inventory to ensure that, at that margin, expected return on investment in inventory is acceptable.

THE REQUIRED RETURN ON INVESTMENT IN RECEIVABLES AND INVENTORY

From the perspective of the financial manager, our approach to the management of accounts receivable and inventory has centered on calculating expected return on in-

---

[8]See Richard I. Levin and Charles A. Kirkpatrick, *Quantitative Approaches to Management*, 3rd ed. (New York: McGraw-Hill, 1975), Chapters 7 and 8.

Finance in Practice 20–1

Asset Management and Inventories

"Mindful of the high cost of borrowing and the long lead time before technological investments yield payback, management has placed increased emphasis on the effective employment of assets. Internal measurements of managerial performance emphasize return on invested capital, inventory turnover, cash flow, payback and other indices of asset management."

The above quotation from IBM's 1981 annual report reflects a theme heard in many U.S. cor-

porations in the early 1980s—the importance of *asset management*. *Asset management* is the attempt to keep assets, such as inventories, needed for operation at an optimal level. This emphasis has been in place for all sorts of firms—publishers, retailers, manufacturers—not just high-technology firms such as IBM. Why has there been an increase in the emphasis on asset management?

Part of the answer is right out of basic finance. As market interest rates and the costs of obtaining funds go up, as they did in the United States during the 1960s and 1970s, firms must impose higher required rates of return on their investments in all sorts of assets. For many firms, inventories represent large dollar investments. For example, IBM reported 1981 inventories in excess

of \$2.8 billion. Cutting inventory by even a few percentage points can save large dollar amounts. Suppose a firm could reduce inventories by \$200 million. At an annual 10 percent interest rate, the financing-cost savings would be \$20 million a year—a tidy sum.

Figure 20–6 displays the finance of the situation. As market required rates of return increase, the required rate of return line in Figure 20–6 shifts up vertically, implying a higher required rate of return at each level of investment. The new required-return line will intersect the marginal-expected-return line at a point to the left of I^*, implying a new but lower optimal level of investment. Asset management is the process of getting to that optimal level of investment.

Operating cash flows— are the flows arising from the project itself, such as sales, cost of goods sold, advertising, and selling, and exclude the cash flows associated with how the project is financed.

Operating return— is the ratio of operating profit to investment.

The **required rate of return**—is the minimum return prospective investors will accept in order to make an investment.

vestment at the margin. In each case, we identified policy alternatives, determined incremental investment and operating earnings, and calculated the marginal expected rate of return.

An important feature of our analysis was that we excluded financing costs. We considered only **operating cash flows**; hence, our result was the expected **operating return**. We found in the case of both receivables and inventory that, as the level of investment increases, marginal operating return declines. In each case, we were left with the question of how far to expand. We noted that the optimum—that is, the point at which the value of the firm is maximized—lies at the point where marginal operating return just equals the **required rate of return**, or the return necessary to compensate those who supply the funds for investment.

The required rate of return is not the rate at which the firm can borrow because the borrowing rate is determined by the lenders to cover the risk of the firm *as a whole* from their own perspective and not the component uses to which the borrowed funds may be put. Each individual investment—for example, marketable securities, accounts receivable, or inventory—has a different risk. The higher the risk, the higher should be the required return on that specific use of funds. Thus, the overall borrowing rate may not adequately account for the risk of investment in receivables and inventory. In the case of receivables, accounts obtained by loosening credit policy become progressively more risky. Starting with a very tight policy, the cash flows associated with the first increments of expansion of receivables may be subject to little uncertainty, be-

Figure 20–6
Optimal Investment in Receivables and Inventory

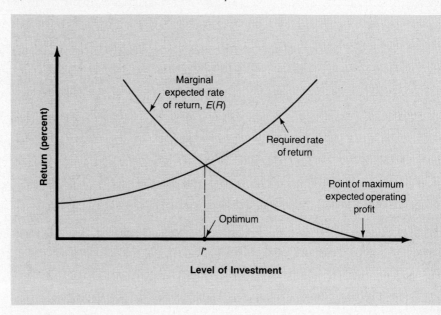

cause only the very best customers are granted credit. As policy becomes progressively looser, accounts become subject to an increasing probability of default. By the same token, cash flows associated with expansion of inventory also are uncertain. Recapture of lost sales is not guaranteed, and as inventory is expanded, the degree of uncertainty regarding such recapture increases. We can conclude that, at the margin, the cash flows and, therefore, the expected return attributable to additional investment in receivables and inventory may be subject to considerable uncertainty.

How is the required rate of return related to risk? In Part Two, we found that lenders and investors are risk-averse and require compensation for both time and risk. The more risky the investment opportunity, the higher is the return demanded by suppliers of funds. In other words, as risk increases, the required rate of return increases.

As the investment in accounts receivable and inventory is increased, two things happen. First, marginal expected return falls. Second, risk increases, so the required rate of return increases. We can diagram the relationships as shown in Figure 20–6. The marginal expected return and the required rate of return must be determined separately for accounts receivable and inventory. Each will have its own marginal-expected-return and required-rate-of-return schedules and its own optimum as diagrammed in Figure 20–6. In each case, the optimum lies at a level of investment below that which maximizes expected operating profit. In Figure 20–6, expected operating profit is maximized at the point at which operating return is zero, but the optimum level of investment occurs at I^*, where the marginal expected rate of return just equals the required rate of return.

In practice, determining the required rate of return is not easy. We know that it slopes upward from the rate on riskless investment, usually taken to be the rate on

Finance in Practice 20-2

Inventories in the Automobile Business

In 1981, General Motors executives measured their worldwide inventory and found it to be worth a whopping $9.7 billion. Facing large cash needs because of sagging profitability and needed capital expenditures, GM executives decided to cut down on inventory. As GM president F. James McDonald stated, "the incentive came from a dire need to accumulate capital without borrowing to keep our forward product schedules going." In other words, GM decided that it had too much invested in inventory and decided to cut back on inventory to free funds for other investment purposes.

How could GM cut back on inventory without reducing the efficiency of the automobile production process? Part of the answer, so GM thought, was to adopt a different concept of supplier/producer relationships—the *kanban* concept proved effective by Japanese manufacturers. *Kanban* or "just-in-time" inventory control brings parts and components to the assembly plant hours or even minutes before cars are built instead of weeks or months earlier to be stockpiled as inventory. With kanban inventory control, GM can have a constant stream of materials delivered with a drastic reduction in the inventory GM actually keeps on hand. One GM program manager at GM's Buick division estimated that kanban inventory control can reduce inventory costs by 50 percent. With multibillion dollar inventory levels, such a reduction would represent huge dollar savings.

Moving to kanban inventory control will have major effects on the way GM does business. As an example, officials from GM's Buick division said that a new facility based on the kanban approach will need only about half the space previously required to produce a given number of cars because less space will be required for parts storage. In addition, the kanban approach puts a new premium on higher quality in parts. Without a stockpile of hundreds of parts to draw upon, the arrival of a supply truck full of defective parts could bring the whole automobile production facility to a standstill. The kanban approach also means that suppliers will need to locate closer to automobile production facilities to reduce the transportation costs of the many deliveries. According to Herb Stone, a program manager for GM, "we're working to get suppliers to build closer for three to four times daily delivery versus once a week as before." As a reflection of this need for closer location, in planning a Buick plant in Flint, Michigan to replace outdated facilities, the GM blueprints allowed for an industrial park across from the plant's loading bays where suppliers can locate.

To induce suppliers to produce higher-quality parts and locate close to automobile-production facilities, GM is prepared to give suppliers long-term contracts and to consider rewarding quality suppliers by naming them as the single source of a particular component.

In short, the kanban approach will change the nature of relationships with suppliers to make suppliers an integral part of the process.

The kanban approach to inventory control is only part of the overhaul taking place in U.S. automobile manufacture (along with the use of robots in production and the fuel-efficient redesign of cars), but it is an important part. The decision to adopt the kanban approach not only reduced GM's investment in inventories, but it required that GM change its basic business relationships with its suppliers.

Source: Adapted from J. Mateja, "'Buick City' Aims at Japanese-Style Cost-Cutting" and "GM Chief: The Dollar Made Us Do It," *The Chicago Tribune*, June 26, 1983.

U.S. Treasury obligations. One workable approach to determining the required rate is to categorize investments into risk classes. In the case of receivables, accounts might be classified as low, medium, and high risk, and a different required rate established for each. Similarly, estimates of risk might be made for different increments in inventory.

KEY CONCEPTS

1. From the perspective of financial management, the proper level of accounts receivable and inventory should be viewed as an investment decision.
2. The appropriate credit policy is determined by trading off costs of analysis, collection, and bad debts against opportunity costs of lost sales.
3. Accounts-receivable policy can be set by calculating the rate of return on the incremental investment in receivables.
4. The basic function of inventories is to decouple the major activities of the firm—purchasing, production, and sales—so that all do not have to proceed at the same rate.

5. The economic order quantity (EOQ) takes into account usage rate, ordering costs, and carrying costs.
6. Safety stocks are held to deal with uncertainty in usage rates and delivery times.
7. The optimal inventory level is determined by trading off carrying costs against ordering and stockout costs.
8. Inventory policy can be set by calculating the rate of return on the incremental investment in inventories and comparing this to the required rate of return.

SUMMARY

The financial manager should view the expansion of accounts receivable and inventories as *investment decisions*, using value maximization as the decision criterion. Receivables and inventories should be expanded to the point where the marginal expected return on additional investment equals the return required by suppliers of funds.

A firm's credit policy includes credit standards, credit terms, and collection procedures. Taken together, the three elements of credit policy determine the size of the firm's investment in accounts receivable and the return on that investment. As credit policy is loosened, accounts receivable expand. Costs of analysis, collection, and bad debts rise, while opportunity costs of lost sales decline. Where the sum of the costs is minimized, operating profit is maximized. The optimal credit policy, however, is more restrictive because it must consider return on investment rather than operating profits alone. The expected return on incremental investment in accounts receivable can be calculated using data on costs of servicing different categories of accounts.

Once overall credit policy has been formulated using a return-on-investment approach, the policy must be implemented by means of decisions on individual accounts. A return-on-investment approach can be utilized but often is too expensive for individual accounts. Analytical techniques such as discriminant analysis and credit scoring may be useful. Payment patterns must be monitored to detect changes requiring management attention.

As in the case of receivables, the financial manager should be concerned with the return on investment in inventories. Inventories serve as buffers to decouple the purchasing, production, and sales activities of the firm so that all do not have to proceed at the same rate and so that unexpected events are not disruptive. Such buffers are necessary because of transaction costs (friction losses) and uncertainty. As inventories are expanded, some costs rise and others decline. Costs that rise with increases in inventory (or carrying costs) include financing costs, storage costs, servicing costs, and risk of loss in value. Costs that decline with increases in inventory include costs of ordering, production, and lost sales.

Inventory theory provides a framework for analyzing inventory costs. The economic order quantity (EOQ) represents a trade-off between carrying costs and ordering costs. The control-limit model trades off carrying costs against the cost of being out of required stocks. Minimizing the sum of all inventory costs leads to the point of optimal inventory investment. As in the case of accounts receivable, the optimal inventory policy must consider not operating profit alone, but return on investment. The expected return on incremental investment in inventory can be calculated by identifying the various elements of operating cost associated with different inventory levels, calculating incremental operating profit, and dividing by the required incremental investment.

The objective of both credit policy and inventory policy is to maximize the value of the firm. In both cases, the policy that accomplishes this objective lies at the point where marginal expected operating return just equals the return necessary to compensate suppliers of funds.

QUESTIONS

1. With respect to accounts receivable, how might the perspective of the financial manager differ from that of the credit manager?

2. Is the credit policy that maximizes expected operating profit the optimal credit policy? Explain.

3. What is the objective of credit policy?

4. Discuss the problem of monitoring payment patterns in seasonal firms.

5. Suppose that the Delta Electric Company described in this chapter and a local bank both are considering extending credit to the same customer. Why might Delta and the bank arrive at different decisions?

6. Describe the functions of the three major types of inventory.

7. What are the principal costs of holding inventories?

8. What two questions does inventory theory try to answer?

9. On what does the optimal size of the safety stock depend?

10. "The function of the safety stock is to prevent stockouts." Is this statement true or false? Explain.

11. Why is the expected return on an investment in accounts receivable subject to uncertainty? Why is the expected return on an investment in inventory subject to uncertainty?

12. "Considering inventory and receivables separately, the optimal level of investment is the point at which the expected operating profit is maximized." Is this statement true or false? Explain.

PROBLEMS

1. Lenk, Inc., a manufacturer of office equipment, expects to have sales of $20 million under current operating policies. Variable costs comprise 80 percent of sales, and the company's cost of capital is 16 percent. Currently, Lenk's credit policy is net 25, but its average collection period is 30 days. This concerns the financial manager, who would like the company to consider tightening the credit policy in an effort to crack down on delinquent accounts. The sales manager, on the other hand, has suggested loosening the credit policy in order to increase sales volume.

In response to these arguments, the credit manager is considering two alternative proposals for changing Lenk's credit policy. Proposal A would lengthen the credit period to net 40, and is expected to increase sales by $4,350,000 and to increase days sales outstanding (DSO) on all sales to 45 days. Proposal B would shorten the credit period to net 20, and is expected to decrease sales volume by $2,570,000 and to decrease DSO to 22 days on all sales. All other costs are identical under the current and proposed policies. Which proposal should be adopted?

2. The Candee Corporation is considering liberalizing its credit policies to allow higher-risk customers to buy on credit terms of net 30. The credit department has been informed that variable costs will remain at 80 percent of sales over the new potential sales levels. All new sales will be on credit, and the projected information for each risk class is as shown in Table A. The scale of required returns reflects the increased risk perceived for each risk class of customers. Which, if any, of the risk classes should Candee allow to buy on credit? (Assume a 365-day year and a 50 percent tax rate.)

Table A

Risk Class	Required Return (percent)	Average Collection Period (days)	New Sales (thousands of dollars)
3	0.12	38	500
4	0.15	45	400
5	0.19	58	300
6	0.25	70	200

3. Assume the credit department for Candee Corporation realized it had failed to include all the relevant costs in problem (1), and the additional information in Table B is submitted. Which risk classes should Candee allow to buy on credit?

4. The CBM Company currently offers credit terms of 1/10, net 30, on annual credit sales of $3,000,000. An average of 50 percent of the current customers take the discount, and the average collection period has consistently remained at 35 days. The percentage default rate has been 1 percent. The company is considering two alternative changes in credit terms as outlined in Table C. If sales are projected to remain stable under either alternative and the required rate of return on investment in accounts receivable is 0.20, what strategy would you recommend for CBM? (Assume a 50 percent tax rate.)

5. Delta Electric Company is considering a request from Bill's Electronics for open-account credit in the amount of $1,000 (figured at Delta's selling price). Delta's gross margin on the particular merchandise to be purchased by Bill's is 17 percent. Delta's salesperson expects Bill's to purchase $5,000 of merchandise annually. On all sales, Delta will incur variable expenses of 2 percent for the salesperson's commissions and 1.5 percent for warehousing.

a. Calculate the annual expected return on the prospective account with Bill's.

b. Suppose Delta establishes 30 percent as the required rate of return on accounts in the risk class in which Bill's falls. Suppose also that there are two possible outcomes: (1) Bill's makes all payments on time, or (2) Bill's defaults immediately and Delta loses its entire investment. What must be the minimum probability of outcome (1) in order to give an expected return of 30 percent? (For simplicity, assume that there are no taxes.)

6. A firm has a $50 per year carrying cost (including costs of financing) on each unit of inventory, an annual usage rate of 10,000 units, and an ordering cost of $100 per order. Ignore any potential stockout costs.

a. Calculate the economic order quantity for the firm.

b. What would be the total annual inventory costs of the firm if it orders in this quantity?

7. Assume that the supplier for the firm in problem (5) offers a quantity discount of $0.30 per unit if the firm orders in lots of 400 units. Should the firm accept the quantity discount?

8. The management of Bland Company is concerned about the seemingly large losses it has been experiencing in lost sales due to frequent stockouts. The company has been carrying a finished-goods inventory of $150,000 and has estimated lost sales at $525,000 per year. Variable costs have consistently remained at 75 percent of sales, and carrying costs of inventory (excluding financing costs) are 4 percent annually. Assuming a tax rate of 46 percent, an after-tax required rate of return of 15

Table B

Risk Class	Default Rate (percent)	Increased Credit Department Expense
3	4	$5,000
4	7	$5,000
5	12	$5,000
6	20	$5,000

Table C

Credit Terms	Customers Taking Discount (percent)	Average Collection Period (days)	Default Rate (percent)
2/10, net 30	75	18	0.005
3/10, net 20	98	12	0.001

percent on investment in inventory, and the projected figures shown in Table D (in thousands of dollars), determine the optimal level of inventory for the company.

9. Marston Industries is reviewing its inventory policy regarding one of its essential raw materials. The production manager has compiled the following information: orders must be placed in multiples of 100 units; usage for the year is 280,000 units; the purchase price per unit is $7.50; carrying costs (including financing costs) are 30 percent of the purchase price of the goods; order costs per order are $150.00; desired safety stock is 35,000 units, which is the amount currently in inventory; 10 days are required for delivery. The credit manager has asked you to provide the following information:

  a. What is the economic order quantity?

  b. How many orders should Marston place per year?

  c. At what level of inventory would these orders be placed?

10. The Broyhill Finishing Company uses 1,000 gallons of dye #704 per day. The dye can be purchased in drums containing 100 gallons for $50 per drum or in 1,000 gallon drums for $450 per drum. Ordering costs are $10 per order. The company's accountant has estimated the following costs associated with carrying inventory: The required rate of return for funds invested in inventory is 15 percent; depreciation and property tax on warehouse space occupied are $100 per month (there is no alternative use for this warehouse space at the present time); and insurance on inventory is 5 percent of cost per year.

  a. What is the economic order quantity assuming that only 100 gallon drums can be ordered? Assume 250 working days per year.

  b. What is the economic order quantity assuming that only 1,000 gallon drums can be ordered?

  c. Assuming that the firm must order one size or the other and not mix them, which drum size and ordering policy would you recommend?

11. Jackson Manufacturing Company uses inventory turnover as one performance measure to evaluate its production manager. Currently, Jackson's inventory turnover (CGS/inventory) is ten times per year compared with an industry average of four. Average sales are $450,000 per year. Variable costs have consistently remained at 70 percent of sales with fixed costs of $10,000. Carrying costs of inventory (excluding financing costs) are 5 percent annually. Jackson's sales force has complained that low inventory levels are resulting in lost sales due to stockouts. The sales manager has made the estimates based on stockout reports which appear in Table E. On the basis of these estimates, assuming a 46 percent tax rate and an after-tax required rate of return of 15 percent on investment in inventory, what inventory policy would you recommend?

Table D

Policy	Inventory Level (thousands of dollars)	Annual Lost Sales (thousands of dollars)
Current	150	525
A	200	375
B	250	250
C	300	150
D	350	75
E	400	25
F	450	0

Table E

Inventory Policy	Inventory Turnover	Sales (thousands of dollars)
Current	10	450
A	8	500
B	6	540
C	4	565

Table F

Policy	Terms (days)	Sales (thousands of dollars)
Current	75	1,200
A	60	1,130
B	45	1,050
C	30	950

12. The financial officers of MVB, Inc. are concerned that the firm's current credit policy of 75-day terms may be too loose when compared with MVB's competitors' 30-day credit terms. MVB's annual average sales are $1.2 million. Variable costs are 75 percent of sales with fixed costs of $100,000. MVB is considering several alternative credit policies as shown in Table F. Assuming a required rate of return on investment in accounts receivable of 20 percent, which policy would you recommend? (Assume a 360-day year and that all sales are on credit with the average collection period equal to the terms given. For simplicity, assume that there are no taxes.)

REFERENCES

Baumol, W. J. "The Transactions Demand for Cash—An Inventory-Theoretic Approach." *Quarterly Journal of Economics* 65 (November 1952): 545–556.

Carpenter, M. D., and J. E. Miller. "A Reliable Framework for Monitoring Accounts Receivable." *Financial Management* 8 (Winter 1979): 37–41.

Hill, N. C., and K. D. Riener. "Determining the Cash Discount in the Firm's Credit Policy." *Financial Management* 8 (Spring 1979): 68–73.

Levin, R. I., and C. A. Kirkpatrick. *Quantitative Approaches to Management.* 3d ed. New York: McGraw-Hill, 1975.

Lewellen, W. G. "Finance Subsidiaries and Corporate Borrowing Capacity." *Financial Management* 1 (Spring 1972): 21–32.

Lewellen, W. G., and R. W. Johnson. "Better Way to Monitor Accounts Receivable." *Harvard Business Review* 50 (May–June 1972): 21–32.

Magee, J. F. "Guides to Inventory Policy, I–III." *Harvard Business Review* 34 (Jan.–Feb. 1956): 49–60; (Mar.–Apr. 1956): 103–116; (May–June 1956): 57–70.

Mehta, D. R. *Working Capital Management.* Englewood Cliffs, N.J.: Prentice-Hall, 1974.

Miller, M., and D. Orr. "A Model of the Demand for Money by Firms." *Quarterly Journal of Economics* 80 (August 1966): 413–435.

Orgler, Y. E. *Cash Management.* Belmont, Ca.: Wadsworth, 1970.

Shapiro, A. "Optimal Inventory and Credit Granting Strategies Under Inflation and Devaluation." *Journal of Financial and Quantitative Analysis* 8 (Jan. 1973): 37–46.

Snyder, A. "Principles of Inventory Management." *Financial Executive* 32 (Apr. 1964): 12–21.

Stone, B. K. "The Payments-Pattern Approach to the Forecasting and Control of Accounts Receivable." *Financial Management* 5 (Autumn 1976): 65–82.

Wrightsman, D. W. "Optimal Credit Terms for Accounts Receivable." *Quarterly Review of Economics and Business* (Summer 1969): 59–66.

Appendix 20A

Derivation of the Economic Order Quantity

The economic order quantity (EOQ) is determined by trading off ordering (or setup) costs against carrying costs. A larger order quantity reduces the frequency of ordering and, therefore, reduces total ordering costs but increases the average inventory and, therefore, increases carrying costs. Assuming usage to be constant over each period, the average inventory can be expressed as

$$\text{Average inventory} = Q/2,$$

where Q = the order quantity.

Total carrying cost per period, then, is the average number of units times carrying cost per unit:

$$\text{Total carrying cost} = (Q/2) \times C,$$

where C = the carrying cost per period.

The number of orders placed per period is total usage divided by units per order:

$$\text{Orders per period} = R/Q,$$

where R = usage per period.

Total ordering cost per period, then, is orders placed times cost per order:

$$\text{Total ordering cost} = (R/Q) \times O,$$

where O = order cost per order.

Total inventory cost (T) per period, then, is the sum of total carrying cost and total ordering cost and can be expressed as

$$T = \frac{CQ}{2} + \frac{RO}{Q}$$

The optimal order size, or EOQ, is that which minimizes total cost, T. To determine EOQ, we differentiate the equation above with respect to Q, set the result equal to zero, and solve for Q, as follows:

$$\frac{dT}{dQ} = \frac{C}{2} - \frac{RO}{Q^2}$$

$$\frac{C}{2} - \frac{RO}{Q^2} = 0$$

$$Q^2 = \frac{2RO}{C}$$

$$Q = EOQ = \sqrt{\frac{2RO}{C}}$$

Thus, the economic order quantity (EOC) can be expressed as shown in Equation (A–1).

The optimal order size, or economic order quantity (EOQ), can be determined as

$$EOQ = \sqrt{\frac{2RO}{C}} \tag{A–1}$$

where R = usage per period, O = order cost per order, and C = carrying cost per period.

Part Seven

Special Topics in Financial Management

We have now covered the basics of financial management. We covered the fundamentals of time and risk in Part Two, financial analysis and planning in Part Three, investment decisions in Part Four, financing decisions in Part Five, and working-capital management in Part Six. In these six prior parts of the book, we covered the concepts, tools, and techniques of financial management.

In Part Seven, we take up two special topics: international finance in Chapter 21 and mergers and acquisitions in Chapter 22. These chapters represent applications to two specialized areas of the fundamental concepts of financial management presented in Parts One through Six. International investment decisions are analyzed using the same tools as are purely domestic investment decisions. With the increasing internationalization of business, international decisions are becoming important for more and more financial managers. An acquisition opportunity, also known as a merger, is analyzed using the same techniques of discounted cash flow that we use for any investment opportunity. In both of these chapters, it is the institutional and descriptive material that is specialized, not the concepts.

Chapter

21

International Financial Management

In this chapter, we will discuss some of the basic issues of doing business in a foreign country. We will learn about foreign-exchange markets, foreign-exchange rates, and how managers can hedge against the risk of unexpected changes in exchange rates. We will also learn how managers view investment decisions in foreign countries and how funds are raised in international capital markets.

So far, we have discussed financial-management decisions focusing on operations only within the domestic U.S. economy. Many firms do business outside the United States. Such multinational operations can take many forms, including the sale of products in foreign markets that were manufactured domestically, the manufacture of products in foreign countries and then sale in foreign or domestic markets, and the raising of funds in foreign capital markets.

The basic concepts and techniques of financial management are just as applicable to firms operating in foreign markets as they are to purely domestic firms, but there are two important things that are different for the multinational firm. First, when a firm does business in a foreign country, it must operate within the laws, customs, and political institutions of that country. It must deal with local financial institutions, buy from local suppliers, hire local workers and managers, and sell to local customers. To succeed, the firm must be as well schooled in these matters as are its local competitors. But these are not issues that are addressed by the theory and practices of financial management, so we will not discuss them in any depth in this chapter.

> **The basic concepts and techniques of financial management are just as applicable to firms operating in foreign markets as they are to purely domestic firms.**

A **foreign-exchange rate**—is the price of one currency expressed in terms of another.

The multinational firms must deal with a second set of issues that are financial in character and, therefore, are addressed in this chapter. Two factors are most important: currency exchange rates and interest rates. **Foreign-exchange rates** are the conversion ratio between, say, U.S. dollars and Mexican pesos or British pounds. A firm doing business in Mexico or the United Kingdom ultimately wants to convert the proceeds of transactions into its native currency. The currency exchange rate is an important factor in determining how much ultimately will be received.

Another important financial factor is the relationship between domestic interest rates and those in the foreign country. In October 1985, short-term interest rates were around 8 percent in the United States and just under 5 percent in West Germany. Why do such differences exist, and what are the implications of the difference in interest rates for firms doing international business?

We will address a number of issues related to currency exchange rates and interest rates in this chapter. What causes exchange rates to behave as they do? How are exchange rates and interest rates related? How can a firm protect itself against fluctuations in exchange rates? When should firms raise needed funds in foreign capital markets rather than at home in domestic markets? What additional factors must a firm consider when it is contemplating an investment, such as building a new plant, in a foreign country? Before turning to these questions, we will briefly review the scope of international activities of U.S. firms and the history of the present international financial system.

SCOPE OF MULTINATIONAL OPERATIONS

Over the past three decades, world trade and investment have grown dramatically. In 1965, total world exports and imports amounted to about $350 billion. By 1984, the total had grown to more than $3,600 billion. In the mid-1960s, the *Eurocurrency market*, which we will discuss in more depth later, totaled about $11 billion in gross liabilities.[1] By mid-1985 it had grown to almost $2,500 billion.

---

[1]See R. M. Kubarych, *Foreign Exchange Markets in the United States*, Federal Reserve Bank of New York, 1978. Kubarych provides an excellent discussion of foreign-exchange markets and other aspects of international finance.

Table 21-1
Export Sales for the Top 20, U.S. Exporting Firms, 1984

Firm	Export Sales (millions of dollars)	Percent of Total Sales
Boeing	4,819	43
General Electric	3,639	14
United Technologies	2,383	16
Du Pont	2,303	7
McDonnell Douglas	2,105	26
Caterpillar	1,584	29
Hewlett-Packard	1,420	23
Westinghouse	1,335	14
Philip Morris	970	10
Archer Daniels Midland	883	18
Weyerhaeuser	870	18
Occidental Petroleum	803	4
Signal	670	11
Allied	637	6
Raytheon	627	11
Lockheed	594	9
Pittston	505	41
Dresser Industries	486	14
FMC	483	14
Union Carbide	482	5

Note: Data are excerpted from Standard & Poors Compustat Services, Inc.
Source: John Pearson, "Strong Dollar or No, There's Money to be Made Abroad," *Business Week.*
   (March 22, 1985).

International trade has become more important to the U.S. economy also. In 1965, the sum of exports and imports in the United States represented just over 7 percent of that year's gross national product. By mid-1985, exports and imports had grown to a point where their sum totaled 15 percent of the gross national product. The past three decades also have brought rapid growth in foreign investments by U.S. firms and in profits earned by foreign subsidiaries of U.S. companies. Table 21-1 shows the importance of foreign sales for the most active U.S. participants in foreign trade.

The Bretton Woods System

In 1949, the major trading nations of the world got together and established a system of managing exchange rates among their currencies known as the Bretton Woods system. Under this system, each nation subscribing to the agreement was required to fix the rate of exchange of its own currency against the U.S. dollar and to maintain that rate within a narrow band above and below. The dollar, thus, served as the linchpin of the system, and its value was tied directly to the price of gold. Gold was regarded as the ultimate store of value and was widely accepted as the proper foundation of the entire system. Thus, all currency values were tied, directly or indirectly, to the price of gold.

Fixed exchange rates—are foreign-exchange rates that are set administratively by governments and changed infrequently according to agreed-upon rules.

From time to time during this period of **fixed exchange rates**, certain member nations found that they were unable to maintain the value of their currencies and were forced to *devalue* relative to the dollar. This **currency devaluation** usually happened after a sustained period of inflation at rates above those of other nations. Exchange rates ultimately must reflect the reality of the relative values of goods and services in one country versus another. So when inflation in one country ran ahead of that in other countries for an extended period, exchange rates would get out of line with prices of goods and services, and devaluation would become necessary. Devaluations took the form of changes in the official exchange rate. Only once did a **currency revaluation**—that is, a raising of the currency's value against the dollar—take place, and that revaluation occurred in the case of the West German deutsche mark.

Currency devaluation—is a reduction in the value of a country's currency stated in terms of other currencies.

Currency revaluation—is an increase in the value of a country's currency stated in terms of other currencies.

Even with these occasional changes, most exchange rates were remarkably stable from 1949, when Bretton Woods took effect, until 1971. The exchange rate between the dollar and the Japanese yen, for example, remained unchanged for the entire 22-year period. France, West Germany, and the United Kingdom together changed their exchange rates against the dollar only a total of four times. This kind of stability was true of most other countries in Europe.

Floating Rates

A big change came in 1971. In that year, the Nixon administration decided that, because of persistent inflation (at rates of 4 to 6 percent, considered intolerable at that time) and other domestic economic problems, the dollar had to be devalued against gold. After two years of futile attempts to set and maintain a new set of fixed exchange rates, the world moved in 1973 to a totally different system of **floating exchange rates**. Under this system, which has remained in effect to the present time, exchange rates were allowed to move against one another in response to market forces. The result has been continuous and sizable shifts, as illustrated in Figure 21–1, which shows changes in the exchange rate of the U.S. dollar against a weighted average of 10 foreign currencies.

Floating exchange rates—are foreign-exchange rates that are set by free-market forces.

Thus, we see that, under a system of fixed exchange rates, rates are set administratively by governments and changed only infrequently according to agreed-upon rules. Under a floating system, rates are set by free-market forces. The issue of fixed versus floating rates is a very important one for managers of companies that do business internationally. Under fixed rates, during normal times a manager can negotiate a transaction with someone in another country with some assurance regarding the amount ultimately to be paid or received in units of domestic currency. Of course, this assurance would evaporate if the exchange rate were changed by one of the governments after the contract was negotiated but before payment. But rate changes under the Bretton Woods system were relatively infrequent.

Under a floating system, a manager faces an element of uncertainty in addition to the normal risks of doing business: if payment is to be made at some future date in a foreign currency, there is no assurance as to what the exchange rate will be on that date. So there is uncertainty regarding the amount ultimately to be received in units of

Figure 21-1

The Ups and Downs of the Floating Dollar

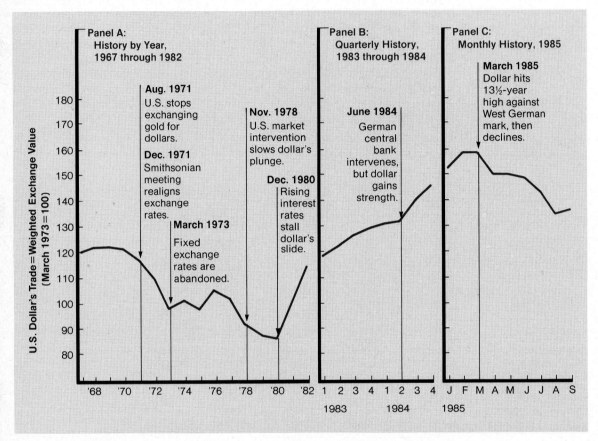

Source: The Federal Reserve System.

Exchange-rate risk—is
the risk of loss in value
due to changes in foreign-
exchange rates.

domestic currency. Later in this chapter, we will explore some of the ways managers deal with this **exchange-rate risk**.

Some economists and business managers believe that a fixed-rate system is preferable to a floating-rate system, although there is great disagreement on this point, even among experts. But it is certainly possible that the major trading nations of the world could return to a fixed system. We may see a good deal of discussion of the merits of returning to fixed rates in the financial press in the late 1980s. In fact, some nations have gone a step back toward a fixed system by periodically intervening in foreign-exchange markets to try to influence exchange rates. Such intervention in a system that is supposed to be floating sometimes is called a "dirty float." We will return later to the matter of central-bank intervention and its effects on foreign-exchange markets.

Because the world for the most part now operates under a system of floating rates, we now will go into more detail regarding just how such a system works.

THE FOREIGN-EXCHANGE MARKET

Most individuals become involved with foreign exchange in only one way: as tourists. An American tourist traveling in the United Kingdom buys British pounds with dollars, using either currency or, more likely, traveler's checks.

These pounds are usually bought at a local bank, hotel, or perhaps a store and are then used to buy things in local markets. A tourist also might use an internationally recognized credit card to make payments abroad. The credit-card company then makes payment to the seller in the local currency and then converts the amount into dollars on the cardholder's monthly statement. Individuals also purchase goods directly from abroad and pay for them using drafts (similar to checks) that are purchased from a domestic commercial bank and denominated in the appropriate foreign currency. In all these transactions, the credit-card company, bank, or other organization that actually makes the currency conversion does so at an exchange rate that, under the system of floating rates in effect since 1973, fluctuates in response to market forces.

Foreign-exchange transactions arising out of the activities of individual tourists involve relatively small amounts and, for most individuals, occur infrequently but in the aggregate add up to substantial amounts. In contrast, transactions arising out of international trade and investment frequently are large and recurrent. A large exporter, for example, likely would generate a large number of transactions, some for substantial amounts, in the course of a single business day. Corporations with international operations, financial institutions, central banks, and various kinds of international organizations all generate large volumes of foreign-exchange transactions in the course of their activities.

The **foreign-exchange market** is a loosely connected group of banks and foreign-exchange brokers who communicate by telephone and mail over great distances to buy and sell different currencies. Market participants are located in the major worldwide financial centers: New York, London, Zurich, Paris, Frankfurt, Tokyo, Toronto, and others.

The supply and demand for foreign currencies originates with commercial transactions between corporations, investors, importers, exporters, and tourists doing business throughout the United States and other countries. Large commercial banks in the major financial centers maintain inventories of foreign currencies and serve as wholesalers for the firms and individuals engaging in the underlying commercial transactions. These banks make the market by buying and selling currencies for their own account—that is, from their own inventories of foreign currencies. In New York, a dozen or so commercial banks trade currencies, normally going through foreign-currency brokers in order to preserve the anonymity of the transacting parties. Central banks, such as the U.S. Federal Reserve, also are active transactors in foreign currencies, as we will discuss later.

The Nature of Foreign-Exchange Transactions

For an individual, a foreign-exchange transaction typically involves swapping traveler's checks for local currency. For corporations, financial institutions, and governmental units, **foreign exchange** is bank deposits denominated in different currencies, and foreign-exchange transactions are executed by exchanging one bank deposit for an-

The **foreign-exchange market**—is a loosely connected group of major banks and foreign-exchange brokers who communicate by telephone and mail over great distances to buy and sell different currencies.

Foreign exchange—consists of money denominated in different currencies.

Finance in Practice 21–1

The Value of the Dollar

The dollar was front-page news during much of the early 1980s. Measured against an average of 10 other currencies, from a low of 88 in 1979 the dollar climbed steadily to a peak of 165 on February 25, 1985. Here we are measuring the dollar's value as an index with 1973 the base year; that is, its 1973 value equals 100. The rise of nearly 90 percent during 1979–85 was not only large enough to make the newspapers, it had very important effects on many Americans. Exports became more difficult as U.S. products became more expensive in foreign markets. Some U.S. firms moved production facilities overseas to take advantage of the dollar's greater purchasing power (a given number of dollars would purchase more foreign labor). Many experts argued that these two developments cost U.S. workers thousands of jobs.

At the same time, the strong dollar made imports cheaper, and foreign products flooded into the United States. Cheaper imports had several effects—some good, some bad. On the plus side, intense foreign competition held prices down in the United States, and many experts feel that the strong dollar contributed to the favorable inflation picture in this country during the early 1980s. On the other side, the U.S. merchandise trade deficit—the excess of our imports over our exports—increased to more than $100 billion by 1985 from about $25 billion in the late 1970s. That trade deficit had to be financed in part by borrowing dollars abroad, which many feel contributed to high real interest rates (relative to inflation) during the early 1980s. During 1984 and early 1985, rather than pointing to the strong dollar with pride as politicians sometimes do, most politicians were complaining that the dollar had gone too far, and many economists agreed.

However, looking at the period since 1980 tells only part of the story, for history did not begin in 1980. After a period of stability during the 1960s, resulting

other. All of these transactions, however, are alike in that each is simply an exchange of one country's money for that of another.

Most foreign-exchange transactions involving individuals and firms have another common feature; they usually are motivated not by a desire to trade the currencies for their own sake, but by a desire to buy or sell goods, services, or financial assets. Foreign-exchange transactions, thus, are a basic part of the international payments mechanism, just as transactions involving checking accounts are a part of the domestic payments mechanism. Unlike individuals and firms, as we noted earlier, central banks often do trade currencies for their own sake when they intervene to prevent exchange rates from fluctuating too much over short periods.

> **Most foreign-exchange transactions for both individuals and firms are undertaken in the process of buying and selling goods, services, or financial assets.**

Because foreign-exchange transactions are part of the payments mechanism, individuals and firms traditionally have called on commercial banks to execute transactions

largely from the system of fixed exchange rates, the dollar went through a long period of decline from 1970 to 1980 after the world moved to a system of floating rates, falling 28 percent from 122 to 88 (see Figure 21–1) as the United States lost its leadership position in the world economy. So the rebound since 1980 started from the dollar's lowest point since World War II.

Economists point to several factors to explain the dollar's strong performance in the early 1980s. First, monetary policy was relatively tighter during much of the period, as the Federal Reserve battled inflation. The resulting high interest rates made dollar investments more attractive relative to investments in other currencies. Second, the 1981 tax cuts initiated by the Reagan administration made business investment

more profitable, raising rates of return generally. Finally, the large deficits in the Federal budget during the early 1980s, projected to continue throughout the decade, contributed to high real rates of interest, again making the dollar attractive.

After peaking in February of 1985, the dollar began to fall against other currencies. Many experts welcomed the decline, feeling that the dollar had been overvalued for some time, at least in part because of high real interest rates in the United States. At its position in the mid-1980s, the dollar stood well above its 1980 low, but some of its strong performance during the early 1980s appears to be a correction of an earlier period of weakness during the 1970s.

The fall in the dollar continued unabated throughout the rest of

1985 and into early 1986. By February, 1986, the dollar had fallen more than 20 percent from its high of a year earlier. Some now began to feel things had gone far enough. Paul Volcker, the influential chairman of the Federal Reserve Board, told the House Banking Committee on February 19, 1986, that the dollar "has fallen enough." Only time will tell whether the decline indeed was enough and whether it would have a positive impact on the U.S. trade deficit and on real rates of interest.

Sources: John Rutledge, "The Dollar Will Keep on Flying," *Fortune*, April 16, 1984, pp. 155–58; Martin Feldstein, "Depressing the Dollar, Gently," *Wall Street Journal*, November 9, 1984; Bruce Steinberg, "Trying to Haul Down the Dollar," *Fortune*, April 15, 1985; "Why the World Loves the Dollar," *Fortune*, February 18, 1985; and the *Wall Street Journal*, September 23, 1985 and February 20, 1986.

for them and make the necessary currency conversions. An importer who needs Japanese yen to pay for a shipment could try to find an exporter with just the right amount of yen for sale, but that would be inconvenient and costly. It is far more convenient and efficient for a bank to act as intermediary, just as banks do in facilitating the flow of funds between lenders and borrowers in domestic transactions. Let us now examine foreign-exchange rates in more detail.

The Spot Market

The **spot rate**—is the price of one currency in terms of another when purchased for immediate delivery.

Table 21–2 shows foreign-exchange rates on a particular day—July 12—in 1985. The rate shown in the first column for the British pound, 1.3885, means that one pound can be purchased for $1.3885. This **spot rate** is the rate applicable for purchasing pounds for *immediate delivery*. In the spot market, "immediate delivery" normally means delivery within two business days to allow time for the necessary accounting and paperwork to be done, although sometimes spot transactions are executed in one day under special circumstances. Just as the pound was quoted spot at $1.3885 on July 12, 1985, the Japanese yen was $0.004155, the Mexican peso was $0.003003, the Italian lira was $0.0005349, and so on.

Table 21–2

Foreign Exchange Rates for Friday, July 12, 1985

	U.S. Dollar Equivalent		Currency per U.S. Dollar	
Country	Friday	Thursday	Friday	Thursday
Argentina (Austral)	1.2422	1.2422	0.805	0.805
Australia (Dollar)	0.7020	0.7025	1.4245	1.4235
Austria (Schilling)	0.04938	0.04892	20.25	20.44
Belgium (Franc)				
Commercial rate	0.01724	0.01702	58.02	58.770
Financial rate	0.01709	0.01688	58.50	59.250
Brazil (Cruzeiro)	0.0001669	0.0001669	5990.00	5990.00
Britain (Pound)	1.3885	1.3785	0.7202	0.7254
30-Day Forward	1.3834	1.3734	0.7229	0.7282
90-Day Forward	1.3746	1.3641	0.7275	0.7331
180-Day Forward	1.3640	1.3533	0.7331	0.7389
Canada (Dollar)	0.7395	0.7389	1.3522	1.3533
30-Day Forward	0.7387	0.7380	1.3538	1.3550
90-Day Forward	0.7369	0.7360	1.3570	1.3587
180-Day Forward	0.7348	0.7338	1.3610	1.3628
Chile (Official rate)	0.005914	0.005914	169.09	169.09
China (Yuan)	0.3491	0.3491	2.8649	2.8649
Colombia (Peso)	0.006990	0.006990	143.06	143.06
Denmark (Krone)	0.09657	0.09542	10.3550	10.4800
Ecuador (Sucre)				
Official rate	0.01489	0.01489	67.18	67.18
Floating rate	0.008881	0.008881	112.60	112.60
Finland (Mark)	0.1659	0.1645	6.0275	6.0800
France (Francs)	0.1141	0.1127	8.7615	8.8750
30-Day Forward	0.118	0.1125	8.7775	8.8910
90-Day Forward	0.1135	0.1120	8.8130	8.9300
180-Day Forward	0.1128	0.1113	8.8635	8.9825
Greece (Drachma)	0.007722	0.007634	129.50	131.00
Hong Kong (Dollar)	0.1290	0.1289	7.7490	7.7560
India (Rupee)	0.08333	0.08333	12.00	12.00
Indonesia (Rupiah)	0.0008993	0.0008993	1112.00	1112.00
Ireland (Punt)	1.0860	1.0660	0.9280	0.9381
Israel (Shekel)	0.0006667	0.0006667	1500.00	1500.00
Italy (Lira)	0.0005349	0.0005328	1869.50	1877.00
Japan (Yen)	0.004155	0.004117	240.65	242.90
30-Day Forward	0.004162	0.004123	240.29	242.56
90-Day Forward	0.004173	0.004134	239.64	241.90
180-Day Forward	0.004194	0.004152	240.65	240.80

Note: The New York foreign-exchange selling rates above apply to trading among banks in amounts of $1 million and more, as quoted at 3 P.M. Eastern time by Bankers Trust Co. Retail transactions provide fewer units of foreign currency per dollar.

Source: *Wall Street Journal*, July 15, 1985.

Country	U.S. Dollar Equivalent		Currency per U.S. Dollar	
	Friday	Thursday	Friday	Thursday
Jordan (Dinar)	2.5820	2.5820	0.3873	0.3873
Kuwait (Dinar)	3.3014	3.3014	0.3029	0.3029
Lebanon (Pound)	0.06325	0.0633	15.81	15.81
Malaysia (Ringgit)	0.4069	0.4065	2.4575	2.4600
Malta (Lira)	2.1254	2.1254	0.4705	0.4705
Mexico (Peso)				
Floating rate	0.003003	0.003175	333.00	315.00
Netherlands (Guilder)	0.3082	0.3046	3.2445	3.2825
New Zealand (Dollar)	0.4855	0.4845	2.0597	2.0640
Norway (Krone)	0.1195	0.1183	8.3700	8.4500
Pakistan (Rupee)	0.06369	0.06349	15.70	15.75
Peru (Sol)	0.00008804	0.00008804	11358.00	11358.00
Philippines (Peso)	0.05411	0.05411	18.48	18.48
Portugal (Escudo)	0.006006	0.005952	166.50	168.00
Saudi Arabia (Riyal)	0.2740	0.2740	3.6495	3.6500
Singapore (Dollar)	0.4535	0.4525	2.2050	2.2100
South Africa (Rand)	0.5245	0.5205	1.9066	1.9212
South Korea (Won)	0.001144	0.001144	874.30	874.30
Spain (Peseta)	0.006017	0.005963	166.20	167.70
Sweden (Krona)	0.1189	0.1181	8.4100	8.4700
Switzerland (Franc)	0.4174	0.4110	2.3955	2.4330
30-Day Forward	0.4186	0.4121	2.3892	2.4267
90-Day Forward	0.4206	0.4140	2.3777	2.4154
180-Day Forward	0.4238	0.4169	2.3598	2.3985
Taiwan (Dollar)	0.025	0.025	40.00	40.00
Thailand (Baht)	0.03656	0.03656	27.35	27.35
United Arab (Dirham)	0.2723	0.2723	3.673	3.673
Uruguay (New Peso)				
Financial	0.01030	0.01030	97.13	97.13
Venezuela (Bolivar)				
Official rate	0.1333	0.1333	7.50	7.50
Floating rate	0.07418	0.07418	13.48	13.48
West Germany (Mark)	0.3468	0.3428	2.8835	2.9170
30-Day Forward	0.3477	0.3436	2.8764	2.9100
90-Day Forward	0.3494	0.3453	2.8623	2.8961
180-Day Forward	0.3520	0.3476	2.8410	2.8765

Table 21–2 shows four spot quotations for each currency. The first two columns give the rate in dollars. The French franc, for example, was quoted at $0.1141 per franc on Friday, July 12, 1985, and $0.1127 per franc the day before. The two additional columns on the right state the exchange the other way, in francs per dollar for each of the two dates—8.7615 francs on July 12 and 8.8750 francs the day before. The dollar/franc rate is simply the reciprocal of the franc/dollar rate.

The Forward Market

The **forward rate**—is the price of one currency in terms of another when purchased for future delivery.

Besides the entries for spot rates in Table 21–2, there are three additional sets of **forward rates** for the British pound. Similarly, for other principal currencies, including the Canadian dollar, French franc, Japanese yen, Swiss franc, and West German mark, listings of forward rates appear. Whereas spot transactions are for immediate delivery (allowing two days for paperwork), forward transactions are made on one date for execution at some future date—normally either 30, 90, or 180 days in the future. For currencies without forward-market quotations in Table 21–2, forward-market transactions still take place, but the market is not as well developed.

Thus, on July 12, 1985, an importer might arrange to purchase British pounds 90 days hence, on October 12, 1985. According to Table 21–2, the rate would be $1.3746. In entering into the transaction, the importer has agreed on July 12, 1985, to purchase pounds on October 12, 1985. The critical point is that the exchange rate is agreed upon on the date of the transaction (July 12), rather than waiting until October 12 to execute the transaction at the spot rate on that date.

What function does the forward market serve? Suppose on July 12, 1985, a U.S. company orders a piece of machinery from a Japanese supplier that will not be delivered until October 12. No one knows what the spot exchange rate will be on October 12. If between July 12 and October 12 the dollar declines in value against the yen, on October 12 it will take more dollars than originally anticipated to pay for the shipment. If the buying company does not want to risk having to pay more, it can fix the exchange rate at the time the order is placed by purchasing yen in the forward market for delivery on October 12. Then the buyer knows exactly what he or she will have to pay. We will talk more about such hedging transactions later in this chapter.

HOW FOREIGN-EXCHANGE RATES ARE DETERMINED

What determines that exactly $0.3468 should be required to purchase one West German DM (deutsche mark) on July 12, 1985? One day earlier, the rate was slightly different at $0.3428. Three years earlier the DM rate was more than $0.4300. What factors determine spot exchange rates, and why do spot rates change over time? It is clear from Table 21–2 that forward and spot rates on a given date are different. Why should this be so, and what factors determine the *forward/spot differential*? As one might guess, the relationship between forward and spot rates is important, and understanding the various factors at work provides insights into how foreign-exchange markets work.

> **Exchange rates are determined by the same forces that determine prices in all competitive markets: the actions of market participants competing against one another—in short, by the forces of supply and demand.**

What factors influence the thousands of individual decisions to buy or sell a currency? Before proceeding, let us note that there are hundreds of different exchange rates. There is the dollar/DM rate, the yen/peso rate, the Swiss franc/Saudi riyal rate, and so on—an exchange rate for each pair of the currencies listed in Table 21–2, and then some. The dollar market for each currency is normally the most active, and most trading activity finds the U.S. dollar on one side of the trade. So we will confine our attention to relationships between the dollar and other currencies.

The Forward/Spot Differential

Note from Table 21–2 that marks for future delivery cost more on July 12, 1985, than marks in the spot market. On that date, the forward DM sold at a *premium* relative to the spot DM, and the longer the contract, the higher was the premium. In contrast, the forward franc sold at a *discount* relative to the spot franc.

Why should the forward mark sell at a premium on July 12, 1985, and the forward franc at a discount? In order to explore this question, Equation (1) shows how to express the spot/forward relationship in quantitative terms. As in the case of interest rates, foreign-exchange premiums and discounts normally are expressed in terms of percent per year.

> The percentage annual premium (or discount, if negative), P, of a forward rate relative to a spot rate can be expressed as
>
> $$P = \frac{F - S}{S} \times \frac{12}{n} \times 100 \tag{1}$$
>
> where F = the forward rate, S = the spot rate, and n = the number of months forward.

In words, the percentage premium is the difference between the forward and spot rates, divided by the spot rate, then multiplied by $12/n$ to annualize it, and multiplied by 100 to put it in percentage terms.

We can now calculate the premium for the 180-day forward mark on July 12, 1985 as

$$P = \frac{0.3520 - 0.3468}{0.3468} \times \frac{12}{6} \times 100 = 3.00 \text{ percent per year.}$$

A similar calculation for the French franc would give

$$P = \frac{0.1128 - 0.1141}{0.1141} \times \frac{12}{6} \times 100 = -2.28 \text{ percent per year.}$$

Thus, the 180-day forward DM is selling at a *premium* of 3.00 percent, and the 180-day forward franc is selling at a *discount* of 2.28 percent. (A discount is a negative premium.)

Why does one currency sell at a forward premium while another simultaneously sells at a forward discount? Is it because the market expected the mark to rise against the dollar over the next six months and the franc to fall? It is possible to view the forward exchange rate in a currency as a forecast of future spot exchange rates. Also very important is the outlook for inflation in the countries involved in the rate relationship. Most important is the *difference* in inflation rates between the countries—the United States and West Germany in the case of dollar/DM exchange rates and the United States and France in the case of the dollar/franc exchange rates.

Dealing with anticipated inflation directly is difficult because of the problem of getting reliable forecasts of future inflation rates, but we can take inflation and its relationship to forward exchange rates into account indirectly by looking at interest rates. As we know from earlier chapters, interest rates contain an inflation premium, which represents the market's consensus forecast of future inflation rates. It is, therefore, possible to explain a great deal about forward exchange rates by examining their relationship to interest rates. This important relationship is described by the **interest-rate-parity theorem**.

The **interest-rate-parity theorem**—shows the relationship between spot and forward exchange rates and interest rates in two currencies.

The Interest-Rate-Parity Theorem

Because the world's major financial centers are linked by telephone, the foreign-exchange market functions essentially as a single market. Therefore, an investor in New York should receive the same interest return on a six-month deposit no matter whether the funds are invested in dollars or deutsche marks—that is the message of the interest-rate-parity theorem.

Suppose someone has money to invest in New York—say, an amount of A dollars—and is considering two options: investing in dollars or in deutsche marks. If this New York investor invests in dollars for a period of n months at an annual interest rate of i ($), the return would be calculated as

$$\text{Return} = \$A[1 + i(\$)(n/12)]$$

where $(n/12)$ represents the fraction of the year the money is invested.

Alternatively, the New York investor could first convert dollars to deutsche marks at the spot rate of DM, S, and receive $\$A/S$ deutsche marks, then invest the deutsche marks for n months at the German annual interest rate of i (DM), and then convert back to dollars at the forward rate, F. The return in this case would be calculated as

$$\text{Return} = \$A/S[1 + i(DM)(n/12)]F.$$

If international currency markets work well, competition would insure that we get the same return no matter which of the above options we pick. If we equate the two expressions for return above and simplify, we get an expression for the interest-rate-parity theorem, as shown in Equations (2) and (3).

According to the interest-rate-parity theorem, the relationship between forward and spot exchange rates and interest rates for any two currencies (here, dollars and deutsche marks are used as an example) can be expressed as

$$\frac{F}{S} = \frac{1 + i(\$)(n/12)}{1 + i(DM)\,n/12} \tag{2}$$

where F = the forward rate in \$/DM, S is the spot rate in \$/DM, $i(\$)$ = the annual interest rate on dollar-denominated deposits, $i(DM)$ = the annual interest rate on DM-denominated deposits, and n = the number of months forward.

According to the interest-rate-parity theorem, the relationship between spot and forward exchange rates and interest rates can also be expressed, by rearranging Equation (2), as

$$\frac{F - S}{S} \times \frac{12}{n} \times 100 = \frac{i(\$) - i(DM)}{1 + i(DM)(n/12)}. \tag{3}$$

When we compare Equation (3) to Equation (1), we see that the interest-rate-parity theorem tells us that the premium on the forward DM for any period of time (say, 90 days) equals the difference between the interest rates in the United States and West Germany for the same period of time divided by one plus the West German interest rate. The premium—on the left side of Equation (3)—is annualized, as are the interest rates, and the denominator of the right side is also adjusted for the time period.

Let us check the accuracy of the theorem. On July 12, 1985, the rate of interest on large six-month **Eurocurrency** deposits denominated in dollars was 8 percent per year. (Eurocurrencies are a form of international money to which we will return later in this chapter.) The corresponding rate on deposits denominated in marks on July 12, 1985, was 5.25 percent per year. We calculated the left side of Equation (2) earlier (the six-month forward premium on the mark) and got 3 percent, or 0.0300. Calculating the right side, we get 0.0268, or 2.68 percent. The difference between the 3.00 and 2.68 percent figures results partly from the fact that in our calculations we are ignoring commissions charged by foreign-exchange traders and other transaction costs.

Thus, the interest-rate-parity theorem helps us understand how interest rates and exchange rates are related. The fact that we earn a lower interest rate in DM (5.25 percent versus 8 percent) than in dollars is offset by the fact that there is a forward premium on the mark. As shown in Table 21–2, the mark is worth more in terms of dollars on the 180-day forward market (\$0.3520 per mark) than it is on the spot market (\$0.3468).

The market process through which the relationships in the interest-rate-parity theorem come into being is known as **covered-interest arbitrage**. Suppose a U.S. corporation had \$100,000 of excess cash on July 12, 1985, and knew that it would not need to use the funds for 180 days. It could invest the funds in a Eurocurrency deposit denominated in dollars and receive interest over the 180-day period at the then-current

A **Eurocurrency**—is a deposit denominated in a given country's currency and that is held in a bank outside that country.

Covered-interest arbitrage—is the market process through which the relationships in the interest-rate-parity theorem are enforced.

Table 21–3
Covered Interest Arbitrage

Panel A: Alternative A
1. Invest $100,000 in dollar-denominated certificate of deposit (CD) for 180 days at 8 percent per year (= 4.0* = 8 ÷ 2 for six months).

July 1985
1. Buy $100,000 CD

January 1986
1. Receive $100,000(1 + 0.04) = $104,000

Panel B: Alternative B
1. In spot market, buy deutsche marks (DM) worth $100,000.
2. Buy CD denominated in marks, at 2.625* percent for six months.
3. In forward market, sell DM for dollars.

July 1985
1. In spot market: $100,000 × 2.8835 = 288,350 DM (exchange rate from Table 21–2).
2. Buy CD for 288,350 DM, which in 6 months will return (288,350 DM) × (1.02625) = 295,919 DM
3. In forward market: Buy dollars for delivery in November, (295,919 DM) × (0.3520) = $104,163.

January 1986
1. Collect 295,919 DM from the investment in the CD.
2. Deliver the 295,919 DM to honor the contract in the forward market, receiving (295,919 DM) × (0.3520) = $104,163 as planned.

*To simplify matters, the percent rate of return has been rounded. All exchange rates are for Friday, July 12, 1985, and come from Table 21–2.

U.S. CD (certificate of deposit) rate of 8.00 percent, for a return of 8.00/2 = 4.00 percent during the six-month period.[2] Alternatively, the firm's treasurer could buy DM spot and invest the proceeds in a CD denominated in DM at an interest rate of 5.25 percent, or 2.625 percent for six months. These two alternatives are outlined in Table 21–3.

At first glance the choice looks pretty clear-cut. The treasurer can earn 4.00 percent in the dollar-denominated CD and only 2.625 percent in the DM-denominated CD. The U.S. CD initially looks better as an investment, but before the treasurer can reach a final conclusion, he or she has to remember that the 2.625 percent is a return in DM. To be directly comparable to the 4.00 percent on the dollar-denominated CD, the marks must be converted to dollars.

The treasurer knows that the marks have to be converted back to dollars in the following January when the foreign CD matures and the dollars are needed for other purposes. Suppose the exchange rate between the two currencies changed between July and January. A change in one direction would make the firm worse off, and a change

---

[2]To simplify matters, we round interest rates to the nearest one hundredth of a percent and assume compounding once per year.

in the other direction would make the firm better off. The treasurer could remove this uncertainty from the transaction by selling marks in July for delivery in January in the forward market because he or she knows in July just how much he or she will have in marks in January—that sum being the original amount plus the interest he or she will earn on the marks between July and January. Such a transaction in the forward market is known as *covering*.

Table 21–3 summarizes the results of the entire series of transactions. Panel A shows the direct investment in a dollar-denominated CD. Panel B shows the steps necessary to perform covered-interest arbitrage. Note that in Panel B, three transactions must be made in July 1985: buying marks in the spot market, buying the DM-denominated CD, and buying dollars in the forward market. In January, 1986, Panel A shows a dollar return of $104,000. Panel B shows a dollar return of $104,163 in January. Note that the figures are very close, just as the interest-rate-parity theorem in Equation (2) suggests. The lower interest rate in Germany was effectively converted to a higher interest rate (in dollar terms) because the forward mark was at a premium. In other words, the interest rates shown in Panels A and B of Table 21–3 are effectively almost the same once the foreign-exchange market is considered—the interest rates are *in parity*.

What should the treasurer do? According to the calculations in Table 21–3, slightly more money can be obtained by the strategy in Panel B, but this result ignores transactions costs. It is highly likely that the extra $163 earned by going from A to B would not be enough to offset the extra transactions costs, in which case, the treasurer should invest the money in a dollar-denominated CD.

> **Covered-interest arbitrage is the market process that enforces the relationships in the interest-rate-parity theorem.**

If the dollar/deutsche mark exchange rate and interest rates in the two countries were *not* related as in Equation (2), investors could earn a profit by entering into covered transactions similar to the one described above. Because all exchange rates were set at the time of the transaction, there would be no risk (ignoring the slight risk of a default or bankruptcy by one of the banks involved). But opportunities for riskless profits do not go unnoticed for long, so we can expect the relationships embodied in the interest-rate-parity theorem in Equation (2) to hold very closely.

We noted earlier that relationships between exchange rates depend on a number of factors. One of the most important factors affecting both exchange rates and interest rates is the inflation rate expected in the future. Differences between inflation rates in two countries—say, the United States and West Germany—have a great deal to do with the way exchange rates between currencies of the two countries behave over time. If the inflation rate were higher in the United States than in West Germany over an extended period, the dollar would decline relative to the mark: the spot exchange rate between the two currencies would change. Suppose the investors and companies engaged in trade between the United States and West Germany expected inflation rates in the two countries to differ in the future. Dollar/DM exchange rates would be affected, but the effects would be felt primarily in forward rates rather than in spot rates. But, as noted earlier, these expectations of future inflation are captured in interest rates, so we take anticipated inflation into account implicitly when we use the interest-rate-parity theorem.[3]

Central-Bank Intervention

In practice, exchange rates are not determined solely by the actions of individuals and firms. Central banks—which are, for practical purposes, arms of governments—also have an important influence. In the United States, the Federal Reserve plays the role of central bank.

Because major currencies began floating against one another in 1973, central banks of different countries have intervened in foreign-exchange markets in varying degrees and for varying reasons. Such intervention takes the form of buying and selling one currency against another. In the case of the United States, intervention by the Federal Reserve typically has been aimed at smoothing out fluctuations in exchange rates rather than trying to maintain a particular exchange rate or to push rates to a new level. This motive might be described as countering disorderly market conditions in order to stabilize the market.

Some governments from time to time may intervene in order to resist an appreciation of their currency that could erode the position of their exports in world markets. Or a government might intervene in the other direction to resist depreciation of its currency that would cause prices of imports to rise and, thereby, increase domestic inflation. In the resulting "dirty float," rates are technically floating, but not freely. The extent to which governments have succeeded in resisting changes in exchange rates to new levels is open to question, although there is no doubt that trading by a central bank can dampen short-term fluctuations.

DEALING WITH FOREIGN-EXCHANGE EXPOSURE

Exchange-rate risk is the inevitable consequence of trading in a world in which foreign-currency values fluctuate in response to forces of supply and demand. Suppose a U.S. electronics manufacturer buys solid-state memory chips from a Japanese supplier. The sales contract could be expressed either in U.S. dollars or Japanese yen—a matter subject to negotiation by the two parties. In a world of floating rates, one of the two parties will wind up bearing the exchange-rate risk. If the contract is in dollars, the Japanese firm bears the risk; if the contract is in yen, the American firm bears the risk. For the party bearing the risk, it is exactly as if the final price to be paid is left

---

[3]There is an important relationship, known as the *purchasing-power-parity theorem*, or less formally as the *law of one price*, that states that a single good must sell at the same price everywhere, adjusting for transportation costs. The theorem also implies that prices of a given good in the future should be the same everywhere. When applied to foreign-exchange markets, the purchasing-power-parity theorem implies that expected differences in inflation rates between two countries should be related in a precise way to expected changes in spot exchange rates. The expectations theory of forward rates in turn calls for a precise relationship between forward rates and expected changes in spot rates. At the same time, expected inflation rates are related to interest rates. Thus, spot exchange rates, forward rates, inflation rates, interest rates, and expectations regarding future values of these variables all are closely related. All of these various relationships can be examined independently, but for our purposes here, much of what is important in foreign-exchange markets can be discussed by focusing on just two factors—exchange rates and interest rates—by means of the interest-rate-parity theorem.

uncertain. Let us now consider how firms and other organizations can deal with the foreign-exchange risk to which they are exposed by virtue of owning assets or owning liabilities denominated in another currency.[4]

Hedging

Hedging—is an attempt to reduce the risk associated with future price fluctuations.

A widely used method of reducing foreign-exchange risk is **hedging** through the use of forward contracts. A hedge is an arrangement designed to reduce the risk from future price fluctuations. Hedging is widely used in connection with commodities as a way for producers and consumers to "lay off" the risk of price fluctuations. Producers of commodities, such as farmers in the case of agricultural commodities or mining companies in the case of metals, regularly hedge against future price fluctuations by selling their production for future delivery. A wheat farmer, for example, in January might sell wheat for delivery in May at a specified price. The farmer is now obligated to deliver a specified amount of wheat and, hence, is subject to business risk but has laid off the risk of price fluctuations.

Consumers of commodities also hedge by buying in the futures market. A manufacturer of chocolate candy might buy cocoa beans in the futures market in order to be assured of a supply at a known price.

In such cases the producers and consumers of the commodities are hedging; they concentrate on what they are best at—growing wheat or manufacturing candy—and let others bear the risk of price fluctuations. The risk bearers are known as **speculators** because they willingly seek to bear the risk, with the prospect of large gains if things turn out favorably for them. Speculators in commodities and foreign exchange perform a socially necessary and desirable function. Through speculation, those willing and able to bear risk do so and those who wish to avoid it have a means of meeting their objectives as well.

Speculators—are people who willingly bear risk, with the prospect of large gains if things turn out favorably for them.

> **Through hedging, the risk of changes in foreign-exchange rates can be eliminated in many international transactions.**

In foreign exchange, the uncertain future price is the exchange rate between two currencies at some future date. Consider an American automobile manufacturer that decided to sell a small foreign subsidiary located in France in order to raise needed cash for domestic use. The subsidiary was sold to a French buyer for 4.5 million French francs (FF). The contract was signed on July 12, 1985, with payment to be made in francs on the closing date six months hence, on January 12, 1986.

The spot exchange rate on July 12, 1985, was $0.1141 (Table 21–2), so if payment could have been received on that date, it would have yielded $0.1141 × 4,500,000 = $513,450. But the funds were not available on July 12 and would not be available for six months. If, between July and January, the franc declines relative to the dollar, the U.S. company will get less than $513,450; if it rises, the company will get more. The automobile company needs the money and does not wish to run the risk of an adverse movement in exchange rates. What should the management do?

The American company can lay off the uncertainty by selling 4.5 million francs

---

[4]For a discussion of ways companies deal with foreign-exchange risk, see R. M. Rodriguez, "Corporate Exchange Risk Management," *Journal of Finance* 36 (May 1981): 427–38.

forward for delivery in six months on January 12, 1986. Such a hedge is called a *forward hedge* because it is being accomplished through the forward currency market. On July 12, the 180-day forward rate was $0.1128, so by hedging the company could be assured of receiving $0.1128 × 4,500,000 = $507,600 in January. Alas, the company will get less by hedging, but this difference simply reflects the fact that, in July 1985, interest rates were higher in France than in the United States. The franc was selling at a forward discount, which implies an expectation that the spot rate relative to the dollar would decline over the coming months.

The American firm has two choices. It can do nothing and simply wait until January, receive the 4.5 million french francs, and convert to dollars at the spot rate on that date—recognizing that the most likely outlook (implied by the current forward discount in the franc) is a declining spot rate. Alternatively, the company can sell the francs now and eliminate the uncertainty. So the choice is between a likely decline of uncertain magnitude and a certain discount now.

The automobile manufacturer was considering hedging against a decline in the price of an asset denominated in a foreign currency. Consider now the opposite case in which an obligation exists to make a payment in a foreign currency at some future date. The Chapel of the Cross, an Episcopal church in Chapel Hill, North Carolina, was given a substantial sum with the stipulation by the donor that it be used to purchase a new organ of first quality. After a lengthy search, a contract was negotiated with a West German company to build and install the organ. Payment was to be made in deutsche marks in installments over a two-year period.

At the spot exchange rate at the time the contract was negotiated, the church had enough dollars to purchase the marks necessary to settle the contract. But what if the dollar declined relative to the mark while the organ was being constructed, a period of more than a year? At the time, the dollar looked weak, and a decline could leave the church with insufficient funds to pay the organ builder. So the church vestry decided to buy marks forward and eliminate the uncertainty. Churches are not regular participants in the foreign-exchange market, but in this case, *not* to have hedged would have been, in effect, to speculate.

In some cases, not to hedge is, in effect, to speculate.

Other Techniques for Reducing Risk

A forward hedge such as that described above will not work in cases where there is no functioning forward market. Forward markets are well-developed in only a few of the world's major currencies: the U.S. dollar, British pound, Canadian dollar, French franc, Japanese yen, Swiss franc, and West German deutsche mark. Table 21–2 showed forward quotes for only these currencies.

In currencies with no forward market, it is sometimes possible to arrange a special forward contract with a large financial intermediary. One cannot count on this, however, and in such cases one often must look to other methods. What other methods can a company use to reduce foreign-exchange risk in transactions involving currencies with no forward market?

One method, called *leading and lagging*, is simply to try to hasten or slow down payments and prospective receipts depending on the likely direction of changes in exchange rates. If a company owed 100,000 Mexican pesos (a currency for which no forward-market quotes appear in Table 21–2) in 90 days, and expected the peso to rise relative to the dollar, the company might find it advantageous to go ahead and settle the bill sooner.

Another device is to borrow or lend in the local currency. Suppose the automobile manufacturer described above with the subsidiary in France instead were selling a subsidiary located in Mexico. The company could not hedge the transaction by selling pesos forward. Instead it could employ a *spot hedge* involving a loan in Mexican pesos. The company would first determine how many pesos it will receive on the closing date, January 12, 1986. It could then borrow that amount from a bank in Mexico, convert the pesos it borrows to dollars in the spot market, and invest the dollars in U.S. Treasury bills or some other dollar-denominated deposit with a maturity of January 12, 1986. On the closing date, January 12, 1986, the company receives payment in pesos for its subsidiary and uses the proceeds to pay off its loan to the Mexican bank. Earlier, by investing in the dollar-denominated deposit, the company locked in the dollar amount of the transaction and so was not exposed to exchange-rate risk during the six-month period.

A third method of reducing exchange-rate risk is by means of a *parallel loan*. Suppose one company expects a payment in 60 days from a subsidiary located in a country for whose currency no forward market exists. At the same time, another company plans to begin building a new plant in that country on about the same date and must make an outlay to start construction. One company wants to sell the foreign currency in 60 days, and the other wants to buy it. The two firms could work out an arrangement that would protect them both from changes in the spot exchange rate. In effect, the two companies create their own foreign-exchange market. Such transactions require that amounts and timing match up and so are relatively rare, but the parallel-loan device can be beneficial in some cases.

Currency Options

In some situations, hedging is not possible using the spot or forward markets. There are also cases in which individuals or firms want to hedge against the risk of a move in one direction without giving up potential profits if the move is the other way.

A **currency option**—is a financial claim that gives one the right but not the obligation to buy or sell a foreign currency.

A new device, called a **currency option**, has come into being recently to fill these needs. Under a forward contract, the buyer or seller is obligated to complete the transaction. With an option, the option buyer has the *right* but not the obligation to buy or sell the currency. We discussed options on securities in Appendix 16A. Here we will focus specifically on currency options.

Consider the following case in which an option might be used. An American firm bids on a contract in the United Kingdom on August 1, 1986. The contract requires that the firm install a security system in a British factory. Most of the materials and labor will be purchased in the United States, but payment will be made in British pounds. Bids must be submitted by August 1, 1986; the contract will be awarded on October 1, 1986; the work must be completed by April 1, 1987; payment will be made on April 1, 1987.

If the firm wins the contract on October 1, at that point it can hedge against changes in the dollar/pound exchange rate by selling pounds forward for delivery on April 1, 1987. It uses the pounds received from its British customer to settle the forward currency contract.

The forward contract will work fine on October 1 once the firm knows for sure that it has the contract. But what can it do on August 1, when winning the contract is not assured? If it sells pounds then and subsequently does not get the contract, it is at risk; if it does not sell pounds and then does get the contract, it is again at risk. There is no way using the forward currency market to hedge against risk during the period from August 1 to October 1.

Enter the currency option. On August 1, when it submits the bid, the firm buys a put option on the pound giving it the right, *but not the obligation*, to sell pounds on or before April 1, 1987, at an agreed-upon price. If it wins the bid, it is assured of the exchange rate at the completion of the contract. If it loses the bid, it simply does not exercise the option. If it wins the bid and the pound moves to the firm's advantage, it can forgo the option and simply sell pounds in the spot market on April 1, 1987.

The option is ideal for situations in which the need for foreign currency is not certain. The buyer of the option pays a price—an option fee that normally ranges from 1.5 to 1.75 percent of the amount of the option. A company using options in its commercial operations obviously would have to build the cost of options into its bids.

Currency options are a recent innovation and only became a significant factor in commercial transactions in 1984. That year the value of contracts outstanding grew rapidly to an estimated $5 billion. Options are now available in the United States in five major foreign currencies: the pound, the deutsche mark, the yen, the Canadian dollar, and the Swiss franc. The typical option has a face amount of $5 to $10 million for three to six months. Banks reportedly have been asked to quote on options for as much as $650 million and for periods as long as two and a half years, although such transactions are unusual.[5]

Credit risk—is the risk that a borrower will default on a loan.

Options are traded on several exchanges, including the Philadelphia Stock Exchange and the Chicago Mercantile Exchange. Commercial banks in major money centers and some major investment-banking firms are also active participants.

> **Currency options sometimes can be used to reduce risk in cases in which hedging in the forward currency markets does not work.**

Other Risks

Foreign-exchange risk is not the only risk to which multinational firms are exposed. If a transaction with a foreign firm involves a loan, there is the standard **credit risk** that the borrower may default. Even if the borrower is a foreign government, credit risk may still be a factor. In 1982, the Polish government was unable to meet maturing loan obligations to western banks. Although the loans were never declared by the banks to be in default, the fact remains that payments were not made according to schedule and loans had to be restructured with new maturities and interest rates.

Country risk—is the risk that a foreign government or foreign politics will interfere with international transactions. At the extreme, country risk includes the possibility that a foreign government may expropriate the firm's property or that a war may ensue.

A second important factor is **country risk**. At one time or another in its history, virtually every government has interfered with international transactions. Such interference has taken the form of regulation of the local foreign-exchange market, restrictions on amounts of currency that can be converted, restrictions on foreign investment by residents, and restrictions on *repatriation* of funds by local subsidiaries of foreign companies (restricting the payment of dividends to the parent company by the subsid-

---

[5] *Wall Street Journal*, April 20, 1984, p. 25.

iary). Such restrictions may be designed to improve control over the domestic banking system, to conserve foreign exchange, to smooth out fluctuations in the exchange rate, or even to try to influence its level. At any rate, restrictions such as these are sometimes a fact of life, and participants in international transactions must take them into account. Actions by foreign governments also affect the basic business risk of operating internationally. At the extreme, the likelihood of war or of expropriation of property affect basic business decisions made across international boundaries.

MULTINATIONAL INVESTMENT AND FINANCING DECISIONS

A **multinational firm**—is a firm that operates or invests in two or more countries.

Thus far we have discussed primarily transactions between two parties—for example, one company buying something from another. Complex problems also arise in the case of a single company that operates in two or more countries, the so-called **multinational firm**. The multinational firm must make long-term investments and pay for them in local currencies. It must invest for short periods its idle cash balances held in local currencies. It may find it advantageous to raise funds in local or international capital markets (see Finance in Practice 21–2). And it must have a way of repatriating the earnings of foreign subsidiaries back to its native country. All such transactions potentially involve foreign-exchange risk.

Long-Term Investment Decisions

Multinational companies invest funds in long-term assets in many countries around the world. They build plants to produce products, replace equipment as it wears out, install new equipment to reduce costs, and invest in transportation and distribution networks. These decisions have the same basic economic characteristics that domestic investment decisions do; namely, they involve making an outlay in the present with the prospect of generating future cash flows.

The analytical techniques that we discussed in Part Four apply to international investment decisions as well as to domestic ones. Discounted-cash-flow techniques can be applied, using valuation as the basic decision framework. This process involves the same steps: estimating cash flows, choosing a decision criterion, and setting a return target.

However, the evaluation process is more complicated when capital flows across international boundaries. Suppose a U.S. firm is contemplating building a plant in France. To evaluate its domestic investment decisions, the firm has been using a weighted-average required return calculated from return data on its outstanding common stock and long-term bonds in the United States. Does it use the same required rate of return to evaluate the French plant? Suppose interest rates are higher in France, and suppose part of the needed capital is to be raised in European capital markets.

Even more complex situations can occur when the contemplated investment differs substantially in risk from the firm's typical investment and the firm attempts to use the capital-asset-pricing model (CAPM) to estimate risk premiums.[6] How does the firm determine the relevant benchmark portfolio? Is the portfolio of U.S. securities used in

---

[6]See Chapter 5 for a discussion of the capital-asset-pricing model (CAPM).

applying the CAPM to domestic decisions appropriate for international investments? Or do we need an international market portfolio, and does such a portfolio exist?

These are complex questions, and even the experts disagree on the answers. The state of the art in such matters is still very primitive, and no one really can say with assurance that the extra complexity introduced by trying to take these special factors into account in setting return targets produces significantly better answers.[7]

Besides additional complexity in setting return targets, estimating cash flows also is more complex. In projecting the cash flows expected from a project several years into the future, what assumptions do we make about changes in foreign-exchange rates? The cash inflows from an international project may well be denominated in a foreign currency. Should we hedge against unfavorable exchange-rate shifts by selling foreign exchange forward each year? There are ways to deal with these questions, but they complicate the analysis.

There are other complicating factors in international investment decisions that are essentially political rather than financial. Earlier, in discussing foreign-exchange risk, we described country risk as the risk that foreign governments will intervene in international financial transactions. Another risk in the same category that applies more to long-term investments is the risk of expropriation of property, sometimes called *nationalization*, either with or without compensation. In the early 1970s, the Chilean government expropriated Anaconda Company's copper mines located there. Other less severe steps that foreign governments sometimes take include prohibitions on repatriation of funds back to the home country, taxation, direct controls over prices and wages, restrictions on local borrowing, and any number of other operating matters. In some countries, there is also the risk of war or local insurrections where almost anything can happen.

In 1969 the U.S. government provided some insurance for multinational firms against some of these risks by establishing a special corporation known as the Overseas Private Investment Corporation. OPIC insures U.S.-owned investments against certain risks, including expropriation, restrictions on currency convertibility, and war and insurrection.

Short-Term Investments

Subsidiaries of international firms have temporarily idle cash balances just as most firms do. Suppose a U.S. firm has a subsidiary in West Germany that has 1 million deutsche marks in a German bank that will not be needed for six months. The funds could be invested in a DM-denominated certificate of deposit with a six-month maturity. Alternatively, the treasurer could buy U.S. dollars on the spot market, invest in a six-month CD denominated in dollars, and sell the dollars (including the prospective interest) six months forward to hedge the transaction and eliminate exchange-rate risk. In fact, the treasurer could do the same thing with any of the major currencies for which an active forward market exists: the British pound, Canadian dollar, French franc, Japanese yen, or the Swiss franc.

A firm does not have to operate internationally to exercise this option; any firm can

---

[7]For a discussion of an approach to evaluating foreign investment projects, see D. R. Lessard, "Evaluating Foreign Projects—An Adjusted Present Value Approach," *International Financial Management: Theory and Application*, 2nd ed. (New York: John Wiley & Sons, 1985).

do it. But firms that operate internationally are more likely to explore such alternatives simply because they are more familiar with the territory.

The fact that any firm can invest cash in any major currency should tell us that the likely returns should all be about the same because competition drives foreign-exchange rates—both spot and forward—into relationships with one another and with interest rates such that one comes out about the same investing in a local CD as converting, investing elsewhere, and then converting back. This is the lesson of the interest-rate-parity theorem, which we discussed earlier.

To illustrate, assume that a firm has $1 million in a bank that it wishes to invest for six months. It could buy a dollar-denominated CD or, alternatively, invest in any of the major currencies by converting spot, investing, and covering in the forward market. In order to use the foreign-exchange rates in Table 21–2, let us assume that it is now July 12, 1985. The six-month rate on dollar-denominated Eurocurrency deposits is 8.0 percent. Taking the DM as an alternative investment vehicle, we find that the six-month DM rate is 5.25 percent. The six-month forward premium on the DM, which we calculated earlier, is 3.00 percent.[8] We can approximate the covered interest rate on an investment in DM by simply adding the forward premium to the DM interest rate. We get $5.25 + 3.00 = 8.25$ percent—not far from the U.S. interest rate of 8.0 percent. If we invest in the dollar-denominated CD, we earn 8.0 percent; if we convert to DM and cover ourselves forward, we earn 8.25 percent. The 0.25 percent spread calculated above overstates the difference in returns because we have ignored transactions costs and made some approximations in our calculations.

If we do the same kind of calculation for other major currencies we get the same result—a covered interest rate close to the U.S. interest rate, which is the result we would expect in a well-functioning market.[9]

Do we conclude that it does not matter, that all the alternatives for investing idle funds yield the same result? Not quite. For amounts of less than $1 million or so, the differences in prospective earnings are too small to make the transaction worthwhile, but on a transaction involving hundreds of millions of dollars, a difference of even 0.01 percent can yield a tidy profit. For this reason, very large firms maintain a staff of individuals expert in foreign exchange. This activity of large firms also explains why the covered interest rates in different countries are so close—the fact that large firms exploit the differences insures that the differences never get very large.

Financing Foreign Operations

Firms doing business in foreign countries face many alternatives for financing those activities.[10] A U.S. firm with a subsidiary in France, for example, could raise funds

---

[8]Note that all of the rates are annualized. Table 21–3 works this same example using actual dollar figures over a 6-month period.

[9]We took a shortcut above in calculating the covered-interest rate. We used only the numerator of the right side of Equation (2) in the calculation. To be strictly correct, the forward premium on the DM should be multiplied by $(1 + i\text{DM } n/12)$ and then added to $i\text{DM}$ to calculate the covered-interest rate on DM. The method above gives a quick-and-dirty approximation adequate for many purposes. But when amounts are large, the full calculation should be made. The calculations shown in Table 21–3 show the exact dollar figures involved.

[10]For a discussion, see A. A. Robichek and M. R. Eaker, "Debt Denomination and Exchange Risk in European Capital Markets," *Financial Management* 5 (Autumn 1976): 11–18.

Finance in Practice 21–2

The Euroequity Market

The Eurocurrency market has been around for a good while, beginning with dollars in the 1950s. Eurobonds came later, providing firms the opportunity to sell bonds denominated in dollars or other currencies in foreign capital markets.

In the mid-1980s, a new "Euro" market, called by some the "Euroequity" market, came into being. Prior to 1980, few companies issued stock outside their own domestic capital markets, in spite of the fact that Eurocurrencies and Eurobonds were used routinely. Since 1980, nearly 60 companies have issued stock simultaneously in two or more countries, and the pace is accelerating: 23 of those issues— more than a third of the total— were issued during the first five months of 1986. The accompanying table shows the development of the Euroequity market since 1983.

Year	Number of Issues of Stock in The Euroequity Market	Amount of Stock Issued in the Euroequity Market (millions of dollars)
1983	4	116.6
1984	5	305.8
1985	26	3,185.6
1986 (Jan. thru May)	23	1,733.6

U.S. companies accounted for 11 of the 23 issues in 1986, compared to 3 issues in 1985 and 1 in 1984. The 11 U.S. issues raised a total of $605 million in the European capital markets. Some investment bankers already are predicting that, before too long, a part of almost every U.S. equity issue will be sold in Europe. One of the U.S. offerings in 1986 was issued by Chrysler Corporation, which sold its holdings in the French automobile manufacturer, Peugeot, through stock offerings in six national markets. Black and Decker recently sold 8.5 million new shares, with 2.0 million of the total going into the European market. In an earlier offering in 1983, Black and Decker had not even considered Europe, but in this latest offering, the company instructed its investment bankers "to get as much of the stock as possible into Europe."

Investment bankers state that the advantage of selling stock in multiple markets is wider distribution, increased demand, and if possible a better price for the issuing company. A company that recently issued 31 percent of its total offering in Europe stated that "the price would have been lower if we had done the deal just in the U.S." One investment banker, whose firm has tripled the size of its staff in London in the past two years, optimistically predicts that "within five years, everybody who issues equity is going to look to the European market."

Source: Adapted from "U.S. Firms Offering Stock Look Overseas," *Wall Street Journal*, June 16, 1986, p. 17.

in U.S. capital markets and transfer them to the subsidiary, where the funds would be converted to francs and used for local purposes. The original financing instrument would be denominated in dollars. Alternatively, the firm or its subsidiary could raise funds locally in France, with the obligation denominated in francs.

Still a third alternative would be to finance in the Eurocurrency market. Eurocurrencies began with Eurodollars back in the 1950s. A *Eurodollar* is simply a dollar-denominated deposit in a bank outside the United States. Such deposits began in banks in Europe—hence, the name. After the Eurodollar was invented, other Eurocurrencies came into being. A Euromark, for example, is simply a deposit denominated in marks in a bank outside West Germany.

The interesting thing about Eurocurrencies is that they are not regulated by any government. In the United States, the Federal Reserve regulates the money supply and controls its size by means of reserve requirements imposed on deposits in commercial banks and by other techniques. Central banks in other countries likewise control the size of their domestic money supplies, but nobody controls Eurocurrencies. If the British government attempted to control Eurodollar deposits in British banks, the deposits would simply move to another country. To gain control of Eurocurrencies would require the collaboration of practically every government in the world—something not likely any time soon.

Eurocurrencies remain an unregulated and truly international currency. No one has exact figures on just how large the Eurocurrency market is, but the total was believed to have been roughly $2,500 billion in mid-1985, with Eurodollars making up 80 percent, or about $2,000 billion, of the market. The Eurocurrency market has become very important in international trade and finance and an important source of financing for many multinational firms. Firms can borrow Eurodollars or other Eurocurrencies in the short term or raise long-term funds in the Eurobond market. Rates of interest parallel those in corresponding domestic markets, but deviations do occur and offer opportunities for cheaper financing to sharp-penciled treasurers.

Accounting and Reporting Requirements

As one might imagine, measuring the performance and financial position of a firm engaged in international operations gets very complicated. Added to the problem of accounting for domestic operations are all the complexities of foreign exchange and dealing with foreign-exchange gains and losses.

Foreign-currency **translation**—is the conversion of accounting information denominated in one currency into accounting information denominated in another currency.

There is the problem of foreign-currency **translation**. Suppose a multinational firm has subsidiaries in several countries. To keep things simple, assume for the moment that during a particular accounting period there were no capital flows between parent and subsidiaries and no foreign-exchange transactions of any kind. The firm still must deal with foreign exchange if it wants to produce a consolidated accounting statement combining the operations of the entire multinational enterprise. The financial statements of the French subsidiary are denominated in francs; the statements of the Japanese subsidiary are denominated in yen. To produce consolidated statements, all of these figures must be converted into dollars.

It sounds simple at first, but it is not. Should an asset acquired in 1980 be converted at today's exchange rate or that existing at the time the asset was acquired? Where thousands of individual assets are involved, this problem quickly gets out of hand. This and other similarly nettlesome questions have driven accountants and managers to distraction over the past two decades. The Financial Accounting Standards Board, the rule-making body that sets the standards for accounting in the United States, made its initial attempt at standards for foreign-exchange translation with FASB #8, issued in 1975. The rules were complex and unsatisfactory to many managers. After several years of controversy, a new set of rules, embodied in FASB #52, was issued in 1982. The new rules also caused controversy, and the issue remains unsettled.

Translation is a very complicated and important matter, but it affects only one part of the overall problem of managing foreign operations—the preparation of consolidated financial statements by multinational firms. Nevertheless, this reporting problem can be important, as IBM's experience recently showed.

In April of 1985, IBM reported earnings of $1.61 per share for the first quarter of 1985, down 18 percent from the figure of $1.97 for first quarter 1984. Revenues were essentially flat: $9.77 billion in 1985 versus $9.59 billion in 1984. In its press release, IBM blamed the earnings decline partly on internal factors and partly on the U.S. dollar. The dollar rose strongly against other major currencies during the period from early 1984 to early 1985. According to IBM, if exchange rates had remained stable, the company would have reported a revenue increase of 9 percent and a decline in profits of only 7 percent, versus the 18 percent decline actually reported.

We can see why IBM and other companies consider the accounting rules an important matter, but they are too complex and unsettled to discuss in detail here.

KEY CONCEPTS

1. International operations have become steadily more important in the U.S. economy during the past two decades.

2. The major trading nations of the world operated under a system of fixed exchange rates, called the Bretton Woods system, from 1949 to 1971. In 1973, a system of floating rates was adopted.

3. Under a fixed-rate system, foreign-exchange rates are set administratively by governments. Under a floating-rate system, rates are set by market forces.

4. A foreign-exchange rate is the price of one currency in terms of another.

5. The *spot* foreign-exchange market is the market for immediate delivery of one currency in exchange for another. The *forward* market is the market for delivery at some future date.

6. The difference between the spot and forward rates, the *forward premium* or *forward discount*, depends on the expectations of investors regarding future changes in exchange rates and depends indirectly on relative interest rates and inflation rates in the two countries. The relationship between spot and forward rates is formally described by the interest-rate-parity theorem.

7. Covered-interest arbitrage is the market process that results in the rate relationships described by the interest-rate-parity theorem.

8. Managers can insure against the risk of changes in exchange rates by hedging—that is, by buying or selling currencies in forward markets.

9. International investment and financing decisions involve credit risk, country risk, and foreign-exchange risk.

10. International money and capital markets offer managers additional flexibility, but at the cost of additional complexity.

SUMMARY

Firms that do business in more than one country must make transactions in currencies other than their own. Managers of such firms, therefore, must deal with the complexities of foreign-exchange rates and foreign-exchange risk.

Spot foreign-exchange rates are the prices of one currency in terms of another for immediate delivery. Forward rates are present prices for transactions at future dates—that is, funds for future delivery. One currency may sell at a forward premium or discount relative to another, depending on expectations regarding future changes in the spot rate and also on relative rates of interest in the two countries.

The interest-rate-parity theorem describes a relationship of fundamental importance in understanding foreign-exchange markets. The theorem relates the forward/spot differential for two currencies to relative rates of interest in the two countries.

Most companies doing business internationally try to insure against losses resulting from movements in exchange rates. The most common technique is to hedge using the forward markets. Both asset and liability positions can be hedged with the appropriate sales or purchases in the forward market.

International investment decisions ought to be analyzed using the same basic framework applicable to domestic decisions. When the standard procedures are applied, however, they become more complex because of the extra complication of foreign exchange.

QUESTIONS

1. How does the financial manager's task change when the company engages in foreign operations?
2. Describe the difference between a fixed-exchange-rate system and a floating-exchange-rate system.
3. Which of the two systems is a business manager likely to prefer and why?
4. Distinguish between the spot and forward foreign-exchange markets.
5. What factors account for the forward/spot differential?

6. Describe how a corporate treasurer can hedge against the chance of an exchange-rate loss on an asset held in French francs.
7. Describe how a corporate treasurer can hedge against the chance of an exchange-rate loss on a long-term liability denominated in Swiss francs.
8. What is the interest-rate-parity theorem?
9. What is covered-interest arbitrage?

PROBLEMS

1. Refer to the exchange rates in Table 21–2 to answer the following:
   a. Is the French franc at a premium or discount to the U.S. dollar?
   b. What is the premium/discount on an annual basis for the 180-day forward franc?
   c. What does this information tell you about relative interest rates and inflation rates in France and the United States?
2. It is July 12, 1985. Using the exchange rates quoted in Table 21-2, how would you, the firm's international-currency expert, respond to the following inquiry from your boss, the firm's treasurer: "We have agreed to advance our West German subsidiary 1,000,000 deutsche marks (DM) on October 12, 1985. My neighbor, an economist, predicts that the spot rate, for dollars per deutsche mark, will be $0.3460 at that time. That means we will need $346,000 to purchase the necessary foreign currency. What do you think?"
3. On January 3, 1986, the U.S. dollar/Canadian dollar spot rate was $0.7121 and the U.S. dollar/Dutch gilder spot rate was $0.3599. On that date, our Canadian affiliate had to arrange to pay its Dutch supplier 150,000 gilders. How many Canadian dollars were required to make the payment?
4. On January 3, 1986, the three-month Eurodollar interest rate was 7.94 percent. The spot and forward rates for West German deutsche marks (DM) per U.S. dollar are given in Table A. What rate would you expect to receive on a three-month Euro-deutsche-mark deposit? What would you do if

Euro-deutsche-mark deposits were offered at 6 percent?

5. ABC Corp. is evaluating a cost-reduction proposal by its Japanese affiliate. The project would increase the amount of funds which could be paid to ABC Corp. by its Japanese affiliate in the form of dividends. The project costs 2,383,500,000 yen. The increased after-tax cash flow available for dividend payments to ABC Corp. would be 476,700,000 yen per year for 10 years. ABC Corp.'s required rate of return on cost-reduction proposals is 15 percent. If the dollar/yen spot rate was currently $0.004195, would the project be acceptable? If the spot rate were to depreciate by 5 percent next week and remain at that level from now on, would you accept this project? Is the current spot rate appropriate for the decision? What factors would you advise someone to consider when evaluating this project?

6. The British pound/U.S. dollar spot rate is currently £0.67 (0.67 pounds per dollar) in New York. If a

Table A

Foreign Exchange Market	West German Deutsche Marks (DM) per U.S. Dollar
Spot	2.4580
30-day forward	2.4504
90-day forward	2.4377
180-day forward	2.4182

Table B

Current spot rate (U.S. dollar equivalent)	0.4834
90-day forward rate (U.S. dollar equivalent)	0.4883
3-month Eurocurrency rate for dollar-denominated deposits	4.0 percent per year
3-month Eurocurrency rate for deposits denominated in Swiss Francs	7.9 percent per year

London currency dealer offered you pounds for $1.47, what action would you take? If other traders followed your example, what would happen to pound/dollar rates in New York and London?

7. It is July 12, 1985, and you have just come into a large inheritance. You want to invest the money at the highest-possible rate for six months while you and your financial advisors develop a long-term investment strategy. Six-month U.S.-dollar deposits in London offer an annual rate of approximately 7.7 percent. Your bank tells you that six-month Swiss-franc deposits in London offer annual rates of approximately 5.0 percent, and six-month French-franc deposits in London offer annual rates of approximately 10.3 percent. Would you make your deposit in U.S. dollars, Swiss francs, or French francs? The exchange rates needed to answer this question can be found in Table 21–2.

8. You are a financial analyst for a large firm in the business of gourmet frozen entrees. The entrees are prepared using only the finest ingredients, many of which are imported from abroad. It is January 3, 1986, and the procurement department has just placed an order with a supplier in Switzerland for Swiss cheese. The cheese has not yet aged sufficiently and, therefore, will not be delivered for three months. Upon delivery, your firm will be required to pay 62,500 Swiss francs (Sw. Fr.) to the supplier. Given that your firm bears the exchange rate risk, you have been asked to hedge the company's position. You have at your disposal the information regarding Sw. Fr. given in Table B. You are considering three alternatives: (i) buy Swiss francs today and invest the proceeds in a Eurocurrency deposit for three months, (ii) buy Swiss francs forward, making an investment today in Eurocurrency deposits to ensure the availability of sufficient funds to honor the contract in April, (iii) buy a call option today on 62,500 Swiss francs, simultaneously investing the dollars to be needed in April in Eurocurrency deposits. (The option expires in March and has an exercise price of 0.4700. Such an option is currently selling for $1,293.75.) Which alternative would you recommend? How would your answer change if your firm's contract with the Swiss supplier provided for refusal of acceptance of the cheese if it is of questionable quality? (*Note:* For simplicity, disregard the fact that the March option will expire shortly before the contract is settled in early April.)

REFERENCES

Dufey, G., and I. H. Giddy. *The International Money Market.* Prentice-Hall Foundations of Finance Series. Englewood Cliffs, N.J.: Prentice-Hall, 1978.

Eiteman, D. K., and A. I. Stonehill. *Multinational Business Finance.* Reading, Mass.: Addison-Wesley, 1982.

Feldstein, Martin. "Depressing the Dollar, Gently." *Wall Street Journal.* (November 9, 1984).

Lessard, D. R. *International Financial Management: Theory and Application,* 2nd ed. New York: John Wiley & Sons, 1985.

Lessard, D. R., and J. L. Paddock. "Evaluating International Projects: Weighted Average Cost of Capital versus Valuation by Components." Working Paper. Sloan School of Management, M. I. T. (October 1983).

Oblak, D. J., and R. J. Helm Jr. "Survey and Analysis of Capital Budgeting Methods Used by Multinationals." *Financial Management* 9 (Winter 1980): 37–41.

Pearson, John. "Strong Dollar or No, There's Money to be Made Abroad." *Business Week* (March 22, 1985).

Rodriguez, R. M. , and E. E. Carter. *International Financial Management.* 2d ed. Englewood Cliffs, N.J.: Prentice-Hall, 1979.

Shapiro, A. *Multinational Financial Management.* Boston: Allyn and Bacon, 1986.

Steinberg, Bruce, "Trying to Haul Down the Dollar." *Fortune* (April 15, 1985).

"Why the World Loves the Dollar." *Fortune* (February 18, 1985).

Chapter

22

Mergers and Acquisitions

In this chapter, we will discuss a phenomenon that has been prominent in the financial press in recent years—namely, mergers and acquisitions. We will begin with some history. Next we will focus on how and why mergers may create value for shareholders and on various possible motives for merging, including creation of value. Then we will learn how to evaluate mergers by applying the technique of discounted cash flow that we learned earlier. Following the DCF discussion, we will examine another consideration in evaluating a merger: its effect on the reported earnings per share of the acquiring firm. We will also look at the effects of a merger on the balance sheet of the firm. Next we will examine some evidence regarding effects of mergers on returns to shareholders of both acquiring and acquired firms. Finally, we will examine the merger phenomenon from a public-policy perspective.

Table 22-1

Biggest Deals of 1985

Rank Companies/Transaction	Industry	Price Paid for Acquired Company (thousands of dollars)	Percent of Book Value of Acquired Company
1. Royal Dutch acquires Shell Oil	Oil and gas / Oil and gas	5,700,118	147.7
2. Philip Morris acquires General Foods	Cigarettes and beverages / Food	5,627,671	286.1
3. Allied merges with Signal Cos.	Multi-industry / Multi-industry	4,944,967	178.5
4. R. J. Reynolds acquires Nabisco	Tobacco, food, consumer products / Food	4,889,051	309.0
5. General Motors acquires Hughes Aircraft	Automobiles / Defense electronics	4,712,500	431.2
6. Baxter Travenol acquires American Hospital Supply	Health care products / Health care products	3,737,181	235.5
7. Nestlé acquires Carnation	Food / Food	2,940,661	241.8
8. Monsanto acquires G. D. Searle	Chemicals and related products / Drugs and consumer products	2,744,950	522.5
9. Coastal acquires American Natural Resources	Energy / Natural gas transmission	2,461,961	215.1
10. SCI Holdings acquires Storer Communications	Multi-industry / Broadcast and cable television	2,358,528	625.4

A **statutory merger**—is a combination of two or more firms in which one company survives under its own name while any others cease to exist as legal entities.

A **statutory consolidation**—is a merger in which all the combining companies cease to exist as legal entities and in which a new corporation is created.

Corporate mergers have played a prominent role in shaping the structure of U.S. corporations. For example, in 1984 Chevron purchased Gulf Oil and paid more than $13 billion in cash for the privilege. In addition, Chevron and Gulf Oil paid financial advisors in excess of $60 million for advice about the merger. This large merger is one of many. In 1984 alone, 2999 separate acquisitions occurred in the United States.[1] In fact, mergers became such publicized events that even cartoon strips carried some of the news.

Technically speaking, there are a number of different ways two (or more) firms can combine. For example, in a **statutory merger**, when two or more firms combine, one company survives under its own name and the others cease to exist as legal entities. In a **statutory consolidation**, on the other hand, all the combining companies cease to exist as legal entities, and a new corporation is created as a result of the consolidation. In addition, corporate combinations differ in their tax treatment and accounting treatment, depending upon rules laid down by the Internal Revenue Service and the accounting profession.

Some mergers are consummated after amicable negotiation between managers of acquiring and acquired firms. Other business combinations occur despite bitter dis-

---

[1] The source for the number of mergers is *Mergers and Acquisitions*, January/February 1986.

A **hostile takeover**—occurs when the acquired firm's management resists the acquisition, and the acquiring firm goes over their heads by buying stock directly from shareholders.

A **tender offer**—is an acquiring firm's offer to pay existing shareholders some specified amount of cash or securities if these shareholders will sell (tender) their shares of stock to the acquiring firm.

A **golden parachute**—is a provision in the employment contract of top-level management that provides for severance pay or other compensation should the manager lose his or her job as the result of a takeover.

agreement between two sets of managers. In such **hostile takeovers**, the acquiring firm often goes over the heads of the acquired firm's management to the shareholders by means of a **tender offer**. A tender offer is an offer to pay existing shareholders some specified amount of cash or securities if these shareholders will sell (tender) their shares of stock to the acquiring firm. For present purposes, we will use the broader term *merger* to refer to combinations of firms without making these detailed distinctions.

One of the most notorious deals of the early 1980s was a four-cornered fight among Bendix, Martin Marrietta, Allied, and United Technologies. Ultimately, in 1982 Allied acquired Bendix for $1.8 billion, but before the takeover could be completed tender offers by Bendix and Martin Marrietta for each other had to be unraveled. In the heat of the Bendix/Martin Marrietta takeover battle, the board of Bendix voted its Chairman Bill Agee a **golden parachute**. The contract guaranteed him an annual salary of $825,000 for five years if Bendix were acquired. The public fighting of such major U.S. corporations was a catalyst for many critics of such takeover activity spurring an outcry for new and stronger federal legislation to control mergers. Yet the merger activity continued. Table 22–1 shows the largest deals of 1985. In 1985 alone there were almost 3,000 separate acquisitions in the United States, according to the magazine *Mergers and Acquisitions*.

The desirability of mergers remains a key topic of public debate. In addition, corporate managers are investing time and resources in buying firms or in fighting off unwanted suitors.

All of this activity raises basic financial questions. Do mergers create value to the owners of merging firms? As we have discussed throughout this book, financial managers should strive to make decisions that increase the value of the firm to existing shareholders. Do mergers further this objective of value maximization? Mergers also raise other questions for public-policy makers. Do mergers increase or decrease competition in U.S. markets? Do mergers allow firms to take advantage of certain cost-saving techniques? Are mergers in the best interests of society? Before we address some of these questions, let us take a look at the history of mergers.

HISTORY OF MERGERS IN THE UNITED STATES

While the current wave of mergers is certainly an important event, it is not unprecedented. In fact, today's activity is the fourth major wave of mergers in U.S. financial history. Mergers tend to occur in large waves with lulls without significant merger activity coming between the waves. The first large mergers in U.S. history began in the late 1800s. During that period, U.S. Steel became the first billion-dollar corporation in U.S. history as the result of many smaller steel firms combining into one corporate giant. Most of the mergers during this period combined companies in the same industry, leading to one dominant firm in that particular industry.

This first merger wave ended around 1903 as the U.S. economy took a downturn. A result of that merger activity, however, was a public outcry against the formation of these large firms, sometimes called *trusts*. This factor contributed to the passage of additional antitrust laws in the first part of the 20th century. Such laws were directed at a corporation's attempts to monopolize industries or fix prices.

The second wave of merger activity occurred after World War I, through the 1920s.

Figure 22–1

Mergers of Exchange-Listed Companies, 1955–1984

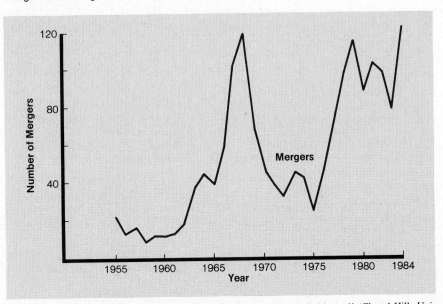

Source: J. R. Franks and R. S. Harris, ''Merger Waves: Theory and Evidence,'' (Chapel Hill, University of North Carolina, Working Paper, 1986).

An **oligopoly**—is an industry that has a few large firms rather than a single large firm or numerous smaller firms and that possesses some competitive characteristics and some monopolistic ones.

A **conglomerate merger**—is a merger that combines firms in different industries.

A **horizontal merger**—is a merger that combines firms operating in the same business line.

A **vertical merger**—is a merger that combines firms that have some customer/supplier relationship.

These mergers, however, did not lead to the large dominant firms in an industry that occurred in the first merger wave. George Stigler, Nobel Prize winner in economics, considers this second wave to have been ''mergers for oligopoly.'' An **oligopoly** is an industry that has a few large firms rather than a single dominant firm. In the merger wave after the first World War, there were typically a number of large firms left in an industry after the mergers.

The third merger wave began after World War II and ran through the late 1960s. Looking at Figure 22–1, we can see some measures of the annual merger activity during this period. While the data in Figure 22–1 are only for stocks traded on the American and New York Stock Exchanges, the figure still portrays the trends in overall merger activity in the United States. One major difference between mergers after World War II and earlier mergers is that mergers after World War II were largely **conglomerate mergers**, or mergers between firms in different industries. In contrast, **horizontal mergers** combine firms operating in the same business line, and **vertical mergers** combine firms that have some customer/supplier relationship. For example, a chemical company buying a sports-equipment manufacturer would be a conglomerate merger. A clothing manufacturer buying a firm that makes fabrics would be a vertical merger. This third merger wave peaked in the late 1960s, as Figure 22–1 shows.

During the 1960s, merger activity was extremely hectic. In a one-month period, one firm, Automatic Sprinkler, acquired four other firms. The mergers also involved a number of innovative financing schemes. In addition, there was public outcry against the mergers. In the late 1960s, the Justice Department issued major guidelines in an

Finance in Practice 22–1

The Language of the Merger Market

No reader of the financial press in the 1980s could fail to notice the frequent accounts of one large company buying another. Corporate America had entered a merger boom sometimes likened to a feeding frenzy of sharks. The question in managers' minds was whether their company was the next deal in the merger market.

Suppose you encountered a newspaper headline reading: "Poison Pill Not Effective; White Knight to the Rescue." Although you might expect an account of a fairy tale to follow, most likely the story would be about an attempted takeover being resisted by the management of the target company. Here are a few definitions to help the confused reader decipher the meaning of some of the language used to describe the merger market.

Crown jewel—the most valued asset held by an acquisition target; divestiture of this asset is frequently a sufficient defense to discourage takeover.

Greenmail—the premium paid by a targeted company to a raider in exchange for the raider's shares of the targeted company.

Maiden—the target company toward which a takeover attempt is directed.

Poison pill—a provision giving stockholders other than those involved in a hostile takeover the right to purchase securities at a very favorable price in the event of a takeover.

Raider—the person or company attempting the takeover of another company.

Shark repellants—antitakeover corporate-charter amendments.

Stripper—a successful raider who sells off some of the assets of the target company once the target is acquired.

White knight—a merger partner (solicited by management of a target) who offers an alternative merger plan to that offered by the raider and who protects the target company from attempted takeover by the raider.

Source: Mack Ott and G. J. Santoni, "Mergers and Takeovers—The Value of Predators' Information," The Federal Reserve Bank of St. Louis, December 1985.

---

attempt to designate when mergers would be in violation of antitrust laws and, thus, subject to legal action by the U.S. government. The decline in mergers, leading into the early 1970s, was a result of a combination of factors including the economic downturn in the economy and the fact that some of the mergers pursued in the 1960s appeared to have less than favorable outcomes.

As Figure 22–1 shows, mergers again started to increase in the 1970s and crescendoed into the 1980s. In 1985 alone there were almost 3,000 corporate acquisitions. The most recent wave of mergers has some different characteristics from the earlier mergers.

As Table 22–2 displays, in many of the recent mergers the acquiring firm focused on the particular assets being purchased (for example, Chevron purchases of oil reserves owned by Gulf) without an exclusive focus on earnings per share. As we'll show later in this chapter, many earlier mergers appear to have been motivated by desires to manipulate earnings-per-share figures. The means of payment in recent mergers have also differed. In the 1960s, most mergers were accomplished through the payment of the acquiring firm's stock or convertible securities (for example, convertible bonds) to the acquired firm's shareholders in exchange for their stock in the acquired firm. More recently, many more mergers were accomplished with payment in cash. Later in this chapter we'll discuss the differences associated with means of

Table 22–2

Comparison of Merger Characteristics and Activity of the 1960s with That of the 1970s and Early 1980s

Mergers in the 1960s	Mergers in the 1970s and 1980s
1. Focus on earnings per share	1. Focus on underlying assets
2. Payment with stock and convertible securities	2. Payment with cash
3. Few hostile takeovers	3. Frequent unfriendly raids
4. Mostly conglomerate mergers	4. Many horizontal mergers

payment. Table 22–2 also indicates that many recent mergers were unfriendly, which means that the acquired firm's management resisted the takeover, and the acquiring firm went over their heads by buying stock directly from shareholders. Such a hostile takeover differs from friendly mergers, where managers of both firms come to terms on the details of the merger. Finally, in recent years there have been many mergers between firms in the same industry. These horizontal mergers have substantially reshaped many U.S. industries. For example, in 1984 the three largest mergers of U.S. companies all involved horizontal mergers in the oil business: Chevron acquiring Gulf, Texaco buying Getty Oil, and Mobil acquiring Superior Oil.

MERGER MOTIVES

A basic question to be answered is: What motivates mergers? One possible motive is that mergers create value for the owners of the acquiring and acquired firms. If such value is created, then we may view mergers as being in the best interest of shareholders and consistent with good capital-budgeting decisions made by firms. On the other hand, some authorities have argued that mergers are simply ways for managers of corporations to further their own interest even at the expense of shareholders. For example, if a manager's compensation and psychic rewards are based on the size of the company, he or she would have an interest in acquiring another firm and, thus, increasing the size of the corporation. If he or she were able to carry out these desires, he or she might acquire another company even if that acquisition cost more than the benefits it could give to shareholders. Thus, a first question is whether mergers create value or whether they are motivated by the personal interests of managers. Do merger projects have a positive net present value (*NPV*) for shareholders in the participating firms?

Even if value is created in mergers, however, we must look a bit further. We have to see if there is extra value in a merger for shareholders of both acquiring and acquired firms. That is, do mergers have a positive net present value for *both* sets of owners? It is possible that acquired-firm shareholders would receive a price in the merger that was sufficiently high to make them better off, while acquiring-firm shareholders would have paid too high a price. In this case, the merger would have a positive net present value for acquired-firm shareholders but a negative *NPV* for acquiring-firm shareholders.

Table 22-3
Merger Motives

Cost Savings
Monopoly power
Avoiding bankruptcy
Tax considerations
Retirement planning
Diversification
Increased debt capacity
Undervalued assets
Manipulating earnings per share
Management desires
Replacing inefficient management

How can mergers increase value? Table 22–3 lists some of the more frequently cited merger motives. One motive is that mergers sometimes allow companies to take advantage of certain cost-saving techniques that may be available only when two firms combine. For example, the merging firms may be able to consolidate some administrative functions (such as accounting staffs) and save money. A merger may also allow certain scale economies in production if prior to the merger the firms were too small to be efficient. Cost savings may also occur if firms with different strengths combine through a merger. An example might be a small firm with the latest technology that merges with a larger company that knows how to mass produce the product and market it nationwide. Alternatively, both combining companies could be small but one might have the technical knowhow while the other has the sales expertise. For example, in 1982 SmithKline Corporation, a major company in the health-care industry, acquired Beckman Instruments, a firm that designs, manufactures, and markets laboratory instruments, related chemical supplies, and industrial components. Among other things, the combination eliminated duplicate fundamental research and, through SmithKline's marketing expertise and access to the health-care distribution system, provided an improved commercial outlet for Beckman's products. Management of the two firms had hopes that the merger would create **synergy**—the result of a combination in which the combined firm is worth more than the sum of the values of the separate firms.

Synergy—is the effect achieved when the whole is greater than the sum of its parts.

Value may also be increased when a combination of two firms allows them to exercise more monopoly power and keep their prices well in excess of costs. Such higher prices that increase profits and cash flow to the firm could also lead to increases in value. This benefit might be achieved when two firms in the same industry combine, reducing the number of effective competitors by one. Of course, the ability to keep higher prices in the long run depends on how easily other firms can enter the market. Unless there are **barriers to entry**, excess profits are not likely to persist over time. New firms will enter the market, and prices and profits will be forced down. In recent years, the potential entrants to markets have increasingly come from abroad as the world economy has become more integrated—as demonstrated by the developments in the automobile, textile, and steel industries.

Barriers to entry—are features of a particular industry, such as economies of scale, high levels of initial investment, or technological sophistication that make it difficult for new entrants to enter the market.

There are many other reasons why individual mergers can lead to increases in value. Some mergers are the best way for one company to avoid some of the high cost associated with the failure of one firm. For example, in early 1983 United American Bank of Knoxville failed—resulting in the fourth largest bank failure in U.S. history. Instead of long and costly delays, United American was taken over by another bank, First Tennessee National Corporation, almost immediately.

Tax laws also provide merger motives in some instances. If one company has tax losses that it cannot presently use (for example, it doesn't have income against which it can deduct taxable expenses), there may be a motive for a merger. After the merger, those tax losses can lead to tax savings when applied to the income of some other company. These tax savings can increase value. Thus, mergers, like leases discussed in Chapter 16, can provide a mechanism whereby corporations take best advantage of tax laws. As an example, Bangor Punta had substantial tax losses after the expropriation of its sugar plantations in Cuba. Because it couldn't use these losses, it combined with other firms that did have taxable income.[2]

Another consideration leading to the acquisition of many smaller firms is planning for retirement by acquired-company owners or managers. An acquisition may be a perfect way for the founder of a company to cash in his or her investment. When all of an individual's wealth is tied up in one company, the person is not well diversified and does not, therefore, gain the risk-reducing benefits of portfolio diversification. When that person is vitally involved in the management of the business, he or she may be prepared to accept such a lack of diversification. In planning for retirement, however, the individual may desire to diversify. One way to achieve that diversification is to sell the company in a merger. The seller may obtain cash that could be invested elsewhere. Alternatively, he or she could receive readily marketable stock in a larger, more diversified acquiring firm.[3]

A reason often given for mergers is the benefit of diversification, but we must be careful because the word *diversification* is sometimes used to mean two quite different things. First, managers sometimes use the term *diversification* to refer to a firm that decides to branch out of its existing lines of business because they no longer offer new investment opportunities for expansion. As an example, a cash-rich company, but one with no new internally profitable investments, may view acquisitions of other lines of business as alternatives to paying increased dividends or repurchasing shares of its own stock. Because dividend payments impose extra personal-income taxes on shareholders, as we discussed in Chapter 15, the acquisition route may be attractive—as long as the merger premium paid is not too high. Acquisitions may be preferable to share repurchase because the Internal Revenue Service may classify large systematic repurchases as taxable if the motive is purely to avoid the paying of personal taxes on dividend income. This type of diversification is based on basic changes in the actual cash flows involved (perhaps motivated by taxes) and may create value. This usage is not the traditional financial definition of diversification, which depends on risk.

---

[2]The Internal Revenue Service does have rules against pursuing mergers solely to use tax losses. In practice, however, these rules allow for some tax benefits to be realized by virtue of two firms combining to take advantage of what would otherwise be unused tax losses.

[3]In fact, tax laws often provide an incentive for owner/managers who are selling their companies to prefer being paid in common stock rather than in cash. Under certain conditions, the capital gain on the stock received in the merger is not taxed until the stock is actually sold, whereas capital-gains taxes would be levied immediately if cash is received.

The second meaning of *diversification* refers to risk. Do mergers diversify risks? As we saw when we discussed risk earlier, as long as returns to two businesses are not perfectly correlated, the combination of the two by merger can produce a firm with lower variability of returns, as we saw when we combined two or more stocks in a portfolio. Mergers can, thus, reduce the variability of a firm's returns.

Is this diversification valuable? The answer depends on how well the firm's shareholders are diversified in the first place. Suppose a shareholder already owned shares in both firms; the firm's diversification might do nothing more than the shareholder has already done. If such were the case, the diversification accomplished through a merger would provide no new diversification benefits. In general, if shareholders are already well diversified, the diversification in the merger will provide no new substantial diversification benefits. For a person who owns stock in only one company, however, the diversification in the merger might be of benefit.

In addition, an indirect benefit of diversification can result if it increases the company's ability to borrow money, allowing it to benefit further from the use of financial leverage. As we saw in Chapters 13 and 14, the use of financial leverage can increase the value of a firm, although firms must trade off the benefits of leverage (for example, the tax-deductibility of interest) against the risks introduced by leverage. Thus, prudence dictates using leverage only up to a point because of leverage-induced risks. Diversification by means of a merger may make the combined entity subject to less variability in operating flows than existed in either of the premerger firms. As a result, the post-merger firm may find that its best capital structure involves using more debt than the combined debt of the two premerger firms. The increased use of debt may increase value.[4]

Especially in a depressed stock market, one frequently stated reason for merger is that the earning power and assets of the acquired company are undervalued by the stock market. If so, the assets of the acquired firm can be bought at a bargain price in a merger. The question then arises: Can managers of an acquiring firm have a better idea of the value of a company than do other investors who buy and sell stocks? If acquiring-firm managers have some inside information, unknown to the general public, then they may in fact know when a company is undervalued. For example, if company A knows that company B is on the verge of discovering a cure for the common cold, but the general investing public does not have this information, company A may know that company B is currently undervalued in the market. There is no doubt that the stock market undervalues some companies and overvalues others relative to the cash flows that the companies will eventually produce. The challenge for a potential acquiring firm is to find some way of knowing how to separate one group of firms from the other. After all, the market value represents the consensus value of thousands of well-informed investors about the current value of *expected* future outcomes.

Three last motives for merger deserve mention. First, as we'll analyze later in this chapter, acquisitions may provide a means to increase earnings per share (at least in the short run). Second, acquisitions may not be motivated by shareholder interests at

---

[4]This increase in debt capacity was suggested by W. G. Lewellen, ''A Pure Financial Rationale for the Conglomerate Merger,'' *Journal of Finance*, May 1971, pp. 521–45. For a more thorough analysis of the issues, see R. C. Higgins and L. D. Schall, ''Corporate Bankruptcy and Conglomerate Merger,'' *Journal of Finance*, March 1975, pp. 93–113.

all but rather may be a result of managers' desire to manage larger and growing firms even if such size and growth come at the expense of shareholder value. Third, some argue that acquisitions are one way that inefficient managers may be replaced. It may be very difficult, and in fact often is difficult, to replace the entire upper level of management. If managers of a company are not doing a good job, someone can buy the company and substitute better management and, in this way, increase value.

While Table 22–3 contains the major merger motives, one could find others that fit certain business combinations.[5] What is important from a financial manager's point of view is to make an estimate of whether the merger can lead to increased value, regardless of the source of that value.

> **The financial manager is interested in estimating whether a merger can increase value, regardless of the source of that value.**

FINANCIAL EVALUATION Of MERGERS

One useful way to view a merger is from the perspective of the acquiring firm. From such a perspective, buying another firm is like investing in a new project. There is a certain outlay associated with the merger. This outlay will be the amount paid to the acquired firm's shareholders, or the value of the securities traded to those shareholders in exchange for obtaining the company. In exchange for this outlay, the acquiring firm will expect to receive certain cash-flow benefits from the acquired firm. These cash flows will occur in future periods as the assets and labor force of the firm that has been purchased generate cash flows from operations.

Alternatively, these cash flows could come from cost savings to the acquiring firm as a result of buying a new entity. Or these cash flows could come from selling off some of the assets of the corporation that has been bought. In any case, we can view the merger as an investment proposal. There is an initial outlay to obtain another company. There are some cash benefits, mostly in the future, of undertaking the merger. Thus, from the perspective of an acquiring firm, a merger can be viewed as an *investment decision*, and we can use the standard discounted-cash-flow techniques developed in earlier chapters to analyze such an acquisition. The questions for the acquiring managers are: Does the merger investment have a positive net present value (*NPV*)? Is the *NPV* of the merger larger than the *NPV* of other mutually exclusive investment alternatives?

> **From the perspective of an acquiring firm, a merger can be viewed as an investment decision where standard discounted-cash-flow techniques can be used.**

[5] See F. M. Scherer, *Industrial Market Structure and Economic Performance*, 2nd ed. (Chicago: Rand McNally, 1982); T. E. Copeland and J. F. Weston, *Financial Theory and Corporate Policy*, 2nd ed. (Reading, Mass.: Addison-Wesley, 1983).

Similarly, the net present value of the merger can also be analyzed from the perspective of the acquired firm. From the acquired firm's perspective, the benefits of selling out the firm are primarily in the present, whereas the costs of the merger are the forgone cash flows that might have been received in future periods. In many cases, this analysis can be simplified because the future cash flows that were expected to be received by acquired-firm shareholders have already been given a value in the market represented by the current market value of the stock of the acquired firm. In such a case, the acquired firm's shareholders must compare the value of money or securities promised by the acquiring firm to the present market value of the stock owned. The difference, the **merger premium**, is a stockholder's incentive to sell out the company. This merger premium must be weighed against whatever other factors the acquired firm's shareholders believe are involved in selling the company.

A **merger premium**—is the difference between the value of the money or securities offered by an acquiring firm and the present value of the stock owned by the shareholders of the firm to be acquired.

Mergers and Discounted Cash Flow

Like other financial-management decisions, acquisitions are not made simply by plugging numbers into equations. Decisions to merge involve complicated judgments about growth and profit potential of specific product markets, the quality of a company's management, and the compatibility of the two organizations that are planning to merge. For these reasons, many of the difficult decisions about mergers involve nonfinancial and nonquantifiable factors. Many firms first approach the subject of making acquisitions by seeing how an acquisition fits a broad corporate strategy. For example, one firm may see itself as specializing in high-technology areas and, as a result, will consider acquisitions only of other high-technology firms. Another firm may be seeking to diversify out of its existing lines of business and will, therefore, look only at certain types of corporations as potential acquisitions.

Realizing this, finance still plays a critical role in acquisitions. To decide whether buying another company makes sense, managers ultimately have to be able to set a value on a company they might buy. If the company can be purchased for less than this value, the acquisition has a positive net present value to the acquiring firm. The challenge is establishing such a value. Fortunately, the discounted-cash-flow techniques we developed in earlier chapters are useful here. An acquisition can be viewed as an investment proposal with cash traded today in hopes of receiving cash in future periods. Equation (1) restates our basic calculation of net present value developed in Chapter 9, with one change. The original outlay, C_0, is separated and is shown as a negative number to emphasize that it is money going out at time zero.

The net present value, *NPV*, of an investment decision to acquire another company can be calculated as

$$NPV = -C_0 + \sum_{t=1}^{N} \frac{C_t}{(1 + K)^t} \tag{1}$$

where C_0 = the market value of all the securities and cash paid in the acquisition plus the market value of all debt liabilities assumed as a result of the acquisition, C_t = the incremental after-tax operating cash flows that are ultimately available to the acquiring company as a result of buying the acquired company, and K = the required return.

In the context of an acquisition, each of the terms in Equation (1) must be interpreted with care.[6] First, C_0 is the dollar value to be paid to the acquired company. If the acquiring company pays in cash and assumes no liabilities as a result of the acquisition, C_0 is the amount of cash paid—but things are not always so clear-cut. For example, in 1984 General Motors (GM) acquired Electronic Data Systems (EDS) by giving cash, common stock, and notes to EDS. The total value of the securities plus cash was $2.555 billion. How would we treat this amount in Equation (1)? One useful way is to set C_0 equal to the full $2.555 billion as if it were a cash outlay even though we know part of the payment was in common stock and notes. The rationale for this approach is that the cash equivalent of GM's offer was $2.555 billion. By using notes and common stock in this acquisition, GM gave up the opportunity to raise cash by selling those securities. Adding their value into C_0 reflects this forgone opportunity.

There may be yet another complication. Suppose GM also assumed some of EDS's debts as a result of the acquisition—a common practice when the acquiring company does not want to retire the acquired company's debt immediately but prefers to pay it off by honoring the interest and principal payments. If the acquiring company assumes these debt obligations, it receives cash flows from the acquisition only after honoring these obligations. We can incorporate this debt in Equation (1) if we define C_0 as including not only the value of the payments (cash plus securities) made by the acquiring firm but also the value of the liabilities (debt) assumed by the acquiring firm. Because the market value of debt appropriately captures this value, C_0 also includes the market value of the acquired-company debt that is assumed by the acquiring company as a result of the acquisition. In Equation (1), then, C_0 represents the market value of all the securities and cash paid in the acquisition plus the market value of all debt liabilities assumed as a result of the acquisition.

The cash flows, C_t, in Equation (1) also deserve attention. Just as in our capital-budgeting analysis in Chapter 9, these flows are incremental after-tax operating cash flows. In other words, they are the cash flows that are ultimately available to one company as a result of buying another company. These cash flows would include the cash flows from the acquired company's operations plus any special cash flows that can be realized only as a result of the acquisition. Even though the cash flows would conceivably extend indefinitely into the future if the firm is a going concern, it is often useful to project cash flows for only a number of years and then assign a lump-sum terminal value to the acquired company. (See Sample Problem 22–1 below.) Also, it is important to remember that these flows are operating cash flows prior to interest charges, just as we calculated in Chapter 9.

Finally, the required return, K, in Equation (1) must reflect the riskiness of the cash flows being analyzed. If these cash flows are of the same risk as the *acquiring* company's existing operations and if the acquiring company plans no change in its financing mix relative to the premerger mix, then we could use the acquiring company's after-tax weighted-average required return (as calculated in Chapter 10) as the appropriate required return in Equation (1). Sometimes, this may be a reasonable assump-

---

[6]We separate financing and investment in using Equation (1), in keeping with our development of net present value in Chapter 9. Other ways to use Equation (1) are discussed in D. Chambers, R. Harris, and J. Pringle, "Treatment of Financing Mix in Analyzing Investment Opportunities," *Financial Management*, Summer 1982, pp. 24–41.

tion. For example, in a horizontal merger the business risk of the acquired firm may be essentially the same as the risk of the acquiring firm.

In most cases, however, the cash flows in Equation (1) are associated with risks related to the business of the acquired company, not the acquiring company. As a result, we would expect financial markets to require a different rate of return on these than on the acquiring company. For example, when Aetna Life and Casualty, a firm primarily involved in insurance and other financial services, acquired Geosource, a company in the oil-exploration-equipment business, it would have been inappropriate to use a required return based on Aetna's existing operations to value cash flows coming from Geosource. In some cases, we could argue that the cash flows in Equation (1) are of essentially the same risk as the acquired firm and, hence, might base K on the required returns that the market appears to have placed on the acquired firm's business.

In practice, a financial manager needs to pay special attention to risks associated with the cash flows that are being acquired. As discussed in Chapter 11, some of the tools for dealing with risk (for example, sensitivity analysis) need to be used in merger valuations.

Sample Problem 22–1

Calculating the Net Present Value of Union Amalgamated's Purchase of Pearsall Manufacturing

In December 1986, Union Amalgamated was considering the purchase of Pearsall Manufacturing, Inc. Union's investment banker has advised Union's chief financial officer that Pearsall's common stock can be bought for $50 million cash plus 1 million shares of Union's stock, which is presently selling for $30 a share. In addition, Union will assume Pearsall's debt, which has a book value of $10 million and a coupon rate of 7 percent. Presently the debt has a market value of $8 million because market interest rates are above 7 percent. Union has made the projections shown in Table 22–4.

Table 22–4
Pro Forma Results for Pearsall Manufacturing, Inc., 1987–89 (millions of dollars)

	1987	1988	1989
Sales	100	130	170
minus			
Cash expenses	−58	−80	−110
minus			
Depreciation	−10	−13	−17
equals			
Earnings before interest and taxes (EBIT)	32	37	43
minus			
Interest	−7	−7	−7
equals			
Profit before taxes (PBT)	25	30	36
minus			
Taxes at 40 percent	−10	−12	−14.4
equals			
Profit after taxes (PAT)	15	18	21.6

Union has also estimated that capital expenditures necessary to maintain this level of operation for Pearsall will be $8 million per year for the next three years. Finally, Union analysts project that Pearsall's assets can be sold at year-end 1989 to net the company $60 million after paying tax obligations. (In this projection we have not dealt with working capital, which is typically relevant in such a decision. We are assuming it away here to keep things simple. See Appendix 9B for a treatment of how to handle working capital.) Union management has traditionally used a weighted-average required return of 12 percent, but feels that because the Pearsall acquisition is somewhat riskier than current operations a 15 percent required return is appropriate. Calculate the net present value of the acquisition. Is the acquisition of Pearsall a sound investment?

Solution

We can use Equation (1) to calculate the net present value of the acquisition. First, we need to calculate the cash flows associated with the purchase of Pearsall. These cash flows are after-tax operating (pre-interest) cash flows and can be calculated as

$$C = \text{EBIT}(1 - T) + \text{Depreciation} - \text{Capital expenditures.}$$

For example in 1987 (in millions of dollars),

$$C = 32(1 - 0.4) + 10 - 8 = 21.2.$$

Note that we must subtract capital expenditures because these are dollars that must be reinvested in Pearsall to produce the cash flows in future periods and justify the estimated $60 million selling price in 1989. Using the data from the problem, we can determine that cash flow from operations will be $21.2 million in 1987, $27.2 million in 1988, and $34.8 million in 1989 and that the cash flow from sales in 1989 will be $60 million.

Note that this $60 million in 1989 would be prior to paying off Pearsall's debt. Because Pearsall's debt is going to be included in C_0 (as a liability assumed), the cash flows should include dollars available to pay off this debt as well as to yield cash to Union.

Second, we must calculate the cash-equivalent outlay for Pearsall, which is composed of three parts: the cash outlay of $50 million; the market value of the stock given to Pearsall's present stockholders, which is 10 million shares × $30 per share = $30 million; and the market value of Pearsall's debt that is assumed, which is $8 million. Thus, $C_0 = \$50$ million + $30 million + $8 million = $88 million.

This $88 million is the amount effectively paid for the operating cash flows of Pearsall—$80 million for Pearsall's common stock plus the assumption of $8 million of debt. In essence, Union would have to pay $88 million to buy all of Pearsall's cash flows with $8 million of the total to pay off debt. Using $K = 15$ percent, we can now use Equation (1) to calculate the net present value (in millions of dollars) as

$$NPV = -\$88 + \frac{\$21.2}{(1 + 0.15)} + \frac{\$27.2}{(1 + 0.15)^2} + \frac{\$34.8}{(1 + 0.15)^3} + \frac{\$60}{(1 + 0.15)^3}$$

$$= -\$88 + \$21.2\,(0.870) + \$27.2\,(0.756) + \$34.8\,(0.658) + \$60\,(0.658)$$

$$= -\$88 + \$101.39$$

$$= \$13.39$$

As the calculations show, the acquisition yields a positive net present value of $13.39 million and appears to be a good investment. Union is paying $88 million for cash flows worth $101.39 million. Stated another way, given current assumptions, Union could afford to pay up to $101.39 million to buy Pearsall and still have the acquisition make financial sense. This price would be $101.39 million − $8 million = $93.39 million in excess of the $8 million debt assumed. Before making a final decision on the acquisition, Union must also make sure that no other mutually exclusive investment alternatives (for example, internal expansion to provide the same benefits as those available from acquiring Pearsall) offer a net present value greater than $13.39 million. ∎

Sample Problem 22–2

Sensitivity Analysis of Union Amalgamated's Acquisition of Pearsall Manufacturing

A. Suppose you thought Union's staff had overestimated all the cash flows from Pearsall by 20 percent. Would the acquisition still look good to you?

B. Suppose that Union thought that acquisition of Pearsall, in addition to the cash flows already calculated and the adjustment in (A) above, would allow Union to cut its own advertising expenditures by $500,000 a year for the next three years because of Pearsall's excellent reputation, which is expected to spill over and help Union's sales. How would this assumption affect your analysis of acquiring Pearsall?

Solution

A. We need to do a sensitivity analysis by cutting the cash flows figured in Sample Problem 22–1 by 20 percent. As a result, we get the cash flows listed in Table 22–5. Using the right-hand column of numbers we can recalculate net present value from Equation (1), in millions of dollars, as

$$NPV = -\$88 + \frac{\$16.96}{(1 + 0.15)} + \frac{\$21.76}{(1 + 0.15)^2} + \frac{\$75.84}{(1 + 0.15)^3}$$

$$= -\$88 + \$16.96 \,(0.870) + \$21.76 \,(0.756) + \$75.84 \,(0.658)$$

$$= -\$88 + \$81.1$$

$$= -\$6.9$$

Table 22–5
Sensitivity Analysis of Pearson Manufacturing's Estimated 1987–89 Cash Flows (millions of dollars)

Year	Original Cash Flow	Original Cash Flow Minus 20 Percent
1987	21.2	16.96
1988	27.2	21.76
1989	34.8 + 60	75.84

With these lower expected cash flows, the net present value of acquiring Pearsall is negative (−$6.9 million), so Pearsall should not be acquired. The maximum that could be paid for Pearsall, given the current assumptions, is $81.1 million, which is $73.1 million in excess of the $8 million debt assumed.

B. The $500,000 advertising savings would save Union $500,000 (1 − 0.4) = $300,000 a year on an after-tax basis for each of the next three years and would increase the calculated net present value of the acquisition by a dollar value of

$$\frac{\$300,000}{(1 + 0.15)} + \frac{\$300,000}{(1 + 0.15)^2} + \frac{\$300,000}{(1 + 0.15)^3} = \$685,200.$$

Compared to the net present value of −$6.9 million found in part (A), the new net present value would be −$6,900,000 + $685,200 = −$6,214,800. Because this *NPV* is still negative, the acquisition does not look good. Note that one might argue for using a discount rate lower than 15 percent for the advertising cost savings if they are fairly safe. Even with a lower discount rate, however, these savings would not overcome the −$6.9 million net present value calculated in part (A). ∎

While discounted-cash-flow analysis provides an extremely useful tool in assessing the value of a company, it is not the only important means of assessing the financial effects of mergers. Mergers also have effects on the basic accounting information that companies present to the financial community because an acquiring company must restate its income statement and balance sheet to reflect the operations, assets, and liabilities of the company being acquired.

Mergers and Earnings per Share

One important effect of an acquisition is on the reported earnings per share (EPS) of the acquiring company. Because analysts in the financial community follow EPS, a thorough analysis of a merger should include a calculation of the impact of the acquisition on EPS.

To calculate the effects on EPS, recall that EPS is calculated as profits after taxes (PAT) divided by the number of shares of common stock.[7] To calculate projected EPS, then, we need to project PAT and the number of shares of stock after the acquisition.

Sample Problem 22–3

EPS Effects of Franklin's Acquisition of Stove Enterprises

In December 1986, Franklin Inc. was planning an acquisition of Stove Enterprises. Franklin's financial staff had prepared the PAT projections that the two companies would have without the acquisition, as shown in Table 22–6. As a preliminary stage of analysis, Franklin is assuming that if the acquisition goes through, the post-merger

---

[7]In Chapter 13, when discussing the effects of financial leverage on the firm, we presented a more thorough discussion of calculating earnings per share. If the company has preferred stock, we subtract preferred dividends from profits after taxes before calculating EPS for common shareholders.

Table 22–6
Projected Profit after Taxes (PAT) for Franklin Inc. and Stove Enterprises without a Merger, 1986–89 (millions of dollars)

Year	Franklin PAT	Stove PAT
1986	20	10
1987	26	12
1988	33.8	14.4
1989	43.9	17.28

profits will simply be the sum of the profits of the two companies if they had not merged. Presently, Franklin has 10 million shares of stock selling at $30 per share. Stove has 4 million shares of stock selling at $20 per share. Last year (1985), Franklin's earnings per share were $1.54.

After negotiations, Franklin has offered to give one share of its stock for each share of Stove Stock. Assuming Franklin's stock price doesn't drop as a result of the offer, Franklin is offering $30 worth of stock in exchange for $20 worth of stock. This offer represents a 50 percent increase for Stove shareholders, and they are quite delighted with the prospect. Paying a 50 percent premium is not uncommon in acquisitions. Such a premium may be necessary to induce Stove shareholders to agree to the merger, especially if other firms are waiting in the wings to make a bid for Stove. What are the effects of the acquisition on Franklin's EPS?

A. Calculate Franklin's EPS without the merger.
B. Calculate Franklin's EPS with the merger.

Solution
To calculate EPS, we need to divide PAT by the number of shares of stock, N.

    A. Without the merger we get the results shown in Table 22–7.

Table 22–7
Calculation of Estimated Earnings per Share (EPS) for Franklin Inc. without a Merger, 1986–1989

Year	PAT (millions of dollars) (1)	Number of Shares of Stock, N (millions) (2)	EPS (3) = (1) ÷ (2)
1986	20	10	$2.00
1987	26	10	$2.60
1988	33.8	10	$3.38
1989	43.9	10	$4.39

Table 22–8

Calculation of Estimated Earnings per Share (EPS) for Franklin Inc. with a Merger, 1986–89

Year	PAT (millions of dollars)	Number of Shares of Stock, N (millions)	EPS
1986	30	14	$2.14
1987	38	14	$2.71
1988	48.2	14	$3.44
1989	61.18	14	$4.37

B. With the merger, the number of shares of stock (N) = Franklin's old shares + new shares issued in acquisition = 10 million + 4 million = 14 million. Note that one new share is issued for each old share of Stove. We can find Franklin's PAT (with the merger) by adding the projected PAT figures for Franklin and Stove. For example, in 1986 PAT will be $20 million + $10 million = $30 million. Summarizing, Franklin's earnings per share are projected as shown in Table 22–8 and Table 22–9.

Note that Franklin's earnings per share initially increase as a result of the acquisition (from $2.00 to $2.14 in 1986), but by 1989 Franklin finds its expected earnings per share are actually lower as a result of the acquisition ($4.37 versus $4.39). Franklin, thus, faces a trade-off. The acquisition initially increases EPS but lowers EPS in the more distant future.

Before leaving this example, let us ask an important question. Would Franklin's stock price be expected to drop below $30 per share once it announced its offer? The answer depends on investors' valuation of the investment Franklin is making by buying Stove Enterprises. If investors think no value is created in the takeover, they would certainly think Franklin is making a mistake offering any premium, so Franklin's stock price would drop. This drop of stock price would make the offer less attractive to Stove stockholders who have been promised a share of Franklin stock for each share of Stove they presently own. ∎

Table 22–9

Comparison of Estimated Earnings per Share (EPS) for Franklin Inc. with and without a Merger, 1986–89

Year	EPS Without Merger	EPS With Merger
1986	$2.00	$2.14
1987	$2.60	$2.71
1988	$3.38	$3.44
1989	$4.39	$4.37

As Sample Problem 22–3 shows, EPS can be changed as a result of an acquisition. The key to understanding the nature of the change is to look at these important factors: the way the acquisition is financed, the price/earnings (PE) ratios of the acquiring and acquired firms, and the expected growth in earnings for the acquired and acquiring firms.

The financing of the acquisition has an important effect on EPS if the financing causes a shift in the mix of debt and equity financing used by the merging firms, because of the effects of financial leverage that we studied in detail in Chapters 13 and 14. For example, suppose an acquiring firm borrows cash to buy the stock of another firm and simultaneously assumes the debt of that firm. These actions would substantially increase the financial leverage of the acquiring firm. The likely effect would be to increase not only the expected EPS but also the risk of those earnings. In some cases, mergers involve large shifts in financing mix, which may have dramatic effects on reported earnings. Even without changes in financial leverage, however, acquisitions can affect EPS, as we'll see below.

A second important factor is the relationship of the price/earnings (PE) ratio of the acquiring firm to that of the acquired firm. If a company with a high PE ratio exchanges its stock for stock of a company with a low PE ratio, short-run EPS typically will increase. To illustrate, let's return to the data for Franklin and Stove in Sample Problem 22–3. Franklin's stock price of $30 per share based on a $2.00 EPS reflects a PE ratio of $30/$2.00 = 15. Stove's (pre-acquisition) EPS is $10 million/4 million = $2.50 and, with a stock price of $20, this produces a PE ratio of $20/$2.50 = 8. Why the difference between the PE ratios? The likely explanation is that Franklin is expected to grow faster than Stove or is less risky than Stove. One other PE ratio is important to examine—namely, the PE ratio Franklin "paid" for Stove. Franklin offered one share of its stock ($30 value) for each share of Stove stock ($2.50 of earnings). As a result, the PE ratio paid was $30/$2.50 = 12.

Now we can see the importance of the PE ratios when a merger is consummated by an exchange of stock. Because Stove was trading at a PE ratio of 8, $8 of share price per $1 of earning, Franklin would have to pay in excess of $8 to Stove's owners per dollar of earnings to make the offer attractive to Stove's shareholders. In other words, Franklin has to pay a merger premium. On the other hand, as long as Franklin pays a PE ratio less than 15 (its current PE), it can buy earnings relatively cheaply and see its EPS rise in the short run. By relatively cheaply, we mean that Franklin will get more earnings per $15 paid in the merger than the earnings its current shareholders get per $15 of their share price. In the actual transaction, Franklin paid a PE ratio of 12, which gave Stove shareholders a merger premium of 50 percent but also increased Franklin's EPS.

Does this analysis mean that mergers necessarily create benefits to both acquiring and acquired firms? The answer is no. It is not EPS that is ultimately important to shareholders but the price per share of the stock they own. Observing an increase in current EPS does not necessarily correspond to an increase in share price.

To get some insight into the problem, we can graph the EPS calculations we made in Sample Problem 22–3, as shown in Figure 22–2. As Figure 22–2 shows, earnings per share with the merger (colored line) are initially higher than EPS without the merger (black line), but the growth rates in EPS are lower with the merger. Looking

Figure 22-2
Earnings Per Share and Mergers

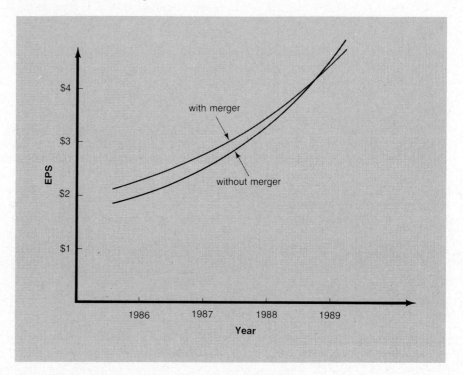

back at the figures for Franklin and Stove, this result is no surprise. Franklin was expecting 30 percent annual growth in earnings, whereas Stove was expecting only 20 percent. The merged firms should reasonably expect growth somewhere between 20 percent and 30 percent. In fact, the post-merger growth turns out to be at a 27 percent annual rate.

As we know from our discussion of stock valuation, stock prices depend not only on the initial level of earnings and dividends but also on their expected growth and the risk associated with these flows.

Because Franklin shareholders expected growth in EPS to drop as a result of this merger, we would expect the PE ratio of Franklin stock to drop. The question is: How far will the PE ratio drop? Looking at the data, we see that 1986 EPS will go from $2 to $2.14 as a result of the merger. The PE ratio necessary to keep Franklin's stock at its current $30 price, when multiplied by Franklin's EPS of $2.14, must equal $30.00. That is, 2.14(PE) = $30.00. Therefore, PE = $30.00/$2.14 = 14.02.

If Franklin's PE ratio right after the merger (that is, the PE of the new combined firm) remains above 14.02, Franklin's share price will go up from its current level of $30. If the share price increases, the merger has served the financial manager's objective—increasing the value of the firm to its owners.

One can pause to ask whether Franklin's current PE is likely to stay above 14.02

and, as a result, whether the merger will increase value to Franklin's shareholders. If the merger itself creates no value, Franklin's PE should drop below 14.02 because Franklin paid a 50 percent premium for Stove's stock. A direct way to estimate whether value will be created from Franklin is to use DCF techniques to analyze the net present value of the acquisition, just as we did earlier in this chapter. If the *NPV* is positive, the merger should benefit the acquiring firm.

Looking back at the effects of mergers on EPS we see that one has to be very careful in analyzing EPS data for merging firms. If we had expected Franklin's EPS without the acquisition to be $2.00 in 1986 and now saw reported 1986 EPS of $2.14 after the merger, we might be tempted to conclude that Franklin had increased its growth rate in EPS from 30 percent (from 1.54 to 2.00) without the merger to 39 percent (from 1.54 to 2.14) with the merger.

In reality, Franklin did increase its *short-run* growth rate in EPS from 30 percent to 39 percent because it bought a company with a lower PE ratio. The danger lies in extrapolating this growth rate into the future. We know from Figure 22–2 and earlier calculations that Franklin's *long-term* growth rate in EPS is actually lowered by this acquisition from 30 percent to 27 percent because Stove, as its lower PE suggests, is not expected to grow as fast as Franklin's existing operations. In making judgments about the merger, it is critical to look beyond the short-run effect on EPS and take into account the long-run effects.

In fact, investors have not always been so careful in looking at EPS figures. In the 1960s a number of acquiring firms with high PE ratios were able to increase short-run growth in EPS by making acquisitions of low-PE companies. The acquiring companies made a series of acquisitions and over the course of a few years were able to produce earnings per share that were growing at outstanding rates. The acquisitions were much like a chain letter. What happened?

For a while, investors in the stock market appeared to extrapolate these short-term growth rates into the distant future. As a result, the acquiring firms maintained their high PE ratios. The problem is that the chain letters couldn't go on forever and eventually earnings growth began to fall off, just as Figure 22–2 suggests will happen if Franklin acquires Stove.

Investors aren't fooled forever, and in the late 1960s they caught on to the chain-letter game of short-run increases in EPS. Acquiring-company PE ratios and stock prices plummeted, and acquisition activity came to a grinding halt. Given this earlier experience and investors' awareness of it, the chain-letter game is not played much these days. Companies and investors appear to focus on both the short-run and long-run effects of acquisitions.

Mergers and Balance Sheets

Pooling of interests—is an accounting method for reporting a merger in which the balance sheets of the two combining companies are added together to produce the balance sheet of the surviving company.

Purchase of assets—is an accounting method for reporting a merger in which the assets of the acquired company are revalued to reflect the amount of money actually paid for the acquired entity.

The balance sheet of the merging corporations can also be affected by mergers. The nature of these effects depends upon the treatment of complex accounting issues. The accounting profession has defined two primary ways to account for acquisitions. In a **pooling of interests**, the balance sheets of the two combining companies are simply added together to produce the balance sheet of the surviving company. In a **purchase of assets**, the assets of the acquired company are revalued to reflect the amount of money actually paid for the acquired entity, which involves taking into account differences between the current book value of assets and the amount paid for the company.

Table 22–10

Comparison of Two Major Methods of Accounting for Mergers (millions of dollars)

Panel A: Pre-Merger Balance Sheets

Franklin Inc.

Current assets	80	Debt	10
Fixed assets	120	Equity	190
Total assets	**200**	**Total debt and equity**	**200**

Stove Enterprises

Current assets	40	Debt	0
Fixed assets	60	Equity	100
Total assets	**100**	**Total debt and equity**	**100**

Panel B: Post-Merger Balance Sheet

Pooling of Interests Method

Current assets	120	Debt	10
Fixed assets	180	Equity	290
Total assets	**300**	**Total debt and equity**	**300**

Assumes Franklin pays 4,000,000 shares at $30 share, or $120 million, and acquisition is pooling of interests.

Purchase Method

Current assets	120	Debt	10
Fixed assets	180	Equity	310
Goodwill	20		
Total assets	**320**	**Total debt and equity**	**320**

Assumes Franklin pays $120 million and acquisition is treated as a purchase of assets.

For example, consider the balance sheets for Franklin and Stove shown in Table 22–10. If the merger is treated as a pooling of interests, the premerger balance sheets are simply added together. Though the details of the requirements for pooling are lengthy, in essence, poolings occur when one company exchanges its stock for the stock of another company. The shareholders of the acquired firm now have a shareholder interest in the new firm.

In a purchase of assets, the balance sheet in Table 22–10 is adjusted for the fact that Franklin paid $120 million, which is $20 million in excess of the book value of Stove's assets. The difference of $20 million could reflect the fact that Stove's tangible assets are actually worth more than their book value—for example, as a result of increased prices of equipment carried on Stove's books at historical costs. In such a case we would have to revalue these tangible assets in producing the post-merger balance sheet.

In the example in Table 22–10, we have assumed that the entire $20 million is paid for intangible assets of Stove that are not listed on the balance sheet. These assets might include Stove's management expertise or its reputation as a producer of quality products. The $20 million is entered as a new asset account called **goodwill**.

Just as other long-term assets are depreciated, this goodwill account must be amortized. This amortization must be done over a period not exceeding 40 years and

Goodwill—is the excess of the price paid for a going concern over the book value of its tangible assets; an intangible asset of the firm.

reduces reported income. For example, the figures in Table 22–10 would lead to an annual amortization charge of $20,000,000/40 = $500,000, which would reduce Franklin's reported income by $500,000 for each of the next 40 years, as compared to pooling-of-interests accounting, which creates no goodwill account. As a result, many managers prefer pooling-of-interest accounting when they pay in excess of the book value of the assets.[8]

On the other hand, goodwill-amortization charges are not cash flows nor are they tax-deductible. As a result, while affecting reported income, goodwill-amortization charges have no effect on the underlying cash flow. If they don't affect this cash flow, our DCF valuation techniques suggest that they should not affect value. Thus, the choice of pooling versus purchase accounting should not affect the value of the acquisition if it has no effect on cash flows.[9]

EFFECTS OF MERGERS

Owners' Perspective

If both sets of shareholders expect a positive net present value, then the merger is expected to create some value, perhaps through cost savings. We can examine past mergers to see if there is any evidence that such value has been created.

There have been a number of studies that have analyzed the effects of mergers on the shareholders of the participating firms.[10] Have shareholders in acquiring firms benefited? Have acquired-firm shareholders benefited? On balance, has there been net increase in value as a result of mergers?

There are a number of difficult issues in trying to answer such questions. For example, if we want to decide whether an acquired shareholder benefits, we need to figure out what sort of value and return such a shareholder would have had in the absence of a merger and compare those to the returns they actually did receive as a result of the merger.[11]

Without going into the details of the techniques used in studies of mergers, we can

---

[8]H. Hong, G. Mandelker, and R. S. Kaplan, "Pooling vs. Purchase: The Effects of Accounting for Mergers on Stock Prices," *Accounting Review*, January 1978, pp. 31–47.

[9]Hong, Mandelker, and Kaplan, "Pooling vs. Purchase." Note that if part of the excess of purchase price over book value is allocated to tangible assets (unlike our example in Table 22–10), tax-deductible depreciation charges will be affected. The ultimate effect of this approach on value depends not only on tax deductions to the acquiring firm but also on the tax status of the selling firm and involves tax issues beyond the scope of our discussion. See B. I. Bittker and J. Eustice, *Fundamentals of Federal Income Taxation of Corporations and Shareholders* (New York: Warren, Gorham and Lamont, 1980).

[10]Two useful review articles are Paul Halpern, "Corporate Acquisitions: A Theory of Special Cases? A Review of Event Studies Applied to Acquisitions," *Journal of Finance*, May 1983, pp. 297–318; and M. Jensen and R. Ruback, "The Market for Corporate Control: The Scientific Evidence," *Journal of Financial Economics*, April 1983.

[11]Halpern, "Corporate Acquisitions"; Jensen and Ruback, "The Market for Corporate Control." Both sources discuss in detail many of the difficulties of structuring a test to see whether mergers benefit shareholders and survey past studies and the results of those studies.

briefly summarize the results. First, shareholders of acquired firms do seem to have benefited. This result is not extremely surprising because acquired-firm shareholders are typically paid a price in excess of the market price of their stock. In the last few years it has not been unusual for shareholders to be paid 50 percent in excess of the market value of their stock in a merger.

Second, shareholders of acquiring firms do not seem to have been harmed by mergers, but the evidence is not so clear that they have been helped. A final judgment involves some interpretation, and authors differ in their conclusions. A reading of the evidence, however, suggests that acquiring firms, on average, have not received large value increases (positive *NPV*s) in mergers. One possible explanation of this result is that the market in which acquiring firms acquire other firms is quite competitive. Acquiring firms will have to pay a price to buy another firm. This price will have to be high enough to outbid other potential acquiring firms. As the price they pay goes up, the net present value to the acquiring firm goes down. In fact, in a highly competitive market, we would expect the price paid to go just high enough that most of the benefits of the merger to the acquiring firm are eliminated. This expectation seems to be consistent with the evidence. The evidence also suggests that acquiring firms should look for acquisitions in which they will have some advantage over other potential acquiring firms.

Thus, mergers seem to have created value for acquired-firm shareholders and at least have not harmed acquiring-firm shareholders. As a result, it appears that mergers in the last few decades have increased value to the shareholders of participating firms. Unfortunately, we cannot be sure that mergers in the future will also be value-increasing. In addition, the results stated above were averages over large samples of mergers. Clearly, some mergers have not increased value for shareholders while others have.

Public-Policy Perspective

One of the remaining issues is whether or not the increases in value that appear to have resulted from mergers are in the best interests of the economy. If the increase in value is from realization of cost savings and efficient production techniques, the merger would benefit not only the owners of the merging firms but could potentially provide lower prices to consumers and release resources for uses elsewhere in the economy. If, on the other hand, the increase in value is the result of increased monopoly power as the merged firms charge higher prices for the goods and services they sell, the merger value would come at the expense of those consumers buying the goods and services of the firm. In short, observing an increase in value is not sufficient to judge whether the merger is in the best interest of society at large. This judgment depends also upon the motives for merger and the effects of mergers on others in the economy.

Who Gets Acquired.   One possible way of getting some insight into the motives for mergers is to look at the types of firms that get acquired. From the numerous studies of the characteristics of firms that get bought, some general features have emerged. Smaller firms are acquired more often than are large firms. In addition, the lower is the price/earning ratio of a firm, the greater is the probability that the firm will be

Finance in Practice 22–2

Mergers in the United Kingdom

Year	Number of Firms Acquired	Value in Historic Prices (millions of pounds)	Value in 1985 Prices (millions of pounds)
1963	888	352	2,429
1964	940	505	3,371
1965	1,000	517	3,295
1966	807	500	3,077
1967	763	822	4,928
1968	946	1,946	11,145
1969	846	1,069	5,794
1970	793	1,122	5,730
1971	884	911	4,255
1972	1,210	2,532	11,023
1973	1,205	1,304	5,197
1974	504	508	1,749
1975	315	291	806
1976	353	448	1,064
1977	481	824	1,690
1978	567	1,140	2,159
1979	534	1,656	2,763
1980	469	1,475	2,087
1981	452	1,144	1,447
1982	463	2,206	2,569
1983	447	2,343	2,608
1984	568	5,474	5,806
1985	474	7,090	7,090

In the 1980s major U.S. investment-banking firms were beefing up their London operations. Why? One reason was that merger activity in the United Kingdom offered a real growth market for their mergers-and-acquisitions (M&A) groups. The prospects of attractive fees for merger advice and assistance was a powerful incentive for U.S. investment bankers. At the same time, London *merchant bankers* (the British term for investment bankers) were increasing their M&A operations. The accompanying table chronicles acquisition activity in the United Kingdom in terms of both numbers and value for the period 1963 to 1985. As the table shows, in terms of the value (in pounds) of acquisitions, merger activity increased sharply in 1984 and 1985. Adjusted for inflation, however, United Kingdom merger activity was still below its 1968 peak—as indicated in the column where all values are in terms of 1985 prices.

As the table shows, mergers have not been restricted to U.S. borders. In fact, during 1985 there were 709 acquisitions in Germany, 712 in Canada, and 318 in the Netherlands. The merger boom is an international business.

Many of the concerns about mergers felt in the United States are also shared by the United Kingdom. Do mergers serve shareholders' interest? Do they reduce competition? The analysis of these and other questions is complex. One comprehensive study of benefits of British mergers to shareholders found results quite similar to those found in U.S. studies. Acquiree shareholders experienced value gains of 20 to 30 percent around the merger date and acquiror shareholders either had zero or small gains. Thus, on average, British mergers appear to benefit shareholders at least around the merger date. Whether or not a particular acquisition is good and whether or not anticipated merger benefits will actually materialize are questions that require close study. What is clear is that financial managers around the globe are operating in a busy merger market.

Source: Data on United Kingdom mergers over time are from the British Department of Trade and Industry. Estimates of effects of mergers on shareholders are from J. Franks and R. Harris, "The Wealth Effects of Corporate Takeovers: the U.K. Experience 1955–1985" (Working paper, University of North Carolina at Chapel Hill, 1986).

acquired.[12] Unfortunately, however, further generalizations are difficult. It appears that mergers are not all alike. There are enough differences in mergers that it's hard to characterize what sorts of firms get acquired or don't get acquired. It does not appear that particularly profitable or unprofitable firms are typically bought or that firms with a lot of debt or a very small amount of debt are typically bought. Many recent mergers have been concentrated in certain industries—oil, gas, transportation, and finance. However, mergers have included everything from the 1984 acquisition of Gulf for which Chevron paid in excess of $13 billion to acquisitions of dime stores for considerably smaller dollar amounts.

Concentration in Particular Markets.   Another factor to examine in assessing the motives for and effects of mergers is to look at the concentration of producers in particular product markets. One measure of industry concentration is the **concentration ratio**. For example, a 4-firm concentration ratio would be the percentage of total sales controlled by the top four firms in an industry. If there were only four firms in the industry, of course, the 4-firm concentration ratio would be 100 percent. The higher is the concentration ratio, the less likely it is that there will be competitive behavior in this particular market and the more likely it is that there would be some monopoly power and, as a result, abnormally high profits earned by firms in that industry. One criticism of certain mergers is that they increase concentration in a particular product market. The most obvious example for such an increase would be a horizontal merger of two firms in the same industry. The ability of firms to earn abnormally high profits for any prolonged period of time is, however, affected by likely entrants into a market as well as the concentration of existing producers. As long as there are no barriers to entry into the market by other firms, the exercise of monopoly power is likely to be rather short-lived.

> A **concentration ratio**—is the percentage of sales, production volume, or any other variable to be measured accounted for the by the x largest firms in an industry.

Since World War II and prior to the 1980s, most of the mergers in the United States were between firms in different industries. These conglomerate mergers do not themselves increase concentration in a particular industry. Furthermore, a number of experts have noted that concentration in particular product markets, at least as measured by average 4-firm concentration ratios, has been remarkably stable over the past few decades (through the 1970s) of U.S. economic history.[13] The recent set of mergers of firms in the same industry has renewed concern in some camps about the desirability of mergers. Some experts believe that mergers of firms in the same industry often provide cost savings and that the vigor of competition (especially given substantial competition from foreign firms in many industries) is strong. These opinions appear to have won in shaping U.S. governmental policy toward mergers, which has become more lenient in the last decade. Many horizontal mergers of the 1980s would have not gone unchallenged by antitrust authorities in the 1960s and early 1970s. On the other hand, critics of merger activity are concerned about the possible exercise of monopoly power if industries have fewer firms. Though the public debate goes on, the full evidence on who is correct is not yet in.

---

[12]See R. Harris, J. Stewart, D. Guilkey, and W. Carleton, "Characteristics of Acquired Firms: Fixed and Random Coefficient Profit Analysis," *Southern Economic Journal*, July 1982, pp. 164–84.

[13]See Scherer, *Industrial Market Structure*. In addition to the 4-firm concentration ratio, investigators use other measures of industry concentration such as the Herfindahl index.

Aggregate Concentration.   Another factor to consider in mergers is the sheer size of firms. Is being big bad? Some argue that mergers leading to large firms are not in the best interest of the economy because they tend to concentrate economic and political power. This argument against being big does not depend solely on a firm's having power in a particular product market. Some argue that very large firms are more likely to wield political power and, hence, will have an undue influence on both economic and political outcomes in the economy. Paraphrasing critics of mergers on these grounds, "Big is bad."

It is extremely difficult to measure aggregate concentration—the amount of economic activity in the hands of a few individuals or firms in the United States. One way to gauge aggregate concentration is to look at the total percentage of certain economic aggregates that are controlled by particular groups of firms. In a study of such aggregate concentration in the entire private sector, L. J. White showed that aggregate concentration (measured by either employment or corporate profits) was not increasing throughout the 1970s despite the large number of mergers in the last part of that decade.[14] For example, White found that in 1980 the largest 100 U.S. companies controlled 16.6 percent of private-sector employment, down from 18.2 percent in 1972.

While aggregate concentration ratios would have fallen without mergers, it appears that basing the case against mergers by arguing that they have increased aggregate concentration is not consistent with the historical evidence, at least for the 1970s. In fact, policymakers in Washington seem to have concluded that mergers are not likely to have damaging effects simply because larger firms are created. Most of the merger legislation in the early 1980s assumed that big is not necessarily bad.

Mergers and Policies.   A large number of government regulations apply to mergers and acquisitions. These include regulations enforced by the Securities and Exchange Commission (SEC), provisions of the Sherman and Clayton Antitrust laws in the United States, and numerous laws issued by states. The antitrust laws, in effect, state that mergers will not be allowed if their effect is to substantially lessen competition in the provision and sale of goods and services in the U.S. economy. They do not emphasize the pure size of the corporation but rather its size relative to each market.

In the 1980s, the Justice Department became more lenient in its policies about stopping mergers for antitrust reasons. This shift allowed both vertical and horizontal mergers to take place that would have been challenged in earlier years. As of this writing, Congress is reviewing proposals to revise some of the antitrust laws about mergers. Any fundamental changes could affect the future course of merger activity in the United States.

The SEC has important responsibilities for governing corporate conduct as it affects the well-being of shareholders. In the merger area, these responsibilities include setting standards for the nature and timing of takeover offers that one firm can make to acquire another. These standards are especially important in hostile takeovers when a potential acquiror, despite resistance from the target company's management, makes a tender offer.

---

[14]These data are drawn from the work of Lawrence J. White. See, for example, L. J. White, "Mergers and Aggregate Concentration," in M. Keenan and L. White, eds., *Mergers and Acquisitions* (Lexington, Mass.: Lexington Books, 1982).

Merger activity in recent years has also been affected by governmental policies to deregulate certain industries. For example, acquisitions in both the banking sector and the airline industry have been spurred by fundamental changes in those industries that have accompanied deregulation.

In addition, tax laws affect mergers in numerous ways. An acquisition is classified as either taxable or tax-free. In tax-free mergers, shareholders of the acquired firm receive shares in the post-merger firm and do not have to pay any capital-gains taxes until they choose to sell the new shares (which suggests that such mergers might better be described as "tax-deferred").

In a taxable merger, the sellers of the acquired firm must recognize any gains or losses immediately and be subject to the applicable taxes. Taxable mergers generally occur whenever shareholders in the acquired firm receive something other than shares of stock (for example, cash or bonds) in exchange for their shares of stock. The taxable versus tax-free status can also affect corporate taxes levied on the post-merger firms. The details of the tax laws are actually quite complicated on this point and are beyond the scope of this text.[15]

KEY CONCEPTS

1. The latest wave of mergers is the fourth in U.S. history.

2. To be good investments, mergers must create value for shareholders. The basic question is whether acquisitions have positive net present values to shareholders.

3. There are many possible motives for mergers, each of which may explain at least some mergers.

4. Mergers can be viewed as investment proposals and analyzed with discounted-cash-flow techniques.

5. Companies with high PE ratios may increase short-term earnings per share by acquiring companies with low PE ratios. Such short-term increases in EPS may not raise share price, however, because they typically come with a reduction in the expected long-term growth of EPS.

6. Mergers have become a public-policy concern in the U.S. economy.

SUMMARY

Mergers have had a long history in U.S. business. From a financial manager's perspective, mergers can be viewed as investment proposals. The fundamental question is whether mergers can create value. While numerous motives for mergers have been suggested, most of them can be thought of as factors that could increase the value of the firm to shareholders.

From the acquiring company's perspective, discounted-cash-flow analysis is a useful way to analyze mergers because it allows the acquiring firm to see if a proposed merger is a good investment. In addition, the analysis provides useful information on the maximum price that can be paid for another company that would still make the acquisition a good investment for the acquiring company.

In addition to DCF analysis, it is also useful to calculate the effects of mergers on the firm's balance sheet and on its earnings per share. In many cases

---

[15]See Bittker and Eustice, *Fundamentals of Federal Income Taxation of Corporations and Shareholders.*

firms with high PE ratios may be able to increase earnings per share in the short run by acquiring firms with low PE ratios. This short-run increase usually comes at the cost of EPS growth in the future.

In addition to the tremendous concern in the business community about mergers and acquisitions, mergers have been a focus of much public-policy debate. This debate extends to the effects of mergers on monopoly power in product markets and on aggregate concentration, in addition to the effects of mergers on shareholders of participating firms.

While each merger is different, past evidence suggests that, on average, acquired-firm shareholders have benefited from mergers because of the large premiums paid. Acquiring-firm shareholders, on the other hand, often appear to have paid a sufficiently high price such that most, if not all, of any value created in a merger goes to the acquired firm.

QUESTIONS

1. What are the differences between horizontal, vertical, and conglomerate mergers?

2. If the value of the post-merger company is larger than the combined values of the two premerger companies, does the merger have a positive net present value as an investment for the acquiring firm?

3. Is diversification through merger likely to lead to increases in value?

4. How can companies with high PE ratios increase earnings per share when they buy companies with low PE ratios?

5. Do merger-induced increases in earnings per share always benefit the shareholders?

6. What is the difference between pooling of interests and purchase of assets as accounting methods for reporting on mergers?

7. In the past, have mergers benefited shareholders of acquired firms? Have mergers benefited shareholders of acquiring firms?

8. Compare mergers in the 1960s to mergers today?

9. How are acquisitions similar to other investment proposals analyzed by firms? How are they different?

PROBLEMS

1. Suppose XYZ corporation's stock is trading for $50 a share while ABC stock goes for $25 a share. XYZ has earnings per share (EPS) of $1 while ABC has EPS of $2.50. Currently neither company has debt, and each has 1,000,000 shares of stock outstanding.

   a. If the merger takes place based on an exchange of stock, which company should be the acquiring firm in order to see an increase in EPS? Explain.

   b. If XYZ buys ABC and pays a premium of 20 percent (20 percent in excess of ABC's current market value), how many shares of XYZ must be given to ABC shareholders for each of their shares? (Use current market prices in your calculations.)

   c. Based on your calculations above, what will be XYZ's EPS after it acquires ABC?

   d. Would you expect XYZ's price/earnings ratio to remain at its current level of $50 divided by $1 = 50 if the merger goes through? Why?

   e. If ABC were to acquire XYZ and offer a 20 percent premium, how many shares of stock would ABC have to offer? What would be the effect on ABC's EPS?

   f. What do the above calculations indicate about which company should acquire the other? (Assume there is to be an acquisition.)

2. The sample problem in the text analyzes Union's acquisition of Pearsall. Answer the following questions using the data provided in that problem. (Do each part separately.)

   a. Should Union buy Pearsall if it has to pay $120 million (cash plus stock) for Pearsall's common stock? Calculate net present value (NPV).

   b. If Pearsall's debt had a market value of $6 mil-

Table A

Dunkirk Enterprises, 1986 (millions of dollars)

Current assets	70	Current liabilities	20
Fixed assets	80	Long-term debt	0
Total assets	**150**	**Equity**	**130**
		Total liabilities and debt	**150**

Statistical Labs, 1986 (millions of dollars)

Current assets	200	Current liabilities	200
Fixed assets	400	Long-term debt	100
Total assets	**600**	Equity	300
		Total liabilities and debt	**600**

lion, what would be the maximum amount of money Union could pay for Pearsall?

c. How much could Union pay for Pearsall's common stock assuming that cash flows were expected to be 25 percent higher than originally projected?

d. How much could Union pay for Pearsall's common stock assuming that cash flows were expected to be 25 percent higher but the required rate of return was 18 percent rather than 15 percent?

e. Suppose that instead of assuming a sale price of $60 million in 1989, you thought that Pearsall's operating cash flows in that year could be maintained indefinitely. Assuming a required return of 15 percent, what would Pearsall be worth in 1986? (Hint: use a perpetuity.) Given this calculation, how would this affect the NPV of buying Pearsall?

3. You are given the premerger (1986) balance sheets for Statistical Labs Amalgamated and Dunkirk Enterprises as shown in Table A. Statistical Labs is planning to acquire Dunkirk, paying $160 million to Dunkirk shareholders and assuming the current liabilities of $20 million for a total "cash equivalent" price of $180 million.

a. Prepare the balance sheet of postmerger company (SLAM-DUNK) if the transaction is a pooling of interests.

b. Prepare a balance sheet for SLAM-DUNK if the acquisition is a purchase of assets. Assume that Dunkirk's tangible assets are not revalued as the result of acquisition.

c. Suppose SLAM-DUNK's 1987 profits after taxes were anticipated to be $5 million if pooling-of-interests accounting is used. What would the reported profits be if the acquisition is a purchase of assets? How would this affect cash flow?

4. Schubert Shoe is considering the acquisition of Lipstein Leather for $6.5 million. Schubert would also assume Lipstein's liabilities of $3.2 million. Half of the merger premium is due to the fact that Lipstein's assets are carried on the books at $6.2 million, which is below their fair market value. The remainder of the premium reflects the unusually strong reputation of Lipstein as a fine-leather manufacturer. Pro-forma analysis predicts pre-tax cash flows from Lipstein of $2.9 million per year for 35 years. Lipstein's assets are to be depreciated on a straight-line basis over 35 years, with zero salvage value anticipated. The goodwill arising from the merger will be amortized over a 35-year period. Schubert is taxed at a rate of 50 percent, and requires a 16 percent return on investments of a risk similar to the Lipstein investment.

a. If the merger must be treated as a purchase for

Table B

Year	Profit after Taxes (PAT) (millions of dollars)
1987	15.0
1988	18.0
1989	21.6

Table C

Year	Profit after Taxes (PAT) (millions of dollars)
1987	40
1988	50
1989	60

accounting purposes, should Lipstein be acquired?

b. If the merger must be treated as a pooling of interests for accounting purposes, should Lipstein be acquired?

5. Rework Franklin's acquisition of Stove (see Sample Problem 22–3) assuming that Franklin's original share price was $20 per share [a price/earnings ratio (P/E) of 10] rather than $30 per share. Assume that Franklin still planned to pay a 50 percent premium and hence was going to offer $30 of its stock for each share of Stove's stock.

a. How many shares of Franklin stock must be offered for each share of Stove stock?

b. What will the EPS be after the merger?

c. Explain why your results are different from those in the sample problem. (*Hint:* Focus on the relevance of Franklin's P/E ratio, the P/E ratio "paid" for Stove, and Stove's P/E ratio.)

6. Let's return to Union Amalgamated's proposed acquisition of Pearsall in Sample Problems 22–1 and 22–2. There we had projected that Pearsall, if acquired, would have profits after taxes (PAT) as shown in Table B. In addition, to buy Pearsall's common stock, Union was planning to pay $50,000,000 cash plus 1,000,000 shares of Union common stock. Now we need to supply information on Union's existing financial situation. Suppose Union had 20,000,000 shares of stock outstanding. Also suppose that Union would raise the $50,000,000 cash by issuing long-term bonds that had an interest rate of 10 percent. Also suppose that Union's PAT without the merger (and also without the borrowing) was projected to be as shown in Table C.

a. Calculate Union's PAT in each of the next three years if it acquires Pearsall.

b. Calculate Union's EPS in each of the next three years if Union buys Pearsall.

c. What happens to Union's EPS as a result of buying Pearsall?

REFERENCES

Bittker, B. I., and J. S. Eustice. *Fundamentals of Federal Income Taxation of Corporations and Shareholders*. New York: Warren, Gorham and Lamont, 1980.

Chambers, D., R. Harris, and J. Pringle. "Treatment of Financing Mix in Analyzing Investment Opportunities." *Financial Management*. (Summer 1982): 24–41.

Copeland, T. E., and J. F. Weston. *Financial Theory and Corporate Policy*. 2nd ed. Reading, Mass.: Addison-Wesley Publishing Company, 1983.

Halpern, P. "Corporate Acquisitions: A Theory of Special Cases? A Review of Event Studies Applied to Acquisitions." *Journal of Finance*. (May 1983): 297–318.

Harris, R. S., J. F. Stewart, D. K. Guilkey, and W. T. Carleton. "Characteristics of Acquired Firms: Fixed and Random Coefficients Profit Analyses." *Southern Economic Journal*. (July 1982): 164–84.

Higgins, R. C., and L. D. Schall. "Corporate Bankruptcy and Conglomerate Merger." *Journal of Finance* (March 1975): 93–113.

Hong, H., G. Mandelker, and R. S. Kaplan. "Pooling vs. Purchase: The Effects of Accounting for Mergers on Stock Prices." *Accounting Review* (January 1978): 31–47.

Jensen, M., and R. Ruback. "The Market for Corporate Control: The Scientific Evidence." *Journal of Financial Economics* (April 1983).

Keenan, M., and L. White. ed. *Mergers and Acquisitions*. Lexington, Mass.: Lexington Books, 1982.

Lewellen, W. G. "A Pure Financial Rationale for the Conglomerate Merger." *Journal of Finance* (May 1971): 521–45.

Scherer, F. M. *Industrial Market Structure and Economic Performance*. 2nd ed. Chicago: Rand McNally and Company, 1980.

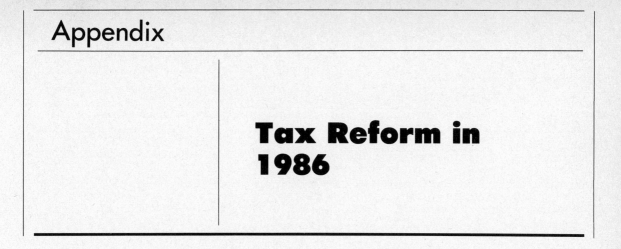

Appendix

Tax Reform in 1986

The U.S. tax code has been in a continuous state of evolution throughout this century. Tax rates reached a peak in the 1940s and 1950s (the top rate for individuals reached a peak of 94 percent during World War II!) and then began a slow and irregular decline over the next two decades. Maximum rates during the 1970s were 48 percent for corporations and, for individuals, 50 percent on "earned" income (wages and salary) and 70 percent on "unearned" income (interest and dividends).

During the late 1970s many economists and political leaders argued that high marginal tax rates distorted economic decisions and reduced efficiency. In 1981, the Reagan Administration proposed and Congress passed a major tax bill that lowered tax rates and also significantly reduced the total tax burden of both individuals and business. The resulting reduction in tax revenue to the government was a major factor in the very large deficits run by the federal government during the early 1980s.

Many believed that rates should be reduced even further and that the tax code should be simplified and made more equitable. A bill with these objectives was introduced in the Senate in 1982, and a similar bill was introduced in the House of Representatives in 1984. The Reagan Administration made tax reform its most important domestic priority at the beginning of its second term in 1984, and in late 1984 sent a bill to the Congress proposing a major overhaul of the entire tax code. The principal objectives of the overhaul were (1) to lower marginal tax rates while holding total tax revenue constant and (2) to simplify the code and reduce inequities.

The Congress debated tax reform throughout 1985 and into 1986. The House passed a bill in December 1985 that embodied the broad outlines of the Reagan proposal, and the Senate passed a similar bill in June of 1986. The differences between the two were resolved and the President signed a new tax bill into law in late 1986. Major features of the new bill are outlined in the accompanying table.

The central feature of the legislation is lower marginal tax rates—from 46 percent to 34 percent for corporations and from 50 percent to 28 percent for individuals. The reductions in rates are "paid for" (in order to avoid reducing total tax revenue) by eliminating a large number of special preferences and deductions and by sharply curtailing the attractiveness of tax shelters. The table shows some of the more important changes. Although total tax revenues are not projected to change as a result of the bill, total taxes on business are expected to rise by approximately $120 billion over five years and taxes on individuals are expected to fall by a like amount.

How Tax Reform Changes the Rules

	Law Through 1986	*New Tax Provisions*
Corporations		
Corporate rate	46 percent	34 percent
Minimum tax	15 percent, but rarely applicable	20 percent on broadened definition of income
Depreciation	Accelerated, far faster than asset life	Accelerated, less generous than current law
Investment tax credit	10 percent	Repealed
Capital gains	28 percent rate	Preference repealed, gains treated as ordinary income
Tax-exempt bonds	Allowed for public and some private purposes	Issuance for private purposes restricted
Research and development	25 percent credit on R&D spending (expired Dec. 31, 1985)	20 percent credit
Travel and entertainment	Fully deductible	Only 80 percent of meal costs deductible; some luxury charges restricted
Individuals		
Tax rate	14 brackets, indexed to inflation, top rate 50 percent	Two brackets, 15 percent and 28 percent; 5 percent surcharge for high-income taxpayers. Special interim rates for 1987
Exemption	$1,080, indexed	Rises in steps to $2,000 in 1989, indexed thereafter
Standard deduction	$3,670 for couples	$5,000 for couples
Marriage penalty relief	Deduction allowed to $3,000	Repealed
Mortgage interest	Deductible	Deductible on first and second homes
Consumer interest	Deductible	Not deductible
Other itemized deductions	Allowed for miscellaneous expenses	Most miscellaneous deductions repealed
Individual retirement accounts	Deductible up to $2,250 (individual and spouse)	Deductible only if income is below certain limits or employee is not covered by company pension
Company retirement plans	401(k) contributions up to $30,000 deductible	Deduction limited to $7,000
Tax shelters	Unlimited ability to offset investment income with "passive" losses	"Passive" losses may be charged only against passive income
Capital gains	20 percent effective maximum rate	Taxed as ordinary income (28 percent maximum rate)

Source: Adapted from "Tax Reform—At Last," *Business Week,* September 1, 1986.

Throughout this book, tax considerations were prominent in almost every decision that we analyzed (except those decisions made by tax-exempt organizations). If marginal tax rates fall, then firms keep more of every revenue dollar (66 cents per dollar versus 54 cents previously). Likewise, firms bear 66 cents of every dollar of expense, versus 54 cents under the old system. The result should be better decisions: efficiency and good decisions are rewarded; waste and mistakes are more costly.

The elimination of the investment tax credit (ITC) will raise the after-tax outlay in capital-investment decisions and, thereby, reduce incentives to invest (the hope is that lower marginal tax rates will more than offset the loss of the ITC). Depreciation will be taken over longer periods, with the result that the present value of depreciation tax shields will decline. While business overall will pay $120 billion more in taxes during 1987–91, some industries will be affected far more than others, and some will pay less taxes. Capital-intensive industries will be hurt by the elimination of the investment tax credit and the changes in depreciation. Service industries generally will benefit from the lower tax rates, although some, such as the banking industry, will lose specific preferences. Overall, for all businesses, tax considerations will become less important, and the underlying economic considerations more important. Most people think this reorientation will be a big improvement.

Individuals will also get much lower tax rates, but in the bargain they must give up preferential treatment of capital gains, tax shelters, and a large number of deductions, including consumer-loan interest, sales taxes, and contributions to individual retirement accounts (IRAs) beyond a certain ceiling amount. High-income individuals will now keep 72 cents of each additional dollar earned versus only 50 cents under current law. Many decisions will be affected, such as owning versus renting a home, saving and investing decisions, and retirement plans.

The 1986 tax-reform bill will have far-reaching implications for the economy, affecting business, individuals, and even tax-exempt organizations (because they transact in an economy heavily influenced by tax considerations). Some economists are worried that the transition to the new system could produce major dislocations in business in 1987 and possibly even trigger a recession. Others dispute this view, but few disagree that final passage of the 1986 tax-reform act should indeed be considered an historic event.

Appendix Table I

Present Value* (at *i* per period) of $1 Received at the End of *n* Periods

n	i = 1%	2%	3%	4%	5%	6%	7%	8%	9%	10%
1	0.990	0.980	0.970	0.962	0.952	0.943	0.935	0.926	0.917	0.909
2	0.980	0.961	0.943	0.925	0.907	0.890	0.873	0.857	0.842	0.826
3	0.971	0.942	0.915	0.889	0.864	0.840	0.816	0.794	0.772	0.751
4	0.961	0.924	0.888	0.855	0.823	0.792	0.763	0.735	0.708	0.683
5	0.951	0.906	0.863	0.822	0.784	0.747	0.713	0.681	0.650	0.621
6	0.942	0.888	0.837	0.790	0.746	0.705	0.666	0.630	0.596	0.564
7	0.933	0.871	0.813	0.760	0.711	0.665	0.623	0.583	0.547	0.513
8	0.923	0.853	0.789	0.731	0.677	0.627	0.582	0.540	0.502	0.467
9	0.914	0.837	0.766	0.703	0.645	0.592	0.544	0.500	0.460	0.424
10	0.905	0.820	0.744	0.676	0.614	0.558	0.508	0.463	0.422	0.386
11	0.896	0.804	0.722	0.650	0.585	0.527	0.475	0.429	0.388	0.350
12	0.887	0.788	0.701	0.625	0.557	0.497	0.444	0.397	0.356	0.319
13	0.879	0.773	0.681	0.601	0.530	0.469	0.415	0.368	0.326	0.290
14	0.870	0.758	0.661	0.577	0.505	0.442	0.388	0.340	0.299	0.263
15	0.861	0.743	0.642	0.555	0.481	0.417	0.362	0.315	0.275	0.239
16	0.853	0.728	0.623	0.534	0.458	0.394	0.339	0.299	0.252	0.218
17	0.844	0.714	0.605	0.513	0.436	0.371	0.317	0.270	0.231	0.198
18	0.836	0.700	0.587	0.494	0.416	0.350	0.296	0.250	0.212	0.180
19	0.828	0.686	0.570	0.475	0.396	0.331	0.277	0.232	0.194	0.164
20	0.820	0.673	0.554	0.456	0.377	0.312	0.258	0.215	0.178	0.149
21	0.811	0.660	0.538	0.439	0.359	0.294	0.242	0.199	0.164	0.135
22	0.803	0.647	0.522	0.422	0.342	0.278	0.226	0.184	0.150	0.123
23	0.795	0.634	0.507	0.406	0.326	0.262	0.211	0.170	0.138	0.112
24	0.788	0.622	0.492	0.390	0.310	0.247	0.197	0.158	0.126	0.102
25	0.780	0.610	0.478	0.375	0.295	0.233	0.184	0.146	0.116	0.092
30	0.742	0.552	0.412	0.308	0.231	0.174	0.131	0.099	0.075	0.057
35	0.706	0.500	0.355	0.253	0.181	0.130	0.094	0.068	0.049	0.036
40	0.672	0.453	0.307	0.208	0.142	0.097	0.067	0.046	0.032	0.022
45	0.639	0.410	0.264	0.171	0.111	0.073	0.048	0.031	0.021	0.014
50	0.608	0.372	0.228	0.141	0.087	0.054	0.034	0.021	0.013	0.009

*Value is calculated as $\dfrac{1}{(1 + i)^n}$.

Appendix Table I
(continued)

n	i = 11%	12%	13%	14%	15%	16%	17%	18%	19%	20%
1	0.901	0.893	0.885	0.877	0.870	0.862	0.855	0.847	0.840	0.833
2	0.812	0.797	0.783	0.769	0.756	0.743	0.731	0.718	0.706	0.694
3	0.731	0.712	0.693	0.675	0.658	0.641	0.624	0.609	0.593	0.579
4	0.659	0.636	0.613	0.592	0.572	0.552	0.534	0.516	0.499	0.482
5	0.593	0.567	0.543	0.519	0.497	0.476	0.456	0.437	0.419	0.402
6	0.535	0.507	0.480	0.456	0.432	0.410	0.390	0.370	0.352	0.333
7	0.482	0.452	0.425	0.400	0.376	0.354	0.333	0.314	0.296	0.279
8	0.434	0.404	0.376	0.351	0.327	0.305	0.285	0.266	0.249	0.233
9	0.391	0.361	0.333	0.308	0.284	0.263	0.243	0.225	0.209	0.194
10	0.352	0.322	0.295	0.270	0.247	0.227	0.208	0.191	0.176	0.162
11	0.317	0.287	0.261	0.237	0.215	0.195	0.178	0.162	0.148	0.135
12	0.286	0.257	0.231	0.208	0.187	0.168	0.152	0.137	0.124	0.112
13	0.258	0.229	0.204	0.182	0.163	0.145	0.130	0.116	0.104	0.093
14	0.232	0.205	0.181	0.160	0.141	0.125	0.111	0.099	0.088	0.078
15	0.209	0.183	0.160	0.140	0.123	0.108	0.095	0.084	0.074	0.065
16	0.188	0.163	0.142	0.123	0.107	0.093	0.081	0.071	0.062	0.054
17	0.170	0.146	0.125	0.108	0.093	0.080	0.069	0.060	0.052	0.045
18	0.153	0.130	0.111	0.095	0.081	0.069	0.059	0.051	0.044	0.038
19	0.138	0.116	0.098	0.083	0.070	0.060	0.051	0.043	0.037	0.031
20	0.124	0.104	0.087	0.073	0.061	0.051	0.043	0.037	0.031	0.026
21	0.112	0.093	0.077	0.064	0.053	0.044	0.037	0.031	0.026	0.022
22	0.101	0.083	0.068	0.056	0.046	0.038	0.032	0.026	0.022	0.018
23	0.091	0.074	0.060	0.049	0.040	0.033	0.027	0.022	0.018	0.015
24	0.082	0.066	0.053	0.043	0.035	0.028	0.023	0.019	0.015	0.013
25	0.074	0.059	0.047	0.038	0.030	0.024	0.020	0.016	0.013	0.010
30	0.044	0.033	0.026	0.020	0.015	0.012	0.009	0.007	0.005	0.004
35	0.026	0.019	0.014	0.010	0.008	0.006	0.004	0.003	0.002	0.002
40	0.015	0.011	0.008	0.005	0.004	0.003	0.002	0.001	0.001	0.001
45	0.009	0.006	0.004	0.003	0.002	0.001	0.001	0.001	*	*
50	0.005	0.003	0.002	0.001	0.001	0.001	*	*	*	*

*Value less than 0.001.

Appendix Table 1
(continued)

n	i = 21%	22%	23%	24%	25%	26%	27%	28%	29%	30%
1	0.826	0.820	0.813	0.806	0.800	0.794	0.787	0.781	0.775	0.769
2	0.683	0.672	0.661	0.650	0.640	0.630	0.620	0.610	0.601	0.592
3	0.564	0.551	0.537	0.524	0.512	0.500	0.488	0.477	0.466	0.455
4	0.467	0.451	0.437	0.423	0.410	0.397	0.384	0.373	0.361	0.350
5	0.386	0.370	0.355	0.341	0.328	0.315	0.303	0.291	0.280	0.269
6	0.319	0.303	0.289	0.275	0.262	0.250	0.238	0.227	0.217	0.207
7	0.263	0.249	0.235	0.222	0.210	0.198	0.188	0.178	0.168	0.159
8	0.218	0.204	0.191	0.179	0.168	0.157	0.148	0.139	0.130	0.123
9	0.180	0.167	0.155	0.144	0.134	0.125	0.116	0.108	0.101	0.094
10	0.149	0.137	0.126	0.116	0.107	0.099	0.092	0.085	0.078	0.073
11	0.123	0.112	0.103	0.094	0.086	0.079	0.072	0.066	0.061	0.056
12	0.102	0.092	0.083	0.076	0.069	0.062	0.057	0.052	0.047	0.043
13	0.084	0.075	0.068	0.061	0.055	0.050	0.045	0.040	0.037	0.033
14	0.069	0.062	0.055	0.049	0.044	0.039	0.035	0.032	0.028	0.025
15	0.057	0.051	0.045	0.040	0.035	0.031	0.028	0.025	0.022	0.020
16	0.047	0.042	0.036	0.032	0.028	0.025	0.022	0.019	0.017	0.015
17	0.039	0.034	0.030	0.026	0.023	0.020	0.017	0.015	0.013	0.012
18	0.032	0.028	0.024	0.021	0.018	0.016	0.014	0.012	0.010	0.009
19	0.027	0.023	0.020	0.017	0.014	0.012	0.011	0.009	0.008	0.007
20	0.022	0.019	0.016	0.014	0.012	0.010	0.008	0.007	0.006	0.005
21	0.018	0.015	0.013	0.011	0.009	0.008	0.007	0.006	0.005	0.004
22	0.015	0.013	0.011	0.009	0.007	0.006	0.005	0.004	0.004	0.003
23	0.012	0.010	0.009	0.007	0.006	0.005	0.004	0.003	0.003	0.002
24	0.010	0.008	0.007	0.006	0.005	0.004	0.003	0.003	0.002	0.002
25	0.009	0.007	0.006	0.005	0.004	0.003	0.003	0.002	0.002	0.001
30	0.003	0.003	0.002	0.002	0.001	0.001	0.001	0.001	*	*
35	0.001	0.001	0.001	0.001	*	*	*	*	*	*
40	*	*	*	*	*	*	*	*	*	*

Appendix Table I

(continued)

n	i = 31%	32%	33%	34%	35%	36%	37%	38%	39%	40%	50%
1	0.763	0.758	0.752	0.746	0.741	0.735	0.730	0.725	0.719	0.714	0.667
2	0.583	0.574	0.565	0.557	0.549	0.541	0.533	0.525	0.518	0.510	0.444
3	0.445	0.435	0.425	0.416	0.406	0.398	0.389	0.381	0.372	0.364	0.296
4	0.340	0.329	0.320	0.310	0.301	0.292	0.284	0.276	0.268	0.260	0.198
5	0.259	0.250	0.240	0.231	0.223	0.215	0.207	0.200	0.193	0.186	0.132
6	0.198	0.189	0.181	0.173	0.165	0.158	0.151	0.145	0.139	0.133	0.088
7	0.151	0.143	0.136	0.129	0.122	0.116	0.110	0.105	0.100	0.095	0.059
8	0.115	0.108	0.102	0.096	0.091	0.085	0.081	0.076	0.072	0.068	0.039
9	0.088	0.082	0.077	0.072	0.067	0.063	0.059	0.055	0.052	0.048	0.026
10	0.067	0.062	0.058	0.054	0.050	0.046	0.043	0.040	0.037	0.035	0.017
11	0.051	0.047	0.043	0.040	0.037	0.034	0.031	0.029	0.027	0.025	0.012
12	0.039	0.036	0.033	0.030	0.027	0.025	0.023	0.021	0.019	0.018	0.008
13	0.030	0.027	0.025	0.022	0.020	0.018	0.017	0.015	0.014	0.013	0.005
14	0.023	0.021	0.018	0.017	0.015	0.014	0.012	0.011	0.010	0.009	0.003
15	0.017	0.016	0.014	0.012	0.011	0.010	0.009	0.008	0.007	0.006	0.002
16	0.013	0.012	0.010	0.009	0.008	0.007	0.006	0.006	0.005	0.005	0.002
17	0.010	0.009	0.008	0.007	0.006	0.005	0.005	0.004	0.004	0.003	0.001
18	0.008	0.007	0.006	0.005	0.005	0.004	0.003	0.003	0.003	0.002	0.001
19	0.006	0.005	0.004	0.004	0.003	0.003	0.003	0.002	0.002	0.002	*
20	0.005	0.004	0.003	0.003	0.002	0.002	0.002	0.002	0.001	0.001	*
21	0.003	0.003	0.003	0.002	0.002	0.002	0.001	0.001	0.001	0.001	*
22	0.003	0.002	0.002	0.002	0.001	0.001	0.001	0.001	0.001	0.001	*
23	0.002	0.002	0.001	0.001	0.001	0.001	0.001	0.001	0.001	*	*
24	0.002	0.001	0.001	0.001	0.001	0.001	0.001	*	*	*	*
25	0.001	0.001	0.001	0.001	0.001	*	*	*	*	*	*
30	*	*	*	*	*	*	*	*	*	*	*

Appendix Table II

Present Value* (at i per period) of $1 Received per Period for Each of n Periods

n	$i = 1\%$	2%	3%	4%	5%	6%	7%	8%	9%	10%
1	0.990	0.980	0.971	0.962	0.952	0.943	0.935	0.926	0.917	0.909
2	1.970	1.942	1.914	1.886	1.859	1.833	1.808	1.783	1.759	1.736
3	2.941	2.884	2.829	2.775	2.723	2.673	2.624	2.577	2.531	2.487
4	3.902	3.808	3.717	3.630	3.546	3.465	3.387	3.312	3.240	3.170
5	4.854	4.713	4.580	4.452	4.330	4.212	4.100	3.993	3.890	3.791
6	5.796	5.601	5.417	5.242	5.076	4.917	4.767	4.623	4.486	4.355
7	6.728	6.472	6.230	6.002	5.786	5.582	5.389	5.206	5.033	4.868
8	7.652	7.325	7.020	6.733	6.463	6.210	5.971	5.747	5.535	5.335
9	8.566	8.162	7.786	7.435	7.108	6.802	6.515	6.247	5.985	5.759
10	9.471	8.983	8.530	8.111	7.722	7.360	7.024	6.710	6.418	6.145
11	10.368	9.787	9.253	8.760	8.036	7.887	7.499	7.139	6.805	6.495
12	11.255	10.575	9.954	9.385	8.863	8.384	7.943	7.536	7.161	6.814
13	12.134	11.348	10.635	9.986	9.394	8.853	8.358	7.904	7.487	7.103
14	13.004	12.106	11.296	10.563	9.899	9.295	8.745	8.244	7.786	7.367
15	13.865	12.849	11.938	11.118	10.380	9.712	9.108	8.560	8.061	7.606
16	14.718	13.578	12.561	11.652	10.838	10.106	9.447	8.851	8.313	7.824
17	15.562	14.292	13.166	12.166	11.274	10.477	9.763	9.122	8.544	8.022
18	16.398	14.992	13.753	12.659	11.690	10.828	10.059	9.372	8.756	8.201
19	17.226	15.678	14.324	13.134	12.085	11.158	10.336	9.604	8.950	8.365
20	18.046	16.351	14.877	13.590	12.462	11.470	10.594	9.818	9.129	8.514
21	18.857	17.011	15.415	14.029	12.821	11.764	10.836	10.017	9.292	8.649
22	19.661	17.658	15.937	14.451	13.163	12.042	11.061	10.201	9.442	8.772
23	20.456	18.292	16.444	14.857	13.489	12.303	11.272	10.371	9.580	8.883
24	21.244	18.914	16.936	15.247	13.799	12.550	11.469	10.529	9.707	8.985
25	22.023	19.523	17.413	15.622	14.094	12.783	11.654	10.675	9.823	9.077
30	25.808	22.396	19.600	17.292	15.372	13.765	12.409	11.258	10.274	9.427
35	29.409	24.999	21.487	18.665	16.374	14.498	12.948	11.655	10.567	9.644
40	32.835	27.355	23.115	19.793	17.159	15.046	13.332	11.925	10.757	9.779
45	36.095	29.490	24.519	20.720	17.774	15.456	13.606	12.108	10.881	9.863
50	39.196	31.424	25.730	21.482	18.256	15.762	13.801	12.233	10.962	9.915

*Value is calculated as $\left(\dfrac{1}{(1 + i)} + \dfrac{1}{(1 + i)^2} + \ldots + \dfrac{1}{(1 + i)^n} \right)$.

Appendix Table II

(continued)

n	i = 11%	12%	13%	14%	15%	16%	17%	18%	19%	20%
1	0.901	0.893	0.885	0.377	0.870	0.862	0.855	0.848	0.840	0.833
2	1.713	1.690	1.668	1.647	1.626	1.605	1.585	1.566	1.547	1.528
3	2.444	2.402	2.361	2.322	2.283	2.246	2.210	2.174	2.140	2.107
4	3.102	3.037	2.975	2.914	2.855	2.798	2.743	2.690	2.639	2.589
5	3.696	3.605	3.517	3.433	3.352	3.274	3.199	3.127	3.058	2.991
6	4.231	4.111	3.998	3.889	3.785	3.685	3.589	3.498	3.410	3.326
7	4.712	4.564	4.423	4.288	4.160	4.029	3.922	3.812	3.706	3.605
9	5.537	5.328	5.132	4.946	4.772	4.607	4.451	4.303	4.163	4.031
10	5.889	5.650	5.426	5.216	5.019	4.833	4.659	4.404	4.339	4.193
11	6.207	5.938	5.687	5.453	5.234	5.029	4.836	4.656	4.487	4.327
12	6.492	6.194	5.918	5.660	5.421	5.197	4.988	4.793	4.611	4.439
13	6.750	6.424	6.122	5.842	5.583	5.342	5.118	4.910	4.715	4.533
14	6.982	6.628	6.303	6.002	5.725	5.468	5.229	5.008	4.802	4.611
15	7.191	6.811	6.462	6.142	5.847	5.576	5.324	5.092	4.876	4.676
16	7.379	6.974	6.604	6.265	5.954	5.669	5.405	5.162	4.938	4.730
17	7.549	7.120	6.729	6.373	6.047	5.749	5.475	5.222	4.990	4.775
18	7.702	7.250	6.840	6.467	6.128	5.818	5.534	5.273	5.033	4.812
19	7.839	7.366	6.938	6.550	6.198	5.878	5.585	5.316	5.070	4.844
20	7.963	7.469	7.025	6.623	6.259	5.929	5.628	5.353	5.101	4.870
21	8.075	7.562	7.102	6.687	6.313	5.973	5.665	5.384	5.127	4.891
22	8.176	7.534	7.170	6.743	6.359	6.011	5.696	5.410	5.149	4.909
23	8.266	7.718	7.230	6.792	6.399	6.044	5.723	5.432	5.167	4.925
24	8.348	7.784	7.283	6.835	6.434	6.073	5.747	5.451	5.182	4.937
25	8.422	7.843	7.330	6.873	6.464	6.097	5.766	5.467	5.195	4.948
30	8.694	8.055	7.496	7.003	6.566	6.177	5.829	5.517	5.235	4.979
35	8.855	8.176	7.586	7.070	6.617	6.215	5.858	5.539	5.251	4.992
40	8.951	8.244	7.634	7.105	6.642	6.233	5.871	5.548	5.258	4.997
45	9.008	8.283	7.661	7.123	6.654	6.242	5.877	5.552	5.261	4.999
50	9.042	8.304	7.675	7.133	6.661	6.246	5.880	5.554	5.262	4.999

Appendix Table II

(continued)

n	i = 21%	22%	23%	24%	25%	26%	27%	28%	29%	30%
1	0.826	0.820	0.813	0.807	0.800	0.794	0.787	0.781	0.775	0.769
2	1.510	1.492	1.474	1.457	1.440	1.424	1.407	1.392	1.376	1.361
3	2.074	2.042	2.011	1.981	1.952	1.923	1.896	1.868	1.842	1.816
4	2.540	2.494	2.448	2.404	2.362	2.320	2.280	2.241	2.203	2.166
5	2.926	2.864	2.804	2.745	2.689	2.635	2.583	2.532	2.483	2.436
6	3.245	3.167	3.092	3.021	2.951	2.885	2.821	2.759	2.700	2.643
7	3.508	3.416	3.327	3.242	3.161	3.083	3.009	2.937	2.868	2.802
8	3.726	3.619	3.518	3.421	3.329	3.241	3.156	3.076	2.999	2.925
9	3.905	3.786	3.673	3.566	3.463	3.366	3.273	3.184	3.010	3.019
10	4.054	3.923	3.799	3.682	3.571	3.465	3.364	3.269	3.178	3.092
11	4.177	4.035	3.902	3.776	3.656	3.544	3.437	3.335	3.239	3.147
12	4.279	4.127	3.985	3.851	3.725	3.606	3.493	3.387	3.286	3.190
13	4.362	4.203	4.053	3.912	3.780	3.656	3.638	3.427	3.322	3.223
14	4.432	4.265	4.108	3.962	3.824	3.695	3.573	3.459	3.351	3.249
15	4.489	4.315	4.153	4.001	3.859	3.726	3.601	3.483	3.373	3.268
16	4.536	4.357	4.189	4.033	3.887	3.751	3.623	3.503	3.390	3.283
17	4.576	4.391	4.219	4.059	3.910	3.771	3.640	3.518	3.403	3.295
18	4.608	4.419	4.243	4.080	3.928	3.786	3.654	3.529	3.413	3.304
19	4.635	4.442	4.263	4.097	3.942	3.799	3.664	3.539	3.421	3.311
20	4.657	4.460	4.279	4.110	3.954	3.808	3.673	3.546	3.427	3.316
21	4.675	4.476	4.292	4.121	3.963	3.816	3.679	3.551	3.432	3.320
22	4.690	4.488	4.302	4.130	3.971	3.822	3.684	3.556	3.436	3.323
23	4.703	4.499	4.311	4.137	3.976	3.827	3.689	3.559	3.438	3.325
24	4.713	4.507	4.318	4.143	3.981	3.831	3.692	3.562	3.441	3.327
25	4.721	4.514	4.323	4.147	3.985	3.834	3.694	3.564	3.442	3.329
30	4.746	4.534	4.339	4.160	3.995	3.842	3.701	3.569	3.447	3.332
35	4.756	4.541	4.345	4.164	3.998	3.845	3.703	3.571	3.448	3.333
40	4.760	4.544	4.347	4.166	3.999	3.846	3.703	3.571	3.448	3.333
45	4.761	4.545	4.347	4.166	4.000	3.846	3.704	3.571	3.448	3.333
50	4.762	4.545	4.348	4.167	4.000	3.846	3.704	3.571	3.448	3.333

Appendix Table II
(continued)

n	i = 31%	32%	33%	34%	35%	36%	37%	38%	39%	40%	50%
1	0.763	0.758	0.752	0.746	0.741	0.735	0.730	0.725	0.719	0.714	0.667
2	1.346	1.332	1.317	1.303	1.289	1.276	1.263	1.250	1.237	1.225	1.111
3	1.791	1.766	1.742	1.719	1.696	1.674	1.652	1.630	1.609	1.589	1.407
4	2.131	2.096	2.062	2.029	1.997	1.966	1.936	1.906	1.877	1.849	1.605
5	2.390	2.345	2.302	2.260	2.220	2.181	2.143	2.106	2.070	2.935	1.737
6	2.588	2.534	2.483	2.433	2.386	2.339	2.294	2.251	2.209	2.168	1.824
7	2.739	2.678	2.619	2.562	2.508	2.455	2.404	2.356	2.308	2.263	1.883
8	2.854	2.786	2.721	2.658	2.598	2.540	2.485	2.432	2.380	2.331	1.922
9	2.942	2.868	2.798	2.730	2.665	2.603	2.544	2.487	2.432	2.379	1.948
10	3.009	2.930	2.855	2.784	2.715	2.650	2.587	2.527	2.469	2.414	1.965
11	3.060	2.978	2.899	2.924	2.752	2.683	2.618	2.556	2.496	2.438	1.977
12	3.100	3.012	2.931	2.853	2.779	2.708	2.641	2.576	2.515	2.456	1.985
13	3.129	3.040	2.956	2.876	2.799	2.727	2.658	2.592	2.469	1.990	
14	3.152	3.061	2.974	2.892	2.814	2.740	2.670	2.603	2.539	2.478	1.993
15	3.170	3.076	2.988	2.905	2.826	2.750	2.679	2.611	2.546	2.484	1.995
16	3.183	3.088	2.999	2.914	2.834	2.758	2.685	2.616	2.551	2.489	1.997
17	3.193	3.097	3.007	2.921	2.840	2.763	2.690	2.621	2.555	2.492	1.998
18	3.201	3.104	3.012	2.926	2.844	2.767	2.693	2.624	2.557	2.494	1.999
19	3.207	3.109	3.017	2.930	2.848	2.770	2.696	2.626	2.559	2.496	1.999
20	3.211	3.113	3.020	2.933	2.850	2.772	2.698	2.627	2.561	2.497	1.999
21	3.215	3.116	3.023	2.935	2.852	2.773	2.699	2.629	2.562	2.498	2.000
22	3.217	3.118	3.025	2.937	2.853	2.775	2.700	2.629	2.562	2.499	2.000
23	3.219	3.120	3.026	2.938	2.854	2.775	2.701	2.630	2.563	2.499	2.000
24	3.221	3.121	3.027	2.939	2.855	2.776	2.701	2.630	2.563	2.499	2.000
25	3.222	3.122	3.028	2.939	2.856	2.777	2.702	2.631	2.563	2.499	2.000
30	3.225	3.124	3.030	2.941	2.857	2.778	2.702	2.631	2.564	2.500	2,000
35	3.226	3.125	3.030	2.941	2.857	2.778	2.702	2.632	2.564	2.500	2.000
40	3.226	3.125	3.030	2.941	2.857	2.778	2.702	2.632	2.564	2.500	2.000
45	3.226	3.125	3.030	2.941	2.857	2.778	2.702	2.632	2.564	2.500	2.000
50	3.226	3.125	3.030	2.941	2.857	2.778	2.702	2.632	2.564	2.500	2.000

Appendix Table III

Future Value* (at *i* per period) at the End of *n* Periods of $1 Invested Today

n	i = 1%	2%	3%	4%	5%	6%	7%	8%	9%	10%
1	1.010	1.020	1.030	1.040	1.050	1.060	1.070	1.080	1.090	1.100
2	1.020	1.040	1.061	1.082	1.103	1.124	1.145	1.166	1.188	1.210
3	1.030	1.061	1.093	1.125	1.158	1.191	1.225	1.260	1.295	1.331
4	1.041	1.082	1.126	1.170	1.216	1.263	1.311	1.361	1.417	1.464
5	1.051	1.104	1.159	1.217	1.276	1.338	1.403	1.469	1.539	1.611
6	1.062	1.126	1.194	1.265	1.340	1.519	1.501	1.587	1.677	1.772
7	1.072	1.149	1.230	1.316	1.407	1.504	1.606	1.714	1.828	1.949
8	1.083	1.172	1.267	1.369	1.478	1.594	1.718	1.851	1.993	2.144
9	1.094	1.195	1.305	1.423	1.551	1.690	1.839	1.999	2.172	2.358
10	1.105	1.219	1.344	1.480	1.629	1.791	1.967	2.159	2.367	2.594
11	1.116	1.243	1.384	1.540	1.710	1.898	2.105	2.332	2.580	2.853
12	1.127	1.268	1.426	1.602	1.796	2.012	2.252	2.518	2.813	3.138
13	1.138	1.294	1.469	1.665	1.886	2.133	2.410	2.720	3.066	3.452
14	1.150	1.320	1.513	1.732	1.980	2.261	2.579	2.927	3.342	3.798
15	1.161	1.346	1.558	1.801	2.079	2.397	2.759	3.172	3.643	4.177
16	1.173	1.373	1.605	1.873	2.183	2.540	2.952	3.426	3.970	4.595
17	1.184	1.400	1.653	1.948	2.292	2.693	3.159	3.700	4.328	5.054
18	1.196	1.428	1.702	2.026	2.407	2.854	3.380	3.996	4.717	5.560
19	1.208	1.457	1.754	2.107	2.527	3.026	3.617	4.316	5.142	6.116
20	1.220	1.486	1.806	2.191	2.653	3.207	3.870	4.661	5.604	6.728
21	1.232	1.516	1.860	2.279	2.786	3.400	4.141	5.034	6.109	7.400
22	1.245	1.546	1.916	2.370	2.925	3.604	4.430	5.437	6.659	8.140
23	1.257	1.577	1.974	2.465	3.072	3.820	4.741	5.871	7.258	8.954
24	1.270	1.608	2.033	2.563	3.225	4.049	5.072	6.341	7.911	9.850
25	1.282	1.641	2.094	2.666	3.386	4.292	5.427	6.849	8.623	10.835
30	1.348	1.811	2.427	3.243	4.322	5.743	7.612	10.063	13.268	17.449
35	1.417	2.000	2.813	3.946	5.516	7.686	10.677	14.785	20.414	28.102
40	1.489	2.208	3.262	4.801	7.040	10.286	14.974	21.725	31.409	45.259
45	1.565	2.438	3.782	5.841	8.985	13.765	21.002	31.920	48.327	72.890
50	1.645	2.692	4.384	7.107	11.467	18.420	29.457	46.902	74.357	117.391

*Value is calculated as $(1 + i)^n$.

Appendix Table III

(continued)

n	i = 11%	12%	13%	14%	15%	16%	17%	18%	19%	20%
1	1.110	1.120	1.130	1.140	1.150	1.160	1.170	1.180	1.190	1.200
2	1.232	1.254	1.277	1.300	1.323	1.346	1.369	1.392	1.416	1.440
3	1.368	1.405	1.443	1.482	1.521	1.561	1.602	1.643	1.685	1.728
4	1.518	1.574	1.631	1.689	1.749	1.811	1.874	1.939	2.005	2.074
5	1.685	1.762	1.842	1.925	2.011	2.100	2.193	2.288	2.386	2.488
6	1.870	1.974	2.082	2.195	2.313	2.436	2.565	2.700	2.840	2.986
7	2.076	2.211	2.353	2.502	2.660	2.826	3.001	3.186	3.379	3.583
8	2.305	2.476	2.658	2.853	3.059	3.278	3.512	3.759	4.021	4.300
9	2.558	2.773	3.004	3.252	3.518	3.803	4.108	4.436	4.786	5.160
10	2.839	3.106	3.395	3.707	4.046	4.411	4.807	5.234	5.695	6.192
11	3.152	3.479	3.836	4.226	4.652	5.117	5.624	6.176	6.777	7.430
12	3.499	3.896	4.335	4.818	5.350	5.936	6.580	7.288	8.064	8.916
13	3.883	4.364	4.898	5.492	6.153	6.886	7.699	8.599	9.597	10.699
14	4.310	4.887	5.535	6.262	7.076	7.988	9.008	10.147	11.420	12.839
15	4.785	5.474	6.254	7.138	8.137	9.266	10.539	11.974	13.590	15.407
16	5.311	6.130	7.067	8.137	9.358	10.748	12.330	14.129	16.172	18.488
17	5.895	6.866	7.986	9.277	10.761	12.468	14.427	16.672	19.244	22.186
18	6.544	7.690	9.024	10.575	12.376	14.463	16.879	19.673	22.901	26.623
19	7.263	8.613	10.107	12.056	14.232	16.777	19.748	23.214	27.252	31.948
20	8.062	9.646	11.523	13.744	16.367	19.461	23.106	27.393	32.429	38.338
21	8.949	10.804	13.021	15.668	18.822	22.575	27.034	32.324	38.591	46.005
22	9.934	12.100	14.714	17.861	21.645	26.186	31.629	38.142	45.923	55.206
23	11.026	13.552	16.627	20.362	24.892	30.376	37.006	45.008	54.649	66.247
24	12.239	15.179	18.788	23.212	28.625	35.236	43.297	53.109	65.032	79.497
25	13.586	17.000	21.232	26.462	32.919	40.874	50.658	62.669	77.388	95.396
30	22.892	29.960	39.116	50.590	66.212	85.850	111.065	143.371	184.675	237.376
35	38.575	52.780	72.069	98.100	133.176	180.314	243.503	327.997	440.701	590.688
40	65.001	93.051	132.781	188.884	267.864	378.721	533.869	750.378	1051.668	1469.772
45	109.530	163.988	244.641	363.679	538.769	795.444	1170.479	1716.684	2509.651	3657.262
50	184.565	289.002	450.736	700.233	1083.657	1670.704	2566.215	3927.357	5988.914	9100.438

Appendix Table IV

Future Value* (at *i* per period) of $1 Invested per Period for Each of *n* Periods

n	i = 1%	2%	3%	4%	5%	6%	7%	8%	9%	10%
1	1.000	1.000	1.000	1.000	1.000	1.000	1.000	1.000	1.000	1.000
2	2.010	2.020	2.030	2.040	2.050	2.060	2.070	2.080	2.090	2.100
3	3.030	3.060	3.091	3.122	3.153	3.183	3.214	3.246	3.278	3.310
4	4.060	4.122	4.184	4.246	4.310	4.375	4.440	4.506	4.573	4.641
5	5.101	5.204	5.309	5.416	5.526	5.637	5.718	5.866	5.984	6.105
6	6.152	6.308	6.468	6.633	6.802	6.975	7.153	7.336	7.523	7.716
7	7.214	7.434	7.663	7.898	8.142	8.393	8.654	8.923	9.200	9.487
8	8.286	8.583	8.892	9.214	9.549	9.898	10.260	10.637	11.028	11.436
9	9.369	9.755	10.159	10.583	11.027	11.491	11.978	12.488	13.021	13.579
10	10.462	10.950	11.464	12.006	12.578	13.181	13.816	14.487	15.193	15.937
11	11.567	12.169	12.808	13.486	14.207	14.972	15.784	16.645	17.560	18.531
12	12.683	13.412	14.192	15.026	15.917	16.870	17.888	18.977	20.141	21.384
13	13.809	14.680	15.618	16.627	17.713	18.882	20.141	21.495	22.953	24.523
14	14.947	15.974	17.086	18.292	19.599	21.051	22.550	24.215	26.019	27.975
15	16.097	17.293	18.599	20.024	21.579	23.276	25.129	27.152	29.361	31.772
16	17.258	18.639	20.157	21.825	23.657	25.673	27.888	30.324	33.003	35.950
17	18.430	20.012	21.762	23.698	25.840	28.213	30.840	33.750	36.973	40.545
18	19.615	21.412	23.414	25.645	28.132	30.906	33.999	37.450	41.301	45.599
19	20.811	22.841	25.117	27.671	30.539	33.760	37.379	41.446	46.019	51.159
20	22.019	24.297	26.870	29.778	33.066	36.766	40.995	45.762	51.160	57.275
21	23.239	25.783	28.676	31.969	35.719	39.993	44.865	50.423	56.764	64.002
22	24.472	27.299	30.537	34.248	38.505	42.392	49.006	55.457	62.873	71.403
23	25.716	28.845	32.453	36.618	41.430	46.996	53.436	60.893	69.532	79.543
24	26.973	30.422	34.426	39.083	44.502	50.816	58.177	66.765	76.790	88.497
25	28.243	32.030	36.459	41.646	47.727	54.865	63.249	73.106	84.701	98.347
30	34.785	40.568	45.575	56.085	66.439	79.058	94.461	113.283	136.308	164.494
35	41.660	49.995	60.462	73.652	90.320	111.435	138.237	172.317	215.711	271.024
40	48.886	60.402	75.401	95.026	120.800	154.762	199.635	259.057	337.882	442.593
45	56.481	71.893	92.720	121.030	159.700	212.744	285.749	386.506	525.859	718.905
50	64.463	84.579	112.797	152.667	209.348	290.336	406.529	573.770	815.084	1163.909

*Value is calculated as $[(1 + i)^{n-1} + (1 + i)^{n-2} + \ldots + (1 + i)^{n-n}]$.

Appendix Table IV

(continued)

n	i = 11%	12%	13%	14%	15%	16%	17%	18%	19%	20%
1	1.000	1.000	1.000	1.000	1.000	1.000	1.000	1.000	1.000	1.000
2	2.110	2.120	2.130	2.140	2.150	2.160	2.170	2.180	2.190	2.200
3	3.342	3.374	3.401	3.439	3.472	3.501	3.539	3.572	3.606	3.640
4	4.710	4.779	4.850	4.921	4.993	5.067	5.141	5.216	5.290	5.368
5	6.229	6.353	6.480	6.610	6l742	6.877	7.015	7.154	7.297	7.442
6	7.913	8.115	8.323	8.536	8.754	8.978	9.207	9.442	9.683	9.930
7	9.784	10.089	10.405	10.730	11.067	11.414	11.772	12.142	12.523	12.916
8	11.859	12.300	12.757	13.233	13.723	14.240	14.774	15.327	15.902	16.499
9	14.164	15.415	16.085	16.786	17.518	18.285	19.086	19.924	20.799	
10	16.722	17.549	18.420	19.337	20.304	21.321	22.393	23.521	24.709	25.959
11	19.562	20.655	21.815	23.044	24.349	25.733	27.200	28.755	30.404	32.150
12	22.714	24.133	25.650	27.271	29.002	30.850	32.824	34.931	37.180	39.580
13	26.212	28.029	29.985	32.089	34.352	36.786	39.404	42.219	45.245	48.497
14	30.095	32.393	34.883	37.581	40.505	43.672	47.103	50.818	54.842	59.196
15	34.405	37.280	40.418	43.842	47.581	51.659	56.112	60.965	66.263	72.035
16	39.190	42.753	46.672	50.981	55.717	60.925	66.647	72.939	79.853	87.440
17	44.501	48.883	53.739	59.118	65.073	71.675	78.984	87.067	96.021	105.931
18	50.696	55.750	61.725	68.393	75.840	84.144	93.406	103.740	115.266	128.117
19	56.939	63.440	70.054	78.971	88.213	98.606	110.285	123.414	138.166	154.740
20	64.203	72.053	80.946	91.029	102.444	115.380	130.033	146.628	165.418	186.688
21	72.265	81.709	92.469	104.768	118.810	134.841	153.139	174.021	197.847	225.026
22	81.214	92.500	105.491	120.436	137.632	157.415	180.172	206.345	236.438	271.031
23	91.145	104.603	120.205	138.297	159.276	183.601	211.801	244.487	282.362	326.237
24	102.174	118.155	136.831	158.659	184.168	213.978	248.808	289.494	337.010	392.484
25	114.413	133.334	155.620	181.871	212.793	249.214	292.105	342.603	402.042	471.981
30	199.021	241.333	293.199	356.787	434.745	530.312	647.439	790.948	966.712	1181.882
35	341.590	431.664	546.681	693.573	881.170	1120.713	1426.491	1816.652	2314.214	2948.341
40	581.826	767.091	1013.704	1342.025	1779.090	2360.757	3134.522	4163.213	5529.829	7343.858
45	986.639	1358.230	1874.165	2590.565	3585.129	4965.274	6879.291	9531.577	13,203.424	18,281.310
50	1668.771	2400.018	3459.507	4994.521	7217.716	10,435.649	15,089.502	21,813.093	31,515.336	45,497.191

Glossary

Accelerated method of depreciation allocates the cost of an asset over a period of years according to a schedule that allows a greater fraction of the historical cost to be allocated to earlier years and a smaller fraction of the historical cost to be allocated to later years. **(9)**

Account see **accrual accounts, concentration account, money-market deposit account, open account.**

Accounting is the system of recording and summarizing business and financial transactions as well as analyzing, verifying, and reporting the results. **(6)**

Accounting income is the income figure that results from the application of generally accepted accounting principles to the problem of allocating receipts and expenditures to particular time periods. **(6)**

Accounting system see **accrual accounting system, cash accounting system.**

Accounts payable are amounts of money owed by a firm to its trade creditors and listed under current liabilities on the balance sheet. **(6, 18)**

Accounts receivable are amounts of money owed to a firm by customers and listed under current assets on the balance sheet. **(6, 18)**

Accrual accounting system is an accounting system that assigns revenues and expenses to particular time periods according to a predetermined set of rules. **(6)**

Accrual accounts are accounts, such as those for the payment of wages or taxes, in which money accumulates over short, regular periods to be paid out at regular intervals. **(18)**

Acid-test ratio, or quick ratio, is a more stringent measure of liquidity than the current ratio because it includes only the most liquid of current assets and is calculated as cash plus marketable securities plus receivables, divided by current liabilities. **(7)**

Actual rate of return on an investment project is the return that investors in fact receive, as distinct from the return they decide to require before undertaking the investment. **(4)**

Agency costs are the costs arising from the separation of ownership and management by the hiring of professional managers. **(13)**

Note: Chapter numbers appear in parentheses.

Agency issues see **federal-agency issues.**

Agent, in economic terms, is an individual or organization that acts in behalf of and to promote the interests of another party, usually referred to as the *principal.* **(10)**

Aging schedule is a technique for analyzing accounts receivable by cataloging receivables outstanding according to the length of time outstanding. **(7, 20)**

Alternatives see **mutually exclusive alternatives.**

Analysis see **break-even analysis, cash-flow analysis, discriminant analysis, EBIT/EPS analysis, economic analysis, incremental analysis, pro-forma analysis, ratio analysis, sensitivity analysis, strategic analysis, worst-case analysis.**

Annual return see **compound annual return.**

Annuity is a stream of equal payments at regular time intervals. **(3)**

Arbitrage see **covered-interest arbitrage.**

Arithmetic average is a summary measure obtained by adding the values observed and dividing their sum by the number of values. **(5, 10)**

AROI approach is a method of analyzing capital investments that relies on an accounting-based measure of return on investment, calculated as some measure of accounting profit divided by some measure of accounting investment. **(9)**

Asset-pricing model see **capital-asset-pricing model.**

Assets see **current assets, liquid assets, net liquid assets, purchase of assets, return on assets, value of an asset.**

Auction market is a market in which buyers and sellers state their terms and intermediaries act to bring the buyers and sellers together. **(17)**

Audit see **post audit.**

Average see **arithmetic average.**

Average tax rate is a taxpayer's payment divided by taxable income. **(2)**

Bad-debt expense is the cost associated with customers who default on their payments. **(20)**

Balance see **compensating balance, working-cash balance.**

Balance sheet is a "snapshot" summary of the firm's financial position at a single point in time. **(6)** See also **pro-forma balance sheet.**

Bank see **commercial bank.**

Banker see **investment banker, mortgage banker.**

Bankruptcy is the failure to meet contractual obligations that results in court action to have the firm administered for the benefit of the firm's creditors; **(17)** also a legal procedure for reorganizing or liquidating a firm that is in financial difficulty, carried out under the supervision of the courts. **(13)**

Barriers to entry are features of a particular industry, such as economies of scale, high levels of initial investment, or technological sophistication that make it difficult for new entrants to enter the market. **(22)**

Beta coefficient is a measure of the risk of an asset relative to the market portfolio. **(5)**

Bills and notes see **U.S. Treasury bills and notes.**

Bond see **corporate bond, exchangeable bond, foreign bond, par value of a bond, zero-coupon bond.**

Bond dealers see **government-bond dealers.**

Bonds are long-term debt claims entitling the holder to periodic interest and principal payments and full repayment of principal by the firm received in exchange for investment funds. **(12)** See also **Eurobonds, junk bonds, original-issue, deep-discount bonds.**

Bond value of a convertible bond is the present value of future interest and principal payments. **(16)**

Book ratio see **market/book ratio.**

Book value of a firm is a measure of net asset value (after all liabilities), valued at historical cost. **(7)**

Book value of stock is the total of book value of net assets available for common shareholders after subtracting claims of creditors and preferred shareholders. **(12)**

Break-even analysis is a technique for analyzing the relationship between revenue and profit that examines the proportion of fixed costs to total costs. **(7)**

Break-even level of EBIT see **EPS break-even level of EBIT, UEPS break-even level of EBIT.**

Break-even point is that quantity of firm output at which sales revenues just cover total fixed costs, or the quantity of output at which revenue equals operating costs and operating profit is zero. **(7)**

Brokers and dealers see **securities brokers and dealers.**

Budget is a time-phased schedule of activities, events, or transactions, usually in dollar terms. **(8)** See also **cash budget.**

Budgeting see **capital budgeting.**

Business failure is the situation that results (1) when the firm is unable to meet its contractual financial obligations even though the value of the firm's assets exceeds its liabilities, (also known as *technical insolvency)* or (2) when the firm's liabilities exceed the value of its assets as a going concern. **(17)**

Business risk see **operating risk.**

Buyout see **leveraged buyout.**

Capacity see **debt capacity.**

Capital see **cost of capital, marginal cost of capital, net working capital, ratio of long-term debt to total capital, total capital.**

Capital-asset-pricing model (CAPM) provides useful insights about how market values and discount rates are determined in financial markets, describes the valuation process in a portfolio context, and analyzes how risk/return trade-offs work in financial markets. **(5)**

Capital budgeting is the process of analyzing capital investment opportunities and deciding which (if any) to undertake; it includes the creative search for investment opportunities, the gathering of data and making of forecasts, the economic analysis, the decision, and the implementation. **(9)**

Capital formation is investment in real assets, such as new buildings, machinery or technology, and is facilitated by financial markets. **(2)**

Capital gain is the difference between the sale price and the purchase price of certain assets; **(9)** also a gain that results from the increase in the value of an asset, or the difference between the purchase price and the sale price. **(10)**

Capital-gains tax is the tax applied to the gain on a sale of assets not used or bought and sold in the ordinary course of the firm's business. **(2)**

Capitalization rate or *discount rate*, is the rate of exchange between various time periods. **(4, 10)**

Capital lease is a lease that, for accounting purposes, must be capitalized on the lessee's balance sheet as an asset and an obligation. **(16)**

Capital market is the market for transactions in longer-term debt issues and stock. **(2)**

Capital value is the present value of a stream of expected cash flows. **(4)**

CAPM see **capital-asset-pricing model.**

Carrying costs rise as inventories increase and include the costs of financing, storage, servicing, and the risk of loss in value. **(20)**

Case analysis see **worst-case analysis.**

Cash for purposes of cash management is total liquid assets: cash plus near-cash. **(19)**

Cash accounting system is an accounting system that assigns revenues and expenses to particular time periods according to the timing of receipts and expenditures. **(6)**

Cash balance see **working-cash balance.**

Cash budget is a time-phased schedule of cash receipts and disbursements. **(8)**

Cash cycle is the process whereby cash is used to purchase materials from which goods are produced that are then sold to customers, who later pay their bills. **(19)**

Cash flow is the total change in the firm's cash account, the actual cash flowing into and out of a firm over a particular time period, and is measured as operating cash flow plus all balance-sheet charges. **(6)** See also **discounted cash flow.**

Cash-flow analysis of debt capacity is the comparison of cash-flow patterns under adverse, or recession, conditions at various levels of leverage in order to determine the level of debt that will allow the firm to meet its contractual obligations in a recession (or other set of adverse circumstances). **(14)**

Cash flows see **financing cash flows, incremental after-tax cash flows, initial-investment cash flows, operating cash flows.**

Cash-management policy is the set of decisions related to (1) managing collections and disbursements of cash, (2) determining the appropriate working-cash balance, and (3) investing idle cash. **(19)**

Categories see **risk categories.**

CD see **certificate of deposit.**

Certificate of deposit (CD) is a fixed-maturity time deposit; **(19)** also a bank's promise to make certain future cash payments to the person who buys the CD for a stated price. **(1)**

Chart see **EBIT/EPS chart.**

Chattel mortgage is a security claim against equipment (or anything other than land or buildings) used in providing collateral for a loan. **(12)**

Claim see **contractual claim, residual claim, financial claims.**

Clientele see **investor clientele.**

Codes see **standard industrial codes.**

Coefficient see **beta coefficient, correlation coefficient.**

Coefficient of variation is the standard deviation divided by the expected value and is a measure of risk relative to return. **(5)**

Collateral is any asset pledged as security for a loan; **(18)** also property pledged by a borrower to protect the interests of the lender. **(12)**

Collection policy is the set of procedures undertaken to collect accounts that have not been paid within a specified period. **(20)**

Commercial bank is a depository financial institution that offers checking-account services, accepts savings and other types of deposits, and makes loans. **(2)**

Commercial loan is the transfer of funds from a bank to a business firm in exchange for the firm's promise to repay the funds with interest, according to a specified schedule; **(2)** also funds borrowed by a business from a bank or lending institution in exchange for a promise to repay at a specified schedule and rate of interest. **(12)**

Commercial paper is unsecured short-term promissory notes issued by firms with the highest credit ratings. **(2, 18, 19)**

Commercial strategy is a firm's definition of the products and services it will produce and the markets it will serve. **(8)**

Commission see **Securities and Exchange Commission.**

Common stock is a perpetual ownership claim that has no maturity. **(12)**

Compensating balance is a minimum checking-account balance required by a bank as a condition for granting a loan to a firm. **(18)**

Compound annual return, or *geometric-average return,* for a specific time period is calculated by multiplying together annual returns and applying discounted-cash-flow techniques. **(10)**

Compounding is the evaluation of how a certain interest rate will cause a certain present dollar amount to grow in the future. **(3)**

Compounding period is the calendar period over which compounding occurs. **(3)**

Compound interest is interest figured on both the initial principal and interest earned in prior periods. Interest earned on interest is the key feature of compound interest. **(3)**

Concentration account is a centralized bank account in which disbursement funds from different branches, divisions, or franchises of a company can be pooled so that the firm's aggregate working-balance requirement is lower than it would be if balances were maintained at each branch. **(19)**

Concentration ratio is the percentage of sales, production volume, or any other variable to be measured, accounted for by the x largest firms in an industry. **(22)**

Conditional sales contract is an installment equipment-purchase contract under which title to the equipment remains with the lender until all payments are made. **(12, 16)**

Conglomerate merger is a merger that combines firms in different industries. **(22)**

Consolidation see **statutory consolidation.**

Constant-growth dividend-valuation model is a method for valuing stock that assumes that the dividend will grow at a constant rate. **(4)**

Contract see **conditional sales contract, financial futures contract, futures contract, interest-rate futures contract.**

Contractual claim is a claim that is an enforceable contract, such as debt. **(12)**

Conversion premium is the amount by which a convertible bond's market price exceeds the higher of its bond value or its conversion value. **(16)**

Conversion value of a convertible bond is the market value of the common stock into which the bond is convertible. **(16)**

Convertible security is a claim that begins as a debenture or as preferred stock but that can later be converted *at the holder's option* and at a specified rate into shares of the issuing company's common stock; **(12)** also a security that can be converted at the option of the holder into a security of the same firm but of another type. **(16)**

Corporate bond is a long-term debt claim representing a corporation's promise to repay with interest money borrowed from a bond holder. **(2)**

Corporation is an entity created by law that owns assets, incurs liabilities, enters into contracts, and engages in ongoing activities. **(2)** See also **Subchapter S corporation.**

Correlation is the relationship between variables indicating how they move relative to each other. **(5)**

Correlation coefficient is a measure of the degree of correlation that exists between two variables. **(5)**

Cost see **equivalent interest cost, opportunity cost, sunk cost.**

Cost minimization is the goal of making a firm's costs as low as possible and can be used as a criterion for making financial-management decisions. **(1)**

Cost of capital is another name for the *required rate of return.* **(10)** See also **marginal cost of capital.**

Cost of equity capital see **required return on equity.**

Costs see **agency costs, carrying costs, fixed costs, flotation costs, ordering costs, variable costs.**

Counter see **over-the-counter market.**

Country risk is the risk that a foreign government or foreign politics will interfere with international transactions. At the extreme, country risk includes the possibility that a foreign government may expropriate the firm's property or that a war may ensue. **(21)**

Coupon bond see **zero-coupon bond.**

Coupon rate is the stated percentage of the face value of a bond or note paid in interest each period; **(4)** the contractual rate of interest paid on a bond. **(12)**

Coverage ratios are measures of indebtedness calculated using income-statement data that reflect a firm's ability to meet periodic payments due on its debt obligations. **(7)** See also **interest coverage ratio, fixed-charge-coverage (FCC) ratio, sinking-fund coverage ratio.**

Covered-interest arbitrage is the market process through which the relationships in the interest-rate-parity theorem are enforced. **(21)**

Credit see **investment tax credit, line of credit, trade credit.**

Credit agreement see **revolving-credit agreement.**

Credit policy is the set of decisions made about credit standards, credit terms, and collection policy. **(20)**

Credit risk is the risk that a borrower will default on a loan. **(21)**

Credit scoring is a technique for discriminating between good and bad accounts in which selection criteria are developed by relating past default experience to certain characteristics of the applicant. Applicants are scored, and a decision is made based on a predetermined cut-off point. **(20)**

Credit standards are criteria and guidelines used by a firm to decide to which accounts it will extend credit. **(20)**

Credit terms include the length of the credit period and the discount offered. **(20)**

Currency see **Eurocurrency.**

Currency devaluation is a reduction in the value of a country's currency stated in terms of other currencies. **(21)**

Currency option is a financial claim that gives one the right but not the obligation to buy or sell a foreign currency. **(21)**

Currency revaluation is an increase in the value of a country's currency stated in terms of other currencies. **(21)**

Currency translation see **foreign-currency translation.**

Current assets   are assets with a maturity of less than one year and include a firm's holdings of cash, accounts receivable, and inventories. **(6, 19)**

Current liabilities   are the short-term debt obligations of a firm, with maturities of less than one year. **(6).**

Current ratio   is a measure of liquidity that is calculated as current assets divided by current liabilities. **(7)**

Current saving   is any income not spent on consumption in the current period. **(2)**

Curve   see **demand curve, supply curve.**

Cycle   see **cash cycle.**

Days purchases outstanding (DPO)   is a measure of how promptly a firm pays its bills. DPO is calculated as accounts payable divided by purchases per day (also known as the *average payment period*). **(7)**

Days sales outstanding (DSO)   is the ratio of accounts receivable to credit sales per day and is also called the *average collection period.* **(7, 20)**

DCF   see **discounted cash flow.**

Dealers   see **government-bond dealers, securities brokers and dealers.**

Debentures   are unsecured bonds with no particular assets pledged as security. **(12)**

Debt   is the contractual liability of a firm to lenders consisting of a promise to make periodic interest payments and to repay the principal according to an agreed-upon schedule. **(12)** See also **intermediate-term debt, long-term debt, ratio of debt to total assets, required return on debt, secured debt, short-term debt, unsecured debt.**

Debt capacity   is the amount of debt that is optimal for shareholders. **(14)**

Debt/equity ratio   see **debt/net worth ratio.**

Debt/net worth ratio,   or *debt/equity ratio,* is a variation of the ratio of debt to total assets and is calculated as total liabilities divided by net worth. **(7)**

Debt ratios   are measures of indebtedness calculated using balance-sheet data and reflect the degree to which creditors are protected in the event of the liquidation of the firm. **(7)**

Deductible expenses   see **tax-deductible expenses.**

Deep-discount bonds   see **original-issue, deep-discount bonds.**

Default risk   is the risk that the firm will not make specified contractual payments at the specified times; **(12)** the possibility that interest or principal might not be paid on time and in the amount promised; **(19)** the risk that the issuer of a bond will not meet promised payments. **(4)**

Deficit spending units   are individuals, companies, or government bodies who need funds. **(2)**

Degree of financial leverage (DFL)   is the percentage change in PAT divided by the percentage change in EBIT, and represents the extent to which changes in operating results affect shareholders. **(13)**

Degree of operating leverage (DOL)   is the percentage change in EBIT divided by the percentage change in sales. **(13)**

Demand curve   for a good or service shows the amounts of the good or service buyers are prepared to purchase at different prices during a specified time period. **(4)**

Deposit   see **certificate of deposit.**

Deposit account   see **money-market deposit account.**

Depreciation   is the allocation of the cost of a long-lived asset to different time periods over the life of the asset. **(2, 6)** See also **accelerated method of depreciation, straight-line method of depreciation.**

Depreciation tax shield   is the tax savings resulting from the subtraction of depreciation in calculating taxable income; it can be calculated as the tax rate multiplied by the amount of the depreciation charge. **(9, 16)**

Devaluation   see **currency devaluation.**

DFL   see **degree of financial leverage.**

Direct finance   is the direct transfer of funds from savers to investors without going through a financial intermediary. **(2)**

Discount bonds   see **original-issue, deep-discount bonds.**

Discounted cash flow (DCF)   is a method of estimating the value of an asset by taking the cash flows associated with the asset and discounting them for time and risk. **(3)**

Discounting   is the evaluation of how a certain discount rate will decrease the value of a certain future dollar amount to convert it to its present value. **(3)**

Discount rate   is the rate of exchange between the future and the present time period, or the interest rate used in the discounting process. **(3)** See also **capitalization rate, risk-adjusted discount rate.**

Discounts   see **prompt-payment discounts.**

Discrete random variable   is a variable that can take on a finite number of possible values. **(5)**

Discriminant analysis   is a technique for discriminating between good and bad accounts based on certain readily available financial data, such as firm size, acid-test ratio, or accounts-payable payment period. **(20)**

Distress see **financial distress.**

Distribution see **probability distribution.**

Diversifiable risk is project-specific risk, such as that deriving from uncertainty over entry of competitors, strikes, or technological advances; **(11)** also called *specific risk,* diversifiable risk is the part of total risk that is unique to the company or asset and is, therefore, the risk that *can* be eliminated by diversification. **(5)**

Diversification is investing in more than one type of asset in order to reduce risk. When risky assets are combined in a portfolio, risk reduction is achieved through diversification. **(5)**

Dividend decision is the choice between retention and investment of earnings on the one hand, and the payout of earnings to shareholders as dividends on the other hand. **(15)**

Dividend-payout ratio is the percentage of earnings a firm pays out as dividends. **(15)**

Dividend rate, or *dividend yield,* is the dividend divided by the price of the stock. **(4)**

Dividend-reinvestment plan is the policy of allowing shareholders to apply their periodic dividend receipts automatically to the purchase of new shares. **(17)**

Dividend-valuation model is the discounted-cash-flow model applied to the valuation of stock, or equity. **(4)** See also **constant-growth dividend-valuation model, variable-growth dividend-valuation model.**

Dividend yield see **dividend rate.**

DOL see **degree of operating leverage.**

Dollar see **profits per dollar.**

DSO see **days sales outstanding.**

Earned ratio see **times-interest-earned ratio.**

Earnings see **residual in earnings.**

Earnings before interest and taxes (EBIT) is a measure of operating earnings. **(13)** See also **operating profit.**

Earnings (P/E) ratio see **price/earnings (P/E) ratio.**

Earnings per share (EPS) is profit after taxes (PAT) divided by the number of shares of stock outstanding and is a widely used performance measure. **(7)** See also **uncommitted earnings per share.**

EBIT see **earnings before interest and taxes, EPS break-even level of EBIT, UEPS break-even level of EBIT.**

EBIT/EPS analysis is an examination of the impact on earnings per share of a given financing alternative at different levels of earnings before interest and taxes. **(14)**

EBIT/EPS chart is a graph of the relationship between operating outcomes (as measured by earnings before interest and taxes) and financial results to shareholders (as measured by earnings per share) for a given financing alternative. **(14)**

Economic analysis is the process of gathering and evaluating quantitative information about the costs and benefits of an investment project. **(9)**

Economic income of an economic unit during a period of time is the change in the net worth of that economic unit during the period. **(6)**

Economic order quantity (EOG) is the optimal quantity of goods to be ordered and is determined by trading off ordering costs (or setup costs) against carrying costs. **(20)**

Economy see **market economy.**

Effective interest rate is the rate compounded *once* per interest period that provides the same dollar payoff as a financial contract (such as a bank account). **(3, 18)**

Effects see **information effects.**

Efficient frontier is the line that represents the set of portfolios that provides the most expected return for a given level of risk. **(5)**

Efficient market is one in which market prices fully reflect all the information that is available about the assets being traded; **(12)** a market in which current market prices impound all available information and are a fair reflection of the true value of a financial asset. **(4)**

EIC see **equivalent interest cost.**

Entry see **barriers to entry.**

EOQ see **economic order quantity.**

EPS see **earnings per share.**

EPS analysis see **EBIT/EPS analysis.**

EPS break-even level of EBIT is the level of earnings before interest and taxes that equates earnings per share for two financing alternatives. **(14)**

EPS chart see **EBIT/EPS chart.**

Equilibrium see **market equilibrium.**

Equilibrium price is the price that equates quantity supplied and quantity demanded for a particular good or service; **(1)** also called the market-clearing price of a good or service, it is the price at which the quantity demanded equals the quantity supplied. **(4)**

Equity is ownership in a firm—specifically, the claims of preferred and common stockholders. **(12)** See also **required return on equity, return on equity.**

Equivalent interest cost (EIC) is the rate that discounts all cash flows of any financing plan such that their present values equal exactly zero. **(16)**

Eurobonds are bonds that are sold mainly in countries other than the country in whose currency the interest and principal payments are to be denominated. **(12)**

Eurocurrency is a deposit denominated in a given country's currency and that is held in a bank outside that country. **(21)**

Exchange see **foreign exchange.**

Exchangeable bond is a bond that can be exchanged for another type of security *at the option of the issuer*. **(12)**

Exchange market see **foreign-exchange market.**

Exchange rate see **foreign-exchange rate.**

Exchange-rate risk is the risk of loss in value due to changes in foreign-exchange rates. **(21)**

Exchange rates see **fixed exchange rates, floating exchange rates.**

Exchanges are actual organizations with physical locations where financial claims are bought and sold. **(2)** See also **stock exchanges.**

Expected rate of return is the rate of return an investor expects to gain from an investment; the mean value of the probability distribution of expected returns. **(20)**

Expected return is the rate of return expected to be earned in the future. **(20)**

Expected-return trade-off see **risk/expected-return trade-off.**

Expected value, or mean, is the weighted average of the possible outcomes, where the weights are the probabilities of the outcomes, and provides a measure of the expected outcome of a random variable. **(4, 5)**

Expected-value operator, the letter E in the expected-value equation, is a signal to take the probability-weighted average of the outcomes. **(5)**

Expenditures are all cash outflows. **(6)**

Expense see **bad-debt expense.**

Expenses are only those expenditures that appear in the income statement (only those that affect net worth). **(6)** See also **tax-deductible expenses.**

Factor see **present-value factor.**

Failure see **business failure.**

FCC see **fixed-charge-coverage ratio.**

Federal-agency issues are short-term obligations of agencies of the federal government. **(19)**

Federal-funds market is the market in which excess bank reserves are borrowed and lent by federal banks. **(2)**

Finance see **direct finance.**

Financial claims are promises to pay money in the future and are exchanged in financial markets for money. Examples are stocks, bonds and loans. **(2)**

Financial distress occurs when a firm has difficulty meeting contractual obligations to its creditors. **(13)**

Financial friction is the cost for search, acquisition, analysis, and sale involved with financial transactions; **(20)** the additional cost of financial transactions, such as commissions paid by investors to buy or sell securities, flotation costs of issuing new securities, information costs of financial decision making, and costs associated with financial distress. **(2, 13, 15)**

Financial futures contract is an agreement between a buyer and seller to buy or sell a financial security at some future date but with the price set at the time of the contract. **(12)**

Financial institution is an institution such as an insurance company, a leasing company, a mutual fund, a savings-and-loan association, or a commercial bank, that channels funds from savers to borrowers. **(2)**

Financial intermediary is a financial go-between, such as a bank, that makes possible the easy transfer of funds from savers to spenders. Financial intermediaries gather funds, analyze credit possibilities, evaluate risk, and handle administrative and legal details for borrowers and lenders. **(2)**

Financial lease is a noncancellable, fully amortized contract typically covering intermediate to long terms where the lessee (user) normally is responsible for maintenance, insurance, and taxes; also known as a *net lease*. **(16)**

Financial leverage is the use of debt, or borrowing, to finance investment. **(4, 13)** See also **degree of financial leverage.**

Financial market is a market where firms can raise funds and where their securities are, if they are publicly owned, valued. It is a vast network linking institutions, instruments, and submarkets; it brings together millions of buyers and sellers of financial instruments. **(1, 2)**

Financial-modeling programs are computer programs specially designed to do *What if?* analysis by calculating the consequences of changing assumptions. **(11)**

Financial plan describes in dollar terms the activities that a firm intends to engage in over some future period. An income statement and balance sheet are key components of the financial plan. **(8)**

Financial planning is part of a larger planning process within an organization; the complete planning system begins at the highest policy level with the statement of the firm's key goal or purpose. **(8)**

Financial risk is the increased risk to shareholders that arises from the use of debt; **(13)** the additional risk to shareholders, over and above operating risk, that results from the use of debt (or debtlike) financing. **(4)**

Financial securities are financial claims, such as bonds and stocks. **(17)**

Financing cash flows are the cash flows, such as interest, principal payments, and dividends to stockholders, arising from the financing arrangements associated with an investment project. **(9)**

Financing instruments are claims against the firm's income and assets. **(12)**

Financing mix is the proportion of debt and equity used to finance investments. **(13)**

Finished goods are completed products awaiting sale. **(20)**

Firm see **multinational firms.**

Fixed-charge-coverage (FCC) ratio is a more comprehensive coverage measure than the times-interest-earned ratio because it measures the margin by which a firm's current earnings can cover debt and all other contractual obligations, including lease payments. **(7)**

Fixed costs are costs that remain the same over a given wide range of production. **(7)**

Fixed exchange rates are foreign-exchange rates that are set administratively by governments and changed infrequently according to agreed-upon rules. **(21)**

Float is the product of the time delay in collecting funds and the dollars collected. **(19)**

Floating exchange rates are foreign-exchange rates that are set by free-market forces. **(21)**

Floating-rate notes (FRNs) are debt instruments for which the interest rate is adjusted periodically with the rise and fall of interest rates generally. **(12)**

Flotation costs are the cash costs associated with the issuance of a company's new long-term debt or stock. **(10, 15)**

Flows see **financing cash flows, incremental after-tax cash flows, investment cash flows, operating cash flows.**

Flow variable is a variable whose value is measured during a period of time. **(6)**

Foreign bond is a bond sold in a foreign country by a home-country borrower and is denominated in the currency of the foreign country. **(12)**

Foreign-currency translation is the conversion of accounting information denominated in one currency into accounting information denominated in another currency. **(21)**

Foreign exchange consists of money denominated in different currencies. **(21)**

Foreign-exchange market is a loosely connected group of major banks and foreign-exchange brokers who communicate by telephone and mail over great distances to buy and sell different currencies. **(21)**

Foreign-exchange rate is the price of one currency expressed in terms of another. **(21)**

Formation see **capital formation.**

Forward rate is the price of one currency in terms of another when purchased for future delivery. **(21)**

Friction see **financial friction.**

Frictionless market is a market in which there are no costs, such as commissions or information costs, involved in financial transactions. **(5)**

Frontier see **efficient frontier.**

FRNs see **floating-rate notes.**

Fund see **sinking fund.**

Fund payment see **sinking-fund payment.**

Funds see **intermediate-term funds, money-market mutual funds, short-term funds, sources of funds, uses of funds.**

Funds market see **federal-funds market.**

Futures contract is an agreement between a buyer and seller to buy or sell something, such as a commodity, at some future date but with the price set at the time of the contract. **(12)** See also **financial futures contract, interest-rate futures contract.**

Future value (FV) is the value of a certain current dollar amount compounded forward through time at an appropriate interest rate. It is the amount to which a payment or series of payments will grow by a given future date. **(3)**

Future-value factor for a single cash flow is the number by which a given present value is multiplied to determine the amount into which that present value will grow in the future (future value). A future-value factor is calculated as $(1 + i)^n$. **(3)**

FV see **future value.**

Gain see **capital gain.**

General partnership is a partnership in which all partners have unlimited liability for the debts and actions of the firm. **(2)**

Geometric-average return see **compound annual return.**

Golden parachute is a provision in the employment contract of top-level management that provides for severance pay or other compensation should the manager lose his or her job as the result of a takeover. **(22)**

Goods see **finished goods.**

Goodwill is the excess of the price paid for a going concern over the book value of its tangible assets; an intangible asset of the firm. **(22)**

Government-bond dealers are financial intermediaries that buy and sell government bonds. **(2)**

Hedging is an attempt to reduce the risk associated with future price fluctuations. **(21)**

Horizontal merger   is a merger that combines firms operating in the same business line. **(22)**

Hostile takeover   occurs when the acquired firm's management resists the acquisition, and the acquiring firm goes over their heads by buying stock directly from shareholders. **(22)**

Hurdle rate   is the return target to which an investment project's internal rate of return is compared in determining whether or not the investment project is acceptable to the firm. **(10)**

Income   see **accounting income, economic income, net income.**

Income statement, or *profit-and-loss statement,* is a record of financial events between two points in time. The income statement is an attempt to measure the change in net worth over time. **(6)** See also **normalized income statement, pro-forma income statement.**

Incremental after-tax cash flows   are the after-tax cash flows directly attributable to the investment and are necessary information for performing a discounted-cash-flow analysis of an investment decision. **(9)**

Incremental analysis   is the evaluation of an investment decision that focuses only on differences in after-tax cash flows that result from the decision in question. **(9)**

Indebtedness,   or financial leverage, is the mix of debt and equity used to finance a firm's activities. **(7)**

Index   see **profitability index.**

Industrial codes   see **standard industrial codes.**

Inflation   is the general rate of increase in the level of prices of goods and services in the economy. **(2)**

Inflation premium   is an addition to the real rate of return required by investors to compensate them for the change in the value of the investment that results from anticipated inflation; **(10)** an additional charge for anticipated or expected inflation that investors add to the real rate of return they are requiring. **(2)**

Information effects   are the change in stock price that results from the market's knowledge that the dividend is to change. **(15)**

Initial-investment cash flows   are the one-time outlays necessary to acquire the land, buildings, and equipment necessary to implement an investment project. **(9)**

Installment equipment-purchase contract   see **conditional sales contract.**

Institution   see **financial**

Institution   see **financial institution, thrift institution.**

Instruments   see **financing instruments.**

Interest   see **compound interest, risk-free rate of interest.**

Interest arbitrage   see **covered-interest arbitrage.**

Interest cost   see **equivalent interest cost.**

Interest coverage ratio   is the number of times interest payments are covered by EBIT and is calculated as EBIT divided by pretax interest. **(14)**

Interest period   is the calendar period over which an interest rate is named. **(3)**

Interest rate   is the price of borrowing funds over time, usually a percentage of the amount borrowed; **(2)** the rate at which individuals or firms will be compensated for exchanging money now for money to be received later. **(3)** See also **effective interest rate, nominal interest rate, real interest rate.**

Interest-rate futures contract   is an agreement to buy or sell a financial security in the future at an agreed-upon price, and allows a manager to hedge against the risk of future rises or falls in interest rates by locking in the price that must be paid in the future. **(19)**

Interest-rate-parity theorem   shows the relationship between spot and forward exchange rates and interest rates in two currencies. **(21)**

Interest-rate risk   is uncertainty about future interest rates as they affect future value; **(4)** the risk that the price of a security may fall due to a rise in the level of interest rates; **(19)** or the risk arising because bond prices change as market interest rates change; the risk that a bond may have to be sold before maturity at a price lower than the price paid for it because of changing interest rates. **(12)**

Interest-rate swap   is an agreement between two companies in which each takes on the obligation of paying interest on the debt of the other company. **(12)**

Interest tax shield   is the reduction in taxes that results from the tax-deductibility of interest. **(13)**

Intermediary   see **financial intermediary.**

Intermediate-term debt   is debt with a maturity of between 1 year and 5–7 years. Intermediate-term financing usually is used to finance part of a firm's fixed assets or permanent additions to working capital. **(12)**

Intermediate-term funds   are funds borrowed for periods between 1 and perhaps 8 or 10 years. **(18)**

Internal rate of return *(IRR)*   of an investment is the rate that discounts all of the cash flows of an investment, including all outlays, to exactly zero; it is the discount rate that makes the net present value of the project equal to zero; it is the discounted-cash-flow measure of the expected rate of return to be earned on an investment. **(9)**

Inventory control   is the determination of economic order quantities, safety stocks, and reorder points for every individual item stocked along with ordering, receiving, handling, storing, protecting, and issuing inventory. **(20)**

Inventory theory is the theory of how much should be ordered and when it should be ordered. **(20)**

Inventory-turnover ratio is a measure of the efficiency with which inventories are utilized and is calculated as the cost of goods sold divided by average inventory. **(7)**

Investment see **return on investments.**

Investment banker is a financial intermediary that underwrites and distributes new securities offerings and helps a business obtain financing. **(2)**

Investment cash flows see **initial-investment cash flows.**

Investment plan is the set of decisions a firm makes about what products to produce, what manufacturing process to use, and what plant and equipment will be required as these questions relate to the acquisition of assets. **(8)**

Investment tax credit (ITC) is a specified percentage of capital expenditures that a firm is permitted to subtract from its tax liability; **(2)** the deduction of a percentage of money spent on certain types of investments from a firm's tax liability. **(16)**

Investor clientele is a group of investors who are attracted to a certain stock investment because of a particular characteristic, such as the company's dividend policy. **(15)**

IRR see **internal rate of return.**

Issued shares are those shares of stock that have been issued at one time or another by the firm to investors. **(12)**

Issues see **federal-agency issues, new issues.**

Issues market see **new-issues market.**

ITC see **investment tax credit.**

Junk bonds are bonds with low credit ratings and high interest rates that play a role in corporate buyouts and takeovers. **(12)**

Lease is a contractual arrangement for financing equipment under which the lessee (the firm) has the right to use the equipment in return for making periodic payments to the lessor (the owner of the equipment); **(12, 16)** see also **capital lease, financial lease, leveraged lease, operating lease.**

Leaseback agreement see **sale-and-leaseback agreement.**

Leasing is a specialized means of acquiring the use of assets without owning the assets. **(16)**

Level of EBIT see **EPS break-even level of EBIT, UEPS break-even level of EBIT.**

Leverage see **degree of financial leverage, degree of operating leverage, financial leverage, operating leverage.**

Leveraged buyout is a transaction in which a firm is purchased using borrowed funds, with the firm's own assets or stock pledged as collateral to secure the loan and with the firm's own cash flows used to pay off the loan. **(14)**

Levered lease is a lease agreement in which the lessor borrows a substantial part of the purchase price of the asset to be leased. **(16)**

Leveraged shares are shares of stock in a company that uses debt. **(13)**

Liability see **tax liability.**

Limited partnership is a partnership in which there is at least one general partner and one or more limited partners. Limited partners contribute capital, share in the profits, have limited liability for debts, and have no voice in directing the firm. **(2)**

Line of credit is a noncontractual loan agreement between a bank or other lender and a firm in which the firm can borrow up to an agreed-upon maximum amount at any time during a specified period. **(18)**

Liquid assets are assets, such as marketable securities, that can be converted to cash almost immediately without having to sell at a price well below their value. **(18, 19)** See also **net liquid assets.**

Liquidation is the dissolution of a firm by selling its assets and distributing the proceeds to creditors and shareholders on the basis of seniority. **(17)**

Liquidity measures a firm's ability to come up with cash quickly to meet expected and unexpected cash requirements. **(7)** See also **marketability.**

Loan see **commercial loan, secured loan, unsecured loan.**

Loans see **seasonal loans, term loans.**

Lock-box system is a collection system in which payments are mailed to a post-office box and emptied several times a day by a bank, which then deposits the payments and updates accounting records. **(19)**

Long-run target payout ratio is the ratio of residual funds to total earnings after taxes over a relatively long planning horizon. **(15)**

Long-term debt (LTD) is debt with a maturity of 8–10 years or longer; **(12)** includes both secured and unsecured debt maturing beyond one year. **(7)** See also **ratio of long-term debt to total capital.**

Maintenance lease see **operating lease.**

Management see **voice in management.**

Marginal cost of capital   is another name for the *return target* for an investment project. **(10)**

Marginal expected return   is the expected rate of return on incremental investment. **(20)**

Marginal tax rate   is the tax rate on the last dollar of income, or the change in a taxpayer's tax payment divided by the change in taxable income. **(2)**

Market   see **auction market, capital market, efficient market, federal-funds market, financial market, foreign-exchange market, frictionless market, money market, new-issues market, over-the-counter (OTC) market, secondary market.**

Marketability   refers to the ease with which an asset can be converted to cash on short notice (also known as *liquidity*). **(19)**

Market/book ratio   is the ratio of share price to book value per share and relates to shareholders the value of the firm's future cash flows (market value) to the historical costs to shareholders of acquiring the firm's assets. **(7)**

Market-clearing price   see **equilibrium price.**

Market economy   is an economic system in which resources are allocated and prices are determined through the interaction of buyers and sellers in markets. **(1)**

Market equilibrium   in the market for risky capital assets is achieved when investors buy and sell assets until each asset offers the same reward/risk ratio. In market equilibrium, the market risk premium per unit of nondiversifiable risk is the same for all risky assets. **(5)**

Market line   shows the relationship between required return and risk. **(5)**

Market portfolio   is the portfolio that includes all risky assets. **(5)**

Market-related risk   see **nondiversifiable risk.**

Market risk   see **nondiversifiable risk.**

Market risk/return schedule   for a given investment project shows the return required by investors at different levels of risk. **(4)**

Market standard   is the rate of return per unit of risk against which all risky investments are judged. **(5)**

Market value   of a firm is the value placed by investors on the future cash flows it is expected to generate. **(7)**

Market value of stock   is the price at which stock is being traded in the marketplace. **(12)**

Materials   see **raw materials.**

Maturity   is the time period over which interest and principal payments are to be made on a loan or bond. **(2, 12, 19)** See also **yield to maturity.**

Maximization   see **profit maximization, value maximization.**

Mean   see **expected value.**

Merger   see **conglomerate merger, horizontal merger, statutory merger, vertical merger.**

Merger premium   is the difference between the value of the money or securities offered by an acquiring firm and the present value of the stock owned by the shareholders of the firm to be acquired. **(22)**

Method of depreciation   see **accelerated method of depreciation, straight-line method of depreciation.**

Minimization   see **cost minimization.**

Mix   see **financing mix.**

MMDA   see **money-market deposit account.**

Modeling programs   see **financial-modeling programs.**

Money market   is the market for transactions in short-term loans. **(2)**

Money-market deposit account (MMDA)   is a deposit account offered by a bank or depository institution that offers money-market interest rates but restricts check writing. **(2)**

Money-market mutual funds   are funds set up to allow small investors to pool their funds to invest in money-market instruments in the required large denominations. **(19)**

Money-market securities   are interest-bearing assets that have low default risk, short maturity, and ready marketability. **(19)**

Mortgage   is a bond that has particular assets, usually buildings or equipment, pledged as security against default on interest or principal payments; **(12)** a loan in which designated property is pledged as security. **(2)** See also **chattel mortgage.**

Mortgage banker   is a financial intermediary who transfers funds from institutions who want to invest in mortgages to institutions or individuals who wish to borrow mortgage funds. **(2)**

Motive   see **precautionary motive, transactions motive.**

Multinational firm   is a firm that operates or invests in two or more countries. **(21)**

Mutual funds   see **money-market mutual funds.**

Mutually exclusive alternatives   are two or more alternatives such that if one is chosen, no other can be chosen. **(1)**

Negotiable-order-of-withdrawal (NOW)   account is a type of checking account at a depository institution that pays interest. **(2)**

Net income is a firm's revenues minus its expenses. **(2)**

Net lease see **financial lease.**

Net liquid assets is a more stringent dollar measure of liquidity than net working capital and is calculated as short-term marketable securities minus discretionary debt maturing in less than one year. **(7)**

Net operating capital is current assets minus operating liabilities (those liabilities that arise directly out of a firm's operations, such as taxes payable). **(6)**

Net operating return on assets (NOROA) is a measure of return on investment that subtracts from operating assets all current liabilities. NOROA is calculated as operating profit divided by net operating assets. **(7)**

Net period is the period within which an invoice is to be paid. **(18)**

Net present value *(NPV)* of an investment is the present value of the cash inflows less (net of) the required outlay. **(9)**

Net working capital (NWC) is a dollar measure of liquidity and is calculated as current assets minus current liabilities. **(6, 7)**

Net worth of a firm is the value of total assets minus total liabilities, or the value of the owners' claim on assets. **(6)**

New issues are the initial public offering of a security of a given class. **(17)**

New-issues market, or primary market, is the market in which issues of new securities are offered for sale by companies to investors. **(2)**

Nominal interest rate is the interest rate observed in financial markets. **(2)**

Nominal rate of return is the contract or observed rate of return. **(10)**

Nondiversifiable risk is market-related risk, the risk that cannot be eliminated by diversification. It depends on how a project's cash flows are related to changes in general economic and market conditions, such as interest rates, GNP growth, or inflation. **(5, 11)**

Normalized income statement is an income statement in which all items are expressed as percentages of sales. **(7)**

Note see **promissory note.**

Notes see **floating-rate notes, U.S. Treasury bills and notes.**

NOW see **negotiable-order-of-withdrawal account.**

NPV see **net present value.**

NWC see **net working capital.**

Offering see **rights offering, public offerings.**

Oligopoly is an industry that has a few large firms rather than a single large firm or numerous smaller firms. It possesses some competitive and some monopolistic characteristics. **(22)**

Open account is a credit arrangement under which no promissory note is normally given, and the purchaser agrees to make payment at a later date under terms specified in the agreement. **(18)**

Operating cash flows are the cash flows, such as sales, cost of goods sold, advertising, and taxes, generated by the operations associated with an investment project. **(6, 9, 20)**.

Operating lease is a contract covering intermediate to short terms where the lessor (owner) typically is responsible for maintenance, insurance, and property taxes; also known as a *maintenance lease* or *service lease.* **(16)**

Operating leverage is the relationship between fixed and variable operating expenses and measures the sensitivity of operating profit to changes in sales; **(13)** measures the sensitivity of operating profit to changes in sales and can be calculated as the percentage change in operating profits divided by the percentage change in sales; **(7)** See also **degree of operating leverage.**

Operating plan describes in detail the activities which the firm plans to engage in and consists of the sales, production, marketing, research-and-development, and personnel plans required to carry out the firm's commercial strategy. **(8)**

Operating profit, or earnings before interest and taxes (EBIT), measures the firm's performance before the effects of financing or taxes. **(7)**

Operating return is the ratio of operating profit to investment; **(20)** the internal rate of return for an investment project, calculated considering only operating cash flows. **(10)**

Operating return on assets (OROA) is a measure of return on investment that reflects the total dollars of profit from operations relative to the assets devoted to those operations, OROA is calculated as *operating profit,* or earnings before interest and taxes (EBIT) divided by total assets. **(7)**

Operating risk is the uncertainty about future profitability that arises from the basic nature of the business and operation of a company, the business risk inherent in the firm's operations **(13)** known as *business risk,* the risk to shareholders that arises from uncertainty about a firm's product markets or operations; **(4)** also the risk inherent in the firm's commercial activities. Operating risk affects the variability of operating profits over time. **(7)**

Operator see **expected-value operator.**

Opportunity cost is the return on the best alternative investment forgone by making the chosen investment; **(3)** the return an investor could have earned on the next best alternative investment forgone. **(10)**

Opportunity rate see **required rate of return.**

Option see **currency option.**

Ordering costs decline as inventories increase and include the costs of placing orders and unit purchase costs. **(20)**

Order quantity see **economic order quantity.**

Original-issue, deep-discount bonds (OIDs) are bonds issued at 40 to 55 percent of face value with very low coupon rates, and have appealed to buyers who believe that interest rates will trend downward. **(12)**

OTC see **over-the-counter market.**

Outstanding see **days sales outstanding.**

Outstanding shares are those shares of stock held by investors at a given time. **(12)**

Over-the-counter (OTC) markets are facilities, such as investment firms, that trade in securities not listed on organized security exchanges; **(17)** the network of buyers, sellers, and brokers who interact by means of telecommunication and deal in securities not listed on an organized exchange. **(2)**

Paper see **commercial paper.**

Parachute see **golden parachute.**

Parity theorem see **interest-rate-parity theorem.**

Partnership is an unincorporated business owned by two or more persons. **(2)** See also **general partnership, limited partnership.**

Par value of a bond is the value that is equal to the principal amount. **(12)**

Par value of stock is the nominal or face value of the share of stock. **(12)**

PAT see **profit after taxes.**

Payable see **accounts payable.**

Payback approach is a method of analyzing investment opportunities that determines how long it will take the cash inflows expected from an investment to repay (pay back) the initial outlay. **(9)**

Payment see **sinking-fund payment.**

Payment discounts see **prompt-payment discounts.**

Payments see **stream of payments.**

Payout ratio see **dividend-payout ratio, long-run target payout ratio.**

Period see **compounding period, interest period, net period.**

P/E ratio see **price/earnings (P/E) ratio.**

Perpetuity is an annuity that continues forever. **(3)**

PI see **profitability index.**

Plan see **financial plan, investment plan, operating plan, sales plan.**

Planning see **financial planning.**

Policy see **collection policy, credit policy.**

Pooling of interests is an accounting method for reporting a merger in which the balance sheets of the two combining companies are added together to produce the balance sheet of the surviving company. **(22)**

Portfolio is the collection of securities (stocks, bonds, loans, etc.) held by an investor; **(2)** the combination of securities held by any one investor. **(5)** See also **market portfolio.**

Post audit is a review of the performance of an investment project in the years following its implementation, or a comparison of actual returns to projected returns. **(9)**

Precautionary motive for holding cash concerns the use of liquid assets as a reserve for contingencies in an uncertain world. **(19)**

Preemptive right is a provision in corporate bylaws and charters giving existing common stockholders the right to purchase new issues of common or convertible securities on a prorated basis. **(17)**

Preferred stock is long-term equity that pays a fixed dividend. Preferred stock is senior to common stock with respect to both income (preferred dividends come ahead of common) and assets. **(12)**

Premium see **conversion premium, inflation premium, merger premium, risk premium.**

Present value is the value today of a future payment or stream of payments, discounted at the appropriate interest rate. **(3, 1)** See also **net present value.**

Present-value factor is the number by which a given future value is multiplied to determine that future value's present value and is calculated as $(1 + i)^{-n}$. **(3)**

Price see **equilibrium price.**

Price/earnings (P/E) ratio is the ratio of current market price per share to the most recently reported annual earnings per share, and gives an indication of the market's assessment of a company's growth prospects and riskiness. **(7)**

Price system is the coordination of economic activity through free trading of goods and services at prices set in markets by producers and consumers. **(1)**

Primary market see **new-issues market.**

Prime rate is the benchmark rate set by the banking industry as the rate for the class of borrowers deemed most creditworthy. **(18)**

Principal is the initial amount of money loaned or borrowed; **(3)** a dollar amount borrowed, loaned, or deposited upon which interest is owed or earned. **(1)** See also **agent.**

Priority, or seniority, is the order in which types of financial claims are satisfied. **(12)**

Private placements are offerings of new securities in which firms sell securities directly to one investor or to a small group of investors rather than to the public. **(17)**

Privileged subscription is the practice of offering new securities to existing shareholders first, before any public offering is made. **(17)**

Probability distribution is a function that assigns probabilities to the possible values of a random variable. **(5)**

Process see **work in process.**

Profit is the excess of revenues over costs for a given project or time period. **(1, 6)** See also **operating profit.**

Profitability index *(PI)* is a ratio measure of an investment's benefits in relation to its costs that is calculated using discounted-cash-flow techniques. **(9)**

Profit after taxes (PAT) is a dollar measure of firm profit. **(7, 13)**

Profit-and-loss statement see **income statement.**

Profit maximization is the goal of making a firm's profits as large as possible and can be used as a criterion for making financial-management decisions. **(1)**

Profits per dollar of sales is a useful measure of a firm's performance that measures profits in relation to the sales necessary to generate those profits. **(7)**

Pro-forma analysis is the projection into the future or past of a firm's financial statements to depict a firm's financial condition as if certain prospective events (such as a given sales and production plan) had taken place. **(8)**

Pro-forma balance sheet is a balance sheet constructed by projecting the firm's financial condition as if a certain sales and production plan had taken place. **(8)**

Pro-forma income statement is an income statement constructed by projecting as if a certain sales and production plan had taken place. **(8)**

Progressive tax rates are tax rates where the higher is the amount of taxable income, the higher is the percentage payable as taxes. **(2)**

Project-specific risk see **diversifiable risk.**

Promissory note is a document specifying the conditions of a loan, including amount, interest rate, and repayment schedule. It is a legally enforceable "promise to pay." **(18)**

Prompt-payment discounts are discounts given for prompt payment of an invoice, within a specified time period. **(18)**

Proprietorship see **sole proprietorship.**

Prospectus is a document filed with the Securities and Exchange Commission that provides a summary of the financial and commercial-strategy information contained in a registration statement and is composed when large amounts of securities are being issued by a firm. (The registration statement contains information on the firm's history, management, financial data, a description of the securities to be offered, uses to which the proceeds will be put, and legal and accounting opinions.) **(17)**

Protective covenants are restrictions, made as part of a loan agreement, that are placed on dividend payments, capital expenditures, or other actions of firm management, designed to protect the position of lenders. **(12)**

Public offerings are security offerings in which securities are made available to the public and are sold to large numbers of buyers. **(17)**

Purchase of assets is an accounting method for reporting a merger in which the assets of the acquired company are revalued to reflect the amount of money actually paid for the acquired entity. **(22)**

Purchasing-power risk is the risk that a bond may not bring the expected *real* rate of return because unexpected inflation will have diminished the purchasing power of dollars received; **(12)** the risk that money received in the future will not purchase the same goods and services as it can today, or the risk that inflation will decrease the value of future cash flows. **(4)**

Pure-play technique calculates risk-adjusted discount rates by matching a particular investment to one or more publicly traded companies that have risks comparable to those of the investment. **(11)**

PV see **present value.**

Quantity see **economic order quantity.**

Random variable see **discrete random variable.**

Rate see **average tax rate, capitalization rate, coupon rate, discount rate, effective interest rate, foreign-exchange rate, forward rate, hurdle rate, interest rate, marginal tax rate, nominal interest rate, prime rate, real interest rate, retention rate, risk-adjusted discount rate, spot rate.**

Rate of interest see **risk-free rate of interest.**

Rate of return on an investment project is the percentage benefit earned per dollar invested. **(3)** See also **actual rate of return, expected rate of return, internal rate of return, nominal rate of return, real rate of return, required rate of return, risk-free rate of return.**

Rates   see **fixed exchange rates, floating exchange rates.**

Ratio   see **concentration ratio, debt/net worth ratio, dividend-payout ratio, interest coverage ratio, long-run target payout ratio, market/book ratio, price/earnings (P/E) ratio, reward/risk ratio, sinking-fund coverage ratio, times-interest-earned ratio.**

Ratio analysis   is the analysis of financial performance based on the comparison of one financial variable to another. **(7)**

Ratio of debt to total assets   measures percentage of total assets financed by creditors and is calculated as total liabilities (current liabilities plus long-term debt) divided by total assets. **(7)**

Ratio of long-term debt to total capital   measures the proportion of total long-term funds supplied by creditors as opposed to owners and is calculated as long-term debt divided by the sum of long-term debt and net worth. **(7)**

Ratios   see **coverage ratios, debt ratios.**

Raw materials   are materials, parts, and subassemblies that are purchased from others and that become part of the final product a firm produces. **(20)**

Real interest rate   is the rate of increase in the ability to purchase goods and services, or the nominal interest rate minus the expected rate of inflation. **(2)**

Real rate of return   is the difference between the nominal rate and the inflation rate. **(10)**

Receipts   are all cash inflows. **(6)**

Receivable   see **accounts receivable.**

Redemption   see **serial redemption.**

Reinvestment   see **dividend-reinvestment plan.**

Reorganization   is the restructuring of liabilities so that a firm's anticipated cash flows are sufficient to meet them. **(17)**

Required rate of return   is the minimum acceptable return on any investment and is the rate forgone on the next best alternative investment opportunity of comparable risk; it is an *opportunity rate* **(10)**; the *minimum* return prospective investors should accept evaluating an investment. **(4, 20)** See also **cost of capital.**

Required return on debt   is the internal rate of return that equates the price of a bond (or debt instrument) to the present value of the expected future cash benefits of

owning the bond (or debt instrument). **(10)** See also **yield to maturity.**

Required return on equity   equates the price of a stock to the present value of the expected future cash benefits of owning the stock; also known as the *cost of equity capital.* **(10)**

Residual claim   is a claim, such as common stock, to what is left after contractual claims are settled. **(12)**

Residual   in earnings is the amount of earnings available for retention or distribution as dividends after all desirable investment opportunities are undertaken and after a target debt/equity ratio has been reached. **(15)**

Residual value   is the value of leased property at the close of the lease term. **(16)** See also **risk-adjusted residual value.**

Retention rate   is dollars retained divided by profits after taxes. **(8)**

Return   see **actual rate of return, compound annual return, expected rate of return, internal rate of return, marginal expected return, nominal rate of return, operating return, rate of return, real rate of return, required rate of return, risk-free rate of return, target return.**

Return on assets (ROA)   is one measure of return on investment in which investment is defined as the total assets of the firm. ROA is calculated as profit after taxes divided by total assets. **(7)**

Return on debt   see **required return on debt.**

Return on equity (ROE)   is a percentage measure of the rate of return on an investment and equals income available to common stockholders divided by common equity. **(7, 13)** See also **required return on equity.**

Return on investment (ROI)   is the return per dollar of investment per unit of time, a measure of the efficiency with which the firm utilizes capital. **(7)**

Return schedule   see **market risk/return schedule.**

Return target or **target return**   is the minimum acceptable expected return on an investment. **(10)** See also **marginal cost of capital.**

Revaluation   see **currency revaluation.**

Revenues   are only those receipts that appear in the income statement (only those that affect net worth). **(6)**

Revolving-credit agreement   is a contractual agreement by the bank to provide funds. **(18)**

Reward/risk ratio   is the expected risk premium per unit of risk and equals the market risk premium (expected rate of return on the market portfolio minus the risk-free rate of return) divided by the risk of the market portfolio. **(5)**

Right   see **preemptive right.**

Rights offering   is the offering of new securities on the basis of privileged subscription. **(17)**

Risk   is the degree of uncertainty about future events or outcomes and is very difficult to measure accurately or quantitatively. **(4, 11)** See also **country risk, credit risk, default risk, diversifiable risk, exchange-rate risk, financial risk, interest-rate risk, nondiversifiable risk, operating risk, purchasing-power risk.**

Risk-adjusted discount rate   is a return target that reflects the risk of the investment being analyzed. **(11)**

Risk-adjusted residual value   is the minimum residual value that reasonably can be anticipated. **(16)**

Risk categories   are groups of investment projects of similar risk. **(11)**

Risk/expected-return trade-off   is that the greater is the risk of an investment opportunity, the greater is the return required by an investor. **(4)**

Risk-free rate of interest   is the interest rate on a relatively riskless asset. **(13)**

Risk-free rate of return   is the rate of return that would be received on a riskless asset and is estimated using a current interest rate on a U.S. Treasury bond or note, the closest available approximation of a riskless asset. **(5)**

Risk premium *(rp)*   is the extra return required as compensation for risk; **(4)** the difference between the required rate of return on a particular risky asset and the rate of return on a riskless asset with the same expected life. **(5, 10, 13)**

Risk-premium approach   bases estimates of required returns on risk-premium data. **(10)**

Risk/return schedule   see **market risk/return schedule.**

ROA   see **return on assets.**

ROE   see **return on equity.**

ROI   see **return on investment.**

rp   see **risk premium.**

Safety stock   is additional inventory over and above that prescribed by the EOQ formula. **(20)**

Sale-and-leaseback agreement   is an arrangement in which a firm or individual owning an asset sells it to another party and then leases it back. **(16)**

Sales contract   see **conditional sales contract.**

Sales outstanding   see **days sales outstanding.**

Sales plan   is the projection of sales into the future for a specifed period and forms the basis for planning production levels, marketing programs, and other firm activities. **(8)**

Saving   see **current saving.**

Schedule   see **aging schedule.**

Scoring   see **credit scoring.**

Seasonality   is the annually recurring pattern of changes within a year. **(8)**

Seasonal loans   are funds that are borrowed for use during a part of a year and that are repaid out of seasonal inflows of funds. **(12)**

SEC   see **Securities and Exchange Commission.**

Secondary market   is the market where existing financial claims (such as stocks or bonds), as compared to new claims, can be bought and sold. **(2)**

Secured debt   is debt against which certain property is pledged to satisfy the debt in the event of borrower default. **(7)**

Secured loan   is a loan against which specific assets are pledged as collateral by the borrower. **(18)**

Securities   are claims to ownership, such as stocks and bonds. **(1)** See also **financial securities, money-market securities.**

Securities and Exchange Commission (SEC)   regulates (1) the markets where stocks and bonds are traded, (2) the issuance of new securities, and (3) the merger of firms. **(2)**

Securities brokers and dealers   are financial intermediaries that buy and sell stocks, bonds, and other financial claims in return for a commission fee. **(2)**

Security   see **convertible security.**

Seniority   see **priority.**

Sensitivity analysis   is a technique for examining the impact on return and net present value of variations in underlying factors and can show the consequences of different possible outcomes. **(11)**

Serial redemption   is the retirement each year as they mature of bonds that have been issued with serial maturity dates. **(17)**

Service lease   see **operating lease.**

Share   see **uncommitted earnings per share.**

Shares   see **issued shares, levered shares, outstanding shares, treasury shares, unlevered shares.**

Shelter   see **tax shelter.**

Shield   see **depreciation tax shield, interest tax shield, tax shield.**

Short-term debt   is debt with a maturity of less than one year. **(12)**

Short-term funds   are funds borrowed for less than one year. **(18)**

SICs   see **standard industrial codes.**

Sinking fund   is an arrangement in which firms make periodic repayments of principal to the trustees of a bond issue, who retire a specified number of bonds by open-market purchases or by calling certain bonds at a previously agreed-upon price. **(17)**

Sinking-fund coverage ratio   is the number of times interest-plus-sinking-fund payments are covered by EBIT. **(14)**

Sinking-fund payment   is the scheduled, periodic payment of principal to the trustee of a bond issue for the purpose of retiring a specific number of bonds by open-market purchase or by calling certain bonds at a previously agreed-upon price. **(14)**

Sole proprietorship   is a business owned and operated by a single individual that is not incorporated. **(2)**

Solvency   is the ability to pay all legal debts. **(14)**

Source-and-use-of-funds statement   is a summary of the flow of the financial activity of the firm, as recorded in the income statement and the balance sheet, that shows where a firm obtains cash and how it uses it. **(6)**

Sources of funds   are (1) increases in liabilities, (2) increases in net worth through retained earnings or additional capital contributions by owners, and (3) reductions in assets. **(6)**

Specific risk   see **diversifiable risk.**

Speculators   are people who willingly bear risk, with the prospect of large gains if things turn out favorably for them. **(21)**

Spending units   see **deficit spending units, surplus spending units.**

Spot rate   is the price of one currency in terms of another when purchased for immediate delivery. **(21)**

Standard   see **market standard.**

Standard deviation   is the probability-weighted measure of the dispersion of possible outcomes around an expected value and is a statistical measure of variability, or risk. **(5)**

Standard industrial codes (SICS)   are systems for classifying companies by their primary line of business. **(11)**

Standards   see **credit standards.**

Statutory consolidation   is a merger in which all the combining companies cease to exist as legal entities and a new corporation is created. **(22)**

Statutory merger   is a combination of two or more firms in which one company survives under its own name while any others cease to exist as legal entities. **(22)**

Stock   is the legal claim to ownership of a business corporation and is divided into shares and represented by certificates that can be transferred from one owner to another. **(1, 2)** See also **book value of stock, common stock, market value of stock, par value of stock, preferred stock, safety stock.**

Stock exchanges   are formal organizations that act as auction markets in the trading of financial securities. **(17)**

Stockout   occurs when there is insufficient inventory to fill orders. **(20)**

Stock variable   is a variable whose value is measured at a given moment in time. **(6)**

Straight-line method of depreciation   allocates the cost of an asset equally over a period of years by dividing the historical cost of the asset by the number of years and allocating that equal fraction of the cost to each year in the recovery period. **(9)**

Strategic analysis   is the process of making fundamental decisions about a firm's basic goal or purpose and about the products or services it will produce and the markets it will serve. **(9)**

Stream of payments   is a series of cash payments at specified, although not necessarily regular, intervals of specified (although not always the same) amounts. **(3)**

Subchapter S corporation   is a small corporation that may legally be treated as if it were a partnership for income-tax purposes. **(2)**

Subscription   see **privileged subscription.**

Sunk cost   is an expenditure made before a decision has been made and is unaffected by the decision under evaluation; it is not part of an investment's capital outlay and, in general, should be ignored in analyzing the investment. **(9)**

Supply curve   for a good or service shows the amounts of the good or service suppliers are willing to offer for sale at different prices during a specified time period. **(4)**

Surplus spending units   are individuals, companies, or government bodies who have excess funds. **(2)**

Swap   see **interest-rate swap.**

Synergy   is the effect achieved when the whole is greater than the sum of its parts. **(22)**

System   see **price system.**

Takeover   see **hostile takeover.**

Target payout ratio   see **long-run target payout ratio.**

Target return   is the rate of return required by the suppliers of funds to the investment project and is the rate with which the investment project's internal rate of return is compared, to determine whether the project will return enough to satisfy those providing the funds. **(9)** See also **Target return** see **return target.**

Tax   see **capital-gains tax, investment tax credit.**

Tax-deductible expenses are expenses that can legally be subtracted from total income to determine taxable income. (**2**)

Taxes see **profit after taxes.**

Tax liability is the amount of tax a taxpayer must pay in a given period. (**2**)

Tax rate see **average tax rate, marginal tax rate, progressive tax rates.**

Tax shelter is an investment opportunity that protects the investor from paying some or all of the taxes the investor would otherwise have to pay on the funds invested. (**15**)

Tax shield is the tax saving a firm generates by using debt because interest on debt is tax-deductible. For example, if a firm has a marginal tax rate of 46 percent, each dollar of interest generates a tax shield of 46 cents. (**10**) See also **depreciation tax shield, interest tax shield.**

Technical insolvency see **business failure.**

Tender offer is an acquiring firm's offer to pay existing shareholders some specified amount of cash or securities if these shareholders will sell (tender) their shares of stock to the acquiring firm. (**22**)

Terminal value of an investment project is an estimate of the cash flows generated beyond the terminal point of the analysis and is treated as a cash inflow in the final year of the analysis. (**9**)

Term loans are secured loans made by banks, insurance companies, or other lending institutions that must be repaid, usually within 3 to 7 years. (**12**)

Terms see **credit terms.**

Theory see **inventory theory.**

Thrift institution is a financial intermediary that accepts savings deposits and makes certain types of loans. (**2**)

Times-interest-earned (TIE) ratio measures the margin by which current earnings cover interest charges on debt and is calculated as current earnings divided by interest charges. (**7**)

Time value of money is the opportunity to earn interest on money one receives now rather than later. Because of the time value of money, a dollar today is worth more than a dollar in the future. (**3**)

Total capital is the sum of long-term debt and net worth, where net worth includes common stock, paid-in surplus, retained earnings, and preferred stock, if any. (**7**)

Trade credit is short-term credit extended by a supplier in connection with goods purchased for ultimate resale; used by nearly all firms to some extent as a source of short-term funds. (**18**)

Trade-off see **risk/expected-return trade-off.**

Transactions motive for holding cash concerns the use of cash to pay bills. (**19**)

Translation see **foreign-currency translation.**

Treasury bills and notes see **U.S. Treasury bills and notes.**

Treasury shares are previously issued shares of stock that a firm repurchases; they are issued but not outstanding shares. (**12**)

UEPS see **uncommitted earnings per share.**

UEPS break-even level of EBIT is the level of earnings before interest and taxes that equates uncommitted earnings per share for two financing alternatives. (**14**)

Uncommitted earnings per share (UEPS) are earnings remaining after the required sinking-fund payment for a bond issue. (**14**)

Unlevered shares are shares of stock in a company that uses no debt. (**13**)

Unsecured debt is debt that is not backed with a pledge of property in the event of borrower default. (**7**)

Unsecured loan is a loan against which no specific assets are pledged as collateral. (**18**)

Uses of funds are (1) reductions in liabilities, (2) reductions in net worth through the payment of dividends, retirement of stock, or operating losses, and (3) increases in assets. (**6**)

U.S. Treasury bills and notes are short-term obligations of the U.S. government. (**19**)

Valuation model see **constant-growth dividend-valuation model, variable-growth dividend-valuation model.**

Value see **bond value, book value, capital value, conversion value, expected value, future value, market value, net present value, par value of a bond, par value of a stock, present value, residual value, risk-adjusted residual value, terminal value, time value.**

Value of an asset is the dollar amount a person would have to receive today to be just as well off as he or she would be owning the asset. (**1**)

Value of stock see **book value of stock, market value of stock.**

Value maximization is the goal of making a firm's value as large as possible and can be used as a criterion for making financial-management decisions. (**1**)

Variable   see **discrete random variable, flow variable, stock variable.**

Variable costs   are costs that vary directly with changes in production volume. **(7)**

Variable-growth dividend-valuation model is a method for valuing stock that assumes that a rapid growth in the dividend can continue for only a short period and will then decline to a more normal growth level. **(4)**

Variation   see **coefficient of variation.**

Vertical merger   is a merger that combines firms that have some customer/supplier relationship. **(22)**

Voice in management   is the extent to which various financial-claim holders can influence the policies of a firm. **(12)**

WACC   see **weighted-average cost of capital.**

WARR   see **weighted-average required return.**

Warrant   is an option to purchase a specified number of shares of common stock at a specified price for a specified period of time, is typically issued in connection with bonds, and is usually detachable. **(16)**

Weighted-average cost of capital *(WACC)*   is another name for the *weighted-average required return (WARR).* **(10)**

Weighted-average required return *(WARR)*   is the required return for an investment project based on an average of equity and debt returns, where the weights are the respective proportions of equity and of debt used by the firm. **(10)** See also **weighted-average cost of capital** *(WACC).*

Working capital   see **net working capital.**

Work in process   is goods in various stages of production. **(20)**

Working-cash balance   is currency plus checking-account balances. **(19)**

Worst-case analysis   tells management how low a return could fall under adverse circumstances by calculating net present value and internal rate of return under the worst conditions likely to be encountered, such as highest possible cost and lowest possible sales. The return target for evaluating the worst case should not include a risk premium for bearing risk. **(11)**

Worth   see **net worth.**

Yield to maturity (YTM)   is the rate that could be earned on a bond or note if the investor bought it at the current price, held it to maturity, and received all the cash flows promised; **(4)** the internal rate of return that equates the price of a bond (or debt instrument) to the present value of the expected future cash benefits of owning the bond (or debt instrument); also known as the *required return on debt.* **(10, 12)**

Zero-coupon bond   is a bond that pays no interest but is issued at a large discount and later redeemed at face value. **(12)**

Answers to Odd-Numbered Questions

Chapter 1

1. The role of business firms in a market economy is to produce the goods and services desired by society as efficiently as possible. *Profit maximization* as a practical criterion suffers from three principal shortcomings: (1) it does not account of uncertainty, (2) it does not take account of the time value of money, and (3) it is ambiguous. *Value maximization* is the extension of profit maximization to a world that is uncertain and multiperiodic in nature. When the time period is short and the degree of uncertainty is not great, value maximization and profit maximization amount to essentially the same thing.

3. Because we assume that most individuals are risk-averse, a promise of return that involves greater uncertainty as to the actual amount of return will have a lower value than a comparable promise of return that is less uncertain.

Chapter 2

1. The three basic forms of organization are sole proprietorship, partnership, and corporation. *Proprietorships* and *partnerships* represent an extension of the activities of individuals into the sphere of commerce. Except in the case of limited partnerships, proprietors and partners have unlimited liability for the acts and debts of their firms. A *corporation,* on the other hand, is an entity created by law that is empowered to own assets, incur liabilities, and engage in certain specified activities. The liability of owners for acts and debts of the firm is limited to their investments. The corporate form also permits easier transfer of ownership and better access to capital markets. Finally, there are important differences in the way these organizational forms are taxed.

3. Corporate income is subject to taxation, with the taxes paid by the corporation. If dividends are paid, the dividends are then subject to taxation as income received by individuals. The taxes on dividends are paid by the individuals.

5. Taxation of income affects incentives. The lower is the marginal tax rate, the more of each incremental dollar of revenue an individual is able to keep, and (presumably) the harder he or she will work to earn an additional dollar. Conversely, when expenses are deductible, the net cost of each expense is only a part of the gross outlay. The lower is the marginal tax rate, the greater will be the portion of the net expense borne by the individual and the more careful he or she will be about expenses. For example, a lower marginal tax rate might reduce the total amount spent by businesses for entertainment.

7. In the aggregate, the net providers of funds in the U.S. economy are households. Business firms, in the aggregate, are net users of funds. When it incurs a deficit, government (federal as well as state and local) also is a net user of funds.

9. Commercial banks, mutual-saving banks, savings-and-loan associations, and credit unions are the major types of depository financial intermediaries. Insurance companies and pension and retirement funds are the major contractual types. Also included are mutual funds, finance companies, and real-estate investment trusts.

11. If lenders anticipate a certain level of inflation, they will add an inflation premium to the interest rate they charge borrowers in order to obtain their required *real* return. Likewise, borrowers will be willing to pay an inflation premium because they anticipate an inflated return on the money borrowed. Thus, anticipated inflation is incorporated into market interest rates.

Chapter 3

1. Money has time value because a dollar today is worth more to the holder than a dollar received at some time in the future. A dollar now can be invested over the time period to earn a profit.

3. The effective rate increases with frequency of compounding.

5. When interest is compounded daily, there will be more opportunity to earn interest on interest; therefore, the account paying 5 percent compounded daily will provide a higher effective rate of interest and should be selected.

Chapter 4

1. The value of an asset depends upon the size, timing, and degree of uncertainty attached to the stream of future payments the owner expects to receive.

3. Risk aversion is the dislike for risk, whereas risk preference is the desire to take on risk. Risk neutrality is indifference to the element of risk. A risk-averse individual requires com-

pensation for bearing risk, whereas a risk-neutral person does not.

5. The dividend-valuation model is a discounted-cash-flow model applied to the valuation of a firm, taking into consideration the cash flows expected to be received by the owners.

7. A market is efficient when market prices reflect all available information. While financial markets may not be perfectly efficient at all times, the competition of thousands of well-informed investors assures that market prices quickly adjust to new information.

Chapter 5

1. The standard deviation of returns is a measure of the variability of *past* returns. We cannot always assume that future variability will be the same. In addition, the standard deviation of returns on an asset does not take into account the relationships among returns on various assets. If assets' returns are not perfectly positively correlated, investors can achieve risk reduction by investing in a portfolio of assets. Therefore, a better measure of risk for a single asset may be the variability that the asset contributes to the variability of the portfolio.

3. The CAPM is a model that relates return on assets in financial markets to nondiversifiable risk. It assumes that investors are risk averse and that market prices will reflect the relative riskiness of assets. The CAPM may be useful for evaluating investment in both physical and financial assets.

5. Because investors can purchase any assets available in the market in any unit desired and because these assets are considered risk averse, under the assumptions of the CAPM investors can be expected to hold diversified portfolios and, therefore, to eliminate diversifiable risk. Nondiversifiable risk then becomes the only possible risk, and, in market equilibrium, securities will be priced to compensate investors for nondiversifiable risk only.

7. The beta coefficient is a measure of the volatility of the firm's return relative to that of the market portfolio. A beta greater than one indicates a firm with greater-than-average volatility in returns relative to the market. A beta of less than one indicates a firm with less volatile returns, and a beta of one indicates a firm with average volatility of returns. Under the assumptions of the CAPM, beta can be used to calculate the required rate of return on a stock as $K_j = R_f + (K_m - R_f)\beta_j$, where R_f is the risk-free rate and K_m is the required return on the market.

9. If the goal of the firm is to maximize shareholder wealth and the firm's cash flows can be improved by concentrating on health books, Farquhar may be correct in suggesting that they concentrate their resources in that area. After all, investors can diversify by holding other stocks and eliminate the risk that health-book publishing may decline. On the other hand, MacTavish can make a strong case that, by diversifying and reducing the riskiness of returns, they will better satisfy the risk-return requirements of shareholders and also reduce the risk of bankruptcy that can result in dead-weight losses of resources. The company must decide what its commercial strategy is, whether it is to be a publisher of health books or popular books, and then proceed from there.

Chapter 6

1. Except for dividends, any transaction that changes net worth appears in the income statement.

3. *Working capital* refers to the firm's current assets, *net working capital* to current assets less current liabilities, and *net operating capital* to current assets less the current liabilities that arise directly out of the firm's operations (such as accounts payable and various accruals.)

5. *Sources of funds* include increases in liabilities, increases in net worth, and reductions in assets. *Uses of funds* include reductions in liabilities, reductions in net worth, and increases in assets.

Chapter 7

1. Return on investment is sometimes an ambiguous measure of performance because it can be calculated in many ways. Return can be calculated either pretax or after-tax, or as an average over several years. Investment can be defined either as the initial outlay or as the average book investment over the period in question.

3. In a seasonal firm, variation in the sales rate over the year will cause the days-of-sales-outstanding (DSO) figure to vary even when there is no change in the underlying collection rate. In such a firm, the averaging period of sales must be selected carefully and the results interpreted with caution. Similarly, seasonality in sales and purchasing may cause the inventory turnover rate to vary over the year.

5. Yes. If a firm is growing rapidly, all of its profits may be absorbed by necessary increases in current assets, leaving the firm always short of cash.

7. *Fixed costs* refer to those that are constant in total over some specified range of output, usually in terms of sales volume. *Variable costs* are those that vary in total as output varies. Costs that are labeled "fixed" over some range of output usually become variable outside that range.

9. Where depreciation is included as an expense, break-even on a cash basis always will be lower than break-even on a profit basis. Less revenue is required to cover cash operating expenses than full operating expenses, which include depreciation.

11. Operating leverage is determined by the firm's cost structure (the ratio of fixed operating costs to total operating costs) and, therefore, by the nature of the business. *Financial leverage* is determined by the mix of debt and equity used to finance the firm's assets. In flow terms, financial leverage depends on the portion of EBIT that is paid in interest.

Chapter 8

1. The planning process begins with the firm's basic goal or purpose. From this is derived the commercial strategy, which

defines products, markets, and production technology. Supporting policies then are developed in production, marketing, research and development, accounting, finance, and personnel.

3. Whereas the percent-of-sales approach often can be used in nonseasonal companies for estimating major items, more refined techniques usually must be employed where seasonality is present. Also, quarterly or even monthly statements often are necessary in highly seasonal firms.

5. In principle, commercial strategy comes first, and financing is tailored to fit. Often an operating plan must be modified to take account of availability of funds. In theory, operating plans and financing requirements should be determined jointly. In practice, however, an iterative process often is appropriate whereby an operating plan is formulated, financing feasibility determined, and the process repeated if necessary.

7. All three financial statements are mutually interdependent. With consistent assumptions and accurate presentation, all of the figures will mesh. For example, collections must be consistent with sales and accounts receivable; accounts payable, purchases, inventory, and cost of goods sold must be consistent with each other; tax payments must be consistent with tax expense on the income statement and with taxes payable on the balance sheet.

9. Inflation generally increases the need for outside financing. Inflation can have very large effects on a firm's need for funding. In trying to meet these funding requirements, managers face important financial-policy questions about dividend policy and the mix of debt and equity financing.

Chapter 9

1. Cash flows relevant to the analysis of an investment opportunity are those *directly attributable to the investment*. Only the cash flows that will differ depending on the decision made should be considered. Thus, previous investments are sunk costs and can be ignored. Also, cash flows that will be identical under alternative decisions can be ignored.

3. Depreciation is relevant in a discounted-cash-flow analysis only as it affects taxes. In an organization that does not pay taxes, depreciation would not be relevant.

5. The appropriate time period depends on the nature of the decision, its size and importance, and the time and effort that can be devoted to the analysis. Any choice of decision horizon is essentially arbitrary. In the final year of the analysis, any remaining value of the project must be taken into account.

7. The *IRR* is the rate that discounts all the cash flows of the investment, including the outlay, to exactly zero.

9. Only expenses that actually will change because of the decision being evaluated should be included. If overhead, for example, will increase or decrease because of the decision at hand, the change in overhead expense should be included in the cash-flow analysis.

11. Payback ignores the time value of money and the cash flows beyond the end of the payback period. Establishing the required payback period is essentially an arbitrary judgment, because payback cannot be related to a more general criterion such as profit maximization or value maximization.

13. Discounted-cash-flow techniques do not consider the impact of an investment on accounting profits. Where performance is measured using accounting profits and accounting return on investment, the use of DCF techniques for decision making may cause conflicts.

Chapter 10

1. In undertaking any investment opportunity, the investor forgoes the return that could be earned on other alternative investments. Rates available on alternative opportunities, thus, establish the minimum acceptable rate of return on any given investment.

3. False. The required rate is that on the next best opportunity forgone by the *shareholders,* rather than by the firm itself. Thus, the required return is established by the alternative opportunities of *shareholders*.

5. Required rates of return are established in the financial markets by the actions of investors competing among themselves. Because all investors have access to the financial markets, a standard set of opportunity rates is established that is the same for all investors. Given risk aversion, those opportunity rates increase with risk.

7. Suppliers and users of capital react to inflation in a way that incorporates anticipated inflation into all market-determined required rates of return. Required rates, thus, reflect the rate of inflation expected in the future.

9. The required rate of return on the firm's outstanding securities represents the required return given the overall or combined risk of all investments undertaken in the past and expected by the market in the future. The required return on a single prospective investment opportunity would be the same as the required return on the firm's outstanding securities only if the riskiness of the prospective investment opportunity equaled the average risk of the firm as a whole.

11. The best source is market data on risk and return on financial assets.

13. First, determine the target financing mix—that is, the proportions of common equity, preferred stock, and various forms of debt that will provide capital to the firm in the future. Second, determine the required rate of return on each component, making certain to adjust for the tax-deductibility of interest. Third, multiply the tax-adjusted required rates of return by their proportions, and add them to obtain the *WARR.*

15. In calculating $K_e,$ we have to make an estimate of the required return of stockholders in a company. This boils down to making some very difficult assumptions. A number of models exist to calculate $K_e,$ including the use of historical risk premia and the dividend-growth model (both finite and infinite growth). In using dividend-growth models, we have to estimate what shareholders expect to happen in the future.

That is, we have to estimate *future* dividends. In using the historical-risk-premium approach, we have to assume that the long-run risk premia earned in the past are expected to be earned in the future. In addition, we have to adjust the risk premium for the length of the time period because arithmetic and geometric averages differ. In short, estimating K_e is a difficult business, and, in practice, it is usually prudent to try a number of different models to calculate K_e.

Chapter 11

1. Two approaches to dealing with risk in capital budgeting are sensitivity analysis on project cash flows and risk-adjusted discount rates. Sensitivity analysis requires recalculating the internal rate of return (or net present value) for a range of possible sales levels and costs, in addition to calculating for the most likely case. This approach allows the manager to focus on how variability in certain factors may affect the success of the project. The alternative approach requires that cash flows be discounted at required rates of return that reflect their relative riskiness. Thus, higher discount rates are used for more uncertain cash flows. This approach is the risk-adjusted discount-rate method.

3. In a worst-case analysis, the riskiness of cash flows has been accounted for. Because the cash flows are likely to be higher than the worst-case projections, there is no risk that must be compensated for by requiring a higher return. Therefore, these cash flows are discounted at a required rate of return that does not include a risk premium.

5. By assigning investment projects to different categories that depend on the riskiness of the cash flows, the firm could use a modified form of the CAPM to derive an estimate of the required rate of return on an unlevered firm. Betas of 0.5, 1, and 1.5, for example, could be assigned to projects of low, average, and high risk. To adjust the required returns for debt financing, the firm could also weight the firm's debt ratio in relation to the riskiness of the project, with the riskiest project having a weight of 0 placed on the firm's debt ratio and average projects having a weight of 1 placed on the firm's debt ratio in equation (7).

7. In theory, the use of a single discount rate to evaluate projects of varying risk will lead to acceptance of some high-risk projects that should be rejected and rejection of some low-risk projects that should be accepted. Over time, the firm's average risk level may be increased as a result of this bias. Also, acceptance of high-risk projects that do not provide sufficient return will, in the long run, reduce the firm's profitability and its market value.

Chapter 12

1. Financial claims issued by firms differ with respect to *maturity, seniority* (priority), whether they are *contractual* or *residual,* whether *collateral* is involved, and *tax treatment.* Because of differences in risks, the financial markets require different rates of return on different types of securities.

3. The agreement between a debt holder and a firm (or other borrower) represents an enforceable contract. If the obligor fails to meet the terms of the agreement with respect to repayment or other matters, the claim holder can take legal action to enforce the claim.

5. Within major categories, some contractual claims may be junior to others. In such cases, the junior claims often are referred to as *subordinated.*

7. A *mortgage bond* is normally secured by a specific asset or assets, usually buildings or equipment, that are pledged as security against default on interest or principal payments. *Debentures,* on the other hand, are not secured by specific assets, but rather by all the assets of the firm collectively.

9. The yield to maturity (YTM) is the rate that discounts all interest and principal payments on a bond to an amount exactly equal to the price of the bond. In the case of publicly traded bonds, price—and, therefore, yield to maturity—is determined in the financial markets.

11. Common stockholders have final responsibility for policy and a residual claim to income and assets, behind preferred shareholders and debt holders. Common stock is a perpetual claim, having no maturity. Common stockholders have limited liability. Under the laws of most states, common stockholders have the right to amend the corporate charter, adopt and amend bylaws, elect the directors, enter into mergers with other firms, change the number of authorized shares outstanding, and authorize the issuance of senior claims such as preferred stock and long-term debt.

13. The book value of common stock is the amount of net assets available for common shareholders, that is, total assets less claims of creditors and preferred shareholders. Market value is the price at which the stock can be sold on the open market, usually the most recent price at which the stock was traded.

15. *Weak-form efficiency* results when market prices reflect all information contained in historic prices. *Semistrong-form efficiency* results when market prices reflect all publicly available information. *Strong-form efficiency* results when market prices reflect *all* information—both public and private.

17. Semistrong-form efficiency does imply weak-form efficiency because past information on security prices is part of public information. Semistrong-form efficiency does not, however, imply strong-form efficiency because public information would not include inside information.

Chapter 13

1. *Operating leverage* is determined by the relationship between fixed and variable operating expenses, which include expenses related to the firm's operations and exclude interest and taxes. The higher is the ratio of fixed operating cost to total operating cost, the higher is the operating leverage. *Financial leverage* refers to the mix of debt and equity used to finance the firm's activities. The higher is the proportion of debt funds to total funds, the higher is the financial leverage. Thus, operating leverage is determined by the nature of the

business and its cost structure, whereas financial leverage is determined by the financing mix.

3. Financial leverage has no effect on the variability of dollar operating returns (no effect on range or standard deviation). Financial leverage does affect the variability of earnings per share and percentage return on equity.

5. When earnings-per-share (EPS) data are used as criteria for financing decisions, the analysis is nearly always carried out in terms of expected values. Earnings per share as criteria, thus, ignore risk and result in a bias toward the use of debt in lieu of equity. If applied strictly, the EPS criterion nearly always leads to the choice of debt rather than equity and can lead to excessive use of debt.

7. *Accounting return on equity* is defined as accounting profit (pretax or after tax) divided by book net worth. *Return to shareholders* is composed of dividends plus capital gains or losses. Excessive use of debt financing will simultaneously increase accounting return on equity and reduce return to shareholders by lowering stock price.

9. Since, for any given firm, debt is always cheaper than equity, strict application of the cost criterion would always lead to a choice of debt over equity. Debt and equity perform different functions, so a strict comparison of cost is insufficient for choosing between the two.

11. In theory, market value is a function of both expected return and risk. The higher is the expected return, the greater is the value, whereas the higher is the risk, the lower is the value. Since an increase in financial leverage increases both expected return and risk, market value theoretically deals with the trade-offs between the two.

13. Tax-deductibility reduces the share of EBIT going to the government and increases by a like amount the share going to equity holders. The share going to debt holders is unchanged.

15. Even if interest were not tax-deductible, some firms might use debt in order to exploit potentially favorable effects of financial leverage. Firms having no access to the equity market would find debt their only source of funds and would use debt regardless of whether interest were deductible. Short-term debt would find use by firms for financing short-term requirements. Debt might also be preferred to equity to avoid dilution of ownership and control.

Chapter 14

1. A firm's operating risk manifests itself in variability of earnings before interest and taxes (EBIT). Variability of EBIT is determined by variability of sales revenue, variability of operating expenses, degree of operating leverage, and composition of the firm's assets. All these factors in turn derive from the characteristics of the industry and company and the technology of the business in which the company is engaged.

3. Yes, short-term debt should be considered. Debt increases risk regardless of whether it is short-term or long-term debt. In fact, an argrument can be made that short-term debt is riskier than long-term debt. In this chapter, the distinction

between short-term and long-term debt is ignored, and all debt is treated the same for determining the optimal level of debt. The question of maturity structure is treated in Chapter 18.

5. Very little can be said about a firm's exposure to risk of financial distress without knowing the maturity of the debt and the schedule for repayment of principal. A complete analysis also requires information on the firm's cash flows, both those from operations and those generated by changes in investment policy, asset structure, and discretionary financial payments (dividends).

7. In general, a firm should not extend the debt level indicated as safe by a cash-flow analysis. A firm should maintain a substantial reserve borrowing capacity to provide flexibility for changes in its commercial strategy and also a reserve for contingencies. Uncertainty about future rates of inflation provides a further reason for maintaining reserve borrowing power.

Chapter 15

1. True. Dividends are treated as a residual. Fluctuating dividends cause no problems for investors in a frictionless world. If the firm errs and pays out too much in dividends, it simply issues new securities to replace the funds, incurring no costs in the process.

3. Shareholders are subject to transaction costs resulting from commissions on purchases and sales of securities and from the time, effort, and inconvenience of altering their personal portfolios. The combined effect of all such costs is significant and may constitute quite a large percentage of small transactions. A second general category includes transaction costs incurred in issuing new securities by firms.

5. Investment, debt/equity, and dividend decisions cannot all be treated as active policy variables unless the firm is prepared to place no constraints on external financing. A constraint on external financing means that one of the three major policy variables must be treated as a residual.

7. Dividend policy should be treated as residual. Any other choice requires that the firm either consciously plan to forgo attractive investments, operate at a nonoptimal debt/equity ratio, or finance dividend payments by selling stock.

9. Dividend policies must be planned over a relatively long time horizon because investment opportunities cannot be foreseen with complete accuracy each year, nor can earnings be forecast accurately each year. In a world of uncertainty and considerable financial friction, dividend policy must be based on trend values over relatively long time periods.

Chapter 16

1. Discounted-cash-flow (DCF) techniques can be used to calculate an equivalent interest cost *(EIC)* of any financing plan. Where financing alternatives affect the risk of the firm in a comparable way, the *EIC* of the alternatives can be directly compared.

3. Take the investment decision (the decision to use the asset) as given. The equivalent interest cost of a lease plan then can be calculated and compared directly to the cost of 100 percent debt financing.

5. Normally, the call feature is included to provide the issuer with a means of forcing conversion.

7. A convertible security may fail to convert if the firm does not do as well as originally anticipated, and its common-stock price does not rise to the levels at which conversion can be forced. A hung convertible issue leaves the firm with a capital structure different from what it had planned and may considerably reduce its flexibility for subsequent external financing.

9. A high degree of competition in financial markets does not imply that convertibles and warrants cannot be used to advantage. It does imply that the firm will pay full price for whatever advantages do accrue.

Chapter 17

1. The three principal methods of issuing securities to the public are public offerings through investment bankers, public offerings by a privileged subscription, and private placements.

3. A privileged subscription is a new offering of securities in which existing security holders (usually stockholders) are given the right to purchase their pro-rata shares of securities before the securities are offered to the general public. The right of shareholders to have first refusal is called a *preemptive* right.

5. The primary purpose of federal and state regulation of security markets is to protect investors against misinformation and fraud.

7. Some issue costs vary with the size of the issue and some costs are fixed. To the extent that some costs are fixed, issue costs as a percentage of funds raised will vary with the size of the issue. Raising small amounts of money, therefore, is uneconomical; firms tend to raise money in larger blocks.

9. Keeping investors and other participants in the financial markets informed about major policies, investments, and financing decisions is of great importance in the pricing of a firm's securities. The factors that determine security prices are future oriented. The better informed the market is kept about the policies and future plans, the more the market relies on facts and substantive information and the less it is forced to draw inferences from other actions. For example, based on an announcement of a major financing decision or a change in dividend policy, the market might draw inferences about the firm's investment opportunities. Depending on the nature of the inferences, stock price may be affected in one direction or the other. Where possible, management should communicate its policies and plans to the market so that prices are based on facts and information rather than inferences.

11. The term *sinking fund* refers to an arrangement whereby a firm makes periodic payments, usually annually or semi-annually, to the trustee of a bond or preferred-stock issue. The trustee then uses the funds to retire a specified number of bonds periodically either by open-market purchase or by calling certain bonds at previously agreed-upon prices.

13. The option to call an entire issue prior to maturity can be advantageous to a firm to permit changes in capital structure or to permit refunding of the issue at a lower interest rate. Whatever advantage accrues from the call privilege accrues to shareholders and represents a corresponding disadvantage to bondholders. Bondholders normally insist on being compensated by a higher interest rate for the call privilege.

15. Four motives exist for a firm to repurchase stock. First, a firm might elect to repurchase its stock in lieu of paying a dividend. However, internal revenue regulations require that such a repurchase be taxed as a dividend. Secondly, repurchase sometimes is justified as a means of accumulating shares of stock for use in future acquisition or for employee stock options, but any advantage of repurchase for this purpose is illusory. A third motive is to effect a partial return of capital to the shareholders or a partial liquidation of the firm. A final motive for repurchase is to bring about a change in the firm's debt/equity ratio.

17. Financial difficulty may result from a number of causes including failures of management, changes in technology or markets, or overallocation of resources to a particular economic activity. In all three cases, profits are a yardstick for judging performance, and society is sending a message that changes are necessary. If technology or markets change, management must make the necessary adjustments. If errors were made by management in the past, they should be corrected; if excessive resources are allocated to the particular activity, resources must be withdrawn and reallocated to other uses.

19. The appropriate remedy when a firm encounters financial difficulty depends on the nature of the difficulty. In cases of technical insolvency, creditors usually are better off to accommodate the firm's short-run liquidity difficulty and to allow it to remain in operation. Such problems usually are worked out either by an extension of maturities, or by a composition, under which all creditors agree to accept a partial payment. Where the appropriate remedy cannot be agreed upon informally, relief can be sought either by the firm or its creditors in the courts. Such relief usually takes the form of a reorganization under the provisions of the Bankruptcy Act. In situations in which the value of a firm as a going concern is less than its liquidation value, liquidation of assets usually is the appropriate remedy.

Chapter 18

1. The firm is exposed to the risk of having short-term creditors either significantly raise the interest rate on funds or refuse to renew the credit. Thus, the firm might face either a significant increase in costs or the necessity of having to reduce its operating assets and alter its commercial strategy accordingly. For reasons of risk and cost, financing permanent requirements with long-term funds is a sensible general rule to follow. Some firms do not have access to long-term capital

markets and, therefore, may be forced to finance certain permanent requirements with short-term debt.

3. Two major alternative methods of financing asset requirements that vary over time are to borrow short term as required, or to select a liquid-asset buffer financed by long-term funds.

5. The liquidity of a firm depends both on its holdings of liquid assets and on the maturity structure of its liabilities. The shorter is the maturity of the firm's assets, and the longer is the maturity of its liabilities, the higher will be the firm's liquidity.

7. The short- and immediate-suppliers are other business firms, commercial banks, finance companies, insurance companies, pension funds, and others to whom firms may become obligated for one reason or another. All of these suppliers are themselves only intermediaries in the chain of finance, because they require financing also. Ultimately, the suppliers of all business funds are individuals, who, by consuming less than they earn, have excess funds to save and invest.

9. Through the financial plan, the borrower communicates to the bank information about the nature of the financing requirement, the amount and timing of the need, the uses to which the funds will be put, and the timing and means of repayment. The fact that a financial plan has been prepared is important in that it communicates to the bank that the firm's management is competent.

11. Collateral permits a lender to make a loan that, when unsecured, is too risky in relation to the rate that can be charged, and yet still has reasonable prospects of being repaid.

13. Short-term lenders are less concerned with earning power than intermediate-term lenders because repayment of a term loan must come from profits over a period of several years rather than from liquidations of the assets financed by the loan.

Chapter 19

1. Principal motives for holding cash and liquid assets include the transactions motive, for making payments, and a precautionary motive, for responding to unexpected problems or opportunities requiring funds on short notice.

3. Concentration banking permits a firm to pool its requirements for working balances in a single account and, thereby, to reduce the aggregate requirements.

5. Under conditions of certainty, finding the optimal working balance represents a trade-off between the costs of too little cash (transaction costs) and the costs of too much cash (opportunity costs).

7. A firm might have idle cash as a matter of policy for either of two reasons: First, a seasonal firm might have temporarily idle balances during parts of the year; second, a firm might hold precautionary balances to finance unpredictable requirements. In both cases, the firm probably would find it advantageous to invest the idle balances temporarily in liquid assets.

Chapter 20

1. The credit manager is responsible primarily for administering credit policy—that is, administering the credit standards, credit terms, and collection policy established by the firm. The financial manager, on the other hand, is concerned primarily with the expected rate of return on the investment in accounts receivable, and, therefore, is concerned with establishing credit policy rather than administering it.

3. The theoretical objective of credit policy is to maximize the value of the firm by setting credit policy at the point at which the marginal expected operating return on the investment in accounts receivable equals the rate of return required by suppliers of funds, given the riskiness of the investment in receivables.

5. The expected return to Delta Electric on an investment in trade credit likely would far exceed the expected return to a bank on a loan to the same customer. Thus, the expected return to Delta might well be sufficient to compensate for the risk involved, whereas the expected return to the bank might be too low given the risk. For this reason, suppliers often are willing to extend trade credit to customers considered too risky to qualify for bank credit.

7. Carrying costs such as financing, storage, servicing, and risks of loss in value due to obsolescence, fire, and theft rise with increases in the level of inventory. A second category of costs that decline with the level of inventory includes ordering costs, unit purchase costs, production costs, and opportunity costs of lost sales.

9. The optimal amount of safety stock varies directly with stockout costs, uncertainty of usage or sales rates, and uncertainty of delivery times. The optimum varies inversely with inventory carrying costs.

11. At the margin, investment in accounts receivable is risky because of the possibility of customer default. Similarly, incremental investment in inventory is risky because of uncertainty surrounding the extent to which lost sales will be recaptured by holding additional inventory.

Chapter 21

1. The basic concepts of finance do not change. They are just as applicable for firms doing business in foreign markets. However, the financial officer will now have additional elements to consider in financial decisions—specifically, currency-exchange rates, both current and future, and interest rates applicable to those currencies.

3. The floating system creates more uncertainty (risk) for the businessmanagers doing business in foreign countries. Even though some businessmanagers might benefit occasionally from changes under a floating system, a fixed system is preferable—all other things being equal—because people are risk averse. There are ways this risk can be reduced, but these methods create transaction costs in both time and money. In practice, all other things are not equal. In the long run, a floating rate system may be more responsive to underlying

economic changes around the world. In short, there is no easy answer for which system is better. It is clear, however, that a floating-rate system introduces new risks to business.

5. The most important factor that accounts for forward-spot differentials is the difference between the inflation rates of the countries involved. Differences in interest rates paid for the country's currency, to the extent those rates reflect anticipated inflation, also affect the differential. Central banks can also have an impact.

7. The process would be just the reverse of that described in answer (6). The treasurer would purchase forward the amount of Swiss francs needed in order to guarantee the availability at the required time. This purchase could result in his or her actually paying more or less, depending on relative inflation rates, but would protect against further fluctuations.

9. Covered-interest arbitrage is the market process through which the relationships in the interest-rate-parity theorem come into being. This process is used to cover one's position by buying or selling forward the currencies involved.

Chapter 22

1. Horizontal mergers combine firms operating in the same business line. Vertical mergers combine firms that have some customer/supplier relationship. Conglomerate mergers combine firms in different industries.

3. Diversification through merger may lead to increases in value, depending on the circumstances of the merger. If the stockholders of the acquiring firm have diversified portfolios, it is not likely that the merger will create value for them. But there are circumstances, such as mergers, that actually change cash flows, increase borrowing power, or take advantage of an undervalued situation, in which value can be created.

5. Merger-induced increases in earning per share (EPS) do not always benefit shareholders. It is not EPS that is ultimately important to shareholders but the price per share of the stock they own. The EPS increase may or may not translate into an increased share price, depending on how the market views the value of the merged firm.

7. Studies indicate that shareholders of acquired firms have benefited. The picture is not so clear for shareholders of the acquiring firm. Evidence suggests that they have not been harmed by mergers.

9. An acquisition is similar to other investment proposals, since a stream of cash flows is being purchased for some outlay. It is different from other investments only in that it may be much more complicated from a financial, tax, or business perspective. There may be more intangibles involved, and a firm may be going outside its area of expertise where there is more uncertainty.

Solutions to Odd-Numbered Problems

Chapter 3

Problems preceded by one asterisk(*) assume knowledge of Appendix 3A.

1. The application of Equation (1) from the text (these problems could be solved using the reciprocal from Appendix Table I at the end of the textbook or figures from Appendix Table III when available) provides the following results:
   a. $\$100(1 + 0.10)^3 = \$133.10$.
   b. $\$100(1 + 0.30)^3 = \$219.70$.
   c. $\$100(1 + 0)^3 = \$100.00$.
3. The application of the annuity present-value table (Appendix Table II at the end of the textbook) provides the following results:
   a. $\$500(2.775) = \$1,387.50$.
   b. $\$500(1.952) = \$976.00$.
5. The application of present-value table (Appendix Table I at the end of the textbook) provides the following results:
   a. $\$100(0.943) + \$400(0.890) + \$800(0.840)$
      $= \$1,122.30$.
   b. $\$100(0.833) + \$400(0.694) + \$800(0.579) = \$824.10$.
7. The solutions require the use of the compounding portion of Equation (1) to find the effective rate.

   a. $\left(1 + \dfrac{0.08}{2}\right)^2 = 1.0816$; effective rate $= 8.16$ percent.

   b. $\left(1 + \dfrac{0.08}{4}\right)^4 = 1.0824$; effective rate $= 8.24$ percent.

   c. $\left(1 + \dfrac{0.08}{12}\right)^{12} = 1.0830$; effective rate $= 8.30$ percent.

9. The application of Equation (2) provides the following results:

   a. $\dfrac{1,000}{(1 + 0.06)^2} = \dfrac{\$1,000}{1.12360} = \$890.00$

   b. $\dfrac{\$4,000}{\left(1 + \dfrac{0.04}{4}\right)^4} = \dfrac{\$4,000}{1.0406} = \$3,843.94$.

   c. $\dfrac{\$1,000}{\left(1 + \dfrac{0.12}{12}\right)^6} = \dfrac{\$1,000}{1.0615} = \$942.06$.

   d. $\dfrac{\$3,000}{\left(1 + \dfrac{0.08}{2}\right)^4} = \dfrac{\$3,000}{1.1699} = \$2,564.32$.

11. Applying Equation (3) and the present-value tables at the back of the book provides the results shown in Table S–1.
13. The problem could be solved by looking up the individual present-value factors for each of the 16 periods. However, problems of this type can usually be shortened considerably by breaking them down into an annuity plus several individual inflows. One such division is given in Table S–2.

Table S–1

Period	Cash Flow (dollars)	Present-Value Factor at 4 Percent	Present Value at 4 Percent (dollars)	Present-Value Factor at 8 Percent	Present Value at 8 Percent (dollars)	Present-Value Factor at 12 Percent	Present Value at 12 Percent (dollars)
1	300	0.962	288.60	0.926	277.80	0.893	267.90
2	400	0.925	370.00	0.857	342.80	0.797	318.80
3	600	0.889	533.40	0.794	476.40	0.712	427.20
4	100	0.855	85.50	0.735	73.50	0.636	63.60
			1,277.50		1,170.50		1,077.50

Table S–2

Year	Cash flow (dollars)	Factor at 8 Percent	Present Value (dollars)
1–16	100 (annuity)	8.851	885.10
5	100	0.681	68.10
6	200	0.630	126.00
16	300	0.292	87.60
			1,166.80

15. This problem is intended to demonstrate the usefulness of discounted cash flow in moving cash flows around through time while maintaining value equivalence. The solutions are as follows:

   a. $100(0.909) + $300(0.826) + $200(0.751) = $488.90.

   b. $100 + $300(0.909) + $200(0.826) = $537.90.

   c. $100(1 + 0.10) + $300 + $200(0.909) = $591.80.

   d. $100(1 + 0.10)^2 + $300(1 + 0.10) + $200 = $651.00.

   Note: Solutions (b), (c), and (d) could also be found by compounding $488.90 forward for one, two, and three years respectively at 10 percent.

17. The application of Appendix Table II at the end of the textbook provides the following result:

$$PV = [1 + (\text{Annuity factor}, n = 3, i = 10 \text{ percent})] \, \$600$$
$$= [1 + (2.487)](\$600)$$
$$= \$2092.20.$$

19. The solution requires the use of the compounding-portion of Equation (1) to find the effective rate:

$$\left(1 + \frac{0.06}{4}\right)^4 = 1.0614; \text{ effective rate} = 6.14 \text{ percent.}$$

21. The future value of $2,000 in two years at 10 percent can be determined as follows: $2,000 (Future value factor) = $2,000(1.21) = $2,420. Your savings, thus invested, would fall short of the $2,500 required.

23. This problem requires the students to solve for the amount of an annuity, given the present value, discount rate, and time horizon. The determination of the maximum amount requires equating the lump-sum amount to the present value of an annuity, solving for the payment:

   (Payment) × (Annuity factor, n = 4, r = 7 percent)
      = $8,000.00.
   Payment = $8,000.00/3.387
      = $2,361.97.

25. This is a fairly straightforward problem, requiring the student to calculate the effective interest rate (r) on a loan as follows:

   (Annuity factor, n = 5) × ($4,161) = $15,000.
   Annuity factor = $15,000/$4,161 = 3.605.

Referring to Appendix Table II at the end of the textbook enables the student to determine that r = 12 percent.

27. Assuming semiannual compounding, the market rate of interest is 4.5 percent per half-year. The value of the bond, therefore, is the present value of an infinite stream of $20 per half-year capitalized at 4.5 percent, or 20/0.045 = $444.44.

29. See Figure S–1 which graphically depicts the dividend income from this investment. It is first necessary to find a rate of return (r) such that the present value of the dividends plus the present value of the final selling price are equal to the purchase price. The formula, using present-value (PV) factors, is as follows:

$1,000 = $60 (PV annuity factor for 7 years at r precent) + $30 (PV annuity factor for 5 years at r percent) (PV factor for 7 years at r percent) + $860 (PV factor for 12 years at r percent)

The next step is to solve by trial and error. Eventually, the use of 4 percent will yield these results: $60(6.002) + $30(4.452)(0.760) + $860(0.625) = 999.1256. The conclusion is that r ≈ 4 percent. Notice that the five-year $30 annuity is collapsed into a single value that represents its present value at the end of the seventh year. Then this sum is discounted back to time zero by applying the seven-year present-value factor.

31. The following is an analysis of your two alternatives: *Alternative 1—Keep the certificate.* A deposit of $500 in a certificate receives 5 percent interest semiannually, $500(1.05)^2 = $551.25, while an average balance of $450 in a checking account receives no interest. The total funds available at year's end = $551.25 + $450.00 = $1,001.25. *Alternative 2—Switch to a NOW account.* A deposit of $500 in savings receives $\dfrac{0.055}{365}$ in interest daily, or

$$\$500 \left(1 + \frac{0.055}{365}\right)^{365} = \$500(1.05653) = \$528.27.$$

An average balance of $450 in checking also receives $\dfrac{0.055}{365}$ in interest daily, or

$$\$450 \left(1 + \frac{0.055}{365}\right)^{365} = \$459(1.05653) = \$465.44.$$

Figure S–1

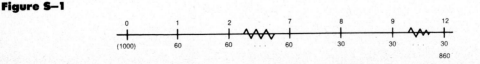

Figure S–2

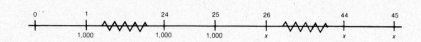

The total funds available at year's end = $528.27 + $475.44 = $1,003.71.

33. The cash flows are given in Figure S-2, a time line along which $t = 0$ corresponds to your 35th birthday, $t = 25$ corresponds to your 60th birthday, and $t = 45$ corresponds to your 80th birthday. As can be seen from the time line, there are two annuities—one with payments of $1,000 and one with withdrawals of x. It is convenient to focus on $t = 25$ (your 60th birthday and anticipated date of retirement). We can calculate the future value of the first annuity ($1,000 payments for 25 years) and the present value (at $t = 25$) of the second annuity ($x withdrawals for 20 years). These two amounts must be equal. Note that $t = 25$ is the terminal date for the first annuity and the beginning date for the second annuity. The calculations to determine the value of x are as follows:

$1,000 (Future-value annuity factor for 25 years at 5 percent) = x (Present-value annuity factor for 20 years at 5 percent)

$$\frac{\$1000 \text{ (Future-value annuity factor for 25 years at 5 percent)}}{\text{(Present-value annuity factor for 20 years at 5 percent)}} = x$$

$$\frac{\$1,000(47.727)}{(12.462)} = x$$

$$\$3,829.80 = x$$

35. The student is required to calculate the amount of an annuity necessary to produce a specified future value and to consider the effects of inflation upon purchasing power.

a. The calculations to determine the annuity required to produce $6,000 in year 5 are:

(Amount of annuity) ×
(FV-annuity factor $n = 1$, $n = 6$ percent) = $6,000.00.
Amount of annuity = $6,000.00/5.637
= $1,064.40.

b. The calculations to determine the annuity required to produce $6,000 in year 5, with the last payment in year 4 are:

(Amount of annuity) ×
(FV-annuity factor, $n = 4$, $r = 6$ percent) ×
(FV factor, $n = 1$, $r = 6$ percent = $6,000.00.
Amount of annuity = $6,000.00/(4.375 × 1.06)
= $6,000/4.6375
= $1,293.80.

37. The calculations are as follows:

(Annuity factor for $i = 6$ percent)($7,000) = $80,500.

$$\text{Annuity factor} = \frac{\$80,500}{\$7,000} = 11.5.$$

The application of Appendix Table II at the end of the text-book determines that n = approximately 20 years. Consequently, Hoe will be about 60 + 20 = 80 years old when his money runs out.

*39. The cash flows are given in Figure S–3. To find the effective interest rate, set the present value of the loan equal to $2,000 and solve for the monthly interest rate:

$P_o = \$2,000 = \$189.17$ (PV annuity factor for 12 months at r^*).
$$\frac{\$2,000}{\$189.17} = \text{(Present-value annuity factor)} = 10.57.$$

(*Note:* Both the 12 and the r^* *must* refer to the same time period. As shown in the appendix tables at the end of the textbook, a factor of 10.57 corresponds to an interest rate of 2 percent *monthly*. On an annual basis, r_A^* is such that $(1 + 0.02)^{12} = 1 + r_A^*$ with $r_A^* = (1 + 0.02)^{12} - 1 = 26.8$ percent annually.)

Chapter 4

1. A review of Table 4–2 in the textbook provides information for the following responses.
a. Expected return of plan A = 0.5(0.20) + 0.5(0.05)
= 0.10 + 0.025
= 0.125 = 12.5 percent.
b. Expected return of plan B = 0.5(1.10) + 0.5(−0.40)
= 0.55 − 0.20
= 0.35.

c. The better strategy depends upon each firm's risk/return trade-off. Plan B has the highest expected value, but it is also a riskier strategy due to the higher variability of possible returns.

3. The purpose of Problems 2 and 3 is to clarify the concepts of *risk* and *risk aversion*. The expected value of each of the four lotteries is $500. The problems put the student in the position of already owning the lottery tickets, rather than having to buy them, so as to avoid having students refuse to answer because of lack of funds. Where the gamble is very small in relation to the decision maker's wealth, the selling price if rights are already owned approximately equals the purchase price if the rights are not owned. Where the gamble

Figure S–3

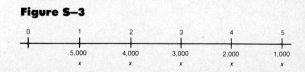

Table S–3

Heads on Throw Number	Probability	Payoff	Weighted Outcome
1	$\frac{1}{2}$	1	$\frac{1}{2}$
2	$\frac{1}{4}$	2	$\frac{1}{2}$
3	$\frac{1}{8}$	4	$\frac{1}{2}$
4	$\frac{1}{16}$	8	$\frac{1}{2}$
5	$\frac{1}{32}$	16	$\frac{1}{2}$
.	.	.	.
.	.	.	.
.	.	.	.
n	$\frac{1}{2}^{n}$	2^{n-1}	$\frac{1}{2}$
.	.	.	.
.	.	.	.
.	.	.	.

Table S–4

Wealth (dollars)	Maximum Payment to Play (dollars)
0	2
10	3
100	4
1,000	6

$$SP = \text{Value} = \frac{E(V)}{1 + K}$$

where E/V is the expected value in dollars and where K is the required rate of return *(RRR)*.

5. This problem is intended only for more advanced students with good grounding in probability theory. The mathematical expectation of the gamble (from Paul's viewpoint) is infinite, as shown in Table S–3. Thus, the following equation is applicable:

$$\text{Expected value} = \frac{1}{2} + \frac{1}{2} + \frac{1}{2} + \ldots = \infty$$

Bernoulli used this problem to expose the fallacy in choosing among uncertain prospects solely on the basis of expected value, pointing out that such an approach ignores the riskiness of the gamble and the decision maker's attitude toward risk. He went on to suggest that decision makers' risk preferences might be approximated by a logarithmic utility function, a suggestion that has spawned research that continues to this day. Assuming that a player's utility function was logarithmic, Bernoulli showed that the maximum amount he would pay for a chance to play the game is a function of his wealth (in ducats), as shown in Table S–4. A risk-averse person offering the gamble to others would charge an entry fee that depended on his initial wealth; the lower is the wealth, the higher would be the fee.

7. If interest rates on government bonds have fallen to 12 percent, the value of the 10 semiannual payments and the repayment of principal is recalculated as follows:

$$P_1 = PV = \sum_{t=1}^{N} \frac{C_t}{(1 + R)^t} = \sum_{t=1}^{10} \frac{\$41.25}{(1.06)^t} + \frac{\$1,000}{(1.06)^{10}}$$

$$= \$41.25 \left(PV \text{ annuity factor for 10 periods at } \frac{0.12}{2} \right)$$

= 6 percent + $1,000 (*PV* factor for 10 periods at 6 percent)
= $41.25(7.360) + $1,000(0.558)
= $861.60.

Now solve for return *(R)* such that

$$P_0 = \$798.75 = \sum_{t=1}^{2} \frac{C_t}{(1 + R)^t} = \frac{\$41.25}{(1 + R)} + \frac{\$41.25 + \$861.60}{(1 + R)^2}.$$

is not small in relation to wealth, in general the selling price would be greater than the purchase price. The manner in which the lottery tickets were obtained is, of course, unimportant; any costs are sunk. The sale price for rights to a given lottery represents the seller's certainty equivalent for the uncertain prospect. Risk-averse individuals will assign a value to the lotteries less than the expected value and risk preferent individuals a value greater. Risk-averse individuals assign progressively lower values as the lotteries become more risky. In solving this problem, the following two questions have been found useful:

a. Why would a given individual assign different values (different certainty equivalents) to different lotteries? This action would be taken because the lotteries vary in riskiness.

b. Why would different individuals assign different values to the same lottery? These actions would be taken because of differences in attitude toward risk.

By posing the questions in this way, the student can see a clear distinction between *risk*—a function of the investment opportunity (probabilities and payoffs) having nothing to do with the investor—and *attitude toward risk*—a function of the preferences of the investor. Use of expected value for decision making is inadequate, because it ignores investors' attitudes toward risk. The student can make the connection between risk, risk aversion, and the required rate of return by noting the following:

$$1 + \text{Expected return (percent)} = \frac{\text{Expected value (dollars)}}{SP}$$

where *SP* is the selling price set by the individual. The individual is willing to forgo an amount just under *SP* in order to retain rights to the lottery. By retaining the lottery, the individual establishes his or her expected return. Presumably, the *SP* will be set so that the expected return equals the individual's required return. Rearranging the elements of the equation yields this result:

Table S–5

State (1)	Probability (2)	(Probability) × (R_X) (3)	$R_X - E(R_X)$ (4)	$[R_X - E(R_X)]^2$ (5)	σ_X^2 (6) = (5) × (2)	σ_X
A	0.2	= 8	25	625	125	
B	0.2	− 2	− 25	625	125	
C	0.2	7	20	400	80	
D	0.2	− 1	− 20	400	80	
E	0.2	3	0	0	0	
		$E(R_X) = 15$		2,050	410	20.24

By trial and error, the following result is generated:

$$R \cong 0.09/6 \text{ months}$$
$$= 0.18/\text{year.}$$

Notice that when market interest rates dropped from 13.22 percent to 12 percent, the price of the bond rose from $798.75 to $861.60. The return to someone who bought the bond at $798.75 consisted of interest payments plus a capital gain on the sale of the bond, for a total return of 18 percent.

9. Application of the simple earnings model in Appendix 4A should generate the following results:

$$D_1 = (1.25)(1.20) = 1.50.$$
$$D_2 = (1.25)(1.20)^2 = 1.80.$$
$$D_3 = (1.25)(1.20)^3 = 2.16.$$
$$P_3 = \frac{D_4}{K - g} = \frac{2.16(1.10)}{0.14 - 0.10} = \$59.40.$$
$$P_0 = \frac{1.50}{(1.14)} + \frac{1.80}{(1.14)^2} + \frac{2.16}{(1.14)^3} + \frac{59.40}{(1.14)^3}$$
$$= 1.32 + 1.39 + 1.46 + 40.09$$
$$= \$44.26.$$

11. The earnings model assumes no growth and 100 percent payout of earnings, whereas the dividend-growth model assumes that part of the earnings stream is reinvested each year, causing the earnings stream to be a growing stream. Because of the large change in inflation from 1966 to 1979 (actual inflation as well as anticipated future inflation), the use of historical data from these years to project future growth is highly questionable. In this case, the simple earnings model probably provides the better estimate of the market required return.

13. Application of the earnings-valuation model generates the following result:

$$K = \frac{E}{PV} = \frac{1}{12} = 8.333 \text{ percent.}$$

However, Kodak does not pay out 100 percent of its earnings, and the market undoubtedly expects some real growth in the earnings stream due to reinvestment. So the earnings model likely understates the return the market expects on Kodak.

15. If the ACC bond were equal in risk to government bonds, we would expect the price to be equal to the present value of the $120 coupons and the face value of $1,000 discounted at the risk-free 9 percent rate of return.

$$P_b = \$120 \ (6.418) + \$1,000(0.422)$$
$$= \$1,192.16.$$

That is, the bond sells for $192.16 less because it is more risky.

Chapter 5

1. The expected return and standard deviation in each case can be calculated as follows:

$$E(R_A) = 0.10(0.10) + 0.20(0.12) + 0.30(0.15) + 0.40(0.20)$$
$$= 0.159$$

Table S–6

State (1)	Probability (2)	(Probability) × (R_Y) (3)	$R_Y - E(R_Y)$ (4)	$[R_Y - E(R_Y)]^2$ (5)	σ_Y^2 (6) = (5) × (2)	σ_Y
A	0.2	5.6	13	169	33.8	
B	0.2	4.0	5	25	5.0	
C	0.2	8.2	26	676	135.2	
D	0.2	− 3.4	− 32	1,024	204.8	
E	0.2	0.6	− 12	144	28.8	
		$E(R_Y) = 15$		2,030	407.6	20.19

$\sigma_A = \sqrt{(0.10 - 0.159)^2\, 0.10 + (0.12 - 0.159)^2\, 0.20 + (0.15 - 0.159)^2\, 0.30 + (0.20 - 0.159)^2\, 0.40}$

$= 0.0367$

$E(R_B) = 0.15(0.08) + 0.15(0.10) + 0.15(0.18) + 0.55(0.24)$

$= 0.186$

$\sigma_B = \sqrt{(0.08 - 0.186)^2\, 0.15 + (0.10 - 0.186)^2\, 0.15 + (0.18 - 0.186)^2\, 0.15 + (0.24 - 0.186)^2\, 0.55}$

$= 0.0664$

Investment B has the larger standard deviation of returns, so it appears to be riskier. The ratio of risk to return (referred to as the coefficient of variation) is also higher for B.

$$CV_A = \frac{\sigma_A}{E(R_A)} = \frac{0.0367}{0.159} = 0.23$$

$$CV_B = \frac{\sigma_B}{E(R_B)} = \frac{0.0664}{0.186} = 0.36$$

3. a. See Tables S-5 and S-6.
   b. See Table S-7.

$$\rho = \frac{\text{cov}\,(R_X, R_Y)}{\sigma_X\,\sigma_Y} = \frac{\sigma_{XY}^2}{\sigma_X\,\sigma_Y} = \frac{272}{(20.24)(20.19)}$$

$$= \frac{272}{408.65} = 0.67$$

$E(R_p) = 0.5\,[E(R_X)] + 0.5\,[E(R_Y)]$

$= 0.5(15) + 0.5(15)$

$= 15$ percent.

$\sigma_p^2 = X^2\,\sigma_X^2 + (1 - X)^2\,\sigma_Y^2 + 2(X)(1 - X)\,\sigma_{XY}^2$ or

$\sigma_p^2 = X^2\,\sigma_X^2 + (1 - X)^2\,\sigma_Y^2 + 2(X)(1 - X)\,\rho\,\sigma_X\,\sigma_Y$

$= (5)^2(410) + (0.5)^2(407.6) + 2(0.5)(0.5)(0.67)(20.24)(20.19)$

$= (0.25)(410) + (0.25)(407.6) + 2(0.25)(0.67)(20.24)(20.19)$

$= 102.5 + 101.9 + 136.90$

$= 341.3.$

$\sigma_p = \sigma_p^2 = 18.47$

c. Results of the calculations are summarized in Table S–8.

d. A risk-averse investor would always choose portfolio XY because it provides the same return as X and Y but with less risk. If risk were measured along the horizontal axis and expected return were measured along the vertical axis, point XY, point Y, and point X would points along an imaginary horizontal line at an expected return of 15 percent, but XY would be furthest to the left (lowest in risk), Y would be in the middle, and X would be furthest to the right (highest in risk).

Table S-7

State (1)	Probability (2)	$R_X - E(R_X)$ (3)	$R_Y - E(R_Y)$ (4)	$(5) = (3) \times (4)$	σ_{XY}^2 $(6) = (2) \times (5)$
A	0.2	25	13	325	65
B	0.2	-25	5	-125	-25
C	0.2	20	26	520	104
D	0.2	-20	-32	640	128
E	0.2	0	-12	0	0
		$E(R_Y) = 15$		1,360	272

Table S–8

	E(R) (percent)	σ^2	σ
X	15	410.0	20.24
Y	15	407.6	20.19
XY	15	341.3	18.47

Table S–9

	Year 1	Year 2	Year 3	Year 4
Working capital	15,800	20,100	24,300	26,400
Net working capital	250	4,000	8,400	6,900
Net operating capital	5,800	9,700	12,900	12,500

Table S–10

	Year 1	Year 2	Year 3	Year 4
Sales	48,200	60,600	72,500	81,400
Cost of goods sold	(35,600)	(46,000)	(56,200)	(63,100)
Selling, general, and administrative expense	(4,100)	(5,500)	(7,100)	(7,700)
Interest	(1,525)	(1,650)	(1,530)	(1,686)
Taxes	(2,100)	(2,200)	(2,400)	(2,700)
After-tax cash flow	4,875	5,250	5,270	6,214

Table S–11

	Year 1	Year 2	Year 3	Year 4
Profit after tax	2,475	2,650	2,670	3,114
Depreciation	2,200	2,400	2,400	2,900
Amortization of goodwill	200	200	200	200
After-tax cash flow	4,875	5,250	5,270	6,214

Chapter 6

Note: Goodwill is included in the Acme financial statements to provide another non-cash charge in addition to depreciation and to include an intangible asset. Amortization of goodwill is not tax deductible and is not reflected in the taxes shown in the income statements.

1. Knowledge of the following relationships is essential in solving this problem:

   Working capital = current assets.
   Net working capital = current assets − current liabilities.
   Net operating capital = current assets − (current liabilities − notes payable).

   See Table S–9 for the amounts (in thousands of dollars) attributed to capital for years 1 through 4.
3. Revenues less cash expenses (in thousands of dollars) are calculated as shown in Table S–10. The shortcut method is shown in the figures (again in thousands of dollars) in Table S–11.
5. See Table S–12 for a source-and-use-of-funds statement for Fuelish Motors, Inc. for the year ending December 31, 1986.
7. An analysis of balance-sheet changes over the period is the first step in determining the sources and uses of funds, as shown in Table S–13. Using the balance-sheet analysis, a source-and-use statement for the year ending December 31, 1982, can be prepared, modeled after Table 6–10, as shown in Table S–14.

9. Following the format in Table 6–12, the source-and-use statement for year 2 (in thousands of dollars) is given in Table S–15. The statements for years 3 and 4 appear as Tables S–16 and S–17 (also in thousands of dollars).

Table S–12

Sources	
Increase in accounts payable	$ 395,200
Increase in other current liabilities	567,500
Increase in accrued liabilities	166,200
Increase in long-term debt	499,700
Decrease in marketable securities	276,100
Total sources	**$1,904,700**
Uses	
Increase in accounts receivable	$ 378,300
Increase in inventory	660,300
Increase in other current assets	89,400
Increase in net fixed assets	491,300
Increase in other assets	76,600
Decrease in taxes payable	150,800
Decrease in deferred income tax	94,400
Decrease in common stock	32,600
Decrease in retained earnings	131,200
Total uses	**$2,104,900**
Decrease in cash	**$ 200,200**

Table S–13

	1985	1986	Change
Assets			
Cash	$ 10,850	$ 431	− $10,419
Accounts receivable	41,614	68,313	+ 26,699
Inventory	82,892	80,710	− 2,182
Miscellaneous current assets	7,681	6,413	− 1,268
Total current assets	$143,037	$155,867	+ $12,830
Land	$ 42,000	$ 42,000	$ 0
Plant and equipment, net	180,759	189,805	+ 9,046
Total Assets	**$365,796**	**$387,672**	**+ $21,876**
Liabilities and net worth			
Accounts payable	$ 52,218	$ 50,946	− $ 1,272
Taxes payable	18,416	22,840	+ 4,424
Accrued expenses	15,823	13,908	− 1,915
Total current liabilities	$ 86,457	$ 87,694	+ $ 1,237
Mortgage payable	$110,000	$103,500	− $ 6,500
Paid-in capital	95,000	105,000	+ 10,000
Retained earnings	74,339	91,478	+ 17,139
Total liabilities and net worth	**$365,796**	**$387,672**	**+ $21,876**

Chapter 7

1. See Table S–18. The normalized income statement (in thousands of dollars) shows that cost of goods sold and selling, general, and administrative expenses increased in years 2 and 3. Management should investigate the reasons. The decline in interest expense may indicate less reliance on debt financing.

3. The company is obviously enjoying a healthy increase in sales and profits, although the return on assets (ROA) seems to imply that things could be even better. We know that ROA = margin × turnover, and, because we know ROA and can find the margin from the information given, we can solve for turnover as shown in Table S–19. It appears that Beech's problems are due to both declining margins and slower turnover. Part of its rapid sales growth may actually be due to the lower margins and, although this area still war-

Table S–14

Sources	
Increase in taxes payable	$ 4,424
Increase in paid-in capital	10,000
Decrease in inventory	2,182
Decrease in miscellaneous current assets	1,268
Retained earnings	17,139
Total sources	**$35,013**
Uses	
Increase in accounts receivable	$26,699
Increase in net plant and equipment	9,046
Decrease in accounts payable	1,272
Decrease in accrued expenses	1,915
Decrease in mortgage payable	6,500
Total uses	**$45,432**
Decrease in cash	**$10,419**

Table S–15

Sources		
Notes payable (5,700 − 5,550)		150
Accruals (2,900 − 2,600)		300
Tax payable (1,200 − 900)		300
Senior debentures (9,000 − 7,000)		2,000
Funds from operations		
Profit after taxes	2,650	
Depreciation	2,400	
Amortization of goodwill	200	5,250
Total sources		**8,000**
Uses		
Accounts receivable (9,600 − 7,900)		1,700
Inventory (6,600 − 5,000)		1,600
Other current assets (1,100 − 1,000)		100
Plant and equipment (45,500 − 42,000)		3,500
Accounts payable (6,500 − 6,300)		200
Total uses*		**7,100**
Increase in cash (2,800 − 1,900)		**900**

*Dividends = net income − change in retained earnings = $2,650 − ($14,100 − $11,450) = 0.

Table S–16

Sources		
Accounts payable (7,400 − 6,300)		1,100
Accruals (3,000 − 2,900)		100
Funds from operations:		
Profit after taxes	2,670	
Depreciation	2,400	
Amortization of goodwill	200	5,270
Total sources		**6,470**
Uses		
Accounts receivable (11,400 − 9,600)		1,800
Inventory (7,200 − 6,600)		600
Notes payable (5,700 − 4,500)		1,200
Tax payable (1,200 − 1,000)		200
Dividends*		870
Total uses		**4,670**
Increase in cash (4,600 − 2,800)		**1,800**

*Dividends = $2,670 − ($15,900 − $14,100) = $870.

rants further investigation, the more severe problem appears to be in the rapid decline in turnover. The company seems to be employing an inordinate amount of assets, and the investigation should begin there. An analysis of changes in inventory and accounts receivable would be a good place to start.

5. a. The troublesome ratios, in terms of both trend and comparison to the industry norms, appear to be inventory turnover (ITO), days of purchases outstanding (DPO), current ratio (CR), acid-test ratio (ATR), debt to total assets (DTA), and times interest earned (TIE). The low and declining ITO indicates that the company does have an inventory problem. If we assume that sales are growing, we can conclude that inventories are too high. The truth of this conclusion is partially confirmed by the rapid decline

Table S–18

	Year 1	Year 2	Year 3	Year 4
Sales (percent)	100.0	100.0	100.0	100.0
Cost of goods sold	73.9	75.9	77.5	77.5
Gross profit	26.1	24.1	22.5	22.5
Depreciation	4.6	4.0	3.3	3.6
Amortization of goodwill	0.4	0.3	0.3	0.2
Selling, general, administrative	8.5	9.1	9.8	9.5
Income from operations	12.6	10.7	9.1	9.2
Interest	3.2	2.7	2.1	2.1
Taxable income	9.4	8.0	7.0	7.1
Taxes	4.3	3.6	3.3	3.3
New income	5.1	4.4	3.7	3.8

Table S–17

Sources		
Notes payable (5,600 − 4,500)		1,100
Inventory (8,900 − 7,400)		1,500
Accruals (3,200 − 3,000)		200
Tax payable (1,800 − 1,000)		800
Subordinated debentures (9 percent)		
(8,000 − 7,000)		1,000
Common stock and surplus		
(12,500 − 10,500)		2,000
Funds from operations		
Profit after taxes	3,114	
Depreciaion	2,900	
Amortization of goodwill	200	6,214
Total sources		**12,814**
Uses		
Accounts receivable		
(13,600 − 11,400)		2,200
Inventory (8,900 − 7,200)		1,700
Other current assets		
(1,200 − 1,100)		100
Plant and equipment		
[54,500 − (45,500 − 600)]		9,600
Dividends*		1,114
Total uses		**14,714**
Decrease in cash (4,600 − 2,700)		**1,900**

*Dividends = $3,114 − ($17,900 − $15,900) = $1,114.

in the CR coupled with a somewhat less severe decline in the ATR. That the ATR is also declining does hint at the possibility that some other current account is also involved, and the high and increasing DPO indicates that the accounts payable may be too high. Finally, the high and increasing DTA ratio coupled with a steady debt/net worth ratio implies that debt is expanding faster than assets. The declining TIE could be attributed to lower profits and higher debt, and, thus, does not supply much new information. In short, the company appears to be expanding inventory too rapidly and relying too heavily on trade credit. The analysis should probably begin with these two accounts.

b. First, every company is unique, and it is difficult to set up

Table S–19

	1982	1983	1984	1985	1986
Margin (percent)	5.0	4.9	4.7	4.5	4.2
Turnover	1.68	1.63	1.53	1.07	0.74
Return on assets	8.4	8.0	7.2	4.8	3.1

Table S–20

	1985	1986	Change
Assets			
Cash	$ 4,000	$ 5,000	+$1,000
Accounts receivable	5,000	4,000	– 1,000
Inventory	10,000	14,000	+ 4,000
Total current assets	**$19,000**	**$23,000**	**+ $4,000**
Liabilities			
Accounts payable	$ 3,000	$ 5,000	+$2,000
Notes payable (short-term)	4,000	3,000	– 1,000
Total current liabilities	**$ 7,000**	**$ 8,000**	**+$1,000**
Net working capital	**$12,000**	**$15,000**	**+$3,000**

a specific classification. Second, companies differ in a number of accounting practices such as depreciation, inventory evaluation, and recognition of income. Finally, median ratios are not necessarily optimal.

7. a. Evaluating current position requires examining liquidity ratios.

Current ratio:

$$\text{Company A: } \frac{\$1,000 + \$4,000}{\$1,000} = \frac{\$5,000}{\$1,000} = 5.0$$

$$\text{Company B: } \frac{\$4,000 + \$2,000}{\$2,000} = \frac{\$6,000}{\$2,000} = 3.0$$

Acid-test ratio:

$$\text{Company A: } \frac{\$1,000}{\$1,000} = 1.0$$

$$\text{Company B: } \frac{\$4,000}{\$2,000} = 2.0$$

Company A appears to have a better current position when one includes inventory in the current category. However, disregarding the inventory as a liquid source of funds, company B appears to have the better current position.

b. This problem requires the student to calculate a ratio that has no formula provided in the text material, thus encouraging creativity in using ratio analysis. A working-capital turnover ratio can be formulated as follows:

$$\text{Working-capital turnover} = \frac{\text{Sales}}{\text{Net working capital}}.$$

This is very similar to the asset-turnover ratio provided in the text. For each company, therefore, the working capital turnover rates are:

$$\text{Company A: } \frac{\$3,000}{\$4,000} = 0.75 \text{ times}$$

$$\text{Company B: } \frac{\$9,000}{\$4,000} = 2.25 \text{ times}$$

c. The profit margin for both firms is calculated as follows:

Table S–21

Dividends	
Retained earnings, December 31, 1985	$12,000
plus	
Net income for 1986	+ 10,000
minus	
Retained earnings, December 31, 1986	– 18,000
equals	
Dividends paid during 1986	$4,000
Depreciation	
Fixed assets, December 31, 1985	$25,000
plus	
Fixed assets purchased during 1986	+ 5,000
minus	
Fixed assets, December 31, 1986	– 28,000
equals	
Depreciation during 1986	$2,000

$$\text{Company A: } \frac{(\$3,000 - \$1,900 - \$400 - \$10 - \$240)}{\$3,000}$$

$$= \frac{\$450}{\$3,000} = 15 \text{ percent}$$

$$\text{Company B: } \frac{(\$9,000 - \$6,900 - \$1,600 - \$110 - \$300)}{\$9,000}$$

$$= \frac{\$90}{\$9,000} = 1 \text{ percent}$$

The profit margin of company A is much greater than that of company B.

d. Book value (A) per share = $310. Book value (B) = $118.

e. Return on assets is calculated as follows:

$$\text{Company A: } \frac{(\$3,000 - \$1,900 - \$400 - \$10 - \$240)}{(\$1,000 + \$4,000 + \$5,000 + \$400)}$$

$$= \frac{\$450}{\$10,400} = 4.33 \text{ percent}$$

$$\text{Company B: } \frac{(\$9,000 - \$6,900 - \$1,600 - \$110 - \$300)}{(\$4,000 + \$2,000 + \$19,000 + \$100)}$$

$$= \frac{\$90}{\$25,100} = 0.36 \text{ percent}$$

Company A provides a better return on the utilization of assets, as measured by the return on assets.

9. a. The change in working capital is determined by first identifying the working capital accounts and then calculating the net change in these accounts over the period, as shown in Table S–20 (in thousands of dollars).

b. A detailed source-and-use statement requires the computation of dividends paid and depreciation, as shown in Table S–21, along with changes in the balance sheet over the period as shown in Table S–22. The resulting source-and-use statement appears as Table S–23. (Figures in these tables are shown in thousands of dollars.)

Table S–22

	1985	1986	Change
Assets			
Cash	$ 4,000	$ 5,000	+$1,000
Accounts receivable	5,000	4,000	− 1,000
Inventory	10,000	14,000	+ 4,000
Net fixed assets	25,000	28,000	+ 3,000
Total Assets	**$44,000**	**$51,000**	**+$7,000**
Liabilities and net worth			
Accounts payable	$ 3,000	$ 5,000	+$2,000
Notes payable	4,000	3,000	− 1,000
Long-term notes payable	10,000	6,000	− 4,000
Common stock	15,000	19,000	+ 4,000
Retained earnings	12,000	18,000	+ 6,000
Total liabilities and net worth	**$44,000**	**$51,000**	**+$7,000**

Table S–23

Sources		
Increase in accounts payable		$ 2,000
Decrease in accounts receivable		1,000
Common stock		4,000
Funds from operations		
Profit after taxes	$10,000	
Depreciation	2,000	12,000
Total sources		**$19,000**
Uses		
Increases in inventory		$ 4,000
Increase in gross fixed assets		5,000
Decrease in short-term notes payable		1,000
Decrease in long-term notes payable		4,000
Dividends		4,000
Total uses		**$18,000**
Increase in cash		**$ 1,000**

11. The break-even point in units can be calculated from Equation (15):

$$Q_b = \frac{FC}{P - VC} = \frac{\$3,000,000}{\$30 - \$18} = 250,000 \text{ units.}$$

The break-even point on a cash basis can be calculated from Equation (16):

$$Q_c = \frac{FC_C}{P - VC} = \frac{\$3,000,000 - \$900,000}{\$30 - \$18} = 175,000 \text{ units.}$$

13. The following formula is used to solve this problem:

$$DOL = \frac{S - VC}{S - VC - FC}.$$

The calculations proceed as follows:

Sales at 300,000 units = 300,000 × $30 = $9,000,000.
Sales at 400,000 units = 400,000 × $30 = $12,000,000.
VC at 300,000 units = 300,000 × $18 = $5,400,000.
VC at 400,000 units = 400,000 × $18 = $7,200,000.

DOL at 300,000 units

$$= \frac{\$9,000,000 - \$5,400,000}{\$9,000,000 - \$5,400,000 - \$3,000,000} = 6.$$

DOL at 400,000 units

$$= \frac{\$12,000,000 - \$7,200,000}{\$12,000,000 - \$7,200,000 - \$3,000,000} = 2.67.$$

15. a. The break-even chart in Figure S–4 indicates a break-even volume of approximately 13,500,000 units. Using the formula provided, break-even volume is calculated as follows:

Contribution to profit = $1.00 − 0.4036 = $0.5964/unit.

$$Q_b = \frac{FC}{P - VC} = \frac{\$8,125,000}{\$0.5964} = 13,623,407 \text{ units.}$$

b. An increase in sales price decreases break-even volume and increases the contribution to profit.

Contribution to profit = $1.05 − 0.4036 = 0.6464/unit.

$$\text{Break-even volume} = \frac{\$8,125,000}{\$0.6464} = 12,569,616 \text{ units.}$$

Profit increases by 14 million × $0.05 = $700,000. The break-even point declines by 1,053,791 units.

c. A decrease in fixed costs increases profits by the amount of the decrease ($406,250) and decreases break-even volume.

$$\text{Break-even volume} = \frac{\$8,125,000 - 0.05(\$8,125,000)}{\$0.5964}$$
$$= 12,942,237 \text{ units.}$$

FIGURE S–4

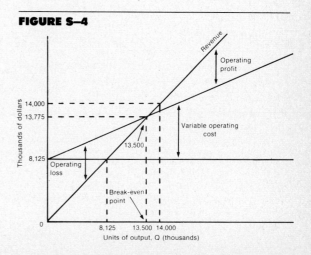

Table S–24

Sales		$20,000,000
Cost of sales		
Fixed	$4,060,000	
Variable[a]	7,000,000	11,060,000
Gross margin		$ 8,940,000
Selling and general expenses	$2,845,000	
Fixed		
Variable[b]	3,200,000	6,045,000
Net income		$ 2,895,000

[a]Variable cost of sales per unit = $\dfrac{\$4,240,000}{12,200,000}$ = $0.35/unit.

[b]Variable selling and general expenses = $\dfrac{\$1,950,000}{12,200,000}$ = $0.16/unit.

d. A decrease in variable costs decreases break-even volume and increases the contribution to profit.

Contribution to profit = $1.00 − [0.4036 − 0.05(0.4036)]
= $0.6166/unit.

Break-even volume = $\dfrac{\$8,125,000}{\$0.6166}$ = 13,177,000 units.

Profit increases by 0.05(0.4036)(14,000,000) = $282,520.

e. All three methods, implemented simultaneously, would have the effect of decreasing break-even volume, increasing per-unit contribution to profit, and increasing profit directly.

Contribution to profit = $1.05 − [0.4036 − 0.05 (0.4036)]
= $0.6666/unit.

Total increase in contribution at 14,000,000 units = (0.6666 − 0.5964) × 14,000,000 = $982,800.

Break-even volume = $\dfrac{\$8,125,000 - 0.05(\$8,125,000)}{\$0.6666}$

= 11,579,283 units.

Direct increase in profits = (0.05)($8,125,000) = $406,250.
Total increase in profit = $406,250 + $982,800 = $1,389,050.

17. a. See Table S–24 for projected income for 1987. It is necessary to classify the expenses listed as either fixed or variable expenses.

b. The break-even point at present (1986) operating levels is calculated as follows:

P = $1.00/unit.
VC = $0.35 + 0.16 = $0.51/unit.
FC = $3,910,000 + $1,500,000 = $5,410,000.

Break-even volume = $\dfrac{FC}{P - VC}$ = $\dfrac{\$5,410,000}{\$1.00 - \$0.51}$

= 11,040,816 units.

Table S–25

Sales	$2,025,000
Cost of goods sold	1,335,000
Gross profit	$ 690,000
Depreciation	136,000
Selling and administrative	240,000
Interest	40,000
Profit before taxes	$ 274,000
Tax at 46 percent	126,040
Net income	$ 147,960

The break-even point at projected (1987) operating levels is calculated as follows:

FC = $4,060,000 + $2,845,000 = $6,905,000.

Break-even volume = $\dfrac{\$6,905,000}{\$0.49}$ = 14,091,837 units.

c. After expansion, the fixed costs will reduce the profit level by $1,495,000. If sales volume were to remain at the current level of 12,200,000 units, there would be a net loss of $895,000.

Chapter 8

1. See Table S–25 for a pro-forma income statement for Hi-Tech Manufacturing for 1987.
3. See Table S–26 for a pro-forma balance sheet for Hi-Tech Manufacturing for 1987.
5. a. The pro-forma balance sheet for December 31, 1987 is given in Table S–27. Major items were calculated as follows:

Table S–26

Assets	
Cash	$ 67,042
Accounts receivable	305,137
Inventory	124,186
Total current assets	$ 496,365
Gross plant and equipment	1,975,000
Less depreciation	1,099,000
Net plant and equipment	$ 876,000
Total assets	**$1,372,365**
Liabilities and Net Worth	
Bank loan	$ 0
Accounts payable	59,905
Accrued labor	60,000
Taxes payable	0
Accrued overhead	10,000
Total current liabilities	$ 129,905
Debentures	500,000
Common stock	300,000
Retained earnings	442,460
Total liabilities and net worth	**$1,372,365**

Table S–27

Assets		Liabilities and Deferred Taxes	
		Current liabilities	$ 6,208.00
		Deferred taxes	3,685.50
		Long-term debt	18,036.00
		Common stock par	575.00
Total assets	$66.508.00	Capital (excess of par)	7,945.00
		Retained earnings	18,664.00
		Total (preliminary)	$55,113.50
		Balancing source	11,394.50
		Total liabilities and deferred taxes	$66,508.00

Assets = [$51,250/$46,235] × $60,000 = $66,508.
Current liabilities = [$4,784/$46,235] × $60,000 = $6,208.
Deferred taxes = [$2,840/$46,235] × $60,000 = $3,685.50.
Retained earnings = 1986 RE + Profit after taxes (PAT)
= $17,070 + $1,594 = $18,664, where PAT
= [$1,228/$46,235] × $60,000 = $1,594.

b. Harrington would need to have a profit after taxes (PAT) such that retained earnings would total $18,664 plus the shortfall of $11,394.50. That is, retained earnings would have to be $30,058.50 for there to be no need for external financing. This figure would represent an increase of $30,058 − $17,070 = $12,988.50 over 1986 retained earnings. For PAT to be $12,988.50, the after-tax profit margin would have to be $12,988.50/$60,000 = 0.216.

c. Since dividends would represent addtional outflows (reducing increments to retained earnings out of any given PAT), more financing would be needed (dollar for dollar) as dividends were paid.

d. The approach outlined above misses seasonal financing needs and fails to distinguish between cash and noncash items. As a result, the calculated figure of $11,394.50 should be viewed as a starting point for planning the financing. Further (more detailed) analysis is needed.

7. On December 31, 1987, there will be an accounts receivable balance of $76,959 composed of:

15 percent of October sales	$ 7,190
65 percent of November sales	28,769
100 percent of December sales	41,000
Balance	$76,959

9. See Table S–28 for pro-forma income statements for Hi-Tech for each month of 1987 (in thousands of dollars).

11. See Table S–29 for a pro-forma monthly cash budget for Hi-Tech for 1987 (in thousands of dollars).

Chapter 9

1. a. See Tables S–30 and S–31. Calculating the depreciation tax shield for machine A is done as follows:

Depreciation = $10,000/5 = $2,000.
Depreciation tax shield = $2,000 × 0.40 = $800.

Applying the same formula to machine B yields the following result:

$$\text{Depreciation tax shield} = \frac{\$7,500}{5} \times 0.040 = \$600.$$

b. If one of the machines must be selected, it should be machine A; otherwise, neither should be chosen because both have a negative net present value.

3. a. Project X should be chosen because it generates the highest net present value (NPV).

b. Project X again should be chosen. The combination of projects W and Y exhausts the $300 budget but provides a total NPV of $55, lower than the $70 provided by project X. Note that the choice of project X leaves $100 in the budget, but this $100 cannot be spent profitably. Using it to invest in project Z would decrease the value of the firm by $10. Therefore, the $100 should be invested for use next period or paid out to investors as a dividend.

5. The key to this problem is to recognize that the cost of the building and the renovation expense are sunk costs while depreciation and property taxes have no incremental influence. Thus, all these items can be ignored in the analysis. The major changes that occur with the warehousing alternative as the base are: (1) Accepting the lease decreases upkeep expense by $25,000, for a cash flow of $25,000(1 − 0.40) = $15,000. (2) Accepting the lease increases revenue by $300,000, for a cash flow of $300,000(1 − 0.40) = $180,000. (3) Accepting the lease increases costs by $400,000, for a cash flow of ($400,000)(1 − 0.40) = ($240,000), a result based on the assumption that Chatham would revert to its existing storage arrangements. In summary, the cash-flow table would show a net outflow of $15,000 + $180,000 − $240,000 = ($45,000) per year for each of the 30 years. Thus, the lease alternative would result in a net disadvantage and should be rejected.

7. a. 0 = $27,000 + $4,000 (PV annuity factor for 13 years).
$27,000 = $4,000 (Present-value annuity factor).
$$\frac{\$27,000}{\$4,000} = \text{Present-value annuity factor.}$$
6.75 = Present-value annuity factor.

Table S-28

	January	February	March	April	May	June	July	August	September	October	November	December	1987
Sales	$ 180	$ 150	$ 130	$ 120	$130	$ 160	$ 175	$ 200	$ 180	$ 160	$ 200	$ 240	$ 2,025
Cost of goods sold													
Material expense	54	45	39	36	39	48	52.5	60	54	48	60	72	607.5
Labor expense	54	45	39	36	39	48	52.5	60	54	48	60	72	607.5
Overhead	10	10	10	10	10	10	10	10	10	10	10	10	120
Total cost of goods sold	$ 118	$ 100	$ 88	$ 82	$ 88	$ 106	$ 115	$ 130	$ 118	$ 106	$ 130	$ 154	$ 1,335
Gross profit	$62	$50	$42	$38	$42	$54	$60	$70	$118	$54	$70	$86	$690
Depreciation	10	10	10	10	12	12	12	12	12	12	12	12	136
Selling and administrative	20	20	20	20	20	20	20	20	20	20	20	20	240
Interest	0	0	0	0	0	20	0	0	0	0	0	20	40
Profit before taxes	$32	$20	$12	$8	$10	$2	$28	$38	$30	$22	$38	$34	$274
Tax (at 46 percent)	14.72	9.2	5.52	3.68	4.6	0.92	12.88	17.48	13.8	10.12	17.48	15.64	126.04
Net income	$17.28	$10.8	$6.48	$4.32	$5.4	$1.08	$15.12	$20.52	$16.2	$11.88	$20.52	$18.36	$147.96

Table S-29

	January	February	March	April	May	June	July	August	September	October	November	December
Receipts												
Cash sales	$ 18	$ 15	$ 13	$ 12	$ 13	$ 16	$ 17.5	$ 20	$ 18	$ 16	$ 20	$ 24
Accounts receivable (1 month)	103.5	81	67.5	58.5	54	58.5	72	78.75	90	81	72	90
Accounts receivable (2 months)	85.5	103.5	81	67.5	58.5	54	58.5	72	78.75	90	81	72
Total receipts	$207.0	$199.5	$161.5	$138.0	$125.5	$128.5	$148.0	$170.75	$186.75	$187.0	$173.0	$186.0
Disbursements												
Payment of accounts payable	54	45	39	36	39	48	52.5	60	54	48	60	72
Payment of labor	54	45	39	36	39	48	52.5	60	54	48	60	72
Overhead	10	10	10	10	10	10	10	10	10	10	10	10
Bond interest						20						20
Capital expense				175								
Selling and administrative	20	20	20	20	20	20	20	20	20	20	20	20
Tax payments				33.12		5.52			44.16			43.24
Total disbursements	$138.0	$120.0	$108.0	$310.12	$108.0	$151.52	$135.0	$150.0	$182.16	$126.0	$150.0	$237.24
Receipts less disbursements	$ 69.0	$ 79.5	$ 53.5	($172.12)	$ 17.5	($ 23.02)	$ 13.0	$ 20.75	$ 4.59	$ 61.0	$ 23.0	($ 51.24)
Add beginning cash balance	20.0	39.0	118.5	172.0	20.0	20.0	20.0	20.0	28.11	32.70	93.70	116.70
	$ 89.0	$118.5	$172.0	($ 0.12)	$ 37.5	($ 3.02)	$ 33.0	$ 40.75	$32.70	$ 93.76	$116.70	$ 65.46
Loan increase (decrease)	($50.0)	$118.5	$172.0	$ 20.12	($17.5)	$23.02	($13.0)	($12.64)	$32.70	$93.76	$116.70	$65.46
Ending cash balance	$39.0			$20.0	$20.0	$20.0	$20.0	$28.11	$ 0	$ 0	$ 0	$ 0
Ending loan	$ 0	$ 0	$ 0	$ 0	$2.62	$25.64	$12.64	$ 0				

Table S–30

Year	Outlay	Depreciation Tax Shield	After-Tax Savings	After-Tax Cash Flow	Present Value Factor at 10 percent	Present Value
0	($10,000)			($10,000)	1.000	($10,000)
1		$800	$1,800	$ 2,600	0.909	$ 2,363
2		$800	$1,800	$ 2,600	0.826	$ 2,148
3		$800	$1,800	$ 2,600	0.751	$ 1,953
4		$800	$1,500	$ 2,300	0.683	$ 1,571
5		$800	$1,500	$ 2,300	0.621	$ 1,428
					Net Present Value at 10 percent =	($537)

Reading across the annuity factor for 13 years in Appendix Table II at the end of the textbook enables the student to see that the annuity factor = 6.75 at 11 percent.

b. $27,000 = $3,000 (Present-value annuity factor for 16 years).

$$\frac{\$27,000}{\$3,000} = \text{Present-value annuity factor.}$$

$$9 = \text{Present-value annuity factor.}$$

For 16 years the annuity factor is 9.447 at 7 percent and 8.851 at 8 percent. Interpolating provides the following result:

$$\left(\frac{9.447 - 9.000}{9.447 - 8.851}\right) = \frac{0.447}{0.596} = 0.75.$$

Thus, the internal rate of return = 7.75 percent.

c. $7,070 = $1,400 (PV annuity factor for 16 years).

$$\frac{\$7,070}{\$1,400} = \text{Present-value annuity factor.}$$

$$5.05 = \text{Present-value annuity factor.}$$

For 16 years the annuity factor is 5.162 at 18 percent and 4.938 at 19 percent. Interpolating provides the following result:

$$\left(\frac{5.162 - 5.05}{5.162 - 4.938}\right) = \frac{0.112}{0.224} = 0.5.$$

Thus, the internal rate of return = 18.5 percent.

9. The net present value (NPV) for the investment described in Part (a) of Problem (6) is calculated as follows:

$$
\begin{aligned}
NPV &= \$4,000 \ (PV \text{ factor for 13 years at 12 percent}) - \$27,000 \\
&= \$4,000 \ (6.424) - \$27,000 \\
&= \$25,696 - \$27,000 \\
&= -\$1,304.
\end{aligned}
$$

The NPV for the investment described in Part (b) of Problem (6) is calculated as follows:

$$
\begin{aligned}
NPV &= \$3,000 \ (PV \text{ factor for 16 years at 12 percent}) - \$27,000 \\
&= \$3,000 \ (6.974) - \$27,000 \\
&= -\$6,078.
\end{aligned}
$$

The NPV for the investment described in Part (c) of Problem (6) is calculated as follows:

$$
\begin{aligned}
NPV &= \$1,400 \ (PV \text{ factor for 16 years at 12 percent}) - \$7,070 \\
&= \$1,400 \ (6.974) - \$7,070 \\
&= \$2,693.60.
\end{aligned}
$$

Based on these results, the investment described in Part (c) is the one that should be accepted.

11. a. See Table S–32.
    b. Using Part (a) as the first trial, select a higher rate because the net present value (NPV) > 0 at 10 percent. The use of 15 percent as the discount rate generates the results shown

Table S–31

Year	Outlay	Depreciation Tax Shield	After-Tax Savings	After-Tax Cash Flow	Present Value Factor (10 percent)	Present Value
0	($7,500)			($7,500)	1.000	($7,500)
1		$600	$1,200	$1,800	0.909	$1,636
2		$600	$1,200	$1,800	0.826	$1,487
3		$600	$1,200	$1,800	0.751	$1,352
4		$600	$1,200	$1,800	0.683	$1,229
5		$600	$1,200	$1,800	0.621	$1,118
					Net Present Value at 10 percent =	($678)

Table S–32

Year	Cash Flow	Present Value Factor (percent)	Present Value
0	($1,000)	1.000	($1,000.00)
1	($500)	0.909	($454.50)
2	$600	0.826	$495.60
3	$800	0.751	$600.80
4	$800	0.683	$546.50
		Net present value =	$ 188.30

Table S–33

Present Value Factor	Present Value
1.000	($1,000.00)
1.000	($435.00)
0.756	$453.60
0.658	$526.40
0.572	$457.60
Net present value =	$ 2.60

in Table S–33, indicating that the internal rate of return *(IRR)* is slightly over 15 percent. Interpolating yields the following as the change in *NPV* for a 1 percent change in the discount rate:

$$\frac{\$188.30 - \$2.60}{10 - 15} = \$37.14.$$

Then solve for the *IRR* as follows:

$$IRR = 15 + \frac{\$2.60}{\$37.14} = 15.07 \text{ percent.}$$

13. a. This problem demonstrates the usefulness of DCF in evaluating financing decisions. The effective interest cost for the single-payment alternative is calculated as follows:

$$\$1,000 = \text{Present value factor } (\$1,259.45).$$
Present value factor = 0.794.

Check Appendix Table II at the end of the textbook in the row for three years to learn that the effective interest cost = 8 per cent. The effective interest cost for the annual payment alternatives is calculated as follows:

$$\$1,000 = PV \text{ annuity factor } (\$402.09).$$
Present value annuity factor = 2.487.

Check Appendix Table I at the end of the textbook in the row for three years to learn that the effective interest cost = 10 percent.

b. The single-payment alternative is preferred because it has a lower effective interest cost.

15. The maximum one should pay for the higher grade of insulation material is the present value. Use Appendix Table II at the end of the textbook to determine the present value annuity factor and solve for the present value as follows:

Present value = $650 (*PV* annuity factor for 10 years at 15 percent)
= $650 (5.019)
= $3,262.35.

17. Because the annual cash inflows are equal, the following can be concluded:

$$\text{Payback period} = \frac{\text{Outlay}}{\text{Inflow}}.$$

$$\text{Payback period} = \frac{\$5,000}{\$2,000} = 2.5 \text{ years}$$

If the $5,000 outlay is used as the investment, then the accounting-based return on investment (AROI) is calculated as follows:

$$\text{AROI} = \frac{\$1,000}{\$5,000} = 20 \text{ percent.}$$

If average investment is used, then the following is true:

$$\text{AROI} = \frac{\$1,000}{\$5,000/2} = 40 \text{ percent.}$$

20. a. Figure the payback period as follows:

$$\frac{\$1,000}{\$301.93} = 3.312 \text{ years.}$$

b. The net present value is calculated as follows:

$$\$301.93(3.312) - \$1,000 = 0.$$

c. The present value factor in Appendix Table II at the back of the textbook for *R* percent and *N* years represents the maximum payback period that an *N*-year investment can

Table S–34

Investment	Payback Period (years)
A	2
B	2.33
C	2.11

Table S–35

Net Present Values at Various Discount Rates for Investment A

Discount Rate (percent)	NPV
14	$363
15	$218
16	$67
17	− $74

Table S-36
Net Present Values at Various Discount Rates for Investment B

Discount Rate (percent)	NPV
15	$988
20	$278
22	$26
23	-$99

have and provide an internal rate of return of R percent. This interpretation is possible only for investments generating level cash inflows.

21. This problem requires the student to calculate the internal rate of return *(IRR)*, the net present value *(NPV)* and the payback period for three mutually exclusive investments. In this problem, *NPV* and *IRR* do not give the same ranking among investments because of differences in initial outlays and patterns of subsequent cash flows.

    a. Table S-34 gives the payback period for each investment. See Tables S-35 and S-36 for the net present values at various discount rates of investments A and B. $IRR_{(A)}$ is between 16 and 17 percent. Interpolating yields the following result:

Table S-37

Investment	Net Present Value
A	$218
B	$988
C	$1,255

$$\frac{74}{141} \times 1.0 \text{ percent} = 0.52 \text{ percent.}$$

$IRR_A = 17 \text{ percent} = 0.52 \text{ percent} = 16.48 \text{ percent.}$

IRR_B is between 22 and 23 percent. Interpolating yields the following result:

$$\frac{99}{125} \times 1.0 \text{ percent} = 0.79 \text{ percent.}$$

$IRR_B = 23 \text{ percent} - 0.79 \text{ percent} = 22.21 \text{ percent.}$

Similarly, the internal rate of return for investment C can be generated as follows:

$15,000 = $7,120$ (Annuity factor, r percent, $n = 3$).

$$\frac{\$15,000}{\$7,120} = 2.107.$$

$IRR_C = 20 \text{ percent.}$

Table S-38

	Project A			Project B	
Year	Cash Flow		CF × IF*	Cash Flow	CF × IF*
0	($200)		($224.98)	($200)	($224.98)
1	$200		$216.32	$100	$108.16
2	0		0	$100	$104.00
3	0		0	$100	$100.00
		Terminal value =	$ 8.66	Terminal value =	$ 87.18

	Project C			Project D	
Year	Cash Flow		CF × IF*	Cash Flow	CF × IF*
0	($200)		($224.98)	($200)	($224.98)
1	$ 20		$ 21.63	$200	$216.32
2	$100		$104.00	$ 20	$ 20.80
3	$300		$300.00	$ 20	$ 20.00
		Terminal value =	$200.65	Terminal value =	$ 32.14

	Project E			Project F	
Year	Cash Flow		CF × IF*	Cash Flow	CF × IF*
0	($200)		($224.98)	($200)	($224.98)
1	$140		$151.42	$160	$173.06
2	$ 60		$ 62.40	$160	$166.40
3	$100		$100.00	$ 80	$ 80.00
		Terminal value =	$ 88.84	Terminal value =	$194.48

*Cash flow (CF), Interest factor (IF).

Table S–39

			Cash Flow × Interest Factor			
Year	Project A	Project B	Project C	Project D	Project E	Project F
0	($675.00)	($675.00)	($675.00)	($675.00)	($675.00)	($675.00)
1	$450.00	$225.00	$ 45.00	$450.00	$315.00	$360.00
2	0	$150.00	$150.00	$ 30.00	$ 90.00	$240.00
3	0	$100.00	$300.00	$ 20.00	$100.00	$ 80.00
Terminal value =	($225.00)	($200.00)	($180.00)	($175.00)	($170.00)	$ 5.00

b. See Table S–37 for the net present value *(NPV)* for each investment at 15 percent. Investment C should be chosen, using the *NPV* criterion, since it provides the greatest *NPV* at the firm's required rate of return. However, if the internal-rate-of-return *(IRR)* criterion were used, investment B would be selected because it has the greatest *IRR*.

23. a. See Table S–38. The compound-interest factors at 4 percent are:

$$\text{Year 0: } (1 + 0.04)^3 = 1.1249.$$
$$\text{Year 1: } (1 + 0.04)^2 = 1.0816.$$
$$\text{Year 2: } (1 + 0.04)^1 = 1.0400.$$
$$\text{Year 3: } (1 + 0.04)^0 = 1.0000.$$

b. See Table S–39. The compound-interest factors at 50 percent are:

$$\text{Year 0: } (1 + 0.5)^3 = 3.375.$$
$$\text{Year 1: } (1 + 0.5)^2 = 2.250.$$
$$\text{Year 2: } (1 + 0.5)^1 = 1.500.$$
$$\text{Year 3: } (1 + 0.5)^0 = 1.000.$$

c. See Table S–40. The rankings are the same as those obtained for Problem (22). The conclusion is that terminal value and net present value will yield the same rankings using identical interest rates.

*25. The purpose of this problem is to stress that the new projects frequently involve some investment for increasing working capital and that a part of the required increase in current assets often is financed by increases in current liabilities. Here, 0.40 ($1,000,000) = $400,000 represents the increased investment in current assets because current assets (cash plus receivables plus inventory) are 40 percent of sales. However, increases in current liabilities are estimated at 0.14 ($1,000,000) = $140,000. Thus, $400,000 − $140,000 = $260,000 is the amount of the required investment in net working capital. When this $260,000 outflow will occur de-

Table S–41

Sale of old machine	
Proceeds from sale	$ 3,000
Book value	2,100
Taxable gain	$ 900
Tax at 40 percent	360
Cash flow: proceeds	3,000
	− 360
Net cash flow after tax	$ 2,640

Outlay for new machine	
Purchase price	$16,500
Freight	900
Installation	600
Total outlay	$18,000
Depreciation	
Old machine, $2,100/3 years	$ 700/year
New machine, $18,000/3 years	6,000/year
Difference	$ 5,300

Table S–40

Project	Rank at an Interest Rate of 4 Percent	Rank at an Interest Rate of 50 Percent
A	6	6
B	4	5
C	1	4
D	5	3
E	3	2
F	2	1

Table S–42

Savings Attributable to New Machine	Year 1	Years 2–3
Direct cash savings	$9,600	$8,400
Increase in depreciation	5,300	5,300
Taxable savings	$4,300	$3,100
Tax at 40 percent	$1,720	$1,240
Cash flow: Direct savings	$9,600	$8,400
Less tax	1,720	1,240
Net cash flow after tax	$7,880	$7,160

Table S–43

Year	Cash from Sale of Old Machine	Cash Outlay for Purchase of New Machine	Savings	Total Cash Flow	Present Value Factor at 10 Percent (percent)	Present Value
0	$2,640	($18,000)		($15,360)	1.000	($15,360)
1			$7,800	$ 7,800	0.909	$ 7,169.92
2			$7,160	$ 7,160	0.826	$ 5,914.16
3			$7,160	$ 7,160	0.751	$ 5,377.16
				Net present value at 10 percent =		$ 3,101.24

pends on when the new sales are expected. This is normally budgeted in period 0, but may well be appropriately divided between period 0 and period 1.

27. a. See Table S–41 for a comparison of the cash flows and depreciation of the new and old machines. Table S–42 shows the savings attributable to the new machine, and Table S–43 provides a calculation of the net present value (NPV) of the investment opportunity at a discount rate of 10 percent. The internal rate of return (IRR) is calculated as follows:

$$NPV \text{ at } 22 \text{ percent} = (141.72).$$
$$NPV \text{ at } 20 \text{ percent} = 318.72.$$

Interpolating provides the following result:

$$\frac{318.72 - 0}{318.72 - (-141.72)} \text{ times 2 percent} = 1.38.$$
$$IRR = 20 \text{ percent} + 1.38 \text{ percent} = 21.38.$$

So, if 10 percent is the minimal acceptable rate of return, the machine should be replaced.

b. See Table S–44 for a revised depreciation schedule. The savings attributable to the new machine are shown in Table S–45, and the calculation of net present value is presented in Table S–46. The IRR is calculated as follows:

$$NPV \text{ at } 25 \text{ percent} = (\$52.48).$$
$$NPV \text{ at } 24 \text{ percent} = \$177.12.$$

Interpolating provides the following result:

$$\frac{\$177.12 - 0}{\$177.12 - (-\$52.48)} \times 1 \text{ percent} = 0.77.$$
$$IRR = 24 \text{ percent} + 0.77 \text{ percent} = 24.77 \text{ percent}.$$

c. The cash outflow at time 0 now = $15,360 + $2,500 = $17,860. Year 3 cash flows = $7,160 + $2,500 =

Table S–44

Revised depreciation schedule	
Outlay for new machine	$18,000
Estimated salvage	3,000
Depreciable amount	$15,000
Depreciation per year (÷ 3)	5,000
Depreciation of old machine	700
Increase in depreciation	$ 4,300

Table S–45

	Year 1	Years 2–3
Direct cash savings	$9,600	$8,400
Increase in depreciation	4,300	4,300
Taxable savings	$5,300	$4,100
Tax at 40 percent	2,120	1,640
Cash flow: Direct savings	9,600	8,400
Less tax	−2,120	−1,640
Net cash flow after tax	$7,480	$6,760

Table S–46

Year	Cash from Sale of Old Machine	Cash Outlay for Purchase of New Machine	Salvage Value	Savings	Total Cash Flow	Present-Value Factor at 10 Percent	Present Value
0	$2,640	($18,000)	—		$(15,360)	1.000	($15,360)
1				$7,480	$7,480	0.909	$6,799.32
2				$6,760	$6,760	0.826	$5,583.76
3			$3,000	$6,760	$9,760	0.751	$7,329.76
					Net present value at 10 percent =		$4,352.84

Table S-47

	Year 0	Year 1	Year 2	Year 3	Year 4	Year 5
			Relevant Cash Flows			
Initial outlay	($50,000)	—	—	—	—	—
Change in sales	—	$200,000	$200,000	$200,000	$135,000	$60,000
Change in maintenance expenses	—	(1,000)	(1,000)	(1,000)	(1,000)	(1,000)
Change in materials and packaging expenses	—	(20,000)	(20,000)	(16,250)	(15,000)	(6,500)
Change in marketing expenses	—	(150,000)	(160,000)	(80,000)	(50,000)	(20,000)
Change in depreciation	—	(10,000)	(10,000)	(10,000)	(10,000)	(10,000)
Change in profit before taxes	—	$ 19,000	$ 9,000	$ 92,750	$ 59,000	$22,500
Taxes on incremental profit	—	$ 9,500	$ 4,500	$ 46,375	$ 29,500	$11,250
Net cash flow	($50,000)	$ 19,500	$ 14,500	$ 56,375	$ 39,500	$21,250

$9,660. Cash outflows in years 1 and 2 remain $7,880 and $7,160, respectively.

$$NPV \text{ at 18 percent} = (\$161.82).$$
$$NPV \text{ at 16 percent} = \$444.52.$$

Interpolating provides the following result:

$$\frac{\$444.52 - 0}{\$444.52 - (-\$161.82)} \times 2 \text{ percent} = 1.466 \text{ percent.}$$

$$IRR = 16 \text{ percent} + 1.466 \text{ percent} = 17.466 \text{ percent.}$$

Table S-48

Year	Cash Flow	Present Value Factor at 20 Percent	Present Value
0	($50,000)	1.000	($50,000)
1	$19,500	0.833	$16,244
2	$14,500	0.694	$10,063
3	$56,375	0.579	$32,641
4	$39,500	0.482	$19,039
5	$21,250	0.402	$ 8,543
		Net present value =	$36,530

29. This problem requires the student to evaluate the information and determine the relevant cash flows. The $75,000 development and testing expenditures are sunk costs and, therefore, are not relevant. The $20,000 depreciation on existing equipment will be the same under either decision and, therefore, need not be included in the analysis.

a. See Table S-47 for relevant cash flows associated with the "Jasper" fragrance line introduction.

b. Incremental net present value *(NPV)* is calculated in Table S-48.

31. This problem can be approached by calculating the net present value *(NPV)* for each alternative and selecting the alternative with the highest *NPV*. The rent alternative for years 1 through 15 has, on an annual basis, rental income of $12,000; depreciation of ($7,500); profit before taxes of $4,500; a tax of $2,250, and a net cash flow of $9,750. The *NPV* at 12 percent = $66,407. See Tables S-49 and S-50 for similar financial data for the two product alternatives. A comparison of the three alternatives available makes it apparent that the rent alternative should be chosen because it provides the greatest *NPV*. A case could be made that the three opportunities are not equally risky, and, hence, the same discount rate should not be used. This question is best deferred until Chapters 13 and 14. If a lower rate were used for the rent alternative (on grounds that it is less risky), its *NPV* advantage would be even greater. Whether renting is less risky depends on who the lessee is.

Table S-49
Net Present Value for Product A

Year	Outlay	Revenue	Expenditures	Depreciation— Buildings	Depreciation— Equipment	Profit before Taxes	Tax	Net Cash Flow
0	($180,000)	—	—	—	—	—	—	($180,000)
1–14	—	$105,000	($60,000)	($7,500)	($12,000)	$25,500	$12,750	$ 32,250
15	($3,750)	$105,000	($60,000)	($7,500)	($12,000)	$21,750	$10,875	$ 30,375
			Net present value at 12 percent = $39,312					

Table S-50
Net Present Value for Product B

Year	Outlay	Revenue	Expenditures	Depreciation—Buildings	Depreciation—Equipment	Profit before Taxes	Tax	Net Cash Flow
0	($216,000)	—	—	—	—	—	—	($216,000)
1–14	—	$127,500	($75,000)	($7,500)	($14,400)	$30,600	$15,300	$ 37,200
15	($28,125)	$127,500	($75,000)	($7,500)	($14,400)	$ 2,475	$ 1,237	$ 23,135

Net present value at 12 percent = $34,795

*33. a. Annual after-tax cash flows from operations are shown (in thousands of dollars) in Table S–51.
  b. The net present value *(NPV)* at 16 percent is shown (in thousands of dollars) in Table S–52.
  c. The internal rate of return *(IRR)* is 26.49 percent. The *NPV* at 26 percent = $8,850 and at 28 percent = −$27,270.
  d. Demand 10 percent below management's expectations would reduce units sold from 5,000,000 to 4,500,000.

The resulting annual after-tax cash flows from operations are shown (in thousands of dollars) in Table S–53. The effect on net present value is shown (in thousands of dollars) in Table S–54. The IRR is 19 percent.
  e. If production costs were to average 70 percent of revenues rather than 60 percent production costs would be $1,400,000 rather than $1,200,000. Annual after-tax cash flows from operations would then be as shown (in thousands of dollars) in Table S–55. The effect on net present

Table S-51

Net revenues = 5,000,000 units at $0.40	$2,000
minus	
Production costs (60 percent of revenues)	−1,200
equals	
Gross profit	$800
minus	
Overhead and sales expense	−500
minus	
Depreciation ($400,000 ÷ 10)	−40
equals	
Profit before taxes	$260
minus	
Taxes (at 50 per cent)	−130
equals	
Profit after taxes	$130
plus	
Depreciation	+40
equals	
Annual cash flow from operations, years 1–10	$170

Table S-53

Net revenues = 4,500,000 units at $0.40	$1,800
minus	
Production costs (60 percent of revenues)	−1,080
equals	
Gross profit	$720
minus	
Overhead and sales expense	−500
minus	
Depreciation	−40
equals	
Profit before taxes	$180
minus	
Taxes (at 50 percent)	−90
equals	
Profit after taxes	$ 90
plus	
Depreciation	+40
equals	
Annual cash flow from operations, years 1–10	$130

Table S-52

Year(s)	Investment in Equipment	Working Capital	Cash Flow from Operations	Total Cash Flows	Present Value Factor at 16 Percent	Present Value
0	($400)	($200)	—	($600)	1.000	($600)
1–9	—	—	$170	$170	4.607	$783.19
10	—	$200	$170	$370	0.227	$ 83.99
					Net present value =	$267.18

Table S–54

Year(s)	Investment in Equipment	Working Capital	Cash Flow from Operations	Total Cash Flows	Present Value Factor at 16 Percent	Present Value
0	($400)	($200)		($600)	1.000	($600)
1–9			$130	$130	4.607	$598.91
10		$200	$130	$330	0.227	$ 74.91
					Net present value =	$ 73.82

value would be as shown (in thousands of dollars) in Table S–56. The *IRR* is 6.8 percent. The *NPV* at 7 percent = $26.8 and at 6 percent = $6.79.

f. At expected levels of demand and cost, the Tasty project is attractive on economic grounds. The *IRR* is about 26.5 percent versus a required rate of return of 16 percent, resulting in an *NPV* of $267,180. At a level of demand 10 percent below the expected level as called for in Part (d), the project is considerably less attractive (*IRR* = 19 per

Table S–55

Net revenues = 5,000,000 units at $0.40	$2,000
minus	
Production costs (70 percent of revenues)	−1,400
equals	
Gross profit	$600
minus	
Overhead and sales expense	−500
minus	
Depreciation	− 40
equals	
Profit before taxes	$ 60
minus	
Taxes (at 50 percent)	− 30
equals	
Profit after taxes	$ 30
plus	
Depreciation	+ 40
equals	
Annual cash flow from operations, years 1–10	$ 70

cent) but still quite acceptable on economic grounds. If production costs were to rise to 70 percent of revenues as called for in Part (e), the project would become clearly unacceptable, returning only about 6.8 percent. The sensitivity analysis thus indicates that a 10 percent shortfall in revenues would not render the project unacceptable, provided production costs remained at 60 percent of revenues.

35. Because all projects have positive net present values, you would want to select the *combination* of projects that has the highest combined net present value and yet still meets the $350,000 constraint. The combination of ABCE has a net present value of $56,000, which is the highest attainable. Assuming there are no other factors that affect the decision, this is the combination that should be accepted.

37. Net cash outflows in year 0 remain at $54,500. Cash flows in years 1–10 would be as shown in Table S–57. The net present value of the new machine is calculated as follows:

Salvage value = $13,000 $(1.05)^9$ = $20,150.
Tax on capital gain = ($20,150 − $13,000)(0.50) = $3,575.
Net salvage = $20,150 − $3,575 = $16,575.
Net present value = $102,854 − $54,500 = $48,354.

a. Because the net present value is positive, it appears that the new machine should be purchased. Notice, however, that the required rate of return has not been adjusted for inflation.

b. The cost reduction provides an annuity of $9,000 after tax per year. The present value of the cost reduction would be = $9,000 (present-value annuity factor) (5.216) = $46,944. This still leaves a positive net present value of $48,354 − $46,944 = $1,410.

Table S–56

Year	Investment in Equipment	Working Capital	Cash Flow from Operations	Total Cash Flows	Present Value Factor at 16 Percent	Present Value
0	($400)	($200)		($600)	1.000	($600)
1–9			$70	70	4.607	$322.49
10		$200	$70	$270	0.227	$ 61.29
				Net present value =		($216.22)

Table S–57

Year	Increase in Sales	Reduction in Costs	Increase in Depreciation	Change in Profit before Taxes	Change in Profit after Taxes	Net Cash Flow	Present Value at 14 Percent
1	$15,000	$18,000	$1,800	$31,200	$15,600	$17,400	$ 15,260
2	$15,750	$18,000	$1,800	$31,950	$15,975	$17,775	$ 13,669
3	$16,538	$18,000	$1,800	$32,738	$16,369	$18,169	$ 12,264
4	$17,365	$18,000	$1,800	$33,565	$16,783	$18,583	$ 11,001
5	$18,233	$18,000	$1,800	$34,433	$17,217	$19,017	$ 9,870
6	$19,145	$18,000	$1,800	$35,345	$17,673	$19,473	$ 8,879
7	$20,102	$18,000	$1,800	$36,302	$18,151	$19,951	$ 7,980
8	$21,107	$18,000	$1,800	$37,307	$18,654	$20,454	$ 7,179
9	$22,162	$18,000	$1,800	$38,362	$19,181	$20,981	$ 6,462
10	$23,271	$18,000	$1,800	$39,471	$19,736	$38,111	$ 10,290
						Present value =	$102,854

Chapter 10

1. The after-tax equivalent required return (K) on each of these sources of funds is as follows:

$K_{\text{Bank debt}} = 0.14(1 - 0.46) = 0.0756 = 7.56$ percent.
$K_{\text{Long-term debt}} = 0.125 (1 - 0.46) = 0.0675 = 6.75$ percent.
$K_{\text{Preferred stock}} = 0.135(1) = 0.135 = 13.5$ percent.

3. a. We can calculate K_e using the dividend-growth model as follows:

$$K_e = \frac{D_1}{P_0} + g.$$

In this case, the figures would be:

$D_1 = \$0.60(1 + 0.05) = \$0.63.$
$P_0 = \$10.$
$g = 0.05.$
$K_e = \dfrac{\$0.63}{\$10.00} + 0.05 = 0.113 = 11.3$ percent.

Note that by year 1, dividends are expected to have grown to 63 cents per share.

b. If government-bond rates were 12 percent, a K_e of 11.3 percent would be too low. K_e should include a risk premium over and above the government-bond rate. A likely possibility is that the current market price of $10 is based on higher expected growth than was the past growth of dividends. For example, assume growth is expected to be 12 percent. We can calculate K_e as follows:

$$K_e = \frac{D_1}{P_0} + g = \frac{\$0.60(1 + 0.12)}{\$10.00} + 0.12 = 0.187.$$

This 18.7 percent figure is higher than the 12 percent rate on bonds.

5. Because the firm intends to maintain its current capital structure, the weights ascribed to its various forms of financing are as follows:

$$\text{Bank Debt} = \frac{\$8,000}{\$52,000} = 0.154$$

$$\text{Long-term debt} = \frac{\$7,000}{\$52,000} = 0.135$$

$$\text{Preferred stock} = \frac{\$4,000}{\$52,000} = 0.077$$

$$\text{Common equity} = \frac{\$8,000 + \$25,000}{\$52,000} = 0.635$$

Note that accounts payable and accruals are excluded, because they are short-term non-interest-bearing forms of financing. Using the after-tax required rate of return for each component from Table 10–12 makes it possible to calculate the weighted-average required return as shown in Table S–58.

Table S–58

Source of Funds	Required Rate of Return (percent)	Weight (proportion of whole)	Weighted Required Rate of Return (percent)
Bank debt, K_l	6.5	0.154	1.00
Long-term debt, K_d	5.8	0.135	0.78
Preferred stock, K_p	11.5	0.077	0.89
Common equity, K_e	16.4	0.635	10.41
Weighted-Average Required Return = K_w =			13.08

Table S–59

| | Book Value | | | | Market Value | | |
	Weight	After-Tax Required Rate of Return (percent)	Weighted Required Rate of Return (percent)		Weight	After-Tax Required Rate of Return (percent)	Weighted Required Rate of Return (percent)
Equity	0.50	18.0	9.0		0.60	18.0	10.8
Debt	0.50	6.48	3.24		0.40	6.58	2.592
	Weighted-average required return =		12.24		Weighted-average required return =		13.392

Note: Long-term debt = $10,000. For book value, common equity (1,000 shares) = $10,000; for market value, common equity (1,000 shares at $15 a share) = $15,000.

7. When firms wish to raise additional equity, they will sell stock at market value, not book value, and the return expected by shareholders is in relation to market value because this is what they have invested. For example, whenever the book value of common stock is less than its market value, using book value weights will result in underweighting the required rate of return of shareholders. Since the required rate to equity is higher than that of debt, this will result in an underestimate of the weighted-average required return as illustrated in Table S–59. The example in the table assumes that the market and book values of debt are equal. In practice, both debt and equity may have market values different from book values. In such cases, the use of market-value weights is theoretically correct. These market-value weights reflect the market's valuation of the company.

9. This problem requires that the cost of equity capital be recalculated to allow for flotation costs. See Table S–60 for a recalculation of the weighted-average required return *(WARR)* with flotation costs. If all equity financing is through retained earnings, it is appropriate to use the weighted-average required return calculated without consideration of flotation costs: *WARR* = 13.08 percent.

*11. a. The after-tax cost of debt, K_d = (Before-tax cost) × (1.0 − Tax rate) = 0.08 × (1 − 0.4) = 0.048 = 4.8 per-

cent. The cost of new preferred stock is:

$$K_p = \frac{D_p}{NP_p} = \frac{\$5}{\$52.50 - \$2.50} = 0.10 = 10 \text{ percent.}$$

$$K_e = \frac{D_1}{P_0} + g.$$

Calculating g is done as follows:

(1977 earnings per share) $(1 + g)^9$ = 1986 earnings per share

or $\$2(1 + g)^9 = 4.$

$$(1 + g)^9 = \frac{4}{2} = 2.$$

Refer to Appendix Table III at the end of the text and see that this result represents a growth rate of approximately 8 percent [that is, $(1 + 0.08)^9 \cong 2$]. The cost of equity, K_e, is then calculated as follows:

$$K_e = \frac{\$2.00}{\$50.00} + 0.08 = 0.12 = 12 \text{ percent.}$$

b. See Table S–61.

c. In order for the capital structure to remain optimal, retained earnings must comprise 70 percent of total new financing before external equity is sold. Retained earnings for 1986 are calculated as follows:

Table S–60

Sources of funds	Required Rate of Return	Weight	Weighted Required Rate of Return
Bank debt, K_l	0.065	0.154	0.0100
Long-term debt, K_d	0.058	0.135	0.0078
Preferred stock, K_p	0.115	0.077	0.0089
Common equity, K_e	0.169	0.635	0.1073
			0.1340

Weighted-average required return with flotation costs = 13.40 percent.

Table S–61

Sources of Funds	Percent of Total Funds Sources (1)	After-tax Cost (2)	Component Cost (3) = (1) × (2)
Debt	0.25	0.048	0.0120
Preferred stock	0.05	0.100	0.005
Common equity	0.70	0.120	0.084
	1.00	Weighted-average required return =	0.1010 = 10.10 percent.

Retained earnings
= (Earnings per share − Current dividend) × (Number of shares)
= ($4.00 − $2.00) × (140,000 shares) = $280,000.

   If X = Total capital investment before external equity is sold, then $280,000/2 = 0.7X$. Thus, $200,000 = X$.

d. First, the marginal cost of equity, K_e, must be calculated. It can be determined from Part (a) of this problem that $D_1 = 2.00$ and $g = 8$ percent. Thus, the following calculation can be made:

$$K_e = \frac{D_1}{NP} + g$$

$$= \frac{\$2.00}{\$45.00} + 0.08$$

$$= 0.0444 + 0.08$$

$$= 0.1244 = 12.44 \text{ percent.}$$

Then the marginal cost of capital must be calculated, as shown in Table S–62. The cost of capital, WARR, is, thus, slightly higher (10.41 percent versus 10.1 percent) if new equity must be issued.

13. a. The calculations for the weighted-average required return (WARR) are as follows:

$$K_d = 0.16(1 − 0.40) = 0.096.$$
$$K_e = D_1/P_0 + g$$
$$= 4/40 + 0.12 = 0.22.$$

The following information comes from the balance sheet:

Debt (D) = 40.
Stock (S) = 5 + 35 = 40.
Firm value (V) = D + S = 80.

$D/V = 1/2.$
$S/V = 1/2.$

Greensboro's WARR for 1986 is generated as follows:

$$WARR = (D/V) K_d + (S/V) K_e$$
$$= 0.50 (0.096) + (0.50) (0.22)$$
$$= 0.158 = 15.8 \text{ percent.}$$

b. To calculate K_e, use the security market line as follows:

$$K_e = R_f + (K_m − R_f)\beta$$
$$= 0.14 + 1.5 (0.20 − 0.14)$$
$$= 0.23.$$

The difference between the 22 percent and 23 percent figures for K_e might be a result of imprecise estimates of β, g, and K_m. The difference neither proves nor disproves the validity of the CAPM.

c. The project under consideration must have the same business risk as Greensboro's existing operations and the firm must maintain its present mix of 50 percent debt and 50 percent stock financing.

Chapter 11

1. After the fifth year, cash flows are the same under the two alternatives, so the decision needs to be analyzed only over five years. Since the two-step alternative involves a fixed-price contract, the second outlay of $350,000 is subject to little uncertainty (assuming only that the contractor remains in business). Maintenance and utilities also are subject to little uncertainty. Therefore, a case can be made for discounting all cash flows at the risk-free rate, 10 percent. The problem is to pick the low-cost alternative. Because the hospital

Table S–62

Sources of Funds	Percent of Total Funds Sources (1)	After-tax Cost (2)	Component Cost (3) = (1) × (2)
Debt	0.25	0.048	0.0120
Preferred stock	0.05	0.100	0.0050
Common equity	0.70	0.1244	0.0871
	1.00	Weighted-average required return =	0.1041 = 10.41 percent.

Table S-63

		Cash Flows	
	Year	Alternative A	Alternative B
0		(500)	(300)
1		(10)	(5)
2		(10)	(5)
3		(10)	(5)
4		(10)	(5)
5		(10)	(355)
Present value at 10 percent =		(537.91)	(536.28)

is not taxed, depreciation is not a factor. Cash flows for the first five years and their present values are shown (in thousands of dollars) in Table S-63. Note that plan B, which delays construction of half the facility, is the less expensive of the two alternatives, but the costs are quite close in present-value terms.

3. The following equation is used to solve this problem: $K_j = R_f + (K_m - R_f)$(Project risk ratio). Return targets are calculated as follows:

$$K_{\text{cost reduction}} = 10 + 7.2(0.40) = 12.88 \text{ percent.}$$
$$K_{\text{expansion}} = 10 + 7.2(1.00) = 17.20 \text{ percent.}$$
$$K_{\text{new-existing}} = 10 + 7.2(1.75) = 22.60 \text{ percent.}$$
$$K_{\text{new-new}} = 10 + 7.2(3.00) = 31.60 \text{ percent.}$$

5. The following equation is used to solve this problem: $K_j = R_f + (K_m - R_f)$(Project risk ratio). See Table S-64 for return targets for each division, assuming a government bond rate of 11 percent.

7. To solve this problem, the following calculations must be made:

Present value of $115/year in years 1–10 at 13 percent
$$= 5.426 (\$115) = \$623.99$$
Present value of $1000/year in year 10 at 18 percent
$$= 0.191(\$1,000) = \underline{\$191.00}$$
Present value $814.99

Net present value = $814,990 − $1,000,000 = −$185,010.

Atlantic should not undertake the project.

Table S-64

	Return Targets (percent)		
Category	Electric Motors Division	Electrical Components Division	Microelectronics Division
Cost reduction	14.60	13.16	16.76
Expansion	18.20	18.20	21.80
New products	25.40	21.80	36.20

9. a. See Table S-65. The pattern shown in the table seems unreasonable because the risk premium should decrease over time as the product becomes more accepted.
   b. See Table S-66. The pattern shown in this table also seems unreasonable. The operating costs of the machinery are well known and will only become more certain over time as the light bulbs are produced.
   c. In this case, the appropriate discount rate decreases over time.

11. a. Assuming the tractor lasts eight years, the following calculations can be made:

$$\text{Depreciation} = \frac{\$50,000}{8} = \$6,250/\text{year.}$$

Additional profit ($16,000 − $6,250)	$9,750
Less taxes at 40 percent	− 3,900
	$5,850
Plus depreciation	+ 6,250
Incremental cash flow	$12,100

$$NPV = \$12,100 (4.639) - \$50,000$$
$$= \$6,131.90.$$

   b. If the tractor lasts only five years and has a market value = 0 at that time, there is a capital loss of the book value = $50,000 − 5($6,250) = $18,750. The tax shield on the loss = $18,750(0.40) = $7,500.

$$NPV = \$12,100 (3.433) - \$50,000 + \$7,500 (0.519)$$
$$= -\$4,568.20.$$

Table S-65

Year	PV factor at 11 percent (1)	PV factor at 16 percent (2)	Risk Premium per dollar (3) = (1) − (2)
1	0.901	0.862	0.039
2	0.812	0.743	0.069
3	0.731	0.641	0.090
4	0.659	0.552	0.107
5	0.593	0.476	0.117

Table S-66

Year	Cash Inflow (1)	Risk Premium (2)	Dollar Risk Premium (3) = (1) × (2)
1	$5,000	0.05	$250.00
2	$5,050	0.05	$252.50
3	$6,020	0.05	$301.00
4	$6,900	0.05	$345.00
5	$7,300	0.05	$365.00

Table S–67

Book value of old machine ($93,800 − $26,800)	$67,000
minus	
Salvage value	−20,000
equals	
Loss on sale of old machine	$47,000
times	
Tax rate	× 0.50
equals	
Tax shield	$23,500
Cost of new machine	$98,000
minus	
Tax shield on old machine	−23,500
minus	
Salvage value of old machine	−20,000
equals	
Net cash flow at year 0	$54,500

c. If the tractor lasts ten years, there will be two additional years of cash flow equal to $16,000 − $16,000 (0.40) = $9,600.

$$NPV = \$6,131.90 + \$9,600 (0.308) + \$9,600 (0.270)$$
$$= \$11,680.70.$$

d. Again, the tractor should be purchased if its life is expected to be eight years or greater. Under the assumptions of higher cost and higher revenues presented in this problem, the variability of the net present value increases. That is, the net present value is higher than it was in Problem 34 of Chapter 9 if the life turns out to be eight years or greater. It is also more negative if the life turns out to be only five years.

13. a. The required return appropriate for examining worst-case scenarios is the riskless rate of 14 percent − 5 percent = 9 percent. The net cash flow for year 0 if sales increase by only $9,000 annually is calculated in Table S-67. The net present value of cash flows for years 1–10 is shown in Table S-68. Because the net present value > 0, the purchase of the new machine is recommended.

Table S–69

Book value of old machine ($93,800 − $26,800)	$67,000
minus	
Salvage value	−20,000
equals	
Loss on sale of old machine	$47,000
times	
Tax rate	× 0.50
equals	
Tax shield	$23,500
Cost of new machine	$98,000
minus	
Tax shield on old machine	−23,500
minus	
Salvage value of old machine	−20,000
Net cash flow at year 0	$54,500

b. If annual operating costs are reduced by only $10,000 annually, the net cash flow is calculated as shown in Table S-69. The net present value of cash flows for years 1–10 is shown in Table S-70. Because the net present value > 0, the purchase of the new machine is still recommended.

Chapter 13

1. a. See Table S–71 for calculation of earnings per share based on debt financing. Note that total debt interest = 0.10($5,000,000) + 0.08($6,000,000) = $980,000, and shares outstanding = 400,000. See Table S–72 for calculation of earnings per share based on equity financing. Note that, in this case, interest = 0.08($5,000,000) = $480,000, and shares outstanding = $5,000,000/$20 + 400,000 = 650,000.

b. The answer here depends on the expected level of earnings before interest and taxes (EBIT) and its variance. Above EBIT of $1.78 million, debt produces higher earnings per share (EPS). Below $1.78 million, equity gives higher EPS. The EBIT/EPS analysis makes explicit the risk/return trade-off, but does not identify the superior plan.

Table S–68

Year(s)	Increase in Sales	Reduction in Costs	Increase in Depreciation	Change in Profit Before Taxes	Tax	Change in Profit after Taxes	Salvage Value	Net Cash Flow	Present Value Factor	Present Value
1–9	$9,000	$18,000	($1,800)	$25,200	$12,600	$12,600	—	$14,400	5.985	$86,184
10	$9,000	$18,000	($1,800)	$25,200	$12,600	$12,600	$13,000	$27,400	0.422	$11,563
										$97,747
										($54,500)
								Net present value =		$43,247

Table S–70

Year	Increase in Sales	Reduction in Costs	Increase in Depreciation	Change in Profit Before Taxes	Tax	Change in Profit after Taxes	Salvage Value	Net Cash Flow	Present Value Factor	Present Value
1–9	$15,000	$10,000	($1,800)	$23,200	$11,600	$11,600	—	$13,400	5.985	$80,199
10	$15,000	$10,000	($1,800)	$23,200	$11,600	$11,600	$13,000	$26,400	0.422	$11,141
										$91,340
										($54,500)
								Net present value =		$36,840

3. See Table S–73. The figures show that, to get a higher expected return, the investor must accept greater risk—that is, greater uncertainty about the return and increased probability of unfavorable outcomes.

5. a. The value of the firm after issuing debt, V_L, can be calculated as follows (with V_U = the value of the debt-free firm and TD = corporate tax on debt): $V_L = V_U + TD = \$1,000 + 0.4(\$300) = \$1,120$.

   b. The stock is now worth $820 as shown below:

$$V_L = \text{Stock} + \text{Debt}.$$
$$\$1120 = \text{Stock} + \$300.$$
$$\text{Stock} = \$1,120 - \$300 = \$820.$$

   Note that shareholders can be made better off if the $300 raised through debt can be given to shareholders (for example, through an equity repurchase) so equity owners have $820 of stock *plus* $300 in cash, or a total value of $1120.

   Alternatively, the company could leave $300 cash in the company in which case the following would be true:

$$V_L = \$1,000 + \$300 + TD$$
$$= \$1,300 + 0.4(\$300)$$
$$= \$1,420.$$
$$\text{Stock} = V_L - \text{Debt} = \$1,420 - \$300 = \$1,120.$$

   c. The stock's beta will increase due to the financial risk introduced by the use of debt. Stockholders' returns are now more risky.

Chapter 14

1. For debt financing, the earnings-before-interest-and-taxes/earnings-per-share (EBIT/EPS) calculations are:

Total debt interest
$$= 0.10(\$5,000,000) + 0.08(\$6,000,000) = \$980.000.$$
$$\text{Shares outstanding} = 400,000.$$
$$\text{At EPS} = 0, \text{EBIT} = \$980,000.$$

At EBIT = $2,000,000,
$$\text{EPS} = \frac{(1 - 0.48)(\$2,000,000 - \$980,000)}{400,000} = \$1.33.$$

Table S–71

Earnings before Interest and Taxes	$1,000,000	$2,000,000	$3,000,000	$4,000,000
less				
Interest	−980,000	−980,000	−980,000	−980,000
equals				
Profit before taxes	$ 20,000	$1,020,000	$2,020,000	$3,020,000
less				
Tax at 48 percent	9,600	489,600	969,600	1,449,600
equals				
Profit after taxes	$ 10,400	$ 530,400	$1,050,400	$1,570,400
Earnings per share	$0.03	$1.33	$2.63	$3.93

Table S–72

EBIT	$1,000,000	$2,000,000	$3,000,000	$4,000,000
less				
Interest	480,000	480,000	480,000	480,000
equals				
Profit before taxes	$ 520,000	$1,520,000	$2,520,000	$3,520,000
less				
Tax at 48 percent	249,600	729,600	1,209,600	1,689,600
equals				
Profit after taxes	$ 270,400	$ 790,400	$1,310,400	$1,830,400
Earnings per share	$0.42	$1.22	$2.02	$2.82

For equity financing, the EBIT/EPS calculations are:

Total debt interest $= 0.08(\$,600,000) = \$480,000$.

$$\text{Shares outstanding} = \frac{\$5,000,000}{\$20} + 400,000 = 650,000.$$

At EPS $= 0$, EBIT $= \$480,000$.

At EBIT $= \$2,000,000$,

$$\text{EPS} = \frac{(1 - 0.48)(\$2,000,000 - \$480,000)}{650,000} = \$1.22.$$

The recommended financing alternative depends on the expected level of EBIT and its variance. Figure S–5 shows, in terms of expected EPS, that debt is better above the point of intersection, whereas equity is better below that point. The point of intersection is at EBIT = $1,780,000, calculated algebraically in problem (2).

3. a. The equation representing the preferred stock alternative in year 1 is developed as follows:

Table S–73

Possible Terminal Value (TV)	Probability	Outcome × Probability	$(TV_1 - EV)^2$	Probability × $(TV_1 - EV)^2$
Levered:				
$1,195.00	0.25	$ 298.75	$12,656.25	$3,164.0625
$1,082.50	0.50	541.25	0	0
$ 970.00	0.25	242.50	$12,656.25	3,164.0625
		Expected Value (EV) = $1,082.50		$\sigma^2 = \overline{\$6,328.125}$
				$\sigma = \$ 79.55$
Unlevered:				
$1,150.00	0.25	$ 287.50	$ 5,625.00	$1,406.25
$1,075.00	0.50	537.50	0	0
$1,000.00	0.25	250.00	$ 5,625.00	$1,406.25
		EV = $1,075.00		$\sigma^2 = \overline{\$2,812.50}$
				$\sigma = \$ 53.03$
Half and half:				
$1,100.00	0.25	$ 275.00	$ 1,406.25	$ 351.5625
$1,062.50	0.50	531.25	0	0
$1,025.00	0.25	256.25	$ 1,406.25	351.5625
		EV = $1,062.50		$\sigma^2 = \overline{\$ 703.125}$
				$\sigma = \$ 26.52$

FIGURE S–5

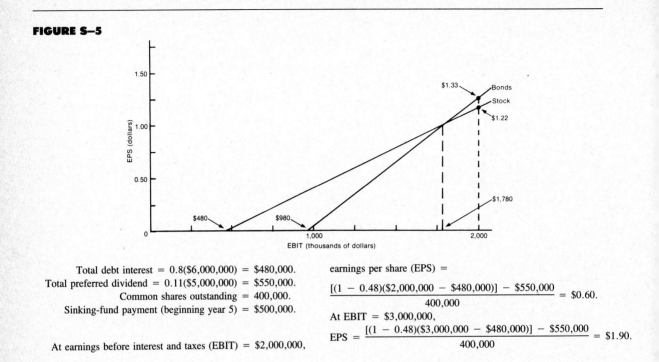

Total debt interest = 0.8($6,000,000) = $480,000.
Total preferred dividend = 0.11($5,000,000) = $550,000.
Common shares outstanding = 400,000.
Sinking-fund payment (beginning year 5) = $500,000.

At earnings before interest and taxes (EBIT) = $2,000,000,

earnings per share (EPS) =

$$\frac{[(1 - 0.48)(\$2,000,000 - \$480,000)] - \$550,000}{400,000} = \$0.60.$$

At EBIT = $3,000,000,

$$EPS = \frac{[(1 - 0.48)(\$3,000,000 - \$480,000)] - \$550,000}{400,000} = \$1.90.$$

FIGURE S–6

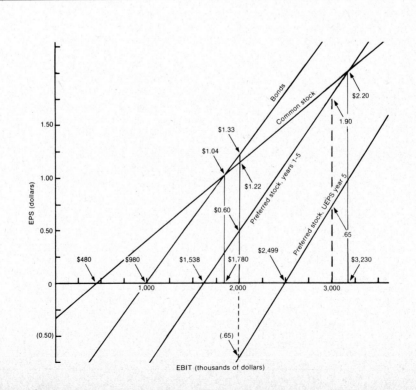

Table S–74

Coverage	Pretax Burden	Times Covered
Interest (bond plan)	$1,775,000	1.09
Interest plus sinking fund	$2,684,090	0.72
Interest (stock plan)	$ 800,000	2.41

In year 1, uncommitted earnings per share (UEPS) = EPS. The preferred-stock alternative in year 5 is generated as follows:

At EBIT = $2,000,000, UEPS =

$$\frac{[(1 - 0.48)(\$2,000,000 - \$480,000)] - \$550,000 - \$500,000}{400,000}$$
$$= -\$(0.65).$$

At EBIT = $3,000,000, UEPS =

$$\frac{[(1 - 0.48)(\$3,000,000 - \$480,000)] - \$550,000 - \$500,000}{400,000}$$
$$= \$0.65.$$

Figure S–6 shows the comparison of preferred-stock alternatives in years 1 and 5.

b. EPS break-even points for the preferred-stock plan compared with the common-stock plan are as follows:

EPS—preferred stock = EPS—common stock
$$\frac{(EBIT - \$480,000)(1 - 0.48) - \$550,000}{400,000}$$
$$= \frac{(EBIT - \$480,000)(1 - 0.48)}{650,000}$$

Solving for EBIT, we find break-even at EBIT = $3,230,000. At that level, EPS = $2.20 under both plans. UEPS break-even points are as follows:

UEPS—preferred stock = UEPS—common stock
$$\frac{[(EBIT - \$480,000)(1 - 0.48)] - \$550,000 - \$500,000}{400,000}$$
$$= \frac{(EBIT - \$480,000)(1 - 0.48)}{650,000}$$

Solving for EBIT, we find break-even at EBIT = $5,729,923. At that level, UEPS = $4.20 under both plans.

c. The preferred-stock plan is not attractive. At all levels of EBIT, it will result in lower EPS than will the bond plan, and its UEPS break-even with the common-stock plan is beyond the current range of EBIT levels.

5. a. We can calculate the key figures under the stock (S) and bond (B) plans and then calculate the break-even (BE) level of EBIT as follows:

$$N_S = \frac{\$7,200,000}{\$4} + \frac{\$7,500,000}{\$6.25} = 3,000,000 \text{ shares.}$$
$$I_S = 0.08(\$10,000,000) = \$800,000.$$
$$N_B = \frac{\$7,200,000}{\$4} = 1,800,000 \text{ shares.}$$
$$I_B = 0.08(\$10,000,000) + 0.13(\$7,500,000) = \$1,775,000.$$
$$EBIT_{BE} = \frac{[3,000,000(\$1,775,000)] - [(1,800,000)(\$800,000)]}{3,000,000 - 1,800,000}$$
$$= \$3,237,500.$$

b. From Equation (2), modified to include the interest on existing bonds, the uncommitted-earnings-per-share (UEPS) break-even level of EBIT is:

$$\frac{[(EBIT - \$1,775,000)(1 - 0.45)] - \$500,000}{1,800,000}$$
$$= \frac{(EBIT - \$800,000)(1 - 0.45)}{3,000,000}$$
$$EBIT_{BE} = \$5,510,227.$$

The necessity to cover sinking-fund payments makes common stock more attractive. In fact, since after-tax earnings are only $539,000 at the projected level of sales, it is unlikely that the firm will be able to meet its contractual obligations if the debt alternative is selected.

c. Following the format of Table 14–2 for an expected EBIT level of $1,930,500(0.033 × $58,500,000), Table S–74 shows that the inclusion of a sinking-fund payment under the bond plan results in a lower coverage ratio.

With the new contract, EBIT will be below the break-even point ($3,237,500). The firm can barely cover the interest payments if the bond plan is used and cannot cover the sinking-fund payments. The stock plan is the only reasonable alternative.

Table S–75

	Year Prior 0	Recession Year 1	2	3	4
Sales at stable prices	$126.5	$113.9	$94.9	$88.6	$113.9
Percent of year 0 sales	100	90	75	70	90
Sales assuming 3 percent price decline	$126.5	$110.5	$92.1	$85.9	$110.5
Cash operating expenses	$101.6	$ 90.7	$84.4	$82.6	$101.6
Net cash inflow from operations	$ 24.9	$ 19.8	$ 7.7	$ 3.3	$ 8.9

Table S–76

	Year Prior 0	Recession Year 1	2	3	4
Current capital structure					
1. Nonfinancial flows	$ 13.4	$ 9.4	$ 3.5	$ (1.2)	$ (4.5)
2. Financial flows	(11.2)	(10.5)	(9.9)	(10.3)	(10.7)
3. Change in cash balance	2.2	(1.1)	(6.4)	(11.5)	(15.2)
4. Cumulative change	2.2	1.1	(5.3)	(16.8)	(32.0)
5. Change in cash with dividend eliminated in year 1	2.2	1.9	(3.4)	(8.5)	(12.2)
6. Cumulative change	2.2	4.1	0.7	(7.8)	(20.0)
Alternative A, 35 percent debt					
7. Financial flows	(12.3)	(11.5)	(10.8)	(11.1)	(11.5)
8. Change in cash	1.1	(2.1)	(7.3)	(12.3)	(16.0)
9. Cumulative change	1.1	(1.0)	(8.3)	(20.6)	(36.6)
10. Change in cash with dividend eliminated in year 1	1.1	0.3	(4.9)	(9.9)	(13.6)
11. Cumulative change	1.1	1.4	(3.5)	(13.4)	(27.0)
Alternative B, 50 percent debt					
12. Financial flows	(13.3)	(12.4)	(11.6)	(11.8)	(12.1)
13. Change in cash	0.1	(3.0)	(8.1)	(13.0)	(16.6)
14. Cumulative change	0.1	(2.9)	(11.0)	(24.0)	(40.6)
15. Change in cash with dividend eliminated in year 1	0.1	1.1	(6.2)	(11.1)	(14.7)
16. Cumulative change	0.1	1.0	(7.2)	(18.3)	(33.0)

7. a. Assumptions regarding operating cash flows under future recession conditions are detailed (in millions of dollars) in Table S–75. Alternate debt policies are reflected (in millions of dollars) in Table S–76.

   b. With the current capital structure of 20 percent debt, Omega will run a cumulative cash deficit beginning in year 2 of the recession, assuming no cut in dividends. If dividends are cut in year 1, the cumulative deficit will begin in year 3. Under alternatives A and B, the cumulative cash deficits begin earlier and are more severe than under the current capital structure. Even under the most conservative of the three capital structures (the current structure), the cash deficits become unmanageable, whereas the company could survive the less severe recession analyzed in the text with the current capital structure. The revised analysis suggests that if the more severe recession is a serious possibility, the firm should reduce its long-term debt rather than increase it. Even with a reduction in debt from existing levels, survival of the more severe recession probably would require even more drastic cuts in operating expenses and capital expenditures, and deferral of the planned resumption in capital outlays in year 5 rather than year 4.

9. a. By converting all payments to a pretax basis, the earnings before interest and taxes (EBIT) required to cover interest, sinking funds and dividend payments are reflected in Table S–77.

   b. Earnings-per-share (EPS) break-even points for the bond plan compared with the stock plan for year 1 are calculated as follows:

$$Stock = Bond$$
$$\frac{(EBIT - 155)(0.52)}{360} = \frac{(EBIT - 506)(0.52)}{200}$$

Table S–77

Bond Plan:	
Interest on existing debt	$ 155,000[a]
Interest on new debt	351,000[b]
Debt retirement	
Old, pretax basis	240,385[c]
New, pretax basis	384,615
Common stock dividends, pretax	192,308
Required EBIT	$1,323,308
Stock Plan:	
Interest on existing debt	$ 155,000
Debt retirement, pretax	240,385
Common stock dividends, pretax	346,154
Required EBIT	$ 741,539

[a] $\left(\$2,000,000 - \dfrac{\$125,000}{2} \right)(0.08) = \$155,000$

[b] $\left(\$4,000,000 - \dfrac{\$200,000}{2} \right)(0.09) = \$351,000$

[c] $\dfrac{125,000}{0.52} = \$240,385$

Table S-78

| | All Equity | | All Debt | |
	Continued Growth	Slow Down	Continued Growth	Slow Down
Sales	$24,000	$17,000	$24,000	$17,000
Variable operating expenses	9,600	6,800	9,600	6,800
Fixed operating expenses	9,800	9,800	9,800	9,800
Earnings before interest and taxes	$ 4,600	$ 400	$ 4,600	$ 400
Interest	100	100	820	820
Profit before tax	$ 4,500	$ 300	$ 3,780	($420)
Tax at 50 percent	2,250	150	1,890	(210)
Profit after tax	$ 2,250	$ 150	$ 1,890	($210)
Shares	700	700	500	500
Equity	$92,250	$90,150	$85,890	$83,770
Earnings per share (dollars)	$3.21	$0.21	$3.78	($0.42)
Return on equity (percent)	2.44	0.17	2.20	−0.25

$$104 \text{ EBIT} - 16,120 = 187.2 \text{ EBIT} - 94,723.2.$$
$$83.2 \text{ EBIT} = 78,603.2.$$
$$\text{EBIT} = 944.75 \text{ thousand}$$
$$= \$944,750.$$

c. The expected earnings before interest and taxes (EBIT) are not much higher than the earnings-per-share (EPS) break-even point, suggesting that the stock plan may be preferred. Assuming that EBIT is distributed normally, a 68 percent probability corresponds to one standard deviation about the mean of the distribution. Standardizing the distance between the expected EBIT level and the break-even level (assuming a standard deviation of 200 thousand):

$$\frac{1033 - 945}{200} = 0.44.$$

Using a normal distribution table, this corresponds to approximately a 33 percent probability that the actual EBIT will be below $944,750, again suggesting that the stock plan may be preferred. (That is, there is a 33 percent chance EBIT will be more than 0.44 standard deviations below its expected level.)

d. The uncommitted-earnings-per-share (UEPS) break-even point for the two plans is generated as follows:

$$\text{UEPS—Stock} = \text{UEPS—Bond}$$
$$\frac{(\text{EBIT} - 155)(0.52) - 125}{360} = \frac{(\text{EBIT} - 506)(0.52) - 325}{200}.$$
$$104 \text{ EBIT} - 16,120 - 25,000$$
$$= 187.2 \text{ EBIT} - 94,723.2 - 117,000.$$
$$83.2 \text{ EBIT} = 170,603.2.$$
$$\text{EBIT} = 2,050 \text{ thousand}$$
$$= \$2,050,000.$$

The UEPS break-even point reinforces the answer provided in part (c). Based on the probability data in part (c), it is virtually certain that EBIT will be below UEPS break-

even ($2,050,000 is more than 5 standard deviations above the expected EBIT of $1,033,000). Given the company's policies about dividends, the stock plan is preferable.

11. This problem considers the effects of operating leverage on a firm's operating profits. The new cost structure posed here represents a higher degree of operating leverage as the ratio of fixed costs to variable costs = 1.125 (compared to a ratio of 0.42 in the previous problem). This higher level of operating leverage increases the variability of the firm's earnings before interest and taxes (EBIT) and earnings per share (EPS), as shown (in thousands of dollars) in Table S-78. The implication for financing policy is that the higher is the degree of *operating* leverage, the lower is the optimal level of *financial* leverage.

Chapter 15

1. a. The declaration date is April 16, the record date is May 18, the ex-dividend date is May 12, and the payment date is June 18.

b. (1) The dividend increase from $4.00 to $5.00 must have been perceived by the market as a favorable sign, because the stock price rises around the announcement date (April 17). Note that the stock price rises on the meeting date of April 16, indicating some information leakage prior to the announcement in the *Wall Street Journal* on April 17. (2) The stock price drops on May 12 by slightly less than the magnitude of the $5.00 dividend. This occurs because those purchasing the stock on May 12 and after would not be entitled to the $5.00 dividend, so the value of the claim is less than it was prior to May 12. The stock price does not fall by the full amount of the dividend, probably due in part to changes in general market conditions. (3) Theoretically, no stock price changes related to the dividend are expected in June, because all reaction took place around the announcement date and the record date. There-

Table S-79

	No Residual	No External Equity Debt/Equity Residual	Dividend Residual
		Policies (thousands of dollars)	
Before external financing			
Debt	14,000	14,000	14,000
Equity	40,000	40,000	40,000
Investment opportunities	30,000	30,000	30,000
Earnings	25,000	25,000	25,000
Payout ratio (percent)	0.4	0.4	0.12
Dividends	10,000	10,000	3,000
Earnings retained	15,000	15,000	22,000
External financing	15,000	15,000	8,000
Debt	8,000	15,000	8,000
Equity	7,000	0	0
After external financing			
Debt	22,000	29,000	22,000
Equity	62,000	55,000	62,000
Debt/equity (percent)	0.35	0.53	0.35

fore, the decline in price in the middle of June is most likely related to factors external to the dividend payment.

3. This problem considers the effects of dividend policy on external financing requirements and the trade-offs between alternative dividend financing policies.

a. The dividend paid = $2.50/share × 4,000,000 shares = $10,000,000. This result implies a payout ratio of:

$$\frac{\$10,000,000}{\$25,000,000} = 40 \text{ percent.}$$

Table S-79, similar to Table 15-3, is helpful in answering parts (b) and (c) of this question.

Table S-80

Year	Earnings (millions of dollars)
1	10.50
2	11.03
3	11.58
4	12.16
5	12.76
	58.03

b. To maintain the dividend-payout ratio of 40 percent and undertake the new investment, $15 million in external financing will be required. To maintain the target debt/equity ratio of 35 percent, $7 million in new equity is required. The number of new shares required is calculated as follows:

$$\frac{\$7,000,000}{\$40/\text{share}} = 175,000 \text{ shares.}$$

The dollar dividend per share can then be determined.

$$\text{Before new issue: } \frac{\$10,000,000}{4,000,000 \text{ shares}} = \$2.50/\text{share.}$$

$$\text{After new issue: } \frac{\$10,000,000}{4,175,000 \text{ shares}} = \$2.40/\text{share.}$$

c. There are two alternative policies available. One policy would be to maintain the dividend-payout ratio and to raise the $15 million through new debt. This action would increase Troxler's debt/equity ratio to 53 percent. The other alternative is to raise $8 million in new debt and the balance through retained earnings by reducing the dividend-payout ratio to 12 percent.

The principal advantage of the policy to use no new

Table S-81

	Year 0	Year 1	Year 2	Year 3	Year 4	Year 5	5-Year Total
				(millions of dollars)			
Earnings	—	7.00	5.00	3.00	6.50	3.50	25.00
Dividends	—	1.62	1.62	1.62	1.62	1.62	8.10
Earnings retained	—	5.38	3.38	1.38	4.88	1.88	16.90
Total equity	200.00	205.38	208.76	210.14	215.02	216.90	—
New debt	—	—	5.10	—	—	—	5.10
Total debt	60.00	60.00	65.10	65.10	65.10	65.10	—
Debt/equity ratio	0.30	0.29	0.31	0.31	0.31	0.30	—
Dividend-payout ratio	—	0.23	0.32	0.54	0.25	0.46	0.32
Funds available for interest							
Retained earnings	—	5.38	3.38	1.38	4.88	1.88	16.90
New debt	—	—	5.10	—	—	—	5.10
Cumulative total		5.38	13.86	15.24	20.12	22.00	22.00
Cumulative investment requirements	—	4.00	9.00	13.00	18.00	22.00	22.00

Table S–82

	Year 0	Year 1	Year 2	Year 3	Year 4	Year 5	5-Year Total
				(millions of dollars)			
Earnings	—	7.00	5.00	3.00	6.50	3.50	25.00
Dividends	—	1.74	1.74	1.74	1.74	1.74	8.70
Earnings retained	—	5.26	3.26	1.26	4.76	1.76	16.30
Total equity	200.00	205.26	208.52	209.78	214.54	216.30	—
New debt	—	—	5.70	—	—	—	5.70
Total debt	70.00	70.00	75.70	75.70	75.70	75.70	—
Debt/equity ratio	0.35	0.34	0.36	0.36	0.35	0.35	—
Dividend payout ratio	—	0.25	0.35	0.58	0.27	0.50	0.35
Funds available for investment							
Retained earnings	—	5.26	3.26	1.26	4.76	1.76	16.30
New debt	—	—	5.70	—	—	—	5.70
Cumulative total	—	5.26	14.22	15.48	20.24	22.00	22.00
Cumulative investment requirements	—	4.00	9.00	13.00	18.00	22.00	22.00

external equity financing is that it allows Troxler to maintain its dividend policy. To the extent that a stable dividend policy carries informational effects, this may be important to Troxler. There are two major disadvantages to this policy: (1) it increases the riskiness of the firm to shareholders and may have an adverse effect on the market's valuation of the stock, and (2) it reduces Troxler's future flexibiilty. These two disadvantages may be especially important as the firm enters a new, higher-risk area of operation.

Reducing the dividend-payout ratio alters what has been a stable dividend policy. Without a careful explanation to the market by management of why this change in policy is necessary, the market may react adversely to it. The new investment opportunities for Troxler may signal increased earnings growth, justifying a change in current dividend policy.

5. Wingo requires $45 million in funds over the next five years for net new investment of $45 million. Because new common stock will not be issued, the $45 million must be raised through new debt and retained earnings: New debt + new retained earnings = $45 million. To achieve the desired debt/equity ratio of 0.35, calculate as follows:

(New debt + Old debt) = 0.35 (New RE + Existing equity).
(New debt + $34 million) = 0.35 (New RE + $86 million).
New debt + $34 million = 0.35 New RE + $30.1 million.

Then solve the two equations simultaneously for the following result:

1.35 (New retained earnings) = $48.9 million.
New retained earnings = $36.22 million.

Expected earnings over the next five years are shown in Table S-80. Of the total expected earnings of $58.03 million over the next five years, $36.22 million must be used to finance new investment, leaving $21.81 million for dividends.

If investment expenditures are spread evenly over the five-year period, Wingo would be able to pay dividends of $4.36 million ($0.87 per share) per year or gradually increase dividends from the current level of $3.5 million ($0.70 per share) per year.

The minimum aggregate level of earnings after tax required over the five years to meet the financial and policy demands is $53.72 million, calculated (in millions of dollars) as follows:

Retained earnings required for investments	$36.22
Dividends (if kept at current level)	17.50
Minimum aggregate level of earnings	$53.72

7. a. An aggregate investment requirement of $22 million with a debt/equity ratio of 0.30 is shown in Table S-81. Calculate debt requirement as follows:

1.30 retained earnings = $22 million.
Retained earnings = $16.90 million.
Total dividends (5 years) = $25.00 − $16.90 = $8.10 million.

$$\text{Annual dividend} = \frac{\$8.1}{5} = \$1.62 \text{ million.}$$

Debt required = $22.00 − $16.90 = $5.1 million.

b. An aggregate investment requirement of $22 million with a debt/equity rate of 0.35 is shown in Table S-82. Calculate debt requirement as follows:

1.35 retained earnings = $22 million.
Retained earnings = $16.30 million.
Total dividends (5 years) = $25.00 − $16.30 = $8.7 million.

$$\text{Annual dividend} = \frac{\$8.7}{5} = \$1.74 \text{ million.}$$

Debt required = $22.00 − $16.30 = $5.70 million.

Chapter 16

1. Table S–83 demonstrates the calculation of the equivalent interest cost (EIC) via several simple examples involving dif-

Table S–83

	Year	Cash Flows	PV Factor at 8 percent	Present Value
(a)				
	0	$1,000	1.000	$1,000
	1	($1,080)	0.926	(1,000)
		EIC = 8 percent		$ 0
(b)				
	0	$1,000	1.000	$1,000
	1–4	($80)	3.312	(265)
	5	($1,080)	0.681	(735)
		EIC = 8 percent		$ 0
(c)				
	0	$1,000	1.000	$1,000
	1–5	($250.44)	3.993	(1,000)
		EIC = 8 percent		$ 0
(d)				
	0	$1,000	1.000	$1,000
	1	($280)	0.926	(259)
	2	($264)	0.857	(226)
	3	($248)	0.794	(197)
	4	($232)	0.735	(171)
	5	($216)	0.681	(147)
		EIC = 8 percent		$ 0

ferent repayment patterns. In each case, the EIC is the rate that discounts the cash flows to zero.

3. Mudville has three alternatives for obtaining the use of the computer for the eight-year period: purchase, lease for years 1–4 and purchase at the end of year 4, or lease for years 1–8. Viewing the latter two as financing alternatives, Table S–84 compares them to borrow/purchase. (Table figures are in thousands of dollars.)

Viewing the renewal option in isolation. Mudville could avoid an outlay of $40,000 (to purchase at the end of year 4)

by paying $18,000 per year during years 5–8 ($30,000 lease payment less $12,000 maintenance). The equivalent interest cost (EIC) for this arrangement is 28.5 percent.

The option of leasing for years 1–4 and purchasing at the end of year 4 has an EIC of 7.6 percent, which is less than Mudville's borrowing cost of 9 percent. Because this arrangement is less expensive than borrowing and purchasing, it is preferable on strict economic grounds. The renewal option definitely should be ruled out, because it has an EIC of 28.5. (Note: We do not have to deal with taxes because Mudville is tax exempt.)

Table S–84

	Year	Acquisition Cost	Maintenance	Lease Payment	Purchase	Total Cash Flow
Lease/purchase	0	150				150
	1–4		12	(48)		(36)
	4				(40)	(40)
					Net present value at 7 percent = −2.46	
					Net present value at 8 percent = +1.36	
					Equivalent interest cost = 7.6 percent	
Lease	0	150				150
	1–4		12	(48)		(36)
	5–8		12	(30)		(18)
					Net present value at 10 percent = −3.09	
					Net present value at 11 percent = +1.53	
					Equivalent interest cost = 10.7 percent	

Table S–85

Year	Acquisition Cost	After-Tax Lease Payment	Deprecia-tion Tax Shield	After-Tax Maintenance	After-Tax Residual Value	Total Cash Flow
Lesase Decision						
0	$112,500	—	—	—	—	$112,500
1–5	—	($19,440)	(15,750)	$2,700	—	($22,490)
6–9	—	($12,960)	($5,750)	12,700	—	($16,010)
10	—	($12,960)	($5,750)	$2,700	($3,240)	($19,250)
Lease/Purchase Decision						
0	$112,500	—	—	—	—	$112,500
1–4	—	($19,440)	($5,750)	$2,700	—	($22,490)
5	($50,000)	($19,440)	($5,750)	$2,700	—	($72,490)
6–10	—	—	($1,150)[a]	—	—	($1,150)

[a]Depreciation during years 6–10 under the lease/purchase option is 50,000 ÷ 5 = $10,000. The tax shield is $4,600. The incremental tax shield compared to purchase option (at year 0) then is 5,750 − 4,600 = $1,150 outflow.

5. a. This problem involves a complicated lease/purchase decision. The firm has three options: purchase initially, lease for five years and then purchase, or lease for ten years. Following the format of Table 16–2, the lease and lease/purchase options are analyzed over ten years using the purchase option as a bench mark in Table S–85. The present value *(PV)* tables at the end of the textbook are useful in calculating the following net present values (NPV):

NPV for the lease option at 12 percent = − $2,344
NPV for the lease option at 13 percent = $1,873
Equivalent interest cost = 12.6 percent
NPV for the lease/purchase option at 11 percent = − $2,793
NPV for the lease/purchase option at 12 percent = $ 723
Equivalent interest cost = 11.8

The firm's after-tax cost of debt is 6.48 percent. Hence, both the lease and the lease/purchase options are more expensive. Lease/purchase is slightly less expensive than leasing for the full ten years, indicating that, if the firm enters into the lease (for other than economic reasons), it should not renew at the end of year 5, but should exercise the purchase option at that point. This point can be seen more clearly if the renewal option is analyzed in isolation. If the firm renews at year 5, it avoids the $50,000 outlay, obligates itself for lease payments in years 6–10, gives up the tax shield and residual, and saves the maintenance expense. The analysis is shown in Table S–86.

b. Using accelerated depreciation does not change the total cash flows, but it does alter the timing of the cash flows. The tax shield forgone from leasing rather than purchasing will be greater in the early years and less in later years.

Table S–86

Year	Acquisition Cost	After-Tax Lease Payment	Deprecia-tion Tax Shield	After-Tax Maintenance	After-Tax Residual Value	Total Cash Flow
5	$50,000					$50,000
6–9		($12,960)	($4,600)	$2,700		($14,860)
10		($12,960)	($4,600)	$2,700	($3,240)	($18,100)

Net present value at 16 percent = − $193
Net present value at 17 percent = $985
Equivalent interest cost = 16.2 percent

Table S–87

Initial Outlay

Cost of calling old bonds (40,000 bonds at $1,160)	− $46,400,000
Receipts from new bond issue	40,000,000
(1) Net outlay	− $ 6,400,000

Expenses

(2) Flotation costs on new bonds	− 450,000
	− $ 6,850,000

Tax savings

(3) Unamortized flotation cost on old bonds 0.46(300,000)	+ 138,000
Net cash flows	− $ 6,712,000

Annual cash flows (15 years)

(4) After-tax interest *expense* on new bonds (0.12)(1 − 0.46)($40,000,000)	− $ 2,592,000
(5) After-tax interest *savings* on retired bonds (0.16)(1 − 0.46)($40,000,000)	+ 3,456,000
(6) Net after-tax savings	+ $ 864,000

Tax effects on flotation costs

(7) Loss of tax shield on amortization of old bonds 0.46($20,000)	− 9,200
(8) Tax shield on amortization of flotation costs on new bond 0.46($30,000)	+ 13,800
Total annual cash flow	$ 868,600

c. Rapidly changing technology increases the risk of purchasing the machine and may make leasing more attractive. If the risk of owning the machine increases, however, the lessor would be expected to require greater compensation for the use of the machine to compensate for bearing those risks. The relatively high equivalent interest costs *(EIC)* in this case are indicative of just such a situation.

7. a. Although the exercise price exceeds the current stock price, it is possible that the situation will reverse prior to the expiration date of the call. Therefore, the call certainly does have value.

b. The call will only be of value if the stock price exceeds the exercise price prior to expiration of the contract. Therefore, the investor must expect the stock price to *rise* in the future.

c. There would still be a market for the contract, but because there are only two months remaining before expiration, there is less of a chance that the stock price will rise above the exercise price. Because all other factors (including stock price) are the same, the price of the contract will be less than it was one month ago.

d. There would still be a market for the call, because the stock price could rise above $43.50 in a week. This is more likely to happen as the stock price is more volatile, so the variability of the stock price is a key factor. Also

important are the short remaining time to expiration (one week) and the opportunity cost of funds to investors.

e. The value of the call = $N(P − E)$ = 100 ($45.25 − $43.50) = $175.

f. The value of the call contract is zero, because $E > P$.

Chapter 17

1. a. To raise $10,000,000 at $80 per share, the firm must issue $10,000,000/$80 = 125,000 shares.

b. Since one right is issued for every share outstanding, 1,000,000 rights will be issued to distribute 125,000 shares. Thus 1,000,000/125,000 = 8 rights will be required along with the subscription price to purchase each share.

c. The total value will be equal to the old price times the old number of shares plus the subscription price times the new number of shares, or

$$V_1 = P_0Y + SX$$
$$= (\$100 \times 1,000,000) + (\$80 \times 125,000)$$
$$= \$110,000,000.$$

The new price per share will be the total value divided by the total number of shares, or

$$\frac{\$110,000,000}{1,125,000} = \$97.78.$$

d. Theoretically, the price of the stock drops by the value of the right, so

$$R = P_0 - P_1 = \$100 - \$97.78$$
$$= \$2.22.$$

3. Follow the format of Table 17–1 in the text to develop Table S–87. For an initial outlay of $6,712,000, the firm can obtain cash flows of $868,600 per year for 15 years. The after-tax cost of new debt is $0.12(1 - 0.46) = 0.065$, which is used as the discount rate.

$$NPV = -\$6,712,000 + \sum_{t=1}^{15} \frac{\$868,600}{(1 + 0.065)^{t}}.$$

The average of the present value annuity factors for 6 percent and 7 percent can be used as an approximation, so that $NPV = -\$6,712,000 + \$868,600(9.4) = \$1,452,840$. Since the NPV is positive, the firm should undertake the refunding.

Chapter 18

1. Note that the dollar value of the invoice (P) is not required in these calculations, since it shows up in both the numerator and the denominator and, thus, cancels out of the equations.

a. $\dfrac{0.02P}{0.98P} \times \dfrac{365}{30} = 0.2483 = 24.8$ percent.

b. $\dfrac{0.03P}{0.97P} \times \dfrac{365}{20} = 0.5644 = 56.4$ percent.

c. $\dfrac{0.01P}{0.99P} \times \dfrac{365}{25} = 0.1475 = 14.8$ percent.

d. $\dfrac{0.02P}{0.98P} \times \dfrac{365}{30} = 0.2483 = 24.8$ percent.

3. a. The firm would effectively be borrowing money for 40 days (from day 15 to day 55). As a result, the effective annual interest cost is

$$\frac{0.02P}{0.98P} \times \frac{365}{40} = 0.186 = 18.6 \text{ percent.}$$

b. If paid on time, the firm would only have a 30-day loan. The effective annual interest cost is

$$\frac{0.02P}{0.98P} \times \frac{365}{30} = 0.248 = 24.8 \text{ percent.}$$

Note that the effective annual interest rate is lower in Part (a) (18.6 percent versus 24.8 percent) because of the extra ten days by which the firm delayed payment.

5. a. To obtain the use of $10,000, the firm must borrow

$$\frac{\$10,000}{(1 - 0.1)} = \$11,111.11$$

This loan would cost $0.15(\$11,111.11) = \$1,666.67$.

Effective annual rate $= \dfrac{\$1,666.67}{\$10,000} = 16.67$ percent.

b. To obtain the use of $250,000, the firm must borrow

$$\frac{\$250,000}{(1 - 0.15)} = \$294,117.65.$$

This loan would cost $0.16(\$294,117.65) = \$47,058.82$.

Effective annual rate $= \dfrac{\$47,058.82}{\$250,000} = 18.82$ percent.

7. a. In this case, MSM is only using the credit for 10 days, since they are paying 20 days after delivery. The effective annual rate is

$$\frac{0.01P}{0.99P} \times \frac{365}{10} = 36.87 \text{ percent.}$$

b. If MSM is to forgo the discount, then they should postpone payment until the 45th day, which would result in an effective annual rate of

$$\frac{0.01P}{0.99P} \times \frac{365}{35} = 10.53 \text{ percent.}$$

Thus, MSM's optimal strategy is to forgo the discount and not pay until the 45th day, since the interest rate on the bank loan exceeds the cost of not taking the discount.

9. In order to choose between the two loan arrangements, it is necessary to compare the effective interest rate of each. To increase funds by $2,000,000 with a 16 percent discount loan (Loan A), $2,380,952 must be borrowed, as can be seen in the following calculation:

$$\text{Loan} - 0.16(\text{Loan}) = \$2,000,000$$
$$0.84(\text{Loan}) = \$2,000,000$$
$$\text{Loan} = (\$2,000,000)/0.84$$
$$\text{Loan} = \$2,380,952.30$$

The effective interest rate for loan A is calculated as follows:

$$\frac{\text{Discount}}{\text{Proceeds}} = \frac{\$2,380,952.30 - \$2,000,000}{\$2,000,000}$$
$$= \frac{\$380,952.30}{\$2,000,000}$$
$$= 19.05 \text{ percent.}$$

To increase funds by $2,000,000 with a 10 percent compensating balance (Loan B), $2,222,222 must be borrowed, as shown in the following calculation:

$$\text{Loan} - 0.10(\text{Loan}) = \$2,000,000$$
$$\text{Loan} = \$2,222,222$$

Interest paid is 16 percent of $2,222,222, or $355,555.52. The effective interest rate for Loan B is therefore:

$$\frac{\text{Interest}}{\text{Proceeds}} = \frac{\$355,555.52}{\$2,000,000}$$
$$= 17.78 \text{ percent.}$$

Table S–88

Sales	$5,000
Cost of goods sold (83 percent)	−4,150
Gross profit	$ 850
Sales commission (2 percent)	− 100
Warehousing (1.5 percent)	− 75
Profit before tax	$ 675

Loan B offers the lower effective interest rate and is the preferred loan arrangement.

Chapter 19

1. Reduction in funds tied up in accounts receivable = $8,000 × 1 day = $8,000. Annual savings = 0.012($8,000) = $960.

3. Purchases of $3 million per year = $8,219.18 per day. Payment five days later increases accounts payable by $8,219.18 × 5 = $41,096, which, at 11 percent per year, gives annual savings of $4,520.56.

5. a. Total float = $300,000(5 days) = $1,500,000. Cost = 0.12($1,500,000) = $180,000/year.
   b. Reduced expense of float = 0.12(2.5 days)($300,000) = $90,000. Total reduced costs = $90,000 + $30,000 = $120,000.

   $$\text{Maximum acceptable compensating balances} = \frac{\$120,000}{0.12} =$$
   $$\$1,000,000.$$

7. a. The cost of the current system is calculated as follows:

   $$\$20,000 + 0.05\left(\frac{\$50,000,000}{\$1,000}\right) = \$22,500.$$

   The savings under the lock-box system are calculated as follows:

   Savings from float reduction
   = (Average daily collections)(Reduction float days)
   (Opportunity cost of short-term funds)

   $$= \left(\frac{\$50,000,000}{250}\right)(2)(0.11)$$
   = $44,000.

   Savings from reduced check clearing costs
   = (Average number of checks/year)(Savings per check)

   $$= \left(\frac{\$50,000,000}{\$1,000}\right)(0.02)$$
   = $1,000.

   The bank's offer of lock-boxes is acceptable as a cost-savings measure.

   Opportunity cost of compensating balances
   = ($300,000)(0.11)
   = $33,000.

Table S–89

Goods delivered	$1,000
Less profit (17 percent)	− 170
Cost of goods sold	$ 830
Sales commission (2 percent)	− 20
Investment	$ 850

Net savings = $44,000 + 1,000 − 33,000 = $12,000.

b. The break-even compensating balance is determined as follows:

$$\text{Net savings} = 0.$$
$$\$44,000 + 1,000 - 0.11(\text{Compensating balance}) = 0.$$
$$\text{Break-even compensating balance} = \$409,090.90.$$

Flyer would accept compensating balances for the lockbox system no greater than $409,090.90.

Chapter 20

1. Policy A provides the following expected incremental dollar return:

(Pre-tax profit margin) × (Change in sales) × (1-tax rate) =
0.20 ($4,350,000) 0.5 = $435,000.

The required incremental dollar investment includes the additional investment in accounts receivable from incremental sales, plus the effect of the change in average collection period (ACP) on original sales:

[(1-pre-tax profit margin) × (New sales per day) × ACP)]
   + [(Change in ACP) × (Original sales per day)]

= 0.8 ($4,350,000/365) 45 + 15 ($20,000,000/365)
= $429,041.10 + $821,917.81
= $1,250,958.91.

The cost of the incremental investment is K × (Incremental investment) = 0.16 ($1,250,958.91) = $200,153.43. The net profit from Policy A, therefore, is $435,000.000 − $200,153.43 = $234,846.57.

Policy B provides the following expected reduction in dollar return:

0.20 ($2,570,000)0.5 = $257,000.

The reduction in required dollar investment is as follows:

0.8($2,750,000/365)(22) + (8) ($20,000,000/365)
= $132,602.74 + $438,356.16
= $570,958.90.

The savings from carrying the reduced investment is 0.16($570,958.90) = $91,353.42. Because the reduced profit from Policy B exceeds the savings from reduced investment, Policy B is unacceptable. Policy A generates in-

Table S–90

Policy	Turnover	Inventory Level	Sales	Cost of Goods Sold	Contribution	Carrying Cost	Incremental Operating Profit Before Tax	Incremental Operating Profit After Tax	Incremental Investment	E(R) Incremental Investment (percent)
Current	10	32.50	$450	$325	$125	$1.625	—	—	—	—
A	8	45.00	$500	$360	$140	$2.25	$14.375	$7.763	$12.50	62.10
B	6	64.67	$540	$388	$152	$3.233	$11.020	$5.951	$19.67	30.25
C	4	101.38	$565	$405.50	$159.50	$5.069	$ 5.664	$3.058	$36.71	8.33

cremental dollar returns that exceed the cost of the incremental investment and, therefore, should be adopted.

3. The required return remains the same while the expected return declines. For risk class 3, bad debt expense = 0.04($500,000) = $20,000. Expected dollar return = ($100,000 − $20,000 − $5,000)(0.50) = $75,000(0.50) = $37,500. On the basis of these results, risk class 3 is still accepted.

   The expected dollar return is equal to the pretax profit—based on a 0.20 profit margin and $500,000 of new sales, 0.20 × $500,000 = $100,000—adjusted downward to reflect bad debt expense ($20,000) and credit department expense ($5,000). All of this is then converted to an after-tax figure by multiplying by (1 − tax rate): 1 − 0.5 = 0.50. For risk class 4, bad debt expense = 0.07($400,000) = $28,000. Expected dollar return = ($80,000 − $28,000 − $5,000)(0.50) = $47,000(0.50) = $23,500. Risk class 4 is still accepted.
   For risk class 5, bad debt expense = 0.12($300,000) = $36,000. Expected dollar return = ($60,000 − $36,000 − $5,000)(0.50) = $19,000(0.50) = $9,500. Risk class 5 is still accepted.
   For risk class 6, bad debt expense = 0.20($200,000) = $40,000. Expected dollar return = ($40,000 − $40,000 − $5,000)(0.50) = −$5,000(0.50) = −$2,500. Risk class is rejected.

5. a. The increased annual profit to Delta is shown in Table S–88. Investment by Delta is illustrated in Table S–89.

   Annual expected return = $\dfrac{\$675}{\$850}$ = 79.41 percent (before tax).

   b. The probability of outcome (1) P_1 would be found from $P_1 \times (0.7941) = 0.30$, or $P_1 = 0.38$. For an expected return of 30 percent or better, there must be a probability of 0.38 or better that Bill's will make all payments over a period of one year.

7. If the firm accepts the quantity discount, the annual savings are $0.30(10,000) = $3,000. Purchasing 400 units results in 10,000/400 = 25 orders per year for a total ordering cost of 25($100) = $2,500. The average inventory of 400/2 = 200 units results in total carrying costs of $50(200) = $10,000. Thus, total annual inventory costs are $12,500, a $2,500 in-

crease; but the firm saves $3,000 on the discounts, for a net advantage of $500. The firm should take the quantity discounts.

9. a. EOQ = $\sqrt{\dfrac{2RO}{C}}$

   = $\sqrt{\dfrac{2(280,000)(150)}{(0.30)(7.50)}}$

   = 6110.10; 6,200 would be ordered.

   b. Number of orders (assuming 6,200 units ordered) per year

   = $\dfrac{280,000}{6,200}$ = 45.16.

   c. Daily usage rate = $\dfrac{280,000}{365}$ = 767.12 units per day.

   Reorder point = [Safety stock) + [(Usage per day) × (Days till delivery)]
   = 35,000 + (767.12)(10)
   = 42,671.2.

   Therefore, reorder at 42,672 units.

11. This problem considers the trade-offs between inventory-carrying costs and lost sales. It brings up the issues of the use of accounting ratios as performance measures and the potential for conflicting policies among departments within a firm. An analysis is shown in tabular form (in thousands of dollars) in Table S–90. The expected return exceeds the 15 percent required rate of return through Policy B, indicating that the firm should aim for an inventory turnover of 6 with an inventory level of $64,667.

Chapter 21

1. a. The French franc is at a discount.

   b. $\dfrac{F-S}{S} \times \dfrac{12}{6} \times 100 = \dfrac{0.1128-0.1141}{0.1141} \times 200 = -2.28$ percent.

   c. Interest rates and inflation rates in France are greater than in the United States.

3. C$/US$ = 1.4043.
   US$/G = 0.3599.

Table S–91

Current assets	$270	Current liabilities	$220
Fixed assets	480	Long-term debt	100
Total	$750	Equity	430
		Total	$750

1.4043 × 0.3599 = C$/G = 0.5054.
0.5054 × 150,000 gilder = 75,810 Canadian dollars.

5. 2,383,500,000 yen = $11,714,903.00 at $0.004915/yen.
   476,700,000 yen = $2,342,980.50 at $0.004915/yen.
   476,700,000 yen = $2,225,712.30 at $0.004669/yen.

The present value *(PV)* of $2,342,980.50 for 10 years at 15 percent = $2,342,980.50 × 5.019 = $11,759,419. The *PV* of $2,225,712.30 for 10 years at 15 percent = $2,225,712.30 × 5.019 = $11,170,850. This project is not acceptable if the yen devalues by 5 percent since $11,170,850 is less than $11,714,903. Spot rates are not appropriate when evaluating long-term projects. Some forecast of exchange rates over the life of the project is needed to convert cash flows to a dollar basis. This requires estimates of relative inflation rates, as well as an evaluation of government policy and conditions for foreign investment in Japan.

7. US$: $1\left(1 + \dfrac{0.077}{2}\right)$ = $1.0385/Dollar invested.

SwFr: $2.3955\left(1 + \dfrac{0.05}{2}\right)$ × 0.4238 = $1.0406/Dollar

FrFr: $8.7615\left(1 + \dfrac{0.103}{2}\right)0.1128$ = $1.0392/Dollar invested.

The rates on both the Swiss franc and the French franc more than compensate for future expected changes in the value of the dollar, but the Swiss franc seems to be the best deal. Neither rate is likely to exist for long, as arbitrage will force them into equilibrium.

Chapter 22

1. a. We need to look at price/earnings (P/E) ratios to answer this question.

P/E of XYZ = $50/$1.00 = 50.
P/E of ABC = $25/$2.50 = 10.

Table S–92

Current assets	$270	Current liabilities	$220
Fixed assets	480	Long-term debt	100
Goodwill	30	Equity	460
Total	$780	Total	$780

XYZ's expected earnings = $1 × 1,000,000 = $1,000,000
ABC's expected earnings = $2.50 × 1,000,000 = 2,500,000
Expected earnings of merged firm = $3,500,000

Our rule of thumb says the firm with the high price/earnings ratio should acquire the firm with the low P/E.

If, in a perfect world, XYZ can acquire ABC for stock in an exchange based on market value, it should offer 1 share of XYZ for every 2 shares of ABC. Thus, the offer would require 1,000,000 ÷ 2 = 500,000 new shares of XYZ, making its total shares outstanding 1,500,000.

With expected earnings of $3,500,000 and 1,500,000 shares, the earnings per share (EPS) for the merged firm is expected to be $2.33, a nice increase for XYZ's premerger EPS of $1.00.

Checking this by working the problem with ABC doing the acquiring in the same perfect world results in a postmerger EPS for ABC of $1.17, ($3,500,000/3,000,000), quite a decrease from the $2.50 EPS.

b. Paying a 20 percent premium is equivalent to treating the $25.00 market price as if it were $30. Thus, instead of giving ABC's shareholders 1 share for every 2 shares, we now must give them $60 ÷ $50 = 1.2 shares for every 2 shares (a 20 percent increase). Or we could have calculated $30 ÷ $50 = 0.6, 0.6 of a share of XYZ for each share of ABC. The total number of shares XYZ must now give becomes 0.6 × 1,000,000 = 600,000, a 20 percent or 100,000 share increase over Part (a).

c. Using the assumptions in Part (b), the merged firm would have 1,000,000 + 600,000 = 1,600,000 shares with expected earnings of 3,500,000. Thus, expected earnings per share (EPS) would be $2.1875.

d. No, XYZ's earnings per share (EPS) did not remain at their current level. Even though EPS rises initially, share price may not increase, and may actually fall, because ex-

Table S–93

Year	Profit after Tax	Number of shares (millions)	Earnings per Share	Sample Problem Merger Earnings per Share
1986	$30	16	$1.875	$2.14
1987	$38	16	$2.375	$2.71
1988	$48.2	16	$3.013	$3.44
1989	$61.18	16	$3.824	$4.37

perience has shown that mergers often reduce the expected long-term growth rate of EPS.

e. As we saw in Part (b), if ABC offered a 20 percent premium for XYZ, it would be treating XYZ's stock as if it were worth $50 × 1.2 = $60/share. Thus, it would require $60 ÷ 25 = 2.4 shares of ABC stock for each share of XYZ. ABC would have to give 2.4 × 1,000,000 = 2,400,000 shares to XYZ's stockholders. Its new total shares outstanding would be 3,400,000. With expected earnings of $3,500,000, new EPS would be $1.03.

f. The calculations alone indicate that XYZ should acquire ABC because its EPS increases significantly. However, a merger decision should not be based on EPS considerations alone. Many other factors will determine whether a merger is appropriate and, if so, who should purchase whom.

3. a. The Slam-Dunk postmerger balance sheet reflecting pooling of interests is shown in Table S–91.

b. The Slam-Dunk postmerger balance sheet based on purchase of assets is illustrated in Table S–92. Here the difference in the value of Dunkirk's assets ($150) and the value of Statistical Lab's offer ($180) is $30 and is treated as goodwill and added to equity.

c. The purchase method would have no effect on cash flow in this example, but it would affect profits, depending on the period over which the goodwill was amortized. For example, if goodwill of $30 were amortized over 30 years, operating profits each year would be reduced by $1 million.

5. a. If Franklin's stock is valued at $20, it will have to offer 1.5 shares of its stock for each share of Stove in order to produce the $30-per-share purchase price. Since Stove has 4,000,000 shares of stock, Franklin will have to give 6,000,000 shares of its stock to complete the merger.

b. The new company will now have 10 + 6 million = 16 million shares and expected earnings per share as shown in Table S–93.

c. In the same problem, Franklin had a 1986 price/earnings ratio (P/E) of 15 and Stove had a P/E of 8. Franklin's offer of $30 per share for Stove was an effective P/E of 12 ($30 ÷ 2.5 = 12).

The P/E of Franklin is now 10, which is still higher than the Franklin market P/E of 8. However, the actual P/E of this offer is 12, which is higher than Franklin's P/E of 10. Thus, the earnings Franklin is buying are no longer cheap as they were in the sample problem, and it does not get the short-term increase in earnings per share (EPS). In fact, postmerger EPS drops below the premerger EPS level of $2.00 immediately.

Name Index

Subject Index

Present Value* (at *i* per period) of $1 Received per Period for Each of *n* Periods

n	i = 1%	2%	3%	4%	5%	6%	7%	8%	9%	10%
1	0.990	0.980	0.971	0.962	0.952	0.943	0.935	0.926	0.917	0.909
2	1.970	1.942	1.914	1.886	1.859	1.833	1.808	1.783	1.759	1.736
3	2.941	2.884	2.829	2.775	2.723	2.673	2.624	2.577	2.531	2.487
4	3.902	3.808	3.717	3.630	3.546	3.465	3.387	3.312	3.240	3.170
5	4.854	4.713	4.580	4.452	4.330	4.212	4.100	3.993	3.890	3.791
6	5.796	5.601	5.417	5.242	5.076	4.917	4.767	4.623	4.486	4.355
7	6.728	6.472	6.230	6.002	5.786	5.582	5.389	5.206	5.033	4.868
8	7.652	7.325	7.020	6.733	6.463	6.210	5.971	5.747	5.535	5.335
9	8.566	8.162	7.786	7.435	7.108	6.802	6.515	6.247	5.985	5.759
10	9.471	8.983	8.530	8.111	7.722	7.360	7.024	6.710	6.418	6.145
11	10.368	9.787	9.253	8.760	8.036	7.887	7.499	7.139	6.805	6.495
12	11.255	10.575	9.954	9.385	8.863	8.384	7.943	7.536	7.161	6.814
13	12.134	11.348	10.635	9.986	9.394	8.853	8.358	7.904	7.487	7.103
14	13.004	12.106	11.296	10.563	9.899	9.295	8.745	8.244	7.786	7.367
15	13.865	12.849	11.938	11.118	10.380	9.712	9.108	8.560	8.061	7.606
16	14.718	13.578	12.561	11.652	10.838	10.106	9.447	8.851	8.313	7.824
17	15.562	14.292	13.166	12.166	11.274	10.477	9.763	9.122	8.544	8.022
18	16.398	14.992	13.753	12.659	11.690	10.828	10.059	9.372	8.756	8.201
19	17.226	15.678	14.324	13.134	12.085	11.158	10.336	9.604	8.950	8.365
20	18.046	16.351	14.877	13.590	12.462	11.470	10.594	9.818	9.129	8.514
21	18.857	17.011	15.415	14.029	12.821	11.764	10.836	10.017	9.292	8.649
22	19.661	17.658	15.937	14.451	13.163	12.042	11.061	10.201	9.442	8.772
23	20.456	18.292	16.444	14.857	13.489	12.303	11.272	10.371	9.580	8.883
24	21.244	18.914	16.936	15.247	13.799	12.550	11.469	10.529	9.707	8.985
25	22.023	19.523	17.413	15.622	14.094	12.783	11.654	10.675	9.823	9.077
30	25.808	22.396	19.600	17.292	15.372	13.765	12.409	11.258	10.274	9.427
35	29.409	24.999	21.487	18.665	16.374	14.498	12.948	11.655	10.567	9.644
40	32.835	27.355	23.115	19.793	17.159	15.046	13.332	11.925	10.757	9.779
45	36.095	29.490	24.519	20.720	17.774	15.456	13.606	12.108	10.881	9.863
50	39.196	31.424	25.730	21.482	18.256	15.762	13.801	12.233	10.962	9.915

*Value is calculated as $\left(\dfrac{1}{(1 + i)} + \dfrac{1}{(1 + i)^2} + \ldots + \dfrac{1}{(1 + i)^n} \right)$.